Shankle, George E

American nicknames

R
929
Sha
c.1

AMERICAN NICKNAMES

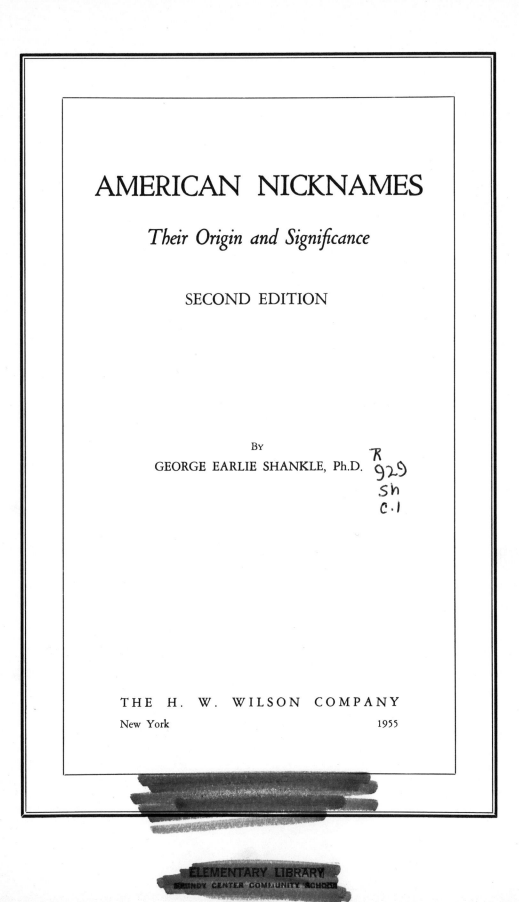

AMERICAN NICKNAMES

Their Origin and Significance

SECOND EDITION

By

GEORGE EARLIE SHANKLE, Ph.D.

THE H. W. WILSON COMPANY

New York   1955

PREFACE TO THE SECOND EDITION

The revised edition of *American Nicknames* comprises a consolidation of much of the material in the original edition plus new information about nicknames of recent or contemporary interest. In order to confine the new edition to a single volume of manageable length, many of the items from the original edition have been considerably abbreviated, and a change has been made in footnote style. This arrangement, while retaining all valuable source material, has permitted the condensation of references to any one source.

References to the nicknames of athletic teams of state teachers colleges and junior colleges have been largely eliminated in this edition, as have been such self-explanatory nicknames as "Doc" or "Red" for individuals or "Aggies" for teams belonging to agricultural colleges. Information about contemporaries mentioned in the 1937 edition has been brought up to date wherever possible. Supplementary information is given wherever the individual has continued to remain in the public eye. Nicknames of nationally prominent people since 1937 include such personalities as President Eisenhower, the late General Joseph Stilwell, and Mrs. Anna Moses.

The author again acknowledges a debt of gratitude to the various librarians and officials of the Library of Congress, where the research and the writing of most of the revised edition were done, for their kindness, consideration, and assistance in securing source material difficult to obtain; to the reference librarians at the central desk in the Library of Congress who often reported nicknames which they found in connection with their work; to the many individuals who took the time to answer questionnaires and to supply data otherwise; to Paul Thorne of Troy, Tenn., who interviewed, for the author, some prominent West Tennesseans to gather needed information; and to Captain Victor Hunt Harding, Secretary of the National Democratic Congress Reelection Committee at Washington, D.C., who kindly supplied data on the nicknames of contemporary United States senators and congressmen.

GEORGE EARLIE SHANKLE

PREFACE TO THE FIRST EDITION

Americans doubtless use more nicknames than any other peoples today. They give them to their wives, husbands, children, friends, enemies, and to almost every object they see or use. No name is too sacred or too base for them to shorten or modify into an affectionate, humorous, or abusive sobriquet. There are literally thousands of them employed in the daily conversations or in the writings of the American people.

The sobriquets of ball teams will disclose to the persons who take the time to study them carefully that in the baseball or football world nicknames are almost as numerous as are spectators who witness athletic contests. There are few baseball or football players who do not possess one or more of these appellations. Often they displace the real names of the persons to whom they have been attributed. The nicknames of ball players record traits or characteristics both personal and professional. Sometimes they are complimentary, and again they are intended to satirize or caricature those to whom they are given.

The sobriquets of towns and cities are equally interesting to those of historical or humorous turn of mind. They give an insight into the historical development of towns and cities in various parts of the United States, into humorous civic and personal struggles, or into the commercial and social development of these places.

The nicknames of the miscellaneous items are perhaps the most amusing of the entire collection. This class of sobriquets ranges from the most ordinary objects of life to complex religious and political organizations.

The finding of and accounting for the origin and the significance of the sobriquets of men and women required most painstaking research because they are interwoven with the biographies and accomplishments of these personages. It is instructive and often amusing to note the vast number of nicknames some have and to see how they reflect an attempt to berate or to elevate the individual.

The sobriquets of the states and of their inhabitants disclose a wealth of historical and traditional data along with facts that reveal discoveries, settlements, and later development of these civic units and of the lives of their inhabitants.

The writing of this book was suggested to the author by the references to various sobriquets in the source material which he used in working out the data for the chapter on the nicknames of the states and of their inhabitants in his book entitled *State Names, Flags, Seals, Songs, Birds, Flowers, and Other Symbols.* The writer consistently followed the plan used in this book both as to organization and as to the method of employing bibliographical footnotes.

Notwithstanding the comprehensiveness of the volume, it cannot be asserted that it contains all the American nicknames in use today, for they are constantly being originated; and, too, it is probable that they were not all discovered in the process of research. The writer, with the aid of a research assistant, spent more than three years in the Library of Congress, turning the pages of thousands of books while he was locating this assemblage of nicknames and accounting for their origin and significance. The data dealing with the sobriquets of athletic teams, and many of the other nicknames had to be collected by means of personal letters or by questionnaires; hence much of this information appears in print for the first time in this publication.

As used in this book, the term nickname signifies a sobriquet or an appellation used instead of the real name of a person, place, or object; consequently, the subject matter deals with recognized and widely used nicknames. No attempt has been made to include slang expressions, however great the overlapping may be between these and nicknames, for there have been published some excellent dictionaries of slang which the general reader or the researcher will find in most reference libraries.

A debt of gratitude is hereby acknowledged to the librarians and to the officials of the Library of Congress for their kindness, consideration, and assistance; to the many individuals who took the time and trouble to answer questionnaires or otherwise to furnish information; and to the following young women, former students of the author, who were employed to assist with the clerical work: Miss Margaret Rose Kalnen of Castle Hayne, North Carolina, who assisted both with the locating and with the assembling of the reference material, with the checking of the first draft of the copy, and also with the proof-reading of the galley-proofs and of the page proofs; Mrs. Elizabeth Glenn Boley, who typed the greater part of the final copy of the manuscript; and also to Mrs. Levera Hume of Nashville, Tennessee, who aided in arranging the data in dictionary form.

GEORGE EARLIE SHANKLE

American Nicknames

Abbe, Cleveland

Cleveland Abbe was nicknamed *Old Probabilities* and *Old Prob.*[1] At Cincinnati, Ohio, in 1869, Abbe began to forecast the weather in that locality, issuing daily bulletins dealing with the "probable" weather to be expected. These weather forecasts, called *Probabilities,* were later published throughout the country as official weather bulletins signed *Old Prob,* and the author was nicknamed *Old Probabilities* or *Old Prob.*

Cleveland Abbe was born at New York City, on December 3, 1838, and died at Chevy Chase, Md., on October 28, 1916.

[1] *The National Cyclopaedia of American Biography.* (James T. White and Co., New York, 1900) vol. 8: p. 264.

Abbitt, Jim

Jim Abbitt, who played halfback in national league football, was nicknamed *Jackrabbit*[1] by the sports writers in 1937 because he was a fast and elusive runner. It is almost inevitable that a fast runner named J. Abbitt would be called *Jackrabbit.*

Jim Abbitt was born at Roxboro, N.C., on April 24, 1916.

[1] A communication from George P. Marshall, President-treasurer of the Washington Club of the National Football League, Washington, D.C., March 20, 1939.

ABC's of the New Deal

Because the various bureaus, agencies, and administrations of the New Deal were often designated by the initial letters of their names, numerous New Deal agencies have been called the *ABC's of the New Deal* and *Alphabet Soup.*

Abilene, Texas

Abilene is nicknamed the *Athens of the West*[1] because of the numerous schools and colleges, its homes and churches, and its agricultural and business activities.

[1] *Flashlights on Texas,* Lillie Terrell Shaver and Willie Williamson Rogers (A. C. Baldwin and Sons, Austin, Tex., 1928) p. 121-2.

Abraham Lincoln of the Sea. See Furuseth, Andrew

Academic Pharisee. See Bonaparte, C. J.

Ace. See Sorrell, V. G.; Wilson, James (Athlete)

Aces. See Evansville College

Accidental President. See Adams, J. Q.; Fillmore, Millard; Tyler, John

Accounts Warren. See Warren, L. C.

Adams, Albert J.

Albert J. Adams, a famous gambler of New York City, was nicknamed the *Policy King.*[1] For some time prior to his death Adams was absolute boss of the policy or "numbers" racket of New York City.

Adams came to New York City from Rhode Island about 1871, when he was twenty-seven years of age. He was first employed by the New York, New Haven and Hartford Railroad as a brakeman, then later as a runner for a policy game conducted by Zachariah Simmons. He afterward became a partner, and after Simmons' death became the boss of the New York policy game. His activities became so notorious that the police finally raided his headquarters on December 14, 1901. Adams was convicted and sent to Sing Sing, where he spent more than a year.

After his release from prison he amassed a fortune in money and land. He lived apart from his family in luxury at the Ansonia Hotel in New York City. It was said that he lived alone in order that his family might share his shame as little as possible. He committed suicide in his apartment on October 1, 1907.

[1] *Washington Post,* Washington D.C. October 2, 1906. p. 1.
[2] *New York Times,* October 2, 1906. p.2.

Adams, John

John Adams, the second President of the United States, has the following sobriquets: *Atlas of Independence, Colossus of Ameri-*

Adams, John—Continued

can Independence, Colossus of Debate, Duke of Braintree, Father of American Independence, Father of the American Navy.

John Adams was nicknamed the *Atlas of Independence*,[1] the *Colossus of American Independence* and the *Father of American Independence*[2] because he was one of the chief agents in securing the adoption of the Declaration of Independence and was consistently one of the strongest supporters among the colonists of the struggle for independence.

The sobriquet the *Colossus of Debate*[2] was applied to John Adams because he showed such outstanding ability in debating. The nickname is said to have been originated by Thomas Jefferson, who accredited Adams with being a colossal figure in the animated debates which preceded the ratification of the Declaration of Independence. Adams' eloquent and persuasive argument in favor of adopting this document was an important factor in causing its final ratification.

At the age of sixty-five John Adams retired from politics and settled in his home at Braintree, Mass. His friends and acquaintances at Braintree and elsewhere nicknamed him the *Duke of Braintree*[2] because he lived the life of a retired gentleman, devoted much of his time to the study of history and philosophy, and was outstanding in the town as a literary and philosophical leader.

John Adams was widely known as the *Father of the American Navy*.[3] During the early years of the Revolutionary War, Adams prepared a war vessel to guard the towns along the Atlantic coast in New England against British plunderers, and as a delegate to the Continental Congress which met at Philadelphia, in 1775, he was instrumental in getting an appropriation for the aid of the national navy which was to be placed in charge of George Washington. When trouble with France occurred in 1798 regarding the conditions of Jay's treaty made between the United States and England in 1795, President Adams organized the Navy Department and ordered ships to be built or bought.

Old Sink or Swim[4] is the nickname given to John Adams by historians, and originated in a statement Adams made to Jonathan Sewell early in the Revolutionary struggle for independence. Sewell, a Royalist, was urging Adams to give up his support of the colonists. Adams replied, "Sink or swim, live or die, survive or perish, I am with my country from this day on."

John Adams was born at Braintree, Mass., on October 19, 1735, and died at Quincy, Mass., on July 4, 1826.

[1] *The Founders of America in the Days of the Revolution; the Lives and Deeds of the Great Patriots Who Gave This Nation Its Independence*, Edwin Wildman (L. C. Page and Company, Inc., Boston, 1924) p. 211. *The Cyclopaedia of American Biography*, ed. by James Grant Wilson and John Fiske (Press Association Compilers, Inc., New York, 1915) vol. 1, p. 23.
[2] "John Adams" by Clifford Smyth, in *Builders of America* (Funk and Wagnalls, New York, 1931) vol. 13, p. 140, 165-6.
[3] *The Cyclopaedia of American Biographies. Comprising the Men and Women of the United States Who Have Been Identified with the Growth of the Nation*, ed. by John Howard Brown (The Cyclopaedia Publishing Company, Boston, 1897) vol. 1, p. 24.
[4] *John Adams and the American Revolution*, Catherine Drinker Bowen, Little Brown and Co., Boston, 1950. p. 457.

Adams, John Quincy

John Quincy Adams was called the *Accidental President* and *Old Man Eloquent*.

In the presidential election of 1824, he received thirteen of the twenty-four votes cast; consequently he was designated by his contemporaries the *Accidental President*,[1] since they felt that his getting a majority of one vote was an accident.

Because of his great ability to debate effectively, and his oratorical powers, John Quincy Adams was called *Old Man Eloquent*[2] during the later years of his life. He was born at Braintree, Mass., on July 11, 1767, and died at Washington, D.C., on February 23, 1848.

[1] *American Leaders*, Mabel Ansley Murphy (Union Press, Philadelphia, 1920) p. 106.
[2] *Complete School History of the United States*, Edward S. Ellis (Porter and Coates, Philadelphia, 1892) p. 136.

Adams, Samuel

The following nicknames have been applied to Samuel Adams: *Amendment Monger, American Cato, Brain of the Revolution, Chief Incendiary of the House, Cromwell of New England, Father of America, Father of the American Revolution, Man of the Town Meeting, Psalm Singer, Sam the Maltster, Samuel the Publican, Tribune of the People,* and *Would-Be Cromwell of America.*

When the Massachusetts State Convention met at Boston on January 9, 1788, to study the draft of the Constitution of the United States with a view to ratifying it, Samuel Adams, one of the more prominent delegates, discussed its weaknesses and offered several amendments which were instrumental in securing its ratification by the Massachusetts Convention. His political enemies and others who opposed the adoption of the Constitution nicknamed him an *Amendment Monger.*[1,2]

The sobriquet, the *American Cato,*[3] was attributed to Samuel Adams in commemoration of his zeal in defending the American colonists against the encroachment of England on their rights. In this respect he was comparable to Marcus Porcius Cato, called Cato the Younger, a Roman patriot who lived from 95 to 46 B.C., and who so ably defended Rome against conspirators.

Samuel Adams has been designated the *Brain of the Revolution*[4] because he was so active in defending the liberty and the rights of the colonists against the attempts of the British Government to force them into subjection, because he argued so ardently for the liberty of the colonists, and took the initiative in planning much of the colonial action against British oppression.

About 1771 he was nicknamed the *Chief Incendiary of the House* as a result of his having analyzed and ardently argued against British tyranny in his speeches before the House of the General Court of the Province of Massachusetts.

The ardor of Samuel Adams in urging the colonists to fight for freedom from British oppression caused a London journal to designate him the *Cromwell of New England,*[2] signifying that Adams was comparable to Oliver Cromwell in advocating and in defending the cause of liberty. The English loyalists expressed their hatred for him by calling him the *Would-Be Cromwell of America* because he so bitterly opposed the oppressive measures of the British King and his Parliament. For the same activity, Stephen Sayre, a London banker, in a communication dated September 18, 1770, called Adams the *Father of America,*[2] signifying that American freedom and liberty were founded largely upon the principles advocated by Adams.

In announcing the death of Samuel Adams, which occurred on October 3, 1803, the newspapers of the time spoke of him as the *Father of the American Revolution.*[2] This was suggested by the prominent part he took in resisting the British Government and by his attempts to arouse the colonists to fight for their liberty.

Because he took such an active part in the town meetings of his generation, Samuel Adams was nicknamed the *Man of the Town Meeting.*[5]

He often assisted in the choir of the New South Church at Boston, Mass.; therefore, the Loyalists designated him the *Psalm Singer.*[2]

In 1748, Adams engaged in the brewing business, the occupation of his father. Later critical writers referred to him as *Sam the Maltster.*[2]

In 1763 he was one of the tax collectors for the Massachusetts colonists in Boston and its vicinity, and spent much time in visiting schools and conversing with his fellow colonists about the political questions of the day. The Royalists expressed their disapproval of him and of his official position by calling him *Samuel the Publican.*[2] In the days of ancient Rome a publican was a taxgatherer who was often hated bitterly because of his oppressive manner.

Because he ardently championed the rights and liberties of the people and served in public office so ably and efficiently, he was sometimes nicknamed the *Tribune of the People.*[6] In Roman civilization, a tribune was an officer chosen by the people to protect them from the tyranny or maltreatment of the patricians.

Samuel Adams was born at Boston, Mass., on September 27, 1722, and died there on October 2, 1803.

[1] *A History of the People of the United States, from the Revolution to the Civil War,* John Bach McMaster (D. Appleton, New York, 1883) vol. 1, p. 532.
[2] *The Life and Public Services of Samuel Adams, Being a Narrative of His Acts and Opinions, and of His Agency in Producing and Forwarding the American Revolution, with Extracts from His Correspondence, State Papers, and Political Essays,* William V. Wells (Little, Brown, Boston, 1865) vol. 1, p. 24, 36, 375, 426, 427, 450; vol. 2, p. 333; vol. 3, p. 250-67.
[3] *A Book of Nicknames,* John Goff (Courier-Journal Job Printing Company, Louisville, Ky., 1892) p. 21.
[4] *Makers of the Nation,* Fanny E. Coe (American Book Company, New York, 1914) p. 19.
[5] *Samuel Adams,* James K. Hosmer (Houghton Mifflin and Company, Boston, 1885) p. 352.
[6] *Samuel Adams, a Character Sketch with Anecdotes, Characteristics, and Chronology,* Samuel Fallows (University Association, Chicago, 1898) p. 15.

Addicks, John Edward O'Sullivan

John Edward O'Sullivan Addicks, an economic adventurer and politician, was nicknamed *Gas Addicks* and the *Napoleon of Gas*[1] because of his interest in promoting the public interest in gas to be used for illuminating purposes, and in building gas works. He built gas works in Jersey City, Chicago, and in Brooklyn. In 1882 he was instrumental in organizing the Chicago Gas Trust; and in 1884 he was elected President of the Bay State Gas Company.

Addicks, J. E. O.—Continued

John Edward O'Sullivan Addicks was born at Philadelphia, Pa., on November 21, 1841, and died at New York City, on August 7, 1919.

¹ *Dictionary of American Biography,* ed. by Allen Johnson (Charles Scribner's Sons, New York, 1928) vol. 1, p. 104.

Admiral. See Hoffman, Michael

Admiral of the Trinity. See Hatfield, B. M.

Advance Agent of Emancipation. See Mott, Lucretia

Advertiser. See Barton, Bruce

Advertising King. See Barton, Bruce

Affidavit Boies. See Boies, Horace

African Astronomer. See Banneker, Benjamin

African Roscius. See Aldridge, Ira

Agricultural and Mechanical College (Magnolia, Arkansas)

The nickname, the *Muleriders,*¹ has been applied to the athletes on the teams of the Agricultural and Mechanical College, at Magnolia, Ark. When the college was founded, about 1810, there were few roads and fewer athletic teams in the vicinity. The boys, most of whom worked on the school farm, stopped their work at noon each Saturday and frequently scheduled baseball games with teams from the surrounding communities. The students rode the school farm mules to the games so they were nicknamed the *Muleriders.*

¹ A letter from Sage McLean, Director of Athletics at the Agricultural and Mechanical College, Magnolia, Ark., June 14, 1935.

Agricultural and Mechanical College (Monticello, Arkansas)

The athletic teams of the Agricultural and Mechanical College, at Monticello, Ark., were designated the *Boll Weevils,*¹ about 1912 or 1913 by rival athletic teams. The boll weevil was at that time just beginning

to come to the Arkansas cotton fields. At first the teams resented the name but in 1914 the student body adopted it as their official nickname. They also named their college annual the *Boll Weevil.*

¹ A communication from Frank Horsfall, President of the Agricultural and Mechanical College, Monticello, Ark., November 17, 1935.

Agricultural Jones. See Jones, Marvin

Agricultural Moses. See Tillman, B. R.

Ain't Gonna Rain No Mo Man. See Lee, E. D.

Airdales. See Lincoln Memorial University

Airplane Ears. See Anderson, J. Z.

Ajax. See Aven, A. J.

Akron, Ohio

Akron has three sobriquets, the *Rubber Capital of the United States, Summit City,* and the *Tire City of the United States.* It is nicknamed the *Rubber Capital of the United States* ¹ because of its extensive rubber manufacturing industries. Akron surpasses all other American cities in its production of manufactured rubber goods. The sobriquet, *Summit City* ² originated in the fact that the Greek word ἄκρον, from which the name Akron is derived, signifies a mountaintop, and that Akron is located upon the hilly crest of the water-shed between the Ohio River and Lake Erie, one of the highest spots in the state. The *Tire City of the United States* ³ is appropriate because this city is outstanding in the manufacture of automobile tires.

¹ *Our World To-day: A Textbook in the New Geography,* De Forest Stull and Roy W. Hatch (Allyn and Bacon, New York and Boston, 1932) p. 605.
Industrial and Commercial Geography, New Edition, J. Russell Smith (Henry Holt and Company, New York, 1930) p. 585.
Industrial Geography, Production, Manufacture, Commerce, Ray Hughes Whitbeck (American Book Company, New York and Boston, 1931) p. 571.
A Book of Nicknames, John Goff (Courier-Journal Job Printing Company, Louisville, Ky., 1892) p. 17.
² *History of Summit County, with an Outline Sketch of Ohio,* ed. by William Henry Perrin (Baskin and Battey, Historical Publishers, Chicago, 1881) p. 330.
A Greek-English Lexicon, Eighth Edition, comp. by Henry George Liddell and Robert Scott (American Book Company, New York, 1882) p. 53.
³ *The Earth and Its People: Our State and Continent,* Wallace W. Atwood and Helen Goss Thomas, with the collaboration of Marion B. Forsythe (Ginn and Company, Boston, 1929) p. 196.

Alabama

Alabama is the possessor of four nicknames: the *Cotton Plantation State, Cotton State, Heart of the New Industrial South, Lizard State,* and the *Yellowhammer State.* Alabama is called the *Cotton Plantation State* and the *Cotton State* just as the other cotton-producing states generally in the South are referred to under the name of Cottonia and Cottondom.[1] Alabama was nicknamed the *Heart of the New Industrial South*[2] because of its great industrial importance. During earlier times lizards were numerous along Alabama streams, hence the state came to be called the *Lizard State.*[3] The *Yellowhammer State*[4] became a nickname of Alabama during the War between the States because the gray uniforms of the Confederate soldiers, having been home-dyed, had a yellowish tinge.

[1] *More About Names,* Leopold Wagner (T. Fisher Unwin, London, 1893) p. 28.
[2] *Compton's Pictured Encyclopedia.* (F. E. Compton, vol. 1, p. 96.
[3] *U. S.: An Index to the United States of America,* comp. by Malcolm Townsend (D. Lothrop Company, Boston, 1890) p. 75.
[4] A letter from Marie B. Owen, Director of the Department of State Archives and History, Montgomery, Ala., March 18, 1930.

Alabama on Wheels

In 1888 Reuben F. Kolb, then commissioner of agriculture and the leader of the Farmer's Alliance in Alabama, through the courtesy of the Louisville and Nashville Railroad, exhibited what was popularly called *Alabama on Wheels,*[1] that is, a special railroad car equipped with specimens or reproductions of the numerous natural resources found in the state and exhibitions particularly of the agricultural products of Alabama. *Alabama on Wheels* was shown throughout the central, western, and north-western sections of the United States.

[1] *History of Alabama and Her People,* Albert Burton Moore, assisted by an advisory council (The American Historical Society, New York and Chicago, 1927) vol. 1, p. 677.

Alabamians

The Alabamians are called *Lizards* and *Yellowhammers* for the same reasons that the state was called the *Lizard State* and the *Yellowhammer State. See* Alabama.

Alamo

The Alamo, the historic garrison located at San Antonio, Texas, is nicknamed the *Thermopylae of America*[1] because it was here that Lieutenant Colonel William Barret Travis, James Bowie, Davy Crockett, and one hundred and eighty-three others withstood the attacks of the Mexican forces under the command of General Santa Anna from February 23 until March 6, 1836. It has been estimated that the Mexican forces numbered four to six thousand men. The six surviving Texans were murdered by the Mexican soldiers after they had captured the garrison.

[1] *World Book Encyclopedia.* (Quarrie Corporation, Chicago, 1938) vol. 1, p. 165.

Alameda County. See Gold Medal County

Alamo City. See San Antonio, Tex.

Alaska

In 1867, when Alaska was sold to the United States by Russia, the majority of Americans, considering it an unprofitable business deal, gave to the newly acquired territory the derisive nicknames, *America's Ice Box,*[1] *Frozen Wilderness*[2] and *Seward's Ice Box*[1] because people believed that the region was covered with snow and ice the year around. It was called *Seward's Folly*[1] and *Johnson's Polar Bear Garden*[1] because William H. Seward was the Secretary of State and Andrew Johnson President when the purchase was made.

[1] *Reminiscences of a War-time Statesman and Diplomat, 1830-1915,* Frederick W. Seward (G. P. Putnam's Sons, New York, 1916) p. 201, 363.
[2] *The Growth of the American People and Nation,* Mary G. Kelty (Ginn, Boston, 1931) p. 200.

Albany, New York

The *Edinburgh of America*[1] is a sobriquet given to Albany because it is similar to Edinburgh, Scotland, in regard to its location, its public buildings, its numerous educational institutions, private, public, and parochial, and its general interest in literary accomplishments.

[1] *More About Names,* Leopold Wagner (T. Fisher Unwin, London, 1893) p. 246.
History of Albany County, New York: Bi-Centennial History of Albany: History of the County of Albany, New York, from 1609-1886, with Portraits, Biographies, and Illustrations, George Rogers Howell and Jonathan Tenny (W. W. Munsell and Company, New York, 1886) p. 677-8, 679-702, 739, 742-5.

Albany Beef

The sturgeon which abounds in the Hudson river and is eaten to a great extent in Albany, N. Y., is humorously termed *Albany*

Albany Beef—Continued

Beef.[1] It is said to resemble beef in texture and appearance.

[1] *A Dictionary of Americanisms,* Fourth Edition, John Russell Bartlett (Little, Brown and Company, Boston, 1877) p. 6.

Albion College

The athletic teams of Albion College, at Albion, Mich., are called the *Britons.* Albion is a poetic name for England, the inhabitants of which are called Britons.

Alcatraz Federal Prison

The *Rock*[1] and *America's Devil's Island*[2] are the nicknames commonly applied to Alcatraz Federal Prison, on Alcatraz Island, a twelve-acre rock in San Francisco Bay four miles north of San Francisco, California. These sobriquets were applied to the prison because it is on a rock and because of the strict discipline and the vigilant guarding of those imprisoned there.

Alcatraz Island is comparable to Devil's Island, a small island in the Atlantic Ocean off the coast of French Guiana, South America, used by the French as a penal settlement because of the difficulty of escape. Alcatraz Island rises one hundred and thirty feet above the level of the water. Upon it is situated one of the most powerful lighthouses on the Pacific Coast.

[1] *Times-Herald,* Washington, D.C., June 8, 1939. p. 10.

[2] *Washington Herald,* October 15, 1933. p. 9.

Alcott, Amos Bronson

Amos Bronson Alcott was nicknamed the *Sage of Concord*[1] because he was a learned scholar who attained prominence as a philosopher and educator, and lived at Concord, Mass. He was born at Wolcott, Conn., on November 29, 1799, and died at Boston, Mass., on March 4, 1888.

[1] *A Woman of the Century: Fourteen Hundred Seventy Biographical Sketches Accompanied by Portraits of Leading American Women in All Walks of Life,* ed. by Frances E. Willard and Mary A. Livermore (Charles Wells Moulton, New York and Chicago, 1893) p. 12.

Alden, Henry Mills

Henry Mills Alden, an editor and author, was nicknamed *Metaphysics*[1] while he was a student at Williams College, at Williamstown, Mass., in 1857, because of his absorbing interest in philosophy, religion, and literature.

Henry Mills Alden was born at Mt. Tabor, Vt., on November 11, 1836, and died at New York City, on October 7, 1919.

[1] *Dictionary of American Biography,* ed. by Allen Johnson (Scribner's, New York, 1928) vol. 1 p. 144.

Aldrich, Louis

Louis Aldrich, an actor, was nicknamed the *Ohio Roscius*[1] because, while he was still a boy, he played with great success the part of Richard III in Shakespeare's drama. He was compared to Roscius, a Roman slave who early in life took up the profession of acting, and was so successful that he made his master a wealthy man, and later accumulated money enough to purchase his own freedom. Roscius was born at Colonium, near Lanuvium, Rome, in 134 B.C., and died about 61 B.C.

Louis Aldrich was born at sea on October 1, 1843, while his mother was on her way from Germany to the United States. He was later adopted by a family living at Cincinnati, Ohio, and died in Kennebunkport, Me., on June 17, 1901.

[1] *Dictionary of American Biography,* ed. by Allen Johnson (Scribner's, New York, 1928) vol. 1, p. 151.

Aldridge, Ira

Ira Aldridge, a Negro tragedian, was nicknamed the *African Roscius*[1] because like Roscius, the Roman slave actor, his success on the stage was most extraordinary.

Some biographers say that Aldridge was a mulatto who was born in Baltimore; that he was first apprenticed to a ship-carpenter and later accompanied the actor Edmund Kean to England as his servant. While there he developed a remarkable liking for the stage.

Others say that he was born in New York City and that his father was a native chieftain of Senegal in West Africa who came to the United States, was converted to Christianity and became the pastor of a Negro church in New York City. He wanted his son to follow the same profession and sent him to England to be educated for the ministry. After Aldridge had spent some time in training for this profession, his desire to become an actor caused him to abandon his ministerial training. After studying to become an actor, Aldridge appeared as Othello at the Covent Garden Theatre in London where he achieved immediate success. He proved to be one of the best interpreters of Shakespeare's plays.

Roscius was a Roman slave who early in life took up the profession of acting, was so successful that he made his master a wealthy man, and later accumulated money enough to buy his own freedom. Roscius was born at Colonium, near Lanuvium, Rome, in 134, B.C. and died about 61 B.C.

Ira Aldridge was born probably at Bellair, near Baltimore, Md., about 1810, and died at Lodz, Poland, on August 7, 1867.

[1] *Appleton's Cyclopaedia of American Biography*, ed. by James Grant Wilson and John Fiske (D. Appleton, New York, 1895) vol. 1, p. 44.

Alexander, Charles W.
Charles W. Alexander, who lived at Fort Laramie, Wyo., about 1876, was nicknamed *Wild Horse Charlie* because he earned his living by catching and breaking mustang horses.

Alexander, Grover Cleveland
Grover Cleveland Alexander, who was born at Saint Paul, Neb., on February 26, 1887, and who was a pitcher in the National League for twenty years was nicknamed *Pete*.[1]

[1] *Who's Who in Major League Base Ball*, comp. by Harold (Speed) Johnson (Buxton Publishing Company, Chicago, 1933) p. 482.

Alexander the Coppersmith. See Hamilton, Alexander

Alexander the Great. See Williams, Alex

Alfalfa Bill. See Murray, W. H.

Alfalfa Joe. See Wing, J. E.

Alfred University
The athletic teams of Alfred University, located at Alfred, N.Y., were nicknamed the *Saxons*[1] and the *Saxon Warriors* about 1922 because "the University was named after Alfred, King of the West Saxons." It is the only American "institution of higher learning named after him."

[1] A communication from J. Nelson Norwood, President of Alfred University, Alfred, N.Y., November 23, 1935.

Alger, Horatio
Horatio Alger was nicknamed *Holy Horatio*[1] while he was a boy because his father, the Reverend Horatio Alger, a strict Unitarian clergyman, reared him in such a conscientious religious manner that young Alger was a facsimile of his father morally and religiously.

Horatio Alger was born at Revere, Mass., on January 13, 1834, and died at the home of his sister at Natick, Mass., on July 18, 1899.

[1] *Dictionary of American Biography*, ed. by Allen Johnson (Scribner's, New York, 1928) vol. 1, p. 178.

All American Division. See Eighty-second Airborne Division of World War II

All Eyes. See Webster, Daniel

Alleghany Johnson. See Johnson, Edward

Allegheny College
The athletic teams of Allegheny College, at Meadville, Pa., are nicknamed the *Alligators*[1] and the *Gators*. The sobriquets were chosen by the college students.

[1] A communication from J. R. Schultz, Professor of English at Allegheny College, Meadville, Pa., May 14, 1935.

Allen, Ethan
Ethan Allen has been called the *Robin Hood of the Forest*[1] because he so fearlessly led the frontier soldiers from the Green Mountains of Vermont into the forests between the Green Mountains and Lake Champlain to fight the British troops at Fort Ticonderoga in 1775. Allen led his soldiers much in the fashion that Robin Hood led his band of foresters. Ethan Allen was born at Litchfield, Conn., on January 10, 1737, and died at Burlington, Vt. on February 13, 1789.

[1] *The Makers of America*, New Edition; Revised and Enlarged, James A. Woodburn and Thomas F. Moran (Longmans, Green and Company, New York and Boston, 1922) p. 60.

Allen, Ira
Ira Allen has been nicknamed the *Founder of Vermont*[1] because of his outstanding services in founding the state, his unselfish interests in guiding its early activities, and his marked influence upon its subsequent development.

Having removed to the Vermont Territory in 1772,[2] Allen actively aided the New Hampshire grantees in this territory in maintaining their grants. In 1777 he was

Allen, Ira—Continued

a leader in the convention which met at Windsor to draw up the constitution of the state, and wrote the preamble to this document. After the adoption of this constitution in 1777, Allen became a member of the Governor's Council, and in 1778 he became the first Secretary of State of Vermont. Later he became the Treasurer and Surveyor General of Vermont.

In 1789 Ira Allen aided in organizing the University of Vermont. He served as a delegate to the territorial convention which approved the Constitution of the United States prior to the admission of Vermont to the Union in February 1791.

Ira Allen was born at Cornwall, Conn., on May 1, 1751, and died at Philadelphia, Pa., on January 15, 1814.

[1] *Ira Allen, Founder of Vermont, 1751-1814*, James Benjamin Wilbur (Houghton Mifflin Company, New York and Boston, 1928) vol. 1, p. 1.
[2] *Dictionary of American Biography under the Auspices of the American Council of Learned Societies*, ed. by Allen Johnson (Charles Scribner's Sons, New York, 1928) vol. 1, p. 194-5.
"Life, Character and Times of Ira Allen" by Daniel P. Thompson, in *Proceedings of the Vermont Historical Society for the Years 1908-1909* (Published by the Society at Montpelier, Vt., 1909) p. 87-172.

Allen, John Mills

The nickname *Private John* [1] was given to John Mills Allen while he was serving as Representative from Mississippi in the United States Congress from 1885 to 1901. Shortly after his election to Congress in 1885, Representative Allen remarked in a speech before the House that during the Civil War he was "the only private in the Confederate Army." This statement created a great deal of merriment among his colleagues. It is a national joke that all of the southerners who served in the Confederate Army became officers. *Private John,* as he was thereafter called, served throughout the Civil War.

John Mills Allen was born in Tishomingo County, Miss., on July 8, 1846, and died at Tupelo, Miss., on October 30, 1917.

[1] *The Book of Birmingham,* John R. Hornady (Dodd, Mead, New York, 1921) p. 339.

Allen, Thomas

The Reverend Thomas Allen was nicknamed the *Fighting Parson* [1] and the *Fighting Parson of Bennington Fields,*[2] because of the courageous manner in which he led his band of volunteer soldiers from Pittsfield, Mass., to fight the Battle of Benning-

ton on August 16, 1777. The Reverend Allen was born at Pittsfield, Mass., in 1743 and died there in 1811.

[1] *The Bennington Battle Monument, Its Story and Its Meaning,* John Spargo (Tuttle Company, Rutland, Vt., 1925) p. 48.
[2] *The National Cyclopaedia of American Biography* (James T. White, New York, 1907) vol. 5, p. 318.

Allen, William

The following nicknames were applied to William Allen, who was a Democratic United States Senator from Ohio from 1837 to 1849, *Earthquake Allen,* the *Fog Horn,* the *Ohio Gong, Petticoat Allen,* and *Rise up William Allen.*

Earthquake Allen had its origin in a speech he made before the United States Senate in 1841, in which he opposed the bill proposing the distribution of the money received from the sale of public lands among the various states. In this speech Allen made the statement that such a procedure would bring about an "Earthquake of indignation from one end of the Union to the other." [1]

During his twelve years in the United States Senate, his colleagues called him the *Ohio Gong* [2] and the *Fog Horn* [3] because of his stentorian voice. The *Fog Horn* originated at a Democratic mass meeting where he made himself heard despite the fact that political opponents kept a steam whistle blowing in the vicinity.

William Allen received the sobriquet *Petticoat Allen* [4] during the exciting Log-cabin and Hard-cider Campaign of 1840, at which time he opposed William Henry Harrison, the Whig presidential candidate. In one of his speeches Allen made the statement that an elderly lady had donated a petticoat to be used in the making of Harrison's presidential campaign banner. He further stated that it was an emblem of Harrison's want of spirit in answering the challenges of his political opponents, and of his inability to make known to the people his attitude toward the political issues of the campaign.

In 1874, many years after his withdrawal from politics, the Democrats, hoping that they could induce him to become the candidate for governor, published an editorial concluding with, "Rise up, William Allen." As a result of this editorial, Allen received the nickname, *Rise Up William Allen.* [5] He served as Governor of the State of Ohio from 1874 to 1876.

William Allen was born at Edenton, N.C., in 1806, and died at his estate called Fruit Hill, near Chillicothe, Ohio, on July 11, 1879.

[1] *Appleton's Cyclopaedia of American Biography*, ed. by James Grant Wilson and John Fiske (D. Appleton, New York, 1891) vol. 1, p. 56.
[2] *The Encyclopedia Americana* (Americana Corporation, New York and Chicago, 1927) vol. 1, p. 416.
[3] *A History of Scioto County, Ohio, together with a Pioneer Record of Scioto County*, Nelson W. Evans (Nelson W. Evans, Portsmouth, Ohio, 1903) p. 173.
[4] *Fifty Years on the Old Frontier at Cowboy, Hunter, Guide, Scout, and Ranchman*, James H. Cook (Yale University Press, New Haven, Conn., 1923) p. 124.
[5] *U.S. "Snap Shots": An Independent, National, and Memorial Encyclopedia . . .: A Gazetteer of National Industries . . . National and State Politics, Parties and Statesmen, Interesting Reminiscences, Anecdotes, Songs, . . . of Famous Campaigns, . . . Chronicle Outline of American History from 986 to 1892, with a Description of the World's Columbian Exposition, Facts about Presidents and Biographical Stories, Anecdotes, and Reminiscences of the . . . Nominees of the Republican and Democratic Parties*, . . . Oliver McKee (A. M. Thayer, Boston, Mass., 1892) p. 244-6.

Allen, William Franklin
William Franklin Allen, a Representative from Delaware to the United States Congress from 1937 to 1939, was nicknamed *Lovebird Allen* [1] by his colleagues in the national House of Representatives because he so frequently said, "I love my country, I love my people," and other similar expressions.

William Franklin Allen was born at Bridgeville, Del., on January 19, 1883, and died at Lewes, Del., on June 14, 1946.

[1] An interview with Captain Victor Hunt Harding, Secretary of the National Democratic Congress Reelection Committee, Washington, D.C., April 10, 1939.

Allen, William Vincent
William Vincent Allen, a Populist Senator from Nebraska from 1893 to 1901, was nicknamed the *Intellectual Giant of Populism* [1] because, while he was in the United States Senate he demonstrated such mental ability in his senatorial career and in his filibuster against the repeal of the Sherman Silver Purchase Act.

William Vincent Allen was born at Midway, Ohio, on January 28, 1847, and died at Madison, Neb., on January 12, 1924.

[1] *Dictionary of American Biography*, ed. by Allen Johnson (Scribner's, New York, 1928) vol. 1, p. 214.

Allerton, Isaac
Isaac Allerton was designated the *Father of New England Commerce*,[1] because for many years after he moved to New Haven, Conn., in 1646, he and his son Isaac carried on an extensive trade with Boston, New Amsterdam, towns along the Delaware Bay, towns in Virginia, and those on the Barbados Islands. He came to be looked upon as the founder and the promoter of the commerce which the New England States now engage in so extensively. Allerton was born in England, about 1583, and died at New Haven, Conn., on February 12, 1659.

[1] *The National Cyclopaedia of American Biography* (James T. White, New York, 1929) vol. 6, p. 105.

Allgood, Miles Clayton
Miles Clayton Allgood is popularly called *Simon* [1] because his surname Allgood is synonymous with the expression "simon pure." Allgood was born at Allgood, Ala., on February 22, 1872. He served as Representative from Alabama to the United States Congress from 1923 to 1935.

[1] *The Washington Post Magazine.* Washington, D.C. March 4, 1934. p. 4.

Alligator State. See Florida

Alligators. See Allegheny College; Floridians, University of Florida

Alline, Henry
Henry Alline was nicknamed the *Whitfield of Nova Scotia* [1] because his success as an itinerant preacher in Nova Scotia was comparable to that of George Whitfield, the great Methodist Evangelist, who assisted Charles Wesley in his religious activities both in England and in the United States. At the age of twelve, Alline emigrated from New England to Nova Scotia where he spent his life as an itinerant preacher and religious leader.

Henry Alline was born at Newport, R.I., on June 14, 1748, and died at North Hampton, N.H., on February 2, 1784, while visiting friends there.

[1] *Dictionary of American Biography*, ed. by Allen Johnson (Scribner's, New York, 1928) vol. 1, p. 219.

Allotters
John Winthrop, Governor of the Massachusetts and the Plymouth Colonies, and six other persons, in November 1634, were nicknamed the *Allotters* [1] because they were empowered by the court to divide and dispose of the lands in Boston which were not in the possession of any person in particular, and to leave as much of this land for future comers as they might deem necessary.

[1] *Warning Out in New England, 1656-1817*, Josiah Henry Benton (W. B. Clarke Company, Boston, 1911) p. 19.

Allston, Washington

Washington Allston was nicknamed the *American Titian* [1] because his paintings were characterized by a marked imaginative power, and because he was unusually talented as a colorist, in which respect he was comparable to Tiziano Vecellio or Titian, the great Venetian painter, who was one of the world's most renowned colorists.

Washington Allston was born at Waccamaw, S.C., on November 5, 1779, and died at Cambridge, Mass., on July 9, 1843.

[1] *The National Cyclopaedia of American Biography* (James T. White and Company, New York, 1907) vol. 5, p. 383.

Alma College

The *Scots* is the nickname of the athletic teams of Alma College, at Alma, Mich. It was selected by means of a contest conducted by *The Almanian*, the student weekly publication, in November 1931. Alma College is a Presbyterian school and most of the faculty and student body are of Scotch descent which doubtless influenced the selection of the nickname.[1]

[1] A communication from Ward Campbell, Athletic Coach at Alma College, Alma, Mich., June 18, 1935.

Alphabet Soup. See *ABC's of the New Deal*

Alpine, Texas

Alpine is called the *Roof Garden of Texas* [1] because it is located in Brewster County amidst natural scenic beauty said to be comparable to that of the Alps in Italy.

[1] *Texas As It Is Today,* Alfred E. Menn (Gammel's Book Store, Austin, Tex., 1925) p. 53.

Alton, Illinois

The *City That Came Back* and *Tusselburgh* are the nicknames applied to Alton. It has been called the *City That Came Back* [1] because, after its incorporation in 1833, it allowed other cities to push ahead of it for about fifty years, but since that time it has forged to the front among other modern American cities. *Tusselburgh* [2] is a nickname also given to Alton.

[1] *Alton, Illinois: A Graphic Sketch of a Picturesque and Busy City, Its Leading Points of Interest and Some Characteristic Phases of Its Life* (James Allan Reid, Book Maker, Saint Louis, Mo., and Alton, Ill., 1912) p. 9.
[2] *A Book of Nicknames,* John Goff (Courier-Journal Job Printing Company, Louisville, Ky., 1892) p. 15.

Ambassador of Good Will. See Rogers, Will

Ambassador of the Air. See Lindbergh, C. A.

Ambulance Brigade

When, in 1862, the One Hundred and Thirty-seventh Infantry of New York Volunteers found it necessary to move their place of encampment from Fairfax Station, Va., to another part of the general encampment, there were so many sick men in the regiment that the ambulances were kept busy moving them. Because of this fact the Forty-ninth Regiment, also encamped at Fairfax Station, nicknamed them the *Ambulance Brigade.*[1]

[1] *Memoirs of the 149th Regiment of the New York Volunteer Infantry,* Captain George Knapp Collins (Published by the author, Syracuse, N.Y., 1891) p. 74.

Amen Corner

The *Amen Corner* [1] was applied to a part of the main corridor in the Fifth Avenue Hotel in New York City. From 1859 until 1908 the *Amen Corner* served as a meeting place for the managers of the Republican party to discuss party plans and platforms. The origin of this nickname was credited to W. J. Chamberlain, a reporter for the *New York Sun* who applied the term, the *Amen Corner*, to this meeting place.

The *Amen Corner* in churches is near the altar where the devout sit and say "Amen" to denote approval.

[1] *The Autobiography of Thomas Collier Platt,* comp. and ed. by Louis J. Lang (B. W. Dodge and Company, New York, 1910) p. 487, 492-4.

Amendment-monger. See Adams, Samuel

Ameners

The *Ameners* [1] is a term applied to those people who participated in the meetings formerly held in a corridor at the Fifth Avenue Hotel in New York City. See *Amen Corner.*

[1] *The Autobiography of Thomas Collier Platt,* comp. and ed. by Louis J. Lang (B. W. Dodge and Company, New York, 1910) p. 489.

American Addison. See Dennie, Joseph

American Athens. See Boston, Mass.

American Bernhardt. See Carter, Mrs. Leslie

American Blackstone. See Tucker, S. G.

American Caesar. See Grant, U. S.

American Cato. See Adams, Samuel

American Chesterfield. See Riker, Richard

American Cicero. See Berrien, J. M.; Lee, R. H.

American Cossacks
During the period of strikes and labor troubles in the United States, which culminated in the great Pullman strike in 1906, as a means of insuring order the national guard of Pennsylvania and several other states were organized into units of mounted constabulary. These mounted officers were promptly nicknamed the *American Cossacks* [1] by the supporters of labor unions.

[1] "The Armies of Labor, a Chronicle of the Organized Wage-earners", by Samuel P. Orth, in *The Chronicles of America Series*, Abraham Lincoln Edition, Allen Johnson, editor (Yale University Press, New Haven, Conn. 1919) vol. 40, p. 254.

American Cruikshank. See Johnston, D. C.

American Devil. See McDougal, D. S.

American Fabius. See Washington, George

American Goldsmith. See Irving, Washington

American Hemans. See Sigourney, L. H.

American Howard. See Eddy, Thomas

American International College
The *Amerks*, the *Internats*, and the *Yellow Jackets* [1] are the nicknames which have been given to the athletic teams of the American International College, located at Springfield, Mass. The *Amerks*, the least widely used of the three nicknames, was originated by the sports writers for the New York and the Boston newspapers about 1933 or 1934.

The *Internats* is widely used by the athletic teams. This nickname was originated by sports writers.

The *Yellow Jackets* was first applied to the basketball teams in 1933 or 1934 by Dick Good, a sports writer for the *Springfield Evening Union*, because at that time the members of the teams wore solid yellow jerseys.

[1] A letter from W. G. McGown, Faculty Adviser of Athletics at the American International College, Springfield, Mass., November 20, 1935.

American Kipling. See London, Jack

American Louis Philippe. See Fillmore, Millard

American Maupassant. See Porter, W. S.

American Meissonier. See Watrous, H. W.

American Nehemiah. See Winthrop, John

American Nile
The Saint Johns River which flows from Lake Helen Blazes through northeast Florida to the Atlantic Ocean, a distance of approximately three hundred and fifty miles, has been called the *American Nile* [1] because it has its source in a lake and along its banks grow reeds and tropical vegetation not unlike the Egyptian Nile.

[1] *The World Book Encyclopedia* (W. F. Quarrie and Company, Chicago, 1929) vol. 6, p. 2477.

American Party. See Know-nothing party; Know ye party

American Pitt. See Stevens, Thaddeus

American Prodigy. See Sauvolle, Le Moine

American Professor. See Felton, C. C.

American Sappho. See Morton, S. W. A.

American Scott. See Cooper, J. F.

American Titian. See Allston, Washington

American Woodman. See Audubon, J. J. F.

American Wordsworth. See Bryant, W. C.

America's Bermuda. See New Shoreham or Block Island

America's Devil's Island. See Alcatraz Federal Prison

America's First Citizen. See Eliot, C. W.

America's Great Winter Garden

The Imperial Valley in Southern California is popularly called *America's Great Winter Garden* [1] because during the winter months it produces large quantities of vegetables and fruits which are distributed throughout the United States and in Canada.

[1] *California of the South, a History,* John Stevens McGroarty (S. J. Clarke Publishing Company, Chicago and Los Angeles, 1933) vol. 1, p. 490.

America's Ice Box. See Alaska

America's Most Historic City. See Charleston, S. C.; Fredericksburg, Va.; Petersburg, Va.

America's One-man Newspaper. See Winchell, Walter

America's Premier Air Woman. See Putnam, A. E.

America's Sweetheart. See Pickford, Mary

Amerks. See American International College

Amherst College

About 1910 sports writers began to apply the nicknames *Lord Jeffs* and *The Sabrinas* [1] to the athletic teams of Amherst College, at Amherst, Mass. *Lord Jeffs* is an abbreviated form of the name Lord Jeffery Amherst, a British hero in the French and Indian Wars, after whom the town of Amherst was named. *The Sabrinas* is derived from Sabrina, a British river goddess, a statue of whom was for many years a college mascot and the object of interclass rivalries.

[1] A letter from Walter A. Dyer, Director of the Amherst College Press, Amherst, Mass., June 22, 1935.

Ammonia King. See Mallinckrodt, Edward

Ananias Club

This name was used by Theodore Roosevelt to describe a hypothetical club of newspaper men who published information given them in confidence.

In 1899, after Theodore Roosevelt had been inaugurated as Governor of New York State, he told the newspaper men that he would discuss with them his views or plans regarding his future political activities. However, he said that some parts of the information he would give them he would not want made public, and that if they insisted on printing such information, he would promptly deny its truthfulness. This policy Roosevelt continued after he became President of the United States, not only with newspaper men, but also with members of Congress and others whom he saw fit to take into his confidence. [1]

Ananias was a biblical character who attempted to deceive the Apostle Peter. Ananias and his wife, Sapphira, sold a possession and withheld a part of the money they had received for it and lied about it.

[1] *People and Politics, Observed by a Massachusetts Editor,* Solomon Bulkley Griffin (Little, Brown and Company, Boston, 1923) p. 399.
 Recent History of the United States, 1865-1929, Revised and Enlarged Edition, Frederic L. Paxson (Houghton Mifflin Company, Boston, 1929) p. 373.

Ancient. See Lincoln, Abraham

Ancient Dominion. See Virginia

Anderson, George Thomas

Brigadier General George Thomas Anderson was popularly nicknamed *Old Tige.* [1] This name originated during the Civil War because he fought with the ferocity, tenacity, and fearlessness of a tiger.

George Thomas Anderson was born at Covington, Ga., on February 3, 1824, and died at Anniston, Ala., on April 4, 1901.

[1] *The National Cyclopaedia of American Biography* (James T. White and Company, New York, 1906) vol. 13, p. 247.

Anderson, James

James Anderson, a pioneer who settled on the Red River near Fargo, N.D., about 1859, was called *Robinson Crusoe Anderson* [1] because like Robinson Crusoe he was the only person living there.

[1] *North Dakota, History and People: Outlines of American History,* Colonel Clement A. Lounsberry (S. J. Clarke Publishing Company, Chicago, 1917) vol. 1, p. 229-30.

Anderson, John Z.

John Z. Anderson, a politician, was nicknamed *Airplane Ears* [1] by his fellow members in the national House of Representatives because he has large ears.

John Z. Anderson was born at Oakland, Calif., on March 22, 1904.

[1] An interview with Captain Victor Harding, Secretary of the National Democratic Congress Reelection Committee, Washington, D.C., April 10, 1939.

Anderson, Richard Heron

Lieutenant General Richard Heron Anderson, a prominent Confederate soldier, was known as *Fighting Dick.* [1] This nickname was given to Anderson at the Battle of Fair Oaks or Seven Pines, which occurred near Richmond, Va., on May 31 and June 1, 1862, when he was in charge of several brigades under Lieutenant General James Longstreet. During the battle Anderson was outstandingly gallant and so successful in inspiring his soldiers that he was favorably commended by Longstreet, and acclaimed by the soldiers as their *Fighting Dick.*

Richard Heron Anderson was born at Statesburg, S.C., on October 7, 1821, and died at Beaufort, S.C., on June 25, 1879.

[1] *The Life of Lieutenant-General Richard Heron Anderson of the Confederate States Army,* Cornelius I. Walker (Art Publishing Company, Charleston, S.C., 1917) p. 77, 268.

Andrews, Ivy Paul

Ivy Paul Andrews, who was born at Dora, Ala., on May 6, 1908, and was a pitcher in major league baseball, was nicknamed *Poison Ivy.* [1]

[1] *Who's Who in Major League Base Ball,* comp. by Harold (Speed) Johnson (Buxton Publishing Company, Chicago, 1933) p. 67.

Angel of the Battlefield. See Barton, Clara

Angel of the Prisons. See Tutwiler, J. S.

Angels. See Eleventh Airborne Division of World War II

Angels of the Battlefield

The members of the Catholic sisterhood, such as the Sisters of Charity, the Sisters of Mercy, the Sisters of St. Joseph, and the Sisters of the Holy Cross, who served as nurses during the Civil War, were generally described by the soldiers as the *Angels of the Battlefield* [1] because they administered to the needs of the wounded soldiers.

[1] *Angels of the Batlefield: A History of the Labors of the Catholic Sisterhoods in the Late Civil War,* George Barton (The Catholic Art Publishing Company, Philadelphia, 1897) p. 17.

Ann the Word. See Lee, Ann

Anniston, Alabama

Anniston is often called the *Brooklyn of the South,* the *City of Churches,* and the *Magic City.* It has been designated the *Brooklyn of the South,* or the *City of Churches,* [1] because, like Brooklyn, it has such a vast number of churches. The rapid increase in the populataon of Anniston from 1880 to 1890 caused it to be nicknamed the *Magic City.* [2] During this decade the population increased from about nine hundred and fifty to approximately ten thousand.

[1] *History of Alabama and Dictionary of Alabama Biography,* Thomas McAdory Owen (S. J. Clarke Publishing Company, Chicago, 1921) vol. 1, p. 48.
[2] *Alabama of To-day, 1904: An Industrial Review of the General Business Interests of Birmingham and the Cities and Towns Comprising the Great State of Alabama* (Published by Post B—Alabama Division Travelers Protective Association of America, Birmingham, Ala., 1905) p. 62.
History of Alabama and Dictionary of Alabama Biography, Thomas McAdory Owen (S. J. Clarke Publishing Company, Chicago, 1921) vol. 1, p. 48.

Antelope State. See Nebraska

Anthony, John Alston

John Alston Anthony was widely known as *Shelby's Man of Faith.* [1] Anthony was elected Superintendent of Schools at Shelby, N.C., about 1900, and he served for about twenty years. Despite limited funds and equipment, Anthony was competent in dealing with the problems of school administration and displayed confidence in the character of the school boys and girls. He was nicknamed *Shelby's Man of Faith.*

John Alston Anthony was born at York, S.C., on October 23, 1854, and died at Shelby, N.C., on March 23, 1927.

[1] *Encyclopedia of American Biography: American Biography, a New Cyclopedia,* (Published under the direction of The American Historical Society, Inc., New York, 1933) vol. 52, p. 216-17.

Anti-chain-store Patman. See Patman, Wright

Anti-expansionists. See *Anti-imperialists*

Anti-federal Junto

When the Constitution of the United States was submitted to the people for their approval on September 8, 1787, to the surprise of his Anti-federal colleagues, George Clymer, a delegate who had been sent to the Federal Convention at Philadelphia, Pa., arose and moved that the Pennsylvania State Convention give consideration to the adoption of the Constitution. He had given no notice of the fact that he had expected to bring the matter up then; the Constitution was adopted by a vote of forty-three to nineteen. At four o'clock, when the House reassembled, only forty-five members were present. This number did not constitute a quorum so the sergeant-at-arms was sent out to find the missing members. They were found at the home of a Mr. Boyd, but firmly refused to return to the House; consequently, they have come to be known as the *Anti-federal Junto.*[1]

[1] *A History of the People of the United States, from the Revolution to the Civil War,* John Bach McMaster (D. Appleton and Company, New York, 1883) vol. 1, p. 460.

Anti-imperialists

The *Anti-imperialists*[1] were those people who were opposed to President McKinley's plan to "extend the military rule of the United States over the whole of the Philippine Islands" in 1899. They termed him an emperor or imperialist because they believed he would force American rule regardless of what the Filipino people wanted. They were also opposed to the annexation of the Philippines and were therefore called *Anti-expansionists.*

[1] *Twenty Years of the Republic, 1885-1905,* Harry Thurston Peck (Dodd, Mead and Company, New York, 1907) p. 611.

Anti-McFarlane. See McFarlane, W. D.

Anti-slickers

Anti-slickers[1] was a nickname given to an organization perfected about 1845 in St. Charles County, Mo., to oppose the *Slickers* of Lincoln County and counteract the work that they were doing there. The *Slickers* were a group of men who organized to rid the county of horse thieves and counterfeiters. Offenders were "slicked down" and given a certain number of hours in which to leave the county.

[1] *Centennial History of Missouri (The Center State) One Hundred Years in the Union, 1820-1921,* Walter B. Stevens (S. J. Clarke Publishing Company, St. Louis, Mo. and Chicago, 1921) vol. 2, p. 240.

Anti-snappers

Anti-snappers[1] were a group of Democrats who would take no part in a snap convention fostered by David B. Hill, the governor of New York, in 1892 for the purpose of preventing Grover Cleveland from being nominated the Democratic candidate for President of the United States.

[1] *Twenty Years of the Republic, 1885-1905,* Harry Thurston Peck (Dodd, Mead and Company, New York, 1907) p. 280-1.

Anti-war Knutson. See Knutson, Harold

Apache State. See Arizona

Apostle of Accomac. See Makemie, Francis

Apostle of California. See De Salvatierra, J. M.

Apostle of Disunion. See Julian, G. W.

Apostle of Free Coinage for Silver. See St. John, W. P.

Apostle of Light and Power. See Lieb, J. W.

Apostle of Methodism. See Lee, Jesse

Apostle of Oregon. See Blanchet, F. H.

Apostle of Peace. See Ladd, William

Apostle of Persia. See Perkins, Justin

Apostle of Prohibition. See Hill, W. B.

Apostle of South America. See Fowler, C. H.

Apostle of Sunshine. See Taylor, R. L.

Apostle of Temperance. See Murphy, Francis

Apostle of the Alleghanies. See Gallitzin, D. A.

Apostle of the Indians. See Eliot, John

Apostle of the Rocky Mountains. See De Smet, P. J.

Apostle of the Wilderness. See Breck, J. L.

Apostle to the Germans. See Guldin, J. C.

Apostle to the Sioux Indians. See Hare, W. H.

Apostle to the Slavs. See Schauffler, H. A.

Apple King. See Wellhouse, Frederick

Apple Pie Ridge

The neighborhood adjoining the farm of W. S. Miller near Gerrardstown in Berkeley County, W.Va., is known as *Apple Pie Ridge* [1] because since Miller planted his orchard in 1851 many other orchards have been added until the ridge is outstanding for its apples (for pies, of course).

[1] *History of West Virginia, Old and New*, James Morton Callahan (American Historical Society, Inc., New York and Chicago, 1923) vol. 1, p. 527.

Applejack

Brandy made from the distilled and fermented juices of apples, flavored with peach kernels, was called *Applejack* [1] probably because it was served in a jack—an English measure holding about half a pint. *Applejohn* is a natural variant of *Applejack.*

[1] *A New Dictionary of Americanisms*, Sylva Clapin (Louis Weiss and Company, New York, 1903) p. 22.

Applejohn. See *Applejack.*

Aqueduct City. See Rochester, N. Y.

Arch Priest of Anti-Masonry. See Stevens, Thaddeus

Area Bird

Area Bird [1] is a name applied to a military cadet who is compelled to walk around or over a definite plot or area in punishment for the violation of regulations.

[1] *Unit Projects in Modern Literature* (Educational Press, Inc., Columbus, Ohio) March 1-14, 1935, p. 12.

Argonauts of Eighteen Forty-nine

People who went to California by boat around Cape Horn in 1849 in search of gold were sometimes called the *Argonauts of Eighteen Forty-nine.* [1] According to Greek mythology, the Argonauts led by Jason voyaged to Colchis in search of the golden fleece.

[1] *The National Cyclopaedia of American Biography* (James T. White and Company, New York, 1897) vol. 4, p. 107.

Arizona

Arizona has ten nicknames: the *Apache State*, the *Aztec State*, the *Baby State*, the *Copper State*, the *Grand Canyon State*, the *Italy of America*, the *Sand Hill State*, the *Sunset State* or the *Sunset Land*, and the *Valentine State*. The nickname the *Apache State* [2] was applied to Arizona, doubtless, from the great numbers of Apache Indians originally inhabiting this territory.

Arizona was nicknamed the *Grand Canyon State* [1] because the Grand Canyon of the Colorado River lies mostly in northern Arizona, and the *Copper State* [1] because it produces more copper than any other state in the Union.

Arizona is called the *Aztec State* [3] from the fact that many of the old ruins in the Gila River and the Salt River valleys and in other parts of Arizona have Aztec names, and were erroneously considered to have been built by the Aztecs. The *Baby State* [4] refers to Arizona's being the last state to come into the Union. It was admitted to statehood on February 14, 1912.

Arizona is nicknamed the *Italy of America* [4] because the state is mountainous and contains some of the most beautiful scenic regions of America.

Arizona is designated the *Sand Hill State* [5] from the desert-like appearance of many regions of the state. The nickname the *Sunset State* or the *Sunset Land* [6] was given to Arizona because of her spectacular sunsets, especially those in the Grand Canyon.

Arizona—Continued

Arizona is often called the *Valentine State* [7] "because she was admitted to statehood on February the fourteenth."

[1] *The World Book* (The Quarrie Corporation, Chicago, 1947) vol. 1, p. 394, 401.
[2] *The Encyclopedia Americana* (Americana Corporation, New York and Chicago, 1929) vol. 2, p. 51.
[3] *A Book of Nicknames*, John Goff (Courier-Journal Job Printing Company, Louisville, Ky., 1892) p. 13.
[4] *Arizona, the Youngest State: Arizona, Prehistoric-Aboriginal-Pioneer-Modern, The Nation's Commonwealth within a Land of Ancient Culture*, James H. McClintock (The S. J. Clarke Publishing Company, Chicago, 1916) vol. 1, p. 6, 7.
[5] *The New International Encyclopaedia*, Second Edition (Dodd Mead and Company, New York, 1930) vol. 2, p. 116.
[6] *The Resources of Arizona*, Third Edition, Patrick Hamilton (A. L. Bancroft and Company Printers, San Francisco Calif., 1894) p. 141.
[7] *Our Arizona*, Ida Flood Dodge (Charles Scribner's Sons, New York and Boston, 1929) p. 134.

Arizonians

The only nickname applied to the residents of the State of Arizona is *Sand Cutters,* [1] because of the sand on the plains.

[1] *A Book of Nicknames*, John Goff (Courier-Journal Job Printing Company, Louisville, Ky., 1892) p. 19.

Arkansans

The people of Arkansas were formerly called *Toothpicks* [1] because outsiders alleged that the early settlers used their bowie knives as toothpicks.

See Arkansas.

[1] *A Pictorial History of Arkansas*, Fay Hempstead (N. D. Thompson Publishing Company, St. Louis and New York, 1890) p. 212.
King's Handbook of the United States, M. F. Sweetser, planned and ed. by Moses King (Moses King Corporation, Buffalo, N.Y., 1891-1892) p. 61.
More About Names, Leopold Wagner (T. Fisher Unwin, London, 1893) p. 31.

Arkansas

Arkansas is known as the *Bear State*, the *Bowie State*, the *Diamond State*, the *Guinea Pig State*, the *Hot Water State*, the *Toothpick State*, and the *Wonder State*.

The nickname the *Bear State* [1] (pronounced Bar) was given to Arkansas because of the number of bears in pioneer days.

The *Bowie State* was a nickname applied to Arkansas because of the prevalence of bowie knives [1] during its frontier times.

Bowie knives that could be shut up into handles, were ironically designated Arkansas toothpicks, from which the nickname *Toothpick State* is derived.

The *Diamond State* signifies that diamonds are found in Arkansas.

It has acquired an additional appellation, the *Guinea Pig State*,[2] as a result of the state's willingness to become a proving

ground for the agricultural experiments of the Roosevelt Administration.

The *Hot Water State* alludes to the many hot springs.

Arkansas adopted the name *Wonder State* [3] on January 26, 1923, because it excels all others in natural resources, its store of mineral wealth, its vast forests of pine and hardwoods, and its agricultural and horticultural prowess.

[1] *Americanisms: The English of the New World*, M. Schele De Vere (Scribner's, New York, 1872) p. 322, 658.
[2] *Washington Post*, Washington, D.C., February 6, 1935, p. 8.
[3] *Acts of Arkansas, 1923: General Acts and Joint and Concurrent Resolutions and Memorials and Proposed Constitutional Amendments of the Forty-fourth General Assembly of the State of Arkansas, Passed at the Session at the Capitol, in the City of Little Rock, Arkansas, Commencing on the 8th Day of January, 1923, and Ending on the 18th Day of March, 1923*, by authority (Democrat Printing and Lithographing Company, Little Rock, Ark., 1923) p. 803, 804.

Arkie. See Vaughan, F. E.

Arm-in-arm Convention

The National Union Convention which met at Philadelphia, Pa., on August 14, 1886, was popularly nicknamed the *Arm-in-arm Convention* [1] because the meeting was opened in a somewhat sensational manner when the delegates from the States of South Carolina and Massachusetts entered the assembly room arm-in-arm. These two states had been antagonists over the issues of slavery and secession.

[1] *Scribners Popular History of the United States from the Earliest Discoveries of the Western Hemisphere by the Northmen to the Present Time*, William Cullen Bryant, Sidney Howard Gay, and Noah Brooks (Charles Scribner's Sons, New York, 1896) vol. 5, p. 384.

Armistead, George

During the War of 1812, Lieutenant Colonel George Armistead was nicknamed the *Hero of Fort McHenry* [1] because of his success in withstanding the assaults of the British fleet upon Fort McHenry, near Baltimore, Md., and preventing the British forces from capturing Baltimore.

George Armistead was born at Newmarket, Va., on April 10, 1780, and died at Baltimore, Md., on April 25, 1818.

[1] *The National Cyclopaedia of American Biography* (James T. White and Company, New York, 1906) vol. 13, p. 324.

Armour Institute of Technology

The *Packers* and the *Tech Hawks* are the nicknames which have been given to the athletic teams of Armour Institute of

Technology, at Chicago. They are called the *Packers* because the Institute is named for and supported by the Armour Packing Company. The nickname *Tech Hawks* [1] was selected by a vote of the student body.

[1] A letter from John J Schourmer, Director of Athletics at Armour Institute of Technology, Chicago, Ill., November 19, 1935.

Army Team. See United States Military Academy

Aroostook County, Maine
Aroostook County has been designated the *Garden of Maine* [1] because it produces quantities of fruits and potatoes annually. Aroostook County has an area of about 4,352,000 acres, has a delightfully mild spring and summer climate, and fertile soil.

[1] *Maine of the Sea and Pines*, Nathan Haskell Dole and Irwin Leslie Gordon (L. C. Page and Company, Boston, 1926) p. 218.

Aroostook Potato. See Brewster, R. O.

Artesian State. See South Dakota

Arthur, Chester Alan
Chester Alan Arthur, the twenty-first President of the United States, has the following sobriquets: *Arthur the Gentleman, Dude President, First Gentleman of the Land, His Accidency,* and *Prince Arthur.*

The nicknames *Arthur the Gentleman,*[1] the *Dude President,*[3] *First Gentleman of the Land,*[2] and *Prince Arthur* [1] were attributed to President Arthur because he was a well-dressed and handsome man, who possessed charm, grace, affability, and hospitality to a marked degree.

His Accidency [4] was applied to President Arthur because he had become President after the assassination of President James A. Garfield.

[1] *Pen Pictures of the Presidents*, Fred T. Wilson (Southwestern Company, Nashville, Tenn. 1932) p. 352.
[2] *U.S. "Snap Shots": An Independent, National, and Memorial Encyclopedia . . .*, Oliver McKee (A. M. Thayer and Company, Boston, 1892) p. 310, 319.
[3] *A Book of Nicknames*, John Goff (Courier-Journal Job Printing Company, Louisville, Ky. 1892) p. 28.
[4] *The Heart of Roosevelt: An Intimate Life-story of Theodore Roosevelt*, Wayne Whipple (John C. Winston Company, Chicago and Philadelphia, 1924) p. 163.

Arthur the Gentleman. See Arthur, C. A.

Artist of Damnation. See Edwards, Jonathan

Asbury, Francis
Francis Asbury has been called the *Saint Francis of Methodism* [1] because he took an active part in preaching and teaching the doctrines of Methodism, in ordaining preachers, and in founding Methodist churches especially in the eastern and southern parts of the United States. He is said to have ordained several thousand Methodist preachers, to have preached over fifteen thousand sermons, and to have traveled more than twenty-five thousand miles on foot or on horseback. He was the first bishop in the Methodist Episcopal Church in the United States. John Wesley had sent Asbury to America as a Methodist missionary about 1770.

Francis Asbury was born at Handsworth, England, on August 20, 1745, and died at Spottsylvania, Va., on March 31, 1816.

[1] *The Hall of Fame, Being the Official Book Authorized by the New York University Senate as a Statement of the Origin and Constitution of the Hall of Fame, and of Its History up to the Close of the Year 1900*, Henry Mitchell MacCracken (G. P. Putnam's Sons, New York and London, 1901) p. 19.

Ashurst, Henry Fountain
Henry Fountain Ashurst, a Democratic Senator from Arizona, was called the *Fountain* [1] because of his fluency and his middle name.

He was nicknamed the *Cowboy Senator* [2] because he had been a ranger for several years and was a typical westerner.

Henry Fountain Ashurst was born at Winnemucca, Nev., on September 13, 1874.

[1] An interview with Captain Victor Hunt Harding, Secretary of the National Democratic Congress Reelection Committee, Washington, D.C., April 10, 1939.
[2] *Washington Herald*, Washington, D.C., April 21, 1912. p. 5.

Athens of Alabama. See Tuscaloosa, Ala.

Athens of America. See Boston, Mass.

Athens of Arkansas. See Fayetteville, Ark.

Athens of Texas. See Waco, Tex.

Athens of the New World. See Boston, Mass.

Athens of the Northwest. See Faribault, Minn.

Athens of the South. See Nashville, Tenn.

Athens of the United States. See Boston, Mass.

Athens of the West. See Abilene, Tex.; Lexington, Ky.

Athens of Virginia. See Lexington, Va.; Westmoreland County, Va.

Atherton, Charles Gordon

Charles Gordon Atherton was frequently called *Gag Atherton* [1] because while he was a Democratic Representative from New Hampshire to the United States Congress, he introduced, on December 11, 1838, a bill known as the *Gag Resolution,* or *Atherton's Gag,* which specified that bills pertaining to slavery introduced into either the Senate or the House should be tabled. The Gag Resolution was adopted in 1838, but it was repealed in 1844.

Charles Gordon Atherton was born at Amherst, N.H., on July 4, 1804, and died at Manchester, N.H., on November 15, 1853.

[1] *The Statue of John P. Hale, Erected in Front of the Capitol and Presented to the State of New Hampshire by William E. Chandler of Concord; an Account of the Unveiling Ceremonies on August 3, 1892, with a Report of the Addresses Delivered by the Donor and His Excellency Governor Hiram A. Tuttle . . .* (Published by direction of the Governor and Council, Republican Press Association, Concord, N.H. 1892) p. 163.

Atherton's Gag. See Atherton, C. G.

Atlanta, Georgia

Atlanta is nicknamed the *Gate City,* or the *Gate City of the South,* and the *Manufacturing and Industrial Metropolis of the Southeast.* This city is known as the *Gate City,*[1] or the *Gate City of the South,*[2] because it is a railroad and trade center through which much of the commerce of the South passes. On account of its great manufacturing and industrial interests, the citizens of this city designate it the *Manufacturing and Industrial Metropolis of the Southeast.*[3]

[1] *Industries of Atlanta: Her Trade, Commerce, Manufactures, and Representative Establishments,* Andrew Morrison (J. M. Eltsner and Company, Atlanta, Ga. 1886) p. 10.
[2] *Manual of Useful Information,* comp. under the direction of J. C. Thomas (The Werner Company, Chicago, 1893) p. 22.
[3] *Encyclopedia Americana* (Americana Corporation, New York, 1927) vol. 2, p. 501.

Atlas of America. See Washington, George

Atlas of Independence. See Adams, John

Attorney General for Runaway Slaves. See Chase, S. P.

Auctioneer Mayor. See Shank, S. L.

Audubon, John James Fougère

John James Fougère Audubon was called the *American Woodman* [1] because he spent many years of his life in forests, especially in Pennsylvania, Kentucky, and Louisiana while he was engaged in ornithological observations.

He was born at Les Cayes, Santo Domingo, now Haiti, on April 26, 1785, and died at New York City, on January 27, 1851.

[1] *National Cyclopaedia of American Biography* (James T. White and Company, New York, 1929) vol. 6, p. 75, 76.

Augusta, Georgia

The *Lowell of the South* [1] has been applied to Augusta because it is the site of many large cotton mills, just as Lowell, Mass., is.

[1] *Principles of Geography and the Continents,* Richard Elwood Dodge and William E. Grady (Rand McNally, Chicago, 1914) p. 147.

Augustana College

Vikings is the nickname given to the athletic teams of Augustana College, at Sioux Falls, S.D., because it is a Lutheran school founded by people of Nordic descent,[1] and most of its students are Scandinavians.

[1] A communication from L. A. Olson, Director of Athletics at Augustana College, Sioux Falls, S.D. June 13, 1935.

Augustana College and Theological Seminary

The athletic teams of Augustana College and Theological Seminary, at Rock Island, Ill., are popularly designated *Norsemen* and *Vikings* because the college was founded by men of Scandinavian ancestry.[1]

[1] A communication from A. V. Svedberg, Director of Athletics at Augustana College and Theological Seminary, Rock Island, Ill., November 15, 1935,

Augustine

The sobriquet an *Augustine* [1] is commonly applied to a cadet who enters the Military Academy at West Point, N.Y., in August.

[1] *Unit Projects in Modern Literature* (Educational Press, Columbus, Ohio) March 1-14, 1935, p. 12.

Auker, Elden Leroy

Big Six [1] was a nickname applied to Elden Leroy Auker who pitched in major league baseball. He acquired this nickname while he was an undergraduate student at the Kansas State College of Agriculture and Applied Sciences, at Manhattan, Kans.

Elden Leroy Auker was born at Norcatur, Kans., on September 21, 1910, and pitched in major league baseball.

[1] *Who's Who in The American League*, 1935 Edition, Harold (Speed) Johnson (B. E. Callahan, Chicago, 1935) p. 15.

Aunt Rachel. See Jackson, R. D.

Austin, Freeman

Freeman Austin was nicknamed *Old Kill Devil*,[1] from his rifle which he called *Kill Devil*. He was at one time a neighbor to John Brown, the famous abolitionist, while he was living on his claim on Mosquito Creek near Ossawatomie, Kans. He died in service during the Civil War, near Helena, Ark., on July 30, 1862.

[1] *Kansas Historical Collections, 1903-1904: Transactions of the Kansas State Historical Society, 1903-1904, together with Addresses at Annual Meetings, Miscellaneous Papers, and a Roster of Kansas for Fifty Years,* ed. by George W. Martin, Secretary (George A. Clark, State Printer, Topeka, Kans., 1904) vol. 8, p. 279.

Austin, James Philip

James Philip Austin, who was born at Swansea, Wales, on December 8, 1879, and who coached major league baseball, was popularly known as *Pepper* [1] because of his enthusiasm and speed.

[1] *Who's Who in Major League Base Ball*, comp. by Harold (Speed) Johnson (Buxton Publishing Company, Chicago, 1933) p. 431.

Austin, Stephen Fuller

Stephen Fuller Austin has been designated the *Father of Texas* [4] because he was one of the outstanding pioneers who settled in Texas. He founded the city of Austin. He was born in Wythe County, Va., in 1792, and died at Columbus, Tex., on December 27, 1836.

[1] *Story of Texas*, Joseph L. Clark (Row, Peterson, New York and Philadelphia, 1933) p. 70.

Austin, Texas

Austin is termed the *City of the Violet Crown* [1] because it is in the center of a chain of beautiful mountains which are violet in the distance.

[1] *Flashlights on Texas*, Lillie Terrell Shaver and Willie Williamson Rogers (A. C. Baldwin and Sons, Austin, Tex., 1928) p. 63.

Author of the New Deal. See Burke, E. R.

Auto State. See Michigan

Autocrat of the Quacks. See Headley, J. T.

Automatic. See Karamatic, George; Manders, Jack

Automobile City. See Detroit, Mich.

Automobile City of the World. See Detroit, Mich.

Automobile Wizard. See Ford, Henry

Aven, Algernon Jasper

Doctor Algernon Jasper Aven was widely known as *Ajax* and the *Seer and Sage of Mississippi College.*

Doctor Aven was Professor of Latin in Mississippi College at Clinton, Miss., for forty-four years. His students came to call him *Ajax* because of his prowess as a Latin scholar, comparable to Ajax and his prowess as a Greek warrior.

The *Seer and Sage of Mississippi College* [1] was applied to Doctor Aven because he was considered one of the most scholarly men on the campus, with insight into life and human nature.

Algernon Jasper Aven was born at Graysport, Granada County, Miss., on August 25, 1858, and died at his home in Clinton, Miss., on February 20, 1935.

[1] *The Clarion Ledger*, Jackson, Miss. February 28, 1935, p. 1.

Axis Sally. See Gillars, Mildred

Ayres, Agnes

Agnes Ayres, an American motion picture actress, was nicknamed the *O. Henry Girl* [1] because she played in a great many of the screen versions of O. Henry's stories.

Ayres, Agnes—Continued

She was born on April 4, 1898, at Carbondale, Ill., but she now lives in San Francisco, Calif.

[1] *The Blue Book of the Screen*, Ruth Wing, Editor, (The Blue Book of the Screen, Hollywood, Calif., 1923) p. 8.

B

Babe. See Herman, F. C.

Babe Ruth. See Ruth, G. H.

Babe Ruth of the New Deal. See Johnson, H. S.

Babes. See Chicago National League Baseball Company

Baby Bonds

About 1878 the Georgia Legislature authorized the issuing of five hundred thousand dollars worth of bonds bearing four per cent interest. These bonds were nicknamed *Baby Bonds* [1] because they were not only much smaller in size than those printed previously, but also in denomination, ranging from five dollars to a hundred dollars in value.

During the First World War, 1914-19, the Treasury Department of the United States Government issued twenty-five cent stamps, and government certificates of five dollar denomination. These were called *Baby Bonds* also.

[1] *National Cyclopaedia of American Biography*, (James T. White and Company, New York, 1893) vol. 3, p. 270.

Baby Boys

During the Civil War the newly recruited soldiers, upon their arrival at the camps of the veteran soldiers, were humorously called by the latter the *Baby Boys* [1] in allusion to their youthfulness.

[1] *Dedication of the New York State Monument on the Battlefield of Antietam*, by the New York State Monuments Commission for the Battlefields of Gettysburg, Chattanooga, and Antietam (J. B. Lyon Company, Albany, N.Y. 1923) p. 80.

Baby Chocs. See Mississippi College

Baby Face Nelson. See Nelson, George

Baby McKee's Grandfather. See Harrison, Benjamin

Baby of the Cabinet

When the Department of Agriculture was first created in 1899, the Secretary of Agriculture was designated the *Baby of the Cabinet* [1] because he was the most recent addition to the Cabinet of the President of the United States.

[1] *My Quarter Century of American Politics*, Champ Clark (Harper and Brothers, New York and London, 1920) vol. 1, p. 249.

Baby State. See Arizona

Baby Vamp. See West, Mae

Baby-doll. See Sorrell, V. G.

Bacharach, Isaac

Isaac Bacharach was sometimes jokingly called *Boardwalk Ike* [1] because for many years he made his home at Atlantic City, N.J., which is famous for its splendid boardwalk. Isaac Bacharach was born at Philadelphia, Pa., on January 5, 1870, and was a Representative from the State of New Jersey to the United States Congress from 1915 to 1937.

[1] *The Washington Post Magazine*, Washington, D.C., March 4, 1934, p. 4.

Bachelor Governor. See Hill, D. B.

Bachelor President. See Buchanan, James

Bachelor Ticket

The New York State Democratic ticket, which in 1881 listed Grover Cleveland and David Bennett Hill as candidates for the offices of governor and lieutenant governor respectively, was nicknamed the *Bachelor Ticket* [1] because both candidates were unmarried.

[1] *Grover Cleveland, as Buffalo Knew Him*, Charles H. Armitage (Buffalo Evening News, Buffalo, N.Y., 1926) p. 212.

Backbone of North America. See Rocky Mountains

Backbone of the Confederacy

During the Civil War the Mississippi River was described as the *Backbone of the Confederacy*.[1] When Union ships blockaded the eastern coast, the Mississippi River became the Confederates' chief means of securing supplies. Commodities were exchanged and exported through New Orleans.

For hundreds of miles upstream the Mississippi River was guarded by a chain of fortifications. The Confederate cause was dealt a severe blow when Vicksburg, Miss., was captured on July 4, 1863.

[1] *History of the United States Navy from 1775 to 1901*, Edgar Stanton Maclay, with technical revision by Roy C. Smith (D. Appleton and Company, New York, 1901) vol. 2, p. 267.

Backbone of the Continent. See Rocky Mountains

Bacon, Leonard

Leonard Bacon, a Congregational clergyman and writer, was called the *Congregational Pope of New England* and the *Nestor of Congregationalism.*

The name, the *Congregational Pope of New England,*[1] was given to him because of the prominence he attained in his religious activities.

During the latter years of his life, Leonard Bacon was widely called the *Nestor of Congregationalism.*[2] In 1825 he became pastor of the First Congregational Church at New Haven, Conn., and held that position officially, if not always actively, until the time of his death in 1881. Nestor according to Greek legend was a Trojan hero distinguished for his longevity, sagacity, and prudence. Because of these same qualities Bacon was nicknamed the *Nestor of Congregationalism.*

He was born at Detroit, Mich., on February 19, 1802, and died at New Haven, Conn., on December 24, 1881.

[1] *The Encyclopaedia Britannica,* Fourteenth Edition (Encyclopaedia Britannica, Inc., New York, 1929) vol. 2, p. 888.
[2] *The National Cyclopaedia of American Biography* (James T. White and Company, New York, 1898) vol. 1, p. 176.

Bacon, Nathaniel

Nathaniel Bacon, a colonial leader, was designated the *Virginia Rebel*[1] because of his prominence in the uprising commonly known as Bacon's Rebellion. In 1676 the planters in the Virginia Colony were dissatisfied with the indifference of the Royal Governor, Sir William Berkeley, in failing to check Indian depredations and refusing to allow the inequalities of the colonial law system to be reformed by the Colonial Assembly.

When Bacon and his irate Virginians came in conflict with Berkeley's soldiers, the latter fled to the Eastern Shore. Bacon's men then burned Jamestown and prepared to bring about the much-needed reforms in their government. The *Virginia Rebel,* as Bacon was then called, became fatally ill, and the rebels were soon subdued by Governor Berkeley.

Nathaniel Bacon was born at Friston Hall in Suffolk, England, on January 2, 1647, and died in Gloucester County, Va., on October 26, 1676.

[1] *Appleton's Cyclopaedia of American Biography,* ed. by James Grant Wilson and John Fiske (D. Appleton and Company, New York, 1895) vol. 1, p. 131.

Bad Land Babies

The *Bad Land Babies*[1] was a term applied to the babies of the Seward and the Dow families on Elkhorn Ranch belonging to Theodore Roosevelt, near Medora, N.D., in the Bad Lands. The first babies born on the ranch were nicknamed by the cowboys the *Bad Land Babies.*

[1] *Jungle Roads and Other Trails of Roosevelt,* Daniel Henderson (E. P. Dutton and Company, New York, 1920) p. 94.

Bad Lands

Bad Lands[1] is a nickname applied to vast regions of arid land in the western part of the Dakotas and central Wyoming, because these regions are waste lands consisting of dry desert country, rocky ridges having no soil, and gullies and ravines. They were so named by the Indians of the region.

[1] *The Encyclopedia Americana* (Americana Corporation, New York and Chicago, 1932) vol. 3, p. 31.

Baden-Baden of America. See Hot Springs, Ark.

Badger State. See Wisconsin

Badgers. See Pacific University; University of Wisconsin; Wisconsin Inhabitants

Bailey, Anna Warner

Mrs. Anna Warner Bailey was nicknamed the *Heroine of Groton* and *Mother Bailey.*

On July 13, 1813, a detachment of British ships appeared in the harbor of New London, Conn. The citizens of Groton feared that these ships were preparing to attack their town, which was separated from New London by the Thames river. During

Bailey, A. W.—Continued

the hurried preparations for defense, it was learned that there was not enough flannel cloth, which was essential for the loading of muskets.

When Mrs. Bailey heard of this she began to canvass the homes of Groton for flannel and even donated the flannel petticoat she was wearing. Her ardent patriotic zeal was an inspiration to the soldiers and to the inhabitants of the town who caused her to be nicknamed the *Heroine of Groton* [1] and *Mother Bailey*.[2]

Mrs. Anna Warner Bailey was born at Groton, Conn., in 1758, and died there in 1850.

[1] *Women in American History: The Part Taken by Women in American History,* Mrs. John A. Logan (The Perry-Nalle Publishing Company, Wilmington, Del. 1912) p. 175.
[2] *Appleton's Cyclopaedia of American Biography,* ed. by James Grant Wilson and John Fiske (D. Appleton and Company, New York, 1891) vol. 1, p. 136.

Bailey, Anne Hennis Trotter

Mrs. Anne Hennis Trotter Bailey was often designated *Mad Anne* [1] by the settlers of Gallipolis, Ohio, and by the frontiersmen on the adjacent Virginia border because her unconventionality and her courage at times seemed to border on madness.

After Mrs. Trotter's husband, Richard Trotter, had been killed in 1774 during an Indian skirmish, Mrs. Trotter dressed in men's clothes, and joined a band of soldiers on the Kanawha River at the present site of Charleston, W.Va., hoping to avenge the death of her husband.

When the Revolutionary War broke out, she inspired a great number of men to join the Continental Army. She became an expert in the use of firearms, and was invaluable as a messenger between the forts and in securing ammunition and supplies for these garrisons.

Because she was so unconventional in her dress and in engaging in the activities of war, she was considered to be abnormal or insane and was called *Mad Anne*.

Mrs. Anne Hennis Trotter Bailey was born at Liverpool, England, about 1742, and died at Gallipolis, in what is now the State of Ohio, on November 22, 1825. Mrs. Trotter was married to John Bailey, a frontier soldier, on November 3, 1785.

[1] *Women in American History* . . . , Mrs. John A. Logan (The Perry-Nalle Publishing Company, Wilmington, Del. 1912) p. 65.
Anne Bailey: Life and Times of Anne Bailey, the Pioneer Heroine of the Great Kanawha Valley, Virgil A. Lewis (The Butler Printing Company, Charleston, W. Va., 1891) p. 26-8, 40-2.

Bailey, Howard Henry

Howard Henry Bailey, who played in national league football, was nicknamed *Screeno* [1] by his college friends while he was once deeply interested in watching the performances in a circus.

He was born at Birmingham, Ala., on January 10, 1913, was graduated with the degree of Bachelor of Science from the University of Tennessee, at Knoxville, Tenn., in 1935, after which he joined the *Chicago Bears,* a team belonging to The National Football League.

[1] *Who's Who in Major League Football,* comp. by Harold (Speed) Johnson and Wilfrid Smith (B. V. Callahan, Chicago, 1935) p. 23.

Bailey, James Montgomery

James Montgomery Bailey, a humorous journalist, was nicknamed the *Father of the "Colyumnist"* and the *Danbury News Man* [1] because he introduced humor as a new feature in journalism and wrote humorous columns for many newspapers of his day. He began writing for the New York *Sunday Mercury* about 1860, and in partnership with Timothy Donovan, purchased the Danbury *Times,* to which he contributed columns of humorous writings.

James Montgomery Bailey was born at Albany, N.Y., on September 25, 1841, and died at Danbury, Conn., on March 4, 1894.

[1] *Dictionary of American Biography under the Auspices of the American Council of Learned Societies,* ed. by Allen Johnson (Charles Scribner's Sons, New York, 1928) vol. 1, p. 499.

Bainbridge, Ohio

Bainbridge, in Ross County, has been designated the *Cradle of Dental Education.* [1] While studying medicine at Bainbridge, Chapin Aaron Harris and James Taylor envisioned the possibilities of dentistry and in 1840 Harris founded the Baltimore College of Dental Surgery, the first dental college in America. He also edited the first dental journal published in America. In 1845 Taylor founded the Ohio College of Dental Surgery at Cincinnati, Ohio, and edited the second dental journal published in America.

[1] *Ohio Archaeological and Historical Quarterly,* published by the Society (F. J. Heer Printing Company, Columbus, Ohio, 1926) 35, no2:382, 394. April 1926.

Baked Bean State. See Massachusetts

Baked Beans. See Massachusetts Inhabitants

Baker, Alpheus

Alpheus Baker was widely known as the *Silver-tongued Orator of the South* [1] because he was an unusually eloquent and polished orator.

Alpheus Baker was born at Abbeville Court House, S.C., on May 23, 1825, and died at Louisville, Ky., on October 2, 1891.

[1] *History of Eufala, Alabama,* Eugenia Persons Smartt (Roberts and Son, Birmingham, Ala., 1933) p. 238.

Baker, Anderson Yancey

Anderson Yancey Baker was nicknamed the *Millionaire Sheriff* [1] because he was a multimillionaire at the time he was serving as the sheriff of Hidalgo County, Tex., from 1912 to 1930.

Baker was prominent in the movement which secured irrigation for this arid but fertile land and was successful in securing good roads, schools, public buildings, churches, and transportation facilities. He was prominent in the political affairs of Hidalgo County, but gained even more recognition for developing its resources.

He was born at Uvalde, Tex., on January 16, 1876, and died at Edinburg, Tex., on November 1, 1930.

[1] *The National Cyclopaedia of American Biography* (James T. White and Company, New York, 1932) vol. 22, p. 270.

Baker, George

George Baker, founder of the Negro Peace Mission Movement, is widely known as *Father Divine* [1], a name which he chose himself. In 1915 he became a disciple of the Reverend St. Bishop, The Vine, who brought the "God-within" doctrine to the colored people of New York City. At first Devine was his spiritual name, but after his religious cult found favor in the Harlem section of New York City he changed his legal name to Morgan J. Divine, and discarded the name of Baker.

George Baker was born on a rice plantation on Hutchinson's Island, lying in the Savannah river at Savannah, Ga., about 1878. His father and mother had been slaves.

[1] *Time: The Weekly Newsmagazine,* Chicago, August 8, 1938, col. 3, p. 7.

Baker, John Franklin

John Franklin Baker, who was born at Trappe, Md., on March 13, 1886, was nicknamed *Home Run Baker* [1] in 1911 because he made nine home runs during the championship season and then followed that record with two home runs in the World Series.

[1] *Who's Who in Major League Base Ball,* comp. by Harold (Speed) Johnson (Buxton Publishing Company, Chicago, 1933) p. 475.

Baker, Johnny

Johnny Baker, the son of Lew Baker of North Platte, Neb., made the acquaintance of William Frederick Cody in North Platte when Johnny was about nine years of age, and about five years later he joined Cody's Wild West Show. He was soon nicknamed the *Cowboy Kid* [1] because, as a youth he did roughriding and shooting with Cody's roughriders. Johnny Baker later became Cody's foster son. His specialty was the breaking of glass balls by shooting them with a rifle held in various positions.

[1] *The Making of Buffalo Bill: A Study in Heroics,* Richard J. Walsh in collaboration with Milton S. Salsbury (The Bobbs Merrill Company, Indianapolis, Ind., 1928) p. 214, 245-7.

Balch, Benjamin

Benjamin Balch was nicknamed the *Fighting Parson* [1] because in 1781 during the battle between the American frigate *Alliance* and a British ship and brig, Balch, who was chaplain on the *Alliance,* "seized a musket" and fought valiantly.

Benjamin Balch was born at Dedham, Mass., on February 12, 1743, and died at Barrington, N.H., on May 4, 1816.

[1] *Genealogy of the Balch Families in America,* Galusha B. Balch (Eben Putnam, Salem, Mass., 1887) p. 88.

Bald Eagle. See Gary, M. W.

Bald Eagle of Edgefield. See Gary, M. W.

Bald Eagle of Westchester. See Husted, J. W.

Baldwin, Elias Jackson

Lucky Baldwin [1] is the nickname widely applied to Elias Jackson Baldwin, a California pioneer, miner, and ranchman because he accumulated his vast wealth by luck. He bought mining stocks when they were selling at a low price and sold them when they were on a boom. He also bred race horses on a large scale, owned and operated a brick yard, and operated hotels and ranches,

Baldwin, E. J.—Continued

Elias Jackson Baldwin was born in Butler County, Ohio, on April 3, 1828, and died on his ranch at Arcadia, Calif., on March 1, 1909.

[1] The National Cyclopaedia of American Biography (James T. White and Company, New York, 1932) vol. 22, p. 381-2.
Lucky Baldwin: The Story of an Unconventional Success, Carl Burgess Glasscock (The Bobbs-Merrill Company, Indianapolis. Ind., 1923).

Baldy. See Smith, W. F.

Balloon Tytler. See Tytler, James

Ballou, Hosea

Hosea Ballou was nicknamed the *Father of American Universalism* [1] because he was the chief expositor of that belief, principally in magazines and reviews which he founded and edited for that purpose.

He was born at Richmond, N.H., on April 30, 1771, and died at Boston, Mass., on June 7, 1852.

[1] The Encyclopaedia Britannica, Fourteenth Edition (Encyclopaedia Britannica, Inc., New York, 1929) vol. 2, p. 1011.

Baloney Dollar

The *Baloney Dollar* [1] was the name given to the proposed devalued dollar when America went off the gold standard on April 19, 1933. The content of the gold dollar was reduced from twenty-five and eight hundredths grains of gold to not less than half that amount. The devaluated American dollar was said to be like baloney because, cut it as thin as one may, it still has the essential characteristics of the original.

[1] The Roosevelt Year: A Photographic Record, ed. by Pare Lorentz (Funk and Wagnalls Company, New York and London, 1934) p. 142.
The New York Times, New York, November 29, 1933, vol. 4, p. 18.

Baltimore, Maryland

Baltimore is nicknamed the *Monument City* [1] because of the numerous monuments to be found throughout the city. The name is said to have originated in 1815 when the graceful Doric column surmounted by a figure of George Washington was erected at the intersection of North Charles Street with Mount Vernon Place.

[1] Reminiscences of Baltimore, Jacob Frey (Maryland Book Concern, Baltimore, Md., 1893) p. 380.
Guide to the City of Baltimore, J. H. Hollander (John Murphy and Company, Baltimore, Md., 1893) p. 154-5.
Baltimore, Its History and Its People, Clayton Colman Hall, General Editor (Lewis Historical Publishing Company, New York and Chicago, 1912) vol. 1, p. 129.

Baltimore Orioles. See Saint Louis American League Baseball Company.

Bambino. See Ruth, G. H.

Bangor, Maine

Bangor is known as the *Lumber City,* the *Metropolis of the Northeast,* and the *Queen City of the East.* The *Lumber City* [1] originated in connection with the enormous lumber industry which developed at Bangor during the nineteenth century. The nickname is not unappropriate at the present time for Bangor's chief interests are manufacturing wood-pulp and paper-making. Its importance in manufacturing, shipping, and commercial activities have merited for it the name of the *Metropolis of the Northeast.*

Bangor is nicknamed the *Queen City of the East* [2] because its location on the Penobscot River, its magnificent residences, and its extensive commercial activities have caused it to become outstanding among the cities of eastern Maine.

[1] Manual of Useful Information, comp. under the direction of J. C. Thomas (The Werner Company, Chicago, 1893) p. 22.
[2] Bangor and Vicinity, Illustrated . . . , comp. and pub. by Edward Mitchell Blanding (Press of the Industrial Journal, Bangor, Maine, 1899) p. 63.

Banished Preacher. See Williams, Roger

Bank Holiday

On March 6, 1933, President Franklin Delano Roosevelt ordered all banks in the various states closed until Congress, which was scheduled to meet on March 9, should decide what was the best way to handle the financial crisis. March 6 to March 9, 1933, was called the *Bank Holiday.* [1]

[1] American History, Illustrated—Complete Edition, from the Discovery of America to the Present Day, Gertrude Van Duyn Southworth and John Van Duyn Southworth (Iroquois Publishing Company, Inc., Syracuse, N.Y., 1933) p. 279.

Bank Parlour Negotiations

When the United States Government's reserve of gold was reduced to sixty-six million dollars on January 31, 1893, John G. Carlisle, Secretary of the Treasury in President Grover Cleveland's second Cabinet, went to New York and arranged with the bankers of that city to exchange their gold for Government bonds to supplement the Government's supply of gold. This has been termed the *Bank Parlour Negotiations.* [1] The plan proved to be detrimental to the purpose of increasing the Government's supply of gold because many of the bankers withdrew gold from the United States Treasury by cashing some of their bonds, which were payable in gold, to furnish the Government with gold in exchange for other bonds. These negotiations had to be handled largely on the terms of the bankers.

[1] *Twenty Years of the Republic, 1885-1905*, Harry Thurston Peck (Dodd, Mead and Company, New York, 1907) p. 404.

Bankhead, William Brockman

William Brockman Bankhead, Speaker of the National House of Representatives from 1917 to 1940, was nicknamed *Tallulah's Papa* [1] because his daughter, Tallulah, is an outstanding American actress.

William Brockman Bankhead was born at Moscow, Ala., on August 12, 1874, and died on September 15, 1940.

[1] An interview with Captain Victor Hunt Harding, Secretary of the National Democratic Congress Reelection Committee, Washington, D.C., April 10, 1939.

Banks, Nathaniel Prentiss

Nathaniel Prentiss Banks, Congressman, Governor of Massachusetts, and Union soldier, was sometimes called the *Bobbin Boy,* [1] because as a youth he worked as a bobbin boy in a cotton factory at Waltham, Mass. He was born at Waltham, on January 30, 1816, and died there on September 1, 1894.

[1] *History of the Cabinet of the United States of America from President Washington to President Coolidge. . .* , William Henry Smith (The Industrial Printing Company, Baltimore, Md., 1925) p. 504.
The National Cyclopaedia of American Biography (James T. White and Company, New York, 1897) vol. 4, p. 222.

Banneker, Benjamin

Benjamin Banneker, a Negro mathematician, was called the *African Astronomer* [1] because he devoted the latter half of his life to the study of astronomy and the making of almanacs.

Benjamin Banneker was born at Ellicott's, Md., on November 9, 1731, and died at Baltimore, Md., in the autumn of 1806.

[1] *The National Cyclopaedia of American Biography* (James T. White and Company, New York, 1907) vol. 5, p. 36.

Banner State. See Texas

Bantams. See Louisville Municipal College for Negroes

Banty. See Hancock, C. E.

Baptists. See Franklin College of Indiana

Bara, Theda (Theodosia Goodman)

Theda Bara was nicknamed the *Original Glamour Girl* and the *Queen of the Vampires,* [1] because she was the first actress to attain fame by portraying the character of a vampire with glamor in motion pictures.

Theda Bara (Theodosia Goodman) was born at Cincinnati, Ohio, in 1890. She married motion picture producer Charles J. Brabin in 1921. Theda Bara died April 7, 1955, in Los Angeles, California.

[1] *Washington Herald*, Washington, D.C., March 15, 1934, p. 30.
Famous Film Folk: A Gallery of Life Portraits and Biographies, Charles Donald Fox (George H. Doran Company, New York, 1925) p. 211.

Barbour, William Warren

William Warren Barbour, a New Jersey manufacturer and politician was nicknamed the *Champ* [1] because in 1910 he had been the national heavy weight boxing champion. He was a Republican Senator from New Jersey to the United States Senate from December 1, 1931 until 1937.

William Warren Barbour was born at Monmouth Beach, N.J., on July 31, 1888, and died November 22, 1943.

[1] An interview with Captain Victor Hunt Harding, Secretary of the National Democratic Congress Reelection Committee, Washington, D.C., April 10, 1939.

Barkley, Alben William

Alben William Barkley, a Kentucky politician and statesman, was nicknamed *Dear Alben* and *Veep*. *Dear Alben* [1] had its origin in a letter written to Senator Barkley by President Franklin Delano Roosevelt on July 15, 1937, in which he urged Senator Barkley, as acting majority leader of the Senate to use his influence to get favorable action on the Supreme Court Reform Bill. Journalists began to apply this nickname to Senator Barkley at that time, but it was during the Democratic primary senatorial campaign in Kentucky between Senator Barkley and Governor Albert Benjamin (Happy) Chandler, in 1938, that it became popular.

He was nicknamed *Little Alby* [2] by his colleagues in the United States Congress and *Veep* after he was elected Vice President in 1948. He is the first Vice President to be popularly called the *Veep*.

Barkley, A. W.—Continued

Alben William Barkley was born in Graves County, Ky., on November 24, 1877, and makes his home at Paducah, Ky.

[1] *Time: The Weekly Newsmagazine,* Chicago, August 1, 1938, p. 16.
Washington Herald, Washington, D.C., July 16, 1937, col. 6, p. 1. and col. 2, p. 2.
[2] An interview with Captain Victor Hunt Harding, Secretary of the National Democratic Congress Reelection Committee, Washington, D.C., April 10, 1939.

Barley King. See Buerger, John

Barlow, Joel. See *Hartford Wits*

Barnacle Bill. See Sutphin, W. H.

Barnburners

About 1844 the Democratic party consisted of two factions differing on the question of slavery. The anti-slavery faction were termed *Barnburners* [1] because the methods they endorsed were considered so dangerous that they were compared to the man who burned his barn to rid it of rats.

[1] *"Lewis Cass"* by Andrew C. McLaughlin, in *American Statesmen,* ed. by John T. Morse, Junior, (Houghton Mifflin and Company, Boston and New York, 1899) p. 59.

Barney. See Shotton, B. E.; Johnson, W. P.

Barnum, Phineas Taylor

Phineas Taylor Barnum was nicknamed the *Prince of Humbugs* [1] because he tricked the public so often with fake shows in his circus. He believed the public loved to be fooled.

Barnum was born at Bethel, Conn., July 5, 1810, and died at Bridgeport, Conn., April 7, 1891.

[1] *Compton's Pictured Encyclopedia,* F. E. Compton and Company, Chicago, 1947, vol. 2, p. 491.

Barnum, William Henry

William Henry Barnum was nicknamed *Seven Mule Barnum* [1] because, while he was Chairman of the Democratic National Committee in 1876, he sent a cipher code message to some of his colleagues in which he used the words *seven mules,* meaning seven thousand dollars.

William Henry Barnum was born at Boston Corner, N.Y., on September 17, 1818, and died at Lime Rock, Conn., on April 30, 1889.

[1] *U. S. "Snap Shots": An Independent, National, and Memorial Encyclopedia . . . ,* Oliver McKee (A. M. Thayer and Company, Boston, 1892) p. 246.

Barnwell, John

John Barnwell was nicknamed *Tuscarora John* [1] because in 1712 he dealt a crushing defeat to the Tuscarora Indians who had conspired to exterminate the Roanoke settlement in North Carolina. The Tuscaroras were so badly beaten that they left the Carolinas and joined the Five Nations in New York.

John Barnwell was born in Ireland, about 1671, and died at Brookfield, S.C., in 1724.

[1] *Appleton's Cyclopaedia of American Biography* (D. Appleton and Company, New York, 1891) vol. 1, p. 173.

Baron von Stiegel. See Stiegel, H. W.

Barrett, George Hooker (or Horton)

George Hooker Barrett or George Horton Barrett, a comedian, was widely known as *Gentleman George* [1] because of his striking physique and his elegant manners and attire. He acted chiefly in comedies and burlesques.

George Hooker or George Horton Barrett was born at Exeter, England, on June 9, 1794, and died at New York City on September 5, 1860.

[1] *Appleton's Cyclopaedia of American Biography,* ed. by James Grant Wilson and John Fiske (D. Appleton and Company, New York, 1895) vol. 1, p. 175.

Barry, John

Commodore John Barry has been called the *Father of the American Navy* [1] because he served skillfully and courageously as a captain in the naval forces during the Revolutionary War, and also in the brief war with France in 1790. He was the first commander commissioned by the Continental Congress, and trained many of the men who later became renowned in the naval service of the United States.

Commodore Barry was born at Wexford, Ireland, in 1745, and died at Philadelphia, Pa., on September 13, 1803.

[1] *Commodore John Barry, Father of the American Navy,* Joseph Gurn (P. J. Kennedy and Sons, New York, 1931) p. 3.
The Port Folio, Third Series, Oliver Oldschool (Joseph Dennie) (H. Maxwell, Philadelphia, 1813) vol. 2, no. 1, July, 1813, p. 1.

Barry, Wesley

Wesley Barry, who was born at Hollywood, Calif., on August 10, 1907, and who was a well-known motion picture actor, was nicknamed *Freckles* [1] because his face was extremely freckled.

[1] *The Blue Book of the Screen,* Ruth Wing, Editor (The Blue Book of the Screen, Inc., Hollywood, Calif., 1923) p. 14.

Barrymore of the Brain Trust. See Tugwell, R. G.

Bartell, Richard

Richard Bartell, who was born at Chicago, Ill., on November 22, 1907, and who played shortshop in major league baseball, has been nicknamed *Pepper Box.*[1]

[1] *Who's Who in Major League Base Ball,* comp. by Harold (Speed) Johnson (Buxton Publishing Company, Chicago, 1933) p. 70.

Barton, Bruce

Bruce Barton, an author, advertising agent, and politician, was nicknamed the *Advertiser,* the *Advertising King,* and the *Great Repealer*[1] by his colleagues in the National House of Representatives because he was an expert in the advertising business and because, while he was a member of the United States Congress, he constantly advocated repealing New Deal legislation. He was a Republican Representative from New York State from 1937 until 1941.

Bruce Barton was born at Robbins, Tenn., on August 5, 1886.

[1] An interview with Captain Victor Hunt Harding, Secretary of the National Democratic Congress Reelection Committee, Washington, D.C., April 10, 1939.

Barton, Clara

Clara Barton is widely known as the *Angel of the Battlefields* and the *Mother of the Red Cross.*

The *Angel of the Battlefields*[1] was given to her as a tribute to her self-sacrificing work as a nurse on the battlefields where she ministered to the sick and wounded soldiers and organized military hospitals.

She was designated the *Mother of the Red Cross*[2] for her work in organizing the American Red Cross Society in 1881. She was elected the first president of the organization and continued to serve until 1904.

Clara Barton was born at Oxford, Mass., in 1821, and died at Glen Echo, Md., on April 12, 1912.

[1] *Ten American Girls from History,* Kate Dickinson Sweetser (Harper and Brothers, New York and London, 1917) p. 143, 157-72.
[2] *Worcester, City of Prosperity,* Donald Tulloch (The Commonwealth Press, Worcester, Mass., 1914) p. 289.

Barton, David

David Barton was nicknamed *Little Red*[2] while serving as Senator from Missouri from 1821 to 1831. One day Barton was making a heated speech in the Senate chamber, de-

nouncing the Jacksonian policies and principles. At the close of his speech, a Missouri frontiersman in the gallery excitedly shouted "Hurrah for the little red!" "Little red" was a famous fighting cock which the frontiersman owned. The newspapers took it up and the nickname stuck.

David Barton was born in what is now Greene County, Tennessee, on December 14, 1783, and died at Booneville, Mo., on September 28, 1837.

[1] *Centennial History of Missouri (The Center State) One Hundred Years in the Union, 1820-1921,* Walter B. Stevens (The S. J. Clarke Publishing Company, Chicago and Saint Louis, 1921) vol. 1, p. 187.

Bartow, Florida

Bartow, in Polk County, Florida, has been called the *City of Oaks*[1] because of the prevalence of fine specimens of oak trees in its parks and along its residential streets.

[1] *Florida in the Making,* Frank Parker Stockbridge and John Holliday Perry (The de Bower Publishing Company, New York and Jacksonville, Fla., 1925) p. 244.

Bartram, John

John Bartram is called the *Father of American Botany*[1] because of his oustanding work as a pioneer in the field. He established at Kingssessing, Pa., the first botanical garden in the United States. He was born in Chester County, Pa., on March 23, 1699, and died at Kingssessing, Pa., on September 22, 1777.

[1] *New Standard Encyclopedia of Universal Knowledge,* prepared under the editorial direction of Frank H. Vizetelly (Funk and Wagnalls Company, New York and London, 1931) vol. 3, p. 10.

Baseball

Baseball in America is commonly designated the *National Pastime* because it has probably become this country's most popular sport since its invention sometime during the first half of the nineteenth century. Today's major league games attract vast numbers of spectators to the ball park and many follow the pennant races on radio and television. The game further merits its nickname because it has long been a major recreation of American schoolboys.

Baseball itself developed from several games played in colonial America on village greens, in parks and on school playing fields. Although Abner Doubleday is officially honored as the man who laid out the first diamond and devised the original rules in Cooperstown, N.Y., in 1839, the best evidence seems to indicate that baseball was played in various cruder forms somewhat

Baseball—Continued

earlier than the official date. These earlier games, however, were not sufficiently well-organized to permit all players a chance at bat, hence a game with more bases, a limited number of fielders, and a ball harder to hit was not long in becoming popular.

Prior to the Civil War the game gained adherents as a *Gentlemen's Pastime* [2] and spread throughout New York and the northeastern states. During the Civil War great crowds of men witnessed baseball for the first time in the huge army posts; Union soldiers played it when they had time to relax and taught it to their guards in Confederate prisons. In 1868 the first professional team paying regular salaries was formed—the Cincinnati Red Stockings—and baseball as America's *National Pastime* was well-established.[2]

[1] *Baseball; a historical narrative of the game, the men who have played it, and its place in American life*, by Robert M. Smith (Simon & Schuster, New York, 1947) p.26-48.

[2] *The Story of Baseball*, by John Durant (Hastings House, New York, 1947) p.1-44.

Baseball Eddy. See Kelly, E. A.

Basin Cats

The schoolboys at Richmond, Va., in 1856, were fond of fighting. Groups from the various sections of the city were termed *cats* with the name of the section in which they lived added, e.g. *Basin Cats*.[1]

[1] *The End of an Era*, John S. Wise (Houghton Mifflin and Company, New York and Boston, 1899) p. 59.

Bates, William Gelston

William Gelston Bates has been called the *Father of the Hampden County Bar*, the *Historian of the Hampden County Bar*, and the *Nestor of the Hampden County Bar*.

The *Father of the Hampden County Bar* [1] was attributed to him because he practiced law at Westfield, Hampden County, Mass., for almost half a century, and took a fatherly interest in the lawyers and in the legal interests of that county.

Bates was called the *Historian of the Hampden County Bar* [2] because his long term of practicing law in Hampden County had enabled him to gather a wealth of information about the legal, social, and civic activities of this county. The public considered him the authority on such matters.

The *Nestor of the Hampden County Bar* [2] was the nickname given to Bates in allusion to his oratorical ability and trustworthiness as a counselor. Nestor was one of the heroes of Troy renowned for his eloquence and sagacity.

William Gelston Bates was born at Westfield, Mass., in 1803, and died there in 1880.

[1] *Contemporary American Biography: Biographical Sketches of Representative Men of the Day, Representatives of Modern Thought, and Progress, of the Pulpit, the Press, the Bench and Bar. of Legislation, Invention, and the Great Industrial Interests of the Country* (Atlantic Publishing and Engraving Company, New York, 1902) vol. 3, p. 76.

[2] *"Our County and Its People": A History of Hampden County, Massachusetts*, Alfred Minot Copeland, Editor (The Century Memorial Publishing Company, Boston, 1902) vol. 1, p. 320, 321.

Battery Dan. See Finn, D. E.

Battle above the Clouds

The *Battle above the Clouds* [1] and the *Battle in the Clouds* [2] were nicknames given to the Battle of Chattanooga, fought on Lookout Mountain near Chattanooga, Tenn., on November 24, 1863, because Lookout Mountain is so high that clouds are often lower than its summit on which the fighting took place. In this battle it is said the troops were sometimes concealed by the clouds.

[1] *A History of the United States for Schools with an Introductory History of the Discovery and English Colonization of North America*, Alexander Johnston (Henry Holt and Company, New York, 1897) p. 333.

[2] *History of the United States of America, under the Constitution*, James Schouler (Dodd, Mead and Company, New York, 1899) vol. 6, p. 512.

Battle Axe Division. See Sixty-fifth Infantry Division of World War II

Battle Axe Gleason. See Gleason, P. J.

Battle Creek, Michigan

Battle Creek is widely known as the *Breakfast Food City* [1] because it has achieved a national reputation for the manufacture of breakfast cereals. The Battle Creek Sanitarium was one of the pioneers in developing ready-to-eat breakfast foods.

[1] *Our State of Michigan*, Revised Edition, Arthur Dondineau and Leah A. Spencer (The Macmillan Company, New York, 1930) p. 117.

Battle Hymn of the Republic. See Marseillaise of the Unemotional Yankee

Battle-born State. See Nevada

Battle Month

April has been nicknamed the *Battle Month* [1] because so many important battles in American history have been fought in that month.

[1] *Nicknames: A Dictionary of Words and Phrases*, by George T. Odell, distributed by the Washington Bureau, Washington, D.C., p. 1.

Battle of the Giants

In 1858 Stephen Arnold Douglas, a Democrat, and Abraham Lincoln, a Republican, were candidates to represent Illinois in the United States Senate. They toured the state speaking to large audiences. Because Douglas and Lincoln were both able and accomplished orators, their campaign was designated the *Battle of the Giants*.[1]

[1] *The Growth of a Nation, the United States of America*, Revised Edition, Eugene C. Barker, Walter P. Webb, and William E. Dodd (Row, Peterson and Company, Evanston, Ill., 1934) p. 448.

Battle of the Kegs

In 1777, during the Revolutionary War, a group of rebelling colonists, led by David Bushnell, loaded a number of kegs with gun powder and set them afloat on the Delaware river in an attempt to blow up the British frigate *Cerberus* and other British vessels anchored at Philadelphia. As a result of this maneuver a British boat was blown up. Alarmed by the occurrence, the occupants of the other British ships detailed a number of soldiers to the wharves. In their excitement these soldiers zealously fired at everything that they saw floating on the river, including the wooden kegs. Historians, in writing of this "battle," have generally designated it *The Battle of the Kegs*.[1] Francis Hopkinson, an American patriot, commemorated the affair in a somewhat satirical and humorous poem entitled *The Battle of the Kegs*.

[1] *History of Eastern Connecticut Embracing the Counties of Tolland, Windham, Middlesex and New London*, Pliny LeRoy Harwood (The Pioneer Historical Publishing Company, Chicago, and New Haven, Conn., 1932) vol. 2, p. 771.

Battle of the Prayer-books

During the Civil War the southern people omitted from their church services the customary prayer for the President of the United States. At New Orleans, Brigadier General Benjamin Franklin Butler, who served as the Federal military governor of that city from May 1 until December 16, 1862, ordered the churches to offer a prayer for President Abraham Lincoln as a part of their Sunday services while the Union troops occupied the city. At St. Paul's Episcopal Church, when the Reverend Elijah Guion chose to omit this prayer, he was seized by Federal soldiers who had been posted at the churches to enforce this order. As the soldiers marched down the aisle to arrest the minister, the women of the congregation threw their prayer-books and hymnals at them. This came to be known as the *Battle of the Prayer-books*.[1]

[1] *Jefferson Davis, Political Soldier*, Elisabeth Cutting (Dodd, Mead and Company, New York, 1930) p. 193. *Some Old Southern Letters*, Grace Lea Hunt (The Raeder Company, Wilkes-Barre, Pa., 1924) p. 33.

Battle of the Rocks

On August 30, 1862, during the Second Battle of Bull Run, at Manassas, in Virginia, the Montgomery Guards of Louisiana found that in the midst of the severe fighting their ammunition had become exhausted. Seeing a quantity of blasted and broken rock Captain Rice ordered his men to throw the rocks at the oncoming Federal soldiers. Other units adopted similar tactics and held the enemy in check till reinforcements arrived. This was termed the *Battle of the Rocks*.[1]

[1] *Confederate Military History, a Library of Confederate States History, in Twelve Volumes, Written by Distinguished Men of the South, and Edited by General Clement A. Evans of Georgia* (Confederate Publishing Company, Atlanta, Ca., 1899) vol. 10, p. 225, 234.

Battlefield Angel. See Hancock, Cornelia

Battleground of Freedom. See Kansas

Battling Bishops. See Ohio Wesleyan University

Battling Bob. See La Follette, R. M., Sr.

Baugh, Samuel Adrian

Samuel Adrian Baugh, who played halfback in national league football, was nicknamed *Slinging Sammy* [1] when he was an all-American baseball player before he became internationally known as a football star. The nickname was further popularized because of his skillful forward passing.

Samuel Adrian Baugh was born at Temple, Tex., on March 17, 1915.

[1] A communication from Jack Espey, General Manager of The Washington Club of The National Football League, Washington, D.C., April 10, 1939.

Bawling Jenkins. See Jenkins, James

Bay Horse. See Boston, Mass.

Bay State. See Massachusetts

Bay Staters. See Massachusetts Inhabitants

Bayard, James Asheton
James Asheton Bayard was widely known as the *Goliath of His Party* and the *High Priest of the Constitution.*

The *Goliath of His Party* [1] was attributed to him because he championed the principles and activities of the Federal party while he was United States Senator from Delaware from 1804 to 1813. The giant Goliath in the Bible story stood as the defender of the Philistines against the Israelites.

Bayard was nicknamed the *High Priest of the Constitution* [2] because he served as an outstanding constitutional lawyer, upholding and defending the Constitution of the United States.

He was born at Philadelphia, Pa., on July 28, 1767, and died at Washington, Del., on August 6, 1815.

[1] *The American Portrait Gallery . . .* , A. D. Jones (J. M. Emerson and Company, New York, 1855) p. 160.

Bayard of the Press. See Pleasants, J. H.

Bayard of the Revolution. See Laurens, John

Bayard of the Sea. See Jones, J. P.

Bayard of the South. See Marion, Francis

Bayou State. See Mississippi

Beadles. See Virginians

Beagles. See Virginians

Beal, Abraham
Abraham Beal, a philanthropist, was called the *Prisoner's Friend* [1] because of his active interest in criminals in England, particularly those convicted of being intoxicated. After his emigration to the United States in 1848 he resumed his work of advocating temperance and of encouraging unfortunate prisoners to lead more respectable lives after their prison terms were over.

Abraham Beal was born at Chatham, England, about 1803, and died at Brooklyn, N. Y., on February 25, 1872.

[1] *Appleton's Cyclopaedia of American Biography,* ed. by James Grant Wilson and John Fiske (D. Appleton and Company, New York, 1895) vol. 1, p. 203.

Beanpole Jimmy. See Jones, J. C.

Beans. See Reardon, J. E.

Bear Cats. See Southwest Baptist College

Bear Party
The *Bear Party* [1] and the *Bears* are names given to a group of thirty-three Americans who, on June 10, 1846, captured the Mexican settlement, Sonoma in what is now Sonoma County, California. This nickname was given to the group because, after they captured the settlement, they called the territory the Californian Republic and displayed their flag, on which was depicted a grizzly bear.

[1] *Our First War in Mexico,* Farnham Bishop (Charles Scribner's Sons, New York, 1916) p. 106.

Bear State. See Arkansas; Kentucky

Bearcats. See University of Cincinnati; Williamette University

Bears. See *Bear Party;* Kentuckians; Ursinus College; Washington University; White Plains Bears Football Club

Beast. See Butler, B. F.

Beast Butler. See Butler, B. F.

Beau. See Dawson, John

Beau Brummel of the Army. See MacArthur, Douglas

Beau Brummel of the Senate. See Lewis, J. H.

Beau Jonathan. See Hazard, J. J.

Beau Neill. See Neill, T. H.

Beauregard, Pierre Gustave Toutant

Pierre Beauregard was nicknamed the *Hero of Fort Sumter*,[1] *Old Bore, Old Alphabet*[2] because he had more than the usual number of initials, and *Prince John*.[2] His bravery and leadership at the Battle of Fort Sumter in Charleston Harbor gave him the nickname the *Hero of Fort Sumter*. His soldiers affectionately called him *Old Bore*, a corruption of his name; and his associates named him *Prince John*.

Pierre Gustave Toutant Beauregard was born in St. Bernard Parish near New Orleans, La., on May 28, 1818, of French ancestry, and died February 20, 1893.

[1] *Lee's Lieutenants*, Douglas Southall Freeman, Charles Scribner's Sons, New York, 1943, vol. 5, p. xxxi-xxxii.
[2] *A Book of Nicknames*, John Goff (Courier-Journal Job Printing Company, Louisville, Ky., 1892, p. 26.

Beautiful Bob. See Taylor, Robert

Beautiful City. See Cincinnati, Ohio

Beautiful City by the Sea. See Portland, Me.

Beauty Stuart. See Stuart, J. E. B.

Beaver State. See Oregon

Beavers. See College of the City of New York; Oregon State College; Oregonians

Beck, Walter William

Walter William Beck, who was born at Decatur, Ill., on October 16, 1906, and who was a pitcher in major league baseball, was nicknamed *Elmer the Great*[1] by his colleagues among the Brooklyn Dodgers.

[1] *Who's Who in Major League Base Ball*, comp. by Harold (Speed) Johnson (Buxton Publishing Company, Chicago, 1933) p. 72.

Beech Seal

From 1764 until about 1789, during the dispute between New York and New Hampshire over the Vermont Territory, the settlers who had received their land grant from New Hampshire resented the surveyors from New York who insisted that grants must carry the New York seal. In retaliation those with grants from New Hampshire applied what they called a *Beech Seal*[1] to the New York representatives—bundles of newly cut beech rods were used to whip them out of the neighborhood.

[1] *The Mountain Hero and His Associates*, Henry W. De Puy (Dayton and Wentworth, Boston, 1855) p. 176.

Bee Hive State. See Utah

Beecher, Lyman

Lyman Beecher, a theologian, was called the *Father of More Brains Than Any Other Man in America*[1] because so many of his thirteen children gained national and international prominence. He was born at New Haven, Conn., on October 12, 1775, and died at Brooklyn, N.Y., on January 10, 1863.

[1] *Encyclopedia Americana* (Americana Corporation, New York and Chicago, 1932) vol. 3, p. 427.

Beecher, Thomas Kinnicut

Thomas Kinnicut Beecher, a Congregational clergyman, was commonly designated *Father Tom*[1] by his parishioners and acquaintances in Elmira, N.Y. He was greatly loved by all who knew him.

Thomas Kinnicut Beecher was born at Litchfield, Conn., on February 10, 1824, and died at Elmira, N.Y., on March 14, 1900.

[1] *Dictionary of American Biography under the Auspices of the American Council of Learned Societies*, ed. by Allen Johnson (Charles Scribner's Sons, New York, 1928) vol. 1, p. 137.

Beecher's Bibles

About 1849 or 1850, while the question of whether or not Kansas would be admitted as a slave-holding state was under discussion, the New England Emigrant Aid Society, composed of men in the New England states who were opposed to slavery gathered money and guns to be used by the anti-slavery emigrants in Kansas Territory. The rifles, because they were considered to have been collected for use in a holy cause, were called *Beecher's Bibles*.[1] They were probably named after Henry Ward Beecher, a preacher and ardent opponent of slavery.

[1] *The American Nation*, Richard J. Purcell (Ginn and Company, New York and Boston, 1929) p. 427.

Beedle. See Smith, W. B.

Beef Barons

The nickname *Beef Barons*[1] has been widely used by journalists to refer to the American meat packing firms which control

Beef Barons—Continued
the packing and distribution of meats and meat products. The term is commonly applied to Armour, Swift, Cudahy, and Morris.

[1] *St. Louis Daily Globe-Democrat*, St. Louis, Mo., October 1, 1905, p. 4.
The Washington Post, Washington, D.C., October 1, 1905, p. 2.

Beef State. See Texas

Beef-heads. See Texans

Bee-hive of Industry. See Providence, R. I.

Beer Keg Battery
The battery of sweet gum cannon located at Spanish Fort, Ala., during the spring of 1865, were designated the *Beer Keg Battery* [1] because they discharged six and twelve pound shells coated with turpentine, which resembled beer kegs. They were also called the *Sweet Gum Battery, (q.v)*.

[1] *Centennial History of Missouri (The Center State) One Hundred Years in the Union, 1820-1921*, Walter B. Stevens (The S. I. Clarke Publishing Company, St. Louis, Mo., and Chicago, 1921) vol. 2, p. 5.

Bees. See University of Baltimore

Beetle. See Smith, W. B.

Belasco, David
David Belasco was commonly known as the *Wizard of American Drama* [1] because of his dramatic ability and for his cleverness in devising stage lighting.

He was born at San Francisco, Calif., on July 25, 1859, and died at New York City, on May 14, 1931.

[1] *Encyclopedia of American Biography: American Biography, a New Cyclopedia* (Published under the direction of The American Historical Society, Inc., New York, 1925) vol. 22, p. 192.

Belfast Chicken. See Clark, William

Belford, James Burns
James Burns Belford was nicknamed the *Red-headed Rooster of the Rockies* [1] while he was a Representative from Colorado to the United States Congress in the 1870's. Belford had red hair, was fiery, outspoken, and fearless in debate, and lived in the Rocky Mountain region.

James Burns Belford was born at Lewiston, Pa., on September 28, 1837, and died at Denver, Colo., on January 7, 1910.

[1] *My Quarter Century of American Politics*, Champ Clark (Harper and Brothers, New York, 1920) vol. 2, p. 221.

Bell, Alexander Graham
Alexander Graham Bell, who was born at Edinburgh, Scotland, on March 3, 1847, and who died at Barreck, Nova Scotia, on August 2, 1922, has been designated the *Father of the Telephone* [1] because he invented the telephone, in July 1875.

[1] *A Book of Nicknames*, John Goff (Courier-Journal Job Printing Company, Louisville, Ky., 1892) p. 29.

Bell, Charles Jasper
Charles Jasper Bell, a Missouri lawyer and politician, was nicknamed the *Investigator* [1] because he was Chairman of the Special Congressional Committee to investigate the Townsend Old Age Pension Plan and the Townsend organizations in the late 1930's.

[1] An interview with Captain Victor Hunt Harding, Secretary of the National Democratic Congress Reelection Committee, Washington, D.C., April 10, 1939.

Bell, Joshua Fry
Joshua Fry Bell, who was born at Danville, Ky., on November 25, 1811, and who died there on August 17, 1870, was popularly called the *Silver-tongued Orator* [1] because of his eloquence and outstanding success as an orator.

[1] *The National Cyclopaedia of American Biography* (James T. White and Company, New York, 1906) vol. 13, p. 581.

Bell and Everett Party
The Constitutional Union party formed in 1860 was often termed the *Bell and Everett Party* [1] because John Bell was the candidate for the presidency, and Edward Everett, the candidate for the vice presidency.

[1] *The Encyclopaedia Britannica*, Fourteenth Edition (Encyclopaedia Britannica Inc., 1929) vol. 3, p. 372.

Belle City. See Racine, Wis.

Belle City of the Bluegrass Regions. See Lexington, Ky.

Belle City of the Lakes. See Racine, Wis.

Belle of the Union. See Le Vert, O. W.

Bellona. See Eaton, M. O.

Beloved Dean. See Moore, W. H.

Beloved Jailer. See Whitman, J. L.

Beloved Man of the Four Nations.
See Hawkins, Benjamin

Belshazzar's Feast

The term *Belshazzar's Feast* [1] was applied
to a costly and elaborate banquet given on
October 29, 1884, at Delmonico's in New
York City, by a group of Wall Street financiers and other prominent men in honor of
James Gillespie Blaine, the Republican candidate for President of the United States. The
nickname originated in the caption of a cartoon by W. H. McDougall in the New York
World on October 30, 1884, entitled *The
Royal Feast of Belshazzar Blaine and th.
Money Kings.* The biblical account of the
feast of Belshazzar is in the book of Daniel

[1] *Blaine of Maine, His Life and Times,* Charles Ed-
ward Russell (Cosmopolitan Book Corporation, New
York, 1931) p. 399.
New York *World,* October 30, 1884, p. 1.

Ben Turpin. See Turpin, C. M.

Bender, Charles Albert

Charles Albert Bender, a Chippewa Indian, who was born at Brainerd, Minn., and
who coached in major league baseball, was
called *Chief* [1] because he was an Indian.

[1] *Who's Who in Major League Base Ball,* comp. by
Harold (Speed) Johnson (Buxton Publishing Company,
Chicago, 1933) p. 473.

Benedict Arnold

In American parlance a *Benedict Arnold*
is equivalent to a Judas, a betrayer. The
original Benedict Arnold forsook his post
as Major General in the Revolutionary
Army to join the British forces in 1780. He
was born at Norwick, Conn., on January 14,
1741, and died at London, England, on
June 14, 1801.

Bengal Tiger. See Twiggs, D. E.

Bengals. See Louisiana State University

Benge, Ray Adelphia

Ray Adelphia Benge, who was born at
Jacksonville, Tex., on April 22, 1905, and
who pitched in major league baseball, was
called *Silent Cal* [1] because he talked so little.
This was the nickname of Calvin Coolidge
who was President at that time.

[1] *Who's Who in Major League Base Ball,* comp. by
Harold (Speed) Johnson (Buxton Publishing Company,
Chicago, 1933, p. 473.

Benjamin, Judah Philip

Judah Philip Benjamin was nicknamed
the *Brains of the Confederacy* [1] because he
was Attorney General of the Southern Confederacy until the close of the Civil War in
1865.

He was born at Saint Croix, West Indies,
on August 11, 1811, and died at Paris,
France, on May 7, 1884.

[1] *The Source Book* (Perpetual Encyclopedia Corporation, Chicago, 1932) vol. 1, p. 284.

Benning, Henry Lewis

Brigadier General Henry Lewis Benning
was designated *Old Rock* [1] during the Civil
War because of his calm and intrepid spirit
on the battlefield.

He was born in Columbia County, Ga.,
on April 2, 1814, and died at Columbus,
Ohio, on July 10, 1875.

[1] *Dictionary of American Biography, under the Auspices of the American Council of Learned Societies,* ed.
by Dumas Malone (Charles Scribner's Sons, New York,
1929) vol. 2, p. 203.

Benton, Thomas Hart

Thomas Hart Benton was called the *Gold
Bug, Gold Humbug, Old Bullion, Old
Humbug,* and the *Old Roman.*

When a United States Senator from
Missouri from 1821 until 1851, he urged
that the United States adopt only metallic
currency. His opponents registered their disapproval of him and his monetary policies
by nicknaming him *Gold Bug,* [1] *Gold Humbug* [2] *Old Humbug* [3] and *Old Bullion.* [4]
During the 1830's when Benton was most
active in advocating the exclusive use of
metal for currency, gold coins were frequently called *Benton's Mint Drops.*

The *Old Roman* [4] was given as a nickname to Senator Benton because of his fondness for alluding to the classics, especially
to Roman history.

Benton, T. H.—Continued

Thomas Hart Benton was born near Hillsboro, N.C., on March 14, 1782, and died at Washington, D.C., on April 10, 1858.

[1] *The Life of Thomas Hart Benton,* William M. Meigs (J. B. Lippincott Company, Philadelphia, 1904) p. 262.
[2] "Thomas H. Benton" by Joseph M. Rogers, in *American Crisis Biographies,* ed. by Ellis Paxson Oberholtzer (George W. Jacobs and Company, Philadelphia, 1905) p. 184.
[3] *Men and Events of Forty Years: Autobiographical Reminiscences of an Active Career from 1850 to 1890,* Josiah Bushnell Grinnell (D. Lothrop Company, Boston, 1891) p. 59.
[4] "Thomas Hart Benton" by Theodore Roosevelt, in *American Statesmen,* ed. by John T. Morse, Junior (Houghton Mifflin and Company, New York and Boston, 1903) p. 93.

Benton's Mint-drops. See Benton, Thomas Hart

Berea College

The athletic teams of Berea College, at Berea, Ky., were designated the *Mountaineers* [1] because the college serves the mountain sections of the Southern Appalachian Mountains.

[1] A communication from Rexford C. Quimby, Berea College, Berea, Ky., January 4, 1936.

Berlin, New Hampshire

Berlin has been called the *Chemical City* [1] because it is the site of manufacturing establishments which produce various chemicals, the principal one being chloroform. At one time two thirds of the chloroform used in the United States was manutured at Berlin. Some of the chemicals it produces are by-products of Berlin's chief manufactures which are sulphite pulp and paper.

[1] *New Hampshire, Resources, Attractions, and Its People, a History,* Hobart Pillsbury (The Lewis Historical Publishing Company, Inc., New York, 1927) vol. 3, p. 671.

Bernicia Boy. See Heenan, J. C.

Berrien, John MacPherson

John MacPherson Berrien was nicknamed the *American Cicero* [1] because of his manner of speaking in Congress when he was Senator from Georgia in the 1920's.

John MacPherson Berrien was born near Princeton, N.J., on August 23, 1781, and died at Savannah, Ga., on January 1, 1856.

[1] *Appleton's Cyclopaedia of American Biography,* ed. by James Grant Wilson and John Fiske (D. Appleton and Company, New York, 1895) vol. 1, p. 249.

Best Friend

The first locomotive built in the United States for actual railroad service has been designated the *Best Friend* [1] because people felt that it would render invaluable service in revolutionizing transportation. This locomotive was built at West Point Foundry in New York in 1830, and was used on the Baltimore and Ohio Railroad.

[1] *The National Cyclopaedia of American Biography* (James T. White and Company, New York, 1893) vol. 3, p. 115.

Bet-a-million-Gates. See Gates, J. W.

Bethany College (Lindsborg, Kans.)

The athletic teams of Bethany College at Lindsborg, Kans., were called the *Swedes* and the *Terrible Swedes* because most of the football players were of Swedish descent.

[1] A communication from George C. Carlson, Director of Athletics at Bethany College, Lindsborg, Kans., June 12, 1935.

Bethel College

The *Bethel Corporals* [1] is the nickname given during World War I to the athletic teams of Bethel College, at McKenzie, Tenn., because like Napoleon they were small but valiant.

[1] A communication from Leonard L. Thomas, President of Bethel College, McKenzie, Tenn., November 25, 1935.

Bethel Corporals. See Bethel College

Bethel Hill. See Hill, D. H.

Bethune, Thomas Green

Thomas Greene Bethune was widely known as *Blind Tom.* [1] Despite the fact that he was blind and was practically an idiot, *Blind Tom* was exhibited throughout the United States and in Europe as a musical prodigy because of his remarkable ability to play on the piano popular or classic compositions after having heard them. He was also successful in imitating animals, birds, and the sounds of a number of musical instruments.

He was born of slave parents near Columbia, Ga., in 1849 and was named after a former master. He died at New York City in 1908.

[1] *The National Cyclopaedia of American Biography* (James T. White and Company, New York, 1900) vol. 10, p. 198.

Bettis Academy

The athletic teams of Bettis Academy, at Trenton, S.C., were nicknamed *Red Devils*,[1] and *Skullions*; *Red Devils* because they wore red helmets and red jerseys, and *Skullions* because they used their heads to assist in making tackles.[1]

[5] A communication from F. M. Jones, Coach of Athletics at Bettis Academy, Trenton, S.C., December 18, 1935.

Betts, Walter M.

Walter M. Betts, who was born at Millsboro, Del., on February 18, 1898, and who pitched in major league baseball was popularly called *Huck*[1] short for *Huckleberry* as newspaper writers had nicknamed him.

[1] *Who's Who in Major League Base Ball*, comp. by Harold (Speed) Johnson (Buxton Publishing Company, Chicago, 1933) p. 80.

Bible-class Man. See Stuart, J. E. B.

Bickerdyke, Mary Ann Ball

Mrs. Mary Ann Ball Bickerdyke was nicknamed the *Brigadier Commanding Hospitals*[1] and *Mother Bickerdyke*.[2]

She was given the first nickname during the Civil War by the officers and doctors while she was a nurse. The soldiers whom she nursed called her *Mother Bickerdyke*.

Mary Ann Ball Bickerdyke was born in Knox County, Ohio, on July 19, 1817, and died at Galesburg, Ill., on November 8, 1901.

[1] *Mary A. Bickerdyke, "Mother,"* Julia A. Chase (Published under the Auspices of the Woman's Relief Corps, Department of Kansas, by the Journal Publishing House, Lawrence, Kans., 1896) p. 28.
Mother Bickerdyke and the Soldier: The Woman who Battled for the Boys in Blue: Mother Bickerdyke, Her Life and Labors for the Relief of Our Soldiers, Sketches of Battle Scenes and Incidents of the Sanitary Service, Margaret B. Davis (A. T. Dewey, San Francisco, Calif., 1886) p. 13.
Mother Bickerdyke as I Knew Her, Florence Shaw Kellogg, with an introduction by Jenkin Lloyd Jones (Unity Publishing Company, Chicago, 1907) p. 27.
[2] *Mary A. Bickerdyke, "Mother,"* Julia A. Chase (Published under the Auspices of the Woman's Relief Corps, Department of Kansas, by the Journal Publishing House, Lawrence, Kans., 1896) p. 43.

Bickmore, Albert Smith

Albert Smith Bickmore, an educator and naturalist, was designated the *Father of the Museum*[1] because it was largely through him that the American Museum of Nattural History in New York City was founded. He received his inspiration for such a museum while he was a student under Jean Louis Rodolphe Agassiz at Har-

vard University about 1861. Bickmore travelled extensively collecting specimens of marine animals for the Museum.

Albert Smith Bickmore was born at Tenant's Harbor, Me., on March 1, 1839, and died at Nonquitt, Mass., on August 12, 1914.

[1] *Dictionary of American Biography under the Auspices of the American Council of Learned Societies,* ed. by Allen Johnson (Charles Scribner's Sons, New York, 1929) vol. 2, p. 239.

Bicknell, Joshua

Joshua Bicknell, a statesman who enjoyed a long and honorable career in the political affairs of his native Rhode Island, was often designated *Old Aristides*[1] because of his unblemished character, his honesty and the fairness of his judicial decisions.

Bicknell was born at Barrington, R.I., on January 14, 1759, and died there in December, 1837.

[1] *The National Cyclopaedia of American Biography* (James T. White and Company, New York, 1900) vol. 8, p. 45.

Biddle, Clement

Clement Biddle was nicknamed *Quaker Soldier*[1] because, although Quakers do not advocate war or warlike activities, Biddle led a company of Quaker volunteers against the Paxton Boys, a band of ruffians who threatened to attack Philadelphia in 1764, for protecting friendly Indians from the desperadoes. When the Revolutionary War broke out Biddle assisted in organizing a Quaker Company of Volunteers which joined the Continental Army.

Clement Biddle was born at Philadelphia, Pa., on May 10, 1740, and died there on July 14, 1814.

[1] *Appleton's Cyclopaedia of American Biography,* ed. by James Grant Wilson and John Fiske (D. Appleton and Company, New York, 1895) vol. 1, p. 255.

Biddle, Nicholas

Nicholas Biddle was nicknamed *Emperor Nick of the Bribery Bank*[1] by those who opposed the maintenance of the National Bank and the political power Biddle exerted as president of the bank. It was charged that certain newspapers were influenced by Biddle's financial contributions. Biddle became President of the Second Bank of the United States in 1823.

Nicholas Biddle was born at Philadelphia, Pa., on January 8, 1786, and died there on February 27, 1844.

[1] *The Godlike Daniel,* Samuel Hopkins Adams (Sears Publishing Company, Inc., New York, 1930) p. 108,

Biddy. See Reed, T. B.

Bierce, Ambrose

Ambrose Bierce was nicknamed *Bitter Bierce* [1] because of the sarcastic humor in much of his writing. He was born in Meiggs County, Ohio, on June 24, 1842. The date of his death is not known for he went to Mexico in 1913 and was never heard of afterwards.

[1] *The Encyclopaedia Britannica,* Fourteenth Edition (Encyclopaedia Britannica Inc., 1929) vol. 3, p. 549-50.

Big Bend State. See Tennessee

Big Benders. See Tennesseans

Big Buckeye. See Sproat, Ebenezer

Big Bugs

In a letter to his wife written about 1833 Amos Kendal from Massachusetts, one of Andrew Jackson's Cabinet members, spoke of the Washington society people and of the officials themselves as *Big Bugs*.[1]

[1] *Our Nation in the Building,* Helen Nicolay (The Century Company, New York, 1916) p. 192.

Big Captain. See Crawford, William

Big Chief. See Curtis, Charles

Big Dan. See Tobin, D. J.

Big Feller. See Sullivan, T. D.

Big Five

The *Big Five* [1] is a term applied to a group of men present at the Peace Conference in Paris, on January 12, 1919. This group was to a great extent responsible for the Versailles Treaty.

The representatives of the United States, the British Empire, France, Italy, and Japan were known as the *Big Five.*

During World War II the *Big Five* were the United States, Great Britain, France, Russia and China. (See also the *Big Four* and the *Big Three.*)

[1] *The Encyclopedia Americana* (Americana Corporation, New York and Chicago, 1927) vol. 28, p. 514.

Big Five Packers

The Armour, Swift, Wilson, Cudahy, and Morris packing companies have been designated the *Big Five Packers*.[1] An investigation by Attorney General Alexander Mitchell Palmer in 1919 revealed that they were controlling the following industries: meat packing, butter and eggs, oleomargarine, fertilizer, cottonseed oil, perfumes, and leather novelties. They were also attempting to get a monopoly on the grocery business. On February 27, 1920, by a decree of the Supreme Court the packing companies discontinued their operating of those interests not essential to the meat packing industry.

[1] *The National Cyclopaedia of American Biography* (James T. White and Company, New York, 1924) Current Volume A, p. 45.

Big Four

Collis P. Huntington, Leland Stanford, Charles Crocker, and Mark Hopkins have been designated by California historians the *Big Four* [1] because they were chiefly responsible for the construction of the first transcontinental railroad to California, the Central Pacific and the Union Pacific Railroads. They met near Promontory, Nev., on May 10, 1869, to complete this tremendous project which linked the East and the West and gave an added impetus to the growth of the West Coast.

The *Big Four* [2] is also applied to the representatives of the United States, Great Britain, France and Italy at the Peace Conference which convened at Paris on January 12, 1919. These were Woodrow Wilson, Lloyd George, Georges Benjamin Eugene Clemenceau, and Vittorio Emanuele Orlando.

[1] *History of the San Francisco Bay Region,* Bailey Millard (The American Historical Society, Inc., New York and Chicago, 1924) vol. 1, p. 213.

[2] *History of America,* Carl Russell Fish (American Book Company, New York and Boston, 1928) p. 545.

The Growth of a Nation, the United States of America, Revised Edition, Eugene L. Barker, Walter P. Webb, and William E. Dodd (Row, Peterson and Company, New York and San Francisco, 1934) p. 652.

Big-game Hunter. See Tinkham, G. H.

Big Greens. See Marshall College

Big Jim. See Farley, J. A.

Big Judge Powell. See Powell, J. S.

Big Knife or Big Knives

The early white settlers in Virginia and in what is now Pennsylvania were called *Big Knife* [1] or *Big Knives* by the Indians because the pioneer hunters carried long knives and the officers of the militia wore swords.

[1] *Fort Ligonier and Its Times; a History of the First English Fort West of the Allegheny Mountains. . . ,* First Edition, C. Hale Sipe (The Telegraph Press, Harrisburg, Pa., 1933) p. 75.

Big Man from Little Egypt. See Keller, K. E.

Big Medicine. See Kelly, C. W.

Big Moose. See Earnshaw, G. L.; Walsh, E. A.

Big-Navy Claude. See Swanson, C. A.

Big Poison. See Waner, L. J. and Waner, P. G.

Big Reds. See Denison University; University of Miami

Big Sister Policy

In 1888 the United States announced that its policy toward the countries of South America was one of peace, friendship, and commercial enlargement; this was nicknamed the *Big Sister Policy*.[1]

[1] *Dollar Diplomacy: A Study in American Imperialism,* Scott Nearing and Joseph Freeman (B. W. Huebsch and the Viking Press, New York, 1925) p. 243.

Big Six

A union of printers in New York City known as Typographical Union Number Six in 1885 termed itself the *Big Six* [1] because of its strength in competing against non-union organizations or individuals in the printing industry.

[1] *Grover Cleveland, the Man and the Statesman,* Robert McElroy (Harper and Brothers, New York and London, 1923) p. 96.

Big Six. See Auker, E. L.; Mathewson, Christopher

Big Steve. See Owen, Stephen

Big Stick Policy

While Theodore Roosevelt was President of the United States, he made a speech at Chicago in 1902 in which he quoted an old saying, "Speak softly and carry a big stick, and you will go far." [1] The way in which he dealt with trusts, monopolies, the conservation of human and natural resources, and with various other critical domestic and foreign situations was the *Big Stick Policy*.[1] President Theodore Roosevelt was often pictured by cartoonists as carrying a large club.

[1] *Theodore Roosevelt, the Boy and the Man,* New Edition, ed. James Morgan (The Macmillan Company, New York, 1919) p. 216-17.
The Boy's Life of Theodore Roosevelt, Hermann Hagedorn (Harper and Brothers, New York and London, 1918) p. 282-3.
T. R. in Cartoon: Four Hundred Illustrations by Leading Cartoonists of the Daily and Weekly Press All over the World, collected and ed. by Raymond Gros (The Saalfield Publishing Company, New York and Chicago, 1910) p. 85.

Big Ten

The *Big Ten* were a group of men at the Peace Conference in Paris, in 1919, who were to a great extent responsible for framing the final draft of the Versailles Treaty. The prime ministers and foreign secretaries of the United States, the British Empire, France, Italy and Japan made up the *Big Ten*.

[1] *The Encyclopedia Americana* (Americana Corporation, New York and Chicago, 1927) vol. 28, p. 514.
A Short Story of the American People, 1860-1921, Robert Granville Caldwell (G. P. Putnam's Sons, New York and London, 1927) p. 532.

Big Three

Woodrow Wilson, Lloyd George, and Georges Clemenceau were the outstanding figures and exerted so much influence at the Peace Conference in Paris, in 1919, that they were termed The *Big Three*.[1]

During World War II the *Big Three* were President Franklin Delano Roosevelt, Prime Minister Winston S. Churchill and Marshal Joseph Stalin.

[1] *Socialized History of the United States,* Charles Garrett Vannest and Henry Lester Smith (Charles Scribner's Sons, New York and Boston, 1931) p. 574.

Big Thunder. See Wayne, Anthony

Big Tim. See Sullivan, T. D.

Big Train. See Sisk, John; Johnson, W. P.

Biggs, Benjamin Thomas

Governor Benjamin Thomas Biggs of Delaware was often called the *Delaware Plowboy* [1] because as a young man he engaged in agricultural pursuits. He was Governor of Delaware from 1887 to 1891.

He was born near Summit Bridge, Del., on October 1, 1821, and died at Middleton, Del., on December 25, 1893.

[1] *The National Cyclopaedia of American Biography* (James T. White and Company, New York, 1909) vol. 11, p. 537.

Bilbo, Theodore Gilmore

Theodore Gilmore Bilbo has been called the *Two-edged Knife* [1] because of his ability to defend his position in debate and to meet the arguments of his opponents.

He was born at Juniper, Miss., on October 13, 1877, and was a Senator from Mississippi from 1934 until the time of his death on August 21, 1947.

[1] *Washington Herald*, Washington, D.C., June 6, 1935, col. 6, p. 5.

Bill Cody the Scout. See Cody, W. F.

Bill Cody the Wagonmaster. See Cody, W. F.

Bill the Builder. See McAdoo, W. G.

Billie the Kid. See Bonney, William; Russell, W. E.

Billikens. See Saint Louis University

Billings, Montana

Billings, the county seat of Yellowstone County, Mont., was nicknamed the *Magic City* [1] soon after the town was laid out in 1882, because of its rapid increase in population and in property value.

[1] *Montana, the Land and the People*, Robert George Raymer (The Lewis Publishing Company, New York and Chicago, 1930) vol. 1, p. 321.

Billings Polytechnic Institute

The *Crusaders* is the nickname given to the athletic teams of Billings Polytechnic Institute, at Billings, Mont.

Billion-dollar Congress

The Fifty-first Congress of the United States was nicknamed the *Billion-Dollar Congress* [1] because its appropriations from 1889 to 1891 totaled over a billion dollars. This was the first time appropriations had reached the billion dollar mark.

[1] *American History for Colleges*, David Saville Muzzey and John A. Krout (Ginn and Company, New York and London, 1933) p. 513.

Billy Kids. See Daniel Baker College

Bingham, Henry Harrison

Henry Harrison Bingham was known as the *Father of the House* [1] because of his unusually long, continuous term of office as a Representative from Pennsylvania which totaled a period of thirty-three years and nineteen days, the longest continuous service in the House of Representatives up to that time. He served from 1879 to 1912.

He was born at Philadelphia, Pa., on December 4, 1841, and died there on March 22, 1912.

[1] *My Quarter Century of American Politics*, Champ Clark (Harper and Brothers, New York and London, 1920) vol. 1, p. 222.

Biographical Directory of the American Congress, 1774-1927; The Continental Congress, September 5, 1774 to October 21, 1788 and The Congress of the United States, from the First to the Sixty-ninth Congress, March 4, 1789 to March 3, 1927, Inclusive (Government Printing Office, Washington, D.C., 1928) House Document number 783, vol. 16, p. 701.

Bird, Francis William

Francis William Bird was called the *Sage of Walpole* [1] because he spent the greater part of his life at East Walpole, Mass., was considered a wise, scholarly, prudent, and public-spirited citizen.

He was born at Dedham, Mass., on October 22, 1809, and died at East Walpole, on May 23, 1894.

[1] *The National Cyclopaedia of American Biography* (James T. White and Company, New York, 1932) vol. 22. p. 32.

Francis William Bird, a Biographical Sketch (Privately printed at Boston, 1897) p. 2, 110.

Birmingham, Alabama

Birmingham is called *City of Executives,* the *Industrial Center of the Great South,* the *Industrial City of Dixie,* the *Inland Metropolis,* the *Magic City,* the *Magic City of the South,* the *Mineral City of the South,* and the *Pittsburgh of the South.*

Because many men prominent in executive positions make their homes in Birmingham, it has come to be called *City of Executives.* [1] It is widely known as the *Industrial Center of the Great South* [2] because it is one of the outstanding southern industrial cities. The factors that have developed Birmingham into the *Industrial Center of the Great South* are as follows: (1) the city is located amidst the deposits of iron ore, coal, and other mineral products which are essential for the manufacturing of iron and steel; (2) available electric power is supplied by the hydro-electricity plants located on the Coosa and the Tallapoosa rivers, and on the Tennessee river at Muscle Shoals; (3) vast quantities of commercial commodities are manufactured, such as cast iron, wire, nails, steel cars, steel rails, cotton gins, lumber products, cotton goods, rubber tires, chemicals, and explosives. Birmingham is styled the *Industrial City of Dixie* [3] because it is the leading industrial city of the South. This city is nicknamed the *Inland Metropolis* [4] in commemoration of the fact that it is the industrial capital of the State. Not being located on a river or bay, it owes its importance not to harbors or to shipping facilities by water, but to the development of its natural resources.

Birmingham is designated the *Magic City* [5] or the *Magic City of the South* [4] because of its growth in population, wealth, and commercial importance [3]; the *Mineral City of the South* [4] because it is located in a region in which are found iron ore, coal, limestone, shales, clays, marble, graphite, asphalt, bauxite, mica, dolomites, gravel, barites, and sandstone. There are also mineral springs in the vicinity of Birmingham. It is also known as the *Pittsburgh of the South* because it is the chief regional center of the coal and iron industry. [6]

[1] *The Book of Birmingham*, John R. Hornady (Dodd, Mead and Company, New York, 1921) p. 328.

[2] *Alabama of To-day, 1904: An Industrial Review of the General Business Interests of Birmingham and the Cities and Towns Comprising the Great State of Alabama* (Published by Post B—Alabama Division Travelers Protective Association of America, Birmingham, Ala., 1905) p. 12-13.
   The Encyclopaedia Britannica, Fourteenth Edition (Encyclopaedia Britannica, Inc., New York, 1932) vol. 3, p. 644.
   History of Alabama and Dictionary of Alabama Biography, Thomas McAdory Owen (The S. J. Clarke Publishing Company, Chicago, 1921) vol. 1, p. 140-2.

[3] *Minute Glimpses of American Cities*, Herbert S. Kates (Grosset and Dunlap, New York, 1933) p. 19.

[4] *The Shoppers' Guide of Greater Birmingham, the Center of Alabama* (The Davis Advertising and Sales Company, Publicity Publishers, Birmingham, Ala., 1909) p. 5, 113.
   Alabama: History of Alabama and Her People, Albert Burton Moore, assisted by an advisory council, *Alabama Biography* by a special staff of writers (The American Historical Society, Inc., Chicago and New York, 1927) vol. 1, p. 868.

[5] *Birmingham Unique in Natural Resources: Views of Birmingham Alabama with a Glimpse at Some of the Natural Resources of the Birmingham District and the Industries Based Thereon* (Isidore Newman and Son, Bankers, New York and New Orleans, 1909) p. 1.
   Address of the President of the United States at the Celebration of the Semicentennial of the Founding of

the City of Birmingham, Alabama, October 26, 1921 (Government Printing Office, Washington, D.C. 1921) p. 3.
   The Mineral Wealth of Alabama and Birmingham Illustrated, J. W. DuBose (N. T. Green and Company, Birmingham, Ala., 1886) p. 48.

[6] *The Encyclopedia Americana* (Americana Corporation, New York and Chicago, 1932) vol. 4, p. 5.
   King's Handbook of the United States, planned and ed. by Moses King, text by M. F. Sweetser (Moses King Corporation, Buffalo, N.Y., 1891) p. 35-6.

Birmingham of America. See Pittsburgh, Pa.

Birthplace of American Liberty. See Lexington, Mass.; Philadelphia, Pa.

Birthplace of Baseball. See Cooperstown, N. Y.

Birthplace of California. See San Diego, Calif.

Birthplace of Liberty. See Independence Hall

Birthplace of Technology. See Rensselaer Polytechnic Institute

Bishop, Max Frederick
Max Frederick Bishop, who was born at Waynesboro, Pa., on September 5, 1899, and who played in major league baseball, was nicknamed *Lillie*. [1]

[1] *Who's Who in Major League Base Ball*, comp. by Harold (Speed) Johnson (Burton Publishing Company, Chicago, 1933) p. 81.

Bishop of All Outdoors. See Jackson, Sheldon

Bishop of Congregational Churches. See Weeden, C. F.

Bison City. See Buffalo, N. Y.

Bison's. See Oklahoma Baptist University; Southwestern University; University of Buffalo

Bitter Bierce. See Bierce, Ambrose

Bitter-enders
During the World War I people in the United States who refused to consider a negotiated peace with the Central Powers in Europe were called the *Bitter-enders* [1] be-

Bitter-enders—Continued
cause they preferred that the Allied Powers
should continue fighting the Central Powers
to the "bitter end."

After the close of World War I in 1918,
the name,[1] *Bitter-enders,* was chiefly applied
to those senators who were opposed to President Wilson's proposal that the United States
become a member of the League of Nations.

[1] *A Desk-book of Idioms and Idiomatic Phrases in
English Speech and Literature,* Frank H. Vizetelly and
Leander J. De Bekker (Funk and Wagnalls Company,
New York and London, 1923) p. 41.

The Life of Woodrow Wilson, 1856-1924, Josephus
Daniels (The John C. Winston Company, Chicago and
Philadelphia, 1924) p. 318-19.

*Wilson the Unknown, an Explanation of an Enigma
of History,* Wells Wells (pseudonym) (Charles Scribner's
Sons, New York and London, 1931) p. 255, 297.

Bixby, Horace Ezra

Horace Ezra Bixby, a former steamboat
pilot on the Mississippi River, was nicknamed the *Lightning Pilot* [1] because he knew
the art of piloting a steamboat so well and
possessed such good judgment and accurate
knowledge of the Mississippi River that he
was able to make unusually good time in
running large passenger boats between St.
Louis and New Orleans. He was a pilot on
the Mississippi River between 1844 and
1912.

Horace Ezra Bixby was born at Geneseo,
N.Y., on May 8, 1829, and died at Maplewood, Mo., on August 1, 1912.

[1] *Dictionary of American Biography under the Auspices
of the American Council of Learned Societies,* ed. by
Allen Johnson (Charles Scribner's Sons, New York,
1929) vol. 2, p. 306.

Black and Tans

During the closing years of the Reconstruction Period the members of the Republican party who were unwilling to abandon
the Negro as the basis of this party's power
in the State of Alabama were called the
Black and Tans.[1]

[1] *Civil War and Reconstruction in Alabama,* Walter L.
Fleming (Columbia University Press, New York, 1905)
p. 799.

Black Bears. See University of Maine

Black Belt

The tract of land in Alabama, which
crosses the state somewhat south of its center
in a direction roughly east to west and some
eight miles in width, is the wealthiest and
most productive agricultural region of Alabama and is popularly called the *Black Belt* [1]
because of the black soil. This tract is also
called the *Black Belt* because the Negro
population is very large.

Slaves in the Southern slave-holding states
were very unevenly distributed. The region
in Virginia between the James River and the
border line of North Carolina was also
known as the *Black Belt* [2] because of the
concentration of slaves there, and the whole
of the slave-holding South is sometimes popularly spoken of as the *Black Belt.*

[1] *The Book of Birmingham,* John R. Hornady (Dodd,
Mead and Company, New York, 1921) p. 205.

[2] *Virginia's Attitude toward Slavery and Secession,*
Beverly B. Munford (Longmans, Green and Company,
New York and London, 1909) p. 126.

Black Billy Sunday. See Willbanks, Alexander

Black Cat Division. See Thirteenth Armored Division of World War II

Black Code

Following the Civil War, in order to curb
the newly acquired freedom and power of
the Negroes, the white people of the South
passed laws which discriminated against the
Negroes politically and socially and were
known as the *Black Code* [1] and the *Black
Laws.*

[1] *History of the United States of America, Its Beginning, Progress, and Modern Development, in Ten Volumes,* Jesse Ames Spencer, ed. by Edwin Wiley and
Irving E. Rines (American Educational Alliance, New
York, 1913) vol. 9, p. 372.

*The Abolitionists, together with Personal Memories
of the Struggle for Human Rights, 1830-1864,* John F.
Hume (G. P. Putnam's Sons, New York and London,
1905) p. 35.

Black Dan. See McFarland, Daniel; Webster, Daniel

Black David. See Forman, David

Black Dragons

The steam engines used on the first rail-
roads built in America at the beginning of
the nineteenth century were nicknamed the
*Black Dragons, Devil Wagons, Flaming
Mercuries, Hell on Wheels, Puffing Billies,
Race Horses on Wheels, Snorting Race
Horses,* and *Wonder Devils on Wheels* [1] be-
cause of their speed and noise.

[1] *The Romance of the Rails; The Story of the American Railroads,* Agnes C. Laut, (Tudor Publishing Company, New York, 1936), p. 13, 74, 215.

Black Eagle of Illinois. See Logan, J. A.

Black-eyed Susan

In Texas and other Western states during frontier days, a revolver or a pistol was nicknamed a *Black-eyed Susan* [1] because, when looked at from the muzzle end, it seemed to have one black eye.

[1] *A New Dictionary of Americanisms*, Sylva Clapin (Louis Weiss and Company, New York, 1903) p. 54.

Black Friday

September 24, 1869, was long remembered as *Black Friday* [1] because this day climaxed an orgy of speculation in gold which caused a money panic throughout the United States. The Wall Street firm of Jay Gould and James Fisk had tried to corner all the gold in the United States except that which actually was in the Treasury. They tried to influence President Grant not to interfere, but on September 24, he ordered the sub-treasury of the United States to sell gold. This broke the corner of the speculators. The panic disrupted trade, paralyzed business, and shook the confidence of the public.

[1] *History of the United States of America, Its Beginning, Progress, and Modern Development, in Ten Volumes*, Jesse Ames Spencer, ed. by Edwin Riley and Irving E. Rines (American Educational Alliance, New York, 1910) vol. 6, p. 58.

The American People; a New History for High Schools, The Story of American Democracy, Political and Industrial, Willis Mason West (Allyn and Bacon, New York and Boston, 1933) p. 520.

Black Friday of New England

Friday, May 19, 1780, has been called the *Black Friday of New England* [1] in allusion to the darkness of the day, to the gloom and consternation that prevailed among the people. The darkness was caused by a great forest fire in the vicinity.

[1] *The Encyclopedia Americana* (Americana Corporation, New York and Chicago, 1927) vol. 8, p. 478.

Black Friday of San Francisco

Friday, February 23, 1855, has been generally recorded by California historians as the *Black Friday of San Francisco* [1] because it climaxed a period of acute financial depression attended by the closing of banks, the failures of business firms, and the panic usually characteristic of a financial crisis.

[1] *New California, the Golden*, Rockwell D. Hunt (Silver, Burdett and Company, New York, Chicago, and San Francisco, Calif., 1933) p. 274.

Black Giant. See Webster, Daniel

Black Gold

Petroleum has been called *Black Gold* [1] because of the money it brings to individuals and nations who own it.

[1] *The World Book Encyclopedia* (The Quarrie Corporation, Chicago, 1938) vol. 13, p. 5521.

Black Gowns or Black Robes

The Jesuits who founded missions along the Pacific Coast, in the Mississippi and Great Lakes regions and in other parts of the United States, were called the *Black Gowns* [1] or *Black Robes* [2] by the Indians among whom they worked, because of their black robes.

[1] *The Jesuit Relations and Allied Documents: Travels and Explorations of the Jesuit Missionaries in North America (1610-1791)*, with an introduction by Reuben Gold Thwaites, selected and ed. by Edna Kenton (Albert and Charles Boni, New York, 1925) p. 11, 348. 426, 427.

[2] *Washakie and Defense of Settlers of Northwest: Washakie, An Account of Indian Resistance of the Covered Wagon and Union Pacific Railroad Invasions of Their Territory*, Grace Raymond Hebard (The Arthur H. Clark Company, Cleveland, Ohio, and Glendale, Calif., 1930) p. 44.

Black Hat Brigade

During the Civil War the United States Volunteer Infantrymen commanded by Brigadier General John Gibbon came to be nicknamed the *Black Hat Brigade*. [1]

Black hats were regularly worn in the volunteer service. After the Battle of Gainsville, Md., on June 27, 1862, the Confederate prisoners inquired who the black-hatted men were with whom they had fought. This was the origin of the nickname of the *Black Hat Brigade*.

[1] *Personal Recollections of the Civil War*, John Gibbon (G. P. Putnam's Sons, New York and London, 1928) p. 93.

Black Hawk Division. See Eighty-sixth Infantry Division of World War II

Black Horse Cavalry

Those legislators who could be influenced to vote for or against legislation by corporations or individuals whose interests would be advanced by such votes, were nicknamed the *Black Horse Cavalry* [1] by Theodore Roosevelt while he was a member of the New York State Assembly from 1881 to 1884. People who can be influenced to act without exercising their own judgment, or contrary to their own convictions, are said to be riding a black horse.

[1] *Theodore Roosevelt and His Times: A Chronicle of the Progressive Movement*, Harold Howland (Yale University Press, New Haven, Conn., 1921) p. 11.

Black Jack. See Logan, J. A.

Black Jack Pershing. See Pershing, J. J.

Black John Brown. See Vesey, Denmark

Black Knight of the Border. See Malone, P. L.

Black Laws. See *Black Code.*

Black List
  The roster containing the names of those employees who are liable to be troublesome especially during strikes has been called the *Black List.*[1] Persons in bad standing, disfavor, or disgrace are said to be on the *Black List.* On President F. D. Roosevelt's *Black List* were the Democrats who had opposed his scheme for "packing" the Supreme Court.

  [1] *A History of the United States,* Allen C. Thomas (D. C. Heath and Company, Boston, 1894) p. 378.

Black Panther Division. See Sixty-sixth Infantry Division of World War II

Black Patti. See Jones, S. J.

Black Republican
  During the controversy over the slavery issue an adherent of the Republican party who favored the liberation of the slaves was called a *Black Republican.*[1] The *Black Republicans* were found chiefly in the central and the Northern states of the Union, but the nickname was applied to them mostly by their Southern political opponents.

  [1] *History of the United States of America, under the Constitution,* Revised Edition, James Schouler (Dodd, Mead and Company, New York, 1904) vol. 5, p. 431, 437.

Black Republican. See Blair, F. P., Jr.

Black Republican Blair. See Blair, F. P., Jr.

Black Robes. See *Black Gowns.*

Black Snake. See Wayne, Anthony

Black Snakes
  Black Snakes[1] was a term applied to a notorious and lawless gang in Baltimore, Md., from about 1857 to 1861. The purpose of the group was to influence elections by intimidating voters through the use of force.

  [1] *Contemporary American Biography: Biographical Sketches of Representative Men of the Day . . .* (Atlantic Publishing and Engraving Company, New York, 1895) vol. 1, p. 39.

Black Sox. See Chicago American League Baseball Company

Black Spurgeon of America. See Walker, C. T.

Black Swan. See Greenfield, E. T.

Black Tom. See Corwin, Thomas

Blackberry Pickers
  During the Civil War the term the *Blackberry Pickers*[1] was applied to half-hearted Union soldiers who would straggle behind the regular army, stopping to pick blackberries, thereby offering opportunity for the enemy to capture them. This nickname appears to have been originated by the Confederates. It was bitterly resented by the Federal prisoners who had not been captured because they picked blackberries.
  See also *Coffee-boilers*

  [1] *Andersonville: A story of Rebel Military Prisons, Fifteen Months a Guest of the So-called Southern Confederacy; a Private Soldier's Experience in Richmond, Andersonville, Savannah, Blackshear, and Florence,* John McElroy (D. R. Locke, Toledo, Ohio, 1879) p. 427.

Blackbirds. See Long Island University

Blackburne, Russell
  Russell Blackburne, who was born at Clifton Heights, Pa., on October 23, 1886, and who coached in major league baseball, was nicknamed *Lena.*[1]

  [1] *Who's Who in Major League Base Ball,* comp. by Harold (Speed) Johnson (Buxton Publishing Company, Chicago, 1933) p. 423.

Blackguard Charlie. See Pinckney, Charles

Blackie. See Mancuso, A. R.

Blackwater State. See Nebraska

Blacky. See Mangum, L. A.

Blaine, James Gillespie

James Gillespie Blaine has the following nicknames: *Gladstone of America, Guano Statesman, Henry of Navarre, Magnetic Man, Magnetic Statesman, Man from Maine, Plumed Knight, Premier Blaine, Tattooed Knight, Tattooed Man,* and *Uncrowned King.*

James Gillespie Blaine was called the *Gladstone of America* [1] because he was an outstanding orator and statesman.

The *Guano Statesman,* [2] has been applied to Blaine because of his attempted mediation between Chile and Peru while he was Secretary of State in President James A. Garfield's Cabinet in 1881.

He was sometimes designated *Henry of Navarre* [3] because of his eminence in directing the political affairs of the United States, both national and international, and his outstanding patriotism and statesmanship in public office.

Blaine was known as the *Magnetic Man* [1] and the *Magnetic Statesman* because of his forceful personality.

He was called *The Man from Maine* [5] because he made his home in Augusta, Me., from 1854 until the time of his death in 1893.

Robert G. Ingersoll in 1876 referred to him as the *Plumed Knight* [6] in an address before the Republican Convention in Cincinnati, Ohio, where he nominated Blaine the Republican presidential candidate. Ingersoll described Blaine as an eloquent orator and as a plumed knight who, in Congress, challenged to a fair fight his political opponents or others who were disposed to slander his character.

He was called *Premier Blaine* [4] because the office of the Prime Minister of Great Britain corresponds to the office of the American Secretary of State.

James Gillespie Blaine was nicknamed the *Plumed Knight* by his admirers, and the *Tattooed Man* by his opponents. The latter also called him the *Tattooed Knight,* [7] a combination of the two other names. The *Tattooed Man* [4] had its origin in a cartoon in a New York weekly illustrated magazine representing Mr. Blaine as Phryne before the Athenian judges tattooed with the names of the political scandals with which his name had been connected.

Blaine was often called the *Uncrowned King* [4] because, as Secretary of State in the Cabinet of President Benjamin Harrison from 1889 to 1892, he was generally considered the power behind the throne.

James Gillespie Blaine was born at West Brownsville, Pa., on January 31, 1830, and died at Washington, D.C., on January 27, 1893.

[1] *The Sage of Sinnissippi, Being a Brief Sketch of the Life of Congressman Frank Orren Lowden, of Oregon, Illinois, Brief Sketches of His Rivals in Political Battles, a Short Article Relating to His Availablity as a Presidential Candidate for 1908, and an Official and Authentic Account of State Elections in Ilinois, Statistically, Combined with a Roll of Honor of the Nation, the State, the County, and the Home of the Author, with Illustrations,* Kinnie A. Osterwig (J. A. Nolan, Shabbona, Ill., 1907) p. 162.

[2] *A Book of Nicknames,* John Goff (Courier-Journal Job Printing Company, Louisville, Ky., 1892) p. 22.

[3] *The Autobiography of Thomas Collier Platt,* comp. and ed. by Louis J. Lang (B. W. Dodge and Company, New York, 1910) p. 185.

[4] *U.S. "Snap Shots": An Independent, National, and Memorial Encyclopedia . . . ,* Oliver McKee (A. M. Thayer and Company, Boston, 1892) p. 244.

[5] *Blaine of Maine: His Life and Times,* Charles Edward Russell (Cosmopolitan Book Corporation, New York, 1935) p. 314-15.

[6] *Political Americanisms,* Charles Ledyard Norton (Longmans, Green and Company, New York and London, 1890) p. 88.

[7] *The World,* New York, October 30, 1884, p. 2.

Blaine's Irishman. See Egan, Patrick

Blair, Francis Preston, Junior

Francis Preston Blair, Junior, was sometimes called the *Black Republican,* [1] or *Black Republican Blair.* This nickname was applied to him about 1858 by the followers of John Caldwell Calhoun, who favored slavery and states rights. At this time Blair was serving in Congress as a Free Soil Democratic Representative from the State of Missouri. Blair was accused of being a *Black Republican* because he favored a policy of gradual and voluntary emancipation rather than war. This policy was bitterly resented by the slaveholding Democrats. They felt he was like those members of the Republican Party who advocated the liberation of the slaves and were called *Black Republicans.*

Francis Preston Blair, Junior, was born at Lexington, Ky., on February 19, 1821, and died at St. Louis, Mo., on July 8, 1875.

[1] *The Francis Preston Blair Family in Politics,* William Ernest Smith (The Macmillan Company, New York, 1933) p. 429, 430, 443.

Blake, John Fred

John Fred Blake, a pitcher in major league baseball, was nicknamed *Sheriff Blake.* [1] In

Blake, J. F.—Continued

1924, he and his teammates were discussing the Chicago revenue officers and bootleggers when one of his colleagues called him sheriff, and *Sheriff Blake* he continued to be.

John Fred Blake was born at Ansted, W.Va., on September 17, 1889.

[1] *Baseball Magazine* (The Baseball Magazine Company, New York, 1927-1928) vol. 40-41, 1928, p. 350.

Blanchet, Francis Herbert

Francis Herbert Blanchet was nicknamed the *Apostle of Oregon* [1] because he was the first Roman Catholic archbishop of Oregon, and was one of the earliest missionaries to preach Christianity to the Indians in that region. He served as archbishop in Oregon from 1850 to 1880.

He was born near Quebec, Canada, in 1795, and died at Portland, Ore., on June 18, 1883.

[1] *The National Cyclopaedia of American Biography* (James T. White and Company, New York, 1906) vol. 13, p. 32.

Bland, Richard

Richard Bland was sometimes referred to as the *Cato of the Revolution* [1] because of the devotion and wisdom with which he served his country.

Bland early became identified as one of the pioneer leaders [2] in the rebellion of the American colonies. He opposed the Stamp Act of 1765; agreed to boycott English goods; and served as a delegate to the Continental Congress.

Richard Bland was born at Williamsburg, Va., on May 6, 1710, and died there on October 26, 1776.

[1] *The National Cyclopaedia of American Biography* (James T. White and Company, New York, 1904) vol. 12, p. 172.
[2] *Dictionary of American Biography under the Auspices of the American Council of Learned Societies,* ed. by Allen Johnson (Charles Scribner's Sons, New York, 1929) vol. 2, p. 354.

Bland, Richard Parks

Richard Parks Bland was nicknamed the *Father of Free Silver* [1] and *Silver Dick* because while he was a Representative from Missouri in the House of Representatives he was one of the outstanding leaders of the Free Silver movement, and the author of the Bland Silver Bill of 1878.

This bill required the government to coin silver dollars amounting to not less than two million nor more than four million monthly. It was passed over the veto of President Rutherford Birchard Hayes.

Richard Parks Bland was born near Hartford, Ky., on August 19, 1835, and died at Lebanon, Mo., on June 15, 1899.

[1] "The Agrarian Crusade, a Chronicle of the Farmer in Politics" by Solon J. Buck, in *The Chronicles of America Series,* Abraham Lincoln Edition, Allen Johnson, Editor (Yale University Press, New Haven, Conn., 1920) vol. 45, p. 181.
Dictionary of American Biography under the Auspices of the American Council of Learned Societies, ed. by Allen Johnson (Charles Scribner's Sons, New York, 1929) vol. 2, p. 355.

Bland, Schuyler Otis

Schuyler Otis Bland is known as *Bridge Builder Bland* [1] because he promoted a number of bills appropriating money for the construction of bridges while he was a Representative from Virginia to Congress between 1918 and 1935.

He was born in Gloucester County, Va., on May 4, 1872.

[1] *The Washington Post Magazine,* Washington, D.C., March 4, 1934, p. 4.

Blankenburg, Rudolph

Rudolph Blankenburg was nicknamed the *Old War Horse of Reform* [1] and *Old Dutch Cleanser* because of his active participation and influence in defending the rights and privileges of the downtrodden and oppressed of Philadelphia. He was outstanding in civic affairs from about 1881 to the time of his death in 1918. He was Mayor of Philadelphia from 1911 to 1915.

Rudolph Blankenburg was born at Brantrup, Germany, on February 16, 1843, and died at Philadelphia, Pa., on April 12, 1918.

[1] *Dictionary of American Biography under the Auspices of the American Council of Learned Societies,* ed. by Allen Johnson (Charles Scribner's Sons, New York, 1929) vol. 2, p. 358.

Blanton, Thomas Lindsay

Thomas Lindsay Blanton was called the *Czar of the District, Hold That Line,* the *Scourge of the District Police, Talkative Tom,* and the *Watchdog of the Treasury.*

Representative Blanton was designated the *Czar of the District* [1] because of his adverseness to the appropriations asked for by the people of the District of Columbia during the session of the Seventy-fourth Congress of the United States in 1935-36.

The nickname, the *Scourge of the District Police,* [2] signifies that he took an active part in investigating the administration of affairs in the police courts of the District of Columbia.

He is known as *Hold That Line* [2] because of his firmness and tenacity in upholding his political principles.

Mr. Blanton was nicknamed *Talkative Tom,* [3] doubtless because of his loquaciousness.

He was designated the *Watchdog of the Treasury* [4] because he was opposed to any unnecessary expenditures of public money.

Thomas Lindsay Blanton was born at Houston, Tex., on October 25, 1872, and served as a Representative from Texas to the United States Congress from 1917 to 1937.

[1] *Washington Herald,* Washington, D.C., August 23, 1935, p. 4-A, col. 1.
[2] *The Washington Post Magazine,* Washington, D.C., March 4, 1934, p. 4.
[3] *The Washington Times,* Washington, D.C., August 22, 1936, Editorial page, col. 1.
[4] *The Washington Post Magazine,* Washington, D.C., March 4, 1934, p. 4.

Blasters. See New Mexico School of Mines

Bleeding Kansas

Following the passage of the Kansas-Nebraska Bill on May 30, 1854, which created the territories of Kansas and Nebraska and allowed the people in these territories to decide whether or not they would become free or slave-holding territories, Kansas was frequently referred to by the newspapers as *Bleeding Kansas.*[1] There was constant fighting between the pro-slavery and anti-slavery factions until Kansas was finally admitted to the Union.

[1] *Barnes' Popular History of the United States of America,* Revised to date, Joel Dorman Steele and Esther Baker Steele (A. L. Burt Company, New York, 1914) p. 474.
Political Americanisms, Charles Ledyard Norton (Longmans, Green and Company, New York and London, 1890) p. 13-14.

Blind Boss Buckley. See Buckley, C. A.

Blind Man Eloquent. See West, W. H.

Blind Minister. See Woodbridge, Timothy

Blind Pigs

About 1858 the State of Virginia had at its capital city, Richmond, an armory with a detachment of soldiers numbering about one hundred men, this unit being called the Public Guard, popularly termed *Blind Pigs.*[1] On the hats of the soldiers were the letters *P. G.* for Public Guard.

PG is pig without an I; a pig without an eye is a blind pig, so the Public Guards were called *Blind Pigs.*

Saloons which sold intoxicating liquor surreptitiously in the United States after it became illegal to do so were also called *Blind Pigs.*[2]

[1] *The End of an Era,* John S. Wise (Houghton Mifflin and Company, New York and Boston, 1899) p. 59.
[2] *A Brief History of North Dakota,* Herbert Clay Fish and R. M. Clack (American Book Company, New York, 1925) p. 148.

Blind Pool

Blind Pool[1] is the term given to a transaction in which several people place in the hands of a selected person funds over which he has complete control. This form of speculation is carried on with the utmost secrecy.

[1] *The Encyclopaedia Britannica,* Fourteenth Edition (Encyclopaedia Britannica, Inc., New York, 1929) vol. 3, p. 732.

Blind Preacher. See Milburn, W. H.; Waddel, James

Blind Savant. See Gore, T. P.

Blind Tiger

Blind Tiger[1] was a nickname for a place in which liquor was stored temporarily for sale to "friends" of the proprietor.

[1] *An American Glossary,* Richard H. Thornton (Francis and Company, London, 1912) vol. 1, p. 70.

Blind Tom. See Bethune, T. G.

Blizzard State. See South Dakota; Texas

Blizzards. See Texans

Blond Beauty of the Lakes. See Milwaukee, Wis.

Blood and Fire Division. See Sixty-third Infantry Division of World War II

Blood Inks

Blood Inks[1] is a nickname applied to notorious gangs in Baltimore and Philadelphia which tried influencing elections by using such brutal methods that the voters were afraid to come to the polls. This gang reached the acme of its power from about

Blood Inks—Continued
1857 to 1861, but its influence on cor-
ruptible politicians did not wane for nearly
a decade.

[1] "The Irrepressible Conflict, 1850-1865" by Arthur
Charles Cole, in *A History of American Life*, Arthur
M. Schlesinger and Dixon Ryan Fox, Editors (The Mac-
millan Company, New York, 1934) vol. 7, p. 154.

Blood Suckers
After President Grover Cleveland vetoed
the Dependent Pension Bill on February 11,
1887, which granted a pension of twelve
dollars monthly to every honourably discharged veteran of the Civil War, there
was a great deal of criticism directed against
his action. The veterans who wanted the
pension were called *Blood Suckers*.[1]

[1] *Twenty Years of the Republic, 1885-1905*, Harry
Thurston Peck (Dodd, Mead and Company, New York,
1907) p. 144.

Bloody Angle
Some of the bloodiest fighting of the
Civil War occurred during Grant's Campaign in the Wilderness near Chancellorsville, Va. There was a plot on the Spottsylvania battlefield known as the *Bloody
Angle*[1] because here throughout the day of
May 12, 1864, Confederate and Federal
soldiers engaged in close combat until the
dead and wounded were piled up on one
another.

[1] *On the Trail of Grant and Lee: A Narrative History
of the Boyhood of Two Great Americans, Based upon
Their Own Writings, Official Records, and Other Au-
thoritative Information*, Frederick Trevor Hill (D. Apple-
ton and Company, New York, 1911) p. 233.
*The History of the Confederate War, Its Causes and
Its Conduct, A Narrative and Critical History*, George
Cary Eggleston (Sturgis and Walton Company, New
York, 1910) vol. 2, p. 242-7.

Bloody Bridge
The bridge over the Walloomsac River
in Bennington County, Vt., some thirty-five
miles from Troy, N.Y., was known as the
Bloody Bridge[1] for many years following
the Battle of Bennington or the Battle of
Walloomsac, which was fought on August
16, 1777. The Walloomsac River is crossed
today at this point by a covered railroad
bridge on the Rutland railroad.

[1] *Memoir and Official Correspondence of General John
Stark, with Notices of Several Other Officers of the Revo-
lution, Also, a Biography of Captain Phinehas Stevens,
and of Colonel Robert Rogers, with an Account of His
Services in America During the Seven Years' War*, Caleb
Stark (G. Parker Lyon, Concord, N.H., 1860) p. 319.
*Battle of Bennington: Centennial Anniversary of the
Independence of the State of Vermont and the Battle of
Bennington, August 15, and 16, 1877*, Westminster—
Hubbardton—Windsor (Tuttle and Company, Rutland,
Vt., 1879) p. 173.

Bloody Bridles Waite. See Waite,
D. H.

Bloody Bucket Division. See Twenty-
eighth Infantry Division of World
War II

Bloody Eights
Bloody Eights[1] is a term applied to a
notorious gang in Baltimore, Md., which
appears to have reached the acme of its
power from about 1857 to 1867. Their purpose was to influence elections by intimidating voters through the use of force.

[1] "The Irrepressible Conflict, 1850-1865" by Arthur
Charles Cole, in *A History of American Life*, Arthur M.
Schlesinger and Dixon Ryan Fox, Editors (The Macmil-
lan Company, New York, 1934) vol. 7, p. 154.

Bloody Fifth
In 1882 the Fifth Congressional District
of Minnesota became known as the *Bloody
Fifth*[1] as a result of the animosity which
characterized the campaign to elect a representative to Congress. The term was first
applied to the district by the *St. Paul Globe*.
Knute Nelson and Charles F. Kindred were
the candidates.

[6] *The Life of Knute Nelson*, Martin W. Odland (The
Lund Press, Inc., Minneapolis, Minn., 1926) p. 111.

Bloody First
In 1847 during their participation in the
War with Mexico, the First Regiment of
Tennessee Volunteer Infantrymen, under the
command of Colonel William Bowen Campbell, was designated the *Bloody First*[1] because of the fierce and aggressive fighting
in which so many were killed or wounded.

[7] *Tennessee, the Volunteer State, 1769-1923*, John
Trotwood Moore and Austin P. Foster (The S. J.
Clarke Publishing Company, Chicago, and Nashville,
Tenn., 1923) vol. 1, p. 438.

Bloody Law
From 1764 until about 1789, during the
controversy between New York and New
Hampshire over the Vermont Territory, the
New York Assembly, on March 9, 1774,
enacted a law invoking the death penalty
for resisting arrest by a sheriff from New
York or for taking part in a riot. This law
was popularly called the *Bloody Law*[1] by
the settlers in the Vermont Territory against
whom it had been directed.

[1] *The Mountain Hero and His Associates*, Henry W.
De Puy (Dayton and Wentworth, Boston, 1855) p. 181.

Bloody Monday

The first Monday of the fall term of 1827 at Harvard University was known as *Bloody Monday* [1] because of the bitterly fought ball game which took place between the freshman and the sophomore teams.

August 6, 1855, has also been referred to by Kentucky historians as *Bloody Monday* [2] because on that election day a bloody fight occurred at Louisville, Ky., between the members of the American, or Knownothing Party, and their opponents who were running for state and national offices. This fight resulted in the death of twentytwo people and in the destruction, chiefly by fire, of a considerable amount of property.

[1] *American Sports (1785-1835)*, Jennie Holliman (The Seeman Press, Durham, N.C., 1931) p. 70.
[2] *Collins' Historical Sketches of Kentucky: History of Kentucky*, by Lewis Collins, *Revised, Enlarged Fourfold, and Brought Down to the Year 1874 . . .,* Richard H. Collins (Collins and Company, Covington, Ky., 1874) vol. 1, p. 75.
Life of Walter Quintin Gresham, 1832-1895, Matilda Gresham (Rand McNally and Company, Chicago, 1919) p. 61-2.

Bloody Ninth

From about 1885 to 1895 the Ninth Congressional District of the State of Missouri was generally spoken of as the *Bloody Ninth* [1] because of the bitter factionalism which raged between the candidates for public offices and their supporters and their opponents.

[1] *My Quarter Century of American Politics*, Champ Clark (Harper and Brothers, New York and London, 1920) vol. 1, p. 164.

Bloody Pond

The sinister appellation, the *Bloody Pond*,[1] has been given to a pool near Fort Edward, N.Y., which became the grave of a large number of soldiers killed in an encounter between the British forces under Colonel Ephraim Williams and the French under Baron Ludwig A. Dieskau, during the French and Indian War which lasted from 1754 to 1763. The British forces were victorious in this encounter but the losses were heavy on both sides. The dead were thrown into the pond.

[1] *American Biography*, ed. by Jared Sparks; *John Stark* by Edward Everett, *William Pinkney* by Henry Wheaton (Harper and Brothers, New York and London, 1902) vol. 5, p. 22.
A History of the United States of America, Intended for Students in Schools, Academies, Colleges, Universities and at Home, and for General Readers, Robert Reid Howison (Everett Waddey Company, Richmond, Va., 1892) p. 287.

Bloody Shirt Foraker. See Foraker, J. B.

Bloody Tubs

The *Bloody Tubs* [1] was the name of one of the factional political gangs which was active in Baltimore, Md., from 1857 until 1861. They were so nicknamed because they were said to have been in the habit of ducking political opponents in the slaughterhouse tubs.

[1] *Life and Liberty in America: Or, Sketches of a Tour in the United States and Canada, in 1857-8*, Charles Mackay (Smith Elder and Company, London, 1859) vol. 1, p. 164.
Political Americanisms, Charles Ledyard Norton (Longmans, Green and Company, New York and London, 1890) p. 15.

Bloody Year

The year 1777 was designated the *Bloody Year* [1] by the settlers along the western frontiers of Kentucky, Pennsylvania, Virginia, and Michigan because that year the frontiersmen were continually harassed by the attacks of the Indians who bitterly fought the encroaching settlers.

[1] *The Centennial History of Illinois: The Illinois Country, 1673-1818*, Clarence Walworth Alvord (Illinois Centennial Commission, Springfield, Ill., 1920) vol. 1, p. 313.

Bloom, Sol

Sol Bloom, a journalist, publisher, and politician, was nicknamed *George Washington Bloom* and the *Savior of the Constitution* while he was Congressman from New York in the House of Representatives, because he was Director of the George Washington Bicentennial Celebration Commission in 1931 and Director General of the United States Constitution Sesquicentennial Commission.

Sol Bloom was born at Pekin, Ill., on March 9, 1870, and died in New York City on March 7, 1949.

[1] An interview with Captain Victor Hunt Harding, Secretary of the National Democratic Congress Reelection Committee, Washington, D.C., April 10, 1939.

Bloomington, Illinois

Bloomington has been styled the *Prairie City* [1] because it is built on a great stretch of prairie land.

[1] *A Book of Nicknames*, John Goff (Courier-Journal Job Printing Company, Louisville, Ky., 1892) p. 16.
History of Bloomington and Normal, in McLean County, Illinois, J. H. Burnham (J. H. Burnham, Bloomington, Ill., 1879) p. 8, 9.

Blow, Susan Elizabeth

Susan Elizabeth Blow, who was born at St. Louis, Mo., on June 7, 1843, and who died at New York City on March 26, 1916, was nicknamed the *Mother of the Kindergarten* [1] because of her outstanding work in establishing kindergartens in the United States. Her first school was opened in St. Louis, Mo., in 1873.

[1] *The Encyclopedia Americana* (Americana Corporation, New York and Chicago, 1927) vol. 4, p. 118-19.

Blue and Gray

During the Civil War the Federal soldiers were dressed in blue and the Confederate soldiers were dressed in gray; consequently, these armies were spoken of as the *Blue* and the *Gray*.[1]

[1] *The Growth of the American People and Nation*, Mary G. Kelty (Ginn and Company, New York and Boston, 1931) p. 344.

Blue and Gray Division. See Twenty-ninth Infantry Division of World War II

Blue Bellies

During the Civil War the Southern soldiers nicknamed the Northern soldiers the *Blue Bellies* [1] because they wore blue uniforms.

[1] *Americanisms—Old and New*, John S. Farmer (Privately printed by Thomas Poulter and Sons, London, 1889) p. 67-8.

Blue Birds

General Alexander Hays, who was born at Franklin, Pa., on July 8, 1819, and who died from a wound received in the Battle of the Wilderness near Chancellorsville, Va., on May 5, 1864, called his soldiers the *Blue Birds* [1] because they wore a blue trefoil as their division badge.

[1] *Life and Letters of Alexander Hays, Brevet Colonel United States Army, Brigadier General and Brevet Major General United States Volunteers*, ed. and arranged with notes and contemporary history by George Thornton Fleming from data compiled by Gilbert Adams Hays (Gilbert Adams Hays, Pittsburgh, Pa., 1919) p. 470.

Blue Devil Division. See Eighty-eighth Infantry Division of World War II

Blue Devils. See Duke University; Long Island University

Blue Dog

During the depression of 1840 to 1843 the city of St. Louis, Mo., became flooded with worthless paper currency which was termed *Blue Dog,* or *Blue Pup,*[1] because it was often decorated with dogs stamped in blue.

[1] *Centennial History of Missouri (The Center State) One Hundred Years in the Union, 1820-1921*, Walter B. Stevens (The S. J. Clarke Publishing Company, St. Louis, Mo., and Chicago, 1921) vol. 2, p. 447.

Blue Grass State. See Kentucky

Blue Hen State. See Deleware

Blue Hen's Chickens. See Delawareans; University of Delaware

Blue Hen's Chickens State. See Delaware

Blue Imps. See Duke University

Blue Jays. See Westminster College

Blue Jeans Williams. See Williams, J. D.

Blue Law State. See Connecticut

Blue Laws

The Puritans in Connecticut during its early colonial days drew up many stern and rigid laws governing the religious, moral, and social life of the colonists. The first collection of these laws, published in book form in 1650, was bound in blue paper covers and so they were designated *Blue Laws.*[1]

[1] *Our Great Continent; Sketches, Picturesque and Historic: Within and Beyond the States*, Benson J. Lossing and George J. Hagar (Gay Brothers and Company, New York, 1890) p. 90.

Blue Light Elder. See Jackson, T. J.

Blue-light Federalists

In December 1813 when Stephen Decatur was attempting to slip his two frigates through the British blockade of the New London, Conn., harbor, his movements were signaled to the British by two blue lights at the mouth of the harbor. Thereafter those who were, or were suspected of being, pro-British were called *Blue-light Federalists.*[1]

[1] *History of the United States of America, under the Constitution*, James Schouler (William H. Morrison, Washington, D.C., 1887) vol. 2, p. 467.
The History of the United States of America, Richard Hildreth (Harper and Brothers, New York, 1852) vol. 6, p. 468.

Blue Pup. See *Blue Dog*

Blue Ridge Division. See Eightieth Infantry Division of World War II

Blue Sky Laws

Laws that have been passed by the state and national governments to prevent the marketing of deceitful securities or shares in worthless or non-existent enterprises have been designated *Blue Sky Laws.* The origin is accredited to a Kansas legislative committeeman who remarked that the restraints laid on investment concerns "should be as far reaching as the blue sky."[1] It is also said that these laws have been popularly termed *Blue Sky Laws* because the agent selling fraudulent securities is marketing something that exists only in the sky.

[1] *The Encyclopedia Americana* (Americana Corporation, New York and Chicago, 1927) vol. 4, p. 127.
Community Life in Minnesota, Maude L. Lindquist and James W. Clark (Charles Scribner's Sons, New York, Chicago, and San Francisco, Calif., 1933) p. 272.

Blue Stocking

Blue Stocking[1] has long been applied to a woman who spends her time reading books and studying and who makes a needless display of knowledge.

It is thought by some that the name of *Blue Stockings* was first applied to a group of Venetian literary men and women who organized themselves into a society about 1400 to discuss literature, and who wore blue stockings. The term came to be commonly applied to groups of English literary men and women about 1746, when Mrs. Agmondesham Vesey at Bath, England, began to invite them to evening assemblies at her home for literary conversation, card playing having been prohibited. In 1750 Mrs. Elizabeth Montagu initiated the custom of inviting groups to her home for literary breakfast parties, and of having elaborate evening assemblies known as conversation parties, where card playing was prohibited and the guests were encouraged to discuss literary topics. Benjamin Stillingfleet, one of her most prominent guests, habitually appeared wearing blue worsted stockings instead of black silk ones and he was nicknamed *Blue Stockings.* The nickname was soon applied to all the guests.[2] Lady Boscawen, the wife of Admiral Edward Boscawen, regularly attended these conversation parties, and held similar gatherings in her own home. Admiral Boscawen, scornful of his wife's social ambitions, applied the nickname *Blue Stockings* to all high brow women.

[1] *Putnam's Everyday Sayings: Their Meanings Explained; Their Origins Given,* Charles N. Lurie (A. L. Burt Company, Publishers, New York, 1928) p. 55.
[2] *Dictionary of National Biography* (Smith, Elder, and Company, London, 1898) vol. 38, p. 241; vol. 54, p. 374.

Blue Stockings. See Presbyterian College

Blue Streakers. See John Carroll University

Bluebacks

Because they were printed in blue on the reverse side, the paper currency bills of the Southern Confederacy were called *Bluebacks*[1] in contradistinction to *Greenbacks,* the paper currency of the United States, which is printed in green.

[1] *Americanisms—Old and New,* John S. Farmer (Privately printed by Thomas Poulter and Sons, London, 1889) p. 67.

Bluege, Otto Adam

Otto Adam Bluege, who was born at Chicago, Ill., on July 20, 1910, and who was an infielder in major league baseball, was called *Squeaky.*[1]

[1] *Who's Who in Major League Base Ball,* comp. by Harold (Speed) Johnson (Buxton Publishing Company, Chicago, 1933) p. 84.

Bluegrass Capital. See Lexington, Ky.

Blues. See Washburn College

Bluff Ben Wade. See Wade, B. F.

Bluff City. See Hannibal, Mo.; Memphis, Tenn.; Natchez, Miss.

Board Fight

The nickname *Board Fight*[1] is commonly attributed by the cadets at a military academy to a recitation at which all the cadets belonging to a class section are required to write for a limited time answering the same questions.

[1] *Unit Projects in Modern Literature* (Educational Press, Inc., Columbus, Ohio) March 1-14, 1935, p. 12.

Board of Buzzards

About 1883, an investigation into the affairs of the Philadelphia almshouse disclosed that the members of the board had shamefully neglected it, were incapable of

Board of Buzzards—Continued

administering its affairs efficiently, and had greedily appropriated to their own use the institution's money and property entrusted to their care. The indignant public nicknamed them the *Board of Buzzards*[1].

[1] *The Blankenburgs of Philadelphia*, Lucretia L. Blankenburg (The John C. Winston Company, Chicago and Philadelphia, 1928) p. 9.

Boardwalk Ike. See Bacharach, Isaac

Boat Load of Knowledge

The *Boat Load of Knowledge*[1] was a keel boat which took a group of eminent people from Pittsburgh, Pa., to New Harmony, Ind., in 1825. Among the group were prominent scientists, men of letters, educators, artists, and musicians, all on their way to Robert Owen's new communistic settlement. The nickname *The Boat Load of Knowledge* is said to have superseded the original name of the boat, *The Philanthropist*.[2]

[1] *Our Foreigners, a Chronicle of Americans in the Making* by Samuel P. Orth, in The Chronicles of America Series, Allen Johnson, Editor (Yale University Press, New Haven, Conn., 1920) vol. 35, p. 94.

[2] *Thomas Say, Early American Naturalist*, Harry B. Weiss and Grace M. Ziegler (Charles C. Thomas, Springfield, Ill., and Baltimore, Md., 1931) p. 123.

Bobbin Boy. See Banks, N. P.

Bobby the Cofferer. See Morris, Robert

Bobby the Treasurer. See Morris, Robert

Bobcats. See Southwestern College (Tenn.); West Virginia Wesleyan College

Boies, Horace

Horace Boies was nicknamed *Affidavit Boies*[1] because he had such an honest face. He was elected Governor of Iowa in 1884 after changing his political affiliation from the Republican party to that of the Democratic party, and was a prominent western Democratic candidate for the office of President of the United States in 1892.

Horace Boies was born in Aurora township in Erie County, N.Y., on December 7, 1827, and died at Long Beach, Calif., on April 4, 1923.

[1] *Appleton's Cyclopaedia of American Biography*, ed. by James Grant Wilson and John Fiske (D. Appleton and Company, New York, 1900) vol. 7, p. 28.

Boilermakers. See Purdue University

Boiling Water. See Lee, Charles

Bok, Edward William

Edward William Bok, an American journalist, was nicknamed *A Lay Preacher to the Largest Congregation in the United States*[1] while he was editor in chief of *The Ladies' Home Journal* from 1889 until 1919, because he advocated numerous civic and humanitarian movements through the editorial pages of this widely circulated magazine.

Edward William Bok was born at Helder, Netherlands, on October 9, 1863 and died near Lake Wales, Fla., on January 9, 1930.

[1] *The World Book Encyclopedia* (The Quarrie Corporation, Chicago, 1938) vol. 2, p. 816.

Boll Weevils. See Agricultural and Mechanical College (Monticello, Ark.)

Bonanza Farms

The large wheat farms in the vicinity of Fargo, N.D., in the Valley of the Red River of the North, are called *Bonanza Farms*[1] because they produce enormous crops.

[1] *Seeing the Middle West*, John T. Faris (J. B. Lippincott Company, Philadelphia, 1923) p. 74.

Bonanza State. See Montana

Bonaparte, Charles Joseph

Charles Joseph Bonaparte was nicknamed the *Academic Pharisee*, the *Imperial Peacock of Park Avenue*, and *Souphouse Charlie*.

He was called the *Academic Pharisee*[1] because he had the reputation of being a brilliant scholar and lawyer whose interest in reforms was presumed to be simulated or pharisaical.

Bonaparte was nicknamed the *Imperial Peacock of Park Avenue*[1] in a sarcastic allusion to his ancestry, his grandfather having been the brother of Napoleon Bonaparte, and to the fact that he lived on Park Avenue and Center Street, an exclusive residential section of Baltimore, Md.

Souphouse Charlie[1] was a reference to his generosity and interest in societies of a charitable or humanitarian character, the "souphouse" where food was distributed to the hungry being a characteristic feature of such institutions.

Charles Joseph Bonaparte was born at Baltimore, Md., on June 9, 1851, and died near there on June 28, 1921.

[1] *Charles Joseph Bonaparte; His Life and Public Services,* Joseph Bucklin Bishop (Charles Scribner's Sons, New York, 1922) p. 103, 292.

Bone-head. See Merkle, F. C.

Bonney, William

The nickname *Billie the Kid* [1] was given to the notorious outlaw, William Bonney, by his outlaw companions. He was born in the slums of the East Side, New York City, on November 23, 1859, and was shot to death at Lincoln, N.M., by the sheriff of that county, on May 13, 1881.

[1] *Trigger Fingers,* Owen P. White (G. P. Putnam's Sons, New York and London, 1926) p. 209, 258-60.

Bonny Brown Wife. See Jackson, R. D.

Boodle

Money which is used by politicians, usually to buy votes or to gain an unfair political advantage, is frequently called *Boodle.* [1] Campaign funds are often so called. The term is also used to denote money obtained by any secret or underhanded manner, and was used by the early Dutch in the sense of loot. [2] Thieves use the expression to signify money that is counterfeit. Postal clerks use the term to designate a valuable letter or package. [2]

[1] *Americanisms—Old and New,* John S. Farmer (Privately printed by Thomas Poulter and Sons, London, 1889) p. 76-7.
[2] *American Language,* H. L. Mencken (A. A. Knopf, New York, 1936) 4th ed. p. 108.; *Supplement One* (1945) p. 295; *Supplement Two* (1948) p. 767.

Boodle Banquet

On October 29, 1884, a costly and elaborate banquet was given at Delmonico's, one of New York City's famous cafés, in honor of James Gillespie Blaine, then the Republican candidate for the office of President of the United States. Because the dinner was to raise campaign funds it was called the *Boodle Banquet.* [1]

[1] *James G. Blaine, a Political Idol of Other Days,* David Saville Muzzey (Dodd, Mead and Company, New York, 1934) p. 319.

Boodle Fight

In the patois of military cadets a *Boodle Fight* [1] is a social gathering at which are served such refreshments as candy, cake, and ice cream, the word *boodle* signifying *loot* or *graft.*

[1] *Unit Projects in Modern Literature* (Educational Press, Inc., Columbus, Ohio), March 1-14, 1935, p. 12.

Boomer's Paradise. See Oklahoma

Boots. See Grantham, G. F.

Borah, William Edgar

The nicknames commonly applied to Senator William Edgar Borah of Idaho by newspaper and magazine writers were the *Lion of the Senate,* the *Lone Lion,* and the *Idaho Lion.* [1]

Senator William Edgar Borah was born at Farfield, Ill., on June 29, 1865, and died January 19, 1940.

[1] *The Washington Herald* (Washington, D.C., June 10, 1936) p. 28.
The Literary Digest, January to March, 1930 (Funk and Wagnalls Company, New York, 1930), vol. 104, March 8, 1930, p. 41.
The Washington Herald (Washington, D.C., June 10, 1936) p. 13.

Borax King. See Smith, F. M.

Borax Smith. See Smith, F. M.

Border-eagle State. See Mississippi

Border Ruffians

The *Border Ruffians* were men who, during the Civil War, declared themselves to be neutral and professed to be occupied in their usual vocations. In reality they availed themselves of every opportunity to attack soldiers, either Federal or Confederate, and to harass their neighbors who differed with them. These marauders were called *Border Ruffians* [1] because they were especially prevalent along the border between adjoining states which differed in their political alignment, the frontiers of Kansas and of Missouri in particular.

[1] *The Life of Horace Greeley, Founder of the New York Tribune, with Extended Notices of Many of His Contemporary Statesmen and Journalists,* L. D. Ingersoll (Union Publishing Company, New York and Chicago, 1873) p. 307.

Border State. See Maine

Border Town. See Rye, N. Y.

Bosox. See Boston American League Baseball Company

Boss. See Roosevelt, F. D.

Boss Hague. See Hague, Frank

Boss Kelly. See Kelly, John

Boston, Massachusetts

Boston is called the *Athens of America, Athens of the New World, Athens of the United States, American Athens, Modern Athens, Bay Horse, City of Baked Beans, City of Kind Hearts, City of Notions, Classic City, The Hub,* or *Hub of the Universe, Hub of New England, Hub of the Solar System, Literary Emporium, Metropolis of New England, Puritan City,* and *Trimountain City.*

Boston has been designated the *Athens of America,*[1] *Modern Athens, Athens of the New World, Athens of the United States,* and *American Athens* because of its prominence as an educational and literary center, comparable to Athens.

About 1635 Boston was nicknamed the *Bay Horse.*[2] It is termed the *City of Baked Beans* because it is nationally known for its beans and brown bread which were served in the Puritan homes, and still are, for the Saturday night meal and for Sunday breakfast.

Helen Keller called Boston the *City of Kind Hearts*[3] because her teacher, Miss Anne Mansfield Sullivan, came to her from Boston, and because so many of her friends and those who helped and inspired her during her life were from there.

Boston has been facetiously designated *The City of Notions* by non-residents because it manufactures and sells, both wholesale and retail, such quantities and varieties of small articles or commodities generally known as notions.

Boston has been termed the *Classic City*[4] because during the nineteenth century it was the American cultural and literary center. It is also widely known as *The Hub,*[5] *Hub of New England,* or *Hub of the Universe,* and *Hub of the Solar System* from Oliver Wendell Holmes' *Autocrat of the Breakfast Table.*

Boston is nicknamed the *Literary Emporium*[6] because of its vast literary activities, that is, colleges and publishing houses, and because of its extensive trade and industrial interests. Boston well merits the sobriquet,

The Metropolis of New England,[7] because it is the largest city in the New England group of states.

It is called *The Puritan City*[8] because its early settlers were Puritans. *The Trimountain City*[9] had its origin in the fact that the city was founded in 1630 on three hills: Fort's Hill on the east, Copp's Hill on the north, and Beacon Hill on the west.

[1] *Bacon's Dictionary of Boston with an Historical Introduction,* George E. Ellis (Houghton Mifflin and Company, Boston and New York, 1886) p. 30.

Letters on the Eastern States, Second Edition, William Tudor (Wells and Lilly, Boston, 1821) p. 364-5.

Americanisms—Old and New, John S. Farmer (Privatel printed by Thomas Poulter and Sons, London, 1889) p. 25, 1949.

The Inner Life of the United States, Monsignor Count Vay De Vaya and Lusod (John Murray, London, 1908) p. 215.

[2] *New Hampshire, an Epitome of Popular Government,* Frank B. Sanborn (Houghton Mifflin and Company, New York and Boston, 1904) p. 16.

A New Dictionary of Americanisms, Sylva Clapin (Louis Weiss and Company, New York, 1903) p. 117.

U.S.: An Index to the United States of America, comp. by Malcolm Townsend (D. Lothrop Company, Boston, 1890) p. 69-70.

[3] *Fifty Years of Boston, 1880-1930: Fifty Years of Boston, a Memorial Volume Issued in Commemoration of the Tercentenary of 1930,* comp. by the Subcommittee on Memorial History of the Boston Tercentenary Committee, Elizabeth M. Herlihy, Chairman and Editor (Allied Printing, Boston, 1932) p. xv, 332.

The Story of My Life, New School Edition, Helen Keller (Houghton Mifflin Company, Boston and New York, 1928) p. 45.

[4] *Americanisms; The English of the New World,* M. Schele De Vere (Charles Scribner and Company, New York, 1872) p. 662.

Boston, the Place and the People, M. A. DeWolfe Howe (The Macmillan Company, New York, 1903) p. 222-49.

[5] *More About Names,* Leopold Wagner (T. Fisher Unwin, London, 1893) p. 243.

Our Singing Strength: An Outline of American Poetry (1620-1930) Alfred Kreymborg (Coward-McCann, Inc., New York, 1929) p. 134.

The Autocrat of the Breakfast Table, Oliver Wendell Holmes, ed. with an introduction by Franklin T. Baker (The Macmillan Company, New York, 1928) p. 138.

Commercial Structure of New England, Edward F. Gerish, Part II of *The Commerce Survey of New England,* Charles E. Artman, in charge, *Domestic Commerce Series—Number Twenty-six* (United States Department of Commerce, Government Printing Office, Washington, D.C., 1929) p. 16, 68-9.

[6] *Manual of Useful Information,* comp. under the direction of J. C. Thomas (The Werner Company, Chicago, 1893) p. 22.

[7] *Illustrated Boston, The Metropolis of New England* (American Publishing and Engraving Company, New York, 1889) p. 33.

Population and Its Distribution: Population of the United States by States and Principal Cities: Population Federal, Individual Income Tax Returns and Automobile Registrations by Counties: Retail Shopping Areas, comp. by J. Walter Thompson Company (Harper and Brothers, New York and London, 1931) p. 6.

Walks and Talks About Historic Boston, comp. and ed. by Albert W. Mann (The Mann Publishing Company, Boston, 1916) p. 1-2.

[8] *A Dictionary of English Phrases, Phraseological Allusions, Catchwords, Stereotyped Modes of Speech and Metaphors, Nicknames, Sobriquets, Derivations from Personal Names, Etc., with Explanations and Thousands of Exact References to Their Sources or Early Usage,* Albert M. Hyamson (George Routledge and Sons, Ltd., London) p. 284.

[9] *The Romantic Story of the Puritan Fathers and Their Founding of New Boston and the Massachusetts Bay Colony together with Some Account of the Conditions Which Led to Their Departure from Old Boston and the Neighboring Town in England,* Albert C. Addison (L. G. Page and Company, Boston, 1912) p. 22-4.

A Topographical and Historical Description of Boston, Third Edition, Nathaniel B. Shurtleff (Published by order of the common council, Rockwell and Churchill, City Printers, Boston, 1891) p. 158-9, 170-1.

Metropolitan Boston: A Modern History, Albert P. Langtry, Editor-in-chief (Lewis Historical Publishing Company, Inc., New York, 1929) vol. 1, p. 16-17.

King's Hand Book of Boston, Third Edition (Moses King, Harvard College, Cambridge, Mass., 1897) p. 1.

Boston American League Baseball Company

The *Boston Red Sox* [1] was the name given to the team of the Boston American League Baseball Company in 1904 by John I. Taylor, president of the organization at that time, because the players wore red stockings. They are also called *Bosox.*

[1] A communication from Hi W. Mason, Secretary of The Boston American League Baseball Company, Boston, Mass., June 25, 1935.

Boston Braves. See Boston National League Baseball Company

Boston National League Baseball Company

James E. Gaffney, who was president of the Boston National League Baseball Company from 1912 to 1915, nicknamed the men of this company the *Boston Braves.*[1] On March 18, 1953, the franchise was shifted from Boston to Milwaukee, Wis., and the team became the *Milwaukee Braves.*[2]

[1] A communication from E. P. Cunningham, Secretary on The Boston National League Baseball Company, Boston, Mass., July 16, 1935.
[2] *New York Times* (New York City) March 19, 1953, p. 1.

Boston Red Sox. See Boston American League Baseball Company

Boston Tea Party

On the evening of December 16, 1773, in the harbor of Boston, Mass., a group of colonists disguised as Indians went aboard three ships belonging to the East India Company, broke open the three hundred and forty-two tea chests thereon, and quietly threw about seventy thousand dollars worth of tea into the harbor. This act, a retaliatory measure against the British decree of a threepence tax on every pound of tea, is generally called the *Boston Tea Party.*[1]

[1] *The New Complete History of the United States of America,* Official Edition, John Clark Ridpath (The Jones Brothers Publishing Company, Cincinnati, Ohio, 1905) vol. 6, p. 2405.

Boston Tim. See Sullivan, T. P.

Botany Bay

Union College, now Union University, at Schenectady, N.Y., is a nonsectarian institution. During the administration of Doctor Eliphalet Nott from 1804 to 1866, this college was nicknamed *Botany Bay* because it welcomed students who had little scholarship, and even students who had been expelled from other colleges, it is said. Students who could not secure admission into other colleges for various reasons were readily admitted to Union College. Botany Bay, in New South Wales, was in former times a convict settlement. The name Botany Bay was given to the settlement by Captain James Cook because of the great variety of plants to be found there. *Botany Bay* was applied to Union College because its student body was composed of such a variety of individuals as to previous training and qualifications.

[1] *The Shorter Oxford English Dictionary of Historical Principles,* prepared by William Little, Revised and Enlarged Edition by C. T. Onions (The Clarendon Press, Oxford, England, 1933) vol. 1, p. 206.

Memoirs of Eliphalet Nott, D.D., LI.D., for Sixty-two Years President of Union College, C. Van Santvoord and Taylor Lewis (Sheldon and Company, New York, 1876) p. 152-3.

Botetourt, Norborne Berkeley

Lord Norborne Berkeley Botetourt was called the *Good Governor of Virginia* [1] because, while he was the Royal Governor of the colony from 1768 to 1770, he consistently opposed the arbitrary measures of the British ministry for colonial taxation,[2] and aligned himself with the colonists in their cherished ideals of freedom and liberty. When George III refused to withdraw objectionable imposts levied on the Virginia colonists Botetourt resigned his governorship.

Norborne Berkeley Botetourt was born in England in 1718, and died at Williamsburg, Va., on October 15, 1770.

[1] *Virginia,* comp. and ed. by Charlotte Allen (Published by the Department of Agriculture and Immigration of the State of Virginia, under the direction of George W. Koiner, Commissioner, Department of Purchase and Printing, Richmond, Va., 1937) p. 131.

The New International Cyclopaedia (Dodd, Mead and Company, New York, 1911) vol. 3, p. 346.

Bouck, William C.

William C. Bouck was popularly designated the *Farmer Governor* [1] because, previous to his election in 1842 as Governor of

Bouck, W. C.—Continued
New York, he had been a farmer on the
land where he had been born. He was born
at Fulton, N.Y., on January 7, 1786, and
died there on April 19, 1859.

[1] *Memorial Encyclopedia of the State of New York, a
Life Record of Men and Women of the Past Whose
Sterling Character and Energy and Industry Have Made
Them Preeminent in Their Own and Many Other States,*
Charles Elliott Fitch (The American Historical Society,
Inc., New York and Chicago, 1916) vol. 1, p. 114.

Bounty Jumpers

During the latter part of the Civil War
the northern officials offered a bounty to
anyone who would enlist in the Union
Army. Men who enlisted to collect the
bounty and then deserted were known as
Bounty Jumpers.[1]

[1] *The Founders of the American Republic, A History
and Biography with a Supplementary Chapter on Ultra-
democracy,* Charles Mackay (William Blackwood and
Sons, Edinburgh and London, 1885) p. 398.
   Webster's Unabridged Dictionary (G. & C. Merriam
Co., Springfield, Mass., 1942)

Bowdoin College

The athletic teams of Bowdoin College,
at Brunswick Me., are called *Polar Bears*
because of the white uniforms which they
wear and because the Arctic explorers Robert
Edwin Peary and Donald Baxter MacMillan
graduated from this college. A polar bear
was once given to the college as a mascot.

[6] A letter from Malcolm E. Morrell, Director of Athletics at Bowdoin College, Brunswick, Me., June 17,
1935.

Bowen, George

George Bowen, an American missionary
to India from 1848 to 1888, was nicknamed
the *Nestor of the Methodist Conference in
India.*[1] He lived simply among the poorest
of the natives while he went about his labors
as a missionary to the Bombay district.

George Bowen was born at Middlebury,
Vt., on April 13, 1816, and died at Bombay,
India, on February 3, 1888.

[1] *Appleton's Cyclopaedia of American Biography,* ed.
by James Grant Wilson and John Fiske (D. Appleton
and Company, New York, 1900) vol. 7, p. 31.

Bowery Boys

During the early 1860's the unlawful element in several cities organized themselves
into gangs for intimidating voters and keeping them away from the polls at election
time. One of the most prominent of these
gangs in New York City was the *Bowery
Boys.*[1]

[1] "The Irrepressible Conflict, 1850-1865," by Arthur
Charles Cole, in *A History of American Life,* Arthur M.
Schlesinger and Dixon Ryan Fox, Editors (The Mac-
millan Company, New York, 1934) vol. 7, p. 154.

Bowie State. See Arkansas

Bowie-knife Potter. See Potter, J. F.

Box Office Girl. See Gray, Gilda

Boxers

During the controversy over a proposed
tariff reduction affecting trade between Cuba
and the United States about 1901, a number
of Republicans, calling themselves *Boxers,*[1]
banded together to oppose such a reduction.
They claimed such a procedure would be
harmful to the beet-sugar and the cane-sugar
industries in the United States.

[2] *An Old-fashioned Senator, Orville H. Platt of Con-
necticut; the Story of a Life Unselfishly Devoted to the
Public Service,* Louis A. Coolidge (G. P. Putnam's Sons,
New York and London, 1910) p. 374.

Boy General. See Custer, G. A.

Boy Geologist of Michigan.   See
Houghton, Douglass

Boy Governor. See Mason, S. T.

Boy Guard. See Whitman, J. L.

Boy-hero of the Confederacy.   See
Davis, Sam

Boy Major. See Pelham, John

Boy Mayor. See Russell, W. E.

Boy Orator. See Lee, J. B.

Boy Orator of the Platte. See Bryan,
W. J.

Boy Preacher. See Furman, Richard;
Kennedy, Crammond; Lipscomb, A. A.

Boy Producer. See Thalberg, I. G.

Boy Wonder. See Lee, J. B.

*Boyhood Home of George Washing-
ton.* See Fredericksburg, Va.

Boys in Blue

In 1868 the Republicans banded themselves into a number of political organizations to campaign for General Ulysses Simp-

son Grant for President of the United States. A prominent group of this nature was known as the *Boys in Blue* [1] because, when they were on parade or campaigning, they wore blue capes of a somewhat military cut and carried blue banners and torches. Blue was chosen because Grant's Union soldiers during the Civil War wore blue uniforms.

[3] "The Election of 1868, the Democratic Effort to Regain Control" by Charles H. Coleman, in *Studies in History, Economics, and Public Law, Number 392,* ed. by the faculty of political science of Columbia University (Columbia University Press, New York, 1933) p. 306.

Braddock, James J.

James J. Braddock, a heavyweight prize fighter, has been nicknamed the *Cinderella Man* [1] and the *Forgotten Man* [2] because he twice fought his way back to prominence in the field of prize fighting from a place of obscurity. These contests were fought on the following dates: on March 23, 1935, he defeated Art Lasky; on June 13, 1935, he won the victory over Max Baer; and on January 22, 1938, he defeated Tommy Farr.

Between 1930 when he was first prominent as a prize fighter, and 1938 when he won his last major victory, he had made and lost a fortune and had been on relief.

[1] *The Washington Post,* Washington, D.C., January 23, 1938, col. 5, p. 3.
[2] *Relief to Royalty: The Story of James J. Braddock, World's Heavyweight Champion,* Ludwig Shabazian (Printed by the Hudson Dispatch, Union City, N.J., 1936) p. 47, 141.

Bradford, John

The name *Franklin of the West* [1] was often applied to John Bradford because in August 1787, he established at Lexington, Ky., the *Kentucky Gazette,* a pioneer newspaper in that region. For nearly half a century he was one of the most prominent journalists in what was then considered the Western United States and was an exemplary citizen who devoted his services to bettering the welfare of his state and country.

John Bradford was born in Virginia, in 1749, and died in Fayette County, Ky., in March, 1830.

[1] *History of Kentucky, from 1803 to 1928,* Samuel M. Wilson (The S. J. Clarke Publishing Company, Chicago, and Louisville, Ky., 1928) vol. 2, p. 451.
History of Kentucky, William Elsey Connelley and E. M. Coulter, Charles Kerr, Editor (The American Historical Society, New York and Chicago, 1922) vol. 5, p. 625.

Bradford, William

William Bradford has been designated the *Father of American History.*[1] He was the author of a number of historical writings of inestimable value as source material for the early history of the Plymouth Colony. His *History of the Plymouth Plantation* is an authentic, connected history of this colony from its beginning in 1602 in England until 1647. Bradford's journal entitled *Mourt's Relation* and his *Letter Book* are also valuable source materials for the Plymouth Plantation during the first decades of its existence.

William Bradford was born at Austerfield, Yorkshire, England, in 1590, and died at the Plymouth Plantation on May 9, 1657.

[2] *Old Colony Days,* May Alden Ward (Robert Brothers, Boston, 1896) p. 11-17.

Bradley, Omar Nelson

General Omar Nelson Bradley is nicknamed the *Doughboy's General.*[1] He was born at Clark, Mo., on Feb. 12, 1893, was graduated from the United States Military Academy at West Point, N.Y., in 1915. He is now Chief of Staff of the American Army.

[1] *The World Book,* The Quarrie Corporation, Chicago, 1947, vol. 2, p. 954.

Bradstreet, Anne

Anne Bradstreet was called the *Tenth Muse* [1] by her contemporaries because of her poetic talents.

She was born at Northampton, England, in 1612, and died at Andover, Mass., on September 16, 1672.

[1] *Commonwealth History of Massachusetts,* ed. by Albert Bushnell Hart (The States History Company, New York, 1927) vol. 1, p. 320.

Brady, James Buchanan

The nickname *Diamond Jim* [1] was given to James Buchanan Brady because of his collection of valuable jewels, among which were a great number of expensive diamonds that he constantly wore.

At New York City he was a stockholder and a director in the firm of Manning, Maxwell, and Moore, who manufactured railway machinery and equipment; and in 1902 he was elected vice president of the Standard Car Company. He founded the Brady Urological Institute of Johns Hopkins Hospital in Baltimore, Md., and donated generously toward its upkeep.

He was born at New York City on August 12, 1856, and died at Atlantic City, N.J., on April 13, 1917.

[1] *The National Cyclopaedia of American Biography* (James T. White and Company, New York, 1926) vol. 19, p. 412.

Brahmin Caste of New England

The aristocratic class of people in New England came to be called *Brahmins* and the *Brahmin Caste of New England*[1] in the early 1840's because these aristocrats, like the Brahmins of India, were the dominant personages of New England who largely controlled social prestige and considered themselves superior to the rest of the people.

[1] *U.S. "Snap Shots": An Independent, National, and Memorial Encyclopedia . . . ,* Oliver McKee (A. M. Thayer and Company, Boston, 1892) p. 60.

Brain of the Revolution. See Adams, Samuel

Brain Trust

The *Brain Trust*,[1] and *Brain Trusters* were the names applied to the group of men who served as research assistants to Franklin Delano Roosevelt in 1932 while he was preparing for his presidential campaign, and who later constituted a board of economic strategy. The *Brain Trust* was a fitting name because the group was composed chiefly of college professors and research men who served to advise President Roosevelt in matters that his political advisors did not handle. Many of them later became members of his cabinet and heads of special boards. (See *ABC's of the New Deal.*)

[1] *The Roosevelt Revolution, First Phase,* Ernest K. Lindley (The Viking Press, New York, 1933) p. 21, 26.

Brainerd, Minnesota

Brainerd, being located in the "geographical center" of the state, is termed the *Hub City.*[1]

[1] *My Minnesota,* Antoinette E. Ford (Lyons and Carnahan, New York and Chicago, 1929) p. 369.

Brains of the Confederacy. See Benjamin, J. P.

Brandeis, Louis Dembitz

Associate Justice Louis Dembitz Brandeis of the United States Supreme Court was called the *People's Lawyer*[1] while he was practicing law in Boston, Mass., because he defended the rights of the working man against industrial trusts and combines of big business.

Louis Dembitz Brandeis was born at Louisville, Ky., on November 13, 1856, and died at Washington, D.C., on October 5, 1941.

[1] *Time: The Weekly Newsmagazine,* Chicago, February 20, 1939, col. 3, p. 11.

Brass Kettle Campaign

The political campaign of 1878 in the Third Congressional District of Minnesota was called the *Brass Kettle Campaign.*[1] Because this was a great wheat-producing area, campaigners often made references to the raising and selling of wheat, and to the two-quart "brass kettle" or measure used in grading wheat.

[1] *The Life of Knute Nelson,* Martin W. Odland (The Lund Press, Inc., Minneapolis ,Minn., 1926) p. 96.

Braves. See Ottawa University

Bread and Butter Rebellion

The *Bread and Butter Rebellion*[1] was the nickname given to the agitation by students of Yale University, at New Haven, Conn., in 1828 or 1829, to secure better food in the university dining hall.

[1] *Dictionary of American Biography under the Auspices of the American Council of Learned Societies,* ed. by Allen Johnson (Charles Scribner's Sons, New York, 1928) vol. 1, p. 622.

Bread and Butter State. See Minnesota

Bread Basket of the World. See Minnesota

Bread-father. See Sower, Christopher

Breakfast Food City. See Battle Creek, Mich.

Breck, James Lloyd

James Lloyd Breck, an Episcopal clergyman and missionary, was nicknamed the *Apostle of the Wilderness.*[1] He spent the greater part of his life in Minnesota and the northwestern territories doing missionary work among the settlers and Indians, establishing missions, founding Christian schools, and establishing a Theological Seminary at Nashotah, Minn.

James Lloyd Breck was born near Philadelphia, Pa., on June 27, 1818, and died at Benicia, Calif., on March 30, 1876.

[1] *Dictionary of American Biography under the Auspices of the American Council of Learned Societies,* ed. by Allen Johnson (Charles Scribner's Sons, New York, 1929) vol. 3, p. 4.

Bresnahan, Roger P.

Roger P. Bresnahan, who was a famous catcher for the New York Giants, was called the *Duke of Tralee.*[1]

[1] *Who's Who in Major League Base Ball,* comp. by Harold (Speed) Johnson (Buxton Publishing Company, Chicago, 1933) p. 472.

Brewster, Ralph Owen

Ralph Owen Brewster, a Maine politician, was nicknamed the *Aroostook Potato* [1] by his colleagues in the House of Representatives because his congressional district included Aroostook County, which is famous for its potatoes. He kept potatoes on display in his office and gave them away by the sackful for advertising purposes.

Ralph Owen Brewster was born at Dexter, Me., on February 22, 1888.

[1] An interview with Captain Victor Hunt Harding, Secretary of the Democratic Congress Reelection Committee, Washington, D.C., April 10, 1939

Brick. See Owens, C. B.

Bricker, John William

John William Bricker, Governor of Ohio, is widely known as *Honest John* [1] because of his reputation for being honest and fair in his dealings. During his first year as governor he reduced the budget of the state by three million dollars.

John William Bricker was born in Madison County, Ohio, on September 6, 1893.

[1] *Time: The Weekly Newsmagazine*, Chicago, May 15, 1939, col. 3, p. 20.

Bridge Builder Bland. See Bland, S. O.

Bridger, James

The nickname *Daniel Boone of the Rocky Mountains* [1] was applied to James Bridger because he was a scout, hunter, and early settler in the Rocky Mountain regions.

He was born at Richmond, Va., on March 17, 1804, and died at Washington, Mo., on July 17, 1881.

[1] *Contributions to the Historical Society of Montana with Its Transactions, Officers, and Members* (State Publishing Company, Helena, Mont., 1900) vol. 3, p. 175.

Brigadier Commanding Hospitals. See Bickerdyke, M. A. B.

Brigadiers. See Washington and Lee University

Brimstone Hill

Andover Hill at Andover, Mass., has been called *Brimstone Hill* [1] because in the Calvinist Theological Seminary, located there, predictions of the tortuous punishments by fire and brimstone which the sinful would suffer after the Judgment Day were made.

[1] *John Marsh, Pioneer, the Life Story of a Trail-blazer on Six Frontiers*, George D. Lyman (Charles Scribner's Sons, New York, 1930) p. 26.

Brindles

In 1871 when Powell Clayton, who was governor of Arkansas, was elected to the United States Senate, a contest developed between his supporters and those of the lieutenant governor James M. Johnson, one of whom was Joseph Brooks.

The term *Brindles*,[1] or *Brindle Tails* originated in a remark by John Agery, a Negro orator, that Joseph Brooks' voice and manners made him think of "an old brindle tail bull" which made so much noise it frightened the other cattle.

The expression *Brindles* or *Brindle Tails* was again widely used in 1872 during the campaign for the next governor of Arkansas.

[1] *The Brooks and Baxter War, a History of the Reconstruction Period in Arkansas*, John M. Harrell (Slawson Printing Company, St. Louis, Mo., 1893) p 96, 99.
Centennial History of Arkansas, Dallas T. Herndon (The S. J. Clarke Publishing Company, Chicago and Little Rock, Ark., 1922) vol. 1, p. 299.
"Reconstruction in Arkansas, 1862-1874" by Thomas S. Staples, in *Studies in History, Economics, and Public Law*, ed. by the Faculty of Political Science of Columbia University (Columbia University Press, New York, 1923) p. 389.

Bristol, Virginia and Tennessee

Bristol is called *The Twin City* [1] because it is divided into two units by the state line separating Virginia from Tennessee. The part situated in Tennessee is separated from the part located in Virginia by a white line placed along the center of State Street. The two sections of Bristol have separate governments and laws, but in other respects they are considered one town.

[1] *Virginia*, comp. and ed. by Charlotte Allen (Published by the Department of Agriculture and Immigration of the State of Virginia under the direction of George W. Koiner, Commissioner, Division of Purchase and Printing, Richmond, Va., 1937) p. 103.

Britons. See Albion College

Broadcloth Mob

The *Broadcloth Mob* [1] was a crowd of some three thousand men of social rank and wealth (mostly dressed in broadcloth) who had gathered to protest against a lecture by the English abolitionist George Thompson, which was to have been given before a meeting of the Boston Female Anti-Slavery Society on October 21, 1835. The lecturer had been warned, however, of the intention of the crowd to tar and feather him, and had left town.

The crowd, frustrated in its original intention, decided to wreak vengeance upon Wil-

Broadcloth Mob—Continued
liam Lloyd Garrison whose anti-slavery news-paper *Liberator* was published in the same building. He was seized by the anti-aboli-tionist crowd, bound with ropes and taken for some distance before he was rescued by friends and police who rushed him to the city jail for safety for the night.

The disturbance was also designated the *Gentlemen's Riot.*

[1] "William Lloyd Garrison the Abolitionist," by Archi-bald H. Grimké, in *American Reformers and Orators,* ed. by Carlos Martyn (Funk and Wagnalls, New York and London, 1891) p. 235.
History of the United States, from the Compromise of 1850, James Ford Rhodes (Harper and Brothers, New York, 1899) vol. 1, p. 61.
[2] *Papers Relating to the Garrison Mob,* ed. by Theodore Lyman (Welch, Bigelow and Company, Cam-bridge, Mass., 1870) p.5.

Broadway, New York City. See Grand Canyon of American Business

Brock, William Emerson
William Emerson Brock is nicknamed the *Candy Kid* [1] because he is the president of the Brock Candy Company at Chattanooga, Tenn. He was born at Farmington, N.C., on March 14, 1872, and was a United States Senator from Tennessee from 1931 to 1937.

[1] *The Literary Digest, January to March, 1930* (Funk and Wagnalls Company, New York, 1930) vol. 3, p. 41.

Brod-vater. See Sower, Christopher

Broken Hints
During the Revolutionary War Joseph Hawley, a lawyer and statesman, took a prominent part in the cause of the colonists. Because he could not get in personal touch with the Massachusetts delegates to the Con-tinental Congress of 1774, he wrote them what he called *Broken Hints*, inciting them to resist the British. They were conveyed as *hints* to prevent the complete betrayal of their author in case the letters miscarried.

[1] *Joseph Hawley, Colonial Radical,* E. Francis Brown (Columbia University Press, New York, 1931) p. 138.

Broncho Charlie or Carlos. See Miller, Charles

Broncos. See University of Santa Clara

Brood of the Constitution
The members of the class who were grad-uated from the United States Naval Acad-emy, at Annapolis, Md., in 1864, were the

first to use the battleship *Constitution*, pop-ularly known as *Old Ironsides*, as a training vessel. They were therefore called the *Brood of the Constitution*.[1]

[1] *Dictionary of American Biography under the Aus-pices of the American Council of Learned Societies,* ed. by Dumas Malone (Charles Scribner's Sons, New York, 1934) vol. 13, p. 172.

Brookline, Massachusetts
Brookline now almost surrounded by Boston, was formerly nicknamed the *Muddy River Hamlet* [1] because it is situated on an arm of the Charles River, which before the days of paved streets and sewerage doubtless warranted the name.

[1] *The Source Book* (Source Research Council, Inc., Chicago, 1936) vol. 1, p. 393.

Brooklyn, New York
Brooklyn is the possessor of three nick-names, *City of Churches, City of Homes,* and *Dormitory of New York.* It was known as *City of Churches* [1] because it had such a great number of churches in proportion to its population. The *City of Homes* [2] and the *Dormitory of New York,* are applied to Brooklyn because so many of the people who work in Manhattan live in Brooklyn.

[1] *History of Brooklyn: A History of the City of Brooklyn, Including the Old Town and Village of Brooklyn, the Town of Bushwick, and the Village and City of Williamsburgh,* Henry R. Stiles (Published by subscription, Joel Munsell, Printer, Albany, N.Y., 1870) vol. 3, p. 504.
[2] *The Encyclopaedia Britannica,* Fourteenth Edition (Encyclopaedia Britannica, Inc., New York, 1932) vol. 4, p. 256.

Brooklyn College
In 1931 the *Kingsmen* [1] was given as a nickname to the athletic teams of Brooklyn College, Brooklyn, N.Y. It was selected by a vote of the student body because the borough of Brooklyn in New York City covers the entire Kings County in New York State.

[1] A communication from Richard Jo Neil, Director of Athletics at Brooklyn College, Brooklyn, N.Y., Novem-ber 25, 1935.

Brooklyn Dodgers. See Brooklyn Dodgers Football Club; Brooklyn National League Baseball Company

Brooklyn Dodgers Football Club
Brooklyn Dodgers [1] is the nickname com-monly applied to the teams of the Brooklyn Dodgers Football Club, a member of the National Football League, located at Brook-lyn, N.Y. This name was borrowed from the Brooklyn National League Baseball

Company whose players have been called the *Brooklyn Dodgers* since about 1904. For the origin of the nickname see the Brooklyn National League Baseball Company.

[1] A communication from Daniel R. Topping, President-secretary of the Brooklyn National League Football Club, Brooklyn, N.Y., March 20, 1939.

Brooklyn National League Baseball Company

The nickname *Brooklyn Dodgers* [4] was given to the Brooklyn National League Baseball Company about 1904 by newspaper writers because at that time Brooklyn was noted for its many trolley lines and Brooklynites were referred to as trolley dodgers.

[1] A communication from James A. Mulvey, vice-President and Secretary of the Brooklyn National League Baseball Company, Brooklyn, N.Y., June 27, 1935.

Brooklyn of the South. See Anniston, Ala.

Brooks, Preston Smith

On May 22, 1856, Senator Charles Sumner of Massachusetts made an anti-slavery speech in the United States Senate offensive to Senator Preston Smith Brooks of South Carolina. After the Senate had adjourned Senator Brooks attacked Senator Sumner with his cane while the latter was seated at his desk engaged in writing. Because of the severity of his assault and because Sumner, seated at his desk, was unable to defend himself, Brooks was called *Bully Brooks*.[1] Brooks later apologized and admitted publicly that he had taken an unfair advantage of his opponent.

Preston Smith Brooks was born at Edgefield, S.C., on August 4, 1819, and died at Washington. D.C., on January 27, 1857.

[1] *The Age of Hate, Andrew Johnson and the Radicals,* George Fort Milton (Coward-McCann, Inc., New York, 1930) p. 34.
"Sumner—Brooks—Burlingame or the Last of the Great Challenges" by James E. Campbell, in the *Ohio Archaeological and Historical Quarterly October, 1925* (Published by the Society, The F. J. Herr Printing Company, Columbus, Ohio, 1925) vol. 34, no. 4, p. 515.

Brooks and Baxter War

In 1872 Elisha Baxter and Joseph Brooks were the candidates for governor of Arkansas. Baxter was inaugurated in January 1873; but Brooks, contending that the election had been dishonestly conducted, attempted to eject him from his office. Thereupon their followers armed themselves, and

Little Rock took on a warlike aspect. Baxter was upheld in his office by President Ulysses S. Grant and continued to serve as governor. This dispute has been called the *Brooks and Baxter War*.[1]

[1] *The Brooks and Baxter War, a History of the Reconstruction Period in Arkansas,* John M. Harrell (Slawson Printing Company, St. Louis, Mo., 1893) p. 95, 214-59.
A History of the United States Since the Civil War, Ellis Paxson Oberholtzer (The Macmillan Company, New York, 1926) vol. 3, p. 205.

Brother Jonathan

Brother Jonathan [1] has been used as a symbol of the people of the United States for nearly two centuries much as the figure of Uncle Sam has been. The most prevalent explanation of its origin is that in 1776, when Washington took charge of the New England Revolutionary forces, he found the army in great need of arms, supplies, and more men. In meeting this emergency he turned for aid to his old friend, Jonathan Trumbull, Governor 'of Connecticut from 1769 to 1783, familiarly known to him as Brother Jonathan, remarking that "We must consult Brother Jonathan." Washington's frequent use of this expression when he went to Trumbull for advice and aid caused it to come into popular use. The American people as a whole possessed the resourcefulness and reliability that had characterized Trumbull; consequently, *Brother Jonathan* gradually came to be applied to the people of the United States in general.

See also Trumbull, Jonathan

[1] *The New England History, from the Discovery of the Continent by the Northmen, A.D. 986, to the Period When the Colonies Declared Their Independence, A.D. 1776,* Charles W. Elliott (Charles Scribner, New York, 1857) vol. 2, p. 36.
King's Handbook of the United States, planned and ed. by Moses King, text by M. F. Sweetser (Moses King Corporation, Buffalo, N.Y., 1891) p. 119.
The Encyclopaedia Britannica, Fourteenth Edition (Encyclopaedia Britannica, Inc., New York, 1932) vol. 4, p. 259.

Brown, David

David Brown, who died at Newfane, Vt., on January 31, 1873, was nicknamed the *Hermit of Newfane* [1] because he lived the life of a recluse, devoting his time to study and book collecting. When he died, he left one of the largest libraries in the state of Vermont.

[1] *Appleton's Cyclopaedia of American Biography,* ed. by James Grant Wilson and John Fiske (D. Appleton and Company, New York, 1895) vol. 1, p. 397,

Brown, John

John Brown was nicknamed the *Martyr Hero, Old Ossawatomie,* and *Ossawatomie Brown.* He was sometimes designated the *Martyr Hero* [1] by the abolitionists because he sacrificed his life in endeavoring to incite slaves to revolt against their masters and to become free.

John Brown was nicknamed *Old Ossawatomie* [2] and *Ossawatomie Brown* [3] because he and his sons settled near Ossawatomie, Kans. where he engaged in continual hostilities against the pro-slavery forces in Kansas and other western states until his death.

John Brown was born at Torrington, Conn., on May 9, 1800, and was executed in Charlestown, in what is now West Virginia, on December 2, 1859.

[1] *Griswold—a History, Being a History of the Town of Griswold, Connecticut from the Earliest Times to the Entrance of Our Country into the World War in 1917,* Daniel L. Phillips (The Tuttle, Morehouse and Taylor Company, New Haven, Conn., 1929) p. 173.

[2] *Fifty Years and Over of Akron and Summit County,* Samuel A. Lane (Beacon Job Department, Akron, Ohio, 1892) p. 588.

[3] *U.S. "Snap Shots": An Independent, National, and Memorial Encyclopedia . . . ,* Oliver McKee (A. M. Thayer and Company, Boston, 1892) p. 243.

Brown, John Jackson

John Jackson Brown was called the *Cyclopaedia of Science* [1] when he became professor of chemistry and industrial mechanics at Cornell University at Ithaca, N.Y., in 1870, because of his profound knowledge.

John Jackson Brown was born at Amenia, N.Y., on February 7, 1820, and died at Syracuse, N.Y., on August 15, 1891.

[1] *The National Cyclopaedia of American Biography* (James T. White and Company, New York, 1899) vol. 2, p. 141.

Brown, Mordecai Peter Centennial

Mordecai Peter Centennial Brown, pitcher with the first outstanding team of modern baseball, the Chicago Cubs of 1906-1910, was nicknamed *Three Fingered Brown.* [1] He lost half of the index finger on his right hand in a cornshredder when he was a boy, but the accident proved a boon to his pitching for the stub enabled him to put a super spin on the ball, and permitted him to develop one of the widest curves ever seen. His pitching ability won for him enduring reputation as one of the great early modern baseball heroes.

Mordecai Brown was born at Nyesville, Ind., on October 19, 1876, and died February 14, 1948.

[1] *The Story of Baseball,* by John Durant (Hastings House, New York, 1947) p. 151.

Brown, William John

William John Brown was called *Done Brown* because while he was a Representative from Indiana during the 1840's he aspired to become the Speaker of the House. When he failed to attain the office, he wrote to a friend describing himself as being "done," and his political opponents promptly designated him *Done Brown.*

William John Brown was born near Washington, Ky., on August 15, 1805, and died near Indianapolis, Ind., on March 18, 1857.

[1] *The National Cyclopaedia of American Biography* (James T. White and Company, New York, 1909) vol. 11, p. 562.

Brown Bomber. See Louis, Joe

Brownell, Henry Howard

Oliver Wendell Holmes is said to have nicknamed Henry Howard Brownell *Our Battle Laureate* [1] because he wrote a poetical version of Admiral David Farragut's orders to his fleet, in 1862, on preparing for the passage of the forts below New Orleans, entitled *The River Fight,* and a description of the fight in Mobile bay, called *The Bay Fight,* in which Brownell had taken part.

Henry Howard Brownell was born at Providence, R.I., on February 6, 1820, and died at Hartford, Conn., on October 31, 1879.

[1] *The Fight for the Republic: A Narrative of the More Noteworthy Events in the War of Secession, Presenting the Great Contest in Its Dramatic Aspects,* Rossiter [Edwin Rossiter] Johnson (G. P. Putnam's Sons, New York and London, 1917) p. 101.
Dictionary of American Biography, ed by Allen Johnson (Charles Scribner's Sons, New York, 1929) vol. 3, p. 171.

Brownlow, William Gannaway

William Gannaway Brownlow was nicknamed the *Fighting Parson.* [1] For many years Brownlow was a Methodist minister who often expressed his political views from his pulpit. He was of an aggressive and critical temperament and his editorials in a newspaper known as *The Whig* were of an independent nature.

In 1839 he went to Jonesboro, Tenn., where he continued to preach and to edit *The Whig* until 1849, when he moved to

Knoxville, Tenn., and supplanted his duties as minister and editor with political activities. The fact that he was loyal to the Union during the Civil War and the Reconstruction provided him with ample opportunity to display his antagonism toward the Confederate cause.

W. G. Brownlow was born near Wytheville, Va., on August 29, 1805, and died at Knoxville, Tenn., on April 29, 1877.

[1] *Colonel Alexander K. McClure's Recollections of a Half-Century*, Alexander K. McClure (The Salem Press Company, Salem, Mass., 1902) p. 223.
Biographical Directory of the American Congress, 1774-1927; The Continental Congress, September 5, 1774, to October 21, 1788, and The Congress of the United States, from the First to the Sixty-ninth Congress March 4, 1789, of March 3, 1927, Inclusive (Government Printing Office, Washington, D.C., 1928) House Document number 783, vol. 16, p. 750.

Brownstone State. See Connecticut

Brownsville, Texas

The two nicknames of Brownsville are: *Metropolis of the Magic Valley* and *Where Mexico Meets Uncle Sam*. Brownsville is called the *Metropolis of the Magic Valley* [1] because it is located at the southern extremity of the Rio Grande Valley on the border between the United States and Mexico, which gives tourists easy contact with the old world atmosphere of Mexico. Because Brownsville is opposite the city of Matamoras in Mexico, it is designated *Where Mexico Meets Uncle Sam*. [2]

[1] *Flashlights on Texas*, Lillie Terrell Shaver and Willie Williamson Rogers (A. C. Baldwin and Sons, Austin, Tex., 1928) p. 60-2.
[2] *Texas As It Is Today*, Alfred E. Menn (Gammel's Book Store, Austin, Tex., 1925) p. 67.

Bruins. See University of California at Los Angeles

Brumbaugh, Carl

Carl Brumbaugh, who coached in national league football, was nicknamed *Little Napoleon* in 1934 by a sports writer on the Chicago *Daily News*, because of his special ability as a quarterback. He was born at West Milton, Ohio, on September 22, 1907.

[1] A communication from George S. Halas, President-treasurer of The Chicago Bears Football Club, Inc., Chicago, March 21, 1939

Brumm, George Franklin

George Franklin Brumm, Representative from Pennsylvania in 1923-27 and 1929-39, became widely known as *Three-minute Brumm* [1] because his speeches in the national House of Representatives were habitually that long. He was born at Minersville, Pa., on January 24, 1878.

[1] *The Washington Post Magazine*, Washington, D.C., March 4, 1934, p. 4.

Brunswick Arithmetic

The report of the committee of the Maine Constitutional Convention which convened at Brunswick, Me., on September 30, 1816, has been called *Brunswick Arithmetic* [1] because the report of the convention was presented in such a way that it showed the greater number of those attending the convention voted to separate the District of Maine from the Commonwealth of Massachusetts in spite of the fact that the majority of those composing the convention did not vote for the separation.

[1] *Collections of the Maine Historical Society*, Third Series (Published by the Society at the Press of the Lefavor-Tower Company, Portland, Me., 1906) vol. 2, p. 424.

Bryan, William Jennings

William Jennings Bryan was nicknamed the *Boy Orator of the Platte'*, the *Great Commoner*, and the *Silver-tongued Orator*.

The *Boy Orator of the Platte* [1] was applied to him by Republican newspapers during his campaign for the office of President of the United States in 1896. He was an unusually passionate and eloquent orator, and being only about thirty-six years of age, was a very young aspirant for the office.

William Jennings Bryan was designated the *Great Commoner* [2] because of his interest in politics which would benefit the common man. In 1900 he founded a weekly journal, *The Commoner*, which was devoted to discussing the political issues of the day. He was nicknamed the *Silver-tongued Orator* because of his great oratorical ability.

He was born at Salem, Ill., on March 19, 1860, and died at Dayton, Tenn., on July 26, 1935.

[1] *Twenty Years of the Republic, 1885-1905*, Harry Thurston Peck (Dodd, Mead and Company, New York, 1907) p. 506.
[2] *The Source Book* (Perpetual Encyclopedia Corporation, Chicago, 1932) vol. 1, p. 403.

Bryan Lassies. See William Jennings Bryan University

Bryan Lions. See William Jennings Bryan University

Bryant, William Cullen

William Cullen Bryant was known as the *American Wordsworth* and the *Father of American Poets*.

He was sometimes called the *American Wordsworth* [1] because he was one of the great nature poets of America and was inspired by the philosophy and writings of William Wordsworth.

Father of American Poets [2] was a nickname given to Bryant because he is generally considered to be the first noteworthy American poet.

William Cullen Bryant was born at Cummington, Mass., on November 3, 1794, and died at New York City, on June 12, 1878.

[1] *American Literary Readings with Introduction, Notes, Biographical Sketches, Some Thought Questions, and Outline of American Literature and a Brief Essay on English Metrics*, ed. by Leonidas Warren Payne (Rand McNally and Company, New York and Chicago, 1917) p. 56.

[2] *The World Book*, M. V. O'Shea, Editor-in-chief (Hanson-Roach-Fowler Company, Chicago, 1917) vol. 2, p. 965.

Buchanan, James

James Buchanan was called the *Bachelor President, Old Buck, Old Public Functionary, Sage of Wheatland,* and *Ten-cent Jimmy*.

President Buchanan was referred to as the *Bachelor President* [1] because he remained a bachelor throughout his life.

Buck [2] is a commonly used nickname for *Buchanan* and *Old Buck* was applied in a spirit of familiarity and affection.

During Buchanan's term as President there was such confusion in Congress over the John Brown disturbance and the repeal of the Missouri Compromise that no official matters could be considered in an orderly manner. President Buchanan was referred to as *Old Public Functionary* [3] because in a message to Congress he pleaded for cessation from "sectional strife" and for orderly consideration of official business saying his advice came from the head of *an old public functionary*.

James Buchanan was nicknamed the *Sage of Wheatland* [4] after he retired to his home at Wheatland near Lancaster, Pa., where he spent the remaining years of his life.

Ten-cent Jimmy [5] was applied to Buchanan because he advocated low tariff and low wages.

He was born near Mercersburg, Pa., on April 23, 1791, and died near Lancaster, Pa., on June 1, 1868.

[1] *The Story of the Great Republic*, New Edition, Hélène A. Guerber (The American Book Company, New York and Chicago, 1927) p. 156.

[2] *U.S. "Snap Shots": An Independent, National, and Memorial Encyclopedia . . .*, Oliver McKee (A. M. Thayer and Company, Boston, 1892) p. 309.

[3] *A Political History of Slavery: Being an Account of the Slavery Controversy from the Earliest Agitations in the Eighteenth Century in the Close of the Reconstruction Period in America*, William Henry Smith (G. P. Putnam's Sons, New York, 1903) p. 268.

[4] *The Life and Public Services of James Buchanan, Late Minister to England and Formerly Minister to Russia, Senator and Representative in Congress, and Secretary of State: Including the Most Important of His State Papers*, Authorized Edition, R. G. Horton (Derby and Jackson, New York, 1856) p. 424, 427.

[5] *The Congressional Globe, August 5, 1856* (Government Printing Office, Washington, D.C., 1856) p. 1169.

Buck Private's Gary Cooper. See MacArthur, Douglas

Buckeye Division. See Thirty-seventh Infantry Division of World War II

Buckeye State. See Ohio

Buckeyes. See Ohians; Ohio State University

Buckingham, William Alfred

William Alfred Buckingham was nicknamed *Staunch Buckingham* [1] during the Civil War because of his loyalty to the Union while he was Governor of Connecticut, 1858-65. He was born at Lebanon, Conn., on May 28, 1804, and died at Norwich, Conn., on February 3, 1875.

[1] *History of Eastern Connecticut Embracing the Counties of Tolland, Windham, Middlesex, and New London*, Pliny LeRoy Harwood (The Pioneer Historical Publishing Company, Chicago, and New Haven, Conn., 1932) vol. 2, p. 727.

Buckland Races

In October 1863, a division of Union soldiers under the command of Major General Hugh Judson Kilpatrick was decoyed into following an apparently retreating division of Confederate soldiers under the command of Lieutenant General Wade Hampton. At this time a number of Confederate soldiers lying in wait suddenly attacked the Union soldiers. In order to prevent being annihilated, the Union soldiers retreated rapidly from Warrenton into Buckland, Va. The hasty flight of one Union brigade and the almost equal celerity with which another Union brigade moved from Warrenton to

Buckland caused the Confederate soldiers to jocularly nickname this episode the *Buckland Races.*[1]

[1] *The Crisis of the Confederacy, a History of Gettysburg and the Wilderness,* Cecil W. Battine (Longmans, Green and Company, New York and London, 1905) p. 322.

Buckley, Christopher A.

Christopher A. Buckley was known as *Blind Boss Buckley.*[1] From 1872 to 1890 he controlled the Democratic political machine of San Francisco completely. In spite of the fact that his word was inviolate, that he contributed much to charity, and that he held taxes down, his regime is credited with being a corrupt one.

In 1882 Buckley was stricken blind.

He was born in County Claire, Ireland, in 1845, and died at San Francisco, Calif., on April 22, 1922.

[1] *California: An Intimate History,* Revised and Enlarged Edition, Gertrude Atherton (Boni and Liveright, New York, 1927) p. 309.
California: California and Californians, ed. by Rockwell D. Hunt assisted by an advisory board (The Lewis Publishing Company, San Francisco and New York, 1930) vol. 4, p. 509.
"The Boss and the Machine, a Chronicle of the Politicians and Party Organization," by Samuel Peter Orth, in *The Chronicles of America Series,* Abraham Lincoln Edition, Allen Johnson, Editor (Yale University Press, New Haven, Conn., 1919) vol. 43, p. 107.
The History of San Francisco, Lewis Francis Byington, Supervising Editor, and Oscar Lewis, Associate Editor (The S. J. Clarke Publishing Company, Chicago and San Francisco, Calif., 1931) vol. 1, p. 369-71.

Bucks. See Ohio State University

Bucks of America

About 1776 in the army of General George Washington, there was a company of Massachusetts Negroes commanded by a Colonel Middleton. This company was called the *Bucks of America.*[1]

[4] *In Freedom's Birthplace: A Study of the Boston Negroes,* John Daniels (Houghton Mifflin Company, Boston and New York, 1914) p. 13.

Buckshot. See Wright, F. G.

Buckshot War

The *Buckshot War*[1] is a name applied to a disturbance in 1838 between the Whig and the Democratic factions over the election of a Pennsylvania state governor. The guns used by the troops called out to help settle the disturbance were loaded with buckshot.

[1] *The Tragic Era: The Revolution after Lincoln,* Claude G. Bowers (Houghton Mifflin Company, New York and Boston, 1929) p. 69.

Buckshots

A secret society in the mining regions of Pennsylvania from about 1854 to 1877 was known as the *Buckshots.*[1] The members were desperate miners who by threats or violence jeopardized the property and personnel of the local mining corporations because they saw no other way of adjusting labor difficulties between employer and employee. They probably carried guns loaded with buckshot.

[1] *The Molly Maguires; the Origin, Growth, and Character of the Organization,* F. P. Dewees (J. B. Lippincott and Company, Philadelphia, 1877) p. 30.

Bucktails

Bucktails[1] were members of a political faction active about 1815 which, influenced by the Tammany Society, opposed the activities of Governor De Witt Clinton of New York. The name was in use as early as 1791 when a bucktail worn on the headgear was adopted as the "official badge" of the Tammany Society. The wearing of the bucktail was said to have been suggested by its appearance in the costume of the Tammany Indians in the vicinity of New York.

During the Civil War the members of the Forty-second Regiment of Pennsylvania Infantrymen were widely known in the Union Army as *Bucktails*[1] because each soldier wore a bucktail in his hat. The flagstaff of the companies which formed the nucleus of this regiment was a green hickory pole surmounted by a bucktail.

[1] *Americanisms: The English of the New World,* M. Schele DeVere (Charles Scribner and Company, New York, 1872) p. 279.
Barne's Popular History of the United States of America, from Pre-historic America to the Present Time, Revised to Date, Joel Dorman Steele and Esther Baker Steele (A. L. Burt Company, New York, 1914) p. 357.
History of Pennsylvania Volunteers, 1861-65; Prepared in Compliance with Acts of the Legislature, Samuel P. Bates (B. Singerly, State Printer, Harrisburg, Pa., 1869) vol. 1, p. 908.

Bucky. See Harris, S. R.; Jordan, B. B.

Buerger, John

John Buerger was known to his contemporaries as the *Barley King*[1] because he was a prominent grain merchant who specialized in the buying and selling of barley. He emigrated from Westphalia, Germany, to the United States in 1866 and soon afterwards established himself at Mil-

Buerger, John—Continued
waukee, Wis. He died on July 23, 1927,
at the age of eighty-two.

[1] *Encyclopedia of American Biography: American Biography, a New Cyclopedia,* comp. under the editorial supervision of a notable advisory board (Published under the direction of The American Historical Society, Inc., New York, 1929) vol. 37, p. 79.

Buffalo, New York

Buffalo is known as the *Bison City, City of Flour, Electric City of the Future, Queen of the Lakes,* and *Queen City of the Lakes.*

Buffalo is frequently spoken of as the *Bison City* [1] since buffalo is the popular name for the North American bison. Buffalo was so called from a creek flowing through it which the Indians called Buffalo Creek. Some claim that the creek and the Indian village came to be called Buffalo because herds of buffaloes came to the salt lick there.

Buffalo is designated the *City of Flour* [2] because it is the second largest flour milling center in the United States. [3] This city is known as the *Electric City of the Future* [4] because Niagara Falls is the site of an immense power plant. The terms, *Queen of the Lakes,* [5] and *Queen City of the Lakes,* [5] are given to this city because its location, at the eastern extremity of Lake Erie and the upper end of the Niagara river, makes it a natural junction for water and railroad transportation [5] and an important commercial and industrial center for the lake regions.

[1] *Municipality of Buffalo, New York: A History, 1720-1923,* Henry Wayland Hill, Editor-in-chief (Lewis Historical Publishing Company, Inc., New York and Chicago, 1923) vol. 1, p. 54-7; vol. 2, p. 492, 837-8, 844.

[2] *A Book of Nicknames,* John Goff (Courier-Journal Job Printing Company, Louisville, Ky., 1892) p. 15.

[3] *Industrial and Commercial Geography,* J. Russell Smith, New Edition (Henry Holt and Company, New York, 1930) p. 67.
Industrial Geography, Production, Manufacture, Commerce, Ray Hughes Whitbeck (American Book Company, New York and Boston, 1931) p. 61.

[4] *Queen of the Lakes, Buffalo, the Electric City of the Future, Souvenir of the Tenth Convention of the National Association of Builders* (The Courier Company, Buffalo, N.Y., 1896) p. 173, 176.

[5] *The New Wonder of the World, Buffalo: The Electric City,* A. E. Richmond (The Matthews-Northrup Company, Buffalo, N.Y., 1892) p. 5, 12.

Buffalo Bill. See Cody, W. F.; Matthewson, William

Buffalo Chips. See White, James

Buffalo Division. See Ninety-second Infantry Division of World War II

Buffalo Hangman. See Cleveland, Grover

Buffalo Jones. See Jones, C. J.

Buffalo Killer. See Matthewson, William

Buffalo Plains State. See Colorado

Buffalo Sheriff. See Cleveland, Grover

Buffalos. See University of Colorado

Buffoon. See Lincoln, Abraham

Bug-eaters. See Nebraskans

Bug-eating State. See Nebraska

Bugs on the White House Doormat

About 1897 the newspapers of New York and elsewhere began to speak of the circle of President Theodore Roosevelt's immediate friends and political office seekers, especially in Washington, as *Bugs on the White House Doormat,* [1] as an expression of resentment for what they considered favoritism in appointing his personal friends and political adherents to positions that should have been filled by those who had demonstrated their worthiness.

[1] *Twenty Years of the Republic, 1885-1905,* Harry Thurston Peck (Dodd, Mead and Company, New York, 1907) p. 706.

Builder of Chattanooga. See Ochs, A. S.

Builder of the City of Houston. See Wilson, W. A.

Bull. See Durham, E. F.

Bull Boats

The fur traders along the Missouri used dried buffalo hides to make rude boats upon which they transported their furs. The boats were designated *Bull Boats* [1] because they were made of buffalo bull hides.

[1] *The Way to the West and the Lives of Three Early Americans, Boone—Crockett—Carson,* Emerson Hough (The Bobbs-Merrill Company, Indianapolis, Ind., 1903) p. 197.

Bull City. See Durham, N.C.

Bull dogs. See Butler University; Southwestern Louisiana Institute; Tennessee Wesleyan College; Union University; University of Georgia; University of Redlands; Wilberforce University

Bull Montana. See Montagne, Luigi

Bull Moose. See Roosevelt, Theodore

Bull Moose Party. See Roosevelt, Theodore

Bull Moosers. See Roosevelt, Theodore

Bull Nelson. See Nelson, William

Bull of the Woods. See Sumner, Charles

Bull-Outfit

The wagon trains which operated on the western prairies from about 1850 to 1870 were called *Bull-outfits* [1] because the wagons composing the train were frequently drawn by oxen.

[2] *The Great Salt Lake Trail,* Colonel Henry Inman and Colonel William F. Cody (The Macmillan Company, New York, 1898) p. 389.

Bull-wagon Boss

The leader of a western wagon train was called the *Bull-wagon Boss* [1] because the wagons making up the train over which he was absolute lord were frequently pulled by oxen.

[1] *The Adventures of Buffalo Bill,* Colonel William F. Cody (Buffalo Bill) (Harper and Brothers, New York, 1904) p. 11.

Bull-whackers

The teamsters who drove the ox wagons in the wagon trains on the western prairies about the middle of the nineteenth century were called *Bull-whackers* [1] because they drove the oxen with long whips which they cracked over their backs. Any driver of ox teams has come to be termed a *bull-whacker.*

[1] *The Great Salt Lake Trail,* Colonel Henry Inman and Colonel William F. Cody (The Macmillan Company, New York, 1898) p. 389.

Bulldog. See Longstreet, James; Smith, W. B.

Bulldog Cheatham. See Cheatham, B. F.

Bulldogs

The athletic teams of many schools and colleges are called *Bulldogs.* See Bull dogs.

Bullets. See Gettysburg College

Bullion State. See Missouri

Bullitt, John Christian

The *Father of Greater Philadelphia* [1] was applied to John Christian Bullitt in commemoration of his services in promoting the growth of Philadelphia, Pa.

In 1849 Bullitt went to live at Philadelphia where he soon became a prominent lawyer. In 1882 he advocated a new municipal charter, advancing a plan for consolidating several administrative departments, thus increasing their efficiency. In 1885 Bullitt drew up a measure known as the Bullitt Bill which was passed by the municipal board of the city. This measure outlined a course of procedure to promote the economic development and social welfare of Philadelphia and its vicinity, often designated *Greater Philadelphia.* This brought him the nickname of the *Father of Greater Philadelphia.*

John Christian Bullitt was born near Louisville, Ky., on February 10, 1824, and died at Paoli, Pa., on August 25, 1902.

[1] *The National Cyclopaedia of American Biography* (James T. White and Company, New York, 1932) vol. 22, p. 423.

Bullpups. See Union University

Bulls. See University of Buffalo

Bulls. See Durham Baseball Club

Bulls and Bears

The people in the Stock Exchange in New York City who try to increase and to hold prices up are called *Bulls* [1] and those who try to pull prices down and to keep them down are called *Bears,* because (the story goes) the bull uses his horns to toss things up and the bear uses his claws to tear them down.

[1] *The Source Book: An International Encyclopedic Authority Written from the New World Viewpoint,* Prepared by Over Two Hundred Authorities in the Fields of Literature, Art and Science (Perpetual Encyclopedia Corporation, Chicago, 1932) vol. 1, p. 417.

Bully Brooks. See Brooks, P. S.

Bump. See Hadley, I. D.

Bums

After President Grover Cleveland vetoed the Dependent Pension Bill on February 11, 1887, which "granted a pension of twelve dollars monthly to every honorably discharged veteran of the Civil War," there was a great deal of criticism directed against him. The veterans who wanted the pension were called *Bums*[1] by those who favored Cleveland's veto.

[1] *Twenty Years of the Republic, 1885-1905*, Harry Thurston Peck (Dodd, Mead and Company, New York 1907) p. 144.

Buncombe. See *Bunkum*

Buncome. See *Bunkum*

Bungtown. See Cold Spring Harbor, N.Y.

Bunkum

Bunkum,[1] *Buncome*, or *Buncombe*, is a name applied to a speech which is nonsenical or absurd. It is said to have originated with Felix Walker, a member of Congress from Buncombe County, N.C. When his fellow members could not understand why he was making a speech in Congress, he would explain that he was making it for Buncombe.

[1] *Americanisms—Old and New*, John S. Farmer (Privately printed by Thomas Poulter, London, 1889) p. 105.

Burbank, Luther

Luther Burbank was called the *Plant Wizard*[1] because of his outstanding work in crossing plants to produce hybrids, and the great scientific information he contributed as a result of his experiments.

Luther Burbank was born at Lancaster, Mass., on March 7, 1849, and died at Santa Rosa, Calif., on April 11, 1926.

[1] *The Growth of the American People and Nation*, Mary G. Kelty (Ginn and Company, New York and Boston, 1931) p. 496.

Burchard, Samuel Dickinson

Samuel Dickinson Burchard, a Presbyterian clergyman, was widely known as the *Student Nurse of Danville*[1] because in 1832, while he was a student at Centre College, at Danville, Ky., a deadly epidemic of cholera broke out. He was almost the only student who was not afflicted with this disease, and untiringly nursed those who were stricken.

Samuel Dickinson Burchard was born at Steuben, N.Y., on September 6, 1812, and died at Saratoga, N.Y., on September 25, 1891.

[1] *Dictionary of American Biography under the Auspices of the American Council of Learned Societies*, ed. by Allen Johnson (Charles Scribner's Sons, New York, 1929) vol. 3, p. 271.

Burdick, Usher L.

Usher L. Burdick, Representative from North Dakota, lawyer and politician, was nicknamed *Chief Burdick*[1] by his colleagues in the House of Representatives because he is of Indian descent.

Usher L. Burdick was born at Owatonna, Minn., on February 21, 1879, and was brought up among the Sioux Indians.

[1] An interview with Captain Victor Hunt Harding, Secretary of the National Democratic Congress Reelection Committee, Washington, D.C., April 10, 1939.

Bureaucratic Czars

During the administrations of Franklin Delano Roosevelt, President of the United States from 1933 to 1941, those persons within the Civil Service of the United States who were directors or managers of certain bureaus or government agencies not controlled by Civil Service regulations have been called *Bureaucratic Czars*[1] because they were often accused of influencing the appointment of their personal friends or political allies, or of securing salary advancements for their friends and relatives.

[1] *Washington Herald*, Washington, D.C., January 25, 1938, col. 7, p. 1.

Burgers. See Wartburg College

Burke, Edward Raymond

Edward Raymond Burke, a Nebraska lawyer and politician, was nicknamed the *Author of the New Deal*[1] by his colleagues in the United States Senate because he was one of the first to define the term *New Deal*.

Edward Raymond Burke was born at Running Water, S.D., on November 28, 1880.

[1] An interview with Captain Victor Hunt Harding, Secretary of the National Democratic Congress Reelection Committee, Washington, D.C., April 10, 1939.

Burke, William

William Burke was nicknamed the *Prince of Flatworkers*[1] and *Philadelphia's Jean Valjean*.[2] The former was attributed to him because he was an expert robber, having robbed some three or four hundred houses and apartments in Boston. He was nicknamed *Philadelphia's Jean Valjean* because after he had served a seven-year prison sentence under an assumed name in the state penitentiary, at Charlestown, Mass., he went to Philadelphia and lived the life of an honest man, saved his money, opened a cigar store, married, and in 1911 was elected a member of the City Council on the reform ticket. He might have continued to live an upright life in Philadelphia had it not been that a former convict, who had served a prison sentence with him in the Charlestown penitentiary and who recognized him, blackmailed him until he resigned from the City Council and confessed his criminal record.

William Burke was born on the East Side of New York City about 1870.

[1] *Evening Star*, Washington, D.C., August 16, 1912.
[2] *Washington Post*, Washington, D.C., August 17, 1912.

Burlington, Iowa

Burlington is called the *Orchard City*[1] and the *Porkopolis of Iowa*[2] because it is located amidst a rich agricultural and horticultural region and one of its chief industries is pork packing.

[1] *Manual of Useful Information*, comp. under the direction of J. C. Thomas (The Werner Company, Chicago, 1893) p. 22.
[2] *History of Des Moines County, Iowa, and Its People*, Augustine M. Antrobus (The S. J. Clarke Publishing Company, Chicago, 1915) vol. 1, p. 111.

Burns, John

John Burns was popularly called the *Hero of the Battle of Gettysburg*[1] because of his courageous services there on July 1, 2, and 3, 1863, when his conduct was an inspiration to his fellows.

He was born at Burlington, N.J., on September 5, 1793, and died at Gettysburg, Pa., on February 7, 1872.

[1] *Appleton's Cyclopaedia of American Biography*, ed. by James Grant Wilson and John Fiske (D. Appleton and Company, New York, 1887) vol. 1, p. 461.

Burns, John Irving

John Irving Burns, who was born at Cambridge, Mass., on August 31, 1907, and who played first base in major league baseball, was known as *Slugger*[1] because of his batting ability.

[1] *Who's Who in Major League Base Ball*, comp. by Harold (Speed) Johnson (Buxton Publishing Company, Chicago, 1933) p. 97.

Burns of America. See Riley, J. W.; Whittier, J. G.

Burns of the Green Mountains. See Eastman, C. G.

Burnside's Peripatetic Geography Class

During the Civil War Major General Ambrose Everett Burnside's Ninth Corps of the Army of the Potomac came to be nicknamed *Burnside's Peripatetic Geography Class*.[1] During its campaign marches, this particular corps had traveled chiefly on foot throughout the states of Maryland, Pennsylvania, Virginia, and Kentucky, providing ample opportunity for the soldiers to get first-hand knowledge of their geography.

[1] *The Seventy-ninth Highlanders; New York Volunteers in the War of Rebellion, 1861-1865*, William Todd (Brandow, Barton and Company, Albany, N.Y., 1886) p. 295.

Burnside's Slaughter Pen

The Battle on Marye's Heights, at Fredericksburg, Va., has been called *Burnside's Slaughter Pen*[1] because it was here that Major General Ambrose Everett Burnside on December 13, 1862, sacrificed a hundred thousand soldiers of the Army of the Potomac in his attempt to dislodge the Confederate Army under General Robert E. Lee.

[1] *A History of the Sixth Iowa Infantry*, Henry H. Wright (Published by The State Historical Society of Iowa, The Torch Press, Cedar Rapids, Iowa, 1923) p. 468.
The Fiery Epoch, 1830-1877, Charles Willis Thompson (The Bobbs-Merrill Company, Indianapolis, Ind., 1931) p. 233.

Burritt, Elihu

Elihu Burritt, who was born at New Britain, Conn., on December 8, 1811, and who died there on March 9, 1879, was designated the *Learned Blacksmith*[1] because he was an outstanding Biblical scholar and reformer and while a young man was for several years a blacksmith.

[1] *The Encyclopedia Americana* (Americana Corporation, New York and Chicago, 1934), vol. 5, p. 65.

Burroughs, John

The nicknames usually attributed to John Burroughs are *Gray-crested Flycatcher, Her-*

Burroughs, John—Continued
mit of Slabsides, John O'Birds, and *Laird of Woodchuck Lodge.*

During World War I, the members of John Burroughs' family nicknamed him the *Gray-crested Fly-catcher* [1] because though a gray-headed man, he would eagerly read the daily papers to see if the allies were winning the war; if they weren't he would busily kill the flies buzzing about him. Burroughs spent much of his time alone in his slab-built retreat near West Park, N.Y., and was called the *Hermit of Slabsides. John O'Birds* designates that Burroughs loved to be among and to study birds. The nickname, *The Laird of Woodchuck Lodge* originated in the fact that Burroughs after 1918 usually spent his summers in his farm house near Roxbury, N.Y., which was called Woodchuck Lodge.

Burroughs was born at Roxbury, N.Y., on April 3, 1837, and died there on March 29, 1921.

[1] *John Burroughs, Boy and Man,* Clara Barrus (Doubleday, Page and Company, Garden City, N.Y., 1920), p. 25, 287, 347, 356.

Busby of New England. See Lovell, John

Bush Arbor Meeting
The *Bush Arbor Meeting* [1] was a political gathering of Democrats at Atlanta, Ga., on July 23, 1868, for the purpose of initiating the Democratic campaign of Horatio Seymour and Frank Preston Blair, Junior, who were candidates for President and Vice President of the United States. The speakers' stand was protected from the sun's rays by an immense bush arbor built for that purpose.

[1] *Benjamin H. Hill; Secession and Reconstruction,* Haywood J. Pearce (The University of Chicago Press, Chicago, 1928) p. 173, 175.

Bushnell's Turtle
In 1775 David Bushnell built a man-propelled oak submarine at Saybrook, Conn., to demonstrate that gun powder could be exploded under water. The submarine looked like two turtle shells fastened together and was nicknamed *Bushnell's Turtle.* [1]

[1] *Dictionary of American Biography under the Auspices of the American Council of Learned Societies,* ed. by Allen Johnson (Charles Scribner's Sons, New York, 1929) vol. 3, p. 349.

Bushwhackers
The *Bushwhackers* [1] were those men who, during the Civil War, declared themselves neutral and professed to be occupied with their usual vocations, but who availed themselves of every opportunity to attack soldiers, either Federal or Confederate, and to harass their neighbors who differed from them on the question of slavery and secession. The *Bushwhackers* were found as a rule in the states in which the Civil War was actively carried on; many of the people living in the Southern states who were in sympathy with the Union cause were accused of belonging to this group. The men operated outdoors in wooded regions where the underbrush aided them in effecting an assault or an escape.

[1] *Life-struggles in Rebel Prisons; a Record of the Sufferings, Escapes, Adventures and Starvation of the Union Prisoners, Containing an Appendix with the Names, Regiments, and Date of Death of Pennsylvania Soldiers Who Died at Andersonville,* Joseph Ferguson (James M. Ferguson, Philadelphia, 1865) p. 189.

Busted Aristocrat
In cadet slang a *Busted Aristocrat* [1] is a cadet officer who has been demoted in rank.

[1] *Unit Projects in Modern Literature* (Educational Press, Inc., Columbus, Ohio), March 1-14, 1935, p. 12.

Butch. See La Guardia, F. H.

Butcher from Galena. See Grant, U. S.

Butcher Grant. See Grant, U. S.

Butcher Hood. See Hood, J. B.

Butler, Benjamin Franklin
Benjamin Franklin Butler is known as The *Beast, Beast Butler, Old Cockeye, Silver Spoon Butler, Spoon Butler,* and *Spoon Stealer.*

General Butler, a Union man who had been put in charge of New Orleans in May 1862, was sometimes called *The Beast* [1] or *Beast Butler* by the Southerners because they considered him brutal, coarse, and devoid of reason and moral feeling in his methods of governing the city. He fastened upon it a stern, military form of government. The inhabitants of New Orleans were so hostile and unsympathetic toward Butler and his Union soldiers that he issued a number of proclamations regulating the conduct of the civilians. Among these his Order number twenty-eight attracted special attention and criticism because it decreed that women who publicly insulted Union soldiers were to be regarded as women of the street.

General Butler was nicknamed *Old Cock-eye* [2] from the fact that his eyes were decidedly prominent.

Butler was also called *Silver Spoon Butler,* [3] *Spoon Butler,* and *Spoon Stealer* because it was alleged that he took the silver from the home in New Orleans which he had used as his headquarters.

General Butler was born at Deerfield, N.H., on November 5, 1818, and died at Washington, D.C., on January 11, 1893.

[1] *The Lost Cause; a New Southern History of the War of the Confederates Comprising a Full and Authentic Account of the Rise and Progress of the Late Southern Confederacy—the Campaigns, Battles, Incidents, and Adventures of the Most Gigantic Struggle of the World's History, Drawn from Official Sources, and Approved by the Most Distinguished Confederate Leaders,* Edward A. Pollard (E. B. Treat and Company, New York, 1867) p. 257.

Jefferson Davis, Political Soldier, Elizabeth Cutting (Dodd, Mead and Company, New York, 1930) p. 192.

General Butler in New Orleans: History of the Administration of the Department of the Gulf in the Year 1862; with an Account of the Capture of New Orleans, and a Sketch of the Previous Career of the General, Civil and Military, James Parton (Mason Brothers, New York, 1864) p. 192.

[2] *A Book of Nicknames,* John Goff (Courier-Journal Job Printing Company, Louisville, Ky., 1892) p. 26.

[3] *The Age of Hate, Andrew Johnson and the Radicals,* George Fort Milton (Coward-McCann, Inc., New York, 1930) p. 25.

Dictionary of American Biography under the Auspices of the American Learned Societies, ed. by Allen Johnson (Charles Scribner's Sons, New York, 1929) vol. 3, p. 358.

Butler, Marion

Marion Butler was nicknamed the *Father of Rural Free Delivery* [1] because he took such an active part in getting laws passed by the United States Senate for experimental rural free delivery of mail. He was a Senator from North Carolina from 1896 to 1901, and was the author of the act passed by Congress in 1902, which authorized the establishing of the present rural free delivery of mail.

Marion Butler was born in Sampson County, N.C., on May 20, 1863, and died June 3, 1938.

[1] *The Father of Rural Free Delivery,* William Eaton Chandler (The News-Dispatch, Clinton, N.C., 1915) p. 2, 4.

Butler, Smedley Darlington

Major General Smedley Darlington Butler is known as *Duckboard, Hell's Devil Butler,* and *Old Gimlet Eye.*

General Butler is called *Duckboard* [1] and *Hell's Devil Butler* [1] by his soldiers because of his exacting ways.

While in command of the Third Battalion of Marines stationed at Panama from 1909 to 1914, at a parley with some rebel officers of Nicaragua. General Butler's eyes appeared unusually fierce and glaring and the Marines nicknamed him *Old Gimlet Eye,* [2] which clung to him throughout his service. It was said among his men that *Old Gimlet Eye* could tell in the dark whether or not the buttons on their uniforms had been polished.

General Butler was born at West Chester, Pa., on July 30, 1881, and died at Philadelphia on June 21, 1940.

[1] *Encyclopedia of American Biography; American Biography; a New Cyclopedia,* comp. under the editorial supervision of a notable advisory board (Published under the direction of The American Historical Society, Inc., New York, 1926) vol. 25, p. 243.

[2] *Old Gimlet Eye: The Adventures of Smedley D. Butler, As Told to Lowell Thomas* (Farrar and Rinehart, New York, 1933) p. 2, 157-8, 300.

Butler, Thomas

Colonel Thomas Butler was nicknamed the *Navarre of the American Revolution.* [1] He distinguished himself during the Revolutionary War by his personal bravery, ingenuity on the battlefield, and devotion to the colonies. Henry of Navarre, or Henry IV, King of France, was beloved for his unselfish and devoted service as a soldier and a statesman.

Thomas Butler was born near Dublin, Ireland, on May 28, 1748, and was brought to America while he was a baby.

[1] *The National Cyclopaedia of American Biography* (James T. White and Company, New York, 1900) vol. 8, p. 84.

Butler's Ditch

About 1862 Major General Benjamin Franklin Butler ordered a canal [1] cut across the peninsula opposite the city of Vicksburg, Miss., with a view of effecting an artificial cut-off across the peninsula opposite Vicksburg, through which transports, troops, and supplies might safely pass to the river below the enemy's batteries at that place. This canal was designated by the soldiers of General William Tecumseh Sherman as *Butler's Ditch.*

[1] *Sherman and His Campaigns: A Military Biography,* Colonel S. M. Bowman and Lieutenant Colonel R. B. Irwin (Charles B. Richardson, New York, 1865) p. 98.

Military Essays and Recollections (Published by order of the Commandery. The Dial Press, Chicago, 1899) vol. 3, p. 252.

Butt Enders

The *Butt Enders* [1] is a term applied to a lawless gang which operated in Baltimore,

Butt Enders—Continued

Md., from about 1857 to 1861. The purpose of the gang was to intimidate voters who favored candidates not desirable to this group so that they would be afraid to go to the polls and vote on election day. The gang used the butt ends of their revolvers as weapons.

[1] "The Irrepressible Conflict, 1850-1865" by Arthur Charles Cole in *A History of American Life*, Arthur M. Schlesinger and Dixon Ryan Fox, Editors (The Macmillan Company, New York, 1934) vol. 7, p. 154.
History of the United States of America, under the Constitution, James Schouler (Dodd, Mead and Company, New York, 1891) vol. 5, p. 426-7.

Butter Capital of the World. See Owatonna, Minn.

Butter-nuts. See Tennesseeans

Butterflies

During the Civil War the Third Cavalry of New Jersey troops were nicknamed *Butterflies* [1] because of their bright, showy uniforms. Yellow stripes were used on the legs of the pantaloons, gold braid was profusely used on the blue jackets, a yellow colored cloth lined the jackets, and the caps were also of a golden hue.

[1] *Andersonville: A Story of Rebel Military Prisons, Fifteen Months a Guest of the So-called Southern Confederacy; a Private Soldier's Experience in Richmond, Andersonville, Savannah, Millen, Blackshear, and Florence*, John McElroy (D. R. Locke, Toledo, Ohio, 1879) p. 434.

Butternuts

Those members of the Democratic party in the northern states who were opposed to the Civil War were called *Butternuts* [1] by the Union men who favored the war. The term was first applied to poor farmers whose outer garments were dyed with the juice of butternut hulls.

[1] *History of the United States from the Compromise of 1850*, James Ford Rhodes (Harper and Brothers, New York and London, 1899) vol. 4, p. 224.

Button Order

About 1865, following the Civil War, many unreasonable and militaristic laws were decreed by the northerners, one of them being the so-called *Button Order* [1] which forbade the southern people to use old Confederate buttons on their clothes except in the case of dire necessity. In that case, the buttons could be used provided they were covered.

[1] *History of the United States of America*, Jesse Ames Spencer, ed. by Edwin Wiley with the assistance of Irving E. Rines (American Educational Alliance, New York, 1910) vol. 6, p. 6.

Buzzard Dollar

The American dollar is sometimes designated the *Buzzard Dollar* [1] because the American Eagle on the silver dollar looks like a buzzard.

[1] *A New Dictionary of Americanisms*, Sylva Clapin (Louis Weiss and Company, New York, 1903) p. 89.

Buzzard State. See Georgia

Buzzards. See Georgians

Buzzy. See Wares, Clyde

By Ganny Cross. See Cross, O. H.

C

C.C.C. Highway

The highway extending from Cleveland, Ohio, through Columbus to Cincinnati, Ohio, is commonly called *The C.C.C. Highway*,[1] or *The Three C's Highway*.

[1] *The Encyclopaedia Britannica*, Fourteenth Edition (Encyclopaedia Britannica Inc., New York, 1932) vol. 5, p. 82.

Cactus Division. See One Hundred and Third Infantry Division of World War II

Cactus Jack. See Garner, J. N.

Cactus State. See New Mexico

Cadets. See College of Saint Thomas; United States Coast Guard Academy

Caesar. See Lincoln, Abraham

Caesar of Football. See Little, Louis

Caesar's Bread

Those who oppose unemployment insurance, believing that it increases the number of unemployed, have nicknamed it *Caesar's Bread* [1] because the Roman citizens were given grain gratuitously in the time of the Caesars.

[1] *Social Aspects of Industry: A Survey of Labor Problems and Causes of Industrial Unrest*, S. Howard Patterson (McGraw-Hill Book Company, Inc., New York, 1929) p. 306.

Cain, Merritt Patrick

Merritt Patrick Cain, who was born at Macon, Ga., on April 5, 1908, and who pitched in major league baseball was nicknamed *Sugar* [1] or *Sugar Cain*.

[1] *Who's Who in Major League Base Ball*, comp. by Harold (Speed) Johnson. (Buxton Printing Company, Chicago, 1933), p. 101.

Calamity Howlers

During the presidential campaign of 1889 members of the Farmer's Alliance, the Grange, the American Federation of Labor, and other similar organizations were called *Calamity Howlers* [1] by the newspapers in the eastern states because of their descriptions of the wretchedness of economic conditions in the West and their dire predictions unless the evils were remedied.

[1] *Twenty Years of the Republic, 1885-1905*, Harry Thurston Peck (Dodd, Mead and Company, New York, 1907) p. 269.

Calamity Jane. See Canary, M. J.

Caldron Linn

The rapids below the American Falls in the Snake river, near Milner, Idaho, were nicknamed the *Caldron Linn* and the *Devil's Scuttle Hole* [1] by Wilson Price Hunt in 1810 after one member of his party, which was exploring that region, had been drowned in these rapids. *Linn* means a waterfall.

[1] *Compton's Pictured Encyclopedia* (F. E. Compton and Company, Chicago, 1933) vol. 7, p. 9.

Caldwell, James

The *Fighting Chaplain* [1] and the *Soldier Parson* [2] were nicknames applied to James Caldwell by the British soldiers and Tories. He was the pastor of the Presbyterian Church at Elizabethtown, N.J., and served as a chaplain in the Continental Army during the Revolutionary War.

James Caldwell was born in Virginia in April 1734, and died at Elizabethtown Point, N.J., on November 24, 1781.

[1] *The Romance of Forgotten Men*, John T. Faris (Harper and Brothers, New York, 1928) p. 64.
[2] *Dictionary of American Biography under the Auspices of the American Council of Learned Societies*, ed. by Allen Johnson (Charles Scribner's Sons, New York, 1929) vol. 3, p. 409.

Caldwell, Kansas

Caldwell, in Sumner County, has been nicknamed the *Queen City of the Border* [1] because its advantageous location near the border betwen Kansas and Oklahoma and its railway and highway facilities make it a center of trade and travel.

[1] *Riata and Spurs, the Story of a Lifetime Spent in the Saddle as Cowboy and Ranger*, Revised Edition, Charles A. Siringo (Houghton Mifflin Company, New York and Boston, 1927) p. 112.

Calhoun, John Caldwell

John Caldwell Calhoun was popularly known as the *Eagle Orator of South Carolina*, the *Father of States' Rights*, the *Great Nullifier*, and the *Napoleon of Slavery*.

The *Eagle Orator of South Carolina* [1] is a nickname given to Calhoun because of his eloquence, skill, and clarity of expression as an orator.

He was widely known as the *Father of States' Rights* and the *Great Nullifier* [1] because of his prominence in asserting and defending the principles of nullification.

William Lloyd Garrison, the editor of *The Liberator* from 1831 to 1866 called Calhoun the *Napoleon of Slavery* [2] because he felt that Calhoun, an ardent champion of slavery, would be ultimately defeated by his opponents as was Napoleon at Waterloo on June 18, 1815.

John Caldwell Calhoun was born in the Abbeville District of South Carolina on March 18, 1782, and died at Washington, D.C. on March 31, 1850.

See *Great Triumvirate*.

[1] *A Book of Nicknames*, John Goff (Courier-Journal Job Printing Company, Louisville, Ky., 1892), p. 21, 22
[2] *William Lloyd Garrison, 1805-1879: The Story of His Life Told by His Children*, W. P. Garrison and F. J. Garrison (The Century Company, New York, 1889), vol. 3, p. 217.
Life of John C. Calhoun, Presenting a Condensed History of Political Events from 1811 to 1843, together with a Selection from His Speeches, Reports, and Other Writings Subsequent to His Election as vice-President of the United States, Including His Leading Speech on the Late War Delivered in 1811, Robert Mercer Taliaferro Hunter (Harper and Brothers, New York, 1843) p. 73.
"A Study of Nullification in South Carolina" by David Franklin Houston, in *Harvard Historical Studies* (Longmans, Green and Company, New York, 1896) vol. 3, p. 80-2.
Calhoun and the South Carolina Nullification Movement, Frederic Bancroft (The Johns Hopkins Press, Baltimore, Md., 1928) p. 45-7.

Calhoun, J. C. See Great Triumvirate

Caliban of Science. See Ramsey, Alexander

California

California was called the *El Dorado State* and the *Golden State* and the *Land of Gold* [1] because of the discovery and extensive mining of gold there.

California—Continued

California is designated as the *Grape State* because of the vast quantities of grapes grown there. It is also referred to as the *Eureka State* because of the state motto, *Eureka*.

[1] *Spanish and Indian Place Names of California, Their Meaning and Their Romance*, Nellie Van De Grift Sanchez (A. M. Robertson, San Francisco, Calif., 1914) p. 300, 303.
The Century Dictionary and Cyclopedia (The Century Company, New York, 1906) vol. 3, p. 1865.
U.S.: An Index to the United States of America, comp. by Malcolm Townsend (D. Lothrop Company, Boston, 1890) p. 66.
King's Handbook of the United States, planned and ed. by Moses King, text by M. F. Sweetser (Moses King Corporation, Buffalo, N.Y., 1891) p. 84.

California Bears. See University of California

California Joe. See Milner, M. E.

Californians

The inhabitants of California are called *Gold Diggers* [1] and *Gold Hunters* because many of the early settlers were gold miners who came after the discovery of gold in 1849. People who were born there are called *Native Sons* and *Native Daughters* to distinguish them from more recent comers.

[1] *U.S.: An Index to the United States of America*, comp. by Malcolm Townsend (D. Lothrop Company, Boston, 1890) p. 75.

Calvin College and Seminary

The basketball teams of Calvin College and Seminary, at Grand Rapids, Mich., are frequently called the *Calvin Knights*.[1]

[1] A communication from H. G. Dekker, Calvin College and Seminary, Grand Rapids, Mich., November 21, 1935.

Calvin Knights. See Calvin College and Seminary

Cambridge, Massachusetts

Cambridge is called the *University City* [1] because it is prominent as an educational center, being the site of Harvard University, Massachusetts Institute of Technology, Radcliffe College, and several theological seminaries, or divinity schools.

[1] *Commercial Structure of New England*, Edward F. Gerish, *Part II of The Commerce Survey of New England*, Charles E. Artman, in charge. *Domestic Commerce Series—number twenty-six* (United States Department of Commerce, Government Printing Office, Washington, D.C., 1929) p. 17.
A History of Cambridge, Massachusetts (1630-1913) Samuel Atkins Eliot (The Cambridge Tribune, Cambridge, Mass., 1913) p. 120, 123, 236.

Camden and Amboy State. See New Jersey

Cameron, Simon

Simon Cameron was often called the *Czar of Pennsylvania Politics* [1] because he exercised dictatorial control over the activities of the Republican party in Pennsylvania. He was a United States Senator from Pennsylvania from 1867 to 1877, and was conspicuous for his opposition to the civil service reforms proposed by President Rutherford Birchard Hayes.

Simon Cameron was born at Donegal, Pa., on March 8, 1799, and died there on June 26, 1889.

[1] *Appleton's Cyclopaedia of American Biography*, ed. by James Grant Wilson and John Fiske (D. Appleton and Company, New York, 1888) vol. 1, p. 509.

Camp, Walter

The Father of American Football [1] and *The Dean of American Football* are nicknames given to Walter Camp because he was a pioneer in establishing and developing football as one of the major sports in America. He was considered an authority on the rules and ethics of the game, and was the author of a large number of books and articles dealing with football.

Walter Camp was born at New Haven, Conn., on April 7, 1859, and died at New York City, on March 14, 1925.

[1] *The Encyclopedia Americana* (Americana Corporation, New York and Chicago, 1927) vol. 5, p. 270.

Campaign of the Three H's

The Republican political campaign of 1904 in the State of Ohio, which resulted in the election of Marcus Alonzo Hanna as Senator, Myron T. Herrick as Governor, and Warren Gamaliel Harding as Lieutenant Governor, was popularly nicknamed the *Campaign of the Three H's* [1] because all their names began with H.

[1] *Myron T. Herrick, Friend of France, an Autobiographical Biography*, T. Bentley Mott (Doubleday, Doran and Company, Inc., Garden City, N.Y., 1929) p. 80.

Campbell, Bruce Douglas

Bruce Douglas Campbell, who was born at Chicago, Ill., on October 20, 1909, and who played outfielder in major league baseball, was nicknamed *Hump* [1] because his name Campbell is suggestive of the camel's hump.

[1] *Who's Who in Major League Baseball*, comp. by Harold (Speed) Johnson, (Buxton Publishing Company, Chicago, 1933) p. 102.

Camp's Ditch

The Sackets Harbor Canal which extended from Huntingville to Sackets Harbor, Jefferson County, N.Y., was popularly called *Camp's Ditch*.[1] Elisha Camp of the Jefferson County Canal Company was chiefly responsible for the planning, construction, and operation of the canal. It was completed in 1832 and used for about ten years.

[1] *The North Country, a History Embracing Jefferson, St. Lawrence, Oswego, Lewis, and Franklin Counties, New York*, Harry F. Landon (Historical Publishing Company, Indianapolis, Ind., 1932) vol. 1, p. 293.

Canal Boy. See Garfield, J. A.

Canal Ring

The *Canal Ring*[1] was the name given to a group of men who made contracts to construct canals. They and their political supporters received pay for constructing the canals but actually the work was never done. Samuel Jones Tilden exposed them and their corrupt schemes soon after he was inaugurated as Governor of New York in 1874.

[1] *The Encyclopedia Americana* (Americana Corporation, Chicago and New York, 1927) vol. 26, p. 624.

Canary, Martha Jane

Martha Jane Canary, a frontier adventuress, who is said to have been born at Princeton, Mo., on May 1, 1852, and who died at Terraville near Deadwood, S.D., in early August 1903, is commonly known as *Calamity Jane*.[1] It is the consensus that she acquired this nickname because she was unlucky in her nefarious activities and brought catastrophe of some kind to her most intimate associates. Eleven of her twelve husbands suffered untimely deaths because of her. Wherever she went she was certain to cause trouble as a result of her unrestrained and intemperate conduct.

[1] *Calamity Jane and the Lady Wildcats*, Duncan Aikman (Henry Holt and Company, New York, 1927), p. 67.

Candy Kid. See Brock, W. E.

Canisius College

The *Grenadiers*[1] is the appellation given to the athletic teams of Canisius College, at Buffalo, N.Y.

[1] A communication from James H. Crowde, Graduate Manager of Athletics, Canisius College, Buffalo, N.Y., June 15, 1935.

Cannon, Clarence

Clarence Cannon, a Missouri educator and politician was nicknamed *Parliamentary Procedure*[1] because he is a great authority on parliamentary procedure and was the parliamentarian at the Democratic National Conventions which met at San Francisco, Calif., in 1920, and at New York City in 1924. He has been a Democratic Representative from Missouri since 1935, and is the author of *Cannon's Procedure* and *National Convention Parliamentary Manual*.

Clarence Cannon was born at Elsberry, Mo., on April 11, 1879.

[1] An interview with Captain Victor Hunt Harding, Secretary of the National Democratic Congress Reelection Committee, Washington, D.C., April 10, 1939.

Cannon, James, Jr.

Bishop James Cannon, Jr., was called the *Dry Bishop from Virginia*[1] because he was an ardent advocate of national prohibition and took an active part in the affairs of anti-saloon organizations. He was a bishop in the Methodist Episcopal Church in Virginia from 1918 to the time of his death.

Bishop Cannon was born at Salisbury, Md., on November 13, 1864, and died Sept. 6, 1944.

[1] *The American Scene*, Edwin C. Hill (Witmark Educational Publications, Department of M. Witmark and Sons, New York, 1933), p. 397.

Cannon, Joseph Gurney

Joseph Gurney Cannon was widely known as *Uncle Joe*[1] and the *Watchdog of the Treasury*.[2]

He was known throughout the country as *Uncle Joe* during the time from 1903 to 1911 when he was Speaker of the House of Representatives.

Joseph Gurney Cannon was for twenty-two years a member of the committee on appropriations in the House of Representatives and for eight years the chairman of this committee, during which time he opposed extravagances in the dispensing of the funds of the United States Treasury, and was called the *Watchdog of the Treasury*.

Cannon was born at New Garden, near Guilford, N.C., on May 7, 1836, and died at Danville, Ill., on November 12, 1926.

[1] *Encyclopedia of American Biography*, New Series, ed. by Winfield Scott Downs (The American Historical Society, Inc., New York, 1934) vol. 1, p. 84.

[2] *The National Cyclopaedia of American Biography*, (James T. White and Company, New York, 1932) vol. 22, p. 5.

Cape Cod Turkey

Along Cape Cod Bay in Massachusetts, cod fish is sometimes called *Cape Cod Turkey*.[1]

See also *Marblehead Turkey*.

[1] *Dictionary of Americanisms*, Fourth Edition, John Russell Bartlett (Little, Brown and Company, Boston, 1877) p. 383.

Capital University

In 1925 sports editors gave the nickname, *Fighting Lutherans*,[1] to the athletic teams of Capital University, at Columbus, Ohio, because this school is a Lutheran College.

[1] A communication from William Bernlohr, Director of Athletics at Capital University, Columbus, Ohio, June 13, 1935.

Capper, Arthur

The nickname *Farmer's Friend* [1] has been applied to Arthur Capper because he was owner, editor, and publisher of *Capper's Weekly* and other farm papers and magazines from 1892 until 1915, when he was elected governor of Kansas.

Capper was born at Garnett, Kan., on July 14, 1865, and his present home is at Topeka, Kan. He was Governor of Kansas from 1915 to 1919, and was a United States Senator from Kansas from 1919 to 1949.

[1] *The Washington Post Magazine*, Washington, D.C., March 4, 1923, p. 4.

Capital City. See Washington, D.C.

Capital of the Blue Grass Region. See Lexington, Ky.

Capital of Vacation Land. See Newport, R.I.

Capstone of Negro Education. See Howard University

Captain

Clocks in the Jesuit mission houses in North America were called the *Captain* [1] by the native Indians. The clock was a constant source of wonder and admiration to the savages who would sit for hours just to hear one strike or chime. A clock was to them the *Captain* probably because it seemed to govern the actions of the Jesuit monks.

[1] *The Jesuits in North America in the Seventeenth Century*, Eighth Edition, Francis Parkman (Little, Brown and Company, Boston, 1874) p. 61.
The Beginning of the American People and Nation, Mary G. Kelty (Ginn and Company, New York and London, 1930) p. 342.

Captain Billy. See McCue, William

Captain Molly. See McCauley, M. L. H.

Captains of Industry

Immediately following the passage of the Currency Bill by Congress on March 14, 1900, the big speculators in stocks and bonds and other commodities sold on Wall Street in New York City came to be designated by the newspapers and by people in general as the *Captains of Industry*.[1] These speculators exerted a tremendous influence on the industrial world and were able to dominate the financial and industrial activities of America.

[1] *Twenty Years of the Republic, 1885-1905*, Harry Thurston Peck (Dodd, Mead and Company, New York, 1907) p. 634.

Caraway, Hattie Wyatt

Hattie Wyatt Caraway was nicknamed *Knitting Hattie* [1] by her colleagues in the United States Senate because she frequently carried her knitting with her to the Senate chamber. She was appointed a Senator from Arkansas to fill out the unexpired term of her husband who died on November 5, 1931, and was elected to the position in a special election held January 12, 1933.

Hattie Wyatt Caraway was born at Bakerville, Tenn., on February 1, 1878, and died on December 21, 1950.

[1] An interview with Captain Victor Hunt Harding, Secretary of the National Democratic Congress Reelection Committee, Washington, D.C., April 10, 1939.

Cardinals. See Catholic University; Saint Louis National League Baseball Club; Saint Procopius College; Stanford University; University of Louisville; William Jewel College.

Carey, Max George

Max George Carey, who was born at Terre Haute, Ind., on January 11, 1890, and who is now president of the All-American Girls' Baseball League, was nicknamed *Carnarius* [1] while he was studying for the ministry at Concordia College at Fort Wayne, Ind., in 1909.

[1] *Who's Who in Major League Base Ball*, comp. by Harold (Speed) Johnson (Buxton Publishing Company, Chicago, 1933), p. 105.

Carleton, James O.

Tex [1] is the sobriquet acquired by James Carleton, who pitched in major league baseball, because he was born and reared in Texas. This nickname was given to him when he became a member of the Syracuse Club of the International League in 1926.

James O. Carleton was born at Comanche, Tex., on August 19, 1906.

[1] *Who's Who in Major League Baseball*, comp. by Harold (Speed) Johnson (Buxton Publishing Company, Chicago, 1933)

Carleton College

The *Carls* and the *Maize and Blues* are the nicknames of the athletic teams of Carleton College, at Northfield, Minn. The *Carls* [1] is obvious, and the *Maize and Blues* [2] is from the college colors.

[1] A communication from Ralph L. Henry, Director of Publicity, Carleton College, Northfield, Minn., November 20, 1935.
[2] A communication from Max E. Hannum, Director of Publicity, Carleton College, Northfield, Minn., November 20, 1935.

Carley, Patrick J.

The Honorable Patrick J. Carley, who served in Congress from 1927 to 1935 as a Representative from New York was called *Fire Chief* [1] because for a number of years he was a volunteer fireman in the town of New Utrecht, N.Y.

He was born in Roscommon County, Ireland, in 1866, and died February 25, 1936.

[1] *The Washington Post Magazine*, Washington, D.C., March 4, 1934, p. 4.

Carls. See Carleton College

Carlsbad of America. See French Lick Springs, Ind.

Carlson, Jules

Jules Carlson, formerly a member of the Chicago Bears Football Club and now football coach of West Virginia University, at Morgantown, W.Va., was nicknamed *Old Reliable* [1] by sports writers in 1934 because he was such a dependable player. He was born at Isaca, Idaho, on November 4, 1904.

[1] A communication from George S. Halas, President-treasurer of The Chicago Bears Football Club, Inc., Chicago, March 21, 1939.

Carnarius. See Carey, M. G.

Carnegie, Andrew

Andrew Carnegie, the American manufacturer, philanthropist, and millionaire, was nicknamed the *Laird of Skibo* [1] or the *Laird* of *Skibo Castle* after he and his family took up their residence in Skibo Castle, on Dornoch Firth in Scotland, in 1898.

Andrew Carnegie was born at Dunfermline, Scotland, on November 25, 1835, and died at his summer home, Shadowbrook, Mass., on August 11, 1919.

[1] *The Life of Andrew Carnegie*, Burton J. Hendrick (Doubleday, Doran and Company, Inc., Garden City, N.Y., 1932), vol. 2, p. 147.

Carnegie Institute of Technology

Sports writers have given the teams of Carnegie Institute of Technology, at Pittsburgh, Pa., the nicknames of the *Plaids*,[1] the *Scots*, the *Skibos*, and the *Tartans*, because Andrew Carnegie who founded the Institute was born in Scotland and at one time lived at Skibo Castle in Scotland.

[1] A communication from Max E. Hannum, Director of Publicity, Carnegie Institute of Technology, Pittsburgh, Pa., June 7, 1935.

Carolinian Gamecock. See Sumter, Thomas

Carpenter, Terry McGovern

Cut Rate Carpenter [1] is the nickname given to Terry M. Carpenter, who served as a United States Representative from Nebraska from 1933 to 1935, because for several years prior to his election he operated a "cut-rate" gasoline station in Nebraska.

Terry McGovern Carpenter was born at Cedar Rapids, Iowa, on March 28, 1900, and now resides at Scottsbluff, Neb.

[2] *The Washington Post Magazine*, Washington, D.C., March 4, 1934, p. 4.

Carpetbaggers

The *Carpetbaggers* [1] were politicians from the North who came into the southern states after the close of the Civil War for the purpose of getting political control of the South and of enriching themselves at the expense of the poverty-stricken southerners. The term had its origin in the fact that these men had no property interest in the South, but only personal belongings which could be packed into a cloth bag.

[1] *The Growth of the American People and Nation*, Mary G. Kelty (Ginn and Company, New York and Boston, 1931) p. 381.

Carrigan, William F.

William F. Carrigan, who was born at Lewison, Me., and who was formerly man-

Carrigan, W. F.—Continued

ager and catcher of the *Boston Red Sox,* was nicknamed *Rough,*[1] during his early days in the American League.

[4] *Who's Who in Major League Base Ball,* comp. by Harold (Speed) Johnson (Buxton Publishing Company, Chicago, 1933), p. 466.

Carrington, Edward

While he was serving in the Continental Army, Quartermaster General Edward Carrington was called *Old Agamemnon*[1] because his manners were stately and imposing and his leadership inspiring. Agamemnon was a Greek hero in Homer's *Iliad.*

[1] *The National Cyclopaedia of American Biography* (James T. White and Company, New York, 1907), vol. 5, p. 55.

Carroll College

The *Pioneers*[1] is the nickname of the teams of Carroll College, at Waukesha, Wis., because Carroll College is the pioneer institution of learning in Wisconsin, having been chartered in 1836 and founded in 1840.

[1] A communication from Mrs. Grace H. Mullen, Director of Publicity at Carroll College, Waukesha, Wis., June 11, 1935.

Carrots. See Gish, Lillian

Carson, Christopher

Father Kit, the *Monarch of the Prairies,* and the *Nestor of the Rocky Mountains,* are nicknames given to Christopher Carson, usually spoken of as Kit Carson.

In 1853 Carson was appointed Indian agent to the Territory of New Mexico where the Indians came to call him *Father Kit*[1] because he treated them kindly and justly, and took a fatherly interest in their activities.

The *Monarch of the Prairies*[2] was a nickname applied to Carson because of his success in outwitting and fighting Indians.

Because of his ability and experience in overcoming the difficulties of the pioneers in settling the Rocky Mountain regions, Christopher Carson was called the *Nestor of the Rocky Mountains.*[3] In Greek legend Nestor was a hero in the Trojan War, distinguished for his wisdom.

Christopher Carson was born in Madison County, Ky., on December 24, 1809, and died at Fort Lyon, Colo., on May 23, 1868.

[1] *American Hero Stories,* Eva March Tappan (Houghton Mifflin and Company, New York and Boston, 1906) p. 238.

[2] *Seventy Years on the Frontier: Alexander Majors' Memoirs of a Lifetime on the Border,* with a preface by

Buffalo Bill (General W. F. Cody), ed. by Colonel Prentiss Ingraham (Rand McNally and Company, Chicago and New York) 1893) p. 114.

[3] *The Encyclopaedia Britannica,* Fourteenth Edition (Encyclopaedia Britannica, Inc., New York, 1929), vol. 4, p. 934.

Carson, John Miller

John Miller Carson, a veteran newspaper man, was nicknamed the *Father and Nursing Mother of the Gridiron Club*[1] because he was largely responsible for the organization of the Gridiron Club, originated the name of the organization, was the first charter member, and was President of the Club in 1887 and again in 1895.

The Gridiron Club is an organization of owners, editors, and correspondents of Washington and out-of-town newspapers, who annually entertain the President of the United States at a banquet. During the festivities the members of the Club present skits burlesquing acts of the President and other prominent politicians and public men.

John Miller Carson was born at Philadelphia, Pa., on June 18, 1838, and died there on September 29, 1912.

[1] *Forty-eight Gridiron Years: A Chronicle Written from Its Records for the Use of Members of the Gridiron Club,* Ernest George Walker (Privately printed at the Press of W. F. Roberts Company, Inc., Washington, D. C., 1933) page opposite the title page.

Carson, Walter Lloyd

Walter Lloyd Carson, who was born at Colton, Calif., on November 15, 1913, and who played infield in major league baseball, was nicknamed *Kit*[1] in honor of Christopher Carson, the American scout and frontiersman on the western plains.

[1] *Who's Who in The Major League,* 1935 Edition, Harold (Speed) Johnson (B. E. Callahan, Chicago, 1935) p. 40.

Carter, Mrs. Leslie

Mrs. Leslie Carter (Mrs. William Louis Payne) was nicknamed the *American Bernhardt*[1] by dramatic critics after she had played the leading role in an adaptation of the French play, *Zaza,* at the Lafayette Square Opera House, now the Schubert-Belasco Theatre, at Washington, D.C., on the opening night, December 26, 1898. Mrs. Carter was similar to Sarah Bernhardt (Rosine Bernard) the great French actress, in her emotional appeal and magnetic personality.

Mrs. Carter made her theatrical debut at the Broadway Theatre in New York City on November 10, 1890, in the leading role in *The Ugly Duckling.*

Mrs. Leslie Carter was born Caroline Louise Dudly, at Louisville, Ky., on June 10, 1862, and died at Santa Monica, Calif., on November 13, 1937.

[1] *The New York Times*, New York, November 14, 1937, cols. 1 and 2, p. LN 11.
Who's Who on the Stage, 1908, ed. by Walter Browne and E. DeRoy Koch (R. B. Dodge and Company, New York, 1908) p. 78.

Carter, Robert
Robert Carter was often called *King Carter*[1] because he was a very wealthy man, owned a great deal of land, and was prominent in the political affairs of the colonies. He was Governor of the Virginia Colony from 1726 to 1727.

Robert Carter was born in Virginia, in 1663, and died in Lancaster County, Va., on August 4, 1732.

[1] *The National Cyclopaedia of American Biography* (James T. White and Company, New York, 1906), vol. 13, p. 388.

Carter, Vincent
Nick Carter[1] is the nickname of Vincent Carter, doubtless applied to him because he is a native of the West which was the scene of the triumphs of *Nick Carter*, a character in western fiction who as a detective always succeeded in bringing frontier desperados to justice.

Vincent Carter served as a United States Representative from Wyoming from 1933 to 1935. He was born at St. Clair, Wyo., on November 6, 1891, and now lives at Kemmerer, Wyo.

[1] *The Washington Post Magazine*, Washington, D.C., March 4, 1934, p. 4.

Carthage College
The athletes of Carthage College, at Carthage, Ill., were designated the *Redmen*[1] and the *Lutherans* because the college colors are red and white and because the school belongs to the Lutheran denomination.

[1] A communication from Lewis Omer, Director of Athletics at Carthage College, Carthage, Ill., June 21, 1935.

Cartwheel. See Cartwright, Wilburn

Cartwright, Alexander Joy
Alexander J. Cartwright, who was born at New York City early in 1800, and who died at Honolulu in 1892, was often called the *Father of Modern Baseball*[1] because in 1845 he organized the Knickerbocker Club of New York, the first baseball club in the

world. Cartwright also set the bases ninety feet apart, and established nine innings as a game and nine players as a team, thus creating baseball as it is played today. He spent the remainder of his life in promoting baseball as a national sport.

[1] *America's National Game: Historic Facts Concerning the Beginning, Evolution, Development and Popularity of Baseball, with Personal Reminiscences of Its Vicissitudes, Its Victories and Its Votaries*, Albert G. Spalding (American Sports Publishing Company, New York, 1911) p. 52-3.
Baseball in Cincinnati, a History, Harry Ellard (Press of Johnson and Hardin, Cincinnati, Ohio, 1907) p. 21.

Cartwright, Wilburn
Wilburn Cartwright, an Oklahoma lawyer and politician, was nicknamed *Good Roads Cartwright*[1] because he was at one time the Chairman of the Congressional Committee on Roads in the House of Representatives. He was also called *Cartwheel*, a corruption of his surname.

Wilbur Cartwright was born at Georgetown, Tenn., on January 12, 1891.

[1] An interview with Captain Victor Hunt Harding, Secretary of the National Democratic Congress Reelection Committee, Washington, D.C., April 10, 1939.

Cary, Alice
Alice Cary, who was born near Cincinnati, Ohio, on April 20, 1820, and who died in New York City, on February 12, 1871, has been called the *Jean Ingelow of America*[1] because she wrote simple, homely verse and children's poetry, similar to Jean Ingelow's.

[1] *A Book of Nicknames*, John Goff (Courier-Journal Job Printing Company, Louisville, Ky., 1892) p. 29.

Case School of Applied Science
The athletic teams of the Case School of Applied Science, at Cleveland, Ohio, were formerly nicknamed the *Scientists*. In 1930 they were called the *Rough-Riders*[1] because the name of their coach at that time was Ray A. Ride.

[1] A communication from Ray A. Ride, Director of Athletics at the Case School of Applied Science, Cleveland, Ohio, June 12, 1935.

Casey. See Stengel, C. D.

Casey Jones. See Jones, J. L.

Casket Girls
During the early decades of the eighteenth century girls who emigrated to the Louisiana Colony from France and who brought with them clothes and other personal belongings

Casket Girls—Continued

packed in small trunks, commonly called caskets, were called the *Casket Girls*,[1] the French term being *Filles à la Cassette.*

[1] *A History of Louisiana, Wilderness—Colony—Province—Territory—State—People,* Henry E. Chambers (The American Historical Society, Inc., New York and Chicago, 1925) vol. 1, p. 117.

Cass, Lewis

The *Great Father at Detroit* [1] was the name given to Lewis Cass by the Indians in the Michigan Territory while he was serving from 1813 until July 1831, as the Superintendent of Indian affairs of this territory. The Indians referred to him by this nickname because he treated them kindly and won their respect and affection.

Lewis Cass was born at Exeter, N.H., on October 9, 1782, and died at Detroit, Mich., on June 17, 1866.

[1] "Lewis Cass" by Andrew C. McLaughlin, in *American Statesmen,* ed. by John T. Morse, Junior (Houghton Mifflin and Company, New York and Boston, 1891), vol. 24, p. 120.

Cassandra of the Columnists. See Thompson, Dorothy

Castle Defiance

About 1797 and 1798, when Robert Morris's creditors were pressing him to pay his debts, he nicknamed his home on the Schuylkill River *Castle Defiance* [1] because it was here that he shut himself in and defied his creditors.

[1] *Robert Morris, Patriot and Financier,* Ellis Paxson Oberholtzer (The Macmillan Company, New York, 1903) p. 340-52.

Castor and Pollux of Georgia. See Stephens, A. H. and Robert Toombs

Catamounts. See University of Vermont

Catawba College

The *Indians* [1] is the name given to the athletic teams of Catawba College, at Salisbury, N.C., because the Catawbas were a tribe of Indians who once lived in this territory.

[1] A communication from Milton Whitener, Secretary of Catawba College, Salisbury, N.C., November 21, 1935.

Cathedral of Learning. See University of Pittsburgh

Catholic University

The *Cardinals* is the name given to the athletes of the Catholic University, at Brookland Station, Washington, D.C. The school colors, red and black, are the same as those employed by a Cardinal. Cardinals are connected with the Catholic Church.

[1] A letter from Arthur J. Bergman, Director of Athletics at the Catholic University, Brookland Station, Washington, D.C., June 8, 1935.

Cato of America. See White, H. L.

Cato of the Revolution. See Bland, Richard

Cato of the Senate. See White, H. L.; Wright, Silas

Cattle King. See Kleberg, R. M.

Cattle Kings

Men who amassed fortunes by grazing cattle in the West from 1870 to 1890 were called *Cattle Kings.*[1]

[1] *The Growth of the American People and Nation,* Mary G. Kelty (Ginn and Company, New York and Boston, 1931) p. 410.

Cavalier. See Hunter, T. L.

Cavalier State. See Virginia

Cavaliers. See Virginians; University of Virginia

Cavalry Troopers. See First Cavalry Division of World War II

Cave Wilson. See Wilson, John

Cedar Rapids, Iowa

Cedar Rapids is frequently designated the *Cereal City* [1] because two of the largest cereal factories in the United States are located there.

[1] *The World Book Encyclopedia* (The Quarrie Corporation, Chicago, 1938) vol. 3, p. 1266.

Celery City. See Kalamazoo, Mich.

Celestial City. See Pekin, Ill.

Cellar Houses

The early Dutch settlers on Manhattan who did not have the means to build complete houses generally built what were commonly called *Cellar Houses*.[1] A cellar was dug, the sides boarded up, a plank floor laid, and a roof of beams erected on which was laid bark of trees and a thick covering of sod. As their owners prospered these were often used as the cellars over which they built their permanent homes.

[1] *Hudson River Landings*, First Edition, Paul Wilstach (The Bobbs-Merrill Company, Indianapolis, Ind., 1933) p. 60.

Centenary College of Louisiana

In 1921 the athletic teams of Centenary College, at Shreveport, La., were called the *Gentlemen*.[1] This nickname originated in a conference between the coach and the president of the college, during which the former stated that he wanted the football players to be gentlemen on all occasions and asked the president to assist him. It is often shortened to the *Gents*.

[1] A letter from Curtis Parker, Director of Athletics at Centenary College of Louisiana, Shreveport, La., June 11, 1935.

Centennial State. See Colorado

Centennials. See Coloradans

Central City. See Syracuse, N.Y.

Central College (Fayette, Mo.)

The *Eagles* and the *Rinkydinks* are the nicknames given to the athletic teams of Central College, at Fayette, Mo. The *Eagles* originated about 1925 when a farmer saw an eagle whipping a whole flock of blue jays. The eagle was injured in the battle and the farmer took it to Central where it was nursed by students and became the pet of the campus. The athletic teams of Westminster College which are the traditional rivals of the members of the teams of Central College, are called the *Blue Jays*. After the eagle became their pet Central College adopted the *Eagles* as their official nickname.

The reserve teams of the college are known on the campus as *Rinkydinks,* from the team of the same name in the Sunday cartoon series called "Perry Winkle."

[1] A communication from Robert H. Ruff, President of Central College, Fayette, Mo., November 22, 1935.

Central College (Pella, Iowa)

The athletes of Central College, at Pella, Iowa, were designated the *Flying Dutch-*

men [1] by sports writers because the town of Pella is composed of Hollanders.

[1] A communication from L. A. Winter, Director of Athletics at Central College, Pella, Iowa, November 30, 1935.

Central Falls and Pawtucket, Rhode Island

Central Falls and Pawtucket are commonly called the *Twin Cities* [1] because the land between the two cities has come to be so thickly settled that they seem to be one continuous municipality.

[1] *Know Rhode Island: Facts Concerning the Land of Roger Williams*, Sixth Edition, comp. and distributed by the Office of the Secretary of State (State of Rhode Island and Providence Plantations, Providence, R.I., 1936) p. 10.

Central State. See Kansas

Centre College of Kentucky

The upper-classmen athletic teams of Centre College of Kentucky, at Danville, Ky., were nicknamed the *Colonels*,[1] an obvious reference to the Kentucky Colonels. The freshman teams are designated the *Lieutenants.*

[1] A communication from Charles J. Turck, President of Centre College of Kentucky, Danville, Ky., November 15, 1935.

Century Division. See One Hundredth Infantry Division of World War II

Cerberus of the Treasury. See Ellsworth, Oliver

Cereal City. See Cedar Rapids, Iowa

Chad. See Kimsey, Clyde

Chadwick, Henry

Henry Chadwick was widely known as the *Father of Baseball*,[1] because he worked for many years in organizing professional baseball in America, developed the rules of the game, and collected valuable material relating to the history of baseball.

Henry Chadwick, who was born at Exeter, England, on October 5, 1824, immigrated to the United States about 1837, and died at Brooklyn, N.Y., on April 20, 1908.

[1] *Dictionary of American Biography under the Auspices of the American Council of Learned Societies*, ed. by Allen Johnson (Charles Scribner's Sons, New York, 1929) vol. 3, p. 587.
Baseball and Baseball Players; a History of the National Game of America and Important Events Connected Therewith From Its Origin Down to the Present Time, Elwood A. Roff (E. A. Roff, Chicago, 1912) p. 178.

Chamberlain, Joshua Lawrence

Because he fought gallantly for the defense of Little Round Top in the battle of Gettysburg, on July 2, 1863, General Joshua Lawrence Chamberlain was called the *Hero of Little Round Top* [1]

General Chamberlain was born at Brewer, Me., on September 8, 1828, and died at Brunswick, Me., on January 24, 1914.

[1] *Maine, My State,* The Maine Writers Research Club (The Journal Print Shop, Lawiston, Me., 1919) p. 272.

Champ. See Barbour, W. W.

Champaign and Urbana, Illinois

Champaign and Urbana, located in Champaign County, Illinois, in the east-central part of the state, have been nicknamed the *Twin Cities* [1] because they are close together and the campus of the University of Illinois lies partly in each of them.

[1] *The World Book Encyclopedia* (The Quarrie Corporation, Chicago, 1938) vol. 9, p. 3353.

Champion Buffalo Hunter of the Plains. See Cody, W. F.

Champion City. See Springfield, Ohio

Chance, Frank LeRoy

Frank LeRoy Chance, who was born at Fresno, Calif., on September 9, 1877, and who died at Los Angeles, Calif., on September 14, 1924, was known as the *Peerless Leader* [1] in baseball circles because of his outstanding ability and leadership.

[1] *Who's Who in Major League Base Ball,* comp. by Harold (Speed) Johnson (Buxton Publishing Company, Chicago, 1933) p. 463.

Chandler, Albert Benjamin

Albert Benjamin Chandler, former Governor of Kentucky, is widely known by his nickname, *Happy Chandler,* [1] which originated in the fact that he is a happy, jovial man. He resigned as Governor of Kentucky and was appointed a United States Senator from Kentucky in 1939. From 1945 to 1951 he was High Commissioner of baseball.

Albert Benjamin Chandler was born at Corydon, Ky., on July 14, 1898.

[1] *Newsweek: The Magazine of News Significance,* Chicago, January 31, 1938, p. 15.

Chandler, William Eaton

William Eaton Chandler, formerly a United States Senator from New Hampshire and Secretary of the United States Navy, was nicknamed the *Father of Our Modern Navy* [1] because while he was Secretary of the Navy he began to build steel battleships and to modernize the old ones. He was called a *Stormy Petrel* [2] because he was a disturbing force as a politician and journalist in New Hampshire.

He was born at Concord, N.H., on December 28, 1835, and died there on November 30, 1917.

[1] *The Father of Rural Free Delivery,* William Eaton Chandler (The News Dispatch, Clinton, N.C., 1915) p. 6.

[2] Dictionary of American Biography under the auspices of the American Council of Learned Societies, ed. by Allen Johnson (Charles Scribner's Sons, New York, 1929) vol. 3, p. 617.

Chaney, Lon

The *Man of a Thousand Faces* [1] was a nickname applied to Lon Chaney because of his unusual ability in assuming the qualities of various types and nationalities of people through the skillful use of make-up.

He was born on April 1, 1883, at Colorado Springs, Colo., and died at Los Angeles, Calif., on August 26, 1930.

[1] *The Blue Book of the Screen,* Ruth Wing, Editor (The Blue Book of the Screen, Inc., Hollywood, Calif., 1923), p. 47.

Channing, William Ellery

William Ellery Channing was often called *Little King Pepin* [1] and the *Peacemaker.*

Little King Pepin was a sobriquet given to Channing because of his self-control, gentleness, and his religious zeal and fervor, comparable to Pepin the Short, who was crowned the first Carolingian king of the Franks by Saint Boniface in 751 A.D.

During his youth at Newport, R.I., he was called the *Peacemaker* because he was a great factor in maintaining peace among his playmates.

William Ellery Channing was born at Newport, R.I., on April 7, 1780, and died at Bennington, Vt., on October 2, 1842.

[1] *The Story of the Hall of Fame, Including the Lives and Portraits of the Elect and of Those Who Barely Missed Election. Also a List of America's Most Eligible Women,* Louis Albert Banks (The Christian Herald, New York, 1902) p. 311.

Chaplin, Charles Spencer

Motion picture comedian Charlie Chaplin was once nicknamed a *Twentieth Century Moses* [1] because he contributed large sums of money to enable Jews to leave Germany and the persecutions of the Nazi regime, like

Moses who delivered the children of Israel from Egyptian bondage.

Charles Spencer Chaplin was born at London, England, on April 16, 1889.

[1] *Times-Herald*, Washington, D.C., July 30, 1939, col. 1, p. 4-A.

Chapman, John

Johnny Appleseed [1] and the *Patron Saint of American Orchards* [2] are nicknames appropriately applied to John Chapman.

He was nicknamed *Johnny Appleseed* because he was always planting appleseeds or giving them to others to plant. This also lead to his being called the *Patron Saint of American Orchards.*

John Chapman was born near Boston, Mass., in 1775 according to some historians, but according to others he was born near Springfield, Mass., on May 11, 1768, died near Fort Wayne, Ind., on March 11, 1847.

This well-known wanderer of the American frontier wilderness began his journeyings among the western pioneer settlers about 1788, and by 1803 he was actively engaged in his chosen mission of planting and caring for apple trees in the frontier settlements beyond the Allegheny Mountains. It was here that he spent the remaining years of his life planting and giving appleseeds to others to plant, setting young apple trees, establishing and caring for nurseries, and distributing apples.

[1] *The National Cyclopaedia of American Biography* (James T. White and Company, New York, 1909) vol. 11, p. 98.
[2] *Seeing the Middle West*, John T. Faris (J. B. Lippincott Company, Philadelphia, 1923) p. 241.
Johnny Appleseed, the True Story of Jonathan Chapman, 1775-1846, James Lattimore Himrod (TenBrook-Viquesney Company, Chicago, 1926. For sale at Chicago Historical Society, Chicago) p. 8.
Johnny Appleseed and His Time, an Historical Romance, Henry A. Pershing (Shenandoah Publishing House, Inc., Strasburg, Va., 1930) p. 5.

Charcoals

Shortly after Missouri was admitted into the Union as a slave-holding state in 1821, the people who favored the abolition of slavery were called *Charcoals* [1] because they busied themselves with the interests of the Negro.

[1] *The Abolitionists together with Personal Memories of the Struggle for Human Rights, 1830-1884*, John F. Hume (G. P. Putnam's Sons, New York and London, 1905) p. 159.

Charleston, South Carolina

Charleston is known as *America's Most Historic City, City by the Sea, City of Seces-*sion, *Cradle of Secession, Earthquake City, Palmetto City,* and *Plumb Line Port to Panama.* It is called *America's Most Historic City* [1] because of its historic buildings and traditions. Charleston is fittingly designated the *City by the Sea* [2] because it is situated on the Atlantic Coast. The nicknames *City of Secession* and *Cradle of Secession* [3] were applied to Charleston because in this city was passed on December 20, 1860, the ordinance of secession, by which South Carolina was the first state to withdraw from the national Union, and because that city continued to be an important focal point for the activities of the Confederate states.

The *Earthquake City* [4] has been applied to Charleston in allusion to the devastating earthquake which occurred there on August 31, 1886. This city is also known as the *Palmetto City* [5] because numerous palmetto trees are to be found growing in the city and its neighboring vicinity. It is called the *Plumb Line Port to Panama* [6] because its harbor is in a straight line directly north of Panama.

[1] *History, Legends, Traditions, Street Strolls around Charleston, South Carolina: Street Strolls around Charleston, South Carolina, America's Most Historic City, Giving the History, Legends, Traditions*, Miriam Bellangee Wilson (Charleston, S.C., 1930) Booklet No. 2, Blue and Gray Historical Series, p. 7.
[2] *Short Sketch of Charleston, South Carolina: How It Fared in Two Wars and an Earthquake*, Third Edition. issued by The Atlantic Coast Line (Wynkoop Hallembeck Crawford Company, New York, 1900) p. 14.
Stories of Charleston Harbor, Catherine Drayton Simons (The State Company, Columbia, S.C., 1930) p. 133.
Commercial Atlas: Rand McNally Commercial Atlas, Fifty-eighth Edition (Rand McNally, New York, 1927) p. 265.
[3] *Lee and His Lieutenants: Comprising the Early Life, Public Services and Campaigns of General Robert E. Lee and His Companions in Arms, with a Record of Their Campaigns and Heroic Deeds*, Edward A. Pollard (E. B. Treat and Company, New York, 1867) p. 257.
The Seventy-ninth Highlanders New York Volunteers in the War of Rebellion, 1861-1865, William Todd (Brandow, Barton and Company, New York, 1886) p. 88.
A Book of Nicknames, John Goff (Courier-Journal Job Printing Company, Louisville, Ky., 1892) p. 16.
[4] *History of Charleston County, South Carolina, Narrative and Biographical*, Thomas Petigru Lesesne (A. H. Cawston—Managing Editor and Publisher, Charleston, S.C., 1931) p. 99-100.
[5] *History of South Carolina*, ed. by Yates Snowden in collaboration with H. G. Cutler, General Historian and an editorial advisory board including special contributors (The Lewis Publishing Company, New York and Chicago, 1920) vol. 2, p. 985-92.
Manual of Useful Information, comp. under the direction of J. C. Thomas (The Werner Company, Chicago, 1893) p. 22.
[6] *Charleston, "The Plumbline Port of Panama,"* comp. by Charleston Chamber of Commerce, arranged by George A. Simms (Walker, Evans and Cogswell Company, Charleston Chamber of Commerce, Charleston, S.C., 1915) p. 2, 19.

Charlotte, North Carolina

Charlotte was nicknamed the *Hornet's Nest* [1] by Major General Charles Cornwallis

Charlotte, N.C.—Continued

in the fall of 1780, while he was in command of the British Army with headquarters in that city, because the citizens displayed such vigorous opposition to the British. The *Mecklenburg Declaration of Independence* was signed in this city on May 20, 1775.

It was also a center of opposition to the northern forces during the Civil War. The hornet's nest was later adopted as the emblem of the city of Charlotte.

[1] *The Source Book* (Source Research Council, Inc., Chicago, 1936) vol. 2, p. 354.

Charter Oak City. See Hartford, Conn.

Chase, Salmon Portland

The nicknames *Attorney General for Runaway Slaves, Father of Greenbacks,* and *Ferry Boy,* have all been given to Salmon Portland Chase. He was sometimes derisively called the *Attorney General for Runaway Slaves* [1] by his political opponents because he was an abolitionist and acted on numerous occasions as attorney for runaway slaves.

The *Father of Greenbacks* [2] was applied to Salmon P. Chase because it was largely through his efforts that the Legal Tender Act was passed by Congress and paper money became legal tender.

As a boy while living on the Cuyahoga River, he had often amused himself by acting as a ferryman for people who wished to cross the river to Cleveland. Because of this he was nicknamed the *Ferry Boy.*[3]

[1] *The National Cyclopaedia of American Biography* (James T. White and Company, New York, 1898) vol. 1, p. 29.
[2] *Manual of Useful Information,* comp. under the direction of J. C. Thomas (The Werner Company, Chicago, 1893) p. 23.
Representative Men: Sketches of Representative Men, North and South . . . ed. by Augustus C. Rogers (Atlantic Publishing Company, New York, 1872) p. 130.
[3] *An Account of the Private Life and Public Services of Salmon Portland Chase,* Robert B. Warden (Wilstach, Baldwin and Company, Cincinnati, Ohio, 1874) p. 69.

Chattanooga, Tennessee

Chattanooga, an important railroad, trade, and manufacturing center, is sometimes spoken of as the *Gate City* [1] because it serves as the gateway for commerce between Alabama, Georgia, and Tennessee, and serves as the passageway for much of the trade from the East through the South into Mexico.

[1] *From Trail to Railway Through the Appalachians,* Albert Perry Brigham (Ginn and Company, New York, Chicago, and London, 1907) p. 174.

Cheatham, Benjamin Franklin

Major General Benjamin Franklin Cheatham was known as *Bulldog Cheatham, Ney of the Confederacy,* and *Old Frank.*

The popular nickname *Bulldog Cheatham* [1] particularly applied to General Cheatham by his soldiers and fellow officers, commemorated his fierce manner of fighting.

Because as an officer in charge of the Army of the Tennessee, he distinguished himself by taking a prominent part in many important battles of the Civil War, General Cheatham was designated the *Ney of the Confederacy.*[2] Michael Ney was Marshal of France and Duke of Elchingen.

Major General Cheatham was called *Old Frank* [3] by his soldiers. Although he was stern, his fairness won the respect of all.

Benjamin Franklin Cheatham was born at Nashville, Tenn., on October 20, 1820, and died there on September 4, 1886.

[1] *Fighting Tennesseans,* George Towns Gaines (Kingsport Press, Kingsport, Tenn., 1931) p. 57.
[2] *The National Cyclopaedia of American Biography* (James T. White and Company, New York, 1909) vol. 11, p. 90.
[3] *A History of Tennessee from 1663 to 1924,* Gentry R. McGee, revised and enlarged by C. B. Ijams (American Book Company, New York, 1924) p. 211.

Checkerboard Division. See Ninety-ninth Infantry Division of World War II

Cheese Box on a Raft

The *Monitor,* a Federal war vessel designed by Captain John Ericsson and built in 1861 by a firm from Troy, N.Y., at Greenpoint, L.I., was nicknamed the *Cheese Box on a Raft,* or the *Yankee Cheese Box on a Raft.*[1] The sobriquet is said to have been given to the *Monitor* during the battle between it and the *Merrimac* in Hampton Roads on March 9, 1862, because the revolving iron gun turret built on the flat deck looked like a cheesebox.

[1] *The Story of Our Country,* Ruth West and Willis Mason West (Allyn and Bacon, New York and Boston, 1933) p. 380.
The Encyclopaedia Britannica, Fourteenth Edition (Encyclopaedia Britannica, Inc., New York, 1932) vol. 15, p. 723; vol. 19, p. 358.
History of the United States of America, under the Constitution James Schouler (Dodd, Mead and Company, New York, 1899) vol. 5, p. 190.

Chemical City. See Berlin, N.H.

Cheney, Sophie H. (Bissell)

Santa Claus of the Manchester Poor [1] was a name frequently applied to Mrs. Richard Otis Cheney, of Manchester, Conn., because of the generous donations made by her to the poor of Manchester.

Mrs. Cheney, prior to her marriage to Richard Otis Cheney on June 2, 1863, was Sophie H. Bissell, daughter of Major Lewis Bissell, of Saint Louis, Mo.

[1] *The National Cyclopaedia of American Biography* (James T. White and Company, New York, 1926) vol. 19, p. 76.

Cherokee. See Johnson, R. L.

Cherokee Bill. See Hastings, W. W.

Cherokee Kid. See Rogers, Will

Chesterfield of the Navy. See Le Roy, W. E.

Chicago, Illinois

The following are the nicknames of Chicago: *City of the Lake and Prairies, Garden City, Packing Town, Porkopolis, Pork City, Rail Center of America, Tower City, White City, Windy City,* and *City of Winds.* This city, located on the shore of Lake Michigan in close proximity to the great prairie lands of the West, is called the *City of the Lake and Prairies.*[1] It has merited the name of *Garden City,*[2] by virtue of its magnificent public and private gardens.

The fact that Chicago is the largest livestock and meat-packing center in the world has caused it to be called the *Packing Town, Porkopolis,*[3] and *Pork City.* Chicago is called the *Tower City* because of its many buildings with towers.

The *White City* [4] often applied to Chicago was originally attributed to the assemblage of white buildings on the Columbian Exposition grounds, on which the World's Fair was celebrated in 1893.

It is called the *Rail Center of America* because it is the terminus of many of the large eastern as well as western railroads.

Chicago is termed the *Windy City,*[5] or *City of Winds* because it is located at the southwest extremity of Lake Michigan, which is almost constantly swept by winds varying in velocity from gentle breezes to gales.

[1] *Little Journeys in America,* Rose Henderson (The Southern Publishing Company, Dallas, Tex., 1922) p. 152.
Westward by Rail: A Journey to San Francisco and Back and a Visit to the Mormons, W. F. Rae (Longmans, Green and Company, London, 1871) p. 34, 40, 48.

[2] *Chicago, The Garden City, Its Magnificent Parks, Boulevards, and Cemeteries, Together with Other Descriptive Views and Sketches,* comp. and ed. by Andreas Simon (The Franz Gindele Printing Company, Chicago, 1893) p. 9-10.
Chicago Welcomes You, Alfred Granger, with an introduction by Rufus C. Dawes, and original illustrations by Leion R. Peschert (A. Kroch, Chicago, 1933) p. 213, 214.
Our City—Chicago, Edna Fay Campbell, Fanny R. Smith, and Clarence F. Jones (Charles Scribner's Sons, New York, 1930) p. 282.
[3] *Industrial and Commercial Geography,* J. Russell Smith, New Edition (Henry Holt and Company, New York, 1930) p. 151.
Chicago's Accomplishments and Leaders, comp. and published by Glenn A. Bishop in collaboration with Paul T. Gilbert, drawings on biographical pages by Raymond E. Craig (Bishop Publishing Company, Chicago, 1933) p. 298.
More About Names, Leopold Wagner (T. Fisher Unwin, London, 1893) p. 245.
The Shorter Oxford English Dictionary on Historical Principles, prepared by William Little, H. W. Fowler, and J. Coulson, Sir James Augustus Henry Murray, Editor, rev. and ed. by C. T. Onions (Clarendon Press, Oxford, England, 1933) vol. 2, p. 1536.
[4] *The White City as It Was; The Story of the World's Columbian Exposition Illustrated by a Series of Eighty Perfect Pictures from Photographs by W. H. Jackson,* text by Selim H. Peabody and Stanley Wood (The White City Art Company, Chicago, 1894) p. 1-2.
Zigzag Journeys in the White City with Visits to the Neighboring Metropolis, Hezekiah Butterworth (Estes and Lauriat, Boston, 1894) p. 89-95.
[5] *The Weather and Climate of Chicago,* Henry J. Cox and John H. Armington, *The Geographic Society of Chicago, Bulletin number four* (Published for The Geographic Society of Chicago by The University of Chicago Press, Chicago, 1914) p. xxiv.

Chicago American League Baseball Company

In 1899 the two chief baseball associations were the National League, formed in 1876, and the American Association, formed in 1881.[1] Since the latter organization had outlived its efficiency, Charles Comiskey and Ban Johnson reorganized the more profitable baseball clubs in the association into a new western league. Thus, at the turn of the century, the American League came into existence.[2]

In Chicago, which prior to that time had harbored only the *Cubs* of the National League, Comiskey established a rival American League team christened the *White Stockings,* later shortened in news headlines to *White Sox* and *Chisox.*[3] The name had originally belonged to the National League club but had been dropped by them. (See Chicago National League Baseball Company.)

Within five years the new club rose to top position in its own league, taking the league pennant in 1906, and becoming a contender with the Chicago *Cubs,* the National League champions, for the World's Series. The World's Series had been inaugurated in 1903 and the 1906 event was the first in series history in which both championship teams represented the same city.

Chicago American League Baseball Company—Continued

The championship Chicago team which lost to the *Cincinnati Reds* in the 1919 World's Series received the nickname *Black Sox* because eight of the players had taken bribes from gamblers to throw the Series. These eight were forever barred from playing professional baseball by baseball Commissioner Landis.

[1] *Baseball*, by Robert Smith (Simon and Schuster, New York, 1947) p. 97.
[2] *The Chicago White Sox*, by Warren Brown (G. P. Putnam's Sons, New York, 1952) p. 10-11, 13.
[3] *Balldom: "The Britannica of Baseball."* Comprising Growth of the Game in Detail; a Complete History of the National and American Leagues; First and Only Authentic Chronology Ever Published; Voluminous Records and Absolutely Accurate Statistics; Fascinating Facts for Fans of America's Greatest Sport from 1845 to 1914, George L. Moreland (Balldom Publishing Company, New York, 1914) p. 30-1.
Baseball and Baseball Players; A History of the National Game of America and Important Events Connected Therewith from Its Origin Down to the Present Time, Elwood A. Roff (E. A. Roff, Chicago, 1912) p. 13.

Chicago Cardinals Football Club

The Redbirds [1] is the nickname commonly attributed to the teams of the Chicago Cardinals Football Club, Incorporated, at Chicago, Ill. The emblem of the club is the cardinal or redbird.

[1] A communication from Charles W. Bidwell, President of The Chicago Cardinals Football Club, Inc., Chicago, Ill., March 29, 1939.

Chicago National League Baseball Company

The Chicago National League Club founded by William A. Hulbert and A. G. Spalding in 1876 was originally dubbed *White Stockings*. This was also the year of the founding of the National League by the same two men and it was Hulbert who gave each team in the league distinguishing colors.

Adrian *Pop* Anson managed the Chicago team from 1878 through 1897, piloting them to five straight championships during the first six years. He was so thoroughly identified with the team that they were known as the *Orphans* when he left them.[1] In 1890, the year in which the Players' League was in existence, so many of the regular players resigned to join the League that Anson had to hire a batch of rookies; it was then that the team began to be called *Pop* Anson's *Colts, Babes* or *Cubs*.[1]

By 1906 they were well-known for the invincible infield combination to whom Franklin P. Adams referred as a "trio of bear cubs": Joe Tinker, Johnny Evers, and Frank Chance.[1]

[1] *The Chicago Cubs*, by Warren Brown (G. P. Putnam's Sons, New York, 1946) p. 19, 20, 36.

Chicago of the South. See Okeechobee, Fla.

Chicago's Grand Old Lady. See Hudlun, A. E.

Chief. See Bender, C. A.; Hale, A. O.; Harder, M. L.; Hogsett, E. C.; Hoover, H. C.

Chief Burdick. See Burdick, U. L.

Chief Executioner. See Roper, D. C.

Chief Incendiary of the House. See Adams, Samuel

Chief Old Woman. See Stevens, Thaddeus

Chief Who Never Sleeps. See Wayne, Anthony

Child of the Mississippi. See Louisiana

Children's Poet. See Longfellow, H. W.

Childress, Texas

Childress is designated a *City of the Plains* [1] because it is located amidst great stretches of flat prairies in the central basin of Texas.

[1] *The Geography of Texas, Physical and Political*, Revised Edition, Frederic William Simonds (Ginn and Company, New York and Boston, 1914) p. 22.

Chillicothe Business College

The athletic teams of the Chillicothe Business College, at Chillicothe, Mo., are popularly designated *The Ducks* because swimming meets constitute a large part of their athletic programs.

Chimneyville. See Jackson, Miss.

Chinese Harrison. See Harrison, Benjamin

Chink. See Outen, W. A.

Chinook State. See Washington

Chip Robert. See Robert, L. W., Jr.

Chisellers

From 1933 to 1935, the nickname *Chisellers*[1] was applied to merchants and heads of business firms who refused to sign the codes of the National Recovery Administration, or violated these codes, or who were accused of unfair business practices.

Chisox. See Chicago American League Baseball Company

Choctaws. See Mississippi College

Choirmaster of the House. See Woodrum, C. A.

Christian Statesman. See Frelinghuysen, Theodore

Christmas Conference

The first conference of the Methodist Episcopal Church met at Baltimore, Md., on December 24, 1784, and was in session for ten days. The Methodist Episcopal Church of the United States was formally organized and the first Discipline of the Methodist Episcopal Church was adopted at this conference which is commonly designated the *Christmas Conference.*[1]

[1] *Francis Asbury, the Prophet of the Long Road,* Ezra Squier Tipple (The Methodist Book Concern, New York and Cincinnati, 1916) p. 145.

Christy, William

William Christy became nicknamed the *Hero of Fort Meigs*[1] during the War of 1812, because of his outstanding courage and gallantry during a battle fought in the vicinity of Fort Meigs on the Maumee River in Ohio between a body of American soldiers under Major General William Henry Harrison and a group of Indians led by Tecumseh. Although badly wounded, Christy ran to Fort Meigs and secured aid to save the soldiers still engaged in battle with the Indians.

William Christy was born at Georgetown, Ky., on December 6, 1791, and died at New Orleans, La., on November 7, 1865.

[1] *The National Cyclopaedia of American Biography* (James T. White and Company, New York, 1909) vol. 11, p. 456.

Chuck Wagon

The wagon which carries food to the cowboys on the western plains of the United States is called the *Chuck Wagon*[1] by the cowboys, *chuck* being a slang word for food, and is used in various parts of the United States today for wagons that haul food and other supplies to gangs of workmen.

[1] *Seeing the Middle West,* John T. Faris (J. B. Lippincott Company, Philadelphia, 1923) p. 122 under the picture opposite.

Church Hill Cats

The school boys at Richmond, Va., about 1856 are said to have been especially fond of fighting. They organized into bands in the various sections of the city where they lived. These bands were called *cats* with the name of the section in which it was located attached. The *Church Hill Cats*[1] were named in this manner.

[1] *The End of an Era,* John S. Wise (Houghton Mifflin and Company, New York and Boston, 1889) p. 59.

Cicero of America. See Livingston, R. R.

Cincinnati, Ohio

Cincinnati has nine nicknames: *Beautiful City, City of Personality, Conservative Cincinnati, Contented City, Paris of America, Porkopolis, Queen City, Queen City of the West,* and *Queen of the West.* The descriptive appellation *Beautiful City,*[1] has been applied to this city because it is picturesquely located in an amphitheatre surrounded by many hills adorned with the beauties of nature, on the Ohio River the Indian name for which means *the fair and beautiful.*

Cincinnati has been termed the *City of Personality*[2] from the charm of its natural scenery, composed of a beautiful expanse of river, hills rising in stately grandeur, and spacious parks, and by its civic pride.

The *Conservative City,*[3] and the *Contented City* were applied to Cincinnati following the Civil War when there was but very little growth or development taking place in this city.

This city justly merits the name of the *Paris of America*[4] from the fact that it offers pleasure seekers a great variety of attractions, such as excursions, concerts, lectures, theatrical shows, museums, and diverse forms of entertainment at the amusement parks.

Cincinnati was formerly called *Porkopolis*[3] from the fact that for many years it was outstanding in the pork-packing industry. It is now surpassed in this industry by a number of other cities.

Cincinnati, Ohio—Continued

Cincinnati was appropriately nicknamed the *Queen City* [4] and the *Queen City of the West* because of its lovely surroundings, excellent climate, fertile soil of the neighborhood, and the bright prospects for the future greatness of the city.

Longfellow, in his poem entitled *Catawba Wine*, refers to Cincinnati as the *Queen of the West*:

And this song of the vine,
This greeting of mine,
The winds and the birds shall deliver
To the queen of the west,
In her garlands dressed,
On the banks of the beautiful river.[5]

[1] *The Town of the Beautiful River*, E. R. Kellogg, etching by E. T. Hurley (U. P. James, Cincinnati, Ohio, 1915) p. ii.
The Queen City in 1869, The City of Cincinnati. A Summary of Its Attractions, Advantages, Institutions, and Internal Improvements, with a Statement of Its Public Charities, George E. Stevens (George S. Blanchard and Company, Cincinnati, Ohio, 1869) p. 9, 12.
Historical Collections of Ohio, Henry Howe (Published for the author by Derby, Bradley and Company, Cincinnati, Ohio, 1847) p. 574.

[2] *Cincinnati, the City of Personality*, Thomas B. Frank (Thomas B. Frank, Cincinnati, Ohio, 1930) p. 6.
King's Handbook of the United States, planned and ed. by Moses King, text by M. F. Sweetser (Moses King Corporation, Buffalo, N.Y., 1891) p. 676-677.
The Citizens Book, Editors, Charles R. Hebble and Frank P. Goodwin, published under auspices of the Cincinnati Chamber of Commerce (Stewart and Kidd Company, Cincinnati, Ohio, 1916) p. 184-192.

[3] *Illustrated Cincinnati: A Pictorial Hand-book of the Queen City Comprising Its Architecture, Manufacture, Trade; Its Social, Literary, Scientific, and Charitable Institutions; Its Churches, Schools, and Colleges; and All Other Principal Points of Interest to the Visitor and Resident together with an Account of the Most Attractive Suburbs*, D. J. Kenny (Robert Clarke and Company, Cincinnati, Ohio, 1875) p. 12.
Cincinnati, The Queen City, 1788-1912, Reverend Charles Frederick Goss, illustrated by A. O. Kraemer (The S. J. Clarke Publishing Company, Chicago, and Cincinnati, Ohio, 1912) vol. 1, p. 227; vol. 2, p. 236, 334, 533.

[4] *King's Pocket-book of Cincinnati*, ed. and published by Moses King (Harvard College, Cambridge, Mass., 1897) p. 62, 69.
Cincinnati and Vicinity with Map and Illustrations: An Alphabetically Arranged Index and Descriptive Guide to Places, Institutions, Societies, Amusements, Resorts, Etc., in and about the City of Cincinnati, comp. by F. W. Brown (C. J. Drehbiel and Company, Cincinnati, Ohio, 1898) p. 6-7.

[5] *Poems*, New Revised Edition with numerous illustrations, Henry Wadsworth Longfellow (James R. Osgood and Company, Boston, 1877) p. 222.

Cincinnati National League Baseball Company

The Cincinnati Baseball Club, organized in 1869, was the first group of professional baseball players in America. They were popularly nicknamed *Red Stockings* [1] or *Cincinnati Reds* because they wore bright red stockings with their uniforms. The nickname of the team in the present day is *Redlegs*.

[1] *Centennial History of Cincinnati and Representative Citizens*, Charles Theodore Greve (Biographical Publishing Company, Chicago, 1904) vol. 1, p. 850-1.

[Balldom: "The Britannica of Baseball," Comprising Growth of the Game in Detail . . . , George L. Moreland (Balldom Publishing Company, New York, 1914) p. 13, 69.
Baseball in Cincinnati, a History, Harry Ellard (Johnson and Hardin, Cincinnati, Ohio, 1907) p. 83.]

Cincinnati Oysters

Pigs' feet are humorously nicknamed *Cincinnati Oysters* [1] because there were so many pigs' feet to be had from the packing companies in Cincinnati, Ohio, and because, when fried in batter they had an appearance somewhat similar to that of fried oysters.

[1] *Dictionary of Nicknames*, Fourth Edition, John Russel Bartlett (Little, Brown and Company, Boston, 1877) p. 121.

Cincinnati Redlegs. See Cincinnati National League Baseball Company

Cincinnati Reds. See Cincinnati National League Baseball Company

Cincinnatus of the West. See Washington, George

Cinderella Man. See Braddock, J. J.

CIO Hoffman. See Hoffman, C. E.

Cipher Officer

Cipher Officer [1] is a sobriquet given to the Vice President of the United States because he usually has but little to do or to say in governmental affairs.

[1] *A Book of Nicknames*, John Goff (Courier-Journal Job Printing Company, Louisville, Ky., 1892) p. 44.

Circuit Rider

Circuit Rider [7] was a name given to a preacher who served churches in different localities. This type of preacher usually rode a horse and went to the same group of churches annually in rotation; consequently, he came to be thought of as riding a circuit. Francis Asbury, a follower of John Wesley, is said to have instituted this custom in the United States.

[1] *The Encyclopaedia Britannica*, Fourteenth Edition (Encyclopaedia Britannica, Inc., New York, 1932) vol. 5, p. 719.

Circus King. See Ringling, John

Cissie Patterson. See Patterson, E. M.

City Beautiful. See Hartford, Conn.; Milwaukee Wis.; Nashville, Tenn.; San Francisco, Calif.; Uvalde, Tex.

City Beautiful in the Land o' Lakes. See Fergus Falls, Minn.

City Built by Hands. See Rochester, N.Y.

City by Accident. See Yoakum, Tex.

City by the Falls. See Louisville, Ky.

City by the Sea. See Charleston, S.C.; Newport, R.I.

City Cosmopolitan. See San Francisco, Calif.

City of Angels. See San Angelo, Tex.

City of Baked Beans. See Boston, Mass.

City of Beautiful Churches. See Louisville, Ky.

City of Black Diamonds. See Scranton, Pa.

City of Brick. See Pullman, Ill.

City of Brotherly Love. See Philadelphia, Pa.

City of Churches. See Anniston, Ala.; Brooklyn, N.Y.

City of Conventions. See Syracuse, N.Y.

City of Elms. See New Haven, Conn.

City of Executives. See Birmingham, Ala.

City of Five Flags. See Mobile, Ala.

City of Flour. See Buffalo, N.Y.

City of Flowers and Sunshine. See Los Angeles, Calif.

City of Health. See Dawson Springs, Ky.

City of Hills. See Lynchburg, Va.

City of Homes. See Brooklyn, N.Y.; Dallas, Tex.; Louisville, Ky.; Milwaukee, Wis.; Philadelphia, Pa.; Rochester, N.Y.

City of Homes, Schools, and Churches. See Yoakum, Tex.

City of Houses Without Streets. See Washington, D.C.

City of Isms. See Syracuse, N.Y.

City of Kind Hearts. See Boston, Mass.

City of Magic. See Lowell, Mass.

City of Magnificent Distances. See Washington, D.C.

City of Notions. See Boston, Mass.

City of Oaks. See Bartow, Fla.; Raleigh, N.C.; Tuscaloosa, Ala.

City of One Hundred Hills. See San Francisco, Calif.

City of Opportunities. See Miami, Fla.

City of Palms. See Fort Myers, Fla.

City of Peace. See Salem, Mass.

City of Penn. See Philadelphia, Pa.

City of People. See Demopolis, Ala.

City of Personality. See Cincinnati, Ohio

City of Prosperity. See Worcester, Mass.

City of Receptions. See Washington, D.C.

City of Rocks. See Nashville, Tenn.

City of Roses. See Little Rock, Ark.

City of Salt. See Syracuse, N.Y.

City of Secession. See Charleston, S.C.

City of Shoes. See Lynn, Mass.

City of Soles. See Lynn, Mass.

City of Steel. See Pittsburgh, Pa.

City of Straits. See Detroit, Mich.

City of Streets Without Houses. See Washington, D.C.

City of the Falls. See Louisville, Ky.

City of the Lake and Prairies. See Chicago, Ill.

City of the Plains. See Childress, Tex. Denver, Colo.; Syracuse, N.Y.

City of the Saints. See Salt Lake City, Utah

City of the Violet Crown. See Austin, Tex.

City of Towers. See New York City

City of Varied Industries. See Rochester, N.Y.

City of Winds. See Chicago, Ill.

City of Witches. See Salem, Mass.

City That Built Its Seaport. See Houston, Tex.

City That Came Back. See Alton, Ill.

City That Lights and Hauls the World. See Schenectady, N.Y.

City Within a City

The Union Terminal buildings in Cleveland, Ohio, are called *A City Within a City;* they cover about thirty-five acres of ground and contain a fifty-two story terminal tower, a department store, a hotel, an office building, the Medical Arts Building, and the Builders Exchange Building.

[1] *The Source Book* (Source Research Council, Inc., Chicago, 1936) vol. 2, p. 618.

Claiborne, William

The *Evil Genius of Maryland* [1] was the nickname attributed to William Claiborne, because he took up arms to enforce his claim to Kent Island, land which both Virginia and Maryland claimed and because he was instrumental in having all Catholics in Maryland removed from public office.

William Claiborne was born at Westmorland, England, about 1589, and died in New Kent County, Va., about 1676.

[1] *The National Cyclopaedia of American Biography* (James T. White and Company, New York, 1909) vol. 11, p. 421.

Claimant. See Cleveland, Grover

Clam Grabbers. See Washington Inhabitants

Clam State. See New Jersey

Clam-catchers. See New Jerseyans

Clams. See New Jerseyans

Clark, Abraham

Because Abraham Clark often acted as legal advisor and was very generous to those unable to afford the fees of an attorney, the sobriquet the *Poor Man's Counsellor* [1] was sometimes applied to him.

Abraham Clark was born near Elizabethtown, N.J., on February 15, 1726, and died at Rahway, N.J., on September 15, 1794. He was one of the signers of the Declaration of Independence.

[1] *The National Cyclopaedia of American Biography* (James T. White and Company, New York, 1893) vol. 3, p. 302.

Clark, David Lytle

David Lytle Clark, a chewing gum and candy manufacturer, was nicknamed the *Pittsburgh Candy King* [1] because he acquired a vast fortune manufacturing and selling chewing gum, candy, and candy-coated popcorn.

David Lytle Clark was born in Derry County, Ireland, in 1864, and died at Pittsburgh, Pa., on February 3, 1939.

[1] *The Evening Star*, Washington, D.C., February 5, 1939, col. 7, p. A-14.

Clark, Earl

Earl Clark, who was a coach in national league football, is commonly called *Dutch Clark*.[1] His brother gave him this sobriquet when Clark was a small boy.

Earl Clark was born at Fowler, Colo., on October 11, 1906.

[1] A communication from M. G. Shaver, Vice-President of The National League Football Club, Inc., Detroit, Mich., April 13, 1939.

Clark, George

George Clark, a coach in national league football, was popularly called *Potsy*[1] by sports writers. This nickname was originated by the foreman of the farm on which Clark was living when he was about six years of age.

George Clark was born at Carthage, Ill., on March 20, 1896.

[1] A communication from Daniel R. Topping, President-Secretary of The Brooklyn National League Football Club, Brooklyn, N.Y., March 20, 1939.

Clark, George Rogers

Brigadier General George Rogers Clark was nicknamed the *Hero of Vincennes*[1] and the *Washington of the West*.[2] Both these names were applied to Clark because of the brilliant leadership he displayed in capturing Vincennes, then Fort Sackville, in what is now Indiana, from the British forces under Colonel Henry Hamilton, on February 25, 1779.

George Rogers Clark was born at Monticello, Va., on November 19, 1752, and died at Louisville, Ky., on February 13, 1818.

[1] *The Hero of Vincennes, the Story of George Rogers Clark*, Lowell Thomas (Houghton Mifflin Company, Boston and New York, 1929), p. 1.
[2] *The Encyclopaedia Britannica*, Fourteenth Edition (Encyclopaedia Britannica, Inc., New York, 1932), vol. 5, p. 764.

Clark, M. Jerome

Sue Mundy was a nickname applied to M. Jerome Clark, a bandit associated with the guerillas under the direction of William Clark Quantrill in the Civil War.

While he was a member of the cavalry of General John M. Morgan, he was crowned Queen of the May in a May Day farce in camp. He was chosen for his girlish face and long curly hair and was nicknamed *Sue Mundy*.[1] He was known by this nickname the rest of his life.

[1] *My Quarter Century of American Politics*, Champ Clark (Harper and Brothers, New York and London, 1920) vol. 1, p. 53.

Clark, Richard

Richard Clark, a South Dakota pioneer, was nicknamed *Deadwood Dick*[1] because during pioneer days he drove a stage coach on a line which terminated at Deadwood, S.D., where he made his headquarters.

Richard Clark was born at Hansborough, England, on December 15, 1845, came to America in 1861, and died at Deadwood, S.D., on May 6, 1930.

[1] *The Washington Post*, Washington, D.C., May 6, 1930, col. 2, p. 1.

Clark, William

William Clark, an Irish prize fighter and swimming instructor, was nicknamed the *Belfast Chicken*[1] because he was a native of Belfast, Ireland, and because he seemed to be a much younger man than he was. Before he came to the United States in 1845, Clark was a prize fighter both in Ireland and in England.

William Clark was born in Belfast, Ireland, in January, 1828.

[1] *The Washington Post*, Washington, D.C., January 26, 1908, Sporting Section, col. 3, p. 3.

Clarke, John

John Clarke has been called the *Father of American Baptists* and the *Father of Rhode Island*.

The nickname, the *Father of American Baptists*,[1] is attributed to him because in 1644 he founded the second Baptist Church in America at Newport, R.I. The First Baptist John Clarke Memorial Church is the oldest orthodox Baptist Church in America. Clarke was pastor of this church much of the time until his death in 1676.

In 1638 John Clarke assisted Roger Williams in establishing a settlement on Acquidneck Island and in 1651 went to England and procured a charter from Charles II for the colony of Rhode Island. This charter gave each person in the colony the right to abide by the dictates of his own conscience in matters pertaining to religious convictions. He took an active part in the

Clarke, John—Continued
civil and ecclesiastical affairs of the colony
of Rhode Island. He was known as the
Father of Rhode Island.[2]

[1] *Appleton's Cyclopaedia of American Biography*, ed.
by James Grant Wilson and John Fiske (D. Appleton
and Company, New York, 1891) vol. 1, p. 634.
[2] *Story of Dr. John Clarke: "His Grand Motive
A Just Liberty to All Men's Spirits in Spiritual Matters";
Roger Williams On Dr. John Clarke: Story of Dr. John
Clarke, the Founder of the First Free Commonwealth of
the World on the Basis of "Full Liberty in Religious
Concernments,"* First Edition, Thomas W. Bicknell,
(Published by the Author, Providence, R.I., 1915),
p. 83.

Clarke, McDonald
The *Mad Poet* and the *Mad Poet of New
York*[1] are nicknames which have been applied to McDonald Clarke because his poems
often displayed erratic flights of imagination
and his style of writing paid little heed to
fixed rules of composition and even went
beyond the freedom in structure allowed by
poetic license. His usually keen mind was
sometimes affected by periods of despond-
ency and marked tendencies toward in-
sanity.

Clarke made his home in New York City
during the greater part of his life. He was
born at Bath, Me., on June 18, 1798, and
died at New York City, on March 5, 1842.

[1] *The National Cyclopaedia of American Biography*
(James T. White and Company, New York, 1929)
vol. 6, p. 406.
Sketch of M'Donald Clarke, "The Mad Poet," Clark
Jillson (Privately printed, Worcester, Mass., 1878) p. 4,
8.

Clarkson, James Sullivan
The Democratic newspapers nicknamed
James Sullivan Clarkson *Headsman Clarkson*[1] because as First Assistant Postmaster
General from 1889 to 1890, in twenty
months under President Benjamin Harrison,
he removed 32,335 Democratic appointees
from fourth class Post Office positions.

James Sullivan Clarkson was born at
Brookville, Ind., on May 17, 1842, and
died at Newark, N.J., on May 31, 1918.

[1] *U.S. "Snap Shots": An Independent, National, and
Memorial Encyclopedia . . .*, Oliver McKee (A. M.
Thayer and Company, Boston, 1892), p. 242.
The Republican Party: A History, William Starr
Myers (The Century Company, New York and London,
1928) p. 306.

Classic City. See Boston, Mass.

Clay, Cassius Marcellus, Senior
Cassius Marcellus Clay, Senior, who was
born in Madison County, Ky., on October
19, 1810, and who died there on July 21,

1903, has been designated the *Kentucky
Duel Fighter*[1] because he fought a number
of duels to settle his difficulties.

[1] *A Book of Nicknames*, John Goff (Courier-Journal
Job Printing Company, Louisville, Ky., 1892) p. 22.

Clay, Henry
The following are nicknames which have
been given to Henry Clay: the *Father of
the National Road*, the *Father of the Protective Policy*, the *Great Commoner*, the
Great Compromiser, the *Great Pacificator*,
the *Mill Boy of the Slashes*, the *President
Maker*, the *Sage of Ashland*, and the *Same
Old Coon*.

In 1825 Henry Clay urgently advocated
that the national road, which extended from
the point where navigation ceased to be
possible on the Potomac River in Maryland,
to Wheeling, Ohio, on the Ohio River, be
extended with government funds through
the states of Ohio, Indiana, and Illinois as
far as the Mississippi River. Because of his
interest in this undertaking, Clay has been
called the *Father of the National Road*.[1]

The *Father of the Protective Policy*[2] was
applied to him because he was the outstanding advocate of the first protective
tariff bill passed by Congress in 1816. As a
representative of the agricultural state of
Kentucky, Clay recognized the value of improved nation-wide transportation facilities
to stimulate the flow of farm products to
manufacturing centers and vice versa. This
question, coupled with the protective tariff
issue, was Clay's "American System."

The *Great Commoner*,[3] one of the most
popular of the nicknames by which Henry
Clay is designated, refers to the zeal with
which he championed the cause of the common people in opposing the Sedition Laws,
passed about 1798-99.

His personal influence and political prominence in bringing about compromises such
as the Missouri Compromise of 1820, the
compromise on tariff in 1833, and the group
of acts known collectively as the Compromise of 1850, won for him the nicknames, the *Great Compromiser*,[4] and the
Great Pacificator.[3]

Henry Clay grew up in Virginia in a district known as the Slashes. He often took
grain to the mill to be ground. During his
campaign for the presidency in 1824, the
Mill Boy of the Slashes[5] was one of the
nicknames used. In this election no candidate received a majority of the electoral

votes. Clay, running fourth, gave his support to elect John Quincy Adams and became known as the *President Maker*.[6]

Later the nickname, the *Sage of Ashland*,[7] was applied to Henry Clay because he made his home at Ashland, near Lexington, Ky.

During the presidential campaign of 1840, when William Henry Harrison was the Whig candidate, the coon became the emblem of the Whig Party. The Democrats attempted to use against Harrison the fact that he had lived in a log cabin which had a coon skin stretched on the door to dry. The Whigs adopted the log cabin and the coon as emblems of their party.

When Henry Clay ran for the presidency again in 1844, his political opponents spoke of him as forever hunting after "that same old coon," and the Whigs carried cartoons and banners depicting coons with the head and face of Clay, labeled the *Same Old Coon*.[7]

Henry Clay was born at Ashland, Va., on April 12, 1777, and died at Washington, D.C., on June 29, 1852.

See also *Great Triumvirate*.

[1] *The Leading Facts of American History*, Revised Edition, D. H. Montgomery (Ginn and Company, New York and Boston, 1910) p. 216.
[2] *American History and Government, a Text-book on the History and Civil Government of the United States*, James Albert Woodburn and Thomas Francis Moran (Longmans, Green and Company, New York, 1908) p. 279.
[3] *Life of Henry Clay: The Life and Public Services of Henry Clay, Down to 1848*, Epes Sargeant, ed. and completed at Mr. Clay's death by Horace Greeley (Porter and Coates, Philadelphia, 1852) p. 22, 94, 354-5.
"Henry Clay" by Carl Schurz, in *American Statesmen*, ed. by John T. Morse, Junior (Houghton Mifflin Company, New York and Boston, 1899) vol. 1, p. 178, 194.
[4] "Life of Henry Clay" by Carl Schurz, in *American Statesmen*, ed. by John T. Morse, Junior (Houghton Mifflin and Company, New York and Boston, 1887) vol. 1, p. 4, vol. 2, p. 329.
A Book of Nicknames, John Goff (Courier-Journal Job Printing Company, Louisville, Ky., 1892) p. 22.
[5] *The Life and Speeches of the Honorable Henry Clay*, Sixth Edition, comp. and ed. by Daniel Mallory (Van Amringe and Bixby, New York, 1844) vol. 1, p. 10.
[6] *The New International Encyclopaedia*, Second Edition (Dodd, Mead and Company, New York, 1930) vol. 5, p. 429.
[7] *Stephen A. Douglas: His Life, Public Services, Speeches, and Patriotism*, Clark E. Carr (A. C. McClurg and Company, Chicago, 1909) p. 38, 194.
The Life of Horace Greeley, Founder of the New York Tribune, with Extended Notices of Many of His Contemporary Statesmen and Journalists, L. D. Ingersoll, (Union Publishing Company, New York and Chicago, 1873) p. 164.
The True Henry Clay, Joseph M. Rogers (J. B. Lippincott Company, Philadelphia, 1904) p. 195.
Henry Clay by his grandson, Thomas Hart Clay, completed by Ellis Paxson Oberholtzer (George W. Jacobs and Company, Philadelphia, 1910) p. 83, 173, 229.

Claybanks

When Missouri was admitted to the Union in 1821, slavery was a vital issue. The nickname *Claybanks*[1] was applied to those Republicans, Democrats, and Semi-Unionists who favored the continuation of slavery because of the variegated complexion of the political mixture.

[1] *The Abolitionists Together with Personal Memories of the Struggle for Human Rights, 1830-1884*, John F. Hume (G. P. Putnam's Sons, New York and London, 1905) p. 159.

Clay-eaters. See South Carolinians

Clay's Rags

In January 1832, Henry Clay introduced a bill in the United States Senate to renew the charter of the Bank of the United States, thus advocating the circulation of bank notes. In the presidential campaign that year, the political opponents referred to the notes of the Bank of the United States as *Clay's Rags*,[1] implying that they were worthless.

[1] *Andrew Jackson, the Fighting President*, Helen Nicolay (The Century Company, New York, 1929) p. 303.

Cleaveland, Parker

Because Parker Cleaveland was a pioneer worker in American mineralogy, he has been called the *Father of American Mineralogy*.[1] He was recognized internationally as an authority on this branch of science. Cleaveland gave lectures and wrote on mineralogy and geology which stimulated widespread interest in these subjects.

Parker Cleaveland was born at Rowley, Mass., on January 15, 1780, and died at Brunswick, Me., on October 15, 1858.

[1] *The National Cyclopaedia of America Biography* (James T. White and Company, New York, 1906) vol. 13, p. 56.
America: An Encyclopedia of Its History and Biography, Arranged in Chronological Paragraphs, with Full Accounts of Prehistoric America and the Indians, and Notes on Contemporaneous History . . . in the Discovery and Development of North and South America, with Biographies of the Leaders Thereof, Stephen Morrell Newman (The Coburn and Newman Publishing Company, Chicago, 1881) p. 531.

Clemens, Samuel Langhorne

Samuel Langhorne Clemens, better known by his pen name *Mark Twain*, was called the *Prince of Humorists*[1] because he was an outstanding humorous writer in American literature, and because his writings are so widely read.

Samuel Langhorne Clemens was born at Florida, Mo., on November 30, 1835, and died at Redding, Conn., on April 21, 1910.

[1] *Compton's Pictured Encyclopedia* (F. E. Compton and Company, Chicago, 1931) vol. 1, p. 115.

Cleveland, Benjamin

The *Hero of King's Mountain* and *Old Round About* are nicknames by which Colonel Benjamin Cleveland has often been designated.

The *Hero of King's Mountain* [1] has been applied to Colonel Cleveland in commemoration of the conspicuous services he rendered at the Battle of King's Mountain, in North Carolina, on October 7, 1780. Cleveland's regiment of volunteer riflemen were popularly acclaimed *Cleveland's Heroes* [2] and *Cleveland's Bulldogs* because of their heroic fighting. The Tories called these men *Cleveland's Devils*.

Colonel Cleveland was popularly called *Old Round About* [1] because the place at which he lived was named Old Round About, and probably also in allusion to his pronounced roundness, his weight in his elderly years being well over four hundred pounds.

Colonel Benjamin Cleveland was born at Bull Run, Va., on March 26, 1738, and died in Tugalo Valley, Oconee County, S.C., in October, 1806.

[1] *The National Cyclopaedia of American Biography* (James T. White and Company, New York, 1898) vol. 1, p. 508.

King's Mountain and Its Heroes: History of the Battle of King's Mountain, October 7, 1780, and the Events Which Led to It, Lyman C. Draper (Peter G. Thomson, Cincinnati, 1881) p. 246-55, 285-8.

[2] *The National Cyclopaedia of American Biography* (James T. White and Company, New York, 1898) vol. 1, p. 508.

Commanders at King's Mountain, James D. Bailey (Edward H. Decamp, Gaffney, S.C., 1926) p. 163, 167.

Cleveland, Grover

The *Buffalo Hangman*, the *Hangman of Buffalo*, the *Buffalo Sheriff*, the *Claimant*, the *Dumb Prophet, Old Grover, Our Grover, His Accidency, Man of Destiny*, the *People's President*, the *Perpetual Candidate*, the *Pretender*, the *Reform Governor*, the *Sage of Princeton*, the *Stuffed Prophet, Uncle Jumbo*, the *Veto Governor*, the *Veto Mayor, Old Veto* are nicknames which have been attributed to Grover Cleveland.

The *Buffalo Hangman*,[1] and the *Hangman of Buffalo*,[2] and the *Buffalo Sheriff* [2] were applied to Grover Cleveland by the Republicans during the bitter presidential campaign of 1884, when he was the Democratic candidate. These nicknames alluded to the fact that while Cleveland was sheriff of Erie County, N.Y., with his office at Buffalo, he was required to hang a man convicted of murder.

Because Grover Cleveland advocated high ideals and standards, he was accused of being insincere; therefore, he was called, the *Claimant*,[1] and the *Pretender*.[1]

The *Dumb prophet* [1] was applied to him because he refused to express himself publicly on some question.

Grover Cleveland was popularly known as *Old Grover* and *Our Grover* [1] to his numerous friends.

His Accidency [8] is a nickname which was sometimes given to Cleveland because his election to the presidency of the United States in 1884 was unexpected for he had not been a man widely known to the public, and his Republican rival, James Gillespie Blaine, was the favored candidate.

The Man of Destiny [7] was considered an appropriate sobriquet for Grover Cleveland because of his remarkable rise from comparative obscurity to power and influence in the political world despite his policy of placing duty, loyalty, and even devotion to country above that of political or partisan obligations.

Because he advocated those policies which best served the needs and the interests of the people as an entirety, Cleveland was known as the *People's President*.[4]

He was nicknamed *The Perpetual Candidate* [5] because he ran for president in 1880, 1884, 1888 and again in 1892.

Because of the fact that Cleveland inaugurated a number of needed improvements in the managing of public affairs and public property while he was Governor of the State of New York from 1883 to 1885, he became widely known as the *Reform Governor*.[6]

At the close of his last term as the President of the United States in 1897, Grover Cleveland retired to Princeton, N.J., and became known as *The Sage of Princeton*.[7]

In 1907, when it was proposed that the plaza on the Manhattan bridge be named Cleveland Square in honor of Grover Cleveland, who had just celebrated his seventieth birthday, an alderman stated that he did not care to perpetuate the name of Cleveland, calling him the Democratic party's *Stuffed Prophet*.[7] Tammany Hall never forgave Cleveland for the fact that he had refused to be domineered by them during his political life. The *Stuffed Prophet* was afterwards applied to him by his political enemies.

Cleveland was sometimes jestingly called *Uncle Jumbo* [8] by the members of his family in allusion to his corpulence.

While serving as Governor of the State of New York from 1883 until he resigned in 1885 to become the President of the United States, Cleveland was often called the *Veto Governor,* [1] or *Old Veto,* because he vetoed bills passed by the legislature that he considered unconstitutional or harmful to the best interests of the people.

In 1882 soon after he was elected Mayor of Buffalo, N.Y., Cleveland was nicknamed the *Veto Mayer* [3] because he ruthlessly vetoed measures passed by the politicians influenced by personal or by party claims. By his wise use of the veto power, he saved the city of Buffalo a million dollars in public expenditures by preventing the passage of fraudulent schemes. He earned the gratitude of the people irrespective of party affiliations.

Grover Cleveland was born at Caldwell, N.J., on March 18, 1837, and died at Princeton, N.J., on June 24, 1908, was President of the United States from 1885 to 1889, and again from 1893 to 1897.

[1] *U.S. "Snap Shots": An Independent, National, and Memorial Encyclopedia . . . ,* Oliver McKee (A. M. Thayer and Company, Boston, 1892) p. 314, 511.

[2] "Grover Cleveland," by Clifford Smyth, in *Builders of America* (Funk and Wagnalls Company, New York and London, 1931) vol. 22, p. 36, 38, 52, 54-5.

[3] *Grover Cleveland, the Man and the Statesman,* First Edition, Robert McElroy (Harper and Brothers, New York and London, 1923) vol. 1, p. 95.

Pen Pictures of the Presidents, Fred T. Wilson (Southwestern Company, Nashville, Tenn., 1932) p. 358, 359, 360, 364-5.

[4] *History of the United States for Schools,* Hubert R. Cornish and Thomas H. Hughes (Hinds, Hayden and Eldredge, Inc., New York and Chicago, 1929) p. 455.

[5] *Twenty Years of the Republic, 1885-1905,* Harry Thurston Peck (Dodd, Mead and Company, New York, 1907) p. 264.

[6] *Contemporary American Biography: Biographical Sketches of Representative Men of the Day; Representatives of Modern Thought and Progress of the Pulpit, the Press, the Bench and Bar, of Legislation, Invention, and the Great Industrial Interests of the Country* (Atlantic Publishing and Engraving Company, New York, 1895) vol. 1, p. 160.

[7] *Grover Cleveland, a Man Four-square,* Denis Tilden Lynch (Horace Liveright, Inc., New York, 1932) p. 64, 367, 538.

[8] *Grover Cleveland, a Study in Courage,* Allan Nevins (Dodd, Mead and Company, New York, 1932) p. 66.

Cleveland, Ohio

Cleveland is nicknamed the *Forest City* [1] because of the great number of shade trees growing throughout the city.

[1] *All About Cleveland: A City Cyclopedia: The Cleveland Cicerone,* Charles Orr, Editor (The Whitworth Brothers Company, Cleveland, Ohio, 1908) p. 29.

Centennial History of Cleveland, C. A. Urann (Press of J. B. Savage, Cleveland, Ohio, 1896) p. 120.

Cleveland American League Baseball Company

The *Cleveland Indians* [1] is a nickname given the Cleveland American League Baseball Company in 1916 by James C. Dunn who was the president of the club at that time, in honor of Sax Elexis, [2] a full blooded Indian who played on the team.

[1] A letter from W. M. McNichols, Business Manager of The Cleveland American League Baseball Company, Cleveland, Ohio, June 21, 1935.

[2] Interview with Clark C. Griffith, President of the Washington Nationals, Washington, D.C., on July 29, 1935.

Cleveland Indians. See Cleveland American League Baseball Company

Cleveland Rams. See Cleveland Rams Football Club, Inc.

Cleveland Rams Football Club, Incorporated

The *Cleveland Rams* [1] is the name commonly applied to the teams of the Cleveland Rams Football Club, Inc., a member of the National Football League, located at Cleveland, Ohio.

[1] A communication from Thomas E. Lipscomb, President of The Cleveland Rams Football Club, Inc., Cleveland, Ohio, March 21, 1939.

Cleveland's Bulldogs

The soldiers who fought under Colonel Benjamin Cleveland in the Battle of King's Mountain, in North Carolina, on October 7, 1780, have been termed *Cleveland's Bulldogs* [1] because of the tenacity which characterized their fighting. The Tories called them *Cleveland's Devils* [1] and they were also known as *Cleveland's Heroes* [1] because of their heroic fighting spirit.

See Cleveland, Benjamin.

[1] *The National Cyclopaedia of American Biography* (James T. White and Company, New York, 1898) vol. 1, p. 508.

Cleveland's Devils. See *Cleveland's Bulldogs*

Cleveland's Heroes. See *Cleveland's Bulldogs*

Clevemen. See Concordia College

Cliff-dwellers. See University of Portland

Clifton, Herman E.

Herman E. Clifton was nicknamed *Flea* [1] in 1932 because as infielder of the Texas League Baseball Club at Beaumont, Tex., he moved about with the agility of a flea.

Herman E. Clifton was born at Cincinnati, Ohio, on December 12, 1910, and was employed as utility infielder by the American League Baseball Company at Detroit, Mich., in 1934.

[1] *Who's Who in the Major Leagues,* Nineteen-hundred-thirty-five Edition, Harold (Speed) Johnson (B. E. Callahan, Chicago, 1935) p. 18.

Clinch, Joseph

Joseph Clinch became known as the *Terror of the Tories* [1] while he was serving as a first lieutenant in the Revolutionary Army. His zeal in fighting gave rise to the nickname.

He at one time lived at Ard-Lamont, N.C.

[1] *The National Cyclopaedia of American Biography* (James T. White and Company, New York, 1904) vol. 12, p. 63.

Clinton, George

The nickname, the *Father of the Barge Canal* [1] has been given to George Clinton because late in the nineteenth century he was a pioneer in securing the construction of a canal in New York State large enough for the accommodation of modern barges.

George Clinton was born at Buffalo, N.Y., on September 7, 1846, and practiced law at Buffalo for more than fifty years. He served on a number of committees to investigate the proper apportioning of funds for inland waterways in New York State. He was a member of the International Waterways Commission from 1903 until 1913.

[1] *De Witt Clinton,* Dorothie Bobbé (Minton, Balch and Company, New York, 1933) p. 297.

Clinton's Big Ditch. See *Clinton's Ditch*

Clinton's Ditch

About 1815, those who doubted the possibility or the probability of building the canal from Lake Erie and Lake Champlain to the Hudson river called the embryonic enterprise *Clinton's Ditch,* [1] or *Clinton's Big Ditch,* because a prominent New York legislator and governor of New York from 1820 to 1823, De Witt Clinton, advocated the construction of such a canal.

[1] *De Witt Clinton,* Dorothie Bobbé (Minton, Balch and Company, New York, 1933) p. 171, 184, 211, 280. *American Achievements,* Library Edition, Elisha Jay Edwards, "Holland," completed and published by Miriam Hewitt Hall (New York and London Press Association, Inc., New York, 1926) vol. 1, p. 95.

Clodknockers

About 1890, in Laurens County, South Carolina, a political group of reformers who taught agrarianism nicknamed the farm laborers who had only their labor to sell the *Clodknockers* [1] because their labor consisted chiefly of cultivating the soil.

[1] *The State That Forgot: South Carolina's Surrender to Democracy,* William Watts Ball (The Bobbs-Merrill Company, Indianapolis, Ind., 1932) p. 207.

Cluett, Ernest Harold

Ernest Harold Cluett, a New York manufacturer and politician, was nicknamed *Collars and Cuffs* [1] in the House of Representatives because he had formerly been the treasurer of Cluett, Peabody, and Company, Inc., at Troy, N.Y., one of the largest collar and cuff manufacturers in the world. He was a Republican Representative from New York State to Congress in 1937.

Ernest Harold Cluett was born at Troy, N.Y., on July 13, 1874.

[1] An interview with Captain Victor Hunt Harding, Secretary of the National Democratic Congress Reëlection Committee, Washington, D.C., April 10, 1939.

Coal State. See Pennsylvania

Cobb, Tyrus Raymond

Ty, the *Georgia Peach,* and the *Idol of Baseball Fandom* are nicknames which have been applied to Tyrus Raymond Cobb.

Because he is a native of the state of Georgia, Cobb became known as the *Georgia Peach.* [1] He is also popularly designated the *Idol of Baseball Fandom* [1] because his record during his twenty-four years as a professional baseball player led all others in hitting, base-stealing, run making, and all-round dynamic playing. The record of his brilliant career continues to excite admiration.

Tyrus Raymond Cobb, was born at Narrows, Banks County, Georgia, on December 18, 1886.

[1] *Who's Who in Major League Base Ball,* comp. by Harold (Speed) Johnson (Buxton Publishing Company, Chicago, 1933) p. 456.

Cobbers. See Concordia College

Cobbler. See Wilson, Henry

Cobwallis. See Cornwallis, Charles

Cochrane, Clark Betton

The sobriquet, *The Great Pacificator*,[2] was given to Clark Betton Cochrane by his associates in the New York State Legislature because he was unusually successful in pacifying or reconciling those who became engaged in violent debates upon the floor of the House.

Clark Betton Cochrane was born in 1817 and died in 1867.

[1] *Appleton's Cyclopaedia of American Biography*, ed. by James Grant Wilson and John Fiske (D. Appleton and Company, New York, 1891) vol. 1, p. 671.
Memorial of Clark B. Cochrane (Joel Munsell, Albany, N.Y., 1867) p. 13.

Cochrane, Gordon Stanley

Gordon Stanley Cochrane is familiarly known by the nickname *Mickey*,[1] probably in allusion to his Scotch-Irish descent. Mick or Mickey is often used as a nickname for any Irishman.

Cochrane, who was born at Bridgewater, Mass., on April 6, 1903, is now a manager in major league baseball.

[1] *Who's Who in Major League Base Ball*, comp. by Harold (Speed) Johnson (Buxton Publishing Company, Chicago, 1933) p. 113.

Cockade City. See Petersburg, Va.; Richmond, Va.

Cockade State. See Maryland

Cockle-bur Bill. See Murray, W. H.

Cohees. See Pennsylvanians

Cody, William Frederick

Following is a list of the sobriquets which have been applied to William Frederick Cody: *Bill Cody the Scout; Bill Cody the Wagonmaster; Buffalo Bill; the Champion Buffalo Hunter of the Plains; the Last of the Great Scouts; Little Billy Cody the Messenger; Pahaska, or Pa-he-haska;* and *Wild Bill the Pony Express Rider.*

William Frederick Cody was called *Bill Cody the Scout* [1] because he frequently served in the capacity of a scout while a member of the Seventh Regiment of Kansas Cavalry Volunteers for the United States Army; and a scout in the Army from 1868 to 1872, during which time he was appointed Chief of the Scouts at Fort Hays by General Philip H. Sheridan.

The nickname, *Bill Cody the Wagonmaster*,[2] originated in the fact that Cody had been assistant wagonmaster to Buck Bomer in 1858; and, while acting as Chief of Scouts, it is probable that he was in charge of some of the wagon trains which were numerous about this time in the West.

The particular incident which brought into wide prominence the sobriquet, *Buffalo Bill*,[3] took place one day when officers from Fort Hays, Kansas, asked Cody to join them in a buffalo hunt. Riding bare-back, Cody shot down eleven buffaloes with a dozen shots before the astonished officers had fired even one shot.

William Frederick Cody and William Comstock were so widely known as expert buffalo hunters that each of them was pronounced the champion of that sport. At Fort Wallace, Kans., where William Comstock was Chief of the United States Scouts, post guide and interpreter his officers believed that he was a better buffalo hunter than Cody, and arranged to hold a contest between the two on the prairies east of Sheridan, Kans. Vast crowds assembled for the occasion. Referees were appointed to trail Comstock and Cody from eight o'clock in the morning until four o'clock in the afternoon to keep count of the buffaloes killed. When the referees totaled their counts, Cody had killed sixty-nine and Comstock forty-six. They, therefore, declared William F. Cody the winner of the five hundred dollar wager and of the championship; consequently, he became known as *The Champion Buffalo Hunter of the Plains.*[3]

Colonel Cody played a prominent role in the capacity of scout, hunter, and Indian fighter from 1861 to 1888, during the period of frontier life in the prairie sections of the Far West; and because he was the last of the outstanding men in this part of the country to engage in these activities he came to be known as *The Last of the Great Scouts.*[4]

The sobriquet, *Little Billy Cody the Messenger*,[3] was attributed to Cody when he was about twelve or fourteen years of age. Cody was riding as a messenger in the

Cody, W. F.—Continued

service of the wagon trains of Russell, Majors, and Waddell, traversing the great stretches of wilderness between the Missouri river and the western coast. These were composed of from twenty-five to fifty enormous wagons accompanied by a large number of mounted men. The prairie schooners often became separated by many miles and messengers were employed to deliver dispatches from one wagon train to another.

Yellow Hand, a chief of the Cheyenne Indians, nicknamed Colonel Cody *Pahaska,*[3] or *Pa-he-haska,*[5] because of the heavy mass of lustrous brown hair which Cody wore long as was the custom of scouts on the western plains, the Indian word *Pahaska,* or *Pa-he-haska,* signifying *long hair.*[6]

William Frederick Cody was nicknamed *Wild Bill the Pony Express Rider* [3] because, as a lad of fourteen or fifteen he was one of the most daring but trustworthy riders of the pony express, which carried messages, mail, and small packages from St. Joseph, Mo., to San Francisco, Calif.

[1] *The Adventures of Buffalo Bill,* Colonel William F. Cody (Buffalo Bill) (Harper and Brothers, New York, 1904) p. 137-40.

The Encyclopaedia Britannica, Fourteenth Edition (Encyclopaedia Britannica, Inc., New York, 1929) vol. 5, p. 960.

[2] *Seventy Years on the Frontier: Alexander Majors' Memoirs of a Lifetime on the Border with a Preface by Buffalo Bill (General W. F. Cody)* ed. by Colonel Prentiss Ingraham (Rand, McNally and Company, New York and Chicago, 1893) p. 243, 244.

The Great Salt Lake Trail, by Henry Inman and William F. Cody (The Macmillan Company, New York, 1898) p. 399.

[3] *Last of the Great Scouts: The Life Story of Colonel William F. Cody (Buffalo Bill),* Helen Cody Wetmore (The Duluth Press Printing Company, Duluth, Minn., 1899) p. 135, 138, 265.

Buffalo Bill's Own Story of His Life and Deeds, Memorial Edition (Homewood Press, Chicago, 1917) p. 107, 115, 342

The Making of Buffalo Bill; A Study in Heroics, Richard J. Walsh in collaboration with Milton S. Salsbury (The Bobbs-Merrill Company, Indianapolis, Ind., 1928) p. 67, 117-18, 191.

The Encyclopedia Americana (Americana Corporation, New York, 1932) vol. 7, p. 198.

The New International Encyclopaedia, Second Edition (Dodd, Mead and Company, New York, 1917) vol. 5, p. 544.

[5] *Boys' Book of Frontier Fighters,* Edwin L. Sabin (George W. Jacobs and Company, Philadelphia, 1919) p. 351.

[6] *Buffalo Bill as I knew Him,* Frank Winch (Tiffin Press, Inc., Tiffin, Ohio, 1928) p. 4.

Coe College

The appellation, *The Kohawks,*[1] is the nickname given the teams of Coe College, at Cedar Rapids, Iowa, by Professor C. W.

Perkins in 1922. It is a combination of the name of the college and a part of the state nickname of Iowa, *Hawkeye.*

[1] A communication from Moray L. Eby, Director of Athletics at Coe College, Cedar Rapids, Iowa, June 13, 1935.

Coffee-boilers

After President Grover Cleveland vetoed the Dependent Pension Bill on February 11, 1887, which would have granted a pension of twelve dollars monthly to every honorably discharged veteran of the Civil War, there was a great deal of criticism directed against his action. The veterans who wanted the pension were called *Coffee-boilers* [1] by those who favored the President's action in the matter. The term *Coffee-boiler* originated during the Civil War when the nickname was applied to Union soldiers who, because they were only half hearted about fighting, would straggle behind the regular army, stopping to boil coffee. They did this so that the enemy could easily capture and imprison them, thus preventing them from having to engage in additional battles.

See also Blackberry Pickers

[1] *Twenty Years of the Republic, 1885-1905,* Harry Thurston Peck (Dodd, Mead and Company, New York, 1907) p. 144.

[2] *Andersonville: A Story of Rebel Military Prisons, Fifteen Months a Guest of the So-called Southern Confederacy; a Private Soldier's Experience in Richmond, Andersonville, Savannah, Blackshear, and Florence,* John McElroy (D. R. Locke, Toledo, Ohio, 1879) p. 427.

Coin Harvey. See Harvey, W. H.

Coiner of Weasel Words. See Wilson, Woodrow

Cold Spring Harbor, New York

Early in the nineteenth century, the western section of Cold Spring Harbor, N.Y., was the site of many cooper shops which made casks and barrels. This side of the town was popularly called *Bungtown,*[1] a nickname which clung to it long after the business declined. A bung is a stopper for a cask or barrel.

[1] *Long Island's Story,* Jacqueline Overton (Doubleday, Doran and Company, Garden City, N.Y., 1929) p. 220.

Cold Water Administration

The administration of Rutherford Birchard Hayes as President of the United States from 1877 to 1881 has been called the *Cold Water Administration,*[1] because refreshments served at the White House social functions during President Hayes' administration were non-intoxicating.

[1] *Autobiographed Portraits, Collection of Joseph G. Butler, Junior* (The Butler Art Institute, Publishers, The Vindicator Printing Company, Youngstown, Ohio, 1927) p. 416.

Cole, Ambrose N.

Ambrose N. Cole was nicknamed *Father Cole* and the *Father of the Republican Party*.

At Friendship, in Alleghany County, N.Y., on May 16, 1854, Cole was the chief instigator of the caucus of antislavery men who organized a party and named it the Republican party at the suggestion of Horace Greeley. Because of this he was designated the *Father of the Republican Party*,[1] and *Father Cole*.

The origin of the present Republican party is not clear, some claiming it was founded at Ripon, Wis., others at Jackson, Mich., and still others at Friendship, N.Y.

[1] *The National Cyclopaedia of American Biography* (James T. White and Company, New York, 1899) vol. 2, p. 446.
The Republican Party: A History of Its Fifty Years' Existence and a Record of its Measures and Leaders, 1854-1904, Francis Curtis (G. P. Putnam's Sons, New York, 1904) vol. 1, p. 1-2, 202-3.
The Republican Party: A History, William Starr Myers (The Century Company, New York, 1928) p. 56.
A History of the Republican Party, George W. Platt (C. J. Krehbiel and Company, Cincinnati, Ohio, 1904) p. 74-81.

Coleman, Leighton

Leighton Coleman, an Episcopal bishop, was nicknamed *Santa Claus*[1] by the children of Wilmington, Del. He was a genial, lovable old gentleman with a long white beard, and was very friendly both to children and to grown people.

Leighton Coleman was born at Philadelphia, Pa., on May 3, 1837, and died at Wilmington, Del., on December 14, 1907.

[1] *Dictionary of American Biography under the Auspices of the American Council of Learned Societies,* ed. by Allen Johnson and Dumas Malone (Charles Scribner's Sons, New York, 1930) vol. 4, p. 293.

Colgate University

The *Little Giants of Chenango,* the *Mad Magicians,* the *Maroons,* and the *Red Raiders* are the nicknames which have been given to the athletes of Colgate University, at Hamilton, N.Y. They were designated the *Little Giants of Chenango*[1] because most of them in the early days came from the Chenango Valley in New York. The *Mad Magicians* was applied to them because of the extensive use of the lateral pass which was a comparatively new play then. These teams have never been officially designated *The Maroons,*[1] but sports writers have so called them because the university colors are maroon and white. The *Red Raiders*[1] is the nickname by which the Colgate athletes prefer to be known.

[1] A letter from William A. Reid, Graduate Manager of Athletics at Colgate University, Hamilton, N.Y., June 11, 1935.

Collar Capital of the World. See Troy, N.Y.

Collars and Cuffs. See Cluett, E. H.

College of the City of New York

The athletic teams of the College of the City of New York, at New York City, are popularly known as the *Saint Nicks*[1] and the *Beavers.* The former nickname was given them about 1907 because the college is located on St. Nicholas Terrace. The *Beavers* was chosen by a vote of the student body in 1934.

[1] A communication from Irving Rosenthal, Director of Publicity at the College of the City of New York, New York City, June 7, 1935.

College of Emporia

The *Fighting Presbyterians* is the nickname applied to the athletic teams of the College of Emporia, at Emporia, Kans., because it is a Presbyterian college.

College of the Holy Cross

The athletic teams of the College of the Holy Cross, at Worcester, Mass., were called *Crusaders*[1] about 1925 by a vote of the student body because of the obvious connection between the Holy Cross and Crusades.

[1] A communication from the Secretary of the Athletic Association at the College of the Holy Cross, Worcester, Mass., June 13, 1935.

College of the Ozarks

The *Mountaineers*[1] was chosen by a vote of the students and teachers to designate the athletic teams of the College of the Ozarks, at Clarksville, Ark., because the college is located in the Ozark Mountains.

[1] A letter from Wiley Lin Hurie, President of the College of the Ozarks, Clarksville, Ark., August 12, 1935.

College of Paterson

In 1934 the members of the athletic teams of the College of Paterson, at Paterson, N.J., were nicknamed *The Cops*[1] by a sports

College of Paterson—Continued
writer who simply used the initials of the college, COP.

[1] A letter from Herbert Spencer Robinson, President of the College of Paterson, N.J., November 25, 1935.

College of Puget Sound
The athletic teams of the College of Puget Sound, at Tacoma, Wash., were called the *Loggers* [1] because lumbering is the chief industry in Tacoma. The name was chosen by the students.

[1] A letter from Edward H. Todd, President of the College of Puget Sound, Tacoma, Wash., June 25, 1935.

College of Saint Thomas
The athletic teams of the College of Saint Thomas, at St. Paul, Minn., are popularly called the *Cadets* [1] because the school was at one time a military college.

[1] A communication from J. M. Boland, Director of Athletics at the College of Saint Thomas, St. Paul, Minn., June 11, 1935.

College of William and Mary
The Indians and *The Looneys* [1] are nicknames given to the athletic teams of the College of William and Mary, at Williamsburg, Va. The *Indians* was given them because Brafferton School for Indians, the first Indian school in America, was situated on the present campus of William and Mary. Prior to 1912 the teams were called *Looneys* because the Eastern State Hospital for the Insane is located at Williamsburg.

[1] A letter from William S. Gooch, Junior, Manager of Athletics at the College of William and Mary, Williamsburg, Va., June 19, 1935.

College of Wooster
The *Scots* [1] is the nickname given to the athletic teams of the College of Wooster, at Wooster, Ohio, in 1932 by a vote of the student body because it is a Scotch Presbyterian college.

[1] A communication from Arthur Murray, Director of the Wooster News Service, College of Wooster, Wooster, Ohio, November 18, 1935.

College Puritan. See Sherman, John (Clergyman)

Collins, James Anthony
Ripper [4] is the familiar nickname of James Anthony Collins, given him because of his great ability to play baseball. *Ripper* is American slang for great or wonderful.

James Anthony Collins was born at Altoona, Pa., on March 30, 1905, and played first baseman in major league baseball.

[1] *Who's Who in Major League Base Ball,* comp. by Harold (Speed) Johnson (Buxton Publishing Company, Chicago, 1933) p. 116.
[2] *The Century Dictionary and Cyclopedia* (The Century Company, New York, 1906) vol. 6, p. 5191.

Collins, Phil Eugene
Phil Eugene Collins, who was born at Chicago, Ill., on August 27, 1903, and who pitched in major league baseball, is nicknamed *Fidgety* [1] because he was so fidgety while pitching.

[1] *Who's Who in Major League Base Ball,* comp. by Harold (Speed) Johnson (Buxton Publishing Company, Chicago, 1933) p. 117.

Colonel. See Fickinger, J. A.; Meek, J. L.; Ruppert, Jacob, Sr.

Colonel Jack. See Krohn, J. A.

Colonels. See Centre College of Kentucky

Colonial Wallis. See Wallis, F. E.

Coloradans
The people of Colorado are sometimes designated *Silverines, Rovers,* and *Centennials.* [1] The first nickname alludes to the great silver mines in the state, from which many amassed fortunes. The second commemorates the roving disposition of the settlers at the time of the Pike's Peak gold fever. The inhabitants of Colorado are named *Centennials* because the state was admitted to the Union in 1876.

[1] *U.S.: An index to the United States of America,* comp. by Malcolm Townsend (D. Lothrop Company, Boston, 1890) p. 75.

Colorado
Colorado is known by seven nicknames: the *Buffalo Plains State,* the *Centennial State,* the *Lead State,* the *Mountain State,* the *Silver State,* the *Switzerland of America,* and the *Treasure State of the Rockies.*

Colorado was formerly known as the *Buffalo Plains State,* [1] but since the buffalo has disappeared this is now seldom used.

It was called the *Centennial State* [2] because it was admitted to the Union on August 1, 1876, one hundred years after the Declaration of Independence was signed. Colorado is designated the *Lead State,* because of the large quantity of lead mined there. The output reached its peak during World War I.

Colorado is now seldom spoken of as the *Silver State*,[3] but it was given that name at the time of the great silver agitation during the 1890's.

The *Switzerland of America* and the *Mountain State* are attributed to Colorado because of its magnificent natural beauty. It contains some of the most spectacular mountain scenery in the western part of the United States.

Colorado is called the *Treasure State of the Rockies*[4] because it is located in the Rocky Mountain regions and because of its gold, silver, and other mineral products.

[1] *More About Names,* Leopold Wagner (T. Fisher Unwin, London, 1893) p. 34.
[2] *U.S.: An Index to the United States of America,* comp. by Malcolm Townsend (D. Lothrop Company, Boston, 1890) p. 66.
[3] *The New International Encyclopaedia,* Second Edition (Dodd, Mead and Company, New York, 1930) vol. 5, p. 612.
A letter from Albert R. Sanford, Assistant Curator of History, State Historical Society, State Museum, Denver, Colo., March 24, 1930.
The Making of Colorado: A Historical Sketch, Eugene Parsons (A. Flanagan Company, Chicago, 1908) p. 6.
[4] *Compton's Pictured Encyclopedia* (F. E. Compton and Company, Chicago, 1931) vol. 3, p. 839.

Colorado School of Mines
The athletic teams of the Colorado School of Mines, at Golden, Colo., are called *Miners* and *Orediggers* because this school teaches the science of mining.

Colossus of American Independence. See Adams, John

Colossus of Debate. See Adams, John

Colossus of Roads. See Harriman, E. H.

Colston, Raleigh Edward
Raleigh Edward Colston who was born in France, was the son of wealthy Virginians who had gone to France to live.

He was nicknamed *Old Allegheny, Old Club, Old Clubby, Old Polly* or *Old Parlez*.[1] He was called *Old Club,* and *Old Clubby* because he was lame and used a long walking stick. The students in the Virginia Military Institute at Lexington, Va., nicknamed him *Old Polly* (a corruption of *parlez*) and *Old Parlez* because he taught French

there, before becoming a Brigadier General in the Confederate Army.

Raleigh Edward Colston was born in Paris, France, on October 31, 1825, and died at Richmond, Va., on July 29, 1896.

[1] *The End of an Era,* John S. Wise (Houghton Mifflin and Company, New York, 1889) p. 261.
Lee's Lieutenants, Douglas Southall Freeman (Charles Scribner's Sons, New York, 1943) vol. 2, p. xlv.

Colts. See Chicago National League Baseball Company

Columbia College of Dubuque
The *Duhawks*[1] is the nickname applied to the athletic teams of Columbia College of Dubuque, at Dubuque, Iowa. The nickname was formed by combining the first syllable of Dubuque with the first syllable of Hawkeye, the nickname of the State of Iowa.

[1] A communication from G. W. Heitkamp, Director of Athletics at Columbia College of Dubuque, Dubuque, Iowa, June 14, 1935.

Columbus of Modern Thought. See Emerson, R. W.

Columella of the New England States. See Lowell, John, Jr.

Comiskey, Charles Albert
Commy, and the *Old Roman* are nicknames which have been applied to Charles Albert Comiskey.

Commy is simply a shortened form of the name Comiskey.

The *Old Roman*[1] was bestowed on him because of his many bright sayings and his appearance while he was the famous first baseman of the St. Louis Browns between 1882 and 1891.

Charles Albert Comiskey was born in Chicago, Ill., on August 15, 1859, and died at his summer home at Eagle River, Wis., October·26, 1931.

[1] *"Commy": The Life Story of Charles A. Comiskey, the Grand Old Roman of Baseball and for Nineteen Years President and Owner of the American League Baseball Team, the White Sox,* told by G. W. Axelson (The Railly and Lee Company, Chicago, 1919) p. 10.
The Baseball Magazine (The Baseball Magazine Company, Boston, June, 1908) vol. 1, no. 2, p. 47.

Commercial Emporium. See New York City

Commercial Metropolis of West Tennessee. See Memphis, Tenn.

Commodore Van Santvoord. See Van Santvoord, Alfred

Commodores. See Vanderbilt University

Commoners. See William Jennings Bryan University

Commy. See Comiskey, C. A.

Compson, Betty

Betty Compson, who was born at Salt Lake City, Utah, on March 18, 1897, was called the *Minx of the Movies* [1] when she made her first appearance in the Christy comedies, because of her happy, fun-loving disposition.

[1] *Twinkle, Twinkle, Movie Star,* Harry T. Brunbride (E. P. Dutton and Company, Inc., 1930) p. 61.

Compton, California

Compton, in Los Angeles County, is popularly called the *Hub City* [1] because it is located in the geographical center of the industrial area of that county, accessible by excellent railway lines and highways.

[1] *California of the South, a History,* John Steven McGroarty (The S. J. Clarke Publishing Company, Inc., Chicago and Los Angeles, Calif., 1933) vol. 1, p. 458.

Comstock, Peter

Because he was as prominent a man in the economic affairs of the northern states as was Napoleon Bonaparte in French military activities, Peter Comstock was nicknamed the *Napoleon of the North.* [1]

He was a very influential business man of Comstock, Washington County, N.Y., about 1840.

[1] *The National Cyclopaedia of American Biography* (James T. White and Company, New York, 1899) vol. 2, p. 150.

Concordia College

The Clevemen, The Cobbers, and *The Concordians* are the names given to the athletic teams of Concordia College, at Moorhead, Minn.

They were called *Clevemen* [1] in 1926 because their coach was Frank Cleve. They were nicknamed *Cobbers* because when the college was founded, it was on the outskirts of the city with cornfields all around the campus. *The Concordians* originated in the word Concordia.

[1] A communication from Norman Wallin, Director of the Concordia College News Bureau, Moorhead, Minn., November 19, 1935.

Concordians. See Concordia College

Coney Island of Boston. See Revere, Mass.

Congregational Pope of New England. See Bacon, Leonard

Congress of the Rough Riders of the World

William Frederick Cody called a group of riders in his Wild West Show in 1893, *A Congress of Rough Riders of the World* [1] because the group was made up of Indians, American cowboys, and skilled riders from all over the world, including Mexico, France, England and Russia.

[1] *Last of the Great Scouts: The Life of Colonel William F. Cody (Buffalo Bill),* Helen Cody Wetmore (The Duluth Printing Company, Duluth, Minn.) p. 247.

Congressional Playboy. See Zioncheck, M. A.

Conkling, Roscoe

Roscoe Conkling was designated the *Peacock Senator.* [1] This nickname had its origin about 1881 in a debate between Senator Conkling and Senator James Gillespie Blaine, in the United States Senate, over the subject of the reestablishment of American shipping, at which time Senator Blaine referred to Senator Conkling as a "peacock." The reference was probably suggested by the fact that Conkling had been an orator of national reputation since the speech he made in Congress in 1862 on the military blunder of Ball's Bluff.

Roscoe Conkling, who was born at Canajoharie, N.Y., on August 22, 1816, and who died at New York City, on September 18, 1891, served as a Senator from the State of New York to the United States Congress from 1867 until 1881.

[1] *U.S. "Snap Shots": An Independent, National, and Memorial Encyclopedia . . . ,* Oliver McKee (A. M. Thayer and Company, Boston, 1892) p. 243-4.

Connally, George Walter

Sarge, Rubber Arm, Rip and Snorter are sobriquets which have been given to George Walter Connally.

He has been called *Sarge* [1] because he was a sergeant in the Marine Corps during World War I.

Because he has the ability to pitch a game of ball without having "warmed up," he has been nicknamed, *Rubber Arm*.[1] *Rip and Snorter*[1] is the sobriquet given to Connally because of his excellent playing ability, this nickname signifying in American slang "an efficient or a large person or thing."

George Walter Connally, who was born at McGregor, Tex., on August 31, 1898, was a pitcher in major league baseball.

[1] *Who's Who in Major League Base Ball*, comp. by Harold (Speed) Johnson (Buxton Publishing Company, Chicago, 1933) p. 120.

Connally, Thomas Terry

Thomas Terry Connally, a Texas lawyer and politican, was nicknamed *Texas Tom*[1] to distinguish him from other senators with the name Thomas or Tom. He was a Democratic Representative from Texas to the United States Congress from 1917 until 1929, and has been a United States Senator from Texas since 1929.

Thomas Terry Connally was born in McLennan County, Tex., on August 19, 1877.

[1] An interview with Captain Victor Hunt Harding, Secretary of the National Democratic Congress Reelection Committee, Washington, D.C., April 10, 1939.

Connecticut

The sobriquet, the *Nutmeg State*,[1] is applied to Connecticut because its early inhabitants had the reputation of being so shrewd that they could sell wooden nutmegs. Connecticut people have not generally resented the nickname, but have used the wooden nutmegs as souvenirs and emblems with a certain amusement.

Connecticut, the Constitution State, was given as a motto on a charter oak, frame and tablet, exhibited in the Connecticut State building, at the Louisiana Purchase Exposition, in 1904. There seems to be some authority for this nickname in various historical works. In 1639, at Hartford, the Fundamental Orders were drawn up, largely the work of Thomas Hooker. These orders are stated to be the first written constitution drawn up by the people, and the Constitution of the United States is said to be in lineal descent more nearly related to that of Connecticut than to that of any other of the thirteen colonies.

Connecticut was nicknamed the *Blue Law State*[2] in commemoration of the unenviable fame acquired by the first government of New Haven Plantation, in framing the famous Blue Laws of that colony.

Connecticut was formerly nicknamed the *Brownstone State* because of the brownstone quarries at Portland, and the *Freestone State* because of her freestone quarries which were formerly valuable. The *Land of Steady Habits*[2] is another name applied to Connecticut because of the staid deportment and excellent morals of its inhabitants.

[1] A letter from George S. Godard, Librarian, Connecticut State Library, Hartford, Conn., March 18, 1930.
[2] *A New Dictionary of Americanisms*, Sylva Clapin (Louis Weiss and Company, New York, 1903) p. 61, 254.
The New International Encyclopaedia, Second Edition (Dodd, Mead and Company, New York, 1930) vol. 3, p. 425.

Connecticut Inhabitants

The nicknames *Nutmegs* and *Wooden Nutmegs* applied to the inhabitants of Connecticut had their origin in the shrewdness and alleged ability of Connecticut traders to sell anything, even wooden nutmegs.

Connecticut State College

Because Connecticut' is the Nutmeg State, students of Connecticut State College at Storrs, Conn., are called *Nutmegs* and *Nutmeggers*.

Connecticut Wits

The *Connecticut Wits*,[1] or *Hartford Wits*, were a group of writers who, during the last quarter of the eighteenth century, lived at Hartford, Conn., which was then for a short time the literary capital of the country. Their purpose was to produce literature that would be more American in treatment, in subject matter, and in nationalist spirit than any produced before. They wrote poetry characterized by a certain liveliness and dry humour not to be found in the usual solemn and theological literature of their predecessors. The more prominent men representative of this group were John Trumbull, Timothy Dwight, and Joel Barlow.

See also Hartford Wits.

[1] *American Literature, an Interpretative Survey*, Ernest Erwin Leisy (Thomas Y. Crowell Company, New York, 1929) p. 39.
A Literary History of America, Barrett Wendell (Charles Scribner's Sons, New York, 1900) p. 123.

Connie Mack. See McGillicuddy, Cornelius

Connolly, Richard

Richard Connolly was known by the nickname *Slippery Dick*[1] because of the elusive and tricky character which he is said to

Connolly, Richard—Continued
have shown in his connection with the
Tweed Ring. With William Marcy Tweed
as its chief, this group in 1871 robbed the
treasury of New York City by corrupt man-
ipulation of its municipal expenses.

[1] *Social and Economic History of the United States:
The Rise of Industrialism, 1820 to 1875*, Harry J. Car-
man (D. C. Heath and Company, New York and Boston, 1934) vol. 2, 645.

Conscience Fund

Several hundred thousand dollars which
has been paid into the United States Treasury
since 1811 by people who had defrauded
or thought that they had defrauded the
government, has been designated the *Conscience Fund*.[1]

[1] *The Washington Post*, Washington, D.C., January
28, 1935, col. 6, p. 2.

Conscience Whigs

About 1840, those members of the Whig
party who opposed slavery because they
could not reconcile it with the dictates of
their conscience were nicknamed the *Conscience Whigs*.[1]

[1] *Dictionary of United States History, 1492-1900: Four
Centuries of History, Written Concisely and Arranged
Alphabetically in Dictionary Form*, J. Franklin Jameson
(History Publishing Company, Boston, 1900) p. 157.

Conservative Cincinnati. See Cincin-
nati, Ohio

Constitution State. See Connecticut

Contemporary Cassandra. See Thomp-
son, Dorothy

Contented City. See Cincinnati, Ohio

Continentals. See Hamilton College

Convention City. See Denver, Colo.

Convention City. See Louisville, Ky.

Coodies

This nickname was applied to the members of the Federalist party in New York
who favored the War of 1812. The group
split from the party over the issue of support for the United States Government in
the prosecution of the war. One of the
leaders of the faction, Gulian C. Verplanck,
wrote for publication under the name of

Abimelech Coody,[1] and the entire group
was soon identified by his pseudonym.

[1] *The Encyclopedia Americana* (The Encyclopedia
Americana Corporation, New York, Chicago, 1922)
vol. VII, p. 620.

Cook, Philip

Because he served during the Civil War
with such distinction and gallantry, Philip
Cook was nicknamed the *Old War Horse*.[1]
He was born in Twiggs County, Ga., on
July 31, 1817, and died at Atlanta, Ga., on
May 22, 1894.

[1] *The National Cyclopaedia of American Biography*
(James T. White and Company, New York, 1897)
vol. 4, p. 182.

Cooke, Allen Lindsey

Allen Lindsey Cooke, who was born at
Swepsonville, N.C., on June 23, 1907, and
who played outfield in major league baseball,
was popularly known as *Dusty*,[1] probably
because his hair is light, and perhaps, too,
because he is such a swift runner that he
"dusts the onlookers."

[1] *Who's Who in Major League Base Ball*, comp. by
Harold (Speed) Johnson (Buxton Publishing Company,
Chicago, 1933) p. 121.

Coolbrith, Ina Donna, Bret Harte,
and Charles Warren Stoddard

Ina Donna Coolbrith, Bret Harte, and
Charles Warren Stoddard, three American
writers, have been designated the *Golden
Gate Trinity*[1] and the *Overland Three*[1]
because they contributed prolifically for several years to the *Overland Monthly* soon
after it was founded in 1868 by Bret Harte
in San Francisco, Calif. All three were then
living at San Francisco, the *Golden Gate
City*.

[1] *The National Cyclopaedia of American Biography*
(James T. White and Company, New York, 1906) vol.
13, p. 512.

Coolidge, Calvin

The sobriquets, *Red* and *Silent Cal*, have
been attributed to President Calvin Coolidge.
He was nicknamed *Red* because as a boy his
hair was red.

Calvin Coolidge was known as *Silent Cal*[1]
because he was exceedingly reticent about his
plans and politics, his philosophy being that
what he left unsaid would never harm him.

Coolidge was born at Plymouth, Vt., on
July 4, 1872, and died at Northampton,

Mass., on January 5, 1933. He was the thirtieth President of the United States, serving from 1923 to 1929.

[1] *Encyclopedia of American Biography: American Biography, a New Cyclopedia,* comp. under the editorial supervision of a notable advisory board (Published under the direction of The American Historical Society, Inc., New York, 1922) vol. 19, p. 23, 25.

Coolidge of the West. See Landon, A. M.

Cooling off Treaties

The *Cooling Off Treaties* [1] was a name applied by William Jennings Bryan to the peace treaties made between the United States and thirty other nations while Bryan was Secretary of State during President Woodrow Wilson's administration from 1913 to 1921. These treaties were designated the *Cooling Off Treaties* because the countries signing them agreed to wait a year before declaring war upon any of the other signatories, to provide time for settling any controversies that might have arisen.

[1] *Democracy at the Crossroads, a Symposium,* W. A. Ayre, H. Parker Willis, Brand Whitlock, and others; arranged by Ellis Meredith (Brewer, Warren and Putnam, New York, 1932) p. 24.

Coonskin Library

A large case of much-used books at Ames in Athens County, Ohio, was long popularly termed the *Coonskin Library* [1] because the pioneer settlers of this region trapped coons and other animals and sent the skins to Boston, Mass., in exchange for the books in this collection. The *Coonskin Library* was the genesis of the present public library of Ames.

[1] *Ohio Archaeological and Historical Quarterly,* July, 1926, Published by the Society (The F. J. Heer Printing Company, Columbus, Ohio, 1926) vol. 35, no. 3, p. 557.

Cooper, James Fenimore

The *American Scott* [1] is a nickname applied to James Fenimore Cooper in allusion to his having literary characteristics similar to Walter Scott's. Cooper was inspired by Scott's literary productions; like Scott he was very fond of a life in the outdoors; both authors used a similar style of writing.

James Fenimore Cooper was born at Burlington, N.J., on September 15, 1789, and died at Cooperstown, N.Y., on September 14, 1851.

[1] *American Literary Readings, with Introduction, Notes, Biographical Sketches, Some Thought Questions, an Outline of American Literature, and a Brief Essay on English Metrics,* ed. by Leonidas Warren Payne (Rand McNally and Company, New York and Chicago, 1917) p. 38.

Cooper, Peter

Peter Cooper has been called the *Father of Railroads* [1] because in 1830 he built the first successful locomotive engine, *Tom Thumb,* which was demonstrated on the Baltimore and Ohio railroad.

He was born at New York City, on February 12, 1791, and died there on April 4, 1883.

[1] *A Book of Nicknames,* John Goff (Courier-Journal Job Printing Company, Louisville, Ky., 1892) p. 29.
The National Cyclopaedia of American Biography (James T. White and Company, New York, 1893), vol. 3, p. 114.

Cooper of the South. See Simms, W. G.

Cooperstown, New York

Cooperstown, N.Y., is widely known as the *Birthplace of Baseball* [1] because it was originally supposed to have been the site of the first baseball diamond in the United States, having been designed by Abner Doubleday in 1839. Although subsequent evidence has shown that baseball was played earlier in various forms in this country, Doubleday Field in Cooperstown is the official home of the game, and is the site of the Baseball Hall of Fame which houses trophies and equipment made famous in the history of the game.

[1] *Times-Herald,* Washington, D.C., May 7, 1939, Sport Section, col. 3, p. B-1.

Copper State. See Wisconsin

Copperheads

Members of the Democratic party in the northern states who were opposed to the Civil War were denounced by the Union men who favored the war as *Copperheads,* [1] an allusion to cooperhead snakes, which strike from their hiding places without giving any warning. As a rule *Copperheads* were not sympathetic toward the southerners, but they contended that the prosecution of the Civil War was illegal. These Peace Democrats generally wore a button made of the head of the Goddess of Liberty cut out of a copper cent, which may have given rise to their nickname. Or they may have used the button because of the name. The sobriquet *Copperheads* is said to have been first used on October 1, 1862, in an article appearing in the *Cincinnati Commercial.*

[3] *History of the United States from the Compromise of 1850,* James Ford Rhodes (Harper and Brothers, New York and London, 1899) vol. 4, p. 224.

Cops. See College of Paterson

Corbett, James John

The sobriquet *Gentleman Jim* [1] has been given to James John Corbett because he was a bank clerk before he took up prize fighting, went to social functions dressed in evening clothes, and read and discussed freely the great English classics.

James John Corbett, who was born at San Francisco, Calif., on September 1, 1866, won the heavyweight championship from John L. Sullivan on March 18, 1893. He died at Bayside, Long Island, N.Y., on February 18, 1933.

[1] *The Ring, World's Foremost Boxing Magazine* (Published Monthly by The Ring, Inc., Dunellen, N.J.) April, 1931, p. 17.

Corcoran, Thomas Gardiner

Thomas Gardiner Corcoran, who was an unofficial advisor of President Franklin Delano Roosevelt and was active in drafting much of the New Deal legislation, was nicknamed *Tommy the Cork* [1] and *White House Tommy.* [2] President Roosevelt gave him the first sobriquet which is a pun on his names, Thomas and Corcoran. The latter nickname was attributed to Corcoran because of his close contact with President Roosevelt and the White House from 1933 until 1941.

Thomas Gardiner Corcoran was born at Pawtucket, R. I., on December 10, 1900.

[1] *Washington Times-Herald,* Washington, D.C., November 13, 1938, col. 6, Editorial page.

[2] *Times-Herald*, Washington, D.C., February 23, 1939, col. 2, p. 1.

Corduroy Roads

During the period of western expansion, roads were sometimes made over swampy lands by cutting down trees and placing them side by side crosswise of the road. Such roads were ridged like corduroy cloth and were therefore nicknamed *Corduroy Roads.* [1]

[1] *The Growth of the American People and Nation,* Mary G. Kelty (Ginn and Company, New York and Boston, 1931) p. 100.

Corn City. See Toledo, Ohio

Corn Rights

The early pioneers, who settled along the New River in northwestern Virginia about 1756, acquired their land by means of the *Corn Rights.* [1] For every acre of ground which a settler planted in corn, he was entitled to one hundred acres of adjoining land.

[1] *Chronicles of Border Warfare or, A History of the Settlement by the Whites, of Northwestern Virginia, and of the Indian Wars and Massacres in That Section of the State, with Reflections, Anecdotes, Etc.,* Alexander Scott Withers: A New Edition, ed. and annotated by Reuben Gold Thwaites, with the addition of a Memoir of the Author, and Several Illustrative Notes by the late Lyman Copeland Draper (The Robert Clarke Company, Cincinnati, Ohio, 1895) p. 60.
History of the Early Settlement and Indian Wars of Western Virginia; Embracing an Account of the Various Expeditions in the West Previous to 1795, also, Biographical Sketches . . . , Wills De Hass (Published by H. Hoblitzell, Wheeling, W.Va., and printed by King and Baird, Philadelphia, 1851) p. 42.

Corn State. See Illinois

Corn-cracker State. See Kentucky

Corn-crackers. See Kentuckians

Cornhuskers. See University of Nebraska

Corn Huskers State. See Nebraska

Corning, Erastus

During his life-time Erastus Corning was nicknamed the *Railway King,* [1] because he devoted his time and money to the development of railroads in New York State, was responsible for the combination of a number of railroads into the New York Central, was president of this corporation, and was a wealthy railway executive and owner of railway stock.

He was born at Norwich, Conn., on December 14, 1794 and died at Albany, N.Y., on April 9, 1872.

[1] *Contemporary American Biography: Biographical Sketches of Representative Men of the Day, Representatives of Modern Thought and Progress, of the Pulpit, the Press, the Bench and Bar, of Legislation, Invention, and the Great Industrial Interests of the Country* (Atlantic Publishing and Engraving Company, New York, 1902) p. 333.

[1] *The Encyclopedia Americana* (American Corporation, New York and Chicago, 1927) vol. 7, p. 714.

Cornwallis, Charles

After his surrender at Yorktown to General George Washington, Isaac Parker, a Virginia Revolutionary soldier, nicknamed Charles Cornwallis, *Cobwallis,* [1] because he humorously said that General Washington "shelled the corn off him in Yorktown."

Charles Cornwallis, British General, was born at London, on December 31, 1738, and died at Ghazipur, Benares, India, on October 5, 1805.

[1] *Personal Recollections of John M. Palmer*, Mrs John M. Palmer (The Robert Clarke Company, Cincinnati, Ohio, 1901) p. 2.

Coroner. See Fernandez, J. O.

Corrigan, Douglas Gorce

Douglas Gorce Corrigan, a California aviator, was nicknamed *Wrong-way Corrigan*[1] after he had made his nonstop transatlantic flight from Brooklyn, N.Y., to Dublin, Ireland, on July 17 and 18, 1938, because when he landed in Dublin without a permit, he said he had intended to fly to Los Angeles, Calif. Corrigan had been refused a permit to fly to Ireland.

Douglas Gorce Corrigan was born at Aransas Pass, Tex., on January 22, 1907.

[1] *The Nashville Tennessean*, Nashville, Tenn., August 11, 1938, col. 1, p. 7.

[2] *Los Angeles Times*, Los Angeles, Calif., July 19, 1938, col. 2, p. 3.

Corwin, Thomas

Thomas Corwin was known by the sobriquets *Black Tom* and the *Wagon Boy*. He was popularly called *Black Tom*[1] in allusion to his very swarthy complexion.

He was called the *Wagon Boy*[2] because as a young man, Corwin was often engaged as a wagoner to haul farm products from Lebanon, Ohio, to Cincinnati and to bring back merchandise for the Lebanon storekeepers, and during the War of 1812 he served as a wagoner in the supply trains of the American Army.

Thomas Corwin was born in Bourbon County, Ky., on July 29, 1794, and died at Washington, D.C., on December 18, 1865.

[1] *My Quarter Century of American Politics*, Champ Clark (Harper and Brothers, New York and London, 1920). vol. 2, p. 187.

[2] *Life and Speeches of Thomas Corwin, Orator, Lawyer, and Statesman*, ed. by Josiah Morrow (W. H. Anderson, Cincinnati, Ohio, 1896) p. 14.

Cosmopolitan San Francisco. See San Francisco, Calif.

Cotton, John

The sobriquet, the *Father and Glory of Boston*[1] was doubtless applied to John Cotton because of his patriarchial interest in the civil and religious life of Boston and his eminence as a scholar and writer.

John Cotton was a prominent preacher and controversialist in England, exhibiting a strong tendency in his doctrinal practices toward the Puritan mode of worship. Because of persecution he fled from England to Boston, Mass., on September 4, 1633, where he served for nearly two decades as the teacher in the New England church and as a colleague to the pastor, John Wilson.

[1] *The New and Complete History of the United States of America*, Official Edition, John Clark Ridpath (The Jones Brothers Publishing Company, Cincinnati, Ohio, 1906) vol. 2, p. 965.

Cotton Bowl. See Football Stadium, Texas State Fair Grounds

Cotton Confederacy

Before the Civil War, the cotton-raising states of the South were sometimes referred to as the *Cotton Confederacy*.[1] The cotton-raising states were united in supporting both slavery and secession.

[1] *Life of Walter Quintin Gresham, 1832-1895*, Matilda Gresham (Rand McNally and Company, Chicago, 1919) vol. 1, p. 114.

Cotton Ed Smith. See Smith, E. D.

Cotton Planation State. See Alabama

Cotton Row

The cotton trading area of the city of Augusta, Ga., is designated the *Cotton Row*[1] because it houses the importers and exporters of cotton, and is the cotton exchange of Augusta.

[1] *Encyclopedia of American Biography: American Biography, a New Cyclopedia*, comp. under the editorial supervision of a notable advisory board (Published under the direction of The American Historical Society, Inc., New York, 1931) vol. 46, p. 286.

Cotton Snobs

The *Cotton Snobs*[1] were people who owned and operated cotton farms in the South prior to the Civil War. Southern cotton planters were too snobbish to associate with tenant farmers or other non-property owners.

[1] *Bedford Forrest and His Critter Company*, Andrew Nelson Lytle (Minton, Balch and Company, New York, 1931) p. 36.

Cotton State. See Alabama; North Carolina

Cotton Whigs

About 1850, in order to maintain peaceful relations with the southern Whigs and harmony between the North and the South, a number of Whigs in the North offered little resistance to the extension of slavery.

Cotton Whigs—Continued

These northerners were termed *Cotton Whigs* [1] because they appeared to be in sympathy with the cotton raisers of the South.

[1] *Dictionary of United States History, 1492-1900; Four Centuries of History, Written Concisely and Arranged Alphabetically in Dictionary Form,* J. Franklin Jameson (History Publishing Company, Boston, 1900) p. 171. "Parties and Slavery, 1850-1859," by Theodore Clarke Smith in *The American Nation: A History,* ed. by Albert Bushnell Hart (Harper and Brothers, New York and London, 1906) vol. 18, p. 265.

Cottonocracy

A group of wealthy manufacturers who operated cotton mills in Boston, Mass., about 1854 were called the *Cottonocracy.* [1] The suffix-*ocracy* is derived from a Greek word meaning to rule.

[1] *The American Nation,* Richard J. Purcell (Ginn and Company, New York and Boston, 1929) p. 412.

Cottonwood City. See Leavenworth, Kans.

Cougars. See State College of Washington; University of Houston

Country. See Warneke, Lonnie

Covenanters. See Geneva College

Couzens, James

The *Croesus of the Senate* and the *Poor Man's Friend* are nicknames which have been applied to James Couzens, United States Senator from Michigan from 1925 to 1935.

The *Croesus of the Senate* [1] is an allusion to his great wealth and social prominence.

The *Poor Man's Friend,* was applied to Senator Couzens because of his generosity to the poor and his donations to philanthropic institutions.

Senator James Couzens was born at Chatham, Ontario, Canada, on August 26, 1872, and died at Detroit, Mich., on October 22, 1936.

[1] *The Washington Post Magazine,* Washington, D.C., March 4, 1934, p. 4.

Covode, John

Because of the integrity and the uprightness which characterized his personality, John Covode, Representative from Pennsylvania to Congress from 1855 to 1863, was called *Honest John Covode.* [1]

John Covode was born in Westmoreland County, Pa., on March 17, 1808, and died at Harrisburg, Pa., on January 11, 1871.

[1] *Appleton's Cyclopaedia of American Biography,* ed. by James Grant Wilson and John Fiske (D. Appleton and Company, New York, 1891) vol. 1, p. 756.

Cowboy Capital. See Prescott, Ariz.

Cowboy Carl. See Hatch, C. A.

Cowboy Kid. See Baker, Johnny

Cowboy Philosopher. See Rogers, Will

Cowboy Senator. See Ashurst, H. F.

Cowboys

During the Revolutionary War, certain Tories were accused of driving off the cattle of the Whigs or patriots on Long Island to replenish the larders of the British forces. These Tories were called *Cowboys* [1] by the colonists.

[1] *Long Island's Story,* Jacqueline Overton (Doubleday, Doran and Company, New York, 1929) p. 133.

Cowboys. See Hardin-Simmons University; Oklahoma Agricultural and Mechanical College; Texans; University of Wyoming

Cowhands. See Hardin-Simmons University

Cox, James R.

James R. Cox, Rector of St. Patrick's Church at Pittsburgh, Pa., has been called the *Pastor of the Poor* [1] because of his sympathy and interest in the poor. In 1932 he led ten thousand hunger marchers to Washington, D.C. In November 1938, he was charged with mail fraud and with conducting a lottery in connection with a contest prize of twenty-five thousand dollars to select a name for the monastery gardens of St. Patrick's Church.

[1] *Newsweek: The Magazine of News Significance,* Rockefeller Center, N.Y., November 23, 1938, col. 3, p. 36.

Cox, Samuel Sullivan

Samuel Sullivan Cox was widely known as the *Letter Carriers' Friend* and *Sunset Cox.*

The *Letter Carriers' Friend* [1] was attributed to Cox while he was a member of Congress because he proposed and was instrumental in getting a bill passed to raise the salaries of letter carriers and to grant them vacations with pay. As a token of their appreciation the letter carriers erected a statue of Representative Cox in Astor Place, New York City.

At Columbus, Ohio, in an article which he published in his paper, the *Ohio Statesman,* on May 19, 1853, entitled "A great old sunset," his other nickname *Sunset Cox* [2] had its origin. The article received wide newspaper publicity. The fact that Cox's initials were S. S. helped to make the nickname endure.

Samuel Sullivan Cox, who was born at Zanesville, Ohio, on September 30, 1824, and died in New York City, on September 10, 1889, served as a Representative from Ohio to Congress from 1857 to 1865, and as a Representative from New York from 1869 until his death.

[1] *The Encyclopedia Americana* (Americana Corporation, New York and Chicago, 1927) vol. 8, p. 141.

[2] *Life of Samuel Sullivan Cox,* William Van Zandt Cox and Milton Harlow Northrup (M. H. Northrup, Syracuse, N.Y., 1899) p. 71.

Coxe, Tench

The *Father of the American Cotton Industry* [1] was sometimes applied to Tench Coxe because he urged the southern people to engage in the production of cotton on an extensive scale, and because as early as 1789 he made an attempt to have an Arkwright spinning machine brought from England to the United States to encourage the home-manufacturing of cotton goods.

Tench Coxe was born at Philadelphia, Pa., on May 22, 1755, and died there on July 17, 1824.

[1] *The National Cyclopaedia of American Biography* (James T. White and Company, New York, 1896) vol. 6, p. 14.

Coxey's Army

Coxey's Army [1] was a name applied to a large body of unemployed men led by Jacob Coxey in 1894 from Massilon, Ohio, to Washington, D.C., to demand that the United States Government give them financial assistance.

[1] *The Leading Facts of American History,* Revised Edition, D. H. Montgomery (Ginn and Company, New York and Boston, 1910) p. 364-5.

Coyote State. See South Dakota

Coyotes. See University of South Dakota

Crack-Down Czar of the NRA. See Johnson, H. S.

Crack-Down Johnson. See Johnson, H. S.

Cracker. See Schalk, R. W.

Cracker Line

In the fall of 1863 at Chattanooga, Tenn., Brigadier General William Starke Rosecrans's Federal Army was for several weeks surrounded by Confederate Forces and was unable to secure provisions. When practically on the verge of starvation, the soldiers received supplies from Bridgeport, Tenn., by means of steamers and wagon-trains which were popularly called the *Cracker Line* [1] by the Union soldiers because their rations often consisted largely of crackers.

[1] *Civil War and Miscellaneous Papers, Papers of the Military Historical Society of Massachusetts* (The Military Historical Society of Massachusetts, Boston, 1918) vol. 14. p. 70.

Cracker State. See Georgia

Crackers. See Early, J. A.; Floridians; Georgians

Cradle of American Liberty. See Independence Hall

Cradle of Aviation. See Dayton, Ohio; Hammondsport, N.Y.

Cradle of Dental Education. See Bainbridge, Ohio

Cradle of Industry. See Springfield, Vt.

Cradle of Liberty

Faneuil Hall in Boston, Mass., is nicknamed the *Cradle of Liberty* [1] because in this historic building the patriotic colonists often met to discuss their grievances against England, to debate the issues relating to their rights as English subjects, and to deliver orations on topics pertaining to their liberty and freedom.

[1] *A History of the United States,* Henry Eldridge Bourne and Elbert Jay Benton (D. C. Heath and Company, New York and Boston, 1913) p. 141.

Cradle of Methodism. See Ebenezer Academy; John Street Methodist Episcopal Church in New York City.

Cradle of Secession. See Charleston, S.C.

Cradle of Texas Liberty. See San Antonio, Tex.

Cradle of the Cotton Manufacturing Business. See Pawtucket, R.I.

Craighill, William Price

William Price Craighill was designated the *Father of Our Modern Fortifications.*[1]

In 1854 and 1855 Craighill superintended the construction of Fort Sumter, S.C., and in 1863 he built defenses for Pittsburgh, Pa. During the Civil War he planned and executed a number of fortifications, and later engaged in the construction of defenses for New York City and Baltimore, Md. On May 10, 1895, he was made the Chief of Engineers of the United States Army with the military rank of Brigadier General.

Craighill was born at Charlestown, in what is now West Virginia, on July 1, 1833, and died there on January 18, 1909.

[1] *The National Cyclopaedia of American Biography* (James T. White and Company, New York, 1922) vol. 18, p. 205.
Who's Who in America, a Biographical Dictionary of Notable Living Men and Women of the United States, 1908-1909, ed. by Albert Nelson Marquis (A. N. Marquis and Company, Chicago, 1908) vol. 5, p. 422.

Cramer, Roger M.

Roger M. Cramer, who was born at Beech Haven, N.J., on July 22, 1906, and who played outfielder in major league baseball, was popularly called *Doc*[1] by his teammates because in his teens he was accustomed to accompanying the physician in Beech Haven on his daily rounds.

[1] *Who's Who in Major League Base Ball,* comp. by Harold (Speed) Johnson (Buxton Publishing Company, Chicago, 1933) p. 123.

Cranberry Gifford. See Gifford, C. L.

Craw-thumpers. See Marylanders

Crawford, Abel

Abel Crawford was affectionately called the *Patriarch of the Hills*[1] and the *Patriarch of the Mountains* because he was one of the earliest settlers in the region of the White Mountains of New Hampshire. He was the progenitor of the well-known Crawfords who established themselves at Crawford Notch near Mount Washington. He settled near Bemis Station, N.H., about 1793, and died there about 1850 at the age of eighty-five.

[1] *The Book of the White Mountains,* John Anderson and Stearns Morse (Minton, Balch and Company, New York, 1930) p. 177.
History of the White Mountains together with Many Interesting Anecdotes Illustrating Life in the Backwoods, Benjamin G. Willey and Frederick Thompson (Isaac N. Andrews, Boston, 1869) p. 96.
The Book of the White Mountains, John Anderson and Stearns Morse (Minton, Balch and Company, New York, 1930) p. 184.

Crawford, Clifford Rankin

It is said that Clifford Rankin Crawford was called *Pat*[1] during his freshman year in college because of his engaging grin. He was born at Society Hill, S.C., on January 28, 1902, and played infielder in major league baseball.

[1] *Who's Who in Major League Base Ball,* comp. by Harold (Speed) Johnson. (Buxton Publishing Company, Chicago, 1933) p. 124.

Crawford, Ethan Allen

The *Giant of the Hills*[1] and the *White Mountain Giant* are names by which Ethan Allen Crawford was popularly known because he was very large, strong man, nearly seven feet tall and of a heavy, powerful build. He lived in the White Mountains of New Hampshire from 1817 until his death.

Ethan Allen Crawford was born at Guildhall, Vt., in 1792, and died at Fabyan House, N.H., in 1848.

[1] *History and Description of New England; New Hampshire,* A. J. Coolidge and J. B. Mansfield (Austin J. Coolidge, Boston, 1860) p. 683.
The Book of the White Mountains, John Anderson and Stearns Morse (Minton, Balch and Company, New York, 1930) p. 182.
History of New Hampshire, Colony, Province, State, 1623-1888, John N. McClintock (B. B. Russell, Boston, 1889) p. 670.

Crawford, William

The nickname of Colonel William Crawford was the *Big Captain.*[1] Crawford was a man of unusual size and strength and was one of the most resourceful of those men who made war against the Indians along the western borders of Virginia, Pennsylvania, Maryland, and Ohio. He was captain of the colonial forces at Fort Du Quesne from 1755 to 1758 under the command of General George Washington.

Colonel Crawford was born in Berkely County, Va., in 1732. On June 5, 1782, he was captured by the Delaware Indians near Upper Sandusky, Ohio, and on June 11, 1782, was tortured to death.

[1] *An Historical Account of the Expedition against Sandusky under Colonel William Crawford in 1782 with Biographical Sketches, Personal Reminiscences and Descriptions of Interesting Localities Including Also, Details of the Disastrous Retreat, the Barbarities of the Savages, and the Awful Death of Crawford by Torture*, C. W. Butterfield (Robert Clarke and Company, Cincinnati, Ohio, 1873) p. 84, 379, 391.

"Colonel William Crawford" by James H. Anderson, in *Ohio Archaeological and Historical Publications* (Published for the Society by John L. Trauger, Columbus, Ohio, 1898) vol. 6, p. 23, 29, 31.

The National Cyclopaedia of American Biography (James T. White and Company, New York, 1907) vol. 9, p. 283.

History of the Early Settlement and Indian Wars of Western Virginia; Embracing an Account of the Various Expeditions in the West, Pervious to 1795, Also, Biographical Sketches of Colonel Ebenezer Zane, Major Samuel M'Colloch, Lewis Wetzel, General Andrew Lewis, General Daniel Brodhead, Captain Samuel Brady, Colonel William Crawford; and Other Distinguished Actors in Our Border Wars, Wills De-Hass (Published by H. Hoblitzell, Wheeling, W.Va., and Printed by King and Baird, Philadelphia, 1851) p. 189-93.

Crawfish Boys

The *Crawfish Boys*[1] were a lawless gang in Cincinnati, Ohio, in the early 1860's organized to influence elections by intimidating voters. Similar gangs have existed at various times and places throughout the history of the United States.

[1] *Contemporary American Biography: Biographical Sketches of Representative Men of the Day, Representatives of Modern Thought and Progress, of the Pulpit, the Press, the Bench and Bar, of Legislation, Invention, and the Great Industrial Interests of the Country* (Atlantic Publishing and Engraving Company, New York, 1895) vol. 1, p. 39.

Crazy Dow. See Dow, Lorenzo

Crazy Marsh. See Marsh, Sylvester

Cream City. See Milwaukee, Wis.

Cream Pitcher of the Nation. See Minnesota

Cream-white City of the Unsalted Seas. See Milwaukee, Wis.

Creole State. See Louisiana

Creoles. See Louisianians

Crescent City. See New Orleans, La.

Crescent City of the Northwest. See Galena, Ill.

Crimson Tides. See University of Alabama

Crittenton, Charles Nelson

Charles Nelson Crittenton was nicknamed the *Merchant Evangelist*.[1] He was a member of the firm of Dunham, Crittenton and Company, and later owner of the Charles N. Crittenton Company, a drug business in New York City. He "experienced conversion" after the death of his four-year-old daughter in 1882 and became an evangelist and mission worker. In her memory he founded the Florence Mission for saving unfortunate women. At the time of his death there were more than sixty such missions, known as Florence Crittenton Homes, in the United States.

Charles Nelson Crittenton was born on a farm in Henderson County, N.Y., on February 20, 1833, and died in a hotel at San Francisco, Calif., on November 16, 1909.

[1] *Dictionary of American Biography under the Auspices of the American Council of Learned Societies*, ed. by Allen Johnson and Dumas Malone (Charles Scribner's Sons, New York, 1930) vol. 14, p. 550.

Crocker, Charles. See *Big Four*

Croesus of the Senate. See Couzens, James

Cromwell of New England. See Adams, Samuel

Crook, George

The Indians, who were given to nicknaming persons for their personal traits called General Crook the *Gray Fox*[1] because of his cunning dealing with them and his gray uniforms.

Major General George Crook was born near Dayton, Ohio, on September 8, 1828, and died at Chicago, Ill., in March, 1890.

[1] *Our Wild Indians: Thirty-Three Years' Personal Experience Among the Red Men of the Great West. A Popular Account of Their Social Life, Religion, Habits, Traits, Customs, Exploits, Etc., with Thrilling Adventures and Experiences on the Great Plains and in the Mountains of Our Wide Frontier*, Colonel Richard Irving Dodge, with an introduction by General Sherman (A. D. Worthington and Company, Hartford, Conn., 1882) p. 231.

The Encyclopedia Americana (Americana Corporation, New York, 1932) vol. 8, p. 226-7.

Cross, Oliver Harlan

Oliver Harlan Cross is widely known as *By Ganny Cross*.[1] This amusing nickname originated in the fact that he habitually prefaced his remarks in the House of Rep-

Cross, O. H.—Continued
resentatives with the expression "by ganny."
He served as a Representative from Texas
from 1929 to 1935.

Oliver Harlan Cross was born at Eutaw,
Ala., on July 13, 1870.

[1] *The Washington Post Magazine,* Washington, D.C.,
March 4, 1934, p. 4.

Cross, Wilbur Lucius
Wilbur Lucius Cross, formerly Governor
of Connecticut and a well-known man of
letters, was widely known as *Uncle Toby,*[1] a
character in Laurence Sterne's novel *Tristram
Shandy.* Governor Cross was an outstanding
student of the writings of Laurence Sterne.
He was a noted scholar and author and was
Governor of Connecticut from 1931 until
1937.

Wilbur Lucius Cross was born at Mansfield, Conn., on April 10, 1862 and died at
New Haven, Conn., on October 5, 1948.

[1] *Newsweek: The Magazine of News Significance,*
Rockefeller Center, N.Y., November 22, 1937, col. 3,
p. 15.

Cross of Gold Speech
The speech of William Jennings Bryan
at the Democratic Convention which met on
July 7, 1896, at Chicago, Ill., is generally
called by historians the *Cross of Gold* [1] or
Crown of Thorns speech. The speech concluded with: "Having behind us the commercial interests, and the laboring interests,
and all the toiling masses, we shall answer
their demands for a gold standard by saying
to them, 'You shall not press down upon
the brow of labor this crown of thorns, you
shall not crucify mankind upon a cross of
gold.'" One of the main issues in this presidential campaign was the free coinage of
silver.

[1] *American History,* Clarence Manion (Allyn and
Bacon, New York and Boston, 1931) p. 438.
Speeches of William Jennings Bryan, revised and
arranged by himself, with a biographical introduction,
by Mary Baird Bryan, his wife (Funk and Wagnalls
Company, New York and London, 1909) vol. 1, p. 238.

Cross of Lorraine Division. See
Seventy-ninth Infantry Division of
World War II

Crosser, Robert
Robert Crosser, an Ohio lawyer and politician, was nicknamed the *Father of Ohio
Labor* [1] while in the House of Representatives. He was the co-author of the Crosser-

Dill Act (Railway Labor Act, 1934) and
of the Crosser-Wheeler Railroad Unemployment Insurance Act of 1938.

Robert Crosser was born at Holytown,
Scotland, on June 7, 1874, and came to
America with his parents in 1881.

[1] An interview with Captain Victor Hunt Harding,
Secretary of the National Democratic Congress Reëlection
Committee, Washington, D.C., April 10, 1939.

Crouch, Jack Albert
Roxey [1] is the nickname by which Jack
Albert Crouch is sometimes called. It was
originated in 1931 by the megaphone announcer in Shibe Park, at Philadelphia, Pa.

Crouch, who was born at Salisbury, N.C.,
on October 12, 1905, was a catcher in major
league baseball.

[1] *Who's Who in Major League Base Ball,* comp. by
Harold (Speed) Johnson (Buxton Publishing Company,
Chicago, 1933) p. 128.

Crowley, James. See *Four Horsemen*

Crown City. See Pasadena, Calif.

Crown City of the Valley. See Pasadena, Calif.

Crown of Thorns Speech. See *Cross
of Gold Speech*

Crown Prince. See McAdoo, W. G.

Crown Prince of the New Deal. See
Roosevelt, James

Crusaders
The *Crusaders* [1] was a name applied to a
group of wealthy and influential men who
formed an association against the prohibition
amendment and who had their headquarters
in Washington, D.C., about 1927. By 1932
it had some 500,000 members and branch
organizations in twenty-four states. They
spent vast sums of money in their crusade
against the amendment.

[1] *The American Scene,* Edwin C. Hill (Witmark Educational Publications Department of M. Witmark and
Sons, New York, 1933) p. 105.

Crusaders. See Billings Polytechnic Institute; College of the Holy Cross;
Wheaton College

Cubs. See Chicago National League Baseball Company

Cumberland, Rhode Island

Cumberland is sometimes designated the *Mineral Pocket of New England* [1] because within the limits of this city, iron, copper, and other minerals have been mined at various times.

[1] *Know Rhode Island: Facts Concerning the Land of Roger Williams.* Sixth Edition, comp. and distributed by the Office of the Secretary of State (State of Rhode Island and Providence Plantations, Providence, R.I., 1936) p. 14.

Cummings, Fred

Fred Cummings, a Colorado farmer and politician, was nicknamed *Sugar Beets* [1] while in the House of Representatives because he took such an active part in sugar beet legislation. He was president of the National Beet Growers Association from 1931 until 1932, and president of the Mountain States Beet Growers Association from 1932 to 1945. He was a Democratic Representative from Colorado to the United States Congress from 1933 to 1945.

Fred Cummings was born in Coos County, N.Y., and died in 1945.

[1] An interview with Captain Victor Hunt Harding, Secretary of the National Democratic Congress Reëlection Committee, Washington, D.C., April 10, 1939.

Cunning President. See Messer, Asa

Cup and Saucer House

Cup and Saucer House [1] was the nickname of a large house located at Cape Vincent, Jefferson County, N.Y., in the early decades of the nineteenth century because of the unusual shape of the building. The first story of the house with its spacious veranda was so much larger than the second story that the building looked like a small cup set in a saucer. According to tradition, the house was built by French sympathizers of the Emperor Napoleon Bonaparte who hoped to rescue him from the island of St. Helena and secrete him there until he could reorganize his political machine.

[1] *The North Country, a History Embracing Jefferson, St. Lawrence, Oswego, Lewis and Franklin Counties, New York,* Harry F. Landon (Historical Publishing Company, Indianapolis, Ind., 1932) vol. 1, p. 272-3.

Currency Famine

On August 1, 1893, during the financial crisis, the banks of the United States put into effect a policy requiring persons who had money on deposit to notify the banks six days before they intended to withdraw money from the banks. The resultant scarcity of money in circulation has been called the *Currency Famine.* [1]

[1] *Twenty Years of the Republic, 1885-1905,* Harry Thurston Peck (Dodd, Mead and Company, New York, 1907) p. 337.

Curtin, Andrew Gregg

During the Civil War, Andrew Gregg Curtin became nicknamed the *Great War Governor* [1] and the *Soldier's Friend.*

Curtin was considered one of the most efficient governors of the Civil War period because he successfully executed the public affairs of the State of Pennsylvania and gave support to the Union Army by raising and equipping a number of regiments of soldiers for the North.

Curtin was interested in the welfare of the Union soldiers, particularly of those from Pennsylvania. He organized voluntary commissions to assist in caring for the sick and wounded soldiers. After the war he secured appropriations for the maintenance of orphaned children and of soldiers. Because of this he was known as the *Soldier's Friend.* [2]

[1] *Andrew Gregg Curtin, His Life and Services,* ed. by William H. Egle (Avil Printing Company, Philadelphia, 1895) p. 451.
[2] *Contemporary American Biography: Biographical Sketches of Representative Men of the Day, Representatives of Modern Thought and Progress, of the Pulpit, the Press, the Bench and Bar, of Legislation, Invention, and the Great Industrial Interests of the Country* (Atlantic Publishing and Engraving Company, New York, 1895) vol. 1, p. 296.

Curtis, Charles

Because of his Indian descent and his importance in politics, Charles Curtis was known as *Big Chief.* [1] He was Vice President of the United States from 1929 to 1933.

Charles Curtis was born at Topeka, Kans., on January 25, 1860, and died at Washington, D.C., on February 8, 1936.

[1] *The Literary Digest, January to March, 1930* (Funk and Wagnalls Company, New York, 1930) vol. 104, March 8, 1930, p. 4.

Cushman, Pauline

Pauline Cushman, an actress, was nicknamed the *Spy of the Cumberland* [1] because she was employed by the Federal Government as a spy in 1862. She was sent out from Nashville, Tenn., on the Cumberland River, to collect military information. She was discovered near Tullahoma, Tenn., tried by a military court, and sentenced to be hanged. After a physical collapse she was removed from the military jail at Tullahoma

Cushman, Pauline—Continued

to Shelbyville, Tenn. When the Confederate forces retreated she was left behind and was sent North where she was acclaimed as the *Spy of the Cumberland,* and was personally praised by President Abraham Lincoln.

Pauline Cushman was born at New Orleans, La., on June 10, 1835, and committed suicide at San Francisco, Calif., on December 2, 1893.

[1] *Dictionary of American Biography under the Auspices of the American Council of Learned Societies,* ed. by Allen Johnson and Dumas Malone (Charles Scribner's Sons, New York, 1930) vol. 5, p. 4.

Custer, George Armstrong

The *Boy General* [1] was often applied to George Armstrong Custer because at the age of 24 he was appointed a Brigadier General of volunteers in the Union Army, only two years after he had graduated from the United States Military Academy at West Point, N.Y.

George Armstrong Custer was born at New Rumley, Ohio, on December 5, 1839, and died in battle near the junction of the Big Horn and Little Big Horn rivers in Montana, on June 25, 1876.

[1] *Representative Men: Sketches of Representative Men, North and South; Representatives of Modern Progress, of the Press, the Pulpit, the Bench, the Bar, the Army and Navy, of Legislation, Invention, and the Great Industrial Interests of the Country,* ed. by Augustus C. Rogers (Atlantic Publishing Company, New York, 1872) p. 178, 179, 182.

Custer Avengers

The *Custer Avengers* [1] were men who, upon hearing of the Custer Massacre of June 25, 1876, enlisted in the American Army that they might avenge the death of Major General George A. Custer and his soldiers.

[1] *Some Memories of a Soldier,* Hugh Lenox Scott (The Century Company, New York and London, 1928) p. 40.

Custer Division. See Eighty-fifth Infantry Division of World War II

Custis, George Washington Parke

In the late years of his life, George Washington Parke Custis, playwright and stepson of George Washington, was nicknamed *Old Man Eloquent* [1] because he was an eloquent speaker.

He was born at Mount Airy, Md., on April 30, 1781, and died at Arlington House in Fairfax County, Virginia, on October 10, 1857.

[1] *Recollections Grave and Gay,* Mrs. Burton Harrison (Charles Scribner's Sons, New York, 1911) p. 33.

Cut Money

During the early part of the nineteenth century, because of the scarcity of silver coin, in small denomination, the pioneer settlers cut silver dollars into eight equal triangular parts, which they called *Cut Money.* [1]

[1] *Michigan Pioneer Collections: Report of the Pioneer Society of the State of Michigan, together with Reports of County, Town, and District Pioneer Societies* (W. S. George and Company, Lansing, Mich., 1877) vol. 1, p. 382.

Cut Rate Carpenter. See Carpenter, T. M.

Cutler, Augustus William

Augustus William Cutler was called the *Father of the Free School System in New Jersey,* [1] because he was the author of a bill providing for free or public schools in New Jersey, which was enacted as a law by the state legislature in 1861. He served from 1854 until 1875 as a member of the Board of Education of Morristown, and worked toward the establishment of free schools throughout New Jersey.

Augustus William Cutler was born at Morristown, N.J., on October 22, 1829, and died there on January 1, 1897.

[1] *A History of Morris County, New Jersey, Embracing Upwards of Two Centuries, 1710-1913* (Leis Historical Publishing Company, New York and Chicago, 1914) vol. 2, p. 2.

Cutler, Manasseh

Manasseh Cutler was called the *Father of Ohio University* [1] because he was instrumental in getting a bill passed by the United States Congress on July 23, 1787, providing that two complete townships in Ohio be given for the purposes of a university. Ohio University was founded with the proceeds derived from the sale of this land.

Doctor Cutler was also known as the *Father of State Universities* [2] because following his suggestion, Congress made grants for school purposes in the parts of the country where it held public land.

Manasseh Cutler was born at Killingly, Conn., on May 3, 1742, and died at Hamilton, Mass., on July 28, 1823.

[1] *Ohio Archaeological and Historical Quarterly* (Press of Fred J. Heer, Columbus, Ohio, 1910) vol. 19, no. 4, October 1910, p. 412-13.

[2] *The Story of Our American People,* Charles F. Horne (H. S. History Publishing Company, New York, 1926) vol. 1, p. 425.

The National Cyclopaedia of American Biography (James T. White and Company, New York, 1893) vol. 3, p. 70.

Cutting, Bronson

Harvard's Gift to the West [1] was a popular nickname of Senator Bronson Cutting, because he was educated at Harvard University and later moved to the West where he became a prominent political figure. He served as a United States Senator from New Mexico from 1910 to 1935.

Senator Cutting was born at Oakdale, Long Island, N.Y., moved to Santa Fe, N.M., in 1910, and was killed in an airplane crash near Atlanta, Mo., on May 6, 1935.

[1] *The Washington Post Magazine*, Washington, D.C., March 4, 1934, p. 4.

Cuyler, Hazen S.

When Hazen S. Cuyler was a lad, his playmates called him *Cuy*. When he went to Nashville, Tenn., with the Southern League in 1923, the newspapers began to spell his nickname *Ki*. This later developed into *KiKi*,[1] a sobriquet by which he was popularly known.

Hazen S. Cuyler was born at Harrisville, Mich., on August 30, 1899, and was an outfielder in major league baseball.

[1] *Who's Who in Major League Base Ball*, comp. by Harold (Speed) Johnson (Buxton Publishing Company, Chicago, 1933) p. 131.

Cy. See Pfirman, C. H.; Rigler, Charles; Young, D. T.

Cyclone Division. See Thirty-eighth Infantry Division of World War II

Cyclones. See Iowa State College

Cyclopaedia of Science. See Brown, J. J.

Cyclone State. See Kansas

Czar of American Baseball. See Landis, K. M.

Czar of Boxing. See Muldoon, William

Czar of Pennsylvania Politics. See Cameron, Simon

Czar of the District. See Blanton, T. L.

Czar of the Liquor Industry. See Morgan, W. F.

Czar of the National Pastime. See Landis, K. M.

Czar Reed. See Reed, T. B.

D

Da Costa, Jacob Mendez

Jacob Mendez Da Costa was nicknamed the *Physician's Physician* because of his deep concern and interest in the welfare and success of physicians in general. He was graduated from the Jefferson Medical College, at Philadelphia, in 1852, and did postgraduate work in Paris, Prague, and Vienna. He was twice President of the College of Physicians of Philadelphia, and was President of the Association of American Physicians in 1897.

Jacob Mendez Da Costa was born on the Island of St. Thomas in the West Indies, on February 7, 1833, and died at Villanova, Pa., on September 11, 1900.

[1] *Dictionary of American Biography under the Auspices of the American Council of Learned Societies*, ed. by Allen Johnson and Dumas Malone (Charles Scribner's Sons, New York, 1930) vol. 5, p. 25.

Dad. See Nelson, William; Price, S. G.; Roberts, Theodore

Daddy Longlegs. See McAdoo, W. G.

Daddy of the Baby. See Johnson, Andrew

Dale, Richard

Commodore Richard Dale distinguished himself by his bravery and fearless fighting on the ship *Bon Homme Richard*; consequently, he was nicknamed *Fighting Dick Dale*.[1]

He was born in Norfolk County, Va., on November 6, 1756, and died at Philadelphia, Pa., on February 26, 1826.

[1] *Robert Morris, Patriot and Financier*, Ellis Paxson Oberholtzer (The Macmillan Company, New York, 1903) p. 102, 283.

Dales. See Hillsdale College

Dallas, Texas

The beautiful and palatial homes in Dallas, Tex., have won for it the name, the *City of Homes*.[1] It is nicknamed the *Metropolis of North Texas* because of its loca-

Dallas, Texas—Continued

tion and of its prominence in the civic, religious, educational, and financial activities of North Texas.

[1] *Flashlights on Texas,* Lillie Terrell Shaver and Willie Williamson Rogers (A. C. Baldwin and Sons, Austin, Tex., 1928) p. 83-8.

Dalzell John

While he was a Representative from Pennsylvania to the United States Congress, John Dalzell was popularly called the *Father of the House* [1] because of his long record of continuous service from 1887 to 1913.

He was born at New York City on April 19, 1845, and died at Altadena, Calif., on October 2, 1927.

[1] *My Quarter Century of American Politics,* Champ Clark (Harper and Brothers, New York and London, 1920) vol. 1, p. 222.

Damariscotta and Newcastle, Maine

Damariscotta and Newcastle, two towns located in Lincoln County, are called *Twin Villages* [1] because they are so closely bound together in business and social activities that they are practically one town separated by the Damariscotta River.

[1] *Maine, Past and Present,* Maine Writers Research Club (D.C. Health and Company, New York and Boston, 1929) p. 41.

Damascus, Virginia

Damascus has been nicknamed the *Little Swiss Town* [1] because it is within the bounds of the Unaka National Forest, a beautiful and attractive Federal forest reserve, which offers recreational facilities such as fishing, hiking, and hunting, comparable to the mountainous country in Switzerland.

[1] *Virginia,* comp. and ed. by Charlotte Allen (Published by the Department of Agriculture and Immigration of the State of Virginia under the direction of George W. Koiner, Commissioner, Division of Purchase and Printing, Richmond, Va.
Industrial Survey of Washington County, Virginia, R. L. Humbert, Director of Surveys in collaboration with R. B. Begg, P. H. McGauhey, J. Elton Lodewick, M. L. Jeffries, W. H. Humbert, and S. C. Andrews (Engineering Extension Division, Virginia Polytechnic Institute, Blacksburg, Va., July, 1929) p. 66.
History of Southwest Virginia, 1746-1786; Washington County 1777-1870, Lewis Preston Summers (J. L. Hill Company, Richmond, Va., 1903) p. 692.

Damon and Pythias of American Verse. See Drake, J. R., and Fitz-Green, Halleck.

Danbury News Man. See Bailey, J. M.

Danbury Trojans Football Club

The athletes of the Danbury Trojans Football Club, a member of the American Professional Football Association, at Danbury, Conn., are commonly known as the *Red Horsemen* and the *Red Raiders* because they wear red uniforms. They are called *Mad Hatters* [1] because Danbury is famous for the manufacturing of hats.

[1] A communication from J. L. Thompson, owner and Coach of The Danbury Trojans Football Club, Danbury, Conn., March 31, 1939.

Dancing Fool. See McAdoo, W. G.

Dandy Little Manager. See Durocher, L. E.

Dandy Wayne. See Wayne, Anthony

Daniel Baker College

The students comprising the athletic teams of Daniel Baker College, located at Brownwood, Tex., were designated the *Hillbillies* [1] and the *Billy Kids* about 1902. The former nickname had its origin as follows.

About 1902 a large uncouth country boy, named Roach, came to Daniel Baker College where the students called him a Hillbilly. He later became an outstanding college athlete. Once in a game someone remarked, "Watch that Hillbilly go." Others joined in, "Watch those Hillbillies go." Then the teams gradually became known as *Hillbillies,* and in 1904 the nickname was officially adopted. The freshman teams are designated the *Billy Kids.* [1]

[1] A letter from R. Guy Davis, President of Daniel Baker College, Brownwood, Tex., December 10, 1935.

Daniel Boone of Southern Kentucky. See Lynn, Benjamin

Daniel Boone of the Rocky Mountains. See Bridger, James

Danville, Virginia

Danville has been called the *Last Capital of the Confederacy* [1] because President Jefferson Davis and his Cabinet used the home of W. T. Sutherland, in Danville, as the headquarters of the Southern Confederacy after Petersburg, Va., had been captured by the Union forces and Richmond, Va., had been evacuated.

[1] *Virginia,* comp. and ed. by Charlotte Allen (Published by the Department of Agriculture and Immigration of the State of Virginia under the direction of George W. Koiner, Commissioner, Division of Purchase and Printing, Richmond, Va., 1927) p. 85.

Dardanelles of the New World

The Detroit River which connects Lake St. Clair with Lake Erie has been called the *Dardanelles of the New World*.[1] The Dardanelles also connects two bodies of water, the Sea of Marmora and the Aegean Sea.

[1] *The Encyclopedia Americana* (Americana Corporation, New York and Chicago, 1927) vol. 9, p. 28.

Dark and Bloody Ground State. See Kentucky

Dark Day

May 19, 1780, has been designated the *Dark Day*[1] in allusion to the darkness of that day, particularly in the New England States. The darkness was so night-like that the animals returned to their resting places, and the people began to fear that the Judgment Day was at hand. It is probable that the darkness was caused by a great forest fire in the region.

[1] *New England, a Human Interest Geographical Reader,* Clifton Johnson (The Macmillan Company, New York and London, 1917) p. 189.

Dark Horse President. See Hayes, R. B.

Dark Lantern Party

The Native American party, which Edward Z. C. Judson organized in 1853 in New York, came to be nicknamed the *Dark Lantern Party*[1] because the meetings were held at night in the woods or other deserted places. The members carried lanterns carefully shaded to protect themselves from being recognized if they should meet anyone who was not a member of this organization.

[1] *Memoirs of Gustave Koerner, 1809-1896; Life-sketches Written at the Suggestion of His Children,* ed. by Thomas J. McCormack (The Torch Press, Cedar Rapids, Iowa, 1909) p. 19.

Darling, Jay Norwood

Jay Norwood Darling, who was born at Norwood, Michigan in 1876, was nicknamed *Ding Darling*.[1] He is famous for his cartoons of wild life which have appeared in the New York Herald Tribune, The Des Moines Register and other newspapers since 1917. In 1934 and 1935, Darling was chief biologist in the Department of Agriculture. He has long been an advocate of conservation policies for the United States.

[1] *The World Book,* The Quarrie Corporation, Chicago, 1947, vol. 4, p. 1877.
[2] *Current Biography 1942, Who's News and Why,* ed. by Maxine Block (The H. W. Wilson Company, New York, 1942) p. 175-77.

Darlington, William

William Darlington was nicknamed the *Nestor of American Botany*[1] because he devoted many years to the study of botanical science, collected and preserved much valuable data relating to the history of early botany in the United States. The nickname signified the veneration in which he was held by American botanists. Nestor, the Trojan hero, was held in similar respect by the Greeks because of his wide learning.

William Darlington was born at Dilworthtown, Pa., on April 28, 1872, and died at Westchester, Pa., on April 23, 1863.

[1] *Dictionary of American Biography under the Auspices of the American Council of Learned Societies,* ed. by Allen Johnson and Dumas Malone (Charles Scribner's Sons, New York, 1930) vol. 5, p. 78.

Dartmouth College

The athletes of Dartmouth College, at Hanover, N.H., are called *Indians*[1] because this college was an outgrowth of Moore's Indian Charity School of Lebanon, Conn. Any full-blooded American Indian who qualifies for admission at Dartmouth is still exempt from tuition.

[1] A letter from Dean Chamberlain, Director of Athletic Information at Dartmouth College, Hanover, N.H., June 17, 1935.

D'Artagnan of the A.E.F. See MacArthur, Douglas

Dashing Phil Kearny. See Kearny, Philip

Daughter of the Confederacy. See Davis, V. A. J.

Daughter of the Stars. See Shenandoah Valley

Daughters of Liberty

Prior to the Boston Tea Party on December 16, 1773, while the colonists were feeling bitter toward King George III and the British Parliament for imposing a tax on tea shipped to the American Colonies, the colonial women banded together for the purpose of refusing to use the English tea and called themselves *Daughters of Liberty*.[1]

[1] *Lives of Celebrated Americans: Comprising Biographies of Three Hundred and Forty Eminent Persons,* Benson J. Lossing (Thomas Belknap, Hartford, Conn., 1869) p. 148.

Davenport, Iowa, Moline, Illinois, and Rock Island, Illinois

The two cities in Illinois, Moline and Rock Island, and Davenport, Iowa, which is opposite Rock Island, are located so near to each other, and are so closely connected by railroads and electric lines, that they are known as the *Tri-cities*.[1]

[1] *Seeing the Middle West*, John T. Faris (J. B. Lippincott Company, Philadelphia, 1923) p. 167.
The New International Cyclopaedia, Second Edition (Dodd, Mead and Company, New York, 1930) vol. 16, p. 110.

Davie, William Richardson

William Richardson Davie, a Revolutionary soldier and politician, was called the *Father of the University of North Carolina*[1] because he had been instrumental in founding, locating, building and financing the University. He chose its early faculty and drafted its first courses of study. He secured the establishment of this university while he represented Halifax Borough in the North Carolina State Assembly from 1786 until 1798.

William Richardson Davie was born at Egremont, England, on June 20, 1756, emigrated to America in 1763, and died in Lancaster County, S.C., on November 29, 1820.

[1] *Dictionary of American Biography under the Auspices of the American Council of Learned Societies*, ed. by Dumas Malone (Charles Scribner's Sons, New York, 1930) vol. 5, p. 98.

Davies, Charles

Old Tush[1] was the nickname applied to Charles Davies at the United States Military Academy at West Point, N.Y., because his teeth projected prominently. From 1816 to 1837 he was professor of mathematics at the Academy.

Charles Davies was born at Washington, Conn., on January 22, 1798, and died at Fishkill Landing, N.Y., on September 18, 1876.

[1] *Robert E. Lee, the West Pointer*, by Charles Dudley Rhodes, Including *Stratford Hall*, by Mrs. Robert Scott Spilman and *The Lineage and Career of Robert E. Lee*, by George S. Wallace (Garrett and Massie, Richmond, Va., 1932) p. 19.
The National Cyclopedia of American Biography (James T. White and Company, New York, 1893) vol. 3, p. 26.

Davies, Charles Stewart

Charles Stewart Davies, a lawyer, was nicknamed *Grecian Davies*[1] while he was a student at Bowdoin College, at Brunswick, Me., because he read so extensively. After he graduated from Bowdoin College in 1807, he studied law and specialized in ad-

miralty law in which he became a nationally known expert.

Charles Stewart Davies was born at Portland, Me., on May 10, 1788, and died there on May 29, 1865.

[1] *Dictionary of American Biography under the Auspices of the American Council of Learned Societies*, ed. by Allen Johnson and Dumas Malone (Charles Scribner's Sons, New York, 1930) vol. 5, p. 81.

Davis, Andrew Jackson

Andrew Jackson Davis, a mesmerist and spiritualist, was called the *Poughkeepsie Seer*[1]. He lived at Poughkeepsie, N.Y., from 1843 until the time of his death and became nationally known as a mesmerist and spiritualist. He claimed to have clairvoyant powers which aided him in the curing of diseases.

Andrew Jackson Davis was born at Blooming Grove, N.Y., on August 11, 1826, and died at Poughkeepsie, N.Y., on January 13, 1910.

[1] *Dictionary of American Biography under the Auspices of the American Council of Learned Societies*, ed. by Allen Johnson and Dumas Malone (Charles Scribner's Sons, New York, 1930) vol. 5, p. 105.

Davis, George Willis

George Willis Davis, who was born at Bridgeport, Conn., on February 12, 1904, and who played outfield in major league baseball, was nicknamed *Kiddo*[1] probably because he was only about twenty-two years of age when he entered professional baseball.

[1] *Who's Who in Major League Base Ball*, comp. by Harold (Speed) Johnson (Buxton Publishing Company, Chicago, 1933) p. 132)

Davis, Harry Albert

Stinky[1] was the nickname applied to Harry Albert Davis by the Rochester team because it was the name of a popular cartoon appearing in the daily papers about 1930 or 1931.

Harry Albert Davis, who was born at Shreveport, La., on May 7, 1910, played first baseman in major league baseball.

[1] *Who's Who in Major League Baseball*, comp. by Harold (Speed) Johnson (Buxton Publishing Company. Chicago, 1933) p. 133.

Davis, Harry Phillips

Harry Phillips Davis has been designated the *Father of Radio Broadcasting*[1] because he initiated radio broadcasting and expanded it within a decade to a great public utility.

A pioneer in radio broadcasting, Harry Phillips Davis was chiefly responsible for establishing, on November 2, 1920, the first radio station in the world to be devoted to broadcasting daily programs for information and recreation. This was Station KDKA at Pittsburgh, Pa., sponsored by the Westinghouse Electric and Manufacturing Company. He became the chairman of the board of the National Broadcasting Company, a director of the Radio Corporation of America and of the Westinghouse Electric and Manufacturing Company.

He was born at Somersworth, N.H., on July 31, 1868, and died at Pittsburgh, Pa., on September 10, 1931.

[1] *Who's Who in America: A Biographical Dictionary of Notable Living Men and Women of the United States, 1930-1931,* ed. by Albert Nelson Marquis (The A. N. Marquis Company, Chicago, 1930-1931) vol. 16, p. 647.
Encyclopedia of American Biography: American Biography, a New Cyclopedia, comp. under the editorial supervision of a notable advisory board (Published under the direction of The American Historical Society, Inc., New York, 1931) vol. 49, p. 9.

Davis, James John
Puddler Jim and the *Welsh Parson* are nicknames of Senator James John Davis of Pennsylvania.

He was known as *Puddler Jim* [1] because when he was a boy he was an assistant puddler in an iron factory at Sharon, Pa., and at sixteen became a full-fledged iron puddler and was admitted to the Union of Iron-workers.

Senator Davis was of Welsh descent, and a very religious person, often quoting verses from the Bible which lead to his being called the *Welsh Parson.*[2]

James John Davis, who was born at Tredegar, South Wales, on October 27, 1873, served as a Senator from Pennsylvania to the United States Congress from 1930 to 1945. He died at Takoma Park, Md., November 22, 1947.

[1] *Our Foreign-born Citizens: What They Have Done for America,* Annie E. S. Beard, revised and enlarged by Frederick Beard (Thomas Y. Crowell Company, New York, 1932) p. 118.
[2] *The Iron Puddler: My Life in the Rolling Mills and What Came of It,* James John Davis, with an introduction by Joseph G. Cannon (The Bobbs-Merrill Company, Indianapolis, Ind., 1922) p. 71, 85, 96.

Davis, Mathew Livingston
Mathew Livingston Davis, a politician and journalist, was designated the *Old Boy in Specs* [1] because he wore spectacles, and was genial and unassuming. He was an active member of the Democratic party both in organizing and formulating the policies of the party.

Mathew Livingston Davis was born at New York City on October 28, 1773, and died at Manhattanville, N.Y., on June 2, 1850.

[1] *Dictionary of American Biography under the Auspices of the American Council of Learned Societies,* ed. by Allen Johnson and Dumas Malone (Charles Scribner's Sons, New York, 1930) vol. 5, p. 138.
Aaron Burr: A Biography Compiled from Rare, and in Many Cases Unpublished, Sources, Samuel H. Windell and Meade Minningerode (G. P. Putnam's Sons, New York, 1925) vol. 1, p. 148.

Davis, Nathan Smith
Nathan Smith Davis, a physician, editor, and lecturer, was internationally known as the *Father of the American Medical Association* [1] because of his outstanding work in organizing the American Medical Association at Philadelphia, Pa., on May 5, 1847. This organization, composed of delegates representing various state medical associations, was formed to promote the science and the art of medicine and disseminate medical knowledge among the members of that profession. Davis was prominent as an organizer of city and state medical societies, was a brilliant lecturer on the science of medicine, and was the founder and editor of numerous medical journals.

Nathan Smith Davis was born at Greene, N.Y., on January 9, 1817, and died at Chicago, Ill., on June 16, 1904.

[1] *Dictionary of American Biography under the Auspices of the American Council of Learned Societies,* ed. by Allen Johnson and Dumas Malone (Charles Scribner's Sons, New York, 1930) vol. 5, p. 139.

Davis, Sam
The nicknames the *Boy-hero of the Confederacy* and the *Nathan Hale of the South* have been given to Sam Davis.

Davis was called the *Boy Hero of the Confederacy* [1] because at twenty-one he was acting as a spy for the Confederacy, carrying papers from Major General Dodge to Lieutenant General Bragg, when he was caught and hanged.

Because he died a martyr to the southern cause he has been designated the *Nathan Hale of the South.*[2]

Sam Davis was born near Smyrna, Tenn., on October 6, 1842, and died at Pulaski, Tenn., on November 27, 1863.

[1] *A School History of Tennessee,* Silas E. Scates (World Book Company, New York and Chicago, 1925) p. 302.
[2] *A History of Tennessee and Tennesseans, the Leaders and Representative Men in Commerce, Industry and Modern Activities,* Will T. Hale and Dixon L. Merritt (The Lewis Publishing Company, New York and Chicago, 1913) vol. 3, p. 707-9.
[2] *The Washington Post,* March 3, 1935, col. 4, p. 5.

Davis, Varina Anne Jefferson

Varina Anne Jefferson Davis who was born at Richmond, Va., on June 27, 1864, and who died at Narragansett Pier, R.I., on September 18, 1898, was called the *Daughter of the Confederacy* [1] because she was the daughter of Jefferson Davis, President of the Confederacy and was born in the Confederate capital.

[1] *The Encyclopedia Americana* (Americana Corporation, New York and Chicago, 1927) vol. 8, p. 513.

Davis, Virgil Lawrence

Spud [1] is the nickname by which Virgil Lawrence Davis was popularly designated because Irish potatoes formed one of the main ingredients of his diet when he was growing up.

He was born at Birmingham, Ala., on December 20, 1904, and was a catcher in major league baseball.

[1] *Who's Who in Major League Base Ball*, comp. by Harold (Speed) Johnson (Buxton Publishing Company, Chicago, 1933) p. 134.

Davis, Walter Alonzo

Walter Alonzo Davis came to be popularly known as the *Marrying Justice of Worcester County* [1] because during his thirty-four years in office as City Clerk in Fitchburg, Worcester County, Mass., he issued over a thousand marriage. licenses and married eight hundred and fifteen couples.

He was born at Fitchburg, Mass., on July 13, 1846, and died there on October 17, 1921.

[1] *Encyclopedia of American Biography: American Biography, a New Cyclopedia*, comp. under the editorial supervision of a notable advisory board (Published under the direction of The American Historical Society, Inc., New York, 1922) vol. 10, p. 166.

Davis, William Morris

The *Father of the Science of Physiography* [1] is a nickname applied to William Morris Davis in commemoration of his achievements in physical geography.

He was Professor of Geology at Harvard University for a number of years. In 1912 he arranged and guided the transcontinental excursion of the Geographical Society of New York, later organizing and conducting field trips in various parts of the world.

William Morris Davis was born at Philadelphia, Pa., on February 12, 1850, and died February 5, 1934.

[1] *The National Cyclopaedia of American Biography* (James T. White and Company, New York, 1927) vol. B, p. 93.
Who's Who in America, A Biographical Dictionary of Notable Living Men and Women of the United States, 1932-1933, ed. by Albert Nelson Marquis (The A. N. Marquis Company, Chicago, 1932) vol. 17, p. 669.

Davis and Elkins College

The athletic teams of Davis and Elkins College, at Elkins, W.Va., are popularly called the *Scarlet Hurricanes* and the *Senators.*

The *Scarlet Hurricanes* [1] was applied to the teams by a sports writer. They were called the *Senators* because the founders of the College, Henry Gassaway Davis and Stephen B. Elkins, were both Senators and lived in the town.

[1] A letter from Charles E. Albert, Acting President of Davis and Elkins College, Elkins, W.Va., November 16, 1935.

Dawes, Henry Laurens

Henry Laurens Dawes, a legislator, was called the *Sage of Pittsfield.* [1] He had achieved nation-wide renown as a lawmaker and he was considered Pittsfield's most influential citizen. Dawes was a Representative from Massachusetts to Congress from 1857 until 1875, and a Senator from 1875 until 1893.

Henry Laurens Dawes was born at Cummington, Mass., on October 30, 1816, and died at Pittsfield, Mass., on February 5, 1903.

[1] *Dictionary of American Biography under the Auspices of the American Council of Learned Societies*, ed. by Allen Johnson and Dumas Malone (Charles Scribner's Sons, New York, 1930) vol. 5, p. 150.

Dawson, John

John Dawson, a statesman, was called *Beau* [1] because of his fastidiousness in dress and his polished and charming manners. Dawson, who took an active part in the adoption of the Federal Constitution in 1781 and in the establishing of the national government, was a Representative from Virginia to the United States Congress from 1797 until 1814.

John Dawson was born in Virginia, in 1762, and died at Washington, D.C., on March 31, 1814.

[1] *Dictionary of American Biography under the Auspices of the American Council of Learned Societies*, ed. by Allen Johnson and Dumas Malone (Charles Scribner's Sons, New York, 1930) vol. 5, p. 153.

Dawson Springs, Kentucky

Dawson Springs has been nicknamed the *City of Health* because it is widely known for its mineral waters and baths.

Day-old Chick. See Wene, E. H.

Day-star of the Revolution. See Hamilton, Andrew

Dayton, Ohio

Dayton, Ohio, is called the *Cradle of Aviation* and the *Gem City of Ohio.* It claims the title the *Cradle of Aviation* [1] because it was the home of Orville and Wilbur Wright, whose experiments with heavier-than-air machines led to the development of aeroplanes and the manufacturing of aeroplanes at Dayton.

This city is called the *Gem City of Ohio* [2] because it is one of the most beautiful and prosperous cities in Ohio. Dayton, located at the confluence of the four streams, the Miami River, the Mad River, the Stillwater River, and the Wolf Creek, is surrounded by fertile valleys which contribute to the importance of the city. It is also prominent as a manufacturing, commercial, industrial and transportation center.

[1] *Dayton and Montgomery County, Resources and People,* Editor, Charlotte Reeve Conover (Lewis Historical Publishing Company, Inc., New York, 1932) vol. 1, p. 293-9.
[2] *A Book of Nicknames,* John Goff (Courier-Journal Job Printing Company, Louisville, Ky., 1892) p. 16.
History of Dayton, Ohio, with Portraits and Biographical Sketches of Some of Its Pioneer and Prominent Citizens, Harvey W. Crew, Proprietor and Managing Publisher (United Brethren Publishing House, Dayton, Ohio, 1889) p. 29.

Dazzy. See Vance, A. C.

Deacon Hatch. See Hatch, C. A.

Deacons. See Hobart College; Wake Forest College

Dead Man's Corner

The Battle of Antietam was fought near the Sharpsburg turnpike and Antietam Creek in Maryland on September 17, 1862. One particularly gruesome spot on this scene of battle was nicknamed *Dead Man's Corner* [1] because of the number of men killed there.

[1] *The Seventy-ninth Highlanders; New York Volunteers in the War of Rebellion, 1861-1865,* William Todd (Press of Brandow, Barton and Company, Albany, N.Y., 1886) p. 236.

Dead Rabbits

The *Dead Rabbits* [1] is a term applied to a gang which existed in Philadelphia, Pa., from about 1857 to 1861. The purpose of the gang was to prevent people who differed from them in their political views from going to the polls on election days.

[1] *Life and Liberty in America: Or Sketches of a Tour in the United States and Canada, in 1857-8,* Charles Mackay (Smith, Elder and Company, London, 1859) vol. 1, p. 164.

Deadeye Division. See Ninety-sixth Infantry Division of World War II

Deadfalls

During the Reconstruction following the Civil War, unscrupulous white men in the southern states established small stores to take in cotton, corn, or other farm products which had been stolen and brought to these stores in return for whiskey, cheap jewelry, and other commodities. These disreputable shops were popularly termed *Deadfalls.* [1] A deadfall is a trap with a weight which falls on and kills an animal getting into it.

[1] *Documentary History of Reconstruction, Political, Military, Social, Religious, Educational and Industrial, 1865 to the Present Time,* Walter L. Fleming (The Arthur H. Clark Company, Cleveland, Ohio, 1907) vol. 2, p. 318.

Deadwood Dick. See' Clark, Richard

Deaf Smith. See Smith, Erasmus

Deafman Eloquent. See Potts, J. H.

Dean, Jay Hanner

Jay Hanner Dean, who was born at Lucas, Ark., on January 16, 1911, and who pitched in major league baseball, is popularly designated *Dizzy Dean* [1] because he "fanned so many of Comiskey's players that he made everyone dizzy." Upon *Dizzy's* retirement from the diamond, he entered the field of sports announcing, and became famous for his inimitable style of broadcasting.

[1] *Who's Who in Major League Base Ball,* comp. by Harold (Speed) Johnson (Buxton Publishing Company, Chicago, 1933) p. 135.

Dean of American Football. See Camp, Walter

Dean of American Popular Music. See Whiteman, Paul

Dean of Community Advertising. See Hatfield, C. F.

Dean of Cotton Row. See Doughty, J. P.

Dean of the Alabama Legislature.
See Tunstall, A. M.

Dean of the American Labor Movement. See Furuseth, Andrew

Dean of the American Stage. See Jefferson, Joseph

Dean of the American Theatre. See Skinner, Otis

Dean of the House. See Sabath, A. J.

Dean of the Liberals. See Norris, G. W.

Dear Alben. See Barkley, A. W.

Death on a Pale Horse. See Wirz, Henry

Death Hole

During the siege of Vicksburg, Miss., in June 1864, a crater caused by an exploded mine near the Confederate defenses was called the *Death Hole*.[1] Federal soldiers had tried to get behind the Confederate lines by means of this hole, but were killed by hand-grenades and shells from higher ground held by Confederates and buried by the toppling debris.

[1] *Military Essays and Recollections; Papers, Read Before the Commanders of the State of Illinois, Military Order of the Loyal Legion of the United States,* published by order of the commandery (A. C. McClurg and Company, Chicago, 1894) p. 342.

Death's Door

The entrance from Lake Michigan into Green Bay in Wisconsin has been designated *Death's Door* [1] because of the treacherous currents and rocks.

[1] *Seeing the Middle West,* John T. Faris (J. B. Lippincott Company, Philadelphia and London, 1923) p. 28.

Defender of the Constitution. See Webster, Daniel

Defender of the Faith. See Roberts, B. H.

Defender of the Union. See Webster, Daniel

De Lancey, James

James De Lancey, a colonial politician and turfman, was nicknamed the *Father of the New York Turf* [1] because he imported from England the first thoroughbred race horses, and assembled the first group of race horses in America. De Lancey was commissioned Lieutenant Governor of New York by George II, King of England, in October 1747.

James De Lancey was born at New York City, in 1732, and died at Bath, England, in April, 1800.

[1] *Dictionary of American Biography under the Auspices of the American Council of Learned Societies,* ed. by Allen Johnson and Dumas Malone (Charles Scribner's Sons, New York, 1930) vol. 5, p. 213.

Delaware

Delaware possesses six nicknames: the *Blue Hen's Chickens State,* the *First State, Blue Hen State, Diamond State, New Sweden (Nya Sveriga),* and *Uncle Sam's Pocket Handkerchief.*

The *Blue Hen's Chickens State* [1] and *Blue Hen State* originated during the Revolutionary War. Captain Caldwell from Kent County, Delaware, took with his company two game cocks of the breed of a certain blue hen, well known in Kent County for their fighting qualities. When put in the ring, these cocks flew at each other with such fury and fought so gamely that a solder cried: "We're sons of the Old Blue Hen and we're game to the end." Thus these Delaware regiments came to be known as "Blue Hen's Chickens." Later this name came to be state wide in its application.

Delaware is called the *Diamond State* [2] because it is small in size but great in importance. It is also called the *First State* [3] because it was the first to ratify the Constitution. The state was nicknamed *New Sweden (Nya Sveriga)* [4] because Peter Minuit built a fort on the present site of Wilmington in 1638 and garrisoned it with Swedes and Finns, after which for many years the peninsula was under Swedish rule. Delaware is sometimes called *Uncle Sam's Pocket Handkerchief,*[5] from the fact that it is so small.

[1] *A History of Delaware,* W. A. Powell (The Christopher Publishing House, Boston, 1928) p. 155.

[2] *A New Dictionary of Americanisms,* Sylva Clapin (Louis Weiss and Company, New York, 1903) p. 158.

[3] *Compton's Pictured Encyclopedia* (F. E. Compton and Company, Chicago, 1947) vol. 4, p. 40.

[4] *King's Handbook of the United States,* planned and ed. by Moses King, text by M. F. Sweetser (Moses King Corporation, Buffalo, N.Y., 1891) p. 143.

[5] *Manual of Useful Information,* comp. under the direction of J. C. Thomas (The Werner Company, Chicago, 1893) p. 22.

Delaware Plowboy. See Biggs, B. T.

Delawareans

The Delawareans are called *Blue Hen's Chickens* and *Muskrats.* They are proud of the sobriquet *Blue Hen's Chickens* because of its historical association as stated above. (See Delaware.) Muskrats were very numerous in Delaware in the early days. From this fact and from the smallness of the state, it was said that only muskrats could get a foothold there and the people of this state became known as *Muskrats.*[1]

[1] *U.S.: An Index to the United States of America,* comp. by Malcolm Townsend (D. Lothrop Company, Boston, 1890) p. 75.

Deliverer of America. See Washington, George

Delmas, Delphin Michael

Delphin Michael Delmas, a lawyer, was widely known as the *Napoleon of the California Bar* [1] and as *The Silver-tongued Spellbinder of the Pacific Coast.*

The *Napoleon of the California Bar* was applied to him because his features were said to be remarkably like those of Napoleon Bonaparte, and because Delmas was a formidable opponent. He was nicknamed the *Silver-tongued Spell-binder of the Pacific Coast* because of his brilliant pleading before courts.

Delphin Michael Delmas was born in France, on April 14, 1844, and died at Santa Monica, Calif., on August 1, 1928.

[1] *Dictionary of American Biography under the Auspices of the American Council of Learned Societies,* ed. by Allen Johnson and Dumas Malone (Charles Scribner's Sons, New York, 1930) vol. 5, p. 226.
Allen Johnson and Dumes Malone (Charles Scribner's

De Longpré, Paul

The *King of Flower Painters* [1] was attributed to Paul De Longpré because he was a master painter of flowers on silk, ivory, and canvas. His pictures were characterized by originality, grace of style, simplicity, and beauty of pattern.

Paul De Longpré was born at Lyons, France, on April 18, 1855, and died at Hollywood, Calif., in 1911 or 1912.

[1] *The National Cyclopaedia of American Biography* (James T. White and Company, New York, 1918) vol. 16, p. 273.

Democratic War Horse. See McMillin, Benton

Democratic War Horse of Tennessee. See McMillin, Benton

Demon Deacons. See Wake Forest College

Demopolis, Alabama

The *City of People* [1] and the *People's City* are the nicknames applied to Demopolis, a direct translation of the Greek name. Contributing perhaps to the fixing of the appellation was the cosmopolitan character of its settlers.

[1] *Alabama: History of Alabama and her People,* Albert Burton Moore, assisted by an advisory council, *Alabama Biography* by a special staff of writers (The American Historical Society, Inc., Chicago and New York, 1927) vol. 1, p. 115.
Demopolis, Alabama, A Pamphlet, Descriptive of Its Location, together with an Accurate Description of Its Surroundings. . . . issued under the auspices of the city council (The Selma Printing Company, Selma, Ala., 1887) p. 4.
"The French Grant in Alabama. A History of the Founding of Demopolis" by Gaius Whitfield, Junior, in *The Alabama Historical Society Collections* (Alabama Historical Society, Birmingham, Ala., 1904) vol. 4, p. 321-55.

Dempsey, Jack

Jack Dempsey, who was born in Kildare County, Ireland, on December 15, 1862, and who was one of the early middleweight American champions, was nicknamed the *Nonpareil.*

Demosthenes of Texas. See Hubbard, R. B.

Demosthens of the Mountains. See Miller, H. V. M.

Dempsey, William Harrison (Jack Dempsey)

William Harrison (Jack) Dempsey, an internationally known heavyweight boxer, is nicknamed the *Manassa Mauler* [1] because he was born at Manassa, Colo. Dempsey was born on June 24, 1895, and now resides at New York City.

[1] *Post Boxing Record* (Post Sports Records Corporation, New York, 1935) p. 81.

Denison, Texas

Denison is called the *Gate City* [1] because of its location at the northern extremity of Texas at the termination of the "black land

Denison, Texas—Continued

belt" of that state where its transportation facilities provide for commerce between Texas, Oklahoma, Louisiana and other states.

[1] *Flashlights on Texas*, Lillie Terrell Shaver and Willie Williamson Rogers (A. C. Baldwin and sons, Austin, Tex., 1928) p. 117.

The Geography of Texas, Physical and Political, Revised Edition, Frederick William Simonds (Ginn and Company, New York and Boston, 1914) p. 195.

Denison University

The *Big Reds*[1] and *Redskins* are the sobriquets given to the athletic teams of Denison University, at Granville, Ohio. Prior to 1925 the nickname *Big Reds* was used because the school colors are red and white. Later the *Redskins* was chosen because this part of Ohio was inhabited by the Miami Indians.

[1] A communication from George L. Rider, Director of Athletics at Denison University, Granville, Ohio, June 18, 1935.

Dennie, Joseph

Joseph Dennie, an American journalist who lived from 1768 to 1812, was often spoken of as the *American Addison*[1] by those who admired his literary contributions and his satirical style.

[1] "Joseph Dennie and His Circle, a Study in American Literature from 1792 to 1812" by Harold Milton Ellis, in *Studies in English, Volumes 3 to 5* (Bulletin of the University of Texas, 1915; Number Forty, Published by the University, Austin, Tex., July, 1915) vol. 3, p. 9; 216, 218-19. 220.

History of the United States of America, under the Constitution, James Schouler (William H. Morrison, Washington, D.C., 1887) vol. 2, p. 261.

Dennison, Aaron Lufkin

Aaron Lufkin Dennison was called the *Father of American Watchmaking*[1] because he was a pioneer watch manufacturer in the United States. With the aid of Edward Howard and Samuel Curtis of Boston, Mass., Dennison set up a plant at Roxbury, Mass., about 1849, where he designed the first factory-made watches in the world. He is accredited with having originated the idea of manufacturing the parts of a watch by machinery so they were interchangeable.

Aaron Lufkin Dennison was born at Freeport, Me., on March 6, 1812, and died at Birmingham, England, on January 9, 1895.

[1] *Dictionary of American Biography under the Auspices of the American Council of Learned Societies*, ed. by Allen Johnson and Dumas Malone (Charles Scribner's Sons, New York, 1930) vol. 5, p. 240.

Denver, Colorado

Denver is known as the *City of the Plains, Convention City*, and *Queen City of the Plains*.

It is frequently called the *Convention City*[1] because its accessibility by railroads and highways and its pleasant climate and scenic surroundings make it an ideal city for the numerous conventions which are held there. The fact that Denver is located on the edge of the Great Plains amidst such scenic beauty as Pike's Peak, Cheyenne Mountain, and Estes Park, and that it was a center of gold mining, have caused it to be designated the *Queen City of the Plains*, and the *City of the Plains*.[1]

[1] *Colorado, the Queen Jewel of the Rockies: A Description of Its Climate and of Its Mountains, Rivers, Forests and Valleys: an Account of Its Explorers; a Review of Its Indians—Past and Present; a Survey of Its Industries, with Some Reference to What It Offers of Delight to the Automobilist, Traveler, Sportsman and Health Seeker*, Mae Lacy Baggs (The Page Company, Boston, 1918) p. 161.

Denver of South Dakota. See Rapid City, S.D.

Depew, Chauncey Mitchell

Chauncey Mitchell Depew, a politician, who was born at Peekskill, N.Y., on April 23, 1834, and who died at New York City on April 15, 1928, was nicknamed the *Peach*.[1] He was elected a Republican United States Senator from New York in 1899. In 1885 he was elected president of the New York Central and Hudson River Railroad. Depew was speaking at a Republican gathering on the Bowery in New York City during the presidential campaign in 1892. When, in an effort to convince his listeners that the United States was still the land of opportunity, he stated that he began his career with only his hands and his head as capital, some one in the audience called out, "That head is a peach, Chaunce." The newspapers began calling him the *Peach*, and he was popularly so called until his death.

[1] *As I Knew Them: Presidents and Politics from Grant to Coolidge*, Henry Luther Stoddard (Harper and Brothers, New York and London, 1927) p. 268-9.

Derby, Elias Hasket

The *Father of American Commerce with India*[1] was the nickname given to Elias Hasket Derby, because in 1799 he established trade relations between the United States and India, his merchant ships being the first to display the American flag in the

Calcutta harbor. Derby was also a pioneer trader with China and the East Indies.

Elias Hasket Derby was born at Salem, Mass., on August 16, 1739, and died there on September 8, 1799.

[1] *The National Cyclopaedia of American Biography* (James T. White and Company, New York, 1907) vol. 5, p. 32.

Derby, George Horatio

George Horatio Derby, a humorist, was nicknamed *Squibob*,[1] from the name of a book which he published in 1859 called *The Squibob Papers*. Derby developed the typical blustering type of western humor while he was living on the Pacific Coast in the 1850's.

George Horatio Derby was born at Dedham, Mass., on April 3, 1823, and died at New York City, on May 15, 1861.

[1] *Dictionary of American Biography under the Auspices of the American Council of Learned Societies*, ed. by Allen Johnson and Dumas Malone (Charles Scribner's Sons, New York, 1930) vol. 5, p. 252.

Derringer, Paul

Paul Derringer, who was born at Springfield, Ky., on October 17, 1907, and who was a pitcher in major league baseball, is nicknamed *Duke*.[1]

[1] *Who's Who in Major League Base Ball*, comp. by Harold (Speed) Johnson (Buxton Publishing Company, Chicago, 1933) p. 138.

De Salvatierra, Juan Maria

Juan Maria De Salvatierra was commonly known as the *Apostle of California*.[1] On October 19, 1697, he founded a Jesuit mission at Loreto in Lower California, and later six other missions along the coast of California.

Juan Maria de Salvatierra was born at Milan, Italy, on November 15, 1648, and died at Guadalajara, Mexico, on July 18, 1717.

[1] *Appleton's Cyclopaedia of American Biography*, ed. by James Grant Wilson and John Fiske (D. Appleton and Company, New York, 1894) vol. 5, p. 381.

Deseret State. See Utah

De Smet, Peter John

The appellation, the *Apostle of the Rocky Mountains*,[1] was applied to Peter John De Smet because he did mission work throughout the regions of the Rocky Mountains.

Peter John De Smet was born in Belgium, on December 31, 1801, was sent to the United States by his Jesuit superiors in 1822, and died at St. Louis, Mo., in May, 1872.

After being ordained a priest about 1838, Peter John De Smet began his activities as a missionary to the Indians. He won the trust and friendship of the Indians, which made him an invaluable agent for the United States during the Sioux War of 1876.

[1] *American History Briefly Told: Book Three, Period of the Revolution and Confederation; Period of the Development of the States to the Civil War: Book Four, Period of the Civil War; Period of Reconstruction and Expansion*, comp. by the Franciscan Sisters of the Perpetual Adoration (St. Rose Convent, La Crosse, Wis., 1912) p. 208.
The National Cyclopaedia of American Biography (James T. White and Company, New York, 1909) vol. 11, p. 454.

Des Moines, Iowa

Des Moines was nicknamed the *Hartford of the West*[1] because like Hartford, Conn., it is an insurance center.

[1] *The World Book*, The Quarrie Corporation, Chicago, 1947, vol. 4, p. 1963.

Des Moines Comets. See Des Moines Pro-football Team, Inc.

Des Moines Pro-football Team, Incorporated

The *Des Moines Comets*[1] is the nickname which was given to the teams of the Des Moines Pro-football Team, Inc., at Des Moines, Iowa. It was selected by a competitive contest.

[1] A communication from A. H. Davis, Manager of The Des Moines Pro-football Team, Inc., Des Moines, Iowa, March 29, 1939.

Despot-in-chief in and over the Rising State of New Jersey. See Livingston, William

Destroying Angels

During the Civil War in Alabama groups of Federal outlaws and sympathizers engaged in burning, plundering, and confiscating the property of the Confederates. These marauding bands called themselves the *Destroying Angels*.[1]

[1] *Civil War and Reconstruction in Alabama*, Walter L. Fleming (The Columbia University Press, New York, 1905), p. 120.

Detroit, Michigan

The following sobriquets are attributed to Detroit: the *Automobile City*, the *Automobile City of the World*, the *Dynamic City*, the *City of Straits*, *Detroit the Beautiful*, and the *Motor Capital of the World*.

Detroit is nicknamed the *Automobile City*[1] and the *Automobile City of the*

Detroit, Michigan—Continued
World [2] because it produces more than sixty per cent of the automobiles built in the United States, and is the largest automobile producing city in the world. It is known as the *Dynamic City* [1] because of its industrial activities.

The sobriquet, *City of Straits,*[6] applied to Detroit, had its origin in the facts that the French word, *détroit,* signifies a strait, a narrow passage, or a sound. The city was founded on the land bordering the Detroit River which connects Lake Erie and Lake St. Claire.

The nickname, *Detroit the Beautiful,*[7] refers to the city's many spacious, well-laid-out parks, gardens filled with shrubs and growing plants, interspersed with colorful flower beds, and numerous playgrounds and boulevards, all of which combine to make it an aesthetically attractive place. *The Motor Capital of the World* [1] is an appellation given to Detroit because it is the greatest automobile producing city in the world.

[1] *History of Wayne County and the City of Detroit, Michigan,* Clarence Monroe Burton and Mary Agnes Burton, Editors, and H. T. O. Blue and Gordon K. Miller, Associate Editors (The S. J. Clarke Publishing Company, Chicago and Detroit, Mich., 1930) vol. 2, p. 1145-54, 1298-9, 1312-23, 1337-46, 1362, 1403, 1426.
[2] *Little Journeys in America,* Rose Henderson (The Southern Publishing Company, Dallas, Tex., 1922) p. 168.
Beautiful Detroit, Illustrated (Detroit Convention and Tourists' Bureau, Detroit, Mich., 1917) p. 34.
[3] *Minute Glimpses of American Cities,* Herbert S. Kates (Grosset and Dunlap, New York, 1933), p. 47.
[4] *Historic Michigan, Land of the Great Lakes, Its Life, Resources, Industries, People, Politics, Government, Wars, Institutions, Achievement, the Press, Schools, Churches, Legendary and Prehistoric Lore,* George N. Fuller, Editor (National Historical Association, Inc., Dayton, Ohio, 1928) vol. 3, p. 752-8.
[5] *Detroit—The Marvel City, Its Makers, Its Men of Action,* Milton R. Palmer, Editor (Industrial Press Association, Detroit, Mich., 1922), p. 147-57, 209-11.
Detroit Illustrated: The Commercial Metropolis of Michigan. . . . (Werner Printing and Lithographing Company, for Hary H. Hook, Detroit, Mich., 1891) p. 39.
[6] *The City of Detroit, Michigan, 1701-1922,* Clarence M. Burton, Editor-in-chief, William Stocking, Associate Editor, Gordon K. Miller, Associate Editor (The S. J. Clarke Publishing Company, Detroit, Mich., and Chicago, 1922) vol. 1, p. 4.
[7] *Detroit, The Beautiful,* ed. and comp. by S. L. Houghton and J. F. Walsh (John Bornman and Son, Detroit, Mich., 1931) p. 3, 6, 47

Detroit American League Baseball Company
The members of this baseball team were first nicknamed *Wolverines* in commemoration of the fact that Michigan is designated the *Wolverine State.*[1] About 1900 the team was renamed *Detroit Tigers* [1] by the Sporting Editor of the Detroit Free Press.

[1] A letter from Charles F. Navin, Secretary and Treasurer of the Detroit Baseball Company, Detroit, Mich., July 19, 1935.

Detroit Institute of Technology
The athletic teams of the Detroit Institute of Technology, at Detroit, Mich., were designated the *Toilers* [1] by a sports writer for the *Detroit Times* because so many of the students were wholly or partially self supporting.

[1] A communication from Paul Hickey, President of the Detroit Institute of Technology, Detroit, Mich., November 18, 1935.

Detroit Lions.   See   Detroit   National League Football Club, Inc.

Detroit National League Football Club, Incorporated
The *Detroit Lions* [1] is the nickname of the Detroit National League Football Club, Inc., a member of the National Football League, located at Detroit, Mich. George A. Richards gave this name to the teams in 1934, when he purchased the franchise of the *Portsmouth Spartans* and took them from Portsmouth, Ohio, to Detroit. Richards selected the nickname *Detroit Lions* because the teams of the Detroit American League Baseball Company are nicknamed the *Detroit Tigers* and the Detroit National League Hockey teams were the *Cougars.*

[1] A communication from M. G. Shaver, vice-President of The National League Football Club, Inc., Detroit, Mich., April 13, 1939.

Detroit River.   See Dardanelles of the New World

Detroit the Beautiful.   See Detroit, Mich.

Detroit Tigers.   See Detroit American League Baseball Company

Detroit's Greatest Traveler.   See Stearns, F. K.

Deutsch-Athens.   See Milwaukee, Wis.

Devil David.   See Forman, David

Devil on Two Sticks.   See Morton, O. H. P. T.

Devil Pete.   See Muhlenberg, J. P. G.

Devil Wagons.   See *Black Dragons*

Devil's Adjutant. See Waller, John

Devil's Half Acre

During the middle decades of the nineteenth century the slum section of Augusta, Me., was termed the *Devil's Half Acre* [1] because it was inhabited chiefly by people of questionable character engaged in unlawful and immoral activities.

[1] *Biographical Encyclopaedia of Maine of the Nineteenth Century*, Henry Clay Williams, Editor (Metropolitan Publishing and Engraving Company, Boston, 1885) p. 13.

Devil's Scuttle Hole. See *Caldron Linn*

Devin, Thomas Casimer

Thomas Casimer Devin was widely known as the *Old War-horse* [1] because he was a soldier in the Union Army during its campaigns against the Indians in the western part of the United States. He entered the army in 1861 and fought the Indians on the western frontiers from 1866 until 1878.

Thomas Casimer Devin was born at New York City, on December 10, 1822, and died there on April 4, 1878.

[1] *Dictionary of American Biography, under the Auspices of the American Council of Learned Societies*, ed. by Allen Johnson and Dumas Malone (Charles Scribner's Sons, New York, 1930) vol. 5, p. 263.

Dewey, George

After the Battle of Manila Bay [1] on May 1, 1898, Admiral George Dewey was designated the *Hero of Manila*. Directed by his skillful military tactics, the squadron under his command defeated the Spanish squadron under Admiral Patricio Montojo and on August 18, the city of Manila was captured, the chief seaport of the Philippine Islands.

Admiral George Dewey was born at Montpelier, Vt., on December 26, 1837, and died at Washington, D.C., on January 16, 1917.

[1] *Autobiography of George Dewey*, Admiral of the Navy (Charles Scribner's Sons, New York, 1913) p. 206-29.
Our Naval Heritage, Fitzhugh Green (Century Company, New York and London, 1925) p. 284-96.
The Hero of Manila, Dewey on the Mississippi and the Pacific, Rossiter Johnson (D. Appleton and Company, New York, 1899) p. 1.

Dewey, Jedediah

Jedediah Dewey, a colonial clergyman, was nicknamed the *Fighting Parson* [1] because he not only preached but also took an active part in the cause of the colonists against the British during the Revolutionary War. He was pastor of a church at Bennington, Vt., from 1763 until the time of his death in 1778.

Jedediah Dewey was born at Westfield, Mass., on April 11, 1714, and died at Bennington, Vt., on December 21, 1778.

[1] *Appleton's Cyclopaedia of American Biography*, ed. by James Grant Wilson and John Fiske (D. Appleton and Company, New York, 1900) vol. 7, p. 91.

Dewey of Manzanillo. See Todd, C. C.

Diamond Jim. See Brady, J. B.

Diamond Lil. See West, Mae

Diamond State. See Arkansas; Delaware

Dickie, George William

The *Father of Ship-building* [1] is the nickname by which George William Dickie was known on the Pacific Coast, in commemoration of his services as a pioneer in developing the ship-building industry.

From 1883 until 1905 Dickie was the general manager of the Union Iron Works at San Francisco, Calif. He drew the designs for a number of privately owned ships and several battleships for the United States Navy. He equipped the United States steamship *Oregon* with hydraulic turret engines later adopted by the British Navy. He designed engines and boilers for merchant ships and battleships, and was a consulting marine engineer and naval architect.

George William Dickie was born at Arbroath, Scotland, on July 27, 1844, and died at Oakland, Calif., on August 17, 1918.

[1] *The National Cyclopaedia of American Biography* (James T. White and Company, New York, 1932) vol. 22, p. 326.

Dickinson, John

The *Penman of the American Revolution* [1] was applied to John Dickinson because he wrote political papers and pamphlets giving expression to many of the ideals and ideas of the American Revolution.

He was born in Talbot County, Md., on November 8, 1732, and died at Wilmington, Del., on February 14, 1808.

[1] *The United States: A History of Three Centuries, 1607-1904, Population, Politics, War, Industry, Civilization, in Ten Parts*, William Estabrook Chancellor and Fletcher Willis Hewes (G. P. Putnam's Sons, New York and London, 1905) vol. 2, p. 473.

Dictator Goebel. See Goebel, William

Dictator of Jersey City. See Hague, Frank

Dictator of Louisiana. See Long, H. P.

Diggers. See Nevadans

Dillinger, John

John Dillinger, a mid-west outlaw, who was killed by Federal agents as he left the Biograph Theatre on Lincoln Avenue in Chicago, Ill., on July 22, 1934, was called *Kill Crazy Dillinger* [1] because of his extensive robbing and murdering during his period of outlawry. The FBI had designated him *Public Enemy Number One.*

[1] *The New York Times,* New York, July 23, 1934, col. 8, p. 1.
Washington Herald, Washington, D.C., March 14, 1934, cols. 2-3, p. 1.

Dimple of the Universe. See Nashville, Tenn.

Ding Darling. See Darling, J. N.

Dingell, John David

John David Dingell, a Michigan journalist, wholesale dealer, and politician, was nicknamed *Witz* and *Owski* because he had changed his Polish family name to Dingell, and often remarked that in doing so he lost his "Witz" and became "Owski."

He has been Democratic Representative from Michigan to the United States Congress since 1933.

John David Dingell was born at Detroit, Mich., on February 2, 1894.

[1] An interview with Captain Victor Hunt Harding, Secretary of the National Democratic Congress Reelection Committee, Washington, D. C., April 10, 1939.

Dinsmoor, Robert

Because his manner of living and his poetic contribution to literature were both characterized by genuine simplicity, artlessness, and a deep love of nature, Robert Dinsmoor was popularly calld the *Rustic Bard.*[1]

He was born at Windham, N.H., on October 7, 1757, and died there on March 16, 1836.

[1] *The National Cyclopaedia of American Biography* (James T. White and Company, New York, 1896) vol. 7, p. 160.

Diplomats. See Franklin and Marshall College

Dirk. See Dirksen, E. M.

Dirksen, Everett McKinley

Everett McKinley Dirksen, an Illinois politician, was nicknamed *Dirk* and the *Distillery King* [1] by his colleagues in the National House of Representatives because his surname is easily contracted into Dirk and because Peoria, Ill., a distillery town, is not far distant from his home town, Pekin, Ill.

He received his elementary and high-school educational training in the public schools of Pekin, and was a student in the College of Law at the University of Minnesota, located at Minneapolis, Minn., from 1913 until 1917. He was in the United States Army from 1917 until 1919, having been seventeen months in the service overseas during that time. He was general manager of the Cook Dredging company from 1922 until 1925, and was Commissioner of Finance for the City of Pekin from 1927 until 1931. He was a Republican Representative from the Sixteenth Congressional District of Illinois to the United States Congress from 1933 to 1949, and was elected a Senator from Illinois in 1950.

Everett McKinley Dirksen was born at Pekin, Ill., on January 4, 1896.

[1] An interview with Captain Victor Hunt Harding, Secretary of the National Democratic Congress Reëlection Committee, Washington, D.C., April 10, 1939.

Disney, Wesley Ernest

Pipe-line Disney [1] is the name by which Wesley Ernest Disney is often referred to as a result of his having enthusiastically advocated a number of bills to separate the pipe lines from the oil industry.

Wesley Ernest Disney, who was born in Shawnee County, Kans., on October 31, 1883, served as a Representative from Oklahoma to the United States Congress from 1931 to 1937.

[1] *The Washington Post Magazine,* Washington, D.C., March 4, 1934, p. 4.

Disraeli of Chiefs of Staff. See MacArthur, Douglas

Distillery King. See Dirksen, E. M.

District of Columbia

The District of Columbia is frequently designated the *Nation's State,* because it is not a separate state; but is owned and administered by the United States Government.[1]

[1] *The Encyclopaedia Americana* (Americana Corporation, New York and Chicago, 1929) vol. 9, p. 193.

Dix, Dorothea Lynde

Dorothea Lynde Dix was called the *Heaven-sent Angel of Mercy and of Prison Reform.*[1] Dorothea Lynde Dix devoted her life to improving conditions for people in houses of correction, prisons, and insane asylums. She called attention to the unsanitary conditions which existed in most of these institutions, and also to the poor food and heating equipment in many of them. It was largely due to her initiative and perseverence that many badly needed reforms were made.

She was born at Hampden, Me., on April 4, 1802, and died at Trenton, N.J., on July 17, 1887.

[1] *True Stories of Famous Men and Women . . . ,* John S. C. Abbott William, Garnett William, W. W. Birdsall, Edward S. Ellis and others (Neither the name of the publisher, the place, nor the date of publication is given) p. 303.

Dixie

The land, or the states south of the Mason and Dixon Line, is termed *Dixie.*[1] There are two stories regarding the origin of the name: one that a slave owner named Dixie lived on Manhattan Island during the latter part of the eighteenth century. After some of his slaves had been sold to southern slave holders, they looked back upon their New York owner's plantation as a land of bliss and called it *Dixie,* or *Dixie's Land.* After they had lived on southern plantations, they began to look upon them in the same way and transferred the name *Dixie.* Another story is that the ten dollar bills issued by the Bank of New Orleans before the Civil War had the French word *dix* printed on them, and that from this the South, and especially Louisiana, came to be called the *Land of Dixie.*[2]

[1] *The Source Book* (Perpetual Encyclopaedia Corporation, Chicago, Winnipeg, Canada, and Toronto, Canada, 1932) vol. 2, p. 837.
[2] *The Encyclopaedia Britannica,* Fourteenth Edition (Encyclopaedia Britannica, Inc., New York, 1929) vol. 7, p. 461.

Dixie. See Walker, Fred; Warneke, Lonnie

Dixie Division. See Thirty-first Infantry Division of World War II

Dixiecrats

Dixiecrats is a nickname given to the Southern Democrats who rebelled against the civil rights program of President Harry S. Truman and his Democratic supporters. The Democratic delegates from Mississippi and Alabama walked out of the National Democratic Convention at Philadelphia in July 1948, called a convention of Southern Democrats at Montgomery, Ala., and nominated their own presidential and vice presidential candidates.

Dixie-Doolittle Convention

Planned by President Andrew Johnson with the cooperation of Senator James M. Dixon and Senator J. R. Doolittle, the National Union Convention met at Philadelphia, Pa., on August 14, 1866, in order to bring about a better understanding between the North and South. The spirit of the meeting was splendid, but the antagonism of the two factions was not improved by the convention. Because of the failure of the convention to bring about harmony between the North and the South the Republicans called the Convention the *Dixie-Doolittle Convention,*[1] implying by the double pun that the convention did little to help the South.

[1] *History of the United States of America under the Constitution,* James Schouler (Dodd, Mead and Company, New York, 1913) vol. 7, p. 68.

Dizzy Dean. See Dean, J. H.

Doc. See Cramer, R. M.; Farrell, E. S.; Newell, Robert

Doc Townsend of Florida. See Hendricks, J. E.

Doc Townsend of Florida. See Hendricks, J. E.

Doctor Charlie. See Mayo, C. H.

Doctor Root's Pill Box

In 1857 Joseph Pomeroy Root, a physician and politician, built a small home at Wyandotte, now Kansas City, Kans. This house came to be known as *Doctor Root's Pill Box*[1] because of its very small size. The house, in a partly assembled form, was

Dr. Root's Pill Box—Continued
carried from Cleveland, Ohio to Wyandotte,
and was accredited with having been the first
house ever built there by a white man.

[1] *The National Cyclopaedia of American Biography*
(James T. White and Company, New York, 1906) vol.
13, p. 309.

Doctor Will. See Mayo, W. J.

Doctor's Mob
On a Sunday in April 1788 in New
York City, a corpse that had been secured
to be dissected by the medical students of
one of the hospitals of that city, was left
in a window exposed to the view of those
passing by. The resentment of those seeing
the body was so strong that they formed a
mob to do violence to the surgeons in the
hospital. Several prominent persons were injured in the riot that followed, among whom
were John Jay and Baron Frederick William
von Steuben. This riot has since been called
the *Doctor's Mob*.[1]

[1] *A History of the People of the United States, from
the Revolution to the Civil War*, John Bach McMaster
(D. Appleton and Company, New York, 1883) vol. 1,
p. 28.
*The Life of John Jay: with Selections from His Cor-
respondence and Miscellaneous Papers*, William Jay (J.
and J. Harper, New York, 1833) vol. 1, p. 261.

Dog Currency
During the depression of 1840 to 1843
the city of St. Louis, Mo., became flooded
with paper currency from other states. This
paper money was worthless and the Bank
of Missouri refused to accept it. It was nicknamed *Dog Currency*[1] probably because it
often had pictures of dogs and other animals.

[1] *Centennial History of Missouri (The Center State)
One Hundred Years in the Union, 1820-1921*, Walter B.
Stevens (The S. J. Clarke Publishing Company, St. Louis,
Mo., and Chicago, 1921) vol. 2, p. 447.

Dog Soldiers
The *Dog Soldiers*[1] were a group of rest-
less, unmanageable Indian braves, the majority of whom were Cheyennes and the rest
Sioux, Arapahoes, or other allied tribes.
Those in the vicinity of the Soloman and
upper Republican rivers were especially hostile and troublesome in 1868, for they bitterly resented the coming of the white settlers and refused to be a party to any friendly advances or peace treaties.

Some authorities say the expression *Dog
Soldiers* had its origin in confusing the Indian word *Cheyenne* with the French term
chien, meaning *dog.* Others say there is no

connection between the two words, but that
Dog Soldiers was a direct translation of an
Indian name given to a group of Cheyenne
Indians called *Hotámita niu,* meaning *dog
soldiers* or *dogmen.*

[1] *Wild Life on the Plains and Horrors of Indian War-
fare. . . ,* General G. A. Custer (Sun Publishing Com-
pany, St. Louis, Mo., 1883) p. 122.
The Adventures of Buffalo Bill, Colonel William F.
Cody (Buffalo Bill) (Harper and Brothers, New York,
1904) p. 28.
*The Cheyenne Indians, Their History and Ways of
Life,* George Bird Grinnell (Yale University Press, New
Haven, Conn., 1923) vol. 1, p. 2.
*Memoirs of the American Anthropological Association:
The Cheyenne Indians,* James Mooney (The New Era
Printing Company, Lancaster, Pa., 1907) vol. 1, pt. 6,
p. 362.
Handbook of American Indians North of Mexico, ed.
by Frederick Webb Hodge, Smithsonian Institution,
Bureau of American Ethnology, Bulletin No. 30 (Govern-
ment Printing Office, Washington, D.C., 1907) pt. 2,
p. 251.

Dogs of War
Because General Robert E. Lee and his
soldiers were so successful in trailing and
locating the Federal armies, his soldiers have
been nicknamed the *Dogs of War*.[1]

[1] *On the Trail of Grant and Lee: A Narrative History
of the Boyhood of Two Great Americans, Based upon
Their Own Writings, Official Records, and Other
Authoritative Information,* Frederick Trevor Hill (D.
Appleton and Company, New York, 1911) p. 124.

Dole, James Drummond
The *Hawaiian Pineapple King*[1] is the
nickname of James Drummond Dole.

He was born at Jamaica Plain, Boston,
Mass., on September 27, 1877, and moved
to Honolulu in 1899, where he became an
extensive pineapple grower. He was responsible for improving the quality of the fruit
grown in Hawaii, and pioneered in the
commercial canning of pineapples.

[1] *The Evening Gazette,* Worcester Mass., November 6,
1934.

Dollar of the Daddies
The old silver dollar in circulation before
1873 was sometimes designated the *Dollar
of the Daddies, the Dollar of the Dads,* and
the *Dollar of the Fathers*.[1] This monetary
unit, coined first in 1794, was in use until
it was demonetized by legislative action in
1873. Because it was used by the founding
fathers of the United States this money came
to be referred to as the *Dollar of the Fathers*.

[1] *History of the United States, from the Earliest Discovery of America to the Present Day,* E. Benjamin
Andrews (Charles Scribner's Sons, New York, 1895)
vol. 4, p. 327.

Dollar Diplomacy
While William Howard Taft was President of the United States from 1909 to 1913,
the diplomatic relations between the United

States and foreign countries, particularly China and Latin America, were dictated by commercial interests. The mercenary character of this diplomacy caused it to be nicknamed *Dollar Diplomacy*.[1]

[1] *Dollar Diplomacy, a Study in American Imperialism,* Scott Nearing and Joseph Freeman (B. W. Huebsch and the Viking Press, New York, 1925) p. 43, 264.
Since the Civil War, Charles Ramsdell Lingley, Revised Edition, (The Century Company, New York, 1920) p. 552.

Dolly. See Stark, A. D.

Dolly Madison. See Madison, D. P. T.

Dominicans. See Providence College

Don Quixote of the Jerseys. See Livingston, William

Done Brown. See Brown, W. J.

Donnelly, Ignatius

Ignatius Donnelly was called the *Sage of Nininger*.[1] He was a scholar and writer who had made his home at Nininger, Dakota County, Pa., from 1857 until his death. He was born at Philadelphia, Pa., on November 3, 1831, and died at Minneapolis, Minn., on January 2, 1901.

[1] *The Life of Knute Nelson,* Martin W. Odland (The Lund Press, Inc., Minneapolis, Minn., 1926) p. 86.

Dons. See University of San Francisco

Dore, John Francis

John Francis Dore, former Mayor of Seattle, Wash., was called the *Labor Mayor*[1] because he was reelected Mayor of Seattle in 1936 on a one hundred per cent labor platform.

Before this campaign he had formed an alliance with Dave Beck, of the Teamsters' Union (AFL), and Harry Bridges of the Committee for Industrial Organization. After the election he publicly announced that the American Federation of Labor would prevail in Seattle, and repudiated the CIO.

John Francis Dore was born at Charleston, Mass., on December 11, 1881, and died at Seattle, Wash., on April 18, 1938.

[1] *Washington Herald,* Washington, D.C., April 19, 1939, col 12, p. 1.
[2] *Seattle Post Intelligencer,* Seattle, Wash., April 19, 1938, col. 5, p. 2.

Dormitory of New York. See Brooklyn, New York.

Doubleday, Abner

Abner Doubleday was nicknamed the *Father of Baseball* and *Old Forty-eight Hours.* He was called the *Father of Baseball*[1] because in the spring of 1839, at Cooperstown, N.Y., he is supposed to have designed the first baseball diamond and made the first rules of the modern game. This original baseball diamond at Cooperstown is now the site of Doubleday Field and the Baseball Hall of Fame.

See also Cooperstown and Baseball in this book.

He was designated *Old Forty-eight Hours*[2] while in the Union Army because he was as calm, slow-moving, and orderly in his activities and in directing his command as though there were forty-eight hours to a day rather than twenty-four.

Abner Doubleday was born at Ballston Spa, N.Y., on June 26, 1819, and died at Mendham, N.J., on January 26, 1893.

[1] *The Sunday Star,* Washington, D.C., April 16, 1939, Sports Section, col. 4, p. E-1.
[2] *Dictionary of American Biography under the Auspices of the American Learned Societies,* ed. by Allen Johnson and Dumas Malone (Charles Scribner's Sons, New York, 1930) vol. 5, p. 302.

Dough Moose. See Perkins, G. W.

Doughboy's General. See Bradley, General O. N.

Dougherty, Daniel

Because he was a skillful and eloquent orator Daniel Dougherty was popularly known as the *Silver-tongued Orator*.[1]

He was born at Philadelphia, Pa., on October 15, 1826, and died there on September 5, 1892.

[1] *The National Cyclopaedia of American Biography* James T. White and Company, New York, 1907) vol. 5, p. 477.

Doughface

About 1840 the Abolitionists designated a northern man who favored slavery a *Doughface*.[1] The term is said to have been originated by John Randolph of Roanoke as early as 1820. He is said to have called them *Doe-faces* in allusion to the "timid, startled look of that animal which is said

Doughface—Continued

to shrink from the reflection of its own face in the water."

[1] *The Abolitionists Together with Personal Memories of the Struggle for Human Rights, 1830-1864*, John F. Hume (G. P. Putnam's Sons, New York and London, 1905) p. 4.

Political Americanisms, Charles Ledyard Norton (Longmans, Green, and Company, New York and London, 1890) p. 36.

Notes and Queries Historical and Genealogical Chiefly Relating to Interior Pennsylvania, Third Series, ed. by William Henry Egle (Harrisburg Publishing Company, Harrisburg, Pa., 1896) vol. 2, p. 172.

Doughton, Robert L.

Farmer Bob and *Muley Doughton* are nicknames which have been applied to Robert L. Doughton.

Doughton was called *Farmer Bob*[1] because he was a successful farmer and livestock raiser on his estate in North Carolina; from 1903 to 1909 he was an outstanding member of the North Carolina State Board of Agriculture, and made every effort to secure legislation beneficial to farmers.

Muley Doughton[2] is a nickname applied to Robert L. Doughton by his political opponents because of his firmness and tenacity of purpose, and because he rode a mule to electioneer for office in his earlier political career.

Robert Doughton was born at Laurel Springs, N.C., on November 7, 1863, and for many years was a Representative from North Carolina to the United States Congress.

[1] *Americanisms—Old and New*, John S. Farmer (Privately printed by Thomas Poulter and Sons, London, 1889) p. 212.

[2] *The Washington Post Magazine*, Washington, D.C., March 4, 1934, p. 4.

Doughty, James P.

James P. Doughty was familiarly known in Augusta, Ga., as the *Dean of Cotton Row* and as *Uncle Jimmie.*

He was designated the *Dean of Cotton Row*[1] because he was the senior member of Augusta's cotton exchange, better known as *Cotton Row*, and an outstanding broker in cotton.

James P. Doughty was affectionately called *Uncle Jimmie* because of his geniality and interest in civic affairs.

He was born at Augusta, Ga., on June 7, 1849, and died there on March 22, 1922.

[1] *Encyclopedia of American Biography: American Biography, a New Cyclopedia*, comp. under the editorial supervision of a notable advisory board (Published under the direction of The American Historical Society, Inc., New York, 1931) vol. 46, p. 132, 286.

Doughty of the South. See Richards, T. A.

Douglas, Stephen Arnold

The *Little Giant*[1] was the nickname given to Stephen Arnold Douglas at Jacksonville, Ill., in 1834, following a debate on the National Bank question. Douglas presented his arguments in such a convincing and forceful manner that he was nicknamed the *Little Giant.*

Stephen Arnold Douglas was born at Brando, Vt., on April 23, 1813, and died at Chicago, Ill., on June 3, 1861.

[1] *Stephen A. Douglas*, Henry Parker Willis (George W. Jacobs and Company, Philadelphia, Pa., 1910) p. 132.

Life of Stephen A. Douglas; William Gardner (Roxburgh Press, Boston, 1905) p. 14.

The Life of Stephen A. Douglas, James W. Sheahan (Harper and Brothers, New York, 1860) p. 19-21.

Douglas Clan

In 1860, when Abraham Lincoln and Stephen A. Douglas were candidates for President of the United States, those Democrats who favored the election of Douglas adopted for themselves the nickname the *Douglas Clan.*[1]

[1] *Political Americanisms*, Charles Ledyard Norton (Longmans, Green and Company, New York, 1890) p. 128.

Douglass, Frederick

Frederick Douglass, who lived in Anacostia, a suburb of Washington, D.C., was given the nickname the *Sage of Anacostia*[1] because he was an intelligent, kind, and just man. During the Period of Reconstruction he wrote and spoke in support of suffrage and civil rights for Negroes. In 1877 he served as marshal for the District of Columbia, and in 1899 was United States Minister to Haiti.

This Negro lecturer and journalist was born at Tuckahoe, Md., in February 1817, and died at Washington, D.C., on February 20, 1895.

[1] *Frederick Douglass*, Booker T. Washington (George W. Jacobs and Company, Philadelphia and London, 1906) p. 338.

Dove Parties

During the interval from 1809 to 1817 when the President was holding meetings of his cabinet, Mrs. James Madison was accustomed to receive the wives of the cabinet members informally. Because these gatherings were attended only by the women, they were called *Dove Parties*.

[1] *Dolly Madison, the Nation's Hostess,* Elizabeth Lippincott Dean (Lothrop, Lee and Shepard Company, Boston, 1928) p. 121.

Dow, Lorenzo

Crazy Dow [1] was the popular sobriquet applied to Lorenzo Dow because he possessed a number of eccentric personal habits, and his preaching was violently outspoken.

He was born at Coventry, Conn., on October 16, 1777, and died at Georgetown, now part of Washington D.C., on February 2, 1834.

[1] *The National Cyclopaedia of American Biography* (James T. White and Company, New York, 1900) vol. 10, p. 472-3.

Dow, Neal

Neal Dow is called the *Father of the Maine Law* and the *Father of Prohibition* [1] because he was instrumental in bringing into existence the first state-wide prohibition law in the United States. He was the author of the act which became known as the Maine Law prohibiting the manufacture and sale of intoxicating liquors in the state of Maine, adopted in 1846.

Neal Dow was born at Portland, Me., on March 20, 1804, and died there on October 2, 1897.

[1] *Prohibition in the United States: A History of the Prohibition Party and of the Prohibition Movement,* David Leigh Colvin (George H. Doran Company, New York, 1926) p. 29.
The Maine Liquor Law: Its Origin, History, and Results, Including a Life of Neal Dow, Henry Stephen Clubb (Published for The Maine Law Statistical Society by Fowler and Wells, New York, 1856) p. 14-19, 47.

Dowager. See Madison, D. P. T.

Down Where the South Begins. See Virginia

Downer, Eliphalet

Eliphalet Downer was nicknamed the *Fighting Surgeon of the Revolution* [1] because he not only fought the British at Lexington, Mass.; but he gave medical attention to the British soldiers who were wounded, and collected money and other commodities for their care. He served as a surgeon in the Twenty-fourth Continental Regiment and as a surgeon on several privateer and continental sloops.

Eliphalet Downer was born at Franklin, Conn., then called Norwich, Conn., and died at Brookline, Mass., on April 3, 1806.

[1] *Dictionary of American Biography under the Auspices of the American Council of Learned Societies,* ed. by Allen Johnson and Dumas Malone (Charles Scribner's Sons, New York, 1930) vol. 5, p. 414.

Draft Dodgers

Those persons who avoided or attempted to avoid being drafted in World War I from 1917 to 1918, and in World War II from 1939 to 1945, were called *Draft Dodgers*.

[1] *The American Nation,* Richard J. Purcell (Ginn and Company, New York and Boston, 1929) p. 677.

Dragonettes. See Lane College

Dragons. See Lane College

Drake, Joseph Rodman and Fitz-Green Halleck

Joseph Rodman Drake and Fitz-Green Halleck were nicknamed the *Damon and Pythias of American Verse* [1] because of their close friendship and because of their co-operative labors in producing satirical sketches in verse, known as the *Croaker Papers,* which began to appear in the *New York Evening Post* about 1819.

Joseph Rodman Drake was born at New York City, on August 7, 1795, and died there on September 21, 1820.

Fitz-Green Halleck was born at Guilford, Conn., on July 8, 1790, and died there on November 19, 1867.

[1] *American Literature,* John Calvin Metcalf (Johnson Publishing Company, Richmond, Va., 1925) p. 167.

Draw Land

In 1800, when the land in the vicinity of Wheelock, N.H., was made accessible to settlers, it was partitioned into one-hundred-acre lots, three of which made a "right," the least amount that a settler could lease. Because the land in the township varied in quality and value it was divided into two classes. The first class land constituted about two-thirds of the township, and second class land constituted the remaining third. A settler was permitted to choose any two one-hundred-acre lots of first class land, and the third one-hundred-acre lot he acquired from the second class tract by drawing of lots.

Draw Land—Continued
This portion of his property was commonly designated *Draw Land.*[1]

[1] *A History of Dartmouth College, 1815-1909, Being the Second Volume of a History of Dartmouth College and the Town of Hanover, N.H., begun by Frederick Chase,* John King Lord (The Rumford Press, Concord, N.H., 1913) p. 227-8.

Dressler, Marie
Because of her popularity as an actress and outstanding professional success, Marie Dressler was nicknamed the *Grand Old Lady of the Movies,* the *Old Trouper,* and *Queen Marie of Hollywood.*[1]
Marie Dressler was born on November 9, 1871, at Cobourg, Canada. Her original surname was Koerber. She died on July 28, 1934, at Montecito, Calif.

[1] *Screen Personalities,* Vincent Trotta and Cliff Lewis (Grosset and Dunlap, New York, 1933) p. 44.

Drexel Dragons. See Drexel Institute

Drexel Institute
The students composing the teams of Drexel Institute, situated at Philadelphia, Pa., were nicknamed *The Drexel Dragons* [3] in 1928 at which time the members of the student body voted to adopt this sobriquet.

[3] A communication from William J. Stevens, Graduate Manager of Athletics at Drexel Institute, Philadelphia, Pa., June 12, 1935.

Driving Force. See Roosevelt, Theodore

Drover Wayne. See Wayne, Anthony

Druid City. See Tuscaloosa, Ala.

Drummer Boy of the Ninth Michigan. See Hendershot, R. H.

Drummer Boy of the Rappahannock. See Hendershot, R. H.

Dry Bishop from Virginia. See Cannon, James, Jr.

Dry Hole Stebbins. See Stebbins, G. C.

Dry Wind. See Guyer, U. S.

Dual Cities. See St. Paul and Minneapolis, Minn.

Duchesne, Rose Philippine
Rose Philippine Duchesne was a founder of Catholic convents, a teacher in mission schools, and a religious leader among the Potawotomi Indians. They called her the *Woman Who Always Prays.*[1] It was her life's desire to work in the missions. Coming from France in 1818, she went to St. Charles, Mo., where she founded her first mission. Six other mission stations were started by her in other parts of the United States. She worked among the Potawotomi at Sugar Creek, Kans., and later went to the Far West, returning to St. Charles in her old age.
Rose Philippine Duchesne was born at Grenoble, France, on August 29, 1769, and died at St. Charles, Mo., on November 18, 1852. She was beatified in 1940.[2]

[1] *Dictionary of American Biography under the Auspices of the American Council of Learned Societies,* ed. by Allen Johnson and Dumas Malone (Charles Scribner's Sons, New York, 1930) vol. 5, p. 478.
[2] *The Book of Saints,* comp. by the Benedictine Monks of St Augustine's Abbey, Ramsgate (Macmillan Company, New York, 1947) p. 517.

Dual Cities. See St. Paul and Minneapolis, Minn.

Duch Bill. See Hickok, J. B.

Duck Bill. See Hickok, J. B.

Duckboard. See Butler, S. D.

Duckie Wuckie. See Medwick, J. M.

Ducks. See Chillicothe Business College

Ducrot
Freshman cadets at military academies are nicknamed *ducrot,*[1] a slang expression for anything momentarily forgotten.

[1] *Unit Projects in Modern Literature* (Educational Press, Inc., Columbus, Ohio) March 1-4, 1935, p. 13.

Dude President. See Arthur, C. A.

Dude Ranches
In the western part of the United States old cattle ranches which have been transformed into fashionable resorts for wealthy people are called *Dude Ranches.* Guests of these so-called ranches are called dudes, and engage in horseback riding and other outdoor sports. A dude is a western expression for a tenderfoot or easterner, and men who work on a dude ranch are dude wranglers.

[1] *The Source Book* (Source Research Council, Inc., Chicago, 1936) vol. 5, p. 2244.

Duel Fighter. See Jackson, Andrew

Duffy. See Lewis, G. E.

Duhawks. See Columbia College of Dubuque

Duke. See Derringer, Paul; Russell, Joseph; Stockton, Richard; and Wickliffe, C. A.

Duke of Birmingham. See Powell, J. R.

Duke of Braintree. See Adams, John

Duke of Summersetts. See Holmes, John

Duke of Tralee. See Bresnahan, R. P.

Duke University

The *Blue Devils* [1] and *The Blue Imps* [1] are the appellations applied to the members of the athletic teams of Duke University, situated at Durham, N.C., *The Blue Devils* being the sobriquet given to the members of the teams of the upper classmen, and *The Blue Imps* being the nickname of the freshman squads.

During the foot-ball season of 1922, Mike Bradshaw, Junior, who was then Associate Editor of the *Duke Chronicle,* the student paper, thus nicknamed the members of the Duke teams, in commemoration of the Blue Devils, the famous French regiment, the members of which distinguished themselves by their bravery in the World War.

[1] A letter from Ted Mann, Publicity Director at Duke University, Durham, N.C., June 11, 1935.

Dukes. See Duquesne University

Duluth, Minnesota

Duluth is called *Zenith City,* [1] or *Zenith City of the Unsalted Seas,* because it is located at the western point of the Great Lakes where the railways from the west converge. From there freight is loaded on steamers for transshipment to eastern states and abroad.

[1] *My Minnesota,* Antoinette E. Ford (Lyons and Carnahan, New York and Chicago, 1929) p. 269.
King's Handbook of the United States, planned and ed. by Moses King, text by M. F. Sweetser (The Matthews-Northrup Company, Buffalo, N.Y., 1896) p. 434.

Dumb Prophet. See Cleveland, Grover

Dunn, Emmet Clarke

Emmet Clarke Dunn, city manager of Alexandria, Va., was nicknamed the *Grand Old Man of Alexandria* [1] because, during the forty-five years that he lived in that city, he distinguished himself for his wisdom, honesty, and business ability. He was largely responsible for the rapid development of the city and for modernizing schools, streets, and sewage systems.

Emmet Clarke Dunn was born at Richmond, Va., in 1860, and died at Alexandria, Va., on February 13, 1938.

[1] *Washington Herald,* Washington, D.C., February 14, 1938, col. 4, p. 5.

Duquesne University

The *Dukes,* the *Iron Dukes,* and the *Night Riders* are the nicknames which have been given to the teams of Duquesne University, Pittsburgh, Pa. The *Dukes* [1] is short for Duquesne and the *Iron Dukes* was a natural corollary, especially as Pittsburg is an iron manufacturing city. They were called *Night Riders* at a time when they were playing night games and were coached by a former member of the "Four Horsemen" of Notre Dame University.

[1] A communication from J. J. Gallahan, President of Duquesne University, Pittsburgh, Pa., November 18, 1935.

Durable Ned. See Kalbfus, E. C.

Durham, Edward Fant

Edward Fant Durham, who was born at Chester, S.C., on August 17, 1908, and who was a pitcher in major league baseball, was called *Bull* [1] because his name suggested the tobacco trade mark *Bull Durham.*

[1] *Who's Who in Major League Base Ball,* comp. by Harold (Speed) Johnson (Buxton Publishing Company, Chicago, 1933) p. 143.

Durham Baseball Club

The *Bulls* [1] is the nickname commonly given by sports writers to the athletes of the Durham Baseball Club, a member of the

Durham Baseball Club—Continued
Piedmont League, at Durham, N.C., because
the famous Bull Durham Tobacco is manufactured at Durham.

[1] A communication from William B. McKechnie, Jr.,
Secretary of The Durham Baseball Club, Durham, N.C.,
March 27, 1939.

Durham, North Carolina
Durham was nicknamed the *Bull City* because Bull Durham Tobacco is manufactured
there.

Durocher, Leo Ernest
Leo Ernest Durocher, shortstop and manager, was tagged *Lippy* [1] at the beginning of
his career in major league baseball because
he was "the cockiest player in the training
field." *The Lip* [1] is famous for his arguments with umpires as well as with fans.

Recognized as an able tactician from the
start of his managerial career in 1938, he is
often referred to as the *Dandy Little Manager.* [2] A more recent sobriquet, *the Little
Shepherd of Coogan's Bluff,* [2] has been
acquired since he became manager of the
New York Giants in 1948. Under his
direction the Giants have won two pennants
and their first World Series in twenty years.
The Giants home field is the Polo Grounds
just under Coogan's Bluff in New York
City. During the 1954 season, which culminated in four straight victories for the
Giants in the World Series, sportswriters
often called Durocher *Leo the Magnificent.* [2]

Leo Ernest Durocher was born at West
Springfield, Mass., on July 27, 1906.

[2] *Current Biography 1950,* Anna Rothe, ed. (H. W.
Wilson Company, New York, 1951) p. 129-30.
[2] New York *Times,* September 30, 1954, p. 41.

Dust Bowl
The *Dust Bowl* is a nickname commonly
applied to the Great Plains lying between
the Mississippi River and the foothills of
the Rocky Mountains, from Canada to Mexico, which suffered a series of severe
droughts in the 1930's.

Dusty. See Cooke, A. L.; Rhodes, J. G.

Dutch Bill. See Hickok, J. B.; Sherman,
Henry

Dutch Clark. See Clark, Earl

Dutch Henry. See Sherman, Henry

Dutch Millionaire. See Philipse,
Frederick

Dutch Pete. See Sherman, Henry

Dutchmen. See Union College

Dutchy. See Provine, J. W.

Duumvirate, or Duumvirs. See Wilson, Woodrow, and E. M. House

Dwarf Statesman. See Stephens, A. H.

Dwight, Timothy. See *Hartford Wits*

Dyer, Mary
Mary Dyer was known as the *Quaker
Martyr.* [1] She was a Quaker who chose to
suffer the death penalty rather than recant.
In 1635 Mary Dyer, with her husband
William Dyer, immigrated from London to
Boston. In 1652 Mary Dyer went back to
England on a visit and became converted to
Quakerism. Upon her return to Boston she
was imprisoned, and then banished. In 1657
she was banished from the New Haven
settlement. At this time the Massachusetts
Bay Colony enacted a law to exclude Quakers, the penalty of a second visit to be the
death sentence. Mary Dyer reentered the
colony to see whether or not this law was
to be enforced. A few months later she was
hanged on the Boston Common, on June 1,
1660.

[1] *Mary Dyer of Rhode Island, the Quaker Martyr That
Was Hanged on Boston Common, June 1, 1660, Horatio
Rogers* (Preston and Rounds, Providence, R.I., 1896)
p. 1, 31-63.

Dynamic City. See Detroit, Mich.

Dynamo of Power. See Roosevelt,
Theodore

E

Eagle of the East. See Webster, Daniel

Eagle Orator. See Henry, G. A.; Stokes,
W. B.

Eagle Orator of South Carolina. See Calhoun, J. C.

Eagle Orator of Tennessee. See Henry, G. A.

Eagle State. See Mississippi

Eagles. See Central College (Fayette, Mo.); Lambuth College; Tennessee Polytechnic Institute

Earlham College

The *Fightin' Quakers* is the nickname of the athletic teams of Earlham College, at Earlham, Ind., because the college is a Quaker school.

Early Birds

The airplane pilots who were trained in America and Europe prior to World War I are popularly known as *Early Birds*[1] because they began to fly before the airplane and aviation began to be used for practical purposes. The *Early Birds* were a comparatively small number of pilots scattered over the United States. When they enlisted in the United States Army for service in 1917, many of the *Early Birds* were commissioned instructors.

[1] *The Encyclopaedia Britannica,* Fourteenth Edition (Encyclopaedia Britannica, Inc., New York, 1938) vol. 2, p. 803.

Early, Jubal Anderson

Crackers, Old Jube, and *Old Jubilee* were nicknames given to Jubal Anderson Early.

Lieutenant General Jubal Anderson Early was popularly called *Crackers.*[1] He was nicknamed *Old Jube*[2] and *Old Jubilee* by his soldiers in the Confederate Army; both are corruptions of Jubal.

Jubal Anderson Early was born in Franklin County, Va., on November 3, 1816, and died at Lynchburg, Va., on March 2, 1894.

[1] *Americanisms; the English of the New World,* M. Schele De Vere (Charles Scribner and Company, New York, 1872) p. 250.
[2] *Lee and His Lieutenants; Comprising the Early Life, Public Services, and Campaigns of General Robert E. Lee and His Companions in Arms, with a Record of Their Campaigns and Heroic Deeds,* Edward A. Pollard (E. B. Treat and Company, New York, 1867) p. 477.

Earnshaw, George Livingston

George Livingston Earnshaw, who was born at New York City, on February 15,

1900, and who pitched in major league baseball, is nicknamed *Moose* or *Big Moose.*[1]

[1] *Who's Who in Major League Base Ball,* comp. by Harold (Speed) Johnson (Buxton Publishing Company, Chicago, 1933) p. 146.

Earthquake Allen. See Allen, William

Earthquake City. See Charleston, S.C.

Easternmost State of the Union. See Maine

Eastman, Charles Gamage

Burns of the Green Mountains[1] was a nickname applied to Charles Gamage Eastman because, like Robert Burns, his poetry dealt chiefly with the everyday life and surroundings of the common man His home was in the Green Mountain regions of Vermont.

Eastman was born at Fryeburg, Me., on June 1, 1816, and died at Burlington, Vt., in 1861.

[1] *The National Cyclopaedia of American Biography* (James T. White and Company, New York, 1907) vol. 9, p. 252-3.

Easy Boss Platt. See Platt, T. C.

Eaton, Margaret O'Neill (Mrs. John H. Eaton)

Margaret O'Neill, the daughter of a Washington inn-keeper and widow of a purser in the Navy, married John H. Eaton who was Secretary of War in President Jackson's Cabinet. The wives of other Cabinet members refused to receive her, the President intervened in her behalf with no effect, and some of the Cabinet threatened to resign. This gave rise to the nickname *Bellona*[1], the goddess of war.

Because Mrs. Eaton was the daughter of a Washington inn-keeper, she was called *Pothouse Peggy*[2] by her enemies. She was called the *Gorgeous Hussy* in Samuel Hopkins Adams' fictional biography of her, and she was spoken of as the *Gorgeous Hussy* by newspaper writers after the screen dramatization of this book appeared in 1936.

[1] *Andrew Jackson, the Fighting President,* Helen Nicolay (The Century Company, New York, 1929) p. 281.
[2] *The Godlike Daniel,* Samuel Hopkins Adams (Sears Publishing Company, Inc., New York, 1930) p. 147.

Ebenezer Academy

The *Cradle of Methodism* [1] is the nickname applied to the old Ebenezer Academy, founded in Brunswick County, Va., in 1796, because it was the first Methodist school in the South and was the school in which many of the earlier Methodist preachers were trained.

[1] *Virginia, comp. and ed. by Charlotte Allen* (Published by the Department of Agriculture and Immigration of the State of Virginia, under the direction of George W. Koiner, Commissioner, Department of Purchase and Printing, Richmond, Va., 1937) p. 197.

Eci. See McConnell, J. P.

Economic Royalists

The *Economic Royalists* [1] is the nickname given to wealthy American business men, manufacturers, and bankers by President Franklin Delano Roosevelt and the New Dealers. They used this nickname in an attempt to lead the American people to believe that these wealthy men were not sympathetic toward the laboring classes, were largely responsible for the depression, and would take unfair advantages of the average American citizen to satisfy their own greed for wealth.

[1] *Washington Herald,* Washington, D.C., July 2, 1936, col. 2, p. 8.

Eddy, Thomas

Thomas Eddy was called the *American Howard* [1] because, like John Howard, he was a philanthropist and reformer.

Thomas Eddy inaugurated a series of reforms in the organization and the administration of New York prisons; put prisoners into separate cells, and secured employment and instruction for them while they were serving their terms. Like Howard, Eddy also interested himself in bettering conditions in houses of correction and institutions for the care of paupers, delinquents, and the insane.

He was born at Philadelphia, Pa., on September 5, 1758, and died at New York City on September 16, 1827.

[1] *The National Cyclopaedia of American Biography* (James T. White and Company, New York, 1893) vol. 3, p. 512.

[2] *The Encyclopedia Americana* (Americana Corporation, New York and Chicago, 1927) vol. 14, p. 452-3.

Edinburgh of America. See Albany, N.Y.

Edison, Thomas Alva

The *Father of the Phonograph, Hugo, Victor,* the *Wizard of Menlo Park,* and the *Wizard of the Wires* are nicknames which have been applied to Thomas Alva Edison.

He was designated the *Father of the Phonograph* [1] because he invented the phonograph, which he exhibited in a very imperfect state at the Paris Exposition in 1878.

While he was a young man, Thomas Alva Edison was sometimes called *Victor* and *Hugo* [2] because he was fond of works of Victor Hugo, particularly *Les Misérables.*

Because Thomas Alva Edison's research laboratory was for some years located at Menlo Park, N.J., and many of his inventions were perfected there, he was known as the *Wizard of Menlo Park.* [3]

Edison was called the *Wizard of the Wires* [1] because of his remarkable inventions in the field of electricity.

Edison was born at Milan, Ohio, on February 11, 1847, and died at East Orange, N.J., on October 17, 1931.

[1] *A Book of Nicknames,* John Goff (Courier-Journal Job Printing Company, Louisville, Ky., 1892) p. 29, 30.

[2] *Contemporary American Biography: Biographical Sketches of Representative Men of the Day, Representatives of Modern Thought and Progress, of the Pulpit, the Press, the Bench and Bar, of Legislation, Invention, and the Great Industrial Interests of the Country* (Atlantic Publishing and Engraving Company, New York, 1895) vol. 1, p. 73.

[3] *The Growth of the American People and Nation,* Mary G. Kelty (Ginn and Company, New York and Boston, 1931) p. 440.

Edmunds, George Franklin

George Franklin Edmunds was nicknamed *St. Jerome* [1] because of his reputed resemblance to the pictures of St. Jerome.

He served as a Senator from Vermont to the United States Congress from 1866 to 1891.

George Franklin Edmunds was born at Richmond, Vt., on February 1, 1829, and died at Pasadena, Calif., on February 28, 1919.

[1] *U.S. "Snap Shots": An Independent, National, and Memorial Encyclopedia . . . ,* Oliver McKee (A. M. Thayer and Company, Boston, 1892) p. 247.
The Fathers for English Readers: Saint Jerome, Fourth Edition, Reverend Edward L. Cutts, Society for Promoting Christian Knowledge, London (E. and J. B. Young and Company, New York, 1897) p. 2.

Edwards, Jonathan

Jonathan Edwards has been described as the *Artist of Damnation* [1] because he pictured so realistically the doctrine of the future punishment of the wicked. The best example of his ability to portray this belief is probably his memorable sermon, *Sinners in the Hands of an Angry God,* delivered in 1741 at Enfield, Conn.

He was born at Windsor, Conn., on October 5, 1703, and died at Princeton, N.J., on March 22, 1758.

[1] *The United States: A History of Three Centuries, 1067-1904, Population, Politics, Wars, Industry, Civilization, in Ten Parts,* William Estabrook Chancellor and Fletcher Willis Hewes (G. P. Putman's Sons, New York and London, 1905) pt. I, p. 476.
The Encyclopedia Americana (Americana Corporation, New York and Chicago, 1927) vol. 9, p. 710.

Egan, Patrick

Blaine's Irishman and the *Escaped Jailbird* were nicknames of Patrick Egan.

He was designated *Blaine's Irishman* [1] by the politicians who disliked James B. Blaine because Blaine was instrumental in having Egan appointed Minister Plenipotentiary to Chile soon after Blaine was made Secretary of State in the Cabinet of President Benjamin Harrison, on March 5, 1889.

The *Escaped Jail-bird* [1] was applied to Patrick Egan by those who criticized the administration of Benjamin Harrison, President of the United States from 1889 to 1893, because Egan, a friend of Harrison's, had been tried for treason in Ireland before he came to America; the courts had acquitted him.

Patrick Egan was born in Longford County, Ireland, in 1841, and died at New York City, on September 30, 1919.

[1] *Twenty Years of the Republic, 1885-1905,* Harry Thurston Peck (Dodd, Mead and Company, New York, 1907) p. 232.

Egypt. See Illinois

Egypt Land

The rich land in Chickasaw County, Miss., has been designated the *Egypt Land* [1] because it produced a great abundance of corn during the Civil War, like Egypt during the seven years of plenty.

[1] *Bedford Forrest and His Critter Company,* Andrew Nelson Lytle (Minton, Balch and Company, New York, 1931) p. 260.

Egyptians. See Illinois Inhabitants

Eighth Armored Division of World War II

The *Iron Snake* [1] was the nickname of the Eighth Armored Division of World War II.

[1] *Combat Divisions of World War II,* (Army of the United States) Army Times Publishing Company, Washington, D.C., 1946, p. 82.

Eighth Infantry Division of World War II

The *Golden Arrow* [1] was the nickname of the Eighth Infantry Division of World War II and the shoulder patch had an upward pointing gold arrow with a silver 8 superimposed.

[1] *Combat Divisions of World War II,* (Army of the United States). Army Times Publishing Company, Washington, D.C., 1946, p. 14.

Eightieth Infantry Division of World War II

The *Blue Ridge Division* [1] was the nickname of the Eightieth Infantry Division of World War II because the division was activated in Virginia in 1917 and the Blue Ridge Mountains are in Virginia.

[1] *Combat Divisions of World War II,* (Army of the United States), Army Times Publishing Company, Washington, D.C., 1946, p. 49.

Eighty-eighth Infantry Division of World War II

The *Blue Devil Division* [1] was the nickname of the Eighty-eighth Infantry Division of World War II because this division was partly trained overseas with the French Seventh Army in 1917, and the French Croix de Guerre was also awarded this division on July 2, 1944. The Blue Devils was the nickname of a famous French regiment, distinguished for bravery in World War I.

[1] *Combat Divisions of World War II,* (Army of the United States), Army Times Publishing Company, Washington. D.C., 1946, p. 56.

Eighty-fifth Infantry Division of World War II

The *Custer Division* [1] was the nickname of the Eighty-fifth Infantry Division of World War II because the division was activated at Camp Custer, Michigan.

[1] *Combat Divisions of World War II,* (Army of the United States), Army Times Publishing Company, Washington, D.C., 1946, p. 53.

Eighty-first Infantry Division of World War II

The *Wildcat Division* [1] was the nickname of the Eighty-first Infantry Division of World War II.

See also Wildcat Division.

[1] *Combat Divisions of World War II,* (Army of the United States), Army Times Publishing Company, Washington, D.C., 1946, p. 50.

Eighty-fourth Infantry Division of World War II

The *Railsplitters* [1] was the nickname of the Eighty-fourth Infantry Division of World War II because it was organized at Camp Taylor, Ky., the home state of Abraham Lincoln, the Rail Splitter.

[1] *Combat Divisions of World War II,* (Army of the United States), Army Times Publishing Company, Washington, D.C., 1946, p. 52.

Eighty-ninth Infantry Division of World War II

The *Rolling W* was the nickname of the Eighty-ninth Infantry Division of World War II. The W stands for West and the rolling signifies the land of rolling prairies.

[1] *Combat Divisions of World War II,* (Army of the United States), Army Times Publishing Company, Washington, D.C., 1946, p. 57.

Eighty-second Airborne Division of World War II

The *All American Division* [1] was the nickname of the Eighty-second Airborne Division of World War II.

[1] *Combat Divisions of World War II,* (Army of the United States), Army Times Publishing Company, Washington, D.C., 1946, p. 94.

Eighty-seventh Infantry Division of World War II

The *Golden Acorn Division* [1] was the nickname of the Eighty-seventh Division of World War II.

[1] *Combat Divisions of World War II,* (Army of the United States), Army Times Publishing Company, Washington, D.C., 1946, p. 55.

Eighty-sixth Infantry Division of World War II

The *Black Hawk Division* [1] was the nickname of the Eighty-sixth Infantry Division of World War II.

[1] *Combat Divisions of World War II,* (Army of the United States), Army Times Publishing Company, Washington, D.C., 1946, p. 54.

Eighty-third Infantry Division of World War II

The *Thunderbolt Division* [1] was the nickname of the Eighty-third Infantry Division of World War II.

[1] *Combat Divisions of World War II,* (Army of the United States), Army Times Publishing Company, Washington, D.C., 1946, p. 51.

Eisenhower, Dwight David

Dwight David Eisenhower is popularly known as *Ike.* [1]

He was born in Denison, Texas on October 14, 1890. He was named Chief of the Allied Forces in World War II in 1942, Supreme Commander of Allied Expeditionary Force in 1943, and Chief of Staff of the United States Army in 1945. He was named commander of North Atlantic Council defense forces on December 19, 1950, and served as Supreme Allied Commander in Europe. In March 1953, he took office as thirty-fourth President of the United States.

[1] *Current Biography, 1948,* Anna Rothe, ed., (The H. W. Wilson Company, New York, 1949) p. 179.

Eldorado, Arkansas

Eldorado was nicknamed the *Oil Capital* [1] because of the great oil boom there in January 1921.

[1] *The World Book,* The Quarrie Corporation, Chicago, 1947, vol. 5. p. 2244.

El Dorado State. See California

Electric City. See Scranton, Pa.

Electric City of the Future. See Buffalo, N.Y.

Elegant Oakey. See Hall, A. O.

Elephant. See Pearson, Eliphalet

Eleventh Airborne Division of World War II

The *Angels* was the nickname of the Eleventh Airborne Division of World War II.

[1] *Combat Divisions of World War II,* (Army of the United States), Army Times Publishing Company, Washington, D.C., 1946, p. 91.

Eleventh Armored Division of World War II

The *Thunderbolt Division* [1] was the nickname of the Eleventh Armored Division of World War II.

[1] *Combat Divisions of World War II,* (Army of the United States), Army Times Publishing Company, Washington, D.C., 1946, p. 85.

Eliot, Charles William

The nickname *America's First Citizen* [1] was attributed to Dr. Charles William Eliot who was president of Harvard University from 1869 to 1900. He was one of the famous speakers and writers of his day concerning educational and social problems, his opinions greatly influencing the trend of American thought.

Dr. Charles William Eliot was born at Boston, Mass., on March 20, 1834, and died at Northeast Harbor, Me., on August 22, 1926.

[1] *Encyclopedia of American Biography: American Biography, a New Cyclopedia,* comp. under the editorial supervision of a notable advisory board. (Published under the direction of The American Historical Society, Inc., New York, 1927) vol. 28, p. 77.

Eliot, John

John Eliot's religious zeal as an evangelist among the Indians well earned for him the sobriquet, the *Apostle of the Indians* [1] given him by Thomas Thorowgood.

He was born in England in 1604, migrated to Boston in 1631, and began to study the Indian language. On October 28, 1646, he first began to preach to the Indians at Nonantum, now Newton, Mass. He translated the Bible into the Algonquin dialect, completing the New Testament in 1661, and the Old Testament in 1663. He died at Roxbury, Mass., on May 21, 1690.

[1] *The National Cyclopaedia of American Biography* (James T. White and Company, New York, 1899) vol. 2, p. 419, 422.
Life and Labors of John Eliot, the Apostle among the Indian Nations of New England, together wtih an Account of the Eliots in England, Robert Boodey Caverly (George M. Elliott, Lowell, Mass., 1881) p. 43.

Elis. See Yale University

Ellenbogen, Henry

Henry Ellenbogen, a Pennsylvania lawyer and politician, was nicknamed *Miss Ellen Bogen* [1] in the House of Representatives. He was a Democratic Representative from Pennsylvania to Congress from 1933 to 1938.

Henry Ellenbogen was born at Vienna, Austria, on April 3, 1900.

[1] An interview with Captain Victor Hunt Harding, Secretary of the National Democratic Congress Reëlection Committee, Washington, D.C., April 10, 1939.

Ellicot, Joseph

The *Father of Buffalo* [1] was the nickname attributed to Joseph Ellicot because of his interest and activities as the agent of the Holland Land Company in surveying the town of Buffalo, N.Y., in 1803.

He was born in Buck County, Pa., on November 1, 1760, and died at Jersey City, N.J., in 1859.

[1] *The Encyclopaedia Britannica,* Fourteenth Edition (Encyclopaedia Britannica, Inc., New York, 1934) vol. 4, p. 342.
A History of Buffalo Delineating the Evolution of the City, by J. N. Larned, *with Sketches of the City of Rochester,* by The Hon. Charles E. Fitch, and *The City of Utica,* by the Honorable Ellis H. Roberts (The Progress of the Empire State Company, New York, 1911) p. 12-13.

Elliott, James Thomas

James Thomas Elliott, who was born at St. Louis, Mo., on October 22, 1901, and pitched in major league baseball, is nicknamed *Jumbo* [1] probably because he weighs about two hundred and twenty pounds.

[1] *Who's Who in Major League Base Ball,* comp. by Harold (Speed) Johnson (Buxton Publishing Company, Chicago, 1933) p. 147.

Ellsworth, George A.

During the Civil War, George A. Ellsworth served as a telegraph operator with Major General John Hunt Morgan and his Confederate cavalry. These soldiers applied the sobriquet *Lightning* [1] to Ellsworth. His interception of the telegraphic messages of the Federal leaders greatly aided General Morgan in harassing them in the Southern states and in misleading them regarding Confederate movements.

[1] *Reminiscences of General Basil W. Duke, C.S.A.* (Doubleday, Page and Company, Garden City, New York, 1911) p. 126, 127.

Ellsworth, Oliver

Oliver Ellsworth was called the *Cerberus of the Treasury.* [1] The nickname originated while Ellsworth served from 1789 to 1796 as a Senator from Connecticut to the newly organized United States Congress because of his constant watchfulness over the disbursements of the national treasury. In Greek mythology, Cerberus was the three-headed dog that guarded the gate of Hades.

Ellsworth, Oliver—Continued

Ellsworth was born at Windsor, Conn. on April 29, 1745, and died there on November 26, 1807.

[1] *Appleton's Cyclopaedia of American Biography*, ed. by James Grant Wilson and John Fiske (D. Appleton and Company, New York, 1888) vol. 3, p. 336.

Elm City. See New Haven, Conn.

Elmer the Great. See Beck, W. W.

Elon College

The athletic teams of Elon College, at Elon College Post Office, N.C., were called the *Fighting Christians* [1] because Elon is a Christian Church school.

[1] A communication from D. C. Walker, Director of Athletics at Elon College, Elon College Post Office, N.C., June 21, 1935.

Ely, William Harvey Johnson

William Harvey Johnson Ely, a former District Court Judge, New Jersey State Senator, and State WPA administrator, was nicknamed *Mickey Mouse* [1] by his Republican opponents during the campaign for state senator in 1938. Ely is small in stature and has a rather prominent nose and large ears.

William Harvey Johnson Ely was born at Rutherford, N.J., on September 18, 1891.

[1] *The Washington Post*, Washington, D.C., November 13, 1938, sec. 3, col. 6, p. 1.

Emancipation President. See Lincoln, Abraham

Embalmed Beef

Refrigerated beef treated with chemicals which made it unwholesome was shipped to Cuba to be used as food by the soldiers in the United States Army during the Spanish American War in 1898. It was nicknamed by the newspapers *Embalmed Beef.* [1]

[1] *Twenty Years of the Republic, 1885-1905*, Harry Thurston Peck (Dodd, Mead and Company, New York, 1907), p. 622.

Embargo Act

Those who opposed the passage of the Embargo Act in 1807 expressed their disapproval by recombining the letters in the word *embargo* thus calling it the *Go-bar-me Act*, [1] the *Mob-rage Act* and *O-grab-me Act*.

See also O-grab-me Pets, Patent Merchants, Presidential Bulls and Indulgences.

[1] *The American People and Nation*, Rolla M. Tryon and Charles R. Lingley (Ginn and Company, New York and Boston, 1929) p. 275.

Emerson, Ralph Waldo

The *Columbus of Modern Thought* and the *Sage of Concord* were names applied to Ralph Waldo Emerson.

He was called the *Columbus of Modern Thought* [1] because he was an original thinker whose expression of ethical truth was a radical departure from the extreme conservative views of his contemporaries.

Ralph Waldo Emerson was designated the *Sage of Concord* [2] because of his philosophical teachings and writings.

Emerson was born at Boston, Mass., on May 25, 1803, and died at Concord, Mass., on April 27, 1882.

[1] *The National Cyclopaedia of American Biography* (James T. White and Company, New York, 1893) vol. 3, p. 416.

[2] *The Child's Book of American Biography*, Mary Stoyell Stimpson (Little, Brown and Company, Boston, 1915) p. 220.

Emory and Henry College

The teams of Emory and Henry College, at Emory, Va., have been designated *The Wasps*. [1] The tradition is that the nickname originated in 1920 at a football game between Emory and Henry and the University of Tennessee. The Emory and Henry players were dressed in gold and blue striped jerseys. The first half of the game ended in a scoreless tie; and when the second half opened, the Emory and Henry players, though small were peppery and rather noticeable for their striped jerseys. Someone remarked, "Those little fellows look and fight like a nest of wasps." Rooters began to yell, "Sting them, Wasps," and from that day to this the team have been *Wasps*.

[1] A letter from J. H. Hillman, President of Emory and Henry College, Emory, Va., December 11, 1935.

Emperor Mackenzie. See Mackenzie, Kenneth

Emperor of the West. See Mackenzie, Kenneth

Emperor Nick of the Bribery Bank. See Biddle, Nicholas

Empire Builder. See Hill, J. J.

Empire City. See New York City

Empire State. See New York

Empire State of the South. See Georgia

Enchanter. See Van Buren, Martin

Endicott, John
Historians have called John Endicott the *Father of New England* [1] because he was instrumental in securing from the Plymouth Council in England a grant or patent for the settlement of the Massachusetts Bay Colony. Upon the establishment of the Massachusetts Bay Colony at Salem in June 1628, he was appointed its first governor, and took an active part in the political and ecclesiastical affairs of the colony.

He was born in Dorchester, England, in 1589, and died at Boston, Mass., on March 15, 1665.

[1] *The American Portrait Gallery; Containing Correct Portraits and Brief Notices of the Principal Actors in American History; Embracing Distinguished Women, Naval and Military Heroes, Statesmen, Civilians, Jurists, Divines, Authors, and Artists; together with Celebrated Indian Chiefs from Christopher Columbus down to the Present Time,* A. D. Jones (J. M. Emerson and Company, New York, 1855) p. 27.
Commonwealth History of Massachusetts Colony, Province and State: Colony of Massachusetts Bay (1605-1689), ed. by Albert Bushell Hart (The States History Company, New York, 1927) vol. 1, p. 19.

Engineers. See Lehigh University; New Mexico School of Mines; Worchester Polytechnic Institute

English, James Edward
While James Edward English was governor of Connecticut from 1867 to 1869, and from 1870 to 1871, he was nicknamed the *Father of the Free School System,* [1] because he was a pioneer trying to institute a system of education which would open the public schools to all the children of the state, impartially, and free of all charges or expenses.

James Edward English was born at New Haven, Conn., on March 13, 1812, and died there on March 2, 1890.

[1] *Sketches of Men of Mark* (New York and Hartford Publishing Company, New York, 1871) p. 116.
The National Cyclopaedia of American Biography (James T. White and Company, New York, 1900) vol. 10, p. 341.

Ens, Jewel
Jewel Ens, who was born at St. Louis, Mo., on August 24, 1889, and who coached in major league baseball, was nicknamed *Mutt* [1].

[1] *Who's Who in Major League Base Ball,* comp. by Harold (Speed) Johnson (Buxton Publishing Company, Chicago, 1933) p. 429.

Episcopalians. See Kenyon College

Equality State. See Wyoming

Era-of-good-feeling President. See Monroe, James

Erbmen. See Humboldt State College

Erskine of the American Bar. See Hoffman, Ogden

Escaped Jail-bird. See Egan, Patrick

Espy, James Pollard
The *Storm King* [1] was the nickname given to James Pollard Espy because he was recognized internationally as an outstanding authority on meteorology, and was especially noted for his information concerning the phenomena of storms. The nickname originated about 1836, when Espy delivered at Columbus, Ohio, a lecture entitled the *Philosophy of Storms* which caused a great deal of interest in, and controversy over, the phenomena of storms.

James Pollard Espy was born in Westmoreland County, Pa., on May 9, 1785, and died at Cincinnati, Ohio, on January 24, 1860.

[1] *The National Cyclopaedia of American Biography* (James T. White and Company, New York, 1929) vol. 6, p. 205.
The Encyclopedia Americana (Americana Corporation, New York and Chicago, 1927) vol. 10, p. 506.

Eternal Flapper. See Hopper, E. W.

Eureka College
About 1923 the athletic teams of Eureka College, at Eureka, Ill., were called the *Golden Tornadoes* and the *Red Devils*. The sobriquet the *Golden Tornadoes* [1] was given to the 'football teams. The *Red Devils* was given the basketball teams about 1923 because they wore red suits. [1]

[1] A communication from Clyde L. Lyon, President of Eureka College, Eureka, Ill., November 16, 1935.

Eureka State. See California

Evans, Robley Dunglison
The nicknames *Fighting Bob* and *Old Gimpy* were attributed to Robley Dunglison Evans.

Evans, R. D.—Continued

Fighting Bob[1] was a sobriquet given to him by the press when Evans, Commander of the United States ship *Yorktown,* was sent to Valparaiso, Chile, following the death there of two American sailors at the hands of a rowdy crowd in 1891.

Old Gimpy[1] originated soon after the victorious Federal assault on Fort Fisher, a Confederate stronghold near Wilmington, N.C. on January 15, 1865. As an ensign of the Union ship *Powhatan,* Evans took a conspicuous part in the storming of the fort and received permanent injuries to both legs which led to his being nicknamed *Old Gimpy.*

Robley Dunglison Evans was born at Floyd Court House, in Floyd County, Va., on August 18, 1847, and died at Washington, D.C., on January 3, 1912.

[1] *Fighting Bob Evans,* Edwin A. Falk (Jonathan Cape and Harrison Smith, New York, 1931) p. 37, 73-4, 76, 164-5.

Evansville College

The *Pioneers*[1] and *Aces*[1] are the nicknames of the athletic teams of Evansville College at Evansville, Ind. *The Pioneers* was given to the members many years ago. The *Aces* or *Purple Aces* originated during the basketball season of 1925-1926, when a Louisville sports writer called two of the star players the *Purple Aces.* (Purple and white were the school colors.) Gradually the *Aces* has come to be used rather than the *Pioneers.*

[1] A communication from William V. Slyker, Director of Athletics at Evansville College, Evansville, Ind., June 12, 1935.

Everglade State. See Florida

Evergreen City. See Sheboygan, Wis.

Evergreen State. See Washington

Evers, John Joseph

John Joseph Evers, who was born at Troy, N.Y., and who played in major league baseball, was nicknamed the *Trojan.*[1]

[1] *Who's Who in Major League Base Ball,* comp. by Harold (Speed) Johnson (Buxton Publishing Company, Chicago, 1933) p. 462.

Evil Genius of Maryland. See Claiborne, William

Excelsior Brigade

The Second Brigade of the Second Division of the Third Corps of the State of New York, which fought in the Battle of Gettysburg on July 1, 2, and 3 1863, was designated the *Excelsior Brigade*[1] because New York is the *Excelsior State.*

[1] *Two Days of War, a Gettysburg Narrative and Other Excursions,* Henry Edwin Tremain (Bonnell, Silver and Bowers, New York, 1905) p. 139.

Excelsior State. See New York

Excelsiors. See New Yorkers

Executive City. See Washington, D.C.

Expansionists

About the time of the proclamation of William McKinley, President of the United States, on January 5, 1899, "to extend the military rule of the United States over the whole of the Philippine Islands" those who favored this action were called *The Expansionists,*[1] the term thus signifying that these people favored the President's action to extend the domain of the United States.

[2] *Twenty Years of the Republic, 1885-1905,* Harry Thurston Peck (Dodd, Mead and Company, New York, 1907) p. 611.

Expounder of the Constitution. See Webster, Daniel

Extra Billy. See Smith, William (Politician)

Extraordinary Chancellor of the Rising State of New Jersey. See Livingston, William

F

F.D. See Roosevelt, F. D.

F.D.R. See Roosevelt, F. D.

FFV's. See Virginians

Fair Deal

The *Fair Deal* is the nickname for the administration of President Harry S. Truman. It was designed to carry on the social and economic policies of the New Deal.

The term was first used by President Truman in his State of the Union message to the members of the 81st Congress on January 6, 1949.

[1] American Year Book; a record of events and progress, year 1948-1949. William M. Schuyler, ed. (Thomas Nelson and Sons, New York, 1950) p. 1.

Fair White City. See Milwaukee, Wis.

Fairbanks, Charles Warren
The reserved and formal manners of Charles Warren Fairbanks, who was Vice President of the United States from 1905 to 1909, caused him to be nicknamed *Icebanks.*[1]

Charles Warren Fairbanks was born near Unionville Center, Ohio, on May 11, 1854, and died at Indianapolis, Ind., on June 4, 1918.

[1] *Twenty Years of the Republic, 1885-1905*, Harry Thurston Peck (Dodd, Mead and Company, New York, 1907) p. 710.

Faithful Andy. See Sommerville, Andrew

Falk, Bibb August
Bibb August Falk, who was born at Austin, Tex., on January 27, 1899, and who coached in major league baseball, is nicknamed *Jockey*[1] because he has ridden horses in the races.

[1] *Who's Who in Major League Base Ball*, comp. by Harold (Speed) Johnson (Buxton Publishing Company, Chicago, 1933) p. 426.

Falls City. See Louisville, Ky.

Fancy Frank. See Powell, D. F.

Fannin, James W.
The *Hero of Conception*[1] was the sobriquet applied to James W. Fannin because of the distinguished service he rendered in the Battle of Conception against the Mexican forces in the struggle for the independence of Texas.

James W. Fannin was born in Georgia, about 1800, moved to Texas in 1834, and was massacred with his men by order of Santa Anna, the Mexican general, after the battle at Soliad, Tex., on March 27, 1836.

[1] *The National Cyclopaedia of American Biography* (James T. White and Company, New York, 1896) vol. 6, p. 71.

Fargo Express. See Petrolle, Billy

Faribault, Minnesota
Faribault is often called the *Athens of the Northwest*[1] because the city is noted for its excellent schools, public, private, and denominational. The Shattuck Military School there for boys is one of the oldest military schools in the United States.

Faribault is called the *Peony Center of the World*[1] because of the abundance of peonies grown in the vicinity of this city and its annual peony festival.

[1] *My Minnesota*, Antoinette E. Ford (Lyons and Carnahan, New York and Chicago, 1929) p. 340.

Farley, James Aloysius
The nicknames, *Big Jim, Four-job Farley, Smiling Jim, A Political Thor,* and *That Candid Spoilsman,* have been applied to James Aloysius Farley.

He has been widely known, especially in political circles, as *Big Jim*[1] because of his physical size and his political influence.

Mr Farley was referred to as *Four-job Farley*[2] because for a time he was Postmaster General of the United States in President Franklin Delano Roosevelt's first cabinet, Chairman of the National Democratic Committee, Chairman of the New York State Democratic Committee, and National Committeeman from New York. Because Mr. Farley was so powerful in the Democratic Party he has been referred to by news writers as a *Political Thor.*[3]

James Aloysius Farley was often called *Smiling Jim*[4] because he was often photographed with a smile.

James Aloysius Farley has been called *That Candid Spoilsman*[5] because he advocates and practices the spoils system. A representative from New York has said that Mr. Farley "has done more to break the civil service, to destroy the merit system, and to build a spoils system than any man who has lived in America."

He was born at Grassy Point, N.Y., on May 30, 1888.

[1] *Encyclopedia of American Biography*, New Series, ed. by Winfield Scott Downs (The American Historical Society, Inc., New York, 1934) p. 24.
[2] *The Washington Times*, Washington, D.C., August 29, 1936, col. 5, p. 3.
[3] *The New York Times*, New York, March 22, 1936, sec. 7, p. 6.
[4] *The American Scene*, Edwin C. Hill (Witmark Educational Publications, Department of M. Witmark and Sons, New York, 1933) p. 48.
[5] *The Washington Post*, Washington, D.C., February 3, 1935, sec. B, col. 6, p. 1.
Congressional Record, Seventy-fourth Congress, First Session, January 28, 1935, vol. 79, no. 18, p. 1111.

Farmer Bob. See Doughton, R. L.; Scott, R. W.

Farmer Governor. See Bouck, W. C.

Farmer President. See Harrison, W. H.; Washington, George

Farmers. See Rhode Island State College; University of Wichita; Utah State Agricultural College

Farmer's Dick. See Oglesby, R. J.

Farmer's Friend. See Capper, Arthur

Farmers' Holiday

In October of 1932 and 1933 farmers in a half dozen states in the midwest withheld their produce from sale in an effort to raise the price at least enough to pay the cost of production and marketing. This market boycott was called the *Farmers' Holiday*.[1] A Farmers' Holiday Association was formed and the movement spread to some twenty states in the middle West.

[1] *The American Scene,* Edwin C. Hill (Witmark Educational Publications, Department of M. Witmark and Sons, New York, 1933) p. 22.
The New York Times, New York, August 7, col. 7, p. 2.

Farragut, David Glasgow

Admiral David Glasgow Farragut was nicknamed the *Hero of Mobile Bay*[1] because on August 5, 1863, he entered Mobile bay and fought a winning battle against the Confederate batteries and gunboats when the odds were against him. Admiral Farragut was also called *Old Salamander*[1] probably because he lived through the hottest of enemy fire on the Mississippi River, particularly at Vicksburg, Miss.

David Glasgow Farragut was born at Campbell's Station, Tenn., on July 5, 1801, and died at Portsmouth, N.H., on August 14, 1870.

[1] *Compton's Pictured Encyclopedia* (F. E. Compton and Company, Chicago, 1931) vol. 5, p. 1225.

Farrell, Edward Stephen

Because he is a dentist by profession, Edward Stephen Farrell, who was born at Johnson City, N.Y., on December 26, 1902,

and who played infield in major league baseball, is nicknamed *Doc*.[1]

[1] *Who's Who in Major League Base Ball,* comp. by Harold (Speed) Johnson (Buxton Publishing Company, Chicago, 1933) p. 150.

Farwell, Charles Benjamin

Senator Charles Benjamin Farwell, who was United States Senator from Illinois from 1887 to 1891, was called *Poker Charley*[1] because it was erroneously believed that he was an expert poker player. However, he denied he knew anything about playing poker.

Senator Farwell was born at Painted Post, N.Y., on July 1, 1823, and died at Lake Forest, Ill., on September 23, 1903.

[1] *U.S. "Snap Shots": An Independent, National, and Memorial Encyclopedia . . . ,* Oliver McKee (A. M. Thayer and Company, Boston, 1892) p. 244.

Fashion Plate. See Lewis, J. H.

Father Abraham. See Lincoln, Abraham

Father and Glory of Boston. See Cotton, John

Father and Nursing Mother of the Gridiron Club. See Carson, J. M.

Father Cole. See Cole, A. N.

Father Divine. See Baker, George

Father Hagerty's Wheel of Fortune. See Industrial Workers of the World

Father Kit. See Carson, Christopher

Father of Abolition. See Hopkins, Samuel

Father of America. See Adams, Samuel

Father of American Anthropology. See Morgan, L. H.

Father of American Apiculture. See Langstroth, L. L.

Father of American Ballad Poetry. See Hewitt, J. H.

Father of American Baptists. See Clarke, John

Father of American Botany. See Bartram, John

Father of American Boxing. See Muldoon, William

Father of American Bridgebuilding. See Whipple, Squire

Father of American Commerce with India. See Derby, E. H.

Father of American Conchology. See Say, Thomas

Father of American Descriptive Entomology. See Say, Thomas

Father of American Engineering. See Wright, Benjamin

Father of American Entomology. See Say, Thomas

Father of American Experimental Physics. See Rood, O. N.

Father of American Football. See Camp, Walter

Father of American Geography. See Morse, Jedidiah

Father of American Geology. See Maclure, William

Father of American History. See Bradford, William

Father of American Independence. See Adams, John

Father of American Literature. See Irving, Washington

Father of American Manufacture. See Slater, Samuel

Father of American Mineralogy. See Cleaveland, Parker

Father of American Minstrelsy. See Rice, T. D.

Father of American Newspapers. See Harris, Benjamin

Father of American Orchestral Music. See Graupner, J. C. G.

Father of American Poets. See Bryant, W. C.

Father of American Prose. See Irving, Washington

Father of American Surgery. See Physick, P. S.

Father of American Universalism. See Ballou, Hosea

Father of American Watchmaking. See Dennison, A. L.

Father of American Zoölogy. See Say, Thomas

Father of Anarchy. See Warren, Josiah

Father of Baseball. See Chadwick, Henry; Doubleday, Abner

Father of Baseball in the West. See Waldo, H. H.

Father of Biblical Learning in America. See Stuart, Moses

Father of Buffalo. See Ellicot, Joseph

Father of Chautauqua County. See Foote, E. T.

Father of Civil Service Reform. See Jenckes, T. A.; Pendleton, George Hunt

Father of Civil Service Reform. See Pendleton, G. H.

Father of Concrete Roads in New York. See Greene, F. S.

Father of Connecticut Jurisprudence. See Ludlow, Roger

Father of English Colonization in America. See Gorges, Ferdinando

Father of Equity in Tennessee. See Green, Nathan

Father of Foreign Mission Work in Christian America. See Mills, S. J.

Father of Free Silver. See Bland, R. P.

Father of Good Roads. See Sproul, W. C.

Father of Greater New York. See Green, A. H.

Father of Greater Philadelphia. See Bullitt, J. C.

Father of Greenbacks. See Chase, S. P.; Spaulding, E. G.

Father of His Country. See Washington, George

Father of Historical Societies in America. See Pintard, John

Father of Homeopathy in America. See Hering, Constantine

Father of Horticulture and Ornamental Gardening. See Henderson, Peter

Father of Iron Shipbuilding in America. See Roach, John

Father of Louisiana Jurisprudence. See Martin, F. X.

Father of Massachusetts. See Winthrop, John

Father of Middle Tennessee. See Robertson, James

Father of Minneapolis. See Stevens, J. H.

Father of Modern Baseball. See Cartwright, A. J.

Father of More Brains Than Any Other Man in America. See Beecher, Lyman

Father of Negro Songs. See Graupner, J. C. G.

Father of New England. See Endicott, John

Father of New England Commerce. See Allerton, Isaac

Father of Niagara Power. See Rankine, W. B.

Father of Ohio Labor. See Crosser, Robert

Father of Ohio University. See Cutler, Manasseh

Father of Organized Alumni Work at Fisk University. See Proctor, H. H.

Father of Our Modern Fortifications. See Craighill, W. P.

Father of Our Modern Navy. See Chandler, W. E.

Father of Pennsylvania. See Penn, William

Father of Pitt Stadium. See Hamilton, A. R.

Father of Pittsburgh. See Washington, George

Father of Presbyterianism in the State of New York. See McNish, George

Father of Presbyterianism in Virginia. See Morris, Samuel

Father of Prison Reform in the United States. See Osborne, G. O.

Father of Prohibition. See Dow, Neal

Father of Public Utility Regulation. See Norris, G. W.

Father of Radio Broadcasting. See Davis, H. P.

Father of Railroads. See Cooper, Peter

Father of Reclamation. See Wisner, Edward

Father of Rhode Island. See Clarke, John

Father of Rural Credit in North Carolina. See Hill, J. S.

Father of Rural Free Delivery. See Butler, Marion

Father of Secession. See Rhett, R. B.

Father of Ship-building. See Dickie, G. W.

Father of State Universities. See Cutler, Manasseh

Father of States' Rights. See Calhoun, J. C.

Father of Steamboat Navigation. See Fulton, Robert

Father of Tacoma. See Wright, C. B.

Father of Texas. See Austin, S. F.; Houston, Samuel

Father of the American Anthracite Iron Industry. See Thomas, David

Father of the American Cotton Industry. See Coxe, Tench

Father of the American Medical Association. See Davis, N. S.

Father of the American Navy. See Adams, John; Barry, John; Humphreys, Joshua

Father of the American Revolution. See Adams, Samuel

Father of the Bar of the State of New York. See Van Vechten, Abraham

Father of the Barge Canal. See Clinton, George

Father of the Blues. See Handy, W. C.

Father of the Bonus. See Patman, Wright, Van Zant, J. E.

Father of the Breaker. See Markle, G. B.

Father of the Brooklyn Institute of Arts and Sciences. See Healy, A. A.

Father of the Code. See Field, D. D.

Father of the "Colyumnist." See Bailey, J. M.

Father of the Constitution. See Madison, James

Father of the Continental Congress. See Franklin, Benjamin

Father of the Cotton Gin. See Whitney, Eli

Father of the Criminal Bar. See Howe, W. F.

Father of the Declaration of Independence. See Jefferson, Thomas

Father of the Dry Plate Process in America. See Newton, H. J.

Father of the Dutch Reformed Church in America. See Livingston, J. H.

Father of the Eighteenth Amendment. See Sheppard, Morris

Father of the Electric Light in Europe. See Lieb, J. W.

Father of the Federal Reserve System. See Glass, G. C.

Father of the Florida Orange Industry. See Harris, J. A.

Father of the Free School System. See English, J. E.

Father of the Free School System in New Jersey. See Cutler, A. W.

Father of the Hampden County Bar. See Bates, W. G.

Father of the Homestead. See Johnson, Andrew

Father of the Homestead Law. See Grow, G. A.

Father of the House. See Bingham, H. H.; Dalzell, John; Gillett, F. H.; Harmer, A. C.; Kelley, W. D.; Macon. Nathaniel; O'Neill, Charles; Williams, Lewis

Father of the Juvenile Court. See Lindsey, B. B.

Father of the Mormons. See Smith, Joseph

Father of the Museum. See Bickmore, A. S.

Father of the National Guard of New York. See Phisterer, Frederick

Father of the National Road. See Clay, Henry

Father of the New York Bar. See Jones, Samuel

Father of the New York State Boxing Bill. See Walker, J. J.

Father of the New York Turf. See De Lancey, James

Father of the North Carolina Bar. See Moore, B. F.

Father of the Patent Office. See Ruggles, John

Father of the Phonograph. See Edison, T. A.

Father of the Plate Glass Industry. See Ford, J. B.

Father of the Protective Policy. See Clay, Henry

Father of the Public School System of Ohio. See Rice, Harvey

Father of the Public School System of Pennsylvania. See Wolf, George

Father of the Public Schools of Alabama. See Meek, A. B.

Father of the Republican Party. See Cole, A. N.

Father of the Science of Physiography. See Davis, W. M.

Father of the Sewing Machine. See Howe, Elias

Father of the Silk Industry. See Ryle, John

Father of the Skyscraper. See Gilbert, Cass

Father of the Steamboat. See Fulton, Robert

Father of the Stove. See Franklin, Benjamin

Father of the System of Common School Education. See Treadwell, John

Father of the Tablet Triturate. See Fuller, R. M.

Father of the Tariff. See Hamilton, Alexander

Father of the Telegraph. See Morse, S. F. B.

Father of the Telephone. See Bell, A. G.

Father of the Tri-borough Bridge. See Franklin, Benjamin (Lawyer)

Father of the Twentieth Amendment to the Constitution. See Norris, G. W.

Father of the Typewriter. See Sholes, C. L.

Father of the Union Party of California. See Van Dyke, Walter

Father of the United States Military Academy. See Thayer, Sylvanus

Father of the University of Minnesota. See Pillsbury, J. S.

Father of the University of North Carolina. See Davie, W. R.

Father of the University of Virginia. See Jefferson, Thomas

Father of the White Line. See Hines, E. N.

Father of Universalism in America. See Murray, John

Father of Virginia. See Smith, John

Father Tom. See Beecher, T. K.

Favorite Son of Texas. See Garner, J. N.

Fayetteville, Arkansas
Fayetteville is termed the *Athens of Arkansas* [1] because the University of Arkansas is located there.

[1] *The Encyclopedia Americana* (Americana Corporation, New York and Chicago, 1927) vol. 11, p. 72.

Featherheads
From about 1875 to 1881, Roscoe Conkling was a prominent leader of the Republican party. Those who opposed his dictatorial political policy and adhered instead to President James Abram Garfield's administration were nicknamed *Featherheads*.[1]

[1] *The Autobiography of Thomas Collier Platt*, comp. and ed. by Louis J. Lang (B. W. Dodge and Company, New York, 1910) p. 164.
The Century Dictionary and Cyclopedia (The Century Publishing Company, New York, 1906) vol. 3, p. 2164.

Febiger, Christian
Christian Febiger, a Revolutionary soldier and general, was popularly designated *Old Denmark* [1] while in the Continental Army during the Revolutionary War.

Christian Febiger was born on the Island of Funen in Denmark, in 1746, and died at Philadelphia, Pa., on September 20, 1796.

[1] *Appleton's Cyclopaedia of American Biography*, ed. by James Grant Wilson and John Fiske (D. Appleton and Company, New York, 1894) vol. 2, p. 424.

Federal Bull-dog. See Martin, Luther

Federal City. See Washington, D.C.

Felton, Cornelius Conway
The *American Professor* [1] was the nickname applied to Cornelius Conway Felton while he was in Greece from 1853 to 1854 visiting its historic antiquities, and studying its past and present history at the University of Athens. He was an eminent professor at Harvard University.

Cornelius Conway Felton was born at Newbury, Mass., on November 6, 1807, and died at Chester, Pa., on February 26, 1862.

[1] *The National Cyclopaedia of American Biography* (James T. White and Company, New York, 1896) vol. 6, p. 419.

Female Petrarch. See Lewis, E. A. B.

Fence-rail Johnson. See Johnson, Edward

Fergus Falls, Minnesota
Fergus Falls is self-styled the *City Beautiful in the Land o'Lakes* because it is situated in the center of the lakes region of the Red River of the North.

[1] *My Minnesota*, Antoinette E. Ford (Lyons and Carnahan, New York and Chicago, 1929) p. 355.

Ferguson, Miriam A.

Miriam A. Ferguson, the former Governor of Texas, who was born in Bell County, Tex., on June 13, 1875, is widely known as *Ma Ferguson* because of her motherly interests in people and in her state, and her initials are M.A.

Fernandez, Joachim Octave

Coroner [1] was a nickname applied to Representative Joachim Octave Fernandez because in Congress he represented a district of Louisiana in which is located New Orleans' municipal morgue.

Representative Fernandez, who was born at New Orleans, La., on August 14, 1896, was a representative from Louisiana to Congress from 1931 to 1941.

[1] *The Washington Post Magazine*, Washington, D.C., March 4, 1934, p. 4.

Ferry Boy. See Chase, S. P.

Fickinger, James Albert

Colonel [1] is the sobriquet by which James Albert Fickinger was generally called in allusion to his capacity for leadership.

During his career as an engineer, he took part in important railroad survey and construction work, particularly in West Virginia and Ohio. He built the great cantilever bridge across the Kanawha River at Point Pleasant, a conspicuous engineering achievement. His talent for organizing and directing the construction of the Ohio River railroad won him the affectionate title of *Colonel,* by which he was known thereafter.

James Albert Fickinger was born at Kingsville, Ohio, on January 31, 1853, and died at Fairmont, W.Va., on January 29, 1903.

[1] *The National Cyclopaedia of American Biography* (James T. White and Company, New York, 1931) vol. 21, p. 358.

Fiddling Bob. See Taylor, R. L.

Fidgety. See Collins, P. E.

Field, David Dudley

David Dudley Field was deservedly called the *Father of the Code* [1] in commemoration of his invaluable services in codifying political, civil, and criminal laws. His codes have been widely used in the United States and have been employed as a guide by foreign nations in the codification of their laws.

In 1857 Field was authorized by the State of New York to codify its civil, penal, and political laws. The penal code was adopted by that state, and other states have made use of three of the codes prepared by him at this time. In 1866 Field was appointed to prepare the outlines of an international code.

Field was born at Haddam, Conn., on February 13, 1805, and died at New York City, on April 13, 1894.

[1] *Contemporary American Biography: Biographical Sketches of Representative Men of the Day, Representatives of Modern Thought and Progress, of the Pulpit, the Press, the Bench and Bar, of Legislation, Invention, and the Great Industrial Interests of the Country* (Atlantic Publishing and Engraving Company, New York, 1902) vol. 3, p. 21.

Field, Eugene

Because so much of his poetry deals with childhood or is written for children, Eugene Field has been called the *Poet of Childhood.* [1]

He was born at St. Louis, Mo., on September 2, 1850, and died at Chicago, Ill., on November 4, 1895.

[1] *Compton's Pictured Encyclopedia* (F. E. Compton and Company, Chicago, 1931) vol. 1, p. 115.

Fifth Armored Division of World War II

V for 5th and Victory [1] was the nickname of the Fifth Armored Division of World War II.

[1] *Combat Divisions of World War II,* (Army of the United States), Army Times Publishing Company, Washington, D.C., 1946, p. 79.

Fifth Infantry Division of World War II

The Fifth Infantry Division of World War II was nicknamed *the Red Diamond Division.* [1]

[1] *Combat Divisions of World War II,* (Army of the United States), Army Times Publishing Company, Washington, D.C., 1946, p. 11.

Fighting Bishop. See Polk, Leonidas

Fighting Bob. See Evans, R. D.

Fighting Cadets. See Marion Institute

Fighting Chaplain. See Caldwell, James

Fighting Christians. See Elon College

Fighting Colonel. See Galbraith, F. W.

Fighting Commissary. See Ginter, Lewis

Fighting Corps

During the Civil War the Second Corps of the Army of the Potomac came to be called The *Fighting Corps* [1] because of the military abilities and the splendid achievements on the field of battle of this unit. According to Lieutenant General Nelson Appleton Miles, who was for a while in command of this corps, the *Fighting* Corps participated in more engagements than any other corps of the Union Army, and was credited with having captured in one day as many battle flags, cannon, and prisoners of the enemy as the corps lost during the entire four years of the Civil War.

[1] *My Little War Experience, with Historical Sketches and Memorabilia,* Edward Spangler (York Daily Publishing Company, York, Pa., 1904) p. 46.
Personal Recollections and Observations of General Nelson A. Miles, Embracing a Brief View of the Civil War or From New England to the Golden Gate and the Story of His Indian Campaigns with Comments on the Exploration, Development and Progress of Our Great Western Empire (The Werner Company, New York and Chicago, 1896) p. 33-4.

Fighting Dick. See Anderson, R. H.; Richardson, I. B.

Fighting Dick Dale. See Dale, Richard

Fighting Doctor. See Reynolds, J. C.

Fighting Engineers. See Rensselaer Polytechnic Institute; Rose Polytechnic Institute

Fighting First. See First Infantry Division of World War II

Fighting Fourth

During the Civil War the Fourth Regiment of Alabama Infantrymen in the Confederate Army were nicknamed the *Fighting Fourth* [1] in commemoration of their marked personal courage and their devotion to duty. The nickname continued to be applied to the Fourth Regiment of Alabama troops in the War with Mexico, and in World War I.

[1] *History of Alabama and Her People,* Albert Burton Moore, Author and Editor (The American Historical Society, Inc., New York and Chicago, 1927) vol. 1, p. 942.

Fighting Hill-toppers. See Hanover College

Fighting Illini. See University of Illinois

Fighting Irish. See University of Notre Dame

Fighting Jack. See Hayes, E. M.

Fighting Jim. See Lane, J. H.

Fighting Joe. See Wheeler, Joseph

Fighting Joe Hooker. See Hooker, Joseph

Fighting Johnnies. See Saint John's University, Minn.

Fighting Lutherans. See Capital University; Wittenberg College

Fighting Marine. See Tunney, J. J.

Fighting Parson. See Allen, Thomas; Balch, Benjamin; Brownlow, W. G.; Dewey, Jedediah; Jones, J. W.; Kelley, D. C.; Moody, Granville

Fighting Parson of Bennington Fields. See Allen, Thomas

Fighting Presbyterians. See College of Emporia

Fighting Quaker. See Greene, Nathanael; Wanton, John

Fighting Quakers. See Earlham College; Nebraska Central College; Wilmington College

Fighting Sixty-ninth. See Sixty-ninth Infantry Division of World War II

Fighting Surgeon of the Revolution. See Downer, Eliphalet

Fighting Tom Hoyne. See Hoyne, Thomas

Fighting Warriors. See Midland College

Fillmore, Millard

An *Accidental President,* the *American Louis Philippe, His Accidency,* and the *Wool-carder President* are nicknames attributed to Millard Fillmore.

President Millard Fillmore was called an *Accidental President* [1] and *His Accidency* [2] because, when President Zachary Taylor died on July 9, 1850, Fillmore automatically became President of the United States.

He was often called the *American Louis Philippe* [3] because of his dignity, aristocratic inclinations, his courtesy, and his refined gentility. President Fillmore is also said to have resembled the French king in physical appearance.

The nickname, *The Wool-carder President* [4] was applied to Millard Fillmore because during his youth he lived on a frontier farm in western New York and helped the family comb the wool from which their clothing was made.

Millard Fillmore was born at Summer Hill, in Cayuga County, N.Y., on February 7, 1800, and died at Buffalo, N.Y., on March 8, 1874.

[1] *The World Book* (Hanson-Roach-Fowler Company, Chicago, Kansas City, and New York, 1917) vol. 3, p. 2170.
[2] *The Heart of Roosevelt: an Intimate Life-story of Theodore Roosevelt,* Wayne Whipple (The John C. Winston Company, Chicago and Philadelphia, 1924) p. 163.
[3] *U.S. "Snap Shots": An Independent, National and Memorial Encyclopedia . . . ,* Oliver McKee (A. M. Thayer and Company, Boston, 1892) p. 309.
The Life and Public Services of Millard Fillmore, W. L. Barre (Wanzer McKim and Company, Buffalo, N.Y., 1856) p. 402-3.
[4] *A Book of Nicknames,* Jonh Goff (Courier-Journal Job Printing Company, Louisville, Ky., 1892) p. 27.

Financier of the American Revolution. See Morris, Robert

Finn, Daniel E.

Daniel E. Finn, a well-known police magistrate and politician of New York City, was nicknamed *Battery Dan* [1] because while he was a member of the State General Assembly in 1885-87, he was instrumental in defeating a bill which would have allowed private corporations to divide Battery Park into pier sites. He was a Representative from New York City to the New York General Assembly for two terms and was police magistrate in his district from 1905 until his death.

Daniel E. Finn was born at Limerick, Ireland, in 1846, came to New York City in 1849, and died there on March 23, 1910.

[1] *The New York Times,* New York, March 24, 1910, col. 1, p. 18.

Finn, Neal Francis

Neal Francis Finn, who was born at New York City on January 24, 1903, and who played second baseman in major league baseball, is known as *Mickey.* [1]

[1] *Who's Who in Major League Base Ball,* comp. by Harold (Speed) Johnson (Buxton Publishing Company, Chicago, 1933) p. 152.

Fire Alarm Foraker. See Foraker, J. B.

Fire Angel. See Hudlun, A. E.

Fire Cake

The colonial soldiers under the command of General George Washington at Valley Forge, Pa., baked bread on the hearths of fireplaces or on the embers of open fires and called it *Fire Cake.* [1]

[1] *American History,* Thomas M. Marshall (The Macmillan Company, New York, 1930) p. 190.

Fire Canoes

When steamboats first began to be seen on the rivers and lakes of America about the beginning of the eighteenth century, the Indians and settlers called them *Milwaukee, Walk-on-the-Water* and *Fire Canoes* [1] because the boats appeared to be mills walking on the water or canoes issuing fire and smoke.

[1] *The Romance of the Rails; The Story of the American Railroads,* Agnes C. Laut (Tudor Publishing Company, New York, 1936) p. 24, 31.

Fire Chief. See Carley, P. J.

Fire-eaters

Prior to the out-break of the Civil War in 1861, the sobriquet *Fire-eaters* [1] was given to southern politicians who held radical views concerning slavery and secession. A fire-eater is a quick-tempered, impetuous person.

[1] *Politics and Pen Pictures at Home and Abroad,* Henry W. Hilliard (G. P. Putnam's Sons, New York and London, 1892) p. 255.

Fire Horse

When the first train arrived over the Union Pacific Railroad at Fort Bridger, Wyo., Washakie, the chief of the Shoshoni Indians, called the locomotive the *Fire Horse* [1] because it ran and smoke and sparks came from its smokestack.

[1] *Washakie, an Account of Indian Resistance of the Covered Wagon and Union Pacific Railroad Invasions of Their Territory*, Grace Raymond Hebard (The Arthur H. Clark Company, Cleveland, Ohio, and Glendale, Calif., 1930) p. 275.

Fire Lands

After the Revolutionary War in 1786, Connecticut ceded to the United States a great deal of land (about three thousand miles in length) which the crown had granted. This grant consisted of a tract of land west of Pennsylvania in northeastern Ohio constituting about three and a half million acres which was called the Western Reserve of Connecticut. In 1792 about five hundred thousand acres of this Reserve land was set aside for those settlers who, during the Revolutionary War, had had their property burned and plundered by the British soldiers. Because of this the Reserve land was popularly termed the *Fire Lands*.[1]

[1] "Connecticut, a Study of a Commonwealth-Democracy" by Alexander Johnston, in *American Commonwealths*, ed. by Horace E. Scudder (Houghton Mifflin and Company, New York and Boston, 1891) p. 282.

Fireside Chats

Immediately after Franklin Delano Roosevelt was inaugurated as President of the United States in March 1933, he began a series of radio broadcasts from the White House to the American people which he called *Fireside Chats*. He chose an early evening hour when whole families would be most likely to be home and could listen together. This was in the midst of the depression and his object was to reassure people and rebuild their morale. The first *Fireside Chat* was on March 12, 1933.

First Cavalry Division of World War II

The *Cavalry Troopers* [1] was the nickname of the First Cavalry Division of the United States Army in World War II.

[1] *Combat Divisions of World War II*, (Army of the United States), Army Times Publishing Company, Washington, D.C., 1946, p. 96.

First Citizen of Brooklyn. See Stranahan, J. S. T.

First Citizen of St. Anthony. See Steele, Franklin

First Dark Horse. See Polk, J. K.

First Gentleman of the Land. See Arthur, C. A.

First Infantry Division of World War II

The First Infantry Division was nicknamed the *Fighting First* [1] and the *Red One*.[1] It was activated on June 8, 1917. The *Red One* is suggested by the division's shoulder emblem.

[1] *Combat Divisions of World War II*, (Army of the United States), Army Times Publishing Company, Washington, D.C., 1946. p. 7.

First Lady of the World. See Wilson, E. B.

First Lord of the Marshes. See Hatfield, B. M.

First Martyr of the Revolution. See Snyder, Christopher

First State. See Delaware

First Tough Girl of the American Drama. See Lewis, Ada

Fish, Hamilton, Junior

Hamilton Fish, Junior, a New York politician, was nicknamed *One Man Patriot* and the *Great All American* [1] in the National House of Representatives. During World War I, having taken an active part in several well-known battles, he was awarded the French Croix de Guerre and the American Silver Star for gallantry. He had been an all-American football player on the Harvard University team from 1909 to 1910. He was a Republican Representative from New York to the United States Congress from 1921 to 1945.

Hamilton Fish, Junior, was born at Garrison, N.Y., on December 7, 1888.

[1] An interview with Captain Victor Hunt Harding, Secretary of the National Democratic Congress Reëlection Committee, Washington, D.C., April 10, 1939.

Fish Hooks. See Stout, A. M.

Fish Palmer. See Palmer, D. D.

Fisher, Hendrick

The *Samuel Adams of New Jersey* [1] was the sobriquet by which Hendrick Fisher was called because, like Adams, he was an outstanding political leader in the New Jersey Colony during the Revolutionary War.

Hendrick Fisher was born in the Province of Lower Palatinate, Germany, in 1697, and died in Somerset County, N.J., on August 16, 1779.

[1] *The National Cyclopaedia of American Biography* (James T. White and Company, New York, 1906) vol. 13, p. 324.

Fisherman's Paradise of the North Atlantic. See New Shoreham or Block Island

Five Brothers

The *Five Brothers* [1] was a nickname given to the five bills proposed in the message of President Woodrow Wilson delivered before the Congress in joint session on January 20, 1914. These proposed laws were to embody: (1) prohibition of interlocking directorates, (2) government supervision of railway financing, (3) exact definition of the Sherman Anti-trust Law, (4) an interstate trade commission to direct and shape corrective processes and inform the public, (5) legislation to reach individuals responsible for corporate wrong-doing. These five bills were eventually combined into the Clayton Act, which was passed by Congress on October 15, 1914.

[1] *The Messages and Papers of Woodrow Wilson*, with editorial notes and an introduction by Albert Shaw (The Review of Reviews Corporation, New York, 1924) vol. 1, p. 47, 48.

Five Years of Slavery

The rule of Sir Thomas Dale over the Virginia Colony was nicknamed the *Five Years of Slavery* [1] because he ruled the people with such strict martial law that the colonists had little if any freedom or self-governing power. Dale held office from May 1611 to 1616, except the period from August 1613 to March 1614.

[1] *The Source Book* (Source Research Council, Inc., Chicago, 1936) vol. 2, p. 773.

Flag-of-truce-fever. See *Flag-of-truce-on-the-brain*

Flag-of-truce-on-the-brain

The Federal soldiers who were in the Confederate Military Prison at Danville, Va., said some of their fellow-prisoners suffered from *Flag-of-truce-on-the-brain*,[1] or *Flag-of-truce-fever*.

These terms were applied to soldiers who believed that if they became patients in the prison hospital they would stand a better chance of being exchanged for Confederate prisoners under a flag of truce. Often such soldiers would pretend to be desperately ill, sometimes making themselves appear prostrated.

[1] *Lights and Shadows in Confederate Prisons; a Personal Experience, 1861-5*, Homer B. Sprague (G. P. Putnam's Sons, New York and London, 1915) p. 107.

Flaming Mercuries. See *Black Dragons*

Flat Boatman. See Lincoln, Abraham

Flea. See Clifton, H. E.; Lee, Fitzhugh

Flea of Conventions. See Folsom, Abigail

Flickertail State. See North Dakota

Flickertails. See University of North Dakota; Wesley College

Flood City. See Johnstown, Pa.

Floods. See University of Mississippi

Florence Nightingale of the Southern Army. See Trader, E. K. N.

Florida

Florida is called the *Alligator State* [1] because alligators are found in its streams and swamps; the *Everglade State* [2] from the numbers of everglades or swamps throughout the state; the *Flower State* or the *Land of Flowers*, from the wild flowers which grow in such abundance and for which the state was given its Spanish name; the *Orange State*,[1] because it has great numbers of orange groves; the *Peninsula State*,[1] because most of its area is the Peninsula of Florida; and the *Gulf State*, because the Gulf of Mexico borders it for such a great distance.

Florida is also known as the *Southern Finger of the United States* [3] because the peninsula of Florida somewhat resembles a finger.

[1] *A Book of Nicknames*, John Goff (Courier-Journal Job Printing Company, Louisville, Ky., 1892) p. 13.

[2] *More About Names*, Leopold Wagner (T. Fisher Unwin, London, 1893) p. 28.

[3] *Compton's Pictured Encyclopedia* (F. E. Compton and Company, Chicago, 1931) vol. 5, p. 1295.

Florida on Wheels

Florida on Wheels [1] was applied to a special railroad car used by the officials of the State of Florida for exhibiting specimens of the state's products in various parts of the United States in 1887 and thereafter. This exhibition car was made especially attractive by the oil paintings on its sides which depicted outstanding bits of coastal and interior Florida scenery.

[1] *The Book of Jacksonville, a History, Being a Series of Descriptive Articles, Historical, Industrial, and Biographical of Jacksonville, Florida*, S. Paul Brown (A. V. Haight, Poughkeepsie, N.Y., 1895) p. 145.

Floridians

The Floridians are nicknamed *Alligators, Crackers,* and *Fly-up-the-Creeks.* They are called *Alligators* because the State is nicknamed the *Alligator State* (See Florida). The nickname *Crackers* [1] is applied to the people of Florida, tradition says, because the planters during the early days cracked their whips over the backs of their mules. Another version is that the term was derived from corn-cracker.

The fly-up-the-creeks are a variety of green heron (*Butorides virescens*) common along the marshy shores throughout the state; consequently, the name was applied to the people. Leopold Wagner says that the Floridians at one time were called *Fly-up-the-Creeks* [2] from their "retiring disposition" on the approach of strangers.

[1] *U.S.: An Index to the United States of America*, comp. by Malcolm Townsend (D. Lothrop Company, Boston, 1890) p. 75.

[2] *More About Names*, Leopold Wagner (T. Fisher Unwin, London, 1893) p. 28.

Flour City. See Minneapolis, Minn.; Rochester, N.Y.

Flower City. See Rochester, N.Y.; Springfield, Ill.

Flower of Quakerism. See Mott, Lucretia

Flower State. See Florida

Flower Town in the Pines. See Summerville, S.C.

Flowers, D'Arcy Raymond

D'Arcy Raymond Flowers, who was born at Cambridge, Md., on March 16, 1902, and who played utility man in major league baseball, is nicknamed *Jake.* [1]

[1] *Who's Who in Major League Base Ball*, comp. by Harold (Speed) Johnson (Buxton Publishing Company, Chicago, 1933) p. 157.

Floyd, Charles

Because of his smooth features and rather handsome face, as well as his attractive form, *Pretty Boy Floyd* [1] was the nickname given to Charles Floyd, a notorious bandit and a member of the Dillinger gang.

Charles Floyd was shot to death by Federal authorities near East Liverpool, Ohio, on October 22, 1934.

[1] *The New York Times*, New York, October 23, 1934, cols. 1 and 2, p. 1.

Flyers. See University of Dayton

Flying Cadets. See Virginia Military Institute

Flying Dutchman. See Wagner, J. H.

Flying Dutchmen. See Central College (Pella, Iowa); Lebanon Valley College

Flying Squadron

The *Flying Squadron* was a nickname applied by journalists to members of the United States Congress who opposed President Franklin Delano Roosevelt's bill presented to them early in 1938, designed to add six more judges to the Supreme Court of the United States. The *Squadron* proposed to speak against the court bill wherever President Roosevelt might speak or might attempt to defeat one of the opponents of the bill in the Democratic primary elections, if the candidates should feel the need of assistance.

The *Flying Squadron* was made up chiefly of Burton K. Wheeler, Democratic Senator from Montana; William Edgar Borah, Republican Senator from Idaho; Joseph C. O'Mahoney, Democratic Senator from Wyoming; Pat McCarran, Democratic Senator from Nevada; David I. Walsh, Democratic Senator from Massachusetts;

Flying Squadron—Continued
Francis T. Maloney, Democratic Senator from Connecticut; and Edward R. Burke, Democratic Senator from Nebraska.

[1] *Washington Herald*, Washington, D.C., May 18, 1938, c. 6, p. 2.

Flying Squadrons. See Virginia Military Institute

Fly-up-the-Creeks. See Floridians

Foghorn. See Allen, William; Funston, E. H.

Folsom, Abigail
Ralph Waldo Emerson humorously nicknamed Mrs. Abigail Folsom the *Flea of Conventions.*[1]

She was a member of the American Antislavery Society and was particularly active as a speaker at its meetings in 1842-45. Although she was a sensible and refined woman, she sometimes made herself conspicuous and a nuisance at conventions by speaking her convictions.

Mrs. Abigail Folsom was born in England, about 1792, emigrated to America in 1837, and died at Rochester, N.Y., in 1867.

[1] *The Complete Writings of Ralph Waldo Emerson, Containing All of His Inspiring Essays, Lectures, Poems, Addresses, Studies, Biographical Sketches and Miscellaneous Works* (William H. Wise and Company, New York, 1929) vo. 2, p. 1063.
The National Cyclopaedia of American Biography (James T. White and Company, New York, 1899) vol. 2, p. 394.

Fool Tom Jackson. See Jackson, T. J.

Football Stadium, Rice Institute
The *Rice Bowl*[1] is the name of the football stadium of Rice Institute, at Houston, Tex. This is a pun on the name of the school.

[1] A communication from George S. Halas, President-treasurer of The Chicago Bears Football Club, Inc., Chicago, March 21, 1939.

Football Stadium, Texas College of Mines and Metallurgy
The football field of the Texas College of Mines and Metallurgy, at El Paso, Tex., was nicknamed the *Sun Bowl*[1] by Dr. C. M. Hendricks of El Paso in 1934 because the city is located in the center of the sunshine belt of the United States. The football game played on New Year's Day on this field as a part of the yearly Sun Carnival is called the Sun Bowl Game.

[1] A communication from Frank Junell, Manager of Athletics at the Texas College of Mines and Metallurgy, El Paso, Tex., May 25, 1939.

Football Stadium, Texas State Fair Grounds
The football stadium in the Texas State Fair grounds at Dallas, Tex., is called the *Cotton Bowl*[1] because cotton is the leading agricultural product of this state. The officials of the Texas State Fair named the stadium in 1936.

[1] A communication from J. H. Stewart, Director of Athletics at the Southern Methodist University, Dallas, Tex., March 15, 1939.

Foot Cavalry
During the Civil War the infantrymen in Lieutenant General Thomas Jonathan Jackson's Confederate Army were known as the *Foot Cavalry*[1] because of their rapidity comparable to that of cavalry.

[1] *The Encyclopedia Americana* (Americana Corporation, New York and Chicago, 1927) vol 15, p. 583.

Foote, Elial Todd
Elial Todd Foote, a physician, was called the *Father of Chautauqua County*[1] because, from 1823 until 1843, he served as the first judge of Chautauqua County, N.Y., because he displayed a keen interest in the religious and economic development of that county, and because he gathered much of the data published later about the early history of Chautauqua County.

He was born at Gill, Mass., on May 1, 1796, and died at New Haven, Conn., on November 17, 1877.

[1] *Appleton's Cyclopaedia of American Biography*, ed. by James Grant Wilson and John Fiske (D. Appleton and Company, New York, 1888) vol. 2, p. 495.

Foote, Henry Stuart
Because of a statement he made in Congress on April 20, 1848, concerning Senator John P. Hale from New Hampshire, Senator Henry Stuart Foote from Mississippi was nicknamed *Hangman Foote.*[1]

In a heated debate hinging on the slavery question, Senator Foote told Senator Hale that if he ever came to Mississippi he would be promptly hanged and that he himself would lend a hand. Thereupon he was called *Hangman Foote.*

Henry Stuart Foote was born in Fauquier County, Va., on February 28, 1804, and died at Nashville, Tenn., on May 20, 1880.

[1] *History of the United States of America, under the Constitution*, James Schouler (Dodd, Mead and Company, New York, 1892) vol. 5, p. 198.
Appendix to the Congressional Globe, for the First Session, Thirtieth Congress: Containing Speeches and Important State Papers, New Series . . . 1847-48 (Printed at the Office of Blair and Rives, Washington, D.C., 1848) p. 502.

Foraker, Joseph B.

Bloody Shirt Foraker and *Fire-alarm Foraker* were nicknames applied to Joseph B. Foraker.

Throughout his term of office as Governor of Ohio from 1886 to 1890, Joseph B. Foraker advocated strict law enforcement and gave expression to many sensational utterances which caused the people to discuss and bring about needed reforms. In 1887, when President Grover Cleveland caused the flags of the various states captured during the Civil War to be returned to these states, Governor Foraker emphatically said, "No rebel flags will be surrendered while I am governor." From the fact that he gave expression to this statement, and from his characteristics named above, he came to be nicknamed *Bloody Shirt Foraker* [1] and *Fire Alarm Foraker*.

Joseph B. Foraker was born near Rainsboro, Ohio, on July 5, 1846, and died at Cincinnati, Ohio, on May 10, 1917.

[1] *Dictionary of American Biography under the Auspices of the American Council of Learned Societies*, ed. by Allen Johnson and Dumas Malone (Charles Scribner's Sons, New York, 1931) vol. 6, p. 503.

Forces. See Wilberforce University

Ford, Henry

Henry Ford has been nicknamed the *Automobile Wizard* and the *Genius of Motordom* [1] because of his ingenuity as an inventor and engineer in the construction and mass production of automobiles. He organized the Ford Motor Company in 1903, the greatest manufacturing establishment of automobiles in the world, and was its president until 1919.

Henry Ford was born at Greenfield, Mich., on July 20, 1863, and died Apr. 7, 1947.

[1] *The Tragedy of Henry Ford*, Jonathan Norton Leonard (G. P. Putnam's Sons, New York and London, 1932) p. 170.

Ford, John Baptiste

John Baptiste Ford was designated the *Father of the Plate Glass Industry* [1] because he was a pioneer manufacturer of plate glass. He established at New Albany, Ind., the first plate glass factory in the United States, and devoted a great deal of time, money, and effort toward its further development. This nickname first appeared as an inscription on a bronze statue dedicated to him by his fellow citizens at Ford City, Pa., in 1891.

J. B. Ford was born at Danville, Ky., on November 17, 1811, and died at Creighton Pa., on May 1, 1903.

[1] *The National Cyclopaedia of American Biography* (James T. White and Company, New York, 1906) vol. 13, p. 505-6.

Fords. See Haverford College

Foreigner State. See New Jersey

Foreigners. See New Jerseyans

Foreman Field, Norfolk, Virginia. See Oyster Bowl

Forest-born Demosthenes. See Henry, Patrick

Forest City. See Cleveland, Ohio; Portland, Me.; Rockford, Ill.; Savannah, Ga.

Forest City of the South. See Savannah, Ga.

Foresters. See Huntington College; Lake Forest College

Forgotten Man

The *Forgotten Man* [1] is a nickname which was used during the depression of the 1930's by those speaking and writing on economic problems for the common working man of America, who had to earn a livelihood. The term was given prominence by President Franklin Delano Roosevelt and his administration with the implication that they were shaping the New Deal to take care of this man and his interest, and that he would not continue to be forgotten.

See also Braddock, J. J.

Forman, David

David Forman was nicknamed *Black David* [1] and *Devil David* [2] because of his cruelty to the Loyalists during the Revolutionary War. He busied himself with the suppression of armed Loyalist refugees along the coast of New Jersey. His brutality and harsh treatment were notorious. He had at one time served in the army under Washington.

David Forman was born near Englishtown in Monmouth County, N.J., on November 3, 1745, and died on September 12, 1797, on board a British privateer which had captured the ship on which Forman was returning from the South.

[1] *Appleton's Cyclopaedia of American Biography*, ed. by James Grant Wilson and John Fiske (D. Appleton and Company, New York, 1894) vol. 2, p. 502.

[2] *Dictionary of American Biography under the Auspices of the American Council of Learned Societies*, ed. by Allen Johnson and Dumas Malone (Charles Scribner's Sons, New York, 1931) vol. 6, p. 524.

Forrest, Nathan Bedford

The *Swamp Fox of Mississippi* and the *Wizard of the Saddle* are nicknames by which Nathan Bedford Forrest has often been called.

Lieutenant General Forrest was known as the *Swamp Fox of Mississippi* [1] because of his cleverness in scattering his forces and carrying on guerrilla warfare in Mississippi in 1864.

The *Wizard of the Saddle* [2] was applied to him because of his skill as a cavalry commander.

Nathan Bedford Forrest was born in Bedford County, Tenn., on July 13, 1821, and died at Memphis, Tenn., on October 29, 1877.

[1] *The American Scene*, Edwin C. Hill (Witmark Educational Publications, Department of M. Witmark and Sons, New York, 1933) p. 49, 50, 130.

A Book of Nicknames, John Goff (Courier-Journal Job Printing Company, Louisville, Ky., 1892) p. 26.

[2] *Bedford Forrest and His Critter Company*, Andrew Nelson Lytle (Minton, Balch and Company, New York, 1931) p. 175.

Fort Myers, Florida

Fort Myers, the county seat of Lee County, is designated by its inhabitants the *City of Palms* [1] because of the profusion of luxuriant tropical palms in its parks, residential sections, and even along its business thoroughfares.

[1] *Florida in the Making*, Frank Parker Stockbridge and John Holliday Perry (The de Bower Publishing Company, New York and Jacksonville, 1925) p. 270.

Fort Wicked. See Godfrey, Hollen

Fortune-seekers. See Idahoans

Fortieth Infantry Division of World War II

The *Sunburst Division* [1] was the nickname of the Fortieth Infantry Division of World War II. It was made up of National Guards from California, Nevada, and Utah.

[1] *Combat Divisions of World War II*, (Army of the United States), Army Times Publishing Company, Washington, D.C., 1946, p. 32.

Forty-eighters

The nickname *Forty-eighters* [1] was applied to the Germans who emigrated to the United States in 1848 because of a political revolution in Germany.

[1] *From Steerage to Congress, Reminiscences and Reflections*, Richard Bartholdt (Dorrance and Company, Inc., Philadelphia, 1930) p. 13.

Forty-fifth Infantry Division of World War II

The *Thunderbird Division* [1] was the nickname of the Forty-fifth Infantry Division of World War II.

[1] *Combat Divisions of World War II*, (Army of the United States), Army Times Publishing Company, Washington, D.C., 1946, p. 37.

Forty-first Infantry Division of World War II

The *Jungleers Division* was the nickname of the Forty-first Infantry Division of World War II because it was made up of National Guard units from Oregon, Washington, Idaho, and Montana which fought in the jungle islands of the Pacific.

[1] *Combat Divisions of World War II* (Army of the United States) Army Times Publishing Company, Washington, D.C., 1946, p. 33.

Forty-niners

The *Forty-niners* [1] was a nickname given to the immigrants who were attracted to California by the discovery of gold in 1849.

[1] *The Story of Our Country*, Ruth West and Willis Mason West (Allyn and Bacon, New York and Boston, 1933) p. 351-2.

The United States, Theodore Calvin Pease (Harcourt, Brace and Company, New York, 1927) p. 375.

Forty-second Division of the AEF.

See Rainbow Division

Forty-second Infantry Division of World War II

The *Rainbow Division* [1] was the nickname of the Forty-second Infantry Division of World War II. It was composed of men from twenty-six states and the District of Columbia.

[1] *Combat Divisions of World War II* (Army of the United States), Army Times Publishing Company, Washington, D.C., 1946, p. 34.

Forty-third Infantry Division of World War II

The *Winged Victory Division* [1] was the nickname of the Forty-third Infantry Division of World War II. It received its nickname on Luzon, the chief island of the Philippine group, from the name of the commanding general, Major General Leonard F. Wing.

[1] *Combat Divisions of World War II* (Army of the United States), Army Times Publishing Company, Washington, D.C., 1946, p. 35.

Founder of the American Navy. See Jones, J. P.

Founder of Vermont. See Allen, Ira

Fountain. See Ashurst, H. F.

Four Eyes. See Roosevelt, Theodore

Four Horsemen

Jim Crowley, Elmer Layden, Don Miller, and Harry Stuhldreyer were the four members of the back field on the Notre Dame football team under Knute Rockne's direction in the 1920's. Their team work was so invincible that sportswriter Grantland Rice referred to them as the *Four Horsemen*,[1] a nickname that immediately caught the public fancy.

[1] *The New York Times* New York, July 14, 1954, p. 27.

Four-job Farley. See Farley, J. A.

Four Lake City. See Madison, Wis.

Four Straight Jake. See Ruppert, Jacob, Sr.

Fourth Infantry Division of World War II

The *Ivy Division* [1] was the nickname of the Fourth Infantry Division of World War II.

[1] *Cambat Divisions of World War II* (Army of the United States), Army Times Publishing Company, Washington, D.C., 1946, p. 10.

Fowler, Charles Henry

The sobriquets, the *Apostle of South America* and the *Great Commoner,* were applied to Charles Henry Fowler.

He was sometimes called the *Apostle of South America* [1] in commemoration of his success as a pioneer missionary in establishing Methodist churches and mission schools in Brazil, Paraguay, and in various other countries in South America.

He was called the *Great Commoner* [2] because of his life-long devotion to serving the common man, regardless of race or creed.

Fowler was born at Burford, Canada, on August 11, 1837, and died at New York City, on March 20, 1908.

[1] *The National Cyclopaedia of American Biography* (James T. White and Company, New York, 1897) vol. 7, p. 311.
[2] *The National Cyclopaedia of American Biography* (James T. White and Company, New York, 1899) vol. 2, p. 61-2.

Fox, Ervin

Pete [1] is the nickname of Ervin Fox, who was born at Evansville, Ind., on March 8, 1909, and who played outfield in major league baseball.

[1] *Who's Who in Major League Base Ball*, comp. by Harold (Speed) Johnson (Buxton Publishing Company, Chicago, 1933) p. 160.

Fox. See Van Buren, Martin

Foxes. See Maine Inhabitants

Fra Elbertus. See Hubbard, Elbert

Frank the Just. See Murphy, Frank

Franklin, Benjamin

The following are nicknames given to Benjamin Franklin: the *Father of the Continental Congress,* the *Father of the Stove,* the *Grand Old Man,* the *Many-sided Franklin,* *Poor Richard,* the *Sage of America,* and the *Tamer of Lightning.*

Benjamin Franklin was a delegate to the Continental Congress and was one of the five persons who drew up the Declaration

Franklin, Benjamin—Continued

of Independence. Because he was determined that agreement should be reached among the colonies, he was called the *Father of the Continental Congress.*[1]

Because he devised the first heating stove in America, Benjamin Franklin has been called the *Father of the Stove.*[1]

Late in his life, Franklin came to be known as the *Grand Old Man*[2] because he could do so many things well, was wise and highly respected both in America and in Europe.

The sobriquet, the *Many-sided Franklin,*[2] was applied to him because he was such a versatile man and rendered valuable service to his country and to humanity in so many different fields.

Benjamin Franklin edited and published *Poor Richard's Almanac,* writing most of the material himself. For this reason, he was nicknamed *Poor Richard.*[3]

He has been designated the *Sage of America*[4] because of his deep insight into life, his practical ability as a statesman, and his scientific learning.

Because of his experiments with bringing lightning from the clouds by means of kite and key, Franklin has been called the *Tamer of Lightning.*[1]

Benjamin Franklin was born at Boston, Mass., on January 17, 1706, and died at Philadelphia, Pa., on April 17, 1790.

[1] *A Book of Nicknames,* John Goff (Courier-Journal Job Printing Company, Louisville, Ky., 1892) p. 21, 29, 30.

[2] *Makers of the Nation,* Fanny E. Coe (American Book Company, New York, 1914) p. 30, 35.

[3] *Manual of Useful Information,* comp. under the direction of J. C. Thomas (The Werner Company, Chicago, 1893) p. 23.

[4] *The Source Book* (Perpetual Encyclopedia Corporation, Chicago, 1932) vol. 3, p. 1091.

Franklin, Benjamin (Lawyer) 1862-

The *Father of the Tri-borough Bridge*[1] is a nickname attributed to Benjamin Franklin because he consistently advocated the building of a bridge with terminals in Queens, upper Manhattan, and the Bronx, three boroughs of New York City. His plans were finally adopted and the bridge was opened for traffic on July 1, 1936.

Benjamin Franklin was born in New York City, on September 8, 1862.

[1] *Encyclopedia of American Biography: American Biography, a New Cyclopedia,* comp. under the editorial supervision of a notable advisory board (Published under the direction of The American Historical Society, Inc., New York, 1927) vol. 30, p. 43.

[2] *The World Almanac and Book of Facts for 1934,* ed. by Robert Hunt Lyman (The New York World-Telegram, New York, 1934) p. 519.

Franklin College of Indiana

The *Baptists* and the *Grizzlies*[1] are the names given to the athletic teams of Franklin College of Indiana, at Franklin, Ind. They are called the *Baptists* because it is a Baptist school. They were called *Grizzlies* in 1925, because Ernest (Griz) Wagner was then the coach.

[1] A communication from Roy E. Tollotson, Director of Athletics at Franklin College of Indiana, Franklin, Ind., June 10, 1935.

Franklin and Marshall College

The athletic teams of Franklin and Marshall College, at Lancaster, Pa., were nicknamed the *Diplomats*[1] because the college is named for Benjamin Franklin and John Marshall, two American diplomats.

[1] A communication from R. W. Bomberger, Dean of Franklin and Marshall College, Lancaster, Pa., November 21, 1935.

Franklin of the West. See Bradford, John

Frasch, Herman

Herman Frasch's eminence as a manufacturer and exporter of sulphur, and his unrivaled position as a pioneer in the sulphur industry of the United States, caused him to be nicknamed the *Sulphur King.*[1]

He was born at Gaildorf, Wurtemberg, Germany, on December 25, 1851, and died at Paris, France, on May 1, 1914.

[1] *The National Cyclopedia of American Biography* (James T. White and Company, New York, 1926) vol. 19, p. 348.

Fraud President. See Hayes, R. B.

Freck. See Owen, M. J.

Freckles. See Barry, Wesley

Fredericksburg, Virginia

Fredericksburg is known as *America's Most Historic City* and the *Boyhood Home of George Washington.* It is styled by its inhabitants *America's Most Historic City.* Although Fredericksburg is rich in historic lore, there are other cities in America whose historic interests are just as pronounced.

Fredericksburg is widely known as the *Boyhood Home of George Washington* because George Washington spent his boy-hood on his father's farm across the Rappa-hanock river from this town.

Freedmen's Village

Freedman's Village [1] is the name which was formerly applied to the settlement of several hundred freed Negro slaves at Arlington, Va. President Abraham Lincoln and the Federal Government provided land for them in 1867 after these freed Negroes had proved unable to support themselves on the Island of Vache in Haiti where the Government had sent them. This settlement was adjacent to the tract of land which George Washington Parke Custis left at his death "to his colored daughter, Maria Syphax."

[1] *Washington; City and Capital: Federal Writers' Project*, American Guide Series, 1937 (Government Printing Office, Washington, D.C., 1937) p. 75.

Freestone State. See Connecticut

Frelinghuysen, Theodore

The sobriquet, the *Christian Statesman*,[1] was applied to Theodore Frelinghuysen because while he was a United States Senator from New Jersey from 1829 to 1835, he advocated that the Indians be placed on reservations and given the fair, honest, and sympathetic treatment they should expect from those who considered themselves Christians.

Theodore Frelinghuysen was born at Millstone, N.J., on March 28, 1787, and died at New Brunswick, N.J., on April 12, 1861.

[1] *The National Cyclopaedia of American Biography* (James T. White and Company, New York, 1893) vol. 3, p. 402.

Frémont, John Charles

The *Gray Mustang* and the *Pathfinder* are nicknames which have been given to John Charles Frémont.

He was called the *Gray Mustang* supposedly because he often rode a mustang pony, or possibly because he was impulsive, and possessed a temperament which resisted restraint.

The *Pathfinder* [1] is a nickname applied to Frémont because his explorations of the lands of the west opened up the route to the northwestern sections of the United States. While serving in the United States Army he made three expeditions in the West, in 1842, 1843, and 1845.

John Charles Frémont was born at Savannah, Ga., on January 31, 1813, and died at New York City, on July 13, 1890.

[1] *A Man Unafraid, The Story of John Charles Frémont*, Herbert Bashford and Harr Wagner (Harr Wagner Publishing Company, San Francisco, Calif., 1927) p. 75.
The Encyclopedia Americana (Americana Corporation, New York and Chicago, 1929) vol. 12, p. 58-9.

French Game-cock. See Lafayette, M. J. P. R. Y. G. du M.

French John See Sioussat, J. P.

French Lick Springs, Indiana

French Lick Springs have been nicknamed the *Carlsbad of America*.[1] The famous Carlsbad Spa in Bohemia, Czechoslovakia, is noted for the medicinal qualities of its mineral springs.

[1] *Book of Louisville and Kentucky*, Robert W. Brown, Editor (Louisville Convention and Publicity League, Inc., Louisville, Ky., 1915) p. 107.

Freneau, Philip

Philip Freneau was called the *Poet of the American Revolution* [1] because he wrote satirical verse against the British, patriotically defending the cause of the rebelling colonists.

He was born at New York City, on January 2, 1752, and died near Freehold, N.J., on December 18, 1832.

[1] *A History of American Literature*, William B. Cairns (Oxford University Press, New York and London, 1930) p. 141.

Fresh Fish

During the Civil War the Union soldiers imprisoned at the Confederate Military Prison at Andersonville, Ga., designated the newly arrived prisoners *Fresh Fish* [1] probably because they were still in an unimpaired condition.

[1] *Andersonville: A Story of Rebel Military Prisons, Fifteen Months a Guest of the So-called Southern Confederacy; a Private Soldier's Experience in Richmond, Andersonville, Savannah, Millen, Blackshear, and Florence*, John McElroy (R. R. Locke, Toledo, Ohio, 1879) p. 433.

Friars. See Providence College

Friend of Helpless Children. See Hoover, H. C.

Friend of the Indian. See Stuart, Robert

Friendliest City. See Rochester, N.Y.

Frisco. See San Francisco, Calif.

Fritz. See Knothe, W. E.

Frozen Wilderness. See Alaska

Fuller, Robert Mason

Robert Mason Fuller, a physician, pharmacist, and inventor, was widely known as the *Father of the Tablet Triturate* [1] because he originated the principle of giving medicine to patients in a compact and palatable form by thoroughly pulverizing it and then putting it up in the form of tablets so that they could be more easily administered.

Robert Mason Fuller was born at Schenectady, N.Y., on October 27, 1845, and died at Schenectady, N.Y., on December 29, 1919.

[1] *Dictionary of American Biography under the Auspices of Learned Societies,* ed. by Allen Johnson and Dumas Malone (Charles Scribner's Sons, New York, 1931) vol. 7, p. 63.

Fulmer, Hampton Pitts

Horsepower [1] is the sobriquet of Hampton Pitts Fulmer, a Senator from South Carolina from 1921 to 1944, because of his initials, H.P.

Senator Hampton Pitts Fulmer was born at Springfield, S.C., on June 23, 1875, and died Oct. 19, 1944.

[1] *The Washington Post Magazine,* Washington, D.C., March 4, 1934, p. 4.

Fulton, Robert

The *Father of Steamboat Navigation,* the *Father of the Steamboat,* and *Quicksilver Bob* are nicknames of Robert Fulton.

He has been called the *Father of Steamboat Navigation* [1] and the *Father of the Steamboat* because he perfected the first steam-propelled boat, the *Clermont,* on August 11 or 12, 1807.

During the Revolutionary War, Fulton was called *Quicksilver Bob* [1] because, while working in the smithery in which government arms were being manufactured, he used as much quicksilver as he could secure for his own personal experiments.

Robert Fulton was born at Little Britain, (now Fulton), Pa., in 1765, and died at New York City, on February 24, 1815.

[1] *Brief History of the United States,* Matthew Page Andrews (J. B. Lippincott Company, Philadelphia, 1924) p. 179.
A Book of Nicknames, John Goff (Courier-Journal Job Printing Company, Louisville, Ky., 1892) p. 29.

[2] *The Story of the Hall of Fame, Including the Lives and Portraits of the Elect and of Those Who Barely Missed Election, Also a List of America's Most Eligible Women,* Louis Albert Banks (The Christian Herald, New York, 1902) p. 129.

Fulton's Folly

In 1807, when Robert Fulton put his newly invented steamboat, the *Clermont,* on the Hudson river in the New York harbor for a trial trip from New York City to Albany, N.Y., people nicknamed it *Fulton's Folly* [1] because they did not believe that a steam propelled ship would be successful.

[1] *The Growth of the American People and Nation,* Mary G. Kelty (Ginn and Company, New York and Boston, 1931) p. 114.

Funston, Edward Hogue

Edward Hogue Funston, a politician, was known as *Foghorn Funston,* [1] because his voice was loud and powerful. Funston was a Representative from Kansas to the United States Congress from 1884 to 1893.

He was born near New Carlisle, Ohio, on September 16, 1836, and died at Iola, Kans., on September 10, 1911.

[1] *Appleton's Cyclopaedia of American Biography,* ed. by James Grant Wilson and John Fiske (D. Appleton and Company, New York, 1900) vol. 7, p. 108.

Furman, Richard

Richard Furman, who was born at New York City, in 1755, and who died at High Hill, S.C., on August 24, 1825, was called the *Boy Preacher* [1] because he began to preach publicly to large audiences when he was scarcely nineteen years of age.

[8] *The National Cyclopaedia of American Biography* (James T. White and Company, New York, 1904) vol. 12, p. 290.

Furman University

The teams of Furman University, at Greenville, S.C., were called the *Purple Hurricanes.* [1] The college colors are purple and white, and their rivals at Georgia Tech were called the *Golden Tornadoes.*

[1] A communication from A. P. McLeod, Director of Athletics at Furman University, Greenville, S.C., June 10, 1935.

Furuseth, Andrew

Andrew Furuseth, a seaman and a leader in the Seamen's Labor Union in America, was nicknamed the *Abraham Lincoln of the Sea,* The *Old Viking,* and The *Dean of the American Labor Movement.* The sobriquet, the *Abraham Lincoln of the*

Sea,[1] commemorated the fact that Furuseth advocated the passage of the Seamen's Bill passed by Congress in 1915, which provided improved working conditions and better life-saving equipment on board ships. This bill was looked upon as the seamen's emancipation act.

The Old Viking commemorated the fact that Furuseth was a Norwegian by birth and fought for the rights of seamen with all the determination of the Vikings of old. Furuseth was designated The *Dean of the American Labor Movement* because he was an outstanding leader in the American labor movement, and took an active part in promoting labor organizations and in securing legislation to protect their interests. He was President of the International Seamen's Union in America from 1908 until the time of his death. He is the only labor leader whose bust stands in the building of the Department of Labor at Washington.

Andrew Furuseth was born at Romedal, Norway, on March 12, 1854, came to America in 1880, and died at Washington, D. C., on January 22, 1938.

[1] *Newsweek: The Magazine of News Significance,* Rockefeller Center, N.Y., January 21, 1938, p. 5.
[2] *The Evening Star,* Washington, D.C., January 22, 1938, cols. 5 and 6, p. 1.

Future Great City of the World. See St. Louis, Mo.

G

G-men. See Gainesville Baseball Association, Incorporated

Gabby. See Street, C. E.; Hartnett, C. L.

Gadsden, Alabama
Gadsden is called the *Queen City of Alabama* [1] because it is surrounded by the exquisite beauty and grandeur of its natural scenery. It is located on a plateau at the southern extremity of Lookout Mountain, with San Mountain to the West, Red Mountain to the South, and the Colvin Mountains to the East.

[1] *Alabama of To-day, 1904: An Industrial Review of the General Business Interests of Birmingham and the Cities and Towns Comprising the Great State of Alabama* (Post B—Alabama Division Travelers Protective Association of America, Birmingham, Ala., 1905) p. 62.

History of Alabama and Dictionary of Alabama Biography, Thomas McAdory Owen (The S. J. Clarke Publishing Company, Chicago, 1921) vol. 1, p. 639.

Gaffney, Margaret
The sobriquet, *Margaret the Orphan's Friend,*[1] was attributed to Margaret Gaffney after she moved to New Orleans, La., and established three large orphan asylums and a home for the sick and aged. She dealt generously and kindly with all orphans, regardless of race or religious creed, and was sympathetic and helpful to all the poor and destitute.

[1] *The National Cyclopaedia of American Biography* (James T. White and Company, New York, 1899) vol. 2, p. 373.

Gag Atherton. See Atherton, C. G.

Gag Resolutions
The *Gag Resolutions* [1] was a nickname given to the resolutions passed by Congress each year from 1836 to 1844 to place all petitions pertaining to slavery on the table to keep from giving consideration to them.

[1] *The American Nation,* Richard J. Purcell (Ginn and Company, New York and Boston, 1929) p. 413.

Gainesville Baseball Association, Incorporated
The athletic teams of The Gainesville Baseball Association, Inc., at Gainesville, Fla., were nicknamed the *G-men* in 1936, by James M. Butler of Gainesville. The sobriquet, an abbreviated form of the Gainesville men, was selected by a competitive contest.

[1] A communication from Ralph B. Kyle, Business Manager of The Gainesville Baseball Association, Inc., Gainesville, Fla., March 31, 1939.

Galbraith, Frederick William
The *Fighting Colonel* [1] is the nickname given to Frederick William Galbraith during World War I.

The *Fighting Colonel's* courage and services were so conspicuous that he was decorated with the Distinguished Service Cross, the Belgian War Cross, the French Croix de Guerre, the cross of the Legion of Honor, and (posthumously) the cross of the Grand Commander of the Legion of Honor.

Frederick William Galbraith was born at Watertown, Mass., on May 6, 1874,

Galbraith, F. W.—Continued
and died at Indianapolis, Ind., on June
9, 1921.

[1] *The National Cyclopaedia of American Biography*
(James T. White and Company, New York, 1926)
vol. 19, p. 170.

Galena, Illinois
Galena is termed the *Crescent City of
the Northwest* [1] because of its remarkably
quick growth and its architecture similar
to that of New Orleans. La., which is
designated the *Crescent City.*

[6] *Americanisms; The English of the New World,* M.
Schele De Vere (Charles Scribner and Company, New
York, 1872) p. 663.
[2] The Encyclopaedia Americana, 1943 edition, vol. 12,
p. 234.

Gallant Pelham. See Pelham, John

Gallatin, Albert
Albert Gallatin was nicknamed the
Watch-dog of the Treasury.[1] While he was
Secretary of the Treasury from 1802 to
1814, he uncompromisingly opposed any
unnecessary expenditures of the public
money. He was born at Geneva, Switzerland, on January 29, 1761, and died at
Astoria, Long Island, N.Y., on August 12,
1849.

[1] *The National Cyclopaedia of American Biography*
(James T. White and Company, New York, 1893)
vol. 3, p. 10.

Gallitzin, Demetrius Augustine
The *Apostle of the Alleghanies* [1] was the
nickname given to Demetrius Augustine
Gallitzin because of his tireless services as
a pastor and missionary to the early settlers
and Indians in the Alleghany Mountains in
Pennsylvania.
Demetrius Augustine Gallitzin was a son
of Ambassador Dimitri Gallitzin and the
heir to extensive wealth, but as a young man
he emigrated to the United States where he
was ordained a Catholic priest in 1795.

[1] *American History Briefly Told: Book Three, Period
of the Revolution and Confederation; Period of the
Development of the States to the Civil War: Book
Four, Period of the Civil War; Period of Reconstruction
and Expansion,* comp. by the Franciscan Sisters of the
Perpetual Adoration (St. Rose Convent, La Crosse, Wis.,
1912) p. 208.
*A Memoir of the Life and Character of the Reverend
Prince Demetrius A. de Gallitzin, Founder of Loretto
and Catholicity, in Cambria County, Pennsylvania,
Apostle of the Alleghanies,* Thomas Heyden (John
Murphy and Company, New York and Boston, 1869)
p. 14.

Galloping Gaels. See Saint Mary's College, Calif.

Galloping Swedes. See Gustavus
Adolphus College

Galloway, Charles Betts
Charles Betts Galloway, a bishop of the
Methodist Episcopal Church South, was
nicknamed the *Golden-mouthed* and *Prince
Charley* [1] because of his polished oratory,
affable disposition, and genteel manners.
Charles Betts Galloway was born at Kos-
ciusko, Miss., on September 1, 1849, and
died at Jackson, Miss., on May 12, 1909.

[1] *Dictionary of American Biography under the Auspices of the American Council of Learned Societies,* ed.
by Allen Johnson and Dumas Malone (Charles Scribner's
Sons, New York, 1931) vol. 7, p. 115.

Gallows Hill
On the outskirts of Salem, Mass., there
is a hill on which were hanged approximately a score of persons in 1692 during the so-
called witchcraft delusion. Since then this
hill has been termed *Gallows Hill.*[1]

[1] *Romance and Reality of the Puritan Coast,* Edmund
H. Garrett (Little, Brown and Company, Boston, 1897)
p. 131.

Galvanized Yankees
In her *War-time Journal of a Georgia
Girl,* under the entries of December 19-24,
1864, Eliza Frances Andrews calls the prisoners or deserters from the northern army
who entered the southern army *Galvanized
Yankees.*[1] By this expression she meant that
these recruits to the southern army were
merely coating their own convictions over
with a thin coat of a different opinion, and
that their true convictions were still with
the cause of the Federal Army, but that for
money or for other reasons they would enlist in the southern army. She gives an insight into what she means by the term when
she says that she has "no faith in Yankees
of any sort, especially these miserable turn-
coats that are ready to sell themselves to
either side." She concludes by saying that
gold cannot galvanize them into respectable
Confederates.

[1] *The War-time Journal of a Georgia Girl, 1864 to
1865,* Eliza Frances Andrews (D. Appleton and Company, New York, 1908) p. 34.

Galveston, Texas
Galveston is known as the *Oleander City,*
the *Oleander City of Texas,* the *Oleander
City by the Sea,* and the *Port of the Southwest.* The *Oleander City,* the *Oleander City
of Texas,* and the *Oleander City by the Sea* [1]

are nicknames attributed to this city because of its numerous and attractive oleander trees which blossom the entire year.

The *Port of the Southwest* [2] is an appropriate sobriquet for Galveston because its advantageous location upon Galveston bay makes it a great seaport for the Southwest.

[1] *A Book of Nicknames,* John Goff (Courier-Journal Job Printing Company, Louisville, Ky., 1892) p. 17.

The Port of Galveston and the State of Texas; The Engelhardt Series: American Cities, Andrew Morrison (Woodward and Tiernan, St. Louis, Mo., 1908) p. 5.

Flashlights on Texas, Lillie Terrell Shaver and Willie Williamson Rogers (A. C. Baldwin and Sons, Austin, Tex., 1928) p. 80.

Galveston, Major General Q. A. Gillmore, U. S. Engineers' (Charles Scribner's Sons, New York, 1879) p. 9.

[2] *History of Galveston, Texas, Narrative and Biographical,* S. C. Griffin (A. H. Cawston, Galveston, Tex., 1931) p. 56-9, 66.

Gamecock. See South Carolina; Sumter, Thomas

Game-cock Brigade

On January 14, 1862, George Edward Pickett was appointed a Brigadier General in the Confederate Army and given charge of a brigade composed of the eighth, eighteenth, nineteenth, twenty-eighth, and fifty-sixth infantry regiments from Virginia. This brigade came to be nicknamed the *Game-cock Brigade* [1] in allusion to the plucky, determined, courageous, and dashing manner in which they distinguished themselves in battle.

Major General George Edward Pickett, a Confederate soldier, was born at Richmond, Va., on January 25, 1825, and died at Norfolk, Va., on July 30, 1875.

[1] *The National Cyclopaedia of American Biography* (James T. White and Company, New York, 1907) vol. 5, p. 49.

Game Cocks. See University of South Carolina

Gans, Joe

Joe Gans, a light-weight Negro boxer, who was born in Baltimore, Md., on November 25, 1874, was nicknamed the *Old Master* because he was outstanding in his boxing technique.

Garden City. See Chicago, Ill.; Savannah, Ga.

Garden of America

The southern part of Rhode Island has been nicknamed the *Garden of America* [1]

because the climate of this section of the state is so mild and the soil is so fertile that the people living there cultivate market gardens, orchards, and greenhouse plants extensively.

[1] *Know Rhode Island: Facts Concerning the Land of Roger Williams,* Sixth Edition, comp. and distributed by the Office of the Secretary of State (State of Rhode Island and Providence Plantations, Providence, R.I., 1936) p. 6.

Garden of Maine. See Aroostook County, Me.

Garden of New England

Guildhall and Lunenburg, Vt., and Lancaster, N.H., are located in an old river basin in the old Coos country region which was described by Major Robert Rogers as the *Garden of New England* [1] in allusion to the fertility of the soil and the grandeur of the scenery. This description was applied to the region by Major Rogers during his participation in the French and Indian War of 1755 to 1763.

[1] *The Connecticut River and the Valley of the Connecticut, Three Hundred and Fifty Miles from Mountain to Sea, Historical and Descriptive,* Edwin M. Bacon (G. P. Putnam's Sons, New York and London, 1906) p. 353.

Garden of Tennessee

Middle Tennessee, located between the Cumberland Plateau and the Tennessee River, is commonly called the *Garden of Tennessee* [1] because it contains the best farming land of the state. It is an elliptical basin containing five thousand square miles, extending practically across the state from northeast to southwest.

[1] *Compton's Pictured Encyclopedia* (F. E. Compton and Company, Chicago, 1933) vol. 14, p. 45.

Garden of the West. See Illinois; Kansas

Garden State. See Kansas; New Jersey

Garfield, James Abram

The *Canal Boy,* the *Martyr President,* the *Preacher President,* and the *Teacher President* are nicknames applied to James Abram Garfield.

While he was a candidate for the office of President of the United States in 1880, he was sometimes referred to as the *Canal Boy* [1] because while he was a young man he was employed as a driver of the horses on the tow-path of the Ohio Canal, and

Garfield, J. A.—Continued

later as the steersman of a canal boat ply-
ing chiefly between Pittsburgh, Pa., and
Cleveland, Ohio.

He has been called the *Martyr President* [2]
because about four months after he was inaugurated President of the United States,
he was shot by Charles Guiteau, a disappointed officeseeker. The shooting occurred
in the Pennsylvania Railroad Station at
Washington, D.C., on July 2, 1881; Garfield died of his wounds at Elberton, N.J.,
on September 19, 1881.

Because he attended Geauga Seminary at
Chester, Ohio, for a time Garfield was nicknamed the *Preacher President*.[3]

The *Teacher President* [2] was applied to
Garfield because, while he was attending
Geauga Academy in 1849, Eclectic Institute
at Hiram, Ohio, from 1851 to 1854, and
Williams College at Williamstown, Mass.,
from 1854 to 1856, he frequently taught
school during a part of the winter months to
earn money to pay his expenses. Later he
also taught the classics, from 1856 to 1857,
at Hiram Institute, Hiram, Ohio.

James Abram Garfield, who was born at
Orange, Ohio, on November 19, 1831, and
who died at Elberton, N.J., on September
19, 1881, was the twentieth President of the
United States.

[1] *U.S. "Snap Shots": An Independent, National and
Memorial Encyclopedia . . . ,* Oliver McKee (A. M.
Thayer and Company, Boston, 1892) p. 310.

[2] *The Life and Letters of James Abram Garfield, 1831-
1877,* Theodore Clarke Smith (University Press, New
Haven, Conn., 1925) vol. 1, p. 21-4, 40-1, 48.

[3] *A Book of Nicknames,* John Goff (Courier-Journal
Job Printing Company, Louisville, Ky., 1892) p. 28.

Garfield Avengers

During the administration of Chester
Alan Arthur who served as President of the
United States from 1881 to 1885, a group
of individuals made it their chief objective
to criticize his public acts and to discredit
his private life by secret rather than open
methods. They called themselves the *Garfield Avengers* [1] because they resented Arthur's taking Garfield's place as President
of the United States.

[1] *Twenty Years of the Republic, 1885-1905,* Harry
Thurston Peck (Dodd, Mead and Company, New York,
1907) p. 7.

Garms, Debs C.

Debs C. Garms, who was born at Bangs,
Tex., on June 26, 1908, and who played
outfield in major league baseball, was nicknamed *Tex* [1] because he was born in Texas.

[1] *Who's Who in Major, League Base Ball,* comp. by
Harold (Speed) Johnson (Buxton Publishing Company,
Chicago, 1933) p. 171.

Garner, John Nance

John Nance Garner has been called *Cactus
Jack,* the *Favorite Son of Texas, Mohair
Jack,* the *Owl, Poker Face,* the *Sage of
Uvalde,* and *Uvalde Jack.*

The nickname *Cactus Jack* [1] was given
to Vice President Garner because he lived
in a section of Texas in which the cactus
grows.

The Favorite Son of Texas [2] was applied
to him because he was not only the Vice
President of the United States, but he had
been a Representative from Texas to Congress from 1903 to 1933.

The nickname *Mohair Jack* [1] alludes to
the fact that John Nance Garner advocated
a tariff in the interests of goat raisers, since
Uvalde is a center of the mohair industry
in Texas.

The Owl and *Poker Face* [1] are doubtless
descriptive of his characteristically imperturb-
able manners and facial expression.

Because of the fact that he was mature in
years and versed in political and practical
lore, he was called the *Sage of Uvalde.
Uvalde Jack* [1] signifies that Mr. Garner lived
in Uvalde, Tex.

John Nance Garner, the thirty-second Vice
President of the United States, was born in
Red River County, Tex., on November 22,
1869.

[1] *The Washington Post Magazine,* Washington, D.C.,
March 4, 1934, p. 4.

[2] *The New York Times,* New York, March 27, 1932,
cols. 4 and 5, p. 6 E.

Garner Buckaroos

The *Garner Buckaroos* [1] is a nickname
which was applied to the conservative faction of the Democratic Party during the
strife between the conservative Democrats
and the New Dealers in Congress during
the session which began on January 3, 1939.
This discord was occasioned by radical legislation recommended by President Franklin
D. Roosevelt and by his appointing radical
New Dealers to key positions in the government. The conservatives were led by Vice

President John Nance Garner and by Senators Harry Flood Byrd and Carter Glass of Virginia.

The fact that Vice President Garner is a Texan and that cowboys in Texas and other western states are sometimes called *buckaroos* gave rise to this nickname. The term *buckaroo* is a corruption of the Spanish word *vaquero* meaning cowboy.

[1]*The Pittsburgh Press*, Pittsburgh, Pa., February 3, 1939, cols. 1 and 2, p. 18.

The American Language: An Inquiry into the Development of English in the United States, Fourth Edition, Corrected, Enlarged and Rewritten, H. L. Mencken (Alfred A. Knopf, New York, 1936) p. 152.

Garnets. See Swarthmore College

Garnier, Baptiste

Baptiste Garnier, a half-blood Sioux Indian, was a well-known army scout and interpreter who lived at Fort Laramie, Wyo., during the last quarter of the nineteenth and the first quarter of the twentieth century. He was called *Little Bat*[1] to distinguish him from a contemporary Indian scout in the same vicinity, Baptiste Pourier, who was commonly designated *Big Bat.* Bat is an abbreviated form of Baptiste.

[1] *Fifty Years on the Old Frontier as Cowboy, Hunter, Guide, Scout, and Ranchman*, James H. Cook (Yale University Press, New Haven, Conn., 1923) p. 194-5.

Garrison Mob

On October 21, 1835, at Boston, Mass., a disorderly throng of people who displayed their antagonism to abolitionists were called the *Garrison Mob*[1] because William Lloyd Garrison, a prominent abolitionist, was the victim. They chose him because he was one of the outstanding persons present at a business meeting of the Boston Female Antislavery Society which was held that day. They intended to tar and feather him. Garrison was seized by the mob and led into the streets before he was rescued by friends and policemen who took him to the city jail where he spent the night in order to be safe from further violence.

[1] *Papers Relating to the Garrison Mob*, ed. by Theodore Lyman (Welch, Bigelow and Company, Cambridge, Mass., 1870) p. 3, 41, 43.

Garrisonians

When the Abolitionists split into two groups in 1839-1840, those who remained true to the doctrines of the original abolitionists were called *Garrisonians*[1] because William Lloyd Garrison was the outstanding champion of that type of abolition.

[1] *American History and Government, a Text-book on the History and Government of the United States*, James Albert Woodburn and Thomas Francis Moran (Longmans, Green and Company, New York, 1906) p. 325.

Gary, Martin Witherspoon

Throughout the southern states, Major General Martin Witherspoon Gary was known as the *Bald Eagle* or the *Bald Eagle of Edgefield*[1] in allusion to the grimly determined manner in which he fought during the Civil War. His home was then at Edgefield, S.C.

Martin Witherspoon Gary was born at Cokesbury, S.C., on March 25, 1831, and died at Edgefield Court House, S.C., on April 9, 1881.

[1] *The Tragic Era: The Revolution after Lincoln*, Claude G. Bowers (Houghton Mifflin Company, New York and Boston, 1929) p. 502-3.

The National Cyclopaedia of American Biography (James T. White and Company, New York, 1932) vol. 22, p. 379.

Gas Addicks. See Addicks, J. E. O.

Gas House Gang

During the 1930's the brilliant, playing of the entire St. Louis Cardinals baseball team made them National League champions for several years and World Series winners twice. The group's invincible technique on the diamond and their highspirited behavior, reminiscent of the rowdy Baltimore Orioles of the nineteenth century, won for them the name of *Gas House Gang*.[1] Among the members of the gang noted for their ability to win games were *Dizzy* and Paul Dean, Frank Frisch, *Pepper* Martin, *Ducky* Medwick, *Lippy* Durocher and *Dazzy* Vance.

[1] *The Story of Baseball*, by John Durant (Hastings House, New York, 1947) p. 190-6.

Gate City. See Atlanta, Ga.; Chattanooga, Tenn.; Denison, Tex.; Keokuk, Iowa; Laredo, Tex.; and Winona, Minn.

Gate City of the South. See Atlanta, Ga.

Gates, Horatio

Horatio Gates was sometimes called the *Hero of Saratoga,* and paradoxically also known as *Granny Gates.*

The *Hero of Saratoga*[1] commemorated the surrender of General Burgoyne to Gates

Gates, Horatio—Continued

near Saratoga Springs, N.Y., on October 17, 1771. Burgoyne surrendered nearly six thousand men and a number of cannons, muskets, and a large quantity of ammunition very useful to the rebelling colonists.

Gates was called *Granny Gates* [1] by people who thought him as timid as an old lady in attacking the British. Gates' victory at Saratoga Springs was made possible by the resourceful strategy of several talented subordinate officers in his command: Morgan of Virginia, Lincoln of Massachusetts, Schuyler of New York, and Benedict Arnold.

Horatio Gates was born at Maldon, Essex, England, in 1728, and died at New York City, on April 10, 1806.

[1] *The Finished Scoundrel: General James Wilkinson, Sometime Commander-in-chief of the Army of the United States, Who Made Intrigue a Trade and Treason a Profession,* Royal Orman Shreve (The Bobbs-Merrill Company, Indianapolis, Ind., 1933) p. 41, 46.

The Turning Point of the Revolution or Burgoyne in America, Hoffman Nickerson (Houghton Mifflin Company, New York and Boston, 1928) p. 364, 427-8.

Gates, John Warne

Bet-a-million Gates, Moonshine Gates, and the *Wire King of America* are sobriquets of John Warne Gates.

He was known as *Bet-a-million Gates* [1] in allusion to his daring speculations.

He was called *Moonshine Gates* [1] because, having infringed upon certain patent rights related to the manufacture of wire fencing in 1879, he constantly traveled about, particularly at night, from state to state to evade the law.

Gates was called the *Wire King of America* [2] because he was a producer of wire and wire fencing and bought up other wire plants until he practically controlled the wire industry in America.

John Warne Gates was born in what is now West Chicago, Ill., on May 8, 1855, and died at Paris, France, on August 9, 1911.

[1] *Bet-A-Million Gates, the Story of a Plunger,* Robert Irving Warshow (Greenberg, New York, 1932) p. 29, 47, 120.

[2] *This Cleveland of Ours,* Wilfred Henry Alburn and Miriam Russell Alburn (The S. J. Clarke Publishing Company, Chicago, and Cleveland, Ohio, 1933) vol. 1, p. 554.

Gateway City. See Minneapolis, Minn.

Gateway City of the Hills. See Rapid City, S.D.

Gateway of the West. See New York

Gateway to the Northwest. See St. Paul, Minn.

Gateway to the South. See Louisville, Ky.

Gatling Gun Parker. See Parker, J. H.

Gators. See Allegheny College; University of Florida

Gehrig, Henry Louis (Lou)

Henry Louis (Lou) Gehrig was known as *The Iron Horse,* the *Iron Man of Baseball* and *Larruping Lou* because of his endurance and speed as batter and as a runner.

Henry Louis (Lou) Gehrig was born at New York City, on June 19, 1903 and died on June 2, 1941. He was considered one of the most valuable first basemen in American League baseball.

Gem City. See Quincy, Ill.; St. Paul, Minn.

Gem City of Ohio. See Dayton, Ohio

Gem City of the West. See Quincy, Ill.

Gem of the Mountains. See Idaho

Gem State. See Idaho

General of the Mackerel Brigade. See McClellan, G. B.

General Tom Thumb. See Stratton, C. S.

Generals. See Washington and Lee University

Geneva College

The athletic teams of Geneva College, at Beaver Falls, Pa., were nicknamed the *Covenanters* [1] because the college is supported by the Reformed Presbyterian Church which is an offshoot of the old Covenanters.

[1] A communication from A. C. Edgecombe, Director of Athletics at Geneva College, Beaver Falls, Pa., June 12, 1935.

Genial Reuben. See Kolb, R. F.

Genius of Motordom. See Ford, Henry

Genius of Romance. See Hawthorne, Nathaniel

Gentle Shepherd of Ohio. See Grosvenor, C. H.

Gentleman from Hale. See Tunstall, A. M.

Gentleman George. See Barrett, G. H.

Gentleman George. See Pendleton, G. H.

Gentleman Jim. See Corbett, J. J.

Gentlemen. See Centenary College of Louisiana

Gentlemen's Pastime. See Baseball

Gentlemen's Riot. See Broadcloth Mob.

Gents. See Centenary College of Louisiana

George, Charlie

Charlie George was called the *Greek*[1] because he is of Greek ancestry. He was born at Waycross, Ga., on December 25, 1912, and was a catcher in major league baseball.

[1] *Who's Who in The Major League,* 1935 Edition, Harold (Speed) Johnson (B. E. Callahan, Chicago, 1935) p. 37.

George the Baker. See Lehman, George

George Washington. See Thomas, G. H.

George Washington Bloom. See Bloom, Sol

George Washington University

The *Colonials*[1] is the nickname of the athletic teams of George Washington University, at Washington, D.C. This nickname arose because of the historical significance of the name of the University.

[1] A letter from Jack Espey, Publicity Director at The George Washington University, Washington, D.C., June 25, 1935.

Georgetown University

The teams of Georgetown University, at Washington, D.C., are popularly called The *Hoyas*[1] because the word *hoya* is a part of their cheer "Hoya Saxa."

[1] A letter from Gabriel Murphy, Graduate Manager of Athletics at Georgetown University, Washington, D.C., June 10, 1935.

Georgia

Georgia is known as the *Buzzard State,* the *Cracker State,* the *Goober State,* the *Empire State of the South,* and the *Yankee Land of the South.* The nickname *Buzzard State* was given to Georgia because of a very strict law enacted in that state for the protection of the buzzards, because they were valuable as scavengers.

As to the origin of the nickname *Cracker State,*[1] authorities differ. Some say it was because the early planters cracked their whips over their mules. Another version is that the term was derived from corncracker, since the poorer people lived largely on corn. Still another version is that the dialect sounds like something being cracked.

Georgia is nicknamed the *Goober State*[2] because goobers or peanuts are commonly grown throughout the State. Georgia is known as the *Empire State of the South,*[3] and the *Yankeeland of the South*[4] in allusion to its rapid industrial development. It stands in the foremost rank of the southern states for the number and value of its manufactures.

[1] *A New Dictionary of Americanisms,* Sylva Clapin (Louis Weiss and Company, New York, 1903) p. 89.

Americanisms—Old and New, John S. Farmer (Privately Printed by Thomas Poulter and Sons, London, 1889) p. 179.

Americanisms; The English of the New World, M. Schele De Vere (Charles Scribner and Company, New York, 1872) p. 659.

[2] *A Book of Nicknames,* John Goff (Courier-Journal Job Printing Company, Louisville, Ky., 1892) p. 13.

[3] *King's Handbook of the United States,* planned and ed. by Moses King, text by M. F. Sweetser (Moses King Corporation, Buffalo, N.Y., 1891) p. 179.

[4] *A Journey in the Seaboard Slave States, with Remarks on Their Economy,* Frederick Law Olmsted (Dix and Edwards, New York, 1856) p. 530.

Georgia Fire-eater. See Toombs, Robert

Georgia Peach. See Cobb, T. R.

Georgia Power Company

The people of Georgia nicknamed the Georgia Power Company *Uncle George*[1] because they are pleased with the economic

Georgia Power Company—Continued
and efficient manner in which the company
has been operating for more than thirty
years.

[1] *Time: The Weekly Newsmagazine,* Chicago, Ill.,
April 29, 1940. col. 2, p. 17.

Georgia State College For Men

The *Rams* is the appellation given to the
individuals composing the athletic teams of
the Georgia State College for men, situated
at Tifton, Ga.; but the writer was unable to
ascertain why they are so called.

Georgia State Industrial College

The athletic teams of the Georgia State
Industrial College, at Industrial College,
Ga., were nicknamed the *Georgia Tigers* [9]
in 1924, doubtless because of the aggressive
and tenacious manner in which these teams
conducted their athletic contests during that
year, going undefeated the entire season.

[9] A communication from M. L. Thomas of Georgia
State Industrial College, Industrial College, Ga., November 25, 1935.

Georgia Tigers. See Georgia State Industrial College

Georgians

The people of the State of Georgia are
called *Buzzards, Crackers, Goober-grabbers,*
and *Sandhillers.* Georgians were nicknamed *Buzzards* and *Crackers* because the
state was called the *Buzzard State* and the
Cracker State.

According to some authorities, the people
of Georgia are called *Crackers* [1] because the
poor white people in the state are said to
eat cracked corn as their principal diet.
Goober-grabbers [1] is applied to the people
of Georgia and Alabama because peanuts or
goobers are so common. The Georgians
were formerly called *Sandhillers* [1] from the
poor and illiterate white people mainly
found in the sandy pine barrens where they
are said to live an idle and wretched life.

[1] *A New Dictionary of Americanisms,* Sylva Clapin
(Louis Weiss and Company, New York, 1903) p. 142,
208. 346.

Gerry, Peter Goelet

Peter Goelet Gerry, a Rhode Island lawyer and politician, was nicknamed the *Millionaire* [1] in the United States Senate because
he belonged to a wealthy family, and married the heiress Edith Stuyvesant Vanderbilt.
He was a Democratic Representative from

Rhode Island to the United States Congress
from 1913 to 1916, and Senator from
Rhode Island from 1917 to 1947.

Peter Goelet Gerry was born at New York
City on September 18, 1879.

[1] An interview with Captain Victor Hunt Harding,
Secretary of the National Democratic Congress Reëlection
Committee, Washington, D.C., April 10, 1939.

Gettysburg College

The athletes of Gettysburg College at
Gettysburg, Pa., were designated the *Bullets* [1] in 1924, by a Sports Editor of the
Gettysburg Times, because the college is
located on the Gettysburg battlefield.

[1] A letter from Charles W. Beachem, Alumni Secretary at Gettysburg College, Gettysburg, Pa., June 29,
1935.

Ghost. See Greeley, Horace

Ghost Cities

The populous towns which grew up in
Nevada and other mining states during the
gold rush days are now called *Ghost Cities* [1]
because they are no longer populous and are
ghosts of what they formerly were.

[1] *The World Book Encyclopedia* (W. F. Quarrie and
Company, Chicago, 1937) vol. 12, p. 4898.

Giant of the Hills. See Crawford, E. A.

Giants. See New York Football Giants,
Incorporated

Gibraltar Brigade

The First Brigade of the Third Division
of the Second Corps of the Army of the
Potomac, commanded by Brigadier General
Nathan Kimball, was known as the *Gibraltar
Brigade.* [1] Distinguished for its brave conduct throughout the Civil War, this brigade
fought with unusually grim determination
and success on September 17, 1862, at the
Battle of Antietam in Maryland, losing many
of its numbers but doggedly holding its
assigned position. It again fought with distinction on December 13, 1862, at the Battle
of Fredericksburg, in Virginia. The nickname *Gibraltar Brigade* likened the brigade's
formidable strength and invincibility to
that of the famous English stronghold of
Gibraltar in the Mediterranean.

[1] *Pennsylvania at Antietam, Report of the Antietam
Memorial Commission of Pennsylvania and Ceremonies
at the Dedication of the Monuments Erected by the
Commonwealth of Pennsylvania to Mark the Position of
Thirteen of the Pennsylvania Commands Engaged in the
Battle* (Harrisburg Publishing Company, State Printer,
Harrisburg, Pa., 1906) p. 197.

Gibraltar in the Pacific. See Hawaii

Gibraltar of America. See Vicksburg, Miss.

Gibraltar of Louisiana. See Vicksburg, Miss.

Gibraltar of the South. See Vicksburg, Miss.

Gibson, Samuel Braxton

Samuel Braxton Gibson, a baseball player, was called *Hoot Gibson* [1] when he was with the Detroit team. The similarity between his name and that of the movie actor, Hoot Gibson, probably gave rise to this nickname.

[1] *The New York Times,* New York, February 1, 1932, col. 4, p. 24.

Gifford, Charles L.

Cranberry Gifford [1] is the nickname of Charles L. Gifford who was a Representative from Massachusetts to the United States Congress from 1921 to 1937. He made his home on Cape Cod noted for the quantities of cranberries produced there.

Charles L. Gifford was born at Cotuit, Mass., on March 15, 1871 and died August 23, 1947.

[8] *The Washington Post Magazine,* Washington, D.C., March 4, 1934, p. 4.

Gilbert, Cass

Cass Gilbert, a noted architect, is designated the *Father of the Skyscraper* [1] because he designed the Woolworth Building, one of the first tall buildings in America, as well as the Custom House at New York City, the Brazier Building at Boston, Mass., the Supreme Court Building at Washington, D.C., several of the state capitols and other well-known buildings.

Cass Gilbert was born at Zanesville, Ohio, on November 28, 1859, and died at Brockenhurst, England, on May 17, 1934.

[1] *The Source Book* (Source Research Council, Inc., Chicago, 1936) vol. 3, p. 1170.

Gilded Age

The last decades of the nineteenth century have been called the *Gilded Age* [1] because the rapid growth of the cities and the inflow of wealthy men and women to the cities caused palatial residences to be built. In these magnificent homes the lux-ury and display of wealth and the entertainments indulged in were such as only those living in a gilded age could afford.

[1] *The Development of the United States since 1865,* Nelson P. Mead (Harcourt, Brace and Company, New York, 1930) p. 193.

Gilded Trap

When the Constitution of the United States was before the states for ratification, people who were not in favor of it designated it the *Gilded Trap* [1] because they thought it favored the wealthy at the expense of the poor.

[1] *A History of the People of the United States from the Revolution to the Civil War,* John Bach McMaster (D. Appleton and Company, New York, 1883) vol. 1, p. 482.

Gillars, Mildred

Mildred Gillars was nicknamed *Axis Sally* during World War II. She was the Nazi radio propagandist from Dec. 11, 1941, through May 6, 1945. Her programs were given under the title *Home Sweet Home* and were designed to persuade American soldiers to lay down their arms and go home. She was a native of Portland, Me.

[1] *The Courier-Journal,* Louisville, Kentucky, August 22, 1948, p. 1, columns 2-3.

Gillett, Frederick Huntington

During his later years as a Representative from Massachusetts to the United States Congress from 1893 to 1925, Frederick Huntington Gillett was called *The Father of the House* [1] in allusion to his length of service. He was Speaker of the House from 1919 to 1925.

Frederick Huntington Gillett was born at Westfield, Mass., on October 16, 1851, and died July 31, 1935.

[1] *My Quarter Century of American Politics,* Champ Clark (Harper and Brothers, New York and London, 1920) vol. 1, p. 222.

Gink. See Hendrick, Harvey

Ginter, Lewis

While he was serving in the Civil War under Major General George Henry Thomas, Lewis Ginter was nicknamed the *Fighting Commissary* [1] because he took every opportunity to participate in the actual fighting outside his line of duty.

Lewis Ginter was born at New York City, on April 4, 1824, and died at his

Ginter, Lewis—Continued
estate, Westbrook, in Henrico County, Va.,
on October 2, 1897.

[1] *The National Cyclopaedia of American Biography*
(James T. White and Company, New York, 1922)
vol. 18, p. 309.

Girl with the Ginger Snap Name. See
Pitts, Zasu

Girty, Simon
The *White Savage* [1] was applied to
Simon Girty because having deserted the
Virginia militia in 1776, he became an
aggressive leader of Indian depredations
on the pioneer settlements, particularly
along the frontiers of Pennsylvania and
Virginia.

Simon Girty was born in what is now
Dauphin County, Pennsylvania, in 1741,
and died in Canada, in 1818.

[1] *Simon Girty, the White Savage,* Thomas A. Boyd
(Minton, Balch and Company, New York, 1928) p. 3.

Gish, Lillian
Because she ate carrots constantly once
while she was attending an outstanding
trial, Lillian Gish, who was born at Springfield, Ohio, on October 14, 1896, and who
now lives at Hollywood, Calif., was nicknamed *Carrots*.[1]

[1] *Doug and Mary and Others,* Allene Talmey (Macy-
Masius, New York, 1927) p. 71.

Glacier Priest. See Hubbard, B. R.

Gladstone of America. See Blaine, J. G.

Glass, George Carter
The nicknames *Father of the Federal
Reserve System, Snapping Turtle, Sound
Money Glass,* and an *Unreconstructed Rebel*
have been applied to George Carter Glass.

Senator Glass has been called the *Father
of the Federal Reserve System* [1] and *Sound
Money Glass* [2] because he drafted the bill
providing for the federal reserve system,
introduced it in the House of Representatives on September 10, 1913, and secured its
adoption with only minor amendments on
December 23, 1913. George Carter Glass
is nicknamed the *Snapping Turtle* [3] because of his quick temper with opponents.

Glass was called an *Unreconstructed Rebel* [4] by President Franklin Delano Roosevelt

during the 1935 session of Congress because
of Glass's opposition to much of the New
Deal program.

George Carter Glass was born at Lynchburg, Va., on January 4, 1858, and died
May 28, 1946. He was a Democratic Representative from Virginia to the United States
Congress from 1902 to 1919, and a Democratic Senator from Virginia from 1919
until the time of his death.

[1] *The National Cyclopaedia of American Biography*
(James T. White and Company, New York, 1924)
current vol. A, p. 37.
[2] *The Washington Post Magazine,* Washington, D.C.,
March 4, 1934, p. 4.
[3] *The New York Times,* New York, January 31, 1932,
Sec. IX, col. 3, p. 2.
[4] *The Washington Post,* Washington, D.C., January
28, 1935, col. 2, p. 2.

Gleason, Patrick Jerome
Patrick Jerome Gleason who was Mayor
of Long Island City, N.Y., was nicknamed
Battle Axe Gleason [1] because in 1888 he
chopped down the railroad fence, gates,
and the ticket office which the Long Island
Railroad Company had built across Front
Street in Long Island City.

Gleason died at Long Island City on May
20, 1901.

[1] *The Boroughs of Brooklyn and Queens, Counties of
Nassau and Suffolk, Long Island, New York, 1609-
1924,* Henry Isham Hazelton (Lewis Historical Publishing Company, Inc., New York and Chicago, 1925)
vol. 2, p. 949.

Gleason, William
William Gleason, a veteran coach of
major league baseball, was nicknamed *Kid
Gleason* [1] because he was small in stature.
It has been said that Gleason played with
baseballs before he learned to walk and
began to play professional baseball when he
was about twenty-one years of age. He
ranks high among the baseball immortals,
and is one of the old players who is well-
known to present-day athletes. Ten of his
twenty-one active years of playing major-
league baseball were spent in the service of
The Philadelphia National League Baseball
Club.

Gleason began to play professional baseball in 1887 when he became pitcher for the
Pennsylvania State League at Williamsport,
Pa. He was pitcher for the Philadelphia National League Baseball Club from 1887 until
1890, having reached the peak of his career
as a National League pitcher in 1890 when
he won thirty-nine out of the fifty-six games
he pitched. He won the National League

pennant for the Baltimore Orioles in 1895 and also in 1896. In 1896 the manager of the Baltimore Orioles traded Gleason to the manager of The New York National League Baseball Company, but he was soon switched to The Philadelphia National League Baseball Club. He played second base on the teams of this club from about 1897 until 1907. Gleason was coach of The Chicago American League Baseball Company under the management of Jimmy Callahan and Clarence Rowland from 1912 until 1917. He was manager of The Chicago American League Baseball Company from December 31, 1918, until the close of the season in 1923. He joined the staff of The Philadelphia American League Baseball Company in 1926.

William Gleason was born at Camden, N.J., on October 26, 1866, and died at Philadelphia, Pa., on January 2, 1933.

[1] *Philadelphia Ledger*, Philadelphia, January 3, 1933, col. 5, p. 13.
Baseball Magazine (The Baseball Magazine Company, New York, 1919-1920) vol. 24-25, June, 1920, p. 324.

Gleason, Tennessee
Gleason is nicknamed the *Tater Town* or *Taterville* because quantities of sweet potatoes are grown there and shipped to market.

Glorious Ninety-two
The *Glorious Ninety-two* [1] were the ninety-two delegates of the Massachusetts House of Representatives who on June 30, 1768, refused to recall a resolution made by the members of the House in February remonstrating against the British system of taxation. The demand that they rescind the February resolution was made by Lord Hillsborough, England's Colonial Secretary. The courage and audacity of these ninety-two men in defying royal authority appealed to the colonists who acclaimed them as the *Glorious Ninety-two*.

[1] *The Life of Artemas Ward, the First Commander-in-chief of the American Revolution*, Charles Martyn (A. Ward, New York, 1921) p. 40.

Goats
During the closing years of the nineteenth century, the Democratic party in Kansas City, Mo., became divided into two factions, one of which was popularly known as the *Goats*,[1] because their leader's home was located on the summit of the highest

hill in the city, the inference being that anyone had to be a mountain goat to get there.

[3] *A Civic History of Kansas City, Missouri*, Roy Ellis The author, State teachers college, Springfield, Mo., 1930) p. 234-5.

Go-bar-me Act. See Embargo Act

Gobblers. See Virginia Polytechnic Institute

Godfrey, Hollen
Because of his bravery and daring in defending his sod house against an Indian attack in the raid of 1865, Hollen Godfrey was designated *Old Wicked* [1] by the Indians, and his sod house was called *Fort Wicked*.[2]

Hollen Godfrey was a noted Indian fighter who lived in the Platte Plains, someplace in the vicinity of Julesburg, Colo.

[1] *Three Thousand Miles through the Rocky Mountains*, A. K. McClure (J. B. Lippincott and Company, Philadelphia, 1869) p. 63.
[2] *A History of the United States since the Civil War*, Ellis Paxson Oberholtzer (The Macmillan Company, New York, 1917) vol. 1, p. 346.

Godless Anne Royall. See Royall, A. N.

God-like Daniel. See Webster, Daniel

Goebel, William
Opponents of William Goebel referred to him as *Dictator Goebel* [1] because of the autocratic manner in which he dominated the Democratic party of Kentucky, and particularly legislation enacted between 1887 and 1899, while he was in the state senate of Kentucky.

William Goebel was born at Carbondale, Pa., on January 4, 1856, and died at Louisville, Ky., on February 3, 1900.

[1] *The Sage of Sinnissippi, Being a Brief Sketch of the Life of Congressman Frank Orren Lowden of Oregon, Illinois, Brief Sketches of His Rivals in Political Battles, a Short Article Relating to His Availability as a Presidential Candidate for 1908, and an Official and Authentic Account of States Elections in Illinois, Statistically, Combined with a Roll of Honor of the Nation, the State, the County, and the Village, the Home of the Author, with Illustrations*, Kinnie A. Ostewig (Press of Joseph A. Nolen, Shabbona, Ill., 1907) p. 162.
Dictionary of American Biography under the Auspices of the American Council of Learned Societies, ed. by Allen Johnson and Dumas Malone (Charles Scribner's Sons, New York, 1931) vol. 7, p. 353.

Gold Bug. See Benton, T. H.

Goldbugs. See Oklahoma City University

Gold Coasters. See Lake Forest College

Gold Corner
September 24, 1869, climaxed an orgy of speculation in gold which caused a money panic throughout the United States. The Wall Street firm of Jay Gould and James Fisk and associates proposed to corner or control all the gold except that in the Federal Treasury. These schemes, known as the *Gold Corner*,[1] were frustrated by the timely action of President Ulysses Simpson Grant.

[1] *Lee at Appomattox, and Other Papers*, Charles Francis Adams (Houghton Mifflin and Company, Boston, 1902) p. 120.

Gold Democrats
In 1896, during the free-silver controversy those Democrats who did not support the free and unlimited coinage of silver by the United States at a certain fixed ratio were called *Gold Democrats*.[1]

[1] *Portrait of an Independent; Moorfield Storey, 1845-1929*, M. A. DeWolfe Howe (Houghton Mifflin Company, New York and Boston, 1932) p. 183.

Gold Diggers. See Califorians

Gold Humbug. See Benton, T. H.

Gold Hunters. See Californians

Gold Medal County
Alameda County in California is often termed the *Gold Medal County*[1] because its agricultural products have so frequently been awarded the gold medal prizes at fairs and exhibits.

[1] *Alameda County, the Ideal Place for Your California Home*, Henry Anderson Lafler (Published by the Alameda Board of Supervisors, Alameda, Calif., 1915) p. 3.

Golden Acorn Division. See Eighty-seventh Infantry Division of World War II

Golden Arrow. See Eighth Infantry Division of World War II

Golden Avalanches. See Marquette University

Golden Bears. See University of California

Golden Calves of the People. See Webster, Daniel, and H. L. White

Golden City. See Sacramento, Calif.

Golden Eagles. See Western Union College

Golden Gate City. See San Francisco, Calif.

Golden Gate Trinity. See Coolbrith, Ina Donna, Bret Harte, and Charles Warren Stoddard

Golden Hurricanes. See University of Tulsa

Golden Lion Division. See One Hundred and Sixth Infantry Division of World War II

Golden-mouthed. See Galloway, C. B.

Golden Rule Jones. See Jones, S. M.

Golden State. See California

Golden Talon Division. See Seventeenth Airborne Division of World War II

Golden Tornadoes. See Eureka College; Storer College

Golden Triangle
The main business section of Pittsburgh, Pa., located in the angle formed by the confluence of the Allegheny and the Monongahela rivers which unite to form the Ohio River, is commonly designated the *Point*.

This area is also called the *Golden Triangle*[1] because the principal wealth of the city including the stores, banks, theatres, and many other business enterprises is centered here.

[1] *The Source Book* (Source Research Council, Inc., Chicago, 1936) vol. 5, p. 2267.

Goliath of His Party. See Bayard, J. A.

Gompers, Samuel
Samuel Gompers, an American labor leader, was nicknamed the *Grand Old Man of Labor*[1] especially during the later years of his life because he was most active in building up the American Federation of Labor. With the exception of the year of 1895, he

was President of that organization from the time it was organized in 1886 until his death.

Samuel Gompers was born in a tenement house at London, England, on January 27, 1850, and died at San Antonio, Tex., on December 13, 1924.

[1] *Washington City and Capital:* Federal Writers' Project, American Guide Series, 1937 (Government Printing Office, Washington, D.C., 1927) p. 539.

Gonzales, Texas

Gonzales is designated the *Lexington of Texas* [1] because the first gun of the Texas Revolution was fired there.

[1] *The Geography of Texas, Physical and Political,* Revised Edition, Frederic William Simonds (Ginn and Company, New York and Boston, 1914) p. 223.

Goober-grabbers. See Georgians

Goober State. See Georgia

Gooch, Wayne R.

Wayne R. Gooch, who was living in Mecklinburg County, Virginia, at the time of his arrest for bootlegging liquor in 1906, was nicknamed the *King of Moonshiners* [1] by the Internal Revenue officers. He was reported to have accumulated a fortune selling "moonshine whiskey."

[1] *The Washington Post,* Washington, D.C., October 13, 1906, c. 2. p. 9.

Good Bishop. See Otey, J. H.

Good Governor of Virginia. See Botetourt, N. B.

Good Gray Poet. See Whitman, Walt

Good-luck House

In the 1880's a wealthy Boston woman, Mrs. Alice N. Lincoln, became interested in slum dwellers. She rented one of the worst tenement houses in a notorious slum, repaired, cleaned and kept it in good condition. She shared her rental profits with the tenants. It came to be known as *Good-luck House.* [1]

[1] *Heroic Personalities,* Louis Albert Banks (Eaton and Mains, New York, 1898) p. 116-20.

Good Physician. See Higbee, C. G.

Good Roads Cartwright. See Cartwright, Wilburn

Good Roads King. See King, C. M.

Goose. See Goslin, L. A.

Goose Egg Congress

The extra session of the Seventy-fifth Congress of the United States from November 15 until December 22, 1937, was nicknamed the *Goose Egg Congress* [1] because during the entire thirty-six days they failed to pass any major legislation.

[1] *The Washington Post,* Washington, D.C., December 22, 1937, col. 1, p. 28.

Gopher State. See Minnesota

Gophers. See Minnesotans; University of Minnesota

Gore, Thomas Pryor

Senator Thomas Pryor Gore of Oklahoma has been designated the *Blind Savant* [1] because of his learning and blindness. He was a Senator from Oklahoma to the United States Congress from 1907 to 1921, and again from 1931 to 1936.

Thomas Pryor Gore was born in Webster County, Miss., on December 10, 1870.

[1] *The Washington Post Magazine,* Washington, D.C., March 4, 1934, p. 4.

Gorgeous Hussy. See Eaton, M. O.

Gorges, Ferdinando

The nickname, the *Father of English Colonization in America,* [1] was applied to Sir Ferdinando Gorges in commemoration of his great influence in establishing a number of early settlements in this country.

Sir Ferdinando Gorges was born at Ashton, Somersetshire, England, about 1565, and died at Ashton Court near Bristol, England, in 1647.

[1] *The Encyclopedia Americana* (Americana Corporation, New York and Chicago, 1927) vol. 13, p. 65.

Goslin, Leon Allen

Leon Allen Goslin, who was born at Salem, N.J., on October 16, 1900, and who played outfield in major league baseball, was given the inevitable nickname of *Goose.* [1]

[1] *Who's Who in Major League Base Ball,* comp. by Harold (Speed) Johnson (Buxton Publishing Company, Chicago, 1933) p. 178.

Gotham. See New York City

Gothamites

The inhabitants of New York City are frequently referred to as *Gothamites* [1] since one of the nicknames of New York City is *Gotham.*

[1] *Dictionary of Americanisms,* Fourth Edition, John Russell Bartlett (Little, Brown and Company, Boston, 1877) p. 255.

Gould, Jay

Jay Gould was nicknamed the *Railroad King* [1] because he amassed much of his fortune in owning railroads and speculating in railroad stocks.

Jay Gould was born at Roxbury, N.Y., on May 27, 1836, and died at New York City, on December 2, 1892.

[1] *A Book of Nicknames,* John Goff (Courier-Journal Job Printing Company, Louisville, Ky., 1892) p. 30.

Grace Darling of America. See Lewis, Ida

Granary of California. See San Joaquin River Valley

Grand Canyon of American Business

Broadway in New York City has been nicknamed the *Grand Canyon of American Business* [1] because it is narrow and the continuous walls of tall buildings shut out the sunlight from it and give it the appearance of a gorge between rock cliffs.

[1] *The World Book Encyclopedia* (W. F. Quarrie and Company, Chicago, 1934) vol. 12, p. 4982.

Grand Canyon State. See Arizona

Grand Old Lady of Opera. See Schumann-Heink, Mme. Ernestine

Grand Old Lady of the Movies. See Dressler, Marie

Grand Old Man. See Franklin, Benjamin; Savage, G. M.

Grand Old Man of Alexandria. See Dunn, E. C.

Grand Old Man of Labor. See Gompers, Samuel

Grand Old Man of Maryland. See Whyte, W. P.

Grand Old Man of Missouri. See Kirk, J. R.

Grand Old Man of the Screen. See Roberts, Theodore

Grand Old Party

The Republican party is known as the *Grand Old Party,* [1] often abbreviated to *GOP.* The Republican party was organized in 1854 and the nickname came into general use shortly after the Civil War.

[1] *Recent History of the United States, 1865-1929,* Revised and Enlarged Edition, Frederic L. Paxson (Houghton Mifflin Company, New York and Boston, 1928) p. 259.

Grandest Roman of Them All. See McMillin, Benton

Grandfather Clause

Following the Period of Reconstruction in the South, several laws were passed which were intended to decrease the political power of the Negro by curtailing his newly acquired right to vote. One of these laws provided that anyone who wished to vote had to furnish proof that he was the descendant of a person who had voted prior to the Civil War, thus disfranchising the Negroes. This clause was termed the *Grandfather Clause.* [2]

[2] *New American History,* Albert Bushnell Hart (American Book Company, New York and Chicago, 1917) p. 594.

Grandfather of all the Missionaries. See Roberts, R. R.

Grandfather of Yale Rowing. See Sheffield, G. St. J.

Grandfather's Hat. See Harrison, Benjamin

Grandma Flapper. See Hopper, E. W.

Grandma Moses. See Moses, A. M. R.

Grandmother of Boston. See Peabody, E. P.

Grange

The *Grange* and *Grangers* [1] were nicknames applied to the Patrons of Husbandry, an organization of farmers founded in Washington, D.C., in 1867 by Oliver Hudson Kelly, who was on the staff of the Department of Agriculture. The purpose of this organization was to improve agricultural conditions especially in the South, to aid in marketing commodities and in purchasing tools, and to assist the farmers in learning more about the technical side of farming.

[1] *The New Nation*, Frederic L. Paxson (Houghton Mifflin Company, New York and Boston, 1927) p. 67.
The Encyclopaedia Britannica, Fourteenth Edition (Encyclopaedia Britannica, Inc., New York, 1932) vol. 10, p. 636.

Grangers. See *Grange*

Granite Boys. See New Hampshire Inhabitants

Granite City. See St. Cloud, Minn.

Granite State. See New Hampshire

·Granny. See Rice, Grantland

Granny Gates. See Gates, Horatio

Granny Hayes. See Hayes, R. B.

Grant, Ulysses Simpson

Following is a list of nicknames designating General Ulysses Simpson Grant: *American Caesar, Butcher Grant, Butcher from Galena, Great Hammerer, Great Peacemaker, Hero of Appomattox, Hero of Fort Donaldson, Hug Grant, Lyss, Old Three Stars, Sam, Silent Man, Tanner President, Texas, Uncle Sam, Uncle Sam Grant, Unconditional Surrender, Uniformed Soldier, Union Safeguard, United States, United States Grant, Unprecedented Strategist, Unquestionably Skilled,* and *Useless Grant.*

Ulysses Simpson Grant was dubbed the *American Caesar* [1] by his political enemies who feared he might be elected President of the United States for a third term, and that he would eventually secure a tyrannical hold upon the United States.

Because his campaigns against the Confederates exacted a tremendous sacrifice of lives on the part of his army, he was called by the Federals *Butcher Grant.* [2] He was also designated the *Butcher from Galena.* [1] He was living in Galena, Ill., at the outbreak of the Civil War.

The *Great Hammerer,* [3,4] is descriptive of Grant's usual military tactics, to pound away at the opposing forces, and by relentless pursuit overcome the enemy.

The *Great Peacemaker* [5] is a nickname applied to Grant because of his efforts to establish a workable peace after the Civil War.

The Federals acclaimed Grant the *Hero of Appomattox* because Lee surrendered to him at Appomattox Court House, Va., on April 9, 1865.

Because of his capture of Fort Donaldson, on the Cumberland River in Tennessee, on February 15, 1862, he has been called the *Hero of Fort Donaldson.* [5]

Ulysses Simpson Grant was named by his parents Hiram Ulysses Grant, consequently his playmates in the vicinity of Georgetown, Ohio, nicknamed him *Hug Grant,* [6] from his initials. He was also called *Lyss,* [7] an abbreviation of Ulysses.

Grant was called *Old Three Stars* [1] by his soldiers because of the silver-embroidered stars on his uniform.

Because he was exceedingly reticent about his plans and his policies, both public and private, Grant was nicknamed the *Silent Man.* [9]

Grant has been called the *Tanner President* [5] because in his youth he assisted his father in the tanning business.

When Grant's father made a long visit to Texas, young Ulysses talked so much about this trip that his friends dubbed him *Texas.* [7]

The change in his given name from Hiram Ulysses to Ulysses Simpson was made because Congressman Thomas L. Hamer, in filling in the papers necessary to secure Grant's appointment to the U.S. Military Academy erroneously gave his name as Ulysses Simpson Grant instead of Hiram Ulysses Grant. Many of his subsequent nicknames were a play on the initials U.S.

The nicknames *United States Grant* and *Uncle Sam* [8, 10, 11] were applied to him while he attended the United States Military Academy at West Point, N.Y., from 1839

Grant, U. S.—Continued
to 1843, and are merely a play upon his initials *U.S. Uncle Sam* was often shortened to *Sam*.

The nickname *Unconditional Surrender* [12] was conferred upon Grant while he was in command at the important Battle of Fort Donaldson on February 15, 1862. The opposing Confederate leaders proposed an armistice, to discuss plans for surrendering. General Grant replied that he would take only immediate and unconditional surrender.

Confederate newspapers altered the nickname *Unconditional Surrender* into such terms as *Uniformed Soldier, Union Safeguard, United States, Unprecedented Strategist*, and *Unquestionably Skilled*.[1]

During his youth near Georgetown, Ohio, he was sometimes called *Useless Grant*,[7] a play upon the word Ulysses.

Ulysses Simpson Grant, who was born at Point Pleasant, Ohio, on April 27, 1822, and who died at Mount McGregor, N.Y., on July 23, 1885, was the eighteenth President of the United States, serving from 1869 to 1877.

[1] *U.S. "Snap Shots": An Independent, National, and Memorial Encyclopedia . . .* , Oliver McKee (A. M. Thayer and Company, Boston, 1892) p. 310, 311.

[2] *Brief Biographies in American History*, Jennie B. Pope, Helen B. Clark and Robert G. Albion (Oxford Book Company, New York, 1930) p. 55.

[3] *History of the United States of America, under the Constitution*, James Schouler (Dodd, Mead and Company, New York, 1889) vol. 6, p. 602.

[4] *The Campaign in Virginia, May and June, 1864*, Thomas Miller Maguire (William Clowes and Sons, Limited, London, 1908) p. 56.

[5] *A Book of Nicknames*, John Goff (Courier-Journal Job Printing Company, Louisville, Ky., 1892) p. 22, 25, 27.

[6] *The Child's Book of American Biography*, Mary Stoyell Stimpson (Little, Brown and Company, Boston, 1915) p. 65, 66.

[7] *Story of the Life of Ulysses S. Grant; His Boyhood, Youth, Manhood, Public and Private Life and Service*, William M. Thayer (Thomas Nelson and Sons, New York and London, 1887) p. 53, 54.

[8] *Life and Letters of Alexander Hays*, ed. and arranged with notes and contemporary history by George Thornton Fleming from data comp. by Gilbert Adams Hays (Pittsburgh, Pa., 1919) p. 96.

[9] *The Book of Pioneers, True Adventures of Famous American Pioneers*, Everett T. Tomlinson (D. Appleton and Company, New York, 1926) p. 47.

[10] *The Encyclopedia Americana* (Americana Corporation, New York and Chicago, 1927) vol. 13, p. 135.

[11] *Pen Pictures of the Presidents*, Fred T. Wilson (Southwestern Company, Nashville, Tenn., 1932) p. 294-5.

[12] "Ulysses S. Grant" by Clifford Smith, in *Builders of America* (Funk and Wagnalls Company, New York and London, 1931) vol. 21, p. 58.

Grantham, George Farley

George Farley Grantham, who was born at Galena, Kans., on May 20, 1900, and

who played second base in major league baseball, was nicknamed *Boots*.[1]

[1] *Who's Who in Major League Base Ball*, comp. by Harold (Speed) Johnson (Buxton Publishing Company, Chicago, 1933) p. 180.

Gran'ther Hoar. See Hoar, G. F.

Grape-juice Diplomacy

When William Jennings Bryan was in President Wilson's cabinet, from 1913 to 1915, he served grape juice instead of alcoholic beverages at all public affairs for which he was host. He advocated and preached total abstinence. The newspapers of the day characterized his diplomatic procedures as *Grapejuice Diplomacy*.[1]

[1] *The National Cyclopaedia of American Biography* (James T. White and Company, New York, 1926) vol. 19, p. 454.

Grape State. See California

Grape-vine Telegraph

During the Civil War, the *Grape-vine Telegraph* [1] was the nickname given to imaginary telegraph lines over which messages came telling of battles that were never fought and giving other information intended to be misleading. Grape vine is common slang for rumor. Some say that the Confederate telegraph lines were called the *Grape-vine Telegraph* [2] because the news received over them was generally given out after dinner along with the bottle containing drinks.

[1] *Americanisms—Old and New*, John S. Farmer (Privately printed by Thomas Poulter and Sons, London, 1889) p. 274.

The Shorter Oxford English Dictionary on Historical Principles, prepared by William Little, revised and ed. by C. T. Onions (The Clarendon Press, Oxford, England, 1933) vol. 1, p. 822.

[2] *Camp, Court and Siege; A Narrative of Personal Adventure and Observation During Two Wars: 1861-1865; 1870-1871*, Wickham Hoffman (Harper and Brothers, New York, 877) p. 29.

Grasshopper State. See Kansas

Grasshopper Year

The year of 1874 has been generally designated by Kansas historians the *Grasshopper Year* [1] because of the swarms of grasshoppers throughout Kansas. Crops were destroyed and famine ensued.

[1] *History of Kansas State and People, Kansas at the First Quarter Post of the Twentieth Century*, written and comp. by William E. Connelley (The American Historical Society, Inc., New York and Chicago, 1928) vol. 2, p. 678.

Grasshoppers. See Kansans

Graupner, Johann Christian Gottlieb

Johann Christian Gottlieb Graupner, a musician and composer, was nicknamed the *Father of American Orchestral Music* [1] because he contributed greatly to the development of orchestral music in America and organized the Philharmonic Society at Boston, Mass., in 1810. He was called the *Father of Negro Songs* [2] because he introduced Negro songs in the Federal Street Theatre at Boston, Mass., on December 30, 1799, when at the end of the second act of *Oroonoko*, Graupner impersonated a Negro and sang *The Gay Negro Boy*, playing his own accompaniment on the banjo.

Johann Christian Gottlieb Graupner was born at Hanover, Germany, on October 6, 1767, became an American citizen in 1808, and died at Boston, in 1836.

[1] *Our American Music, Three Hundred Years of It*, Joseph Tasker Howard (Thomas Y. Crowell, New York, 1931) p. 135.
[2] *Famous First Facts*, Joseph Nathan Kane (The H. W. Wilson Company, New York, 1933) p. 351.

Graveyard of the Atlantic. See North Carolina

Gray, Finly Hutchinson

Finly Hutchinson Gray, a Democratic Representative from Indiana, was nicknamed the *Hoosier Shakespeare* [1] because he was from Indiana and therefore a *Hoosier*, and because his clothing and mannerisms reminded them of Shakespeare's characters.

Finly Hutchinson Gray was born on a farm in Columbia Township in Fayette County, Ind., on July, 1864.

[1] An interview with Captain Victor Hunt Harding, Secretary of the National Democratic Congress Reëlection Committee, Washington, D.C., April 10, 1939.

Gray, Gilda (Marianna Michalska)

The *Box Office Girl* [1] is the nickname attributed to Gilda Gray because she was successful in pleasing the public and in drawing large crowds to her performances.

[1] *Doug and Mary and Others*, Allene Talmey (Macy-Masius, New York, 1927) p. 88.

Graybacks

During the Civil War, the Union soldiers imprisoned at the Confederate military prison at Andersonville, Ga., nicknamed the body lice with which they became infested

Graybacks,[1] because of the color of the backs of these vermin, and in an unflattering allusion to the gray-uniformed Confederate soldiers.

About this time the Confederate money became known as *Graybacks*.[2]

[1] *Andersonville: A Story of Rebel Military Prisons, Fifteen Months a Guest of the So-called Southern Confederacy; a Private Soldier's Experience in Richmond, Andersonville, Savannah, Millen, Blackshear, and Florence*, John McElroy (E. R. Locke, Toledo, Ohio, 1879) p. 414.
[2] *Campaigning with Grant*, Horace Porter (The Century Company, New York, 1897) p. 392.

Gray-beard Regiment

A regiment of soldiers from Iowa who enlisted in the army in 1863 came to be called the *Gray-beard Regiment* [1] because they were from forty-five to sixty years of age.

[1] *The Story of the American Soldier in War and Peace*, Elbridge S. Brooks (D. Lothrop Company, Boston, 1889) p. 261.

Gray-crested Flycatcher. See Burroughs, John

Gray Eagle. See Nye, J. W.

Gray Fox. See Crook, George

Gray Mustang. See Frémont, J. C.

Great All American. See Fish, Hamilton, Jr.

Great American Commoner. See Stevens, Thaddeus

Great American Traveler. See Pratt, Daniel

Great Butter Rebellion

The *Great Butter Rebellion* [1] was staged in 1766 at Harvard College, Cambridge, Mass., when the students openly rebelled against having to eat the rancid butter served to them. They complained to the Board of Harvard College and then for several weeks expressed their indignation by acting in an unruly and disrespectful manner toward the college faculty and officials. The *Great Butter Rebellion* was terminated by Sir Francis Bernard, the Royal Governor of the Massachusetts Bay Colony, who read to

Great Butter Rebellion—Continued
them certain regulations which reminded
them of their obligations to the school, and
so succeeded in restoring order.

[1] *Bits of Harvard History.* Samuel F. Batchelder
(Harvard University Press, Cambridge, Mass., 1924)
p. 135.
   The History of Harvard University, Josiah Quincy
(John Owen, Cambridge, Mass. 1840) vol. 2, p. 99-100.

Great Central State. See North Dakota

Great Commoner. See Bryan, W. J.;
   Clay, Henry; Fowler, C. H.; Hogg,
   J. S.

Great Compromiser. See Clay, Henry

Great Dismal. See Washington, D.C.

Great Emancipator. See Lincoln, Abraham

Great Eye. See Schuyler, P. J.

Great Father at Detroit. See Cass,
   Lewis

Great Financier. See Sherman, John
   (Legislator)

Great Hammerer. See Grant, U. S.

Great Interpreter. See Webster, Daniel

Great Knives
   The white settlers in colonial America
were called the *Great Knives* [1] by the Indians because the pioneer hunters carried
long, heavy knives and the officers of the
militia wore swords.

[1] *Fort Ligonier and Its Times; a History of the
First English Fort West of the Allegheny Mountains and
an Account of Many Thrilling, Tragic, Romantic, Im-
portant but Little Known Colonial and Revolutionary
Events in the Region Where the Winning of the West
Began, Based Primarily on the Pennsylvania Archives
and Colonial Records,* First Edition, C. Hale Sipe (The
Telegraph Press, Harrisburg, Pa., 1933) p. 75.

Great Liberal. See Wheeler, B. K.

Great Marcher. See Sherman, W. T.

Great Nullifier. See Calhoun, J. C.

Great Objector. See Holman, W. S.

Great Ox-bow Route
   Established by an act of Congress in
1857, the Butterfield Overland Mail Route
from St. Louis, Mo., to San Francisco, Calif.,
was called the *Great Ox-bow Route* [1] because it greatly resembled a large ox bow
in shape when it was mapped out.

[1] *The Pony Express: The Record of a Romantic
Adventure in Business,* Arthur Chapman (G. P. Putman's
Sons, New York and London, 1932) p. 70.

Great Pacificator. See Clay, Henry;
   Cochrane, C. B.

Great Peacemaker. See Grant, U. S.

Great Purist. See Norris, G. W.

Great Repealer. See Barton, Bruce

Great River City. See St. Louis, Mo.

Great Smoky National Park
   The Great Smoky National Park has been
nicknamed the *Roof Top of Eastern America* [1] and the *Playground of Two Nations.* [1]
The *Roof Top of Eastern America* means
that the park is on the highest peak of the
Great Smoky Mountains with an elevation
of about 6642 ft. The *Playground of Two
Nations* signifies that the park lies along the
border of North Carolina and Tennessee.

[1] *Compton's Pictured Encyclopedia,* F. E. Compton and
Company, Chicago, 1947, vol. 10, p. 15.

Great South Gate. See New Orleans, La.

Great Stone Face. See Webster, Daniel

Great Thundering Rooster. See Johnson, H. S.

Great Triumvirate
   John Caldwell Calhoun, Henry Clay, and
Daniel Webster were often called the *Great
Triumvirate.* [1] Webster and Calhoun as
leaders of the antislavery and proslavery
factions and Clay as the great compromiser,
were the great law makers of their time in
Congress, and their abilities were best seen
when they were arrayed against each other.
However, they occasionally collaborated for
a common goal. The careers of the three
showed striking parallels: they were about
the same age, became representatives, and
later senators at about the same time, and

each served as Secretary of State. Each had a background in the law, each was at home on the rostrum, and each aspired to the presidency.[2]

[1] *A School History of the United States*, Philip Alexander Bruce (American Book Company, New York and Chicago, 1903) p. 242.

[2] *America: Its History and People*, by Harold Underwood Faulkner and Tyler Kepner (Harper & Brothers, New York and London, 1950) p. 216.

Great War Governor. See Curtin, A. G.

Great White Chief. See Roosevelt, Theodore

Great White Devil. See Van Cortlandt, Philip

Great Wolf. See Tryon, William

Great Wrestler. See Lincoln, Abraham

Greatest American Jurist. See Marshall, John

Greatest Primary Winter Wheat Market. See Kansas City, Mo.

Grecian Davies. See Davies, C. S.

Greek. See George, Charlie

Greeley, Ezekiel

Not because he was a sea-faring man was Ezekiel Greeley called *Old Captain Ezekiel*,[1] but because he was a capable, stern, and uncompromising lawyer and farmer who took a prominent part in the activities of his community and was recognized as a leader.

Ezekiel Greeley, Horace Greeley's grandfather, was born at Haverhill, Mass., on October 21, 1725, and died at what is now Hudson, N.H., then Nottingham West, N.H., on January 21, 1793.

[1] *The Life of Horace Greeley, Editor of the New York Tribune*, James Parton (Fields, Osgood, and Company, Boston, 1869) p. 29.

Genealogy of the Greeley-Greeley Family, George Herain Greeley (Frank Wood, Boston, 1905) p. 80.

Greeley, Horace

Horace Greeley was called the *Ghost*, *Old White Hat*, the *Prince of Journalists*, and the *Sage of Chappaqua*. While he was a young boy, Horace Greeley was nicknamed *The Ghost* [1] because of his exceptionally fair complexion and his long white hair which he wore uncut.

He was often called *Old White Hat* [2] because for many years he wore a high-topped white hat. His lack of interest in the current vogue in clothes caused him to be dressed usually in a somewhat peculiar fashion.

Because of his journalistic work, his genial personality, and his uplifting influence on humanity, Horace Greeley was designated *The Prince of Journalists*.[3]

During the latter part of his lifetime, Greeley was popularly called the *Sage of Chappaqua* [4] because he was an outstanding editor, educator, and moral leader. He purchased a farm at Chappaqua, N.Y., in 1853, and spent as much time there as he could spare from his office.

Horace Greeley was born at Amherst, N.H., on February 3, 1811, and died at Pleasantville, N.Y., on November 29, 1872.

[1] *The National Cyclopaedia of American Biography* (James T. White and Company, New York, 1893) vol. 3, p. 448.

[2] *The "Also Rans"; Great Men Who Missed Making the Presidential Goal*, Don C. Seitz (Thomas Y. Crowell Company, New York, 1928) p. 242.

"Horace Greeley, the Editor" by Francis Nicoll Zabriskie, in *American Orators and Reformers*, ed. by Carlos Martyn (Funk and Wagnalls, New York and London, 1890) p. 351.

[3] *A Book of Nicknames*, John Goff (Courier-Journal Job Printing Company, Louisville, Ky., 1892) p. 30.

[4] *Carl Schurz, Reformer, 1829-1906*, Claude Moore Fuess (Dodd, Mead and Company, New York, 1932) p. 201.

Dictionary of American Biography under the Auspices of the American Council of Learned Societies, ed. by Allen Johnson and Dumas Malone (Charles Scribner's Sons, New York, 1931) vol. 7, p. 531.

Green, Andrew Haswell

The nickname *The Father of Greater New York* [1] commemorated Andrew Haswell Green's outstanding services in increasing the size, wealth, and prestige of New York City. He advocated the consolidation of New York City with its immediate suburbs and boroughs into what is now known as Greater New York. On October 6, 1898, upon the completion of the consolidation, Green was presented with a gold medal inscribed *To The Father of Greater New York*.

[1] *The National Cyclopaedia of American Biography* (James T. White and Company, New York, 1906) vol. 13, p. 70.

Green, Nathan

Nathan Green was deservedly called the *Father of Equity in Tennessee* and the *Hardwicke of Tennessee.*

The sobriquet, the *Father of Equity in Tennessee*,[1] commemorated the fact that while he was Chief Justice of the Supreme Court of Tennessee from 1836 to 1852, he was influential in securing certain reforms in the judicial system and was active in developing the courts of equity.

The *Hardwicke of Tennessee*[2] is a nickname which originated in Green's accomplishments in law which were comparable to those of Phillip Yorke Hardwicke, an outstanding English jurist, who secured numerous reforms pertaining to the courts of equity.

Nathan Green was born in Amelia County, Va., on May 16, 1792, and died at Lebanon, Tenn., on March 30, 1866.

[1] *The National Cyclopaedia of American Biography* (James T. White and Company, New York, 1907) vol. 5, p. 552.

[2] *Tennessee, the Volunteer State*, 1769-1923, John Trotwood Moore and Austin P. Foster (The S. J. Clarke Publishing Company, Chicago, and Nashville, Tenn., 1923) vol. 2, p. 138.

Green Bag Message

In the late fall of 1819 a bitter controversy arose between Governor De Witt Clinton, of New York, and the State Senate because of Clinton's protest against the interference of Federal office holders in New York elections. In replying to the demands of the angry senators that he furnish proofs of his allegations, Clinton, in January 1821, sent a copious message to the Assembly, accompanied by numerous letters, affidavits, and other documents. Governor Clinton had packed the whole thing in a large, green bag. The message was therefore nicknamed The *Green Bag Message*.[2]

[1] *Stagecoach and Tavern Tales of the Old Northwest*, Harry Ellsworth Cole, ed. by Louise Phelps Kellogg (The Arthur H. Clark Company, Cleveland, Ohio, 1930) p. 33.

Green Bay National League Football Club, Incorporated

The *Green Bay Packers*[1] is the nickname commonly applied to the teams of the Green Bay National League Football Club, Inc., a member of the National Football League, at Green Bay, Wis. This name was originated in 1919 by the Acme Packing Company of Green Bay because this company sponsored the first team of the club.

[1] A communication from L. H. Joannes, President of The Green Bay National League Football Club, Inc., Green Bay, Wis., April 7, 1939.

Green Bay Packers. See Green Bay National League Football Club, Incorporated

Green Bay Races

During the settlement of the Northwest Territory in the middle decades of the nineteenth century, several men often desired the same tract of land. The one who became its owner was he who first filed his claim with the Government Land Office. In the vicinity of Green Bay in what is now Brown County, Wis., these contests of speed were popularly called the *Green Bay Races*[1] in allusion to the mad rush individuals would make to the Government Land Office at Green Bay to secure the title to a coveted piece of land.

[1] *History of the State of New York, Political and Governmental*, 1776-1822, ed. by Ray B. Smith and Willis Fletcher Johnson (The Syracuse Press, Inc., Syracuse, N.Y., 1922) vol. 1, p. 445.

Green Knights. See Saint Norbert College

Green Mountain Boys. See Vermonters

Green Mountain City. See Montpelier, Vt.

Green Mountain State. See Vermont

Green Tornadoes. See Wilmington College

Green Wave from Ohio. See Wilberforce University

Green Waves. See Wagner Memorial Lutheran College

Greenbacks

The legal-tender notes, issued originally by the United States Government about 1863, are called *Greenbacks*[1] because the backs are printed in green ink.

[1] *The Republican Party: A History*, William Starr Myers (The Century Company, New York, 1928) p. 139.

Greenbrier White Sulphur Springs, West Virginia

Greenbrier White Sulphur Springs has been nicknamed the *Saratoga of the South* [1] because it is a noted health resort having a great variety of mineral waters.

[1] *Compton's Pictured Encyclopedia* (F. E. Compton and Company, Chicago, 1933) vol. 15, p. 74.

Greene, Frederick Stuart

Frederick Stuart Greene, a civil engineer, was nicknamed the *Father of Concrete Roads in New York* [1] because it was during his administration as Commissioner of Highways of the State of New York from 1919 until 1921, and as Superintendent of Public Works of New York from 1923 until 1939, that he initiated concrete roadbuilding in the state and developed it to its present point of perfection.

Frederick Stuart Greene was born in Rappahannock County, Va., on April 14, 1870, and died in Washington, D.C., on March 26, 1939.

[1] *The Washington Post,* Mail Edition, Washington, D.C., March 28, 1939, col. 5, p. 17.

Greene, Nathanael

The *Fighting Quaker* [1] is a nickname given to Nathanael Greene, one of the ablest American generals under Washington's command. Although brought up a Quaker, Greene took an active part in the military activities of the colonies during the American Revolution. Because of this, he was excommunicated by the Quakers, who opposed war.

Nathanael Greene was born in Warwick County, R.I. on May 27, 1742, and died at Mulberry Grove, Ga., on June 19, 1786.

[1] *Hazen's Elementary History of the United States, a Story and a Lesson,* M. W. Hazen (The Morse Company, New York and Boston, 1903) p. 145.

Memoirs of the Life and Campaigns of the Honorable Nathanael Greene, Major-general in the Army of the United States, and Commander of the Southern Department, in the War of the Revolution, Charles Caldwell (Robert Desilver and Thomas Desilver, Philadelphia, 1819) p. 356.

Greenfield, Elizabeth Taylor

Elizabeth Taylor Greenfield was nicknamed the *Black Swan* [1] because she was a Negro, and a most successful singer both in the United States and in England. She was born a slave, but early in life gave such promise of developing into a singer that her mistress gave her her freedom and educated her.

Elizabeth Taylor Greenfield was born at Natchez, Miss., in 1808, and died at Philadelphia, Pa., in 1876.

[1] *Appleton's Cyclopaedia of American Biography,* ed. by James Grant Wilson and John Fiske (D. Appleton and Company, New York, 1894) vol. 2, p. 755.

Grenadiers. See Canisius College

Grey-eyed Man of Destiny. See Walker, William

Greyhound Regiment

During the Civil War, the Eighty-third Regiment of Ohio Volunteers was called the *Greyhound Regiment* [1] and those composing it were *Greyhounds.* In October 1862, the members of the Twenty-third Regiment of Wisconsin Volunteer Infantrymen referred to the Eighty-third Regiment as *Greyhounds* because they had surpassed the Twenty-third Regiment in marching and had arrived at their destination ahead of the Twenty-third.

[1] *History of the Eighty-third Ohio Volunteer Infantry, The Greyhound Regiment,* T. B. Marshall (The Eighty-third Ohio Volunteer Infantry Association, Cincinnati, Ohio, 1912) p. 1, p. 42.

Greyhounds. See *Greyhound Regiment*

Greyhounds. See Indiana Central College; Loyola College; Yankton College

Gridiron Widows

Gridiron Widows [1] was the name applied to the wives of the members and guests of the Gridiron Club of Washington, D.C., and the newspaper women of Washington, who were entertained each year in the East Room of the White House by Mrs. Franklin D. Roosevelt on the night when the Gridiron Club gave a dinner in honor of the President.

Mrs. Roosevelt inaugurated this entertainment, patterned largely after that of the Gridiron Club, in 1933, because women are not permitted to attend the Gridiron Club dinner.

The Gridiron Club of Washington, organized on January 24, 1885, entertains the President at its annual meeting by presenting skits and giving dramatizations of the President's personal characteristics and policies.

[1] *The Sunday Star,* Washington, D.C., December 18, 1938, Society Section, col. 2, p. D.

The Gridiron Club (Printed by W. F. Roberts Company, Washington, D.C., 1914) Constitution of the Club, art. 1, sec. 2, p. 15-16.

Griffith, Clark

Clark Griffith, a major league pitcher, was nicknamed the *Old Fox* [1] because he was tricky and resourceful. He was born at Clear Creek, Mo., on November 20, 1869.

[1] *Who's Who in Major League Baseball*, comp. by Harold (Speed) Johnson (Buxton Publishing Company, Chicago, 1933) p. 44.

Grim Chieftain. See Lane, J. H.

Grim Old Lion of Athens. See Grosvenor, C. H.

Grimes, Burleigh A.

Burleigh A. Grimes, who was born at Emerald, Wis., on August 18, 1893, and who pitched in major league baseball, was nicknamed *Senator*.[1]

[1] *Who's Who in Major League Baseball*, comp. by Harold (Speed) Johnson (Buxton Publishing Company, Chicago, 1933) p. 44.

Grinnell College

The teams of Grinnell College, at Grinnell, Iowa, were nicknamed the *Pioneers* [1] because it was one of the first colleges established west of the Mississippi River, and had the first athletic teams and first athletic meets in that region.

[1] A communication from John C. Truesdale, Director of Athletics at Grinnell College, Grinnell, Iowa, June 18, 1935.

Grizzlies. See Franklin College of Indiana; State University of Montana

Grosvenor, Charles Henry

The sobriquets, *Gentle Shepherd of Ohio, Grim Old Lion of Athens,* and *Old Figgers* were applied to Charles Henry Grosvenor.

While he was serving as a Republican Representative from Ohio to Congress from 1885 to 1891 and from 1893 to 1907, he took an active part in securing legislation favorable to the sheep-growers in that state. This caused him to be given the nickname of the *Gentle Shepherd of Ohio*.[1]

During his congressional term he was called the *Grim Old Lion of Athens* [1] by his colleagues because he was fierce and formidable as an opponent. He had made his home in Athens, Ohio.

Old Figgers [1] arose from his habit of making forecasts regarding the results of coming elections.

Charles Henry Grosvenor was born at Pomfret, Conn., on September 20, 1833, and died at Athens, Ohio, on October 30, 1917.

[1] *Roosevelt: The Happy Warrior*, Bradley Gilman (Little, Brown and Company, Boston, 1921) p. 111.
[1] *My Quarter Century of American Politics*, Champ Clark (Harper and Brothers, New York and London, 1920) vol. 2, p. 205-6.

Ground-hog State. See Mississippi

Grover, Martin

The *Ragged Lawyer* [1] was the name applied to Martin Grover because for many years, totally indifferent to his personal appearance, he customarily appeared in court and elsewhere dressed in clothes that were old and shabby.

Martin Grover was born at Hartwick, N.Y., in 1811, and died at Angelica, N.Y., on August 23, 1875.

[1] *The National Cyclopaedia of American Biography* (James T. White and Company, New York, 1909) vol. 11, p. 272.

Grow, Galusha Aaron

Galusha Aaron Grow has been called the *Father of the Homestead Law* [1] because he introduced the Homestead Bill into the lower House of Congress on March 30, 1852, and in 1862 finally secured its enactment.

Galusha Aaron Grow, who was born at what is now Eastford, Conn., on August 31, 1823, and who died at Glenwood, Pa., on March 31, 1907, was a Representative from Pennsylvania to Congress from 1850 to 1863, and again from 1894 to 1903.

[1] *Galusha A. Grow, Father of the Homestead Law*, James T. DuBois and Gertrude S. Mathews (Houghton Mifflin Company, New York and Boston, 1917) p. 146, 261.

Grub Wagon

When ranching and grazing were important factors in life on the western plains the wagon which carried food and equipment was called the *Grub Wagon*.[1]

[1] *Jungle Roads and Other Trails of Roosevelt*, Daniel Henderson (E. P. Dutton and Company, New York, 1920) p. 62.

Guano Statesman. See Blaine, J. G.

Guardian Angels

During World War I Americans who traveled as passengers on armed vessels of belligerent powers were called *Guardian*

Angels.[1] In theory other belligerents would hesitate to attack a ship carrying American passengers.

[1] *The Strangest Friendship in History, Woodrow Wilson and Colonel House,* George Sylvester Viereck (Liveright Inc., New York, 1932) p. 182.

Congressional Record, Containing the Proceedings and Debates of the First Session of the Sixty-fourth Congress of the United States of America (Government Printing Office, Washington, D.C., 1916) vol. 534, p. 3120.

Guardian of Civil Service. See Ramspeck, Robert

Guffey, Joseph F.

Joseph F. Guffey has been called the *Kingmaker*[1] because of his influence in the Senate.

Joseph F. Guffey was born in Westmoreland County, Pa., on December 29, 1875. He served as a Senator from Pennsylvania from 1934 to 1947.

[1] *Washington Herald,* Washington, D.C., February 8, 1935, col. 7, p. 8.

Guilford College

The *Quakers* is the appellation applied to the teams of Guilford College, at Guilford College Post Office, N.C., because this is a Quaker college.

Guinan, Mary Louise Cecelia

Mary Louise Cecelia Guinan, a motion picture actress and night-club entertainer, was nicknamed the *Night-club Queen, Texas Guinan,* and the *Two-gun Girl.* She was called *The Night-club Queen*[1] because she was a successful night-club entertainer. *Texas Guinan*[1] was applied to her because she was born in Texas. She was nicknamed *The Two-gun Girl*[1] because she played western cowgirls armed with two revolvers in motion pictures.

Mary Louise Cecelia Guinan was born at Waco, Tex., in 1884, and died at Vancouver, British Columbia, on November 5, 1933.

[1] *The Washington Times,* Washington, D.C., November 6, 1933, col. 5, p. 2.

Guinea Pig State. See Arkansas

Guldin, John C.

John C. Guldin, a clergyman, was known as the *Apostle to the Germans*[1] because he was active as a missionary and preacher to the German immigrants and their descendants in Pennsylvania and in New York State

from 1820 until 1863. He was in charge of the German religious literature published by the American Tract Society, and edited the hymnal since used by the members of the German Presbyterian Churches.

John C. Guldin was born in Bucks County, Pa., in 1799, and died at New York City, in 1863.

[1] *Appleton's Cyclopaedia of American Biography,* ed. by James Grant Wilson and John Fiske (D. Appleton and Company, New York, 1888) vol. 3, p. 12.

Gulf City. See Mobile, Ala.; New Orleans, La.

Gulf State. See Florida

Gumshoe. See Hunter, W. G.

Gunboat. See Hudson, Walter

Gunflints. See Rhode Islanders

Gustavus Adolphus College

The athletic teams of the Gustavus Adolphus College, at St. Peter, Minn., are called the *Shrouds* and the *Galloping Swedes*[1] because most of the players are of Swedish descent.

[1] A communication from O. J. Jackson, President of Gustavus Adolphus College, St. Peter, Minn., November 18, 1935.

Guyer, Ulysses Samuel

Ulysses Samuel Guyer, a Kansas politician, was nicknamed the *Dry Wind* and the *Kansas Dry* in Congress because he was a strong prohibitionist who perennially introduced bills into the House of Representatives to prohibit the sale and use of intoxicating liquors in the District of Columbia.

Ulysses Samuel Guyer was born in Lee County, Ill., on December 13, 1863.

[1] An interview with Captain Victor Hunt Harding, Secretary of the National Democratic Congressional Reëlection Committee, Washington, D.C., April 10, 1939.

Gwaltney, Pembroke Decatur

In commemoration of his services as a pioneer in developing the peanut industry of the South, Pembroke Decatur Gwaltney was called the *Peanut King.*[1] He began to raise peanuts about 1868 in Surry County, Va. Later he bought peanuts which he shelled, cleaned, graded, and marketed and established his first peanut factory at Smithfield. In 1906 he became president of the newly

Gwaltney, P. D.—Continued
established American Peanut Corporation.

Gwaltney was born in Isle of Wight County, Va., September 21, 1836, and died at Smithfield, Va., February 10, 1914.

[1] *The National Cyclopaedia of American Biography* (James T. White and Company, New York, 1920) vol. 17, p. 113.

Gymnasts. See International Young Men's Christian Association College

Gypsy Smith. See Smith, Rodney

H

Haas, George W.
While George W. Haas was playing baseball in the Southern League at Birmingham, Ala., in 1925, baseball writers spoke of his having the "kick of a mule in every wallop," so he was nicknamed *Mule.*[1]

George W. Haas was born at Montclair, N.J., on October 15, 1903, and played outfield in major league baseball.

[1] *Who's Who in Major League Baseball,* comp. by Harold (Speed) Johnson (Buxton Publishing Company, Chicago, 1933) p. 190.

Habeas Corpus Howe. See Howe, W. F.

Hack. See Wilson, L. R.

Hadley, Irving D.
Bump[1] is the nickname given to Irving D. Hadley, who was born at Lynn, Mass., on July 5, 1904, and who pitched in major league baseball.

[1] *Who's Who in Major League Baseball,* comp. by Harold (Speed) Johnson (Buxton Publishing Company, Chicago, 1933) p. 191.

Hagner, Peter
The *Watch-dog of the Treasury*[1] was the nickname given to Peter Hagner while he was auditor of the United States Treasury, beginning in 1817. It is said that he was the first treasury official to whom this sobriquet was applied.

Peter Hagner was born at Philadelphia, Pa., on October 1, 1772, and died at Washington, D.C., on July 16, 1850.

[1] *The National Cyclopaedia of American Biography* (James T. White and Company, New York, 1932) vol. 22, p. 372.

Hague, Frank
Frank Hague, Mayor of Jersey City, N.J., was nicknamed *Boss Hague* and the *Dictator of Jersey City*[1] when he was mayor of that city from 1917 to 1937.

Frank Hague was born at Jersey City, N.J., on January 17, 1876.

[1] *New York Post*, January 24, 1938, p. 1, 8.

Hale, Arnel Odell
Arnel Odell Hale, who was born at Hosston, La., on August 10, 1909, and who played infield in major-league baseball, is nicknamed *Chief.*[1] He had at one time played with the Cleveland Indians.

[1] *Who's Who in Major League Baseball,* comp. by Harold (Speed) Johnson (Buxton Publishing Company, Chicago, 1933) p. 194.

Hale, Sarah Josepha
Sarah Josepha Hale, an author and editor, was nicknamed the *Mother of Thanksgiving*[1] because her editorials on Thanksgiving in *The Lady's Book* influenced President Abraham Lincoln to issue his Thanksgiving proclamation in 1864 declaring the last Thursday in November a national day of thanksgiving for the people of the United States. Since President Lincoln's proclamation, each President of the United States has issued an annual Thanksgiving proclamation following his precedent.

She became the literary editor of *The Lady's Book* in 1837, a magazine established by Louis A. Godey at Philadelphia, Pa., and was the author of "Mary Had a Little Lamb."

Sarah Josepha Hale was born at Newport, N.H., on October 24, 1788, and died at Philadelphia, Pa., on April 30, 1879.

[1] *The Sunday Star*, Washington, D.C., April 9, 1939, part 3, col. 2, p. D-8.

Half-breeds
From about 1875 to 1881, Roscoe Conkling was a prominent leader of the Republican party. Those who only partially supported his direction of the Republican party, adhering to President James Abram Garfield's policies of administration, were nicknamed *Half-breeds.*[1]

[1] *Reconstruction and Union,* 1865-1912, Paul Leland Haworth (Henry Holt and Company, New York, 1912) p. 107.

Hall, Abraham Oakey

Abraham Oakey Hall, a lawyer, politician, and author, was nicknamed *Mayor Von O' Hall* [1] while he was Mayor of New York City from 1868 until 1872, because he was particularly attentive to the wants of the Irish and the German people in order to secure their votes. Hall was also called *Elegant Oakey* because of his fastidious dress, and manners, and his social eminence in New York City.

Abraham Oakey Hall was born at Albany, N.Y., on July 26, 1826, and died at New York City, on October 7, 1898.

[1] *Dictionary of American Biography under the Auspices of the American Council of Learned Societies*, ed. by Dumas Malone (Charles Scribner's Sons, New York, 1932) vol. 8, p. 115.

Hall, Musa L.

The *Madonna of Hall-Moody* was applied to Miss Musa L. Hall at Hall-Moody Institute, at Martin, Tenn., because of her noble ideals and the influence she exerted on the life of the college community.

Miss Hall taught at Hall-Moody Institute from 1904 or 1905 to 1918. She was born in Weakley County, Tenn., on February 15, 1877.

Halleck, Fitz-Green. See Drake, J. R. and Fitz-Green Halleck

Halleck, Henry Wager

The nickname *Old Brains* [1] was given to Major General Henry Wager Halleck in 1861 because of the ability he displayed at the outbreak of the Civil War in reorganizing the Department of the Missouri, then in a state of chaos, and in directing the military activities of the Union Army.

Henry Wager Halleck was born at Westernville, N.Y., on January 16, 1815, and died at Louisville, Ky., on January 19, 1872.

[1] *Men and Things I Saw in Civil War Days*, James F. Rusling (Eaton and Mains, New York, 1899) p. 176.

Ham Young. See Young, W. H.

Hamilton, Alexander

Alexander the Coppersmith, the *Father of the Tariff,* and the *Little Lion* are nicknames attributed to Alexander Hamilton.

When he was Secretary of the Treasury, Alexander Hamilton was called *Alexander the Coppersmith* [1] because he was responsible for the coining of the first copper one-cent pieces.

Hamilton was nicknamed the *Father of the Tariff* [2] because he organized the United States Treasury Department, and devised a system of national taxation and a means of raising and collecting internal revenue. He established the National Bank and the mint, and insisted on paying off the Revolutionary War debts. His zeal in these matters (and his small stature) caused him to be called the *Little Lion.* [3]

Alexander Hamilton was born at Charlestown, West Indies, on January 11, 1757, and died at New York City, on July 12, 1804.

[1] *A History of the People of the United States, from the Revolution to the Civil War*, John Bach McMaster (D. Appleton and Company, New York, 1883) vol. 1, p. 404.

[2] *A Book of Nicknames*, John Goff (Courier-Journal Job Printing Company, Louisville, Ky., 1892) p. 21.

[3] "Alexander Hamilton" by Clifford Smyth, in *Builders of America* (Funk and Wagnalls Company, New York and London, 1931) vol. 14, p. 142, 165.

The United States, Theodore Calvin Pease (Harcourt Brace and Company, New York, 1927) p. 221-4.

Hamilton, Alfred Reed

The nickname the *Father of Pitt Stadium* [1] was applied to Alfred Reed Hamilton because of his leadership in planning the great stadium at the University of Pittsburgh and in selling the bonds to finance it.

Alfred Reed Hamilton was born at Allegheny City, Pa., on July 19, 1872, and died at Pittsburgh, Pa., on March 28, 1927.

[1] *Encyclopedia of American Biography: American Biography, a New Cyclopedia*, comp. under the supervision of a notable advisory board (Published under the direction of The American Historical Society, Inc., New York, 1928) vol. 39, p. 34.

Hamilton, Andrew

Andrew Hamilton was nicknamed the *Day-star of the Revolution* [1] by Gouverneur Morris of New York, because Hamilton was a great advocate of liberty, was one of the purchasers of the ground upon which Independence Hall was built in Philadelphia, Pa., and opposed the arbitrary displacing of judges by the British authorities and the erecting of new courthouses without the consent of the colonists.

Andrew Hamilton was born in Scotland about 1676, and died at Philadelphia, Pa., on August 4, 1741.

[1] *Appleton's Cyclopaedia of American Biography*, ed. by James Grant Wilson and John Fiske (D. Appleton and Company, New York, 1888) vol. 3, p. 61.

Hamilton, John Daniel Miller

John Daniel Miller Hamilton, who was formerly Chairman of the Republican National Committee, and who was campaign manager for Governor Alfred Mossman Landon during the presidential campaign of 1936, was popularly called *Torchy*.[1] Mr. Hamilton has red hair and quick flaring wit.

John Daniel Miller Hamilton was born at Fort Madison, Iowa, on March 2, 1892.

[1] *Washington Herald*, Washington, D.C., June 10, 1936, p. 28.

Hamilton College

The *Continentals*[1] is the nickname given to the athletic teams of Hamilton College, at Clinton, N.Y., because of the connection of Alexander Hamilton with the founding of the college, which grew out of the Hamilton Oneida Academy of which Alexander Hamilton was the first trustee.[1]

[1] A communication from Frederick C. Ferry, President of Hamilton College, Clinton, N.Y., November 21, 1935.

Hamline Pipers. See Hamline University

Hamline University

The athletic teams of Hamline University, at Saint Paul, Minn., are called the *Hamline Pipers*[1] from "The Pied Piper of Hamlin."

[1] A communication from Charles N. Pace, President of Hamline University, Saint Paul, Minn., November 18, 1935.

Hammond, James Henry

James Henry Hammond, a Senator from South Carolina, was frequently referred to as *Mudsill Hammond*[1] in allusion to an unfortunate statement in a speech on the admission of Kansas made in the Senate on March 4, 1858. He said that in all society there had to be people who were unskilled, and fitted only to perform menial labor, that this group was "the mud-sill of society and of political government," and that any attempt to construct a social order on any other foundation than this mud-sill would be like trying to build on the air.

Senator James Henry Hammond was born in Newberry District, S.C., on November 15, 1807, and died at Beech Island, S.C., on November 13, 1864.

[1] *Appleton's Cyclopaedia of American Biography*, ed. by James Grant Wilson and John Fiske (D. Appleton and Company, New York, 1891) vol. 3, p. 67.

[4] *Speech of Honorable James H. Hammond, of South Carolina, on the Admission of Kansas, under the Lecompton Constitution, Delivered in the Senate of the United States, March 4, 1858* (Lemuel Towers, Washington, D.C., 1858) p. 13, 14.

"James Henry Hammond, 1807 to 1864" by Elizabeth Merritt, in the *Johns Hopkins University Studies on Historical and Political Science under the Direction of the Departments of History, Political Economy, and Political Science* (The Johns Hopkins Press, Baltimore, Md., 1923) p. 119.

Hammondsport, New York

Hammondsport was nicknamed the *Cradle of Aviation* because of the pioneer work in aviation done by Glenn Hammond Curtiss there. Curtiss owned a bicycle shop, and he and one of his assistants, Lieutenant Thomas Selfridge, began to experiment with building and flying airplanes in 1908. Selfridge flew his airplane, "The Red Wing," over Lake Keuka near Hammondsport on March 12, 1908, a little more than three years after Orville and Wilbur Wright had flown their biplane successfully at Kittyhawk, N.C., on December 17, 1903. Curtiss created a sensation by flying his "June Bug" over the old racetrack near Hammondsport on July 4, 1908.

[1] *The Evening Star*, Washington, D.C., July 24, 1930, col. 6, p. A-9.

Hampton Institute

The *Seasiders* is the nickname given to the athletic teams of Hampton Institute, at Hampton, Va., because the school is located on the Chesapeake Bay near where it connects with the Atlantic Ocean.

Hancock, Clarence Eugene

Clarence Eugene Hancock, a lawyer and politician, was nicknamed *Banty*[1] when he was a Representative from New York from 1927 to 1947. He was a medium sized man with the characteristics of a game cock.

[1] An interview with Captain Victor Hunt Harding, Secretary of the National Democratic Congress Reelection Committee, Washington, D.C., April 10, 1939.

Hancock, Cornelia

The soldiers in the Battle of Gettysburg nicknamed Cornelia Hancock, who served as a volunteer nurse in the Second Army Corps of the Potomac from July 6, 1863 to May 23, 1865, the *Battlefield Angel*.[1]

[1] *Women in American History: The Part Taken by Women in American History*, Mrs. John A. Logan (The Perry-Nalle Publishing Company, Wilmington, Del., 912) p. 366.

Hancock, John

King Hancock and the *King of the Smugglers* were nicknames given to John Hancock.

He was called *King Hancock* [1] by the British and their sympathizers, because he was a man of wealth, entertained in a lavish manner, and appeared on public occasions richly dressed, attended by servants in showy livery and armed horsemen.

The British also called Hancock the *King of the Smugglers* [2] because, as a ship-owner and a wealthy importer, he was said to be one of the leaders in smuggling goods into the colonies to avoid taxation.

John Hancock was born at Braintree, Mass., on January 23, 1737, and died at Quincy, Mass., on October 8, 1793.

[1] *Metropolitan Boston, a Modern History*, Albert P. Langtry, Editor-in-chief (Lewis Historical Publishing Company, Inc., New York, 1929) vol. 1, p. 195.

[2] *The Story of Our American People; Volume One—The Divided Colonies, Volume Two—The United States,* Charles F. Horne (United States Publishing Company, New York, 1926) vol. 1, p. 340.

Hand and Pen of the Congress. See Thompson, Charlie

Handcuff King. See Houdini, Harry

Handkerchief Moody. See Moody, Joseph

Handsome Jack. See Tucker, J. R.

Handy, William Christopher

William Christopher Handy, a Negro musician, composer, and musical publisher, is called the *Father of the Blues.*[1] The "blues," a type of Negro sorrow song which is now an integral part of modern jazz and accepted in polite musical circles, was popularized largely through the efforts of Handy, who published the *Memphis Blues* in 1912. He has composed and published more than 150 songs, among them the *St. Louis Blues,* the *Yellow Dog Blues* and the *Beale Street Blues.* He is also the author of a number of well-known Negro spirituals.

William Christopher Handy was born in Florence, Ala., November 16, 1873.

[1] *Newsweek: The Magazine of News Significance,* Rockefeller Center, N.Y., November 28, 1938, col. 1, p. 36.

Who's Who in Colored America: a Biographical Dictionary of Notable Living Persons of African Descent in America, 1930-1931-1932, Third Edition (Thomas Yenser, Editor and Publisher, Brooklyn, N.Y., 1933) p. 189.

Handy Andy. See Sommerville, Andrew

Hangman Foote. See Foote, H. S.

Hangman of Buffalo. See Cleveland, Grover

Hannah More of America. See Mercer, Margaret

Hannibal, Missouri

Hannibal is nicknamed the *Bluff City* [1] because it is located upon picturesque bluffs overlooking the Mississippi River and the adjacent country.

[1] *Americanisms; The English of the New World,* M. Schele De Vere (Charles Scribner and Company, New York, 1872) p. 663.

Centennial History of Missouri (The Center State) One Hundred Years in the Union, 1820-1921, Walter B. Stevens (The S. J. Clarke-Publishing Company, St. Louis, Mo., and Chicago, 1921) vol. 1, p. 95.

Encyclopedia of the History of Missouri: A Compendium of History and Biography for Ready Reference, Howard L. Conard, Editor (The Southern History Company, Haldeman, Conard and Company, Proprietors, New York, Louisville, and St. Louis, 1901) vol. 3, p. 167-9.

Hanover College

The *Hillbillies,* the *Hilltoppers,* and the *Panthers* are the nicknames which have been given to the athletic teams of Hanover College, at Hanover, Ind. Until about 1928 they were called *Hilltoppers* [1] because the college is located on a high bluff overlooking the Ohio River. Rival teams changed the nickname to the *Hillbillies.* In 1928 the *Panthers* [2] became the official name of the teams.

[1] A letter from C. V. Money, Director of Athletics at Hanover College, Hanover, Ind., June 19, 1935.

Hansen, Roy Fred

Roy Fred Hansen, who was born at Chicago, Ill., on February 21, 1910, and who pitched in major league baseball, was nicknamed *Snipe* [1] because, while he was at Catalina Island on a training trip with the Chicago Cubs in 1926 or 1927, he went on a traditional snipe hunt.

[1] *Who's Who in Major League Base Ball,* comp. by Harold (Speed) Johnson (Buxton Printing Company, Chicago, 1933) p. 196.

Hanson, Roger Weightman

Roger Weightman Hanson, a Confederate Army officer, was called *Old Flintlock* [1] by his soldiers because of his excellence as a drillmaster and his interest in

Hanson, R. W.—Continued
their welfare. The guns used in the Civil
War were flintlocks.

Roger Weightman Hanson was born at
Winchester, Ky., on August 27, 1827, and
died at Murfreesboro, Tenn., on January 4,
1863.

[1] *Dictionary of American Biography under the Auspices of the American Council of Learned Societies,* ed.
by Dumas Malone (Charles Scribner's Sons, New York,
1932) vol. 8, p. 233.

Happy Chandler. See Chandler, A. B.

Happy Warrior. See Roosevelt,
Theodore; Sheets, F. H.; Smith, A. E.

Happy Valley
During the early decades of the nineteenth century, the pioneer settlers of the
Tennessee Valley commonly called it the
Happy Valley [1] because of its fertility and
productiveness, its natural resources, and
its promise of rapid industrial and cultural
development.

[1] *History of Alabama and Her People,* Albert Burton
Moore, assisted by an advisory council (The American
Historical Society, Inc., New York and Chicago, 1927)
vol. 1, p. 105.

Hard-case State. See Oregon

Hard Cases. See Oregonians

Hard-headed Pete. See Stuyvesant,
Peter

Harder, Melvin Leroy
Chief [1] was the sobriquet by which Melvin
Leroy Harder was often called because those
who have played with the Cleveland Indians are frequently so designated.

Melvin Leroy Harder was born at Beemer,
Neb., on October 15, 1909, and pitched in
major-league baseball.

[1] *Who's Who in Major League Baseball,* comp. by
Harold (Speed) Johnson (Buxton Publishing Company,
Chicago, 1933) p. 197.

Hardin, Benjamin
While he was a Representative from Kentucky to Congress for several terms between
1815 and 1837, Benjamin Hardin was called
the *Terror of the House* [1] because he
aroused fear by scathingly censuring those
who opposed him in debate.

Benjamin Hardin was born in Westmoreland County, Pa., on February 29, 1784,
and died at Bardstown, Ky., on September
24, 1852.

[1] *Our Living Representative Men, from Official and
Original Sources,* John Savage (Childs and Peterson,
Philadelphia, 1860) p. 145.

Hardin-Simmons University
The *Cowboys,* the *Cowhands,* and the
Ranchers are the nicknames given to the
athletic teams of Hardin-Simmons University, at Abilene, Tex. They were chosen by
the student body.

[1] A letter from J. D. Sandefer, President of Hardin-Simmons University, Abilene, Tex., November 20, 1935.

Hardknockers. See South Dakota State
School of Mines

Hardkopping Piet. See Stuyvesant, Peter

Hard Shell Baptists. See *Primitive
Baptists*

Hardware City of the World. See New
Britain, Connecticut

Hardwicke of Tennessee. See Green,
Nathan

Hare, William Hobart
The *Apostle to the Sioux Indians* and
Swift Bird are nicknames given to William
Hobart Hare.

From 1873 to 1904, Hare was missionary
Bishop of the Episcopal Church to the Sioux
Indians. He did missionary work, founded
missions, established schools, and cultivated
Christianity among the Sioux Indians in
South Dakota and was called the *Apostle
to the Sioux Indians.* [1]

Because of the rapidity with which he
made long journeys in his diocese, Bishop
Hare was called *Swift Bird* [1] by the Indians.

William Hobart Hare was born at Princeton, N.J., on May 17, 1838, and died at
Atlantic City, N.J., on October 23, 1909.

[1] *History of South Dakota: South Dakota Sui Generis,
Stressing the Unique and Dramatic in South Dakota
History,* Doane Robinson (The American Historical
Society, Inc., Chicago and New York, 1930) vol. 1,
p. 452, 480.

Hargrave, William McKinley

Because he has red hair, *Pinkey* [1] is the nickname given to William McKinley Hargrave, who was born at New Haven, Ind., on January 31, 1900, and who was catcher in major league baseball.

[1] *Who's Who in Major League Base Ball*, comp. by Harold (Speed) Johnson (Buxton Publishing Company, Chicago, 1933) p. 198.

Harmer, Alfred Crout

The *Father of the House* [1] as applied to Alfred Crout Harmer, commemorated the fact that for more than a quarter century he was a Representative from Pennsylvania to Congress.

Alfred Crout Harmer was born at Germantown, Pa., on August 8, 1825, and died there on March 6, 1900.

[1] *My Quarter Century of American Politics*, Champ Clark (Harper and Brothers, New York and London, 1920) vol. 1, p. 221-2.

Harnett, Cornelius

Cornelius Harnett, a statesman, was called the *Samuel Adams of North Carolina* [1] because he was as prominent in colonial North Carolina as Samuel Adams was in the Massachusetts Bay Colony. The nickname was originated about 1773 when Harnett influenced the North Carolina Colonial Assembly to appoint a committee of correspondence to negotiate with the royal authorities in America and in England concerning the grievances of the colonists. He was active in organizing civil and military opposition to the mother country.

Cornelius Harnett was apparently born in Chowan County, S.C., on April 20, probably in 1723, and died at Wilmington, N.C., on April 28, 1781.

[1] *Dictionary of American Biography under the Auspices of the American Council of Learned Societies*, ed. by Dumas Malone (Charles Scribner's Sons, New York, 1932) vol. 8, p. 279.

Harold (Speed) Johnson. See Johnson, Harold

Haroun-al-Roosevelt. See Roosevelt, Theodore

Harriman, Edward H.

The fact that Edward H. Harriman was a gigantic figure in the financial world and a railroad magnate, caused him to be given the nickname *The Colossus of Roads.* [1] The nickname is a pun on the name of the giant statue which, in ancient times, stood at the harbor entrance of the island of Rhodes in the eastern Mediterranean Sea.

Edward H. Harriman was born at Hempstead, Long Island, N.Y., on February 25, 1848, and died at his home, "Arden," in Orange County, N.Y., on September 9, 1909.

[1] *Builders of Empire*, Floyd L. Darrow (Longmans, Green and Company, New York, 1930) p. 23.

Harrington, Francis C.

Lieutenant Colonel Francis C. Harrington was nicknamed *Pinky* [1] when he entered the United States Military Academy at West Point, N.Y., in 1915, because of his sanguine complexion. He was appointed Administrator of the Works Progress Administration by President Franklin Delano Roosevelt on December 24, 1938, but he still retained his rank as Lieutenant Colonel in the United States Army.

Francis C. Harrington, was born at Bristol, Va., on December 10, 1887, and died September 30, 1940.

[1] *Washington Herald*, Washington, D.C., December 22, 1938, col. 8, p. 1.

Harrington, Vincent Francis

Vincent Francis Harrington, an Iowa educator and politician, was nicknamed *Seven Mules Harrington* [1] in the House of Representatives because he played football at Notre Dame in 1924 when "the *Four Horsemen* and *Seven Mules* constituted the team." He was elected Democratic Representative from Iowa in November 1936, and served from January 1937 until his resignation on September 5, 1942, to accept a commission as major in the Air Corps, U.S. Army.

Vincent Francis Harrington was born at Sioux City, Iowa, on May 16, 1903, and died at Rutlandshire, England, on November 29, 1943, while on active duty.

[1] An interview with Captain Victor Hunt Harding, Secretary of the National Democratic Congress Reëlection Committee, Washington, D.C., April 10, 1939.

Biographical Directory of the American Congress, 1774-1949. (U.S. Govt. Printing Office, Wash., D.C., 1950) p. 1271.

Harris, Benjamin

Benjamin Harris, the first American journalist, a bookseller, author, and publisher, has been nicknamed the *Father of American Newspapers* [1] because he published the first American newspaper, *Public Occurrences, Both Foreign and Domestic,* at Boston,

Harris, Benjamin—Continued

Mass., on September 25, 1690. It was printed for Harris by Richard Pierce, and consisted of three pages of American news, chiefly without advertisements. Harris had planned to publish the *Public Occurrences* monthly, but the first issue so displeased the governor and the Council of the Massachusetts Bay Colony that they forbade its publication because it had been published without a license and because it contained references to the French king and to the Mohawk Indians.[2]

Benjamin Harris began his publishing career at London, in 1673, came to Boston, Mass., in 1686. He died at London but the date is unknown.

[1] *Famous First Facts*, Joseph Nathan Kane (The H. W. Wilson Company, New York, 1933) p. 363.

[2] *The Early Massachusetts Press, 1638-1711*, George Emery Littlefield (The Club of Odd Volumes, Boston, 1907) vol. 2, p. 46.

Harris, David Stanley

David Stanley Harris, who was born on a farm in North Carolina on July 27, 1903, and who played outfield in major-league baseball was nicknamed *Sheriff* [1] because he had been at one time a deputy sheriff in North Carolina.

[1] *Who's Who in Major League Base Ball*, comp. by Harold (Speed) Johnson (Buxton Publishing Company, Chicago, 1933) p. 199.

Harris, James Armstrong

The *Father of the Florida Orange Industry* and the *Orange King* [1] are nicknames by which James Armstrong Harris has been called because he was a pioneer in establishing the orange industry in Florida and came to be the foremost owner of orange groves in that state.

He was interested in improving the flavor and the quality of the oranges and, is credited with being one of the first to popularize grapefruit in the North.

James Armstrong Harris was born at Yalaha-on-Lake Harris, in Lake County, Fla., on February 5, 1847, and died at Crystal River, Fla., on December 30, 1921.

[1] *The National Cyclopaedia of American Biography* (James T. White and Company, New York, 1909) vol. 19, p. 166.

Harris, Joel Chandler

Joel Chandler Harris was widely known as *Uncle Remus* [1] because he had written folk tales which gained for him international reputation using "Uncle Remus" as a

pseuonym. These tales about animals were told by an old Negro called "Uncle Remus."

Harris was born at Eatonton, Ga., on December 8, 1848, and died at Atlanta, Ga., on July 3, 1908.

[1] *Life of Henry W. Grady*, Gentry Dugat (Press of the Valley Printery, Edinburg, Tex., 1927) p. 1.

Harris, Stanley Raymond

Bucky [1] is a nickname of Stanley Raymond Harris, who was born at Port Jervis, N.Y., on November 8, 1896, and who played second base in major-league baseball, and formerly managed the New York Yankees.

[1] *Who's Who in Major League Base Ball*, comp. by Harold (Speed) Johnson (Buxton Publishing Company, Chicago, 1933) p. 200.

Harrison, Benjamin

The sobriquets, *Baby McKee's Grandfather, Chinese Harrison, Grandfather's Hat, Kid-gloves Harrison,* and *Little Ben,* have been attributed to Benjamin Harrison.

He was nicknamed *Baby McKee's Grandfather* [1] in allusion to the attention he lavished upon his young grandson Benjamin Harrison McKee. Because of his opposition to restricting Chinese immigration, Benjamin Harrison has been called *Chinese Harrison.*[2]

While he was serving as President of the United States from 1889 to 1893, Benjamin Harrison was sometimes pictured as wearing a hat as large as himself, which was labeled *Grandfather's Hat* [1] because his grandfather, William Henry Harrison, had held the office of President of the United States from March 4, 1841 until his sudden death on April 4 of the same year.

In 1876, Benjamin Harrison was urged to run for the Governorship of Indiana although he did not seem especially interested. His opponents, noticing his lack of enthusiasm, nicknamed him *Kid-gloves Harrison.*[3]

In allusion to his large stocky body set on small short legs, Harrison was sometimes called *Little Ben* [3] by the soldiers under his command during the Civil War.

Benjamin Harrison, the twenty-third President of the United States, was born at North Bend, Ohio, on August 20, 1833, and died at Indianapolis, Ind., on March 13, 1901.

[1] *U.S. "Snap Shots": An Independent, National, and Memorial Encyclopedia . . . ,* Oliver McKee (A. M. Thayer and Company, Boston, 1892) p. 314.

The Lives of Benjamin Harrison and Levi P. Morton, by Gilbert L. Harney, *with a History of the Republican Party, and a Statement of Its Position on the Great Issues of the Present Day, the Platform of the Party, the Letter of Acceptance of Benjamin Harrison, Statistics of Elections, Etc.,* by Edwin C. Pierce (J. S. and R. A. Reid, Providence, R.I., 1888) p. 176.

[2] *A Book of Nicknames,* John Goff (Courier-Journal Job Printing Company, Louisville, Ky., 1892) p. 21.

[3] *Pen Pictures of the Presidents,* Fred T. Wilson 'Southwestern Company, Nashville, Tenn., 1932) p. 380, 381.

Harrison, William Henry

William Henry Harrison has been called the *Farmer President,* the *Hero of Tippecanoe,* the *Log Cabin Candidate, Old Granny, Old Tippecanoe,* and the *Washington of the West.*

He was spoken of as the *Farmer President* [1] throughout the presidential campaign of 1840 because Harrison was a farmer.

During the exciting *Log-cabin and Hardcider Campaign* of 1840, Harrison was nicknamed the *Log Cabin Candidate* [2] because he came from the western part of the United States where the majority of the people had lived in log cabins, and Harrison's own house had been partly of logs.

While he was in the French and Indian War, Harrison was designated *Old Granny.* [3]

In commemoration of his having defeated tribes of western Indians under the leadership of Tecumseh, on November 7, 1811, in the Battle of Tippecanoe, William Henry Harrison was called *Old Tippecanoe,* and the *Hero of Tippecanoe.* [4]

These nicknames were part of the Whig slogan, "Tippecanoe and Tyler Too," used in the tumultuous *Log-cabin and Hard-cider Campaign* of 1840. Harrison was sometimes called the *Washington of the West* [5] because during the War of 1812, he took an active part in defeating the British.

William Henry Harrison was born at Berkeley, Va., on February 9, 1773, and died at Washington, D.C., on April 4, 1841. He was the ninth President of the United States.

[1] *Our Nation in the Building,* Helen Nicolay (The Century Company, New York, 1916) p. 344.

[2] *Young Folks' History of the United States,* Thomas Wentworth Higginson (Lee and Shepard, Boston, and Charles T. Dillingham, New York, 1875) p. 269.

A Popular School History of the United States, in Which Are Inserted as Part of the Narrative Selections from the Writings of Eminent American Historians, and Other American Writers of Note, to which Are Added the Declaration of Independence, and the Constitution of the United States, with Copious Notes, John Jacob Anderson (Clark and Maynard, New York, 1879) p. 234.

[3] *A Book of Nicknames,* John Goff (Courier-Journal Job Printing Company, Louisville, Ky., 1892) p. 23.

[4] *The Encyclopedia Americana* (Americana Corporation, New York and Chicago, 1932) vol. 26, p. 643.

The American People and Nation, Rolla M. Tryon and Charles R. Lingley (Ginn and Company, New York and Boston, 1929) p. 356.

[5] *U.S. "Snap Shots": An Independent, National, and Memorial Encyclopedia . . . ,* Oliver McKee (A. M. Thayer and Company, Boston, 1892) p. 309.

William Henry Harrison: A Political Biography, Dorothy Burne Goebel (Published by The Historical Bureau of the Indiana Library and Historical Department, Indianapolis, Ind., 1926) p. 164, 180-3.

Harry Percy of the House. See Wise, H. A.

Harry Percy of the Union. See South Carolina

Harte, Bret. See Coolbrith, Ina Donna, Bret Harte, and Charles Warren Stoddard

Harter, Dow Watters

Dow Watters Harter, an Ohio Lawyer and politician, was nicknamed the *Rubber King* [1] in Congress because he lives at Akron, Ohio, the rubber capital of the United States.

He was a Democratic Representative from Ohio to Congress from 1933 to 1943.

Dow Watters Harter was born at Akron, Ohio, on January 2, 1885.

[1] An interview with Captain Victor Hunt Harding, Secretary of the National Democratic Congress Reëlection Committee, Washington, D.C., April 10, 1939.

Hartford, Connecticut

Hartford has three nicknames, the *Charter Oak,* the *City Beautiful,* and the *Insurance City.* It is called the *Charter Oak City* [1] because here stood the historic oak tree known as the Charter Oak in which the colonists hid the Charter of the Colony of Connecticut to keep from surrendering it to King James II of England.

Hartford, the capital of the state, is called the *City Beautiful* [2] because of the architecture, its many well-kept parks, its places of historic interest, and its handsome residential streets.

The *Insurance City* [3] is applied to Hartford because it is the site of some of the largest insurance companies in America.

[1] *Americanisms; The English of the New World,* M. Schele De Vere (Charles Scribner and Company, New York, 1872) p. 663.

Wadsworth or The Charter Oak, W. H. Gocher (W. H. Gocher, Hartford, Conn., 1903) p. 334-8.

A Complete History of Connecticut, Civil and Ecclesiastical, from the Emigration of Its First Planters, from England, in the Year 1650, to the Year 1764; and to the Close of the Indian Wars, Benjamin Trumbull (Maltby, Goldsmith and Company, and Samuel Wadsworth, New Haven, Conn., 1818) vol. 1, p. 371.

The Colonial History of Hartford Gathered from the Original Records, Reverend William DeLoss Love (Published by the Author, Hartford, Conn., 1914) p. 218-19.

Hartford, Conn.—Continued

[2] *The Hartford Monthly* (The Hartford Monthly Publishing Company, Hartford, Conn., 1906) vol. 1, no. 3, August, 1906, p. 103.

[3] *Manual of Useful Information*, J. C. Thomas (The Werner Company, Chicago, 1893) p. 22.

History of Hartford, Connecticut: The Memorial History of Hartford County, Connecticut, 1633-1884, ed. by J. Hammond Trumbull (Edward L. Osgood, Boston, 1886) vol. 1, p. 499-522.

The Encyclopaedia Britannica, Fourteenth Edition (Encyclopaedia Britannica, Inc., New York, 1929) vol. 2, p. 226.

Hartford of the West. See Des Moines, Iowa

Hartford Wits

The nickname *Hartford Wits* [1] was given to Joel Barlow, Timothy Dwight and John Trumbull, leaders of an important group of Revolutionary poets which also included Richard Alsop, Lemuel Hopkins, David Humphries, and Theodore Dwight. They were known first as the "Connecticut Wits" and later as above, although Barlow, Dwight and Trumbull were all Yale (New Haven) graduates.

[1] *The Reader's Encyclopedia*, William Rose Benét, ed. (Thomas Y. Crowell Company, New York) p. 483.
Connecticut Wits, Leon Howard (University of Chicago Press, Chicago)

Hartnett, Charles Leo

Charles Leo Hartnett, who was born at Woonsocket, R.I., on December 20, 1900, and who was a catcher in major-league baseball, was nicknamed *Gabby* [1] because he talked almost incessantly.

[1] *Who's Who in Major League Base Ball*, comp. by Harold (Speed) Johnson (Buxton Publishing Company, Chicago, 1933) p. 202.

Hartwick College

The *Indians,* the *Iroquois,* the *Tribesmen,* and the *Warriors* [10] are the nicknames of the athletic teams of Hartwick College, at Oneonta, N.Y., because the college is located in territory which formerly belonged to the Iroquois Indians.

[1] A communication from Charles W. Leitzell, President of Hartwick College, Oneonta, N.Y., December 2, 1935.

Harvard Crimsons. See Harvard University

Harvard University

The athletic teams of Harvard University, at Cambridge, Mass., are popularly called the *Harvard Crimsons* and the *John

Harvard Boys, because the University colors are crimson and John Harvard founded Harvard College.

Harvard's Gift to the West. See Cutting, Bronson

Harvey, William Hope

William Harvey was called *Coin Harvey* [1] because he displayed a keen interest in the monetary policies of the United States, and helped formulate a number of plans for the coinage of silver.

William Hope Harvey was born at Buffalo, W.Va., on August 16, 1851, and died February 11, 1936.

[1] *John G. Carlisle, Financial Statesman*, James A. Barnes (Dodd, Mead and Company, New York, 1931) p. 473.

Hashknife Simpson. See Simpson, J. N.

Haskell Indians. See Haskell Institute

Haskell Institute

The *Haskell Indians* is the nickname given to the athletic teams of Haskell Institute, at Lawrence, Kan., because this is a school primarily for educating Indians.

Haslam, Robert

Robert Haslam was one of the most daring and expert riders in the famous Pony Express in 1860-61 and was known to his friends as *Pony Bob*.[1]

[1] *A Thrilling and Truthful History of the Pony Express or Blazing the Westward Way and Other Sketches and Incidents of Those Stirring Times*, William Lightfoot Visscher (Rand, McNally and Company, Chicago, 1908) p. 44.

Hastings, William Wirt

Cherokee Bill [1] is the nickname applied to William Wirt Hastings because he was of Cherokee Indian parentage.

William Wirt Hastings, who was born in the Indian Territory, on December 31, 1866, and died April 8, 1938, was a Representative from Oklahoma to Congress from 1915 to 1921, and again from 1923 to 1935.

[1] *The Washington Post Magazine*, Washington, D.C., March 4, 1934, p. 4.

Hatch, Carl Atwood

Carl Atwood Hatch, a Senator and politician, was nicknamed *Cowboy Carl* [1] because he is a native of New Mexico, a state noted for cattle raising and cowboys.

He was also called *Deacon Hatch* [2] because of his interest in reform. The Hatch Bill, passed by Congress in 1940, prohibits employees paid wholly or in part by Federal funds, from engaging in political activities.

Carl Atwood Hatch was born at Kirwin, Kans., on November 27, 1889.

[1] *Time: The Weekly News Magazine,* Chicago, March 18, 1940, col. 3, p. 14.
[2] *The United States News,* Washington, D.C., April 5, 1940, col. 1, p. 37.

Hatfield, Bazil Muse

Bazil Muse Hatfield has the following nicknames: *Admiral of the Trinity, First Lord of the Marshes, Johnny Simmonseed,* and *Master of the Swamps.* He is said to have originated these himself, in connection with his activities in behalf of getting a canal constructed from Fort Worth to Galveston Bay. He built a flat-bottomed scow which he called the "Texas Steer," and made trips to stimulate interest in having the Trinity Valley developed. He traveled by scow, wagon and on foot trying to interest people in opening a canal to develop the lower Trinity Valley.

He called himself *Johnny Simmonseed* [1] because while making these trips he carried his pockets full of persimmon seeds which, like Johnny Appleseed, he scattered wherever he went.

Bazil Muse Hatfield was born on July 4, 1870, at Washington-on-the-Brazos, Texas.

[1] *Who: The Magazine About People,* Gerard Publishing Company, New York City, October, 1941, p. 21.

Hatfield, Charles Folsom

Charles Folsom Hatfield was nicknamed the *Dean of Community Advertising* [1] because he was an authority on publicity and community advertising.

Mr. Hatfield's initiative, winning personality, and executive abilities brought him into great demand as an advertiser for cities and organizations of national importance.

He was born at Warren, Ohio, on May 2, 1862, and for many years made his home at St. Louis, Mo.

[1] *Encyclopedia of American Biography: American Biography, a New Cyclopedia,* comp. under the editorial supervision of a notable board (Published under the direction of The American Historical Society, Inc., New York, 1928) vol. 36, p. 178.

Who's Who in America: A Biographical Dictionary of Notable Living Men and Women of the United States, 1932-33, revised and reissued biennially, ed. by Albert Nelson Marquis (The A. N. Marquis Company, Chicago, 1932) vol. 17, p. 1071.

Hatters. See John B. Stetson University

Havelock of the American Army. See Howard, O. O.

Haverford College

The athletic teams of Haverford College, at Haverford, Pa., are known as the *Fords* and the *Little Quakers.* [1] The college is owned and operated by the Society of Friends or Quakers.

[1] A communication from the Graduate Manager of Athletics at Haverford College, Haverford, Pa., November 18, 1935.

Hawaii

Hawaii was nicknamed the *Paradise of the Pacific* because of its delightful climate, luxuriant vegetation, facilities for pleasure and its abundant fruits. It was also called the *Gibraltar in the Pacific* because of its strongly fortified naval base at Pearl Harbor.

Hawaiian Pineapple King. See Dole, J. D.

Hawkeye State. See Iowa

Hawkeyes. See Iowans; State University of Iowa; University of Iowa

Hawkins, Benjamin

Benjamin Hawkins, a Senator from North Carolina and Indian agent, was called the *Beloved Man of the Four Nations* [1] by the Indians of Georgia, Alabama, and Mississippi among whom he worked as a commissioned agent from 1795 until the outbreak of the War of 1812. His treatment of the Creeks, Choctaws, Chickasaws, and Cherokees had endeared him to these Indians, who during this time maintained the peace.

He was born in what is now Warren County, N.C., on August 15, 1754, and died near Roberta, Ga., on June 6, 1816.

[1] *Dictionary of American Biography under the Auspices of the American Council of Learned Societies,* ed. by Dumas Malone (Charles Scribner's Sons, New York, 1932) vol. 8, p. 414.

Hawks. See Saint Joseph's College

Hawley, John

The wisdom and insight of John Hawley caused him to be called the *Nestor of the Patriots.* [1] He had given timely advice to

Hawley, John—Continued

John Adams about guarding against the haughty and dictatorial policies of certain Massachusetts gentlemen. Nestor was the counselor and advisor of the Greeks in the Trojan War.

[1] "John Adams" by Clifford Smyth, in *Builders of America* (Funk and Wagnalls Company, New York, 1931) vol. 13, p. 58.

Hawthorne, Nathaniel

Nathaniel Hawthorne has been called the *Genius of Romance* [1] because of his writings.

He was born at Salem, Mass., on July 4, 1804, and died at Plymouth, N.H., on May 19, 1864.

[1] *Compton's Pictured Encyclopedia* (F. E. Compton and Company, Chicago, 1931) vol. 1, p. 114.

Hay, John Milton

About 1880, John Milton Hay, who was born at Salem, Ind., on October 8, 1838, and who died near Newbury, N.H., on July 1, 1905, was nicknamed *Little Breeches* [1] by the *Cleveland Plain Dealer* because he wrote the poem "Little Breeches," one of his Pike County Ballads.

[1] *Cleveland Plain Dealer*, Cleveland, Ohio, August 2, 1880.

Hayes, Edward Mortimer

Brigadier General Edward Mortimer Hayes was nicknamed *Fighting Jack*.[1] He enlisted in the United States Army on August 28, 1855, and served in the Second Cavalry in Texas until August 28, 1860. He won the nickname, *Fighting Jack*,[1] because of his courage in engagements against hostile Indians. In 1890 he was breveted a major for gallant services in action against Indians at Beaver Creek, Kansas, on October 25 and 26, 1868.

He was born in New York on December 23, 1842, and died at Morgantown, N.C., August 15, 1912.

[1] *The Evening Star*, Washington, D.C., August 16, 1912, col. 4, p. 18.

Hayes, Lucy Ware Webb

While Rutherford Birchard Hayes was President of the United States from 1877 to 1881, Mrs. Hayes was nicknamed *Lemonade Lucy*.[1]

She did not serve wine or other intoxicating beverages at the White House but instead served soft drinks containing fruit juices. This gave rise to the nickname.

[1] *White House Gossip from Andrew Johnson to Calvin Coolidge*, Edna M. Colman (Doubleday, Page and Company, Garden City, N.Y., 1927) p. 114.

Hayes, Rutherford Birchard

Rutherford Birchard Hayes was known as The *Dark Horse President*, The *Fraud President*, *Granny Hayes*, *Old Eight to Seven*, and the *President de facto*.

During the Hayes-Tilden presidential election of 1876, election returns gave Samuel Jones Tilden one hundred and eighty-four electoral votes, and Rutherford Birchard Hayes one hundred and sixty-three electoral votes. A controversy arose over twenty-two electoral votes and Congress appointed an electoral commission to settle the controversy. Their decision, based on a vote of eight to seven, gave the questioned electoral votes to Hayes, who thus received one hundred and eighty-five electoral votes while Tilden received one hundred and eighty-four. From this arose the nicknames the *Dark Horse President*, The *Fraud President*, *Old Eight to Seven*, and The *President de facto*.[1]

The nickname *Granny Hayes* [2] was applied to Hayes by the Republican party because he insisted on abiding by ethical standards of political conduct which the party bosses considered fussy and out of date.

Rutherford Birchard Hayes, who was born at Delaware, Ohio, on October 4, 1822, and died at Fremont, Ohio, on January 17, 1893, was President of the United States from 1877 until 1881.

[1] *History of the United States*, Second Edition Revised, Emerson David Fite (Henry Holt and Company, New York, 1919) p. 421.

[2] *The Oxford History of the United States, 1783-1917*, S. E. Morison (Oxford University Press, London, 1927) p. 385.

Haymakers. See Phillips University

Hayne, Paul Hamilton

Paul Hamilton Hayne was often called the *Poet Laureate of the South* [1] because he was one of the prominent poets in the South, whose poetry was influenced by southern life and environment.

Paul Hamilton Hayne was born at Charleston, S.C., on January 1, 1830, and died near Augusta, Ga., on July 6, 1886.

[1] *The National Cyclopaedia of American Biography* (James T. White and Company, New York, 1897) vol. 4, p. 307.

Hazard, Jonathan J.

Jonathan J. Hazard, a political leader, was known as *Beau Jonathan* [1] because of his elegant attire, polished manners, and fastidious personal habits. Hazard was active in the political affairs of Rhode Island, and served as a delegate from Charlestown to the Rhode Island House of Representatives in 1776, and as a member of the General Assembly of Rhode Island which passed the statute declaring Rhode Island's independence from Great Britain. He was a member of the Continental Congress in which capacity he opposed the adoption of the Federal Constitution.

Jonathan J. Hazard was born at Newport, Rhode Island, about 1744, and died at Oneida, N.Y., about 1824.

[1] *Dictionary of American Biography under the Auspices of the American Council of Learned Societies,* ed. by Dumas Malone (Charles Scribner's Sons, New York, 1932) vol. 8, p. 470.

Hazelton, James

During the Civil War, James Hazelton was known as the *Red Fox* [1] because of his fox-like skill in eluding his enemies and because of his reddish or sandy hair. He was a member of the Sixty-fifth Regiment of Ohio Volunteers.[2]

[1] *The Story of the Sherman Brigade, the Camp, the March, the Bivouac, the Battle, and How "the Boys" Lived and Died During Four Years of Active Field Service,* Wilbur F. Hinman (Published by the Author, Alliance, Ohio, 1897) p. 641.

[2] *Official Roster of the Soldiers of the State of Ohio in the War of the Rebellion, 1861-1866,* comp. under the direction of the Roster Committee; Joseph B. Foraker, Governor; James S. Robinson, Secretary of the State; and H. A. Axline, Adjutant-general, published by Authority of the General Assembly (The Werner Printing and Manufacturing Company, Akron, Ohio, 1887) vol. 5, 54th-69th Regiments-Infantry, p. 512.

HE Watters. See Watters, H. E.

Headley, Joel Tyler

Joel Tyler Headley, an author, was called the *Autocrat of the Quacks* [1] by Edgar Allan Poe, a contemporary writer, because he considered Headley's publications wordy, florid, and unoriginal. Headley wrote American history, biography, and scenic geography which was so popular that approximately three hundred thousand copies of his books were sold. Critics said that much of his work was only compilation, limited in thought and superficial in expression.

Joel Tyler Headley was born at Walton, N.Y., on December 30, 1813, and died at Newburgh, N.Y., on January 16, 1897.

[1] *Dictionary of American Biography under the Auspices of the American Council of Learned Societies,* ed. by Dumas Malone (Charles Scribner's Sons, New York, 1932) vol. 8, p. 478.

Headsman Clarkson. See Clarkson, J. S.

Headstrong Peter. See Stuyvesant, Peter

Healy, Aaron Augustus

The *Father of the Brooklyn Institute of Arts and Sciences* [1] was applied to Aaron Augustus Healy in commemoration of the facts that he donated funds to the Institute and contributed works of art amounting to several hundred thousand dollars. He often loaned works from his private art collection. In 1895 he became president of the Institute and served as such for twenty-five years, during which time he built up that institution to its present size and scope. He bequeathed to the Institute a large sum of money and many of the finest art productions in his collection.

Aaron Augustus Healy was born at Brooklyn, N.Y., on June 26, 1850, and died at his summer home, Cold Springs-on-the Hudson, N.Y., on September 28, 1921.

[1] *Encyclopedia of American Biography: American Biography, a New Cyclopedia,* comp. under the editorial supervision of a notable advisory board (Published under the direction of The American Historical Society, Inc., New York, 1922) vol. 16, p. 128.

Heart of America. See Kansas City, Mo.

Heart of Georgia. See Macon, Ga.

Heart of the New Industrial South. See Alabama

Heaven-sent Angel of Mercy and of Prison Reform. See Dix, D. L.

Heck, Barbara Ruckle

Barbara Ruckle Heck, who was born at Balligarrene, Ireland, in 1744, and who died in Augusta, Canada, in 1804, was designated the *Mother of Methodism in the United States* [1] because she was instrumental

Heck, B. R.—Continued

in organizing the first Methodist meeting in America and helped build the first Methodist meeting house here.

[1] The National Cyclopaedia of American Biography (James T. White and Company, New York, 1909) vol. 13, p. 115.

Heenan, John Carmel

John Carmel Heenan, a pugilist, was known as the *Bernicia Boy* [1] because he worked for some time in the shops of the Pacific Mail Steamships located at Bernicia, Calif., where he had gone in 1852 to search for gold. From 1858 until 1863, he was one of the most popular boxers in the United States.

John Carmel Heenan was born at West Troy, N.Y., on May 2, 1835, and died at Green River Station, Wyo., on October 25, 1873.

[1] Dictionary of American Biography under the Auspices of the American Council of Learned Societies, ed. by Dumas Malone (Charles Scribner's Sons, New York, 1932) vol. 8, p. 499.

Heidelburg College

The athletic teams of Heidelburg College, at Tiffin, Ohio, are called the *Student Princes*.[1]

[1] A communication from E. R. Butcher, Publicity Director at Heidelburg College, Tiffin, Ohio, June 13, 1935.

Heine. See Meine, H. W.

Heinie. See Manush, H. E.; Schuble, H. G., Jr.

Hell March

In August 1862, the first thousand men recruited in Ohio who formed the One Hundred and Fifth Regiment of Ohio Volunteers were detailed to Lexington, Ky., to join the Army of Kentucky then under the command of Brigadier General William Nelson. This army then made a forced march from Lexington to Louisville, which was designated the *Hell March* [1] in allusion to the acute suffering because of the hot dusty weather, lack of water, insufficient food, and the lack of sleep or rest. During the *Hell March* from August 30 to September 5, 1862, the newly recruited soldiers covered a distance of one hundred and forty

miles, and slept less than thirty hours in the six days.

[1] The Story of a Thousand, Being a History of the Service of the 105th Ohio Volunteer Infantry, in the War for the Union from August 21, 1862, to June 6, 1865, Albion W. Tourgee (S. McGerald and Son, Buffalo, N.Y., 1895) p. 94.

Hell on Wheels

Samuel Bowles, an American journalist who lived in New England from 1826 to 1878, applied the nickname *Hell on Wheels* [1] to the newly formed towns or camps (with their shooting and other frontier excitement) that grew up every few miles along the newly-laid track of the railroads being built across the United States. The tents, lumber, and other materials out of which they were built were shipped to the end of the newly laid track on flat cars, and the towns were built almost as if by magic.

[1] The Making of Buffalo Bill: A Study in Heroics, Richard J. Walsh in collaboration with Milton S. Salisbury (The Bobbs-Merrill Company, Indianapolis, Ind., 1928) p. 106.

Hell on Wheels. See *Black Dragons*

Hellafloat

During the Revolutionary War, the British prison ship, *Jersey*, anchored at what is now the Brooklyn Navy Yard in New York, was nicknamed *Hellafloat* [1] because of the inhumane treatment to which the British subjected the sick and wounded American prisoners aboard this ship.

[1] The Valley of the Hudson, River of Destiny, 1609-1930: Covering the Sixteen New York State Hudson River Counties of New York, Bronx, Westchester, Rockland, Orange, Putnam, Dutchess, Ulster, Greene, Columbia, Albany, Rensselair, Saratoga, Washington, Warren, and Essex, ed. by Nelson Greene (The S. J. Clarke Publishing Company, Chicago, 1931) vol. 1, p. 519.

Hell Upon Earth

The Confederate Military Prison at Andersonville, Ga., was called *Hell Upon Earth* [1] by its inmates because of the hardships and cruelties to which they were exposed. Andersonville prison [2] was enclosed but unsheltered from the inclemencies of the weather. The scarcity of food and clothing, the complete lack of shelter and sanitary facilities, the uncleanliness and unhealthfulness of the vermin-ridden prison caused acute suffering among the inmates and produced a high death rate.

[1] History of O'dea's Famous Picture of Andersonville Prison, as It Appeared August 1st, 1864, When it Contained Thirty-five Thousand Prisoners of War; Graphic

Description of That Famous Locality, with Explanation of Key to Prison and Marginal Scenes, Thomas O'dea (Clark and Foster, Cohoes, N.Y., 1887) p. 4.

[2] *History of the United States of America, under the Constitution, 1861-1865*, James Schouler (Dodd, Mead and Company, New York, 1899) vol. 6, p. 412-14.

Hellcat Division. See Twelfth Armored Division of World War II

Hell's Devil Butler. See Butler, S. D.

Hell's Half Acre

A plot of ground near Spottsylvania where Confederate and Federal soldiers fought throughout May 12, 1864, until dead and wounded were piled one on the other came to be known as *Hell's Half Acre*.[1]

[1] *On the Trail of Grant and Lee: A Narrative History of the Boyhood of Two Great Americans, Based upon Their Own Writings, Official Records, and Other Authoritative Information*, Frederick Trevor Hill (D. Appleton and Company, New York, 911) p. 233.

The History of the Confederate War, Its Causes and Its Conduct, A Narative and Critical History, George Cary Eggleston (Sturgis and Walton Company, New York, 1910) vol. 2, p. 242-7.

Helperite

Hinton Rowan Helper, a white man living in North Carolina, had written and published a book in 1857 entitled the *Impending Crisis*[1] in which he attempted to prove by the use of material from census reports that the South, through its dependence upon slavery, was degenerating. He also made other unfavorable comments about the southern slave-holders. After that *Helperite* was a sobriquet applied to anyone who was accused of treachery to the South in any form.

[1] *Andrew Johnson, Plebian and Patriot*, Robert W. Winston (Henry Holt and Company, New York, 1928) p. 108.

Hemp State. See Kentucky

Hemphill, Joseph

Joseph Hemphill, a legislator and jurist, was nicknamed *Single Speech Hemphill*[1] while he was a Representative from Pennsylvania to Congress, from 1801 until 1803. The nickname originated in the fact that on February 16, 1802, he made his first address before Congress to oppose the repeal of a judiciary act. This speech was so convincing that it was said his single effort was worth all the speeches by his opponents. The nickname was brought into popular usage after he was reelected to Congress in 1819 and again in 1829 when he was noted for his few, but concise, and effective speeches.

Joseph Hemphill was born in Thornbury Township, in what is now Delaware County, Pa., on January 7, 1770, and died at Philadelphia, Pa., on May 29, 1842.

[1] *Dictionary of American Biography under the Auspices of the American Council of Learned Societies*, ed. by Dumas Malone (Charles Scribner's Sons, New York, 1932) vol. 8, p. 521.

Hendershot, Robert Henry

The *Drummer Boy of the Rappahannock*[1] was the nickname of Robert Henry Hendershot, who served during the Civil War as a drummer boy in the Union Army. Some accounts say Hendershot enlisted at Detroit, Mich., on August 19, 1862, as a drummer boy in Company B of the Eighth Infantry of Michigan Volunteers. He joined the regiment at Fredericksburg, Va., on November 28, 1862, and having been wounded in battle was mustered out of service at Falmouth, Va., on December 27, 1862.

Two unofficial accounts say he served as a drummer boy in the Ninth Infantry of Michigan Volunteers, one of them speaking of him as the *Drummer-boy of the Ninth Michigan*.[2]

There is a discrepancy in the place and date of Robert Henry Hendershot's birth. He was born at Moscow, Mich.,[3] on February 27, 1850, according to one author; and another writer states that he was born at Cambridge, Mich.,[2] on December 11, 1850. He is said to have died on December 26, 1925.

[1] *Encyclopedia of American Biography: American Biography, a New Cyclopedia*, comp. under the editorial supervision of a notable advisory board (Published under the direction of The American Historical Society, Inc., New York, 1927) vol. 28, p. 245.

Michigan Adjutant-general's Office Record of Service of Michigan Volunteers in the Civil War, 1861-1865, published by authority of the Senate and House of Representatives of the Michigan Legislature under the direction of Brigadier-general George H. Brown, Adjutant-general (Ihling Brothers and Everard, Kalamazoo, Mich., 1905) p. 67.

[2] *Robert Henry Hendershot; or, the Brave Drummer Boy of the Rappahannock*, William Sumner Dodge (Church and Goodman, Chicago, 1867) p. 16, 51, 78, 96-7, 113.

[3] *American Biography, a New Cyclopedia*, comp. under the editorial supervision of a notable advisory board (Published under the direction of The American Historical Society, Inc., New York, 1927) vol. 28, p. 245.

Henderson, Peter

The nickname the *Father of Horticulture and Ornamental Gardening*[1] has been applied to Peter Henderson because he was a pioneer worker in the American field of

Henderson, Peter—Continued
horticulture. He made several valuable contributions to the methods of cultivating fruits, vegetables, and ornamental plants and was a prominent seed merchant. He contributed articles to horticultural journals and published several books dealing with floriculture and other special branches of horticulture.

Peter Henderson was born at Porthead, Scotland, in 1823 and died at Jersey City, N.J., on January 17, 1890.

[1] *The National Cyclopaedia of American Biography* (James T. White and Company, New York, 1929) vol. 6, p. 144.
The Encyclopedia Americana (Americana Corporation, New York and Chicago, 1927) vol. 14, p. 94.

Hendrick, Harvey

Harvey Hendrick, who was born at Mason, Tenn., on November 9, 1897, and who played first base in major-league baseball, was nicknamed *Gink*.[1]

[1] *Who's Who in Major League Base Ball*, comp. by Harold (Speed) Johnson (Buxton Publishing Company, Chicago, 1933) p. 208.

Hendricks, Joseph Edward

Joseph Edward Hendricks, a politician, was nicknamed the *Doc Townsend of Florida*[1] in the House of Representatives because he advocated California's Townsend Plan for the State of Florida. He was a Democratic Representative from Florida to Congress from 1937 to 1949.

Joseph Edward Hendricks was born at Lake Butler, Fla., on September 24, 1903.

[1] An interview with Captain Victor Hunt Harding, Secretary of the National Democratic Congress Reëlection Committee, Washington, D.C., April 10, 1939.

Hendrix College

The *Warriors*[1] is the nickname given to the athletic teams of Hendrix College, at Conway, Ark. The student body selected this nickname because it is in keeping with the early history and traditions of this section of Arkansas.

[1] A communication from Ivan H. Grove, Director of Athletics at Hendrix College, Conway, Ark., June 11, 1935.

Henry, Gustavus Adolphus

The Eagle Orator[1] or *The Eagle Orator of Tennessee*[2] were nicknames by which Gustavus Adolphus Henry was known throughout the South because he was an eloquent and skillful orator.

Gustavus Adolphus Henry was born at Cherry Springs, Ky., on October 8, 1804, and died at Clarksville, Tenn., on September 10, 1880.

[1] *A History of Tennessee and Tennesseans, the Leaders and Representative Men in Commerce, Industry, and Modern Activities*, Will T. Hale and Dixon L. Merritt (The Lewis Publishing Company, New York and Chicago, 1913) vol. 3, p. 571.
[2] *The National Cyclopaedia of American Biography* (James T. White and Company, New York, 1916) vol. 13, p. 131.

Henry, Patrick

Patrick Henry was known as the *Forest-born Demosthenes*, the *Man of the People*, the *Prophet of the Revolution*, and the *Voice of the Revolution*.

The *Forest-born Demosthenes*[1] alluded to the fact that Patrick Henry was born in the western forest region of the Virginia Colony. He was one of the most outstanding orators in America.

Because of his humble birth and the ardent support he gave to the colonists in their revolt against the English authorities preceding the Revolutionary War, Patrick Henry was called the *Man of the People*.[2]

Henry was known as the *Prophet of the Revolution* because in his speeches analyzing the policies of Great Britain he prophesied as an inevitable consequence, the Revolutionary War.

The *Voice of the Revolution*[3] was applied to him because he was outstanding among the colonial orators in causing the colonists to unite and to fight for their liberty.

Patrick Henry was born in Hanover County, Va., on May 29, 1736, and died in Charlotte County, Va., on June 6, 1799.

[1] *My Quarter Century of American Politics*, Champ Clark (Harper and Brothers, New York and London, 1920) vol. 1, p. 347.
[2] *American Literature*, John Calvin Metcalf (B. F. Johnson Publishing Company, Richmond, Va., 1921) p. 70.
[3] *Virginia; Rebirth of the Old Dominion*, Philip Alexander Bruce (The Lewis Publishing Company, New York and Chicago, 1929) vol. 1, p. 393.

Henry of Navarre. See Blaine, J. G.; Watterson, Henry

Hering, Constantine

Constantine Hering has been called the *Father of Homeopathy in America*[1] because he was one of the leading pioneers of homeopathy in America. In 1835, Constantine Hering with several homeopathists founded the North American Academy of the Homeopathic Healing Art at Allentown, Pa. He returned to Philadelphia, Pa., in 1898 and reestablished his practice there, wrote books, pamphlets, and articles for medical journals on homeopathy, and was responsible for the translation of German textbooks on this subject into English.

He was born at Oschatz, Saxony, Germany, on January 1, 1800, emigrated to Philadelphia, Pa., in 1833, and died there on July 23, 1880.

[1] *The National Cyclopaedia of American Biography* (James T. White and Company, New York, 1893) vol. 3, p. 477.

Herman, Floyd Caves

In 1922, when Floyd Caves Herman joined the Detroit American League Baseball Company, he asked to be nicknamed *Babe* [1] because he said that he was destined to be another *Babe Ruth*.

Floyd Caves Herman was born at Buffalo, N.Y., on June 26, 1903, and played outfield in major-league baseball.

[1] *Who's Who in Major League Base Ball*, comp. by Harold (Speed) Johnson (Buxton Publishing Company, Chicago, 1933) p. 210.

Hermit Author of Palo Alto. See Hoover, H. C.

Hermit of Newfane. See Brown, David

Hermit of Slabsides. See Burroughs, John

Hero of Appomattox. See Grant, U. S.

Hero of Charleston. See Lee, Charles

Hero of Chippewa. See Scott, Winfield

Hero of Conception. See Fannin, J. W.

Hero of Fort Donaldson. See Grant, U. S.

Hero of Fort Fisher. See Lamb, William

Hero of Fort McHenry. See Armistead, George

Hero of Fort Meigs. See Christy, William

Hero of Fort Mifflin. See Thayer, Simeon

Hero of Fort Sumter. See Beauregard, P. G. T.

Hero of Fredericksburg. See Kirkland, R. R.

Hero of King's Mountain. See Cleveland, Benjamin

Hero of Lake Erie. See Perry, O. H.

Hero of Little Round Top. See Chamberlain, J. L.

Hero of Manila. See Dewey, George

Hero of Mobile Bay. See Farragut, D. G.

Hero of New England. See Standish, Miles

Hero of New Orleans. See Jackson, Andrew

Hero of San Juan Hill. See Roosevelt, Theodore

Hero of Saratoga. See Gates, Horatio

Hero of Stony Point. See Wayne, Anthony

Hero of the Battle of Gettysburg. See Burns, John

Hero of the Crater. See Mahone, William

Hero of the Hornet's Nest. See Prentiss, B. M.

Hero of Tippecanoe. See Harrison, W. H.

Hero of Vincennes. See Clark, G. R.

Heroine of Groton. See Bailey, A. W.

Herring, Arthur L.

Arthur L. Herring, who was born at Altus, Okla., on March 1, 1907, and who pitched in major-league baseball, was known as *Sandy*.[1]

[1] *Who's Who in Major League Base Ball*, comp. by Harold (Speed) Johnson (Buxton Publishing Company, Chicago, 1933) p. 212.

Hessian Flies

During the American Revolution the colonists, particularly the farmers, often spoke of the Hessian soldiers in the British Army as being *Hessian Flies*.[1] The British Army sometimes sent the Hessian soldiers out to secure provisions by foraging and plundering the countryside, which was a constant source of annoyance and irritation to the colonists.

[1] *Alexander Hamilton*, Howard H. Hicks (The Macmillan Company, New York, 1928) p. 57.

Hewit, Augustine Francis

The *Newman of America*[1] is the nickname applied to Augustine Francis Hewit because he changed his religious faith and joined the Roman Catholic Church. He attained an eminent position as a teacher in Catholic institutions, as an editor of religious literature relating to the Catholic Church, as an official in this Church, and as a theological scholar. In these respects he was comparable to John Henry Newman, the renowned English author, theologian, preacher, and cardinal in the Roman Catholic Church.

Augustine Francis Hewit was born at Fairfield, Conn., on November 27, 1820, and died at New York City, on July 3, 1897.

[1] *The National Cyclopaedia of American Biography* (James T. White and Company, New York, 1909) vol. 11, p. 358.

Hewit, Nathaniel

Nathaniel Hewit, a clergyman, was nicknamed *Luther of the Early Temperance Reformation* in allusion to his prominence and success as an agent of the American Temperance Society by whom he was invited to undertake a three years' mission in 1827. From 1830 to 1852 he was a minister at Bridgeport, Conn., where he devoted much of his energy to the Temperance Society. The nickname signified that Hewit's activities in behalf of temperance reform were comparable to the work of Martin Luther for religious reform.

Nathaniel Hewit was born at New London, Conn., on August 28, 1788, and died at Bridgeport, Conn., on February 3, 1867.

[1] *Appleton's Cyclopaedia of American Biography*, ed. by James Grant Wilson and John Fiske (D. Appleton and Company, New York, 1888) vol. 3, p. 191.

[2] *National Cyclopaedia of American Biography*, (James T. White and Company, New York, 1909) vol. 11, p. 357.

Hewitt, John Henry (Hill)

John Henry Hewitt has been called *Father of American Ballad Poetry*[1] because he was an early and prolific writer of American ballad poetry. He often composed the music to which he set his verses.

John Henry Hewitt was born in New York on July 11, 1801, and died at Baltimore, Md., on October 7, 1890.

[1] *The National Cyclopaedia of American Biography* (James T. White and Company, New York, 1909) vol. 11, p. 363.

Hibbing, Minnesota

Hibbing is known as the *Iron Ore Capital of the World*, the *Richest Village on Earth*, and the *Town That Moved Overnight*. This town, the largest in the Mesabi Iron Range in St. Louis county, has been nicknamed the *Iron Ore Capital of the World*[1] because it is the principal city in one of the most important iron producing sections in the world. For the same reason Hibbing has been designated the *Richest Village on Earth*.[1] Hibbing has been called the *Town That Moved Overnight* because it was moved after it became a town of considerable size to give access to the magnificent beds of iron ore underneath it.

[1] *My Minnesota*, Antoinette E. Ford (Lyons and Carnahan, New York and Chicago, 1929) p. 252, 255.

Hickok, James Butler

James Butler Hickok was nicknamed *Duck Bill*, *Dutch Bill*. or *Duch Bill*, the *Prince of Pistoleers*, *Shanghai Bill*, and *Wild Bill*.

David McCanles, who disliked Hickok, and who was killed by Hickok at Rock Creek, Neb., in 1861, is said to have given Hickok *Duck Bill* because of the shape of Hickok's nose and upper lip.[1]

This explanation is denied by others.[2] *Duck Bill* was often corrupted to *Dutch Bill* or *Duch Bill*.

The *Prince of Pistoleers*[5] was a nickname applied to Hickok because of his dexterity in the use of pistols. His favorite pistols were two pearl-handled, silver plated, single action forty-four Colt revolvers, the catches of which he honed down until they were very "easy on the trigger."

The origin of *Shanghai Bill* [6] is a matter of controversy. Some say that in 1855 Hickok attempted to join the Red Legs or the Red Leg Rangers, a group of Federal scouts or anti-slavery men at Leavenworth, Kans., but that they refused to admit him. Later he watched the Red Legs at target practice and was so offensive in his ridicule of their inaccuracy that Shanghai Bill, a notorious desperado and a member of the Red Legs, challenged Hickok to better the marksmanship. Hickok hit the bull's eye three times out of three successive shots and the Red Legs made him a member in full standing and transferred the name *Shanghai Bill* [6] to him. This story is denied by the late William Elsey Connelley who refutes the entire account on the grounds that Lane [3] had no military headquarters at Leavenworth; that the Red Legs [3] came into existence just prior to the Civil War; and that Hickok, instead of serving in the then non-existent regiment, soon after his arrival at Leavenworth in 1855, worked near there during the next two years for a man named Richard Butt. [4]

There are several accounts of how James Butler Hickok came to be ·nicknamed *Wild Bill*. [3] According to the explanation [3] given by the late William Elsey Connelley, the sobriquet had its origin in an occurrence which took place at Independence, Mo., sometime between the first and the tenth of August, in 1861.

Hickok, having been appointed wagon-master of a wagon train transporting Government supplies from Sedalia, Mo., to Fort Leavenworth, Kans., had proceeded from Fort Leavenworth with his wagon-train for about three days when a guerilla band consisting of about fifty men captured the train and burned a part of the wagons. Mounted on horseback, Hickok escaped to Independence, Mo.

Upon arriving at Independence, he went to the saloon of one of his friends where he found the bar-tender amidst a crowd of teamsters and ruffians, some threatening his life and others promising to defend him. Hickok pulled out his pistols and challenged the entire crowd to fight him. When they would not accept his challenge, he commanded them to scatter and to leave the

town, threatening that if they did not do so, he would leave them with more corpses than they would be able to bury. The crowd immediately obeyed this command.

The news of what Hickok had done soon spread throughout the town and the inhabitants assembled to express their appreciation to him for having rid the town of a group of trouble-making men. Among the assembled citizens was an unknown woman, who, in expressing her appreciation to Hickok, addressed him as *Wild Bill*. The sobriquet was taken up by others in the assembly who likewise called him *Wild Bill*.

Hickok proceeded to Sedalia, Mo.; but news of his actions in Independence reached Sedalia before he did, and when he arrived there people greeted him as *Wild Bill*, by which name he was widely known thereafter.

Another interesting explanation, but one with a noticeable discrepancy in it, as to how Hickok came to be nicknamed *Wild Bill* is told by William Frederick Cody, better known as *Buffalo Bill*. Cody said that Hickok had an elder brother named William who was wagon-master of a wagon train operating between the western border of the older settlements of the United States and the Pacific Coast. Because this William Hickok was equal to any crisis which arose on the dangerous journeys across the plains to the West Coast, and because he dealt so effectively with the hostile Indians, highwaymen, and other rowdies who sometimes attacked his wagon train, he was nicknamed *Wild Bill Hickok*. His brother, James, following closely the example of William in successfully coping with trying situations, became also known as *Wild Bill Hickok*. [7] It is exceedingly difficult to harmonize this account of the origin of the sobriquet with the fact that Hickok had no brother [3] by the name of William. However, Frank J. Wilstach states that Mrs. Louis Hickok told him that James Butler Hickok had a brother, Lorenzo, [5] who fitted the description given to the William of Cody's account, and that as a youngster, Lorenzo had been called "Billy Barnes," thus there is a possibility that Lorenzo was the original *Wild Bill* who was called William Hickok by Cody.

This incident in the life of James Butler Hickok which has probably received the most notoriety was his fight with the McCanles brothers at Rock Creek, Neb.

Hickok, J. B.—Continued

Some writers assert that immediately after this bloody fight, Hickok told the assembled spectators that when he found himself pitted against a half-dozen desperate men intent upon killing him, he thought that he would surely be killed; therefore, he went wild and slashed everything about him with his knife. The nickname *Wild Bill* is said by these writers [6] to have originated in connection with this statement made by Hickok, himself.

James Butler Hickok was born in La Salle County, Ill., in 1839, and died on August 2, 1870 from a pistol shot fired by Jack McCall at Deadwood, in the Black Hills of South Dakota.

[1] "True Story of Wild Bill-McCanles Affray in Jefferson County, Nebraska, July 12, 1861; Photographic Copies of Original Documents Never Before Published," by George W. Hansen, in the *Nebraska History Magazine, Missouri Number* (Illustrated), Addison E. Sheldon, Editor (Published quarterly by the Nebraska State Historical Society, Lincoln, Neb., January-March, 1925) vol. 8-10, no. 1, p. 79.

[2] "Wild Bill—James Butler Hickok," by William Elsey Connelley, in the *Collections of the Kansas State Historical Society, 1926-1928 together with Addresses, Memorials and Miscellaneous Papers*, ed. by William Elsey Connelley (Kansas State Printing Plant, B. P. Walker, State Printer, Topeka, Kans., 1928) vol. 17, p. 21.

[3] *Wild Bill and His Era: The Life and Adventures of James Butler Hickok*, William Elsey Connelley, with Introduction by Charles Moreau Harger (The Press of the Pioneers, New York, 1933) p. 8-10, 12, 14, 34, 44-6, 216.

[4] *The Pony Express: The Record of Romantic Adventure in Business*, Arthur Chapman (G. P. Putnam's Sons, New York and London, 1932) p. 168.

[5] *Wild Bill Hickok, the Prince of Pistoleers*, Frank J. Wilstach (Doubleday, Page and Company, Garden City, N.Y., 1926) p. 1, 24-6, 39.

"Earlyday Skill with the Six-shooter" in the *Outer's Book, A Magazine of Outdoor Interest* (The Sportsman Publishing Company, Milwaukee, Wis., November, 1912) vol. 24, p. 513-14.

"Rifle and Trap" by R. A. Kane, in the *Outdoor Life, A Sportsman's Magazine of the West*, ed. by J. A. McGuire (Denver, Colo., June, 1906) vol. 17, p. 589-90.

[6] *The Real Wild Bill Hickok, Famous Scout and Knight Chivalric of the Plains—A True Story of Pioneer Life in the Far West*, Wilbert Edwin Eisele (Ross Lyndon) (William H. Andre, Denver, Colo., 1931) p. 21-5, 51.

[7] *True Tales of the Plains*, Buffalo Bill (William F. Cody) (Cupples and Leon Company, New York, 1908) p. 46-7.

Heroes of the Plains, J. W. Buel (Historical Publishing Company, St. Louis, Mo., 1884) p. 49.

Higbee, Chester Goss

Chester Goss Higbee was popularly known as the *Good Physician* [1] in St. Paul, Minn., because he was an unusually skillful physician and surgeon and a man of sterling character.

He was born at Pike, N.Y., on August 5, 1835, and died at St. Paul, Minn., on April 3, 1908.

[1] *The National Cyclopaedia of American Biography* (James T. White and Company, New York, 1920) vol. 17, p. 113.

Higgins, Eugene

Eugene Higgins, a painter of rural life, was nicknamed the *Millet of America* [1] because like Jean François Millet, the painter of French peasant life, Higgins painted rural scenes . His paintings are characterized by the large size of the people and objects he depicts. Their simplicity gives them an unsurpassed reality.

Eugene Higgins was born at Kansas City, Mo., on February 28, 1874.

[1] *Newsweek: The Magazine of News Significance*, Rockefeller Center, N.Y., December 26, 1938, p. 21.

High Priest of the Constitution. See Bayard, J. A.

Highbinders

The *Highbinders* [1] was a nickname given to gangs who allied themselves with political factions prior to the outbreak of the Civil War. When the polls were open for voting they would frequently club the voters with revolvers and clubs to keep them from voting.

[1] *Political Americanisms*, Charles Ledyard Norton Longmans, Green and Company, New York and London, 1890) p. 54.

Highlanders. See Humboldt State College; Maryville College; New York American League Baseball Company

Hill, Daniel Harvey

The nickname *Bethel Hill* [1] was sometimes applied to Daniel Harvey Hill. At Big Bethel, Va.,[2] on June 10, 1861, four regiments of Federal soldiers under Brigadier General Benjamin Franklin Butler, were repulsed by Confederate soldiers under Major General John Bankhead Magruder. Hill, a Confederate colonel, distinguished himself by his courage and leadership and was thereafter often called *Bethel Hill*.

Daniel Harvey Hill was born at Hill's Iron Works, in York District, S.C., in July, 1821, and died at Charlotte, N.C., on September 24, 1889.

[1] *Lee and His Lieutenants; Comprising the Early Life, Public Services, and Campaigns of General Robert E. Lee and His Companions in Arms, with a Record of*

Their Campaigns and Heroic Deeds, Edward A. Pollard (E. B. Treat and Company, New York, 1867) p. 448.
[2] *Lives of Distinguished North Carolinians*, W. J. Peele (The North Carolina Publishing Society, Raleigh, N.C., 1897) p. 531-3.

Hill, David Bennett

The *Bachelor Governor* and *Young Hickory* are nicknames which have been given to David Bennett Hill. Because he was not married when he was Governor of New York, from 1885 to 1891, Hill was known as the *Bachelor Governor*.[1]

The sobriquet *Young Hickory*[1] is said to have originated in 1892, from a statement which David Bennett Hill made about there still being "some old hickory in the Democratic party," and because his views on the spoils system were similar to those of Andrew Jackson.

David Bennett Hill was born at Havana, N.Y., on August 29, 1843, and died at Woorfert's Roost, his country home, near Albany, N.Y., on October 20, 1910.

[1] *U.S. "Snap Shots": An Independent, National, and Memorial Encyclopedia . . . .*, Oliver McKee (A. M. Thayer and Company, Boston, 1892) p. 248.

Hill, George Handel

George Handel Hill was known as *Yankee Hill*[1] because on the stage he was a popular and professional success in the role of a Yankee.

He was born at Boston, Mass., on October 9, 1809, and died at Saratoga, N.Y., on September 27, 1848.

[1] *The National Cyclopaedia of American Biography* (James T. White and Company, New York, 1898) vol. 1, p. 401.

Hill, James Jerome

During the period from 1880 to 1893, James Jerome Hill built and put into operation the Great Northern Railroad connecting Lake Superior with Puget Sound. Be cause this railroad was instrumental in developing the northwestern part of the United States, Hill was called the *Empire Builder*.[1]

James Jerome Hill was born near Guelph, in Wellington, County, Ontario, Canada, on September 16, 1838, and died at St. Paul, Minn., on May 29, 1916.

[1] *The Growth of the American People and Nation*, Mary G. Kelty (Ginn and Company, New York and Boston, 1931) p. 400.

Hill, John Sprunt

The *Father of Rural Credit in North Carolina*[1] is the nickname given to John Sprunt Hill because of the service he rendered as a pioneer in securing for the farmers of North Carolina long-term credit at low rates of interest. He was largely responsible for the Credit Union Act, passed in 1915 by the North Carolina Legislature. He published articles dealing with the problems of farm credits and mortages.

John Sprunt Hill was born near Faison, N.C., on May 17, 1869, and now resides at Durham, N.C.,

[1] *Encyclopedia of American Biography: American Biography, a New Cyclopedia*, comp. under the editorial supervision of a notable advisory board (Published under the direction of The American Historical Society, Inc., New York, 1928) vol. 32, p. 131.

Hill, Walter Barnard

Walter Barnard Hill, a lawyer and educator, was known as the *Scholar of the Georgia Bar* and the *Apostle of Prohibition*.

The *Scholar of the Georgia Bar*[1] was applied to him because he was recognized by the judges in the Georgia courts and by his fellow lawyers for his skill in compiling briefs and in presenting his cases. The *Apostle of Prohibition* was applied to him because he was a pioneer in securing temperence legislation in the state of Georgia.

Walter Barnard Hill was born in Talbott County, Ga., on September 9, 1851, and died at Macon, Ga., on December 28, 1905.

[1] *Dictionary of American Biography under the Auspices of the American Council of Learned Societies*, ed. by Dumas Malone (Charles Scribner's Sons, New York, 1932) vol. 9, p. 48.

Hillbillies. See Daniel Baker College; Hanover College

Hill City. See Lynchburg, Va.; Portland, Me.

Hillhouse, William

William Hillhouse was humorously called the *Sachem*[1] by his friends because, like an Indian, he possessed a swarthy complexion, high cheek bones, a strong physique, and a remarkable power of endurance. Hillhouse occupied a prominent place in the political affairs of Connecticut.

He was born at Montville, Conn., on August 25, 1728, and died there on January 12, 1816.

[1] *The Natoinal Cyclopaedia of American Biography* (James T. White and Company, New York, 1899) vol. 2, p. 9.

Hillsdale College

The athletic teams of Hillsdale College, at Hillsdale, Mich., were nicknamed the *Dales*.[1]

[1] A communication from Dwight B. Harwood, Director of Athletics at Hillsdale College, Hillsdale, Mich., June 20, 1935.

Hilltoppers. See Hanover College; Marquette University; Wartburg College

Hindman, Thomas Carmichael

Thomas Carmichael Hindman was known as the *Lion of the South*[1] because of his outstanding leadership, his courage, and his endurance under adverse conditions.

He served as an officer in both the war with Mexico, and in the Confederate Army during the Civil War. His conduct was conspicuously gallant and resourceful.

Thomas Carmichael Hindman was born at Knoxville, Tenn., on January 28, 1828, and died at Helena, Ark., on September 27, 1868.

[1] *The National Cyclopaedia of American Biography* (James T. White and Company, New York, 1932) vol. 22, p. 130.

Hines, Edward Norris

Edward Norris Hines was nicknamed the *Father of the White Line*[1] because when he was Road Commissioner of Wayne County, Michigan, in 1911, he ordered a white line painted down the center of the bridges and curved roads under his supervision.

Edward Norris Hines was born at St. Louis, Mo., on January 13, 1870.

[1] *This Week: Magazine Section of Herald Tribune*, New York, December 25, 1938, cols. 4, 5, 6, p. 19.

His Accidency. See Arthur, C. A.; Cleveland, Grover; Fillmore, Millard; Johnson, Andrew; Tyler, John

Historian of the Hampden County Bar. See Bates, W. G.

Hoar, George Frisbie

The following are nicknames which have been applied to George Frisbie Hoar: *Gran'ther Hoar*, the *Moon-faced Senator from Worcester*, the *Old Man Eloquent of the Senate*, and *Pre-Adamite*.[1]

The *Boston Globe* designated Senator Hoar *Gran'ther Hoar*[1] because of his long service as a senator.

George Frisbie Hoar was nicknamed the *Moon-faced Senator from Worcester*[2] because of his round face.

Old Man Eloquent of the Senate[2] was applied to Senator Hoar while he was a Senator from Massachusetts from 1877 to 1904 because of his ability as a speaker.

He was nicknamed *Pre-Adamite*[1] because those who politically favored the policy of Adams were commonly called *Adamites*. Senator Hoar's basic principles were not only opposed to those of Adams, but they also antedated them.

George Frisbie Hoar was born at Concord, Mass., on August 29, 1826, and died at Worcester, Mass., on September 30, 1904.

[1] *U.S. "Snap Shots": An Independent, National, and Memorial Encyclopedia . . .* , Oliver McKee (A. M. Thayer and Company, Boston, 1892) p. 244.

[2] *The Encyclopedia Americana* (Americana Corporation, New York and Chicago, 1927) vol. 14, p. 300.

Hobart College

The *Deacons*[1] is the nickname given to the athletic teams of Hobart College, at Geneva, N.Y., because at one time they were coached by Vincent S. Welch whose nickname was *Deacon* or *Deac*.

[1] A letter from Clifford E. Orr, Director of the Hobart College News Bureau, Geneva, N.Y., June 14, 1935.

Hobson, Richmond Pearson

Kissing-bug Hobson and *Parson Hobson* were nicknames of Richmond Pearson Hobson.

Upon his return from Cuba to New York City, as a popular hero in August 1898, he was surrounded by young women who wanted to kiss him. The newspapers played it up and he became known as *Kissing-bug Hobson*.

While Hobson was attending the United States Naval Academy at Annapolis, Md., from 1885 to 1889, he was nicknamed *Parson Hobson*[2] by fellow-cadets because of his participation in religious activities.

Richmond Pearson Hobson was born at Greensboro, Ala., on August 1, 1870.

[1] *The Sage of Sinnissippi . . .* , Kinnie A. Ostewig (Press of Joseph A. Nolen, Shabbona, Ill., 1907) p. 159.

The Age-Herald, Birmingham, Ala., August 9, 1898, col. 4, p. 5.

Twenty Years of the Republic, 1885-1905, Harry Thurston Peck (Dodd, Mead and Company, New York, 1907) p. 626.

[2] *America's War for Humanity Related in Story and Picture Embracing a Complete History of Cuba's Struggle for Liberty and the Glorious Heroism of America's Soldiers and Sailors, Compiled from the Letters and Personal Experience of Noted Writers and Correspondents, a Thrilling and Wonderful Record of Human Heroism and Patriotic Devotion,* introduction by John J. Ingalls (N. D. Thompson Publishing Company, New York and St. Louis, 1898) p. 397.

Hoffman, Clare E.

Clare E. Hoffman, a Michigan lawyer and politician, was nicknamed *CIO Hoffman* and the *Sit-down Striker* in the House of Representatives because he opposed the sit-down strikes and John L. Lewis's labor organizations.

He was a Republican Representative from Michigan from 1935 to 1949.

Clare E. Hoffman was born at Vicksburg, Pa., on September 10, 1875.

[1] An interview with Captain Victor Hunt Harding, Secretary of the National Democratic Congress Reëlection Committee, Washington, D.C., April 10, 1939.

Hoffman, Michael

During his last term in Congress while he was the chairman of the naval affairs committee, Michael Hoffman was nicknamed *Admiral.*[1]

Michael Hoffman, who was born at Clifton Park, N.Y., on October 11, 1787, and who died at Brooklyn, N.Y., on September 27, 1848, was a Representative from New York to Congress from 1825 to 1833.

[1] *The National Cyclopedia of American Biography* (James T. White and Company, New York, 1909) vol. 11, p. 89.

Hoffman, Ogden

Because of his prominence as a successful and learned American criminal and civil lawyer Ogden Hoffman was called the *Erskine of the American Bar.*[1] Thomas Erskine was a Scottish jurist, distinguished as an orator and counsellor at law, who was contemporary with Hoffman.

Ogden Hoffman was born at New York City, on May 3, 1793, and died there on May 1, 1856.

[1] *The National Cyclopedia of American Biography* (James T. White and Company, New York, 1909) vol. 1, p. 85.

Hog and Hominy State. See Tennessee

Hogan, James Francis

James Francis Hogan, who was born at Somerville, Mass., on March 21, 1906, and

who was a catcher in major-league baseball was nicknamed *Shanty.*[1]

[1] *Who's Who in Major League Base Ball,* comp. by Harold (Speed) Johnson (Buxton Publishing Company, Chicago, 1933) p. 218.

Hogg, James Stephen

The *Great Commoner* [1] was the nickname applied to James Stephen Hogg because during his political career he always espoused the cause of the common man.

James Stephen Hogg, who was born near Rusk, Tex., on March 24, 1851, and who died at Austin, Tex., on March 3, 1906, was the nineteenth Governor of Texas.

[1] *The Real Colonel House,* Arthur D. Howden Smith (George H. Doran Company, New York, 1918) p. 47.

Hogsett, Elon Chester

Because he is part Indian, *Chief* [1] was the nickname given to Elon Chester Hogsett, who was born at Brownell, Kans., on November 2 1903, and who pitched in major league baseball.

[1] *Who's Who in Major League Base Ball,* comp. by Harold (Speed) Johnson (Buxton Publishing Company, Chicago, 1933) p. 219.

Holcombe, Solomon

Solomon Holcombe was known as *King Solomon* [1] because of his wealth and the great number of his descendants.

He was born at West Amwell, N.J., on October 4, 1789, and died at Mount Airy, N.J., on March 26, 1871.

[1] *The National Cyclopaedia of American Biography* (James T. White and Company, 1893) vol. 3, p. 313.

Hold That Line. See Blanton, T. L.

Hole in The Sky Speech

During the impeachment trial of President Andrew Johnson from February 24 to May 16, 1868, George Sewell Boutwell, a Representative from Massachusetts who was appointed one of the managers of the impeachment trial, made a speech outlining suitable means of disposing of the President after his conviction. He advocated banishing Johnson to the vacant space in the southern heavens, near the Southern Cross called by the uneducated "hole in the sky." This address was nicknamed the *Hole in the Sky Speech.*

[1] *Andrew Johnson, Plebian and Patriot,* Robert W. Winston (Henry Holt and Company, New York, 1928) p. 443.

Hollingsworth, James M.

In 1861, at the outbreak of the Civil War, Lieutenant Colonel James M. Hollingsworth of the Nineteenth Regiment of Louisiana Infantry was nicknamed *Old Double Quick*.[1]

James M. Hollingsworth was born in Monroe County, Ala., on December 9, 1830, and in 1894 moved to Louisiana.

[1] *The National Cyclopaedia of American Biography* (James T. White and Company, New York, 1900) vol. 10, p. 495.

Holman, William Steele

The *Great Objector* and the *Watchdog of the Treasury* were nicknames given to William Steele Holman.

Because throughout his long career as a United States Representative from Indiana, Holman opposed all unncesssary appropriations, he was nicknamed the *Watchdog of the Treasury*[1] and the *Great Objector*.[2]

William Steele Holman was born at Veraestau, Ind., on September 6, 1822, and died at Washington, D.C., on April 22, 1897.

[1] *The Encyclopedia Americana* (Americana Corporation, New York and Chicago, 1927) vol. 14, p. 321.
[2] *My Quarter Century of American Politics*, Champ Clark (Harper and Brothers, New York and London, 1920) p. 56.

Holmes, John

John Holmes, a lawyer and legislator, was nicknamed the *Duke of Summersetts*[1] because having been an ardent Federalist, in 1811 he became an active Democrat. He was a Representative and later a Senator from Massachusetts.

John Holmes was born at Scituate, Mass., on March 28, 1773, and died at Thomaston, Me., on July , 1843.

[1] *Dictionary of American Biography under the Auspices of the American Council of Learned Societies*, ed. by Dumas Malone (Charles Scribner's Sons, New York, 1932) vol. 9, p. 166.

Holy Horatio. See Alger, Horatio

Holyoke, Massachusetts

Holyoke has been termed the *Paper City*[1] because its chief industry is paper making, in the manufacturing of which the city attained its greatest prominence after the Civil War.

[1] *A History of Paper-Manufacturing in the United States, 1609-1916, Illustrated*, Lyman Horace Weeks (The Lockwood Trade Journal Company, New York, 1918) p. 244, 283-4.

Home Run Baker. See Baker, J. F.

Home, Sweet-home House

The boyhood home of John Howard Payne in Easthampton, Long Island, N.Y., has ben designated the *Home, Sweet-home House*[1] because John Howard Payne wrote the song "Home Sweet Home."

[1] *Manor Houses and Historic Homes of Long Island and Staten Island*, Harold Donaldson Eberlein (J. B. Lippincott Company, Philadelphia and London, 1928) p. 53.

Homesteader's Paradise. See Palestine, Tex.

Honest Abe Lincoln. See Lincoln, Abraham

Honest Harold. See Ickes, H. L.

Honest John. See Bricker, J. W.; Covode, John; Kelly, John; Stephenson, John

Honest Lawyer. See Ogden, Robert

Honest Money

The policy of having a currency consisting of gold, silver, and paper money was written into the Ohio Republican Platform during the presidental campaign in 1896. This was called *Honest Money*[1] because it did not discriminate against any of the three types of currency. William Jennings Bryan was running on the Democratic ticket which advocated free coinage of silver.

[1] *Twenty Years of the Republic, 1885-1905*, Harry Thurston Peck (Dodd, Mead and Company, New York, 1907) p. 482.

Honey. See Walker, William

Honey War

The dispute in 1840 between Iowa and Missouri over the state boundary line in Clark County, Missouri, has been called the *Honey War*[1] because a farmer in Clark County cut down several bee trees located on a narrow strip of land claimed by both states. The incident led to further complications until the two states were on the verge of war. The matter was referred to the United States Supreme Court, and in 1851 markers were erected on the exact boundary line.

[1] *A History of Missouri and Missourians*, Floyd C. Shoemaker (The Walter Ridgway Publishing Company, Columbia, Mo., 1922) p. 212.

Honeyman, John

The American troops nicknamed John Honeyman the *Tory Traitor*.[1] He posed as a Tory in order to gather information from the British forces at Trenton. He then allowed himself to be captured by the American troops and turned his information over to General George Washington. Honeyman rendered most valuable assistance to General Washington.

John Honeyman, a native of Briggstown, N.J., had served as bodyguard to General Wolfe in the Battle of Quebec, on September 13, 1759.

[1] *The Life of James Monroe*, George Morgan (Small, Maynard and Company, Boston, 1921) p. 45-6.

Honeymoon Period

From 1898 to 1902 has been termed the *Honeymoon Period* [1] because during those first years of collective bargaining employer-employee relations were especially harmonious. The waning of the honeymoon began to be noticed about 1902.

[4] *Labor Problems in American Industry*, Carroll R. Daugherty (Houghton Mifflin Company, New York and Boston, 1933) p. 443.

Honorable Company of Goose Catchers

In 1885 the city council of Cleveland, Ohio, was called the *Honorable Company of Goose Catchers* [1] because the chairman of the pound-keepers' committee investigated the records of a pound-keeper who had kept a number of geese at a cost to the city of thirty-nine dollars per goose. The press thereupon originated the nickname for the council.

[1] *Myron T. Herrick, Friend of France*, T. Bentley Mott (Doubleday, Doran and Company, Inc., Garden City, N.Y., 1929) p. 32.

Honus. See Wagner, J. H.

Hood, John Bell

Lieutenant General Hood was sometimes called *Butcher Hood* [1] because he sacrificed so many men in his campaigns in the latter part of the Civil War.

John Bell Hood, a Confederate soldier, was born at Owingsville, Ky., on June 29, 1831, and died at New Orleans, La., on August 30, 1879.

[1] *Hood's Tennessee Campaign*, Thomas Robson Hay (Walter Neale, New York, 1929) p. 41-2.

Sherman's March Through the South, with Sketches and Incidents of the Campaign, David P. Conyngham (Sheldon and Company, New York, 1865) p. 223.

Hoodoo Ship of the Navy

The second-class battleship *Texas*, which fought in the naval battle at Santiago, Cuba, on July 3, 1898, during the Spanish-American War, was nicknamed the *Hoodoo Ship of the Navy* [1] because during its entire existence it suffered one disaster after another.

The battleship *Texas* was the second vessel in the United States Navy which bore that name. The first was an ironclad ram, which was captured when the Federals captured Richmond, Va., on April 4, 1865.

[1] *The Washington Post*, Washington, D.C., January 5, 1908, Miscellany Section, col. 3, p. 5.

Ships Data: U. S. Naval Vessels, C. F. Adams, Secretary of the Navy (Government Printing Office, Washington, D.C., July 1, 1931) p. 314.

Hooey Long. See Long, H. P.

Hooker, Joseph

The nickname *Fighting Joe Hooker* [1] was applied to Joseph Hooker because of his military genius and fighting qualities. The nickname is said to have originated at the Battle of Williamsburg, on May 5, 1862.

Joseph Hooker was born at Hadley, Mass., on November 13, 1814, and died at Garden City, N.Y., on October 31, 1879.

[1] *History of the United States of America, under the Constitution*, James Schouler (Dodd, Mead and Company, New York, 1899) vol. 6, p. 341.

Two Days of War, a Gettysburg Narrative and Other Excursions, Henry Edwin Tremain (Bonnell, Silver and Bowers, New York, 1905) p. 353-4.

The Encyclopaedia Britannica, Fourteenth Edition (Encyclopaedia Britannica, Inc., New York, 1929) vol. 11, p. 728.

Hooker, Thomas

Thomas Hooker was called the *Light of the Western Churches* [1] because he was a prominent colonial clergyman, noted for his zeal, sagacity, and learning. He was not afraid to follow the dictates of his conscience in regard to religious worship and played an important part in the establishment of dissenting churches of New England.

He was born at Markfield, in Leicestershire, England, on July 7, 1586, and died at Hartford, Conn., on July 19, 1641.

[1] *The New and Complete History of the United States of America*, Official Edition, John Clark Ridpath (The Jones Brothers Publishing Company, Cincinnati, Ohio, 1906) vol. 3, p. 966.

Makers of America: Thomas Hooker, Preacher, Founder, Democrat, George Leon Walker (Dodd, Mead and Company, New York, 1891) p. 152-4.

Hooks and Eyes

The Amish, Old and New Order, branches of the Mennonite Church, were nicknamed *Hooks and Eyes* [1] because the people of this sect, forgoing all that they considered ornamental or superfluous even to buttons, used hooks and eyes as fastenings for their clothes. The first Mennonite immigrants from Holland to America settled at Germantown, Pa., in 1863.

[1] "Our Foreigners, A Chronicle of Americans in the Making" by Samuel P. Orth, in *The Chronicles of America Series*, Allen Johnson, Editor (Yale University Press, New Haven, Conn., 1920) p. 68.

Hooper, Robert

It is said that the nickname *King Hooper* [1] was given to Robert Hooper by the fishermen of Marblehead, Mass., because of his wealth and eminence in society and the princely manner in which he contributed to the welfare of less fortunate people.

Robert Hooper was born at Marblehead, Mass., on June 26, 1709, and died there on May 20, 1790.

[1] *The National Cyclopaedia of American Biography* (James T. White and Company, New York, 1926) vol. 19, p. 435.

The Book of Boston, Robert Shockleton (The Penn Publishing Company, Philadelphia, 1916) p. 264.

Hoosier Orator. See Orton, H. S.

Hoosier Poet. See Riley, J. W.

Hoosier Shakespeare. See Gray, F. H.

Hoosier State. See Indiana

Hoosierdom. See Indiana

Hoosiers. See Indianans

Hoosiers. See Indiana University

Hoot Gibson. See Gibson, S. B.

Hoover, Herbert Clark

The *Chief*, the *Friend of Helpless Children*, the *Hermit Author of Palo Alto*, and the *Man of Great Heart* are the nicknames applied to Herbert Clark Hoover.

Because of the influence he exerted as Secretary of Commerce from 1917 to 1921 he was nicknamed the *Chief*.[1]

Hoover served from 1915 to 1916 as the Chairman of the American Relief Committee in London and Chairman of the Commission for Relief in Belgium, in which capacity he distributed millions of dollars worth of food and clothing. In 1919 he aided in the organization of a private charitable organization known as the European Children's Fund which continued in existence until 1922, and fed and clothed approximately two million destitute and orphaned children. In 1927 he directed much of the relief work executed in behalf of the refugees of the Mississippi flood. For this he is known as the *Friend of Helpless Children* [3] and the *Man of Great Heart*.[3]

In the November 1934 issue of *Vanity Fair*, Herbert Clark Hoover was cartooned as the *Hermit Author of Palo Alto*.[3] After his term of office as President of the United States had expired on March 4, 1933, Mr. Hoover lived at Palo Alto, Calif., where he engaged in writing.

Herbert Clark Hoover, who was born at West Branch, Iowa, on August 10, 1874, was the thirty-first President of the United States.

[1] *The Literary Digest, January to March, 1930* (Funk and Wagnalls Company, New York, 1930) vol. 104, March 8, 1930, p. 41.

[2] *The New Pioneers*, Mary H. Wade (Little, Brown and Company, Boston, 1930) p. 113, 152, 160, 161.

[3] *Vanity Fair* (The Conde Nast Publications, Inc., Greenwich, Conn.) November, 1934, p. 20.

Hopkins, Ferdinand T.

The sobriquet, *Sink the Track and Arch It Over*,[1] was applied to Ferdinand T. Hopkins after his active work in securing for the upper part of New York City submerged railroad tracks with the streets arching over them at the crossings.

Ferdinand T. Hopkins was born at Lake Mahopac, in Putnam County, N.Y., on January 16, 1834, and died in Westchester County, N.Y.

[1] *The National Cyclopaedia of American Biography* (James T. White and Company, New York, 1899) vol. 2, p. 215.

Hopkins, Samuel

Because he was one of the earliest advocates of abolishing the slave trade in America, Samuel Hopkins has been designated the *Father of Abolition*.[1] His agitation of this question led to the passage of a law in 1774 forbidding further importation of slaves into the colony of Rhode Island, and to a subsequent act declaring the children of slaves born after March 1, 1785, to be free.

Samuel Hopkins was born at Waterbury, Conn., on September 17, 1721, and died at Newport, R.I., on December 20, 1803.

[1] *The National Cyclopaedia of American Biography* (James T. White and Company, New York, 1897) vol. 7, p. 155.

Hopkins, Mark. See *Big Four*

Hopper, Edna Wallace
Edna Wallace Hopper (Mrs. Albert O. Brown), who was the star of the musical comedy "Floradora" in 1900, was nicknamed the *Eternal Flapper* [1] and the *Grandma Flapper* because she retained her beauty and youthful appearance long after the end of her stage career. She toured the country as a beauty specialist for some years, and settling in New York City became associated with the brokerage firm of L. F. Rothschild and Company.

Edna Wallace Hopper was born at San Francisco, Calif. Suggested dates are January 17, 1864, or 1874, but Miss Hopper prefers to let people speculate.[2]

[1] *Washington Herald*, Washington, D.C., March 18, 1936, col. 3, p. 13; April 14, 1927, col. 2, p. 3.
[2] *New York Times Magazine*, April 19, 1953, p. 47.

Horace Mann of the South. See Ruffner, W. H.

Horan, John Michael
John Michael Horan, at one time the oldest railroad employee in the United States, was nicknamed *Soda Ash Johnny* [1] because he developed a boiler wash containing soda ash for cleaning engine boilers after they had become clogged with lime and other substances dissolved in the water used to produce steam. He had been an employee of the Chicago, Milwaukee, and St. Paul Railroad for eighty-three years at the time of his death.

John Michael Horan was born at Burlington, Vt., on January 23, 1838, and died at Racine, Wis., on February 4, 1938.

[1] *The Racine Journal-Times*, Racine, Wis., January 17, 1938, cols. 4 and 5, p. 1.
The Washington Post, Washington, D.C., February 5, 1938, col. 3, p. 4.

Horned Frogs. See Texas Christian University

Hornet's Nest
The *Hornet's Nest* [1] is a sobriquet given by the Confederates to the slope adjacent to the intersection of the Corinth road and a road cut by the forces of General Mayberry Prentiss where violent and destructive fighting took place between the Union forces under the command of General Ulysses S. Grant and the Confederate forces under the command of General Albert Sidney Johnston during the Battle of Shiloh a short distance from Pittsburg Landing in Tennessee on April 5 and 6, 1862. The nickname suggests that this place was the scene of such vigorous and destructive firing that the bullets flew as thick as hornets.

[2] *Sketches of War History, 1861-1865: Papers Prepared for the Commandery of the State of Ohio, Military Order of the Loyal Legion of the United States, 1896-1903*, ed. by Major W. H. Chamberlin, Brevet Major A. M. Van Dyke, and Captain George A. Thayer, Publication Committee (Published by the Commandery, The Robert Clarke Company, Cincinnati, Ohio, 1903) vol. 5, p. 464.

Hornet's Nest. See Charlotte, N. C.

Hornsby, Rogers
Rogers Hornsby, who was born at Winters, Tex., on April 27, 1896, was nicknamed *Rajah*.[1] This nickname, a corruption of his first name, was acquired as a result of Hornsby's forthright and imperious behavior while he was making baseball history as a hitter and later as a manager in the major leagues.

[3] *Who's Who in Major League Base Ball*, comp. by Harold (Speed) Johnson (Buxton Publishing Company, Chicago, 1933) p. 221.

Horse. See Twiggs, D. E.

Horse-and-Ox Marine. See *Horse Marines*

Horse Marines
During the War of 1812 coastal shipping was interfered with so that goods had to be shipped by wagons drawn by horses, mules, and oxen, or sometimes by a combination of these. The wagon trains were operated as nearly as possible on a schedule. In the columns formerly given over to ship schedules, the newspapers began to list the arrival and the departure of these wagon

Horse Marines—Continued
trains from various towns and cities, calling them *Horse Marines* or *Horse and Ox Marines*.[4]

[7] *A History of the People of the United States, from the Revolution to the Civil War*, John Bach McMaster (D. Appleton and Company, New York, 1895) vol. 4, p. 220.

Horse Meat March

The march of General George Crook and his soldiers in 1876 was nicknamed the *Horse Meat March*.[1] The first column went from the headwaters of the Heart River to Deadwood in the Black Hills of the Dakotas. Crook and his soldiers, in addition to being constantly drenched with cold rains, had scarcely any food except the flesh of horses and ponies which they sometimes had to eat raw because there was often no fuel for fires.

[1] *On the Border with Crook*, John G. Bourke (Charles Scribner's Sons, New York, 1891) p. 362, 368-9, 378.

Horsemen. See Norwich University

Horsepower. See Fulmer, H. P.

Horizontal Bill. See Morrison, W. R.

Hot Oil Marland. See Marland, E. W.

Hot Springs, Arkansas

Hot Springs is called the *Nation's Health Resort*[1] and the *Baden-Baden of America*[2] because the healing properties of the cold and hot springs attract thousands of people from all parts of the United States. Hot Springs is a National Park where the government furnishes free baths to the poor and operates an Army and Navy General Hospital. The city and its surrounding territory offer opportunities for various forms of amusement and recreation which contribute much to its popularity. Baden-Baden in Germany is a famous watering-place noted for its natural hot springs and for its baths.

[1] *Arkansas and Its People, A History, 1541-1930*, David Yancey Thomas (The American Historical Society, Inc., New York, 1930) vol. 2, p. 830.
[2] *The World Book Encyclopedia* (The Quarrie Corporation, Chicago, 1938) vol. 1, p. 397-8.

Hot-water Rebellion

In July 1798, Congress passed a law to raise two million dollars by a direct tax on Negro slaves, houses, and lands. In 1799 when the assessors in Pennsylvania began to estimate the worth of houses by counting and measuring the windows, the farmers and landowners objected and when they reached the most eastern counties of the state, the women of this section railed at them, set the dogs on them, and threw scalding water on them as they attempted to count and measure the windows. This revolt has been nicknamed the *Hot-water Rebellion*.[1]

[1] *A History of the People of the United States, from the Revolution to the Civil War*, John Bach McMaster (D. Appleton and Company, New York, 1885) vol. 2, p. 435.

Hot Water State. See Arkansas

Houdini, Harry

The *Handcuff King*[1] is a name applied to Harry Houdini because of his ability to free himself when bound with cords, or held by handcuffs.

Harry Houdini was born at Appleton, Wis., on April 6, 1874, and died at Detroit, Mich., on October 31, 1926.

[1] *The Encyclopedia Americana* (Americana Corporation, New York and Chicago, 1927) vol. 14, p. 441.

Houdini in the White House. See Roosevelt, F. D.

Houghton, Douglass

Douglass Houghton, a geologist, was called the *Little Doctor*[1] and the *Boy Geologist of Michigan* because of his slight physique and youthful appearance. He had been a physician and surgeon at Detroit, Mich., prior to 1837 when he planned a geological survey of Michigan. In 1842 he was appointed Professor of Geology at the University of Michigan, at Ann Arbor.

Douglass Houghton was born at Troy, N.Y., on September 21, 1809, and was drowned in Lake Superior on October 13, 1845.

[1] *Dictionary of American Biography under the Auspices of the American Council of Learned Societies*, ed. by Dumas Malone (Charles Scribner's Sons, New York, 1932) vol. 9, p. 254.

Hourglass Division. See Seventh Infantry Division of World War II

House, Edward Mandell

See Wilson, Woodrow and Edward Mandell House.

House of Golden Weddings

Located at Quincy, Mass., the old Adams family home has been termed the *House of Golden Weddings*,[1] because in this residence were celebrated the golden wedding anniversaries of Mr. and Mrs. John Adams in 1814; of Mr. and Mrs. John Quincy Adams in 1847; and of Mr. and Mrs. Charles Francis Adams in 1878.

[1] *Mr. and Mrs. John Quincy Adams; an Adventure in Patriotism,* Dorothie Bobbe (Minton, Balch and Company, New York, 1930) p. 297.

House with the Eagles

The home of Captain Churchill, commander of the ship *Yankee,* a well-known privateer, near Bristol, R.I., has been nicknamed the *House with the Eagles* [1] because it has eagles perched on the corners of the balustrade of its roof.

[1] *Know Rhode Island: Facts Concerning the Land of Roger Williams,* Sixth Edition, comp. and distributed by the Office of the Secretary of State (State of Rhode Island and Providence Plantations, Providence, R.I., 1936) p. 62.

Houston, Samuel

Because Samuel Houston took an active part in helping Texas to gain its independence from Mexico, he has been called the *Father of Texas.*[1]

Samuel Houston was born at Timber Ridge Church in Rockbridge County, Va., on March 2, 1793, and died at Huntsville, Texas, on July 26, 1863.

[1] *The Makers of America,* New Edition, Revised and Enlarged, James A. Woodburn and Thomas F. Moran (Longmans, Green and Company, New York and Boston, 1922) p. 231.

Houston, Texas

Houston has two nicknames, the *City That Built Its Seaport* and the *Magnolia City.* It is called the *City That Built Its Seaport* [1] because it enlarged the fifty-mile ship channel to Galveston in order to have access to the gulf. It is called the *Magnolia City* [2] because of the many magnolia trees growing in its residential suburbs and parks.

[1] *Texas As It Is Today,* Alfred E. Menn (Gammel's Book Store, Austin, Tex., 1925) p. 111.

[2] *Flashlights on Texas,* Lillie Terrell Shaver and Willie Williamson Rogers (A. C. Baldwin and Sons, Austin, Tex., 1928) p. 97.

Standard History of Houston, Texas, from a Study of the Original Sources, ed. by B. H. Carroll (H. W. Crew and Company, Knoxville, Tenn., 1912) p. 436.

How, James Eads

James Eads How, the grandson of the builder of Eads Bridge at St. Louis, Mo., was nicknamed the *Millionaire Hobo* [1] and the *Millionaire Tramp.*[2] His mother, Eliza Ann Eads How, left him the heir to two hundred and fifty thousand dollars when she died in 1915 but because he believed that it was wrong to live on money which had not been earned, he traveled on foot through the country working at what he could get.

James Eads How was born at St. Louis, Mo., in 1868, and died in a hospital at Staunton, Va., on July 22, 1930.

[1] *The New York Times,* New York, July 24, 1930, col. 4, p. 23.

[2] *Washington Herald,* Washington, D.C., August 24, 1911, col. 2, p. 3.

St. Louis Post-Dispatch, St. Louis, Mo., July 27, 1930, col. 8, p. 1J.

Howard, Oliver Otis

The nickname the *Havelock of the American Army* [1] was applied to Oliver Otis Howard because for many years he was a prominent soldier in the American Army, distinguished for his activities of a religious and humane nature. Sir Henry Havelock was an English soldier who lived from 1795 to 1857 and whose life was characterized by religious zeal.

Oliver Otis Howard was born at Leeds, Me., on November 8, 1830, and died there on October 26, 1909.

[1] *Dictionary of American Biography* under the Auspices of the American Council of Learned Societies, ed. by Dumas Malone (Charles Scribner's Sons, New York, 1928) vol. 9, p. 279.

[2] *The Encyclopedia Americana* (Americana Corporation, New York and Chicago, 1927) vol. 13, p. 763.

Howard University

Howard University at Washington, D.C., is frequently called the *Capstone of Negro Education* [1] because it is America's largest and best equipped university for Negroes. It has approximately two thousand students.

[1] *Washington City and Capital: Federal Writers' Project,* American Guide Series, 1937 (Government Printing Office, Washington, D.C., 1937) p. 87.

Howe, Edgar Watson

Edgar Watson Howe, a newspaper publisher, editor, author, and philosopher was nicknamed the *Sage of Potato Hill.*[1] He was widely known for his philosophical writings and for his pungent diction. He called his home at Atchison, Kans., "Potato Hill."

Edgar Watson Howe was born near Treaty, Ind., on May 3, 1854, and died at Atchison, Kans., on October 3, 1937.

[1] *The Emporia Gazette,* Emporia, Kans., October 4, 1937, col. 2, 8, p. 1.

Howe, E. W.—Continued

The Topeka Daily Capital, Topeka, Kans., October 4, 1937, col. 2, p. 5.

The Washington Post, Washington, D.C., October 4, 1937, col. 6, p. 1.

Howe, Elias

Elias Howe, who was born at Spencer, Mass., on July 9, 1819, and who died at Brooklyn, N.Y., on October 3, 1867, has been called the *Father of the Sewing Machine* [1] because he invented the sewing machine in April 1845.

[1] A Book of Nicknames, John Goff (Courier-Journal Job Printing Company, Louisville, Ky., 1892) p. 29.

Howe, Samuel Gridley

Samuel Gridley Howe was called the *Lafayette of the Greek Revolution* [1] because from 1824 to 1830 he devoted himself to aiding the revolutionists in Greece. He gave freely of his own money and raised funds in America to relieve the starving people and founded a colony on the isthmus of Corinth for those who had been exiled from Greece for political reasons.

Samuel Gridley Howe was born at Boston, Mass., on November 10, 1801, and died there on January 9, 1876.

[1] The National Cyclopaedia of American Biography (James T. White and Company, New York, 1907) vol. 8, p. 372.

Howe, William Frederick

The *Father of the Criminal Bar* and *Habeas Corpus Howe* were nicknames given to William Frederick Howe.

He was frequently called the *Father of the Criminal Bar* [1] because he was one of the earliest criminal lawyers to gain recognition for his success in defending clients charged with murder.

He was given the nickname *Habeas Corpus Howe* because during the Civil War he obtained the release of a large number of men drafted for service in the Federal Army by means of writs of *habeas corpus,* issued chiefly on the grounds that the men had enlisted while under the influence of intoxicating liquors.

William Frederick Howe was born at Boston, Mass., on July 7, 1828, and died at New York City, on September 1, 1902.

[1] The National Cyclopaedia of American Biography (James T. White and Company, New York, 1932) vol. 22, p. 49.

Dictionary of American Biography under the Auspices of the American Council of Learned Societies, ed. by Dumas Malone (Charles Scribner's Sons, New York, 1932) vol. 9, p. 299.

Howells, William Dean

Because William Dean Howells wrote realistic literature and influenced others to accept his point of view, he has been called the *Master of Realism.* [1]

He was born at Martin's Ferry, Ohio, on March 1, 1837, and died at New York City, on May 11, 1920.

[1] Compton's Pictured Encyclopedia (F. E. Compton and Company, Chicago, 1931) vol. 1, p. 114.

Hoyas. See Georgetown University

Hoyne, Thomas

Thomas Hoyne, a Chicago lawyer and politician, was called *Fighting Tom Hoyne* [1] because of his intolerance of dishonesty and corruption in public offices and institutions. He was for a time District Attorney for Illinois, and served as United States Marshal in that state.

Thomas Hoyne was born at New York City, on February 11, 1817, and died at Carlton station, N.Y., on July 27, 1883.

[1] The National Cyclopaedia of American Biography (James T. White and Company, New York, 1922) vol. 18, p. 62.

Sketch of the Life and Character of Thomas Hoyne, with the Proceedings of Public Bodies on the Occasion of His Death, and Memorial Addresses (Barnard and Gunthrop, Chicago, 1883) p. 40-1, 50-2, 67-8, 80.

Hub. See Boston, Mass.

Hub City. See Brainerd, Minn.; Compton, Calif.

Hub City of South Texas. See Yoakum, Tex.

Hub of New England. See Boston, Mass.

Hub of New York

Columbus Circle, located at Fifty-ninth Street where Broadway intersects Eighth Avenue at the southwest corner of Central Park, is called the *Hub of New York* [1] because distance on all roads leading from New York City is reckoned from this circle.

[1] The World Book Encyclopedia (The Quarrie Corporation, Chicago, 1938) vol. 12, p. 4988.

Hub of the Solar System. See Boston, Mass.

Hub of the Universe. See Boston, Mass.

Hubbard, Bernard Rosecrans

Bernard Rosecrans Hubbard has been nicknamed the *Glacier Priest* [1] and the *Priest of Volcanoes* [2] because of his interest in explorations of volcanoes and glaciers.

He was born at San Francisco, Calif., on November 24, 1888. He was Professor of Geology in the University of Santa Clara, California.

[1] *Who's Who in America: A Biographical Dictionary of Notable Living Men and Women of the United States, 1934-35,* ed. by Albert Nelson Marquis (The A. N. Marquis Company, Chicago, 1934) vol. 18, p. 1218.
The American Scene, Edwin C. Hill (Witmark Educational Publications, Department of M. Witmark and Sons, New York, 1933) p. 347.

Hubbard, Elbert

Elbert Hubbard, an editor, essayist, lecturer, and publisher nicknamed himself *Fra Elbertus* [1] when he began to publish a magazine entitled *The Fra* in 1908. Hubbard first won public attention as a writer in 1895 when he founded the *Philistine;* a monthly magazine written largely by himself. It was extremely popular. *The Fra* was another magazine which he used for the expression of his own cultural and philosophical views. His nickname ("Brother Elbert") was probably used to enhance the educational tone of his essays.

Elbert Hubbard was born at Bloomington, Ill., on June 19, 1856, and died on board the Lusitania, when it was sunk off the Irish coast on May 8, 1915.

[1] *The World Book Encyclopedia* (The Quarrie Corporation, Chicago, 1938) vol. 8, p. 3269.
Twentieth Century Authors, ed. by S. J. Kunitz and Howard Haycraft (The H. W. Wilson Company, New York, 1942) p. 677.

Hubbard, Richard Bennett

Richard Bennett Hubbard, a lawyer, soldier, and politician, was nicknamed the *Demosthenes of Texas* [1] when he was campaigning for the Democratic party in Texas in 1855-56.

Richard Bennett Hubbard was born in Walton County, Ga., on November 1, 1832, and died at Tyler Tex., on July 13, 1901.

[1] *Dictionary of American Biography under the Auspices of the American Council of Learned Societies,* ed. by Dumas Malone (Charles Scribner's Sons, New York, 1932) vol. 9, p. 331.

Huck. See Betts, W. M.

Hudlun, Anna Elizabeth

During the great fire in Chicago in 1871, and again in 1874, at the time of another disastrous fire there, Anna Elizabeth Hudlun, a Negro social welfare worker, earned for herself the sobriquets *Fire Angel* [1] and *Chicago's Grand Old Lady* [1] because she gave food, shelter, and all possible assistance to the victims of the conflagration.

[1] *Homespun Heroines and Other Women of Distinction,* comp. and ed. by Hallie Q. Brown (The Aldine Publishing Company, Xenia, Ohio, 1926), p. 143.

Hudson, Walter

Walter Hudson, who was born at New York City on January 30, 1898, and who was a baseball writer for the *New York Daily Mirror* was nicknamed *Gunboat* [1] by the cartoonist Tom Dorgan because he thought Hudson looked like Gunboat Smith.

[2] *Who's Who in Major League Base Ball,* comp. by Harold (Speed) Johnson (Buxton Publishing Company, Chicago, 1933) p. 493.

Hudson River

The Hudson River, which flows southward through New York State into New York harbor has been nicknamed the *Rhine of America* [1] because, like the Rhine, the Hudson is bordered by steep rocky hills, beautiful natural scenery and fertile slopes. It is called the *River of Steep Hills* because the eastern mountain belt composed of rugged hills and low mountains lies along the eastern bank.

[1] *The World Book Encyclopedia* (W. F. Quarrie and Company, Chicago, 1937) vol. 8, p. 3272, vol. 12, p. 4968.

Hudson Tubes. See McAdoo Tubes

Hug Grant. See Grant, U. S.

Hugo. See Edison, T. A.

Humboldt State College

Erbmen, Highlanders, Lumberjacks, Thunderbolts, and *Thunderboldts* are the nicknames given to the athletic teams of Humboldt State College, at Arcata, Calif. They were called *Erbmen* [1] when Charles Erb was coach. They were called *Highlanders* because the college is located on a plateau, and *Lumberjacks* because the college is located in the heart of the Redwood Country. The latest nicknames are the *Thunderbolts* and the *Thunderboldts* coined by local sports writers from the name Humboldt.

[1] A letter from Maurice Hicklin, Dean of the Lower Division of Humboldt State College, Arcata, Calif., November 23, 1935.

Hump. See Campbell, B. D.

Humphreys, Benjamin Grubb

Benjamin Grubb Humphreys, a soldier and politician, was nicknamed *Old Veto* [1] when he was the Governor of Mississippi in 1865-68. During the Period of Reconstruction the Legislature of Mississippi often passed bills which Humphreys considered unconstitutional and detrimental to the best interests of the state and which he consistently vetoed.

Benjamin Grubb Humphreys was born in Claiborne County, Mississippi Territory, on August 24 or 26, 1808, and died at his plantation in Leflore County, Miss., on December 20, 1882.

[1] *Dictionary of American Biography under the Auspices of the American Council of Learned Societies,* ed. by Dumas Malone (Charles Scribner's Sons, New York, 1932) vol. 9, p. 373.

Humphreys, Joshua

Joshua Humphreys was often called the *Father of the American Navy* [1] because he was the first builder of war vessels for the American colonists and aided in organizing the United States Navy. He was the builder of the famous ship, *Constitution,* popularly known as *Old Ironsides.*

He was born at Haverford, Pa., on June 17, 1751, and died there on January 12, 1838.

[1] *The National Cyclopaedia of American Biography* (James T. White and Company, New York, 1907) vol. 5, p. 111.

Hunger Hollow

Late in 1862 the Thirty-sixth Regiment of Massachusetts Infantry nicknamed their camping ground at Carter's Run, Va., *Hunger Hollow* [1] because of the scarcity of provisions when army supply trains failed to reach the camp.

[1] *Recollections of a Varied Career,* William F. Draper (Little, Brown and Company, Boston, 1908) p. 94.

Hunger Meetings

The panic of 1854 left the United States in such a distressed condition that all phases of financial and industrial life suffered from it. By November 1857, vast numbers of men out of work were meeting in Tompkins Square and in other places in New York City and elsewhere asking for work and food. These meetings were called *Hunger Meetings.* [1]

[1] *A History of the People of the United States, from the Revolution to the Civil War,* John Bach McMaster (D. Appleton and Company, New York, 1913) vol. 8, p. 298-9.

Hungry Hill

In the early part of November 1862, the camping ground of Major [1] General Ambrose Everett Burnside's troops near Warrenton, Va., was nicknamed *Hungry Hill* [1] by the soldiers because of the scarcity of rations allotted them.

[1] *The Seventy-ninth Highlanders; New York Volunteers in the War of the Rebellion, 1861-1865,* William Todd (Brandow, Barton and Company, Albany, N.Y., 1886) p. 253.

Hunkers

Hunkers [1] or *Old Hunkers* [1] was a favorite sobriquet applied to the conservative members of the Democratic party who, about 1844 in New York, decided to adhere to the pro-slavery policy of the Democratic Administration rather than adopt the suggestions of the opposing radical faction. The pro-slavery group were nicknamed *Hunkers* [2] or *Old Hunkers* because, it was alleged, their chief reason for being conservative was that they had a strong "hankering" for office and believed that they could better satisfy this "hankering" by remaining loyal to the old party principles. It is also said that the term *Hunkers* or *Old Hunkers* was applied to this faction to describe their stubborn conservatism and reluctance to adopt new measures. The name is said to have originated from the Dutch word *honk,* meaning *home,* because the conservatives would stay home and remain loyal to old principles rather than go out into a changing world and accept new political doctrines.

[1] "Lewis Cass" by Andrew C. McLaughlin, in *American Statesmen,* ed. by John T. Morse, Junior (Houghton Mifflin and Company, New York, 1891) vol. 24, p. 237.
Political Americanisms, Charles Ledyard Norton (Longmans, Green and Company, New York and London, 1890) p. 55-6.

Hunter, Thomas Lomax

Thomas Lomax Hunter was called the *Cavalier* because he wrote a column in the Richmond *Times Dispatch* over that name. He was Virginia's state poet laureate.

He was born at Belle Grove, Port Conway, in King George County, Va., on March 6, 1875, and died at Fredericksburg, Va., June 19, 1948.

Hunter, Whiteside Godfrey

Whiteside Godfrey Hunter, a politician and legislator, was humorously called *Gumshoe* [1] because he systematized the Republican politician machine in Kentucky effectively but with so little noise and show that it seemed as if he must have worn rubber overshoes. *Gumshoe* in American slang is often used to designate a political campaign which is conducted with some degree of stealth. Hunter was a Representative from Kentucky to the Congress three times between 1887 and 1905.

Whiteside Godfrey Hunter was born near Belfast, Ireland, on December 25, 1841, and died at Louisville, Ky., on November 2, 1917.

[1] *Dictionary of American Biography under the Auspices of the American Council of Learned Societies,* ed. by Dumas Malone (Charles Scribner's Sons, New York, 1932) vol. 9, p. 406.

Hunter-preacher. See Lynn, Benjamin

Huntington, C. P. See *Big Four*

Huntington College

The *Foresters* is the appellation applied to the athletic teams of Huntington College, at Huntington, Ind., by sports writers because of the college colors apple green and scarlet which suggested to them Robin Hood's men.

[1] A letter from Harold C. Mason, President of Huntington College, Ind., July 29, 1935.

Huntsville, Alabama

Huntsville has been designated the *Industrial City of North Alabama* [1] because it is. the chief industrial city in the northern part of the state. It is outstanding in its manufacture of knitted goods, and cotton cloth such as sheets, khaki, drilling, and printing cloth. This city has numerous fibre and planing mills, brick plants, canning factories, grist and flour mills, and mattress factories.

[1] *Alabama of To-day, 1904: An Industrial Review of the General Business Interests of Birmingham and the Cities and Towns Comprising the Great State of Alabama* (Published by Post B—Alabama Division Travelers Protective Association of America, Birmingham, Ala., 1905) p. 65.

The Encyclopedia Americana (Americana Corporation, New York and Chicago, 1932) vol. 14, p. 519-20.

Early History of Huntsville, Alabama, 1804 to 1870, Revised 1916, Edward Chambers Betts (The Brown Printing Company, Montgomery, Ala., 1916) p. 49.

Hurry Up Yost. See Yost, F. H.

Huskies. See Northeastern University; University of Washington

Husted, James William

James William Husted, a politician, was known as the *Bald Eagle of Westchester,* [1] because he was a native of Westchester County, N.Y., and like the bald eagle, was aggressive and fearless. He served from 1872 until 1892 in the New York State Assembly, and was, for many years, the Major General of the Fifth Division of the National Guard of New York State.

James William Husted was born at Bedford, N.Y., on October 31, 1833, and died in New York State, in 1892.

[1] *Appleton's Cyclopaedia of American Biography,* ed. by James Grant Wilson and John Fiske (D. Appleton and Company, New York, 1888) vol. 3, p. 330.

Proceedings of the Legislature of the State of New York in Memory of General James W. Husted, Held at the Capital on March 28, 1893, (James B. Lyon, Printer, Albany, New York, 1893) p. 29.

I

Icebanks. See Fairbanks, C. W.

Ice-bear Kroeger. See Kroeger, Henry

Ice King. See Morse, C. W.; Tudor, Frederic

Ichabods. See Washburn College

Ickes, Harold Le Claire

Harold L. Ickes has been called the *Curmudgeon* and *Honest Harold*. The former nickname was appropriated by Mr. Ickes himself to describe his uncompromising personality in public life and his peppery temperament. [1] He was quite proud of being a "self-made" *Curmudgeon* and did not mind the many names he was called during his contentious public career. The second nickname, the use of which he deprecated as an essentially modest man, was given to him while he was responsible for administering the Public Works Administration. Billions of dollars were spent under his jurisdiction without a breath of scandal. [2]

Harold L. Ickes, Secretary of the Interior from 1933 to 1946, was born in Franks-

Ickes, H. L.—Continued
town Township, Blair County, Pa., on
March 15, 1874, and died on February 4,
1952.

[1] *Autobiography of a Curmudgeon,* by Harold L. Ickes
(Reynal & Hitchcock, New York, 1943) p. 1-13.
[2] *Current Biography, Who's News and Why, 1941,* ed.
by Maxine Block (The H. W. Wilson Company, New
York, 1941) p. 427.

Idaho
Idaho is called the *Gem State* or the *Gem
of the Mountains,*[1] from the State name,
which means *Gem of the Mountains;* and
Little Ida[2] because the state is small in
comparison to many of the other western
states.

[1] *Americanisms; The English of the New World,*
M. Schele De Vere (Charles Scribner and Company,
New York, 1872) p. 18.
[2] *A Book of Nicknames,* John Goff (Courier-Journal
Job Printing Company, Louisville, Ky., 1892) p. 13.

Idaho Lion. See Borah, W. E.

Idahoans
The Idahoans were nicknamed *Fortune-
seekers*[1] because many of the people who
came to Idaho during pioneer days were
prospecting for gold and silver.

[1] *Manual of Useful Information,* comp. under the
direction of J. C. Thomas (The Werner Company, Chicago, 1893) p. 23.

Idol of Baseball Fandom. See Cobb,
T. R.

Idol of Ohio. See McKinley, William

Idol of the American Boy. See Ruth,
G. H.

Ike. See Eisenhower, D. D.

Illinois
The state of Illinois is nicknamed the
Corn State, Egypt, the *Garden of the West,*
the *Prairie State,* and the *Sucker State.* Illinois is called the *Corn State*[1] because it is
one of the most important states in the corn
belt.

The sobriquet *Egypt*[2] was given to the
state of Illinois, because Cairo, Ill., was
named for Cairo, Egypt, and because southern Illinois was settled earlier than the
northern part, and for many years the

northern settlers were dependent on the
south for their corn, and were in the habit
of saying, "we must go down into Egypt
to buy corn."

The state is nicknamed the *Garden of
the West*[3] from its fertile rolling prairies
and cultivated fields.

Illinois is called the *Prairie State* because
so much of its area is prairie land. There
is much conjecture as to the origin of the
nickname, *Sucker State.*[4] One version is
that the miners at the Galena lead mines
were local men who went up to the mines
in the spring and returned in the fall, like
the suckers which go up the rivers in spring
and return in Autumn.

Another version is that in many places on
the western prairies there was little water
except in crawfish holes out of which the
early travellers would suck up the water by
means of long reeds. When a traveller
would find one of these holes, he would
call "a sucker! a sucker!" meaning a reed.

[1] *The Encyclopedia Americana* (Americana Corporation, New York and Chicago, 1929) vol. 14, p. 686.
[2] *More About Names,* Leopold Wagner (T. Fisher
Unwin, London, 1893) p. 32.
The American Language, Sup. 2, by H. L. Mencken
(A. A. Knopf, New York, 1948) p. 615.
[3] *King's Handbook of the United States,* planned and
ed. by Moses King, text by M. F. Sweetser (Moses King
Corporation, Buffalo, N.Y., 1891) p. 203.
[4] *U.S.: An Index to the United States of America,*
comp. by Malcolm Townsend (D. Lothrop Company,
Boston, 1890) p. 67-8.

Illinois Baboon. See Lincoln, Abraham

Illinois Division. See Thirty-third Infantry Division of World War II

Illinois Inhabitants
The inhabitants of Illinois are called
Egyptians, Sandhillers, and *Suckers.* The
Sandhillers was first applied to those who
live on the rolling sandy plains of the state.
For *Egyptians* and *Suckers* see Illinois
above.

Illinois Thunderbolt. See Overlin, Ken

Illinois Wesleyan University
The teams of Illinois Wesleyan University, at Bloomington, Ill., have two nicknames, the *Methodists* and the *Titans.* The
Methodists[1] originated because the Methodist Church controls the board of trustees

of the University. The *Titans* was first used by a sports writer in 1925, a year when the teams were particularly successful.

[1] A letter from William Wallis, Dean of Illinois Wesleyan University, Bloomington, Ill., November 25, 1935.

Illustrious Defender. See Webster, Daniel

Immaterial John Jameson. See Jameson, John

Immortal Thirteen

The *Immortal Thirteen* [1] is the term applied to the thirteen Democratic senators in the Tennessee Legislature in 1841 who prevented a joint session of the two branches of the State Legislature in order to elect two new senators to replace two Whig senators.

[1] *Andrew Johnson, Plebian and Patriot,* Robert W. Winston (Henry Holt and Company, New York, 1928) p. 32.

Immortal Trio

Henry Clay, John Caldwell Calhoun, and Daniel Webster were often called *Immortal Trio.* [1] For many years prior to the Civil War they were the outstanding men in the Senate.

See also Great Triumvirate.

[1] *History of the United States, for Schools and Academies,* New Edition, Joseph T. Derry (J. B. Lippincott Company, Philadelphia, 1885) p. 237.

Immortal Webster. See Webster, Daniel

Impeachment Thomas. See Thomas, J. P.

Imperial Peacock of Park Avenue. See Bonaparte, C. J.

Imperial Valley. See *America's Great Winter Garden*

Independence Hall

Independence Hall, or the Old State House in Philadelphia, Pa., is commonly known as the *Birthplace of Liberty* [1] and the *Cradle of American Liberty* because George Washington accepted his appointment as General of the Continental Army there on June 16, 1775; the Declaration of Independence was adopted there on July 4, 1776; the Second and succeeding Continental Congresses met there; on July 9, 1778, the Articles of Confederation were signed there; and the final draft of the Federal Constitution was completed there on September 17, 1787.

[1] *The Philadelphia Inquirer,* Philadelphia, December 26, 1938, col. 1, p. 10.

Independent Gutherie Greys

In 1861 an independent military company was organized in Cincinnati, Ohio, which called itself the *Independent Gutherie Greys* [1] because they wore grey uniforms and were led by Captain Presley N. Gutherie. It later became the Sixth Regiment of Ohio Volunteer Infantry.

[1] *The Story of a Regiment: A History of the Campaigns, and Associations in the Field of The Sixth Regiment Ohio Volunteer Infantry,* E. Hannaford (Published by the author, Cincinnati, Ohio, 1868) p. 18.

Indian Dan. See Webster, Daniel

Indian Fighter. See Talcott, John

Indian Head Division. See Second Infantry Division of World War II

Indiana

The origin of the nicknames *Hoosier State* and *Hoosierdom* for Indiana is a moot question. One story is that the original form of the word was *Hoozer* signifying hill dweller or highlander as well as something large, later corrupted to mean uncouthness and rusticity, and probably of English origin.[1]

Another explanation is that the nickname *Hoosier* was given to the settlers, who were so inquisitive that they could never pass a house without pulling the latchstring and crying out, "Who's here?"[2]

Still another account is that the early boatmen of Indiana were great fighters, and that one of them after winning a fist fight at New Orleans, La., jumped up and exclaimed, "I'm a Hoosier!" The New Orleans papers printed an account of the affair, and afterwards applied the name to all boatmen from Indiana, and finally to the citizens of the state. According to the story, the word Hoosier means *husher,* or one who can hush his man.[2]

[1] *Indiana and Indianans,* Jacob Piatt Dunn (The American Historical Society, Chicago and New York, 1919) vol. 2, p. 1146.

Indiana—Continued
[2] *Americanisms—Old and New*, John S. Farmer (Privately printed by Thomas Poulter and Sons, London, 1889) p. 304.

The American Language, Sup. 2, H. L. Mencken (A. A. Knopf, New York, 1948) p. 618.

Indiana Central College
The athletic teams of Indiana Central College, at Indianapolis, Ind., were nicknamed *Greyhounds*[1] because of the speed with which they played.

[1] A communication from Irby J. Good, President of Indiana Central College, Indianapolis, Ind., November 13, 1935.

Indiana University
The *Hoosiers*[1] is the nickname applied to the athletic teams of Indiana University, at Bloomington, Ind., because Indiana is called the *Hoosier State.*

[1] A communication from Z. G. Clevenger, Director of Athletics at Indiana University, Bloomington, Ind., June 13, 1935.

Indianans
The Indianans are called *Hoosiers.* For the origin of this nickname see Indiana.

Indianapolis, Indiana
Indianapolis is known as the *Railroad City*[1] because many of the great lines going from the Mississippi valley to the Atlantic coast, and many of those going north and south converge at Indianapolis. Indianapolis is accredited with being the largest interurban railway center in the United States.

[1] *Americanisms; The History of the New World*, M. Schele De Vere (Charles Scribner and Company, New York, 1872) p. 663.

Centennial History and Handbook of Indiana: The Story of the State from Its Beginning to the Close of the Civil War and a General Survey of Progress to the Present Time, George S. Cottman (Max R. Hyman, Indianapolis, Ind., 1915) p. 132, 321, 355-6.

Indiana, One Hundred and Fifty Years of American Development, Charles Roll, assisted by an advisory council (The Lewis Publishing Company, Chicago and New York, 1931) vol. 2, p. 393.

Geography, United States and Canada, Harlan H. Barrows and Edith Putnam Parker (Silver, Burdett and Company, New York and Boston, 1933) p. 208-9.

Indian-Appian Way
Because the Indians and the fur traders made extensive use of the Maunee and Wabash Rivers as an outstanding trade route, these rivers were sometimes termed the *Indian-Appian Way.*[1] The Appian Way, built by the Romans about 300 B.C., extended from Rome to Capua and was one of the most important highways in the Roman Empire.

[1] *Indiana, One Hundred and Fifty Years of American Development*, Charles Roll, assisted by an advisory council (The Lewis Publishing Company, New York and Chicago, 1931) vol. 1, p. 55.

Indianapolis Potato Mayor. See Shank, S. L.

Indiana's Gateway City. See Jeffersonville, Ind.

Indians. See Catawba College; College of William & Mary; Dartmouth College; Hartwick College; Juniata College; Stanford University

Indian's Friend. See Williams, Roger

Industrial Center of the Great South. See Birmingham, Ala.

Industrial City of Dixie. See Birmingham, Ala.

Industrial City of North Alabama. See Huntsville, Ala.

Industrial Workers of the World
Samuel Gompers, the former President of the American Federation of Labor, derisively nicknamed the original plan of the organization of the Industrial Workers of the World *Father Hagerty's Wheel of Fortune.*[1] The Reverend T. J. Hagerty provided the first organizational plan for this revolutionary labor organization founded in 1905 in Chicago. The IWW was bitterly opposed to the AFL on the grounds that the latter was not aggressive enough in organizing labor, and that President Gompers held anti-revolutionary sentiments. The IWW was an aggressive organization from 1909 to 1917 in the United States, acquiring a particularly strong following among northwestern lumberman, and effectively directing the great textile strikes at Lawrence, Mass., and Paterson, N.J. IWW members were nicknamed *Wobblies.*

[1] *The Encyclopaedia Britannica*, Fourteenth Edition (Encyclopaedia Britannica, Inc., New York, 1938) vol. 12, p. 310.

Infant Mississippi River

In 1836 Joseph Nicollet, a French scientist, found that the Mississippi River had its source in Lake Itasca. The Mississippi River when it leaves the lake is only one and a half feet wide and a foot deep; consequently, he spoke of it as the *Infant Mississippi River*.[1] Later it was referred to by othes as *Nicollet's Infant Mississippi River*.

[1] *My Minnesota*, Antoinette E. Ford (Lyons and Carnahan, New York and Chicago, 1929) p. 64-5.

A History of Minnesota, William Watts Folwell (Published by the Minnesota Historical Society, Saint Paul, Minn., 1921) vol. 1, p. 127.

Ingalls, Marilla Baker

Marilla Baker Ingalls, a Baptist missionary to India, was called the *Lady of the Iron Watch Dog*[1] by the natives at Thongze, Lower Burma, where she served as a missionary, nurse, temperance worker, librarian, and friend to the Indians from 1858 to 1900. Because she disapproved of the Indian practice of worshipping idols, she had a great cast-iron dog placed in the yard before her house to show that it had neither good nor bad influence on her activities.

Marilla Baker Ingalls was born at Greenfield Centre, N.Y., on November 25, 1828, and died at Thongze, India, on December 17, 1902.

[1] *Dictionary of American Biography under the auspices of the American Council of Learned Societies*, ed. by Dumas Malone (Charles Scribner's Sons, New York, 1932) vol. 9, p. 463.

Ingersoll, Ralph Isaacs

Ralph Isaacs Ingersoll, a statesman, was nicknamed *Young Hotspur*[1] because he was a spirited debater while in the Connecticut Legislature from 1819 until 1825, and as a Representative from Connecticut to the United States Congress from 1825 to 1833.

Ralph Isaacs Ingersoll was born at New Haven, Conn., on February 8, 1788, and died there on August 26, 1872.

[1] *Appleton's Cyclopaedia of American Biography*, ed. by James Grant Wilson and John Fiske (D. Appleton and Company, New York, 1888) vol. 3, p. 348.

Inland Metropolis. See Birmingham, Ala.

Insurance City. See Hartford, Conn.

Intellectual Awkward Squad

The *Brain Trusters* of President Franklin Delano Roosevelt have also been nicknamed the *Intellectual Awkward Squad*[1] probably referring to the experimentation of this group in Governmental activities, much of which was considered to be awkward and clumsy.

[1] *Washington Herald*, Washington, D.C., September 2, 1934, col. 3, p. 1-A.

Intellectual Giant of Populism. See Allen, W. V.

Intellectual Termites

In 1936, the New Dealers gave the nicknames *Intellectual Termites*[1] and *Political Gadflies* to those who criticized or made complaints against the policies or practices of the administration of President Franklin Delano Roosevelt. Termites destroy a structure by eating away its supporting timbers. Gadflies drive their victims wild by constant biting.

[1] *The Washington Post*, Washington, D.C., February 28, 1936, col. 2, p. 2.

International Young Men's Christian Association College

The nicknames the *Gymnasts,* the *Maroons,* and the *Redmen* have been given to the athletic teams of the International Young Men's Christian Association College, at Springfield, Mass. The *Gymnasts*[1] was given them by sports writers because between the halves of games the boys performed gymnastic stunts. The *Maroons* doubtless originated from the college colors. They are called *Redmen* because the mascot of the college is Chief Massasoit, a North American Indian.

[1] A communication from G. B. Affleck, Director of the Natural Science Division at the International Young Men's Christian Association College, Springfield, Mass., December 5, 1935.

Internats. See American International College

Intolerable Acts

The five acts passed by the British Parliament on March 31, 1774, against Massachusetts, occasioned largely by the action of the *Boston Tea Party,* were called by the colonists the *Intolerable Acts*[1] because they considered them unreasonable and not to be submitted to by any self-respecting citizens. These acts provided (1) that the port of Boston be closed to in-going and out-going ships; (2) that the charter of Massachusetts

Intolerable Acts—Continued

be so altered that, without the King's consent, the citizens could not exercise their right to elect officers, judges of courts, or hold town meetings except under limited conditions; (3) that those acting upon the authority of the King might have the authority to transfer the King's officials, who had committed murder in attempting to enforce the British laws, to Great Britain or to some of the other colonies for trial; (4) that the colonists might be forced to quarter the British troops sent over by the King to enforce the laws imposed on them by Great Britain; and (5) that the boundary of the province of Quebec be extended to include all the territory lying between the Great Lakes and the Ohio River.

[1] *American History and Government, a Textbook on the History and Government of the United States*, James Albert Woodburn and Thomas Francis Moran (Longmans, Green and Company, New York, 1906) p. 129.
The New Century History of the United States, Revised and Enlarged, Edward Eggleston (American Book Company, New York and Boston, 1919) p. 150.

Invalid Corps

During the Civil War the First Division of the Union Army commanded by Brigadier General Daniel Tyler, designated those men who remained at their camps in time of battle as the *Invalid Corps* [1] whether they were sick or did not actively participate in battle for other reasons.

[1] *The Seventy-ninth Highlanders; New York Volunteers in the War of Rebellion, 1861-1865*, William Todd (Press of Brandow, Barton and Company, Albany, N.Y., 1886) p. 18.

Investigator. See Bell, C. J.

Invincible Stonewall. See Jackson, T. J.

Invincible Warrior in Righteous Causes. See Mott, Lucretia

Iodine State. See South Carolina

Iowa

According to some authorities,[1] the *Hawkeye State* came to be the nickname of Iowa from the Indian chief Hawkeye, who was once the terror of travelers along the border. *The New International Encyclopaedia* says that the *Hawkeye State* was applied to Iowa in allusion to J. G. Edwards, familiarly known as "Old Hawkeye," editor of the Burlington *Patriot*, later the *Hawkeye*

and Patriot. The *Land of the Rolling Prairie* was applied to Iowa because of the vast expanse of rolling prairies within the State.

[1] *Americanisms—Old and New*, John S. Farmer (Privately printed by Thomas Poulter and Sons, London, 1889) p. 291.
A New Dictionary of Americanisms, Sylva Clapin (Louis Weiss and Company, New York, 1903) p. 223.
King's Handbook of the United States, planned and ed. by Moses King, text by M. F. Sweetser (Moses King Corporation, Buffalo, N.Y., 1891) p. 225.
More About Names, Leopold Wagner (T. Fisher Unwin, London, 1893) p. 30.
The New International Encyclopaedia, Second Edition (Dodd, Mean and Company, New York, 1930) vol. 21, p. 463.

Iowa State College

The athletic teams of Iowa State College, at Ames, Iowa, are called the *Cyclones*.[1] When the Iowa State College football team played Northwestern University at Evanston, Ill., in 1895, the final score was thirty-six to nothing in favor of Iowa State. In reporting the game, the Chicago papers said that a cyclone from Iowa had struck Northwestern.

[1] A letter from Merle J. Ross, Business Manager of Athletics at Iowa State College, Ames, Iowa, June 26, 1935.

Iowans

For the origin of the nickname *Hawkeyes* applied to the Iowans, see Iowa.

Irish. See University of Portland

Iron Brigade

During the Civil War the brigade of United States Volunteer Infantrymen commanded by Brigadier General John Gibbon came to be nicknamed the *Iron Brigade*.[1] According to Gibbon, the nickname originated soon after the Battle of Antietam in Maryland on September 17, 1862, when this brigade distinguished itself by its endurance and firmness in resisting the enemy.

The First Brigade in the First Division of the First Army Corps of the Army of the Potomac, commanded by Brigadier General Solomon Meredith was also nicknamed the *Iron Brigade* [2] because of their skill and endurance in the Battle of Chancellorsville in Virginia in April 1863, and in the Battle of Gettysburg in Pennsylvania on July 1, 2, and 3, 1863.

The brigade organized and commanded by Brigadier General Rufus King of Milwaukee, Wis., in 1862, likewise has been called the *Iron Brigade* [3] because of its record of endurance in the Civil War.

[1] *Personal Recollections of the Civil War*, John Gibbon (G. P. Putnam's Sons, New York and London, 1928) p. 93.

[2] *The Iron Brigade at Gettysburg: Official Report of the Part Borne by the 1st Brigade, 1st Division, 1st Army Corps, Army of the Potomac in Action at Gettysburg, Pennsylvania, July 1st, 2nd, and 3rd, 1863*, William Wade Dudley, Brevetted Brigadier General, U.S.V. (Peter G. Thomson, Arcade Book Store, Cincinnati, Ohio, 1879) p. 9, 11.

[3] *Wisconsin, Its History and Its People, 1634-1924*, Milo Milton Quaife (The S. J. Clarke Publishing Company, Chicago, 1924) vol. 1, p. 567.

Iron City. See Pittsburgh, Pa.

Iron City on the Tennessee River. See Sheffield, Ala.

Ironclad Oath

On March 27, 1867, Congress passed a law called a Reconstruction Act to the effect that in the Southern states all persons who desired to vote had to take an oath, known as the *Ironclad Oath*,[1] at registration preliminary to voting. The men who took this oath swore that they had taken no part in the Civil War, nor given assistance to the Confederacy. This measure practically eliminated the white people from voting, and offices and legislation came to be controlled by the Negroes. The hard, uncompromising qualities of this act doubtless led to its nickname.

[1] *New School History of the United States*, Revised and Enlarged, Susan Pendleton Lee (B. F. Johnson Publishing Company, Richmond, Va., 1899) p. 377.

Iron Dough-Nuts. See *Jeff Davis Neckties*

Iron Duke. See Muldoon, William

Iron Dukes. See Duquesne University

Iron Horse. See Gehrig, H. L.; Schulmerich, E. W.

Ironman. See Starr, R. F.

Iron Man of Baseball. See Gehrig, H. L. (Lou)

Iron Man of Metz. See Ninety-fifth Infantry Division of World War II

Iron Mountain State. See Missouri

Iron Ore Capital of the World. See Hibbing, Minn.

Iron Scouts

While he was encamped with his brigade of Confederate cavalry in Culpepper County, Va., in the autumn of 1862, Lieutenant General Wade Hampton detailed about twenty men to act as scouts in Prince William County, Va., to secure information regarding the movements of the Federals in that locality. The Federal soldiers nicknamed these men the *Iron Scouts* [1] because of their unusual physical strength and endurance.

[1] *Butler and His Cavalry in the War of Secession, 1861-1865*, U. R. Brooks (The State Company, Columbia, S.C., 1909) p. 136.

Iron Snake. See Eighth Armored Division of World War II

Iron Trail

The connecting of the Central Pacific and the Union Pacific railroads near Ogden, Utah, on May 10, 1869, gave to the western part of the United States eighteen hundred miles of railroad extending from San Francisco, Calif., to Omaha, Neb. Following the custom of designating as trails the roads or routes for travel over this section of the country, the people spoke of the new railroad as the *Iron Trail*.[1]

[1] *The Making of America*, Grace Vollintine (Ginn and Company, New York and Boston, 1925) p. 240.

Iroquois. See Hartwick College

Iroquois Division. See Ninety-eighth Infantry Division of World War II

Irvin, Cecil P.

Cecil P. Irvin, a well-known football player, has been nicknamed *Tex* [1] because he was born and reared in Texas.

He was born at De Leon, Tex., on October 9, 1906, and played tackle in major league football.

[1] *Who's Who in Major League Football*, comp. by Harold (Speed) Johnson and Wilfrid Smith (B. V. Callahan, Chicago, 1935) p. 17.

Irving, Washington

The following nicknames have been applied to Washington Irving: the *American Goldsmith*, the *Father of American Literature*, the *Father of American Prose*, and the *Prince of American Letters*.

Irving, Washington—Continued

He has been called the *American Goldsmith*[1] because he was similar to Oliver Goldsmith in that both wrote a charming style of prose, neither of them ever married, and they both were authors of sketches and essays.

The *Father of American Literature*[2] was applied to him because he was the first American to receive international recognition as a man of letters, and because he was a pioneer in investing the life of his native country with the glamour of romance.

Irving is called the *Father of American Prose*[3] and the *Prince of American Letters*[4] because his *Knickerbocker's History of New York* and his *Sketch Book* gained international fame.

Washington Irving was born at New York City, on April 3, 1783, and died at Tarrytown, N.Y., on November 28, 1859.

[1] *A Book of Nicknames,* John Goff (Courier-Journal Job Printing Company, Louisville, Ky., 1892) p. 29.

[2] *American Literary Readings, with Introduction, Notes, Biographical Sketches, Some Thought Questions, an Outline of American Literature and a Brief Essay on English Metrics,* ed. by Leonidas Warren Payne (Rand McNally and Company, New York and Chicago, 1917) p. 1.

[3] *Compton's Pictured Encyclopedia* (F. E. Compton and Company, Chicago, 1931) vol. 1, p. 112.

[4] *Manual of Useful Information,* comp. under the direction of J. C. Thomas (The Werner Company, Chicago, 1893) p. 23.

Italy of America. See Arizona

Ivy Division. See Fourth Infantry Division of World War II

J

Jack the Giant Killer. See Jackson, R. H.; Randolph (of Roanoke), John

Jackass Express or *Jackass Mail*

The pack trains which carried mail and supplies to the mining camps in California in the early days were nicknamed the *Jackass Express*[1] or *Jackass Mail* because this system of exchange was usually operated by men with burros or mules. Alexander H. Todd is credited with operating the first express of this type, in 1849, to transfer mail from San Francisco and Sacramento to the mining camps. In this manner he helped to relieve the problem of dead letters in California which the Postmaster General

reported to be 2,400 pounds in 1851. It is said that Todd made as much as one thousand dollars a day out of the activities of his pack trains.

[1] *The Pony Express: The Record of a Romantic Adventure in Business,* Arthur Chapman (G. P. Putnam's Sons, New York and London, 1932) p. 33, 34.

Jackrabbit. See Abbitt, Jim.

Jackson, Andrew

The *Duel Fighter*, the *Hero of New Orleans*, *King Andrew the First*, the *Land Hero of 1812*, *Mischievous Andy*, *Old Hickory*, the *People's President*, the *Pointed Arrow*, the *Sage of the Hermitage*, and the *Sharp Knife* are numerous nicknames attributed to Andrew Jackson.

He was called the *Duel Fighter*[1] because more than once he fought a duel. Two of Jackson's noted duels were his duel with Colonel Waightstill Avery near Jonesboro, Tenn., in 1795, and the duel with Charles Dickinson near Harrison's Mill, in Logan County, Ky., in 1806.

Because of his daring and skill in commanding the American forces at the battle of New Orleans on January 8, 1815, he was popularly acclaimed the *Hero of New Orleans*.[2,10]

The political enemies of Andrew Jackson nicknamed him *King Andrew the First*[3,4] because of his determination to follow his own political plans.

Andrew Jackson has been called the *Land Hero of 1812*[5] in commemoration of his conspicuous leadership in the land campaigns against the British in the War of 1812.

During his youth and school days, Jackson was sometimes called *Mischievous Andy*[6] because he was a spirited mischievous youth.

Old Hickory,[4,7] one of Andrew Jackson's most widely known nicknames, originated in 1813, among his soldiers, composed of Tennessee volunteers, in hickory homespun, on the homeward march to Nashville, Tenn. Jackson received orders from the Secretary of War to disband his troops at Natchez, Miss. Jackson considered it unfair to his soldiers to do this and, believing that his first obligation was to his soldiers, ignored the command and marched them back to Nashville, Tenn. Many of the soldiers were ill or disabled. Jackson, disregarding his position of superior rank, turned over his horses to be used by his sick soldiers and walked. His soldiers said he was *tough as hickory* and they began calling him *Old Hickory*,[1,8,9] a sobriquet which Jackson liked very much and which clung to him throughout his life.

The nickname *People's President* [3] had its origin in the fact that Jackson was so well known for military leadership, that he came from the backwoods of Tennessee, and that the people greeted him with enthusiasm on his way to Washington for his inauguration.

In commemoration of his grave dignity and wisdom, when Jackson retired to the Hermitage, his estate near Nashville, Tenn., he was referred to as the *Sage of the Hermitage*.[1]

The *Pointed Arrow* [10] and the *Sharp Knife* [11] were applied to Andrew Jackson by the Indians on the western frontiers of North Carolina, and what is now the state of Florida, sometime between 1789 and 1794, when he was campaigning against the Creek Indians. The pointed arrow and the sharp knife were the weapons of the frontiersmen and the Indians.

Andrew Jackson was born probably near Waxhaw Creek in Lancaster County, N.C., on March 15, 1767, and died at the Hermitage, near Nashville, Tenn., on June 8, 1845.

[1] *A Book of Nicknames*, John Goff (Courier-Journal Job Printing Company, Louisville, Ky., 1892) p. 21, 27.
[2] *Life of Andrew Jackson in Three Volumes*, James Parton (Mason Brothers, New York, 1861) vol. 1, p. 160-2, 381-2; vol. 3, p. 632.
"Andrew Jackson by William Graham Sumner, in *American Statesmen*, ed. by John T. Morse, Junior (Houghton Mifflin Company, Boston and New York, 1924) p. 20, 43-4, 46-7.
The Life of Andrew Jackson, John Spencer Bassett (Doubleday, Page and Company, Garden City, N.Y., 1911) vol. 1, p. 62-4.
History of Andrew Jackson, Pioneer, Patriot, Soldier, Politician, President, Augustus C. Buell (Charles Scribner's Sons, New York, 1904) vol. 1, p. 161-76.
The American People and Nation, Rolla M. Tryon and Charles R. Lingley (Ginn and Company, New York and Boston, 1929) p. 345.
[2] "Andrew Jackson" by Clifford Smyth, in *Builders of America* (Funk and Wagnalls Company, New York, 1931) vol. 17, p. 74-90.
[3] *Andrew Jackson, the Fighting President*, Helen Nicolay (The Century Company, New York, 1929) p. 262, 265, 274.
[4] *Andrew Jackson, an Epic in Homespun*, Gerald W. Johnson (Minton, Balch and Company, New York, 1927) p. 164, 286.
[5] *The Land Hero of 1812*, Chauncey C. Hotchkiss (D. Appleton and Company, New York, 1904) p. 125-31.
[6] *American Leaders and Heroes: A Preliminary Textbook in United States History*, Wilbur F. Gordy (Charles Scribner's Sons, New York, 1905) p. 254.
[7] "The Reign of Andrew Jackson: A Chronicle of the Frontier in Politics" by Frederick Austin Ogg, in *The Chronicles of America Series*, Allen Johnson, Editor (Yale University Press, New Haven, Conn., 1919) vol. 20, p. 30.

[8] *Life and Times of Andrew Jackson, Soldier, Statesman, President*, A. S. Colyar (Marshall and Bruce Company, Nashville, Tenn., 1904) vol. 1, p. 88.
[9] *Tennessee: The Volunteer States, 1769-1923*, John Trotwood Moore and Austin P. Foster (The S. J. Clarke Publishing Company, Chicago and Nashville, Tenn., 1923) vol. 1, p. 154.
[10] *Jackson and New Orleans: An Authentic Narrative of the Memorable Achievements of the American Army, under Andrew Jackson, before New Orleans, in the Winter of 1814, '15*, Alexander Walker (J. C. Derby, New York, 1856) p. 22, 402.
[11] *The Military Heroes of the War of 1812; with a Narrative of the War*, Charles J. Peterson (William A. Leary, Philadelphia, 1848) p. 199.

Jackson, Andrew, and Rachel Donelson Jackson

After Andrew Jackson and his wife, Rachel Donelson Jackson, had moved to the Hermitage, their home near Nashville, Tenn., in 1804, they came to be widely known as the *King and Queen of Hospitality*.[1] The Hermitage was often packed with so many visitors that beds and cots had to be placed in the halls and porch to accommodate them.

[1] *Women in American History: The Part Taken by Women in American History*, Mrs. John A. Logan (The Perry-Nalle Publishing Company, Wilmington, Del., 1912) p. 235.

Jackson, Rachel Donelson

Aunt Rachel and the *Bonny Brown Wife* are nicknames applied to Rachel Donelson Jackson.

She was called *Aunt Rachel* [1] by her neighbors and friends and their children because she was kind and motherly and interested in their welfare and happiness.

The fact that Mrs. Jackson was an attractive lady whose skin was tanned from exposure to the sun and air of the out-of-doors gave rise to the nickname the *Bonny Brown Wife*,[2] which pleased her husband, Andrew Jackson.

Rachel Donelson Jackson (Mrs. Andrew Jackson) was born in Virginia, in 1767, and died at the Hermitage, near Nashville, Tenn., on December 22, 1828.

[1] *Dames and Daughters of the Young Republic*, Geraldine Brooks (Thomas Y. Crowell and Company, New York, 1901) p. 237, 238, 242.
[2] *Women in American History: The Part Taken by Women in American History*, Mrs. John A. Logan (The Perry-Nalle Publishing Company, Wilmington, Del., 1912) p. 235.

Jackson, Robert Houghwout

Robert Houghwout Jackson, while Assistant Attorney General of the United States, was nicknamed *Jack the Giant-Killer* [1] because of his vigorous investigation of Andrew Mellon in 1937 for an alleged de-

Jackson, R. H.—Continued

ficiency in income taxes. After Mellon's death the courts found that there had been no deficiency. Jackson was appointed Assistant Attorney General for the United States in 1936, and Attorney General in 1940. He was born at Spring Creek, Pa., on February 13, 1892.

[1] *The Literary Digest* (Funk and Wagnalls Company, New York) January 5, 1938, p. 5-6.

Jackson, Sheldon

Sheldon Jackson was nicknamed the *Bishop of All Outdoors* [1] because his missionary activities extended throughout the western parts of the United States and Alaska. He is said to have traveled close to a million miles in the course of his work.

He was born at Minaville, N.Y., on May 18, 1834, and died at Asheville, N.C., on May 2, 1909.

[1] *The Alaskan Pathfinder: The Story of Sheldon Jackson*, John T. Faris, with an introduction by John A. Marquis (Fleming H. Revell Company, New York and Chicago, 1926) p. 46.

Sheldon Jackson, Pathfinder and Prospector of the Missionary Vanguard in the Rocky Mountains and Alaska, Robert Laird Stewart (Fleming H. Revell Company, New York and Chicago, 1908) p. 467.

Jackson, Thomas Jonathan

The following sobriquets have been attributed to Thomas Jonathan Jackson: the *Blue Light Elder, Fool Tom Jackson*, the *Invincible Stonewall, Old Jack, Old Tom Jackson, Stonewall Jackson*, and the *Sword of the Confederacy*.

Jackson was accused of being narrow-minded, prejudiced, and sectarian; consequently, he was nicknamed the *Blue Light Elder*.[1] This sobriquet, however, misrepresented the true character of Jackson's religious life, for he was sincere and broad-minded in his religious views. During his participation in the Civil War, he took time to meditate on religion and to pray regularly, which doubtless had more to do with popularizing the nickname than did his alleged religious bigotry.

Fool Tom Jackson,[2] *Old Jack*,[3] and *Old Tom Jackson* were nicknames applied to Thomas Jonathan Jackson by the students of the Virginia Military Institute, at Lexington, Va., where General Jackson was teaching from 1857 to 1861 because of his strict discipline, rigid bearing, and awkward physical appearance.

From Jackson's refusal to admit defeat at Bull Run, in Virginia, on July 21, 1861,

came the nickname *Stonewall Jackson*.[4] Bernard E. Bee, a Confederate general galloped up to Jackson and announced that the Confederate lines were beaten back. Jackson ordered him to use the bayonets. Bee returned to his men and pointing with his sword to Jackson, he exclaimed, "There is Jackson standing like a stone wall." Later this nickname was sometimes changed to *Invincible Stonewall*.[5]

The *Sword of the Confederacy* [6] is an allusion to the destruction and punishment which Jackson inflicted upon the Union Army from 1861 to 1863. This nickname may have originated in a speech of Jackson's in which he remarked that despite his longing that the Union might be preserved, now that war had been declared he was in favor of "drawing the sword and throwing away the scabbard."

Thomas Jonathan Jackson was born at Clarksburg, Va., on January 21, 1824, and died near Chancellorsville, Va., on May 10, 1863.

[1] *Stonewall Jackson: A Military Biography*, John Esten Cooke (D. Appleton and Company, New York, 1876) p. 23.

History of the United States of America, under the Constitution, James Schouler (Dodd, Mead and Company, New York, 1889) vol. 6, p. 76.

[2] *The Military History of the Virginia Military Institute from 1839 to 1865 with Appendix, Maps, and Illustrations*, Jennings C. Wise (J. P. Bell Company, Inc., Lynchburg, Va., 1915) p. 90.

[3] *The End of An Era*, John S. Wise (Houghton Mifflin and Company, New York and Boston, 1889) p. 261.

[4] *Stonewall Jackson and the American Civil War*, New Impression, G. F. R. Henderson (Longmans, Green and Company, New York and London, 1900) p. 145.

Stonewall Jackson: A Military Biography, John Esten Cooke (D. Appleton and Company, New York, 1876) p. 68.

[5] *The Boys in White: the Experience of a Hospital Agent in and Around Washington*, Julia S. Wheelock (Freeman) (Lange and Hillman, New York, 1870) p. 94.

[6] *Lee and His Lieutenants; Comprising the Early Life, Public Services, and Campaigns of General Robert E. Lee and His Companions in Arms, with a Record of Their Campaigns and Heroic Deeds*, Edward A. Pollard (E. B. Treat and Company, New York, 1867) p. 369.

Jackson, William Hicks

William Hicks Jackson, a soldier and stock breeder, was nicknamed *Red Fox Jackson* by the soldiers under his command during the Civil War because he was daring, cunning, and quick in maneuvering his troops on the battlefield. He began his career as a soldier in 1861, later became a Captain of Artillery in the Confederate Army, and attained the rank of Brigadier-general by February, 1865, at that time having been in charge of all the cavalrymen from Tennessee and of a brigade of soldiers from Texas. After the War he was a planter and breeder of thoroughbred horses.

William Hicks Jackson was born at Paris, Tenn., on October 1, 1835, and died at Belle Meade, Tenn., on March 30, 1903.

[1] *Dictionary of American Biography under the Auspices of the American Council of Learned Societies*, ed. by Dumas Malone (Charles Scribner's Sons, New York, 1932) vol. 9, p. 561.

Jackson, Mississippi

Jackson was nicknamed *Chimneyville* [1] because during the Civil War it was destroyed by fire leaving nothing but the chimneys standing.

[1] *The World Book Encyclopedia* (The Quarrie Corporation, Chicago, 1938) vol. 9, p. 3605.

Jackson's Pet Banks

During the second term of Andrew Jackson as President of the United States from 1832 to 1836, he was opposed to the National Bank and did all in his power to bring about its downfall. During this time state banks developed all over the country. Jackson encouraged them by placing government deposits in them; consequently, they were nicknamed *Jackson's Pet Banks* and *Jackson's Pets.*[1]

[1] *Our Nation in the Building*, Helen Nicolay (The Century Company, New York, 1916) p. 168.

Jackson's Pets. See *Jackson's Pet Banks*

Jackson's Yellow Boys

While he was President of the United States from 1828 to 1832, Andrew Jackson opposed the bill to renew the charter of the United States Bank. He favored gold coins instead of bank notes. Gold coins came to be widely known as *Jackson's Yellow Boys.*[1]

[1] *Andrew Jackson, the Fighting President*, Helen Nicolay (The Century Company, New York, 1929) p. 303.

Jacob's Ladder Speech

When Andrew Johnson was inaugurated Governor of the state of Tennessee in 1853, in his inaugural address in presenting his views of what constitutes a Democracy, he spoke of it as a ladder and compared it with the ladder Jacob saw in his vision; consequently, his political opponents nicknamed this inaugural address the *Jacob's Ladder Speech.*[1]

[1] *Andrew Johnson, Plebian and Patriot*, Robert W. Winston (Henry Holt and Company, New York, 1928) p. 79.

Jake. See Flowers, D. R.; Ruppert, Jacob, Sr.

Jameson, John

John Jameson, a lawyer, was elected a Representative from Missouri to the United States Congress in 1838, 1842, and in 1846. His friends and associates called him *Immaterial John Jameson* [1] because when he was a young man he would occasionally become intoxicated, would pretend he was suffering from rheumatism and would bind up his leg with a silk handkerchief. When people expressed sympathy he would assure them that it was immaterial. He was born near Mount Sterling, Ky., on March 6, 1802, and died at Fulton, Mo., in 1855.

[1] *Centennial History of Missouri (The Center State) One Hundred Years in the Union, 1820-1921*, Walter B. Stevens (The S. J. Clarke Publishing Company, St. Louis, Mo., and Chicago, 1921) vol. 2, p. 518.

Jamestown College

The athletic teams of Jamestown College, situated at Jamestown, N.D., are popularly designated the *Jimmies.*[1]

[1] A communication from E. J. Cassell, Director of Athletics at Jamestown College, Jamestown, N.D., November 30, 1935.

Japanese Cherry-trees Nemesis. See Jenckes, V. E.

Jaspers. See Manhattan College

Javelinas. See Texas College of Arts and Industries

Jayhawker State. See Kansas

Jayhawkers. See Kansans; University of Kansas

Jayhawks. See University of Kansas

Jean Ingelow of America. See Cary, Alice

Jeb Stuart. See Stuart, J. E. B.

Jeff Davis Neckties

During Sherman's March to the Sea in the fall of 1864, the railroad leading from Madison, Ga., to Atlanta was completely destroyed by Sherman's men. The iron rails were heated and made into objects which,

Jeff Davis Neckties—Continued
on account of their round shape, were nick-named *Jeff Davis Neck-ties*[1] or *Iron Doughnuts* by Sherman's soldiers.

[1] *Memoirs of the 149th Regiment of the New York Volunteer Infantry*, Captain George Knapp Collins (Published by the author, Syracuse, N.Y., 1891) p. 289.

Jefferson Jim. See Wilson, J. F.

Jefferson, Joseph

Joseph Jefferson was called the *Dean of the American Stage*[1] because he was one of the earliest great American actors. He was on the American stage from about 1837 until 1904. One of his most successful roles was Rip Van Winkle.

Joseph Jefferson was born at Philadelphia, Pa., on February 20, 1829, and died at Palm Beach, Fla., on April 23, 1905.

[1] *The World Book Encyclopedia* (The Quarrie Corporation, Chicago, 1938) vol. 9, p. 3645.

Jefferson, Thomas

Thomas Jefferson has been called the *Father of the Declaration of Independence,* the *Father of the University of Virginia, Long Tom,* the *Man of the People,* the *Pen of the Revolution,* the *Philosopher of Democracy,* the *Sage of Monticello,* and the *Scribe of the Revolution.*

He is well known as the *Father of the Declaration of Independence*[1] because he wrote its original draft.

The *Father of the University of Virginia*[2] is a nickname applied to Thomas Jefferson because he founded this institution, super-intended the erection of the buildings, was the guiding hand in determining its poli-cies and its course of study, and became its first Rector.

Jefferson was called *Long Tom*[3] because he was tall and slender, six feet three inches in height.

Because of his teaching of democracy, his democratic practices, and his interest in the common people. Thomas Jefferson was known as the *Man of the People.*[4]

So many of the messages and documents bearing on the Revolution were written by Jefferson, that he was called the *Pen of the Revolution*[5] and the *Scribe of the Revolution.*[6]

Thomas Jefferson has been called the *Philosopher of Democracy*[7] in commemo-ration of his interests and activities in es-tablishing democratic government. In Vir-

ginia, he succeeded in separating church and state; he advocated the freeing of slaves, and advanced many other democratic ideals regarding civil and religious government, some of which seemed very radical to his contemporaries.

Because of his scholarly attainments, and because he spent the closing years of his life on his estate near Charlottesville, Va., known as Monticello, Jefferson was called the *Sage of Monticello.*[8]

Thomas Jefferson was born at Shadwell, Va., on April 2, 1743, and died at his home Monticello, in Albemarle County, Va., on July 4, 1826. He was President of the United States from 1801 to 1809.

[1] *A Book of Nicknames,* John Goff (Courier-Journal Job Printing Company, Louisville, Ky., 1892) p. 21.

The Life of Thomas Jefferson, Henry S. Randall (J. B. Lippincott Company, Philadelphia, 1888) vol. 1, p. 172, 179.

[2] *Life of Jefferson: Life of Thomas Jefferson, with Selections from the Most Valuable Portions of His Voluminous and Unrivalled Private Correspondence,* B. L. Rayner (Lilly, Wait, Coleman and Holden, Boston, 1834) p. 414-17, 431.

[3] *The Life of James Monroe,* George Morgan (Small, Maynard and Company, Boston, 1921) p. 25.

[4] *The Makers of America,* New Edition, Revised and Enlarged, James A. Woodburn and Thomas F. Moran (Longmans, Green and Company, New York and Boston, 1922) p. 189.

[5] *Virginia, Rebirth of the Old Dominion,* Philip Alexander Bruce (The Lewis Publishing Company, New York and Chicago, 1929) vol. 1, p. 393.

[6] *The Boy's Life of Thomas Jefferson,* Helen Nicolay (D. Appleton-Century Company, Inc., New York, 1933) p. 55.

"Thomas Jefferson" by John T. Morse, Junior, in *American Statesmen,* ed. by John T. Morse, Junior (Houghton Mifflin and Company, Boston, 1883) p. 21-4, 27, 30, 33.

[7] "Thomas Jefferson" by Clifford Smyth, in *Builders of America* (Funk and Wagnalls Company, New York and London, 1931) vol. 15, p. 64-72, 79.

[8] *American Heroes from History,* Inez N. McFee (A. Flanagan Company, Chicago, 1913) p. 143.

Jeffersonville, Indiana

Jeffersonville is called *Indiana's Gateway City*[1] because of its deep and efficient harbor and its connection with Louisville, Ky., Charlestown, Ind., New Albany, Ind., and Indianapolis, Ind.

[1] *The Encyclopedia Americana* (Americana Corporation, New York and Chicago, 1927) vol. 16, p. 6.

Jekyll Island

Jekyll Island, near Brunswick, Ga., the county seat of Glenn County and a seaport, has been nicknamed the *Millionnaires' Re-sort*[1] because it is a well-known summer and winter resort which is visited during both seasons by many wealthy people.

[1] *The Source Book* (Source Research Council, Inc., Chicago, 1936) vol. 1, p. 401.

Jellyfish

During the controversies within the Republican Party in 1881, those who remained neutral were called *Jellyfish*[1] because of their lack of "backbone" in not aligning themselves with one faction or the other.

[1] *Reconstruction and Union, 1865-1912*, Paul Leland Haworth (Henry Holt and Company, New York, 1912) p. 107.

Jenckes, Thomas Allen

In commemoration of his diligence and perseverance in arousing public sentiment to favor and demand the establishment of the Civil Service Department on the merit system, with its provisions for competition and probation, Thomas Allen Jenckes was nicknamed the *Father of Civil Service Reform.*[1]

Thomas Allen Jenckes, who was born at Cumberland, R.I., on November 2, 1818, and who died there on November 4, 1875, was a Representative from Rhode Island to the United States Congress from 1862 to 1871.

[1] *The National Cyclopaedia of American Biography* (James T. White and Company, New York, 1900) vol. 8, p. 35.

Jenckes, Virginia Ellis

Virginia Ellis Jenckes, a farmer and politician, was nicknamed the *Japanese Cherry-trees Nemesis*[1] because she was bitterly opposed to preserving the Japanese cherry trees, planted about the Tidal Basin at Washington, D.C. She was a Democratic Representative from Indiana to the United States Congress from 1933 until 1939.

Virginia Ellis Jenckes was born at Terre Haute, Ind., on November 6, 1882.

[1] An interview with Captain Victor Hunt Harding, Secretary, of the National Democratic Congress Reëlection Committee, Washington, D.C., April 10, 1939.

Jenkins, James

Bawling Jenkins[1] and *Thundering Jimmy* were nicknames applied to James Jenkins because of the violent denunciations and vehement criticisms which characterized his sermons.

James Jenkins was born in Marion County, S.C., on November 29, 1764, and died at Camden, S.C., on January 24, 1847.

[1] *The National Cyclopaedia of American Biography* (James T. White and Company, New York, 1900) vol. 10, p. 442.

Jennison's Monuments

During the Civil War, *Jennison's Monuments*[1] and *Jennison's Tombstones* were nicknames especially prevalent in Missouri where they were first applied to the chimneys of homes destroyed by Lieutenant Colonel Charles R. Jennison who led a campaign of retaliation against pro-slavery activities in Missouri. He was accused of murdering, pillaging, and burning the homes and property not only of the slave owners but also of the people who were opposed to slavery or who were neutrals. The scene of his depredations in 1861-62 was chiefly in the vicinity of Kansas City in Jackson County, Mo., where for miles his destructive route was marked by chimneys standing amidst the ashes of burned homes. The terms *Tombstones* and *Monuments* appear to have been used later in designating the chimneys of homes which were destroyed throughout the Southern states during the Civil War period usually by those who were opposed to slavery.

[1] *A History of the Sixth Iowa Infantry*, Henry H. Wright (Published at Iowa City, Iowa in 1923 by The State Historical Society of Iowa) p. 174.
Rebel Invasion of Missouri and Kansas, and the Campaign of the Army of the Border against General Sterling Price in October and November, 1864, Richard J. Hinton (Church and Goodman, Chicago, 1865) p. 187.
History of Kansas, State and People; Kansas at the First Quarter Post of the Twentieth Century, written and comp. by William E. Connelley (The American Historical Society, Inc., New York and Chicago, 1928) vol. 2, p. 650.
"Jayhawkers in Missouri, 1853-1863" by Hildegarde R. Herklotz, in *The Missouri Historical Review, October, 1923-July, 1924* (Published by The State Historical Society of Missouri, Columbia, Mo., 1924) p. 69-75.

Jennison's Tombstones. See *Jennison's Monuments*

Jenny. See Short, Dewey

Jensen, Forrest

The sobriquet *Woody*[6] is applied to Forrest Jensen, who was born at Seattle, Wash., on August 11, 1909, and who played outfield in major-league baseball, not only because his name is Forrest but also because he once played ball with the Timber League in the State of Washington.

[6] *Who's Who in Major League Base Ball*, comp. by Harold (Speed) Johnson (Buxton Publishing Company, Chicago, 1933) p. 227.

Jephtha. See Rixey, Eppa, Jr.

Jersey Blue State. See New Jersey

Jersey Blues. See New Jerseyans

Jersey Joe. See Stripp, J. V.

Jersey Slick. See Tichenor, Isaac

Jester. See Lincoln, Abraham

Jesuits. See Loyola College

Jewel City of California. See San Diago, Calif.

Jiggs McManus. See McManus, George

Jim Crow

Originally Jim Crow [1] was a Negro slave stable-hand at Louisville, Ky., whose song and hopping dance were mimicked by Thomas Dartmouth Rice, an actor of stock parts in Ludlow and Smith's Southern Theatre at Louisville, in 1828. Rice's impersonation of Jim Crow's antics initiated Negro minstrel shows, and caused the name Jim Crow to be applied to Negroes in general and to the parts of cars, buses, boats and the like which were restricted to the use of colored people in the Southern states.

Jim Crow Laws are enactments of the legislatures of the Southern states to restrict colored people to certain sections of public vehicles, theatres, churches, hotels, schools, and similar places. By an act of Congress in 1947, *Jim Crow Laws* are not applicable to interstate commerce.

[1] *National Cyclopaedia of American Biography* (James T. White and Company, New York, 1909) vol. 11, p. 207.

In Freedom's Birthplace: A Study of the Boston Negroes, John Daniels (Houghton Mifflin Company, Boston and New York, 1914) p. 234.

American History, William H. Mace (Rand McNally and Company, New York and Chicago, 1925) p. 217, appendix, p. xl.

"The New South, a Chronicle of Social and Industrial Evolution" by Holland Thompson, in *The Chronicles of America Series,* Abraham Lincoln Edition, Allen Johnson, Editor (Yale University Press, New Haven, Conn., 1919) vol. 42, p. 133.

The United States in Our Times, 1865-1920, Paul L. Haworth (Charles Scribner's Sons, New York, Chicago, and Boston, 1920) p. 62, 508.

Jim-Jim Crowd

About 1910, James Smith, Junior, and James Nugent, two politicians and public officials, and their followers were termed the *Jim-Jim Crowd* [1] because they were both named James. They united to control the Democratic party in New Jersey. The *Jim-Jim Crowd* was prominent in 1910 in securing the nomination of Woodrow Wilson for the office of Governor of New Jersey.

James Smith, Junior, a Senator from New Jersey from 1893 to 1899, was born at Newark, N.J., on June 12, 1851, and died there on April 1, 1927. James Nugent lived from 1864 to 1927.

[1] *Woodrow Wilson, the Man, His Times and His Task,* William Allen White (Houghton Mifflin Company, New York and Boston, 1924) p. 200-3

Jimmies. See Jamestown College

Jingle Money Smith. See Smith, J. M.

Joan of Arc of the Modern Religious World. See Langkop, Mrs. W. E.

Jockey. See Falk, B. A.

Joe Brown's Pikes

During the Civil War, Governor Joseph Emerson Brown of Georgia, ordered the manufacture of long wooden staffs tipped with pointed steel heads which soon became known as *Joe Brown's Pikes.*[1]

Joseph Emerson Brown was born in South Carolina on April 15, 1821, and died at Atlanta, Ga., on November 30, 1894.

[1] *Reminiscences of the Civil War,* Memorial Edition, General John B. Gordon (Charles Scribner's Sons, New York, 1904) p. 5.

John Barleycorn

John Barleycorn [1] is the nickname for malt liquor. It is said to have had its origin in an old English tract entitled *The Arraignment and Indicting of Sir John Barleycorn Kent* [1] printed for Timothy Tosspot.

[1] *Nicknames: A Dictionary of Words and Phrases,* by George T. Odell, distributed by the Washington Bureau, Washington, D.C., p. 1.

John B. Stetson University

The *Hatters* [1] is the nickname of the athletic teams of John B. Stetson University, at Deland, Fla., because the university was founded by John B. Stetson of Philadelphia, Pa., the manufacturer of Stetson hats.

[1] A letter from W. S. Allen, President of John B. Stetson University, Deland, Fla., November 19, 1935.

John Carroll University

The teams of John Carroll University, at Cleveland, Ohio, were designated the *Blue Streakers* [1] by a sports writer on the *Cleveland News,* because the backfield was fast and the team wore blue uniforms.

[1] A communication from Ralph Vince, Head Football Coach at John Carroll University, Cleveland, Ohio, June 13, 1935.

John Harvard Boys. See Harvard University

John O'Birds. See Burroughs, John '

John Partridge. See Page, John

John Street Methodist Episcopal Church in New York City

John Street Methodist Episcopal Church, at Forty-four John Street in New York City, is known as the *Cradle of Methodism* [1] because it was erected on the site of the first Methodist Church built in America.

[1] *The World Book Encyclopedia* (W. F. Quarrie Company, Chicago, 1934) vol. 12, p. 4986.

John Tarleton Agricultural College

The *Plowboys* [1] is the nickname given to the athletic teams of John Tarleton Agricultural College, at Stephenville, Tex., because John Tarleton is an agricultural college.

[1] A communication from W. J. Wisdom, Director of Athletics at John Tarleton Agricultural College, Stephenville, Tex., June 22, 1935.

John Turncoat. See Thayer, John

Johnnies. See Saint John's University, Minn.

Johnny Appleseed. See Chapman, John

Johnny Reb

Johnny Reb [1] is a sobriquet applied humorously or contemptuously to Confederate soldiers by the soldiers of the Union Army during the Civil War. *Reb* is an abbreviation of *rebel.*

[1] *Drum-beat of the Nation: The First period of the War of the Rebellion from Its Outbreak to the Close of 1862,* Charles Coffin (Harper and Brothers, New York, 1888) p. 463.

Johnny Simmonseed. See Hatfield, B. M.

Johnson, Andrew

The following nicknames have been attributed to Andrew Johnson: the *Daddy of the Baby, the Father of the Homestead Act, His Accidency, King Andy, Old Andy, Sir Veto,* and the *Veto President.*

Andrew Johnson was called the *Father of the Homestead Act* [1] because he framed and was instrumental in securing the passage of the Homestead Bill by Congress on May 19, 1862. The *Daddy of the Baby* was the nickname applied to Johnson because he had nursed the bill through Congress.

He was sometimes referred to as *His Accidency* [2] because as Vice President, he automatically became President upon the death of Lincoln.

After he became President of the United States, Andrew Johnson was called *King Andy* [1] by the radical element in the North because he did not advocate any changes in the Federal Constitution that would prevent the representatives and the senators elected by the Southern states from taking their places again in the House of Representatives and in the Senate after the Civil War was ended. They feared that he and the Southern members of Congress would become strong enough to control congressional action so that the Negro would virtually remain a slave.

While he was President of the United States from 1865 to 1869, Andrew Johnson was nicknamed *Sir Veto* and the *Veto President* [3] by his political enemies because he vetoed many bills during his administration particularly those passed by Congress dealing with reconstruction in the Southern states, which he considered unduly harsh or radical.

Andrew Johnson, the seventeenth President of the United States, was born at Raleigh, N.C., on December 29, 1808, and died at Carter's Station, Tenn., on July 31, 1875.

[1] *Andrew Johnson, Plebian and Patriot,* Robert W. Winston (Henry Holt and Company, New York, 1928) p. 105, 139, 358, 381.
[2] *The American Immortals: The Record of Men Who by Their Achievements in Statecraft, War, Science, Literature, Art, Law, and Commerce, Have Created the American Republic and Whose Names Are Inscribed in the Hall of Fame,* George Cary Eggleston (G. P. Putnam's Sons, New York and London, 1901) p. 223.
[3] *U.S. "Snap Shots": An Independent, National, and Memorial Encyclopedia . . . ,* Oliver McKee (A. M. Thayer and Company, Boston, 1892) p. 310.

Johnson, Edward

At the Battle of Alleghany, on July 2, 1864, Major General Edward Johnson was severely wounded, and in order to walk picked up a rough heavy piece of wood. From this he was called *Alleghany Johnson* and *Fence-rail Johnson*.[1]

Edward Johnson was born in Chesterfield County, Va., on April 16, 1816, and died at Richmond, Va., on February 22, 1873.

[1] *Four Years Under Marse Robert*, Robert Stiles (The Neale Publishing Company, New York and Washington, 1903) p. **218.**

Johnson, Harold

Harold Johnson, who was Editor-in-chief of *Who's Who in Major League Base Ball*, was nicknamed *Speed Magee*,[1] or more commonly, *Harold (Speed) Johnson*.

[1] *Who's Who in Major League Base Ball*, comp. by Harold (Speed) Johnson (Buxton Publishing Company, Chicago, 1933) p. 13.

Johnson, Hugh Samuel

General Hugh Samuel Johnson, a soldier, lawyer, manufacturer, former NRA Administrator, and columnist, was nicknamed the *Babe Ruth of the New Deal*, *Crack-Down Johnson*, *Crack-Down Czar of the NRA*, the *Great Thundering Rooster*, the *King of the Never-Made-Good Crack Downs*, the *NRA Czar*, and *Old Iron Pants*.

He was called the *Babe Ruth of the New Deal*[1] by William E. Street, former Governor of Colorado, in an address before the National Education Association at Washington, D.C., on July 4, 1934. *Crack-down Johnson*,[2] *Crack-down Czar of the NRA*,[3] the *King of the Never-Made-Good Crack-downs*, *NRA Czar*,[4] and *Old Iron Pants* were applied to Johnson because, while he was Administrator of the NRA, he threatened to "crack down" on Henry Ford and other industrialists and business men who refused to sign the NRA Codes, but never took legal action.

After the National Recovery Act was invalidated by the Supreme Court of the United States on May 27, 1935, as a result of legal proceedings brought before this Court by the Schenectady Poultry Firm, former employees of the NRA organized the Sick Chicken Society and called Johnson the *Great Thundering Rooster*, and the temporary board of governors of the organization the *Nine Old Capons* satirizing the "Nine Old Men" of the Supreme Court.

Hugh Samuel Johnson was born at Fort Scott, Kans., on August 5, 1882, and died at Washington, D.C., on April 15, 1943.

[1] *Washington Herald*, Washington, D.C., April 21, 1934, col. 5, p. 8; July 5, 1934, col. 3, p. 5; November 13, 1933, col. 2, p. 1; August 25, 1934, cols. 6-7, p. 1; December 8, 1933, col. 2, p. 2.

[2] *The Evening Star*, Washington, D.C., January 24, 1938, col. 1, p. A-3.

Johnson, John Monroe

John Monroe Johnson, a civil engineer and assistant Secretary of Commerce, was nicknamed *Rowboat Johnson*[1] because he made the statement before a Congressional Investigating Committee in October 1937, that "his knowledge of maritime affairs was limited to rowboats." The Congressional Investigating Committee wanted to know why the Commerce Department had not enforced the law requiring ship companies to install and enforce the "sprinkler rule."

John Monroe Johnson was born in Marion County, S.C., on May 5, 1878.

[1] *Washington Herald*, Washington, D.C., October 21, 1937, col. 7, p. 6.

Johnson, Mary McDonough

After Andrew Johnson's father died, his mother, Mary McDonough Johnson, began to spin and weave cloth on a hand loom to support her two children. She was successful and became known as *Polly The Weaver*[1] in Raleigh, N.C.

[1] *Andrew Johnson, Plebian and Patriot*, Robert W. Winston (Henry Holt and Company, New York, 1928) p. 8.

Johnson, Robert Lee

Because he is a Cherokee Indian, Robert Lee Johnson, who was born at Pryor, Okla., on November 25, 1908, and who played outfield in major-league baseball was called *Cherokee*.[1]

[1] *Who's Who in Major League Base Ball*, comp. by Harold (Speed) Johnson (Buxton Publishing Company, Chicago, 1933) p. 229.

Johnson, Walter Perry

Barney and the *Big Train* are the nicknames given to Walter Perry Johnson, an exceptional pitcher who played with the American League team in Washington. Johnson was active in professional baseball as pitcher and manager from 1907 to 1927. He was born at Humboldt, Kan., on November 6, 1887, and died in 1946.

[1] *Who's Who in Major League Base Ball*, comp. by Harold (Speed) Johnson (Buxton Publishing Company, Chicago, 1933) p. 233.

The Washington Herald, Washington, D.C., August 3, 1934, col. 7, p. 21.

Johnson, William Eugene

About 1907, the people in the Indian Territory and vicinity nicknamed William Eugene Johnson *Pussyfoot Johnson*[1] because of his cat-like methods of outwitting those who broke the prohibition laws.

William Eugene Johnson was born at Coventry, N.Y., on March 25, 1862, and died February 2, 1945.

[1] *The Literary Digest, January to March,* 1920 (Funk and Wagnalls Company, New York, 1920) vol. 64, March 6, 1920, p. 67.

Who's Who in America; A Biographical Dictionary of Notable Men and Women in the United States, 1932-33, ed. by Albert Nelson Marquis (The A. N. Marquis Company, Chicago, 1933) vol. 17, p. 1260.

"Pussyfoot" Johnson, Crusader—Reformer—a Man among Men, F. A. McKenzie (Fleming H. Revell Company, New York, 1920) p. 93.

Johnson, William Ransom

William Ransom Johnson, a sportsman, was known as the *Napoleon of the Turf*[1] because of his success in training horses and running them in the races held between the North and the South from 1823 until 1834. These races were a prominent national sport, and under the leadership of Johnson the southern entries won seventeen of the thirty races in which they participated.

William Ransom Johnson was born in Warren County, N.C., in 1782, and died at Mobile, Ala., on February 10, 1849.

[1] *Dictionary of American Biography under the Auspices of the American Council of Learned Societies,* ed. by Dumas Malone (Charles Scribner's Sons, New York, 1933) vol. 10, p. 130.

Johnson's Popar Bear Garden. See Alaska

Johnston, David Claypoole

David Claypoole Johnston was called the *American Cruikshank*[1] because he was a prominent engraver of original caricatures and published a number of sketchbooks illustrated with humorous sketches and caricatures. George Cruikshank was an English engraver and illustrator, distinguished for his original and amusing caricatures and sketches, many of which he engraved for the novels of Charles Dickens. He lived at London from 1792 until 1878.

David Claypoole Johnston was born at Philadelphia, Pa., in 1797, and died at Dorchester, Mass., on November 8, 1865.

[1] *The National Cyclopaedia of American Biography* (James T. White and Company, New York, 1907) vol. 5, p. 519.

Johnstown, Pennsylvania

Johnstown has frequently been referred to as the *Flood City*[1] because of the great Johnstown flood which was so disastrous to life and property in 1889. There have been many floods at Johnstown since that time.

[1] *A Book of Nicknames,* John Goff (Courier-Journal Job Printing Company, Louisville, Ky., 1892) p. 16.

Official History of the Johnstown Flood, Frank Connelly and George C. Jenks (Journalist Publishing Company, Pittsburgh, Pa., 1889) p. 10.

Jo-Jo. See White, Joyner

Jolly Millionaire. See O'Brien, W. S.

Jones, Charles Jesse

Charles Jesse Jones, a well-known western pioneer, was commonly called *Buffalo Jones,*[1] because he was an expert buffalo hunter. Throughout the eighteen sixties he hunted buffaloes for fifty cents a head chiefly for their hides. In 1875 Jones began experimenting with wild animal sanctuaries in an effort to preserve the buffalo from extermination. He said that he had hunted them from the Rio Grande River to the Canadian border and that his efforts to preserve the remaining ones was largely to atone for having slaughtered them so mercilessly.

In 1885 when it was realized that the buffalo on the western plains were disappearing, eighty-five buffalo calves were captured and domesticated. Of these Jones captured fifty-eight in central Texas and took them to his ranch in Kansas. It has been said that all the existing buffaloes in the United States have descended from these.

On his ranch, Jones has crossbred the buffalo and domestic cattle very successfully. The hybrid "catalo" is superior to both ancestors in quality of flesh and hides.

Charles Jesse Jones was born in Tazwell County, Ill., in 1844. He was appointed Warden of the Yellowstone National Park in 1902.

[1] *The Washington Post,* Washington, D.C., January 14, 1906, col. 3, p. 3.

Buffalo Jones' Forty Years of Adventure, comp. by Colonel Henry Inman (Crane and Company, Topeka, Kans., 1899) p. 14.

Jones, James C.

The nicknames *Beanpole Jimmy*[1] and *Lean Jimmy Jones* were applied to James C. Jones because of his tall, thin, and

Jones, J. C.—Continued

angular physique. He was six feet, two inches in height and weighed only about one hundred and twenty-five pounds. From 1841 to 1845 he was Governor of Tennessee. He was popular with the Tennesseans as a political campaigner because he was an entertaining stump-speaker.

James C. Jones was born near Nashville, Tenn., in 1809, and died at Memphis, Tenn., on October 29, 1859.

[1] *A History of Tennessee and Tennesseans, the Leaders and Representative Men in Commerce, Industry and Modern Activities,* Will T. Hale and Dixon L. Merritt (The Lewis Publishing Company, New York and Chicago, 1913) vol 2, p. 439.

Jones, John Luther

Casey Jones was the nickname of John Luther Jones, an engineer on the Illinois Central Railroad, because he learned railroading in the shops of the Mobile and Ohio Railroad Company, near Cayce, Kentucky. He was widely known as the subject of the famous ballad, *Casey Jones.*

John Luther Jones was born at Hickman, Ky., on March 14, 1864, and was killed in a train wreck near Vaughan, Miss., in the early 1900's. Jones was engineer of the "Cannonball," Illinois Central's famed express, itself the subject of many a railroad legend.

[1] *The Commercial Appeal,* Memphis, Tenn., April 1, 1900, p. 1.

Jones, John Paul

John Paul Jones has been called the *Bayard of the Sea* and the *Founder of the American Navy.*

The Duchess of Chartres, wife of the Duke of Chartres, Louis Phillipe Joseph, whom John Paul Jones met when he carried official dispatches to France in 1777, well designated him the *Bayard of the Sea* [1] because he was even then serving in the Revolutionary War as a captain in the American Navy, winning renown for himself and for his country as one of the greatest of sea fighters in American naval history. Pierre du Terrail Chevalier de Bayard was a French nobleman who, in the sixteenth century, served fearlessly, brilliantly, and most honorably in the aggressive wars of his country.

John Paul Jones was designated the *Founder of the American Navy* [2] in apprecia-

tion of the good use to which he put his master mariner's knowledge and the energy and patriotic zeal with which he worked to establish an American navy. The Continental Congress appointed a Naval Committee which on June 24, 1775, invited Jones to advise and assist them. He became the driving force of this committee, buying, constructing, and equipping vessels destined for war purposes. He also advised Congress as to the personnel of the newly formed navy, and helped to establish many of the underlying principles and philosophies of the present American navy.

John Paul Jones was born at Arbigland, Parish of Kirkbean, Kirkcudbright, Scotland, on July 6, 1747, and died at Paris, France, on July 18, 1792.

[1] *Paul Jones,* Hutchins Hapgood (Houghton Mifflin and Company, Boston and New York, 1901) p. 28.

[2] *Paul Jones, Founder of the American Navy, A History in Two Volumes,* Augustus C. Buell (Charles Scribner's Sons, New York, 1900) vol. 1, p. 1, 27-38.

Jones, John Percival

The *Nevada Commoner* [1] was applied to John Percival Jones by the newspapers of Nevada because while Jones served from 1863 to 1867 as a member of the State Senate of Nevada, and as a Senator from Nevada to the United States Congress from 1873 to 1903, he worked constantly to secure legislation favorable to the interests of the common people of his state. He was unusually popular with the miners.

John Percival Jones was born at The Hay, England, on January 27, 1829, was brought to the United States that same year by his parents, and died at Los Angeles, Calif., on November 27, 1912.

[1] *The National Cyclopaedia of American Biography* (James T. White and Company, New York, 1898) vol. 1, p. 300.

Jones, John William

John William Jones, a Baptist clergyman, soldier, and author, was called the *Fighting Parson* [1] in the South because he joined the Confederate Army in 1861 as a private and served until 1862 when he was appointed a chaplain. He was a leader in the revival meetings conducted in the winter of 1862-63 for the Army of General Robert E. Lee, and continued his work as a chaplain until 1865.

John William Jones was born at Louisa Court House, Va., on September 25, 1836, and died at Columbus, Ga., on March 17, 1909.

[1] *Dictionary of American Biography under the Auspices of the American Council of Learned Societies,* ed. by Dumas Malone (Charles Scribner's Sons, New York, 1933) vol. 10, p. 191.

Jones, Marvin

Marvin Jones, a Texas lawyer and politician, was nicknamed *Agricultural Jones* [1] when he was Chairman of the Agricultural Committee in the House of Representatives. He was a Democratic Representative from Texas to the United States Congress from 1917 to 1941.

Marvin Jones was born on a farm near Valley View, Tex., on February 26, 1886.

[1] An interview with Captain Victor Hunt Harding, Secretary of the National Democratic Congress Re-election Committee, Washington, D. C., April 10, 1939.

Jones, Mary Harris

Mary Harris Jones, a labor leader, was widely known throughout the United States as *Mother Jones.*[1]

After she had lost all her property in 1871 in the great fire at Chicago, Ill., and after she had lost her husband and children in the yellow fever epidemic of 1876 at Memphis, Tenn., she began to devote her time and energy to securing reforms in the social and economic life of laborers in the United States. For over fifty years she was outsanding in her efforts to secure legislation against child labor, unsanitary and dangerous working conditions, and the exploitation of human energy. Because these activities were promoted by genuine humanitarianism, she was popularly called *Mother Jones* and was respected alike by friends and foes.

Mary Harris Jones was born at Cork, Ireland, on May 1, 1830, and died at Silver Springs, Md., on November 30, 1930.

[1] *Dictionary of American Biography under the Auspices of the American Council of Learned Societies,* ed. by Dumas Malone (Charles Scribner's Sons, New York, 1933) vol. 10, p. 195.

Jones, Robert Tyre, Junior (Bobby Jones)

Robert Tyre (Bobby) Jones, Junior, was called the *King of the Links* [1] because of his exceptional record as a golf player. He won national and international championships. He was born at Atlanta, Ga., on March 17, 1902.

[1] *Washington Herald,* Washington, D.C., March 30, 1934, cols. 5-6, p. 24.

Jones, Samuel

Samuel Jones was known as the *Father of the New York Bar* [1] because in 1789 he took a leading part in revising the statutes of New York State. He came to be considered one of the most eminent lawyers of his time in New York.

Jones was born at Fort Hill, Long Island, N.Y., on July 26, 1734, and died at West Neck, N.Y., on November 25, 1819.

[1] *The National Cyclopaedia of American Biography* (James T. White and Company, New York, 1909) vol. 11, p. 489.

Jones, Samuel Milton

Samuel Milton Jones was designated *Golden Rule Jones* [1] in 1893 when he established a manufacturing concern at Toledo, Ohio, because of the consistent way in which he abided by the Golden Rule: "Whatsoever ye would that men should do to you, do ye even so to them." He posted on the walls of his workrooms copies of the Golden Rule instead of the stern, restrictive rules generally found on factory walls. The cordial relations which he succeeded in establishing between himself and his employees, together with his policy of "practicing what he preached" caused him to be given this nickname.

Samuel Milton Jones was born near Bedd Gelert, North Wales, on August 3, 1846, and died at Toledo, Ohio, on July 12, 1904.

[1] *Golden Rule Jones, Mayor of Toledo,* Ernest Crosby The Public Publishing Company, Chicago, 1906) p. 12, 58.
The *National Cyclopaedia of American Biography* (James T. White and Company, New York, 1900) vol. 10, p. 414.

Jones, Samuel Porter

Samuel Porter Jones, an evangelist, lecturer, and author, was nicknamed the *Mountain Evangelist.*[1] During his early years he was a circuit rider in the mountain regions. His evangelistic preaching was so successful that he was called to Memphis, Tenn., in 1884, and in 1885 the Reverend T. DeWitt Talmage engaged him to assist in evangelistic work in Brooklyn, N.Y. From 1885 until his death in 1906, Jones was a nationally known evangelist, who held meetings in most of the large American cities.

Samuel Porter Jones was born in Chambers County, Ala., on October 16, 1847, and died in a Pullman car of the Rock

Jones, S. P.—Continued
Island Railroad, near Perry, Ark., on
October 15, 1906.

[1] *The New International Encyclopaedia,* Second Edition, (Dodd, Mead and Company, New York, 1915) vol. 12, p. 770.
[2] *The Source Book* (Source Research Council, Inc., Chicago, 1936) vol. 4, p. 1518.

Jones, Samuel Pound
Samuel Pound Jones, a major league baseball pitcher, was called *Sad Sam.*[1] He was born at Woodsfield, Ohio, on July 26, 1892.

[1] *Who's Who in Major League Base Ball,* comp. by Harold (Speed) Johnson (Buxton Publishing Company, Chicago, 1933) p. 235.

Jones, Sissierretta Joyner
The *New York Clipper* was the first newspaper to apply the name *Black Patti*[1] to Mrs. Sissierretta Joyner Jones soon after her debut as a singer at Wallack's Theater in New York City. Mrs. Jones possessed a voice characterized by unusual range and volume. She was an effective singer of arias from Italian operas and made a number of successful concert tours of the leading cities in the United States. Adelina Maria Patti was an outstanding Spanish singer who distinguished herself in both Italian and Wagnerian operas.

Sissierretta Joyner Jones was born at Portsmouth, Va., on January 5, 1869.

[1] *The National Cyclopaedia of American Biography* (James T. White and Company, New York, 1906) vol. 13, p. 424.
Women of Distinction, Remarkable in Works and Invincible in Character, Lawson A. Scruggs (L. A. Scruggs, Raleigh, N.C., 1893) p. 327, 328.

Jordan, Baxter Byerley
Bucky[1] is the nickname given to Baxter Byerley Jordan, who was born at Cooleemee, N.C., on January 16, 1908, and who played first base in major league baseball.

[1] *Who's Who in Major League Base Ball,* comp. by Harold (Speed) Johnson (Buxton Publishing Company, Chicago, 1933) p. 236.

Julian, George Washington
The *Apostle of Disunion,* the *Orator of Free Dirt,* and *Wooly-head*[1] were nicknames applied to George Washington Julian because he was one of the founders of the Free Soil Party which came into existence in 1848, and because he advocated the abolition of slavery.

George Washington Julian was born at Centerville, Ind., on May 5, 1817, and died at Irvington, Ind., on July 7, 1899.

[1] "George W. Julian" by Grace Julian Clarke, in *Indiana Biographical Series, Vol. 1* (Published by the Indiana Historical Commission, Indianapolis, Ind., 1923) vol. 1, p. 80.

Jumbo. See Elliott, J. T.

Jumbo State. See Texas

Jumbos. See Tufts College

Jungleers Division. See Forty-first Infantry Division of World War II

Juniata College
The teams of Juniata College, at Huntingdon, Pa., have been designated *Indians*[1] because Huntingdon is located along the Juniata River at a favorite camp site for the Oneida tribe's peace pow-wows.

[1] A communication from J. E. Oller of Juniata College, Huntingdon, Pa., November 18, 1935.

K

Kalamazoo, Michigan
Kalamazoo is called the *Celery City*[1] because it is located in a rich agricultural region, one of the chief products of which is celery.

[1] *Our State of Michigan,* Revised Edition, Arthur Dondineau and Leah A. Spencer (The Macmillan Company, New York, 1925) p. 109.

Kalbfus, Edward Clifford
Edward Kalbfus, a Rear Admiral in the United States Navy, has two nicknames, *Old Man* and *Durable Ned.* The *Old Man* is a nickname conventionally applied to all admirals. *Durable Ned*[1] is the name he uses in radiograms and other messages to his wife.

Edward Clifford Kalbfus was born at Mauch Chunk, Pa., on November 24, 1877.

[1] *Time: The Weekly Newsmagazine,* Chicago, May 8, 1939, col. 3, p. 6.

Kansans
The Kansans are nicknamed *Grasshoppers, Jayhawkers,* and *Sunflowers.* They are called *Grasshoppers* because of a great plague of grasshoppers that almost destroyed the crops of Kansas and her neighboring states in 1874.

The people of Kansas were called *Jay-hawkers*[1] during the slavery controversy prior to the Civil War. The name was applied to guerillas and armed marauders and pillagers. It is said to be derived from jay-hawk, a predatory bird. Another version is that when a New York regiment was stationed in one of the Kansas forts they were called *Gay Yorkers*,[2] which gradually emerged as *Jayhawkers*.

Kansas is known as the *Sunflower State* and the people as *Sunflowers* because of the abundance of sunflowers which grow there.

[1] *U.S.: An Index to the United States of America*, comp. by Malcolm Townsend (D. Lothrop and Company, Boston, 1890) p. 76.
A New Dictionary of Americanisms, Sylva Clapin (Louis Weiss and Company, New York, 1903) p. 243.
[2] *King's Handbook of the United States*, planned and ed. by Moses King, text by M. F. Sweetser (The Matthews-Northrup Company, Buffalo, N.Y., 1896) p. 265.

Kansas

Kansas is known as the *Battleground of Freedom, Central State, Cyclone State, Garden State, Garden of the West, Grasshopper State, Jayhawker State, Navel of the Nation, Squatter State,* and *Sunflower State.*

The State of Kansas was called the *Battleground of Freedom*[1] because for a decade after the passage of the Kansas-Nebraska Bill in 1854 there was contention and political wrangling over whether slavery would be permitted in Kansas.

Because it occupies a central position in the United States Kansas is designated the *Central State* and the *Navel of the Nation.*[2]

The origin of the nickname, the *Cyclone State*[2] is self explanatory when one considers that the great cyclone area of the United States is the central Mississippi Valley, notably in Kansas."

Kansas is called the *Garden State*,[3] and the *Garden of the West*[4] from the rolling prairies and vast cultivated fields which abound in that fertile region.

It is nicknamed the *Grasshopper State*[5] because grasshoppers frequently damage the grain crops.

The *Jayhawker State*[5] is a term applied to Kansas in reference to its territorial troubles.

The term *Jayhawker* was applied along the border at the beginning of the Civil War to irregular troops and pillaging bands on both sides. The *Standard History of Kansas and Kansans* says the origin of the

name is unknown but it was in use in Texas and the West many years before Kansas was a territory.[6]

Kansas is called the *Squatter State*[2] from the hordes of settlers poured into the territory by the proslavery and antislavery factions prior to the Civil War.

The name, the *Sunflower State*,[2] has been applied to Kansas because of the numbers of sunflowers which grow there.

[1] *Seeing the Middle West*, John T. Faris (J. B. Lippincott Company, Philadelphia, 1923) p. 104.
New American History, Albert Bushnell Hart (American Book Company, New York, 1930) p. 388-96.
[2] *The Encyclopedia Americana* (Americana Corporation, New York and Chicago, 1929) vol. 8, p. 362; vol. 16, p. 294; vol. 26, p. 37.
[3] *Americanisms; The English of the New World*, M. Schele De Vere (Charles Scribner and Company, New York, 1872) p. 659, 660.
[4] *U.S.: An Index to the United States of America*, comp. by Malcolm Townsend (D. Lothrop Company, Boston, (1890) p. 68.
[5] *The New International Encyclopaedia*, Second Edition (Dodd, Mead and Company, New York, 1930) vol. 10, p. 263; vol. 21, p. 463.
[6] *A Standard History of Kansas and Kansans*, William E. Connelley (The Lewis Publishing Company, Chicago and New York, 1918) vol. 2, p. 742.

Kansas Bibles

In 1854 the Kansas-Nebraska Bill provided that the settlers in the territory of Kansas would decide whether or not the people of the future State of Kansas would be permitted to own slaves. The abolitionists in the northern and the eastern states wanted Kansas to be a free state, and through various organizations they procured funds for that purpose. Some of the money collected in churches was used to buy rifles which were nicknamed *Kansas Bibles*.[1]

[1] *A School History of the United States*, Susan Pendleton Lee, *with Questions and Summaries for Reviews and Essays*, by Louise Manly (B. F. Johnson Publishing Company, Richmond, Va., 1895) p. 327.

Kansas City, Missouri

Kansas City is nicknamed the *Greatest Primary Winter Wheat Market, Heart of America, Metropolis of the Missouri Valley,* and *Mushroomopolis.*

The fact that the numerous mills and elevators in this city store such vast quantities of wheat, which is shipped to various other milling centers and markets, has caused it to be termed the *Greatest Primary Winter Wheat Market.*[1] It is often spoken of as *The Heart of America*[2] because it is located near the center of the United States, and is a great railroad center, that serves as

Kansas City, Mo.—Continued
an entrance to the West and Southwest from
the North and East.

Kansas City is frequently called the
Metropolis of the Missouri Valley [1] because
of its stock yards and packing houses, its
vast grain and produce markets and its
milling and elevator and shipping facilities.

It is termed *Mushroomopolis* [3] because of
its rapid growth.

[1] *The Encyclopedia Americana* (Americana Corporation, New York and Chicago, 1932) vol. 16, p. 299.

[2] *The Story of Kansas City, Books One, Two and Three*, Emma Serl (Board of Education, School District of Kansas City, Mo., Empire Printing Company, Kansas City, Mo., 1929) book 3, p. 137.

Kansas City in Three Decades: History of Kansas City Illustrated in Three Decades, Being a Chronicle Wherein Is Set Forth the True Account of the Founding, Rise, and Present Position Occupied by Kansas City in Municipal America, William Griffith (Hudson-Kimberly Publishing Company, Kansas City, Mo., 1900) p. 129.

[3] *A Book of Nicknames*, John Goff (Courier-Journal Job Printing Company, Louisville, Ky., 1892) p. 16.

History of Missouri: Missouri, Mother of the West, Walter Williams, Floyd Calvin Shoemaker, assisted by an advisory council (The American Historical Society, Inc., New York and Chicago, 1930) vol. 2, p. 393-8.

Kansas City Athletics. See Philadelphia
American League Baseball Company.

Kansas Coolidge. See Landon, A. M.

Kansas Dry. See Guyer, U. S.

Kansas Hero. See Montgomery, James

Karamatic, George
George Karamatic, who played halfback
in national league football, was nicknamed
Automatic [1] by the sports writers of Spokane, Washington, in 1936, because of the
almost mechanical precision with which he
kicked field goals and touchdowns.

George Karamatic was born at Aberdeen,
Wash., on February 22, 1917.

[1] A communication from George P. Marshall, President-treasurer of the Washington Club of the National Football League, Washington, D.C., March 20, 1939.

Kaw. See *Kaw River*

Kaw River
Those living near the Kansas River commonly refer to it as the *Kaw*, this being a
contraction of Kansas (pronounced kansaw).

[1] *Seeing the Middle West*, John T. Faris (J. B. Lippincott Company, Philadelphia and London, 1923) p. 105.

Kaydets. See United States Coast Guard
Academy

Kearney, Denis
Denis Kearney, an Irish labor agitator,
was nicknamed the *Sand Lot Agitator* [1] because he frequently spoke on vacant lots in
San Francisco, Calif. Kearney was the leading spirit in organizing the Workingmen's
party of California on October 12, 1877.
He was influential in bringing about the
enactment of a law suspending Chinese immigration to the United States.

Denis Kearney was born at Oakmount, in
Cork County, Ireland, on February 1, 1847,
and died at Alameda, Calif., on April 24,
1907.

[1] *The Editorial Review* (Published by The Editorial Review Company, New York, 1909) vol. 1, August to December, p. 127.

Kearny, Philip
In allusion to the manner in which Major
General Philip Kearny conducted himself
on the field of battle, he was sometimes
called *Dashing Phil Kearny*.[1] He was a
member of Winfield Scott's staff, served in
the Mexican War, and as an officer in the
Union Army in the Civil War.

Philip Kearny was born at New York
City, on June 2, 1815, and died near
Chantilly, Va., on September 1, 1862.

[1] *Our First War in Mexico*, Farnham Bishop (Charles Scribner's Sons, New York, 1916) p. 181.

The Encyclopedia Americana (Americana Corporation, New York and Chicago, 1927) vol. 16, p. 327.

Keller, Kent Ellsworth
The *Big Man from Little Egypt* [1] is the
nickname sometimes applied to Kent Ellsworth Keller because of his political
prominence in Illinois, the southern part of
which is often called *Little Egypt*.

Kent Ellsworth Keller, who was born
near Ava, Ill., on June 4, 1867, was a Representative from Illinois to the United States
Congress from 1931 to 1941.

[1] *The Washington Post Magazine*, Washington, D.C., March 4, 1934, p. 4.

Kelley, David Campbell
During the Civil War, Lieutenant Colonel
David Campbell Kelley was nicknamed the
Fighting Parson [1] because he was a minister
in the Methodist Episcopal Church.

David Campbell Kelley was born in Wilson County, Tenn., on December 25, 1833,
and died at Nashville, Tenn., on May 15,
1909.

[1] *Bedford Forrest and His Critter Company*, Andrew Nelson Lytle (Minton, Balch and Company, New York, 1931) p. 312.

Kelley, William Darragh

William Darragh Kelley was designated the *Father of the House* and *Pig Iron Kelley.*

The *Father of the House* [1] originated in the fact that Kelley was a Representative from Pennsylvania to Congress from 1860 to 1890 and was thus the oldest member in point of service at that time.

Pig Iron Kelley [2] was a nickname applied to him because of his interest in fostering and protecting the industries of his state, particularly the manufacture of pig iron.

William Darragh Kelley was born at Philadelphia, Pa., on April 12, 1848, and died at Washington, D.C., on January 9, 1890.

[1] *American Orators and Oratory, Comprising Biographical Sketches of the Representative Men of America, together with Gems of Eloquence upon the Leading Questions that Have Occupied Public Attention from the Foundation of the Republic to the Present Time*, G. M. Whitman, with an introduction by Frank Gilbert (Fairbanks, Palmer and Company, Chicago, 1884) p. 633.

[2] *The American Nation: A History; National Development, 1877-1885*, Edwin Erle Sparks (Harper and Brothers, New York and London, 1907) vol. 23, p. 299.
The National Cyclopaedia of American Biography (James T. White and Company, New York, 1896) vol. 6, p. 140.

Kelly, Clinton Wayne

The Indian-like nickname *Big Medicine* [1] by which Doctor Clinton Wayne Kelly was often called, was applied to him as a result of the wide-spread recognition of his ability as a physician in the city of Louisville, Ky.

Clinton Wayne Kelly was born near Smithville, Ky., on February 12, 1844, and died at Louisville, Ky., on January 26, 1923.

[1] *Encyclopedia of American Biography: American Biography, a New Cyclopedia*, comp. under the editorial supervision of a notable advisory board (Published under the direction of The American Historical Society, Inc., New York, 1928) vol. 21, p. 353.

Kelly, Edward Austin

Edward Austin Kelly, an Illinois politician, was nicknamed *Baseball Eddy* [1] in the House of Representatives because he had formerly played second base in major league baseball. He was a Representative from Illinois to Congress from 1931 to 1947.

Edward Austin Kelly was born at Chicago, Ill., on April 3, 1892.

[1] An interview with Captain Victor Hunt Harding, Secretary of the National Democratic Congress Reëlection Committee, Washington, D.C., April 10, 1939.

Kelly, James Edward

James Edward Kelly has been called the *Sculptor of American History* [1] because he took scenes from American history for many of his sculptures. He was born at New York City, on July 30, 1855 and died on May 25, 1933.

[1] *The Encyclopedia Americana* (Americana Corporation, New York and Chicago, 1927) vol. 16, p. 344.

Kelly, John

The appellations *Boss Kelly* and *Honest John Kelly* were applied to John Kelly, a New York politician.

He was known as *Boss Kelly* [1] when for many years, he was a dominant figure in the political activities of Tammany Hall and the Democratic party in New York City.

The supporters of John Kelly applied the sobriquet *Honest John Kelly* [2] to him because he had assisted in reorganizing Tammany Hall following the exposure of the corrupt Tweed Ring, the activities of which had been closely connected with those of Tammany Hall. This nickname was given to him in 1878, when Kelly had himself nominated for Governor of New York State on an independent ticket.

John Kelly was born at New York City, on April 21, 1821, and died there on June 1, 1886.

[1] *The Development of the United States since 1865*, Nelson P. Mead (Harcourt, Brace and Company, New York, 1930) p. 138.

[2] *Chester A. Arthur, a Quarter-century of Machine Politics*, George Frederick Howe (Dodd, Mead and Company, New York, 1934) p. 54.

Kelly, Michael J.

Michael J. Kelly, a baseball player, was nicknamed *King Kelly* and the *Ten Thousand Dollar Beauty. King Kelly* [1] originated in the fact that he was one of the outstanding players of his time. The *Ten Thousand Dollar Beauty* [1] originated when the Chicago American League Company sold Kelly's services to the Boston Players League Club in 1887 for ten thousand dollars.

Michael J. Kelly was born at Troy, N.Y., on December 31, 1857, and died at Boston, Mass., on November 8, 1894.

[1] *Dictionary of American Biography under the Auspices of the American Council of Learned Societies*, ed. by Dumas Malone (Charles Scribner's Sons, New York, 1933) vol. 10, p. 310.

Kelly, Walter C.

Walter C. Kelly, an actor, was nicknamed the *Virginia Judge* [1] because he made his appearance on the vaudeville stage in 1899, in a skit by that name which he originated.

Kelly, W. C.—Continued

Walter C. Kelly was born at Mineville, N.Y., on October 29, 1873, and died at Philadelphia, Pa., on January 6, 1939.

[1] *Pittsburgh Post-Gazette*, Pittsburgh, Pa., January 7, 1939, col. 4, p. 1.

Who's Who in the Theatre: A Biographical Record of the Contemporary Stage, comp. and ed. by John Parker, Eighth Edition, Revised and Enlarged (Sir Isaac Pitman and Sons, Limited, London, 1936) p. 874.

Kenneally, George V.

George V. Kenneally, a national-league football player, is frequently called the *Old Man of the Gridiron* [1] because he played football for twenty years and more. He was captain and assistant coach for the *Philadelphia Eagles* in the National Football League. He was born at Boston, Mass., on April 12, 1902.

[1] *Who's Who in Major League Football*, comp. by Harold (Speed) Johnson and Wilfrid Smith (B. V. Callahan, Chicago, 1935) p. 85.

Kennedy, Crammond

Crammond Kennedy was nicknamed the *Boy Preacher* [1] while he was delivering religious addresses in New York City between 1857 and 1860, when he was about fifteen years of age. In 1861 he was ordained as a chaplain in the army.

Crammond Kennedy was born at North Berwick, Scotland, on December 29, 1842, and died at Washington, D.C., on February 20, 1918.

[1] *Appleton's Cyclopaedia of American Biography*, ed. by James Grant Wilson and John Fiske (D. Appleton and Company, New York, 1888) vol. 3, p. 516.

Kenney, Edward A.

Edward A. Kenney, a New Jersey real estate dealer and politician, was nicknamed *Lottery Kenney* [1] in the House of Representatives because he introduced many bills designed to legalize federal lotteries. He was a Democratic Representative from New Jersey from 1933 to 1937.

Edward A. Kenney was born at Clinton, Mass., on August 11, 1884.

[1] An interview with Captain Victor Hunt Harding, Secretary of the National Democratic Congress Reëlection Committee, Washington, D.C., April 10, 1939.

Kentuckians

The Kentuckians are called *Bears*, *Corn-crackers*, and *Red Horses*. The nickname *Bears* [1] is applied to Kentuckians because the state is nicknamed the *Bear* State from the prevalence of bears found there in pioneer days. The origin and the significance of the term *Corn-crackers*, applied to the Kentuckians, is explained in connection with the origin of the nickname, *Corn-cracker State*. The sobriquet *Red Horses* [2] given to the people of Kentucky, probably alludes to a kind of fish, a large red sucker commonly found in the Ohio River and its tributaries. See Kentucky.

[1] *Americanisms: The English of the New World*, M. Schele De Vere (Charles Scribner and Company, New York, 1872) p. 660.

[2] *A New Dictionary of Americanisms*, Sylva Clapin (Louis Weiss and Company, New York, 1903) p. 333.

Kentucky

Kentucky is known as the *Bear State*, the *Blue Grass State*, the *Corn-cracker State*, the *Dark and Bloody Ground State*, the *Hemp State*, the *Rock-ribbed State*, and the *Tobacco State*.

Kentucky is called the *Bear State* because bears were very prevalent during pioneer days, and the *Blue Grass State* [1] from the abundant growth of blue grass on its rich limestone soil, especially in the vicinity of Louisville and Lexington.

The *Corn-cracker State* [2,3] was applied to Kentucky in allusion to the poorer class of white people living in the mountainous regions. Another authority says that the name is a corruption of corn-crake, a species of crane, found frequently in Kentucky.

Kentucky was called the *Dark and Bloody Ground*, [2] from the fact that her territory was the battleground between the northern and southern Indian tribes. [6] *Dark and Bloody Ground* is the meaning of the Indian word *Kentucky*.

Because Kentucky has always been the foremost State in the cultivation of hemp, it is known as the *Hemp State*. [4]

Kentucky is referred to as the *Rock-ribbed State*, [5] because of the rocky chain of mountains at its eastern end.

This state is called the *Tobacco State* because so much tobacco is raised within her borders. Kentucky produces about two thirds of the annual American tobacco crop.

[1] *A New Dictionary of Americanisms*, Sylva Clapin (Louis Weiss and Company, New York, 1903) p. 60.

[2] *Dictionary of Americanisms*, Fourth Edition, John Russell Bartlett (Little, Brown and Company, Boston, 1877) p. 147, 168.

[3] *U.S.: An Index to the United States of America*, comp. by Malcolm Townsend (D. Lothrop Company, Boston, 1890) p. 68.

[4] *King's Handbook of the United States*, planned and ed. by Moses King, text by M. F. Sweetser (Moses King Corporation, Buffalo, N.Y., 1891) p. 279.

[5] *American History and Government, a Text-Book on the History and Civil Government of the United States,* James Albert Woodburn and Thomas Francis Moran Longmans, Green and Company, New York and London, 1908) p. 354.

Kentucky Duel Fighter. See Clay, C. M. Sr.

Kentucky State Industrial College

The athletic teams of Kentucky State Industrial College, at Frankfort, Ky., were nicknamed the *Thorobreds* [1] because the college is located in the midst of the thoroughbred horse-breeding districts of Kentucky.

[1] A communication from J. D. Stewart, Kentucky State Industrial College, Frankfort, Ky., November 16, 1935.

Kenyon College

The athletic teams of Kenyon College, at Gambier, Ohio, are called the *Episcopalians* [1] because the college is owned and operated by the Episcopalian Church.

[1] A communication from R. J. Kutler, Director of Athletics at Kenyon College, Gambier, Ohio, November 10, 1935.

Keokuk, Iowa

Keokuk is nicknamed the *Gate City* and the *Power City.* It is termed the *Gate City* [1] because it is situated at the foot of the Des Moines Rapids in the Mississippi River, at which point the river becomes navigable. Keokuk is designated the *Power City* [2] because it is the site of one of the largest hydro-electric power plants in the world. The power is obtained by means of a concrete dam across the Mississippi River, 31 feet high and nearly a mile long.

[1] *Description of Keokuk, The Gate City, Lee County, Iowa,* William Rees (Printed at the Office of the Keokuk Daily and Weekly Times, Keokuk, Iowa, 1855) p. 5.

[2] *The Encyclopedia Americana* (Americana Corporation, New York and Chicago, 1932) vol. 16, p. 373.

[3] *Our World and Ourselves: Our Home, State, and Continent,* Albert Perry Brigham and Charles T. McFarlane (American Book Company, New York, 1933) p. 207.

Key City. See Vicksburg, Miss.

Key of the Great Valley. See New Orleans, La.

Key to the Blue Ridge. See North Wilkesboro, N.C.

Keystone Division. See Twenty-eighth Infantry Division of World War II

Keystone of the South Atlantic Seaboard. See South Carolina

Keystone State. See Pennsylvania

Kid Gleason. See Gleason, William

Kid-gloves Harrison. See Harrison, Benjamin

Kid Sheriff of Nebraska. See Wedgwood, E. A.

Kiddo. See Davis, G. W.

Kiki. See Cuyler, H. S.

Kill Crazy Dillinger. See Dillinger, John

Killefer, William

Because of his speed, *Reindeer* [1] is the nickname given to William Killefer, who was born at Paw Paw, Mich., on October 10, 1888, and who was a manager in major-league baseball.

[1] *Who's Who in Major League Base Ball,* comp. by Harold (Speed) Johnson (Buxton Publishing Company, Chicago, 1933) p. 243.

Kimsey, Clyde

Chad [1] is the sobriquet of Clyde Kimsey, who was born at Copperhill, Tenn., on August 6, 1906, and who pitched in major-league baseball.

[1] *Who's Who in Major League Base Ball,* comp. by Harold (Speed) Johnson (Buxton Publishing Company, Chicago, 1933) p. 244.

Kinderhook Fox. See Van Buren, Martin

King, Cyrus Murdock

The nickname *Good Roads King* [1] was given to Cyrus Murdock King because he devoted much of his time, money, and energy to securing improvements for the old highways in Minnesota and establishing new highways.

Cyrus Murdock King was born at Middleville, Minn., on August 2, 1860, and died at Deer River, Minn., on November 2, 1922.

[1] *The National Cyclopaedia of American Biography* (James T. White and Company, New York 1926) vol. 19, p. 144.

King, William Henry

King of the District, King of Investigators and the *Mormon Bishop* are nicknames which have been applied to William Henry King, a Utah lawyer and politician. He was called the *Mormon Bishop* [1] by his colleagues in the United States Senate, because he came from Salt Lake City. He was a Democratic Senator from Utah from 1897 to 1899, from 1900 to 1901 to fill a vacancy, and from 1917 to 1941.

The *King of the District*, is partly a play on the Senator's surname and partly a description of his power and influence in the District of Columbia, when he was chairman of the committee appointed by Congress to execute the municipal affairs of the District.

Senator King was known as *King of Investigators* [2] because he took a prominent part in the investigations made by the District Commissioners into the milk strikes and other municipal disturbances in Washington, D.C., in 1939.

William Henry King was born at Fillmore City, Utah, on June 3, 1864.

[1] An interview with Captain Victor Hunt Harding, Secretary of the National Democratic Congress Reëlection Committee, Washington, D.C., April 10, 1939.

[2] *The Washington Post Magazine*, Washington, D.C., March 4, 1934, p. 4.

King and Queen County, Virginia

The *Shoe-string* [1] is a nickname often applied to King and Queen County, Va., because it is a long, narrow county situated between the Mattaponi and the Piankitank rivers in the Tidewater section of the State.

[1] *Virginia*, comp. and ed. by Charlotte Allen (Published by the Department of Agriculture and Immigration of the State of Virginia under the direction of George W. Koiner, Commissioner, Department of Purchase and Printing, Richmond, Va., 1937) p. 183.

King and Queen of Hospitality. See Jackson, Andrew, and Rachael Donelson Jackson

King Andrew the First. See Jackson, Andrew

King Andy. See Johnson, Andrew

King Carter. See Carter, Robert

King Caucus. See Stilwell, S. M.

King College

The athletic teams of King College, at Bristol, Tenn, were nicknamed the *Red Tornadoes* [1] by sports writers because the teams wore scarlet uniforms.

[1] A communication from W. A. Richardson, Director of Athletics at King College, Bristol, Tenn., June 19, 1935.

King Coody. See Taney, R. B.

King Cotton

After Eli Whitney had invented the Cotton gin in 1793, cotton came to be the major crop of southern farmers, and was nicknamed *King Cotton.* [1] It is claimed that the expression originated just previous to the Civil War in statements made by southerners that the North could not wage a war upon the South because the North had to have the cotton which was grown in the South.

Senator James Henry Hammond from South Carolina in a speech made on March 4, 1858, remarked that "Cotton is King," [2] and that no one would dare make war upon cotton.

[1] *Stories of American Leaders,* Sarah Dow Heard and M. W. King (The John C. Winston Company, Philadelphia, 1934) p. 123.

[2] *Speech of Honorable James H. Hammond, of South Carolina on the Admission of Kansas under the Lecompton Constitution, Delivered in the Senate of the United States, March 4, 1858* (L. Towers, Washington, D.C., 1858) p. 12.

King Hancock. See Hancock, John

King Hooper. See Hooper, Robert

King Josiah the First. See Quincy, Josiah

King Kelly. See Kelly, M. J.

King Kong. See Kline, R. G.

King Martin the First. See Van Buren, Martin

King of American Clowns. See Rice, Daniel

King of Florida. See Plant, H. B.

King of Flower Painters. See De Longpré, Paul

King of Investigators. See King, W. H.

King of Jazz. See Whiteman, Paul

King of Moonshiners. See Gooch, W. R.

King of Squatters. See Robinson, Solon

King of the District. See King, W. H.

King of the Links. See Jones, R. T. (Bobby) Jr.

King of the Lobby. See Ward, Samuel

King of the Marine Insurance Business. See Townsend, H. N.

King of the Missouri. See Mackenzie, Kenneth

King of the Never-Made-Good Crack-Downs. See Johnson, H. S.

King of the New Dealers. See Minton, Sherman

King of the Quakers. See Pemberton, Israel

King of the Smugglers. See Hancock, John

King Sears. See Sears, Isaac

King Solomon. See Holcombe, Solomon

King Wampum. See Pemberton, Israel

Kingfish. See Long, H. P.

Kingmaker. See Guffey, J. F.

Kingsmen. See Brooklyn College

Kinzie, John

John Kinzie, a fur trader, was nicknamed *Shaw-nee-aw-kee* or the *Silver Man* [1] by the Indians along the Maunee River in Ohio because of his proficiency as a silversmith. His chief occupation, however, was fur trading. Despite his cunning as a merchant, he was fair and was so well liked by the Indians that at the time of the massacre at Fort Dearborn, Mich., in August 1812, he and his family were warned by the Indians and escaped with their lives.

John Kinzie was born at Quebec, Canada, on December 3, 1763, and died at Chicago, Ill., on January 6, 1828.

[1] *Dictionary of American Biography under the Auspices of the American Council of Learned Societies,* ed. by Dumas Malone (Charles Scribner's Sons, New York, 1933) vol. 10, p. 422.

Kirchhoff, Theodore

Theodore Kirchhoff, who was born at Uetersen, Holstein, Germany, on January 8, 1828, and who died at San Francisco, Calif., on March 2, 1899, was called the *Poet of the Golden Gate* [1] because many of his lyrical poems were descriptive of the scenery and life in the vicinity of San Francisco where he made his home. The entrance to the San Francisco harbor is known as the *Golden Gate.*

[1] *The National Cyclopaedia of American Biography* (James T. White and Company, New York, 1909) vol. 11, p. 266.

Kirk, John Robert

Doctor John Robert Kirk, a noted Missouri educator, was called the *Grand Old Man of Missouri* [1] because of his long educational service in the State of Missouri.

He began his educational work as a teacher in the rural schools of Harrison County, Missouri, in 1870. He was State Superintendent of Public Instruction of Missouri for a number of years until he became President of the Northeast Missouri State Teachers College, at Kirksville, Mo. in 1899. He was President Emeritus from 1925 to his death in 1937.

[1] *The Peabody Reflector and Alumni News: A Monthly Magazine Devoted to the Interests of the Alumni of George Peabody College for Teachers* (Published jointly by the College and the Alumni Association of George Peabody College for Teachers, Nashville, Tenn., 1937) vol. 10, no. 11, December 1937, p. 435.

Kirkland, Richard R.

Richard R. Kirkland was acclaimed the *Hero of Fredericksburg* because of an unusually brave and generous act at the Battle of Fredericksburg, Virginia, on December 13, 1862.

At this battle, which was one of the bloodiest and most bitterly contested engagements of the Civil War, Kirkland saw that a large number of badly wounded soldiers had fallen between the two opposing lines of battle. Sergeant Kirkland, unmindful of

Kirkland, R. R.—Continued

his personal safety, carried water to Confederate and Federal alike. He himself escaped injury.

Richard R. Kirkland was born in Kershaw County, S.C., in 1841, and was killed at the Battle of Chickamauga in Georgia, in September, 1863.

[1] *Confederate Military History, a Library of Confederate States History in Twelve Volumes, Written by Distinguished Men of the South, and Edited by General Clement A. Evans* (Confederate Publishing Company, Atlanta, Ga., 1899) vol. 5, p. 697.

Kirkpatrick, John Milton

In allusion to the lucidity and the eloquence with which he delivered his orations or pleaded his cases at the bar, John Milton Kirkpatrick, who was born at Milton, Pa., on December 1, 1825, was widely known as the *Silver Tongued Orator*.[1]

[1] *The National Cyclopaedia of American Biography* (James T. White and Company, New York, 1924) vol. 8, p. 469.

Kiss-of-death Oliver. See Oliver, E. L.

Kissing Bridge

About the middle of the eighteenth century, the *Kissing Bridge*[1] was a sobriquet given to a bridge over De Voor's millstream, located at about Fifty-third Street between Second and Third Avenues in what is now New York City. It was customary for gentlemen to kiss the ladies they were escorting as they crossed this bridge on returning to their homes from picnics and other rural social activities.

[1] *Social New York under the Georges, 1714-1776, Houses, Streets, and Country Homes, with Chapters on Fashions, China, Plate and Manners,* Esther Singleton (D. Appleton and Company, New York, 1902) p. 351.

Kissing-bug Hobson. See Hobson, R. P.

Kit. See Carson, W. L.

Kitchen Cabinet

While he was President of the United States from 1829 to 1837, Andrew Jackson conferred but little with his cabinet officers, but greatly relied upon the judgment of a group of his trusted friends who came to be nicknamed Jackson's *Kitchen Cabinet*[1] because he often held meetings with them in the privacy of his home.

[1] *Andrew Jackson, the Fighting President,* Helen Nicolay (The Century Company, New York, 1929) p. 270.

Kleberg, Richard Miffin

Richard Miffin Kleberg, a Texas ranchman and politician, was nicknamed the *Cattle King*[1] while in the House of Representatives because his grandfather, Richard King, founded one of the largest cattle ranches in the United States. He was a Democratic Representative from Texas to Congress from 1931 to 1945.

Richard Miffin Kleberg was born at Corpus Christi, Tex., on November 18, 1887.

[1] An interview with Captain Victor Hunt Harding, Secretary of the National Democratic Congress Reëlection Committee, Washington, D.C., April 10, 1939.

Kline, Robert George

Robert George Kline, who was born at Enterprise, Ohio, on December 1, 1910, and who pitched in major-league baseball, was popularly called *King Kong*.[1]

[1] *Who's Who in Major League Base Ball,* comp. by Harold (Speed) Johnson (Buxton Publishing Company, Chicago, 1933) p. 246.

Knickerbocker, Herman

The *Prince of Knickerbocker*[1] and the *Prince of Schaghticoke*[2] were applied to Herman Knickerbocker because he lived at Schaghticoke, N.Y., and was liberal with his hospitality.

Herman Knickerbocker was born at Albany, N.Y., on July 27, 1782, and died at Williamsburg, N.Y., on January 30, 1855.

[1] *The Encyclopedia Americana* (Americana Corporation, Chicago and New York, 1927) vol. 16, p. 479.

The National Cyclopaedia of American Biography (James T. White and Company, New York, 1893) vol. 3, p. 466.

Knickerbocker Group

The group of literary men living in or near New York City which became the center of literary activity in America about the second decade of the nineteenth century, were called the *Knickerbocker Group* or the *Knickerbocker School* of writers. The name was suggested by Washington Irving's *Knickerbocker's History of New York*, published in 1809.

[1] *American Literature,* John Calvin Metcalf (B. F. Johnson Publishing Company, Richmond, Va., 1921) p. 106.

Knickerbockers. See New Yorkers

Knight of the Golden Spurs. See Stuart, J. E. B.

Knight of the Most Honorable Order of Starvation. See Livingston, William

Knight of the Red Rose. See Taylor, A. A.

Knight of the White Rose. See Taylor, R. L.

Knights. See Wartburg College

Knitting Hattie. See Caraway, H. W.

Knothe, Wilfred Edgar
While he was a mere lad, Wilfred Edgar Knothe was nicknamed *Fritz* [1] by a younger brother.

Wilfred Edgar Knothe was born at Passaic, N.J., on May 1, 1905, and played infield in major-league baseball.

[1] *Who's Who in Major League Base Ball*, comp. by Harold (Speed) Johnson (Buxton Publishing Company, Chicago, 1933) p. 248.

Know-nothing Party
The *Know-nothing Party* [1] was a term applied to the Native American party, a political association organized by Edward Z. C. Judson in New York in 1853, which existed until about 1860. The party members were called *Know-nothings.* These nicknames arose because the meetings the party were secretly conducted, and the common answer to any question about the organization or its policies to people who were not members was, "I don't know."

[1] *The National Cyclopaedia of American Biography* (James T. White and Company, New York, 1906) vol. 13, p. 194.
The New International Encyclopaedia, Second Edition (Dodd, Mead and Company, New York 1930) vol. 13, p. 310.

Know Ye Party
During the trying period of organizing the thirteen colonies into a nation after the American Revolution, one of the chief political issues was that of currency, the establishing and issuing of which rested then within the jurisdiction of each state. The American Party, nicknamed the *Know Ye Party*,[1] advocated the issuing of paper-money, which their opponents denounced on the grounds that a large amount of money would be without guarantee and would be useless. In Rhode Island the American Party decreed that creditors accept paper money in payment of their debtors. If the creditor demurred, the debtor could free himself from debt by leaving the money at court and printing an announcement of it in the newspapers. Because these advertisements as a rule began with the words *Know Ye*, the American Party was called the *Know Ye Party*.

[1] *The Development of American Nationality,* Carl Russell Fish (American Book Cmpany, New York and Boston, 1913) p. 28.

Knox, Philander Chase
While Philander Chase Knox was Attorney General in President William McKinley's Cabinet from 1901 to 1904, the editors of American newspapers and others who wanted him to prosecute the trusts nicknamed him *Sleepy Phil* [1] because he did not comply with their wishes.

Philander Chase Knox was born at Brownsville, Pa., on May 6, 1853, and died at Washington, D.C., on October 12, 1921.

[1] *Twenty Years of the Republic, 1885-1905,* Harry Thurston Peck (Dodd, Mead and Company, New York, 1907) p. 686.

Knox College
The teams of Knox College, at Galesburg, Ill., were called the *Siwashes* [1] because George Fitch who graduated from Knox College in 1897 wrote books and stories about Siwash College.

[1] A communication from E. R. Jackson, Director of Athletics at Knox College, Galesburg, Ill., June 15, 1935.

Knoxville, Tennessee
Knoxville is called the *Queen City of the Mountains* and the *Metropolis of East Tennessee*. It is referred to as the *Queen City of the Mountains* [1] because it is situated among the forest covered foothills of the Chilhowie and Clinch Mountains, on the Tennessee River, and in the valley between the Great Smoky and the Cumberland Ranges of the Appalachian Mountains.

This city is commonly called the *Metropolis of East Tennessee* [2] because of its size, its natural resources, manufacturing, commericial activities, and educational opportunities.

[1] *More About Names*, Leopold Wagner (T. Fisher Unwin, London, 1893) p. 247.
The Standard Blue Book of Tennessee, 1911-1912, An exclusive edition de luxe, A. J. Peeler (A. J. Peeler and Company, Nashville, Tenn., 1911-12) p. 34.
[2] *The Standard Blue Book of Tennessee, 1911-1912,* An Exclusive Edition de Luxe, A. J. Peeler (A. J. Peeler and Company, Nashville, Tenn., 1911-12) p. 34.

Knutson, Harold

Harold Knutson, a Minnesota journalist and politician, was nicknamed *Anti-war Knutson* [1] in the House of Representatives because he was the only surviving member of that legislative body who voted against the United States entering World War I in 1917. He was a Republican Representative from Minnesota to Congress from 1917 to 1949.

Harold Knutson was born at Skien, Norway, on October 20, 1880, and came to the United States with his parents in 1886.

[1] An interview with Captain Victor Hunt Harding, Secretary of the National Democratic Congress Reëlection Committee, Washington, D.C., April 10, 1939.

Kodak City. See Rochester, N.Y.

Kohawks. See Coe College

Kolb, Reuben Francis

Genial Reuben, Our Patrick Henry, and *Run Forever Kolb* are the nicknames given to Reuben Francis Kolb.

He was popularly called *Genial Reuben* [1] because of his cheerful, kindly personality. Because he was an enthusiastic leader and spokesman for the agricultural movement in Alabama, they called him *Our Patrick Henry.* [2]

Having been four times an unsuccessful candidate for the office of Governor of Alabama, his political opponents dubbed him *Run Forever Kolb,* [2] a nickname suggested by his initials.

He was born at Eufaula, Ala., on April 15, 1839, and died at Montgomery, Ala., on March 23, 1918.

[1] *History of Alabama and Her People,* Albert Burton Moore, Author and Editor (The American Historical Society, Inc., New York and Chicago, 1927) vol. 1, p. 699.

[2] *Dictionary of American Biography under the Auspices of the American Council of Learned Societies,* ed. by Dumas Malone (Charles Scribner's Sons, New York, 1933) vol. 10, p. 492.

Kroeger, Henry

Henry Kroeger, who was born in Westphalia, Prussia, on August 25, 1819, was known as *Ice-bear Kroeger* [1] because he was the first person to conduct an ice business in Milwaukee, Wis. He began his business in 1844.

[1] *History of Milwaukee, Wisconsin,* John G. Gregory (The S. J. Clarke Publishing Company, Chicago and Milwaukee, Wis., 1931) vol. 1, p. 444.

Krohn, John Albert

John Albert Krohn, an American transcontinental walker, was nicknamed *Colonel Jack* [1] when he was walking and pushing a wheelbarrow around the United States. Krohn started on this trip from Portland, Me., on June 1, 1908, and returned to Portland on July 20, 1910, having traveled over a distance of nine thousand and twenty-four miles in three hundred and fifty-seven days of actual walking, for he took many rest periods at various places along the way.

John Albert Krohn was born at Saint Peter, Minn., and was living at Newburyport, Mass., at the time he made his trip around the United States.

[1] *The Washington Post,* Washington, D.C., January 23, 1910, Sports Section, col. 2, p. 1.

The Walk of Colonel Jack: A Story of a Long-distance Walker, John Albert Krohn (Printed by the Newburyport Herald Company, Newburyport, Mass., 1910) p. 5.

L

La Belle Americaine. See Monroe, Mrs. James

Labor Mayor. See Dore, J. F.

Labor's Magna Charta

The Clayton Act, passed by Congress on October 15, 1914, has been termed *Labor's Magna Charta* [1] because the act was intended to check monopolistic tendencies of corporations and the practice of contracting purchasers so that they would refrain from buying from competitive organizations. The Clayton Act, however, contained a clause exempting "fraternal, labor, or agricultural organizations" from the provisions of the act. The name was also applied to the National Labor Relations act passed by Congress in 1935. This act gave labor the right to organize and bargain collectively by means of representatives of its own selection.

[1] *The Quest for Social Justice, 1898-1914,* Harold Underwood Faulkner (The Macmillan Company, New York, 1931) p. 64.

Ladd, William

William Ladd, an ardent advocate of the peace movement in America in 1812, was called the *Apostle of Peace.* [1] He was president of the American Peace Society from

1828 until his death and wrote articles and delivered numerous addresses in its behalf.

William Ladd was born at Exeter, N.H., on May 10, 1778, and died at Portsmouth, N.H., on April 9, 1841.

[1] *Sprague's Journal of Maine History, April, May, June,* 1922 (John Francis Sprague, Dover, Me., 1922) vol. 11, no. 2, p. 53.

Lady Davis

During the Civil War the name *Lady Davis* [1] was given to one of the cannons located at Belmont, Mo., belonging to the Confederate forces encamped there. The cannon was named *Lady Davis* in honor of Mrs. Jefferson Davis, the wife of the President of the Southern Confederacy.

[1] *The Rise of U. S. Grant,* A. L. Conger (The Century Company, New York, 1931) p. 93.

Lady of the Iron Watch Dog. See Ingalls, M. B.

Lady of the Lakes. See Michigan

Lafayette, Marie Jean Paul Roch Yves Gilbert Du Motier

The *French Game-cock* [1] was a nickname applied to Marie Jean Paul Roch Yves Gilbert Du Motier Lafayette during the Revolutionary War with England.

[1] *The Pictorial Field-Book of the Revolution: or Illustrations, by Pen and Pencil, of the History, Biography, Scenery, Relics, and Traditions of the War for Independence,* Benson J. Lossing (Harper and Brothers New York, 1852) vol. 2, p. 466.

Lafayette, Indiana

Lafayette's location on the Wabash River at the farthest point of navigation made this city important. Very early in its existence it came to be nicknamed the *Star City.* [1]

[1] *Indiana, One Hundred and Fifty Years of American Development,* Charles Roll (The Lewis Publishing Company, New York and Chicago, 1931) vol. 1, p. 466.

Past and Present of Tippecanoe County, Indiana, General R. P. DeHart, Editor-in-chief (B. F. Bowe and Company, Indianapolis, Ind., 1909) vol. 1, p. 415.

Lafayette College

The members of the athletic teams of Lafayette College, in Easton, Pa., were nicknamed the *Lafayette Leopards,* [1] about 1929 or 1930 by sports writers, probably because of the alliterative effect [1] produced by combining the names Lafayette and leopards.

[1] A letter from D. L. Reeves, Graduate Manager of Athletics at Lafayette College, Easton, Pa., December 3, 1935.

Lafayette Leopards. See Lafayette College

Lafayette of the Greek Revolution. See Howe, S. G.

La Follette, Robert Marion, Senior

Robert Marion LaFollette, Senior, was nicknamed *Battling Bob* [1] because he fought for the progressive political policies which he advocated, when he was a Representative from Wisconsin, Governor of Wisconsin, and Senator from Wisconsin to the United States Congress.

He was a Republican Representative from Wisconsin to Congress from 1885 to 1891, Governor of Wisconsin from 1901 to 1906, and Senator from Wisconsin from 1906 until his death in 1925.

Robert Marion LaFollette, Senior, was born at Primrose, Wis., on June 14, 1855, and died at Washington, D.C., on June 18, 1925.

[1] *The World Book Encyclopedia* (The W. F. Quarrie and Company, Chicago, vol. 10, p. 3839.

La Guardia, Fiorello H.

Fiorello H. La Guardia, during his three consecutive terms as Mayor of New York City, became especially well-known as *Butch* [1] and the *Little Flower.* [2]

The first nickname characterized his vigorous and aggressive approach to the responsibilities of his office. The latter sobriquet, a translation of his Italian given name, was an apt reference to its owner's small stature, but was often applied humorously in contrast to his fiery personality.

During World War I La Guardia became commander of the United States air forces on the Italian-Austrian front, and subsequently he served ten years as Representative from New York to Congress. He was elected Mayor of New York City in 1933 and reelected for two more terms, administering the affairs of the city during World War II. He retired from office at the end of 1945 and became Director General of the United Nations Relief and Rehabilitation Administration.

La Guardia, F. H.—Continued

Fiorello H. La Guardia was born at New York City on December 11, 1882, and died there on September 20, 1947.

[1] *Survey Graphic,* October, 1947. p. 519.

[2] *Life,* Rockefeller Center, N.Y., March 27, 1939. col. 2, p. 16.

Washington Herald, Washington, D.C., November 8, 1937, col. 7, p. 6.

Laird of Skibo. See Carnegie, Andrew

Laird of Skibo Castle. See Carnegie, Andrew

Laird of Woodchuck Lodge. See Burroughs, John

Lajoie, Napoleon

Napoleon LaJoie, a major-league baseball player, who was born at Woonsocket, R.I., on September 5, 1875, was nicknamed *Larry,*[1] a corruption of his family name. *Larry* Lajoie's plaque in the Baseball Hall of Fame pays tribute to him as "the most graceful and efficient second baseman of his era."

[1] *Who's Who in Major League Base Ball,* comp. by Harold (Speed) Johnson (Buxton Publishing Company, Chicago, 1933) p. 485.

Lake Forest College

The athletic teams of Lake Forest College, at Lake Forest, Ill., were called the *Foresters* and the *Gold Coasters.*[1]

[1] A letter from P. C. Allen, Director of Athletics at Lake Forest College, Lake Forest, Ill., July 26, 1935.

Lake State. See Michigan; Minnesota

Lamb, William

The *Hero of Fort Fisher*[1] is the nickname given Lieutenant Colonel William Lamb because of the way in which he inspired his men to defend the Confederate stronghold of Fort Fisher, N.C., on December 25, 1864.

William Lamb was born at Norfolk, Va., on September 7, 1835, and died there on March 23, 1909.

[1] *The National Cyclopaedia of American Biography* (James T. White and Company, New York, 1898) vol. 1, p. 274.

Lambuth College

The athletic teams of Lambuth College, at Jackson, Tenn., were designated *The Eagles*[1] in 1924 in honor of the present Director of Athletics, M. E. Eagle.

[1] A communication from M. E. Eagle, Dean of Lambuth College, Jackson, Tenn., June 13, 1935.

Lame-duck Congress

The session of Congress which came to a close on the fourth of March in the year following the election of a new President of the United States was nicknamed the *Lame-duck Congress*[1] because many of those making up this session of Congress had been defeated in the November elections and would be replaced by the successful candidates on March 4th. The session of Congress which convened in 1922 was the first to be called a *Lame-duck Congress* and members of this Congress were known as *Lame-ducks.*[1]

The *Lame-duck Congress* was abolished by the Twentieth Amendment to the Constitution in 1933 which provides that Congress shall meet on the third of January and that the President and vice President shall be inaugurated on the twentieth of January following the November election.[2]

[1] *Standard History of America,* Thomas Bonaventure Lawler (Ginn and Company, New York, Boston and San Francisco, 1933) p. 613-14.

Recent History of the United States, 1865-1929, Revised and Enlarged Edition, Frederic L. Paxson (Houghton Mifflin Company, New York, Boston, and San Francisco, 1929) p. 641-2.

[2] *The American Scene.* Edwin C. Hill (Witmark Educational Publications, Department of M. Witmark and Sons, New York, 1933) p. 40.

Lame-ducks. See *Lame-duck Congress*

Lamour, Dorothy

Dorothy Lamour, a motion picture actress and singer, has the following nicknames: the *Sarong Girl,* the *Mary Pickford of this War* (World War II), *Uncle Sam's Favorite Niece,* the *Sweetheart of the Foxholes,* the *Paratrooper Pet,* and *Number One Pin-up Girl.* She was born on December 10, 1914, and first came into prominence as a jungle girl clad in sarong.

[1] *Current Biography,* The H. W. Wilson Company, New York, May, 1946, p. 33.

Land Admiral. See Reeside, James

Land-grabbers

Those men in legislative bodies who make large grants of public lands "to companies chartered to build railways, lay deepsea telegraph lines, or to engage in other great works of national importance," have been termed *Land-grabbers*[1] because often these large tracts of public lands were transferred to such companies without the states or other agencies holding them wanting to dispose of them, the lands merely having been evaluated in many instances and paid for often when those owning or controlling them preferred not to dispose of them.

[1] *Americanisms; The English of the New World*, M. Schele De Vere (Charles Scribner and Company, New York, 1872) p. 261.

Land Hero of 1812. See Jackson, Andrew

Land of Flowers. See Florida

Land of Gold. See California

Land of Hard-cases. See Oregon

Land of Heart's Desire. See New Mexico

Land of Opportunity. See New Mexico

Land of Plenty. See South Dakota

Land of Steady Habits. See Connecticut

Land of Sunshine. See New Mexico

Land of the Cactus. See New Mexico

Land of the Dakotas. See North Dakota

Land of the Delight Makers. See New Mexico

Land of the Mormons. See Utah

Land of the Red People. See Oklahoma

Land of the Rolling Prairie. See Iowa

Land of the Saints. See Utah

Land of the Sky. See North Carolina

Landis, Kenesaw Mountain

Kenesaw Mountain Landis was nicknamed the *Czar of American Baseball* and the *Czar of the National Pastime* [1] because he was Commissioner of the American and the National Leagues of Professional Base Ball Clubs and also of the National Association of Professional Base Ball Leagues from November 12, 1920 until his death. Former Senator Albert B. (*Happy*) Chandler succeeded him as Commissioner of Organized Baseball.

Kenesaw Mountain Landis was born at Melville, Ohio, on November 25, 1866, and died on November 25, 1944.

[1] *Who's Who in The American League, 1935 Edition*, Harold (Speed) Johnson (B. E. Callahan, Chicago, 1935) p. 2.

Landon, Alfred Mossman

Former Governor Alfred Mossman Landon was called the *Coolidge of the West* [1] and the *Kansas Coolidge* by newspaper and magazine writers because his administration as Governor of Kansas had been an economical one, comparable to the administration of Calvin Coolidge as President of the United States.

Alfred Mossman Landon was born at West Middlesex, Pa., on September 9, 1887, and was Governor of Kansas from 1933 to 1936, and Republican nominee for President of the United States in 1936.

[1] *Washington Herald* (Washington, D.C.), October 28, 1935, p. 1.

Time: The Weekly Magazine (Published by Time Inc., New York and Chicago) May 18, 1936, p. 18.

Lane, James Henry

Fighting Jim [1] and the *Grim Chieftain* [2] were nicknames applied to James Henry Lane because he was of a militant and aggressive nature, a fierce champion of the anti-slavery cause.

He served in the Mexican War and as a Brigadier General in the Federal Army during the Civil War.

James Henry Lane was born at Lawrenceburg, Ind., on June 22, 1814, and died at Leavenworth, Kan., on July 11, 1866.

[1] *John Brown, the Making of a Martyr*, Robert Penn Warren (Payson and Clarke, Ltd., New York, 1929) p. 214.

[2] *Kansas Historical Collections: Transactions of the Kansas State Historical Society, 1903-1904; together with Address at Annual Meetings, Miscellaneous Papers, and a Roster of Kansas for Fifty Years*, ed. by George W. Martin (George A. Clark, State Printer, Topeka, Kans., 1904) vol. 8, p. 201.

Lane, Joseph

During the Mexican War Brigadier General Joseph Lane came to be called the *Marion of the Mexican Army*,[1] in allusion to the boldness and speed with which he maneuvered his troops.

Lane, Joseph—Continued

Joseph Lane was born in Buncombe County, N.C., on December 14, 1801, and died in Oregon, on April 19, 1881.

[1] *The National Cyclopaedia of American Biography* (James T. White and Company, New York, 1924) vol. 8, p. 2.

Lane College

The athletic teams of Lane College, at Jackson, Tenn., were nicknamed the *Dragons* and the *Dragonettes.* The upper classmen were designated the *Dragons* [1] and the freshman teams were called the *Dragonettes.*

[1] A communication from J. F. Lane, President of Lane College, Jackson, Tenn., November 18, 1935.

Lane's Chimneys

James Henry Lane, an American politician and soldier, who took an active part in the antislavery affairs of Kansas, in 1856 marked the route of the underground railway from Topeka, Kans., to Nebraska City, Neb., by monuments of stones more or less regularly heaped together somewhat in the form of a chimney. These markers were popularly called *Lane's Chimneys.* [1]

[1] *History of Kansas, State and People, Kansas at the First Quarter Post of the Twentieth Century,* written and comp. by William E. Connelley (The American Historical Society, Inc., New York and Chicago, 1928) vol. 1, p. 33.

Langkop, Mrs. Wilbur E. (Uldine Utley)

Mrs. Wilbur E. Langkop (Uldine Utley), a Methodist Episcopal minister, was nicknamed the *Joan of Arc of the Modern Religious World* [1] by Dr. John Roach Straton of New York City in 1926 because she conducted a successful mass-revival meeting at Madison Square Garden at the age of fourteen. Joan of Arc began her heroic career at about the same age.

Uldine Utley was born at Durant, Okla., on March 16, 1912, and was married to Wilbur E. Langkop at New York City on January 9, 1938.

[1] *Newsweek: The Magazine of News Significance,* Rockefeller Center, N.Y., January 10, 1938, p. 26.

Langstroth, Lorenzo Lorraine

Lorenzo Lorraine Langstroth, an apiarist, educator, and clergyman, was nicknamed the *Father of American Apiculture* [1] because he was an authority on beekeeping, invented the movable-frame beehive which revolutionized both beehives and the methods of beeculture, and was a pioneer in many of the methods of managing bees which later came into general use.

Lorenzo Lorraine Langstroth was born at Philadelphia, Pa., on December 25, 1810, and died at Dayton, Ohio, on October 6, 1895.

[1] *The Washington Star,* Washington, D.C., December 26, 1938, col. 3, p. B—14.

Lanier, Sidney

Sidney Lanier, one of the great Southern poets, has been called the *Sunrise Poet* [1] because he recorded such a vivid impression of the sunrise in his poem of that name in his *Hymns of the Marshes.*

Sidney Lanier was born at Macon, Ga., on February 3, 1842, and died at Lynn, N.C., on September 7, 1881.

[1] *The World Book Encyclopedia* (The Quarrie Corporation, Chicago, 1938) vol. 10, p. 3871.

Lanman, Charles

Washington Irving designated Charles Lanman the *Picturesque Explorer of the United States* [1] because Lanman, visiting the various parts of the United States, reproduced through his paintings and writings much of the picturesque scenery which he observed on his journeys.

Charles Lanman was born at Monroe, Mich., on January 14, 1819, and died at Washington, D.C., on March 4, 1895.

[1] *The National Cyclopaedia of American Biography* (James T. White and Company, New York, 1893) vol. 3, p. 444.

Laredo, Texas

Laredo, the county seat of Webb County, is popularly called the *Gate City* [1] because it is so located that it is a natural gateway from western Texas into Mexico.

[1] *The Geography of Texas, Physical and Political,* Revised Edition, Frederic William Simonds (Ginn and Company, New York and Boston, 1914) p. 194.

Larruping Lou. See Gehrig, H. L.

Larry. See Lajoie, Napoleon

Last Capital of the Confederacy. See Danville, Va.

Last Cocked Hat. See Monroe, James

Last Ditch

During the siege of Knoxville, Tenn., an attack was made on Fort Sanders, near Knoxville, on November 29, 1863. Around the major part of this fort ran a trench several feet deep, dug to make the scaling of the walls of the fort more difficult. This trench was called the *Last Ditch* [1] by the Union defenders of the fort, because it was in fact the last ditch that many of the Confederates ever saw; most of them were killed or wounded in an attempt to cross it.

[1] *The Seventy-ninth Highlanders; New York Volunteers in the War of Rebellion, 1861-1865,* William Todd Press of Brandow, Barton and Company, Albany, N.Y., 1886) p. 391.

Last of the Cocked Hats. See Mease, John

Last of the Great Scouts. See Cody, W. F.

Laughing-gas Man. See Short, Dewey

Laureate of Song. See Longfellow, H. W.

Laurens, John

The nickname *Bayard of the Revolution* [1] was given to John Laurens because of his gallant and daring nature. Pierre Terrail Chevalier De Bayard was a great French soldier of the sixteenth century, noted for his impetuous fighting.

John Laurens was born at Charleston, S.C., on October 28, 1754, and was killed in battle on the Combachee River, in South Carolina, on August 27, 1782.

[1] *The Encyclopaedia Britannica,* Fourteenth Edition (Encyclopaedia Britannica, Inc., New York, 1932) vol. 13, p. 770.

Law, George

Live Oak George [1] was a nickname applied to George Law by his employees, because in Law's shipyard a great deal of live oak lumber was used because he wanted to make his vessels as strong and lasting as possible.

George Law was born at Jackson, N.Y., on October 25, 1806, and died at New York City, on November 18, 1881.

[1] *A Sketch of Events in the Life of George Law, Published in Advance of His Biography* (J. C. Derby, New York, 1855) p. 14.

Appleton's Cyclopedia of American Biography, ed. by James Grant Wilson and John Fiske (D. Appleton and Company, New York, 1888) vol. 3, p. 636.

Law, Sallie Chapman

Mrs. Sallie Chapman Law, nee Sallie Chapman Gordon, who was born in Wilkes County, N.C., on August 27, 1805,

and who died at Memphis, Tenn., on June 28, 1894, was called the *Mother of the Confederacy* [1] because of her "will to do and dare for the Southern soldiers, as well as to ameliorate the sufferings of such Federals as came under her charge."

[1] *A History of Tennessee and Tennesseeans: The Leaders and Representative Men in Commerce, Industry and Modern Activities,* Will T. Hale and Dixon L. Merritt (The Lewis Publishing Company, Chicago and New York, 1913) vol. 3, p. 660-1.

Lawrence College

The nickname *Vikings* [1] was given to the athletes of Lawrence College, at Appleton, Wis., by a vote of the student body.

[1] A communication from A. C. Denny, Director of Athletics at Lawrence College, Appleton, Wis., July 1, 1935.

Lawson, John Daniel

Sitting Bull [1] was the nickname commonly applied to John Daniel Lawson. He was an active member of the Republican party, and served as a delegate from New York State to every Republican National Convention from 1868 to 1892. He was a Representative from New York to Congress from 1873 to 1875.

John Daniel Lawson was born at Montgomery, N.Y., February 18, 1816, and died at New York City, January 24, 1896.

[1] *The Autobiography of Thomas Collier Platt,* comp. and ed. by Louis J. Lang (B. W. Dodge and Company, New York, 1910) p. 103.

Biographical Directory of the American Congress, 1774 to 1927; The Continental Congress September 5, 1774, to October 21, 1788, and the Congress of the United States, from the First to the Sixty-ninth Congress, March 4, 1789, to March 3, 1927, Inclusive (Government Printing Office, Washington, D.C., 1928) House Document no. 783, p. 1210.

Lawyer. See Sorrell, V. G.

Lay Preacher to the Largest Congregation in the United States. See Bok, E. W.

Layden, Elmer. See Four Horsemen

Layers-out

The *Layers-out* [1] were those men who, during the Civil War, declared themselves neutrals and professed to be occupied with their usual vocations, but in reality availed themselves of every opportunity to attack individual or collected bodies of soldiers, either Federal or Confederate, and to harass their neighbors if they differed with them on the question of slavery and secession.

Layers-out—Continued

The term probably described them as "laying-out" for someone whom they could assail, or as "laying-out" of service in either army.

[1] *Life-struggles in Rebel Prisons; a Record of the Sufferings, Escapes, Adventures and Starvation of the Union Prisoners, Containing an Appendix with the Names, Regiments, and Date of Death of Pennsylvania Soldiers Who Died at Andersonville,* Joseph Ferguson (James M. Ferguson, Philadelphia, 1865) p. 189.

Lazzeri, Anthony Michael

The nickname *Push-'em-up Lazzeri* [1] has been applied to Anthony Michael Lazzeri, New York Yankees' famous second baseman from 1925 to 1937. Lazzeri could usually be relied on to advance his teammates around the bases because he was a good hitter, hence the nickname.

Anthony Michael Lazzeri was born at San Francisco, Calif., on December 6, 1903, and died August 6, 1946.

[1] *Who's Who in Major League Base Ball,* comp. by Harold (Speed) Johnson (Buxton Publishing Company, Chicago, 1933) p. 255.

Lea, Clarence Frederick

During his campaign for election to the House of Representatives Clarence Frederick Lea was nicknamed *Triple Threat* [1] because he was running for election on three tickets. He was a Representative from California to Congress from 1917 to 1949, when he retired to take up public relations work in Washington, D.C.

Clarence Frederick Lea was born near Highland Springs, Calif., on July 11, 1874.

[1] *The Washington Post Magazine,* Washington, D.C., March 4, 1934, p. 4.

Lea, Luke

While he was a young man, Luke Lea became known as *Young Thunderbolt* [1] because he was at that time inclined to be somewhat violent and threatening in manner when championing a political principle or policy. He was a Senator from Tennessee from 1911 to 1917.

Luke Lea was born at Nashville, Tenn., on April 12, 1879.

[1] *The Life of John Worth Kern,* Claude G. Bowers (The Hollenbeck Press, Indianapolis, Ind., 1918) p. 211.

Lead State. See Colorado; Missouri

Lean Jimmy Jones. See Jones, J. C.

Learned Blacksmith. See Burritt, Elihu

Learned Shoemaker. See Sherman, Roger

Leatherheads. See Pennsylvanians

Leathernecks

The members of the United States Marine Corps are called the *Leathernecks* because of the leather stock which was once a part of the uniform.

Leavenworth, Kansas

Leavenworth has frequently been termed the *Cottonwood City* [1] because the site of the city was a forest of cottonwood trees, which were sawed into lumber and used in constructing the new town.

[1] *Manual of Useful Information,* under the direction of J. C. Thomas (The Werner Company, Chicago, 1893) p. 22.

Early History of Leavenworth City and County...., H. Miles Moore (Samuel Dobsworth Book Company, Leavenworth, Kan., 1906) p. 34.

Fort Leavenworth and the Soldiers' Home with Sketches of Leavenworth and of the Men and Tragedies That Have Made Her Famous, Valuable to Visitors, of Whom There Are Thousands Annually, Matthew H. Jamison (Hudson-Kimberly Publishing Company, Kansas City, Kan., 1895) p. 27.

Leavitt, Dudley

Dudley Leavitt, an almanac-maker, was known in New Hampshire as *Old Master Leavitt* [1] because for some time he had taught school during the winter months and in the lengthy evenings had written arithmetic and grammar texts and compiled almanacs.

Dudley Leavitt was born at Exeter, N.H., on May 23, 1772, and died at Meredith, N.H., on September 15, 1851.

[1] *Appleton's Cyclopaedia of American Biography,* ed. by James Grant Wilson and John Fiske (D. Appleton and Company, New York, 1888) vol. 3, p. 649.

Lebanon Valley College

The *Flying Dutchmen* [1] is the nickname of the athletic teams of Lebanon Valley College, at Annville, Pa. It was selected by the student body. The reason for the selection can be traced to the fact that Lebanon Valley College is in the heart of the Pennsylvania Dutch section. This, coupled with the traditional prowess of the historic sailing vessel, "The Flying Dutchman," made this nickname an appropriate selection.

[1] A communication from L. P. Clements, Director of Publicity at Lebanon Valley College, Annville, Pa., November 18, 1935.

Lee, Ann

Ann Lee, a religious teacher, who was born at Manchester, England, on February 29, 1736, and who died at Watervliet, N.Y., on September 8, 1784, was sometimes called *Ann the Word*, but more commonly *Mother Lee*. She called herself *Ann the Word*,[1] because she said she had been endowed with such immeasurable and eternal wisdom that she was the "second appearing of Christ," whose religious works and teachings she would parallel in her own life. She was called *Mother Lee*[1] because she founded the Church of Christ's Second Appearing at Watervliet early in 1776.

[1] *Appleton's Cyclopaedia of American Biography*, ed. by James Grant Wilson and John Fiske (D. Appleton and Company, New York, 1894) vol. 3, p. 656.

Lee, Charles

Boiling Water and the *Hero of Charleston* were sobriquets attributed to Charles Lee.

In 1762 the Mohawk Indians nicknamed him *Boiling Water*[1] while he was living with them, because of his fiery traits of character. His vigor and force so pleased the Mohawk Indians that they adopted him and made him a chief of their tribe.

Because he successfully defended Charleston, S.C., when it was threatened with destruction by British land and sea forces, on June 28, 1776, he was popularly known as the *Hero of Charleston*.[2]

Charles Lee was born at Dernhall, Cheshire, England, in 1731, and died at Philadelphia, Pa., on October 2, 1782.

[1] *The American Portrait Gallery: Containing Correct Portraits and Brief Notices of the Principal Actors in American History; Embracing Distinguished Women, Naval and Military Heroes, Statesmen, Civilians, Jurists, Divines, Authors, and Artists; together with Celebrated Indian Chiefs, from Christopher Columbus down to the Present Time*, A. D. Jones (J. M. Emerson and Company, New York, 1855) p. 367.

Lives of Celebrated Americans: Comprising Biographies of Three Hundred and Forty Eminent Persons, Benjamin J. Lossing (Thomas Belknap, Hartford, Conn., 1869) p. 307.

[2] *The Encyclopedia Americana* (Americana Corporation, New York and Chicago, 1929) vol. 17, p. 217.

Lee, Edward D.

Edward D. Lee received the nickname the *Ain't Gonna Rain No Mo Man*[1] from the children at Oswego, N.Y., and at Davenport, Iowa, because he is said to have been fortunate enough to have given these boys and girls delightful picnics annually for about fifty years without having any of these occasions spoiled by rain.

He was born at Oswego, N.Y., on May 2, 1844, and died at Davenport, Iowa, on September 1, 1927.

[1] *Encyclopedia of American Biography: American Biography, a New Cyclopedia*, comp. under the editorial supervision of a notable advisory board (Published under the direction of The American Historical Society, Inc., New York, 1929) vol. 44, p. 140.

Lee, Fitzhugh

While he was attending the United States Military Academy at West Point, N.Y., from 1851 to 1856, Fitzhugh Lee was nicknamed *Flea*[1] by his classmates because he customarily signed his name *F. Lee*.

Fitzhugh Lee was born at Clermont, Va., on November 19, 1835, and died at Washington, D.C., on April 28, 1905.

[1] *Lee and His Lieutenants; Comprising the Early Life, Public Services, and Campaigns of General Robert E. Lee and His Companions in Arms, with a Record of Their Campaigns and Heroic Deeds*, Edward A. Pollard (E. B. Treat and Company, New York, 1867) p. 558.

Lee, Hal Burnham

Sheriff[1] is the nickname given to Hal Burnham Lee, who was born at Ludlow, Miss., on February 15, 1907, and who played outfield in major league baseball.

[1] *Who's Who in Major League Base Ball*, comp. by Harold (Speed) Johnson (Buxton Publishing Company, Chicago, 1933) p. 257.

Lee, Henry

Light-horse Harry and the *Sage of Ashland* were the nicknames of Henry Lee.

Because he was the leader of light cavalry troops which harassed the British during the Revolutionary War, Major General Henry Lee was known as *Light-horse Harry*.[1]

He has been called the *Sage of Ashland*[2] because he was a man of wisdom. He lived on his farm at Ashland, Ky., about a mile and a half northeast of Lexington, Ky.

Henry Lee was born at Leesylvania, Va., on January 27, 1756, and died on Cumberland Island, Ga., on March 25, 1818.

[1] *Light-horse Harry Lee*, Thomas Alexander Boyd (Charles Scribner's Sons, New York, 1931) p. 40, 66-86.

[2] *A Book of Nicknames*, John Goff (Courier-Journal Job Printing Company, Louisville, Ky., 1892) p. 23.

Henry Clay, by his grandson Thomas Hart Clay, completed by Ellis Paxson Oberholtzer (George W. Jacobs and Company, Philadelphia, 1910) p. 28.

Lee, Jesse

In New England, the Reverend Jesse Lee was known as the *Apostle of Methodism*[1] because he was one of the earliest and most outstanding adherents of that faith in that section. He organized the first Methodist congregation, at Stratford, Conn., on Sep-

Lee, Jesse—Continued

tember 26, 1787. Lee's publications regarding the history of Methodism in America have been used as the foundation for a great deal of the history of early Methodism.

He was born in Prince George County, Va., on March 12, 1758, and died at Hillsboro, Md., on September 12, 1816.

[1] *The National Cyclopaedia of American Biography* (James T. White and Company, New York, 1906) vol. 13, p. 187.

Lee, Joshua Bryan

Senator Joshua Bryan Lee has been called the *Boy Orator,* the *Boy Wonder, One Speech Lee,* the *Second William Jennings Bryan,* and *Silver-tongued Josh.* He was called the *Boy Orator* and the *Boy Wonder* [1] because he developed the ability to speak fluently and effectively early in life, the *Second William Jennings Bryan* [1] because like Bryan, he is a fluent and polished orator. He has been called *One Speech Lee* [1] because he has given his favorite antiwar speech several hundred times. The Oklahomans nicknamed him *Silver-tongued Josh* [2] because he is recognized as one of the most polished and effective orators in America.

He was a Representative from Oklahoma to Congress from 1935 to 1937, and was a Senator from Oklahoma from 1937 to 1943. Joshua Bryan Lee was born at Childersburg, Ala., on January 23, 1892.

[1] An interview with Captain Victor Hunt Harding, Secretary of the National Democratic Congress Reëlection Committee, Washington, D.C., April 10, 1939.

[2] *Washington Herald,* Washington, D.C., August 21, 1934, cols. 2 and 3, p. 9.

Lee, Richard Henry

Richard Henry Lee has been designated the *American Cicero* [1] because of the eloquence and forcefulness of his oratory, and because of his graceful, pleasing manner of delivery.

Richard Henry Lee was born in Westmoreland County, Va., on January 20, 1732, and died at Chantilly, Va., on June 19, 1794.

[1] *American Literature,* John Calvin Metcalf (B. F. Johnson Publishing Company, Richmond, Va., 1925) p. 80.

Lee, Robert Edward

Old Ace of Spades, or *Old Spades Lee,* and *Uncle Robert* were nicknames applied to Robert Edward Lee.

Old Ace of Spades [1] and *Old Spades Lee* commemorated the fact that during the Civil War, Lieutenant General Lee deemed it important to dig trenches and throw up breastworks for the defense of his troops. Spades were an essential part of his men's equipment. It is said that these names were originated by Lieutenant General Jubal Anderson Early, one of Lee's most prominent officers in the Confederate Army.

Lee's soldiers and intimate friends affectionately called him *Uncle Robert.* [2]

Robert Edward Lee was born at Stratford, Va., on January 19, 1807, and died at Lexington, Va., on October 12, 1870.

[1] *The Heart of a Soldier As Revealed in the Intimate Letters of General George E. Pickett* (Seth Moyle, Inc., New York, 1908) p. 133.

[2] *Manual of Useful Information,* comp. under the direction of J. C. Thomas (The Werner Company, Chicago, 1893) p. 23.

Lee, William Henry Fitzhugh

The purpose of the appellation *Rooney,* [1] which was given to William Henry Fitzhugh Lee, was to differentiate him from his first cousin, Major General Fitzhugh Lee. The source of the nickname is unknown.

William Henry Fitzhugh Lee, a Confederate soldier, was born at Arlington, Va., on May 31, 1837, and died near Alexandria, Va., on October 15, 1891.

[1] *Dictionary of American Biography,* under the Auspices of the American Council of Learned Societies, ed. by Dumas Malone (Charles Scribner's Sons, New York, 1933) vol. 11, p. 134.

Memorial Addresses on the Life and Character of William H. F. Lee, a Representative from Virginia, delivered in the House of Representatives and in the Senate, Fifty-second Congress, First Session (Published by order of Congress at the Government Printing Office, Washington, D.C., 1892) p. 41, 52.

Lee's Old War-horse. See Longstreet, James

Lee's Ragamuffins

When the Confederate soldiers returned to their homes throughout the South after General Lee had surrendered to General Grant at Appomattox Court House on April 9, 1865, they were often called *Lee's Ragamuffins* [1] because most of them were in rags and were returning to ruins and poverty.

[1] *K.K.K. Sketches, Humorous and Didactic, Treating the More Important Events of the Ku-Klux-Klan Movement in the South with a Discussion of the Causes Which Gave Rise to It, and the Social and Political Issues Emanating from It,* James Melville Beard (Claxton, Remsen and Haffelfinger, Philadelphia, 1877) p. 14.

Leemans, Alphonse

Alphonse Leemans, who played half back in national league football, was nicknamed *Tuffy Leemans* [1] by his playmates while he was a small boy because, although he was much smaller than they, not one of them could beat him in a fight.

He was born at Superior, Wis., on August 24, 1913.

[1] A communication from Timothy J. Mara, Founder and President of The New York Football Giants, Inc., New York City, March 23, 1939.

Lefty. See O'Doul, F. J.; Shaute, J. B.

Lehigh University

The teams of Lehigh University, situated at Bethlehem, Pa., are called the *Engineers* [1] because the majority of the students are enrolled in the School of Engineering.

[1] A communication from Nelson A. Kellogg, Director of Athletics at Lehigh University, Bethlehem, Pa., November 22, 1935.

Lehman, George

George the Baker and *Round House George* were sobriquets applied to George Lehman, a Los Angeles resort proprietor.

He was called *George the Baker* [1] because at one time he had owned a baker's shop in Los Angeles, Calif.

In 1856 Lehman bought property in Los Angeles, on Main Street with a cyclindrical house patterned after a building on the coast of Africa. Lehman transformed the Round House into a beer garden known as the Garden of Paradise which he opened to the public in 1858. The nickname, *Round House George* [1] was given to George Lehman because the Garden of Paradise was such a popular resort, and because he had transformed the Round House into this famous garden.

[1] *Sixty Years in Southern California, 1853-1913, Containing the Reminiscences of Harris Newmark*, ed. by Maurice H. Newmark and Marco R. Newmark (The Knickerbocker Press, New York, 1916) p. 192-3.

Lemke, William

William Lemke, a North Dakota lawyer and politician, was nicknamed *Moratorium Bill* [1] while in the House of Representatives because he was the co-author of the Frazier-Lemke Moratorium Bill which became a Federal law on August 28, 1935, and which provided the suspension of mortgage payments on farm property. He was a Non-Partisan Representative from North Dakota to Congress from 1933 to 1949.

William Lemke was born at Albany, Minn., on August 13, 1878.

[1] An interview with Captain Victor Hunt Harding, Secretary of the National Democratic Congress Reëlection Committee, Washington, D.C., April 10, 1939.

Lemonade Lucy. See Hayes, L. W. W.

Lemons. See Solters, J. J.

Lena. See Blackburne, Russell; Stiles, R. M.

Leo the Lip. See Durocher, L. E.

Leo the Magnificent. See Durocher, L. E.

Leonidas of America. See Stark, John

Le Roy, William Edgar

Because of his poise, refined manners, and fastidious personal appearance, Rear Admiral Le Roy was called the *Chesterfield of the Navy*. [1] Philip Dormer Stanhope, Earl of Chesterfield, lived at London from 1694 to 1773, and was famous for his cultured manners and eminent social position.

William Edgar Le Roy was born at New York City, on March 24, 1818, and died there on December 10, 1888.

[1] *The National Cyclopaedia of American Biography* (James T. White and Company, New York, 1897) vol. 4, p. 413.

Letter-carriers' Friend. See Cox, S. S.

Lettuce Bowl. See Stadium of The Salinas Packers Football Club

Let-ups

During the political campaign of 1868 in West Virginia, the radical Republicans favored the continuance of legislation which discriminated against the ex-Confederates by withholding from them the right to vote. The liberal Republicans who favored a more generous treatment of the ex-Confederates were termed the *Let-ups*. [1]

[1] *The Life and Times of Henry Gassaway Davis, 1823-1916*, Charles M. Pepper (The Century Company, New York, 1920) p. 41.

Le Vert, Octavia Walton

The *Belle of the Union* [1] appears to have been particularly applied to Octavia Walton Le Vert in 1833 and 1834, when she toured the United States, and was the welcome and popular guest of some of the most exclusive and refined society of the country. This nickname was an allusion to her eminent position in society, her personal loveliness, and her charming and cultured manners.

Le Vert, O. W.—Continued

Octavia Walton Le Vert was born at Bellevue, near Augusta, Ga., in 1810, and died at Augusta, Ga., on March 13, 1877.

[1] *The National Cyclopaedia of American Biography* (James T. White and Company, New York, 1896) vol. 6, p. 440.

Lewis, Ada

The *First Tough Girl of the American Drama* [1] was the appellation given to Ada Lewis because she played so successfully the part of the tough girl almost from the beginning of her stage career.

Ada Lewis was born at New York City but moved to San Francisco, Calif. when she was a child and began her stage career there.

[1] *Washington Herald*, Washington, D.C., March 17, 1934. p. 32.

Lewis, David John

David John Lewis, a Maryland coal miner and politician, was nicknamed *Little Davey* and *Little Giant* [1] in the House of Representatives. He was a Democratic Representative from Maryland to Congress from 1911 to 1917, and from 1931 to 1939.

David John Lewis was born at Osceola, Pa., on May 1, 1869.

[1] An interview with Captain Hunt Harding, Secretary of the National Democratic Congress Reëlection Committee, Washington, D.C., April 10, 1939.

Lewis, Estelle Ann Blanche (Robinson)

Estelle Ann Blanche (Robinson) Lewis was sometimes called the *Female Petrarch* and the *Rival of Sappho.*

She was known as the *Female Petrarch* [1] because of the emotion, imagination, and the polished style which characterized her sonnets and other poems. Alphonse Marie Louis de Prat de Lamartine, the French poet and statesman originated the nickname.

Edgar Allan Poe, the American poet and short-story writer, nicknamed her the *Rival of Sappho.*[1] The Greek poetess, Sappho, was considered the greatest of the female poets of classic times.

Estelle Ann Blanche (Robinson) Lewis was born near Baltimore, Md., in April, 1824, and died at London, England, on November 24, 1880.

[1] *The Encyclopedia Americana* (The Americana Corporation, New York and Chicago, 1927) vol. 17, p. 334.
  The National Cyclopaedia of American Biography (James T. White and Company, New York, 1900) vol. 10, p. 449.

Lewis, George Edward

Duffy [1] is the nickname of George Edward Lewis, who was born at San Francisco, Calif., on April 18, 1888, and who was formerly an outfielder in major-league baseball.

[1] *Who's Who in Major League Base Ball,* comp. by Harold (Speed) Johnson (Buxton Publishing Company, Chicago, 1933) p. 468.

Lewis, Ida

Ida Lewis has been called the *Grace Darling of Amberica* [1] because of her bravery and her work as a life saver. Grace Darling, the English heroine, rescued five persons from a steamer wrecked near Longstone lighthouse, on Farne Island off the northeast coast of Northumberland, England, on September 7, 1838.

Acting as assistant to her father, Hosea Lewis, who was the keeper of Lenie Rock lighthouse, Ida Lewis, at the age of seventeen, saved the crew from drowning when a boat was wrecked by a storm near this lighthouse. She received several medals for her bravery, among them a gold medal given her by the United States Government.

Ida Lewis was born at Newport, R. I., on February 25, 1841, and died there.

[1] *Women in American History: The Part Taken by Women in American History,* Mrs. John A. Logan (The Perry-Nalle Publishing Company, Wilmington, Del., 1912) p. 291.

Lewis, James Hamilton

The *Beau Brummel of the Senate,* the *Fashion Plate,* and *Pink Whiskers,* have been applied to Senator James Hamilton Lewis.

He was called the *Beau Brummel of the Senate* [1] because he was not only well dressed but also had charming manners. George Byran Brummel, a famous English man of fashion, was known as *Beau Brummel.*

The Fashion Plate [1] was a nickname also applied to Senator Lewis because he was one of the best dressed men in the Senate. His political opponents called him *Pink Whiskers* because his beard was a lighter shade of red than his hair.

James Hamilton Lewis, who was born at Danville, Va., on May 18, 1866, was a Senator from Illinois from 1913 to 1919, and was reelected in 1930. He died April 9, 1939.

[1] *The Washington Post Magazine,* Washington, D.C., March 4, 1934, p. 4.

Lewis, Meriwether

Long Knife and the *Sublime Dandy* are nicknames by which Meriwether Lewis was known.

The Indians of the northwest called him *Long Knife* [1] because he wore a sword.

The *Sublime Dandy* [1] was applied to Captain Lewis because he was immaculate in his dress, fastidious in his personal habits, and possessed graceful and polished manners.

Meriwether Lewis was born near Charlottesville, Va., on August 18, 1774, and died near Nashville, Tenn., on October 8, 1809.

[1] *Idaho, the Place and Its People; a History of the Gem State from Pre-historic to Present Days*, Byron Defenbach (The American Historical Society, Inc., New York and Chicago, 1933) vol. 1, p. 69, 70.

Lexington, Kentucky

Lexington has been called the *Athens of the West,* the *Belle City of the Bluegrass Regions,* the *Bluegrass Capital,* and the *Capital of the Blue Grass Region.*

As early as 1824 Lexington was nicknamed the *Athens of the West* [1] because even then it was prominent as a center of learning and intellectual culture west of the Alleghany Mountains.

This city has been designated the *Belle City of the Bluegrass Regions* [2] because of its beauty. It is called the *Bluegrass Capital* [2] and the *Capital of the Blue Grass Region* [1] because it is the capital of the state of Kentucky which is known as the *Blue Grass State.*

[1] *History of Fayette County, Kentucky, with an Outline Sketch of the Blue Grass Region*, Robert Peter, ed. by William Henry Perrin (O. L. Baskin and Company, Chicago, 1882) p. 219, 270.

[2] *A Book of Nicknames*, John Goff (Courier-Journal Job Printing Company, Louisville, Ky., 1892) p. 15.

Lexington, Massachusetts

Lexington is designated the *Birthplace of American Liberty* [1] because the Minute Men fought the first battle of the Revolutionary War on the Lexington Commons on April 19, 1775. Major General Thomas Gates, who was Colonial Governor of Massachusetts, had secretly sent British soldiers to Lexington to destroy the provincial stores there and to capture Samuel Adams and John Hancock.

[1] *The Source Book* (Source Research Council, Inc., Chicago, 1936) vol. 4, p. 1626.
The New International Encyclopaedia, Second Edition (Dodd, Mead and Company, New York, 1930) vol. 9, p. 391.

Lexington, Virginia

The *Athens of Virginia* [1] has been applied to Lexington, Va., because it is the site of two prominent educational institutions, the Virginia Military Institute, and the Washington and Lee University.

[1] *A Book of Nicknames*, John Goff (Courier-Journal Job Printing Company. Louisville, Ky., (1892) p. 15.

Lexington of Texas. See Gonzales, Tex.

Lexington of the South

In 1771, North Carolinians in the vicinity of the Alamance River resented the actions of the Royal Governor. Because they refused to submit to Governor William Tryon's authority, the British soldiers fought the local militia in a battle later designated the *Lexington of the South.* [1] The first battle of the Revolutionary War was fought at Lexington, Mass., April 19, 1775. Although fought previous to the one in Massachusetts, the battle near the Alamance River later became known as the *Lexington of the South.*

[1] *History of the United States*, Charles A. Beard and Mary R. Beard (The Macmillan Company, New York, 1921) p. 92.

Liberator. See MacGahan, J. A.

Liberty Bell

In 1752, the Colonial Assembly had a bell weighing about 2080 pounds imported from England and hung in the steeple of the Old State House in Philadelphia, Pa. This bell was inscribed with the motto, "Proclaim liberty throughout the land, and to all the people thereof." [1] It was rung to give out the news of the signing of the Declaration of Independence in 1776, and has come to be known as the *Liberty Bell.* [1]

[1] *Annals of Philadelphia and Pennsylvania, in the Olden Time; Being a Collection of Memoirs, Anecdotes, and Incidents of the City and Its Inhabitants, and of the Earliest Settlements of the Inland Part of Pennsylvania, from the Days of the Founders, Intended to Preserve the Recollections of Olden Times, and to Exhibit Society in Its Changes of Manners and Customs, and the City and Country in Their Local Changes and Improvements, Embellished with Engravings*, by T. H. Mumford, Edition of 1856, John F. Watson (Whiting and Thomas, Philadelphia, 1856) vol. 1, p. 398-9.

Lieb, John William

John William Lieb was called an *Apostle of Light and Power* and the *Father of the Electric Light in Europe.*

He was known as an *Apostle of Light and Power* [1] because he contributed a number of valuable electrical inventions and improvements for using light, heat, and power for domestic and industrial consumption in the United States and in Europe.

On March 3, 1883, the electric switches were thrown at Milan, Italy, putting into operation the first central light and power plant in Europe. Lieb had served as the chief electrician. His later activities in Italy and in other foreign countries in promoting the use of electricity caused him to be nicknamed the *Father of the Electric Light in Europe.* [1]

John William Lieb was born at Newark, N.J., on February 12, 1860, and died at New Rochelle, N.Y., on November 1, 1929.

[1] *Encyclopedia of Amercan Biography: American Biography, a New Cyclopedia,* comp. under the editorial supervision of a notable advisory board (Published under the direction of The American Historical Society, Inc., New York, 1929) vol. 53, p. 120, 122.

Lieutenants. See Centre College of Kentucky

Light of the Western Churches. See Hooker, Thomas

Light-horse Harry. See Lee, Henry.; Watterson, Henry

Lightning. See Ellsworth, G. A.

Lightning Division. See Seventy-eighth Infantry Division of World War II

Lightning Pilot. See Bixby, H. E.

Lillie. See Bishop, M. F.

Lily Whites

During the closing years of the Reconstruction Period, certain Republicans in Alabama desired to eliminate this party's practice of campaigning on the issue of the Negroes' rights and of depending on the votes of the Negroes to make the Republican party the controlling political power in the state. These Republicans were commonly called *Lily Whites* [1] because of their efforts to make the Republican party in Alabama a white man's party.

[1] *Civil War and Reconstruction in Alabama,* Walter L. Fleming (The Columbia University Press, New York, 1905) p. 799.

Lincoln, Abraham

Abraham Lincoln has been nicknamed the *Ancient,* the *Buffoon, Caesar,* the *Emancipation President, Father Abraham,* the *Flatboat Man,* the *Great Emancipator,* the *Great Wrestler, Honest Abe Lincoln,* the *Illinois Baboon,* the *Jester,* the *Long 'Un,* the *Man of the People,* the *Martyr President, Massa Linkum,* the *Rail Splitter,* the *Sage of Springfield,* the *Sectional President,* the *Tycoon,* the *Tyrant,* and *Uncle Abe.*

His private secretaries often spoke of President Abraham Lincoln as the *Ancient,* [1] because they considered him to have the experience and wisdom of age. These men also called him the *Tycoon.* [1]

The *Buffoon* [2] and the *Jester* were applied to President Lincoln by those who were not in sympathy with him or his policies.

Because during the Civil War President Abraham Lincoln deemed it best to suspend the Habeas Corpus Act and to endorse some other measures which interfered with civil liberty, Clement Laird Vallandigham, a Democrat of Ohio, called Lincoln *Caesar.* [4]

He was often called *Father Abraham* [5] by the northern people, especially after the war song, *Three Hundred Thousand More,* [6] by James Sloan Gibbons was published on July 16, 1862, the opening line of the first stanza and the closing line of each of the four stanzas being "We are coming, Father Abra'am—three hundred thousand more!"

Because early in his life he was accustomed to making trips and working on flat boats on the Ohio River, he was nicknamed the *Flatboatman.* [7]

Abraham Lincoln has been called the *Emancipation President* and the *Great Emancipator* [8] because the slaves in America were freed and the system of slavery was abolished during his administration.

The *Great Wrestler* [8] was applied to him because while he was a youth he distinguished himself as a wrestler.

Lincoln's honesty and integrity caused him to be called *Honest Abe Lincoln*,[9] particularly during the first campaign for his election as President of the United States.

Because he was unusually tall, he was sometimes referred to as the *Long 'Un*.[10] This nickname appears to have been used especially when he appeared in the famous debates with Stephen Arnold Douglas when they were often spoken of as the *Long 'Un* and the *Little Giant*.

The *Man of the People* [11] was applied to Lincoln because he was born of humble parentage and was fair and unbiased in dealing with the common people.

President Lincoln, who was assassinated at Ford's Theatre, in Washington, D.C., on April 14, 1865, by John Wilkes Booth, has for that reason been called the *Martyr President*.[12]

After the Emancipation Proclamation had gone into effect, the Negroes of the South called President Lincoln *Massa Linkum* [5] and *Uncle Abe*.[5]

Abraham Lincoln came to be known as the *Rail Splitter* [13] because as a young man, he split rails to earn his living.

Because he lived at Springfield, Ill., for many years before he became President of the United States, and because of his staid wisdom and his deep insight he has been called the *Sage of Springfield*.[8]

The Southerners nicknamed Abraham Lincoln the *Sectional President* [5] because of the position he took on the abolition of slavery and the secession of states from the Federal Union.

The appellation *Tyrant* [2] was given to Lincoln by those people who were dissatisfied with his administration, and who contended that he was harsh and despotic in his conduct of the war.

Abraham Lincoln, the sixteenth President of the United States, was born near Hodgensville, Ky., on February 12, 1808, and died at Washington, D.C., on April 15, 1865.

[1] *The Life and Letters of John Hay*, William Roscoe Thayer (Houghton Mifflin Company, New York and Boston, 1915) vol. 1, p. 93, 101, 105.
[2] *Lincoln and Episodes of the Civil War*, William E. Doster (G. P. Putnam's Sons, New York and London, 1915) p. 15.
[3] *Twenty Years of the Republic, 1885-1905*, Harry Thurston Peck (Dodd, Mead and Company, New York, 1907) p. 112.
[4] *History of the United States*, Charles A. Beard and Mary R. Beard (The Macmillan Company, New York, 1921) p. 360.

[5] *U.S. "Snap Shots": An Independent, National, and Memorial Encyclopedia . . .*, Oliver McKee (A. M. Thayer and Company, Boston, 1892) p. 310.
[6] *Personal and Political Ballads*, arranged and ed. by Frank Moore (George P. Putnam, New York, 1864) p. 330, 335.
[7] *Americanisms: The English of the New World*, M. Schele De Vere (Charles Scribner and Company, New York, 1872) p. 250.
[8] *A Book of Nicknames*, John Goff (Courier-Journal Job Printing Company, Louisville, Ky., 1892) p. 22, 23.
[9] *A History of the People of the United States, from the Revolution to the Civil War*, John Bach McMaster (D. Appleton and Company, New York, 1913) vol. 8, p. 455.
[10] *The Man on a Hill Top*, Sarah J. Day (Ware Brothers Publishing Company, Philadelphia, 1931) p. 111.
[11] *American Leaders*, Mabel Ansley Murphy (The Union Press, Philadelphia, 1920) p. 139.
[12] *Biographical Sketches of Preeminent Americans*, Frederick G. Harrison (E. W. Walker Company, Boston, 1893) vol. 3, p. 152.
[13] *The Republican Party: A History*, William Starr Myers (The Century Company, New York, 1928) p. 90.

Lincoln, Mary Todd

Before her marriage to Abraham Lincoln, Mary Todd was called the *She-wolf* [1] because she so frequently gave way to outbursts of temper.

Mary Todd (Mrs. Abraham Lincoln) was born at Lexington, Ky., on December 12, 1818, and died at Chicago, Ill., on July 16, 1882.

[1] *"Abraham Lincoln"* by Clifford Smyth, in *Builders of America* (Funk and Wagnalls Company, New York, 1931) vol. 19, p. 52.

Lincoln Memorial University

The athletic teams of Lincoln Memorial University, at Harrogate, Tenn., are called the *Airdales* [1] and the *Railsplitters*,[1] although the *Airdales* has been dropped except occasionally. In 1930 the athletic committee of the University adopted the *Railsplitters*, because Abraham Lincoln, in whose honor the school was founded, was called the *Railsplitter*.

[1] A communication from J. D. Alexander, Athletic Director of Lincoln Memorial University, Harrogate, Tenn., July 13, 1935.

Lindbergh, Charles Augustus

The *Ambassador of the Air* and the *Lone Eagle* are nicknames of Charles Augustus Lindbergh.

Because he made good-will tours to Central America, South America, West Indies, and other countries, he has been called the *Ambassador of the Air*.[1]

Colonel Lindbergh was known as the *Lone Eagle* [2] because of his famous first solo flight across the Atlantic.

Lindbergh, C. A.—Continued

Charles Augustus Lindbergh was born at Detroit, Mich., on February 4, 1902.

[1] *The National Encyclopedia* (P. E. Collier and Son Corporation, New York, 1935) vol. 6, p. 241.

[2] *Washington Herald,* Washington, D.C., October 17, 1934, col. 3, p. 2.

Lindsey, Benjamin Barr

Benjamin Barr Lindsey is known as the *Father of the Juvenile Court* [1] because he originated the Juvenile Association for the Protection and Betterment of Children in 1902. The Juvenile Court of Denver, often called the Children's Court, was established in connection with this association.

Judge Lindsey served as judge of the Juvenile Court of Denver from 1900 to 1927. He was an active promoter of the juvenile court system, and the originator of many of its methods of dealing with youthful delinquents.

He was born at Jackson, Tenn., on November 25, 1869, and died March 26, 1943.

[1] *The National Cyclopedia of American Biography* (James T. White and Company, New York, 1916) vol. 15, p. 185.

Who's Who in America, a Biographical Dictionary of Notable Living Men and Women of the United States, 1932-1933, ed. by Albert Nelson Marquis (The A. N. Marquis Company, 1932) vol. 17, p. 1423.

Lion-hearted Thomas. See Thomas, G. H.

Lion Hunter. See Tinkham, G. H.

Lion of the Senate. See Borah, W. E.

Lion of the South. See Hindman, T. C.

Lion's Den State. See Tennessee

Lippy. See Durocher, L. E.

Lipscomb, Andrew Adgate

Andrew Adgate Lipscomb was called the *Boy Preacher* [1] because he entered the Methodist ministry at the age of eighteen.

Andrew Adgate Lipscomb was born at Georgetown, D.C., on September 6, 1816, and died at Athens, Ga., on November 23, 1890.

[1] *The National Cyclopedia of American Biography* (James T. White and Company, New York, 1929) vol. 6, p. 217.

Liquor Czar. See Morgan, W. F.

Literary Emporium. See Boston, Mass.

Little, Louis

The *Caesar of Football* [1] is a nickname applied to Louis Little, who has been head of the Columbia University football coaching Staff since 1930. After coaching Columbia to victory in the 1933 Rose Bowl game, Little was recognized as one of the country's foremost coaches. [2]

Louis Little was born in Leominster, Mass, on December 6, 1893.

[1] *Vanity Fair* (The Condé Nast Publications, Inc., Greenwich, Conn.) November, 1934, p. 57.

[2] *Current Biography, 1945: Who's News and Why,* ed. by Anna Rothe, (The H. W. Wilson Company, New York, 1946) p. 352.

Little Alby. See Barkley, A. W.

Little Aleck. See Stephens, A. H.

Little Bat. See Garnier, Baptiste

Little Ben. See Harrison, Benjamin

Little Billy. See Smith, W. R.; Whiting, W. H. C.

Little Billy Cody the Messenger. See Cody, W. F.

Little Black Dan. See Webster, Daniel

Little Breeches. See Hay, J. M.

Little Chief. See Thatcher, Moses

Little Children's Dower

The buttercup or crowfoot (*Ranunculus acris*), which grows wild and in flower gardens has been called the *Little Children's Dower* [1] because it is the color of gold and children may pick it freely.

[1] *The World Book Encyclopedia* (The Quarrie Corporation, Chicago, 1938) vol. 2, p. 1044.

Little Church Around The Corner

The Church of the Transfiguration in New York City is known as the *Little Church Around the Corner.* [1] It is said the name originated in 1870 after the death of the comedian George Holland. Joseph Jefferson, a friend and fellow-actor of Holland's, asked an Episcopalian minister if he would conduct Holland's funeral in his church. This clergyman declined to do so because Holland was a professional actor, but suggested to Jefferson that probably the minister of the little church around the corner would conduct the funeral for him. This little church was the Church of the Transfiguration, located on Twenty-ninth Street, near Fifth Avenue, which has ever since been widely known as *The Little Church Around the Corner*.

[1] *The Autobiography of Joseph Jefferson* (The Century Company, New York, 1897) p. 340.
The National Cyclopedia of American Biography (James T. White and Company, New York, 1929) vol. 6, p. 9.

Little Corporal. See Nelson, Knute

Little Corporal of Unsought Fields. See McClellan, G. B.

Little Crusaders. See Susquehanna University

Little Davey. See Lewis, D. J.

Little David. See Randolph (of Roanoke), John

Little Doctor. See Houghton, Douglass

Little Feller. See Sullivan, T. P.

Little Flower. See La Guardia, F. H.

Little Generals. See Washington and Lee University

Little Giant. See Douglas, S. A.; Lewis, D. J.

Little Giant of Alexandria. See Nelson, Knute

Little Giants
The Democrats who favored the election of Stephen A. Douglas as President of the United States in 1860 adopted the nickname *Little Giants*[1] because Douglas was known as the *Little Giant*. The Republicans, playing on the name, called them *Little Joints*.[2]

[1] *Political Americanisms*, Charles Ledyard Norton (Longmans, Green and Company, New York, 1890) p. 128.

[2] *The Lyon Campaign in Missouri, Being a History of the First Iowa Infantry, and of the Causes Which Led up to its Organization, and How It Earned the Thanks of Congress Which It Got, together with a Bird's eye View of the Conditions in Iowa Preceding the Great Civil War of 1861*, E. F. Ware (Crane and Company, Topeka, Kans., 1907) p. 66.

Little Giants. See Wabash College

Little Giants of Chenango. See Colgate University

Little Hero. See Wheeler, Joseph

Little Ida. See Idaho

Little Indian Fighter. See Standish, Miles

Little Italy
Because there are so many fruit and vegetable vendors in and around the Old French Market in New Orleans, La., that part of the city is nicknamed *Little Italy*.[1]

[1] *The World Book Encyclopedia* (W. F. Quarrie and Company, Chicago, 1934) vol. 12, p. 4944.

Little Joe. See Wheeler, Joseph

Little Joints. See *Little Giants*

Little King Pepin. See Channing, W. E.

Little Lion. See Hamilton, Alexander

Little Mac. See McClellan, G. B.

Little Mac the Young Napoleon. See McClellan, G. B.

Little Magician. See Van Buren, Martin

Little Missy. See Oakley, Annie

Little Napoleon. See Brumbaugh, Carl.; McClellan, G. B.

Little New Deal
The Democratic state administration of Pennsylvania from 1935 until 1939, the first in forty-four years, has been called the *Little New Deal*[1] because it was patterned closely after the Democratic administration of President Franklin Delano Roosevelt which extended from 1933 until 1945.

Little New Deal—Continued
George Howard Earle was the Governor of Pennsylvania who initiated the *Little New Deal* of Pennsylvania.

[1] *The Washington Daily News,* Washington, D.C., November 9, 1938, col. 3, p. 2.

Little Norwegian. See Nelson, Knute

Little Phil. See Sheridan, P. H.; Thompson, P. B., Jr.

Little Pill Doctor. See Miller, Archie

Little Poison. See Waner, L. J. and Waner, P. G.

Little Quakers. See Haverford College

Little Red. See Barton, David

Little Rhody. See Rhode Island

Little Rock, Arkansas

Little Rock has been designated the *City of Roses* [1] because its climate and natural surroundings are ideal for the growing of roses which abound in its gardens and in its effectively landscaped parks.

[1] *Centennial History of Arkansas,* Dallas T. Herndon, Editor (The S. J. Clarke Publishing Company, Chicago, and Little Rock, Ark., 1922) vol. 1, p. 845.
Arkansas and Its People, A History, 1541-1930, David Yancey Thomas (The American Historical Society, Inc., New York, 1930) vol. 2, p. 798.

Little Senate

A few weeks before December 16, 1773, the date of the *Boston Tea Party,* committees from Boston, Brookline, Cambridge, Charleston, Dorchester, and Roxbury met to protest the landing of several shiploads of tea which were enroute to Boston. This gathering was called a *Little Senate* [1] by Thomas Hutchinson, the Royal Governor of the Massachusetts Bay Colony, because he sensed that it was a legislative body which represented in a fair way the attitude of the colonists on taxation.

[1] "Samuel Adams" by James K. Hosmer, in *American Statesmen,* ed. by John T. Moore, Junior (Houghton Mifflin and Company, New York and Boston, 1885) vol. 2, p. 246.

Little Shepherd of Coogan's Bluff. See Durocher, L. E.

Little Sure Shot. See Oakley, Annie

Little Swiss Town. See Damascus, Va.

Little Switzerland of America. See Rest Island, Minn.

Little Tim. See Sullivan, T. P.

Little Van. See Van Buren, Martin

Little White House

Prior to his inauguration on March 4, 1893, as President of the United States, Grover Cleveland, the twenty-second and the twenty-fourth President of the United States, occupied an unpretentious house at Lakewood, N.J., which was nicknamed the *Little White House* [1] because it housed the President-elect and was painted white. After the close of his second administration, Cleveland and his family often went to stay at the *Little White House,* because it was plain, and reminded him of his home in Caldwell, N.J., where he was born.

The home of Mrs. James Madison, on the corner of Lafayette Square and H Street in Washington, D.C., was often referred to as the *Little White House.*[1] After they had paid their respects to President Monroe at the White House, many prominent people would next call upon Mrs. Madison at her home across Lafayette Square. Mrs. Madison had been very popular and greatly beloved for her tact and graciousness as hostess at the White House while her husband was President of the United States from 1809 to 1817.

[1] *Under Four Administrations; from Cleveland to Taft.* Recollections of Oscar S. Straus (Houghton Mifflin Company, New York and Boston, 1922) p. 112, 118.
Records of the Columbia Historical Society, Washington, D.C., comp. by the Committee on Publication and the Recording Secretary (Published by the Society, Washington, D.C., 1904, at the Press of The New Era Printing Company, Lancaster, Pa.) p. 174.

Live Oak George. See Law, George

Livingston, John Henry

The *Father of the Dutch Reformed Church in America* [1] is applied to John Henry Livingston because of his pioneer work in guiding the early activities of the Dutch Reformed Church in America, and in founding Rutgers College in 1766, and the Theological Seminary of the Reformed Church in America.

John Henry Livingston was born at Poughkeepsie, N.Y., on May 30, 1746, and died at New Brunswick, N.J., on January 20, 1825.

[1] *The National Cyclopaedia of American Biography* (James T. White and Company, New York, 1893) vol. 3, p. 400.

Livingston, Robert R.

Benjamin Franklin described Robert R. Livingston as the *Cicero of America* [1] because Livingston, like the Roman orator Cicero, was an eloquent, skillful, and versatile orator.

Robert R. Livingston was born at New York City, on November 27, 1746, and died at Clermont, N.Y., on February 26, 1813.

[1] *Builders of the Republic: Some Great Americans Who Have Aided in the Making of the Nation,* Margherita Arlina Hamm (James Pott and Company, New York, 1902) p. 314.

Livingston, William

Despot-in-chief in and over the Rising State of New Jersey, Don Quixote of the Jerseys, Extraordinary Chancellor of the Rising State of New Jersey, Knight of the Most Honorable Order of Starvation, and *Spurious Governor* [1] are nicknames by which William Livingston was called during the Revolutionary War by the British and their Tory sympathizers, chiefly through the medium of *Rivington's Gazette,* a New York paper which was the organ of the British party. The nicknames originated because William Livingston, who served as Governor of New Jersey from August 28, 1776, until his death in 1790, was particularly hated by the Tories, who several times attempted to capture him and put an end to his services to the colonies.

William Livingston was born at Albany, N.Y., on November 30, 1723, and died at Elizabethtown, N.J., on July 25, 1790.

[1] *The National Cyclopaedia of American Biography* (James T. White and Company, New York, 1907) vol. 5, p. 202.

Lizard State. See Alabama

Lizards. See Alabamians

Lobos. See University of New Mexico

Locofocos

During a meeting of the Democratic party in Tammany Hall, New York City, in 1835, the opponents of the equal-rights faction of this party turned off the gas lights. The radicals, having anticipated such an act, had provided themselves with locofoco or friction matches and candles which they promptly lighted. When the New York papers published an account of the affair, *The Morning Courier* and *The Evening Enquirer* called the radical faction of the Democratic Party the *Locofocos* [1] and for ten years or more the sobriquet was applied to the entire Democratic party.

[1] *Our Republic, a History of the United States for Grammar Grades,* Revised Edition, Franklin L. Riley, Julian A. C. Chandler, and Joseph G. de Roulhac Hamilton (Row, Peterson and Company, New York and San Francisco, 1932) p. 304.
Political Americanisms, Charles Ledyard Norton (Longmans, Green and Company, New York and London, 1890) p. 66.
The Century Dictionary and Cyclopedia (The Century Company, New York, 1906) vol. 4, p. 3499.

Log-cabin and Hard-cider Campaign

The presidential campaign of 1840 was nicknamed the *Log-cabin and Hard-cider Campaign* [1]. The Democratic candidate was Martin Van Buren and the Whig candidate William Henry Harrison. This nickname grew out of the comment of an eastern Democratic newspaper that all Harrison demanded of life was a log cabin and a barrel of cider. The Whigs immediately adopted the log cabin and barrel of hard cider as their campaign symbols, using miniature log cabins and barrels of hard cider so profusely in the processions and the activities pertaining to Harrison's campaign that it became known as the *Log-cabin and Hard-cider Campaign.*

[1] *Recollections of a Busy Life: Including Reminiscences of American Politics and Politicians, From the Opening of the Missouri Contest to the Downfall of Slavery; to Which are Added Miscellanies. . . ,* Also, a Discussion with Robert Dale Owen of the Law of Divorce, Horace Greeley (J. B. Ford and Company, New York, 1868) p. 132.
The Making of Our United States, R. O. Hughes (Allyn and Bacon, New York and Boston, 1933) p. 215.

Log Cabin Candidate. See Harrison, W. H.

Log Hall Philips. See Philips, M. W.

Logan, John Alexander

The nicknames *Black Eagle of Illinois, Black Jack,* and the *Murat of the Union Army* have been given to Major General John Alexander Logan.

He was known as the *Black Eagle of Illinois* [1] because of his dark complexion,

Logan, J. A.—Continued

his prominence as a soldier, and because he was a native of Illinois.

Black Jack [2] was a sobriquet applied to Logan because of his very dark complexion, his dark eyes, and his black hair.

Logan's military career was so distinguished because of his outstanding personal courage and daring, his inspiring leadership, his prompt and effective decisions in critical situations upon the battlefield, that he was, therefore, called the *Murat of the Union Army*.[3] The French Marshall Joachim Murat was a brilliant cavalry leader under Napoleon Bonaparte.

From 1866 to 1871 he was a Republican Representative from Illinois to Congress, and Senator from 1871 to 1877, and from 1879 until his death.

John Alexander Logan was born at Murphysboro, Ill., on February 9, 1826, and died at Washington, D.C., on December 26, 1886.

[1] *Champ Clark*, N. I. Webb (The Neale Publishing Company, New York, 1912) p. 179.

[2] *Sherman's March Through the South, with Sketches and Incidents of the Campaign*, David P. Conyngham (Sheldon and Company, New York, 1865) p. 54.

[3] *Contemporary American Biography: Biographical Sketches of Representative Men of the Day, Representatives of Modern Thought and Progress, of the Pulpit, the Press, the Bench and Bar, of Legislation, Invention, and the Great Industrial Interests of the Country* (Atlantic Publishing and Engraving Company, New York, 1899) vol. 2, p. 224.

Logan's Slaughter Pen

During the siege of Vicksburg, Miss., the Federal forces under Major General John Alexander Logan on June 25, 1864, exploded a mine which had been laid from their lines to the Confederate defenses. After the explosion a large, cone-like crater appeared which was called *Logan's Slaughter Pen*,[1] because a large number of Federal soldiers had been killed there trying to get inside the Confederate parapets.

[1] *Reminiscences of the Civil War*, Memorial Edition, General John B. Gordon (Charles Scribner's Sons, New York, 1904) p. 186.

Loggers. See College of Puget Sound

Lombardi, Ernest Natali

Because his nose is unduly large, Ernest Natali Lombardi, who was born at Oakland, Calif., on April 6, 1908, and who was a catcher in major-league baseball, is nicknamed *Snozz*.[1]

[1] *Who's Who in Major League Base Ball*, comp. by Harold (Speed) Johnson (Buxton Publishing Company, Chicago, 1933) p. 262.

London, Jack

The *American Kipling* [1] is a nickname applied to Jack London because, like Kipling, he drew upon his varied experiences and those of all classes of people for material for his writing.

Jack London was born at San Francisco, Calif., on January 12, 1876, and died at Glen Ellen, Calif., on November 22, 1916.

[1] *The National Cyclopedia of American Biography* (James T. White and Company, New York, 1906) vol. 13, p. 134.

Lone Eagle. See Lindbergh, C. A.

Lone Lion. See Borah, W. E.

Lone Star. See Starr, Frederick

Lone Star of Civilization. See Santa Fe, N.M.

Lone Star State. See Texas

Lone Wolf of the Underworld. See Millman, Harry

Lonesome Charley. See Reynolds, C. A.

Long, Huey Pierce

The late Huey Pierce Long was called the *Dictator of Louisiana, Hooey Long*, the *Kingfish*, and *Louisiana's Loud Speaker*.

Senator Long was called the *Dictator of Louisiana* [1] because he exercised such power in the government of Louisiana.

Huey Pierce Long's name was often mispronounced as *Hooey*, and he made such grandiose political promises that he was often called *Hooey Long*.[2]

The *Kingfish*,[3] meaning in slang an important person, was applied by Senator Long to himself. While he was Governor of Louisiana, there was a meeting of the highway commission to dispose of some bonds. Officially, he had no right to attend the meeting, but he urged the members of the board to allow him to be present. When they asked him on what grounds, he said, "Call me the *Kingfish*," [3] and this has been his nickname ever since.

Because his speeches in the United States Senate were delivered in a spectacular bombastic manner, Senator Long has been referred to as *Louisiana's Loud Speaker*.[4]

Huey Pierce Long was born at Winnfield, La., on August 30, 1893, was shot at the State Capitol on September 8, 1935, by Dr. Carl Austin Weiss, and died at Our Lady of the Lake Sanitorium in Baton Rouge, La., on September 10, 1935.[5]

[1] *The Washington Post*, Washington, D.C., January 27, 1935, col. 6, p. 1.
[2] "Gallery Glimpses" by Robert C. Albright, in *The Washington Post*, Washington, D.C., February 3, 1935, sec. B, col. 4, p. 1.
[3] *The Washington Post Magazine*, Washington, D.C., March 4, 1934, p. 4.
[4] *The American Scene*, Edwin C. Hill (Witmark Educational Publications, Department of M. Witmark and Sons, New York, 1933) p. 22-3.
[5] *The Times-Picayune*, New Orleans, La., September 10, 1935, p. 1.

Long Bobs

Near the close of the Revolutionary War, such a scarcity of money prevailed that the colonies could not pay their taxes, or their part of the expense of the Revolution. Robert Morris, the colonial Superintendent of Finance, issued notes carrying his own signature to relieve the currency situation. These notes, which were to be redeemed when the colonies were able to do so, were termed *Long Bobs*[1] and *Short Bobs* depending on whether the term of the notes was of long or short duration.

[1] *Makers of Our History*, John T. Faris (Ginn and Company, New York and Boston, 1917) p. 46.

Long Hunters

The *Long Hunters* were a large party of men who in 1769 left the Holston settlement in North Carolina to explore the surrounding woods and mountains. Many of the men were away from their homes for a whole year. When they returned to the settlement they were nicknamed the *Long Hunters*.[1]

Men who came to the territory lying between the Allegheny Mountains and the Mississippi river and made a business of hunting in the 1780's were called also *Long Hunters*.[2] These men spent the fall and winter each year hunting and trading with the Indians and usually returned to their homes east of the Allegheny Mountains in the spring.

[1] *The Germans in Colonial Times*, Lucy Forney Bittinger (J. B. Lippincott Company, Philadelphia and London, 1901) p. 279.
[2] *The Birth and Growth of Our Nation*, Marion G. Clark and Wilbur Fish Gordy (Charles Scribner's Sons, New York and Boston, 1933) p. 266.

Long Island University

The teams of Long Island University, at Brooklyn, N.Y., are known as *Blackbirds, Blue Devils*, and *Mariners*. They were called *Blackbirds*[1] during the years when their uniforms were black and red, and *Blue Devils*[1] when their uniforms were blue. Because the school yearbook was called *The Sound*, the athletic teams were called *Mariners*.[1]

[1] A communication from Clair F. Bee, Director of Athletics at Long Island University, Brooklyn, N.Y., June 12, 1935.

Long John. See Wentworth, John

Long Knife. See Lewis, Meriwether

Long Knives

The *Long Knives*[1] was a name frequently applied to colonial white men by the Indians. There seems to be some difference of opinion about the origin. The usual explanation is that the Indians called white men *Long Knives* because they wore swords, or carried long hunting knives. Another version is that Colonel John Gibson in 1760 in the course of a skirmish with Indians, cut off the head of a chief with one blow of his sword. The surviving Indians called Gibson the *Long Knife Warrior*, and soon all whites were *Long Knives*.

[1] *History of the Early Settlement and Indian Wars of Western Virginia. . . ,* Wills De Hass (Published by H. Hoblitzell, Wheeling, W.Va., printed by King and Baird, Philadelphia, 1851) p. 215.
An *Historical Account of the Expedition against Sandusky under Colonel William Crawford, in 1782 with Biographical Sketches, Personal Reminiscences, and Descriptions of Interesting Localities Including Also, Details of the Disastrous Retreat, the Barbarities of the Savages, and the Awful Death of Crawford, by Torture,* C. W. Butterfield (Robert Clarke and Company, Cincinnati, Ohio, 1873) p. 32-3.
History of the Early Settlement and Indian Wars of Western Virginia. . . , Wills De Hass (Published by H. Hoblitzell, Wheeling, W.Va., printed by King and Baird, Philadelphia, 1851) p. 215-216.

Long Nine

The nine men elected in 1836 from Sangamon County to serve in the Illinois Legislature were called the *Long Nine*[1] because each was six feet or more in height. The *Long Nine* were Senators Job Fletcher and Archer G. Herndon, Representatives John Dawson, Ninian W. Edwards, W. F. Elkin, Abraham Lincoln, Andrew McCormick, Dan Stone, and Robert L. Wilson.

[1] *Illinois: History of Illinois and Her People*, George W. Smith (The American Historical Society, Inc., New York and Chicago, 1927) vol. 2, p. 228-9.

Long Tom. See Jefferson, Thomas

Long Tom Perkins. See Perkins, T. H.

Long 'Un. See Lincoln, Abraham

Longfellow, Henry Wadsworth

The *Children's Poet*, the *Laureate of Song* and the *Poet of the Commonplace* are nicknames applied to Henry Wadsworth Longfellow.

He well merited the nickname of the *Children's Poet* [1] because he wrote many poems for and about children. He was called the *Poet of the Commonplace* because so many of his poems deal with conventional subjects.

The *Laureate of Song* [2] was applied to Longfellow because he was one of the most popular of the Cambridge group of American poets.

Henry Wadsworth Longfellow was born at Portland, Me., on February 27, 1807, and died at Cambridge, Mass., on March 24, 1882.

[1] *Makers of Our History.* John T. Faris (Ginn and Company, New York and Boston, 1917) p. 235.
Henry Wadsworth Longfellow, George Rice Carpenter (Small, Maynard and Company, Boston, 1901) p. 140.
[2] *Compton's Pictured Encyclopedia* (F. E. Compton and Company, Chicago, 1931) vol. 1, p. 113.

Longstreet, James

Lieutenant General James Longstreet was called the *Bulldog, Lee's Old Warhorse, Old Pete, Pete,* and the *Warhorse of the Confederacy.*

He was nicknamed the *Bulldog* [1] by his soldiers in the Confederate Army because he was an aggressive and obstinate fighter and because opposition made him only more determined.

While Longstreet was attending the United States Military Academy, at West Point, N.Y., from 1838 to 1842, his fellow-cadets called him Pete.[2] This nickname continued to be applied to him, and during the Civil War he was familiarly known as *Old Pete.*[3]

Lee's Old Warhorse and the *Warhorse of the Confederacy,*[4] were originated by Robert E. Lee, who called Longstreet his "old war-horse" after the Battle of Antietam in Maryland on September 17, 1862,

when Longstreet distinguished himself by his personal daring and military genius.

James Longstreet was born in Edgefield District, S.C., on January 8, 1821, and died at Gainsville, Ga., on January 2, 1904.

[1] *Lee and His Lieutenants; Comprising the Early Life, Public Services, and Campaigns of General Robert E. Lee and His Companions in Arms, with a Record of Their Campaigns and Heroic Deeds*, Edward A. Pollard (E. B. Treat and Company, New York, 1867) p. 411, 415.
[2] *Life and Letters of Alexander Hays*, ed. and arranged with notes and contemporary history by George Thornton Fleming from data compiled by Gilbert Adams Hays (Pittsburgh, Pa., 1919) p. 96.
[3] *Lee and Longstreet at High Tide; Gettysburg in the Light of the Official Records*, Helen D. Longstreet (Published by the Author at Gainesville, Ga., 1904) p. 222, 223, 228, 250, 251, 257, 272, 276.
[4] *From Manassas to Appomattox; Memoirs of the Civil War in America*, James Longstreet (J. B. Lippincott Company, Philadelphia, 1896) p. 261.

Longworth, Alice Lee (Roosevelt)

Mrs. Alice Lee (Roosevelt) Longworth, the eldest daughter of President Theodore Roosevelt, was nicknamed *Princess Alice* and *Queen Alice.* When she made her debut in Washington on January 5, 1902, Alice Roosevelt was called *Little Miss Roosevelt* by the guests at the White House reception. After her debut, people began calling her the *Princess.*[1] This nickname was publicized while Henry, Prince of Prussia, the brother of Kaiser Wilhelm II of Germany, was visiting the United States in 1902. He and the President's daughter attended many of the same social gatherings during the Prince's visit. Alice Roosevelt, at the request of the Kaiser, christened the Kaiser's yacht *The Meteor* at Sharpshooter's Island in New York Harbor on February 25, 1902.

Mrs. Longworth has long been called *Queen Alice* [2] by society people of Washington because of her gracious manners and queenly bearing, and because her father was President of the United States.

Alice Lee Roosevelt was born on February 12, 1884. She was married to Nicholas Longworth, former Speaker of the National House of Representatives, at the White House on February 17, 1906.

[1] *Famous Girls of the White House*, Revised Edition, Kate Dickinson Sweetser (Thomas Y. Crowell Company, New York, 1937) p. 238-9.
Washington Herald, Washington, D.C., November 9, 1936, col. 3, p. 6.

Looneys. See College of William and Mary

Lord Jeffs. See Amherst College

Loring, William Wing

William Wing Loring, a Confederate officer, was nicknamed *Old Blizzards*.[1] Early in 1863, Major General Loring, while in charge of Fort Pemberton, repulsed a Union attack by land and sea. During this onslaught he climbed to the cotton-bale parapet and yelled, "Give them blizzards, boys! Give them blizzards!" After that he was called *Old Blizzards*.

William Wing Loring was born at Wilmington, N.C., on December 4, 1818, and died at New York City on December 30, 1886.

[1] *Confederate Military History, A Library of Confederate States History, in Twelve Volumes, Written by Distinguished Men of the South, and Edited by General Clement A. Evans of Georgia* (Confederate Publishing Company, Atlanta, Georgia, 1899) vol. 11, p. 205.

Appleton's Cyclopaedia of American Biography, ed. by James Grant Wilson and John Fiske (D. Appleton and Company, New York, 1886) vol. 4, p. 28.

Los Angeles, California

Los Angeles is often called the *City of Flowers and Sunshine*[1] because of the profusion of flowers in the parks and gardens and because of the high percentage of sunshiny weather. It was formerly referred to as the *Queen of the Cow Counties*[2] because it was the center of extensive livestock ranches.

[1] *Little Journeys in America,* Rose Henderson (The Southern Publishing Company, Dallas, Tex., 1922) p. 230-1.

[2] *California and Californians,* ed. by Rockwell D. Hunt, assisted by an advisory board (The Lewis Publishing Company, New York and Chicago, 1930) vol. 2, p. 481-2, 566.

Lost Battalion

During World War I, several hundred American soldiers of the Seventy-seventh Division became separated from their comrades in battle in the Argonne Forest on October 2, 1918, and were surrounded by the Germans. Because they were isolated from the other members of the Seventy-seventh Division, they were called the *Lost Battalion*.[1] Efforts to rescue them were of no avail until October 8 when reinforcements from the Twenty-eighth and the Eighty-second Divisions, after a week of fighting enabled the rest of the Seventy-seventh Division to rescue the hungry and weary soldiers of the *Lost Battalion*.

[1] *My Experiences in the World War,* John J. Pershing (Frederick A. Stokes Company, New York, 1931) p. 324, 330, 331, 392.

Lost Ducks

The nickname, *The Lost Children*, which was applied to the members of the Forty-eighth Regiment of New York Infantrymen during the Civil War, became intentionally, but in a spirit of fun, translated into the sobriquet, *The Lost Ducks*.[1] The appellation, *The Lost Ducks*, may have been a sly allusion to the coats of the uniforms of these soldiers because the two little coat-tails, being only about two inches long, resembled somewhat the abbreviated tail-feathers of a duck.

[1] *Andersonville: A Story of Rebel Military Prisons, Fifteen Months a Guest of the So-called Southern Confederacy; a Private Soldier's Experience in Richmond, Andersonville, Savannah, Millen, Blackshear, and Florence,* John McElroy (D. R. Locke, Toledo, Ohio, 1879) p. 161-2, 434.

Lottery Kenney. See Kenney, E. A.

Louis, Joe

Joe Louis (Joseph Louis Barrow) a heavyweight American Negro champion boxer is nicknamed the *Brown Bomber* because of his heavy and accurate hitting. He was born near Lafayette, Alabama, on May 13, 1914.

Louisiana

Louisiana is nicknamed the *Child of the Mississippi*, the *Creole State*, the *Pelican State*, and the *Sugar State*.

Louisiana was nicknamed *The Child of the Mississippi*[1] because it was built by deposits from the Mississippi River on the bottom of the Gulf of Mexico. The Gulf once extended as far up the river as Cairo, Ill.

Louisiana is named the *Creole State*[2] because of the great number of Creoles, descendants of the French and Spanish settlers living there.

The *Pelican State*[3] was applied to Louisiana because this bird is frequently seen throughout the state. It is the emblem on the state coat of arms.

Louisiana is nicknamed the *Sugar State* because of its numerous sugar plantations and refineries.

[1] *Compton's Pictured Encyclopedia* (F. E. Compton and Company, Chicago, 1947) vol. 8, p. 204.

[2] *A New Dictionary of Americanisms,* Sylva Clapin (Louis Weiss and Company, New York, 1903) p. 145.

[3] *Americanisms: The English of the New World,* M. Schele De Vere (Charles Scribner and Company, New York, 1872) p. 660.

Louisiana Ram. See Mouton, R. L.

Louisiana State University

The *Bengals, Old Lou*, the *Ole War Skule*, and the *Tigers* are nicknames applied to the athletic teams of Louisiana State University, at Baton Rouge, La.

The *Bengals* [1] is a nickname which the students of Louisiana State University do not generally accept. It was used by sports writers as a substitute for the *Tigers*.

Old Lou was originated by sports writers in imitation of *Old Miss*, the nickname of the University of Mississippi teams.

The *Ole War Skule* was applied to the athletic teams of Louisiana State University about 1908 by the students because Lieutenant General William Tecumseh Sherman founded the school and it has always had military training.

The *Tigers* was applied to the athletic teams of Louisiana State University in 1896 by President Thomas D. Boyd and the student body, in commemoration of the fact that General Thomas Jonathan (Stonewall) Jackson applied this nickname to a Louisiana regiment containing many cadets from the school who fought during the Civil War.

[1] A letter from Harry Costello, Director of Publicity at Louisiana State University, Baton Rouge, La., June 21, 1935.

Louisiana Tigers. See Wheat, C. R.

Louisiana's Loud Speaker. See Long, H. P.

Louisianians

The Louisianians are designated *Creoles* and *Pelicans*. For the origin of these nicknames, see Louisiana.

Louisville, Kentucky

Louisville is called the *City of Beautiful Churches, City of Homes, Convention City, Falls City*, or *City of the Falls*, or *City by the Falls, Gateway to the South, Metropolis of the New South*, and *Nation's Thoroughfare*.

Louisville has been called the *City of Beautiful Churches* [1, 2] because there are two hundred and sixty-five churches in the city, many of them beautiful.

It is called the *City of Homes* [3] because of its fine residential sections and the homelike welcome and hospitality extended to guests and visitors. It is frequently spoken of as the *Convention City* [3] because its trans-

portation facilities, hotel accommodations, restaurants, and spacious Convention Hall make it a desirable place for conventions of any kind.

The *Falls City*, [4] or the *City of the Falls*, [5] or the *City by the Falls*, [6] are nicknames applied to Louisville because of its location on the Ohio river at the falls or rapids of that stream. It is sometimes designated the *Gateway to the South* [7] because it is geographically located on the dividing line between the North and the South, and because its excellent railroad and water transportation facilities make access to it easy from all directions.

Because it is the gateway to the South, is outstanding in the marketing and the manufacturing of tobacco and various other products, is the site of the greatest Theological Seminary in the South, and is a center for race horses, it is termed the *Metropolis of the New South*. [8] Louisville is designated the *Nation's Thoroughfare* [3] on the seal of the city because of its transportation facilities.

[1] *Press Reference Book of Prominent Kentuckians, Containing Portraits and Biographical Sketches of Men Prominent in Political, Professional, Manufacturing, Financial, Commercial, Club, Social, and Philanthropic Activity in the State of Kentucky. . . .* Colonel Ben LaBree, Editor-in-chief (The Standard Printing Company, Inc., Louisville, Ky., 1916) p. 43.
[2] *Book of Louisville and Kentucky*, 1915 Edition with Pictures, Robert W. Brown, Editor (Louisville Convention and Publicity League, Inc., Louisville, Ky., 1915) p. 8, 42-3.
[3] *Louisville Today* (Comp. and published by Sam McDowell Anderson, Louisville, Ky., 1912) p. 1, 21.
[4] *History of Kentucky*, by William Elsey Connelley and E. M. Coulter, Judge Charles Kerr, Editor (The American Historical Society, Chicago and New York, 1922) vol. 2, p. 926.
[5] *King's Handbook of the United States*, planned and ed. by Moses King, text by M. F. Sweetser (Moses King Corporation, Buffalo, N.Y., 1891) p. 285.
[6] *Casseday's History of Louisville: The History of Louisville, from Its Earliest Settlement till the Year 1852*, Ben Casseday (Hull and Brother, Louisville, Ky., 1852) p. 15.
[7] *Louisville, Nineteen Hundred and Five* (Published and distributed by the Commercial Club of Louisville, Ky., 1905) p. 1.
History of Kentucky, William Elsey Connelley and E. M. Coulter, Judge Charles Kerr, Editor (The American Historical Society, Chicago and New York, 1922) vol. 2, p. 928-30.
Minute Glimpses of American Cities, Herbert S. Kates (Grosset and Dunlap, New York, 1933) p. 65.
[8] *Brief Facts About Louisville*, issued by the Louisville Commercial Club (H. L. Morrow and Company, Louisville, Ky., 1890) p. 10.

Louisville Municipal College For Negroes

The athletic teams of the Louisville Municipal College for Negroes, at Louisville, Ky., were nicknamed the *Bantams* [1] in 1933, by a student sports writer because the men on the teams were game but small.

[1] A letter from Rufus E. Clement, Dean of Louisville Municipal College for Negroes, Louisville, Ky., November 16, 1935.

Love-bird Allen. See Allen, W. F.

Lovejoy, Elijah Parish

Elijah Parish Lovejoy, a reformer, was designated the *Martyr Abolitionist* [1] because he devoted his life to the abolition of slavery, and was killed as a result of his activities. He began his crusade against slavery in 1835 in his editorials in *The St. Louis Observer*. The hostility of the people of St. Louis to the anti-slavery movement caused Lovejoy to move to Alton, Ill., where he edited *The Alton Observer*, denounced slavery and organized an anti-slavery association. His activities so enraged those who upheld slavery that his printing press was destroyed, and he was fatally shot by a mob of anti-abolitionists.

Elijah Parish Lovejoy was born at Albion, Me., on November 9, 1802, and died at Alton, Ill., on November 7, 1837.

[1] *Dictionary of American Biography under the Auspices of the American Council of Learned Societies*, ed. by Dumas Malone (Charles Scribner's Sons, New York, 1933) vol. 11, p. 434.

Lovell, John

The *Busby of New England* [1] was applied to John Lovell because he was headmaster of the Public Latin School of Boston from 1738 to 1776. Richard Busby was headmaster of Westminster School in London, England.

John Lovell was born at Boston, Mass., on June 16, 1710, and died at Halifax, Nova Scotia, in 1778.

[1] *The National Cyclopedia of American Biography* (James T. White and Company, New York, 1897) vol. 12, p. 428.

Lowden, Frank Orren

The nickname the *Sage of Sinnissippi* [1] was applied to Frank Orren Lowden because he was recognized as a wise, scholarly, and dignified man, and his home is called Sinnissippi.

For many years he was prominent in the political activities of Illinois. He served as a Representative from Illinois to the United States Congress from 1906 to 1911 and as Governor of the state from 1917 to 1921.

Frank Orren Lowden was born at Sunrise, in Chicago County, Minn., on January 26, 1861.

[1] *The Sage of Sinnissippi; Being a Brief Sketch of the Life of Congressman Frank Orren Lowden of Oregon, Illinois, Brief Sketches of His Rivals in Political Battles, a Short Article Relating to His Availability as a Presidential Candidate for 1908, and an Official and Authentic Account of State Elections in Illinois. . . .* Kinnie A. Ostewig (J. A. Nolen, Shabbona, Ill., 1907) p. 170.

Lowell, John, Junior

John Lowell, Junior, a Massachusetts political writer, was nicknamed *Columella of the New England States* [1] because he wrote much on various phases of agriculture, like Lucius Junius Moderatus Columella, a Roman writer on agriculture who flourished about the middle of the First Century A.D. For many years Lowell was president of the Massachusetts Agricultural Society.

John Lowell, Junior, was born at Newburyport, Mass., on June 17, 1743, and died at Boston, Mass., on March 12, 1840.

[1] *Appleton's Cyclopaedia of American Biography*, ed. by James Grant Wilson and John Fiske (D. Appleton and Company, New York, 1894) vol. 4, p. 42.

Lowell, Massachusetts

Lowell is nicknamed the *City of Magic*, the *Manchester of America*, and the *Spindle City*. It has been called the *City of Magic* [1] because of its rapid growth from 1820 to 1860 because of the development of the cotton manufacturing industry which was greatly aided by utilizing the water power from the Pawtucket Falls of the Merrimac River.

Lowell is known as the *Manchester of America* [2] because of its prominence in the manufacturing and dyeing of cotton and woolen textiles, in which respects it closely resembles Manchester, England. It is called the *Spindle City* [3] for the same reason.

[1] *Stories of Massachusetts*, Mara L. Pratt and Anna Temple Lovering (Educational Publishing Company, Boston, 1892) p. 296, 301.

"Industrial Structure of New England," in *Part I of the Commercial Survey of New England*, Charles E. Artman, United States Department of Commerce, Bureau of Foreign and Domestic Commerce (Government Printing Office, Washington, D.C., 1930) p. 288.

[2] *The Encyclopaedia Britannica*, Fourteenth Edition (Encyclopaedia Britannica Inc., New York, 1932) vol. 14, p. 444.

[3] *Manual of Useful Information*, J. C. Thomas (The Werner Company, Chicago, 1893) p. 22.

The Earth and Its People: Our State and Continent, Wallace W. Atwood and Helen Goss Thomas, with the collaboration of Marion B. Forsythe (Ginn and Company, New York, 1929) p. 90.

Scientific American, An Illustrated Journal of Art, Science and Mechanics (Munn and Company, New York, 1857-58) vol. 13, p. 153.

Lowell of the South. See Augusta, Ga.

Loyola College

The *Jesuits* and the *Greyhounds* are the nicknames of the athletic teams of Loyola College, at Baltimore, Md. The *Jesuits* [1] originated in the fact that the college is owned and operated by the Jesuit order of the Roman Catholic church.

The Greyhounds [5] is the nickname given to the teams of Loyola College by sports writers for *The Evening Sun,* Baltimore.

[1] A communication from William Liston, Director of Athletics at Loyola College, Baltimore, Md., November 22, 1935.

Luce, Robert

Robert Luce, a Massachusetts politician, was nicknamed the *Parliamentarian* in the House of Representatives because he was an authority on parliamentary law.

He was Lieutenant Governor of Massachusetts in 1912, and a Republican Representative from Massachusetts to Congress from 1919 to 1935, and again from 1937 to 1941.

Robert Luce was born at Auburn, Me., on December 2, 1862, and died April 7, 1946.

[1] An interview with Captain Victor Hunt Harding, Secretary of the National Democratic Congress Reëlection Committee, Washington, D.C., April 10, 1939.

Luchese, Thomas

During the hearings of the New York State Crime Commission in 1952, it was revealed that Thomas Luchese, known as a well-to-do businessman in the garment industry, was actually a racketeer and a long-time leader in the criminal underworld under the nickname of *Three-Finger Brown.* [1] Luchese earlier lost his right index finger in a machine-shop accident. When he was first arrested under the alias Tommy Brown, a whimsical policeman is supposed to have dubbed him *Three-Finger Brown,* recalling the nickname of the famous baseball pitcher, Mordecai Brown.

Luchese was born Gaetano Luchese in Sicily in 1899. He came to America at the age of 12.

[1] *Newsweek,* Nov. 24, 1952, p. 26-7.

Lucky Baldwin. See Baldwin, E. J.

Lucky Seventh. See Seventh Armored Division of World War II

Ludlow, Louis Leon

Louis Leon Ludlow, an Indiana journalist and politician, was nicknamed *Peace Ludlow* [1] in the House of Representatives because he introduced the Ludlow War Referendum Resolution in 1938 and a bill proposing a naval holiday and arms limitation in the United States.

For many years he was Washington correspondent for a number of newspapers. He was a Democratic Representative from Indiana to Congress from 1929 to 1949.

Louis Leon Ludlow was born on a farm in Fayette County, Ind., on June 24, 1873.

[1] An interview with Captain Victor Hunt Harding, Secretary of the National Democratic Congress Reëlection Committee, Washington, D.C., April 10, 1939.

Ludlow, Roger

The Father of Connecticut Jurisprudence [1] is a sobriquet given to Roger Ludlow because he drafted the Constitution for Connecticut in 1639, and framed the body of laws of Connecticut in 1650, which became known as *Ludlow's Code.*

Roger Ludlow was born at Dorchester, England, on March 7, 1590.

[1] *The National Cyclopaedia of American Biography* (James T. White and Company, New York, 1904) vol. 12, p. 61.

Lumber City. See Bangor, Me.

Lumber State. See Maine

Lumberjacks. See Northland College

Lumbermen. See Maine Inhabitants

Lundy, Benjamin

Benjamin Lundy was known as *Peter-the-Hermit of the Abolitionist Movement* [1] because he was one of the earliest advocates of the abolition of slavery in America, and conducted a continuous crusade against slavery.

Peter the Hermit, who was born in the Diocese of Amiens, about 1050, and died at Neufmountier, near Huy, Belgium, on July 8, 1115, was a preacher of the first crusade. Clad as a hermit, he went about urging the crusade wherever opportunity presented itself.

Benjamin Lundy differed from William Lloyd Garrison and many other advocates of abolition in the fact that he wished to liberate the slaves and colonize them, while Garrison merely wanted them freed.

Benjamin Lundy was born at Hardwick, N.J., on January 4, 1789, and died at Lowell, Ill., on August 22, 1839.

[1] *The Abolitionists, Together with Personal Memories of the Struggle for Human Rights, 1830-1864*, John F. Hume (G. P. Putnam's Sons, New York and London, 1905) p. 26.

Lunenburg County, Virginia

Lunenburg County, Virginia, was nicknamed the *Old Free State of Lunenburg* or the *Old Free State* [1] because in 1861 when prominent citizens were making speeches at Lunenburg Court House advocating the secession of Virginia, Captain C. T. Allen advocated that if Virginia did not secede, Lunenburg county would secede from Virginia, and set up a free state of her own.

This county was also nicknamed *The Mother of Counties* because nine counties have been formed from the original county.

[1] *History of Lunenburg County in World War II*, compiled by Mary Croft Pulley, The Dietz Press, Incorporated, Richmond, Virginia, 1949, p. xvii.

Luther of the Early Temperance Reformation. See Hewit, Nathaniel

Lutherans. See Carthage College

Lynchburg, Virginia

Because Lynchburg is situated in the foothills of the Blue Ridge Mountains it is called the *City of Hills* or the *Hill City*.[1]

[1] *A Book of Nicknames*, John Goff (Courier-Journal Job Printing Company, Louisville, Ky., 1892) p. 15.
South-west Virginia and the Valley, Historical and Biographical Illustrated (Published by A. D. Smith and Company, Roanoke, Va., Edwards and Broughton, Printers, Raleigh, N.C., 1892) p. 23.

Lynn, Benjamin

The *Daniel Boone of Southern Kentucky* and the *Hunter-preacher* were appellations given to Benjamin Lynn.

Like Daniel Boone, Benjamin Lynn was one of the early hunters in the pioneer settlements of southern Kentucky; therefore, he was nicknamed the *Daniel Boone of Southern Kentucky*.[1]

Because he was an active hunter and a preacher in the early settlements along Green River Valley, in Kentucky, about 1782, Lynn was known as the *Hunter-preacher*.[1]

[1] *Appleton's Cyclopaedia of American Biography*, ed. by James Grant Wilson and John Fiske (D. Appleton and Company, New York, 1888) vol. 4, p. 66.

Lynn, Massachusets

The nicknames, *the City of Soles* [1] and *The City of Shoes* [2] applied to Lynn, commemorate the fact that this city manufactures vast quantities of boots, shoes, cut leather, and machinery used in the production of shoes and leather goods.

[1] *Americanisms—Old and New*, John S. Farmer (Privately Printed by Thomas Poulter and Sons, London, 1889) p. 149.
[2] *Lynn and Surroundings*, Clarence W. Hobbs (Lewis and Winship, Lynn, Mass., 1886) p. 16.

Lynxes. See Southwestern College Tennessee

Lyons of America. See Paterson, N.J.

Lyss. See Grant, U. S.

M

Ma Ferguson. See Ferguson, M. A.

Maas, Melvin Joseph

Melvin Joseph Maas, a Minnesota business man and politician, was nicknamed the *Marine Aviator* [1] in the House of Representatives because he served in the Aviation Brigade of the United States Marine Corps from 1917 to 1918.

He was a Republican Representative from Minnesota to Congress from 1927 to 1933, and again from 1935 to 1939.

Melvin Joseph Maas was born at Duluth, Minn., on May 14, 1898.

[1] An interview with Captain Victor Hunt Harding, Secretary of the National Democratic Congress Reëlection Committee, Washingotn, D.C., April 10, 1939.

Mac the Unready. See McClellan, G. B.

McAdoo, William Gibbs

William Gibbs McAdoo, formerly a Senator from California, was nicknamed *Bill the Builder* [1] because of his part in the construction of the Hudson and Manhattan Railroad Company tunnels under the Hudson River. See also *McAdoo Tubes*.

McAdoo was called the *Crown Prince* [1] because while he was Secretary of the Treas-

McAdoo, W. G.—Continued

ury in Wilson's Cabinet he married Eleanor Randolph Wilson, the daughter of President Woodrow Wilson, on May 7, 1914.

The *Dancing Fool, Daddy Longlegs,* and the *World War Croesus,*[2] were applied to Senator McAdoo. The *Dancing Fool* originated in the fact that Senator McAdoo so frequently participated in public dances as a form of recreation. The fact that he was a tall man gave rise to *Daddy Longlegs.* The *World War Croesus* originated in the fact that McAdoo was the Secretary of the Treasury in President Woodrow Wilson's cabinet during World War I where he handled vast sums of money. He was a Senator from California from 1933 to 1939.

William Gibbs McAdoo was born near Marietta, Ga., on October 31, 1863, and died at Washington, D.C., on February 1, 1941.

[1] *The Commentator,* Published monthly at Concord, N.H., June 1937, p. 34, 37.
[2] An interview with Captain Victor Hunt Harding, Secretary of the National Democratic Congress Reëlection Committee, Washington, D.C., April 10, 1939.

McAdoo Tubes

The Hudson and Manhattan Railroad Company tunnels under the Hudson River connect New Jersey with downtown Manhattan. These tunnels have been called *McAdoo Tubes*[1] because William Gibbs McAdoo, President of the company, was greatly influential in securing the interest of J. P. Morgan and other financiers in the undertaking and in organizing stock companies to finance it. The tubes were constructed between 1902 and 1912 at a cost of approximately seventy million dollars.

[1] *The National Cyclopaedia of American Biography* (James T. White and Company, New York, 1924) current volume A, p. 35.

Macalester College

The athletic teams of Macalester College, at Saint Paul, Minn., are called the *Scots*[1] and the *Macs* because the college is a Scotch Presbyterian school.

[1] A communication from John C. Acheson, President of Macalester College, Saint Paul, Minn., December 10, 1935.

MacArthur, Douglas

Douglas MacArthur was nicknamed the *Beau Brummel of the Army,* the *Buck Private's Gary Cooper,* the *D'Artagnan of the A.E.F,* the *Disraeli of Chiefs of Staff,* the *Napoleon of Luzon,* and *The Magnificent.*

He was designated the *Magnificent*[1] by newspaper writers in February, 1942, because of the splendid manner in which he defended the Philippine Islands against the Japanese for twelve weeks following the attack on Pearl Harbor on December 7, 1941.

From 1935 to 1941, while as Field Marshal of the Philippines he was organizing and training a Filipino army, some Americans in Manila who deplored the necessity for defending the islands customarily referred to MacArthur as the *Napoleon of Luzon.* President Franklin Delano Roosevelt appointed him the Commanding General of the United States Armed Forces in the Far East on July 26, 1941.

During his early career as a soldier MacArthur was nicknamed the *Beau Brummel of the Army,*[3] the *Buck Private's Gary Cooper,* the *D'Artagnan of the A.E.F,* and the *Disraeli of Chiefs of Staff* because of his dashing manners and his elegant appearance.

MacArthur was born on January 26, 1880, at Milwaukee, Wis.

[1] *The Washington Post,* Washington, D.C., February 24, 1942, col. 4, p. 1.
[2] *Times-Herald,* Washington, D.C., February 23, 1942, col. 2, p. 1.
[3] *Life,* Chicago, Ill., December 8, 1941, p. 132.

McCabe, Charles Cardwell

Charles Cardwell McCabe was a Methodist Episcopalian minister and chaplain in the Union Army. In 1884 he became the Secretary of the Methodist Episcopal Missionary Society and in 1896 he was made a bishop. He had a voice of unusual resonance and a talent for leading congregational singing, which lead to the nicknames the *Singing Bishop, Singing Chaplain,* and *Singing Secretary.*[1]

Charles Cardwell McCabe was born at Athens, Ohio, on October 11, 1836, and died at New York City, on December 19, 1906.

[1] *The Life of Chaplain McCabe, Bishop of the Methodist Episcopal Church,* Frank Milton Bristol (Fleming H. Revell Company, New York and Chicago, 1908) p. 254-7, 358.

McCarl, John Raymond

John Raymond McCarl, former Comptroller General of the United States, was nicknamed the *Watchdog of the Treasury*[1] by newspapermen because he kept a strict audit on the money spent by the Federal

Government while he was Comptroller General of the United States from 1921 to 1935.

John Raymond McCarl was born at Des Moines, Iowa, on November 27, 1879, and died August 2, 1940.

[1] *Newsweek: The Magazine of News Significance,* Rockefeller Center, N.Y., January 24, 1938, p. 14.

McCarthy, Joseph Vincent

Joseph Vincent McCarthy, who was born at Germantown, Pa., on April 21, 1887, and who was a manager in major league baseball, was nicknamed *Marse Joe.*[1]

[1] *Who's Who in Major League Base Ball,* comp. by Harold (Speed) Johnson (Buxton Publishing Company. Chicago, 1933) p. 269.

McCauley, Mary Ludwig Hays

Captain Molly and *Molly Pitcher* are sobriquets which have been applied to Mrs. Mary Ludwig Hays McCauley.

The soldiers to whom Mrs. Mary Ludwig Hays McCauley (at that time Mrs. John Hays) carried water in a pitcher nicknamed her *Molly Pitcher.*[1] This nickname originated during the Battle of Monmouth in New Jersey, on June 28, 1778, where as usual she was engaged in carrying water to the soldiers. During this battle, her husband, John Hays, who had been firing a cannon, fell mortally wounded. Mrs. Hays took his place as cannoneer and has gone down in history as *Captain Molly* or *Molly Pitcher.*[2]

Mary Ludwig Hays McCauley was born probably at Carlisle, Pa., on October 13, 1744, and died there on January 27, 1823.

[1] *The Battle of Monmouth,* William S. Stryker, ed. by William Starr Myers (Princeton University Press, Princeton, N.J., 1927) p. 191-2.
The Germans in Colonial Times, Lucy Forney Bittinger (J. P. Lippincott Company, Philadelphia and London, 1901) p. 250-1.

[2] *The Essential Facts of American History,* Lawton B. Evans (Benjamin H. Sanborn and Company, New York and Boston, 1914) p. 214.

McClellan, George Brinton

Major General George Brinton McClellan was called the *General of the Mackerel Brigade, Little Corporal of Unsought Fields, Little Mac, Little Mac the Young Napoleon, Little Napoleon,* and *Mac the Unready.*

Even after his army was organized and equipped for war, McClellan hesitated in starting a campaign against the Confederates harassing the Federals on the outskirts of Washington, D.C., with only about a third as many men as McClellan. The northern

people clamored for action but McClellan continued to procrastinate. Because of this, he was called the *General of the Mackerel Brigade, The Little Corporal of Unsought fields,* and *Mac the Unready.*[1]

His soldiers called him *Little Mac*[2] because of his short, stocky physique.

On May 23, 1861, McClellan routed the Confederates from West Virginia, with only a small body of troops. His campaign was so successful that by June, West Virginia was completely isolated from Virginia and the Confederacy. McClellan's display of leadership in carrying out his campaign caused him to be nicknamed *Little Mac the Young Napoleon*[3] and *Little Napoleon.*

George Brinton McClellan was born at Philadelphia, Pa., on December 3, 1826, and died at Orange, N.J., on October 29, 1885.

[1] *The New Complete History of the United States of America,* Official Edition, John Clark Ridpath (The John Brothers Publishing Company, Cincinnati, Ohio, 1906) vol. 10, p. 4780.

[2] *History of the United States of America, under the Constitution,* James Schouler (Dodd, Mead and Company, New York, 1899) vol. 6, p. 133.

[3] *The Encyclopaedia Britannica,* Fourteenth Edition (Encyclopaedia Britannica, Inc., New York, 1929) vol. 14, p. 551.

McClintic, James V.

Rivet McClintic[1] is the nickname applied to former Representative James V. McClintic of Texas. This was given to him because, during the building of the dirigible *Akron,* he demanded that every rivet used be minutely examined and tested.

James V. McClintic was born at Bremond, Tex., on September 8, 1878, and was a Representative from Texas to Congress from 1915 to 1935.

[1] *The Washington Post Magazine,* Washington, D.C., March 4, 1934, p. 4.

McConnell, John Preston

Dr. John Preston McConnell, a Virginia educator and philosopher, was nicknamed *Eci*[1] while he was professor of History and Economics at Emory and Henry College from 1904 to 1913. This sobriquet was originated by the students at the college who recognized that Dr. McConnell was a master at teaching Economics and History.

He was nicknamed the *Serving Knight*[2] because of the diligent manner in which he served his state as teacher and college president.

McConnell, J. P.—Continued

Dr. John Preston McConnell was born in Scott County, and died at Radford, Virginia, on October 11, 1941.

[1] *Virginia Journal of Education* (Virginia Education Association, Richmond, Va., 1937) vol. 31, December, 1937, p. 116.

[2] *Virginia Journal of Education* (Virginia Education Association, Richmond, Va., 1941) vol. 35, November, 1941, p. 94.

McCue, William

William McCue was known in New Orleans, La., as *Captain Billy*,[1] because he was a kind and understanding leader in the civic, religious, and political life of the city.

He was born at New Orleans, La., on April 18, 1874, and died there on November 30, 1913.

[1] *Encyclopedia of American Biography: American Biography, a New Cyclopedia*, comp. under the editorial supervision of a notable advisory board (Published under the direction of The American Historical Society, Inc., New York, 1932) vol. 50, p. 375.

McDaniel, Ira C.

Ira C. McDaniel, a West Tennessee farmer and blooded-stock breeder, was nicknamed *Red Rat* because of his red hair and ruddy complexion. He was born at Troy, Tenn., on August 19, 1877, and died at Union City, Tenn., on January 25, 1954.

McDonald, Joseph Ewing

Joseph Ewing McDonald, an Indiana lawyer and politician, was nicknamed *Old Saddlebags*[1] because as a boy he had been apprenticed to a saddle and harness maker.

Joseph Ewing McDonald was born in Butler County, Ohio, on August 29, 1819, and died at Indianapolis, Ind., on June 21, 1891.

[1] *The National Cyclopedia of American Biography* (James T. White and Company, New York, 1909) vol. 11, p. 504.

McDougal, David Stockton

The appellation, the *American Devil*,[1] given to David Stockton McDougal, originated in the fact that, while the ship "Wyoming" in his command was cruising in Asiatic waters during the Civil War in a search for Confederate privateers, it engaged in an encounter in the straits of Shimoneseki, Japan, on July 16, 1863, with three hostile Japanese vessels which were aided by land batteries. McDougal practically demolished all three of the enemy's vessels and successfully braved the fire from the land batteries, his skillfulness, boldness, and

success in outwitting the Japanese, causing them to speak respectfully of him thereafter as the *American Devil*.

David Stockton McDougal was born at Chillicothe, Ohio, on September 27, 1809, and died at San Francisco, Calif., on August 7, 1882.

[1] *The National Cyclopedia of American Biography* (James T. White and Company, New York, 1906) vol. 13, p. 130.

Dictionary of American Biography (Charles Scribner's Sons, New York, 1933) vol. 12, p. 21.

McDowell, Joseph

Joseph McDowell, a legislator, was nicknamed *Pleasant Gardens Joe*[1] because he owned an estate called *Pleasant Gardens*, near Morganton, N.C. He was a Major in the Revolutionary Army; and a Representative from North Carolina to Congress from 1793 to 1795.

Joseph McDowell was born at Pleasant Gardens, near Morganton, N.C., on February 25, 1758, and died there on March 7, 1799.

[1] *Biographical Directory of the American Congress, 1774-1927; The Continental Congress, September 5, 1774, to October 21, 1788, and The Congress of the United States, from the First to the Sixty-ninth Congress, March 4, 1789, to March 3, 1927, Inclusive* (Government Printing Office, Washington, D.C., 1928) House Document number 783, vol. 16, p. 1261.

McDowell, Joseph

Because he lived at Quaker Meadows, N.C., Major General Joseph McDowell was nicknamed *Quaker Meadows Joe*[1] in order to distinguish him from a cousin Joseph McDowell who was called *Pleasant Gardens Joe*.

Major General McDowell participated in the expeditions against the Indians along the frontier of North Carolina and took part in the Revolutionary War. He was a Representative from North Carolina to Congress from 1797 to 1799.

Joseph McDowell was born at Winchester, Va., on February 25, 1756, and died near Morganton, N.C., on February 5, 1801.

[6] *Appleton's Cyclopedia of American Biography*, ed. by James Grant Wilson and John Fiske (D. Appleton and Company, New York, 1888) vol. 4, p. 109.

Biographical History of North Carolina from Colonial Times to the Present, Samuel A. Ashe and Stephen B. Weeks, Editors (Charles L. Van Noppen, Greensboro, N.C.) vol. 7, p. 307.

McFarland, Daniel

Daniel McFarland, an Ohio politician, was called *Black Dan*[1] because of his dark hair and eyes and very dark complexion.

Daniel McFarland was born at Baltimore, Md., on September 3, 1825, and died at Portsmouth, Ohio, on June 1, 1900.

[1] *A History of Scioto County, Ohio, together with a Pioneer Record of Southern Ohio,* Nelson W. Evans (Nelson W. Evans, Portsmouth, Ohio, 1903) p. 147.

McFarlane, William Doddridge

William Doddridge McFarlane, a Texas lawyer and politician, was nicknamed *Anti-McFarlane* [1] because he was so strongly opposed to the social and economic legislation proposed by the New Deal during the sessions of the Seventy-third through the Seventy-fifth Congresses. He was elected a Democratic Representative from Texas to Congress in 1933.

William Doddridge McFarlane was born at Greenwood, Ark., on July 17, 1894.

[1] An interview with Captain Victor Hunt Harding, Secretary of the National Democratic Congress Reelection Committee, Washington, D.C. April 10, 1939.

MacGahan, Januarius Aloysius

Januarius Aloysius MacGahan, a war correspondent, was nicknamed the *Liberator* [1] because his "Bulgarian Letters" concerning the bashi-bazouk massacre published in *The Daily News* of London, England, during July and August 1876, helped bring about the Russo-Turkish war which resulted in Bulgaria's gaining its independence.

Januarius Aloysius MacGahan was born in Perry County, Ohio, on June 12, 1844, and died at San Stefano, Turkey, on June 9, 1878.

[1] *Dictionary of American Biography under the Auspices of the American Council of Learned Societies,* ed. by Dumas Malone (Charles Scribner's Sons, New York, 1933) vol. 12, p. 46.

McGillicuddy, Cornelius

Cornelius McGillicuddy, a well-known manager of major league baseball, is widely known as *Connie Mack.* [1] He was president and manager of the *Philadelphia Athletics* team, before it was transferred to Kansas City in 1954.

Cornelius McGillicuddy was born at Brookfield, Mass., on December 23, 1862.

[1] *Who's Who in The American League,* 1935 Edition, Harold (Speed) Johnson (B. E. Callahan, Chicago, 1935) p. 56.

McGroarty, John Steven

John Steven McGroarty, a politician, was called the *Poet Laureate of California* and the *Sage of the Verduga Hills.* [1] He was designated the *Poet Laureate of California* because he wrote many poems dealing with

California and a history of California. He was elected Poet Laureate of California by the Legislature of California in 1933. He was nicknamed the *Sage of the Verduga Hills* because he formerly wrote a column in *The Los Angeles Times* entitled "From the Green Verduga Hills." He was a Democratic Representative from California to Congress from 1935 to 1943.

John Steven McGroarty was born in Luzerne County, Pa., on August 20, 1862, and died August 7, 1944, in Los Angeles.

[1] An interview with Captain Victor Hunt Harding, Secretary of the National Democratic Congress Reelection Committee, Washington, D.C., April 10, 1939.

Machiavellian Belshazzar. See Van Buren, Martin

Mackenzie, Kenneth

Kenneth Mackenzie, a fur trader, was nicknamed *King of the Missouri, Emperor Mackenzie,* and *Emperor of the West* [1] because he had trading posts along the Upper Missouri, Yellowstone, Bighorn, Marais, and Mississippi rivers. Fort Union on the Mississippi River was one of the outstanding trading posts of this region.

Kenneth Mackenzie was born in the shire of Ross and Cromarthy in Scotland, on April 15, 1779, and died at St. Louis, Mo., on April 26, 1861.

[1] *Dictionary American Biography under the Auspices of the American Council of Learned Societies,* ed. by Dumas Malone (Charles Scribner's Sons, New York, 1933) vol. 12, p. 95.

McKinley, William

William McKinley was called the *Idol of Ohio, The Napoleon of Protection, Prosperity's Advance Agent,* and *The Stockingfoot Orator.*

Because William McKinley was practically idolized by the people in his state he was called the *Idol of Ohio.* [1]

Writers on the staff of *The New York Sun* nicknamed McKinley the *Napoleon of Protection.* [2] While he was a Representative from Ohio to Congress from 1885 to 1891 he sponsored a noted protective tariff bill, commonly known as the McKinley Bill, which was passed by Congress in 1890.

William McKinley was acclaimed as *Prosperity's Advance Agent* [3] because a period of nationwide prosperity followed close upon his election. The nickname is said to have been used first by Marcus Alonzo Han-

McKinley, William—Continued

na, the Republican presidential campaign manager in 1896, when McKinley was the candidate.

The *Stocking-foot Orator* [4] was applied to William McKinley while he was a student at Polland Seminary, in Mahoning County, Ohio. The mud was so deep in the town of Polland that members of McKinley's debating society removed their shoes and debated in their stocking feet in order to keep the mud off of the carpet.

William McKinley, the twenty-fifth President of the United States, was born at Niles, Ohio, on January 29, 1843. He was assassinated by Leon Czolgosz, an anarchist, at the Pan American Exposition in Buffalo, N.Y., on September 6, 1901, and died at Buffalo, on September 14.

[1] *Contemporary American Biography: Biographical Sketches of Representative Men of the Day, Representatives of Modern Thought and Progress, of the Pulpit, the Press, the Bench and Bar, of Legislation, Invention, and the Great Industrial Interests of the Country* (Atlantic Publishing and Engraving Company, New York, 1899) vol. 2, p. 123.
[2] *U.S. "Snap Shots": An Independent, National, and Memorial Encyclopedia* . . . , Oliver McKee (A. M. Thayer and Company, Boston, 1892) p. 243.
[3] *Barne's Popular History of the United States of America, from Prehistoric America to the Present Time,* Revised to Date, Joel Dorman Steele and Esther Baker Steele (A. L. Burt Company, New York, 1914) p. 667.
[4] *The Boyhoods of the Presidents,* Bessie White Smith (Lothrop, Lee and Shepard Company, Boston, 1929) p. 226, 232-3.

McLellan, Isaac

Isaac McLellan, a New England poet, was nicknamed the *Poet Sportsman* [1] because of his fondness for out-door recreations and because many of his poems deal with field sports.

Isaac McLellan was born at Portland, Me., on May 21, 1806, and died at Greenport on Long Island, N.Y., on August 20, 1899.

[1] *Appleton's Cyclopaedia of American Biography,* ed. by James Grant Wilson and John Fiske (D. Appleton and Company, New York, 1894) vol. 4, p. 145.

Maclure, William

William Maclure was called the *Father of American Geology* [1] because of his extensive research in the field of geology and his generosity in contributing the results of his work to his adopted country.

He was born in Scotland, in 1763, and came to the United States in about 1805 to make a geological survey of this country.

[1] "Our Foreigners, a Chronicle of Americans in the Making" by Samuel P. Orth, in *The Chronicles of America Series,* Allen Johnson, Editor (Yale University Press, New Haven, Conn., 1920) p. 95.
The Encyclopedia Americana (Americana Corporation, New York and Chicago, 1927) vol. 18, p. 81.

A Memoir of William Maclure, Esquire, Late President of the Academy of Natural Sciences of Philadelphia, Second Edition, Samuel George Morton, read July 1, 1841, and published by direction of the Academy (Merrihew and Thompson, Philadelphia, 1844) p. 11, 12, 23.

McManus, George

George McManus, a comic cartoonist, has been called *Jiggs McManus* [1] because for over forty years he has supplied American daily newspapers with the comic strip, *Bringing up Father,* in which Maggie and Jiggs have amused the American people.

George McManus was born at St. Louis, Mo., on January 23, 1884, and died in Santa Monica, Calif., on October 22, 1954.

[1] *Washington Herald,* Washington, D.C., January 25, 1938, col. 1, p. 10.
Newsweek. November 1, 1954. p. 70.

McMillin, Benton

Benton McMillin, Governor of Tennessee, was nicknamed the *Democratic War Horse,* the *Democratic War Horse of Tennessee,* the *Grandest Roman of them all* and the *Noblest Roman of them all.*

He was called the *Democratic War Horse* [1] and the *Democratic War Horse of Tennessee* because he took an active part in the Democratic campaigns in Tennessee and elsewhere, speaking for Democratic candidates. His political allies called him the *Grandest Roman of them all* [2] and the *Noblest Roman of them all* because he advocated the principles of the Democratic party and democratic control of state and national affairs. The latter nickname is from a line spoken in Shakespeare's *Julius Caesar* in allusion to the integrity and patriotism of Brutus. McMillin attended every Democratic National Convention from 1876 to 1932 except the one which met at St. Louis, Mo., in 1916.

Benton McMillin was born in Monroe County, Ky., on September 11, 1845, and died at Nashville, Tenn., on January 8, 1933.

[1] *The Nashville Banner,* Nashville, Tenn., January 9, 1933, col. 2, p. 2.
[2] *The Nashville Tennesseean,* Nashville, Tenn., January 9, 1933, col. 8, p. 1.

McNair, Donald Eric

Donald Eric McNair, who was born at Meridian, Miss., on April 12, 1910, and who played infield in major-league baseball, was nicknamed *Rabbit.* [1]

[1] *Who's Who in Major League Base Ball,* comp. by Harold (Speed) Johnson (Buxton Publishing Company, Chicago, 1933) p. 274.

McNary, Charles Linza

Charles Linza McNary, an Oregon lawyer and politician, was nicknamed *Wise Charley* [1] in the United States Senate because he was an astute political leader. He was a Senator from Oregon to Congress from 1917 to 1943.

Charles Linza McNary was born on a farm near Salem, Ore., June 12, 1874, and died February 25, 1944.

[1] An interview with Captain Victor Hunt Harding, Secretary of the National Democratic Congress Reelection Committee, Washington, D.C., April 10, 1939.

McNish, George

The *Father of Presbyterianism in the State of New York* [1] was an appellation given to George McNish because he championed the cause of Presbyterianism in New York and in the neighboring states while he was pastor of the Presbyterian Church at Jamaica, N.Y., from 1711 until about 1721. He organized the first Presbytery in the state of New York.

George McNish was born either in Ireland or Scotland, about 1660, and died at Newton, N.J., on March 10, 1722.

[1] *Appleton's Cyclopaedia of American Biography*, ed. by James Grant Wilson and John Fiske (D. Appleton and Company, New York, 1888) vol. 4, p. 155.

Macon, Nathaniel

The *Father of the House* [1] was a sobriquet applied to Nathaniel Macon because he was a member of Congress from 1791 to 1828. He was a Representative from North Carolina from 1791 to 1815, serving as Speaker of the House from 1801 to 1806, and was Senator from North Carolina from 1815 to 1828. His services for over three decades caused him to be looked upon as the patriarch of Congress.

Nathaniel Macon was born at Macon Manor, N.C., on December 17, 1758, and died at Buck Springs, N.C., on June 29, 1837.

[1] *The National Cyclopaedia of American Biography* (James T. White and Company, New York, 1907) vol. 5, p. 176.

Macon, Georgia

Macon is known as the *Heart of Georgia* [1] because it is located near the center of the state.

[1] *The Encyclopedia Americana* (Americana Corporation, New York and Chicago, 1927) vol. 18, p. 87.

Macs. See Macalester College

Mad Anne. See Bailey, A. H. T.

Mad Anthony. See Wayne, Anthony

Mad Hatters. See Danbury Trojans Football Club

Mad Jack. See Percival, John

Mad Magicians. See Colgate University

Mad Poet. See Clarke, McDonald

Mad Poet of New York. See Clarke, McDonald

Mad Tom. See Sherman, W. T.

Madison, Dorothy Payne Todd

Dolly Madison, the *Dowager* or the *Queen Dowager,* the *Nation's Hostess, Quaker Dolly,* and *Queen Dolly* are nicknames by which Mrs. Dorothy Payne Todd Madison has been called.

She was generally spoken of as *Dolly Madison* [1] instead of Dorothy Madison or Mrs. James Madison.

When she returned to Washington, D.C., in 1837, after the death of her husband, Mrs. James Madison came to be known as the *Dowager* [2] or the *Queen Dowager* [3] because she was well past middle age, and was a charming, dignified hostess, and a great favorite with the society people of Washington.

Mrs. James Madison has been nicknamed the *Nation's Hostess* [4] and *Queen Dolly* [2] because she had such charming manners as the hostess of the White House, and because she so graciously presided over the numerous balls, dinners, receptions, and other social functions given while her husband was President of the United States from 1809 to 1817.

Because her parents, John and Mary Coles Payne, were Quakers, Mrs. Madison was called *Quaker Dolly.* [2]

Dorothy Payne Todd (Mrs. James Madison) was born in what is now Guilford County, in North Carolina, on May 20, 1772, and died at Washington, D.C., on July 12, 1849.

[1] *The American People and Nation*, Rolla M. Tryon and Charles R. Lingley (Ginn and Company, New York and Boston, 1932) p. 276.

Madison, D. P. T.—Continued

[2] *Some American Ladies: Seven Informal Biographies, Martha Washington, Abigail Adams, Dolly Madison, Elizabeth Monroe, Louisa Adams, Rachel Jackson, Peggy Eaton*, Meade Minnegerode (G. P. Putnam's Sons, New York, 1926) p. 100, 108, 114, 130.

[3] *Women of Colonial and Revolutionary Times: Dolly Madison*, Maude Wilder Goodwin (Charles Scribner's Sons, New York, 1896) p. 261.

[4] *Dolly Madison, the Nation's Hostess*, Elizabeth Lippincott Dean (Lothrop, Lee and Shepard Company, Boston, 1928) p. 13, 115.

Madison, James

The nicknames, the *Father of the Constitution* and the *Sage of Montpelier* were applied to James Madison.

He is widely known as the *Father of the Constitution* [1] because of the prominent part he took in framing and securing the adoption of the Constitution of the United States, at the Constitutional Convention at Philadelphia, Pa., on May 25, 1787.

The *Sage of Montpelier* [2] was applied to James Madison because he spent the latter part of his life at Montpelier, Vt., and because of his mature judgment and learning.

James Madison, who was born at Port Conway, Va., on March 16, 1751, and who died at Montpelier, Vt., on June 28, 1836, was the fourth President of the United States.

[1] *History of the United States*, Charles A. Beard and Mary R. Beard (The Macmillan Company, New York, 1921) p. 145.

"James Madison" by Sydney Howard Gay, in *American Statesmen Series*, ed. by John T. Morse, Junior (Houghton Mifflin and Company, Boston, 1892) p. 88.

[2] *A Book of Nicknames*, John Goff (Courier-Journal Job Printing Company, Louisville, Ky., 1892) p. 23.

Madison, Wisconsin

Madison is designated the *Four Lake City* [1] because it is located in close proximity to four beautiful lakes, Lake Kegonsa, Lake Waubesa, Lake Monona, and Lake Mendota.

[1] *A Book of Nicknames*, John Goff (Courier-Journal Job Printing Company, Louisville, Ky., 1892) p. 16.

History of Madison, Dane County and Surroundings. . . (William J. Park and Company, Madison, Wis., 1877) p. 32-3.

Madison, Our Home: the City of Madison, the Capital of Wisconsin—Seat of the State University—the County Seat of Dane County, Frank A. Gilmore (Issued and copyrighted by the Madison Board of Commerce, Blied Printing Company, Madison, Wis., 1916) p. 48.

Madison's Night Caps

Madison's Night Caps [1] was a nickname given to the tarbarrels used as a protective covering for the wooden masts of American vessels which lay idle in New York harbor in the spring of 1812, because of the strained relations of the United States with France and England, and because of the embargo imposed by Congress on American vessels in port and coming in. The embargo began on April 1, 1812, during President James Madison's administration, and continued for sixty days.

[1] *Women of Colonial and Revolutionary Times: Dolly Madison*, Maud Wilder Goodwin (Charles Scribner's Sons, New York, 1896) p. 151.

"American Statesmen: James Madison" by Sydney Howard Gay, in *American Statesmen* ed. by John T. Morse, Junior (Houghton Mifflin and Company, Boston and New York, 1898) p. 295.

Madonna of Hall-Moody. See Hall, M. L.

Mae West

Actress Mae West (q.v.) has lent her name to several items because of their imagined resemblance to her famed hourglass figure:

(1) An inflatable life-preserver developed during World War II and nicknamed a *Mae West* [1] by fliers in the RAF.

(2) A figure-eight-shaped cruller referred to as a *Mae West* in lunch counters and diners.

[1] *The Language of World War II*, comp. by A. Marjorie Taylor (The H. W. Wilson Company, New York, 1948) p. 127.

Maggot Camp

After the First Battle of Bull Run, near Manassas, Va., on July 21, 1861, the Confederate forces encamped along the banks of the Bull Run called it *Maggot Camp,* because there had been no chance to bury the dead for several days and there were no facilities for the disposal of refuse.

[1] *Stonewall*, Julia Davis Adams (E. P. Dutton and Company, Inc., New York, 1931) p. 86.

Magic City. See Anniston, Ala.; Billings, Mont.; Birmingham, Ala.; Miami, Fla.

Magic City of the South. See Birmingham, Ala.

Magic Mascot of the Plains. See Wichita, Kans.

Magic Valley

The delta region of the Rio Grande Valley in southern Texas is called the *Magic Valley* [1] because of the rapid development of its industries, and its prospects for continued prosperity and expansion.

[1] *The Story of Texas*, Joseph L. Clark (Row, Peterson and Company, New York, Philadelphia, and San Francisco, 1933) p. 306.

Magnetic Man. See Blaine, J. G.

Magnetic Statesman. See Blaine, J. G.

Magnificent. See MacArthur, Douglas; Maretzek, Max

Magnolia City. See Houston, Tex.

Magnolia State. See Mississippi

Mahaffey, Leroy

Probably because he has large brown eyes, *Pop-eye* [1] is the sobriquet given to Leroy Mahaffey, who was born at Belton, S.C., on February 9, 1904, and who pitched in major-league baseball.

[1] *Who's Who in Major League Base Ball*, comp. by Harold (Speed) Johnson (Buxton Publishing Company, Chicago, 1933) p. 276.

Mahone, William

The *Hero of the Crater* [1] came to be applied to William Mahone because during the Battle of the Petersburg Crater, in Virginia on July 30, 1864, he manifested unusual bravery and daring.

William Mahone was born near Monroe, Va., on December 1, 1826, and died at Washington, D.C., on October 8, 1895.

[1] *The National Cyclopaedia of American Biography* (James T. White and Company, New York, 1907) vol. 5, p. 12.

Main Street of America

The Federal Highway U.S.66 is popularly called the *Main Street of America* [1] because it is the most direct automobile highway between Chicago, Ill. and Los Angeles, Calif., and passes through some of the most outstanding agricultural and scenic sections of Illinois, Missouri, Oklahoma, New Mexico, Arizona, and California. This highway provides an east-to-west route about two hundred miles shorter than any other highway.

[1] *The World Book Encyclopedia* (W. F. Quarrie and Company, Chicago, 1934) vol. 11, p. 4232-3.

Maine

The following are the nicknames of Maine: the *Border State*, the *Easternmost State of the Union*, the *Lumber State*, the *Old Dirigo State*, the *Pine Tree State*, the *Polar Star State*, and *The Switzerland of America*.

Maine is called the *Border State* because for many miles it borders on Canada. It is called the *Easternmost State* [1] of the Union because all of the other states lie west of Maine.

The *Lumber State* [2] was applied to Maine because it is still one of the twenty-two states in the Union which produces the bulk of the lumber for the United States.

According to tradition, Maine came to be called the *Old Dirigo State* because the state motto is *Dirigo,* meaning I guide or direct.

Maine is named the *Pine Tree State* [3, 4] because extensive pine forests cover its northern and central parts, and because the pine tree is one of the symbols on the state seal.

Maine is widely known as the *Switzerland of America* [5] because of its mountainous scenery and abundant snowfalls.

Because Maine is the most northern state of the Union, and because the state coat of arms pictures the North Star, it is called the *Polar Star State.*[6]

[1] *Compton's Pictured Encyclopedia* (F. E. Compton and Company, 1947) vol. 9, p. 37.

[2] *Americanisms: The English of the New World,* M. Schele De Vere (Charles Scribner and Company, New York, 1872) p. 660.

[3] *A New Dictionary of Americanisms,* Sylva Clapin (Louis Weiss and Company, New York, 1903) p. 308.

[4] *King's Handbook of the United States,* planned and ed. by Moses King, text by M. F. Sweetser (Moses King Corporation, Buffalo, N.Y., 1891) p. 312.

[5] *Maine, Resources, Attractions, and Its People: A History,* Harrie Badger Coe, Editor The Lewis Historical Publishing Company, Inc., New York, 1928) vol. 1, p. 6.

[6] *Heraldry in America,* Eugene Zieber (Department of Heraldry of The Bailey, Banks and Biddle Company, Philadelphia, 1895) p. 134.

Maine Inhabitants

The Maine folk are commonly known as *Foxes, Lumbermen,* and *Pine Trees.* Regarding the origin of the first nickname, Malcolm Townsend says: "The lives of many of its people being passed in the woods, together with the abundance of foxes, suggested the local application." [1] The state of Maine is called the *Pine Tree State* and the *Lumber State* and from these nicknames the people have come to be called *Pine Trees* and *Lumbermen.*

[1] *U.S.: An Index to the United States of America,* comp. by Malcolm Townsend (D. Lothrop and Company, Boston, 1890) p. 76.

Maize and Blues. See Carleton College

Majorettes. See Millsaps College

Majors. See Millsaps College

Makemie, Francis

The *Apostle of Accomac* and the *Saint Francis of Presbyterianism* are names which have been applied to Francis Makemie.

Because of his religious activities while living in Accomac County, Va., Francis Makemie was known as the *Apostle of Accomac.*[1]

He has been called the *Saint Francis of Presbyterianism*[2] because he was a pioneer of Presbyterians in the United States. He went about all over the southern states preaching and teaching Presbyterian doctrines, and suffered greatly on account of his preaching and teaching, even being imprisoned as a result of his religious activities.

Francis Makemie was born in Ireland, in 1658, and died in Accomac County, Va., in 1708.

[1] *The National Cyclopaedia of American Biography* (James T. White and Company, New York, 1909) vol. 11, p. 384.
[2] *The Hall of Fame, being the Official Book Authorized by the New York University Senate as a Statement of the Origin and Constitution of the Hall of Fame, and of Its History up to the Close of the Year 1900,* Henry Mitchell MacCracken (G. P. Putnam's Sons, New York and London, 1901) p. 18.

Mallinckrodt, Edward

Edward Mallinckrodt, a manufacturer of chemicals, was called the *Ammonia King*[1] by the newsmen of his time because as head of the National Ammonia Company he controlled the international production of ammonia. He had been a pioneer manufacturer of chemicals since 1867, and founded the National Ammonia Company in St. Louis, Mo., in 1889.

Edward Mallinckrodt was born near St. Louis, Mo., on January 21, 1845, and died at St. Louis, Mo., on February 1, 1928.

[1] *Dictionary of American Biography under the Auspices of the American Council of Learned Societies,* ed. by Dumas Malone (Charles Scribner's Sons, New York, 1933) vol. 12, p. 224.

Mallon, Mary

Mary Mallon, an Irish-American cook, was nicknamed *Typhoid Mary*[1] because the medical authorities discovered that her body was a breeding ground for typhoid germs although she herself was immune to them. She was the first person in America who was known to be a typhoid carrier. She is said to have been the source of fifty-one cases of typhoid fever.

Physicians discovered that she was a carrier of typhoid germs in 1904 when an epidemic of typhoid fever in Oyster Bay, N.Y., and adjacent towns was traced to the homes where Mary Mallon had been employed as cook. In 1907 the New York Health Department found her, and, in order to prevent her from spreading the diseases, they isolated her on North Brother Island, in the North River in New York Harbor. She remained in isolation there until her death in 1938 except for a period from 1910 to 1915, when she was released on condition that she would not secure work where she would handle foods. When, in 1915, the health authorities found Mary cooking in a sanitorium at Newfoundland, N.Y., where twenty-five employees were stricken with typhoid fever, she was again committed to North Brother Island until she died at the age of sixty-eight.

[1] *The New York Times,* New York, November 12, 1938, col. 7, p. L+ 17.

Malone, Percy Lay

Percy Lay Malone has been given the nicknames the *Black Knight of the Border* and *Pat.*

While he served at Douglas, Ariz., as a cavalryman in the United States Army, he was nicknamed the *Black Knight of the Border*[1] because he had black hair and patrolled the border-line between the United States and Mexico.

Pat,[2] a popular nickname of Percy Lay Malone, is a corruption of his given name.

Percy Lay Malone was born at Altoona, Pa., on September 26, 1903, and pitched in major-league baseball.

[1] *Who's Who in Major League Base Ball,* comp. by Harold (Speed) Johnson (Buxton Publishing Company, Chicago, 1933) p. 277.

Mamma's Pets

During the Civil War, the newly recruited soldiers, upon their arrival at the camps of the veteran soldiers, were called *Mamma's Pets* and *Baby Boys*[1] because of their youthfulness, inexperience and recent departure from home.

[1] *Dedication of the New York State Monument on the Battlefield of Antietam,* New York State Monuments Commission for the Battlefields of Gettysburg, Chattanooga and Antietam (J. B. Lyon Company, Albany, N.Y., 1923) p. 80.

Man from Maine. See Blaine, J. G.

Man in the Iron Mask. See Moody, W. V.

Man of a Thousand Faces. See Chaney, Lon

Man of Destiny. See Cleveland, Grover

Man of Great Heart. See Hoover, H. C.

Man of the People. See Henry, Patrick; Jefferson, Thomas; Lincoln, Abraham

Man of the Town Meeting. See Adams, Samuel

Man on Horseback. See Roosevelt, Theodore

Man to Whom Hall-Moody Owes Most. See Penick, I. N.

Man Who Can Say Anything and Make Everybody Like it. See Rogers, Will

Man With the Sling. See Randolph (of Roanoke), John

Manassa Mauler. See Dempsey, W. H.

Manchester, New Hampshire

Manchester has been called the *Queen City of the Merrimac Valley* [1] because of its commanding location on the Merrimac River at the mouth of the Piscataqua River overlooking a large area on the Merrimac River valley, its national importance as the center of great cotton and woolen manufacturing, and its attractive parks and public buildings.

[1] *New Hampshire, Resources, Attractions, and Its People, a History,* Hobart Pillsbury (The Lewis Historical Publishing Company, Inc., New York, 1927) vol. 4, p. 1138.

Manchester of America. See Lowell, Mass.

Mancuso, August Rodney

August Rodney Mancuso, who was born at Galveston, Tex., on December 5, 1905, and who was a catcher in major-league baseball, was popularly known as *Blackie* [1] probably because of his black hair.

[1] *Who's Who in Major League Base Ball,* comp. by Harold (Speed) Johnson (Buxton Publishing Company, Chicago, 1933) p. 278.

Manders, Jack

Jack Manders, who played right halfback in national-league football, was nicknamed *Automatic* [1] in 1934 by a sports writer of *The Chicago Evening American,* because of his consistent field goal kicking.

He was born at Milbank, S.D., on January 13, 1909.

[1] A communication from George S. Halas, President-treasurer of The Chicago Bears Football Club, Inc., Chicago, March 21, 1939.

Mangum, Leo Allan

Blacky [1] is the appellation given to Leo Allan Mangum, who was born at Durham, N.C., on May 24, 1900, and who pitched in major league baseball.

[1] *Who's Who in Major League Base Ball,* comp. by Harold (Speed) Johnson (Buxton Publishing Company, Chicago, 1933) p. 279.

Manhattan College

The teams of Manhattan College at New York City, were called *Jaspers* [1] by the students and alumni of the college in honor of the Reverend Brother Jasper who was Athletic Director and Prefect of Studies of the College.

[1] A communication from Reverend Brother Anselm, F. S. C., Director of Athletics at Manhattan College, New York City, June 15, 1935.

Manila, Philippine Islands

Manila, the capital of the Philippine Islands, has been nicknamed the *Pearl of the Orient* [1] because of the beauty of the city and the harbor.

[1] *The Nashville Tennesseean,* Nashville, Tenn., January 3, 1942, col. 7, p. 1.

Manion, Clyde Jennings

The nickname *Pete* [1] has been applied to Clyde Jennings Manion, who was born at St. Louis, Mo., on October 30, 1896, and who was a catcher in major league baseball.

[1] *Who's Who in Major League Base Ball,* comp. by Harold (Speed) Johnson (Buxton Publishing Company, Chicago, 1933) p. 280.

Manning's Folly

The home of Robert Manning, the uncle of Nathaniel Hawthorne, at Raymond, Me., was nicknamed *Manning's Folly* [1] because it was a showy and pretentious mansion compared with the other houses in the village.

[1] *The Story of the Hall of Fame, Including the Lives and Portraits of the Elect and of Those Who Barely Missed Election, Also a List of America's Most Eligible Women,* Louis Albert Banks (The Christian Herald, New York, 1902) p. 213.

Mansfield of the Screen. See Walthall, H. B.

Manufacturing and Industrial Metropolis of the Southeast. See Atlanta, Ga.

Manush, Henry Emmett

Henry Emmett Manush, who was born at Tuscombia, Ala., on July 20, 1901, and who played outfield in major-league baseball, was nicknamed *Heinie*[1] or *Heinrich* in recognition of his German descent. Manush is now a coach in the major leagues.

[1] *Who's Who in Major League Base Ball,* comp. by Harold (Speed) Johnson (Buxton Publishing Company, Chicago, 1933) p. 281.

Many-sided Franklin. See Franklin, Benjamin

Maramen. See New York Football Giants, Inc.

Maranville, Walter James Vincent

Because he was a swift runner and a small sprightly man, *Rabbit*[1] was the nickname of Walter James Vincent Maranville, who played shortstop and second base for twenty-three years in major-league baseball.

The *Rabbit* stood five feet four inches tall and never weighed more than 150 pounds, but he played on long after his huskier contemporaries had retired. He was an outstanding base-runner and stole 291 bases in the majors. He endeared himself to followers of the national pastime throughout his career.

Walter Maranville was born in Springfield, Mass., on November 11, 1891, and died in New York City, on January 5, 1954.

[1] *Who's Who in Major League Base Ball,* comp. by Harold (Speed) Johnson (Buxton Publishing Company, Chicago, 1933) p. 282.
New York *Times,* January 6, 1954. p. 46.

Marberry, Fred

Firpo[1] is the nickname given to Fred Marberry because like Louis Firpo, the prize fighter, he is a large man and weighs over two hundred pounds.

Fred Marberry was born at Streetman, Tex., on November 30, 1899, and pitched in major-league baseball.

[1] *Who's Who in Major League Base Ball,* comp. by Harold (Speed) Johnson (Buxton Publishing Company, Chicago, 1933) p. 283.

Marblehead Turkey

In the vicinity of Marblehead, Mass., cod fish is such a common food commodity that the inhabitants refer to it as *Marblehead Turkey* in the same sense that elsewhere cheese is dubbed Welsh rabbit.

[1] *Dictionary of Americanisms,* Fourth Edition, John Russell Bartlett (Little, Brown and Company, Boston, 1877) p. 383.

Marcantonio, Vito

Vito Marcantonio, a lawyer and politician, was nicknamed the *Firebrand*[1] in the House of Representatives because he was quickly aroused, particularly in support of labor bills introduced into Congress. He was elected as an American Labor Party Representative from New York to Congress in 1935.

Vito Marcantonio was born at New York City on December 10, 1902 and died in New York City, August 9, 1954.

[1] An interview with Captain Victor Hunt Harding, Secretary of the National Democratic Congress Reelection Committee, Washington, D.C., April 10, 1939.

March King. See Sousa, J. P.

Marcy, Oliver

The *Methodist Agassiz*[1] is the name applied to Oliver Marcy. He was a loyal and devoted member of the Methodist Church. He was also a learned scientist particularly interested in zoölogy, botany, geology, and anthropology and was a beloved and inspiring teacher.

Louis Agassiz, a nineteenth century naturalist was renowned for his original contributions to science and his success in awakening interest in the natural sciences.

Oliver Marcy was born at Colerain, Mass., on February 13, 1820, and died at Evanston, Ill., on March 19, 1899.

[1] *The National Cyclopaedia of American Biography* (James T. White and Company, New York, 1906) vol. 13, p. 536.

Margaret the Orphan's Friend. See Gaffney, Margaret

Marietta College

The teams of Marietta College, at Marietta, Ohio, were nicknamed the *Pioneers*[1] because the city of Marietta and the college were founded by pioneers.

[1] A communication from R. D. Pinkerton, Financial Secretary of Marietta College, Marietta, Ohio, June 11, 1935.

Marine Aviator. See Maas, M. J.

Marine Bob. See Mouton, R. L.

Marine Division. See Third Infantry of World War II

Mariners. See Long Island University

Marion, Francis
The *Bayard of the South,* the *Old Swamp Fox,* and the *Swamp Fox of South Carolina* are nicknames of Francis Marion.

Brigadier General Marion was nicknamed the *Bayard of the South* [1] because he did much skillful and effective fighting with small bands of troops in and around South Carolina and resembled in courage and daring, Pierre du Terrail, Chevalier de Bayard, a brave and fearless French soldier of the sixteenth century.

Banaster Tarleton, a British general in the Revolutionary War, is credited with nicknaming Marion the *Old Swamp Fox* [2] or the *Swamp Fox of South Carolina* because he was wily and frequently escaped well-laid traps of the British forces by making his way across the swampy lands of the Carolinas.

Francis Marion was born at Winyah, S.C., in 1732, and died at Pond Bluff, S.C., on February 27, 1795.

[1] *Barnes' Popular History of the United States of America, from Prehistoric America to the Present Time,* Revised to Date, Joel Dorman Steele and Esther Baker Steele (A. L. Burt Company, New York, 1914) p. 287.
[2] *The Story of the Revolution,* Henry Cabot Lodge (Charles Scribner's Sons, New York, 1898) vol. 2, p. 45.
The American People and Nation, Rolla M. Tryon and Charles R. Lingley (Ginn and Company, New York and Boston, 1929) p. 206.

Marion Institute
The athletic teams of Marion Institute, at Marion, Ala., are called *Fighting Cadets* and the *Marion Tigers.* The *Fighting Cadets* [1] was applied to the teams by sports editors because of the spirit and ability displayed in athletic contests. Prior to 1915 they had been called the *Marion Tigers.*

[1] A communication from Captain T. H. Williams, Publicity Director at Marion Institute, Marion, Ala., November 18, 1935.

Marion of the Mexican Army. See Lane, Joseph

Marion Tigers. See Marion Institute

Market Street, San Francisco, Calif. See Path of Gold

Markle, George Busher
About 1858 George Busher Markle invented a machine, commonly known as a *breaker,* for crushing coal or rock, used extensively in the mining of anthracite. Consequently he was nicknamed the *Father of the Breaker.* [1] Markle whittled the model for the device from a piece of wood with his pocket-knife.

George Busher Markle was born at Milton, Pa., on July 1, 1827, and died at Hazelton, Pa., on August 18, 1888.

[1] *The National Cyclopaedia of American Biography* (James T. White and Company, New York, 1897) vol. 7, p. 175.

Marland, Ernest Whitworth
Ernest Whitworth Marland was nicknamed *Hot Oil Marland* [1] because he raised a great deal of controversy regarding an oil bill that came up in Congress while he was a Representative from Oklahoma to Congress between 1933 and 1935.

Ernest Whitworth Marland was born at Pittsburgh, Pa., on May 8, 1874.

[1] *The Washington Post Magazine,* Washington, D.C., March 4, 1934, p. 4.

Maroons. See Roanoke College; University of Chicago

Marquard, Richard W.
Richard W. Marquard, who was born at Cleveland, Ohio, on May 22, 1889, and who coached the *Atlanta Crackers* baseball team in 1932, was nicknamed *Rube.* [1]

[1] *Who's Who in Major League Base Ball,* comp. by Harold (Speed) Johnson (Buxton Publishing Company, Chicago, 1933) p. 471.

Marquette, Michigan
Marquette is called the *Queen City of Lake Superior* [1] because it is excellently located on Lake Superior for lake and inland trade and transportation and is a thriving and attractive city.

[1] *A History of the Northern Peninsula of Michigan and Its People, Its Mining and Agricultural Industries,* Alvah L. Sawyer (The Lewis Publishing Company, Chicago, 1911) vol. 1, p. 415.

Marquette University
The *Golden Avalanches* [1] and the *Hilltoppers* [1] are the popular appellations given to the teams of Marquette University, at Milwaukee, Wis. The latter nickname is applied to the basketball and track squads. The *Golden Avalanches* was applied to the football squads in 1924, after Marquette

Marquette University—Continued
had defeated Annapolis twenty-one to three
in 1924. The sports writer, Jimmy Powers,
wrote an account of how the "gold-clad
team swept down and over everything in its
path" like an golden avalanche.

[1] A letter from Edmund S. Carpenter, Director of the
News Bureau at Marquette University, Milwaukee, Wis.,
June 14, 1935.

*Marrying   Justice   of   Worcester
County.* See Davis, W. A.

Marse Henry. See Watterson, Henry

Marse Joe. See McCarthy, J. V.

*Marseillaise   of   the   Unemotional
Yankee*
The Battle Hymn of the Republic, written by Julia Ward Howe, in 1861, is frequently called *The Marseillaise of the Unemotional Yankee* [1] because it was used by
the Yankees as a camp song in the Civil
War.

[1] *The World Book Encyclopedia* (The Quarrie Corporation, Chicago, 1938) vol. 8, p. 3267.

Marsh, Sylvester
On June 25, 1858, Sylvester Marsh obtained a charter to build a railroad to the
top of Mount Washington, the highest peak
of the White Mountains, in New Hampshire. People who thought this an impos-
sible undertaking called him *Crazy Marsh.*[1]
However, in spite of financial and other
difficulties Marsh succeeded in building the
railroad as far as Jacob's Ladder, which was
formally opened on August 14, 1868. The
entire road was finished in July 1869.
Sylvester Marsh was born at Campton,
N.H., on September 30, 1803, and died at
Concord, N.H., on December 30, 1884.

[1] *Appleton's Cyclopaedia of American Biography,* ed.
by James Grant Wilson and John Fiske (D. Appleton
and Company, New York, 1888) vol. 4, p. 219.

Marshall, John
The *Greatest American Jurist* and *Silver
Heels* are sobriquets which have been ap-
plied to John Marshall.
Because of his ability as a lawyer, and the
many important decisions he made while
Chief Justice of the United States Supreme
Court from 1801 to 1935, John Marshall
has been called the *Greatest American
Jurist.*[1]

The soldiers and fellow-officers in the
Revolutionary War from 1775 to 1779 nicknamed him *Silver Heels.*[2] The occasion was
a foot-race between Marshall and one of his
soldiers. Marshall ran in his stocking feet
and won. His stockings were blue with
white heels.
John Marshall was born at Germantown,
or what is now Midland, Va., on September
24, 1755, and died at Philadelphia, Pa., on
July 6, 1835.

[1] *American History and Government, a Text-book on
the History and Civil Government of the United States,*
James Albert Woodburn and Thomas Francis Moran
(Longmans, Green and Company, New York, 1908)
p. 221.
[2] *The Life of James Monroe,* George Morgan (Small,
Maynard and Company, Boston, 1921) p. 30.
John Marshall, James Bradley Thayer (Houghton
Mifflin and Company, Boston and New York, 1901)
p. 12-13.

Marshall College
The athletic teams of Marshall College,
at Huntington, W.Va., are called the *Big
Greens* [1] and the *Thundering Herd.* The
former nickname was given them because
green and white are the college colors. The
latter was given them by a sports writer in
1926.

[1] A communication from Roy M. Hawley, Director of
Athletics at Marshall College, Huntington, W.Va., June
14, 1935.

Martin, François Xavier
The *Father of Louisiana Jurisprudence* [1]
was a nickname given to François Xavier
Martin because he published in English and
French a digest of the Louisiana Territory
and State laws in 1816.
François Xavier Martin was born at Mar-
seille, France, on March 17, 1762, and died
at New Orleans, La., on December 19, 1846.

[1] *The Encyclopaedia Britannica,* Fourteenth Edition
(Encyclopaedia Britannica, Inc., New York, 1932)
vol. 14, p. 987.

Martin, James Green
James Green Martin, a Confederate sol-
dier, was nicknamed *Old One Wing* [1] dur-
ing the War with Mexico when he lost his
right arm from a wound at the Battle of
Churubusco in Mexico, on August 20, 1847.
He was called by this nickname by the sol-
diers in his brigade in the Confederate
Army during the Civil War.
James Green Martin was born at Elizabeth
City, N.C., on February 14, 1819, and died
at Asheville, N.C., on October 4, 1878.

[1] *Dictionary of American Biography under the Auspices
of the American Council of Learned Societies,* ed. by
Dumas Malone (Charles Scribner's Sons, New York,
1933) vol. 12, p. 341.

Martin, Johnny Leonard

Johnny Leonard Martin, who was born at Temple, Okla., on February 29, 1904, and who played outfield and third base in major-league baseball, was popularly known as *Pepper*.[1] He is said to have acquired this nickname in 1925 because it described his manner of playing on the baseball diamond.[1]

[1] *Who's Who in Major League Base Ball*, comp. by Harold (Speed) Johnson (Buxton Publishing Company, Chicago, 1933) p. 284.

Martin, Luther

Thomas Jefferson nicknamed Luther Martin the *Federal Bull-dog*[1] because Martin was a Federalist and obstinately opposed Jefferson on the adoption of the Constitution. Martin was one of Maryland's representatives to the constitutional Convention of 1787, but opposed the constitution and refused to affix his signiture. He subsequently allied himself with the Federalists. He was a brilliant if somewhat eccentric lawyer.

Luther Martin was born at New Brunswick, N.J., on February 9, 1748, and died at New York City, on July 10, 1826.

[1] *The Encyclopaedia Britannica*, Fourteenth Edition (Encyclopaedia Britannica, Inc., New York, 1932) vol. 14, p. 988.

Martin College

The *Martinettes*[1] is the nickname applied to the athletic teams of Martin College, at Pulaski, Tenn. The sobriquet was first applied to the Martin College Radio Team which was being featured by radio station WSM at Nashville, Tenn.

[1] A communication from Sinclair Daniel, President of Martin College, Pulaski, Tenn., November 18, 1935.

Martinettes. See Martin College

Martling's Long Room

Martling's Long Room and the *Pig Pen* were names given to the second wigwam of the Tammany Society or Columbian Order of New York City. *Martling's Long Room* was a long, low, one-story wooden structure attached to the tavern kept by Abraham Martling, at the corner of Nassau and Spruce Streets. The floor of this long room, originally intended for dancing, was several feet lower than the barroom and kitchen. Later the dilapidated condition of the structure and its general unsightliness caused the opponents of the Tammany Society to refer to it as the *Pig Pen*. The first

Tammany Hall built by the Society in 1811, at Nassau and Frankfort Streets, partly overlapped the site of Martling's Tavern.

[1] *The National Cyclopedia of American Biography* (James T. White and Company, New York, 1893) vol. 3, p. 379, 381.

[2] *Tammany Hall*, Morris Robert Werner (Doubleday, Doran and Company, Incorporated, New York, 1928) p. 16, 17.

Martyr Abolitionist. See Lovejoy, E. P.

Martyr Band

Those who supported President Woodrow Wilson toward the close of his administration in 1921, were sometimes termed the *Martyr Band*[1] because they considered Wilson a martyr persecuted by political opponents because he was the champion of the great cause of serving all mankind.

[1] *Woodrow Wilson: A Character Study*, Robert Edwards Annin (Dodd, Mead and Company, New York, 1924) p. 364-72.

Martyr Hero. See Brown, John

Martyr President. See Garfield, J. A.; Lincoln, Abraham

Mary Pickford of This War. See Lamour, Dorothy

Maryland

Maryland is known as the *Cockade State*, the *Monumental State*, the *Old Line State*, the *Oyster State*, the *Queen State*, and the *Terrapin State*.

The Old Maryland Line was largely made up of patrician young men, who wore brilliant cockades, consequently, Maryland became known as the *Cockade State*.[1]

Maryland is called the *Monumental State*[2] because its largest city, Baltimore, has so many superior monumental trophies.

The *Old Line State*[3] is a popular name for Maryland, which in early Colonial days was the dividing line between the Crown land grants of William Penn and those of Lord Baltimore. Maryland is also called the *Old Line State*[4] from the "Old Line" regiments contributed by Maryland during the Revolution. She was then the only colony that had regular troops of "the line."

The nickname *Oyster State* refers to the large oyster fisheries in the state.

Maryland was named for Henrietta Maria, who was the Queen of Charles I of England and is therefore the *Queen State*.

Maryland—Continued

Maryland is nicknamed the *Terrapin State* because of the extensive diamondback terrapin farms on the Chesapeake Bay.

[1] *King's Handbook of the United States,* planned and ed. by Moses King, text by M. F. Sweetser (Moses King Corporation, Buffalo, N.Y., 1891) p. 324.

[2] *Americanisms—Old and New,* John S. Farmer (Privately printed by Thomas Poulter and Sons, London, 1889) p. 371.

[3] *The Encyclopedia Americana* (Americana Corporation, New York and Chicago, 1929) vol. 20, p. 635.

[4] *A New Dictionary of Americanism,* Sylva Clapin (Louis Weiss and Company, New York, 1903) p. 293.

Marylanders

The Marylanders are called *Crawthumpers, Oysters,* and *Terrapins.* The fishermen of Maryland probably first used the expression *Craw-thumpers* [1] as a nickname for lobsters, after which the nickname was applied to the fishermen themselves, and later to the inhabitants of Maryland. *Craw* is a corruption of the word *claw,* and the phrase refers to the thumping noise made by the pincers of the lobsters as they crawl about in a boat.

The people of Maryland are called *Oysters* [2] because oyster fishing is one of Maryland's chief industries. The Marylanders are frequently designated *Terrapins* because of the extensive terrapin industry along the Chesapeake Bay.

[1] *U.S.: An Index in the United States of America,* comp. by Malcolm Townsend (D. Lothrop and Company, Boston, 1890) p. 76.

[2] *A Book of Nicknames,* John Goff (Courier-Journal Job Printing Company, Louisville, Ky., 1892) p. 19.

Maryville College

The athletic teams of Maryville College, at Maryville, Tenn., are nicknamed *Highlanders,* [1] *Scotties,* and *Scots* because it is a Presbyterian college situated in the mountainous section of Tennessee.

[1] A communication from E. R. Vuntin, Director of Curriculum at Maryville College, Maryville, Tenn., December 13, 1935.

Mason, Stevens Thomson

The *Boy Governor* [1] is a nickname given to Stevens Thomson Mason by the people of Michigan because he became the Secretary and Acting Governor of the Territory of Michigan before he was of age.

Stevens Thomson Mason was born at Leesburg, Va., on October 27, .1811, and died at New York City, on January 4, 1843.

[1] *The Encyclopedia Americana* (Americana Corporation, New York and Chicago, 1927) vol. 18, p. 382.

Mason and Dixon Line

The boundary line separating Pennsylvania from Delaware, Maryland, and Virginia is commonly known as the *Mason and Dixon Line* [1] from the names of the two English astronomers, Charles Mason and Jeremiah Dixon, who surveyed it. When Charles I gave Lord Baltimore the land which is now the State of Maryland, and Charles II made his grant of what is now Pennsylvania to William Penn, their inaccurate knowledge of American geography caused them to make overlapping grants. After several unsatisfactory attempts at a settlement of the dispute, Mason and Dixon were employed (1763 to 1767) to run the line due west from an agreed point on the parallel 39° 43' 26.3" north latitude. They surveyed the line two hundred and forty-four miles west and every five miles set up stones which were engraved on one side with the Coat of Arms of William Penn, and on the other side with the Coat of Arms of Lord Baltimore. Colonel Alexander McLean from Pennsylvania and Joseph Reville from Virginia completed the line, extending it twenty-six miles further west in 1784.

The Mason and Dixon Line became famous as being in part the boundary between the free and slave states.

[1] *Universal Cyclopaedia and Atlas,* A Newly Revised and Enlarged Edition (D. Appleton and Company, 1905) vol. 7, p. 556.

Massa Linkum. See Lincoln, Abraham

Massachusetts

The nicknames of Massachusetts are the *Baked Bean State,* the *Old Colony State,* the *Old Bay State,* or *Bay State,* the *Puritan State,* and the *Rock-ribbed State.*

Massachusetts is called the *Baked Bean State* [1] because Bostonians in Puritan days served beans and brown bread as a regular Sabbath meal because they could be prepared the day before. Baked beans and brown bread are now the traditional Saturday night meal.

The *Old Colony State* [2] is applied to that part of Massachusetts included within the limits of the original Plymouth Colony, which was settled some time before Massachusetts Bay Colony.

The *Bay State* and the *Old Bay State* [2] were given as nicknames to the State of Massachusetts because of its many bays and because the early settlements were on Boston Bay and Cape Cod Bay.

The *Puritan State* was given as a nickname to Massachusetts because it was settled by the Puritans.

Massachusetts has been referred to as the *Rock-ribbed State*,[3] because of its rocky terrain.

[1] *U.S.: An Index to the United States of America*, comp. by Malcolm Townsend (D. Lothrop Company, Boston, 1890) p. 69-70.

[2] A letter from Edward H. Redstone, Librarian, State Library, Boston, Mass., March 18, 1930.

[3] *A New Dictionary of Americanisms*, Sylva Clapin (Louis Weiss and Company, New York, 1903) p. 42.

[3] *American History and Government, a Text-Book on the History and Civil Government of the United States*, James Albert Woodburn and Thomas Francis Moran (Longmans, Green and Company, New York and London, 1908) p. 354.

Massachusetts Giant. See Webster, Daniel

Massachusetts Inhabitants

The people of Massachusetts are called *Baked Beans, Bay Staters,* and *Puritans.* For the origin of these nicknames see Massachusetts.

Massachusetts State College

The *Statesmen* [1] is the nickname of the athletic teams of Massachusetts State College, at Amherst, Mass., because the school is a State College and many prominent statesmen have been graduated from it.

[1] A communication from George E. Smery, Assistant Secretary at Massachusetts State College, Amherst, Mass., November 21, 1935.

Massachusetts Thunderer. See Webster, Daniel

Master of Realism. See Howells, W. D.

Master of the Swamps. See Hatfield, B. M.

Matadors. See Texas Technological College

Mathewson, Christopher

The nickname *Big Six* [1] was applied to Christopher Mathewson, in commemoration of a fire engine by that name in New York City, because he was a powerful pitcher in major-league baseball.

Christopher Mathewson was born at Factoryville, Pa., on August 12, 1880.

[1] *Who's Who in Major League Base Ball*, comp. by Harold (Speed) Johnson (Buxton Publishing Company, Chicago, 1933) p. 470.

Matthews, Joseph W.

Joseph W. Matthews who was Governor of Missouri from 1848 to 1850 was called the *Well-digger* [1] because that had been his occupation for many years. He lived for the greater part of his life in Marshall County, Mo., and died there in 1863 or 1864.

[1] *The National Cyclopaedia of American Biography* (James T. White and Company, New York, 1906) vol. 13, p. 488.

Matthewson, William

In 1860 when the settlers in Kansas were starving because of a drought, William Matthewson, one of the founders of Wichita, Kans., and one of the last of the government scouts on the western plains, killed quantities of buffaloes during the fall and early winter and sent them back to the settlers. He was nicknamed *Buffalo Killer,*[1] but later his close associates called him *Buffalo Bill.* It has been said that he was the original *Buffalo Bill.*

[1] *Portrait and Biographical Album of Sedgwick County, Kansas, Containing Full Page Portraits and Biographical Sketches of Prominent and Representative Citizens of the County, together with Portraits and Biographies of all the Governors of Kansas, and of the Presidents of the United States* (Chapman Brothers, Chicago, 1888) p. 166.

Matty. See Van Buren, Martin

Maury, Mathew Fontaine

Mathew Fontaine Maury, a meteorologist, naval officer, and oceanographer, has been nicknamed the *Pathfinder of the Sea* [1] because it was largely through his studies and research that the winds and ocean currents were first charted. His *Physical Geography of the Sea,* published in 1855, was the first textbook of "modern oceanography."

Mathew Fontaine Maury was born near Fredericksburg, Va., on January 14, 1806, and died at Lexington, Va., on February 1, 1873.

[1] *Makers of Virginia History*, J. A. C. Chandler (Silver, Burdett and Company, New York, 1904) p. 306.

Mavericks

The term *Maverick* was applied to unbranded cattle on the ranges of the West. The word came into use when Samuel Maverick, a Texas cattle-raiser who had failed to brand the cattle on his range, found

Mavericks—Continued

that they had stampeded and mixed in with the branded cattle of other ranges. His ranch being a very extensive one, all the unbranded cattle on the range were considered to belong to Maverick, and were called *Mavericks.*

[1] *Jungle Roads and Other Trails of Roosevelt,* Daniel Henderson (E. P. Dutton and Company, New York, 1920) p. 60.

[2] *The Century Dictionary and Cyclopedia* (The Century Company, New York, 1906) vol. 5, p. 3666.

Mayhew, Thomas

Thomas Mayhew was called the *Patriarch of the Indians* [1] because of his efforts to convert the Indians on the island of Martha's Vineyard to Christianity. He had procured a grant for the settlement of the island in 1641, and later became governor. The Indians reciprocated his interest in them by protecting the white settlers from Indian depredations during King Philip's War.

Thomas Mayhew was born in England, in 1592, and died at Martha's Vineyard, Mass., on March 25, 1862.

[1] *Thomas Mayhew, Patriarch to the Indians, 1593-1682, the Life of the Worshipful Governor and Chief Magistrate of the Island of Martha's Vineyard; Proprietary of Martha's Vineyard, Nantucket and the Elizabeth Island, and Lord of the Manor of Tisbury in North America,* Lloyd C. M. Hare (D. Appleton and Company, New York and London, 1931) p. 1.

Maynard, Horace

Horace Maynard, a legislator and politician, was known as the *Narragansett* [1] because he was a native of Massachusetts, the home of the Narragansett Indians in colonial days. He looked like an Indian, being tall, thin and erect, with dark skin and eyes and black hair. He was said to be of part Indian descent. From 1857 to 1863 and again from 1866 to 1875, he was a Representative from Tennessee to the United States Congress.

Horace Maynard was born at Westboro, Mass., on August 30, 1814, and died at Knoxville, Tenn., on May 3, 1882.

[1] *Dictionary of American Biography under the Auspices of the American Council of Learned Societies,* ed. by Dumas Malone (Charles Scribner's Sons, New York, 1933) vol. 12, p. 460.

Mayo, Charles Horace

Charles Horace Mayo, one of America's noted surgeons, was nicknamed *Doctor Charlie.* [1] Soon after he had received his medical degree, he and his brother, William James Mayo, established the famous Mayo Clinic at Rochester, Minn., in 1889. In 1915 he and his brother founded at Rochester the Mayo Foundation for Medical Education and Research.

Doctor Charles Horace Mayo was born at Rochester, Minn., on July 19, 1865, and died at Chicago, Ill., on May 26, 1939.

[1] *Newsweek: The Magazine of News Significance,* Rockefeller Center, N.Y., June 5, 1939, col. 2, p. 40.

Mayo, William James

William James Mayo, one of America's famous surgeons, was known as *Doctor Will.* [1] He and his brother, Charles Horace Mayo, also a noted surgeon, established the Mayo Clinic at Rochester in 1889, and the Mayo Foundation in 1915.

Doctor William James Mayo was born at La Sueur, Minn., on June 29, 1861, and died at Rochester, Minn., on July 28, 1939.

[1] *Newsweek: The Magazine of News Significance,* Rockefeller Center, N.Y., August 7, 1939, col. 2, p. 37.

Mayor Von O'Hall. See Hall, A. O.

Me Too Platt. See Platt, T. C.

Mease, John

John Mease was called the *Last of the Cocked Hats* [1] because, during the latter years of his life, he continued to wear the old-fashioned three-cornered hat peculiar to the Revolutionary Period. During the Revolutionary War, Mease served in the Continental Army under the direct command of General George Washington.

He was born at Strabane, Ireland, in 1746, emigrated to the United States about 1754, and died at Philadelphia, Pa., in 1826.

[1] *The National Cyclopaedia of American Biography* (James T. White and Company, New York, 1907) vol. 5, p. 516.

Mecca of Telephone Men. See New York City

Medary, Samuel

The nickname *Old Wheel-horse of Democracy* [1] was applied to Samuel Medary because of the active support he gave the Democratic party throughout his life. A wheel-horse is the one nearest to the wheels, therefore anyone who does especially steady and effective work.

Samuel Medary was born in Montgomery County, Pa., on February 25, 1801, and died at Columbus, Ohio, on November 7, 1864.

[1] *The National Cyclopaedia of American Biography* (James T. White and Company, New York, 1900) vol. 8, p. 342.

Medwick, Joseph M.

Duckie Wuckie, and *Mickey* are nick-names which have been applied to Joseph M. Medwick who played outfield in major-league baseball.

He was usually called *Mickey.* The news-papers began nicknaming him *Duckie Wuckie* [1] after a young woman at Houston, Tex., said that he swam like a duck.

Joseph M. Medwick was born at Carteret, N.J., on November 24, 1911.

[1] *Who's Who in Major League Base Ball,* comp. by Harold (Speed) Johnson (Buxton Publishing Company, Chicago, 1933) p. 285.

Meek, Alexander Beaufort

Because he was a pioneer worker in be-half of public schools for Alabama, Alex-ander Beaufort Meek has been called the *Father of the Public Schools of Alabama.* [1]

From 1853 to 1855 Meek represented Mobile County in the Alabama House of Representatives. While he was Chairman of the Committee on Education in the House, he introduced a bill to establish free public schools in Alabama and was active in pro-moting its passage.

Alexander Beaufort Meek was born at Columbia, S.C., on July 17, 1814, and died at Columbus, Miss., on November 7, 1865.

[1] *The National Cyclopaedia of American Biography* (James T. White and Company, New York, 1909) vol. 11, p. 165.
History of Alabama and Her People, Albert Burton Moore, Author and Editor (The American Historical Society, Inc., New York and Chicago, 1927) vol. 1, p. 329-30.

Meek, Joseph L.

Joseph L. Meek, a trapper and pioneer settler, was nicknamed *Colonel* [1] in May 1948, when he appeared before the mem-bers of the Congress at Washington, with an official message from the American set-tlers in the Oregon Territory asking Con-gress to give them civil and military security. He displayed such extravagance of manners and of speech that Congress nicknamed him *Colonel.* He was a pioneer settler in the Oregon Territory in 1840, and devoted his life to its political and economic up-building.

Joseph L. Meek was born in Washington County, Va., on June 20, 1810, and died at Hillsboro, Ore., in 1875.

[1] *Dictionary of American Biography under the Auspices of the American Council of Learned Societies,* ed. by Dumas Malone (Charles Scribner's Sons, New York, 1934) vol. 14, p. 469.

Meine, Henry William

Henry William Meine, who was born at St. Louis, Mo., on May 1, 1899, and who pitched in major baseball was nicknamed *Heine,* [1] or *Heinrich,* which is the German form of Henry. Meine is of German de-scent.

[1] *Who's Who in Major League Base Ball,* comp. by Harold (Speed) Johnson (Buxton Publishing Company, Chicago, 1933) p. 286.

Mell, Patrick Hues

The *Prince of Parliamentarians* [1] is a name applied to Patrick Hues Mell because he was an excellent presiding officer at scores of Baptist Conventions of which he was president.

Patrick Hues Mell was born at Walthour-ville, Ga., on July 19, 1814, and died at Athens, Ga., on January 26, 1888.

[1] *The National Cyclopaedia of American Biography* (James T. White and Company, New York, 1907) vol. 9, p. 181-2.

Melting Pot

The United States of America is often spoken of as the *Melting Pot* [1] because so many people living in it are foreigners who in time become amalgamated with the rest of the population all of whom are them-selves of immigrant descent.

See also New York City.

[1] *What This Country Needs,* Jay Franklin (John Franklin Carter) (Covici, Friede, New York, 1931) p. 251.

Melting Pot Division

During World War I the Seventy-seventh Division of the American Expeditionary Force in France was known as the *Melting Pot Division* [1] because a large part of this division was recruited in New York City and represented many races, creeds, and colors.

[1] *History of New York State, 1523-1927,* James Sulli-van, Editor-in-chief, and E. Melvin Williams, Benedict Fitzpatrick, and Edwin P. Conklin, Associate Editors (Lewis Historical Publishing Company, Inc., New York and Chicago, 1927) vol. 4, p. 1333.

Memphis, Tennessee

Memphis is known as the *Bluff City* and the *Commercial Metropolis of West Ten-nesee.* It has the nickname *Bluff City* [1] be-cause it is built on the historic Chickasaw Bluff overlooking the Mississippi River.

This city has been termed the *Commercial Metropolis of West Tennessee* [1] because it

Memphis, Tenn.—Continued
is one of the principal gateways between the eastern and the western parts of the United States.

[1] *Tennessee State Gazetteer, and Business Directory, for 1860-'61*, John L. Mitchell (John L. Mitchell, Nashville, Tenn., 1860) p. 123.

Memphis Bill. See Terry, W. H.

Memphis of the American Nile. See Saint Louis, Mo.

Mephistopheles of the Ocean. See Schley, W. S.

Mercer, Margaret
Margaret Mercer was known as the *Hannah More of America.* She wrote ethical and religious articles and was active in promulgating Sunday Schools. Hannah More, an English woman who lived from 1745 to 1833, was noted for her moral and religious writings and for her interest in providing educational opportunities for all. With her sisters, she established Sunday Schools in the vicinity of Bristol, England.

Margaret Mercer was born at Annapolis, Md., in 1791, and died at Belmont, Va., in June, 1846.

[1] *The Life of James Monroe*, George Morgan (Small, Maynard and Company, Boston, 1921) p. 69.
[2] *The New International Encyclopaedia* (Dodd, Mead and Company, New York, 1923) vol. 16, p. 242.

Merchant Evangelist. See Crittenton, C. N.

Merchant Prince. See Morris, Robert

Meriden, Connecticut
Meriden, in New Haven Country, is often called the *Silver City* [1] because of its extensive manufacturing of silverware.

[1] *A Modern History of New Haven and Eastern New Haven County*, Everett G. Hill (The S. J. Clarke Publishing Company, New York and Chicago, 1918) vol. 1, p. 287.

Merkle, Frederick C.
Frederick C. Merkle, an outstanding major-league baseball player, has been nicknamed *Bone-head* [1] and *One of the Gamest Players in the Game.* [1] *Bone-head* originated in 1907 while he was playing with the New York National League Baseball Company. He failed to touch the base in making a run which caused the team to lose the game,

the pennant, and a vast sum of money. Later Merkle's good playing helped the *New York Giants* to win three pennants. In 1917 Merkle was transferred to the Chicago National League Baseball Company where his admirers nicknamed him *One of the Gamest Players in the Game.* Few players could have withstood the criticism and censure which he endured without being driven out of professional baseball.

Frederick C. Merkle was born at Watertown, Wis., on December 20, 1888.

[1] *Baseball Magazine* (The Baseball Magazine Company, New York, 1917-1918) vol. 20-21, August, 1918, p. 357, 374.

Messer, Asa
Doctor Asa Messer, who was president of Brown University, at Providence, R.I., from 1804 to 1920, was sometimes referred to as the *Cunning President* [1] because of his cleverness, cunning, and sharpness of wit in administering the affairs of the University.

He was born at Methuen, Mass., in 1769 and died at Providence, R.I., on October 11, 1836.

[1] *The National Cyclopaedia of American Biography* (James T. White and Company, New York, 1924) vol. 8, p. 22.

Metaphysics. See Alden, H. M.

Metcalfe, Thomas
Thomas Metcalfe, who was at various times the Governor, Congressman, and Senator from Kentucky, was called *Old Stone Hammer* [1] because as a young man he had been a stonemason.

He was born in Fauquier County, Va., on March 20, 1780, and died in Nicholas County, Ky., on August 18, 1855.

[1] *The National Cyclopaedia of American Biography* (James T. White and Company, New York, 1906) vol. 13, p. 4.

Methodist Agassiz. See Marcy, Oliver

Methodists. See Illinois Wesleyan University; West Virginia Wesleyan College

Me-Too-ism
Me-too-ism is the name for the acceptance by certain members of the Republican party of the economic domestic policies and the foreign policies of the New Deal and Fair Deal federal administrations. Wendell Willkie, the Republican nominee for Presi-

dent of the United States, who ran against President Franklin D. Roosevelt in 1940 was the first Republican candidate to accept these policies. Thomas E. Dewey who ran against President Roosevelt in 1944 and against President Harry S. Truman in 1948 also accepted them.

Newsweek: The Magazine of News Significance, Rockefeller Center, N.Y., February 21, 1949, p. 72, December 26, 1949, p. 14

Life, 540 West Michigan Avenue, Chicago, Ill., May 26, 1947, p. 25-26.

Metropolis of America. See New York City

Metropolis of East Tennessee. See Knoxville, Tenn.

Metropolis of New England. See Boston, Mass.

Metropolis of North Texas. See Dallas, Tex.

Metropolis of the "Magic Valley." See Brownsville, Tex.

Metropolis of the Missouri Valley. See Kansas City, Mo.

Metropolis of the New South. See Louisville, Ky.

Metropolis of the Northeast. See Bangor, Me.

Metropolitan City. See New York City

Metropolitan Division

The Seventy-seventh Division of the American Expeditionary Forces in France during World War I was called the Metropolitan Division [1] because the majority of the soldiers had come from the five boroughs of the metropolitan district of Greater New York.

[1] History of New York State, 1523-1927, James Sullivan, Editor-in-chief, and E. Melvin Williams, Benedict Fitzpatrick, and Edwin P. Conklin, Associate Editors (Lewis Historical Publishing Company, Inc., New York and Chicago, 1927) vol. 4, p. 1333.

Miami, Florida

Miami is called the City of Opportunities, Magic City, and the Wonder City of the World. It is termed the City of Oppor-

tunities [1] in allusion to the advantages and opportunities it offered to those who took part in the early development of the city.

It is known as the Magic City [2] and the Wonder City of the World [1] because of the remarkably rapid growth of its population and property value since its incorporation in 1896. The name Magic City was originated by Ethan V. Blackman in an issue of the Florida Homeseeker which he edited during the 1920's, a boom period for Florida real estate.

[1] Miami and Dade County, Florida, Its Settlement, Progress, and Achievement, with a Collection of Individual Sketches of Representative Citizens and Genealogical Records of Some of the Old Families, Ethan V. Blackman (Victor Rainbolt, Washington, D.C., 1921) p. 86.

[2] Florida, Old and New, Frederick W. Dau (G. P. Putnam's Sons, New York and London, 1934) p. 302.

Michigan

Michigan is known by five names, the Auto State, the Lady of the Lakes, the Lake State, the Peninsula State, and the Wolverine State.

The Auto State is a nickname recently given to Michigan because of her numerous automobile manufacturing.

Michigan has been called the Lady of the Lakes and the Lake Lady because it is surrounded on three sides by four of the Great Lakes, Lake Superior, Lake Michigan, Lake Huran, and Lake Erie and because it has numerous lakes within its borders.

It is called the Peninsula State because it is largely made up of two great peninsulas, The Upper Peninsula jutting between Lake Superior and Lake Michigan and Huron, and The Lower Peninsula between Lake Huron and Lakes Michigan and Erie.

Michigan was nicknamed the Wolverine State [1] from the number of wolverines which used to abound there.

[1] Americanisms; The English of the New World, M. Schele De Vere (Charles Scribner and Company, New York, 1872) p. 660.

Michigan Inhabitants

The name Wolverines is applied to the people of the state of Michigan. It is told how Conrad Tan Eyck, a tavern keeper, about 1800, made a specialty of wolf steaks. After a person had eaten a lamb chop, or a beef steak, he would ask, "Well, how did you enjoy your wolf steak?" The nickname grew out of the reply of a young girl, who having been told that she had eaten wolf steak, replied, "Then I suppose

Michigan Inhabitants—Continued

I am a Wolverine?" This name is said to have been given first to those who had eaten at this inn, and afterwards it was applied to the inhabitants of the state.[1]

[1] *Detroit Free Press*, Detroit, Mich., November 30, 1918.

Michigan State College

The athletic teams of Michigan State College, at East Lansing, Mich., were called *Spartans* [1] by the sports editors of the Lansing papers about 1915.

[1] A letter from Ralph H. Young, Director of Athletics at Michigan State College, East Lansing, Mich., June 17, 1935.

Mickey. See Cochrane, G. S.; Finn, N. F.; Medwick, J. M.

Mickey Mouse. See Ely, W. H. J.

Middies. See United States Naval Academy

Midland College

The *Fighting Warriors* [1] is the sobriquet given to the athletic teams of Midland College, at Fremont, Neb. They were called the *Warriors* in 1920 by the student body, and sports writers began calling them the *Fighting Warriors* in 1931.

[1] A communication from Karl J. Lawrence, Director of Athletics at Midland College, Fremont, Neb., June 18, 1935.

Midnight Appointees

The *Midnight Appointees* [1] and the *Midnight Judges* [2] were federal judges and other office-holders appointed by the Federalist President, John Adams, in the closing hours of his presidential term in 1801.

[1] *History of the United States*, Charles A. Beard and Mary R. Beard (The Macmillan Company, New York, 1921) p. 187.

[2] *The Story of American Democracy, Political and Industrial*, Willis Mason West (Allyn and Bacon, New York and Boston, 1922) p. 333.

Midnight Judges. See *Midnight Appointees*

Midwayites. See University of Chicago

Mighty Bambino. See Ruth, G H.

Mighty Medicine Man. See Powell, D. F.

Milburn, William Henry

William Henry Milburn, who for several years was chaplain of the House of Representatives and Senate in Washington, was known as the *Blind Preacher* [1]. He became an itinerant Methodist preacher in 1843, and in that capacity was active throughout the South for many years, despite the fact that he was completely blind.

William Henry Milburn was born at Philadelphia, Pa., on September 26, 1823, and died at Santa Barbara, Calif., on April 10, 1903.

[1] *The National Cyclopaedia of American Biography* (James T. White and Company, New York, 1896) vol. 7, p. 137.

Mile of Christmas Trees

Santa Rosa Avenue in Pasadena, Calif., has been nicknamed the *Mile of Christmas Trees* [1] because magnificent evergreen trees form an intertwined archway over this avenue.

[1] *The World Book Encyclopedia* (The Quarrie Corporation, Chicago, 1929) vol. 13, p. 5406.

Milk of Magnesia. See Phillips, A. N., Jr.

Mill Boy of the Slashes. See Clay, Henry

Miller, Archie

The *Little Pill Doctor* [1] is a nickname by which Doctor Archie Miller was known because he was the first homeopathic doctor to practice in the state of Indiana and followed the custom of these doctors of administering their medicines in small doses.

Archie Miller was the father of William Henry Harrison Miller who distinguished himself as a soldier and as an officer in the Civil War.

[1] *The National Cyclopaedia of American Biography* (James T. White and Company, New York, 1918) vol. 16, p. 362.

Miller, Charles

Charles Miller, an adventurer, who was born at Hat Creek in Modoc County, Calif., on January 1, 1850, was called *Broncho Charlie* or *Broncho Carlos* [1] from the age of eight when he succeeded in riding unbroken horses where most of the cowboys were Mexicans.

Miller, who led a varied and adventursome life, became a rider in the Russell, Majors, and Waddell Pony Express when he was scarcely twelve years old. He joined the Wild West Show of William Frederick Cody in New York City in 1885, and although he was sixty-eight years of age, he served as a private in the Eighteenth Hussars in the British Army during World War I.

[1] *Broncho Charlie: A Saga of the Saddle,* Gladys Shaw Erskine (Thomas Y. Crowell Company, New York, 1934), p. 19.

Miller, Cincinnatus Heine

Cincinnatus Heine Miller, better known as Joaquin Miller, was often called the *Poet of the Sierras* [1] because he lived the greater part of his life in the Sierra Nevada mountain region of California. One of his most successful collections of verses, *Songs of the Sierras,* dealt chiefly with that region.

He was born in the Wabash District of Indiana, November 10, 1848, and died at San Francisco, Calif., February 17, 1913.

[1] *California, the Wonderful; Her Romantic History, Her Picturesque People, Her Wild Shores, Her Desert Mystery, Her Valley Loveliness, Her Mountain Glory, Including Her Varied Resources, Her Commercial Greatness. Her Intellectual Achievements, Her Expanding Hopes, with Glimpses of Oregon and Washington, Her Northern Neighbors,* Edwin Markham (Hearst's International Library, New York, 1914) p. 336.

Miller, Donald. See *Four Horsemen*

Miller, Homer Virgil Milton

The *Demosthenes of the Mountains* [1] is a nickname applied to Homer Virgil Milton Miller because he was a talented orator from the mountainous regions of South Carolina.

Homer Virgil Milton Miller was born in Pendelton District, S.C., on April 29, 1814, and died at Atlanta, Ga., on May 31, 1896.

[1] *The National Cyclopaedia of American Biography* (James T. White and Company, New York, 1904) vol. 12, p. 344.

Miller, James Russell

The nickname, *Modern Bunyan,* [1] was attributed to James Russell Miller because he was both an author and a preacher, and because, like Bunyan, in a simple, direct, and clear style, he wrote poetry which dealt with the practical things of everyday life.

James Russell Miller was born at Harshaville, Pa., on March 20, 1840, and died at Philadelphia, Pa., on July 2, 1912.

[1] *National Cyclopedia of American Biography* (James T. White and Company, New York, 1904) vol. 10, p. 19.

Miller, Lowell Otto

Lowell Otto Miller, who was born at Minden, Neb., on June 1, 1889, and who was a catcher in major league baseball, was nicknamed *Mooney.* [1]

[1] *Who's Who in Major League Base Ball,* comp. by Harold (Speed) Johnson (Buxton Publishing Company, Chicago, 1933) p. 428.

Miller, Warner

The Democratic press of New York called Warner Miller *Wood-Pulp Miller* [1] while he was a Senator from New York to the United States Congress from 1881 to 1887 and because for many years he was engaged in the manufacture of paper from wood-pulp at Herkimer, N.Y.

Warner Miller was born in Oswego County, N.Y., on August 12, 1838, and died at New York City on March 21, 1918.

[1] *U.S. "Snap Shots": An Independent, National, and Memorial Encyclopedia . . . ,* Oliver McKee (A. M. Thayer and Company, Boston, 1892) p. 247-8.
The National Cyclopaedia of American Biography (James T. White and Company, New York, 1897) vol. 4, p. 560.

Miller, William

William Miller, a religious leader, was nicknamed the *Poet of Low Hampton* [1] because he wrote poetry which was pleasant in rhyme, subject matter, and rhythm, and during the greater part of his life lived at Low Hampton, N.Y. In 1845, at Albany, N.Y., he founded the religious order known as Adventists or Millerites. The followers of Miller's religious teachings looked in vain for the second coming of Christ in 1843, in 1844, and at various later dates.

William Miller was born at Pittsfield, Mass., on February 5, 1782, and died at Low Hampton, N.Y., on December 20, 1849.

[1] *Appleton's Cyclopaedia of American Biography,* ed. by James Grant Wilson and John Fiske (D. Appleton and Company, New York, 1894) vol. 4, p. 329.

Millet of America. See Higgins, Eugene

Milligan, Maurice Morton

Maurice Morton Milligan, a lawyer and United States Attorney, was nicknamed *Missouri's Tom Dewey* [1] because of the prominent part he took in exposing racketeers and illegal financial procedures in Missouri. in 1939. Thomas Edmund Dewey, as District Attorney of New York County, N.Y., in 1937, successfully prosecuted law breakers and racketeers in New York City.

Milligan, M. M.—Continued

Milligan was admitted to the bar of Missouri in 1908, was attorney for the city of Richmond, Mo., from 1909 to 1913, was Probate Circuit Judge of Ray County, Mo., from 1915 to 1923, and has been United States Attorney of the Western District of Missouri since 1934.

Maurice Morton Milligan was born at Richmond, Mo., on November 23, 1884.

[1] *Newsweek: The Magazine of News Significance,* Rockefeller Center, N.Y., April 17, 1939, col. 2, p. 17.

Millionaire. See Gerry, P. G.

Millionaire Hobo. See How, J. E.

Millionaire Sheriff. See Baker, A. Y.

Millionaire Tramp. See How, J. E.

Millionaires' Resort. See Jekyll Island

Millionaire's Row

During the nineteenth century the highway which extended along the east bank of the Hudson River from New York City to Yonkers in New York, was called *Millionaire's Row* [1] because many wealthy people built magnificent residences along this picturesque drive.

Orange Grove Avenue and Oak Knoll in Pasadena, Calif., are colloquially known as *Millionaire's Row* [2] because along these drives have been built palatial houses amidst magnificent gardens.

[1] *Hudson River Landings,* Paul Wilstach (The Bobbs-Merrill Company, Indianapolis, Ind., 1933) p. 211.

[2] "Land of Homes" by Frank J. Taylor, in *California,* ed. by John Russell McCarthy (Powell Publishing Company, Chicago and San Francisco, Calif., 1930) vol. 6, p. 84.

Millman, Harry

Harry Millman, who at twenty-seven years of age was recognized as the leader of the Purple Gang of Detroit, Mich., was shot to death by assassins in a cocktail grill in Detroit on November 25, 1937. Millman was commonly called the *Lone Wolf of the Underworld* [1] because he was said to have no confidants among the gangsters under him.

[1] *The Washington Post,* Washington, D.C., November 26, 1937, col. 1, p. 7.

Mills, Samuel John

During the latter part of his life, Samuel John Mills was called the *Father of Foreign Mission Work in Christian America* [1] because he was a pioneer missionary to the colored people throughout the United States and was prominent in organizing the United Foreign Missionary Society. He helped to found schools for the training of colored teachers and preachers in New York and in New Jersey.

Samuel John Mills was born at Torringford, Conn., on April 21, 1783, and died at sea, on June 16, 1818.

[1] *The National Cyclopaedia of American Biography* (James T. White and Company, New York, 1906) vol. 13, p. 187.

Millsaps College

The athletes of Millsaps College at Jackson, Miss., are nicknamed *Majors, Minors,* and *Majorettes.* [1] The college was founded by Major Reuben Webster Millsaps, an officer in the Confederate Army. Upper-class athletic teams are called *Majors,* freshman teams are *Minors,* and the women's teams are called *Majorettes.*

[1] A letter from D. M. Key, President of Millsaps College, Jackson, Miss., November 19, 1935.

Milner, Moses Embree

Moses Embree Milner, a frontier scout and adventurer, who was born at Standford, Ky., on May 8, 1829, and died at Fort Robinson, Neb., on October 29, 1876, was nicknamed *California Joe.* [1] He was a scout for the Fifteenth Infantrymen under General Winfield Scott Hancock from 1866 to 1871.

In 1864 while Milner was panning for gold near Virginia City, Nevada, his cabin and premises were taken over by three claims jumpers who, having resisted Milner's orders to leave, were killed by him. Milner, after he had reported to the authorities at Virginia City, was returning to his cabin when he met four strangers who stopped him to exchange greetings. When they asked him his name, thinking that perhaps they were associates of the claim jumpers he had shot, he replied that his name was Joe and that he was from California. So they called him *California Joe,* a nickname by which he was popularly known ever afterwards.

[1] *California Joe, Noted Scout and Indian Fighter,* Joe E. Milner and Earl R. Forrest (The Caxton Printers, Ltd., Caldwell, Idaho, 1935), p. 107.

Milwaukee, Wisconsin

Milwaukee has eight nicknames: the *Blonde Beauty of the Lakes, City Beautiful, City of Homes, Cream City, Cream-white*

City of the Unsalted Seas, Deutsch-Athens, Fair White City, and *Milwaukee the Beautiful.*

Milwaukee is called the *Blonde Beauty of the Lakes,*[1] *Cream City,*[2,3] *Cream-white City of the Unsalted Seas,*[6] and *Fair White City,*[4,5] because the buildings throughout the city are of cream-colored bricks from the native clay. Milwaukee is on the shore of Lake Michigan, one of the Great Lakes which are sometimes called "the unsalted seas."

Milwaukee, unlike many other pioneer settlements, especially of the mining-camp type which were long inhabited by men only, from its beginning was called the *City of Homes.*[3]

This city is termed *Milwaukee the Beautiful*[6] and *City Beautiful*[8] because of its beauty and picturesqueness. It is located on an elevation sloping down to the shores of Lake Michigan, with many trees, splendid residential sections, playgrounds, greens, squares, and parks.

This city was called the *Deutsch-Athens.*[3,7] in 1856 by the German-Americans there. It was the center of music and the theatre throughout that section of the country. The people were preponderantly Germans.

[1] *Illustrated Annual Review of Milwaukee, Its Trades and Industries,* Supplement to the Milwaukee Sentinel, J. L. Kaine (Issued by the Milwaukee Sentinel, Burdic, Armitage and Allen, Printers, Milwaukee, Wis., 1890) p. 1.

[2] *The Chronicles of Milwaukee: Being a Narrative History of the Town from Its Earliest Period to the Present,* A. C. Wheeler (Jermain and Brightman, Milwaukee, Wis., 1861) p. 279, 296-7.

[3] *History of Milwaukee, Wisconsin,* John G. Gregory (The S. J. Clarke Publishing Company, Chicago and Milwaukee, Wis., 1931) vol. 2, p. 1024, 1070, 1315, 1326.

[4] *Milwaukee Illustrated, Its Trade, Commerce, Manufacturing Interests, and Advantages as a Residence City,* Charles B. Harger (W. W. Coleman, Milwaukee, Wis., 1877) p. 36.

[5] *More About Names,* Leopold Wagner (T. Fisher Unwin, London, 1893) p. 244-5, 296.

[6] *Milwaukee: The Beautiful, Official Souvenir of the Biennial Meeting of the General Federation of Women's Clubs* (Published by George H. Yenowine and George W. Peck, Junior, at the Press of the Evening Wisconsin Company, Milwaukee, Wis., 1900) p. 1.

[7] *Memoirs of Henry Villard, Journalist and Financier, 1835-1900,* Henry Villard (Houghton Mifflin and Company, Boston and New York, 1904) vol. 1, p. 48, 49.

[8] *Milwaukee S. A. F.: Greetings from Milwaukee Florists' Club* (Issued by the Milwaukee Florists' Club with compliments to the members of the S.A.F. and O.H. in Nineteenth Annual Convention at Milwaukee, Wis., August 18, 19, 20, and 21, 1903, at the Press of Frederick Pollworth and Brother, Milwaukee, Wis., 1903) p. 2.

Milwaukee. See *Fire Canoes*

Milwaukee Braves. See Boston National League Baseball Company

Milwaukee National League Baseball Club. See Boston National League Baseball Company

Milwaukee the Beautiful. See Milwaukee, Wis.

Mineral City of the South. See Birmingham, Ala.

Mineral Pocket of New England. See Cumberland, R.I.

Mineral Point, Wisconsin

The origin of the nickname *Shake-rag*[1] for Mineral Point, Wis., is obscure. One tradition has it that the wives of the early miners would shake their table cloths to let their husbands know that the meals were ready. Another story is that the men whose turn it was to prepare the meals would shake a dish rag or table cloth at meal time. Some authorities atttribute the origin of the nickname to "Uncle Ab Nichols," one of its early settlers.

[1] *Wisconsin Lore for Boys and Girls,* Susan Burdick Davis (George Banta Publishing Company, Menasha, Wis., 1931) p. 151.

History of Iowa County, Wisconsin. . . . , C. W. Butterfield (Western Historical Company, Chicago, 1881) p. 661.

Miners. See Colorado School of Mines; Nevadans; New Mexico School of Mines; South Dakota State School of Mines

Mining State. See Nevada

Minister's Hotel

The home of Jonathan Andrew, at Windham, Me., was nicknamed the *Minister's Hotel*[1] because of the warm welcome extended to itinerant clergymen. Jonathan Andrew, who lived from 1782 until 1849, made his home in Windham from 1817 to 1837.

[1] *Biographical Sketches of Preeminent Americans,* Frederick G. Harrison (E. W. Walker Company, Boston, 1899) vol. 4, p. 38.

Minneapolis, Minnesota

Minneapolis is known as the *Flour City,* the *Gateway City,* and the *Sawdust City.* It has been termed the *Flour City*[1,2,3] because

Minneapolis, Minn.—Continued
it is the greatest flour manufacturing city in the United States.

It is called the *Gateway City* [1] because it is located near the head of the Mississippi River, is the terminus of nine railway trunk lines, and numerous truck or bus lines.

Minneapolis was nicknamed the *Sawdust City* [1,4] because of the great amount of lumber sawed there prior to 1900.

[1] *History of Minneapolis, Gateway to the Northwest,* ed. by Reverend Marion Daniel Shutter (The S. J. Clarke Printing Company, Chicago and Minneapolis, Minn., 1923) vol. 1, p. 99, 347, 357.

[2] *Industrial and Commercial Geography*, New Edition, J. Russell Smith (Henry Holt and Company, New York, 1930) p. 67.

[3] *Industrial Geography, Production, Manufacture, Commerce*, Ray Hughes Whitbeck (American Book Company, New York and Boston, 1931) p. 61.

[4] *Resources of Minnesota Series: City of Minneapolis. . . . ,* Elmer Epenctus Barton (E. E. Barton, Publisher, Minneapolis, Minn., 1889) p. 17.

Minneapolis and St. Paul, Minnesota.
See St. Paul and Minneapolis, Minn.

Minneapolis of the West. See Spokane, Wash.

Minnesota
Various sobriquets are attributed to Minnesota; the *Bread Basket of the World, Bread and Butter State, Cream Pitcher of the Nation, Gopher State, Lake State, New England of the West, North Star State, Playground of the Nation,* and *Wheat State.*

Minnesota has often been called the *Bread Basket of the World* [1] because of its immense wheat fields and flour mills.

The *Bread and Butter State* [2,3] is applied to Minnesota because of its wheat and dairy products.

Minnesota is called the *Cream Pitcher of the Nation* [1] because of its numerous great dairy farms.

Minnesota is called the *Gopher State* [4] from the striped gopher, a common species throughout the prairie region.

As early as 1854 the settlers discussed whether they would call Minnesota the *Beaver State* or the *Gopher State* [5] but *Gopher* finally won.

The sobriquet, the *Lake State* [6] was given to Minnesota because of its thousands of inland lakes.

The *New England of the West* [7] came to be applied to Minnesota because great numbers of people from New England settled there.

The *North Star State* [6] originated because the state seal has on it *L'Etoile du Nord* (the star of the north).

Because Minnesota has an abundance of natural resources, lakes, beautiful forests, streams filled with fish, game reserves, parks, and resorts it has been nicknamed the *Playground of the Nation.* [1] Much of the credit for advertising the natural beauty of Minnesota belongs to the Ten Thousand Lakes of Minnesota Association formed by a number of progressive business men in St. Paul, Minn., in 1917.

Minnesota is called the *Wheat State* because wheat is one of its main crops.

[1] *My Minnesota*, Antoinette E. Ford (Lyons and Carnahan, New York and Chicago, 1929) p. 194, 400.

[2] *The New International Encyclopaedia*, Second Edition (Dodd, Mead and Company, New York, 1930) vol. 21, p. 463.

[3] "Minnesota Geographical Names" by Warren Upham, in the *Collections of the Minnesota Historical Society* (Published by the Minnesota Historical Society, Saint Paul, Minn., at Colwell Press, Inc., Minneapolis, Minn., 1920) vol. 17, p. 4.

[4] *Minnesota in Three Centuries, 1655-1908*, Semi-Centennial Edition, Warren Upham (The Publishing Society of Minnesota, 1908, Printed by the Free Press Printing Company, Mankato, Minn., 1908) vol. 1, p. 75.

[5] *The History of Minnesota and Tales of the Frontier*, Judge Charles Eugene Flandrau (E. W. Porter, Saint Paul, Minn., 1900) p. 242-4.

[6] *King's Handbook of the United States*, planned and ed. by Moses King, text by M. F. Sweetser (Moses King Corporation, Buffalo, N.Y., 1891) p. 421.

[7] *Americanisms; The English of the New World*, M. Schele De Vere (Charles Scribner and Company, New York, 1872) p. 660.

Minnesotans
The Minnesotans have been called *Gophers* [1] and the state is called the *Gopher State* from the striped gopher, which is commonly found on the prairies of the state.

[1] *History of Minnesota and Tales of the Frontier*, Judge Charles Eugene Flandrau (E. W. Porter, Saint Paul, Minn., 1900) p. 242-4.

Minnesota's First State House
Carver's Cave near St. Paul, Minn., has been called *Minnesota's First State House* [1] because the cave was used by the Sioux Indians as a council chamber where they discussed tribal affairs.

[1] *My Minnesota*, Antoinette E. Ford (Lyons and Carnahan, New York and Chicago, 1929) p. 29.

Minnesota's Potato King. See Schroeder. Henry

Minton, Sherman
Sherman Minton, a lawyer and politician, was nicknamed *King of the New Dealers* [1] in the United States Senate because he supported the New Dealers and New Deal leg-

islation vigorously, and was President Franklin Delano Roosevelt's contact man in the Senate to try to influence other senators to vote for New Deal legislation. He was a Democratic Senator from Indiana to the United States Congress from 1935 to 1941. Sherman Minton was born at Georgetown, Ind., on October 20, 1890.

[1] An interview with Captain Victor Hunt Harding, Secretary of the National Democratic Congress Reëlection Committee, Washington, D.C., April 10, 1939.

Minors. See Millsaps College

Minutemen

Because they were prepared to fight the British soldiers at a minute's notice, the colonial militia were called *Minutemen.*[1] The term was especially applied to the colonists who, during the early stages of the Revolutionary War, fought in Lexington, Mass., and its vicinity. It may be said, however, that other colonies had their share of minutemen.

In Alabama and other southern states just before the outbreak of the Civil War there were organizations called *Minute Men*[2] composed of men who were ready to fight for the right of their state to secede from the Union.

[1] *Commonwealth History of Massachusetts; Province of Massachusetts, 1689-1775*, ed. by Albert Bushnell Hart (The States History Company, New York, 1928) vol. 2, p. 553.
The War of Independence; American Phase, Being the Second Volume of a History of the Founding of the American Republic, Claude H. Van Tyne (Houghton Mifflin Company, Boston and New York, 1929) vol. 2, p. 9.
The History of Massachusetts, from the Landing of the Pilgrims to the Present Time, Including a Narrative of the Persecutions by State and Church in Engand; the Early Voyages to North America; the Explorations of the Early Settlers; Their Hardships, Sufferings, and Conflicts with the Savages; the Rise of Colonial Power; the Birth of Independence; the Formation of the Commonwealth, and the Gradual Progress of the State from Its Earliest Infancy to Its Present High Position, George Lowell Austin (B. B. Russell, Boston, 1884) p. 295-6.
[2] *A History of the People of the United States, from the Revolution to the Civil War*, John Bach McMaster (D. Appleton and Company, New York, 1913) vol. 8, p. 479-80.

Minx of the Movies. See Compson, Betty

Mischievous Andy. See Jackson, Andrew

Miss Ellen Bogen. See Ellenbogen, Henry

Mission City. See San Antonio, Tex.

Missionaries. See Whitman College

Mississippi

Mississippi is called the *Bayou State, Border-eagle State, Eagle State, Ground-hog State, Magnolia State, Mud-cat State,* and *Mud-waddler State.*

It is called the *Bayou State*[1] because of the number of its bayous.

The nicknames of *Border-eagle State*[2] and *Eagle State* originated because the state coat of arms depicts the American eagle.

Mississippi is nicknamed the *Ground-hog State,*[3] presumably because ground hogs are numerous in Mississippi.

The *Magnolia State* is given as a nickname to Mississippi because of the great number of magnolia trees growing within the state.

Mississippi is occasionally spoken of as the *Mud-cat State*[4] because of the many large catfish abounding in the swamps and the mud of the rivers of the state.

Mississippi's sobriquet, the *Mud-waddler State,*[1] is given by John Goff but he does not explain its origin or significance.

[1] *The New International Encyclopaedia*, Second Edition (Dodd, Mead and Company, New York, 1930) vol. 21, p. 463.
[2] *More About Names*, Leopold Wagner (T. Fisher Unwin, London, 1893) p. 30.
[3] *A Book of Nicknames*, John Goff (Courier-Journal Job Printing Company, Louisville, Ky., 1892) p. 14.
[4] *Americanisms; The English of the New World*, M. Schele De Vere (Charles Scribner and Company, New York, 1872) p. 660.

Mississippi Bubble

The *Mississippi Bubble*[1] is the popular name given to a financial scheme of John Law, "a fugitive from English justice," who promised to increase the importance of France in Colonial America, to bring France a great deal of profit, and to increase the importance and value of the Louisiana Territory. Law secured a charter for a bank in 1716, and in 1718 France invested heavily in the notes of this bank, which almost ruined her financially by 1720 when the bubble burst.

[1] *A History of the American People*, Arthur Gilman (D. Lothrop and Company, Boston, 1883) p. 178-9.

Mississippi College

The freshman athletic teams of Mississippi College, at Clinton, Miss., are known as the *Baby Chocs*[1] or the *Papooses* and the

Mississippi College—Continued
upper class teams are called *Choctaws*, because the campus is the site of an old Choctaw Indian encampment.

[1] *The Mississippi Collegian*, Clinton, Miss., November 22, 1935, col. 3, p. 2.

Mississippi River. See *Backbone of the Confederacy*

Mississippians
The Mississippians are called *Mud-cats, Mud-waddlers,* and *Tadpoles*. The state is nicknamed the *Mud-cat State* and the *Mud-waddler State* so the people are *Mud-cats* and *Mud-waddlers*.[1] As to *Tadpoles*,[2] Townsend says that the nickname is "equivalent to the expression Young Frenchmen. . . . Frenchmen were called . . . frogs from their ancient heraldic device, 'three toads erect.'"

[1] *A Book of Nicknames*, John Goff (Courier-Journal Job Printing Company, Louisville, Ky., 1892) p. 19.
[2] *U.S.: An Index to the United States of America*, comp. by Malcolm Townsend (D. Lothrop and Company, Boston, 1890) p. 76.

Missouri
There are eight nicknames given to Missouri: the *Bullion State*, the *Iron Mountain State*, the *Lead State*, the *Mother of the West*, the *Ozark State*, the *Pennsylvania of the West*, the *Puke State*, and the *Show Me State*.

Missouri's nickname, the *Bullion State*,[1] is derived from the sobriquet *Old Bullion*, applied to Senator Thomas Hart Benton because of the stand he took favoring gold and silver currency only.

The nickname *Iron Mountain State* originated because of the large deposits of iron ore in the Iron Mountains in St. François County.

The *Lead State*[1] refers to the productive lead mines in the southeastern part of the state.

The nickname *Ozark State* was given to Missouri from the Ozark mountains. Missouri is called the *Pennsylvania of the West* because of her similarity to Pennsylvania in mining interests and manufacturing.

Concerning Missouri's nickname, the *Puke State*[3] Townsend says that "this inelegant application took place in 1827 at the Galena Lead Mines, where throughout the mining craze so many Missourians had assembled,

that those already there declared the state of Missouri had taken a 'puke.'" (See also under Missourians.)

Missouri is called the *Show Me State*[4] from the expression generally attributed to the late Willard D. Vandiver, a former Representative from Missouri to the United States Congress, "I'm from Missouri, and you've got to show me."

[1] *The New International Encyclopaedia*, Second Edition (Dodd, Mead and Company, New York, 1930) vol. 21, p. 463, 665.
[2] A letter from Floyd C. Shoemaker, Secretary of the State Historical Society of Missouri, Columbia, Mo., March 25, 1930.
[3] *U.S.: An Index to the United States of America*, comp. by Malcolm Townsend (D. Lothrop Company, Boston, 1890) p. 71.
[4] *The Washington Post*, Washington, D. C., May 31, 1932, col. 3, p. 7.

Missourians
With regard to the origin of the nickname *Pukes* applied to the natives of Missouri, Leopold Wagner says that "the natives of Missouri are universally styled *Pukes,* a corruption of the older name *Pikes,* which still obtains in California" to describe the migratory whites from the South owing to the mistaken idea that these originally came from Pike County, Missouri.[1] (See also under Missouri.)

[1] *More About Names*, Leopold Wagner (T. Fisher Unwin, London, 1893) p. 28-9.

Missouri's Tom Dewey. See Milligan, M. M.

Missy. See Walker, William

Mr. American. See Tugwell, R. G.

Mr. Republican. See Taft, R. A.

Mistletoe Politician. See Van Buren, Martin

Mitchel, John Purroy
John Purroy Mitchel, a New York politician, was nicknamed *Young Torquemada*[1] soon after his appointment in 1906 as a special investigator in the office of John F. Ahearn, President of Manhattan Borough. The nickname was applied to Mitchel because, like Juan de Torquemada, a Spanish theologian of the fifteenth century, he distinguished himself as a young leader with marked ability as a debater and speaker.

John Purroy Mitchel was born at Fordham, N.Y., on July 19, 1879, and died at Lake Charles, La., on July 6, 1918.

[1] *Dictionary of American Biography under the Auspices of the American Council of Learned Societies*, ed. by Dumas Malone (Charles Scribner's Sons, New York, 1934) vol. 13, p. 37.

Mitchell, Stephen Mix

The jurist and statesman, Stephen Mix Mitchell, was called the *Stalking Library* [1] because of his encyclopedic knowledge in many fields.

Stephen Mix Mitchell was born in Wethersfield, Conn., on December 9, 1743, and died there on September 30, 1835.

[1] *Dictionary of American Biography under the Auspices of the American Learned Societies*, ed. by Allen Johnson (Charles Scribner's Sons, New York, 1929) vol. 13, p. 65.

Mitchill, Samuel Latham

Samuel Latham Mitchill, a scientist and legislator, was known as the *Nestor of American Science* [1] because of his activities in promoting the study of science in the institutions of higher learning in the United States, because of his scholastic learning and his influence in advancing scientific inquiry and the practical application of science. Mitchill served from 1801 to 1804 as a Representative from New York State to the United States Congress; from 1804 to 1809 as a Senator from New York; and again from 1810 to 1813 as a Representative.

Samuel Latham Mitchill was born at Hempstead, N.Y., on August 20, 1764, and died at New York City, on September 7, 1831.

[1] *Appleton's Cyclopaedia of American Biography*, ed. by James Grant Wilson and John Fiske (D. Appleton and Company, New York, 1894) vol. 4, p. 349.

Mobile, Alabama

Mobile is known as the *City of Five Flags,* the *Gulf City* and the *Picnic City*. Mobile is called the *City of Five Flags* because it had at various times belonged to five countries, Spain, France, Great Britain, Confederate states and the United States. It is designated the *Gulf City* [1,2] because it is located on the Mobile River which flows into the Mobile bay which leads into the Gulf of Mexico.

This city is nicknamed *Picnic City* [3] because its climate makes outdoor sports and outings desirable and there are numbers of northern people who spend a part of the winter months in Mobile.

[1] *Mobile: Her Trade, Commerce and Industries, 1883-4, Manufacturing Advantages, Business and Transportation Facilities, together with Sketches of the*

Principal Business Houses and Manufacturing Concerns in the "Gulf City," Historical and Descriptive Review, John E. Land (Published and copyrighted by the author, Mobile, Ala., 1884) p. 19-20.

[2] *History of Alabama and Dictionary of Alabama Biography*, Thomas McAdory Owen (The S. J. Clarke Publishing Company, Chicago, 1921) vol. 2, p. 1019-20.

[3] *A Book of Nicknames*, John Goff (Courier-Journal Job Printing Company, Louisville, Ky., 1892) p. 16.

Mob-rage Act. See Embargo Act

Moccasins. See University of Chattanooga

Model City. See Quincy, Ill.

Modern Athens. See Boston, Mass.

Modern Bunyan. See Miller, J. R.

Modern Gomorrah. See New York City

Modern Mother of Presidents. See Ohio

Modern Poor Richard's Almanac

George Horace Lorimer's *Letters from a Self-made Merchant to His Son* have been called a *Modern Poor Richard's Almanac* [1] because they are similar to Benjamin Franklin's *Poor Richard's Almanac* in humor and philosophy. They were published serially in the *Saturday Evening Post* from August 3, 1902, to October 11, 1902, and were later published in book form.

[1] *The World Book Encyclopedia* (The Quarrie Corporation, Chicago, 1938) vol. 10, p. 4110.

Modern Rome. See Richmond, Va.

Modern Sisyphus. See Webster, Daniel

Mohair Jack. See Garner, J. N.

Moline, Illinois. See Davenport Iowa, Moline and Rock Island, Ill.

Molly. See Stark, L. C.

Molly Maguires

A secret society which is said to have existed in the mining regions of Pennsylvania from about 1854 to 1877 was known as the *Molly Maguires*.[1] The members were desperate miners who, by threat or violence, jeopardized the property and personnel of local mining corporations because they saw

Molly Maguires—Continued
no other way of adjusting labor difficulties
between employer and employee.

The organization which supposedly furnished the miners with a pattern for their
activities was the *Molly Maguires* society
which existed in Ireland in the nineteenth
century. The members were Irish tenants
who committed acts of violence against their
English landlords. Why *Molly Maguires*
was selected for the name of the Irish organization has several interesting explanations. It is said that the organization was
perfected with the help of an aged woman
by the name of Molly Maguire, at whose
home the members often met. A second
story is that a woman of Amazonian characteristics originated many of the trouble-
making ideas executed by the *Molly Maguires.* Probably the most widely accepted
explanation is that a group of men, mas-
querading in women's apparel, called themselves by that name.

Anthony Bimba asserts that there is no
documentary proof that the rebellious
miners in Pennsylvania had any organization
by the name of *Molly Maguires,* and that
the name was applied by the press and the
public because of the similarity of their
activities to those of the *Molly Maguires.*

[1] *The Molly Maguires; the Origin, Growth, and
Character of the Organization,* F. P. Dewees (J. B.
Lippincott and Company, Philadelphia, 1877) p. 30, 44.

*The Nineteenth Century; Progress of the United States
of America, in the Century,* William P. Trent (The
Linscott Publishing Company, Philadelphia and London,
1901) vol. 5, p. 361.

[2] *The Molly Maguires,* Anthony Bimba (International
Publishers, New York, 1932) p. 9-14.

Molly Pitcher. See McCauley, M. L. H.

Monarch of Hampshire. See Williams,
Israel

Monarch of the Prairies. See Carson,
Christopher

Monitor. See Cheese Box on a Raft

Monkey State. See Tennessee

Monroe, James

The *Era-of-good-feeling President* and
the *Last Cocked Hat* are nicknames applied
to James Monroe.

He has been called the *Era-of-good feeling President* [1] because it was during his ad-

ministration as President of the United
States that the Era of Good Feeling took
place from 1817 to 1825.

During his first term of office as the
Chief Executive of the United States James
Monroe toured the country in 1817 and
again in 1819. On these trips he wore the
uniform of an officer of the Revolutionary
Army, a very conspicuous part of which was
a cocked hat, which by this time was out of
fashion. Monroe retained his polished manners and his military bearing and appeared
to his fellow-countrymen as the exponent
of the later Colonial and Revolutionary
Periods when the cocked hat was in vogue.
He was appropriately nicknamed the *Last
Cocked Hat.*[2]

James Monroe, the fifth President of the
United States, was born in Westmoreland
County, Va., on April 28, 1758, and died
at New York City, on July 4, 1831. He
was the last Chief Executive who had taken
an active part in the Revolutionary War.

[1] *A Book of Nicknames,* John Goff (Courier-Journal
Job Printing Company, Louisville, Ky., 1892) p. 27.

[3] "History of the Life Administration, and Times
of James Monroe, Fifth President of the United States"
by John Robert Ireland, in *The Republic; or, a History
of the United States of America in the Administrations,
from the Monarchic Colonial Days to the Present Times,*
John Robert Ireland (Fairbanks and Palmer Publishing
Company, Chicago, 1887) p. 227.

Dolly Madison, the Nation's Hostess, Elizabeth Lippincott Dean (Lothrop, Lee and Shepard Company,
Boston, 1928) p. 175.

Monroe, Mrs. James

The inhabitants of Paris, France, called
Mrs. James Monroe *La Belle Americaine,*[1]
the beautiful American, when she and her
husband were living in Paris from 1794 to
1796, while Monroe was United States Minister to France.

[1] *Compton's Pictured Encyclopedia* (F. E. Compton
Company, Chicago, 1933) vol. 15, p. 90.

Montagne, Luigi

Moving picture producers nicknamed
Luigi Montagne, an Italian actor and wrestler, *Bull Montana.*[1]

[1] *The Ring, World's Foremost Boxing Magazine* (Published monthly by The Ring, Inc., Dunellen, N.J.,
1931) March, 1931, p. 26.

Montana

Montana is called the *Bonanza State,* the
State of Treasure and Opportunity, the *Stubtoe State,* and the *Treasure State.*

The Montana State Librarian says, "The
names *Bonanza*[1] and *Treasure* are typical

of the mining area of the state, and *Stubtoe* of the mountainous . . . western section," because of its precipitous slopes.[2]

King says that Montana was called the *Bonanza State*[2] by Judge John Wasson Eddy because of its many rich mines, and that name has been generally accepted.

Montana was nicknamed the *State of Treasure and Opportunity*[3] because it is rich in mineral wealth and is less densely populated than some other Western states. Other resources are petroleum, timber, wool, sugar beets, grains, and grazing.

[1] A letter from David Hilger, Librarian of the Historical Society of Montana, Helena, Mont., April 18, 1930.

[2] *King's Handbook of the United States*, planned and ed. by Moses King, text by M. F. Sweetser (Moses King Corporation, Buffalo, N.Y., 1891) p. 510.

[2] *The American Language: Sup. II*, by H. L. Mencken (A. A. Knopf, New York, 1948) p. 635.

[3] *Compton's Pictured Encyclopedia*, F. E. Compton and Company, Chicago, 1947, vol. 9, p. 242.

Montgomery, James

James Montgomery, a Kansas pioneer, was nicknamed the *Kansas Hero*[1] because of the bravery and fairness which he displayed in dealing with the Indians and with rough adventurers in the Kansas and other western frontier settlements.

He was one of the acknowledged leaders in the Free-state cause from 1857 to 1861. It is said that, next to John Brown, he was feared more than any other man. In 1857 he was a Representative from his county to the Kansas Senate.

James Montgomery was born in Ashtabula County, Ohio, on December 22, 1814, and died in Linn County, Kansas, on December 6, 1871.

[1] *Appleton's Cyclopaedia of American Biography*, ed by James Grant Wilson and John Fiske (D. Appleton and Company, New York, 1894) vol. 4, p. 368.

Montpelier, Vermont

Montpelier is called the *Green Mountain City*,[1] because it is situated among the Green Mountains for which the state is also named and nicknamed.

[1] *Americanisms; The English of the New World*, M. Schele De Vere (Charles Scribner and Company, New York, 1872) p. 664.

Monument City. See Baltimore, Md.

Monumental State. See Maryland

Moody, Granville

Granville Moody, a Civil War soldier, was nicknamed the *Fighting Parson*[1] because of his bravery at the Battle of Stone River near Murfreesboro, Tenn., on October 29, 1862. During this encounter he was wounded several times and his horse was shot but he refused to leave the battlefield.

On June 15, 1833, Moody·was licensed to preach by the Methodist Episcopal Church in Norwich, Ohio. He later joined the Conference of the Methodist Episcopal Church in Ohio, and was appointed in 1860 to take charge of Morris Chapel, now St. Paul's Church, in Cincinnati, Ohio. He served in the Union Army from 1861 to May 16, 1863, when he resigned. On March 13, 1865, Colonel Moody was brevetted Brigadier General of Volunteers because of his bravery at the Battle of Stone River.

Granville Moody was born at Portland, Me., on January 2, 1812, and died near Jefferson, Ohio, on June 4, 1887.

[1] *Appleton's Cyclopaedia of American Biography*, ed. by James Grant Wilson and John Fiske (D. Appleton and Company, New York, 1894) vol. 4, p. 378.

Moody, Joseph

In the early part of his life, Reverend Joseph Moody accidentally shot and killed a youthful friend and wore a silk handkerchief over his face as a token of his grief. He became known as *Handkerchief Moody*.[1]

He was pastor of the Second Church in York, Me., from 1732 to 1736, when he became so melancholy that he gave up his ministry.

Joseph Moody was born at York, Me., in 1700, and died there on March 20, 1753.

[1] *Biographical Sketches of the Moody Family: Embracing Notices of Ten Ministers and Several Laymen, from 1633 to 1842*, Charles C. P. Moody (Published by Samuel G. Drake, Boston, 1847) p. 95, 96, 104.

Moody, William Vaughan

William Vaughan Moody, a writer and educator, was called the *Man in the Iron Mask*[1] by the students at the University of Chicago, where he taught English from 1895 to 1899 and from 1901 to 1907. He was unusually reserved and reticent, but kindhearted, dependable, and a leader among his contemporaries.

William Vaughan Moody was born at Spencer, Ind., on July 8, 1869, and died at

Moody, W. V.—Continued
Colorado Springs, Colo., on October 17, 1910.

[1] *Dictionary of American Biography under the Auspices of the American Council of Learned Societies,* ed. by Dumas Malone (Charles Scribner's Sons, New York, 1934) vol. 13, p. 109.

Mooney. See Miller, L. O.

Moon-faced Senator from Worcester. See Hoar, G. F.

Moonshine Gates. See Gates, J. W.

Moore, Bartholomew Figures
Bartholomew Figures Moore has been called the *Father of the North Carolina Bar* [1] because, for over forty years, he was outstanding in the legal profession of North Carolina. In 1848 he took a prominent part in revising the State Laws of North Carolina, which became the *Revised Code of North Carolina.*

He was born near Fishing Creek, in Halifax County, N.C., on January 29, 1801, and died at Raleigh, N.C., on November 27, 1878.

[1] *Encyclopedia of American Biography: American Biography, a New Cyclopedia,* comp. under the editorial supervision of a notable advisory board. (Published under the direction of The American Historical Society, Inc., New York, 1930) vol. 42, p. 51.
Distinguished North Carolinians: Lives of Distinguished North Carolinians with Illustrations and Speeches, collected and comp. by W. J. Peele (Published by the North Carolina Publishing Society, Raleigh, N.C., at the press of The Lord Baltimore Press, The Friedenwald Company, Baltimore, Md., 1898) p. 379-84.

Moore, Walter Homer
Walter Homer Moore was known as the *Beloved Dean* [1] when he was Dean of St. John's Cathedral at Quincy, Ill., from 1892 to 1908. He was a highly cultured man and possessed an agreeable and kindly disposition which endeared him to great numbers of people.

In 1912, he became Rector of St. Luke's Church, at South Glastonbury, and served until his death in 1917.

Walter Homer Moore was born at Warren, R.I., on December 18, 1844, and died at South Glastonbury, Conn., on May 11, 1917.

[1] *The National Cyclopaedia of American Biography* (James T. White and Company, New York, 1922) vol. 18, p. 44.

Moore, William Henry
William Henry Moore, a capitalist and promoter, was nicknamed the *Sphinx of the Rock Island* [1] in 1904, when he succeeded in acquiring a majority of the stock of the Chicago and Alton Railroad Company. He was already in control of the Chicago, Rock Island and Pacific Railway and acquired the new railway with the greatest secrecy.

William Henry Moore was born at Utica, N.Y., on October 25, 1848, and died at New York City, on January 11, 1923.

[1] *Dictionary of American Biography under the Auspices of the American Council of Learned Societies,* ed. by Dumas Malone (Charles Scribner's Sons, New York, 1934) vol. 13, p. 144.

Moorhead, James Kennedy
James Kennedy Moorhead, a legislator, canal builder, and pioneer in commercial telegraphy, was often called *Old Slackwater.* [1] While he was President of the Monongahela Navigation Company at Pittsburgh, P., from 1846 to 1884, he brought about the construction of numerous dams, locks and reservoirs throughout Indiana, Kentucky, and Pennsylvania, which produced immense quantities of slackwater above them.

James Kennedy Moorhead was born at Halifax, Pa., on September 7, 1806, and died at Pittsburgh, Pa., on March 6, 1884.

[1] *Dictionary of American Biography under the Auspices of the American Council of Learned Societies,* ed. by Dumas Malone (Charles Scribner's Sons, New York, 1934) vol. 13, p. 148.

Moose. See Earnshaw, G. L.

Moratorium Bill. See Lemke, William

Morgan, John Hunt
Because he adopted guerrilla warfare to annoy Union commanders, John Hunt Morgan was called the *Raider.* [1]

He was born at Huntsville, Ala., on June 1, 1826, and died at New Greenville, Tenn., on September 4, 1864.

[1] *A Book of Nicknames,* John Goff (Courier-Journal Job Printing Company, Louisville, Ky., 1892) p. 26.

Morgan, Lewis Henry
Lewis Henry Morgan was known as the *Father of American Anthropology.* [1] He published a study in 1851 entitled *The League of the Iroquois,* which is said to have been the first scientific discussion of the social and political organization of the Indians. In order to get first-hand information, Mor-

gan affiliated himself with a secret order known as the Grand Order of the Iroquois, and later was adopted into the tribes of the Senecas and the Iroquois.

Lewis Henry Morgan was born at Aurora, N.Y., on November 21, 1818, and died at Rochester, N.Y., on December 17, 1881.

[1] *Appleton's Cyclopaedia of American Biography,* ed. by James Grant Wilson and John Fiske (D. Appleton and Company, New York, 1888) vol. 4, p. 403.

Morgan, William Forbes

William Forbes Morgan, a New York investment banker and a Democratic politician, was nicknamed the *Liquor Czar* or the *Czar of the Liquor Industry* [1] because he was President of the Distilled Spirits Institute, Incorporated, which regulated a major part of the American liquor industry. Prior to this he was treasurer of the National Democratic Campaign Committee. He was appointed president of the Distilled Spirits Institute on February 16, 1937, but he delayed taking office until March 15, in order to finish his work on the National Democratic Campaign Committee.

William Forbes Morgan was born at New York City, on September 22, 1879, and died at Columbus, Ohio, on April 21, 1937.

[1] *The Washington Post,* Washington, D.C., April 25, 1937, col. 8, p. B-4.

Mormon Bishop. See King, W. H.

Mormon City. See Salt Lake City, Utah

Mormon State. See Utah

Mormons. See Utah Inhabitants

Mormon's Mecca. See Salt Lake City, Utah

Morris, Robert

Bobby the Cofferer, Bobby the Treasurer, Financier of the American Revolution, Merchant Prince, and the *Patriot Financier* are nicknames which were applied to Robert Morris.

He was nicknamed *Bobby the Cofferer* [1] by a writer who signed his articles Lucius, in the *Freeman's Journal* published in 1788, about the time that Morris resigned his office as Superintendent of Finances of the

United States, and when the contest over the adoption of the Federal Constitution was receiving greatest attention.

On February 20, 1781, Robert Morris became Superintendent of Finances of the United States, taking over the management of the United States Treasury in the place of a board that had previously had charge of it, and became known as *Bobby the Treasurer.* [2]

Morris was also called the *Financier of the American Revolution* [1] and the *Patriot Financier* [2] and the *Merchant Prince* [3] because of his services to the colonists during the Revolutionary War. In 1776, he was commissioned by Congress to provide funds for financing the war. He raised the needed money by employing great financial skill, and by even making use of his personal credit.

Robert Morris was born at Liverpool, England, on January 31, 1734, and died at Philadelphia, Pa., on May 8, 1806.

[1] *Robert Morris, Patriot and Financier,* Ellis Paxson Oberholtzer (The Macmillan Company, New York, 1903) p. 1, 16, 18, 30, 52, 55, 193, 209, 255, 258.

[2] *Robert Morris,* William Graham Sumner (Dodd, Mead and Company, New York, 1892) p. 53, 118.

[3] *A History of the United States for Grammar Schools,* Reuben Gold Thwaites and Calvin Noyes Kendall Houghton Mifflin Company, New York, 1912) p. 169-70.

Morris, Samuel

Because he was a pioneer in preaching and teaching the doctrines of the Presbyterian Church in Virginia in Colonial days, Samuel Morris was known as the *Father of Presbyterianism in Virginia.* [1]

Samuel Morris was born in Hanover County, Va., about 1700, and died there about 1770.

[1] *The National Cyclopaedia of American Biography* (James T. White and Company, New York, 1907) vol. 5, p. 516.

Morrison, William Ralls

William Ralls Morrison was nicknamed *Horizontal Bill* [1] because he introduced a bill into Congress on February 4, 1884, which sought to reduce the duty on practically all imported articles by a "horizontal" 20 per cent. The bill was rejected in the House of Representatives on May 6, 1884.

He was a Representative from Illinois to the United States Congress from 1873 to 1887. He was born near the present town

Morrison, W. R.—Continued

of Waterloo, Ill., on September 14, 1825, and died there on September 29, 1909.

[1] *U.S. "Snap Shots": An Independent, National and Memorial Encyclopedia . . . ,* Oliver McKee (A. M. Thayer and Company, Boston) 1892) p. 242.

Morris's Folly

In 1795 Robert Morris bought an entire block of land in Philadelphia, Pa., lying between Seventh and Eighth, and Chestnut and Walnut streets, where he proposed to erect a magnificent residential mansion. Major Pierre Charles L'Enfant, the famous French architect, had charge of the designing and building of this marble palace. Owing to the enormous amount of money spent on materials, labor, and changed plans, and to financial reverses, Morris and his family were never able to live in the partly finished house, which was popularly called *Morris's Folly*.[1]

[1] *Robert Morris, Patriot and Financier,* Ellis Paxson Oberholtzer (The Macmillan Company, New York, 1903) p. 279-9.

Morse, Charles Wyman

Charles Wyman Morse, a business executive, was nicknamed the *Ice King* [1] about 1899 when he established the Consolidated Ice Company at New York City after he had forced the majority of his competitors out of business. He dominated the ice business and doubled the price of ice in 1900. Following a public investigation which proved that leading municipal officials held stock in the enterprise, Morse cleverly withdrew from the corporation some twelve million dollars and devoted the rest of his life to banking, shipping, and speculating in Wall Street.

Charles Wyman Morse was born at Bath, Me., on October 21, 1856, and died there on January 12, 1933.

[1] *Dictionary of American Biography under the Auspices of the American Council of Learned Societies,* ed. by Dumas Malone (Charles Scribner's Sons, New York, 1934) vol. 13, p. 240.

Morse, Jedidiah

The *Father of American Geography* [1] was applied to Jedidiah Morse, a pioneer geographer in the United States. His text-book entitled *Geography Made Easy* which appeared in 1784, was the first of its kind to be published in the United States. He also wrote a number of other books and articles dealing with the study of geography.

Jedidiah Morse was born at Woodstock, Conn., on August 23, 1761, and died at New Haven, Conn., on June 9, 1826.

[1] *The National Cyclopaedia of American Biography* (James T. White and Company, New York, 1906) vol. 13, p. 353.

Morse, Samuel Finley Breese

Because he invented the electro-magnetic telegraph about 1835 or 1837, Samuel Finley Breese Morse was called the *Father of the Telegraph*.[1] He was born at Charlestown, Mass., on April 27, 1791, and died at New York City, on April 2, 1872.

[1] *A Book of Nicknames,* John Goff (Courier-Journal Job Printing Company, Louisville, Ky., 1892) p. 29.

Morton, Oliver Hazard Perry Throck

The *Devil on Two Sticks, Sitting Bull,* and the *War Governor* are appellations which have been given to Oliver Hazard Perry Throck Morton.

While he was a Senator from Indiana to the United States Congress from 1867 until his death in 1877, he came to be known as the *Devil on Two Sticks* and *Sitting Bull.* In October 1865, Morton was stricken with paralysis and was never able to walk again or to stand without the aid of canes. Consequently he usually remained seated while addressing the Senate and was nicknamed *Sitting Bull.*[1]

However, when questions of nation-wide interest and importance arose in the Senate, Morton, partly rising, would prop himself upon his two canes and express his views so forcibly and fearlessly that his political opponents nicknamed him the *Devil on Two Sticks.*[2]

Because he served as Governor of Indiana during the Civil War, he became known as the *War Governor.*[3]

Oliver Hazard Perry Throck Morton was born at Saulsbury, Ind., on August 4, 1823, and died at Indianapolis, Ind., on November 1, 1877.

[1] *U.S. "Snap Shots": An Independent, National, and Memorial Encyclopedia . . . ,* Oliver McKee (A. M. Thayer and Company, Boston, 1892) p. 244.

[2] *The National Cyclopaedia of American Biography* (James T. White and Company, New York, 1906) vol. 13, p. 271.

[3] *The Encyclopaedia Britannica,* Fourteenth Edition (Encyclopaedia Britannica, Inc., New York, 1929) vol. 15, p. 832.

Morton, Sarah Wentworth Apthorp

Sarah Wentworth Apthorp Morton was nicknamed the *American Sappho* [1] by Robert Treat Paine, Junior, because of the quality of the short poems which she contributed to the *Massachusetts Magazine* during the late eighteenth and early nineteenth centuries. Sappho, the Greek poetess, flourished at Mitylene, or Eresus, on the Island of Lesbos, from about 630 to 570 B.C.

Sarah Wentworth Apthorp Morton was born at Braintree, Mass., on August 29, 1759, and died at Quincy, Mass., on May 14, 1846.

[1] *Appleton's Cyclopaedia of American Biography,* ed. by James Grant Wilson and John Fiske (D. Appleton and Company, New York, 1894) vol. 4, p. 430.

Moses, Anna Mary Robertson

Grandma Moses [1] is the nickname of Anna Mary Robertson Moses, a New York State farmwife who began to paint in 1938, at the age of 78.

After a lifetime devoted to raising her ten children and the duties of managing a farm, Mrs. Moses, recalling her childhood pleasure in drawing, took up the use of oils. Her pictures were discovered in a Woman's Exchange exhibit in Hoosick Fall, N. Y., and she soon became known throughout the art world as an "authentic American primitive." Her works have been widely reproduced on Christmas cards which are very popular with the buying public.

Anna Mary Robertson Moses was born September 7, 1860, on a farm in Washington County, N. Y. She lives with her youngest son and his family in Eagle Bridge, N.Y.

[1] *Current Biography, Who's News and Why, 1949* ed. by Anna Rothe (The H. W. Wilson Co., New York, 1950) p. 441-442.

Moses. See Tubman, Harriet

Moses of America. See Wise, I. M.

Mosquito State. See New Jersey

Mother Bailey. See Bailey, A. W.

Mother Bickerdyke. See Bickerdyke, M. A. B.

Mother Church of American Baptists

The First Baptist Church of Providence, R.I., is called the *Mother Church of American Baptists* [1] because it was the first Baptist Church founded in America. It was founded in 1639 by Roger Williams who was its first pastor.

[1] *Corners and Characters of Rhode Island,* George D. Laswell (Printed by the Oxford Press, Providence, R.I., 1924) p. 64.

Mother Jones. See Jones, M. H.

Mother Lee. See Lee, Ann

Mother of All the Doughboys. See Schumann-Heink, Mme. Ernestine

Mother of Counties. See Lunenburg County, Va.

Mother of Methodism in the United States. See Heck, B. R.

Mother of Mischief

Benjamin Franklin nicknamed the Stamp Act the *Mother of Mischief* [1] because he saw that, if it were passed, it would eventually lead to serious trouble between the colonists and the British Government.

[1] *Clark of the Ohio: A Life of George Rogers Clark,* Frederick Palmer (Dodd, Mead and Company, New York, 1929) p. 40.

Mother of Presidents. See Virginia

Mother of Rivers. See New Hampshire

Mother of Southwestern Statesmen. See Tennessee

Mother of States. See Virginia

Mother of Statesmen. See Virginia

Mother of Thanksgiving. See Hale, S. J.

Mother of the American Legion. See Schumann-Heink, Mme. Ernestine

Mother of the Confederacy. See Law, S. C.

Mother of the Kindergarten. See Blow, S. E.

Mother of the Red Cross. See Barton, Clara

Mother of the West. See Missouri

Mother Stewart. See Stewart, E. D.

Mother Wood. See Wood, Mrs. M. R. L.

Mother-in-law of the Navy. See Norfolk, Va.

Motor Capital of the World. See Detroit, Mich.

Mott, James Wheaton

James Wheaton Mott, an Oregon lawyer and politician, was nicknamed *Tonguepoint Mott*[1] because he introduced a bill into the House of Representatives on March 16, 1934, to authorize an appropriation for the further development of the submarine and destroyer base at Tongue Point, Ore.

He was a Republican Representative to the Oregon Legislature from 1922 to 1928, and from 1930 to 1932, and a Republican Representative from Oregon to the United States Congress from 1933 to 1945.

James Wheaton Mott was born on a farm in Clearfield County, Pa., on November 12, 1883, and died Nov. 12, 1945.

[1] An interview with Captain Victor Hunt Harding, Secretary of the National Democratic Congress Reëlection Committee, Washington, D.C., April 10, 1939.

Mott, Lucretia

Mrs. Lucretia Mott was called the *Advance Agent of Emancipation, Invincible Warrior in Righteous Causes, Flower of Quakerism,* and the *Sweet-spirited Advocate of Justice, Love and Humanity.*

She was nicknamed the *Flower of Quakerism*[1] because she was one of the first women of that religious faith in America to preach the gospel in public. Each of the other nicknames were applied to her because of her zeal in striving to protect runaway slaves from unjust punishment, and in helping them to secure their freedom.

Mrs. Lucretia Mott was born at Nantucket, on Nantucket Island, off the coast of Massachusetts, on January 3, 1793, and died near Philadelphia, Pa., on November 11, 1880.

[1] *True Stories of Famous Men and Women of America for Young People, Containing Full Accounts of the Lives and Heroic Deeds of About Half a Hundred Illustrious Men and Women Who Have Made Our Country Great and Our Flag Respected Throughout the World, from the Time of George and Mary Washington to Admiral Dewey and Clara Barton,* John S. C. Abbott, William Garnett, W. W. Birdsall, Edward E. Ellis, and others (Neither the name of the publisher, the place, nor the date of publication is given) p. 312.

Mound City. See St. Louis, Mo.

Moundbuilders. See Southwestern College (Kansas)

Mountain Empire

The southwestern part of the State of Virginia is often designated the *Mountain Empire*[1] because its mountain ranges are rich in scenic beauty and fertile valleys. It is a blue grass region famous for producing fine beef cattle, and is one of the richest sections of the state.

[1] *Virginia,* comp. and ed. by Charlotte Allen (Published by the Department of Agriculture and Immigration of the State of Virginia under the direction of George W. Koiner, Commissioner, Division of Purchase and Printing, Richmond, Va., 1937) p. 99.

Industrial Survey Washington County, Virginia, R. L. Humbert, Director of Surveys, in collaboration with R. B. H. Begg, P. H. McGauhey, J. Elton Podewick, M. L. Jeffries, W. H. Humbert, S. C. Andrews (Engineering Extension Division, Virginia Polytechnic Institute, Blacksburg, Va., July 1929) cover page.

Mountain Evangelist. See Jones, S. P.

Mountain State. See Colorado; West Virginia

Mountaineer Division. See Tenth Mountain Division of World War II

Mountaineers. See College of the Ozarks; West Virginia University; Western State College of Colorado

Mouton, Robert L.

Robert L. Mouton, a Louisiana horticulturalist and politician, was nicknamed *Marine Bob* and *Louisiana Ram*[1] in the National House of Representatives. He was called *Marine Bob* because he had formerly belonged to the United States Marine Corps, and *Louisiana Ram* because his French name, *mouton,* means sheep. He was elected Democratic Representative from Louisiana in 1936.

Robert L. Mouton was born at Duchamp, La., on October 20, 1892.

[1] An interview with Captain Victor Hunt Harding, Secretary of the National Democratic Congress Reëlection Committee, Washington, D.C., April 10, 1939.

Muckers. See New Mexico School of Mines; Texas College of Mines and Metallurgy

Muckrakers

During the second term of office of Theodore Roosevelt as President of the United States from 1905 to 1909, vigorous campaigns for reforms were carried on by magazines and newspapers to expose the corrupt practices of great corporations. A number of writers produced highly sensational articles professing to describe these conditions, but in reality exaggerating or distorting them. President Roosevelt compared them to the Muckraker in *Pilgrim's Progress* who could not stop his muckraking in order to take the crown which a Celestial figure was holding over his head. The expression *Muckrakers* [1] came into popular usage soon after President Roosevelt had made his speech on April 14, 1906, on the subject entitled, "The Man with the Muck Rake" and *muckrake* and *muckraker* came into standard English usage not long after. President Roosevelt, himself an ardent reformer, was out of sympathy with those who brought only unjust and destructive criticism against existing conditions. He also warned his countrymen to weigh carefully the spectacular accusations of corrupt activities made by the *Muckrakers* before they accepted these sensational reports as true.

[1] *A History of the United States*, John Holladay Latané (Allyn and Bacon, New York and Boston, 1926) p. 535.

Mud-cat State. See Mississippi

Mud-cats. See Missippians

Muddy. See Ruel, H. D.

Muddy River Hamlet. See Brookline, Mass.

Mud-heads. See Tennesseeans

Mud March

The march of the Union army under General Ambrose Everett Burnside from Fredericksburg, Va., between January 20 and 22, 1863, to attack General Robert E. Lee at Falmouth, Va., was known as the *Mud March* [1] because heavy rains bogged down both men and equipment.

Another expedition known as the *Mud March* [2] was that of General George Crook in the Black Hills of the Dakotas in 1876. Crook and his men were a part of an expedition sent out under General Philip H. Sheridan by the War Department to force the Sioux Indians and their allies to return to their reservations. They were bogged down in knee-deep mud for some ten days, between the Heart River and the Black Hills.

[1] *The Fiery Epoch, 1830-1877*, Charles Willis Thompson (The Bobbs-Merrill Company, Indianapolis, Ind., 1931) p. 234.

"Captains of the Civil War: A Chronicle of The Blue and The Gray" by William Wood, in *The Chronicles of America Series*, Allen Johnson, Editor, Gerhard R. Lomer and Charles W. Jefferys, Assistant Editors (Yale University Press, New Haven, Conn., 1921) vol. 31, p. 251-2.

[2] *South Dakota Historical Collections*, comp. by the State Historical Society (News Printing Company, Aberdeen, S.D., 1902) vol. 1, p. 145, vol. 2 p. 422-7, vol. 6, p. 493.

The Black Hills: or, The Last Hunting Ground of the Dakotahs: A Complete History of the Black Hills of Dakota from Their First Invasion in 1874 to the Present Time, Comprising a Comprehensive Account of How They Lost Them; of Numerous Adventures of the Early Settlers; Their Heroic Struggles for Supremacy Against the Hostile Dakotah Tribes, and Their Final Victory; The Opening of the Country to White Settlement, and Subsequent Development, Annie D. Tallent (Nixon-Jones Printing Company, St. Louis, Mo., 1899) p. 232.

Mudsill Hammond. See Hammond, J. H.

Mud-waddler State. See Mississippi

Mud-waddlers. See Mississippians

Muggletonians

The *Muggletonians* [1] was a nickname applied during Woodrow Wilson's presidential campaign to his enthusiastic supporters. Oliver Wendell Holmes described the *Muggletonians* and gave several humorous characteristics of them in *The Professor at the Breakfast Table*.[2] A muggletonian is defined by *The Century Dictionary and Cyclopedia* as "a member of a sect founded in England by Ludowick Muggleton and John Reeve about 1651. The members of the sect believed in the prophetic inspiration of its founders."

[1] *Woodrow Wilson: A Character Study*, Robert Edwards Annin (Dodd, Mead and Company, New York, 1924) p. 364-72.

[2] *The Professor at the Breakfast Table*, Oliver Wendell Holmes (Houghton Mifflin and Company, Boston, 1890) p. 421-3.

Mugwumps

The sobriquet, *Mugwumps*,[1] took on political significance in 1884 during the campaign of James Gillespie Blaine as the Republican candidate for President of the United States. The regular Republicans gave

Mugwumps—Continued

the nickname to those who had become alienated from the Republican party because they were not in sympathy with its platform. On June 15, 1884, *The New York Sun* designated the radical members of the Republican party as *Mugwumps.* It is also sometimes applied to Republicans who support a Democratic candidate. Norton points out that the term was colloquially used along the Massachusetts coast before this time and that *The Indianapolis Sentinel* used it in 1872.

Thornton and others point out that mugwump is an Algonquin Indian word, signifying chief or leader. John Eliot, in his translation of the Bible into the Algonquin dialect, used the form *mukquomp.*

[1] *The Republican Party: A History,* William Starr Myers (The Century Company, New York and London, 1928) p. 286-7.

Political Americanisms, Charles Ledyard Norton (Longmans, Green and Company, New York, 1890) p. 74-6.

An American Glossary, Being an Attempt to Illustrate Certain Americanisms upon Historical Principles, Richard H. Thornton (Francis and Company, London, 1912) vol. 2, p. 595.

Natick Dictionary, James Hammond Trumbull, Smithsonian Institution, Bureau of American Ethnology, Bulletin number 25 (Government Printing Office, Washington, D.C., 1903) p. 67.

Muhlenberg, John Peter Gabriel

Major General John Peter Gabriel Muhlenberg was nicknamed *Devil Pete* [1] because of his daring which bordered on recklessness.

He was born at Trappe, Pa., on October 1, 1746, and died at Philadelphia, Pa., on October 1, 1807.

[1] *The Life of Major-general Peter Muhlenberg of the Revolutionary Army,* Henry A. Muhlenberg (Carey and Hart, Philadelphia, 1849) p. 30.

American Leaders, Walter Lefferts (J. B. Lippincott Company, Philadelphia, 1919) vol. 1, p. 190, 191.

The Life of Major-general Peter Muhlenberg of the Revolutionary Army, Henry A. Muhlenberg (Carey and Hart, Philadelphia, 1849) p. 331-3.

Muldoon, William

The *Czar of Boxing, Father of American Boxing, Iron Duke, Old Roman, Solid Man* [1] are nicknames applied to William Muldoon because of his reputation in the boxing world. In addition to being an outstanding boxer, he was an influential member of the New York State Athletic Commission, which exercises control over boxing in New York City.

William Muldoon was born in the Genessee Valley of New York State, on May 25,

1846, and died at White Plains, N.Y., on January 3, 1933.

[1] *Muldoon, the Solid Man of Sport,* Edward Van Every (Frederick A. Stokes Company, New York, 1929), p. vii.

Mule. See Haas, G. W.

Mule Brigade

During the Civil War, a regiment of about five hundred Confederate cavalrymen under the command of Major General James Ewell Brown Stuart became nicknamed the *Mule Brigade* [1] in allusion to the fact that these soldiers were deprived of their horses during the course of the war, and, unable to secure others, were forced to ride mules. The stubborness and undependability of these animals and the difficulties which their riders experienced in attempting to control them upon the battlefield, caused the activities of the *Mule Brigade* to be a source both of amusement and of chagrin to their owners and to other Confederate soldiers.

[1] *The Blue and the Gray: A Graphic History of the Army of the Potomac and That of Northern Virginia, Including the Brilliant Engagements of These Forces from 1861 to 1865; the Campaigns of the Shenandoah Valley and the Army of the James, together with Reminiscences of Tent and Field, Acts of Personal Daring, Deeds of Heroic Suffering and Thrilling Adventure, Coupled with Which Will Be Found Many Tales of Individual Achievements, Army Yarns, and Pen Pictures of Officers and Privates, a Complete Roster of the Two Great Armies and Twenty Full-page Maps,* Theodore Gerrish and John S. Hutchinson (Hoyt, Fogg and Donham, Portland, Me., 1863) p. 338.

Mule Watson. See Watson, Milton

Muleriders. See Agricultural and Mechanical College (Magnolia, Ark.)

Muley Doughton. See Doughton, R. L.

Murat of America. See Wheat, C. R.

Murat of the Union Army. See Logan, J. A.

Murphy, Charles Francis

The appellation, *Silent Charley,* [1] was given to Charles Francis Murphy because he was unusually taciturn with regard to his personal and business activities.

In 1892 Murphy became the leader of the Tammany or Eighteenth Assembly District of New York City. He was the Commissioner of Docks and Ferries from 1897 to 1901, and in 1902 succeeded Richard Croker as the Chief of Tammany Hall, a post he held until his death.

Charles Francis Murphy was born at New York City, on June 20, 1858, and died there on April 25, 1924.

[1] *The National Cyclopaedia of American Biography* (James T. White and Company, New York, 1906) vol. 13, p. 575.

Who's Who in America, a Biographical Dictionary of Notable Living Men and Women of the United States, 1922-1923, ed. by Albert Nelson Marquis (A. N. Marquis and Company, Chicago, 1922) vol. 12, p. 2279.

Murphy, Francis

Francis Murphy, who devoted the major part of his life to the cause of temperance, has been nicknamed the *Apostle of Temperance* [1] because of his outstanding work in connection with the Christian Temperance movement. He secured the signatures of thousands of persons pledging themselves to abstain totally from selling or using intoxicating liquors.

Murphy came from Ireland to America in 1852 and served in the Civil War for three years. In 1865 he moved to Portland, Me., where he opened a bar, became a hard drinker and sank into poverty and want.

In 1870 he was arrested and sent to jail at Portland for drunkeness. While there he was converted to Christianity.

After his conversion and release from prison, Murphy became deeply interested in pledging others to refrain from drinking liquors. He originated a total-abstinence pledge to renounce the use of alcoholic liquors, and was himself the first to sign this pledge. It later became the pledge of the National Christian Temperance Union and read: " 'With malice toward none and charity to all' I, the undersigned, do pledge my word and honor, God helping me, to abstain from all intoxicating liquors as a beverage, and that I will, by all honorable means, encourage others to abstain."[2]

Francis Murphy was born at Tagoat in Wexford County, Ireland, on April 24, 1836, and died at Los Angeles, Calif., on June 30, 1907.

[1] *The Washington Post,* Washington, D.C., July 3, 1907, col. 4, p. 5.

The Los Angeles Times, Los Angeles, Calif., July 1, 1907, col. 7, p. 1 and col. 1, p. 4.

[2] *The True Path; or Gospel Temperance: Being the Life, Work, and Speeches of Francis Murphy, Dr. Henry A. Reynolds, and Their Co-laborers Embracing also a History of the Women's Christian Temperance Union,* J. Samuel Vandersloot (Henry S. Goodspeed and Company, New York, 1878) p. iv, 71.

Murphy, Frank

During the spring of 1939 the New Dealers nicknamed Attorney General Frank Murphy *Frank the Just* [1] because of his reforms in reorganizing the Justice Department of the United States, his aggressiveness in helping to bring to justice political racketeers, and his insistence upon rigorous law enforcement. The New Dealers considered Murphy's legal reorganization and racket-busting activities comparable to the accomplishments of New York's Thomas Dewey; consequently, he was designated *The New Deal's Tom Dewey* [2]

Murphy was graduated from the University of Michigan, at Ann Arbor, Mich., with the degree of Bachelor of Laws in 1914. He studied law at Lincoln's Inn, London, England, and at Trinity College, Dublin, Ireland. He became Attorney General of the United States in January 1939, and was appointed an Associate Justice of the United States Supreme Court in 1940. He conducted the Nuremberg war trials of Nazi officials.

Frank Murphy was born at Harbor Beach, Mich., on April 13, 1893, and died on July 19, 1949.

[1] *The Evening Star,* Washington, D.C., May 27, 1939, col. 2, p. A-9.

[2] *The Washington Post,* Washington, D.C., August 2, 1939, col. 4, p. 9.

Murray, John

The *Father of Universalism in America* [1] is a nickname given to Reverend John Murray. In 1775 he established at Gloucester, Mass., the first Universalist Society in the New World and took an outstanding part in the first Universalist convention which met at Oxford, Mass., in 1785, to organize a Universalist church and adopt articles of faith and form of government. From 1793 until his death in 1815, he was in charge of the Universalist Society at Boston.

John Murray was born at Alton, Hampshire, England, on December 10, 1741, emigrated to America in September 1770, and died at Boston, Mass., on September 3, 1815.

[1] *The National Cyclopaedia of American Biography* (James T. White and Company, New York, 1906) vol. 13, p. 175.

The Life of Reverend John Murray, Preacher of Universal Salvation, New Edition, written by himself, with a continuation by Mrs. Judith Sargent Murray (Universalist Publishing House, Boston, 1833) p. 312. 318.

Murray, William Henry

Alfalfa Bill, Cockle-bur Bill, and the *Sage of Tishomingo* were nicknames applied to William Henry Murray.

Alfalfa Bill [1] was applied to him soon after he had moved to Indian Territory, in 1898, because he was the first man in the Chickasaw Nation to grow alfalfa.

During the constitutional convention at Muskogee, Okla., in 1905, a Wapanucka, Okla., newspaper editor called him *Cockle-bur Bill* [1] because he persisted in his fight to make his home town of Tishomingo the county seat of Johnston County instead of Wapanucka.

Because he was a man of deep insight into the practical and political affairs of his state he was known as the *Sage of Tishomingo.* [1]

William Henry Murray was born at Collinsville, Tex., on November 21, 1869, was Governor of Oklahoma from 1931 to 1935.

[1] *Oklahoma Yesterday—Today—Tomorrow,* ed. by Lerona Rosamond Morris (Cooperative Publishing Company, Guthrie, Okla., 1930) p. 538.

Muscles. See Waner, L. J. and Waner, P. G.

Mushroom City. See San Francisco, Calif.

Mushroomopolis. See Kansas City, Mo.

Musketeers. See Xavier University

Muskrats. See Delawareans

Muslin Palace

The *Muslin Palace* [1] was a name given to a temporary building erected in Judiciary Square at Washington, D.C., to house the inaugural ball of March 4, 1873, when Ulysses Simpson Grant became President of the United States, white muslin was used to cover the walls, ceilings, arches, and columns of the building.

[1] *White House Gossip, from Andrew Johnson to Calvin Coolidge,* Edna M. Colman (Doubleday, Page and Company, Garden City, N.Y., 1927) p. 79, 81.

Mustangs. See Southern Methodist University; University of California Agricultural College

Mutt. See Ens, Jewel

N

NRA Czar. See Johnson, H. S.

Nail City. See Wheeling, W.Va.

Napoleon of Gas. See Addicks, J. E. O.

Napoleon of Luzon. See MacArthur, Douglas

Napoleon of Protection. See McKinley, William

Napoleon of Slavery. See Calhoun, J. C.

Napoleon of the California Bar. See Delmas, D. M.

Napoleon of the North. See Comstock, Peter

Napoleon of the Stump. See Polk, J. K.

Napoleon of the Turf. See Johnson, W. R.

Napoleons of Wall Street

Immediately following the passage of the Currency Bill by the United States Congress on March 14, 1900, the big Wall Street speculators in New York City were called the *Napoleons of Wall Street,* [1] because they dominated the financial activities of America.

[1] *Twenty Years of the Republic, 1885-1905,* Harry Thurston Peck (Dodd, Mead and Company, New York, 1907) p. 634.

Narragansett. See Maynard, Horace

Nashville, Tennessee

Nashville is known as the *Athens of the South,* the *City Beautiful, Dimple of the Universe, Rock City* and *City of Rocks.* It is called the *Athens of the South* [1] because of the number of schools and colleges, of which Vanderbilt University, George Peabody College for Teachers, Ward-Belmont, and Fisk University are outstanding. Situated in Centennial Park, Nashville, stands an excellent reproduction of the Parthenon which crowned the Acropolis at Athens.

Nashville is called the *City Beautiful* [3] because it is located in one of the most beautiful sections of middle Tennessee.

John Trotwood Moore, the late State Historian and Archivist of Tennessee, termed Nashville the *Dimple of the Universe* [4] because it is located in the Great Basin of the Highland Rim of middle Tennessee, called the Nashville Basin.

Nashville is nicknamed the *Rock City* or the *City of Rocks*,[2] because it is built on a series of limestone bluffs on both sides of the Cumberland River.

[1] *The Economic and Social Beginnings of Tennessee*, Albert C. Holt (Published under the auspices of George Peabody College, Nashville, Tenn., 1923) p. 3.

[2] *The Wayne Hand-book of Nashville, and the Tennessee Centennial Exposition, Illustrated: A Complete Guide-Book for Tourists, with Maps, Plans, Etc.* (Wayne Publishing Company, Fort Wayne, Ind., 1897) p. 15.

[3] *Pen and Sunlight Sketches of Nashville* (Comp., illustrated, and published by The American Illustrating Company, Nashville, Tenn., 1911) p. 64.

[4] *All About Nashville: A Complete Historical Guide-Book of the City*, comp. by Ida Clyde Clarke (Marshall and Bruce Company, Nashville, Tenn., 1912) p. 5.

Natchez, Mississippi

Natchez is known as the *Bluff City* [1] because it is situated upon high bluffs, commanding an extensive view of the Mississippi River.

[1] *Natchez, Mississippi on Top, Not "Under the Hill,"* *Adams County and the Neighboring Territory*, C. N. McCormick (Daily Democrat Steam Print, Natchez, Miss., 1897) p. 24.

Proud Old Natchez, History and Romance, Compiled from Ancient Chronicles and Modern Histories, Thomas Reber (Natchez Printing and Stationery Company, Natchez, Miss., 1909) p. 5.

Nathan Hale of the South. See Davis, Sam

Natick Cobbler. See Wilson, Henry

National Pastime. See Baseball

National Training School for Women and Girls

The National Training School for Women and Girls, located on Lincoln Heights, Washington, D.C., is called the *Nickel and Dime School* [1] because it is largely supported by contributions from people who cannot afford to give large sums of money to its maintenance. This school was founded by Nannie Burroughs for the purpose of training Negro women and girls.

[1] *Washington, City and Capital: Federal Writers' Project*, American Guide Series, 1937 (Government Printing Office, Washington, D.C., 1937) p. 87.

Nationals. See Washington American League Baseball Club

Nation's Hostess. See Madison, D. P. T.

Nation's State. See District of Columbia

Nation's Thoroughfare. See Louisville, Ky.

Native American Party. See Dark Lantern Party

Navarre of the American Revolution. See Butler, Thomas

Navel of the Nation. See Kansas

Navy Hill Cats

In the 1850's gangs of boys in Richmond, Va., were called "cats," and those in various parts of the city were known by the name of the district, *Navy Hill Cats* [1] for example.

[1] *The End of an Era*, John S. Wise (Houghton, Mifflin and Company, New York and Boston, 1899) p. 59.

Nebraska

The nicknames given to Nebraska are the *Antelope State, Blackwater State, Bug-eating State, Tree Planters State*, and the *Corn Huskers State*.

The State Historical Society says that the name *Antelope State* [1] was applied to Nebraska because of the abundance of antelopes there in the early days.

Nebraska is called the *Blackwater State* [2] from the color of its streams, darkened by the black soil of the prairie.

The *Bug-eating State* [3] is applied to Nebraska because it has numerous bullbats (*Caprimulgus europaeus*) locally named "bug-eaters."

The nickname, the *Tree Planters State*,[4] was adopted by an act of the Nebraska legislature in 1895. *"Be it Resolved by the Legislature of the State of Nebraska*: That Nebraska shall hereafter in a popular sense be known and referred to as the 'Tree Planters State.' "

The University of Nebraska football team were called *Corn Huskers* [1] and the nickname was later extended to the state.

[1] A letter from Addison E. Sheldon, Secretary and Superintendent of the Nebraska State Historical Society, Lincoln, Neb., March 20, 1930.

Nebraska—Continued

[2] *King's Handbook of the United States,* planned and ed. by Moses King, text by M. F. Sweetser (Moses King Corporation, Buffalo, N.Y., 1891) p. 522.

[3] *U.S.: An Index to the United States of America,* comp. by Malcolm Townsend (D. Lothrop Company, Boston, 1890) p. 77.

[4] *Laws of Nebraska, 1895: Laws, Joint Resolutions, and Memorials Passed by the Legislative Assembly of the State of Nebraska at the Twenty-fourth Session, Begun and Held at the City of Lincoln, January 1, 1895,* published by authority (Omaha Printing Company, State Printers, Omaha, Neb., 1895) p. 441.

Nebraska Central College

The *Quakers, Fighting Quakers,* and *Praying Quakers* [1] are the nicknames of the athletic teams of Nebraska Central College, at Central City, Neb., because the college is owned by the Society of Friends or Quakers.

[1] A communication from O. W. Carrell, President of Nebraska Central College, Central City, Neb., November 30, 1935.

Nebraskans

The people of Nebraska are called *Bug-eaters* and the state is the *Bug-eating State* because of the numerous bull-bats, locally called bug-eaters," found there. (See Nebraska.)

Sylva Clapin says the term comes from "the poverty-stricken appearances of many parts of the state. Indeed, so they say, if one living there were to refuse to eat bugs, he would like Polonius, soon be 'not where he eats, but where he is eaten.' " [1]

[1] *A New Dictionary of Americanisms,* Sylva Clapin (Louis Weiss and Company, New York, 1903) p. 81.

Negro Fort

Following the departure of the British Army from Florida in 1814, a British officer built a fort near the mouth of the Appalachicola River in Florida and left the Seminole Indians in charge of it when he returned to England. Soon afterwards it became a place of refuge for runaway Negro slaves and became known as the *Negro Fort.* [1]

[1] *Scribner's Popular History of the United States from the Earliest Discoveries of the Western Hemispheres by the Northmen to the Present Time,* William Cullen Bryant, Sidney Howard Gay, and Noah Brooks (Charles Scribner's Sons, New York, 1896) vol. 4, p. 248.

Negro Moses. See Tubman, Harriet

Neill, Thomas Hewson

The sobriquet, *Beau Neill,*[1] was applied to Major General Thomas Hewson Neill because he was unusually handsome, refined in manner, and neat in appearance.

Thomas Hewson Neill was born at Philadelphia, Pa., on April 9, 1826, and died there on March 12, 1885. During his participation in the Civil War, he attained the ranks of brevet Brigadier General and brevet Major General of volunteers in the United States Army.

[1] *The National Cyclopaedia of American Biography* (James T. White and Company, New York, 1906) vol. 13, p. 513.

Neily, Harry

While he was in Mexico in 1920 as the guest of former President Alvaro Obregon, a Mexican interpreter, Juan Rentvio, called Harry Neily *El Neily Manoso,* or the *Skillful Neily.*[1] He has been widely called by this nickname. He is also known as *Señor* [1] or *Harry (Señor) Neily.*

Harry (Señor) Neily was born at Spartansburg, Pa., on March 7, 1881, and was associate editor of *Who's Who in Major League Base Ball.*

[1] *Who's Who in Major League Base Ball,* comp. by Harold (Speed) Johnson (Buxton Publishing Company, Chicago, 1933) p. 14.

Nelson, George

Because of his youthful appearance, *Baby Face Nelson* [1] was a nickname given to George Nelson, a notorious bandit who was a member of the Dillinger gang. He became *Public Enemy Number One* instead of *Public Enemy Number Two* after Charles Floyd was killed by federal agents near East Liverpool, Ohio, on October 22, 1934.

[1] *The New York Times,* New York City, October 23, 1934, cols. 1 and 2, p. 1.

Nelson, Knute

The *Little Corporal,* the *Little Giant of Alexandria,* and the *Little Norwegian* were nicknames of Knute Nelson, Populist Governor of Minnesota from 1893 to 1895 and Senator from Minnesota from 1896 to 1923.

He was called the *Little Corporal* [1] in allusion to his somewhat short stature and to his having attained the rank of a corporal in the Wisconsin Cavalry during the Civil War.

The Little Giant of Alexandria [1] was a nickname applied to Knute Nelson because of his small build, and unusual intellectual ability. He made his home at Alexandria, Douglas County, Minn., from 1871 until his death in 1923.

The sobriquet the *Little Norwegian* [1] sometimes attributed to him, was in allusion to his Norwegian descent.

Knute Nelson was born at Voss, Norway, on February 2, 1843, and died near Timonium, Md., on April 28, 1923.

[1] *The Life of Knute Nelson*, Martin W. Odland (The Lund Press, Inc., Minneapolis, Minn., 1926) p. 41, 42, 43, 111.
Roster of Wisconsin Volunteers, War of the Rebellion, 1861-1865, Compiled by Authority of the Legislature Under the Direction of Jeremiah M. Rusk, Governor, and Chandler P. Chapman, Adjutant-general (Democrat Printing Company, State Printers, Madison, Wis., 1886) vol. 1, p. 165.

Nelson, William

The nicknames, *Bull Nelson* and *Dad Nelson*, have been given to William Nelson.

Because he was a powerful, stubborn, and aggressive fighter, he was sometimes called *Bull Nelson*.[1]

Nelson's fellow-cadets at the Virginia Military Institute, at Lexington, Va., nicknamed him *Dad Nelson*[2] because he was younger than the majority of them.

At the outbreak of the Civil War in 1861, Nelson was put in charge of the Union gunboats on the Ohio River, with the rank of Lieutenant Commander. At the Battle of Shiloh, in Tennessee, on April 6 and 7, 1862, as Brigadier General of Volunteers, he commanded the Second Division in Major General Don Carlos Buell's Army of the Ohio.

William Nelson was born at Maysville, Ky., on September 27, 1824, and died at Louisville, Ky., on September 29, 1862.

[1] *Lee and His Lieutenants; Comprising the Early Life, Public Services, and Campaigns of General Robert E. Lee and His Companions in Arms, with a Record of Their Campaigns and Heroic Deeds*, Edward A. Pollard (E. B. Treat and Company, New York, 1867) p. 762.
The End of an Era, John S. Wise (Houghton Mifflin and Company, New York and Boston, 1889) p. 261.
"Major-general William Nelson" by A. M. Ellis, in the *Register of Kentucky State Historical Society* (George G. Fetter Company, Louisville, Ky., 1906) vol. 4, May, 1906, p. 56.

Nestor of American Botany. See Darlington, William

Nestor of American Science. See Mitchill, S. L.; Silliman, Benjamin

Nestor of Congregationalism. See Bacon, Leonard

Nestor of the German-American Journalists. See Preetorius, Emil

Nestor of the Hampden County Bar. See Bates, W. G.

Nestor of the Methodist Conference in India. See Bowen, George

Nestor of the Patriots. See Hawley, John

Nestor of the Rocky Mountains. See Carson, Christopher

Nevada

Nevada's nicknames are the *Battle-born State*, the *Mining State*, the *Sage State*, or the *Sagebrush State*, the *Sagehen State*, and the *Silver State*.

The sobriquet, the *Battle-born State*,[1] commemorates the fact that Nevada was admitted to the Union during the Civil War.

Nevada was called the *Mining State* and the *Silver State* in recognition of its important silver mines.

The *Sage State*, the *Sagebrush State* and the *Sagehen State*[2] were given as nicknames to Nevada because of the prevalence of wild sage (*Artemisia tridentata*) and sagehens throughout the arid regions of the state.

[1] *King's Handbook of the United States*, planned and ed. by Moses King, text by M. F. Sweetser (Moses King Corporation, Buffalo, N.Y., 1891) p. 533.
[2] *More About Names*, Leopold Wagner (T. Fisher Unwin, London, 1893) p. 35.

Nevada Commoner. See Jones, J. P.

Nevadans

Diggers, Miners, and *Sagehens* are nicknames applied to the inhabitants of Nevada. The first two nicknames refer to the mining industries of the state. The people of Nevada are called *Sagehens* because of the prevalence of sagebrush and sagehens throughout the arid regions of the state. (See Nevada.)

New Britain, Connecticut

New Britain was nicknamed the *Hardware City of the World* because in this city are manufactured quantities of hardware which are shipped to all parts of the world.

New Deal

Beginning on March 4, 1933, the administration of Franklin Delano Roosevelt as President of the United States is generally referred to as the *New Deal*[1] because its major efforts were directed toward relief,

New Deal—Continued

recovery, and reform. The President felt that these reforms were necessary because of the depression following the stock market crash of October 1930.

The expression, "a new deal," is said to have been first suggested by Samuel L. Rosenman during the early stages of the Roosevelt campaign. In accepting the nomination for the office of President of the United States, Mr. Roosevelt said that he was going to give the people "a new deal," which became the *New Deal* [1] in President Roosevelt's subsequent talks. He was urged to feature this expression by Dr. Herbert Bayard Swope.

[1] *The Roosevelt Revolution, First Phase*, Ernest K. Lindley (The Viking Press, New York, 1933) p. 26-7.

New Deal's Tom Dewey. See Murphy, Frank

New England Cicero. See Webster, Daniel

New England of the West. See Minnesota

New Hampshire

New Hampshire is called the *Granite State*, the *Mother of Rivers*, the *White Mountain State*, and the *Switzerland of America*.

New Hampshire is called the *Granite State* [1] because of her extensive quarries.

The nickname *Mother of Rivers* [2] is well deserved, for five of the great rivers of New England have their origin among the mountains of New Hampshire.

New Hampshire is called the *White Mountain State* [2] because the White Mountains lie in the northern part of this state.

The nickname *Switzerland of America* [3] is applied to New Hampshire because of her beautiful mountain scenery.

[1] *More About Names*, Leopold Wagner (T. Fisher Unwin, London, 1893) p. 27.
[2] *The Tourists' Guide-Book to the State of New Hampshire*, Second Edition (Published by Frank West Rollins at The Romford Press, Concord, N.H., 1902) p. 5.
[3] *King's Handbook of the United States*, planned and ed. by Moses King, text by M. F. Sweetser (Moses King Corporation, Buffalo, N.Y., 1891) p. 539.

New Hampshire Demosthenes. See Webster, Daniel

New Hampshire Inhabitants

The people of New Hampshire are called *Granite Boys* [1] and the state is nicknamed the *Granite State* because of its extensive granite quarries.

[1] *Manual of Useful Information*, comp. under the direction of J. C. Thomas (The Werner Company, Chicago, 1893) p. 23.

New Haven, Connecticut

The *City of Elms* and the *Elm City*, [1] are fitting nicknames for New Haven, for an interesting aspect of the city is the number and the magnificence of its elm trees.

About 1759 a row of trees was planted to border the village green. The result was so gratifying that in the spring of 1787 James Hillhouse drew up a written agreement, which many citizens signed, to contribute towards beautifying the village green by planting elms.

S. H. Elliot, in his book *Attractions of New Haven*, said, "and New Haven is in goodsooth a very handsome city covered, as it were, with lofty and beautiful elms, arching the streets with their limbs, overshading the walk with their tender foliage. Hence it bears the celebrated *nom de plume*, 'The City of Elms.'" [2]

[1] *History of the City of New Haven to the Present Time, with Biographies, Portraits, and Illustrations*, ed. by Edward E. Atwater (W. W. Munsell and Company, New York, 1887) p. 396.
An Outline History of New Haven (Interspersed with Reminiscences) Henry Howe (O. A. Dorman, New Haven, Conn., 1884) p. 18.
[2] *The Attractions of New Haven, Connecticut: A Guide to the City, with Maps and Illustrations*, S. H. Elliot (N. Tibbals and Company, New York, 1869) p. 2.

New Jersey

People call New Jersey the *Camden and Amboy State* or the *State of Camden and Amboy*, the *Clam State*, the *Foreigner State*, the *Garden State*, the *Jersey Blue State*, the *Mosquito State*, *New Spain*, the *State of Spain*, and the *Switzerland of America*.

New Jersey was designated the *State of Camden and Amboy* [1] when the Camden and Amboy Railroad was prominent.

The quantities of clams taken from the Atlantic Ocean and Delaware Bay in New Jersey and shipped out, give rise to the nickname the *Clam State*.

This state is sometimes called the *Foreigner State*, *New Spain*, and the *State of Spain* because when the fortunes of the Bonaparte family fell, Joseph Bonaparte, then King of Spain, fled to New Jersey about 1812 and bought fourteen hundred acres of land at Bordentown, upon which he built a palatial mansion.

New Jersey has many extensive truck farms, especially in the valley of the Delaware River, catering to the New York and Philadelphia metropolitan areas and is therefore called the *Garden State.*

New Jersey is called the *Jersey Blue State* because the Revolutionary Militia of the colony wore blue uniforms. Possibly the name goes back for its origin to the Blue Laws of the State.

It is called the *Mosquito State* because of the swarms of those insects which breed in the swamps.

New Jersey is often called the *Switzerland of America* [1] because of its mountain scenery in the northwestern part of the state. The most famous of these scenic spots is the Palisades, a line of basaltic precipices extending from Jersey City to the vicinity of Piermont, N. Y., with a twelve-mile frontage along the Hudson River.

[1] *King's Handbook of the United States,* planned and ed. by Moses King, text by M. F. Sweetser (Moses King Corporation, Buffalo, N.Y., 1891) p. 551-3.

New Jerseyans

The New Jerseyans are called *Clam-catchers, Clams, Foreigners, Jersey Blues,* and *Spaniards.* These nicknames originated from the nicknames of the state. (See New Jersey.)

New Mexicans

The inhabitants of New Mexico are called *Spanish Indians* [1] because much of its early population consisted of Indians or Spaniards from Mexico.

[1] *Manual of Useful Information,* comp. under the direction of J. C. Thomas (The Werner Company, Chicago, 1893) p. 23.

New Mexico

New Mexico is called the *Cactus State, Land of the Cactus, Land of the Delight Makers, Land of Heart's Desire, Land of Opportunity, Land of Sunshine, Sunshine State,* and the *Spanish State.*

New Mexico is called the *Cactus State* and the *Land of the Cactus* [1] because little but cactus grows along the Mexican border and on the arid plains of the state.

George Wharton James calls New Mexico *The Land of the Delight Makers,* [2] and says that New Mexico should be so called

because of the influence it has had upon literature and art.

It is very fitting that New Mexico should be named the *Land of Heart's Desire* [3] because its climatic conditions are ideal, and it is yet in the early stages of its development.

New Mexico is the *Land of Opportunity* [3] because of its natural beauty, its ideal climatic conditions, the newness of its civilization, its free lands, and its industries.

From the high percentage of sunshiny weather that it affords, New Mexico well deserves the title of the *Sunshine State.* It gets its nickname, the *Spanish State* because of its nearness to Mexico and the number of people within the State who speak Spanish.

[1] *The New International Encyclopaedia,* Second Edition (Dodd, Mead and Company, New York, 1930) vol. 4, p. 271.

[2] *New Mexico, The Land of the Delight Makers,* George Wharton James (The Page Company, Boston, 1920) p. 6, 7.

[3] "The Land of Heart's Desire," by Paul F. Walter, in *New Mexico, The Land of Opportunity* (A. E. Koehler, Junior, Editor and Publisher, Commissioner of Publicity, New Mexico's Board of Exposition Managers, Santa Fe, N.M., 1915) p. 17.

New Mexico School of Mines

The athletic teams of New Mexico School of Mines, at Socorro, N.M., are commonly designated *Miners, Orediggers, Muckers, Blasters, Ore Boys,* and *Engineers* [1] because the school teaches the science and the art of mining.

[1] A communication from L. C. Butler, Director of Athletics at the New Mexico School of Mines, Socorro, N.M., December 1, 1935.

New Orleans, Louisiana

New Orleans is the possessor of six nicknames, the *Crescent City, Great South Gate, Gulf City, Key of the Great Valley, Old French Town,* and the *Queen of the South.*

It was formerly called the *Crescent City* [1] because when De Pauger designed it in 1718 the Mississippi River curved around it in the form of a crescent. This name is still used in a popular poetic sense though it is no longer as appropriate because the development of the city has expanded it beyond its original crescent shape.

Built where the Mississippi River empties into the Gulf of Mexico, New Orleans is frequently called the *Gulf City.*

It has been called the *Key of the Great Valley* [2] and the *Great South Gate* [3] because it is located near the mouth of the Missis-

New Orleans, La.,—Continued

sippi River and products of the southern states and the Mississippi Valley pass through the port of New Orleans to all parts of the world.

Because it was under French domination during the eighteenth century, and French influence is pronounced at the present time, this city is often termed *Old French Town.*[4]

It has been designated the *Queen of the South*[5] because of its commanding position near the mouth of the Mississippi River, its land and water facilities for travel, its manufacturing interests, and its commerce.

[1] *Louisiana: A History of Louisiana, Wilderness—Colony—Province—Territory—State—People,* Henry Edward Chambers (The American Historical Society, Inc., Chicago and New York, 1925) vol. 1, p. 108.

Our World and Ourselves: Our Home, State and Continent, Albert Perry Brigham and Charles T. McFarlane (American Book Company, New York, 1933) p. 110.

The Crescent City, Dedicated to the People of New Orleans and the Southland, William Horace Rea [n.p.,n.d.] p. 1-7.

Dictionary of Americanisms, Fourth Edition, John Russell Bartlett (Little, Brown and Company, Boston, 1877) p. 160.

[2] *The South-West,* by a Yankee, J. H. Ingraham (Harper and Brothers, New York, 1835) vol. 1, p. 63, 91, 96.

[3] *A Book of Nicknames,* John Goff (Courier-Journal Job Printing Company, Louisville, Ky., 1892) p. 16.

Standard History of New Orleans, Louisiana, Henry Rightor (The Lewis-Publishing Company, Chicago, 1900) p. 57-64, 538-9.

[4] *Little Journeys in America,* Rose Henderson (The Southern Publishing Company, Dallas, Tex., 1922) p. 123.

[5] *Old Louisiana,* Lyle Saxon (The Century Company, New York, 1929) p. 136.

New Shoreham or Block Island

New Shoreham or Block Island, located at the mouth of Long Island Sound, has been nicknamed *America's Bermuda*[1] and the *Fisherman's Paradise of the North Atlantic.*[1] New Shoreham is similar to the Bermuda Islands in that tourists visit it in great numbers, and it is one of North America's most excellent fishing grounds for swordfish, tuna and various other types of fish.

[1] *Know Rhode Island: Facts Concerning the Land of Roger Williams,* Sixth Edition, comp. and distributed by the Office of the Secretary of State (State of Rhode Island and Providence Plantations, Providence, R.I., 1936) p. 29.

New Spain. See New Jersey

New Sweden. See Delaware

New York

The *Empire State,* the *Excelsior State,* and the *Gateway of the West* are nicknames applied to New York.

It is called the *Empire State* in allusion to its "commanding position," "vast wealth," and the enterprise of its people. New York is called the *Excelsior State* because the state motto is *Excelsior.* During the nineteenth century the State of New York was called the *Gateway of the West*[1] after the Hudson River was connected with Lake Erie by the Erie Canal thereby making New York the gateway to and from the West.

[1] *More About Names,* Leopold Wagner (T. Fisher Unwin, London, 1893) p. 27.

[2] *History of the State of New York,* Charles F. Horne, with an introduction by James Austin Holden (D. C. Heath and Company, New York and Chicago, 1916) p. 2.

New York American League Baseball Company

The *New York Yankees*[1] or *Yanks* is the name given to players of the New York American League Baseball Company. They were once called the *Highlanders* because the headquarters of the club was located on the highlands of the Hudson River.

[1] *Who's Who in Major League Baseball,* comp. by Harold (Speed) Johnson (Published by Buxton Publishing Company, Chicago, 1933) p. 38.

New York City, New York

New York City is known as the *City of Towers, Commercial Emporium, Empire City, Gotham, Mecca of Telephone Men, University of Telephony, Melting Pot, Metropolis of America, Metropolitan City,* and *Modern Gomorrah.*

It is termed the *City of Towers*[1] because it is the site of many tall buildings which make a most impressive skyline, especially when viewed from the harbor.

The *Commercial Emporium*[2,3] is a nickname descriptive of the extensive buying and selling which characterize this city and make it the leading commercial center of the United States.

New York City is called the *Empire City*[4] because it is the largest city in the *Empire State.*

The origin of the nickname *Gotham*[5] is attributed to Washington Irving's use of it in *Salmagundi,* published in 1807. The passage in which Irving used this expression is as follows: "The person who played the French horn was very excellent in his way, but 'Sbidlikens could not relish his performance, having some time since heard a gentleman amateur in Gotham play a solo on his *proboscis,* in a style infinitely superior."[6] The term, *Gotham,* is a transfer from the village of that name, in the county of Nottinghamshire, England, whose inhabitants are noted for their shrewd and humorous doings.

The fact that New York City has been the site of extensive development of the telephone has caused it to be designated the *Mecca of Telephone Men* and the *University of Telephony*.[3]

It has been called the *Melting Pot*[7] because it is a chief port of entry for foreign immigrants to the United States and great numbers of them remain in New York City, making it one of the nation's most cosmopolitan cities.

New York City is often termed the *Metropolitan City*[8] and the *Metropolis of America*[2] because of its commerce, population, manufacturing industries, and financial leadership.

For several decades after the close of the Civil War, from about 1865 to 1890, this city became so corrupt that the police force was demoralized and crime and vice raged practically unchecked. Because the city was so crime ridden and full of cheap dance halls, houses of ill-repute and saloons, it was often called the *Modern Gomorrah*[9] in allusion to the Gomorrah of Biblical days, which together with Sodom, in Palestine, was described in the book of Genesis as being so wicked and sinful that they were destroyed by fire and brimstone. The name, *Modern Gomorrah*, was said to have been first applied to New York City in 1875 by the Reverend Thomas DeWitt Talmage in a discourse in the Brooklyn Tabernacle.

[1] *Little Journeys in America*, Rose Henderson (The Southern Publishing Company, Dallas, Tex., 1922) p. 34.

[2] *Manual of Useful Information*, comp. under the direction of J. C. Thomas (The Werner Company, Chicago, 1893) p. 22.

[3] *History of the City of New York, 1609-1909, from the Earliest Discovery to the Hudson-Fulton Celebration together with Brief Biographies of Men Representative of the Business Interests of the City*, John William Leonard (The Journal of Commerce and Commercial Bulletin, New York, 1910) p. 444, 466.

[4] *Americanisms; The English of the New World*, M. Schele De Vere (Charles Scribner and Company, New York, 1872) p. 664.

[5] *Salmagundi*, Knickerbocker Edition, William Irving, James Kirke Paulding, and Washington Irving (G. P. Putnam's Sons, New York, 1897) vol. 1, p. 42.

[6] *Why Gotham? The Story of a Name*, Grosvenor Clarkson (The Gotham National Bank, Broadway at Columbus Circle, New York, 1915) p. 6, 7, 13.

[7] *History of the State of New York*, Charles F. Horne, with an introduction by James Austin Holden (D. C. Heath and Company, New York and Chicago, 1916) p. 3.

[8] *A Book of Nicknames*, John Goff (Courier-Journal Job Printing Company, Louisville, Ky., 1892) p. 16.

[9] *The Gangs of New York, an Informal History of the Underworld*, Herbert Asbury (Alfred A. Knopf, New York and London, 1928) p. 174.

New York City Inhabitants. See Gothamites

New York Division. See Twenty-seventh Division of World War II

New York Football Giants, Incorporated

The *Giants* and the *Maramen*[1] are the nicknames applied to the teams of the New York Football Giants, Inc., a member of the National Football League, in New York City. The former sobriquet was given to them by the sports writers of the New York newspapers because it was short and because it was similar to the *New York Giants,* the name of the teams of the New York National League Baseball Company. They were called *Maramen* because the New York Football Giants, Inc., was owned by Timothy J. Mara and his two sons, John V. and Wellington T.

[1] A communication from Timothy J. Mara, Founder and President of the New York Football Giants, Inc., New York City, March 23, 1939.

New York Giants. See New York National League Baseball Company

New York National League Baseball Company

In 1883 when the ball teams of Troy, N.Y., and of Worcester, Mass., withdrew from the National League and those of New York City and of Philadelphia, Pa., were added, John B. Day and James Mutrie picked out the most stalwart men from the Troy team as a nucleus for the New York City team and called them the *New York Giants*.[2]

[1] *Balldom: "The Britannica of Baseball," Comprising Growth of the Game in Detail; a Complete History of the National and American Leagues; First and Only Authentic Chronology Ever Published; Voluminous Records and Absolutely Accurate Statistics; Fascinating Facts for Fans of America's Greatest Sport from 1845 to 1914*, George L. Moreland (Balldom Publishing Company, New York, 1914) p. 13, 69.

New York University

The *Violets*[1] is the nickname applied to the athletic teams of New York University, at New York City, by the newspaper writers because the college color is violet. Years ago it was the custom to plant violets at the foot of the buttresses of the Washington Square building of New York University, in the yard-wide strip of grass which then

New York University—Continued
served as a campus. It is a generally accepted theory that the selection of violet for the university color may be attributed to this.

[1] A letter from George L. Shiebler, Athletic Publicity Director at New York University, New York City, June 18, 1935.

New York Yankees or Yanks. See New York American League Baseball Company

New Yorkers
The New Yorkers are known both as *Excelsiors* and as *Knickerbockers.* The origin and the significance of *Excelsiors* is explained in the paragraph dealing with the nickname the *Excelsior State.* (See New York State.) The second alludes to "the wide breeches worn by the early Dutch settlers of New York City, or rather New Amsterdam." The application of the nickname *Knickerbockers* [1] to New Yorkers may be traced to Washington Irving's use of the word in his "Knickerbocker's History of New York."

[1] *More About Names,* Leopold Wagner (T. Fisher Unwin, London, 1893) p. 27.

New York's Own. See Seventy Seventh Infantry Division of World War II

Newberry College
The *Newberry Indians* and the *Redmen* are the nicknames given to the athletic teams of Newberry College, at Newberry, S.C. Soon after athletic teams were organized at Newberry College, they were uniformed in bright red and sports writers began to call them *Redmen.* [1] Quite naturally the *Newberry Indians* evolved from this nickname, especially as an Indian head is used as the symbol of the college.

[1] A letter from Mamie B. Hawkins, Secretary to the President of Newberry College, Newberry, S.C., November 19, 1935.

Newberry Indians. See Newberry College

Newcastle and Damariscotta, Maine. See Damariscotta and Newcastle, Me.

Newell, Robert
Robert Newell, a trapper and pioneer settler in the Oregon Territory, was known throughout the extreme Northwestern section of the United States as *Doc* or *Doctor.* [1]

Newell acquired the nickname while he was a young man, and it was applied to him throughout his life. From 1829 until 1840 he trapped in the Rocky Mountain region, then moved with his family and that of Joseph L. Meed to the Willamette Valley near what is now Hillsboro, Ore. In the colonization of Oregon and its establishment as a state, Newell distinguished himself as a leader in its civil and political activities.

Robert Newell was born in Muskingum County, Ohio, on March 30, 1807, and died at Lewiston, Idaho, in November 1869.

[1] *Dictionary of American Biography under the Auspices of the American Council of Learned Societies,* ed. by Dumas Malone (Charles Scribner's Sons, New York, 1934) vol. 13, p. 458.

Newman of America. See Hewitt, A. F.

Newport, Rhode Island
Newport is called the *Capital of Vacation Land, City by the Sea,* and *Queen of Summer Resorts.* It has been called the *Capital of Vacation Land* [1] because of its location, climate, bathing beaches, variety of amusements, and the crowds of people who spend their vacations there each summer.

It is called the *City by the Sea* [2] because it is on Narragansett Bay with daily steamer communication with Providence, R.I., New York City, Fall River, Mass., and is a fashionable pleasure resort.

Newport is frequently designated the *Queen of Summer Resorts* [1] because its location makes it easily accessible by land and water to the large eastern cities. Its natural scenery and climate throughout the summer and autumn make it a desirable place at which to spend the summer months.

[1] *The Book of Rhode Island,* distributed by Rhode Island State Bureau of Information in co-operation with Rhode Island Conference of Business Associations compilers and publishers (Designed and printed by Remington Press, Providence, R.I., 1930) p. 94.

[2] *Representative Men and Old Families of Rhode Island, Genealogical Records and Historical Sketches of Prominent and Representative Citizens and of Many of the Old Families* (J. H. Beers and Company, Chicago, 1908) vol. 1, p. 229.

Newspaper Cabinet
The *Newspaper Cabinet* was applied to the group of newspaper reporters and correspondents assigned to the White House while Theodore Roosevelt was serving from 1901 to 1909 as President of the United States, alluding to the esprit de corps that existed between President Roosevelt and these newspapermen. The nickname continued to be applied to them even after Roose-

velt's office as President of the United States had expired, when they continued to keep Roosevelt almost as prominent a political figure as was the President who succeeded him.

[1] *Roosevelt: The Happy Warrior*, Bradley Gilman (Little, Brown and Company, Boston, 1921) p. 335.

Newt. See Penick, I. N.

Newton, Henry Jotham

Henry Jotham Newton has been designated the *Father of the Dry Plate Process in America.*[1] He invented the first permanent collodion emulsion for producing dry plates for photographic use, in 1875. After this type of plate was popularized, Newton improved upon the process and originated a paraffin paper negative used in developing pictures.

Henry Jotham Newton was born at Hartleton, Pa., on February 23, 1823, and died at New York City, on December 23, 1895.

[1] *The National Cyclopaedia of American Biography* (James T. White and Company, New York, 1897) vol. 7, p. 24.

The Encyclopedia Americana (Americana Corporation, New York and Chicago, 1932) vol. 20, p. 289.

Newton, Massachusetts

It is said that during the first eighteen or twenty years of the existence of Newton, workmen were summoned to their work by the blowing of a tin horn; consequently, this village was nicknamed the *Tin Horn Village.*[1]

[1] *History of Middlesex County, Massachusetts, Containing Carefully Prepared Histories of Every City and Town in the County, by Well-Known Writers; and a General History of the County from the Earliest to the Present Time*, Samuel Adams Drake (Estes and Lauriat, Boston, 1880) vol. 2, p. 247.

Ney of the Confederacy. See Cheatham, B. F.

Niagara of the East

The Grand Falls on the St. John River, located in Aroostook County in the northeastern part of Maine a few miles below Van Buren, Me., are commonly called the *Niagara of the East*[1] because of their grandeur.

[1] *Maine of the Sea and Pines*, Nathan Haskell Dole and Irwin Leslie Gordon (L. C. Page and Company, Boston, 1928) p. 293.

Niccolet's Infant Mississippi River. See *Infant Mississippi River*

Nichols, John Conover

John Conover Nichols, an Oklahoma lawyer and politician, was nicknamed *Oklahoma Jack*[1] by his colleagues in the House of Representatives. He became a Democratic Representative from the Second Congressional District of Oklahoma to the United States Congress in 1935 serving until his resignation in 1943.

John Conover Nichols was born at Joplin, Mo., on August 31, 1896 and died November 7, 1945, in an airplane crash at Asmara, Eritrea.

[1] An interview with Captain Victor Hunt Harding, Secretary of the National Democratic Congress Reëlection Committee, Washington, D.C., April 10, 1939.

Nick Carter. See Carter, Vincent

Nickel and Dime School. See National Training School for Women and Girls

Night-club Queen. See Guinan, M. L. C.

Night Riders. See Duquesne University

Ninetieth Infantry Division of World War II

The *Tough Ombres*[1] was the nickname of the Ninetieth Infantry Division of World War II.

[1] *Combat Divisions of World War II*, (Army of the United States), Army Times Publishing Co., Washington, D.C., 1946. p. 58.

Ninety-eighth Infantry Division of World War II

The *Iroquois Division*[1] was the nickname of the Ninety-eighth Infantry Division of World War II.

[1] *Combat Divisions of World War II*, (Army of the United States), Army Times Publishing Co., Washington, D.C., 1946. p. 66.

Ninety-fifth Infantry Division of World War II

The *Victory and OK Division*[1] was the nickname of the Ninety-fifth Infantry Division of World War II. After the fall of Metz in November 1944 this division was called the *Iron Men of Metz*.

[1] *Combat Divisions of World War II*, (Army of the United States), Army Times Publishing Co., Washington, D.C., 1946. p. 63.

Ninety-first Infantry Division of World War II

The *Powder River Division*[1] was the nickname of the Ninety-first Infantry Di-

Ninety-first Infantry Division of World War II—Continued

vision of World War II because when they were asked in World War I where they were from, they yelled, "Powder River, Let'er Buck."

[1] *Combat Divisions of World War II*, (Army of the United States), Army Times Publishing Co., Washington, D.C., 1946. p. 59.

Ninety-ninth Infantry Division of World War II

The *Checkerboard Division* [1] was the nickname of the Ninety-ninth Infantry Division of World War II because the checkerboard was on the coat of arms of William Pitt, and Pittsburgh, Pa., was the home station of the division when it was organized in 1921.

[1] *Combat Divisions of World War II*, (Army of the United States), Army Times Publishing Co., Washington, D.C., 1946. p. 67.

Ninety-second Infantry Division of World War II

The *Buffalo Division* [1] was the nickname of the Ninety-second Infantry Division of World War II.

[1] *Combat Divisions of World War II*, (Army of the United States), Army Times Publishing Co., Washington, D.C., 1946. p. 60.

Ninety-sixth Infantry Division of World War II

The *Deadeye Division* [1] was the nickname of the Ninety-sixth Infantry Division of World War II.

[1] *Combat Divisions of World War II*, (Army of the United States), Army Times Publishing Co., Washington, D.C., 1946. p. 64.

Ninth Armored Division of World War II

The *Phantom Division* [1] was the nickname given to the Ninth Armored Division of World War II.

[1] *Combat Divisions of World War II*, (Army of the United States), Army Times Publishing Co., Washington, D.C., 1946. p. 83.

Nittany Lions. See Pennsylvania State College

Noah's Ark

The convention hall in which the Republican Party held its National Convention, on August 14, 1866, at Philadelphia, Pa., was popularly ridiculed as *Noah's Ark*[1] because when the delegates assembled they entered the building arm-in-arm two by two like the animals entering the Ark.

One of the boats which took part in the exercises celebrating the opening of the Erie Canal in New York in 1825 was also called *Noah's Ark* [2] because it carried a number of wild animals, many of them in pairs.

[1] *Life of Oliver P. Morton, Including His Important Speeches*, William Dudley Foulke (The Bowen-Merrill Company, Indianapolis, Ind., 1899) vol. 1, p. 483.

[2] *Old New York for Young New Yorkers*, First Edition, Caroline D. Emerson (E. P. Dutton and Company, Inc., New York, 1932) p. 218.

Noblest Roman of Them All. See McMillin, Benton; Thurman, A. G.

Nodaks. See University of North Dakota; Wesley College

No-horse-to-feed-buggy

In 1866 Hosea Waite Libbey, an American inventor, designed and constructed a chain-geared tricycle. The horse and buggy was the popular means of transportation in those days so Libbey nicknamed his invention the *No-horse-to-feed-buggy*. From this tricycle evolved the modern bicycle. Libbey was born at Chichester, N.H., on June 28, 1834, and died at Boston, Mass., on August 18, 1900.

[1] *The National Cyclopaedia of American Biography* (James T. White and Company, New York, 1904) vol. 12, p. 515.

No-man's Land

The territory including what is now the State of Kentucky was called *No-man's Land* [1] during the last half of the eighteenth century. Although used as a hunting ground by both northern and southern tribes of Indians, this region belonged to neither and was therefore nicknamed *No-man's Land*. This territory was more widely known as the *Dark and Bloody Ground*. (See Kentucky.)

No Man's Land was used during World War I to designate the land lying between the trenches of the Allies and those of the Germans, and this is the most popular use of the phrase today.

[1] *The United States: A History of Three Centuries, 1607-1904, Population, Politics, War, Industry, Civilization, in Ten Parts,* William Estabrook Chancellor and Fletcher Willis Hewes (G. P. Putnam's Sons, New York and London, 1905) vol. 2, p. 44.

Nonpareil. See Dempsey, Jack

Norfolk, Virginia

Norfolk is known as the *Mother-in-law of the Navy*[1] and as *Sailor Town.*

Norfolk was named *Sailor Town* because it is the location of one of America's largest shipyards and there are many sailors stationed there.

Norfolk was nicknamed the *Mother-in-law of the Navy*[1] by Rear Admiral J. K. Taussig, Admiral Commandant of the (Norfolk District and Naval Operating Base, because the Norfolk Navy Yard, the oldest and one of the most important in the United States, is located on the Portsmouth side of the Elizabeth River directly opposite Norfolk. The social and civic life of the people of Norfolk are closely interwoven with naval activities. The Hampton Roads Naval Operating Base is located at Sewell Point in northern Norfolk, comprising a naval training station, a naval supply station, the navy's chief fuel-reserve depot, a naval air station, and a submarine base.

[1] *The Washington Post,* Washington, D.C., April 3, 1939, cols. 2, 3 and 4, p. 9.

Norfolk Baseball Club

The athletes of the Norfolk Baseball Club, a member of the Piedmont League, located at Norfolk, Va., were nicknamed the *Tars*[1] because Norfolk and Portsmouth, on the opposite side of the Elizabeth River, constitute the largest naval station in the United States and sailors are popularly called *Tars.*

[1] A communication from H. P. Dawson, Business Manager of The Norfolk Baseball Club, Norfolk, Va., March 27, 1939.

Norris, George William

George William Norris, a Nebraska lawyer and politician, was nicknamed the *Dean of the Liberals,* the *Father of Public Utility Regulation,* the *Great Purist,*[1] and the *Father of the Twentieth Amendment to the Constitution.* He was called the *Dean of the Liberals* because he was the oldest liberal in the United States Congress. He was

called the *Father of Public Utility Regulation* because he sponsored the Muscle Shoals Act, which on May 18, 1933, established the Tennessee Valley Authority to produce and sell electric power. Senator Morris was called the *Great Purist* because he tried to purify politics and to prevent combines and trusts from monopolizing the commercial enterprises of the United States. He was nicknamed the *Father of the Twentieth Amendment to the Constitution*[2] because he was the author of the amendment to have Congress convene on January 3rd of each year, and to have incoming Presidents of the United States inaugurated on January 20th, following their election in November. This amendment was adopted on February 6, 1933, and automatically abolished the so-called "Lame-duck" session of Congress. He was a Republican Representative from Nebraska to the United States Congress from 1903 until 1913, and a Republican Senator from Nebraska from 1913 to 1942.

George William Norris was born on a farm in Sandusky County, Ohio, on July 11, 1861 and died in McCook, Neb. on September 2, 1944.

[1] An interview with Captain Victor Hunt Harding, Secretary of the National Democratic Congress Reëlection Committee, Washington, D.C., April 10, 1939.

[2] *Who's Who in America: A Biographical Dictionary of Notable Living Men and Women of the United States, 1938-1939,* ed. by Albert Nelson Marquis (The A. N. Marquis Company, Chicago, 1938) vol. 20, p. 1873.

Norsemen. See Augustana College and Theological Seminary

North Carolina

North Carolina is nicknamed the *Cotton State,* the *Graveyard of the Atlantic,* the *Land of the Sky,* the *Old North State,* the *Rip Van Winkle State,* the *Tarheel State,* and the *Turpentine State.*

The *Land of the Sky*[1] is applied to North Carolina because of its many lofty mountain peaks.

The *Old North State* was generally applied to North Carolina after the original state was divided into two.

C. J. Thomas's *Manual of Useful Information* on page 22 records without explaining North Carolina's sobriquet, the *Rip Van Winkle State.*

The name *Tarheels* was "given in derision by Mississippians to a brigade of North Carolinians, who, in one of the great

North Carolina—Continued
battles of the Civil War, failed to hold
their position. . . ." [2] Later it came to be
popularly employed, so that North Carolina
is now called the *Tarheel State.*

The *Cotton State* became a nickname of
North Carolina because the state produced
so much cotton.

North Carolina was nicknamed the *Graveyard of the Atlantic* because its long wind-
swept barrier beach is so dangerous to Atlantic shipping.[3]

North Carolina is designated the *Turpentine State* from the fact that vast quantities
of turpentine are produced from its pine
forests.

[1] *King's Handbook of the United States,* planned and
ed. by Moses King, text by M. F. Sweetser (Moses King
Corporation, Buffalo, N.Y., 1891) p. 650.
[2] *Americanisms—Old and New,* John S. Farmer (Privately printed by Thomas Poulter and Sons, London,
1889) p. 528.
*Histories of the Several Regiments and Battalions
from North Carolina in the Great War, 1861-'65,* ed.
by Walter Clark (Nash Brothers, Goldsboro, N.C., 901)
vol. 3, p. 376.
[3] *The World Almanac and Book of Facts,* New York
World Telegram, New York, 1941, p. 362.

North Carolinians

The North Carolinians are called *Tarheels* and *Tuckoes.* The first nickname had
its origin in the same source as the *Tarheel
State.* (See North Carolina.) The name
Tuckoes is a corruption of the common term
Tuckahoe, Tuck-a-hoe, or *Tauquauh,* an Indian word meaning *bread.* This word was
used by the early settlers for the *Schlerotium
giganteum,*[1] a curious truffle-like growth
called Indian bread used by the poor people
of the state for food when poverty drove
them to it. It grows under the ground and
resembles a loaf of coarse brown bread.
This nickname is applied both to the North
Carolinas and to the Virginians.

[1] *U.S.: An Index to the United States of America,*
comp. by Malcolm Townsend (D. Lothrop Company,
Boston, 1890) p. 79.

North Dakota

The sobriquets of North Dakota are:
the *Flickertail State,* the *Great Central State,*
the *Sioux State,* and the *Land of the Dakotas.*

North Dakota is called the *Flickertail
State* [1] from the nickname of the Richardson
ground squirrel (*Citellus richardsonii*)
which is called flickertail because it flicks or
jerks its tail while running or entering its
burrow. North Dakota is the only state in
the Union in which this squirrel is found.

The *Great Central State* is given as a
sobriquet to North Dakota supposedly because it is in the center of the great western
wheat belt and contains "several of the
bonanza-wheat farms of the Red River
Valley.

North Dakota is called the *Sioux State*
and the *Land of the Dakotas* because the
territory now comprising this state was once
the home of the Sioux Indians, who called
themselves Dakotas, meaning allies.

[1] A letter from Mrs. Florence H. Davis, Librarian,
State Historical Library, Bismarck, N.D., March 20,
1930.

North Star City. See Saint Paul, Minn.

North Star State. See Minnesota

North Wilkesboro, North Carolina

North Wilkesboro, a town situated at the
foot of the Blue Ridge Mountains, is commonly known as the *Key to the Blue Ridge*
because its location makes it the point of
entrance to the towns and cities lying within the mountains.

Northeastern University

The *Huskies* [1] is the nickname of the
athletic teams of Northeastern University, at
Boston, Mass. because in March 1927,
Northeastern University was presented with
a full-blooded Siberian husky dog by Leon-
hard Seppala, noted Alaskan musher, who
achieved world fame in his dog-sled dash
to Nome, Alaska, with serum during an
epidemic. King Husky I became the mascot
of the University.

[1] A letter from H. Nelson Raymond, Director of
Publicity at Northeastern University, Boston, Mass., November 22, 1935.

Northland College

The *Lumberjacks* [1] was applied to the
athletic teams of Northland College, at
Ashland, Wis., because Ashland was supposed to be the home of the mythical
lumberjack, Paul Bunyan.

[1] A letter from John T. Kendrigan, Registrar at
Northland College, Ashland, Wis., December 5, 1935.

Norton, Mary Teresa

Mary Teresa Norton, a New Jersey Congresswoman, was nicknamed *Washington's
First Mayoress* [1] when she was Chairman of
the Committee on the District of Columbia,
in which position she was virtually the
mayor of the city of Washington, D.C.

She was a Democratic Representative from New Jersey to the United States Congress from 1925 to 1949. She was the first woman to be elected to Congress by the Democratic party. Mary Teresa Norton was born at Jersey City, N.J., on March 7, 1875.

[1] An interview with Captain Victor Hunt Harding, Secretary of the National Democratic Congress Reëlection Committee. Washington, D.C., April 10, 1939.

Norwich University

The athletic teams of Norwich University, at Northfield, Vt., were designated the *Horsemen* [1] many years ago because the university had a cavalry unit of the Reserved Officers Training Corps.

[1] A communication from Robert D. Guerin, Chairman of the Athletic Council of Norwich University, Northfield, Vt., November 18, 1935.

Nott, Samuel

Samuel Nott, a clergyman and educator, was called the *Patriarch of the New England Clergy* [1] because of his lengthy services in church work in Connecticut. He was the pastor of the Congregational Church at Franklin, Conn., from 1781 to 1852, a total of seventy-one years. During this time, he became prominent as an educator as well as a minister and in 1825, was honored by the degree of Doctor of Divinity conferred upon him by Yale University.

Samuel Nott was born at Saybrook, Conn., on January 23, 1754, and died at Franklin, Conn., on May 26, 1852.

[1] *Appleton's Cyclopaedia of American Biography,* ed. by James Grant Wilson and John Fiske (D. Appleton and Company, New York, 1894) vol. 4, p. 539.

Number One Pin-up Girl. See Lamour, Dorothy

Nutmeg State. See Connecticut

Nutmeggers. See Connecticut State College

Nutmegs. See Connecticut Inhabitants

Nye, James Warren

James Warren Nye, a politician and legislator, was nicknamed *Gray Eagle* [1] because, like the eagle, he possessed unusual vigor, liveliness, and keenness of mind and perception and because his hair was gray. Nye was prominent in the political affairs of Nevada, and from 1864 until 1873 he was a Senator from Nevada to the United States Congress.

James Warren Nye was born in Madison County, N.Y., on June 10, 1814, and died at White Plains, N.Y., on December 25, 1876.

[1] *Dictionary of American Biography under the Auspices of the American Council of Learned Societies,* ed. by Dumas Malone (Charles Scribner's Sons, New York, 1934) vol. 13, p. 600.

O

Oakley, Annie

Little Missy and *Little Sure Shot* are the nicknames of Annie Oakley.

Little Missy [1] originated when William Frederick Cody introduced her to the members of his Wild West Show by saying, " 'Boys, this little missy here is Miss Annie Oakley.' "

In 1881, *Sitting Bull*, chief and medicine man of the Sioux Indians, nicknamed Annie Oakley *Little Sure Shot* [2] when he saw her exhibiting her skill in shooting a rifle in the St. Paul opera house at St. Paul, Minn.

Annie Oakley (Mrs. Frank E. Butler) became internationally known as an expert shot in Cody's Wild West Show.

She was born at Woodland, Ohio, on August 13, 1866, and died at Dayton, Ohio, in 1926.

[1] *The Making of Buffalo Bill: A Study in Heroics,* Richard J. Walsh in collaboration with Milton S. Salsbury (The Bobbs-Merrill Company, Indianapolis, Ind., 1928) p. 248.

[2] *Annie Oakley, Woman at Arms: A Biography,* Courtney Ryley Cooper (Duffield and Company, New York, 1927) p. 76, 100, 101.

Oberlin College

The athletic teams of Oberlin College, at Oberlin, Ohio, are known as the *Yeomen.*

Obici, Amedeo

Amedeo Obici was called the *Peanut King* [1] because he organized the Planters Peanut Company in 1906, and became President of the Planters Nut and Chocolate Company, which developed the peanut business on a large scale not only in America but also overseas.

Amedeo Obici was born at Oderzo, Italy, on July 15, 1877, and died May 21, 1947.

[1] *The Commonwealth,* Richmond, Va., January, 1935, vol. 2, no. 1, p. 17.

O'Brien, William Shoney

William Shoney O'Brien, a capitalist, was widely known as the *Jolly Millionaire* [1] because he was consistently good natured, humorous, and amicable to his friends and to strangers. Soon after gold was discovered in California in 1849, he made his fortune there. By 1875 he had money enough to establish the Nevada Bank at San Francisco, Calif., with a capital stock of five million dollars.

William Shoney O'Brien was born in Queen's County, Ireland, about 1826, and died at San Rafael, Calif., on May 2, 1878.

[1] *Dictionary of American Biography under the Auspices of the American Council of Learned Societies*, ed. by Dumas Malone (Charles Scribner's Sons, New York, 1934) vol. 13, p. 612.

Ochs, Adolph Simon

The *Builder of Chattanooga* and the *Watchdog of Central Park* are nicknames by which Adolph Simon Ochs was called.

He was nicknamed the *Builder of Chattonooga* [1] because he contributed so much to the growth and development of Chattonooga, Tenn., through his civic activities and his publications.

The *Watchdog of Central Park* commemorates Ochs' vigilance in preserving Central Park in New York City as a place of recreation, for which purpose it was originally intended.

Adolph Simon Ochs was born at Cincinnati, Ohio, on March 12, 1858, and died in the Sanitarium at Chattanooga, Tenn., on April 8, 1935.

[1] *The Encyclopaedia Britannica*, Fourteenth Edition (Encyclopaedia Britannica, Inc., New York, 1932) vol. 16, p. 697, 698.

Octagon House

The building on the northeast corner of Eighteenth Street and New York Avenue, Washington, D.C., is known as the *Octagon House* [1] because of its shape. Its erection was begun in 1798 and was completed in 1800. The famous three story building, built of brick trimmed with sandstone, was formerly the property of Colonel John Tayloe. President and Mrs. Madison lived at *Octagon House* from August 1814 until late in 1815, while the White House was being repaired. It was there President Madison signed the Treaty of Ghent, on February 18, 1815, which terminated the War of 1812.

[1] *Dolly Madison, The Nation's Hostess*, Elizabeth Lippincott Dean (Lothrop, Lee and Shepard Company, Boston, 1928) p. 89.

Records of the Columbia Historical Society, Washington, D.C., ed. by John B. Larner (Published by the Society at the Press of W. F. Roberts, Washington, D.C., 1924) vol. 26, p. 100-1.

O'Day, Caroline Godwin

Caroline Godwin O'Day, a New York Congresswoman, was nicknamed the *White House Pet* [1] because of her close personal friendship with Mrs. Franklin Delano Roosevelt, whose bridesmaid she had been. She was elected a Democratic Representative at large from New York State in 1935.

Caroline Godwin O'Day was born at Perry, Ga., on June 22, 1875 and died on January 4, 1943.

[1] An interview with Captain Victor Hunt Harding, Secretary of the National Democratic Congress Reëlection Committee, Washington, D.C., April 10, 1939.

O'Doul, Frank Joseph

Frank Joseph O'Doul, who was born at San Francisco, Calif., on March 4, 1897, and who played left field in major league baseball, was nicknamed *Lefty* [1] because he both throws and bats the ball left-handed.

[1] *Who's Who in Major League Base Ball*, comp. by Harold (Speed) Johnson (Buxton Publishing Company, Chicago, 1933) p. 303.

Ogden, Robert

The *Honest Lawyer* [1] was the nickname by which Robert Ogden was known in the legal profession because he was scrupulously honest and exact in the execution of his legal duties and he was personally characterized by honor and integrity.

Robert Ogden was born at Elizabethtown, N.J., on March 23, 1746, and died at Hamburgh, N.J., on February 14, 1826.

[1] *The National Cyclopaedia of American Biography* (James T. White and Company, New York, 1907) vol. 5, p. 159.

Oglesby, Richard James

The nicknames *Farmers' Dick* and *Uncle Dick* have been given to Richard James Oglesby.

Because he was exceedingly popular with the farmers of the state of Illinois, he was known as *Farmers' Dick*.[1] He had served in the Civil War and devoted many years of his life to the honest and efficient execution of his duties in the public offices which he held. He possessed the genial, kindly and affectionate nature which made appropriate the nickname of *Uncle Dick*.

Richard James Oglesby was born in Oldham County, Ky., on July 25, 1824, and died at Elkhart, Ill., on April 24, 1899. He was Governor of Illinois from 1865 to 1869, and again from 1885 to 1889.

[1] *U.S. "Snap Shots": An Independent, National, and Memorial Encyclopedia . . . ,* Oliver McKee (A. M. Thayer and Company, Boston, 1892) p. 241.

Oglethorpe University

The athletes of Oglethorpe University, at Atlanta, Ga., are nicknamed the *Stormy Petrels*.[1]

[1] A letter from Frank Anderson, Director of Athletics at Oglethorpe University, Atlanta, Ga., June 17, 1935.

O-grab-me Act. See Embargo Act

O-grab-me Pets

In May 1808, President Thomas Jefferson issued a circular letter to the governors of the states, permitting them "to grant permits to respectable merchants to bring in so much flour as might be needed to prevent a bread famine" in the various states. This act was made necessary by the Long Embargo passed by Congress on December 22, 1807. The Federalists, the political enemies of President Jefferson, accused the various governors of commercializing these permits and nicknamed the merchants who used the permits *O-grab-me Pets*.[1] *O-grab-me* is *embargo* spelled backward. (See also Patent Merchants and Presidential Bulls and Indulgences.)

[1] *A History of the People of the United States, from the Revolution to the Civil War,* John Bach McMaster (D. Appleton and Company, New York, 1892) vol. 3, p. 301.

O. Henry Girl. See Ayres, Agnes

Ohio

Ohio's nicknames are the *Buckeye State,* the *Modern Mother of Presidents,* and the *Yankee State.*

Ohio was called the *Buckeye State* from the following historical incident: The first court conducted by the native settlers of Ohio was at Marietta on September 2, 1788. "Colonel Sproat, who led the procession [to the court] with glittering sword, was a very tall, erect man. . . . [He] so impressed a group of onlooking Indians that they shouted "Hetuck, hetuck," meaning Big Buckeye. It was from that incident, coupled with the abundance of the buckeye tree (*Aesculus glabra*), which caused the sobriquet 'Buckeye State' to be applied to Ohio." [1]

William M. Farrar says that "the name [*Buckeye*] never became fully crystallized until 1840, when in the crucible of what is known as the 'bitterest, longest, and most extraordinary political contest ever waged in the United States,' the name *Buckeye* became a fixed sobriquet of the state of Ohio and its people." It cannot be definitely determined just when the nickname, *Buckeye,* first began to be widely applied to Ohio and Ohioans, but Cyrus P. Bradley in his journal of 1835 makes mention of its use.

The nickname, the *Modern Mother of Presidents,* was given to Ohio because this was the birthplace of eight Presidents of the United States.

M. F. Sweetser says that "before 1820 Ohio was generally called the *Yankee State* [2] by Kentuckians and Virginians, because it was largely settled by people from New England.

[1] "Why Is Ohio Called the Buckeye State?" by William M. Farrar, in the *Historical Collections of Ohio, . . . an Encyclopedia of the State,* The Ohio Centennial Edition, Henry Howe (Henry Howe and Sons, Columbus, Ohio, 1890) vol. 1, p. 202.
[2] *King's Handbook of the United States,* planned and ed. by Moses King, text by M. F. Sweetser (Moses King Corporation, Buffalo, N.Y., 1891) p. 665.

Ohio Gong. See Allen, William

Ohio Roscius. See Aldrich, Louis

Ohio State University

The *Buckeyes* or *Bucks* [1] is the nickname given to the athletic teams of Ohio State University, at Columbus, Ohio, because Ohio is popularly known as the *Buckeye State.*

[1] A communication from Henry D. Taylor, Assistant Athletic Director at Ohio State University, Columbus, Ohio, June 13, 1935.

Ohio Wesleyan University

The athletic teams of Ohio Wesleyan University, at Delaware, Ohio, were nicknamed the *Battling Bishops* [1] because Ohio Wesleyan is said to have "trained more Bishops for the Methodist Church than any other college."

[1] A communication from George E. Gauthier, Director of Athletics at Ohio Wesleyan University, Delaware, Ohio, June 17, 1935.

Ohioans

People in Ohio are called *Buckeyes* [1] because the state is known as the *Buckeye State.* (See Ohio.)

[1] *Americanisms; The English of the New World,* M. Schele De Vere (Charles Scribner and Company, New York, 1872) p. 661.

Ohio's Jewels

On the Capitol grounds at Columbus, Ohio, stands a group of statues called *Ohio's Jewels*.[1] It is composed of statues of Ulysses Simpson Grant, William Tecumseh Sherman, Philip Henry Sheridan, Salmon Portland Chase, Edwin McMasters Stanton, James Abram Garfield, and Rutherford Birchard Hayes, all of whom were born in Ohio except Philip Henry Sheridan and Salmon Portland Chase, who were residents of the state for a time.

[1] *The Source Book* (Source Research Council, Inc., Chicago, 1936) vol. 2, p. 663.

Oil Capital. See Eldorado, Ark.

Oil Capital of the World. See Tulsa, Okla.

Oil Dorado

The northwestern part of the state of Pennsylvania, especially in the vicinity of Titusville on Oil Creek in Crawford County has been humorously nicknamed *Oil Dorado*,[1] a corruption of *El Dorado*. *El Dorado* is the name of an imaginary country abounding in gold which the Spaniards of the sixteenth century thought they would locate in South America.

[1] *America, Picturesque and Descriptive*, Joel Cook (Henry T. Coates and Company, Philadelphia, 1900) vol. 1, p. 339.

Oil State. See Pennsylvania

Okeechobee, Florida

Okeechobee, in Okeechobee County, terms itself the *Chicago of the South* [1] because it is located on a lake and on the "southern edge of the old cattle-range country of South Florida," because it is the site of several manufacturing plants, and because its constantly growing transportation facilities are increasing its importance as a commercial center in the South.

[1] *Florida in the Making*, Frank Parker Stockbridge and John Holliday Perry (The de Bower Publishing Company, New York and Jacksonville, 1925) p. 234.

Oklahoma

The *Boomer's Paradise*, the *Land of the Red People*, and the *Sooner State* are the sobriquets applied to Oklahoma.

M. F. Sweetser says that "for years the region [of Oklahoma] has been known as the Boomer's Paradise," because when President Benjamin Harrison opened up this territory for settlement on April 22, 1889, "great processions of 'boomers' poured into the new territory." [2]

Oklahoma has been frequently called the *Land of the Red People* [3] because the word *Oklahoma* is an Indian word meaning *red men* or *red people*.

The sobriquet, *Sooner State*, was given to Oklahoma from the fact that "when the lands of Oklahoma were opened to settlement at a given hour, those who did not await the appointed time but who slipped in clandestinely ahead of time, were dubbed 'sooners' because they did not wait as required by law, but tried to gain an unfair advantage by entering the forbidden precincts too soon."

[1] *King's Handbook of the United States*, planned and ed. by Moses King, text by M. F. Sweetser (Moses King Corporation, Buffalo, N.Y., 1891) p. 693-4.

[2] A letter from Joseph B. Thoburn, Curator, Oklahoma Historical Society, Oklahoma City, Okla., April 15, 1930.

[3] *Seeing the Middle West*, John T. Faris (J. B. Lippincott Company, Philadelphia, 1923) p. 111.

Oklahoma Agricultural and Mechanical College

The athletes on the teams of Oklahoma Agricultural and Mechanical College, located at Stillwater, Okla., were designated the *Cowboys* [1] about 1927 or 1928 to replace the older sobriquet, the *Tigers*,[1] which had fallen into disuse. The nickname *Cowboys*, was first used by a publicity man because of the cowboy traditions in Oklahoma.

[1] A letter from George F. Church, Assistant Professor of Journalism at Oklahoma Agricultural and Mechanical College, Stillwater, Oka., June 17, 1935.

Oklahoma Baptist University

The athletic teams of Oklahoma Baptist University, at Shawnee, Okla., are called the *Bisons*, because bison were formerly numerous throughout the State, and because the skeleton of a large bison was unearthed on the campus while the university buildings were being erected.

Oklahoma City University

The Goldbugs is the appellation given to the athletic teams of Oklahoma City University, at Oklahoma City, Okla.

Oklahoma Jack. See Nichols, J. C.

Oklahomans

Oklahomans are called *Sooners*. When the territory now embracing the state of Oklahoma was opened for settlement, some of the waiting settlers "became so anxious that they disregarded the conditions set forth in the rules prescribed for the opening of the lands to settlement and, eluding the vigilance of the cordon of troops by which the bounds of the district were patrolled, slipped in and concealed themselves at points conveniently near to the best lands so that they would not have far to go when the legal hour of opening arrived." [1]

[1] *A Standard History of Oklahoma*, Joseph B. Thoburn (The American Historical Society, Chicago and New York, 1916) vol. 2, p. 632.

Old Ace of Spades. See Lee, R. E.

Old Agamemnon. See Carrington, Edward

Old Alcalde. See Roberts, O. M.

Old Allegheny. See Colston, R. E.

Old Alphabet. See Beauregard, P. G. T.

Old Andy. See Johnson, Andrew

Old Aristides. See Bicknell, Joshua

Old Bald. See Preston, J. T. L.

Old Bandanna. See Thurman, A. G.

Old Bay State. See Massachusetts

Old Ben Wade. See Wade, B. F.

Old Billie. See Sherman, W. T.

Old Blizzards. See Loring, W. W.

Old Bore. See Beauregard, P. G. T.

Old Boy in Specs. See Davis, M. L.

Old Brains. See Halleck, H. W.

Old Buck. See Buchanan, James

Old Buena Vista. See Taylor, Zachary

Old Bullion. See Benton, T. H.

Old Captain Ezekiel. See Greeley, Ezekiel

Old Chinook. See Wise, H. A.

Old Club; Old Clubby. See Colston, R. E.

Old Cocked Hat

An old house, built in Dock Square or Adams Square in Boston, Mass., about 1860, was nicknamed the *Old Cocked Hat* and the *Old Feather Store*. The house somewhat resembled a cocked hat in shape. For many years it was a market place for those who bought and sold feathers.

[1] *St. Botolph's Town; An Account of Old Boston in Colonial Days*, Mary Caroline Crawford (L. C. Page and Company, Boston, 1908) p. 236.

Old Cockeye. See Butler, B. F.

Old Colony State. See Massachusetts

Old Commoner. See Stevens, Thaddeus

Old Davy. See Twiggs, D. E.

Old Denmark. See Febiger, Christian

Old Dirigo State. See Maine

Old Dominion. See Virginia

Old Double Quick. See Hollingsworth, J. H.

Old Dutch Cleanser. See Blankenburg, Rudolph

Old Eight to Seven. See Hayes, R. B.

Old Feather Store. See *Old Cocked Hat*

Old Figgers. See Grosvenor, C. H.

Old Flintlock. See Hanson, R. W.

Old Forty-eight Hours. See Doubleday, Abner

Old Fox. See Griffith, Clark; Washington, George

Old Frank. See Cheatham, B. F.

Old Free State of Lunenburg, or *Old Free State.* See Lunenburg County, Va.

Old French Town. See New Orleans, La.

Old Fuss and Feathers. See Scott, Winfield

Old Gimlet Eye. See Butler, S. D.

Old Gimpy. See Evans, R. D.

Old Glory
The national flag of the United States is said to have been nicknamed *Old Glory* [1] by William Driver, "a skipper from Salem, Mass., who was in command of the brig, *Charles Doggert* in 1837. When Driver was on the point of setting sail on the *Charles Doggert* for the South Seas, a group of his friends presented him with the United States flag which he immediately called *Old Glory.*

[1] "History of the Flag" by Honorable Homer P. Snyder, in *Papers Read before the Herkimer County Historical Society,* comp. by Arthur Tappan Smith, Secretary of the Society (Herkimer and Ilion, New York, 1924) vol. 5, p. 214-15.

Old Granny. See Harrison, W. H.

Old Grover. See Cleveland, Grover

Old Guard
The managers of the Republican party sometimes have been designated the *Old Guard* [1] in allusion to the watch they keep over members and activities of the party, often joining themselves into an intimate group or gang in order to more successfully control party principles and policies.

[1] *Roosevelt: The Happy Warrior,* Bradley Gilman (Little, Brown and Company, Boston, 1921) p. 230.

Old Hickory. See Jackson, Andrew

Old Hickory Division
During World War I, the Thirtieth Division of the American Expeditionary Forces was popularly called the *Old Hickory Di-* vision [1] because most of its constituents had been recruited in North Carolina, South Carolina, and Tennessee, in the history of which states Andrew Jackson, the soldier and statesman, better known as *Old Hickory,* was a prominent figure. The *Old Hickory Division,* under the command of Major General E. M. Lewis, landed at Calais, France, on May 24, 1918, and became world-renowned as a result of having broken the great Hindenburg Line on September 29, 1918, this division having been officially [2] credited with this accomplishment.

[1] *The History of the 105th Regiment of Engineers, Divisional Engineers of the "Old Hickory" (30th) Division,* comp. by Willard P. Sullivan and Harry Tucker (George H. Doran Company, New York, 1919) p. 3, 7, 9.
[2] *Final Report of the Provost Marshal General to the Secretary of War on the Operations of the Selective Service System to July 15, 1919* (Government Printing Office, Washington, D.C., 1920) p. 288.

Old Hoss. See Stephenson, J. R.

Old Humbug. See Benton, T. H.

Old Hunkers. See *Hunkers*

Old Iron Pants. See Johnson, H. S.

Old Ironsides
The naval battle between the American frigate *Constitution,* and the British frigate, *Guerrière,* occurred on August 18, 1812. When the sailors on board the American vessel saw the balls discharged from the guns of the British ship bouncing off instead of penetrating the two and one-half inch oak armor covering the American vessel, they nicknamed the sturdy ship, *Old Ironsides,* by which sobriquet it has been known ever since.

[1] *The Encyclopaedia Britannica,* Fourteenth Edition (Encyclopaedia Britannica, Inc., New York, 1932) vol. 6, p. 313-14.

Old Ironsides. See Stewart, Charles

Old Jack. See Jackson, T. J.

Old Jeb. See Stuart, J. E. B.

Old Johnny Congress
Colonel Miles Vernon, a Missouri politician of enviable reputation, was born in 1786. In his political speeches, Colonel Ver-

non often referred to the United States government at Washington, D.C., by familiarly calling it *Old Johnny Congress*.[1]

[1] *Centennial History of Missouri (The Center State) One Hundred Years in the Union, 1820-1921,* Walter B. Stevens (The S. J. Clarke Publishing Company, St. Louis, Mo., and Chicago, 1921) vol. 2, p. 528.

Old Jube, or Old Jubilee. See Early, J. A.

Old Kill Devil. See Austin, Freeman

Old Line State. See Maryland

Old Liners. See University of Maryland

Old Lion. See Roosevelt, Theodore

Old Lou. See Louisiana State University

Old Man. See Kalbfus, E. C.

Old Man Eloquent. See Adams, J. Q.; Custis, G. W. P.

Old Man Eloquent of the Senate. See Hoar, G. F.

Old Man of Dixville

The sobriquet, *Old Man of Dixville*,[1] has been applied to a group of massive rocks in the White Mountains at the Dixville Notch about ten miles from Colebrook in Coos County, New Hampshire. When viewed from a distance, they greatly resemble the profile of a man.

[1] *History of Coos County,* New Hampshire, ed. by Georgia Drew Merrill (W. A. Ferguson, Syracuse, N.Y., 1888) p. 37.

Old Man of the Gridiron. See Kenneally, G. V.

Old Man of the Mountain

The Great Stone Face, an enormous profile of a human face about eighty feet long which stands out from the perpendicular cliffs of Profile Mountain, in the White Mountains of New Hampshire, has been nicknamed the *Old Man of the Mountain*.[1]

[1] *The World Book Encyclopedia* (The Quarrie Corporation, Chicago, 1937) vol. 18, p. 7750.

Old Master. See Gans, Joe

Old Master Leavitt. See Leavitt, Dudley

Old Nick's Money

Those who favored abolishing the United States Bank, termed the currency of that institution *Old Nick's Money*.[1] The sobriquet alluded to the fact that Nicholas Biddle was president of this bank from 1823 until 1836, during which time a groundless suspicion[2] had been cast upon his honesty.

[1] *A History of the United States for Schools,* Andrew C. McLaughlin and Claude Halstead Van Tyne (D. Appleton and Company, New York and Chicago, 1919) p. 305.

[2] *The Encyclopedia Americana* (Americana Corporation, New York and Chicago, 1929) vol. 3, p. 687.

Old North State. See North Carolina

Old One Wing. See Martin, J. G.

Old Ossawatomie. See Brown, John

Old Pancake

The Comstock Lode, a silver mine discovered in 1859 near Virginia City in Storey County, Nevada, was nicknamed the *Old Pancake*.[1] While the silver and gold ore in this great vein, four miles in length and varying in breadth from zero to three thousand feet, are very irregular, there is a noticeable tendency in the accumulation of ore to take the form and the shape of a double convex lens.[2] The similarity in shape to that of a pancake doubtless suggested the appellation.

[1] *The Pony Express: The Record of a Romantic Adventure in Business,* Arthur Chapman (G. P. Putnam's Sons, New York and London, 1932) p. 54.

[2] *Universal Cyclopaedia and Atlas,* A Newly Revised and Enlarged Edition, Charles Kendall Adams, Editor-in-chief (D Appleton and Company, New York, 1903) vol. 3, p. 109.

Old Pap Safety See Thomas, G. H.

Old Parlez. See Colston, R. E.

Old Pete. See Longstreet, James

Old Phil. See Thompson, P. B., Sr.

Old Planters

Prior to the arrival of John Endicott in 1628, John Balch, Roger Conant, Peter Palfrey, and John Woodbury, four men who had settled on the Naumkeag peninsula at what is now Salem, Mass., were designated the *Old Planters*.[1] They were among the

Old Planters—Continued
earliest settlers to come to New England to found a permanent colony, and were engaged chiefly in agricultural pursuits.

[1] *Famous Families of Massachusetts*, Mary Caroline Crawford (Little, Brown and Company, Boston, 1930) vol. 1, p. 89.

Old Polly. See Colston, R. E.

Old Prob, or Old Probabilities. See Abbe, Cleveland

Old Public Functionary. See Buchanan, James

Old Put. See Putnam, Israel

Old Ranger. See Reynolds, John

Old Reliable. See Carlson, Jules; Thomas, G. H.

Old Rock. See Benning, H. L.

Old Roman. See Benton, T. H.; Comiskey, C. A.; Muldoon, William; Thurman, A. G.

Old Rosey. See Rosecrans, W. S.

Old Rough and Ready. See Taylor, Zachary

Old Round About. See Cleveland, Benjamin

Old Sacramento

Old Sacramento [1] was the nickname given to the cannon which had been buried on the Bickerton Farm near Lawrence, Kans., by the Free-State men and which was carried to Lawrence and fired at frequent intervals during the night of January 29, 1861, the date on which Kansas became a state in the federal union. The sobriquet commemorates the fact that the cannon was captured at the Battle of Sacramento.

[1] *History of Kansas, State and People: Kansas at the First Quarter of the Twentieth Cenury*, written and comp. by William E. Connelley (The American Historical Society, Inc., Chicago and New York, 1928) vol. 2, p. 607.

Old Saddlebags. See McDonald, J. E.

Old Salamander. See Farragut, D. G.

Old Sanitary. See Yeatman, J. E.

Old Ship

The old square meeting house built at Hingham, Mass., in 1681, is known as the *Old Ship*. [1]

[1] *Social Life in Old New England*, Mary Caroline Crawford (Little, Brown and Company, Boston, 1914) p. 146.

Old Silver Leg. See Stuyvesant, Peter

Old Silver Nails. See Stuyvesant, Peter

Old Slackwater. See Moorhead, J. K.

Old Slow Trot. See Thomas, G. H.

Old Soldiers Clause

The *Old Soldiers Clause* [1] is the name applied to a law passed by the white people during the Period of Reconstruction in the South following the Civil War. This law restricted the privilege of voting to those who had served as soldiers in the land or in the naval forces of the United States, and to their lawful descendants. The abovementioned clause was found particularly in the laws of Alabama and Virginia, having been adopted about 1901 for the purpose of limiting popular suffrage.

[1] *Documentary History of Reconstruction, Political, Military, Social, Religious, Educational and Industrial, 1865 to the Present Time*, Walter L. Fleming (The Arthur H. Clark Company, Cleveland, Ohio, 1907) vol. 2, p. 453.

Old South. See Old South Church

Old South Church

The Old South Church, located at Washington and Milk Streets in Boston, Mass., is widely known as *Old South* and the *Sanctuary of Freedom* [1] because during the pre-Revolutionary period of strife and agitation, it was the scene of speeches, addresses, and public meetings for the purpose of defending and preserving the freedom of the colonists. The present structure was built in 1730 "to replace an older church which had stood on the same site since 1669."

This famous old church is used at the present time as a museum for Revolutionary-War relics and portraits and as a hall for historical and patriotic lectures.

[1] *The World Book Encyclopedia* (The Quarrie Corporation, Chicago, 1938) vol. 2, p. 874,

Old Sow

During the War of 1812, while the British squadron was attempting to capture the American vessel, *Oneida*, in Sackett's Harbor on Lake Ontario, Captain William Vaughan from the fort nearby did the British fleet much damage by firing cannon balls from the *Old Sow*,[1] a cannon so called because, having been very heavy, it had been left on the shore by the crew of the *Oneida* where it lay buried in the mud for some time before it was mounted on the fort for use.

During the Revolutionary War a large cannon, stationed in the mountainous regions near Morristown, N.J., and used by the Continental Army, particularly in a fight there on June 23, 1780, became nicknamed the *Old Sow* [2] because the shock of the recoil following its discharge caused the heavy gun to "root" or dig itself into the ground somewhat in the manner of an old sow.

[1] *When America Became a Nation*, Tudor Jenks (Thomas Y. Crowell and Company, New York, 1910) p. 130.
[2] *Narratives of Newark in New Jersey, from the Days of Its Founding*, 1666-1916, David Lawrence Pierson (Pierson Publishing Company, Newark, N.J., 1917) p. 214.

Old Spades Lee. See Lee, R. E.

Old Spex. See Smith, F. H.

Old Stone Hammer. See Metcalfe, Thomas

Old Straight. See Stewart, A. P.

Old Swamp Fox. See Marion, Francis

Old Tecumseh. See Sherman, W. T.

Old Three Stars. See Grant, U. S.

Old Tige. See Anderson, G. T.

Old Tippecanoe. See Harrison, W. H.

Old Titanic Earth-son. See Webster, Daniel

Old Tom Jackson. See Jackson, T. J.

Old Trooper. See Dressler, Marie

Old Tu'key Neck. See Stilwell, J. W.

Old Tush. See Davies, Charles

Old Tycoon. See Price, S. G.

Old Usufruct. See Tilden, S. J.

Old Veto. See Cleveland, Grover; Humphreys, B. G.

Old Viking. See Furuseth, Andrew

Old War Horse. See Cook, Philip

Old War Horse of Reform. See Blankenburg, Rudolph

Old Wheel-horse of Democracy. See Medary, Samuel

Old Whiskers. See Wiles, G. F.

Old White Hat. See Greeley, Horace

Old Wicked. See Godfrey, Hollen

Old Zach. See Taylor, Zachary

Old Zeb. See Weaver, Zebulon

Ole Miss Teams. See University of Mississippi

Ole War Skule. See Louisiana State University

Oleander City, or *Oleander City by the Sea.* See Galveston, Tex.

Oleander City of Texas. See Galveston, Tex.

Oles. See Saint Olaf College

Olive-branch Petition

The *Olive-branch Petition* [1] was the sobriquet given to an appeal sent to King George III of England by the members of the Continental Congress of 1775, in a last effort to harmonize the disrupted relations between England and the thirteen colonies. The *Olive-branch Petition* was conciliatory

Olive-branch Petition—Continued
in tone, and offered peaceful negotiations
but it was unheeded by the King.

[1] *United States, Its Past and Present*, Henry W. Elson
(American Book Company, New York and Boston,
1926) p. 137.

Oliver, Edna May

Edna May Oliver, a motion picture actress,
who was born at Boston, Mass., was known
as the *Woman Who Always Speaks Her
Mind* [1] because of her frank, straightfor-
ward manner of expressing her opinion. She
was born on November 9, 1883, and died
on November 9, 1942.

[1] *Screen Personalities*, Vincent Trotta and Cliff Lewis
(Grosset and Dunlap, New York, 1933) p. 89.

Oliver, Eli L.

Eli L. Oliver, vice-president of Labor's
Nonpartisan League, was nicknamed *Kiss-
of-death Oliver* [1] because, in some congressional districts during the elections of 1938,
the endorsement of the members of this
league given to a candidate for a political
office was almost sure to result in the defeat of that candidate. The league had the
strong backing of the members of the Congress of Industrial Organization and where
the voters were divided on the labor issue
or where the American Federation of Labor
was exceptionally strong, the backing of
Labor's Nonpartisan League was especially
detrimental to a candidate as the members
of the AFL frequently would not support
a candidate for public office if the members
of the CIO had endorsed him first.

Eli L. Oliver was born at Walker, Minn.,
on May 4, 1899.

[1] *Washington-Herald*, Washington, D.C., July 21,
1938, col. 8, p. 6.

Oliver, Thomas N.

Because he is a southerner, *Rebel* [1] is the
sobriquet of Thomas N. Oliver, who was
born at Montgomery, Ala., on January 15,
1904, and who played outfield in major
league baseball.

[1] *Who's Who in Major League Base Ball*, comp. by
Harold (Speed) Johnson (Buxton Publishing Company,
Chicago, 1933) p. 305.

Oliver Goldsmith of America. See
Taylor, B. F.

Olivet College

The *Olivet Comets* [1] is the appellation
given to the athletic teams of Olivet Col-

lege, at Olivet, Mich., in 1931 or 1932 because it suggested action, and because it was
short and easily symbolized on the athletic
equipment. This nickname was selected from
four or five best ones suggested by members
of the student body in contest.

[1] A letter from Joseph Brewer, President of Olivet
College, Olivet, Mich., November 19, 1935.

Olivet Comets. See Olivet College

Omnibus Bill

The Compromise Bill reported to Congress on May 8, 1850, by Henry Clay, has
been called by historians the *Omnibus Bill* [1]
because it covered many different things:
the admission of California into the Union
as a state, the organization of Utah and
New Mexico into territories subject to
"Squatter Sovereignty," the payment of an
indemnity to Texas for the purpose of
securing her claim to the territory to be
organized into the New Mexican territory
and the abolition of slave trade from the
District of Columbia.

[1] *The Encyclopedia Americana* (Americana Corporation, New York and Chicago, 1927) vol. 7, p. 451.

Onaway Division. See Seventy-sixth Infantry Division of World War II

One-eyed Scribe

In Texas and other western states during
frontier days, a revolver or a pistol was
nicknamed *One-eyed Scribe*,[1] signifying that
the revolver had only one barrel with which
to record its message of death.

[1] *A New Dictionary of Americanisms*, Sylva Clapin
(Louis Weiss and Company, New York, 1903) p. 54.

One Hundred and First Airborne Division of World War II

The *Screaming Eagle Division* [1] was the
nickname of the One Hundred and First Airborne Division of the Combat Divisions of
World War II.

[1] *Combat Divisions of World War II*, (Army of the
United States), Army Times Publishing Company, Washington, D.C., 1946, p. 95.

One Hundred and Fourth Infantry Division of World War II

The *Timberwolf Division* [1] was the nickname of the One Hundred and Fourth Infantry Division of the Combat Divisions of
World War II because this division was
activated in September 1942, at Camp Adair,

Oregon, and the first training was received in California, Colorado, and Oregon, the home of the timber wolves.

[1] *Combat Divisions of World War II,* (Army of the United States), Army Times Publishing Company, Washington, D.C., 1946, p. 71.

One Hundred and Second Infantry Division of World War II

The *Ozark Division* [1] was the nickname of the One Hundred and Second Infantry Division of World War II because the original plans were for the personnel of the division to be drawn from the Ozark Mountain area.

[1] *Combat Divisions of World War II,* (Army of the United States), Army Times Publishing Company, Washington, D.C., 1946, p. 69.

One Hundred and Sixth Infantry Division of World War II

The *Golden Lion Division* [1] was the nickname of the One Hundred and Sixth Infantry Division of the Combat Divisions of World War II.

[1] *Combat Divisions of World War II,* (Army of the United States), Army Times Publishing Company, Washington, D.C., 1946, p. 72.

One Hundred and Third Infantry Division of World War II

The *Cactus Division* [1] was the nickname of the One Hundred and Third Infantry Division of World War II because the personnel of the division was from Arizona, Colorado, and New Mexico.

[1] *Combat Divisions of World War II,* (Army of the United States), Army Times Publishing Company, Washington, D.C., 1946, p. 70.

One Hundredth Infantry Division of World War II

The *Century Division* [1] was the nickname of the One Hundredth Division of the Combat Divisions of World War II, so called because a century is one hundred years.

[1] *Combat Divisions of World War II,* (Army of the United States), Army Times Publishing Company, Washington, D.C., 1946, p. 68.

One-legged Governor. See Stuyvesant, Peter

One Man Patriot. See Fish, Hamilton, Jr.

One Man Trust Company. See Wilson, C. M.

One of the Gamest Players in the Game. See Merkle, F. C.

One Speech Lee. See Lee, J. B.

O'Neill, Charles

Because he served as a Representative from Pennsylvania to the United States Congress from 1863 to 1871, and again from 1873 to 1893, Charles O'Neill was nicknamed the *Father of the House.* [1]

Charles O'Neill was born at Philadelphia, Pa., on March 21, 1821, and died there on November 25, 1893.

[1] *My Quarter Century of American Politics,* Champ Clark (Harper and Brothers, New York and London, 1920) vol. 1, p. 222.

O'Neill, Margaret. See Eaton, M. O.

Orange Bowl. See Roddey Burdine Memorial Stadium of Miami

Orange Empire

Along the foothills west of the Sierra Nevada Mountains, and particularly in the southern region of California, the absence of killing frosts has resulted in the establishment of immense richly productive orange groves and citrus fruit orchards, hence the territory is popularly known as the *Orange Empire.* [1]

[1] "Land of Homes" by Frank J. Taylor, in *California,* ed. by John Russell McCarthy (Powell Publishing Company, Chicago and San Francisco, Calif., 1930) vol. 6, p. 77.

Orange King. See Harris, J. A.

Orange State. See Florida

Orangemen. See Syracuse University

Oranges

Orange is an industrial city in Essex County, four miles northwest of Newark, N.J. [2] · Orange and the surrounding municipalities of East Orange, West Orange, South Orange, and Maplewood form a suburban community called *The Oranges.* [1]

[1] *The World Book,* (The Quarrie Corporation, Chicago, 1947) vol. 5, p. 2174.
[2] *The Columbia Lippincott Gazetteer of the World,* ed. by Leon E. Seltzer (Columbia University Press, New York, 1952) p. 1386.

Orator of Free Dirt. See Julian, G. W.

Orator of Secession. See Yancey, W. L.

Orchard City. See Burlington, Iowa

Ore Boys. See New Mexico School of Mines

Orediggers. See Colorado School of Mines; New Mexico School of Mines

Oregon

Oregon is called the *Beaver State,* the *Hard-case State* or the *Land of Hard-cases,* the *Sunset State,* and the *Webfoot State.*

Oregon "is sometimes called the *Beaver State* [1] because of the prevalence of the little fur-bearing animal in the early history of Oregon and because of the beaver's association with the virtues of intelligence, industry, ingenuity.

The sobriquet, the *Hard-case State* or the *Land of Hard-cases,* attributed to Oregon, has reference to the rough and hardy life led by the early settlers [2] of the state.

Oregon is known as the *Sunset State,* "because it reaches a more westerly point than any other American commonwealth, except Washington." [3]

It is called the *Webfoot State,* because, due to the excessive rainfall during the winter months, the climate at that season is best appreciated by the 'web-foot' animals." [2]

[1] *History of Oregon,* Charles Henry Carey (The Pioneer Historical Publishing Company, Chicago and Portland, Ore., 1922) p. 808.

[2] *U.S.: An Index to the United States of America,* comp. by Malcolm Townsend (D. Lothrop Company, Boston, 1890) p. 72, 79.

[3] *King's Handbook of the United States,* planned and ed. by Moses King, text by M. F. Sweetser (Moses King Corporation, Buffalo, N.Y., 1891) p. 699.

Oregon State College

The nickname *Beavers* [1] has been attributed to the athletic teams of Oregon State College, at Corvallis, Oregon, because Oregon is sometimes called the *Beaver State.* (See Oregon.)

[1] A communication from W. D. Sprandel, Director of Athletics at Olivet College, Olivet, Mich., June 14, 1935.

Oregonians

Oregonians are called *Beavers, Hard Cases,* and *Webfeet.* [1] (See Oregon.)

[1] *The Undeveloped West: or Five Years in the Territories,* J. H. Beadle (National Publishing Company, Philadelphia, Chicago, Cincinnati, Ohio, St, Louis, Mo., 1873) p. 759.

Western Wilds, and The Men Who Redeem Them, an Authentic Narrative, J. H. Beadle (J. C. Chilton Publishing Company, Detroit, Mich., 1882) p. 400.

O'Reilly, Mary M.

Mary M. O'Reilly, former Assistant Director of the Mint of the United States Government, is often designated the *Sweetheart of the Treasury* [1] because she was modest, retiring, and admirable in her dealings with other employees in the Mint.

Miss O'Reilly was in Government service for thirty-six years, having become a Government employee in 1902. She was employed in the Mint in 1905 where she was an expert on coinage and coinage laws. Her work was chiefly administrative and supervisory, and she sanctioned the coinage of new designs of money. The Jefferson five-cent piece was the latest coin she saw sent to the Mint. She is reported to have liked the dime more than any other American coin.

Mary M. O'Reilly was born at Springfield, Mass., in 1865, and retired from Government service on November 29, 1938.

[1] *The Evening Star,* Washington, D.C., October 29, 1938, col. 6, p. 1.

Original Bathing Girl. See Steadman, Vera

Original Glamour Girl. See Bara, Theda

Orphan Brigade

The nickname, *Orphan Brigade,* [1] was applied to the First Brigade [2] of Kentucky Volunteers in the Confederate Army Corps of Central Kentucky which was placed under the command of Brigadier General John Cabell Breckinridge on November 16, 1861. During its participation in the Civil War from 1861 to 1865, this brigade became known as the *Orphan Brigade* because several times it was left temporarily without a commander, the commanding officer having died or having been removed to another post, and because these Confederate soldiers were looked upon as exiles by the majority of the Kentuckians who were loyal to the Union.

[1] *History of the Orphan Brigade,* Ed. (Edwin) Porter Thompson (Caxton Publishing House, Cincinnati, Ohio, 1898) p. 29.

[2] *History of the First Kentucky Brigade,* Ed. (Edwin) Porter Thompson (Caxton Publishing House, Cincinnati, Ohio, 1868) p. 55, 57.

Orton, Harlow S.

For some time, Harlow S. Orton was called the *Hoosier Orator* [1] because he was one of Indiana's most eloquent orators. Indiana is widely known as the *Hoosier State* and its inhabitants are called *Hoosiers.* Orton moved to Wisconsin in 1847.

Harlow S. Orton was born in Niagara County, N.Y., on November 23, 1817, and died at Madison, Wis., on July 4, 1895.

[1] *The National Cyclopaedia of American Biography* (James T. White and Company, New York, 1906) vol. 13, p. 170.

Osborne, George O.

The *Father of Prison Reform in the United States* [1] is an appellation attributed to George O. Osborne in commemoration of the numerous prison reforms he instituted while he was Warden of the New Jersey State Prison at Trenton for more than twenty years.

George O. Osborne was born at Elmira, N.Y., on June 24, 1845, and died at St. Petersburg, Fla., on May 13, 1926.

Some of the reforms inaugurated by Osborne at the New Jersey State Prison which have been widely adopted throughout the country are: the establishing of schools with practical courses of instruction; more attention to the religious life; improvements upon the parole system; and the abolition of certain customs peculiar to prisons such as dark cells, the ball and chain, shaven heads, and striped uniforms. Osborne's pioneer work in this field and the excellent results of his constructive methods have made the sobriquet *Father of Prison Reform in the United States,* not only a nickname but a tribute.

[1] *Encyclopedia of American Biography: American Biography, a New Cyclopedia,* comp. under the editorial supervision of a notable advisory board (Published under the direction of The American Historical Society, Inc., New York, 1930) vol. 41, p. 154.

Ossawotomie Brown. See Brown, John

O'Sullivan, Dennis

Dennis O'Sullivan, at one time an intimate friend of Ulysses Simpson Grant, lived at 128 Park Row in New York City, and was widely known as *The Penny Plug* [1] because it was his custom to buy penny plugs of tobacco.

O'Sullivan, who drew a pension from the Federal Government as an ex-Union soldier, lived at the Cleveland Lodging House, widely known in New York City as the *Flea Bag* because it was so unsanitary.

O'Sullivan lived at the *Flea Bag* from choice. His long residence there caused him to be known throughout that section of the city.

O'Sullivan, a well-educated man, had many friends and acquaintances among prominent people. Before the Civil War, he had kept a shop in St. Louis, Mo. It was here that he met and formed the friendship of Lieutenant General Grant, whom he came to know intimately.

At the beginning of the Civil War in 1861, O'Sullivan enlisted and became one of Lieutenant General Robert E. Lee's staff members. Later he was captured by the Union Army.

After his capture, O'Sullivan became an ardent supporter of the Union cause. He then joined the Union Army, but was captured by the Confederates and imprisoned at the Confederate Military Prison at Andersonville, Ga.

While Ulysses Simpson Grant was President of the United States from 1869 until 1877, he was accustomed to stop at the Astor Hotel when he visited New York City. On such occasions he would invite his old friend, O'Sullivan, to dine with him at the hotel. It is said that on these visits O'Sullivan would address his host as Mr. President, and that President Grant would ask him to call him *Ulix,* the familiar name by which O'Sullivan had called Grant from the time their friendship began.

Dennis O'Sullivan died in New York City, on November 28, 1907, at the age of eighty-nine.

[1] *The Washington Post,* Washington, D.C., November 28, 1907, col. 3, p. 11.

Otey, James Harvey

The people throughout the region of Tennessee, Arkansas, Florida, Louisiana, and Mississippi, spoke of James Harvey Otey in a spirit of appreciation as the *Good Bishop* [1] because he devoted himself to the execution of his numerous duties as Bishop of the Protestant Church in Tennessee, and later as the Provisional Bishop of the Protestant Churches in the above-named states.

James Harvey Otey was born at Liberty, Va., on January 27, 1800, and died at Memphis, Tenn., on April 23, 1863.

[1] *The National Cyclopaedia of American Biography* (James T. White and Company, New York, 1907) vol. 5, p. 487.

Ottawa University

The athletic teams of Ottawa University, at Ottawa, Kans., were designated the *Braves* [1] because the University was founded by John Tecumseh Jones, an Indian.

[1] A communication from Warren P. Behan, Acting President of Ottawa University, Ottawa, Kan., November 13, 1935.

Our Battle Laureate. See Brownell, H. H.

Our Bob. See Reynolds, R. R.; Taylor, R. L.

Our Grover. See Cleveland, Grover

Our Patrick Henry. See Kolb, R. F.

Outdoor Girl of the Films. See Valli, Virginia

Outen, William Austin

In a game of baseball between North Carolina State College and Clemson College, William Austin Outen was called *Plunging Chink,* later shortened to *Chink.* [1]

William Austin Outen was born at Mount Holly, N.C., on June 17, 1905, and was a catcher in major league baseball.

[1] *Who's Who in Major League Base Ball,* comp. by Harold (Speed) Johnson (Buxton Publishing Company, Chicago, 1933) p. 308.

Overland Three. See Coolbrith, Ina Donna, Bret Harte, and Charles Warren Stoddard

Overlin, Ken

Ken Overlin, who was born at Decatur, Ill., in 1910, and who was the all Navy middleweight champion, was nicknamed the *Illinois Thunderbolt* [1] because of his terrific fighting ability, and because he is a native of Illinois.

[1] *Post Boxing Record* (Post Sports Records Corporation, New York, 1935) p. 19.

Overton's Folly

The Maxwell House, a popular hotel located at the intersection of Fourth Avenue and Church Streets in Nashville, Tenn., was nicknamed *Overton's Folly* [1] while it was in the process of being built from 1859 until 1868 because Colonel John Overton built a part of it before the outbreak of the Civil War, and then due to the war and the sub-sequent business decline and disorganization, was unable to complete the building until after the close of the war.

Colonel John Overton was a public-spirited man who, when he saw that Nashville needed a first-class hotel with modern conveniences to meet the needs of a growing commercial center, undertook the building of such a hotel which he named after his wife, Mrs. Harriet Maxwell Overton. "He had borrowed a large sum of money for that work, and just before completion Nashville was taken by the Federal Army. The Government seized the unfinished building and used it for over three years as barracks for prisoners. When it was finally restored to its owner, the damage had been so great that it required more than the original cost to finish and furnish it." [2] Many of the people of Nashville thought that Colonel Overton would never be able to complete this building and that the venture was a foolish one.

Colonel John Overton was born at his ancestral home, Traveler's Rest, in Davidson County, Tenn., on May 25, 1821, and died there on December 12, 1898.

[1] *The Wayne Hand-book of Nashville and the Tennessee Centennial Exposition* (The Wayne Publishing Company, Fort Wayne, Ind., 1907) p. 49.

[2] *Memorial, Colonel John Overton and Mrs. Harriet Maxwell Overton,* James H. McNeilly (Neither publisher nor place of publication given, 1899) p. 33.

Owatonna, Minnesota

Owatonna, in Steele County, has been designated the *Butter Capital of the World* [1] because, located amidst the dairy farms of Minnesota, it handles and markets vast quantities of butter to various parts of the United States and to other countries.

[1] *My Minnesota,* Antoinette E. Ford (Lyons and Carnahan, New York and Chicago, 1929) p. 236.

Owen, Marvin James

Marvin James Owen, who was born at San José, Calif., on March 22, 1908, and who played third base in major league baseball, is popularly known as *Freck,* [1] doubtless because he has freckles on his face.

[1] *Who's Who in Major League Base Ball,* comp. by Harold (Speed) Johnson (Buxton Publishing Company, Chicago, 1933) p. 309.

Owen, Stephen

Stephen Owen, a major league football coach, was commonly designated *Big Steve* [1] because he is five feet and eleven inches in height, and weighs about two hundred and sixty pounds, and was an outstanding player in athletic sports from his college days.

He was born in Missouri in 1900. He joined the New York Football Giants in 1926 and was appointed Coach of the team in 1930.

[1] *Who's Who in Major League Football*, comp. by Harold (Speed) Johnson and Wilfrid Smith (B. E. Callahan, Chicago, 1935) p. 13.

Owens, Clarence B.

Because someone struck him with a brick while he was umpiring a game at Pittsburgh, Kans., *Brick* was the nickname given to Clarence B. Owens, who was born at Milwaukee, Wis., on March 31, 1885, and who was an American League umpire.

[1] *Who's Who in Major League Football*, comp. by Harold (Speed) Johnson and Wilfrid Smith (B. E. Callahan, Chicago, 1935) p. 450.

Owl. See Garner, J. N.

Owl Russell. See Russell, W. H.

Owls. See Tarkio College; Temple University

Owski. See Dingell, J. D.

Oyster Bowl

This is a nickname applied to Foreman Field, Norfolk, Virginia. It is a stadium for the Norfolk Division of the College of William and Mary and the Virginia Polytechnic Institute. The stadium gets its nickname from the oysters beds of the Chesapeake Bay, said to be the most productive in the world. The Lynn Haven oysters found there are famous for their size.

Oyster State. See Maryland

Oysters. See Marylanders

Ozark Division. See One Hundred and Second Infantry Division of World War II

Ozark State. See Missouri

P

Pacific College

The *Quakers* and the *Prune Pickers* are nicknames which have been given to the athletic teams of Pacific College, at New-

berg, Ore. The oldest and most widely used nickname, the *Quakers,* [1] commemorates the fact that Pacific College was established and is maintained by the Society of Friends or Quakers.

Some years ago an effort was made to change the nickname of the teams to *Prune Pickers* [1] because of the enterprise shown by the students in picking thousands of boxes of prunes one day in the orchard of Mr. W. W. Silver who, unable to handle the crop himself, offered to the college the prunes they could pick in a day.

The industriousness of the students added hundreds of dollars to their treasury and to 'that of the college, the proceeds being evenly divided; and it occurred to some of the students to change the nickname of the college athletic teams. The name apparently did not appeal to many, and the old nickname of the *Quakers* is now used almost exclusively.

[1] A letter from Levi T. Pennington, President of Pacific University, Newberg, Ore., November 21, 1935.

Pacific University

The athletic teams of Pacific University, at Forest Grove, Ore., are nicknamed the *Badgers.*

Packers. See Armour Institute of Technology

Packing Town. See Chicago, Ill.

Page, John

John Page, Revolutionary patriot, congressman, and Governor of Virginia, was nicknamed *John Partridge* [1] by his friends because of his interest in astronomy, especially in the prediction of solar eclipses. John Partridge was an English astrologer and almanac maker who lived from 1644 to 1715. John Page, a lifelong friend of Thomas Jefferson, was particularly active in Virginia politics during the colonial and post-Revolutionary periods. He was a Representative from Virginia to the United States Congress from 1789 until 1797.

John Page was born in Gloucester County, Va., on April 17, 1744, and died at Richmond, Va., on October 11, 1808.

[1] *Dictionary of American Biography under the Auspices of the American Council of Learned Societies,* ed. by Dumas Malone (Charles Scribner's Sons, New York, 1934) vol. 14, p. 138.

Pahaska. See Cody, W. F.

Pa-he-haska. See Cody, W. F.

Paige, Leroy Robert

Leroy Robert Paige is familiarly known to baseball fans as *Satchel*.[1] The source of the nickname is not definitely known. Paige says he was first called that by a schoolmaster for an unknown reason. Others conjecture that perhaps the name derives from his suitcase-size shoes for his very large feet, or from his days as a redcap in Mobile, Ala.[2]

Leroy Robert Paige was born from forty to fifty years ago in Mobile, Ala. In July 1948 he became the first Negro pitcher in the American League when the Cleveland Indians signed him to a contract. That same year he participated in the Cleveland World Series games. For twenty-five-odd years prior to that, he had become a celebrity in the Negro leagues because of his phenomenal pitching arm.

[1] *Baseball Register, 1952,* compiled by J. G. Taylor Spink (published by *The Sporting News*) p. 194.

[2] *Baseball Personalities,* by J. J. A. ("Jimmy") Powers, (Rudolph Field, New York, 1949) p. 283-288.

Painter of Presidents. See Stuart, Gilbert

Palestine, Texas

Palestine is known as the *Homesteader's Paradise*[1] because it offered exceptional advantages to farmers who, in the earlier days, were looking for a place to homestead, and later to people seeking advantageous locations for the pursuit of agricultural and business careers.

[1] *Flashlights on Texas,* Lillie Terrell Shaver and Willie Williamson Rogers (A. C. Baldwin and Sons, Austin, Tex., 1928) p. 109.

Palmer, Daniel David

Daniel David Palmer, founder of the Palmer School of Chiropractic, was nicknamed *Fish Palmer*[1] because before beginning to collect and study human bones, he had made a collection of goldfish bones.

He was a Canadian of Scotch-Irish parentage, came to the United States in 1861, and taught school in Illinois and Iowa until he bought a small general store at What Cheer, Iowa. He moved to Burlington, Iowa, in 1883, and began to practice magnetic healing. In 1895 he moved to Davenport, Iowa, where he began to practice osteopathy and to make spinal adjustments. In September 1895 he made his first spinal adjust-

ment on the janitor of the building in which he had his office. In 1898 he founded the Palmer School of Chiropractic which is widely known in all parts of the United States, and in foreign countries.

Daniel David Palmer was born at Lake Skogogg, near Toronto, Canada, on March 7, 1845, and died at Los Angeles, Calif., on October 20, 1913.

[1] *Time: The Weekly Magazine,* Chicago, March 18, 1940, col. 1, p. 55.

Palmer, James Shedden

At the opening of the Civil War James Shedden Palmer was commander of the *Iroquois,* and supported Farragut at the passage of the Vicksburg batteries in 1862. He was promoted to commodore in 1863 and created rear admiral in 1866 for his services during the war.

Admiral Palmer was a man of dignified bearing and fastidious taste, as well as a resolute and skillful commander. He was nicknamed *Piecrust Palmer*[1] and was described as going into battle dressed with scrupulous neatness, "performing the last act of his toilet in buttoning his kid gloves as though he were about to enter a ballroom."

[1] *The National Cyclopaedia of American Biography* (James T. White and Company, New York, 1897) vol. 4, p. 554.

Palmetto City. See Charleston, S.C.

Palmetto Regiment

During the War with Mexico, the South Carolina soldiers who fought in the Battle of Churubusco near Mexico City, Mexico, on August 20, 1847, were nicknamed the *Palmetto Regiment*[1] because they came from South Carolina, the *Palmetto State.*

[1] *Our First War in Mexico,* Farnham Bishop (Charles Scribner's Sons, New York, 1916) p. 179.

Palmetto State. See South Carolina

Palmettoes. See South Carolinians

Pancho. See Snyder, F. J.

Pandora's Box of Evil

The Kansas-Nebraska Bill, passed by Congress on May 30, 1854, was called *Pandora's Box of Evil.*[1] The bill authorized the division of the unorganized Indian territory known as Nebraska (that part of the Louisiana Purchase lying between the Rocky Mountains and Missouri) into the two territories of Kansas and Nebraska. The former, west of Missouri, was to be settled from the older state, and was to permit slavery, while Nebraska was to be free. The bill, reopening the violently disputed issues of the Missouri Compromise and of the Compromise of 1850, stirred up sectional feeling and hatred between the North and South, and was thus likened to Pandora's box, the opening of which had loosed discord and hatred on mankind.

[1] *The Life of Robert Toombs: Robert Toombs, Statesman, Speaker, Soldier, Sage, His Career in Congress and on the Hustings—His Work in the Courts—His Record with the Army—His Life at Home*, Pleasant A. Stovall (Cassell Publishing Company, New York, 1892) p. 149.

Panhandle State. See West Virginia

Pan-handleites. See West Virginians

Panna Maria, Texas

Panna Maria, settled in 1853, is called the *Polish City in Texas* because it is "the oldest Polish settlement in the United States." [1]

[1] *Flashlights on Texas*, Lillie Terrell Shaver and Willie Williamson Rogers (A. C. Baldwin and Sons, Austin, Tex., 1928) p. 136.

Panthers. See Virginia Union University; York College

Pants Rowland. See Rowland, C. H.

Pap. See Price, S. G.; Thomas, G. H.

Paper City. See Holyoke, Mass.

Paper Towns

Prior to the Panic of 1837, on maps and other advertising matter displayed in saloons and public places to catch the attention of those interested in buying property, well laid-out towns were pictured along the shores of Lakes Michigan and Huron; but in reality these towns existed on paper only.

They actually consisted of a poorly-built house or two, and frequently no house at all, hence the nickname *Paper Towns*. [1]

[1] *A History of the People of the United States, from the Revolution to the Civil War*, John Bach McMaster (D Appleton and Company, New York, 1910) vol. 7, p. 198-9.

Papooses. See Mississippi College

Paradise For Hunters

That portion of North America along the Missouri River and its tributaries was designated the *Paradise for Hunters* [1] by H. M. Breckenridge in his *Journal of a Voyage up the River Missouri; Performed in 1811.* Doubtless the nickname suggested itself from the great abundance of game then found throughout this region.

[1] *Journal of a Voyage up the River Missouri; Performed in Eighteen Hundred and Eleven*, Second Edition Revised and Enlarged, H. M. Breckenridge, Esquire (Coale and Maxwell, Baltimore, Md., 1916) p. 152.

The volume named above may be found in *Early Western Travels, 1748-1846*, ed. by Reuben Gold Thwaites (The Arthur H. Clark Company, Cleveland, Ohio, 1904) vol. 6.

Paradise of New England. See Salem, Mass.

Paradise of the Pacific. See Hawaii

Paratrooper Pet. See Lamour, Dorothy

Parcel Post Church

The *Parcel Post Church* [1] is a term applied to the first church built at Orleans, Calif., in 1916. At the time the prices of transporting building materials to Orleans were so exorbitantly high that as many building supplies as possible were conveyed to the town by parcel post. Because much of the material used in building the church had been delivered in this manner, it was nicknamed the *Parcel Post Church*.

[1] *Indian Tribes and Missions; The Church in Story and Pageant; Indian Tribes and Missions: A Handbook of General History of the North American Indians, Early Missionary Efforts, and Missions of the Episcopal Church* (Church Missions Publishing Company, Hartford, Conn., 1926) part 4, p. 46.

Paris of America. See Cincinnati, Ohio

Parker, Francis James

Francis James Parker was nicknamed *Salty* [1] because of his partiality for salted peanuts. He was born at East Saint Louis,

Parker, F. J.—Continued
Ill., on July 8, 1913, and played infield in major league baseball.

[1] *Who's Who in The Major Leagues,* 1935 Edition, Harold (Speed) Johnson (B. E. Callahan, Chicago, 1935) p. 18.

Parker, John Henry
During the Spanish-American War in 1898, John Henry Parker was nicknamed *Gatling Gun Parker* [1] by his fellow-officers because he successfully commanded the Gatling Gun Detachment of the Fifth Army Corps in the Battle of Santiago.[2]

Lieutenant Parker was born near Tipton, Mo., on Sept. 19, 1866.

[1] *Centennial History of Missouri (The Center State) One Hundred Years in the Union, 1820-1921,* Walter B. Stevens (The S. J. Clarke Publishing Company, St. Louis, Mo., and Chicago, 1921) vol. 2, p. 892.
[2] *History of the Gatling Gun Detachment, Fifth Army Corps, at Santiago with a Few Unvarnished Truths Concerning that Expedition,* John H. Parker (Hudson-Kimberly Publishing Company, Kansas City, Mo., 1898) p. 93-151.

Parliamentarian. See Luce, Robert

Parliamentary Procedure. See Cannon, Clarence

Parson Hobson. See Hobson, R. P.

Pasadena, California
Pasadena is nicknamed the *Crown City,*[1] or *Crown City of the Valley.* The name Pasadena comes from a Chippewa Indian word meaning *Crown of the Valley.* [2]

[1] *California and Californians,* ed. by Rockwell D. Hunt, assisted by an advisory board (The Lewis Publishing Company, New York and Chicago, 1930) vol. 2, p. 484. 506.
[2] *The American Language: Supplement II,* by H. L. Mencken (Alfred A. Knopf, New York) p. 554.

Pasadena Stadium
The *Rose Bowl* [1] is the popular nickname given to the Pasadena Stadium or the Tournament of Roses Stadium, in Brookside Park at Pasadena, Calif.[1] The famous amphitheatre was constructed in a dry canyon and is now surrounded by rosebushes.

The nickname was applied to the stadium by Harlan Hall, a Pasadena newspaperman. The Pasadena Tournament of Roses Association presents its pageant of roses in this stadium on New Year's Day each year. From 1923 on, in addition to the pageant, the Rose Bowl has been the scene of the annual East-West football game.

The Pasadena Tournament of Roses Association built the stadium and later deeded it to the city of Pasadena. The first unit of the structure was completed by January 1, 1923. The amphitheatre has since been enlarged to its present seating capacity of 89,090.

[1] A letter from Ray C. Maple, Assistant Manager of The Pasadena Tournament of Roses Association, Pasadena, Calif., April 1, 1939.

Pastor of the Poor. See Cox, J. R.

Pat. See Crawford, C. R.; Malone, P. L.

Patent Merchants
In May 1808, when the states were suffering from privation as a result of the Embargo Act, which had then been in force five months, President Thomas Jefferson issued a circular letter to the state governors allowing them "to grant permits to respectable merchants to bring in so much flour as might be needed to prevent a bread famine." The Federalists, Jefferson's political enemies, called those who used the permits *Patent Merchants* [1] implying that they were unfairly privileged. (See also Presidential Bulls and Indulgences and O-grab-me pets.)

[1] *A History of the People of the United States, from The Revolution to the Civil War,* John Bach McMaster (D. Appleton anl Company, New York, 1892) vol. 3, p. 301.

Pater Universitatis Missouriensis. See Rollins, J. S.

Paterson, New Jersey
Paterson is often called the *Lyons of America* [1] because it is a leading silk-weaving and dyeing center, as- is Lyons, France.

[1] *A History of Industrial Paterson: Being a Compendium of the Establishment, Growth and Present Status in Paterson, N.J., of the Silk, Cotton, Flax, Locomotive, Iron and Miscellaneous Industries; together with Outlines of State, County and Local History, Corporate Records, Biographical Sketches, Incidents of Manufacture, Interesting Facts and Valuable Statistics, Illustrated with Views and Portraits on Steel, and Including a Map of the City, Carefully Revised and Corrected to Date,* L. R. Trumbull (Carleton M. Herrick, Printer, Paterson, N.J., 1882) p. 149.

Path of Gold
Market Street in San Francisco, Calif., is termed the *Path of Gold* [1] because it is one of the greatest commercial thoroughfares of the city and many of the city's leading business firms are located there, and because it is splendidly illuminated at night by an elaborate electric lighting system.

[1] "Land of Homes" by Frank J. Taylor, in *California,* ed. by John Russell McCarthy (Powell Publishing Company, Chicago and San Francisco, Calif., 1930) vol. 6, p. 183.

Pathfinder. See Frémont, J. C.

Pathfinder of the Sea. See Maury, M. F.

Patman, Wright

Wright Patman, cotton farmer, lawyer, and Representative from Texas, was nicknamed *Anti-chain-store Patman* and the *Father of the Bonus* [1] by his colleagues in the House of Representatives because he introduced and worked for passage of anti-chain store legislation, and soldiers' bonus payment ("adjusted compensation") legislation by the House. [2]

He was elected a Democratic Representative from the First Congressional District of Texas to the United States Congress in 1929 and has been reelected for eleven consecutive terms since then.

Wright Patman was born at Hughes Springs, Tex., on August 6, 1893.

[1] An interview with Captain Victor Hunt Harding, Secretary of the National Democratic Congress Reëlection Committee, Washington, D.C., April 10, 1939.

[2] *Current Biography, Who's News and Why, 1946,* ed. by Anne Rothe (The H. W. Wilson Company, New York, 1947) p. 461-4.

Patriarch of Columbia. See Taylor, Thomas

Patriarch of the Hills. See Crawford, Abel

Patriarch of the Mountains. See Crawford, Abel

Patriarch of the New England Clergy. See Nott, Samuel

Patriarch to the Indians. See Mayhew, Thomas

Patriot Financier. See Morris, Robert

Patriot Mother of the Mohawk Valley. See Van Alstine, Mrs. M. J.

Patron Saint of American Orchards. See Chapman, John

Patrons of Husbandry. See Grangers

Patten, George Washington

The sobriquet, *Poet Laureate of the Army* [1] was applied to George Washington Patten after he produced a volume of poems entitled *Voices of the Border,* in 1867. The poems concerned military life, and became very popular among soldiers. Pattern served with the Union Army during the Civil War.

George Washington Patten was born at Newport, R.I., on December 25, 1808, and died at Houlton, Me., on April 28, 1882.

[1] *The National Cyclopaedia of American Biography* (James T. White and Company, New York, 1906) vol. 13, p. 183.

Patter-rollers

Patrols were appointed throughout the South about 1829 or 1830 whose duty it was to catch and to punish Negro slaves who were found off the premises of their masters without a signed permit. The Negroes called these patrols *Patter-rollers,* [1] or *Patter-rolls.* [1]

[1] *Personal Recollections of John M. Palmer,* Mrs. John M. Palmer (The Robert Clarke Company, Cincinnati, Ohio, 1901) p. 8.

Patterson, Eleanor Medill

Eleanor Medill Patterson, newspaper owner and editor known for her spectacular news presentations, was nicknamed *Cissie* [1] by her brother in his youth. New York and Washington society knew her as *Cissie Patterson* throughout her career as the first woman editor-publisher of a large metropolitan daily in the United States.

In 1930, after the death of her second husband, she resumed her maiden name, Patterson, and persuaded William Randolph Hearst, an old friend, into letting her try her hand at editing his *Washington Herald.* [2] Subsequently, Mrs. Patterson became publisher of the *Times-Herald,* Washington, D.C. She was also part owner of the *Chicago Tribune* and the *New York Daily News,* both owned by members of her family.

Mrs. Patterson was born at Chicago, Ill., on November 7, 1884, and died on July 24, 1948. [3]

[1] *The Senator,* Washington, D.C., April 8, 1939, p. 14.

[2] *Current Biography, Who's news and why, 1940,* ed. by Maxine Block. (The H. W. Wilson Company, New York, 1940) p. 634, 6.

[3] *Current Biography, Who's news and why, 1948,* ed. by Anne Rothe (The H. W. Wilson Company, New York, 1949) p. 493.

Paul Jones of the South. See Semmes, Raphael

Pawtucket, Rhode Island

Pawtucket is called the *Cradle of the Cotton Manufacturing Business* [1] because in 1790 Samuel Slater established the first American factory in this city.

[1] *Know Rhode Island: Facts Concerning the Land of Roger Williams*, Sixth Edition, comp. and distributed by the Office of the Secretary of State (State of Rhode Island and Providence Plantations, Providence, R. I., 1936) p. 38.

Peabody, Elizabeth Palmer

Elizabeth Palmer Peabody was called the *Grandmother of Boston* [1] in token of respect and appreciation for her contribution to the cultural life of that city.

Her life interest was teaching and she spent many years both conducting schools, and writing and lecturing for reforms in educational methods. Familiar with the work of Froebel, she opened in Boston in 1860 the first kindergarten in the United States. In Boston for a short time she also owned a book store which became a cultural center and rendezvous for the intellectuals of the city and the leading figures of the Transcendental movement. [2]

She was born at Billerica, Mass., on May 16, 1804, and died at Jamaica Plain, Mass., on January 4, 1894.

[1] *Women in American History: The Part Taken by Women in American History*, Mrs John A. Logan (The Perry-Nalle Publishing Company, Wilmington, Del., 1912) p. 286.

[2] *American Authors 1600-1900*, ed. by S. J. Kunitz and Howard Haycraft. (The H. W. Wilson Company, New York, 1938) p. 604-5.

Peace Ludlow. See Ludlow, L. L.

Peace Maker

In Texas and other western states during frontier days, a revolver or pistol was nicknamed *Peace Maker*,[1] signifying that by means of this weapon all difficulties might be settled.

[1] *A New Dictionary of Americanisms*, Sylva Clapin (Louis Weiss and Company, New York, 1903) p. 54.

Peacemaker. See Channing, W. E.

Peach. See Depew, C. M.

Peacock Senator. See Conkling, Roscoe

Peacocks. See Saint Peter's College; Upper Iowa University

Peak of the Division

During World War I, the Fourth Regiment of Alabama Infantrymen in the American Expeditionary Forces was designated the *Peak of the Division* [1] because of the courage shown by the regiment during some of the most critical military drives.

[1] *History of Alabama and Her People*, Albert Burton Moore, author and editor (The American Historical Society, Inc., New York and Chicago, 1927) vol. 1, p. 945.

Peanut King. See Gwaltney, P. D.; Obici, Amedeo

Pearl of the Orient. See Manila, P.I.

Pearson, Eliphalet

Eliphalet Pearson, educator, was called *Elephant* [1] by his students, though probably not in the classroom. He was of massive build, and his given name, Eliphalet, undoubtedly suggested the nickname. Pearson taught first in a grammar schol at Andover, Mass., and in 1778 became the first principal of the Phillips Academy, established there the same year. In 1786 he became a member of the faculty of Harvard College, at Cambridge, Mass., and remained there until 1806 when he returned to Andover to found the Andover Theological Seminary in 1807.

Eliphalet Pearson was born at Newbury, Mass., on June 11, 1752, and died at Greenland, N.H., on September 12, 1826.

[1] *Dictionary of American Biography under the Auspices of the American Council of Learned Societies*, ed. by Dumas Malone (Charles Scribner's Sons, New York, 1934) vol. 14, p. 358.

Peary, Marie Ahnighito

Marie Ahnighito Peary, the daughter of the Arctic explorer, Robert Edwin Peary, and Mrs. Josephine Diebitsch Peary, was born in Greenland, in September, 1893, while Mrs. Peary was accompanying her husband on an exploring expedition to the North Pole. The natives called her the *Snow Baby*.[1]

[1] *The Growth of the American People and Nation*, Mary G. Kelty (Ginn and Company, New York and Boston, 1931) p. 610.

Peerless Leader. See Chance, F. L.

Pekin, Illinois

Pekin has been termed the *Celestial City* [1] probably because the name is similar to Peking, China, called the *Celestial City*, by the Chinese.

[1] *A Book of Nicknames*, John Goff (Courier-Journal Job Printing Company, Louisville, Ky., 1892) p. 15.

Pelham, John

John Pelham was known as the *Boy Major* [1] and the *Gallant Pelham* [2] because despite his youth, he occupied a responsible position in the Confederate Army, and was a brave but modest soldier.

In July, 1856, Pelham entered the United States Military Academy at West Point, N.Y.; he resigned on April 22, 1861, to join the Confederate Army, was commissioned a lieutenant and sent to Virginia. In November, 1861, at the age of twenty-three, he organized and captained a six-gun battery of horse artillery in Major General James Ewell Brown Stuart's cavalry brigade. Pelham's battery soon became widely known for its efficiency and its youthful captain renowned for his intelligence and initiative. During the Seven Days' Battle near Richmond, Va., from June 25 to July 1, 1862, he displayed such talent in directing the activities of his battery that he was appointed a major on August 16, 1862. At the Battle of Fredericksburg in Virginia, on December 13, 1862, his successful assaults on Federal gunboats and his determined resistance to a superior number of enemy forces, caused Lieutenant General Robert E. Lee to recommend his promotion to Lieutenant Colonel; before the appointment could reach him, he was fatally wounded at Kelly's Ford, Va., on March 17, 1863. It is said that General Lee called him the *Gallant Pelham* after the Battle of Fredericksburg.

John Pelham was born in what is now Calhoun County, Ala., on September 14, 1838, and died at Kelly's Ford, Va., on March 17, 1863.

[1] *Dictionary of American Biography under the Auspices of the American Council of Learned Societies*, ed. by Allen Johnson and Dumas Malone (Charles Scribner's Sons, New York, 1930) vol. 14, p. 408.

[2] *The Life of The Gallant Pelham*, Philip Mercer (The J. W. Burke Company, Macon, Ga., 1929) p. 167, 173, 178.

Pelican State. See Louisiana

Pelicans. See Louisianians

Pemberton, Israel

Israel Pemberton, a Quaker philanthropist, became one of the wealthiest merchants of his time. He was popularly called *King of the Quakers* [1] and *King Wampum* [1] because of the prominent part he played in the affairs of the Pennsylvania Quakers. He was manager of and contributor to Pennsylvania Hospital, and a member of the American Philosophical Society, but the largest share of his time and money went to the Friendly Association for Regaining and Preserving Peace with the Indians by Pacific Measures, an organization sponsored by the Philadelphia Meeting to keep the Delawares and Shawnees from joining the French in 1756.

Israel Pemberton was born at Philadelphia, Pa., in 1715, and died there on April 22, 1779.

[1] *Appleton's Cyclopedia of American Biography*, edited by James Grant Wilson and John Fisk (D. Appleton and Company, New York, 1888) vol. 4, p. 706.

Pen-and-Ink Sermons

The cartoons of John Tinney McCutcheon are known as *Pen-and-ink Sermons* [1] because they depict incidents of every-day life and are designed to illustrate fundamental truths. McCutcheon's first pen-and-ink sermons appeared in 1903 in the *Chicago Tribune*.

[1] *The World Book Encyclopedia* (The Quarrie Corporation, Chicago, 1938) vol. 11, p. 4175.

Pen of the Revolution. See Jefferson, Thomas

Pendleton, George Hunt

Father of Civil Service Reform [1] and *Gentleman George* were the nicknames of George Hunt Pendleton.

He was designated the *Father of Civil Service Reform* [1] because he introduced the Civil Service Bill, called the Pendleton Bill, in the United States Congress, and was instrumental in securing passage of this bill in 1883.

Pendleton was also known as *Gentleman George* [2] because he was unfailingly well-mannered.

He was born at Cincinnati, Ohio, on July 19, 1825, and died at Brussels, Belgium, on November 24, 1889.

[1] *A Book of Nicknames*, John Goff (Courier-Journal Job Printing Company, Louisville, Ky., 1892) p. 21.

[2] *The National Cyclopaedia of American Biography* (James T. White and Company, 1893) vol. 3, p. 278.

Penguins. See Youngstown College

Penick, Isaac Newton

Dr. Isaac Newton Penick, Dean of Theology at Union University, Jackson, Tenn., was nicknamed the *Man to Whom Hall-Moody Owes Most* and *Newt.* The former sobriquet was given to Dr. Penick because he was largely instrumental in the building of Hall-Moody Institute, at Martin, Tenn. *Newt* is an abbreviation of his middle name used by members of his family and intimate friends.

Dr. Penick was pastor of the First Baptist Church at Martin, Tenn, from 1896 to 1918, and was Professor of Theology and Dean of the Theological Department of Union University from 1918.

He was born in Carroll County, Tenn., on October 9, 1859, and died at Jackson, Tenn., in September 1945.

Peninsula State. See Florida; Michigan

Penman of the American Revolution. See Dickinson, John

Penn, William

William Penn is known as the *Father of Pennsylvania* [1] because of his part in founding and settling the original colony. Pennsylvania itself means *Penn's Woods.*

William Penn was born at London, England, on October 14, 1644, and died at Philadelphia, Pa., on July 30, 1718.

[1] *American Leaders,* Mabel Ansley Murphy (The Union Press, Philadelphia, 1920) p. 9.

Penn College

The athletic teams of Penn College, at Oskaloosa, Iowa, are popularly known as the *Quakers.* The college is the property of the Quaker denomination.

Pennamites. See Pennsylvanians

Pennsylvania

Five nicknames are given to Pennsylvania: *Coal State, Keystone State, Oil State, Quaker State,* and *Steel State.*

Coal State, Oil State, and *Steel State* are suggestive of Pennsylvania's three greatest industries. The name, *Keystone State,* is accounted for in two versions: (1) When the Government was moved to Washington, D.C., and the Pennsylvania Avenue Bridge was built, Pennsylvania's initials were put on the thirteenth, or key stone of the arch, the initials of the twelve other original states being carved on the stones at either side;[1] (2) John Morton of Pennsylvania, is said to have cast the last vote for the issuance of the Declaration of Independence. The decision of the thirteen colonies to be henceforth independent was thereby made unanimous, and Pennsylvania's vote was thus of prime importance to the strength of the union, as the keystone is important to the strength of an arch.

The nickname, *Quaker State,* commemorates the fact that Pennsylvania was originally a proprietary colony owned by William Penn, who was a Quaker, and who encouraged Quaker settlement.

[1] *A History of the Origin of the Appellation Keystone State,* John S. Morton (Claxton, Remsen and Hafflefinger, Philadelphia, 1847) p. 13-14, 16.

Pennsylvania of the West. See Missouri

Pennsylvania State College

The *Nittany Lions* [1] is the nickname of the athletic teams of Pennsylvania State College, at State College, Pa. The team wanted a nickname that would distinguish them from other college teams called *Lions,* and mountain lions are still found in the Nittany Mountains not far from the college.

[1] A communication from Pennsylvania State College, State College, Pa., June 24, 1935.

Pennsylvanians

The inhabitants of Pennsylvania are variously called *Cohees, Leatherheads, Pennamites,* and *Quakers.* Settlers in the west of Pennsylvania were "called Cohees, in consequence of their addiction to the old-fashioned phrase 'Quoth he,' generally corrupted into *Qho'he.*" [1] *Leatherheads* alludes to the great hide and tanning industry of Pennsylvania, particularly those in the northwestern part of the state.[2] *Pennamites* is a cant name for the followers or admirers of William Penn.[2] *Quakers* refers to the religion of Penn and of the early settlers of Pennsylvania, and to that of many of their descendants even to this day.

[1] *More About Names,* Leopold Wagner (T. Fisher Unwin, London, 1893) p. 24.

[2] *U.S.: An Index to the United States of America,* comp. by Malcolm Townsend (D. Lothrop Company, Boston, 1890) p. 80.

Penny Plug. See O'Sullivan, Dennis

Pension-leeches

Because of corrupt politics there had been much wastefulness in the awarding of pensions to veterans of the War Between the States and President Grover Cleveland had vetoed the Dependent Pension Bill on February 11, 1887, which would have granted a pension of twelve dollars monthly to every honourably discharged veteran of the Civil War. Veterans who wanted the pension were called *Pension-leeches* [1] by supporters of the veto, implying that these veterans were trying to get money from the Government in a parasitical manner.

[1] *Twenty Years of the Republic, 1885-1905*, Harry Thurston Peck (Dodd, Mead and Company, New York, 1907) p. 144.

Peony Center of the World. See Faribault, Minn.

People's City. See Demopolis, Ala.

People's Lawyer. See Brandeis, L. D.

People's President. See Cleveland, Grover; Jackson, Andrew

Peoria, Illinois

Peoria was formerly designated the *Whiskey Town*, [1] in reference to that city's prominence, during the latter decades of the nineteenth century, in the distilling of wines and alcoholic liquors. [2]

[1] *A Book of Nicknames*, John Goff (Courier-Journal Job Printing Company, Louisville, Ky., 1892) p. 17.

[2] *History of Peoria County, Illinois: The History of Peoria County Illinois, Containing a History of the Northwest—History of Illinois,—History of the County, Its Early Settlement, Growth, Development, Resources, Etc.,—A Sketch of Its Cities and Towns, Their Improvements, Industries, Manufacturers, Churches, Schools, Etc.,—A War Record of Its Volunteers in the Late Rebellion—General and Local Statistics—Biographical Sketches—Portraits of Early Settlers and Prominent Men—Map of Peoria County—Constitution of the United States—Miscellaneous Matters—Tables, Etc.* (Johnson and Company, Chicago, 1880) p. 552.

The History of Peoria, Illinois, C. Ballance (N. C. Nason, Peoria, Ill., 1870) p. 135-8.

Pep. See Young, L. F.

Pepper. See Austin, J. P.; Martin, J. L.

Pepper Box. See Bartell, Richard

Percival, John

Because of "his rough and eccentric manners" John Percival, a naval officer, was nicknamed *Mad Jack*. [1]

John Percival entered the United States Navy in 1809, became a lieutenant in 1814, and was in several important actions during that year of the war with England.

He was born at Barnstable, Mass., on April 3, 1779, and died at Roxbury, Mass., on September 17, 1862.

[1] *The National Cyclopaedia of American Biography* (James T. White and Company, New York, 1909) vol. 11, p. 400.

Perkins, George Douglas

George Douglas Perkins, editor and legislator, was popularly called *Uncle George* by residents of Iowa. He devoted himself throughout his life to the social, economic, and political development of that state. He was the pioneer editor of the *Sioux City Journal*, in Iowa, from 1869 until 1884, and its editor and publisher from 1884 until 1914. He also served from 1891 until 1899 as a Representative from Iowa to the United States Congress.

George Douglas Perkins was born at Holly, N.Y., on February 29, 1840, and died at Sioux City, Iowa, on February 3, 1914.

[1] *Dictionary of American Biography under the Auspices of the American Council of Learned Societies*, ed. by Dumas Malone (Charles Scribner's Sons, New York, 1934) vol. 14, p. 469.

Perkins, George Walbridge

George Walbridge Perkins, a banker, was nicknamed the *Dough Moose* because of his strong financial support to the Progressive Republican party which was nicknamed the *Bull Moose* party.

George Walbridge Perkins was born at Chicago, Ill., on January 31, 1862, and died at Stamford, Conn., on June 18, 1920.

[1] *Crowded Hours: Reminiscences*, Alice Roosevelt Longworth (Charles Scribner's Sons, New York and London, 1933) p. 223.

Perkins, Justin

The *Apostle of Persia* [1] was the nickname of Justin Perkins. One of the earliest missionaries sent to Persia by the Congregational Church of the United States, he was successful in establishing churches and mission schools there.

Justin Perkins was born at West Springfield, Mass., on March 12, 1805, and died at Chicopee, Miss., on December 31, 1869.

[1] *The National Cyclopaedia of American Biography* (James T. White and Company, New York, 1909) vol. 10, p. 45-6.

Perkins, Thomas Handasyd

Long Tom Perkins [1] was the nickname of Thomas Handasyd Perkins, a wealthy merchant and personal friend of Daniel Webster.

Thomas Handasyd Perkins was born at Boston, Mass., on December 15, 1764, and died at Brookline, Mass., on January 11, 1854.

[1] *The Godlike Daniel*, Samuel Hopkins Adams (Sears Publishing Company, Inc., New York, 1930) p. 309.

Perpetual Candidate. See Cleveland, Grover

Perpetual Secretary. See Thompson, Charlie

Perry, Oliver Hazard

Commodore Oliver Hazard Perry was called the *Hero of Lake Erie* [1] because his gallant leadership [2] enabled the American fleet to overcome the British ships in the Battle of Lake Erie on September 10, 1813.

Oliver Hazard Perry was born at South Kingston, R.I., on August 21, 1785, and died at Port of Spain, Trinidad, in the West Indies, on August 23, 1819.

[1] *The American Portrait Gallery; Containing Correct Portraits and Brief Notices of the Principal Actors in American History; Embracing Distinguished Women, Naval and Military Heroes, Statesmen, Civilians, Jurists, Divines, Authors, and Artists; together with Celebrated Indian Chiefs, from Christopher Columbus down to the Present Time*, A. D. Jones (J. M. Emerson and Company, New York, 1855) p. 145.

[2] *Oliver Hazard Perry and the Battle of Lake Erie*, James Cooke Mills (John Phelps, Detroit, Mich., 1913) p. 144-52.

Perry Davis' Pain Killer City. See Providence, R.I.

Persecutor. See Rawson, Edward

Pershing, John Joseph

General John Joseph Pershing was often called *Black Jack Pershing*.[1] Legend has it that he acquired the name early in his career because of his success in working with Negro troops under his command.

He was born in Linn County, Mo., on September 13, 1860, and died at Washington, D.C., on July 15, 1948.

[1] *Time, The Weekly News Magazine.* vol. 52, no.4, p. 17, July 26, 1948.
Life, vol. 25, no. 4, July 26, 1948. p. 33-4.

Pet of the Palace. See Stratton, C. S.

Petaluma, California

Petaluma is widely known as the *World's Egg Basket* [1] because it is the center of a large poultry and egg industry.

Petaluma is about thirty-five miles north of San Francisco, on the navigable Petaluma Creek in Sonoma County, Calif. It has a population of over ten thousand.

[1] *Washington Herald-Times,* Washington, D.C., December 11, 1938, col. 1, p. A-5.
The Columbia Lippincott Gazetteer of the World, ed. by Leon E. Seltzer (Columbia University Press, New York, 1952) p. 1460.

Pete. See Alexander, G. C.; Fox, Ervin; Longstreet, James; Manion, C. J.

Peter-the-Hermit of the Abolitionist Movement. See Lundy, Benjamin

Petersburg, Virginia

Petersburg is known as *America's Most Historic City* and the *Cockade City.* With Fredericksburg, Virginia, it claims the title of *America's Most Historic City* because it is rich in historic lore and traditions.

During the War of 1812, Petersburg came to be nicknamed the *Cockade City* [1] because a company of soldiers recruited there wore, as part of their uniform, cockades in their hats.

[1] *Campaigning with Grant,* Horace Porter (The Century Company, New York, 1897) p. 205.

Petroleum. See *Black Gold*

Petrolle, Billy

The *Fargo Express* [1] was a nickname given to Billy Petrolle, a prize fighter from Fargo, N.D., probably because of his swiftness in the ring.

[1] *The Ring, World's Foremost Boxing Magazine* (The Ring, Inc., Duellen, N.J., 1931) March, 1931, p. 8.

Petticoat Allen. See Allen, William

Petticoat Insurrection

In 1702 on the present location of Mobile, Ala., a French settlement on the Mobile river was established by Pierre le Moyne Iberville and others. The colony was reinforced in 1703 and 1704 by French recruits. In the summer of 1704 twenty-three girls arrived on the ship *Pelican,* and all but one were soon married. Before long, however, the women rebelled against eating the food provided for them because supplies in the colony being limited and scanty, they were of necessity forced to eat foods made of Indian corn. This revolt has been amusingly described by historians as the *Petticoat Insurrection.*[1]

[1] *Colonial Mobile, an Historical Study Largely from Original Sources of the Alabama-Tombigbee Basin and the Old South West from the Discovery of the Spiritu Santa in 1519 until the Demolition of Fort Charlotte in 1821,* Peter J. Hamilton (Houghton Mifflin Company, New York and Boston, 1910) p. 66.
The Encyclopedia Americana (Americana Corporation, New York and Chicago, 927) vol. 19, p. 280.

Petticoat Pet. See Van Buren, Martin

Pewter Mug. See *Pewter Muggers*

Pewter Muggers
About 1828 in New York a group of politicians belonging to the Democratic party refused to support candidates endorsed by Tammany Hall. The members of the faction held most of their political meetings at a Franklin Street tavern known as the *Pewter Mug*[1] where drinks were served from pewter mugs. It was not long, therefore, before they acquired the nickname *Pewter Muggers.*[2]

[1] *The National Cyclopaedia of American Biography* (James T. White and Company, New York, 893) vol. 3, p. 388.
[2] *Encyclopedic Dictionary of American History,* J. Franklin Jameson and J. W. Buel (American History Society, Washington, D.C., 1900) vol. 2, p. 92.

Pfirman, Charles H.
Charles H. Pfirman, who was born in Cincinnati, Ohio, on February 27, 1891, and who was a National League umpire, was popularly known as *Cy*[1] because of his ability in baseball. Outstanding baseball players are frequently honored with the same nickname as that of Denton T. Young.

[1] *Who's Who in Major League Base Ball,* comp. by Harold (Speed) Johnson (Buxton Publishing Company, Chicago, 1933) p. 446.

Phantom Division. See Ninth Armored Division of World War II

Phenomenal Presiding Elder. See Wilson, J. A. B.

Philadelphia, Pennsylvania
Philadelphia has six sobriquets: the *Birthplace of American Liberty, City of Brotherly Love, City of Homes, City of Penn, Quaker City,* and *Rebel Capital.*

This city is proud of the nickname, *Birthplace of American Liberty,*[1] which commemorates the fact that it is the location of Independence Hall, the seat of the Revolutionary Congress and the scene of the signing of the Declaration of Independence. The name *City of Brotherly Love,*[2] is not of recent origin. It appeared in print as early as 1799 in the *Aurora General Advertiser*[3] as follows: "And behold a great wonder appeared in the city which is called Brotherly Love, a creature which arose out of the sea, a very terrible and such as hath not been seen hitherto."

City of Brotherly Love, is a liberal translation of the Greek noun, Φιλαδέλφεια, or *brotherly love.*[4] Philadelphia was the name of a city in Lydia, and comes from a late Latin form, Philadelphia, which is derived from the Greek noun given above. Young says, in speaking of Philadelphia, Pennsylvania, and its founder, William Penn: "Even the name for it, derived probably from the ancient Philadelphia in Asia Minor, to whose church, as John records, he was directed to write, had been in the founder's mind. . . ." And in his letter to Thomas Lloyd, in 1684, from on board ship as he was departing for England after his first visit here, he breaks out in an apostrophe to the infant city: "'And thou Philadelphia . . . named before thou wert born,' etc."[5]

It is designated the *City of Homes*[6] because thousands of industrial workers there own their homes.

Philadelphia is nicknamed the *City of Penn*[7] to commemorate the fact that it was founded by William Penn.[8] It is known as the *Quaker City*[9] because William Penn and his followers belonged to the Society of Friends, or *Quakers.*[10]

The city was often called the *Rebel Capital*[11] by the British because it became, in 1776, at the outbreak of the American Revolution, the capital of the thirteen colonies. In 1800 the seat of government was moved from Philadelphia to Washington, D.C.

[1] *Little Journeys in America,* Rose Henderson (The Southern Publishing Company, Dallas, Tex., 1922) p. 80.
[2] *Americanisms: The English of the New World,* M. Schele De Vere (Charles Scribner and Company, New York, 1872) p. 664.
[3] *Aurora General Advertiser* (Published for the heirs of Benjamin Franklin Bache, at Bristol, Pa., September 28, 1799) col. 5, p. 2.
[4] *The Century Dictionary and Cyclopedia* (The Century Company, New York, 1906) vol. 6, p. 4442.
[5] *Memorial History of the City of Philadelphia, from Its First Settlement to the Year 1895,* ed. by John Russell Young (New York History Company, New York, 1895) vol. 1, p. 9.
[6] *A Book of Nicknames,* John Goff (Courier-Journal Job Printing Company, Louisville, Ky., 1892) p. 15.

Philadelphia, Pa.—Continued

[7] *Manual of Useful Information*, comp. under the direction of J. C. Thomas (The Werner Company, Chicago, 1893) p. 22.

[8] *Philadelphia*, Horace Mather Lippincott, foreword and illustrations by Thornton Oakley (Macrea-Smith Company, Philadelphia, 1926) p. 2.

[9] *History of Philadelphia, 1609-1884*, J. Thomas Scharf and Thomas Wescott (L. H. Everts and Company, Philadelphia, 1884) vol. 2, p. 965.

Americanisms: The English of the New World, M. Schele De Vere (Charles Scribner and Company, New York, 872) p. 664.

[10] *Philadelphia*, Horace Mather Lippincott, foreword and illustrations by Thornton Oakley (Macrea-Smith Company, Philadelphia, 1926) p. 1, 9.

A Quaker Experiment in Government, Isaac Sharpless (Alfred J. Ferris, Philadelphia, 1898) p. 21.

[11] *Alexander Hamilton*, Howard H. Hicks (The Macmillan Company, New York, 1928) p. 43.

Philadelphia American League Baseball Company

About 1901 the Philadelphia American League Baseball Company was called the *Philadelphia Athletics* [1] by baseball writers. A baseball club formed in Philadelphia in the late 1860's had been legally styled the Athletic Club,[2] and this probably inspired the later name.

In November 1954, the club's franchise was officially transferred from Philadelphia to Kansas City.[3]

[1] *Who's Who in Major League Base Ball*, comp. by Harold (Speed) Johnson (Buxton Publishing Company, Chicago, 1933) p. 56.

[2] A communication from James C. Isaminger, a sports writer for the Philadelphia Inquirer and Public Ledger, Philadelphia, Pa., June 20, 1935.

[3] The New York Times, November 10, 1954, p. 47.

Philadelphia Athletics. See Philadelphia American League Baseball Company

Philadelphia National League Baseball Club

The official name, Philadelphia National League Baseball Club, is often abbreviated to *Philadelphia Nationals*.[1] The players are also designated *Phillies* and *Quakers* [2] because they are in the *Quaker City*.

[1] *Who's Who in Major League Base Ball*, comp. by Harold (Speed) Johnson (Buxton Publishing Company, Chicago, 1933) p. 40.

[2] A letter from James H. Hagan, Travelling Secretary for The Philadelphia National League Baseball Club, Philadelphia, June 21, 1935.

Philadelphia Nationals. See Philadelphia National League Baseball Club

Philadelphia's Jean Valjean. See Burke, William

Philippi Races

From about June 1 to 3, 1861, the Confederate forces hurriedly retreated from Philippi, W.Va., to Huttonsville, W.Va., a distance of about forty miles. This march has been designated the *Philippi Races* [1] because of the rapidity with which it was accomplished.

[1] *History of West Virginia*, James Morton Callahan (The American Historical Society, Inc., New York and Chicago, 1923) vol. 1, p. 377.

Philips, Mardin Wilson

Mardin Wilson Philips, writer, reformer and agriculturalist, was widely known as the *Sage of Log Hall*,[1] and *Log Hall Philips*.[1] Log Hall, his plantation in Hinds County, Miss., was profitably and scientifically managed under his direction. He was a scholarly man who worked consistently to raise the standards of education in Mississippi. He contributed numerous articles to farm journals, and from 1867 to 1873 edited a magazine called *Philips' Southern Farmer*, published at Memphis, Tenn.

He was born at Columbia, S.C., on June 17, 1806, and died at Oxford, Miss., on February 26, 1889.

[1] *Dictionary of American Biography under the Auspices of the American Council of Learned Societies*, ed. by Dumas Malone (Charles Scribner's Sons, New York, 1934) vol. 14, p. 537.

Philipse, Frederick

The *Dutch Millionaire* [1] was a nickname given to Frederick Philipse because he was of Dutch descent, and one of the wealthiest men in the town of New York.

He was born at Bolsward, in Friesland, Holland, in 1626, and died at what is now New York City, on November 6, 1702.

[1] *The National Cyclopaedia of American Biography* (James T. White and Company, New York, 1910) vol. 14, p. 275.

Phillies. See Philadelphia National League Baseball Club

Phillips, Alfred Noroton, Jr.

Alfred Noroton Phillips, Jr., was nicknamed *Milk of Magnesia* by his fellow members in the House of Representatives because he was formerly associated with a manufacturer of milk of magnesia.

He was a Democratic Representative from Connecticut to the United States Congress from 1937 until 1939.

Alfred Noroton Phillips, Jr., was born at Darien, Conn., on April 23, 1894.

[1] An interview with Captain Victor Hunt Harding, Secretary of the National Democratic Congress Re-election Committee, Washington, D.C., April 10, 1939.

Phillips University

The athletic teams of Phillips University, at Enid, Okla., are designated the *Haymakers*.[1] This nickname originated in 1908 when the hay had to be cleared "from the newly-mown [athletic] field"[1] before it could be used for athletics.

[1] A communication from I. N. McCash, President of Phillips University, Enid, Okla., November 19, 1935.

Philosopher. See Sorrell, V. G.

Philosopher of Democracy. See Jefferson, Thomas

Philosophy Smith. See Smith, T. V.

Phisterer, Frederick

Frederick Phisterer was appropriately nicknamed *Father of the National Guard of New York*[1] because he worked faithfully to promote the effectiveness of the New York state militia.

In 1892 he was appointed assistant Adjutant General of the State of New York, and in this capacity devoted himself to reorganizing and developing the state militia. He aided in the revision of the New York State military codes and wrote a number of authoritative books and articles relating to military affairs, several of the publications dealing with the national guardsmen of New York State.

He was born at Stuttgart, Würtemberg, Germany, on October 11, 1836, emigrated to the United States in 1855, and died at Albany, N.Y., on July 13, 1909.

[1] The National Cyclopaedia of American Biography (James T. White and Company, New York, 1920) vol. 17, p. 41.

Phrasemaker. See Wilson, Woodrow

Physician's Physician. See Da Costa, J. M.

Physick, Philip Syng

The *Father of American Surgery*[1] is a sobriquet of Dr. Philip Syng Physick because of his notable career[2] as an American surgeon, and as a pioneer teacher of surgery at the University of Pennsylvania. He improved upon several surgical instruments and devised better methods of treating emergency cases.

Philip Syng Physick was born at Philadelphia, Pa., on July 7, 1768, and died there on December 15, 1857.

[1] A Memoir on the Life and Character of Philip Syng Physick, M.D., Jacob Randolph (T. K. and P. G. Collins, Philadelphia, 1839) p. 107.
Lives of Eminent American Physicians and Surgeons of the Nineteenth Century, ed. by Samuel D. Gross (Lindsay and Blakiston, Philadelphia, 1861) p. 404, 459.

[2] A Memoir on the life and Character of Philip Syng Physick, M.D., Jacob Randolph (Printed by T. K. and P. G. Collins, Philadelphia, 1839) p. 36-50.

Piatt, John James and Piatt, Sarah Morgan Bryan

John James Piatt and his wife, Sarah Morgan Bryan Piatt, were sometimes called the *Wedded Poets*[1] because they both attained considerable recognition among the minor American poets, and were joint authors of collections of verse.

John James Piatt was born at James' Mill, Ind., on March 1, 1835, and died at Cincinnati, Ohio, on February 16, 1917. His wife, Sarah Morgan Bryan Piatt, was born at Lexington, Ky., on August 11, 1836, and died probably at Cincinnati, Ohio, on December 24, 1919.

[1] Our Singing Strength: An Outline of American Poetry (1620-1930), Alfred Kreymborg (Coward-McCann, Inc., New York, 1929) p. 175.

Pickens, Andrew

Although Major General Andrew Pickens was a formidable enemy of the Cherokee Indians in wartime, and had severely repulsed them at the battle of Tomassee, in South Carolina, about 1779 or 1780, he was called by them *Skyagunsta*, and the *Wizard of Tomassee*.[1] This latter sobriquet implies that Pickens led the seemingly charmed life of a wizard. He was a courageous soldier and in his treatment of the Cherokee was fair and humane. According to various interpretations, the Indian term, *Skyagunsta*, is said to mean *Great Chief* or *Great Warrior, Chosen Clear-Sky Owl*, or *Chosen Clear-Sky Wizard*, all obviously expressions of esteem.

Andrew Pickens was born at Paxton, Pa., on September 19, 1739, and died in the Pendleton district of South Carolina, on August 17, 1817.

[1] Skyagunsta, the Border Wizard Owl, Major-General Andrew Pickens (1739-1817), Andrew Lee Pickens (Observer Printing Company, Greeenville, S.C., 1934) p. 124-6.

Pickford, Mary (Gladys Smith)

America's Sweetheart [1] and the *World's Sweetheart* [2] are nicknames of Mary Pickford in allusion to her popularity with the movie-going public. She became famous for her portrayals in children's roles.

Mary Pickford was born at Toronto, Canada, on April 8, 1893, and now makes her home at Hollywood, Calif.

[1] *Mary and Doug and Others*, Allene Talmey (Macy-Masius, New York, 1927) p. 30.
[2] *Who's Who in Filmland*, Third Edition, comp. and ed. by Langford Reed and Hetty Spiers (Chapman and Hall, Ltd., London, 1931) p. 242.

Picnic City. See Mobile, Ala.

Picturesque Explorer of the United States. See Lanman, Charles

Pie. See Traynor, H. J.

Piecounter Brigade

Newspapers of New York and elsewhere referred to the circle of President Theodore Roosevelt's immediate friends, at Washington, D.C. especially, as the *Piecounter Brigade*,[1] indicating a feeling of resentment against what they considered favoritism in the appointment of an administrator's personal friends and political adherents to positions that should have been filled by those whose worthiness had been demonstrated. In American slang the sobriquet signifies that those to whom it was applied obtained the best of everything either without paying for or meriting it.

[1] *Twenty Years of the Republic, 1885-1905*, Harry Thurston Peck (Dodd, Mead and Company, New York, 1907) p. 706.

Piecrust Palmer. See Palmer, J. S.

Pietruszka, Anthony Francis

The nicknames, *Tony Piet, Tony the Silent,* and *Whitey* have been given to Anthony Francis Pietruszka.

Tony Piet,[1] is a shortened form of his name.

Because he is rather reticent, he has been nicknamed *Tony the Silent.*[1] He is sometimes called *Whitey*[1] because he has a heavy crop of blonde hair.

Anthony Francis Pietruszka was born at Berwick, Pa., on December 6, 1907, and played infield in major league baseball.

[1] *Who's Who in Major League Base Ball*, comp. by Harold (Speed) Johnson (Buxton Publishing Company, Chicago, 1933) p. 319.

Pig Iron Kelley. See Kelley, W. D.

Pig Pen. See *Martling's Long Room*

Pikers. See Washington University

Pill Box

In Texas and other western states during frontier days, a revolver or a pistol was called a *Pill Box*,[1] implying that the bullets in the revolver were pills.

[1] *A New Dictionary of Americanisms*, Sylva Clapin (Louis Weiss and Company, New York, 1903) p. 54.

Pillar of the Constitution. See Webster, Daniel

Pillsbury, John Sargent

John Sargent Pillsbury, seventh governor of Minnesota, and founder of the Pillsbury Flour Company, was designated *Father of the University*[1] *of Minnesota* because of the personal as well as official interest which he took in the welfare of this institution.

Pillsbury was appointed regent of the University of Minnesota in 1863, and was elected to the state senate the same year. In this dual capacity, he was responsible for the final adjustment of all claims against the university, saving it upwards of 30,000 acres of the land grants made to it by Congress. Later, as governor, he added to the legislature's grant of $100,000 for a new university building a $150,000 personal contribution, and the Pillsbury Hall of Science is the visible result of this generosity.

He was born at Sutton, N.H., on July 29, 1828, and died at Minneapolis, Minn., on October 18, 1901.

[1] *The National Cyclopaedia of American Biography* (James T. White and Company, New York, 1904) vol. 10, p. 65-6.

Pilots. See University of Portland

Pinckney, Charles

Charles Pinckney, statesman, was nicknamed *Blackguard Charlie*[1] by his political opponents in the Federalist party who considered him a demagogue, a disciple of the spoils system, and a man of questionable honesty. To his friends and political constituents, however, he was a demi-god worthy of the presidency by virtue of his work in the drafting of the Constitution of the United States, his staunch support of and leadership in the Jeffersonian Republican party; his efficiency as Governor of South Carolina from 1789 until 1792, and his skill in executing numerous governmental and public offices during his lifetime.

Charles Pinckney was born at Charleston, S.C., on October 26, 1757, and died there on October 29, 1824.

[1] *Dictionary of American Biography under the Auspices of the American Council of Learned Societies,* ed. by Dumas Malone (Charles Scribner's Sons, New York, 1934) vol. 14, p. 613.

Pine Tree State. See Maine

Pine Trees. See Maine Inhabitants

Pineapple Division. See Twenty-fifth Infantry Division of World War II

Pink Whiskers. See Lewis, J. H.

Pinkey. See Hargrave, W. M.; Whitney, A. C.

Pinky. See Harrington, F. C.

Pintard, John

The *Father of Historical Societies in America* [1] is a nickname given to John Pintard to commemorate his success in establishing, at Boston, Mass., in 1791, the Massachusetts Historical Society. This organization was the pattern for numerous historical societies throughout the United States. In 1804 he founded a historical society in New York City, to which he contributed liberal funds and valuable book collections.

John Pintard was born at New York City, on May 18, 1759, and died there on June 21, 1844.

[1] *The National Cyclopaedia of American Biography* (James T. White and Company, New York, 1893) vol. 3, p. 461.

Pioneers. See Carroll College; Evansville College; Grinnell College; Marietta College; University of Denver

Pipe-line Disney. See Disney, W. E.

Pipes. See Whistler, G. W.

Pirates. See Whitworth College

Pirate's Home

The *Pirate's Home* [1] was the term given to the area including the Bay of Barataria

and its many islands, the shoreline of Louisiana along the Gulf of Mexico between the mouth of the Mississippi River and the point where the Bayou LaFourche enters the Gulf, and the island between the Bay of Barataria and the Gulf of Mexico known as Grand Terre. During the first quarter of the nineteenth century privateers, pirates, contrabandists, and smugglers had their hiding place on Grand Terre because they could anchor their ships in the adjacent Bay of Barataria. Merchants from New Orleans and other southern cities would go to the *Pirate's Home* to buy the costly merchandise and various wares which had been plundered from ships carrying goods to and from all parts of the world. The pirates were especially active in the settlement along the Bay of Barataria and its vicinity from about 1810 to 1813; but in 1814 a detachment from the United States Army and Navy effectively destroyed the settlement and put an end to an illicit trade center which was materially interfering with the revenue on incoming goods.

[1] *New Orleans, the Place and the People,* Grace King (The Macmillan Company, New York, 1902) p. 191-2, 194-6, 204.
Life of Andrew Jackson, James Parton (Mason Brothers, New York, 1861) vol. 1, p. 580-90.

Pitched Land

About 1800 the land in the vicinity of the village of Wheelock, N.H., was made accessible to settlers. A settler was permitted to pick any two one-hundred-acre lots of first class land that he desired, and this possession was popularly called *Pitched Land* [1] because, soon after acquiring it, the settler pitched or established a temporary home.

[1] *A History of Dartmouth College, 1815-1902, Being the Second Volume of a History of Dartmouth College and the Town of Hanover, New Hampshire, begun by Frederick Chase,* John King Lord (The Rumford Press, Concord, N.H., 1913) p. 227-8.

Pitchfork Ben. See Tillman, B. R.

Pitchfork Tillman. See Tillman, B. R.

Pittman, Key

Key Pittman, Nevada miner and politician, was nicknamed the *Voice of Silver* [1] by his colleagues in the United States Senate because for a number of years he advocated greater silver coinage and was the originator and sponsor of the Pittman Act (silver coinage) which became a Federal law on April

Pittman, Key—Continued

23, 1918. He later introduced several acts pertaining to silver buying and silver coinage into the United States Senate.

He was in the Northwest Territory and in Alaska from 1897 until 1901, where he worked as a gold miner. He was a Democratic Senator from Nevada to the United States Congress from 1913 to 1940.

Key Pittman was born at Vicksburg, Miss., on September 19, 1872, and died at Reno, Nev., on November 10, 1940.

[1] An interview with Captain Victor Hunt Harding, Secretary of the National Democratic Congress Re-election Committee, Washington, D.C., April 10, 1939.

Pitts, Zasu

The sobriquet, *Girl With the Ginger Snap Name*,[1] was given to Zasu Pitts because of the similarity between Zasu and Zuzu, a popular brand of ginger snaps. The name *Zasu* was created from the first and last syllables of the names of her aunts, Eliza and Susan.

Zasu Pitts was born at Parsons, Kans., on January 3, 1898.

[1] *Who's Who on the Screen*, ed. by Charles D. Fox and Milton L. Silver (Ross Publishing Company, Inc., New York City, 1920) p. 113.

Pittsburgh, Pennsylvania

Pittsburgh is designated the *Birmingham of America, City of Steel*, or the *Steel City, Iron City, Smoky City*, and the *World's Workshop*.

It is termed the *Birmingham of America* [1] because of its extensive manufacturing similar to Birmingham, England. It justly merits the nickname. *Steel City*,[2] or *City of Steel*,[3] because it is the outstanding iron and steel manufacturing city in America, and one of the largest of such centers in the world." [4] Pittsburgh is widely known as the *Iron City* [5] because it is also a great iron manufacturing center. It is named *Smoky City* [6] because of the volumes of smoke produced by the use of bituminous coal in manufacturing plants, railroad engines, and furnaces in private homes. The topography of Pittsburgh and the surrounding region is particularly conducive to the creation of dense fogs made heavier and darker by the smoke emanating from the city. In recent years, the use of electric power, and of coke and gas for fuel, has somewhat decreased the amount of smoke.

The sobriquet, the *World's Workshop*,[7] is applied to this city because it is an immense industrial center, its products going to all parts of the world.

[1] *A Book of Nicknames*, John Goff (Courier-Journal Job Printing Company, Louisville, Ky., 1892) p. 15.

[2] *Minute Glimpses of American Cities*, Herbert S. Kates (Grosset and Dunlap, New York, 1933) p. 99.

[3] *Geography, United States and Canada*, Harlan H. Barrows and Edith Putnam Parker (Silver, Burdett and Company, New York and Boston, 1934) p. 220.

[4] *Journeys Through Our World Today: A Textbook in the New Geography*, De Forest Stull and Ray W. Hatch (Allyn and Bacon, New York and Boston, 1934) p. 22.

[5] *Americanisms; The English of the New World*, M. Schele De Vere (Charles Scribner and Company, New York, 1872) p. 664.

[6] *Minute Glimpses of American Cities*, Herbert S. Kates (Grosset and Dunlap, New York, 1933) p. 99.

[7] *Little Journeys in America*, Rose Henderson (The Southern Publishing Company, Dallas, Tex., 1922) p. 62-4.

Pittsburgh Candy King. See Clark, D. L.

Pittsburgh National League Baseball Company

The Pittsburgh National League Baseball Club acquired the nickname *Pittsburgh Pirates* [1] in 1891.

Prior to that time the National League and the American Association controlled between them all the major baseball clubs. Near the opening of the 1890 baseball season many players, dissatisfied with the conditions of work and pay then prevailing, withdrew from the existing organizations and formed the Brotherhood League which placed clubs in almost all major league cities. Among the men who withdrew were Harry Stovey and Louis Bierbauer, the former joining the Brooklyn Players League Club, and the latter becoming a member of the Philadelphia Athletics.

Eventually an agreement between the Brotherhood League and the two major leagues was reached, one stipulation being that all players who had withdrawn were to be returned automatically to clubs to which they had previously belonged.

A basic regulation of major league baseball is that in October of each year all clubs must submit to the league a reserved list of the players to whom they hold titles. However, when the reserved lists were submitted in October 1891, through an oversight the Philadelphia Athletics failed to include Bierbauer's name. Detecting the omission, the Pittsburgh Club immediately contracted with Bierbauer for his services during the coming season. The Philadelphia Athletics and the American Association quickly registered a protest against this act and stated that Bierbauer's name had been unintentionally omitted. The matter was arbitrated and the Pittsburgh Club was found to have acted strictly within its rights under the rules of major league baseball. However the deed was designated an act of piracy both by the Philadelphia Athletics and by the American Association, and the Pittsburgh club has been nicknamed the *Pirates* ever since.

[1] The information about the origin of the nickname, *The Pittsburgh Pirates*, was condensed from the contents of a letter written by Samuel E. Watters, Vice President and Secretary of The Pittsburgh National League Baseball Club, Pittsburgh, Pa., June 20, 1935.

Pittsburgh of the South. See Birmingham, Ala.

Pittsburgh of the West. See Pueblo, Colo.

Pittsburgh Pirates. See Pittsburgh National League Baseball Company

Pittsburgh Pirates Football Club

The *Steelers* [1] is the nickname given the teams of the Pittsburgh Pirates Football Club, a member of the National Football League, at Pittsburgh, Pennsylvania. This sobriquet was selected for the teams on March 2, from three thousand names submitted by football fans, because it fittingly symbolized Pittsburgh's position as the world's leading steel center.[1]

[1] *Times-Herald*, Washington, D.C., March 3, 1940, Sports Section, col. 5, p. 1.

Plaids. See Carnegie Institute of Technology

Plant, Henry Bradley

Because of the active part he had taken in the industrial development of the state of Florida, Henry Bradley Plant was often referred to as the *King of Florida*.[1]

Plant's chief contribution to Florida was as a builder [2] of railroads in all parts of the state, especially in territories previously considered to be too remote for commercial purposes. He built and controlled over two thousand miles of railway lines; and, by advertising the scenic attractions, latent resources, and commercial and industrial advantages of Florida, he succeeded admirably in developing its industrial and commercial potential. Plant also established regular steamship connections between Tampa, Fla.,

and Cuba, and between seaports of Florida and those of other states on the Gulf of Mexico. In addition to contributing to institutions or organizations of a philanthropic nature, he built hotels and health resorts along the southern coast of Florida.

Henry Bradley Plant was born at Branford, Conn., on October 27, 1819, and died at New York City, on June 23, 1899.

[1] *The National Cyclopaedia of American Biography* (James T. White and Company, New York, 1922) vol. 18, p. 287.

[2] *The Life of Henry Bradley Plant, Founder and President of the Plant System of Railroads and Steamships and Also of the Southern Express Company*, G. Hutchinson Smyth (G. P. Putnam's Sons, New York and London, 1898) p. 113-140.

Plant-cutters

About 1680 and 1681 the tobacco growers in the Virginia Colony produced more tobacco than they could sell. They tried various methods of avoiding the selling of this, their chief commodity, below the cost of production. Finding that none of the proposed methods succeeded, they took their hoes and chopped down great quantities of the crop, hence the nickname *Plant-cutters*.[1]

[1] *Scribner's Popular History of the United States from the Earliest Discoveries of the Western Hemisphere by the Northmen to the Present Time*, William Cullen Bryant, Sidney Howard, and Noah Brooks (Charles Scribner's Sons, New York, 1896) vol. 3, p. 55.

Plant Wizard. See Burbank, Luther

Plantation State. See Rhode Island

Platt, Thomas Collier

Easy Boss Platt and *Me Too Platt* were the sobriquets of Thomas Collier Platt, onetime United States Senator, and a leader of the Republican party from 1884 until 1910.

In his autobiography, Platt states that he was first called *easy boss* [1] by a little news girl, when she thanked him for preventing a rival from forcing her to move her news stand. After relating the incident to his friends, he was constantly referred to as *Easy Boss Platt*.[2] This nickname was also an allusion to his quiet, skillful manner in dealing with men, and to his policy of leading his party in the direction in which it wished to be led rather than having it follow his own course of action.

The nickname, *Me Too Platt*,[3] originated in May, 1881, when Platt and his colleague, Roscoe Conkling, resigned their offices as senators from New York to the United States Congress because President Garfield

Platt, T. C.—Continued
had appointed a collector for the port of
New York without consulting either of them.
It was believed that Platt had been influenced by Conkling to give up his senatorial office, and a cartoon in a paper of
that day picturing their "political death,"
depicted a large tombstone with the inscription *Me Too. T. Platt.* Another cartoon representd him as a small boy pro-
truding from Conkling's pocket, with a
card bearing the inscription *Me Too* [3] fastened to one hand.

Thomas Collier Platt was born at Oswego, N.Y., on July 15, 1833, and died at
New York City, on March 6, 1910.

[1] *The Autobiography of Thomas Collier Platt,* comp.
and ed. by Louis J. Lang (B. W. Dodge and Company,
New York, 1910) p. 525-6.
[2] *Reconstruction and Union, 1865-1912,* Paul Leland
Haworth (Henry Holt and Comany, New York, 1912)
p. 107.
[3] *The Autobiography of Thomas Collier Platt,* comp.
and ed. by Louis L. Lang (B. W. Dodge and Company,
New York, 1910) p. 159.

Platt's Sunday School Classes
From 1859 until 1908 the Fifth Avenue
Hotel in New York City served as a meeting place for managers of the Republican
party, their associates, and many non-Repub-
lican public officials who met there to discuss party policy and to determine strategy.
Legislators and other officeholders in Washington D.C. and elsewhere being occupied
during the week with official duties, they
came to the hotel on Sunday mornings to
discuss their political activities. Because
Thomas Collier Platt was generally the leading spirit in these Sunday conferences, they
were widely known as *Platt's Sunday School
Classes.*[1]

[1] *Boss Platt and His New York Machine, a Study of
the Political Leadership of Thomas C. Platt, Theodore
Roosevelt, and Others,* Harold Foote Gosnell, with an
introduction by Charles E. Merriam (The University of
Chicago Press, Chicago, 1924) p. 57.

Playboy. See Reynolds, R. R.

Playboy of New York. See Walker,
J. J.

Playground of the Nation. See Minnesota

Playground of Two Nations. See Great
Smoky National Park

Pleasant Gardens Joe. See McDowell,
Joseph

Pleasants, John Hampden
Bayard of the Press [1] was the nickname
frequently applied to John Hampden Pleasants, editor. Through the medium of his
publications he vigorously upheld the principles of the Whig party, of which he was
a member, and was fearless in dealing with
his political opponents. The sobriquet alludes to Pierre du Terrail Chevalier de Bayard, an intrepid and loyal French soldier
of the sixteenth century.

John Hampden Pleasants was born in
Goochland County, Va., on January 4, 1797,
and died at Richmond, Va., on February 27,
1846.

[1] *The National Cyclopaedia of American Biography*
(James T. White and Company, New York, 1896)
vol. 7, p. 545.

Plowboys. See John Tarleton Agricultural
College

Plow 'Em Under Wallace. See Wallace, H. A.

Plumb Line Port to Panama. See
Charleston, S.C.

Plumed Knight. See Blaine, J. G.

Plumed Knight of the Confederacy.
See Stuart, J. E. B.

Plunging Chink. See Outen, W. A.

Plutocracy's Bastilles
Because the disorders accompanying the
Pullman strike in 1894 near Chicago, Ill.,
had endangered both life and property,
many states reorganized their state militia
into national guard units, making the state
military forces a part of the regular United
States Army. These units were subject to
call not only in local emergencies but also
for service on a nation-wide scale. The
armories built for the accommodation of
these guardsmen and their weapons came
to be nicknamed *Plutocracy's Bastilles* [1] by
the labor unions because they felt that the
armories protected the interests of the
wealthy class who were attempting to con-

trol the Government. The State prison of France prior to the French Revolution in 1789 was called the Bastille.

[1] "The Armies of Labor, a Chronicle of the Organized Wage-earners" by Samuel P. Orth, in *The Chronicles of America Series*, Abraham Lincoln Edition, Allen Johnson, Editor (Yale University Press, New Haven, Conn., 1919) vol. 40, p. 254.

Plymouth of the West. See San Diego, Calif.

Poage, William Robert
William Robert Poage, a Texas lawyer and congressman, was nicknamed the *Professor* [1] by his colleagues in the House of Representatives because he was formerly an instructor in geology and later in law at Baylor University, at Waco, Tex.

He was a Democratic Representative to the Texas Legislature from 1924 until 1928, Democratic Senator to the Texas Legislature from 1930 until 1936, and has served as Democratic Representative from the Eleventh Congressional District of Texas to the United States Congress from 1937.

William Robert Poage was born at Waco, Tex., on December 28, 1899.

[1] An interview with Captain Victor Hunt Harding, Secretary of the National Democratic Congress Reëlection Committee, Washington, D.C., April 10, 1939.

Pocket Veto
If the President of the United States retains an act of Congress for ten days without signing it, and if Congress adjourns in the meantime, the act is designated a *Pocket Veto*.[1]

[1] *Political Americanisms*, Charles Ledyard Norton (Longmans, Green and Company, New York and London, 1890) p. 88.

Poe, Edgar Allan
Edgar Allan Poe, who was born at Boston, Mass., on January 19, 1809, and who died at Baltimore, Md., on October 7, 1849, has been designated the *Wizard of Word Music* [1] because he wrote poetry of such beautiful rhythm and descriptive power.

[1] *Compton's Pictured Encyclopedia* (F. E. Compton and Company, Chicago, 1931) vol. 1, p. 112.

Poet Laureate of California. See McGroarty, J. S.

Poet Laureate of New England. See Whittier, J. G.

Poet Laureate of the Army. See Patten, G. W.

Poet Laureate of the South. See Hayne, P. H.

Poet Naturalist. See Thoreau, H. D.

Poet of Childhood. See Field, Eugene

Poet of Low Hampton. See Miller, William

Poet of the American Revolution. See Freneau, Philip

Poet of the Commonplace. See Longfellow, H. W.

Poet of the Common People. See Riley, J. W.

Poet of the Golden Gate. See Kirchhoff, Theodor

Poet of the Sierras. See Miller, C. H.

Poet Sportsman. See McLellan, Isaac

Poets. See Whittier College

Point. See *Golden Triangle*

Pointed Arrow. See Jackson, Andrew

Poison Ivy. See Andrews, I. P.

Poison Twins. See Waner, L. J. and Waner, P. G.

Poker Alice Tubbs. See Tubbs, Alice

Poker Charley. See Farwell, C. B.

Poker Face. See Garner, J. N.

Polar Bears. See Bowdoin College

Polar Star State. See Maine

Policy King. See Adams, A. J.

Polish City in Texas. See Panna Maria, Tex.

Political Gadflies. See *Intellectual Termites*

Political Meteor. See Randolph (of Roanoke), John

Political Philosopher. See Smith, T. V.

Political Savior of Virginia. See Walker, G. C.

Political Thor. See Farley, J. A.

Polk, James Knox

The appellations, the *First Dark Horse,* the *Napoleon of the Stump,* and *Young Hickory* have been given to James Knox Polk.

At their convention in Baltimore, Md., in 1844, the Democrats eliminated Martin Van Buren as the candidate for the presidency of the United States and unexpectedly chose to support James Knox Polk. Polk was hence nicknamed the *First Dark Horse.*[1] The phrase, *Dark Horse,*[2] is often used in politics to designate a candidate who is nominated at a convention and wins an unanticipated following. The expressions originated in the language of the race-tracks where it is used to refer to a horse whose strength of achievement or chances of winning a race are not usually known to the public.

Polk was sometimes called the *Napoleon of the Stump* [3] because he was a resourceful, aggressive, and formidable opponent in debate who carried his argument with such power that the opponent's defeat was certain. In this respect Polk was comparable to Napoleon, who by similar traits of character won victory after victory over those who opposed him.

He received the nickname, *Young Hickory,*[4] because like Andrew Jackson, *Old Hickory,* he was born and reared near the North Carolina borderline and experienced the hardships of early frontier life, he later moved to Tennessee where he studied and practiced law, and his political policies were similar to those practiced by Jackson.

James Knox Polk was born in Mecklenburg County, N.C., on November 2, 1795, and died at Nashville, Tenn., on June 15, 1849. He was President of the United States from 1845 to 1849.

[1] *The State of the Nation,* Albert J. Beveridge (The Bobbs-Merrill Company, Indianapolis, Ind., 1924) p. 210.

[2] *The Encyclopedia Americana* (Americana Corporation, New York and Chicago, 1927) vol. 8, p. 478.

[3] *The Presidents of the United States, 1789 to 1914,* John Fiske, Carl Schurz, Robert C. Winthrop, George Ticknor Curtis, George Bancroft, John Hay, and many others, ed. by James Grant Wilson (Charles Scribner's Sons, New York, 1914) vol. 2, p. 93.

[4] *U.S. "Snap Shots": An Independent, National, and Memorial Encyclopedia . . . ,* Oliver McKee (A. M. Thayer and Company, Boston, 1892) p. 309.

Polk, Leonidas

The sobriquet, *Fighting Bishop,*[1] applied to Leonidas Polk, Bishop of the Protestant Episcopal Church in Louisiana in 1841, and a Major General in the Confederate Army in 1861, commemorates his distinguished service during the Civil War.

Leonidas Polk was born at Raleigh, N.C., on April 10, 1806, and died at Pine Mountain, Ga., on June 14, 1864.

[1] *A History of Louisiana, Wilderness—Colony—Province—Territory—State—People,* Henry E. Chambers (The American Historical Society, New York and Chicago 1925) vol. 1, p. 464.

Polly the Weaver. See Johnson, M. M.

Polygamists. See Utah Inhabitants

Pomeroy, Samuel Clarke

While he was a Senator from Kansas to the United States Congress from 1861 to 1873, Samuel Clarke Pomeroy became known as *Subsidy Pomeroy* [1] because he consistently favored the adoption of subsidy measures introduced in the Senate.

Samuel Clarke Pomeroy was born at Southampton, Mass., on January 3, 1816, and died at Whitinsville, Mass., on August 27, 1891.

[1] *The National Cyclopaedia of American Biography* (James T. White and Company, New York, 1904) vol. 12, p. 69.

Pomona College

The athletic teams of Pomona College, at Claremont, Calif., are popularly known as the *Sagehens.*[1] Before World War I the college athletes were sometimes referred to as the *Huns.* After Kaiser William likened his troops to the Huns, the sobriquet became unpopular. A sports writer, however, used the nickname in a news article, but a typesetter used the word hens instead. This mistake suggested the present nickname, *Sagehens.*

[1] A communication from Eugene W. Nixon, Director of Athletics at Pomona College, Claremont, Calif., June 24, 1935.

Pony Bob. See Haslam, Robert

Pooh-bah of the Saddle
The *Pooh-bah of the Saddle* [1] was a nickname given to the mule-riders engaged in messenger service between the outside world and mining camps in California in 1849. The nickname probably arose because the miners were amused by the elaborate methods used by the mule express operators to advertise the speed of their messenger service. This advertising often consisted of decorating the stationery and the envelopes provided by the company with pictures of messengers mounted on swiftly-racing ponies or on skis.

[1] *The Pony Express: The Record of a Romantic Adventure in Business*, Arthur Chapman (G. P. Putnam's Sons, New York and London, 1932) p. 35.

Poor Little Rich Girl. See Vanderbilt, Gloria

Poor Man's Counsellor. See Clark, Abraham

Poor Man's Friend. See Couzens, James

Poor Man's Paradise. See San Francisco, Calif.

Poor Richard. See Franklin, Benjamin

Pop. See Zukor, Adolph

Pop Warner. See Warner, G. S.

Pope's Night
In Boston preceding the outbreak of the Revolutionary War, it was a custom on the fifth of November each year to have an elaborate celebration at the close of which the effigy of the Pope of Rome would be burned. This was called the *Pope's Night.* [1]

[1] *The Irish in the American Revolution and Their Early Influence in the Colonies*, James Haltigan (Patrick J. Haltigan, Publisher, Washington, D.C., Sudwarth Printing Company, 1908) p. 347.

Pop-eye. See Mahaffey, Leroy

Popocrats
During the presidential campaign of 1896, the chief political issue was the silver question. The Populists and the Democrats, both favoring the free coinage of silver, united on the issue. This Populist-Democrat union was popularly known as the *Popocrats,* [1] a combined and abbreviated form of the names of the two parties.

[1] *American History for Colleges*, David Saville Muzzey and John A. Krout (Ginn and Company, New York and London, 1933) p. 548.

Pork Barrels
Pork Barrels [1] was a slang phrase applied to bills passed by Congress during the last half of the nineteenth century authorizing appropriations from the Federal treasury ostensibly to make needed public improvements, but actually appropriated for local patronage. Such a measure, a river and harbor bill authorizing the expenditure of over $18 million, was vetoed by President Chester Alan Arthur in 1882. The nickname, *Pork Barrels,* came to be attributed to such bills supposedly because they contained so many kinds of appropriations, much as a pork barrel contains so many kinds of meats. The term is applied today to graft on the part of government officials.

[1] *Recent American History*, Lester Burrell Shippee (The Macmillan Company, New York, 1930) p. 100.

[2] *A Compilation of the Messages and Papers of the Presidents, Prepared under the Direction of the Joint Committee on Printing, of the House and Senate, Pursuant to an Act of the Fifty-second Congress of the United States*, James D. Richardson (Published by the Bureau of National Literature, Inc., New York, at the Government Printing Office, Washington, D.C., 1890-1899) vol. 10, p. 4707-9.

Pork City. See Chicago, Ill.

Porkopolis. See Chicago, Ill.; Cincinnati, Ohio

Porkopolis of Iowa. See Burlington, Iowa

Port o' Missing Men. See San Francisco, Calif.

Port of the Southwest. See Galveston, Tex.

Porter, William Sydney (O. Henry)
William Sydney Porter has been called the *American Maupassant* [1] because certain characteristics in his writing style are reminiscent of the famous French author. Both

Porter, W. S.—Continued

writers were highly skilled in the technique of the short story and were able dramatists, possessing in common a keen insight into human nature. Their writing is also characterized by realistic detail and frequent use of the "surprise ending." Maupassant was born at Chateau Miromesnil, Seine-Inférieure, France, on August 5, 1850, and died at Paris, France, on July 6, 1893.

William Sydney Porter was born at Greensboro, N.C., on September 11, 1862, and died at New York City, on June 5, 1910.

[1] *The National Cyclopaedia of American Biography* (James T. White and Company, New York, 1916) vol. 15, p. 170.

Porter, William Trotter

York's Tall Son [1] is an appellation given to William Trotter Porter because he made his home in New York City for many years and was six feet, four inches tall. He became famous as a New York journalist and editor. When Horace Greeley first came to New York City, Porter engaged him as a compositor on one of his papers. On December 10, 1831, Porter issued the initial number of the *Spirit of the Times,* the first sporting journal in the United States.

William Trotter Porter was born at Newberry, Vt., on December 24, 1809, and died at New York City, on July 20, 1858.

[1] *Appleton's Cyclopaedia of American Biography*, ed. by James Grant Wilson and John Fiske (D. Appleton and Company, New York, 1888) vol. 5, p. 81.

Portland, Maine

Portland has three nicknames: *Beautiful City by the Sea,* the *Forest City,* and the *Hill City.* The *Beautiful City by the Sea,*[1] is a sobriquet which perhaps had its origin in the line from *My Lost Youth* by Henry Wadsworth Longfellow

"Often I think of the beautiful town
    That is seated by the sea."

This city is proud to be called the *Forest City* [2] because of the stately elms and other shade trees adorning her avenues and public squares.

The finest street in the city is State Street, laid out in 1799. It is one hundred feet wide and is lined on both sides with a double row of beautiful shade trees. Longfellow mentions "the trees which o'er shadow each well known street."

The city is built on a hilly peninsula [3] causing it to be designated the *Hill City.*[4]

[1] *The Beauties of Portland and Scenic Gems of Casco Bay* (G. W. Morris, Portland, Me., 1925) p. 4.

[2] *Hand-Book, Portland, Old Orchard, Cape Elizabeth and Casco Bay, with Maps and Illustrations,* John T. Hull, Editor and Publisher (Southworth Brothers, Printers, Portland, Me., 1888) p. 25.

Portland by the Sea: An Historical Treatise, Augustus F. Moulton (Katahdin Publishing Company, Augusta, Me., 1926) p. 217.

[3] *Portland and Vicinity,* Edward H. Elwell (Loring, Short, and Harmon, and W. S. Jones, Portland, Me., 1876) p. 22.

[4] *Manual of Useful Information,* comp. under the direction of J. C. Thomas (The Werner Company, Chicago, 1893) p. 22.

Portland, Oregon

Portland was nicknamed the *Rose City* [1] because its citizens take pride in beautifying their town by planting roses on the lawns and about the premises of their homes.

[1] *The Encyclopedia Americana* (Americana Corporation, New York and Chicago, 1927) vol. 22, p. 395.

Portrait Painter of Presidents. See Stuart, Gilbert

Possum John Randolph. See Randolph, John

Possum Policy

The *Possum Policy* [1] was a nickname used to describe the policy of the Liberal Republican movement in Missouri about 1870 which was directed by Major General Frank Preston Blair, Jr., and other prominent Liberal Republicans. This movement resulted in the downfall of the Republican party in Missouri, in the election of Benjamin Gratz Brown as Governor, and in the nomination of Horace Greeley in 1872 as a Liberal Republican candidate for President of the United States. The movement was characterized as the *Possum Policy* because the Democrats in Missouri, having at this time agreed to support the Liberal Republicans, did not nominate any candidates from their party or take an active part in promoting their own political ambitions. This seeming lifelessness and inactivity was comparable to the habit of the possum who, in time of danger, lies down, shuts its eyes, and endeavors to create the impression that it is dead.

[1] *My Quarter Century of American Politics*, Champ Clark (Harper and Brothers, New York and London, 1920) vol. 1, p. 21-2.

Potato Mayor. See Shank, S. L.

Pothouse Peggy. See Eaton, M. O.

Potsy. See Clark, George

Potter, John Fox

While he was a Representative from Wisconsin to the United States Congress from 1857 to 1863, John Fox Potter was challenged to a duel by Roger Atkinson Pryor, a Representative from Virginia. The combat, however, failed to take place because Potter, having the privilege of choosing the weapons for the duel, named bowie-knives; but Pryor refused to be party to a condition which he termed "barbarous." [1] In the widespread publicity attending this affair, John Fox Potter was designated *Bowie-knife Potter*,[2] and was popularly known thereafter by this nickname.

[1] *History of Walworth County, Wisconsin, Containing an Account of Its Settlement, Growth, Development and Resources; an Extensive and Minute Sketch of Its Cities, Towns and Villages—Their Improvements, Industries, Manufactures, Churches, Schools and Societies; Its War Record, Biographical Sketches, Portraits of Prominent Men and Early Settlers; the Whole Preceded by a History of Wisconsin, Statistics of the State, and an Abstract of Its Laws and Constitution of the United States* (Western Historical Company, Chicago, 1882) p. 548.

[2] *The Americanization of Carl Schurz*, Chester Verne Easum (The University of Chicago Press, Chicago, 1930) p. 315.

Potts, James Henry

The widely known sobriquet, the *Deafman Eloquent*,[1] was conferred on Dr. James Henry Potts at the general Methodist Conference which met at London, Canada, about 1894. Although Dr. Potts had been deaf for some twenty years, he had proved himself a most powerful orator on several public occasions.

James Henry Potts was born at Norfolk, Ontario, Canada, on June 12, 1848.

[1] *The National Cyclopaedia of American Biography* (James T. White and Company, New York, 1900) vol. 10, p. 317.

Poughkeepsie Seer. See Davis, A. J.

Powder Horn

The little brick building, "having eight sides and a high pointed roof," which stands on the Duke of Gloucester Street in Williamsburg, Va., is widely known as the *Powder Horn*.[1] This sobriquet has been brought down from colonial times because in this building the Virginia colonists stored their supply of gun powder for use during the Revolutionary War.

[1] *A History of Virginia for Boys and Girls*, John W. Wayland (The Macmillan Company, New York, 1930) p. 83.

Powder River Division. See Ninety-first Infantry Division of World War II

Powell, David Frank

Fancy Frank, the *Mighty Medicine Man*, the *Surgeon Scout*, and the *White Beaver* are appellations which have been applied to Dr. David Frank Powell.

The fact that he wore fancy clothes with dash and show gave rise to the nickname *Fancy Frank*.[1]

The sobriquet, *Mighty Medicine man*[1] was doubtless given to Dr. Powell by the Indians because of his knowledge of medicine and his skill in treating his patients both among the Indians and the white people while living on the frontier.

Powell employed his talents as a physician and surgeon on the frontiers of Wyoming, Colorado, and Nebraska, and was therefore known as the *Surgeon Scout*.[1]

While he was an army surgeon, a siege of small-pox broke out among the Indians in the country close to the camp where Dr. Powell was stationed. Although the Indians were hostile to him and to the other white settlers, Dr. Powell went over into their encampment and vaccinated practically the whole tribe, thereby stamping out the epidemic. The Indians were so grateful to their benefactor for this deed that they assembled for a great pow-wow and presented him with a robe made of white beaver skins, the white beaver being their sacred animal, and named him *White Beaver*,[2] by which sobriquet he was popularly known thereafter.

David Frank Powell was born in Kentucky, in 1857, and later in life was a prominent physician of La Crosse, Wis.

[1] *Seventy Years on the Frontier: Alexander Majors' Memoirs of a Lifetime on the Border*, with a preface by Buffalo Bill (General W. F. Cody) ed. by Colonel Prentiss Ingraham (Rand McNally and Company, Chicago and New York, 1893) p. 317.

[2] *Seventy Years on the Frontier: Alexander Majors' Memoirs of a Lifetime on the Border*, with a preface by Buffalo Bill (General W. F. Cody) ed. by Colonel Prentiss Ingraham (Rand McNally and Company, Chicago and New York, 1893) p. 318-19.

Biographical History of La Crosse, Monroe, and Jeneau Counties, Wisconsin (The Lewis Publishing Company, Chicago, 1892) p. 587.

Powell, James Robert

Because of James Robert Powell's great influence in the establishment and development of Birmingham, Ala., and his social and political eminence there, he was called the *Duke of Birmingham*.[1]

Powell, J. R.—Continued

Having moved to Birmingham in 1871, shortly after the town was laid out, and having served as president of the Elyton Land Company, Powell was chiefly responsible for the founding of this great manufacturing city amidst the abundant mineral resources of Jefferson County. He also secured grants of land from this company to be used for parks and as sites for churches and schools.

James Robert Powell was born in Brunswick County, Va., on December 7, 1814, and died at his plantation on the Yazoo River, in Alabama, in the fall of 1883.

[1] *Jefferson County and Birmingham, Alabama, Historical and Biographical*, John Witherspoon Du Bose (Teeple and Smith, Birmingham, Ala., 1887) p. 165.

Powell, John Stephen

In 1902 John Stephen Powell was appointed to the judgeship of Moro Province in the Philippine Islands, and held that position until 1906, at which time he was appointed Judge of the Seventh District at Batangas, where he remained until 1910. He was then appointed Judge at Iloilo, where he served until ill health caused him to retire in September 1917, and to return to the United States. Powell's responsible position and important part in administering justice on the islands caused him to be nicknamed *Big Judge Powell* [1] by the Filipinos.

John Stephen Powell was born at Newnam, Ga., on April 16, 1857, and died there on October 29, 1921.

[1] *The National Cyclopaedia of American Biography* (James T. White and Company, New York, 1926) vol. 19, p. 218.

Powell, Ransom T.

During the Civil War, while he was imprisoned at the Confederate Military Prison at Andersonville, Ga., Ransom T. Powell was called *Red Cap* [1] by the soldiers there in allusion to a showy, gilt-laced, red cap that he constantly wore.

Ransom T. Powell enlisted as a drummer boy in Company I of the Tenth Regiment of West Virginia Infantrymen, on May 9, 1862, at the age of fourteen. On January 3, 1863,[2] he was captured near Petersburg, Va., and in the latter part of 1864, he was sent to the Andersonville prison. He possessed a winning personality and was a favorite with all the men. For several months Powell acted as an orderly to Captain Henry Wirz, Superintendent of the prison.

[1] *Andersonville: A Story of Rebel Military Prisons, Fifteen Months a Guest of the So-called Southern Confederacy; a Private Soldier's Experience in Richmond, Andersonville, Savannah, Millen, Blackshear, and Florence*, John McElroy (D. R. Locke, Toledo, Ohio, 1879) p. 291, 292.

[2] *Annual Report of the Adjutant General of the State of West Virginia for the Year Ending December 31, 1864*, Brigadier-general Francis P. Pierpont (John F. M'Dermot, Public Printer, Wheeling, W.Va., 1865) p. 282.

Power City. See Keokuk, Iowa; Rochester, N.Y.

Prairie Buggy

The *Prairie Buggy* [1] was the sobriquet applied to the travois used by the Shoshoni Indians in Wyoming to carry their children or sick, and to cart supplies. A crude vehicle of transportation, the travois consisted chiefly of two trailing poles harnessed to a horse, the poles serving as shafts upon which a small platform was fastened approximately near the middle of the poles, often with a canopy raised over it, thereby causing the travois to resemble a buggy minus its wheels. Because of this and because the vehicle was commonly used on the prairie-lands, it was nicknamed the *Prairie Buggy.*

[1] *Washakie, an Account of Indian Resistance of the Covered Wagon and Union Pacific Railroad Invasions of Their Territory*, Grace Raymond Hebard (The Arthur H. Clark Company, Cleveland, Ohio, 1930) p. 299.

Prairie City. See Bloomington, Ill.

Prairie Division. See Thirty-third Infantry Division of World War II

Prairie Schooner

The gigantic canvas-covered wagon which was pulled across the western plains by as many as ten mules was designated the *Prairie Schooner.*[1] These enormous wagons were widely used during the second half of the nineteenth century to transport food, merchandise, and other commodities across the western plains of the United States to the frontier settlements. They cost about two thousand dollars apiece, were in charge of a wagon-master, and were accompanied by a pack train of mules which served as a reserve supply, and by a train of teamsters, cooks, and other workers.

[1] *The Great Plains: The Romance of Western American Exploration, Warfare, and Settlement, 1527-1870*, Randall Parrish (A. C. McClurg and Company, Chicago, 1907) p. 136.

Prairie State. See Illinois

Pratt, Daniel

Daniel Pratt was widely known as the *Great American Traveler.*[1] Pratt spent his time rambling about various parts of the United States, especially in New England. He often addressed college gatherings or other public assemblages.

Daniel Pratt was born at Prattville, Mass., about 1809, and died at Boston, Mass., on June 21, 1887.

[1] *Appleton's Cyclopaedia of American Biography*, ed. by James Grant Wilson and John Fiske (D. Appleton and Company, New York, 1888) vol. 5, p. 101.

Praying Indians

The *Praying Indians*[1] was a nickname applied to the Indians converted to Christianity under the preaching of John Eliot and his fellow-workers in Massachusetts. This sobriquet was used to distinguish those who had been converted and who prayed from those who had not been converted to Christianity. From about 1646 to 1716 the Christian Indians were influenced by Eliot and his helpers to settle in townships in various parts of Massachusetts where they were taught to lead a civilized life and to earn a livelihood by means of agricultural pursuits. The Indian settlements disintegrated very rapidly after the outbreak of King Philip's War in 1674 because during this war both Christian and heathen Indians suffered alike at the hands of the British and the colonists.

[1] *The Encyclopedia Americana* (Americana Corporation, New York and Chicago, 1927) vol. 10, p. 243.
The American Indian on the New Trail, Thomas C. Moffett (Missionary Education Movement of the United States and Canada, New York, 1914) p. 66.

Praying Quakers. See Nebraska Central College

Pre-Adamite. See Hoar, G. F.

Preacher. See Short, Dewey

Preacher President. See Garfield, J. A.

Preachers. See Whitworth College

Preaching Woman. See Sprague, A. W.

Preetorius, Emil

Emil Preetorius, a journalist and publicist of German descent, was called the *Nestor of the German-American Journalists,*[1] because of his eminence as an editor of publications which helped to bring about a better understanding between Americans and citizens of German descent. Preetorius worked consistently to enlighten German-Americans regarding the spirit and mechanism of the democratic government of the United States. At the same time he encouraged them to preserve the best in German culture and to contribute it towards American civilization. The sobriquet alludes to Nestor, a Trojan hero, who in Greek legend, was greatly respected for his knowledge and wise counsel.

Emil Preetorius was born at Alzey, Rhenish Hesse, Germany, on March 15, 1827, and died at St. Louis, Mo., on November 19, 1905.

[1] *Dictionary of American Biography under the Auspices of the American Council of Learned Societies*, ed. by Dumas Malone (Charles Scribner's Sons, New York, 1935) vol. 15, p. 185.

Premier Blaine. See Blaine, J. G.

Prentiss, Benjamin Mayberry

Major General Benjamin Mayberry Prentiss was sometimes called the *Hero of the Hornet's Nest*[1] in commemoration of the splendid manner in which he bravely and determinedly held his assigned position at the Battle of Shiloh, near Pittsburgh Landing, in Tennessee, on April 5 and 6, 1862. This battle was often described as a *Hornet's Nest.* Prentiss, Brigadier General at the time, was finally captured, together with most of his command, on the second day of the battle.

Benjamin Mayberry Prentiss was born at Belleville, in what is now the state of West Virginia, on November 23, 1819, and died at Bethany, Mo., on February 8, 1901.

[1] *Reminiscences of the Civil War*, Memorial Edition, General John B. Gordon (Charles Scribner's Sons, New York, 1904) p. 181.

Presbyterian College

The athletic teams of Presbyterian College, at Clinton, S.C., were nicknamed *Blue Stockings* about 1918, by sports writers because the teams wear blue stockings[1] and sweaters.

[1] A letter from Walter A. Johnson, Director of Athletics at Presbyterian College, Clinton, S.C., June 15, 1935.

Prescott, Arizona

Prescott is called the *Cowboy Capital*[1] because it was the capital of the territory

Prescott, Ariz.—Continued
of Arizona, and is located in an important
farming and stock-raising section of Arizona
noted for its picturesque cowboy and Indian life.

¹ *The Source Book* (Source Research Council, Inc.,
Chicago, 1936) vol. 5, p. 2343.

President de facto. See Hayes, R. B.

President Maker. See Clay, Henry

Presidential Bulls and Indulgences
In May 1808, President Thomas Jefferson
issued a circular letter to the state governors
giving them permission "to grant permits
to respectable merchants to bring in so much
flour as might be needed to prevent a bread
famine" in the various states. This act was
made necessary because of the privation suffered as a result of the Embargo which had
been passed by an act of Congress on December 22, 1807. The Federalists, political
enemies of President Jefferson, accused the
various governors of commercializing these
permits and nicknamed them *Presidential
Bulls and Indulgences* ¹ implying that they
considered Jefferson's circular letter comparable to a papal bull.

(See also Patent Merchants and O-grab-
me-pets)

¹ *A History of the People of the United States, from
the Revolution to the Civil War*, John Bach McMaster
(D. Appleton and Company, New York, 1892) vol. 3,
p. 301.

Presidents. See Washington and Jefferson
College

Preston, John Thomas Lewis
Students in the Virginia Military Institute
at Lexington, Va., nicknamed Colonel John
Thomas Lewis Preston *Old Bald* ¹ while he
and other Confederate officers were stationed
there during the winter of 1862-3. Possibly
this appellation was applied to him because
he was bald-headed or because his hair was
very thin.

John Thomas Lewis Preston was a professor in the above-named institution at the
outbreak of the Civil War, and later became
a Colonel in the Confederate Army.

¹ *The End of An Era*, John S. Wise (Houghton
Mifflin and Company, New York and Boston, 1889)
p. 261.

Pretender. See Cleveland, Grover

Pretty Boy Floyd. See Floyd, Charles

Price, Sterling G.
The *Old Tycoon, Dad,* and *Pap* are so-
briquets which have been applied to Sterling
G. Price.

He was called the *Old Tycoon* ¹ in allusion to his prominence and leadership in
the Confederate Army. (*Tycoon* is the title
of the commander-in-chief of the Japanese
Army, the term originating from the Chinese
word *tai-kun*, meaning *great prince*.)

The nicknames *Dad* and *Pap* were applied
to Major General Price because of his paternal interest in the safety and welfare of the
soldiers under his command and because he
was kind and considerate in his dealings
with them. *Pap* is a commonly used southern nickname for father or papa.

Sterling G. Price was born in Prince Edward County, Va., on September 11, 1809,
and died at St. Louis, Mo., on September 29,
1869.

¹ *Lee and His Lieutenants; Comprising the Early Life,
Public Services, and Campaigns of General Robert E. Lee
and His Companions in Arms, with a Record of Their
Campaigns and Heroic Deeds*, Edward A. Pollard (E. B.
Treat and Company, New York, 1867) p. 334.

Priest of the Volcanoes. See Hubbard,
B. R.

Primitive Baptists
The Primitive Baptists were nicknamed
Hard-shells, or *Hard Shell Baptists* ¹ because
they have never given up any of the beliefs
of their founders, nor modernized their beliefs and teachings.

They interpret the Bible literally, have no
Sunday schools, and do not send missionaries to foreign countries. They do not use
musical instruments in connection with their
worship, nor do their ministers believe in
theological training. There are more than
two thousand seven hundred Primitive Baptist churches in the United States.

¹ *Newsweek: The Magazine of News Significance*,
Rockefeller Center, May 6, 1940, p. 36.

Prince Arthur. See Arthur, C. A.

Prince Charley. See Galloway, C. B.

Prince John. See Beauregard, P. G. T.;
Van Buren, John

Prince of America. See Todd, Payne

Prince of American Letters. See Irving, Washington

Prince of Flatworkers. See Burke, William

Prince of Humbugs. See Barnum, P. T.

Prince of Humorists. See Clemens, S. L.

Prince of Journalists. See Greeley, Horace

Prince of Knickerbocker. See Knickerbocker, Herman

Prince of Mail Contractors. See Reeside, James

Prince of Merchants. See Stewart, A. T.

Prince of Parliamentarians. See Mell, P. H.

Prince of Pistoleers. See Hickok, J. B.

Prince of Schaghticoke. See Knickerbocker, Herman

Prince of Wales Party

In 1881 the Republican President of the United States, James Abram Garfield, appointed William H. Robertson a collector for the port of New York without consulting either Thomas Collier Platt or Roscoe Conkling, senators from New York and political leaders in the Republican party. The controversy aroused by this act divided the Republicans into several factions, one of which was called the *Prince of Wales party*.[1] This group consisted of Vice President Chester Arthur's supporters and the sobriquet was apparently an allusion to Vice President Arthur whose marked dignity, refined manners, and elegant attire caused him to be compared with the Prince [2] of Wales.

[1] *Reconstruction and Union, 1865-1912*, Paul Leland Haworth (Henry Holt and Company, New York, 1912) p. 107.
[2] *Chester A. Arthur, a Quarter-century of Machine Politics*, George Frederick Howe (Dodd, Mead and Company, New York, 1934) p. 176.

Prince of Wit and Wisdom. See Rogers, Will

Prince Rupert of the Confederacy. See Stuart, J. E. B.

Princess Alice. See Longworth, A. L. R.

Princeton University

Tigers [1] is the nickname applied to the athletic teams of Princeton University, at Princeton, N.J. Newspaper writers gave this sobriquet to the Princeton teams because of their orange and black striped uniforms, and because of the "so-called 'tiger cheer'" used by the undergraduates. The tiger has been used as a mascot of Princeton University since the late 1870's.

[1] A letter from Frederick S. Osborne, Director of Public Information at Princeton University, Princeton, N.J., June 20, 1935.

Prisoner's Friend. See Beal, Abraham

Private John. See Allen, J. M.

Proctor, Henry Hugh

Henry Hugh Proctor, a Negro clergyman, was nicknamed the *Father of Organized Alumni Work at Fisk University*.[1] He was a pioneer worker in inspiring the alumni of that University, at Nashville, Tenn., to take an active part in the upbuilding of that institution. He was the pastor of the First Congregational Church, located at Atlanta, Ga., from 1894 until 1919, and afterwards he devoted his time to lecturing, preaching, and doing social welfare work among the Negroes of the South. His sole aim was to improve the standards of learning in the schools for Negroes.

Henry Hugh Proctor was born near Fayetteville, Tenn., on December 8, 1868, and died at Atlanta, Ga., on May 12, 1933.

[1] *Dictionary of American Biography under the Auspices of the American Council of Learned Societies*, ed. by Dumas Malone (Charles Scribner's Sons, New York, 1935) vol. 15, p. 243.

Prof. See Weaver, M. M.

Professor. See Poage, W. R.

Prophet. See Tenskwatawa

Prophet of the Revolution. See Henry, Patrick

Prosperity Panic

Following the passage of the Gold Act of 1900, establishing the gold standard, speculation in Wall Street was so great that many companies combined in order that their money power or stocks might be increased. As a result of this gigantic combining movement there was a sharp decline in the stock market, which was nicknamed the *Prosperity Panic* [1] because the decline was only temporary and greater speculative activities followed it.

[1] *Twenty Years of the Republic, 1885-1905*, Harry Thurston Peck (Dodd, Mead and Company, New York, 1907) p. 633.

Prosperity's Advance Agent. See McKinley, William

Providence, Rhode Island

Providence is known as the *Bee-hive of Industry, Perry Davis' Pain Killer City, Roger Williams City,* and the *Southern Gateway of New England.* It is termed the *Bee-hive of Industry* [1] because it is a flourishing industrial city. It has been facetiously called The *Perry Davis' Pain Killer City* [2] because the firm of Perry Davis and Son, makers of Perry Davis' Pain Killer, [3] was located there.

The city was founded by Roger Williams in February, 1631, and is thus designated the *Roger Williams City.* [4] It is situated in the southern part of the New England states, and has an excellent harbor on the Providence River, making it the natural outlet for much of the trade and commerce of the New England region, hence the term *Southern Gateway of New England.* [5]

[1] *King's Handbook of the United States*, planned and ed. by Moses King, text by M. F. Sweetser (The Matthews-Northrup Company, Buffalo, N.Y., 1896) p. 772.

[2] *Manual of Useful Information*, comp. under the direction of J. C. Thomas (The Werner Company, Chicago, 1893) p. 22.

[3] *Pain-killer Almanac and Family Receipt Book* (Perry Davis and Son, Providence, R.I., 1868) p. 3.

[4] *Manual of Useful Information*, comp. under the direction of J. C. Thomas (The Werner Company, Chicago, 1893) p. 22.

[5] *Providence, the Southern Gateway of New England, Commemorating the One Hundred Fiftieth Anniversary of the Independence of the State of Rhode Island* (Published by the Historical Publishing Company, W. S. Solomon, Business Manager, H. A. Barker, Historical Director, Remington Printing Company, Providence, R.I., 1926) p. 16, 20.

Providence College

The athletic teams of Providence College, at Providence, R.I., are generally designated *Dominicans* [1] and *Friars* [1] because the school is operated and the faculty manned by members of The Order of Friars Preachers,

founded by St Dominic in 1218, a religious order of the Catholic Church. The former sobriquet was used by sports writers on the *Providence Journal* about 1926. The newspaper men, wishing a shorter nickname, began calling the teams *Friars* in 1929.

[1] A letter from E. H. Schmitt, O. P. Director of Athletics at Providence College, Providence, R.I., June 15, 1935.

Provine, John William

The nickname, *Dutchy,* was playfully given to Dr. John William Provine by the students at Mississippi College because he had taught German in the college at various times, and had received his Ph.D. from the University of Göttingen, Germany, in 1892.

John William Provine was born at Big Creek, Miss., on June 19, 1866, and was Professor of Chemistry and German at Mississippi College, at Clinton, Miss. He was President of the institution from 1897 to 1898, and again from 1911 to 1932, and died at Clinton, Miss., November 2, 1942.

Prowling Brigades

During the Civil War when the Union Army was fighting in Alabama, groups of deserters from that army or groups of individuals unsympathetic to the Confederates would engage in burning, plundering and confiscating the property of the Confederates. These marauding bands were called the *Prowling Brigades.* [1]

[1] *Civil War and Reconstruction in Alabama*, Walter L. Fleming (The Columbia University Press, New York, 1905) p. 120.

Prune Pickers. See Pacific College

Psalm Singer. See Adams, Samuel

Public Enemy Number One. See Dillinger, John; Nelson, George

Public Enemy Number Two. See Nelson, George

Puddler Jim. See Davis, J. J.

Pueblo, Colorado

Pueblo is called the *Pittsburgh of the West* [1] because of its extensive iron and steel manufacturing industries.

[1] *The Source Book* (Source Research Council, Inc., Chicago, 1936) vol. 6, p. 2368.

Puffing Billies. See *Black Dragons*

Puke State. See Missouri

Pukes. See Missourians

Pullman, Illinois

Pullman was formerly nicknamed the *City of Brick* [1] in allusion to the manufacture and the extensive use of Calumet bricks [2] in the construction of houses there.

[1] *A New Dictionary of Americanisms*, Sylva Clapin (Louis Weiss and Company, New York, 1903) p. 117.
[2] *One Hundred Years in Illinois (1818-1918)*, John McLean (Peterson Linotyping Company, Chicago, 1919) p. 229.

Purdue University

The *Boilermakers* [1] was given as a derogatory nickname to the athletic teams of Purdue University, at Lafayette, Ind., around 1890 by the students from Wabash College because they felt that "engineering as an education was anything but intellectual." [1] Purdue is a technical and professional university and Wabash is a Liberal Arts institution. The nickname no longer carries its derogatory implication.

[1] A letter from Robert C. Woodworth, Assistant Publicity Director at Purdue University, Lafayette, Ind., July 8, 1935.

Puritan City. See Boston, Mass.

Puritan Poet. See Whittier, J. G.

Puritan State. See Massachusetts

Puritans. See Massachusetts Inhabitants

Purple Aces. See Evansville College

Purple Hurricanes. See Furman University

Purple Tornadoes. See University of Washington

Purples. See Mount Union College

Push Buggy

A baby carriage is often humorously designated a *Push Buggy* [1] because one pushes it about from place to place.

[1] *A New Dictionary of Americanisms*, Sylva Clapin (Louis Weiss and Company, New York, 1903) p. 324.

Push-'em-up Lazzeri. See Lazzeri, A. M.

Pussyfoot Johnson. See Johnson, W. E.

Putnam, Amelia Earhart

Newspaper writers have designated Amelia Earhart Putnam *America's Premier Air Woman* [1] because she was the first aviatrix to fly across the Atlantic Ocean. Mrs. Putnam was born at Atchison, Kans., on July 24, 1898. Accompanied by her attendant, Captain Fred J. Noonan, she left Miami, Fla., on June 1, 1937, for a flight around the world. She was lost at sea in the South Pacific Ocean, near Howland Island, latitude 0° 49′ N, and longitude 176° 40′ W. It is thought that her airplane was forced down at sea.

[1] *Washington Herald*, Washington, D.C., February 6, 1935, col. 2, p. 1.

Putnam, Israel

Old Put and *Wolf Putnam* are sobriquets of the American Revolutionary commander, Israel Putnam.

He was called *Old Put* [1] by his fellow soldiers.

In the winter of 1743 a female wolf destroyed a large number of sheep at Pomfrey, Conn., taking a heavy toll of Israel Putnam's excellent flock. The owners of the sheep determined to kill the wolf and hunted it time and again. One night several of the men, including Putnam, tracked the wolf to its lair in a cave. Unable to dislodge it, Putnam took a torch and his gun, crawled into the cave alone and shot the wolf. His daring and success in this affair caused him to be nicknamed *Wolf Putnam*. [2]

Israel Putnam was born in Danvers, Mass., on January 7, 1718, and died at Pomfrey, now Brooklyn, Conn., on May 19, 1790.

[1] *Makers of the World's History and Their Grand Achievements, Containing Graphic Accounts of Men and Women Whose Daring Deeds Have Given Them World-Wide Fame. . .*, Henry Davenport Northrop (National Publishing Company, Philadelphia, 1903) p. 334.
[2] *Once Upon a Time in Connecticut*, Caroline Clifford Newton (Houghton Mifflin Company, New York and Chicago, 1916) p. 83.

Q

Quaker City. See Philadelphia, Pa.

Quaker City of the West. See Richmond, Ind.

Quaker Dolly. See Madison, D. P. T.

Quaker Guns

At the outbreak of the Civil War in 1861, the Confederates mounted sham cannons or *Quaker Guns* [1] upon Munson's Hill in sight of the White House at Washington, D.C., thus deceiving the Federals for nearly a year as to the impregnability of this line of fortification. A *Quaker Gun* was merely a wooden log with a circular spot of black at the end facing the enemy. At a distance, this contrivance resembled the muzzle of a cannon. The false guns were so called probably because the Quakers as a rule were opposed to war and fighting and strongly adhered to peace, hence a *Quaker Gun* would be a harmless, ineffective weapon of warfare.

[1] *The New Complete History of the United States of America*, Official Edition, John Clark Ridpath (The Jones Brothers Publishing Company, Cincinnati, Ohio, 1906) vol. 10, p. 4787.

Quaker Martyr. See Dyer, Mary

Quaker Meadows Joe. See McDowell, Joseph

Quaker Poet. See Whittier, J. G.

Quaker Soldier. See Biddle, Clement

Quaker State. See Pennsylvania

Quakers

The members of the religious organization known as the Society of Friends were commonly called *Quakers*. George Fox, the great English religious leader and the founder of the Society of Friends, recorded in his *Journal* [1] and in his *Great Mystery* [2] that to his knowledge the first man to nickname the Friends *Quakers* was a Justice of the Peace, Gervase Bennett of Derby, England. When Justice Bennett put Fox in prison at Derby on a false charge of blasphemy, the latter bade the former "tremble at the Word of God." It has been affirmed by others that Bennett aided in promulgating the sobriquet, *Quakers,* but that he was not the originator of the expression itself, the term being previously applied to the Friends because they actually trembled [3] or quaked when deeply moved by the preaching or the studying of the Bible. William Penn [1] wrote that the Society of Friends were not ashamed to be designated *Quakers* because they had

trembled at the revelations of God's Word. In the documents of the British Parliament the word *Quakers* is first recorded in 1654 in the Journal of the House of Commons. [4]

[1] *The Journal of George Fox, Edited from the Manuscript*, Norman Penney, with an Introduction by T. Edmund Harvey (The University Press, Cambridge, England, 1911) vol. 1, p. 4, p. 395.

[2] *The Great Mystery of the Great World Unfolded: and Antichrist's Kingdom Revealed unto Destruction in Answer to Many False Doctrines and Principles. . . . Against the Despised People Of the Lord Called Quakers. . .* (George Fox, London, 1659) p. 61, 110.

[3] *Creative Lives*, ed. by Harold E. B. Speight, George Fox, Seeker and Friend, Rufus M. Jones (Harper and Brothers, New York and London, 1930) p. 50, 74.

"William Penn" by Clifford Smith in *Builders of America* (Funk and Wagnalls Company, New York, 1931) vol. 7' p. 35.

[4] *George Fox, an Autobiography*, ed. with an introduction and notes by Rufus M. Jones (Ferris and Leach, Philadelphia, 1903) vol. 1, p. 126.

Quids

From 1806 to about 1811, the *Quids* [1] was a nickname applied to that faction of the Republican party led by John Randolph of Roanoke which attempted to assert itself as a third political party. The members of this group violently opposed the nomination of James Madison as candidate for the office of President of the United States in 1808 and nominated James Monroe for the office [2] and they criticized Thomas Jefferson and his administrative staff on the grounds that they were controlling Congress by unfair means. The members of this faction were called the *tertium quids*, since they stood apart from the conventional two-party system; later the name was abbreviated to the *Quids*.

[1] *The American Nation: A History: The Jeffersonian System, 1801-1811*, Edward Channing (Harper and Brothers, New York and London, 1906) vol. 12, p. 136.

The Making of the Nation, 1783-1817, Francis A. Walker (Charles Scribner's Sons, New York, 1895) vol. 3, p. 215.

[2] *Encyclopedia Dictionary of American History*, J. Franklin Jameson and J. W. Buel (American History Society, Washington, D.C., 1900) vol. 2, p. 144.

Quakers. See Guilford College; Nebraska Central College; Pacific College; Penn College; Pennsylvanians; Philadelphia National League Baseball Club

Quality City. See Rochester, N.Y.

Queen Alice. See Longworth, A. L. R

Queen City. See Cincinnati, Ohio

Queen City of Alabama. See Gadsden, Ala.

Queen City of Lake Superior. See Marquette, Mich.

Queen City of the Border. See Caldwell, Kans.

Queen City of the East. See Bangor, Me.

Queen City of the Iron Range. See Virginia, Minn.

Queen City of the Lakes. See Buffalo, N.Y.

Queen City of the Merrimac Valley. See Manchester, N.H.

Queen City of the Mountains. See Knoxville, Tenn.

Queen City of the Ozarks. See Springfield, Mo.

Queen City of the Pacific Coast. See San Francisco, Calif.

Queen City of the Plains. See Denver, Colo.

Queen City of the South. See Natchez, Miss.; Richmond, Va.

Queen City of the West. See Cincinnati, Ohio

Queen Dolly. See Madison, D. P. T.

Queen Dowager. See Madison, D. P. T.

Queen Marie of Hollywood. See Dressler, Marie

Queen Mother of Oregon. See Wood, Mrs. M. R. L.

Queen of Summer Resorts. See Newport, R.I.

Queen of the Brazos. See Waco, Tex.

Queen of the Cow Counties. See Los Angeles, Calif.

Queen of the Lakes. See Buffalo, N.Y.

Queen of the Missions. See Santa Barbara, Calif.

Queen of the Pacific. See San Francisco, Calif.

Queen of the South. See New Orleans, La.

Queen of the Vampires. See Bara, Theda

Queen of the West. See Cincinnati, Ohio

Queen on the James. See Richmond, Va.

Queen State. See Maryland

Quentin the Eagle. See Roosevelt, Quentin

Quicksilver Bob. See Fulton, Robert

Quill Book

The book used by the officers of a military company to record delinquency is nicknamed the *Quill Book.*

[1] *Unit Projects in Modern Literature* (Educational Press, Inc., Columbus, Ohio), March 1-14, 1935, p. 12.

Quincy, Josiah

In a caricature of Josiah Quincy published in Boston sometime between 1805 and 1813, he was humorously called *King Josiah the First.*[1] Quincy played a dominant role in the Federal party and the affairs of the New England states.

He was an energetic leader, a splendid orator, and an enthusiastic participant in politics. He held many prominent offices, among others that of Representative from Massachusetts to the United States Congress from 1805 to 1813, Mayor of Boston from 1823 to 1828, and president of Harvard University from 1829 to 1845.

Josiah Quincy was born at Boston, Mass., on February 4, 1772, and died at Quincy, Mass., on July 1, 1864.

[1] *Lives of Celebrated Americans: Comprising Biographies of Three Hundred and Forty Eminent Persons,* Benson J. Lossing (Thomas Belknap, Hartford, Conn., 1869) p. 424.

Quincy, Illinois

Quincy is known as the *Gem City*, the *Gem City of the West*, and the *Model City*. It is called *Gem City* [1] and *Gem City of the West* [1] because of its picturesque location upon high bluffs overlooking the Mississippi River, because its picturesqueness is enhanced by the care given to the homes, lawns, and numerous well-laid-out parks.

Quincy has been termed the *Model City* [2] because it is well-laid-out, well-kept, and gives evidence of taste and skill in building and managing both homes and municipality.

[1] *The History of Adams County, Illinois, Containing a History of the County—Its Cities, Towns, etc.* (Murray, Williamson and Phelps, Chicago, 1879) p. 448, 941.

[2] *History of Quincy, and Its Men of Mark, or Facts and Figures Exhibiting Its Advantages and Resources, Manufactures and Commerce*, Pat H. Redmond (Heirs and Russell, Book and Job Printing, Quincy, Ill., 1869) p. 8.

R

Rabbit. See Maranville, W. J.; Warstler, H. B.

Rabbit Shepherds

About 1882 Lawrence Yates Sherman, later United States Senator from Ohio, nicknamed the Ohio state game wardens *Rabbit Shepherds*.[1] Sherman was a gifted coiner of political slang, as this deprecating description of the politically-appointed game wardens illustrates.

[1] *The National Cyclopaedia of American Biography* (James T. White and Company, New York, 1916) vol. 15, p. 101.

Rabbits

During the closing years of the nineteenth century, the Democratic party in Kansas City, Mo., became divided into factions, one of which was popularly known as the *Rabbits*.[1] This nickname was acquired because one of the early leaders of the faction possessed a "peculiar galloping gait" which his political opponents were quick to compare to a rabbit's hopping.

[1] *A Civic History of Kansas City, Missouri*, Roy Ellis (The author, State teachers college, Springfield, Mo., (1930) p. 234-5.

Raccoon Roughs

About the beginning of the Civil War, the members of a company of infantrymen recruited in Jackson County, Ala., by John Brown Gordon were humorously designated the *Raccoon Roughs*.[1] The men were mountaineers from the Raccoon Mountain neighborhood, and were somewhat uncouth in manner and dress, part of their apparel being the raccoon-skin cap.[2]

The *Raccoon Roughs* were part of the Sixth Regiment of Alabama Infantrymen in the Confederate Army, and acquitted themselves well throughout the Civil War.

[1] *Lee and His Lieutenants: Comprising the Early Life, Public Services, and Campaigns of General Robert E. Lee and His Companions in Arms, with a Record of Their Campaigns and Heroic Deeds*, Edward A. Pollard (E. B. Treat and Company, New York, 1867) p. 536.

[2] *Reminiscences of the Civil War*, General John B. Gordon (Charles Scribner's Sons, New York, 1904) p. 9.

Race Horses on Wheels. See *Black Dragons*

Racine, Wisconsin

Racine is nicknamed the *Belle City*, or the *Belle City of the Lakes* [1] because of its excellent location on the Racine River and Lake Michigan, and because of its beautiful homes, its spacious churches, its well-landscaped parks and playgrounds, its harbors and water scenes, and its well-paved streets and boulevards.

[1] *United Commercial Travelers: Racine, an Historical Narrative*, Eugene W. Leach (United Commercial Travelers of America, Racine Council Number 337, Racine, Wis., 1920) p. 5, 6.

Ragged Lawyer. See Grover, Martin

Raider. See Morgan, J. H.

Raiders

During the Civil War, certain Union soldiers imprisoned at the Confederate Military Prison at Andersonville, Ga., were generally spoken of by their fellow-prisoners as the *Raiders*.[1] These men had been recruited from the slum sections of New York City, and the nickname referred to their activities as a gang within the prison walls to rob the other inmates of clothes, food, or other desirable items. The severe punishment administered by prison officials considerably diminished the activity of the *Raiders*.

[1] *Andersonville: A Story of Rebel Military Prisons, Fifteen Months a Guest of the So-called Southern Confederacy; A Private Soldier's Experience in Richmond, Andersonville, Savannah, Millen, Blackshear, and Florence*, John McElroy (D. R. Locke, Toledo, Ohio, 1879) p. 111, 220-4.

Rail Center of America. See Chicago, Ill.

Rail Splitter. See Lincoln, Abraham

Railroad City. See Indianapolis, Ind.

Railroad King. See Gould, Jay

Railroad on Stilts

In 1839 the Ohio Railroad Company began the construction of a railway to extend from Richmond to Manhattan near Toledo, Ohio. Inasmuch as lumber was abundant in the region and the coutryside hilly, it was decided to lay the tracks on an elevated wooden trestle rather than regular roadbeds. The project, nicknamed the *Railroad on Stilts* [1] was abandoned in 1843 because funds ran out and the sixty-three miles of wooden structure built was already rotting.

[1] *This Cleveland of Ours,* Wilfred Henry Alburn and Miriam Russel Alburn (The S. J. Clarke Publishing Company, Chicago and Cleveland, Ohio, 1933) vol. 1, p. 319-21.

Railsplitters. Eighty-fourth Infantry Division of World War II; Lincoln Memorial University

Railway King. See Corning, Erastus

Rainbow Division

The Forty-second Division of the American Expeditionary Forces, organized in August 1917, contained at its inception eight huundred and eighty-seven officers and twenty-six thousand two hundred and sixty-five men drawn from military groups in the District of Columbia and twenty-five states. This group, representing diverse sections, nationalities, religions and viewpoints, but acting as an organized military unit, was nicknamed the *Rainbow Division,*[1] in allusion to the many shadings which make up the whole rainbow.

The insignia of the Forty-second Division was "a rainbow superimposed on a field of black, carried on the left shoulder"; this design was also emblazoned on the division's battle banner.

See also Forty-second Infantry Division of World War II

[1] *The Encyclopedia Americana* (Americana Corporation, New York and Chicago, 1927) vol. 23, p. 183.
[2] *A Brief Story of the Rainbow Division,* Walter B. Wolf (Rand, McNally and Company, Chicago and New York, 1919), p. 13.

Rajah. See Hornsby, Rogers

Raleigh, North Carolina

Raleigh is called the *City of Oaks* [1] because it possesses such an abundance of stately oak trees in Capitol Square Park and throughout the city.

[1] *Historical Raleigh from Its Foundation in 1792, Descriptive, Biographical, Educational, Industrial, Religious, Reminiscences, Reviewed and Carefully Compiled,* Moses N. Amis (Edwards and Broughton, Raleigh, N.C., 1902) p. 49.

Ramblers. See University of Notre Dame

Ramlets. See Rhode Island State College

Rams. See Georgia State College for Men; Rhode Island State College

Ramsey, Alexander

Alexander Ramsey was nicknamed the *Caliban of Science* [1] because of his grotesque appearance and arrogance. He studied medicine under George Cruikshank in London, England, and became famous for his anatomical knowledge. He advocated the use of alkalies for venomous snake bites, but died from the results of experimenting on himself to prove the theory.

Alexander Ramsey was born probably in London, England, in 1754, emigrated to the United States in 1800; and died at Parsonsfield, Me., on November 24, 1824.

[1] *Appleton's Cyclopaedia of American Biography,* ed. by James Grant Wilson and John Fiske (D. Appleton and Company, New York, 1888) vol. 5, p. 168.

Ramspeck, Robert

Robert Ramspeck, lawyer and former congressman, was nicknamed the *Guardian of Civil Service* [1] by his colleagues in the House of Representatives because he fostered Civil Service legislation.

For sixteen years (1929-1945) a Democratic Representative from Georgia, Ramspeck for the last ten of those years served as chairman of the House Civil Service Committee and as such was responsible for introducing or inspiring much legislation of benefit to Federal employees.[2]

Former Representative Ramspeck was appointed by President Truman on February 26, 1951, to serve as Chairman of the United States Civil Service Commission. He

Ramspeck, Robert—Continued

resigned from this position in January 1953 to enter private industry.

[1] An interview with Captain Victor Hunt Harding, Secretary of the National Democratic Congress Reelection Committee, in Washington, D.C., April 10, 1939.

[2] Current Biography, Who's News and Why, 1951, edited by Anna Rothe, (H. W. Wilson Company, New York, 1952) p. 500-2.

Ranchers. See Hardin-Simmons University

Randolph, John

John Randolph, "one of the brothers of Judith and Nancy Randolph," of Bizarre, Va., about 1810, attempted to collect a small debt owed him by John Randolph of Roanoke. He became so enraged at his kinsman from Roanoke that he attacked him with a knife and cut his coat. After this, the Roanoke Randolph signed his name *John Randolph of Roanoke* to distinguish himself from his kinsman who bore the nickname *Possum John Randolph*.[1] This nickname was given him to indicate that he only pretended to be an aristocrat.

[1] *John Randolph of Roanoke, 1773-1833: A Biography Based Largely on New Material*, William Cabell Bruce (G. P. Putnam's Sons, New York and London, 1922) vol. 2, p. 737.

Randolph (of Roanoke), John

Jack the Giant-killer, Little David, the *Man with the Sling,* the *Political Meteor,* and the *Sage of Roanoke* are appellations given to John Randolph (of Roanoke).

He was nicknamed *Jack the Giant-killer,*[1] *Little David,*[2] and the *Man with the Sling*[2] because, while he was debating, he sometimes spoke of himself as David and called his opponent Goliath.

Because of his rapid rise in politics and his fiery eloquence in debate, John Randolph was called the *Political Meteor.*[3]

The *Sage of Roanoke* was applied to John Randolph because he was learned and possessed a philosophical outlook on life. He spent the greater part of his life at Roanoke, Va.

John Randolph was born at Cawsons, Va., on June 2, 1773, and died at Philadelphia, Pa., on May 24, 1833.

[1] *U.S. "Snap Shots": An Independent, National, Memorial Encyclopedia . . . ,* Oliver McKee (A. M. Thayer and Company, Boston, 1892) p. 242.

[2] *A Book of Nicknames,* John Goff (Courier-Journal Job Printing Company, Louisville, Ky., 1892) p. 22, 23.

[3] *Manual of Useful Information,* compiled under the direction of J. C. Thomas (The Werner Company, Chicago, 1893) p. 23.

Randolph Field

Randolph Field, seventeen miles northeast of San Antonio, Tex., is popularly known as the *West Point of the Air*[1] because it is the site of the Air University of the United States Air Force.

[1] *The Source Book* (Source Research Council, Inc., Chicago, 1936) vol. 6, p. 2538.

Randolph-Macon College

The nickname, the *Yellow Jackets,*[1] has been applied to the athletic teams of Randolph-Macon College, at Ashland, Va., by sports writers and others for fifty years or more because the college "colors are lemon and black and suggest the colors of the yellow jacket."[1]

[1] A communication from R. E. Blackwell, President of Randolph-Macon College, Ashland, Va., November 14, 1935.

Rangers. See Texans

Rankin, John Elliott

John Elliott Rankin, a Mississippi lawyer and politician, was nicknamed *TVA Rankin*[1] in the House of Representatives because he was co-author of the bill creating the Tennessee Valley Authority which became law on May 18, 1933.

He was elected a Democratic Representative from Mississippi to the United States Congress from 1921, and has been reelected to succeeding Congresses to date.

John Elliott Rankin was born on a farm near Bolanda, Itawamba Co., Miss., on March 29, 1882.

[1] An Interview with Captain Victor Hunt Harding, Secretary of the National Democratic Congress Reelection Committee in Washington, D.C., April 10, 1939.

Rankine, William Birch

William Birch Rankine was called the *Father of Niagara Power*[1] because in 1890 he was instrumental in founding the first hydroelectric plant at Niagara Falls to generate electricity. This name is engraved on a bust of Rankine in the City Hall Park at Niagara Falls, N.Y., because of his service in utilizing electricity generated by the falls at Niagara.

William Birch Rankine was born at Owego, Tioga Co., N.Y., on January 4, 1858, and died at Niagara Falls, N.Y., on September 30, 1905.

[1] *Dictionary of American Biography under the Auspices of the American Council of Learned Societies,* ed. by Dumas Malone (Charles Scribner's Sons, New York, 1935) vol. 15, p. 376.

Rapid City, South Dakota

Rapid City has been called the *Denver of South Dakota* and the *Gateway City of the Hills*. It has been called the *Denver of South Dakota* [1] because, like Denver, it is a commercial center, has both mines and quarries, and is surrounded by rich grazing lands.

The *Gateway City of the Hills* [2] originated in the fact that in 1886 Rapid City was the first of the newly laid-out towns in the Black Hills to have a railroad connecting it with the older settled parts of the West. It was the center from which incoming freight was distributed to points in the Black Hills.

[1] *King's Handbook of the United States*, planned and ed. by Moses King, text by M. F. Sweetser (The Matthews-Northrup Company, Buffalo, N.Y., 1896) p. 794.
[2] *Seeing the Middle West*, John T. Faris (J. P. Lippincott Company, Philadelphia, 1923) p. 88.
The Black Hills; or, The Last Hunting Grounds of the Dakotas, Annie D. Tallent (Nixon-Jones Printing Company, St. Louis, Mo., 1899) p. 436.

Rattle Snakes

When Abraham Lincoln was elected President of the United States in 1860, there were organizations of men in the southern states who were ready to fight for the right to secede. One of these organizations in Alabama was called *Rattle Snakes*. [1]

[1] *A History of the People of the United States, from the Revolution to the Civil War*, John Bach McMaster (D. Appleton and Company, New York, 1913) vol. 8, p. 479-80.

Rattlers. See Saint Mary's University of San Antonio

Ravens. See Saint Benedict's College

Raw Deal

Franklin Delano Roosevelt's first term of office as President of the United States from 1933 to 1936 was nicknamed the *Raw Deal* [1] by newspaper columnists and editors who disagreed with the social and economic objectives of Roosevelt's administration as expressed in the New Deal policies.

[1] *Washington Herald*, Washington, D.C., August 10, 1935, col. 6, p. 6.

Rawson, Edward

The *Persecutor* [1] was applied to Edward Rawson because he persistently persecuted the Quakers with whom he came in contact at Newberry and Boston, Mass.

He was Secretary of the Boston Colony from 1650 to 1686, was agent of the So-ciety for Propagating the Gospel among the Indians in New England, and was one of the founders of the Old South Church. His intolerant attitude toward the Quakers was consistent with the harsh treatment accorded religious dissenters of the time.

Edward Rawson was born in England, on April 16, 1615, and died at Boston, Mass., on August 27, 1693.

[1] *The American Portrait Gallery, Containing Correct Portraits and Brief Notices of the Principal Actors in American History; Embracing Distinguished Women, Naval and Military Heroes, Statesmen, Civilians, Jurists, Divines, Authors, and Artists; together with Celebrated Indian Chiefs, from Christopher Columbus down to the Present Time*, A. D. Jones (J. M. Emerson and Company, New York, 1855) p. 290.
Proceedings of the Massachusetts Historical Society, 1897-1899, Second Series (Published by the Society, Boston, 1899) vol. 12, p. 219-25.

Razorbacks. See University of Arkansas

Ready Money Spencer. See Spencer, Elihu

Reardon, John E.

John E. Reardon, who was a National League umpire until retirement in 1949, was popularly known as *Beans*. [1]

[1] *Who's Who in Major League Base Ball*, comp. by Harold (Speed) Johnson (Buxton Publishing Company, Chicago, 1933) p. 446.

Rebel. See Oliver, T. N.

Rebel Brigadiers

After President Grover Cleveland vetoed the Dependent Pension Bill on February 11, 1887, which granted a pension of twelve dollars monthly to every honourably discharged veteran of the Civil War, those who opposed the President's veto called those who favored his action the *Rebel Brigadiers*, [1] signifying that in their attempts to destroy the pension bill they were working against the best interests of the veterans.

[1] *Twenty Years of the Republic, 1885-1905*, Harry Thurston Peck (Dodd, Mead and Company, New York, 1907) p. 144.

Rebel Capital. See Philadelphia, Pa.

Rebel Congress

The first session of the Seventy-sixth Congress of the United States, from January 3, to August 6, 1939, was nicknamed the *Rebel Congress* [1] by journalists because during the last three weeks of the session, the members revolted against the leadership of President Franklin Delano Roosevelt and his New

Rebel Congress—Continued
Deal advisors and his spending policies. They completely repudiated the New Deal and challenged all spend-for-recovery practices. Although they appropriated the largest peacetime appropriation ever made by a United States Congress, over thirteen billion dollars, they defeated the New Deal spending-lending bill, the Neutrality Bill, the Federal Housing Bill, and numerous other proposed appropriations. They also passed the Hatch Bill to prevent Federal employees from actively participating in political campaigns, to prevent the coercion of Federal workers to vote for certain candidates, and to forbid the use of relief funds for political purposes, modified the WPA laws so that the Federal Theatre project and some other PWA activities were eliminated, and so that the PWA program was controlled by Congressional provision administered wholly by a Federal PWA administrator.

[1] *The Washington Post*, Washington, D.C., August 6, 1939, p. 1.

Rebel Flag Order
President Grover Cleveland approved a letter written by Adjutant General Richard C. Drum to William C. Endicott, Secretary of War in Cleveland's Cabinet suggesting that both the Union and the Confederate flags which were in the custody of the War Department be returned to the officials of their respective states. Those who opposed the President's approval nicknamed his act the *Rebel Flag Order* [1] because Confederate as well as Union flags were to be returned.

[1] *Twenty Years of the Republic, 1885-1905*, Harry Thurston Peck (Dodd, Mead and Company, New York, 1907) p. 145.

Rebel Governor. See Trumbull, Jonathan

Rebel Ladies
About 1780, while the Revolutionary War was in progress, the women of South Carolina took pride in being called *Rebel Ladies*.[1] These patriotic women took every opportunity to assist their husbands, fathers, and brothers who were fighting in the Continental army.

[1] *History of the United States of America*, ed. by Edwin Wiley, . . . with the assistance of Irving E. Rines (American Educational Alliance, New York, 1909) vol. 2, p. 194.

Rebel of Salem. See Williams, Roger

Red and Blues. See University of Mississippi

Red Arrow Division. See Thirty-second Infantry Division of World War II

Redbirds. See Chicago Cardinals Football Club

Red Bull Division. See Thirty-fourth Infantry Division of World War II

Red Cap. See Powell, R. T.

Red Cats. See Western Reserve University

Red Devils. See Bettis Academy; Eureka College; Temple University

Red Devils of Wittenberg. See Wittenberg College

Red Diamond Division. See Fifth Infantry Division of World War II

Red Fox. See Hazelton, James; Van Buren, Martin

Red Fox Jackson. See Jackson, W. H.

Red-headed Rooster of the Rockies. See Belford, J. B.

Red Horses. See Kentuckians

Red Legs
The *Red Legs* [1] were bands of Union scouts in civilian clothes who wore red or tan buckskin leggings as a means of identification. Against slavery, they banded together during 1862 or 1863 in Kansas, and they were constantly employed to do scouting.

Daniel Webster Wilder says in the *Annals of Kansas* that the *Red Legs,* consisting of one hundred and sixty-three men under the leadership of Colonel George H. Hoyt, were organized in June 1862.[2]

[1] "Memorial Monuments and Tablets in Kansas: A Paper Read at the University of Kansas on the Occasion of Dedicating Markers in Lawrence, on December 4, 1908" by George Martin, Secretary of the State Historical Society, in *Collections (Previous Volumes,*

Transactions) of the Kansas State Historical Society, 1909-1910, ed. by George W. Martin, Secretary (State Printing Office, Topeka, Kan., 1910) vol. 11, p. 279-81.
A Standard History of Kansas and Kansans, written and comp. by William Elsey Connelley (Lewis Publishing Company, New York and Chicago, 1918) vol. 2, p. 742.
[2] The Annals of Kansas, 1541-1885, New Edition, Daniel Webster Wilder (T. Dwight Thacher, Kansas Publishing House, Topeka, Kans., 1886) p. 956.

Redmen. See Carthage College; International Young Men's Christian Association College; Newberry College; Saint Mary's College, Minn.; Saint John's University, N.Y.

Red Necktie. See Wearin, O. D.

Red One. See First Infantry Division of World War II

Red Raiders. See Colgate University; Texas Technological College

Red Rat. See McDaniel, I. C.

Redskins. See Denison University; University of Utah

Redskins
The American Indians were nicknamed *Redskins*[1] by settlers and trappers in the west because of the color of their skins.
[1] Jungle Roads and Other Trails of Roosevelt, Daniel Henderson (E. P. Dutton and Company, New York, 1920) p. 76.

Red Star Division. See Sixth Infantry Division of World War II

Red Sticks
The Creek Indian warriors, who fought in the war of 1813 and 1814, were called the *Red Sticks*. One historian says that this nickname originated because red to the Creeks signified warfare, and their chiefs sent a red stick to the warriors to call them to war. Other writers say that war clubs of the Creeks were painted red.
[1] A History of Alabama for Use in Schools, William Garrott Brown (University Publishing Company, New York and New Orleans, 1900) p. 21.
History of Alabama and Incidentally of Georgia and Mississippi, from the Earliest Period, Albert James Pickett, Annals of Alabama, 1819-1900, Thomas McAdory Owen (The Webb Book Company, Birmingham, Ala., 1900) p. 580.

Red Tornadoes. See King College

Redeemed Captive. See Williams, John

Reed, Thomas Brackett
Biddy, Czar Reed, and the *Terrible Turk* are nicknames of Reed. In his youth, Reed was sometimes called *Biddy,* a nickname often applied to young children.

When he was a Representative from Maine to the United States Congress from 1876 to 1899, Thomas Brackett Reed was referred to by his opponents as *Czar Reed,*[2] because he took such stern measures against "filibustering" in the House. This nickname was originated by John Tyler Morgan, a Democratic Senator from Alabama who called him the *Great White Czar*[3] in allusion to his great physical size, his very white complexion, and his outstanding power as the Speaker of the House, but later this was abbreviated to *Czar Reed.*

During this same time, Reed was also called the *Terrible Turk,*[4] American slang for "wild Irish," because he was a formidable opponent in the House.

The *Great White Father* is an Indian name for the President of the United States, which Indians used when they began going to the President to right their grievances against the United States Government, because they considered him their friend and protector. They also used this term in this sense to apply to other important white people whom they considered friends.

Thomas Brackett Reed was born at Portland, Me., on October 18, 1839, and died at Washington, D.C., on December 7, 1902.

[1] Thomas B. Reed, Parliamentarian, William A. Robinson (Dodd, Mead and Company, New York, 1930) p. 10, 98.
[2] American History for Schools, R. B. Cousins and J. A. Hill (D. C. Heath and Company, New York and Boston, 1913) p. 508.
The Encyclopedia Americana (Americana Corporation, New York and Chicago, 1927) vol. 23, p. 294.
[3] My Quarter Century of American Politics, Champ Clark (Harper and Brothers, New York and London, 1920) p. 278.
[4] The American Language, H. L. Mencken, (Alfred A. Knopf Inc., N.Y., 1948) Supplement 1, p. 312, 603.

Reeside, James
James Reeside came to be known as the *Land Admiral*[1] and the *Prince of Mail Contractors*[2] because of the respect his energy and efficiency had gained for him as a mail contractor.

With the aid of several business men, Reeside established the first regular stage line to carry mail between Baltimore, Md., and Wheeling, W.Va., in 1818. In 1827, Postmaster General John McLean persuaded him to take the contract for transporting

Reeside, James—Continued

mail between Phildelphia and New York City. In about a year, Reeside had materially decreased the time between these points, and increased the efficiency of this service. In a few years he owned the majority of the stage coach lines between Philadelphia and New York City, and was the largest mail contractor in the United States, using over a thousand horses and over four hundred men.

He was born near Paisley, in Renfrew, Scotland, emigrated to Baltimore, Md., in 1789, and died in 1842.

[1] *The Old Pike: A History of the National Road with Incidents, Accidents, and Anecdotes Thereon*, Thomas B. Searight (Published by the Author, Uniontown, Pa., 1894) p. 186.

[2] *The Life and Times of Colonel Richard M. Johnson of Kentucky*, Leland Winfield Meyer (Columbia University Press, New York, 1932) p. 399.

Reform Governor. See Cleveland, Grover

Registry of the Desert

The *Registry of the Desert* [1] is the name often applied to a large granite boulder in Natrona County, Wyo., about fifty-five miles southwest of Casper. It lies on the north bank of the Sweetwater River near the main road between Casper and Rawlins, Wyo. Being on the old Oregon Trail, this rock was the registry of such outstanding pioneers as Benjamin L. E. Bonneville and John Charles Frémont, and the Jesuit priest and explorer, Peter DeSmet. Added to these are the names of scores of pioneers who, as they went westward, rested by the Sweetwater River and chiseled their names on the south end of this natural monument which was named Independence Rock. Because it served as a record of the emigrants who traversed this arid region, Independence Rock came to be known as the *Registry of the Desert*. The origin of this name is accredited to Father DeSmet.

[1] *Washakie, an Account of Indian Resistance of the Covered Wagon and Union Pacific Railroad Invasions of Their Territory*, Grace Raymond Hebard (The Arthur H. Clark Company, Cleveland, Ohio, 1930) p. 59. *Wyoming from Territorial Days to the Present*, under the editorial supervision of Francis Birkhead Board; *Wyoming Biography*, gratuitously published by special staff of writers (The American Historical Society, Inc., New York and Chicago, 1933) vol. 1, p. 52.

Reindeer. See Killefer, William

Rensselaer Polytechnic Institute

Rensselaer Polytechnic Institute, at Troy, N.Y., was nicknamed the *Birthplace of Technology* [1] because it is the oldest engineering school in the United States. It was founded by Stephen Van Rensselaer in 1824. The college creed states that "there shall be excluded from our classrooms all controversial discussions about politics, religion, and sociology . . . that this school has developed and prospered under the capitalistic regime, that it has been endowed by industrial leaders, that it trains men for work in industrial organizations, and that it will glory in being called the 'last refuge of conservatism.' "

The athletic teams of Rensselaer Polytechnic Institute are called the *Fighting Engineers*.[2]

[1] *Time: The Weekly Newsmagazine*, Chicago, July 1, 1939, col. 2, p. 32.

[2] A communication from Harry A. Van Welsor, Director of Athletics at Rensselaer Polytechnic Institute, Troy, N.Y., June 13, 1935.

Republican Elephant

About 1868 in *Harper's Weekly*, Thomas Nast nicknamed the Republican party the *Republican Elephant* [1] because of the clumsiness of the party.

The first Republican elephant cartoon was a drawing by Thomas Nast which appeared in *Harper's Weekly* on November 7, 1874, in connection with a third-term-for-Grant campaign.

[1] *Political Americanisms*, Charles Ledyard Norton (Longmans, Green and Company, New York and London, 1890) p. 40.

Republican party. See Grand Old Party

Rest Island, Minnesota

Rest Island, located at the west side of Lake Pepin in Le Sueur County, has been called the *Little Switzerland of America* [1] because of its natural mountain beauty.

[1] *My Minnesota*, Antoinette E. Ford (Lyons and Carnahan, New York and Chicago, 1929) p. 306.

Revere, Massachusetts

Revere, a residential suburb and a summer resort in Boston, Mass., is commonly designated the *Coney Island of Boston* because it is the resort and aquatic playground of Boston as Coney Island is that of New York City.

[1] *The Source Book* (Source Research Council, Inc., Chicago, 1936) vol. 6, p. 2429.

Reynolds, Charles Alexander

Charles Alexander Reynolds, a hunter, scout, and guide, was known throughout the western part of the United States as

Lonesome Charley [1] because while friendly and kind to all, he was habitually quiet and unassuming. He was a hunter in the Dakota hills from about 1867 until 1873, and for the next three years, a scout and guide in the expeditions of the United States Army against the Indians in the Yellowstone region of the West.

Charles Alexander Reynolds was born probably near Stephensburg, Ky., on March 20, 1842, and was killed in the Battle of the Big Horn at the junction of the Little and the Big Horn Rivers, Montana, on June 25, 1876.

[1] *Dictionary of American Biography under the Auspices of the American Council of Learned Societies*, ed. by Dumas Malone (Charles Scribner's Sons, New York, 1935) vol. 5, p. 517.

Reynolds, John

Because he served for some time as a scout for the American forces during the War of 1812, John Reynolds was nicknamed *Old Ranger*.[1]

John Reynolds was born in Montgomery County, Pa., on February 26, 1788, and died at Belleville, Ill., on May 8, 1865.

[1] *The National Cyclopaedia of American Biography* (James T. White and Company, New York, 1909) vol. 11, p. 44.

Reynolds, John Cromwell

In 1846 and 1847, during the struggle between the United States and Mexico, Dr. John Cromwell Reynolds was the surgeon for the First Regiment of American Volunteers. His invaluable services in this capacity were rendered in such a courageous and soldierly manner that he became known as the *Fighting Doctor*.[1]

John Cromwell Reynolds was born in Cecil County, Md., in 1810, and died at Lewiston, Pa., on February 20, 1849.

[1] *The National Cyclopaedia of American Biography* (James T. White and Company, New York, 1893) vol. 3, p. 223.

Reynolds, Robert Rice

Robert Rice Reynolds was nicknamed *Our Bob* [1] during his term of office as a Senator from North Carolina to the United States Senate from 1933 until 1945, having originated the sobriquet himself in order to popularize himself with the voting public. His colleagues in the United States Senate nicknamed him the *Playboy* [2] because of his jovial nature, easy-going manner of living, and his spectacular manner of delivering speeches on the Senate floor.

Robert Rice Reynolds was born at Asheville, N.C., on June 18, 1884.

[1] *Ken*, Chicago, April 20, 1939, col. 2, p. 16.
[2] An interview with Captain Victor Hunt Harding, Secretary of the National Democratic Congress Reëlection Committee, Washington, D.C., April 10, 1939.

Rhem, Charles Flint

Charles Flint Rhem, who was born at Rhems, S.C., on January 24, 1903, and who pitched in major league baseball, is nicknamed *Shad*.[1]

[1] *Who's Who in Major League Base Ball*, comp. by Harold (Speed) Johnson (Buxton Publishing Company, Chicago, 1933) p. 326.

Rhett, Robert Barnwell

Robert Barnwell Rhett is widely known as the *Father of Secession* [1] because he took an active part in bringing about the secession of South Carolina from the Union, and because he was a firm advocate of state's rights and nullification.[2]

Robert Barnwell Rhett was born at Beaufort, S.C., on December 24, 1800, and died in St. James' Parish, La., on September 14, 1876.

[1] *Robert Barnwell Rhett: Father of Secession*, Laura A. White (The Century Company, New York, 1931) p. 181, 188.
[2] *The Encyclopedia Americana* (Americana Corporation, New York, 1932) vol. 23, p. 459.

Rhine of America. See Hudson River

Rhode Island

Little Rhody and the *Plantation State* are the nicknames applied to Rhode Island.

Rhode Island is sometimes called *Little Rhody* [1] because it is the smallest state in the Union.[2]

The nickname, *Plantation State*, is a shortening of Rhode Island's official title, the *State of Rhode Island and Providence Plantations*.

[1] *More About Names*, Leopold Wagner (T. Fisher Unwin, London, 1893) p. 28.
[2] *Americanisms; The English of the New World*, M. Schele De Vere (Charles Scribner and Company, New York, 1872) p. 661.

Rhode Island State College

The *Farmers, Rams,* and *Ramlets,* are nicknames popularly applied to the athletic teams of Rhode Island State College, at Kingston, R.I.

The college is located at the country town of Kingston, and the school once offered agriculture as the predominating course of study, hence the nickname *Farmers*.[1] *Rams* [1] was chosen for the teams about 1929, be-

Rhode Island State College—Continued

cause they often won the game from their opponents by an unexpected play or attack near the close of the game. College publicity director William G. Mokray coined the diminutive form *Ramlets* [1] for the freshman teams.

[1] A letter from William G. Mokray, Physical Director at Rhode Island State College, Kingston, R.I., June 23, 1935.

Rhode Islanders

The people of Rhode Island are nicknamed *Gunflints*.[1] It is said that the nickname arose through the use of fire arms by its citizens at the time of the Dorr Rebellion of 1842, the arms being mostly old gunflint models from their owners' garrets.[1]

[1] *U.S.: An Index to the United States of America*, comp. by Malcolm Townsend (D. Lothrop Company, Boston, 1890) p. 80.

Rhodes, James Lamar. See Rhodes, J. G.

Rhodes, John Gordon

Ballplayers named Rhodes are inevitably tagged *Dusty*. The first of the line was John Gordon Rhodes, former pitcher, born August 11, 1907 in Salt Lake City, Utah. The latest *Dusty* is outfielder James Lamar Rhodes who came to the majors in 1952. He was born at Mathews, Ala., on May 3, 1927.

[1] *Who's Who in Major League Base Ball*, comp. by Harold (Speed) Johnson (Buxton Publishing Company, Chicago, 1933) p. 328.

Rice, Daniel

The *King of American Clowns* and the *Shakespeare Clown* are nicknames attributed to Daniel Rice.

He was nicknamed *King of American Clowns* [1] because his popularity as a clown was widespread and lasting.

Because he was so well versed in the works of Shakespeare, Rice was also called the *Shakespeare Clown*.[2]

Daniel Rice was born at New York City, in 1822, and died at Long Branch, N.J., on February 22, 1900.

[1] *The Circus, from Rome to Ringling*, Earl Chapin May (Duffield and Green, New York, 1932) p. 62, 66.
[2] *The Encyclopedia Americana* (Americana Corporation, New York and Chicago, 1927) vol. 23, p. 485.

Rice, Grantland

Grantland Rice, the sports writer and authority was affectionately nicknamed *Granny* by his colleagues and friends.

In the 1920's Rice himself coined a nickname which caught the nation's fancy when he referred to the backfield of the Notre Dame football team as the *Four Horsemen* (*q.v.*).

Grantland Rice was born at Murfreesboro, Tenn., and died in New York City, July 13, 1954.

Rice, Harvey

As chairman of the Committee on Schools in the Ohio State Senate, Harvey Rice framed the bill bringing into existence the Ohio public school system, hence he was called the *Father of the Public School System of Ohio*.[1]

As agent for the Western Reserve school lands in 1829, Rice sold the entire amount of ground allotted to this organization, about fifty-six thousand acres, inside of three years, which brought into the State Treasury a school fund of about $150,000.

Harvey Rice was born at Conway, Mass., on June 11, 1800, and died at Cleveland, Ohio, on November 7, 1891.

[1] *The National Cyclopaedia of American Biography* (James T. White and Company, New York, 1906) vol. 13, p. 81.

Rice, Thomas Dartmouth

The actor, Thomas Dartmouth Rice, was known nationally and internationally as the *Father of American Minstrelsy* [1] because he introduced and popularized Negro minstrelsy on the stage in America and Europe.

In 1828, while Rice was lamp lighter, stage carpenter, property man, and a player of minor stock parts in Ludlow and Smith's Southern Theatre in Louisville, Ky., he appeared, in a between-the-acts performance, for the first time in a Negro characterization. It was here that "he sang and jumped *Jim Crow*. This piece of mimicry was based on the song and manner of a local Negro stable hand, a slave called Jim Crow,[2] who, as he went about doing his work, would croon an old melody, and do a curious shuffling step whenever he reached the chorus of his song, with a little jump.

Rice's impersonation was well received by the audience and after that time he acted exclusively as an imitator of colored people. He was the author of many burlesques which became the basis for "skits" in minstrel shows for years to come.

Thomas Dartmouth Rice was born at New York City, on May 20, 1808, and died there on September 19, 1860.

[1] *Dictionary of American Biography under the Auspices of the American Council of Learned Societies*, ed. by Dumas Malone (Charles Scribner's Sons, New York, 1935) vol. 15, p. 545.
[2] *The National Cyclopaedia of American Biography* (James T. White and Company, New York, 1909) vol. 11, p. 207.

Rice Institute

The athletic teams of the Rice Institute, at Houston, Tex., are commonly known as the *Owls* [1] because the shield and seal of the Rice Institute carry the image of three owls taken from an Attic coin of about 480 B. C.

[1] A communication from J. F. McCants, The Rice Institute, Houston, Tex., November 20, 1935.

Rice-birds. See South Carolinians

Rice Bowl. See Football Stadium, Rice Institute

Rice State. See South Carolina

Rich, Robert Fleming

The Honorable Robert Fleming Rich is popularly known as *Woolly Bob* [1] by his colleagues in the United States Congress in humorous allusion to the fact that for some time he was manager of the Woolrich Woolen Mills at Woolrich, Pa.

He was born at Woolrich, Pa., on June 23, 1883, and was a Representative from Pennsylvania to the Seventy-first United States Congress and six succeeding congresses (1930-1943).

[1] *The Washington Post Magazine*, Washington, D.C., March 4, 1934, p. 4.

Richards, Thomas Addison

Horace Greeley nicknamed Thomas Addison Richards the *Doughty of the South* [1] at the appearance of one of Richard's early works, *Georgia Illustrated,* a beautiful quarto volume of fine steel engravings from Richards' original drawings. Thomas Doughty, who lived from 1783 to 1856, was one of the few distinguished painters who, at that early date, drew the American landscape. Richards' specialty throughout his artistic career was landscape painting and many of his American scenes were shown at National Academy exhibitions.

Thomas Addison Richards was born at London, England, on December 3, 1829,

and died at Annapolis, Md., on June 29, 1900.

[1] *The National Cyclopaedia of American Biography* (James T. White and Company, New York, 1900) vol. 8, p. 425.

Richardson, Israel Bush

During the War wth Mexico from 1846 to 1847, Brigadier General Israel Bush Richardson was designated *Fighting Dick* [1] by his fellow soldiers for his courageous action and soldierly conduct on the battlefields.

Israel Bush Richardson was born at Fairfax, Vt., on December 26, 1815, and died at Sharpsburg, Md., on November 3, 1862.

[1] *The National Cyclopaedia of American Biography* (James T. White and Company, New York, 1904) vol. 12, p. 226.

Richest Village on Earth. See Hibbing, Minn.

Richmond, Indiana

Richmond, having been settled and laid out by Friends or Quakers from North Carolina in 1816, has been termed the *Quaker City of the West,* [1] being further west than Philadelphia, the original *Quaker City.*

[1] *Manual of Useful Information*, comp. under the direction of J. C. Thomas (The Werner Company, Chicago, 1893) p. 22.

Richmond, Virginia

Richmond possesses four nicknames: *Cockade City, Modern Rome, Queen City of the South,* and *Queen on the James.* The writer was unable to find why it was designated the *Cockade City.* It is frequently termed the *Modern Rome* [1] because, like Rome, it was built on seven hills.

It is called the *Queen City of the South,* [2] because it is advantageously located on the James River, is easily accessible by highways and railroads, and is the leading center of manufacturing in Virginia and one of the important manufacturing cities of the South.

Richmond is often designated the *Queen of the James* [3] because it is situated "on a succession of hills, which overlook rich lowlands; at a point where the James River breaks over the rocks at 'the falls' and in foam and fury buries itself in the tidal waters of the harbor, the landscape in lines and colors blends the grace and softness of the country with the majesty and vigor of the highlands." [4]

[1] *The Encyclopedia Americana* (Americana Corporation, New York and Chicago, 1932) vol. 23, p. 500.

Richmond, Va.—Continued

[2] *Pen and Sunlight Sketches of Richmond, the Most Progressive Metropolis of the South.* . . (Comp., illustrated and published by The American Illustrating Company, Richmond, Va., 1918) p. 38.
[3] *A Book of Nicknames*, John Goff (Courier-Journal Job Printing Company, Louisville, Ky., 1892) p. 17.
[4] *Guide to Richmond and the Battle-fields*, W. D. Chesterman (James E. Goode, Richmond, Va., 1881) p. 3.

Rider College

The *Rough Riders*[1] is the nickname given the athletic teams of Rider College, at Trenton, N.J., by Claire F. Bee, former athletic coach at the college, because they "ride rough-shod over their opponents."

[1] A communication from Joseph W. Seay, Director of Athletics at Rider College, Trenton, N.J., July 1, 1935.

Right-angled, Tri-angled Thurman.
See Thurman, A. G.

Right Hand Mind. See Robinson, F. M.

Rigler, Charles

Charles Rigler, who was born at Massillon, Ohio, on May 16, 1882, and who was a National League impire, is nicknamed *Cy*.[1]

[1] *Who's Who in Major League Base Ball*, comp. by Harold (Speed) Johnson (Buxton Publishing Company, Chicago, 1933) p. 448.

Riker, Richard

Because of his eminent position in society, and his refined manners and pleasing personality, Richard Riker was given the sobriquet the *American Chesterfield*,[1] by the English actress and author, Fannie Kemble. The nickname refers to Philip Dormer Stanhope, Earl of Chesterfield, who lived at London from 1694 to 1773, and who was distinguished for his polished manners.

Richard Riker was born at Newtown, Long Island, N.Y., on September 9, 1773, and died at New York City on September 26, 1822.

[1] *The National Cyclopaedia of American Biography* (James T. White and Company, New York, 1900) vol. 8, p. 295.

Riley, James Whitcomb

James Whitcomb Riley has been designated the *Burns of America,* the *Hoosier Poet,* and the *Poet of the Common People.*

His verse deals chiefly with the common people and the humorous, pathetic, or common-place incidents of their life; his writings were often in popular dialect, and

his style is simple, clear, and unaffected; in all of these qualities he is comparable to the Scotch poet, Robert Burns.

As a native of Indiana, the Hoosier state, and its most outstanding poet, James Whitcomb Riley has been aptly designated the *Hoosier Poet.*[2]

Because so many of his productions dealt with the common man and his life, Riley is widely known as the *Poet of the Common People.*[3]

James Whitcomb Riley was born at Greenfield, Ind., on October 7, 1853, and died at Indianapolis, Ind., on July 22, 1916.

[1] *The Encyclopedia Americana* (Americana Corporation, New York and Chicago, 1927) vol. 23, p. 524.
[2] *The National Cyclopaedia of American Biography* (James T. White and Company, New York, 1896) vol. 6, p. 31.
[3] *The Encyclopedia Britannica*, Fourteenth Edition (Encyclopaedia Britannica, Inc., New York, 1929) vol. 19, p. 308.

Ringling, John

John Ringling, manager of the world famous Ringling Brothers Show, was nicknamed the *Circus King.*[1]

He was born near Baraboo, Wis., in 1866, and died at New York City, on December 2, 1936.

[1] *The Circus from Rome to Ringling*, Earl Chapin May (Duffield and Green, New York City, 1932) p. 325.

Rinkydinks. See Central College (Fayette, Mo.)

Rip and Snorter. See Connally, G. W.

Ripper. See Collins, J. A.

Rip Van Winkle State. See North Carolina

Rise up William Allen. See Allen, William

Rival of Sappho. See Lewis, E. A. B.

River of Steep Hills. See Hudson River

Rivet McClintic. See McClintic, J. V.

Rixey, Eppa, Jr.

The sobriquet, *Jephtha,*[1] was applied to Eppa Rixey, Jr., by Charles Dryden after Dryden had read about the Biblical character Jephtha.

Eppa Rixey, Jr., was born at Culpepper, Va., on May 3, 1891, and pitched in major league baseball.

[1] *Who's Who in Major League Base Ball*, comp. by Harold (Speed) Johnson (Buxton Publishing Company, Chicago, 1933) p. 333.

Roach, John

The shipbuilder, John Roach, was nicknamed the *Father of Iron Shipbuilding in America*.[1] He was a pioneer builder of iron ships in the United States, and was influential in causing both private and governmental builders of vessels to construct iron ships for commercial and for military use. He was also active in promoting the American merchant marine and was considered well-versed in the organization of its activities.

John Roach was born at Mitchelstown, Cork County, Ireland, on December 25, 1813, and died at New York City, on January 10, 1887.

[1] *Dictionary of American Biography under the Auspices of the American Council of Learned Societies*, ed. by Dumas Malone (Charles Scribner's Sons, New York, 1935) vol. 15, p. 640.

Roanoke College

The nickname, *Maroons,* has been applied to the athletic teams of Roanoke College, at Salem, Va. The college colors are maroon and gray.

Robbie of the Codes. See Robinson, F. M.

Robert, Lawrence Wood, Jr.

Lawrence Wood Robert, Jr., a construction engineer, was nicknamed *Chip Robert,*[1] because his father was called Wood Robert. Robert was Assistant Secretary of the United States Treasury from 1933 until 1936. He was appointed Assistant Treasurer of the Democratic National Committee on April 15, 1936.

Lawrence Wood Robert, Jr., was born at Monticello, Ga., on September 3, 1887.

[1] *Time: The Weekly Newsmagazine*, Chicago, Ill. February 27, 1939, col. 2, p. 18.

Roberts, Brigham Henry

Brigham Henry Roberts, a Mormon leader, was popularly called by the members of that sect the *Defender of the Faith*[1] because he consistently and ardently defended Mormonism in Utah. In 1887 the Congress of the United States disincorporated the Mormon Church in recognition of the final decision of the United States Supreme Court that the law allowing a plurality of wives was invalid. This affair created nationwide controversy between the adherents of the Church of the Latter-Day Saints, that is, the Mormon Church, and its opponents. During this time Roberts' spoken and written support of Mormon doctrines caused him to become nicknamed the *Defender of the Faith.*

Brigham Henry Roberts was born at Warrington in Lancashire, England, on March 13, 1857, and died at Salt Lake City, Utah, on September 27, 1933.

[1] *Dictionary of American Biography under the Auspices of the American Council of Learned Societies*, ed. by Dumas Malone (Charles Scribner's Sons, New York, 1935) vol. 16, p. 4.

Roberts, John

Because he wore a white surplice when he was preaching or administering spiritual aid to the Indians, Reverend John Roberts was nicknamed *White Robe*[1] by them. The Indians called all the Episcopal missionaries *White Robes*[1] because they wore white surplices.

Reverend John Roberts was a missionary to the Shoshoni Indians in the Northwestern part of the United States from 1883 to 1929.

[1] *Washakie and Defense of Settlers of Northwest: Washakie, An Account of the Covered Wagon and Union Pacific Railroad Invasions of Their Territory,* Grace Raymond Hebard (The Arthur H. Clark Company, Cleveland, Ohio, 1930) p. 236, 245.

Roberts, Oran Milo

Oran Milo Roberts, soldier, jurist, and statesman, was widely known as the *Old Alcalde*[1] because of his eminence in the legal profession. He was for many years an outstanding attorney in Texas, and subsequently Chief Justice of the State Supreme Court of Texas from 1874 until his election to the governorship of the state. *Alcalde* is a term of Spanish origin signifying an administrative official, usually a judge.

Oran Milo Roberts was born in the Laurens District of Carolina, in July 1815, and died at Austin, Tex., on May 19, 1898.

[1] *Dictionary of American Biography under the Auspices of the American Council of Learned Societies*, ed. by Dumas Malone (Charles Scribner's Sons, New York, 1935) vol. 16, p. 14.

Roberts, Robert Richford

Elected a Bishop in the Methodist Episcopal Church in 1816, Robert Richford Roberts went to Indiana and spent the remainder of his life preaching and ministering to the Indians and to the scattered settlers of that state. The Indians respectfully called him

Roberts, R. R.—Continued

the *Grandfather of the Missionaries* [1] in allusion to his quiet dignity, sincerity, and deep piety.

Robert Richford Roberts was born in Frederick County, Md., on August 2, 1778, and died in Laurence County, Ind., on March 26, 1843.

[1] *The National Cyclopaedia of American Biography* (James T. White Company, New York, 1907) vol. 9. p. 485.

Roberts, Theodore

Theodore Roberts, who was born at San Francisco, Calif., on October 2, 1861, and who died at Los Angeles, Calif., on December 14, 1928, was known as *Dad* and the *Grand Old Man of the Screen* [1] because of his years in films and his many lovable qualities.

[1] *The Blue Book of the Screen*, Ruth Wing, Editor (The Blue Book of the Screen, Inc., Hollywood, Calif., 1923) p. 228.

Robertson, James

The *Father of Middle Tennessee* [1] is a nickname given to James Robertson because of the prominent part he took in the social and political development of the settlement which later became Nashville, the center of Middle Tennessee.

James Robertson was born in Brunswick County, Va., on June 28, 1742, and died near Memphis, Tenn., on September 1, 1814.

[1] *A History of Tennessee from 1663 to 1924*, Gentry R. McGee, revised and enlarged by C. B. Ijams (American Book Company, New York, 1924) p. 63.

Robin Hood of the Forest. See Allen, Ethan

Robinson, Frances M.

Because she possessed remarkable ability in remembering the seven hundred codes of the N.R.A., the *Right Hand Mind* [1] and *Robbie of the Codes* [1] were sobriquets applied to Frances M. Robinson.

She was born at Troy, N.Y., in 1906, and resigned her position as secretary to General Hugh S. Johnson when he resigned from the directorship of the N.R.A. (National Recovery Act) about September 26, 1934.

[1] *Washington Herald*, Washington, D.C., September 3, 1934, cols. 3-5, p. 13.

Robinson, Solon

Solon Robinson, pioneer, agriculturalist, and author, was nicknamed *King of the Squatters* [1] in 1836 because in the then uncultivated region of northern Indiana called "Robinson's Prairie," he established the Squatters Union to prevent land speculators from seizing this area of the state, thereby deterring settlers from securing it for a nominal sum. The gratitude of the "squatters" for his interest in their welfare and their veneration for him for his continued aid gave rise to the nickname. Robinson was a prolific contributor to newspapers and magazines, particularly regarding the agricultural problems of the Indiana pioneers; he also wrote fiction and travel sketches.

Solon Robinson was born at Tolland, Conn., on October 21, 1803, and died at Jacksonville, Fla., on November 3, 1880.

[1] *Dictionary of American Biography under the Auspices of the American Council of Learned Societies*, ed. by Dumas Malone (Charles Scribner's Sons, New York, 1935) vol. 16, p. 51.

Robinson Crusoe Anderson. See Anderson, James

Rochester, New York

Rochester has been nicknamed the *Aqueduct City*, a *City Built by Hands*, *City of Homes*, *City of Varied Industries*, *Flour City*, *Flower City*, *Friendliest City*, *Kodak City*, *Power City*, and *Quality City*.

It has been called the *Aqueduct City* [1] because of the great aqueduct [2] which supplies the city with water from Hemlock Lake twenty-eight miles away.

It is termed a *City Built by Hands* [3] because it was built by manual labor rather than by machinery, and because it is outstanding in those industries that require manual labor. An early symbol of the city which constituted the official seal was an arm grasping a hammer.

Rochester merits the nickname, *City of Homes*, [4] because, from its earliest days, its inhabitants have taken great pride in owning their homes, about fifty percent of its citizens being home-owners in 1932.

It is often designated the *City of Varied Industries*, [5] a great variety of manufactured articles being produced there.

Rochester was officially nicknamed the *Flour City* [4] as this sobriquet is inscribed on the seal of the city. Flour-producing activities began early in the development of the city, and have continued to be of considerable importance. From 1834 to 1878 Rochester was the leading center [6] of flour production in the United States. When wheat began to be grown on a large scale in the West, its milling activities declined somewhat.

The city is termed the *Flower City* [4] because of its prominence in horticultural activities,[7] being the site of numerous seedhouses and nurseries, from which seeds, bulbs, and plants are shipped throughout the country. Rochester itself contains innumerable flower gardens and many garden clubs [4] which contribute much to its beauty.

Friendliest City [4] is an allusion to the hospitable and friendly attitude of its inhabitants noted by strangers and tourists.

Rochester is called *Kodak City* [4] because it is the site of the Eastman Kodak Company.

This city is outstanding in the production of hydroelectricity, the generating plant being located at the falls of the Genessee River within the city limits; hence the name, *Power City.*[4]

Quality City [4] refers to the high manufacturing standards of the city as implied in the city slogan, *Rochester Made Means Quality.*[5]

[1] *Manual of Useful Information,* comp. under the direction of J. C. Thomas (The Werner Company, Chicago, 1893) p. 22.

[2] *Landmarks of Monroe County, New York. . . ,* William F. Peck, Thomas Raines, and Herman Le Roy Fairchild (The Boston History Company, Boston, 1895) p. 149.

[3] *Centennial History of Rochester, New York: Volume I,* Beginnings, comp. and ed. by Edward R. Foreman (Rochester Historical Society, Rochester, N.Y., 1932) p. 16, 17.

[4] *Centennial History of Rochester, New York: Volume II,* Home Builders, comp. and ed. by Edward R. Foreman (Rochester Historical Society, Rochester, N.Y., 1932) p. 5, 6, 30, 204, 206, 207, 222.

[5] *The Encyclopedia Americana* (Americana Corporation, New York and Chicago, 1932) vol. 23, p. 591.

[6] *The Encyclopedia Britannica,* Fourteenth Edition (Encyclopedia Britannica, Inc., New York, 1932) vol. 19, p. 364.

[7] *Rochester, 1906,* comp. by John M. Ives (Rochester Chamber of Commerce, Press of Union and Advertiser Company, Rochester, N.Y., 1906) p. 31.

Rock. See Alcatraz Federal Prison; Rockne, K. K.

Rock Brigade

Brigadier General Henry Lewis Benning's brigade in the Confederate Army was nicknamed the *Rock Brigade* [1] because, inspired by the steadfastness of their leader, the men of the brigade distinguished themselves by the unyielding and courageous manner in which they fought. The sobriquet was prob-

ably derived from General Benning's nickname, *Old Rock.*

[1] *From Manassas to Appomatox, Memoirs of the Civil War in America,* James Longstreet (J. B. Lippincott Company, Philadelphia, 1896) p. 448.

Rock City. See Nashville, Tenn.

Rock Island, Illinois. See Davenport, Iowa, Moline and Rock Island, Ill.

Rock of Chickamauga. See Thomas, G. H.

Rock of Notre Dame. See Rockne, K. K.

Rockets. See University of Notre Dame; University of Toledo

Rockefeller, John Davison

Standard Oil King [1] was the nickname of John Davison Rockefeller. He organized and became president of the Standard Oil Company, in 1870, and from this organization made his immense fortune. He remained dominant in the oil business until his retirement in 1911.

John Davison Rockefeller was born at Richford, N.Y., on July 8, 1839, and died at Ormond Beach, Fla., on May 23, 1937.

[1] *A Book of Nicknames,* John Goff (Courier-Journal Job Printing Company, Louisville, Ky., 1892) p. 30.

Rockford, Illinois

Rockford was nicknamed the *Forest City* [1] because it is situated on the banks of Rock River, a well-forested region.

[1] *The Source Book* (Source Research Council, Inc., Chicago, 1936) vol. 6, p. 2460.

Rockne, Knute Kenneth

Rock and the *Rock of Notre Dame* are the nicknames given to Knute Kenneth Rockne.

Rock [1] is an abbreviated form of his surname and probably came into use because Knute was difficult to pronounce.

He was called the *Rock of Notre Dame* [2] in commemoration of his firmness in discipline, his strength of character, and his steadiness of purpose during his outstanding career as a football player, and as coach at Notre Dame University.

From 1914 to 1918 Rockne was an assistant to Jesse Harper, football coach at Notre Dame University, South Bend, Ind.

Rockne, K. K.—Continued

He became head football coach of that institute in 1918 and was occupying that position at the time of his death in 1931.

Knute Kenneth Rockne was born at Voss, Norway, on March 4, 1888, and was killed in an airplane crash near Bazaar, Kans., on March 31, 1931.

[1] *Goals: The Life of Knute Rockne*, Huber William Hurt, with an introduction by Lowell Thomas (Murray Book Corporation, New York, 1931) p. 87, 88.

[2] *Our Foreign-born Citizens: What They Have Done for America*, Annie E. S. Beard, revised and enlarged by Frederica Beard (Thomas Y. Crowell Company, New York, 1932) p. 320.

Rock-ribbed State. See Kentucky; Massachusetts

Rocks. See Stone, F. M.

Rocky. See Stone, J. T.

Rocky Mountains

The Rocky Mountains, the major mountain system of western North America, are called the *Backbone of the Continent*,[1] *Backbone of North America*,[2] and the *Roof of the Continent*.[1]

The Rockies extend over 3000 miles from central northern Mexico generally north northwest into western Canada and northern Alaska and reach Bering Strait north of the Arctic Circle. They form the Continental Divide separating Pacific drainage from Atlantic (Gulf of Mexico) and Arctic drainage.[3] They also form a dividing line for the physical features of the continent, separating the Great Plains in the east from the high plateaus, basins and ranges of the intermountain region in the west. The loftiest summits in the Rockies are concentrated in the Colorado region and all reach above 14,000 feet.

[1] *Compton's Pictured Encyclopedia* (F. E. Compton & Company, Chicago, 1933) vol. 12, p. 123.

[2] *The New International Encyclopedia*, 2nd ed. (Dodd, Mead & Company, New York, 1930) vol. 20, p. 68.

[3] *The Columbia Lippincott Gazetteer of the World*, ed. by Leon E. Seltzer (Columbia University Press, New York, 1952) p. 1594.

Roddey, Philip Dale

Philip Dale Roddey, a soldier and merchant, while serving in the Confederate Army during the Civil War, was nicknamed the *Swamp Fox of the Tennessee Valley*.[1] He commanded his swiftly-riding cavalry with such cunning, originality, and unexpectedness of movement that he was compared to the wily swamp fox native to the Tennessee River Valley, the locality in which Roddey was stationed from 1862 until 1865. He enlisted in the Confederate Army in 1861 as a Captain of Cavalrymen, and in 1863 he was made a Brigadier General in that army.

Philip Dale Roddey was born at Moulton, Ala., in 1820, and died at London, England, in August, 1897.

[1] *Dictionary of American Biography under the Auspices of the American Council of Learned Societies*, ed. by Dumas Malone (Charles Scribner's Sons, New York, 1935) vol. 16, p. 70.

Roddey Burdine Memorial Stadium of Miami

The Roddey Burdine Memorial Stadium at Miami, Fla., is called the *Orange Bowl*[1] by sports writers. The nickname undoubtedly owes its origin to the fact that Florida is the *Orange State*.

The stadium was built in 1937 through the cooperation of the United States government, and is the property of the city of Miami. It replaced a smaller wooden structure, is "considered one of the most modern in design and is somewhat like the Olympic Stadium in Berlin, Germany." The lighting system is considered about the best in the United States.

The stadium is used by the football teams of the University of Miami, by the football teams of five local high schools for practically all of their home games, and for the annual Orange Bowl Football Game.

[1] A letter from Jack Harding, Director of Athletics at the University of Miami, Coral Gables, Fla., March 11, 1939.

Roger Williams City. See Providence, R.I.

Rogers, Will

The nicknames which have been applied to Will Rogers are: *Ambassador of Good Will, Cherokee Kid, Cowboy Philosopher*, the *Man Who Can Say Anything And Make Everybody Like it*, and the *Prince of Wit and Wisdom*.

Rogers was called the *Ambassador of Good Will* after his attendance at the Disarmament Conference[1] in London in 1926 as an unofficial ambassador of the United States. For several months in Europe Rogers made contacts with many prominent European officials who received him and the spirit of his mission kindly. About 1900 Clem

Rogers, Will's father, who was one-quarter Cherokee Indian, enrolled himself and his son on the Cherokee rolls of the Indian Territory. Will was nicknamed the *Cherokee Kid,*[1] which is said to have been his favorite sobriquet. *The Cowboy Philosopher* [2] also commemorates his Western origin but he is said not to have liked being called a philosopher.

The Man Who Can Say Anything And Make Everybody Like It [3] was a sobriquet applied to Will Rogers because his wit was so full of humor and goodwill that it was never offensive to anyone. The *Prince of Wit and Wisdom* was a frequent nickname for Will Rogers because of his humorous exposition of philosophical truths.

Will Rogers was born at Oologah, in the Indian Territory, on November 4, 1879, and was killed in an airplane crash at Point Barrow. Alaska, on August 15, 1935.

[1] *An Appreciation of Will Rogers*, David Randolph Milsen (The Naylor Company, San Antonio, Tex., 1935) p. 47, 126.
[2] *Our Will Rogers*, Jack Lait (Greenberg, New York, 1935) p. 106.
[3] *Screen Personalities*, Vincent Trotta and Cliff Lewis (Grossett and Dunlap, New York, 1933) p. 95.

Rolling Green Waves. See Tulane University

Rolling W. See Eighty-ninth Infantry Division of World War II

Rollins, James Sidney

Pater Universitatis Missouriensis and the *Silver-tongued Orator* are nicknames by which James Sidney Rollins has been designated.

He was known as *Pater Universitatis Missouriensis,*[1] or *Father of the University of Missouri,* in commemoration of his outstanding services in reorganizing the University of Missouri. at Columbia, Mo. He was instrumental in securing its recognition as the state university, in establishing an agricultural and mechanical college as a department of the University, and in securing a permanent endowment for the institution, by which the matriculation fee was greatly lessened.

Rollins' speeches were characterized by lucidity and fluency, and his manner of address was pleasing to his audiences, hence the name, *Silver-tongued Orator.*[1]

James Sidney Rollins was born at Richmond, Ky., on April 19, 1812, and died near Columbia, Mo., on January 9, 1888.

[1] *The National Cyclopaedia of American Biography* (James T. White and Company, New York, 1900) vol. 8, p. 182, 183.

Rollins College

The athletes of Rollins College at Winter Park, Fla., were designated the *Tars* [1] about 1920, because at that time the college authorities had two or three small government boats on a lake on the college grounds in connection with a naval training unit.

[1] A letter from Frederick H. Ward, Secretary of the Athletic Committee at Rollins College, Winter Park, Fla., June 25, 1935.

Rood, Ogden Nicholas

The sobriquet, the *Father of American Experimental Physics,*[1] was applied to Ogden Nicholas Rood because he was one of the first American physicists to engage in extensive and detailed experimental research work in physics. The thoroughness of Rood's investigations won for him his reputation as an authentic and reliable investigator. His most outstanding work related to the application of certain principles of physics in the fields of mechanics, optics, acoustics, and electricity. He wrote numerous articles dealing with his experiments in these subjects.

Ogden Nicholas Rood was born at Danbury, Conn., on February 3, 1831, and died at New York City, on November 12, 1902.

[1] *The National Cyclopaedia of American Biography* (James T. White and Company, New York, 1906) vol. 13, p. 507.

Roof Garden of Texas. See Alpine, Tex.

Roof of the Continent. See Rocky Mountains

Roof Top of Eastern America. See Great Smoky National Park

Rooney. See Lee, W. H. F.

Roosevelt, F. D. See Big Three

Roosevelt, Franklin Delano

Franklin Delano Roosevelt, thirty-second President of the United States, was nicknamed the *Boss, F.D.,* or *F. D. R., That Man in the White House,* the *Houdini in the White House,* the *Squire of Hyde Park,* and the *Sphinx.*

Roosevelt, F. D.—Continued

He was designated the *Boss*[1] by supporters of his New Deal policy in the United States Congress during his first administration. At the time he took office Congress delegated emergency powers and authority to Roosevelt in order to cope with the existing economic crisis, and he exerted a tremendous influence on Federal legislation, international affairs, and the actions of civic, financial and industrial groups throughout the country.

President Roosevelt's initials were habitually used in newspaper stories and headlines, and *F.D.* or *F.D.R.* was perhaps the most widely known short form of reference.

Roosevelt acquired nicknames from detractors as well as admirers in the course of twelve consecutive years in office. By the time of the 1934 congressional elections a good deal of dissension had arisen over the New Deal program of his first two years. Newspapers and financial, industrial, and business leaders hostile to his policies referred to him as *That Man in the White House.*[3] Dewey Short, Representative from Missouri, called him the *Houdini in the White House,*[2] probably referring to Roosevelt's seemingly miraculous ability to get out of difficult situations and to the vast public confidence he enjoyed, especially during his first administration when he was able to present fifteen pieces of major legislation for passage by Congress, "a record of . . . effort . . . that has no parallel in the history of American Presidents."[3]

President Roosevelt's family home was an estate in Hyde Park on the Hudson River in New York. He frequently referred to himself as a farmer and he was often called the *Squire of Hyde Park.*

In 1939 he was nicknamed the *Sphinx* because he refused to say whether or not he would seek to be reelected for a third term.

Franklin Delano Roosevelt was born at Hyde Park, New York, on January 30, 1882, and died at Warm Springs, Ga., on April 12, 1945, at the start of his fourth term of office.

[1] *Newsweek: The Magazine of News Significance,* Rockefeller Center, N.Y., December 26, 1938, p. 11.

[2] *The Senator,* Washington, D.C., February 18, 1939, col. 1, p. 15.

[3] *Current Biography, Who's News and Why, 1942,* ed. by Maxine Block (H. W. Wilson Company, New York, 1942) p. 709.

Roosevelt, James

James Roosevelt, the eldest son of Franklin Delano Roosevelt, was nicknamed the *Crown Prince of the New Deal*[1] and *Son Jimmy*[1] by newspapermen while he was his father's assistant and secretary during 1937 and 1938.

The former sobriquet was applied to James Roosevelt because, being the eldest son, hostile critics intimated that his father would use his influence to assist James in seeking to be elected president when President Roosevelt's second term of office expired in 1941. In the monarchical form of government the Crown Prince naturally succeeds his father. The latter nickname came into popular usage because President Roosevelt, as a fond and proud parent, spoke of James so frequently as "my son Jimmy."

On January 6, 1937, James Roosevelt was appointed administrative assistant to his father, and in July of that year became the President's press secretary. It was during this period when he was acting as a clearing house and coordinator of 23 Federal agencies, and receiving as many as 150 phone calls on a typical day, that *Time* magazine nicknamed him a *Modern Mercury.*[2]

Since August 1945, when his war service terminated, Roosevelt has interested himself in California politics. He sought the governorship there in 1950 but was defeated by the incumbent, Republican Governor Earl Warren.

[1] *Washington Herald,* Washington, D.C., April 21, 1938, col. 3, p. 1.

[2] *Current Biography, Who's News and Why, 1950,* edited by Anna Rothe, (H. W. Wilson Company, New York, 1951) p. 503-60

Roosevelt, Quentin

Quentin Roosevelt has been called *Quentin the Eagle*[1] because he died while fighting in the air. His father said of him that he "had fought in high air like an eagle, and, like an eagle, fighting had died."[1]

He was born at Washington, D.C., on November 19, 1897, and died in an airplane fight with the Germans near the village of Dormans, on the Marne river, in France, on July 14, 1918.

[1] *Jungle Roads and Other Trails of Roosevelt,* Daniel Henderson (E. P. Dutton and Company, New York, 1920) p. 213.

Roosevelt, Theodore

The following sobriquets were acquired by Theodore Roosevelt: *Bull Moose,* the *Driving Force,* the *Dynamo of Power, Four*

Eyes, Great White Chief, the Happy Warrior, Haroun-al-Roosevelt, the Hero of San Juan Hill, Man on Horseback, the Old Lion, Telescope Teddy, Theodore the Meddler, the Trust-buster, or the Trust-busting President, and the Typical American.

The nickname Bull Moose originated in June 1912, when Roosevelt, as the leader of the newly-organized Progressive Party and its candidate for the office of President of the United States, went to Chicago, Ill., to deliver his speech accepting the nomination. A number of newspaper reporters who interviewed him at the time of his arrival, noted that he appeared to be in excellent health, but remembering that he was facing a strenuous period of campaigning, asked him how he felt. Roosevelt assured them that he felt "like a bull moose." [1] This conversation, printed in the newspapers, caused his political opponents to attempt to ridicule him as a "bull moose" and the Progressive Party as the "bull moose party." Roosevelt's friends and the adherents of the Progressive Party, however, proudly accepted this nickname for him, declaring that the bull moose, a large male member of the deer family found in the extreme northwestern part of the United States, was one of the largest most powerful, most noble, and sturdiest of American animals. In 1912, during the presidential campaigning activities of the Progressives, Roosevelt was popularly called the Bull Moose, his party the Bull Moose Party, and its constitutents Bull Moosers.[2]

Because Roosevelt was such a forceful personality, and because he usually succeeded in getting people to cooperate with him in carrying out his ideas, he has been described as the Driving Force [3] and the Dynamo of Power.[3]

In 1883 Roosevelt bought an interest in the Elkhorn Ranch, near Medora, N.D., and spent some time there in order to improve his health. People in the vicinity of this ranch nicknamed him Four Eyes,[4] ridiculing the fact that he wore glasses. However, it is said that his conduct and common sense so won the respect of these people that the sobriquet came to be a symbol of their admiration for him.

When Roosevelt arrived at Mombasa on his East African hunting trip in 1909, the African natives designated him the Great White Chief,[5] the usual phrase for a white man who corresponded to a chief of their tribe in power and influence.

Bradley Gilman called Roosevelt the Happy Warrior [6] in allusion to the heroic figure of William Wordsworth's poem, The Character of the Happy Warrior, who fearlessly upheld the right and attacked the wrong. Roosevelt was comparable to this heroic character because during his administration from 1901 to 1909, he was a courageous and enthusiastic champion of things he considered right, and a militant prosecutor of what he considered wrongs and abuses in the administration of public service. Throughout his life, he continued to display these qualities of character. The sobriquet was also used to commemorate his active participation in the Spanish-American War in 1898, at which time Roosevelt organized and lead the famous Rough Riders.

While serving as one of New York City's Police Commissioners from 1894 to 1896, Theodore Roosevelt was nicknamed Haroun-al-Roosevelt [7] by the newspaper reporters of the day who knew that he personally inspected various sections of the city where crime and immorality flourished, in order to secure first-hand information and to see if the municipal police were executing their duties. This sobriquet was a humorous allusion to the renowned Haroun-al-Rashid, Caliph of Baghdad from 786 to 809, A.D., who personally investigated Baghdad in a similar manner and for similar reasons.

Because he led his Rough Riders to victory at the Battle of San Juan Hill during the Spanish-American War he has been designated the Hero of San Juan Hill.[8]

William Jennings Bryan called Roosevelt the Man on Horseback.[9] This appellation had once been given to George Ernest Jean Marie Boulanger, a cavalry officer prominent in the Franco-Prussian War of 1870. Aided by their splendid military records, both men became outstanding in the political activities of their respective countries. The Man on Horseback was an appropriate nickname for Roosevelt because he was very fond of riding horses and was often photographed on horseback.

The Old Lion [10] was an affectionate nickname applied to Theodore Roosevelt by his children. The children, themselves, had often been referred to as lion cubs. At the close of his presidential administration in 1909, Roosevelt went to East Africa on a hunting trip. During his sojourn there and upon his return to the United States, cartoonists made sport of his lion hunting in

Roosevelt, T.—Continued
the African jungles, picturing [11] him as conversing or fighting with the lions. These cartoons doubtless aided in perpetuating the sobriquet. On January 6, 1919, conveying the news of their father's death to his brother, one of Roosevelt's sons sent the message "The Old Lion is dead."

Soon after he went to the West, Roosevelt had his long guns fitted with small telescopes in order that he might do some accurate shooting at long range, hence the nickname *Telescope Teddy* [12] by the cowboys on his ranches in western North Dakota.

During his presidential administration from 1901 to 1909, Roosevelt made it his policy to investigate and intervene in such matters as railroad strikes, coal strikes, the adulteration of foods, the business dealing of trusts and monopolies, the activities of foreign countries, the preservation of public lands and natural resources, and the disclosures of corruption of breaches of trust in the administratiion of public service. His detractors in these affairs, particularly those connected with Wall Street, called him *Theodore the Meddler*.[13]

Theodore Roosevelt made it his policy during his administration to enforce the anti-trust laws and to regulate monopolies, hence he was popularly proclaimed the *Trust-buster*,[14] or the *Trust-busting President*.

Because of his interest in all phases of American life, his devotion to democracy, and his zest for the strenuous life, Theodore Roosevelt was called *The Typical American*.[8]

Theodore Roosevelt, the twenty-sixth President of the United States, was born at New York City, on October 27, 1858, and died at Sagamore Hill, N.Y., on January 6, 1919.

[1] *Roosevelt, the People's Champion for Human Rights Covering Every Phase of the Most Vital Questions of the Day, Including Biographies of Roosevelt and Johnson, Candidates for President and vice-President; The Platform; How Conventions Are Conducted; Great National Issues, Etc., Together with a Portrait Gallery of National Celebrities, Comprising Photo-type and Line Engravings of All Our Presidents and Progressive Statesmen, the Whole Forming a Complete Handbook of Political Information, Voter's Guide, Instructor, Etc.*, compiled by Jay Henry Mowbray (National Publishing Company, Philadelphia, 1912) p. 11.
"Great-heart," the Life Story of Theodore Roosevelt, Daniel M. Henderson (Neil MacIntyre) William Edwin Rudge, New York, 1919) p. 187.
[2] *Funk and Wagnalls New Standard Dictionary of the English Language* (Funk and Wagnalls Company, New York and London, 1933) p. 1610.
[3] *The Makers of America*, New Edition, Revised and Enlarged, Jane A. Woodburn and Thomas F. Moran (Longmans, Green and Company, New York and Boston, 1922) p. 310.

[4] *Seeing the Middle West*, John T. Faris (J. B. Lippincott Company, Philadelphia, 1923) p. 75.
[5] *Jungle Roads and Other Trails of Roosevelt*, Daniel Henderson (E. P. Dutton and Company, New York, 1920) p. 166.
[6] *Roosevelt: The Happy Warrior*, Bradley Gilman (Little, Brown and Company, Boston, 1921) p. 98, 132, 134, 148, 181, 328, 360.
[7] *Theodore Roosevelt, an Intimate Biography*, William Roscoe Thayer (Houghton Mifflin Company, New York and Boston, 1919) p. 103.
[8] *The Makers of America*, New Edition, Revised and Enlarged James A. Woodburn and Thomas F. Moran (Longmans, Green and Company, New York and Boston, 1922) p. 311, 314.
[9] *Pen Pictures of the Presidents*, Fred T. Wilson (Southwestern Company, Nashville, Tenn., 1932) p. 430.
Roosevelt: The Happy Warrior, Bradley Gilman (Little, Brown and Company, Boston, 1921) p. 163.
[10] *Theodore Roosevelt*, Edmund Lester Pearson (The Macmillan Company, New York, 1920) p. 159.
[11] *T.R. in Cartoon; Four Hundred Illustrations by Leading Cartoonists of the Daily and Weekly Press All Over the World*, collected and ed. by Raymond Gros (The Saalfield Publishing Company, New York and Chicago, 1910) p. 290-1, 292-3, 298.
[12] *Jungle Roads and Other Trails of Roosevelt*, Daniel Henderson (E. P. Dutton and Company, New York, 1920) p. 97.
[13] *T.R. in Cartoon; Four Hundred Illustrations by Leading Cartoonists of the Daily and Weekly Press All Over the World*, collected and ed. by Raymond Gros (The Saalfield Publishing Company, New York and Chicago, 1910) p. 21.
[14] *American History for Colleges*, David Saville Muzzey and John A. Krout (Ginn and Company, New York and London, 1933) p. 603.

Roper, Daniel Calhoun

The *Chief Executioner* [1] was a sobriquet applied to Daniel Calhoun Roper, the first Secretary of Commerce in the Cabinet of President Franklin Delano Roosevelt. He was frequently called upon to put into operation plans worked out by the President and other members of his administrative staff.

Daniel Calhoun Roper was born in Marlboro County, S.C., on April 1, 1867.

[1] *Washington and the Revolutionists: A Characterization of Recovery Policies and of the People Who Are Giving Them Effect*, Roger W. Babson (Harper and Brothers, New York and London, 1934) p. 198.

Rose. See Rosenman, S. I.

Rose Bowl. See Pasadena Stadium

Rose City. See Portland, Ore.

Rose Polytechnic Institute

The *Fighting Engineers* is the nickname given to the athletic teams of Rose Polytechnic Institute, at Terre Haute, Ind. Many of these athletes are engineering students.

Rosecrans, William Starke

During the Civil War, Brigadier General William Starke Rosecrans was affectionately called *Old Rosey* [1] by the soldiers under his command. *Rosey* is partly an abbreviation and partly a corruption of his surname.

William Starke Rosecrans was born at Kingston, Ohio, on September 6, 1819, and died near Redondo, Calif., on March 11, 1898.

[1] *The Story of the Sherman Brigade, the Camp, the March, the Bivouac, the Battle, and How "the Boys" Lived and Died during Four Years of Active Field Service*, Wilbur F. Hinman (Published by the Author, Alliance, Ohio, 1897) p. 320, 542.

Rosenman, Samuel Irving

Samuel Irving Rosenman was nicknamed *Sammy the Rose* and *The Rose* [1] by Governor Franklin Delano Roosevelt. Rosenman was counselor to the New York Governor from 1929 until 1932.

Judge Rosenman was a member of the New York legislature from 1922 until 1926, was appointed Justice of the New York Supreme Court in 1932, reappointed in 1933, and in the same year was elected to this office for the full fourteen year term. He was an ardent New Dealer, who exerted much silent influence on Roosevelt's program. During World War II, he was given several important assignments in the national defense program, and such government agencies as the Office of Production Management and the War Manpower Commission were organized as a result of his extensive investigation of national problems during wartime. His book, *Working with Roosevelt,* published in 1952, recalls many of his experiences as "Roosevelt's most intimate adviser." [2]

Samuel Irving Rosenman was born at San Antonio, Texas, on February 13, 1896.

[1] *The Courier-Journal*, Louisville, Ky., August 31, 1941, col. 4, p. 7.
[2] *Current Biography, Who's news and why, 1942*, ed. by Maxine Block, (H. W. Wilson Company, New York, 1942) p. 715-717.

Rosser, Thomas Lafayette

On October 5, 1864, Major General Thomas Lafayette Rosser arrived in the vicinity of Harrisburg, Va., in the Shenandoah Valley, with about six hundred mounted men and took over the command of Brigadier General Fitzhugh Lee's Division. Believing that the Confederate cause in the Shenandoah Valley would be successfully defended under the leadership of Rosser, the soldiers already stationed there nicknamed him the *Savior of the Valley*. [1]

Thomas Lafayette Rosser was born in Campbell County, Va., on October 15, 1836,

and died near Charlottesville, Va., on March 29, 1910.

[1] "General Sheridan" by Henry E. Davies, in *The Great Commanders Series*, ed. by James Grant Wilson (D. Appleton and Company, New York 1895) p. 176. *The Shenandoah Valley in 1864*, George E. Pond (Charles Scribner's Sons, New York, 1883) p. 203.

Rotten Cabbage Rebellion

The students who participated in it applied the sobriquet the *Rotten Cabbage Rebellion* [1] to a disturbance in 1807 at Harvard College in Cambridge, Mass. The students protested vigorously against the quality of the food [2] served to them in the college dining hall, and formally appealed to the college authorities to remedy the matter. Because action was delayed, the lower classmen after several days of rebellious conduct, pledged themselves to be guided in future regarding the food by the judgment of the senior class. Upon smelling and tasting the food served at one of the dinner meals, this group decided that it was unfit to eat and as a body arose and left the dining hall. Finally the majority of them apologized for their conduct, some of those who did not apologize were expelled, and the students returned to the college for their meals.

[1] *The National Cyclopaedia of American Biography* (James T. White and Company, New York, 1907) vol. 7, p. 182.
Bits of Harvard History, Samuel F. Batchelder (Harvard University Press, Cambridge, Mass., 1924) p. 138.
[2] *Harvard University: Universities and Their Sons, Harvard University; Its History, Influence, Equipment and Characteristics with Biographical Sketches and Portraits of Founders, Benefactors, Officers, and Alumni,* Joshua L. Chamberlain, Editor-in-chief (R. Herndon Company, Boston, 1900) p. 181.

Rough. See Carrigan, W. F.

Rough Riders

The *Rough Riders* [1] was the sobriquet given to the First Regiment of the United States Cavalry and to the Second Regiment of United States Volunteer Cavalry which fought in the Spanish-American War in 1898. The nickname was formerly applied to the riders of the Pony Express. The First Regiment consisted of about one thousand soldiers, under the command of Colonel Leonard Wood and Lieutenant Colonel Theodore Roosevelt. Roosevelt later became Colonel.

The term was applied to the regiments because the majority of the men composing them were from ranches in the western United States. Theodore Roosevelt, in his book *The Rough Riders,* [2] says that the public fastened the nickname upon the regi-

Rough Riders—Continued
ment, and that at first its bearers fought against its use. However, as the Division and Brigade Generals used the name in their formal correspondence concerning the regiments, as the people and the newspapers continued to use it, the soldiers finally accepted the nickname without further protest.

[1] *The Standard Reference Work for the Home, School, and Library* (Welles Brothers Publishing Company, Minneapolis, Minn., and Chicago, 1917) vol. 5, p. 534.
[2] *The Rough Riders*, Theodore Roosevelt (Charles Scribner's Sons, New York, 1899) p. 7.

Rough Riders. See Case School of Applied Science

Rough Riders. See Rider College

Round Head Regiment
During the Civil War, the One Hundredth Regiment of Pennsylvania Infantrymen was commonly known as the *Round Head Regiment,*[1] members of this regiment having been recruited in the southwestern part of Pennsylvania. This section was originally settled by *Round Heads* from England and by Scotch-Irish Covenanters, many of whom had left their respective countries as the result of the political revolution in England in 1646.

The *Round Heads* in England were supporters of Oliver Cromwell, and were so called because contrary to the prevailing fashion of wearing wigs, they chose to cut their hair short, revealing the natural contour of their heads.

[1] *History of Pennsylvania Volunteers, 1861-5; Prepared in Compliance with Acts of the Legislature*, Samuel P. Bates (B. Singerly, State Printer, Harrisburg, Pa., 1870) p. 553.

Round House George. See Lehman, George

Rovers. See Coloradans

Rowboat Johnson. See Johnson, J. M.

Rowe, Lynwood Thomas
During a baseball game between the Methodist and the Baptist ball teams at El Dorado, Ark., about 1927, some of the fans cried out, "Don't let that schoolboy strike you out." Ever since this incident, Lynwood Thomas Rowe has been called *Schoolboy Rowe.*[1]

He was born at Waco, Tex., on January 11, 1912, and pitched in major league baseball.

[1] *Who's Who in Major League Base Ball*, comp. by Harold (Speed) Johnson (Buxton Publishing Company, Chicago, 1933) p. 337.

Rowland, Clarence H.
Clarence H. Rowland, who became manager of The Chicago American League Baseball Company in 1914, was nicknamed *Pants*[1] while still a boy. During his youth in Platteville, Wis., he played baseball with the other boys of the town. Not financially able to buy uniforms, they played in the clothing they wore every day, and their parents complained about holes torn in their trousers during the sand-lot games. Young Rowland, in order to avoid unpleasantness, took an old pair of his father's trousers from the garret, rolled up the bottoms, and fastened them up with a string. While he was making a home run during an important sand-lot game the trousers became unfastened,[1] and he ran out of them; he has been nicknamed *Pants Rowland* ever since.

Clarence H. Rowland was born at Platteville, Wis., on February 12, 1879.

[1] *Baseball Magazine* (The Baseball Magazine Company, New York, 1917) p. 200, 248.

Roxey. See Crouch, J. A.

Royall, Anne Newport
Anne Newport Royall, a writer and traveler of the nearly nineteenth century, was noted for her vehemently stated opinions. She was ardently pro-Mason and anti-Evangelical and her position on certain issues acquired for her the nickname *Godless Anne Royall.*[1] She advocated among other things, Sunday mail delivery, no union of church and state, tolerance of Roman Catholics, and state rights in the issue of slavery. As editor of a small independent newspaper in Washington, D.C., she was especially noted for her ability to uncover graft in governmental departments.

She traveled over the United States extensively from 1824 to 1831, and wrote ten books describing people and places of interest visited. Although the violent expression of her likes and dislikes was often tiresome, students of the social history of the United States find her works a valuable source for research.[1]

Anne Newport Royall was born in Maryland on June 11, 1769, and died at Washington, D.C., on October 1, 1854.

[1] *Dictionary of American Biography under the Auspices of the American Council of Learned Societies*, ed. by Dumas Malone (Charles Scribner's Sons, New York, 1935) vol. 16, p. 205.

Rubber Arm. See Connally, G. W.

Rubber Capital of the United States. See Akron, Ohio

Rubber King. See Harter, D. W.

Rubber Stamp Congress

The Seventy-fourth Congress of the United States, convened on January 3, 1935, was frequently designated a *Rubber Stamp Congress* [1] by opponents of President Roosevelt's New Deal policies who objected to Congress' acquiescence in authorizing expenditures for the national recovery program.

It was believed that many of the bills had been framed by President Roosevelt or by his advisers in the *Brain Trust* before being presented to the legislative bodies for formal passage, and that they were given the stamp of approval without considered judgment.

[1] *The Washington Times*, Washington, D.C., July 20, 1935, col. 5, p. 2.

Rubber Wagons

In the first decade of the twentieth century when the Shoshoni Indians in Wyoming first saw the early automobiles in use, they called them *Rubber Wagons* [1] because the automobiles still somewhat resembled buggies or light wagons and the wheel-rims had rubber tires.

[1] *Washakie, an Account of Indian Resistance of the Covered Wagon and Union Pacific Railroad Invasions of Their Territory*, Grace Hammond Hebard (The Arthur H. Clark Company, Cleveland, Ohio, 1930) p. 275.

Rube. See Marquard, R. W.; Waddell, G. E.; Walberg, George

Ruel, Herold D.

Because he once fell in a muddy place when he was a youngster, *Muddy* [1] was the sobriquet given to Herold D. Ruel, who was born at St. Louis, Mo., on February 20, 1896, and who was a catcher in major league baseball.

[1] *Who's Who in Major League Base Ball*, comp. by Harold (Speed) Johnson (Buxton Publishing Company, Chicago, 1933) p. 338.

Ruffner, William Henry

The clergyman and educator, William Henry Ruffner, was often called the *Horace Mann of the South* [1] because he devoted a great deal of time and energy to the development of the public school system in the South. In 1870 he was elected State Superintendent of Education in Virginia, and drafted a system of public education which was enacted by the members of the General Assembly, and which was so practical that it was later used as a model in several other southern states. Horace Mann, who lived from 1796 to 1859, pioneered in reforming the state system of education in Massachusetts.

William Henry Ruffner was born at Lexington, Va., on February 11, 1824, and died at Asheville, N.C., on November 24, 1908.

[1] *Dictionary of American Biography under the Auspices of the American Council of Learned Societies*, ed. by Dumas Malone (Charles Scribner's Sons, New York, 1935) vol. 16, p. 219.

Ruggles, Benjamin

While he was a Senator from Ohio to the United States Congress from 1815 to 1833, Benjamin Ruggles became known as the *Wheel-horse of the Senate* [1] because of his dependability and efficiency during his long term of service.

Benjamin Ruggles was born at Abington, Conn., on February 21, 1783, and died at St. Clairsville, Ohio, on September 2, 1857.

[1] *Appleton's Cyclopaedia of American Biography*, ed. by James Grant Wilson and John Fiske (D. Appleton and Company, New York, 1888) vol. 5, p. 343.

Ruggles, John

The *Father of the Patent Office* [1] is the appropriate nickname given to John Ruggles. He was responsible for the establishment of the present Patent Office in the United States, which has served as a pattern for similar institutions in various foreign countries. On December 31, 1835, while he was a Senator from Maine to the United States Congress he presented a motion that a committee be appointed to investigate the conditions and affairs of the Patent Office then existing. The bill, signed by President Andrew Jackson on July 4, 1836, established the Modern Patent Office with its system of classified departments providing for the investigation of applications for United States patents.

Ruggles, John—Continued

John Ruggles was born at Westboro, Mass., on October 8, 1789, and died at Thomaston, Me., on June 20, 1874.

[1] *The National Cyclopaedia of American Biography* (James T. White and Company, New York, 1904) vol. 12, p. 230.

Run Forever Kolb. See Kolb, R. F.

Ruppert, Jacob, Sr.

Jacob Ruppert, Sr., was commonly known as the *Colonel, Four Straight Jake,*[1] and *Jake*[2] by businessmen and athletes. From 1889 until 1892 Rupert was aide-de-camp with the rank of colonel on the staff of Governor David Bennett Hill of New York. He was a Representative from the Fifteenth Congressional District of New York City to the United States Congress in 1899 until 1907, and manager of the Jacob Ruppert Brewery from 1888 until his death in 1939. In 1914, Colonel Ruppert and Colonel Tillinghast L. Huston of Havana, Cuba, bought the New York American League Baseball Company (Yankees) for $500,000, and in 1923, Colonel Ruppert bought his partners half interest in the club for $1,250,000.[3] The sobriquet, *Four Straight Jake,* was given to Ruppert by sports writers because the New York Yankees won the World Series in four straight games in 1927, 1928, 1932, 1937, and 1938. Colonel Ruppert is said to have liked this nickname better than any other.

Jacob Ruppert, Sr., was born at New York City on August 5, 1867, and died there on January 13, 1939.

[1] *Time: The Weekly Newsmagazine, Chicago,* January 23, 1939, col. 2, p. 34.

[2] *Washington Herald,* Washington, D. C., January 17, 1939, col. 3, 4, 5, 6 and 7, p. 11

[3] *The New York Times,* New York, June 1, 1923, col. 2, p. 15.

Rusk, Jeremiah McLain

While he was Secretary of Agriculture in President Benjamin Harrison's Cabinet from 1889 to 1893, Jeremiah McLain Rusk was affectionately nicknamed *Uncle Jerry*[1] by the general public in admiration of his personal integrity and wit.

Jeremiah McLain Rusk was born at Malta, Ohio, on June 17, 1830, and died near Virginia, Wis., on November 21, 1893.

[1] *Twenty Years of the Republic, 1885-1905,* Harry Thurston Peck (Dodd, Mead and Company, New York, 1907) p. 174.

Russell, Joseph

Joseph Russell, a merchant and shipowner of the eighteenth century, was generally known as *The Duke.*[1] The land on which New Bedford, Massachusetts, was built was originally Russell's farm. He had apportioned the land into lots and sold them to the settlers. The family name of the English dukes of Bedford was Russell, and Joseph Russell was, therefore, nicknamed *The Duke.* He was the founder of the whaling industry of Dartmouth, Mass., and was a pioneer merchant and shipowner.

Joseph Russell was born in Dartmouth township in the Massachusetts Bay Colony, on October 8, 1719, and died at Dartmouth, Mass., on October 16, 1804.

[1] *Dictionary of American Biography under the Auspices of the American Council of Learned Societies,* ed. by Dumas Malone (Charles Scribner's Sons, New York, 1935) vol. 16, p. 246.

Russell, William Eustis

William Eustis Russell was elected Mayor of Cambridge, Mass., at the age of twenty-eight and was called the *Boy Mayor,* or *Billie the Kid.* He served as mayor from 1885 to 1887.

Russell was born at Cambridge, Mass., on January 6, 1857, and died at Little Palos, Quebec, Canada, on July 16, 1896.

[2] *U.S. "Snap Shots": An Independent, National, and Memorial Encyclopedia. . . ,* Oliver McKee (A. M. Thayer and Company, Boston, 1892) p. 241.

Russell, William Henry

William Henry Russell, a politician and California pioneer, was popularly known as *Owl Russell.*[1] One evening he mistook a chorus of hoot-owls for a number of people asking persistently, "Who are you? Who are you?" Russell, who was egotistical by nature and somewhat bombastic, is said to have shouted in answer, " 'Colonel William Russell of Kentucky—a bosom friend of Henry Clay!' " His friends called him *Owl* from then on. From 1841 until 1845 he was United States Marshal of the District of Missouri. In 1846 he emigrated to California where he remained until about 1854, and took an active part in the political growth of that state.

William Henry Russell was born in Nicholas County, Ky., on October 9, 1802, and died at Washington, D.C., on October 13, 1873.

[1] *Dictionary of American Biography under the Auspices of the American Council of Learned Societies,* ed. by Dumas Malone (Charles Scribner's Sons, New York, 1935) vol. 16, p. 252.

Rustic Bard. See Dinsmoor, Robert

Rustlers

To rustle is an Americanism used in the general sense of to forage around for or to put forth effort to collect something.[1]

On the western plains of the United States cattle thieves are called *Rustlers*.[2]

The *Rustlers War*,[3] the conflict between the cattle owners and the thieves, lasted from about 1881 until 1890.

[1] *The American Language Supplement II,* H. L. Mencken (Alfred A. Knopf, New York, 1948) p. 677.
[2] *A New English Dictionary,* ed. by James A. H. Murray (The Clarendon Press, Oxford England) vol. 8. p. 929.
[3] *The Southwestern Historical Quarterly, July 1916 to April, 1917,* Editors, Eugene C. Barker and Herbert E. Bolton (The Texas State Historical Association, Austin, Tex., 1917) vol. 20, p. 11.

Rustler's War. See *Rustlers*

Ruth, George Herman

George Herman Ruth, who established a record as the greatest long-distance hitter in baseball, was known to the public as *Babe Ruth, Bambino, The Mighty Bambino,* the *Sultan of Swat* and the *Idol of the American Boy.*

Ruth joined the Baltimore Orioles baseball team in 1914. Coach Steinman, introducing him to his new teammates, said, "Boys, here's Jack's new Babe," and it is said Ruth's most famous nickname originated then and there.[1] *Bambino* is the diminutive of the Italian *bambo,* meaning baby. Ruth was described as the *Sultan of Swat* [1] by sports writers because of his talent for whacking the ball into the uncharted distances beyond the ballpark. He was virtually the *Idol of the American Boy* [2] because· of his ability as a baseball player and because he himself was always mindful of his duty to his younger public.

George Herman Ruth was born in Baltimore, Md., on February 7, 1894, and died July 29, 1948.

[1] *Who's Who in Major League Base Ball,* comp. by Harold (Speed) Johnson (Buxton Publishing Company, Chicago, 1933) p. 341.
[2] *Babe Ruth, the Idol of the American Boy,* Daniel M. Daniel (Whitman Publishing Company, Racine, Wis., 1930) p. 108.

Rye, New York

Rye, in Westchester County, has often been called the *Border Town*.[1] Founded in 1660 on the border line separating the present states of Connecticut and New York, there was for many years a continual controversy over its boundary line, with the result that several times during its existence, Rye has been located at one time in Connecticut, and at another in New York.

[1] *The Bar of Rye Township, Westchester County, New York, an Historical and Biographical Record, 1600-1918,* Arthur Russell Wilcox (The Knickerbocker Press, New York, 1918) p. 7, 14-19.

Ryle, John

John Ryle has been designated the *Father of the Silk Industry*.[1] He is accredited with having been the first American manufacturer to market sewing silk on spools. The silk manufacturing firm of Murray and Ryle, Paterson, N.J., has contributed much to the development of the American silk manufacturing industry.

John Ryle was born in England, on October 22, 1817, and died there.

[1] *Paterson and Its Environment: History of Paterson and Its Environs (The Silk City),* William Nelson and Charles A. Shriner (Lewis Historical Publishing Company, New York and Chicago, 1920) vol. 1, p. 340-2.

S

Sabath, Adolph Joachim

Adolph Joachim Sabath, congressmen from Illinois who served under eight consecutive presidents of the United States, was nicknamed the *Dean of the House* [1] by his colleagues in the House of Representatives.

Sabath came to America from Zabori, Bohemia, in 1881. He was admitted to the bar of Illinois in 1892, and began to practice law in Chicago. He was made a justice of the peace in Chicago in 1895 and was judge of a municipal court there from 1897 to 1907. He preferred the title of "Judge" even after he became a congressman.[2]

In 1907 he was elected a Democratic Representative from Illinois. He was the first representative in Congress in history to win election to twenty-four consecutive terms.

Adolph Joachim Sabath was born at Zabori, Bohemia, on April 4, 1866, and died November 6, 1952, a few days after his election to the Eighty-third Congress.

[1] An interview with Captain Victor Hunt Harding, Secretary of the National Democratic Congress Reelection Committee, Washington, D. C., April 10, 1939.
[2] *Current Biography, Who's News and Why, 1946,* ed. by Anna Rothe, (The H. W. Wilson Company, New York, 1947) p. 529.

Sabrinas. See Amherst College

Sachem. See Hillhouse, William

Sacramento, California
Sacramento has been designated the *Golden City* [1] probably because of the beauty of the city and its surroundings, and because it is the capital of California, the *Golden State.*

[1] *A Book of Nicknames,* John Goff (Courier-Journal Job Printing Company, Louisville, Ky., 1892) p. 16.

Sad Sam. See Jones, S. P.

Sage of America. See Franklin, Benjamin

Sage of Anacostia. See Douglass, Frederick

Sage of Ashland. See Clay, Henry; Lee, Henry

Sage of Auburn. See Seward, W. H.

Sage of Chappaqua. See Greeley, Horace

Sage of Concord. See Alcott, A. B.; Emerson, R. W.

Sage of Emporia. See White, W. A.

Sage of Gramercy Park. See Tilden, S. J.

Sage of Greystone. See Tilden, S. J.

Sage of Happy Valley. See Taylor, A. A.

Sage of Hickory Hill. See Watson, T. E.

Sage of Kinderhook. See Van Buren, Martin

Sage of Lindenwald. See Van Buren, Martin

Sage of Log Hall. See Philips, M. W.

Sage of McDuffie. See Watson, T. E.

Sage of Monticello. See Jefferson, Thomas

Sage of Montpelier. See Madison, James

Sage of Mt. Vernon. See Washington, George

Sage of Nininger. See Donnelly, Ignatius

Sage of Pittsfield. See Dawes, H. L.

Sage of Potato Hill. See Howe, E. W.

Sage of Princeton. See Cleveland, Grover

Sage of Roanoke. See Randolph (of Roanoke), John

Sage of Sinnissippi. See Lowden, F. O.

Sage of Springfield. See Lincoln, Abraham

Sage of the Hermitage. See Jackson, Andrew

Sage of the Verduga Hills. See McGroarty, J. S.

Sage of Tishomingo. See Murray, W. H.

Sage of Uvalde. See Garner, J. N.

Sage of Walden Pond. See Thoreau, H. D.

Sage of Walpole. See Bird, F. W.

Sage of Wheatland. See Buchanan, James

Sage State. See Nevada

Sagebrush State. See Nevada; Wyoming

Sagehen State. See Nevada

Sagehens. See Nevadans; Pomona College; University of Nevada

Sailor Town. See Norfolk, Va.

Sailor's Bible
Stephen B. Luce's *Textbook of Seamanship* has been nicknamed the *Sailor's Bible* [1] because it has been a standard text in schools

concerned with teaching marine navigation, and has been looked upon by sailors as the highest source of authority on nautical information.

[1] *Fighting Bob Evans,* Edwin A. Falk (Jonathan Cape and Harrison Smith, New York, 1931) p. 39.

Saint Benedict's College

Ravens[1] is the nickname given to the athletic teams of Saint Benedict's College, situated at Atchison, Kans., in 1928 by Bob Schmidt[2] and Reverend Maurus Kennedy, O.S.B.[2] Saint Benedict, the founder of the Benedictine Order was reputed to have been fed by a raven while he was hiding in a cave at Subiaco, Italy, after he had fled from Rome.

[1] A communication from Larry Mullins, Director of Athletics at Saint Benedict's College, Atchison, Kans., July 17, 1935.
[2] A communication from G. H. Mitchell, Senior, Director of Athletics at Saint Augustine's College, Raleigh, N.C., July 2, 1935.

St. Cloud, Minnesota

St. Cloud is termed the *Granite City*[1] because there are many large granite quarries in its immediate vicinity.

[1] *The Development of the Twin Cities (Minneapolis and St. Paul) as a Metropolitan Market: A Thesis Submitted to the Faculty of the Graduate School of the University of Minnesota in Partial Fulfillment of the Requirements for the Degree of Doctor of Philosophy,* Mildred Lucile Martsough (The University of Minnesota Press, Minneapolis, Minn., 1925) p. 189.
My Minnesota, Antoinette E. Ford (Lyons and Carnahan, New York and Chicago, 1929) p. 373, 374.

Saint Edward's Night Hawks. See Saint Edward's University

Saint Edward's Tigers. See Saint Edward's University

Saint Edward's University

The *Saint Edward's Tigers* and the *Saint Edward's Night Hawks* are nicknames attributed to the athletic teams of Saint Edward's University, at Austin, Tex. *Saint Edward's Tigers*[1] was originated by Jack Chevigny,[1] Coach of Athletics at the University in 1933.

Saint Edward's Night Hawks[1] was originated by John *One Play* O'Brien,[1] Head Athletic Coach at the University, because practically all the athletic games at Saint Edward's University are played at night.[1]

[1] A communication from John O'Brien, Head Coach of Athletics at Saint Edward's University, Austin, Tex., November 21, 1935.

Saint Francis of Methodism. See Asbury, Francis

Saint Francis of Presbyterianism. See Makemie, Francis

St. Jerome. See Edmunds, G. F.

St. John, William Pope

The contemporaries of William Pope St. John designated him *The Apostle of Free Coinage for Silver*[1] because he was conspicuous among bankers for his earnestness in advocating the equally free and unlimited coinage of gold and silver in the United States.

William Pope St. John was born at Mobile, Ala., on February 19, 1948, and died there on January 24, 1897.

[1] *The National Cyclopaedia of American Biography* (James T. White and Company, New York, 1899) vol. 2, p. 439.

Saint John's River. See *American Nile*

Saint John's University, Minnesota

Fighting Johnnies and the *Johnnies* are sobriquets given to the athletic teams of Saint John's University, at Collegeville, Minn. The nickname, *Fighting Johnnies,*[1] was attributed to them for a while because "of their inability to win games in the face of continual close defeats."[1]

[1] A communication from Alcuin Deutsch, President of Saint John's University, Collegeville, Minn., November 19, 1935.

Saint John's University, New York

The athletic teams of Saint John's University, at Brooklyn, N.Y., are popularly designated the *Redmen.*[1] College authorities have no record of the origin of the sobriquet.

[1] A communication from Thomas F. Ryan, President of Saint John's University, Brooklyn, New York, November 21, 1935.

Saint Joseph's College

The sobriquet, the *Hawks,*[1] was selected by the students comprising the athletic teams of Saint Joseph's College, at Philadelphia, Pa., in 1928.

[1] A communication from E. A. Thomas, Director of Athletics at Saint Joseph's College, Philadelphia, Pa., June 18, 1935.

St. Louis, Missouri

St. Louis has been called the *Future Great City of the World,* the *Great River City,* *Memphis of the American Nile,* the *Mound City,* and the *Solid City.*

St. Louis, Mo.—Continued

About 1870 the optimistic outlook of its citizens in regard to its future growth and development caused them to designate it the *Future Great City of the World*.[1] In 1875 a book entitled *"Saint Louis: The Future Great City of the World,"*[2] by L. U. Reavis set forth arguments to prove that this city had great prospects. It is today a major transportation center, one of the world's largest raw-fur markets, and an important market for livestock, grain, wool, and lumber.[3]

St. Louis is called the *Great River City*[4] because it is located on the Mississippi River, the largest in America.

H. W. Brackenridge, in his articles entitled "Views of Louisiana," collected and published in book form in 1817, predicted that this city, on account of its location and its importance as a distributing center of merchandise and supplies to the traders of the North and the West, and its position as a probable outlet for commodities to the West Indies by means of its water transportation facilities, would become the *Memphis of the American Nile*,[5] thus providing the city with one of its early nicknames.

It is given the sobriquet, *Mound City*,[6] because it was founded upon a site formerly inhabited by the Indian mound builders, remains of their works being still in evidence.[7]

St. Louis has been termed the *Solid City*[8] because its financial and economic structure has remained relatively unaffected during periods of financial panic and depression.

[1] *Seeing the Middle West*, John T. Faris (J. B. Lippincott Company, Philadelphia, 1923) p. 131.

[2] *Saint Louis: The Future Great City of the World*, Biographical Edition, L. U. Reavis (Gray, Baker and Company, St. Louis, Mo., 1875) p. 79-128.

[3] *The Columbia Lippincott Gazetteer of the World*, ed. by Leon E. Seltzer, (Columbia University Press, New York, 1952) p. 1639.

[4] *Little Journeys in America*, Rose Henderson (The Southern Publishing Company, Dallas, Tex., 1922) p. 178.

[5] *Views of Louisiana; Containing Geographical, Statistical and Historical Notices of That Vast and Important Portion of America*, H. W. Brackenridge, Esquire (Schaeffer and Maund, Baltimore, Md., 1817) p. 224.

[6] *Americanisms; The English of the New World*, M. Schele De Vere (Charles Scribner and Company, New York, 1872) p. 665.

[7] *Mound Builders of Illinois, Descriptive of Certain Mounds and Village Sites in the American Bottoms and Along the Kaskaskia and Illinois Rivers*, Addison J. Thropp (Call Printing Company, East St. Louis, Ill., 1928) p. 76.

[8] *Historic Towns of the Western States*, ed. by Lyman P. Powell (G. P. Putnam's Sons, New York and London, 1901) p. 333.

Saint Louis American League Baseball Company

The Saint Louis American League Baseball Company's team was nicknamed *Saint Louis Browns*[1] because brown caps and stockings were part of their uniforms. In September 1953 the American League approved the transfer of the team's franchise to Baltimore, Md., and it was announced that the *Saint Louis Browns* would henceforth be called the *Baltimore Orioles*.[2] In taking this name they were honoring the original *Baltimore Orioles* who, in the 1890's, made a reputation as an aggressive colorful ball team.

[1] *Balldom: "The Britannica of Baseball," Comprising Growth of the Game in Detail; a Complete History of the National and American Leagues; First and Only Authentic Chronology Ever Published; Voluminous Records and Absolutely Accurate Statistics; Fascinating Facts for Fans of America's Greatest Sport from 1845 to 1914*, George L. Moreland (Balldom Publishing Company, New York, 1914) p. 24.

[2] *New York Times*, (New York City, September 30, 1953) p. 1.

Saint Louis Browns. See Saint Louis American League Baseball Company

Saint Louis Cardinals. See Saint Louis National League Baseball Club

Saint Louis National League Baseball Club

The teammates of the Saint Louis National League Baseball Club were dubbed the *Saint Louis Cardinals*[1] soon after becoming members of the League in 1892 because scarlet caps and stockings are a part of their uniform.

See also Gas House Gang.

[1] *Balldom: "The Britannica of Baseball," Comprising Growth of the Game in Detail; a Complete History of the National and American Leagues; First and Only Authentic Chronology Ever Published; Voluminous Records and Absolutely Accurate Statistics; Fascinating Facts for Fans of America's Greatest Sport from 1845 to 1914*, George L. Moreland (Balldom Publishing Company, New York 1914) p. 24.

Saint Louis University

The athletes of Saint Louis University, at St. Louis, Mo., were nicknamed the *Billikens*[1] by sports writers in 1911. One day at team practice a sports writer for the *St. Louis Post Dispatch*, said that Coach Johnny Bender, "who had a round, moon-shaped face,"[1] looked like a billiken. Other sports writers took up the expression and applied it to the members of the team, and the nickname has been in constant use ever since.

A billiken is a squat, smiling, comic figure used as a mascot.

[1] A letter from Robert L. Finch, Business Manager of Athletics at Saint Louisc University, Saint Louis, Mo., June 18, 1935.

Saint Mary's College, California

The sports editor of the *San Francisco Call-Bulletin* in 1926 gave the nickname the *Galloping Gaels* to the athletic teams of Saint Mary's College, at Saint Mary's College, Calif.

Saint Mary's College, Minnesota

The *Redmen* is the sobriquet given to the athletes of Saint Mary's College, at Winona, Minn.

Saint Mary's University of San Antonio

In 1924 the members of the student body selected the nickname, *Rattlers,*[1] for the athletic teams of Saint Mary's University of San Antonio, at San Antonio, Tex., because rattlesnakes are prevalent "in the mesquite brush" in that section of Texas.

[1] A communication from Alfred H. Rabe, S. M. President of Saint Mary's University of San Antonio, San Antonio, Tex., November 20, 1935.

Saint Nicks. See College of the City of New York

Saint Norbert College

The athletic teams of Saint Norbert College, at West De Pere, Wis., were called *Green Knights*[1] in 1911 by the coach of athletics at that time. The insignia of the college depicts a knight's head,[1] probably that of St. Norbert, who was a nobleman of the early twelfth century, and the college colors are green and gold.[3]

[1] A communication from Reverend M. J. Whirdt, Director of Athletics at St. Norbert College, West De Pere, Wis., November 19, 1935.

Saint Olaf College

The members of the athletic teams of Saint Olaf College, situated at Northfield, Minn., are designated the *Oles*[1] and the *Vikings*[1] because "the majority of the students are of Scandinavian ancestry. *Ole* is one of the forms of the Norwegian name *Olaf*

[1] A letter from George Weida Spohn of Saint Olaf College, Northfield, Minn., November 21, 1935.

St. Paul, Minnesota

St. Paul possesses three sobriquets; *Gateway to the Northwest, Gem City,* and *North Star City.* It is called the *Gateway to the Northwest*[1] because it is located near the head of the Mississippi River and is a commercial, industrial, and transportation center, served by several air lines and numerous railroads.[2]

St. Paul is designated the *Gem City*[3] because of its beautiful situation at the head of the navigable[4] waters of the Mississippi River, and because of its manufacturing, packing, and industrial activities. The nickname *North Star City*[5] alludes to its being the capital of Minnesota, the *North Star State.*

[1] *Saint Paul, Location-Development-Opportunity,* F. C. Miller (Webb Book Publishing Company, St. Paul, Minn., 1928) p. 109, 175.

[2] *The Encyclopaedia Britannica,* Fourteenth Edition (Encyclopaedia Britannica, Inc., New York, 1932) vol. 19, p. 851.

[3] *A Book of Nicknames,* John Goff (Courier-Journal Job Printing Company, Louisville, Ky., 1892) p. 16.

[4] *King's Handbook of the United States,* planned and ed. by Moses King, text by M. F. Sweetser (The Matthews-Northrup Company, Buffalo, N.Y., 1895) p. 431.

[5] *Manual of Useful Information,* comp. under the direction of J. C. Thomas (The Werner Company, Chicago, 1893) p. 23.

St. Paul and Minneapolis, Minnesota

The *Twin City,*[1] *Twin Cities,*[1] the *Dual Cities,*[1] and the *Twins*[1] are sobriquets given to St. Paul and Minneapolis because they are adjacent to each other, their common boundary line often running down the middle of the street. Each city, however, possesses its own municipal government. The nickname, *Twin City,* is attributed to President William Howard Taft[1] who, while visiting St. Paul in 1909, proposed the name when he suggested that St. Paul and Minneapolis combine into one unit.

[1] *History of St. Paul and Vicinity: A Chronicle of Progress and a Narrative Account of the Industries, Institutions and People of the City, and Its Tributary Territory,* Henry A. Castle (The Lewis Publishing Company, Chicago and New York, 1912) vol. 2, p. 639.

Saint Peter's College

Peacocks,[1] was the nickname attributed in 1930 by the Dean of the College to the athletic teams of Saint Peter's College, at Jersey City, N.J. The seal of the college has a peacock emblem on it, and "the first proprietor of the land now occupied by the college was Lord Michael Pauw," Pauw meaning peacock in Dutch.

[1] A communication from Joseph S. Dinneen, President of Saint Peter's College, Jersey City, N.J., November 22, 1935.

St. Petersburg, Florida

St. Petersburg, a popular winter resort on Tampa Bay, is widely known as the *Sunshine City*.[1] This nickname originated in connection with a pledge made on September 1, 1910, by Lew B. Brown, publisher of the *St. Petersburg Independent,* to the effect that he would distribute gratis all copies of his newspaper on any day on which the sun did not shine. From that date until January 1, 1924, the papers were given away only seventy-one times.

[1] *History of St. Petersburg, Historical and Biographical,* Karl H. Grismer (The Tourist News Publishing Company, St. Petersburg, Fla., 1924) p. 35.

Saint Procopius College

The athletic teams of Saint Procopius College, at Lisle, Ill., are designated *Cardinals*[1] because they "dress in cardinal uniforms for all major sports."[1] Sports writers originated the nickname about 1921.

[1] A letter from Robert F. Mastny, Director of Athletics at Saint Procopius College, Lisle, Ill., November 17, 1935.

Saints. See Utah Inhabitants

Salad Bowl of America

Salinas Valley in Monterey County, Calif., is widely known as the *Salad Bowl of America*.[1] Great quantities of lettuce are grown in this section.

[1] *The Literary Digest* (Funk and Wagnalls Company, New York) October 10, 1936, p. 5.

Salary Grab

In 1872 the members of the Forty-second Congress voted to increase their salaries from $5000 to $7500, and to make the act retroactive so that each member would receive $5000 in back pay. Public sentiment was already against many of the congressmen, as they had been accused of corrupt practices and fraud, and the act increasing their compensation was indignantly called the *Salary Grab*.[1]

[1] "Division and Reunion, 1829-1909" by Woodrow Wilson, in *Epochs of American History,* ed. by Albert Bushnell Hart (Longmans, Green and Company, New York and London, 1912) p. 280.

A History of Our Country: A Textbook for Schools, Oscar H. Cooper, Harry F. Estill, and Leonard Limmon (Ginn and Company, Boston and London, 1895) p. 408.

Salem, Massachusetts

Salem is known as the *City of Peace,* the *City of Witches,* the *Witchcraft City,* and the *Paradise of New England*. It is called the *City of Peace*[1] because its name is a variant spelling of the Arabic *salaam,* meaning peace.[2] It was formerly nicknamed the *City of Witches*[3] or *Witchcraft City*[3] because of its connection with the New England witchcraft hysteria of 1692 which resulted in the execution of approximately twenty people.[4]

Salem, the second oldest town in Massachusetts, has been called the *Paradise of New England*.[5] It was partially founded by colonists from other settlements in the state who had fled from previously-established places of abode on account of overlapping claims, jealousies, and other causes of disagreement or dissention. A group of colonists, under the leadership of John Endicott, as governor, in 1628 reinforced the few settlers who had previously fled there, and in this manner the settlement became permanent. The sobriquet supposedly signified that the settlers had found in Salem a place of safety from the discord of their former homes.

[1] *A Book of Nicknames,* John Goff (Courier-Journal Job Printing Company, Louisville, Ky., 1892) p. 16.

[2] *A New History of Old Salem, and the Towns Adjacent—Viz.: Danvers, Beverly, Marblehead, and Lynn,* Ralph Noter, Esq. (Bookstore of John P. Jewett, Salem, Mass., 1842) p. 3.

[3] *Americanisms—New and Old,* John S. Farmer (Privately Printed by Thomas Poulter and Sons, London, 1889) p. 149.

[4] *Historical Collections, Being a General Collection of Interesting Facts, Traditions, Biographical Sketches, Anecdotes, Etc., Relating to the History and Antiquity of Every Town in Massachusets, with Geographical Descriptions,* John Warner Barber (Dorr, Howland and Company, Worcester, Mass., 1839) p. 221.

Historical Sketch of Salem, 1626 to 1879, Charles S. Osgood and H. M. Batchelder (Essex Institute, Salem, Mass., 1879) p. 34.

[5] *Commonwealth History of Massachusetts: Colony of Massachusetts Bay, (1605-1689),* ed. by Albert Bushnell Hart (The States History Company, New York, 1927) vol. 1, p. 19.

Salem College

Salem Tigers, the *Seven Days,* and the *Tenmilers* are sobriquets given to the athletic teams of Salem College, at Salem, W.Va. The first nickname[1] perhaps alludes to their aggressive manner. The *Seven Days,*[1] commemorates the fact that the college is owned and operated by the Seventh Day Adventists. The *Tenmilers,*[1] alludes to the fact that the college is in the Tenmile District of Harrison County, W.Va.

[1] A communication from W. J. Griffith, Director of Publicity at Salem College, Salem, W.Va., November 20, 1935.

Salem Tigers. See Salem College

Salinas Valley, California. See Salad Bowl of America

Salt Boilers

In 1862, while the One Hundred and Forty-ninth Regiment of New York Volunteer Infantry were encamped at Fairfax Station, Va., they were nicknamed the *Salt Boilers* [1] by the One Hundred and Thirty-seventh Regiment of New York Volunteer Infantry because the majority of the men composing the former unit were from Syracuse, N.Y., noted for its salt boiling works.

[1] *Memoirs of the 149th Regiment of the New York Volunteer Infantry,* Captain George Knapp Collins (Published by the author, Syracuse, New York, 1891) p. 75.

Salt City. See Syracuse, N.Y.

Salt Lake City, Utah

Salt Lake City is termed the *City of the Saints*, the *Mormon City*, and the *Mormon's Mecca*. The city was founded by members of the Church of the Latter-Day Saints or Mormons, hence the name *City of the Saints*.[1]

It is designated the *Mormon City* [2] and the *Mormon's Mecca* [3] because it is the home of the Mormon Church and is thus the source of authority to Mormons.

[1] *Westward by Rail: A Journey to San Francisco and Back and a Visit to the Mormons,* Second Edition, W. F. Rae (Longmans, Green, and Company, London, 1871) p. 98.
[2] *Manual of Useful Information,* comp. under the direction of J. C. Thomas (The Werner Company, Chicago, 1893) p. 22.
[3] *Seventy Years on the Frontier: Alexander Majors' Memoirs of a Lifetime on the Border,* with a preface by Buffalo Bill (General W. F. Cody), ed. by Colonel Prentiss Ingraham (Rand McNally and Company, Chicago and New York, 1893) p. 63.

Salt Lake State. See Utah

Saltine Warriors. See Syracuse University

Salty. See Parker, F. J.

Sam. See Grant, U. S.

Sam Adams Regiments

Following the Boston Massacre on March 5, 1770, Samuel Adams was made chairman of a committee appointed by Bostonians to inform Governor Thomas Hutchinson and his council that they had voted to have the two regiments of British soldiers, the Fourteenth and the Twenty-ninth Regiments, removed from within the town limits. The Governor endeavored to effect a compromise and to have one regiment left in Boston, but Adams insisted on the removal of "both regiments or none" and urged the people of Boston to insist likewise until Hutchinson finally yielded. These two groups of British soldiers were thereafter humorously called the *Sam Adams Regiments* [1] the nickname having been originally applied to them by Lord Frederick North, Prime Minister of England during the Revolutionary War.

[1] *Metropolitan Boston, a Modern History,* Albert P. Langtry, Editor-in-chief (Lewis Historical Publishing Company, Inc., New York, 1929) vol. 1, p. 189.
The National Cyclopaedia of American Biography (James T. White and Company, New York, 1898) vol. 1, p. 107.

Sam the Maltster. See Adams, Samuel

Same Old Coon. See Clay, Henry

Same Old Mose. See Weinberger, Moses

Same Young Mose. See Weinberger, Moses

Sammy the Rose. See Rosenman, S. I.

Sams

The members of the American or *Know-nothing Party*, being intensely nationalistic, were often called *Sams* [1] because they professed continually their love for *Uncle Sam*.

[1] *History of Alabama and Her People,* Albert Burton Moore (The American Historical Society, Inc., New York and Chicago, 1927) vol. 1, p. 273.

Samuel Adams of New Jersey. See Fisher, Hendrick

Samuel Adams of North Carolina. See Harnett, Cornelius

Samuel the Publican. See Adams, Samuel

San Angelo, Texas

San Angelo is nicknamed the *City of the Angel*.[1] San Angelo, laid out in 1869 by B. J. DeWitt, was named by him in honor of his sister-in-law, Angela, who was a nun.

[1] *Flashlights on Texas,* Lillie Terrell Shaver and Willie Williamson Rogers (A. C. Baldwin and Sons, Austin, Tex., 1928) p. 125.

San Antonio, Texas

San Antonio is nicknamed the *Alamo City*, the *Cradle of Texas Liberty*, the *Mission City* and the *West Point of the Air*.

It is designated the *Alamo City* [1] and the *Cradle of Texas Liberty* [2] because it is the site of the historic battle of the Alamo of 1836,[3] in which the Mexican forces overpowered and massacred the Texan defenders of the Alamo garrison, thus inspiring the battle cry of the Texan struggle for independence, "Remember the Alamo!"

San Antonio is widely known as the *Mission City* [4] because of its many old missions, founded by the Franciscan Friars when Texan territory was still under Spanish and Mexican rule.

Randolph Field, the *West Point of the Air*,[5] is near by and the city has become associated with the nickname as a number of the largest military airfields in the United States are also in the vicinity.

[1] *A book of Nicknames*, John Goff (Courier-Journal Job Printing Company, Louisville, Ky., 1892) p. 15.
[2] *The Geography of Texas, Physical and Political*, Revised Edition, Frederick William Simonds (Ginn and Company, New York and Boston, 1914) p. 157.
[3] *Texas Under Many Flags*, Clarence R. Wharton, *Texas Biography* by a special staff of writers (The American Historical Society, Inc., New York and Chicago, 1930) vol. 1, p. 259-68.
[4] *Flashlights on Texas*, Lillie Terrell Shaver and Willie Williamson Rogers (A. C. Baldwin and Sons, Austin, Tex., 1928) p. 41-3.
[5] *Compton's Pictured Encyclopedia*, F. E. Compton and Company Chicago, 1947, vol. 13, p. 20.

San Carlos, Arizona

San Carlos, a settlement in Pinal County, at the junction of the Gila and San Carlos rivers was in 1882 the agency of the White Mountain Indian Reservation. The settlement was called *Hell's Forty Acres* [1] by the soldiers because it was extremely hot, dry, dusty, devoid of vegetation, and insect-ridden.

In 1930 [2] the original site was abandoned, being covered by the backwaters of the Coolidge Lake Reservoir, and the Indians were removed to Rice, renamed San Carlos, in nearby Gila County.

[1] *The Truth about Geronimo*, Britton Davis, ed. with an introduction by Milo M. Quaife (Yale University Press, New Haven, Conn., 1929) p. 31.
[2] *The Arizona Year Book, 1930-1931; a Compendium of Historical and Statistical Information Relating to the State of Arizona*, comp. under the direction of Forrest E. Doucette (The Manufacturing Stationers, Phoenix, Ariz., 1930) p. 287.

Sanctuary of Freedom. See *Old South Church*

Sand Cutters. See Arizonians

Sanders, Daniel Jackson

Daniel Jackson Sanders, Presbyterian clergyman, editor, and educator, was nicknamed *Zeus* by the students at Biddle University at Charlotte, N.C. Sanders was the first Negro President of this school, holding office from 1891 until 1907. He was a leader in the education and church world throughout his adult life because of his religious attitudes, his forensic power, and sound logic. (In Greek mythology, Zeus was the king of the gods and was venerated for his wise rule of the universe.)

[1] *Dictionary of American Biography under the Auspices of the American Council of Learned Societies*, ed. by Dumas Malone (Charles Scribner's Sons, New York, 1935) vol. 16, p. 332.

Sand Hill State. See Arizona

Sandhillers. See Georgians; Illinois Inhabitants; South Carolinians

San Diego, California

San Diego is called the *Birthplace of California*, the *Jewel City of California*, and *Plymouth of the West*.[1]

It merits the nickname, *Jewel City of California*,[3] because of its mild climate, the most equable in the United States, as a result of which it has long been a residential and year-round resort city. San Diego was one of the first settlements to be made on the West Coast, Father Junípero Serra having founded the San Diego Mission in 1769, hence the nicknames *Birthplace of California* and *Plymouth of the West*.[2]

[1] "Land of Homes" by Frank J. Taylor in *California*, ed. by John Russell McCarthy (Powell Publishing Company, Chicago and San Francisco, Calif., 1929) p. 128.
[2] *California of the South, A History*, John Stevens McGroarty (The S. J. Clarke Publishing Company, Inc., Chicago and Los Angeles, Calif., 1933) vol. 1, p. 459.
[3] *California and Californians*, ed. by Rockwell D. Hunt, assisted by an advisory board (The Lewis Publishing Company, New York and Chicago, 1930) vol. 2, p. 505.

Sandlapper State. See South Carolina

Sandlappers. See South Carolinians

Sand Lot Agitator. See Kearney, Denis

Sandy. See Herring, A. L.

San Francisco, California

San Francisco has the following nicknames: *City Beautiful, City of One Hundred Hills, Cosmopolitan San Francisco,* or the *City Cosmopolitan, Frisco, Golden Gate City, Mushroom City, Poor Man's Paradise, Port O' Missing Men,* and *Queen of the Pacific,* or the *Queen City of the Pacific Coast.*

City Beautiful[1] refers to the natural charm of its location upon hills[2] overlooking San Francisco Bay and the Golden Gate, and to the general attractiveness of the city with its numerous boulevards, gardens, playgrounds, and extensive parks.[1]

San Francisco was founded upon a series of hills, many of which have since been removed or graded down[2] in order to facilitate transportation and to enable the city to expand; a goodly number of them remain, however, as does the nickname *City of One Hundred Hills.*[3]

Cosmopolitan San Francisco,[4] or the *City Cosmopolitan,*[5] describe one of its chief characteristics; people from all parts of the world may be seen there, often retaining their native dress, language, customs, religion, and manners. The buildings of the city represent many and varied types of architecture,[4] Byzantine, Gothic, English, Spanish, and Modern. The cosmopolitan aspects of the city are especially apparent in the shops, restaurants, and places of amusement.[6]

In various parts of the United States, and especially in the West, the city is known as *Frisco,*[7] an abbreviation of its name which is sometimes deplored by its inhabitants.

It is designated the *Golden Gate City*[7] because it is located along the break in the Coast Range Mountains through which a strait connects the Pacific Ocean with San Francisco Bay, both break and strait being called the *Golden Gate.*[2]

San Francisco was nicknamed the *Mushroom City*[8] because of its overnight growth during the California gold rush in 1849. Its population increased most during the summer and fall of 1849. In February of that year population numbered 2,000; in August, 6,000; but upon the return of the miners in the early winter, the inhabitants increased[9] to 20,000.

The mild climate, and the abundance of fruits and vegetables which may be bought at a low cost, make living expenses cheap.

San Francisco is said to be "the place where the working man can work more days in the year in comfort than he can any place else," hence the term *Poor Man's Paradise.*[10]

It is widely known as the *Port O' Missing Men*[11] because the size and cosmopolitan nature of the population make it easy for one coming to the city to conceal his identity, or to lose touch with family, and friends if he wishes. Too, San Francisco is a large sea port, making it easy to embark on boats bound for distant ports.

Because San Francisco has been said to sit "at the gateway of the sea and gather toll from all the passing ships"[12] and because the wealth of the valleys, mines, and forests of California are poured into her coffers, it is called the *Queen of the Pacific,*[12] and the *Queen City of the Pacific Coast.*[13]

[1] *The Old San Francisco and New: The City Beautiful, San Francisco, Past, Present and Future,* Andrew G. Park (Published by Houston and Harding, at the Press of Commercial Printing House, Los Angeles, Calif., 1906) p. 1.
The History of San Francisco, Lewis Francis Byington, Supervising Editor, Oscar Lewis, Associate Editor (The S. J. Clarke Publishing Company, Chicago and San Francisco, Calif., 1931) vol. 1, p. 474, 485, 517, 518.

[2] *San Francisco, as It Was, as It Is, and How to See It,* Helen Throop Purdy (Paul Elder and Company, San Francisco, Calif., 1912) p. 34, 39, 40, 131-3, 135, 195, 196, 198.

[3] *San Francisco and California* (E. P. Charlton and Company, San Francisco, Calif., 1909) p. 1.

[4] *California, Land of Homes,* Frank J. Taylor (Powell Publishing Company, San Francisco, Calif., Los Angeles, Calif., and Chicago, 1929) p. 167, 168, 171, 193.

[5] *Care-Free San Francisco,* Allen Dunn (A. M. Robertson, San Francisco, Calif., 1913) p. 31.

[6] *San Francisco and Thereabout,* Charles Keeler (The California Promotion Committee, San Francisco, Calif., 1903) p. 54-69.

[7] *The History of the San Francisco Disaster and Mount Vesuvius Horror,* Charles Eugene Banks and Opie Read (Thompson and Thomas, Chicago, 1906) p. 186, 243, 246, 252.

[8] *California Gold Days,* Owen Cochran Coy (Powell Publishing Company, San Francisco, Calif., Los Angeles, Calif., and Chicago, 1929) vol. 3, p. 243.

[9] *Eldorado or Adventures in the Path of Empire, Comprising a Voyage to California, Via Panama; Life in San Francisco and Monterey; Pictures of the Gold Region; and Experiences of Mexican Travel,* Household Edition, Revised, Bayard Taylor (G. P. Putnam's Sons, New York, 1882) p. 203-4, 205.

[10] *San Francisco, Fifteenth Thousand* (Passenger Department, Santa Fe Railroad, Chicago, 1901) p. 50.

[11] *Vignettes of San Francisco,* Almira Bailey (The San Francisco Journal, San Francisco, Calif., 1921) p. 21.

[12] *Modern San Francisco* (Western Press Association, San Francisco, Calif., 1908) p. 102.

[13] *Westward by Rail: A Journey to San Francisco and Back and A Visit to the Mormons,* Second Edition. W. F. Rae (Longmans, Green and Company, London, 1871) p. 263.

San Joaquin River Valley

The valley of the San Joaquin River in California is designated the *Granary of California.*[1] The valley is about thirty miles

San Joaquin River Valley—Continued
wide and two hundred miles long and constitutes the southern end of Central Valley, one of the richest farm regions in the United States. The San Joaquin Valley produces grain and every type of crop grown in California. Its agricultural importance has been greatly increased by the use of irrigation.

[1] *The Source Book* (Source Research Council, Inc., Chicago, 1936) vol. 6, p. 2547.

Santa Barbara, California

The Santa Barbara mission settlement, which was the nucleus of the present Santa Barbara, was widely known as the *Queen of the Missions*.[1] Established in 1786 in a remarkably fertile agricultural region, the productivity of the surrounding country soon brought the mission unusual prosperity, and it became the largest, wealthiest, most powerful, and most cultured of the Spanish settlements in California.

[1] *California, Land of Homes*, Frank J. Taylor, ed. by John Russell McCarthy (Powell Publishing Company, Chicago and San Francisco, Calif., 1930) vol. 1, p. 145.

Santa Claus. See Coleman, Leighton

Santa Claus of the Manchester Poor. See Cheney, S. H. (Bissell)

Santa Fe, New Mexico

Santa Fe, the second oldest city in the United States, was formerly, and still is sometimes, called the *Lone Star of Civilization*[1] because, having been settled by Mexican settlers in the Rio Grande Valley in 1609, it was the only town in "a million square miles of lonely desert, mountains, and plain" for a century or more.

[1] *The Source Book* (Source Research Council, Inc., Chicago, 1936) vol. 6, p. 2550.

Santa Fe Division. See Thirty-fifth Infantry Division of World War II

Saratoga of the South. See Greenbrier White Sulphur Springs, W.Va.

Sarge. See Connally, G. W.

Sarong Girl. See Lamour, Dorothy

Satchel. See Paige, L. R.

Saulsbury, Eli, Gove, and Willard

The three sons of William Saulsbury, of Kent County, Del., Eli, Gove, and Willard Saulsbury, were popularly called the *Saulsbury Triumvirate*[1] because of their prominence in the public affairs of the state of Delaware. All three brothers were lawyers who devoted much of their time and energy to discharge the duties of the public offices to which they had been elected by the people of Delaware. In Roman antiquity, a triumvirate was a coalition of three men united in public office or authority.

The brothers were born at Mispillion Hundred, Del., and they died at Dover, Del. Eli Saulsbury was born on December 29, 1817, and died on March 22, 1893; Gove Saulsbury was born on May 29, 1815, and died on July 31, 1881; Willard Saulsbury was born on June 2, 1820, and died on April 6, 1892.

[1] *Contemporary American Biography: Biographical Sketches of Representative Men of the Day, Representatives of Modern Thought and Progress, of the Pulpit, the Press, the Bench and Bar, of Legislation, Invention, and The Great Industrial Interests of the Country* (Atlantic Publishing and Engraving Company, New York, 1895) vol. 1, p. 297.

Saulsbury Triumvirate. See Saulsbury, Eli, Gove, and Willard

Savior of Babies. See Straus, Nathan

Savior of His Country. See Washington, George

Savior of the Arts. See Sirovich, W. I.

Savior of the Constitution. See Bloom, Sol

Savior of the Valley. See Rosser, T. L.

Sauvolle, Le Moine

Le Moine Sauvolle was nicknamed the *American Prodigy*[1] while he was a student in France because of his ability to make important social contacts and to achieve unusual results. Sauvolle was the first colonial Governor of Louisiana, having been appointed by King Louis XIV of France.

Le Moine Sauvolle was born at Montreal, Canada, about 1617, and died at Biloxi, in what is now Mississippi, on July 22, 1701.

[1] *Appleton's Cyclopaedia of American Biography*, ed. by James Grant Wilson and John Fiske (D. Appleton and Company, New York, 1888) vol. 3, p. 686.

Savage, George Martin

The *Grand Old Man*, and *Union's Grand Old Man* were often-used sobriquets of Dr. George Martin Savage, President Emeritus of Union University, at Jackson, Tenn. These nicknames were used by the students of the University and by his fellow townsmen to show the respect and esteem in which he was held by them.

George Martin Savage was born near Rienzi, Miss., on February 5, 1849. He was prominently connected with Union University as President and as Professor of Bible, Philosophy, and Modern Languages since 1887. He died in June 1938.

Savannah, Georgia

The beautiful old southern city, Savannah, is nicknamed the *Forest City*,[1] or the *Forest City of the South*.[1] The origin and the appropriateness of this sobriquet are evident in the streets and avenues of the city, which are interspersed with squares or parks, and bordered with numerous stately and magnificent shade-trees.[2] It is also known as the *Garden City*[3] because it has so many beautifully laid-out and well-kept parks.

[1] *Savannah: Her Trade, Commerce, and Industries, 1883-4: Manufacturing, Business and Transportation Facilities, and a Delineation of Representative Industrial and Commercial Establishments of the Forest City of the South, Historical and Descriptive Review*, John E. Land (John E. Land, Savannah, Ga., 1884) p. 16.
[2] *A Guide to Strangers Visiting Savannah for Business, Health, or Pleasure*, J. H. Estill (Morning News Steam Printing House, Savannah, Ga., 1881) p. 13.
[3] *Americanisms: The English of the New World*, M. Schele De Vere (Charles Scribner and Company, New York, 1872) p. 665.

Saving Southerners

Senators from the southern states to the United States Congress during, and for some time following, the post-Civil War period, were nicknamed by their colleagues from the northern and eastern states *Saving Southerners*[1] because the poverty undergone by southerners during the postwar and Reconstruction period caused them either to avoid contracting large debts of any kind or to refuse to agree to any kind of long-range financing on a credit basis. This nickname was again applied to the southern senators in the United States Congress during February and March of 1939 because they strongly urged a ten per cent reduction in expenditures of all the departments of the Federal Government.

[1] *Times-Herald*, Washington, D.C., March 5, 1939, col. 2, p. 2-A.

Sawdust City. See Minneapolis, Minn.

Saxon Warriors. See Alfred University

Saxons. See Alfred University

Say, Thomas

Father of American Conchology, Father of American Entomology, Father of American Descriptive Entomology, and *Father of American Zoölogy* are nicknames of Thomas Say.

Say was the first[1] American to publish an article on the subject of conchology, the contribution appearing in the American Edition of *Nicholson's British Cyclopedia* in the winter of 1816-17. This essay may well be called the working basis of conchology in America and Say is therefore credited as the *Father of American Conchology*. However, the merits of his work were not confined to America alone, but were accepted throughout the world of science.

Thomas Say was designated *Father of American Entomology*[1] and *Father of American Descriptive Entomology*[1] in commemoration of his splendid achievements in that branch of zoölogy. He was a pioneer in the field of entomology, and was particularly proficient in discovering and identifying an exceedingly large number of insects. He wrote[2] many descriptive articles on this science, and his three volumes of *American Entomology*, filled with lovely colored engravings, were considered one of the most attractive publications of its type ever printed on an American press at the time. They were published, in 1824, 1825, and 1828, respectively.

He became known as the *Father of American Zoölogy*[3] because he was one of the foremost American natural scientists, particularly in the undeveloped field of zoölogy.

He was one of the charter members[1] of the group who founded the Academy of Natural Sciences at Philadelphia, Pa., in 1812. In 1819 he was chief zoölogist in the United States Survey of the Rocky Mountain region, the scientific expedition made under the command of Major Stephen H. Long. From 1821 to 1825, Say was Professor of Zoölogy in the Philadelphia Museum. He made invaluable contributions to zoölogy, conchology, entomology, ethnology, and paleontology.

Say, Thomas—Continued

Thomas Say was born at Philadelphia, Pa., on July 27, 1787, and died at New Harmony, Ind., on October 10, 1834.

[1] *Thomas Say, Early American Naturalist*, Harry B. Weiss and Grace M. Ziegler (Charles C. Thomas, Springfield, Ill., and Baltimore, Md., 1931) p. 4, 33, 190-2, 197.

[2] *A Biographical Sketch of the Late Thomas Say, Read Before the Academy of Natural Sciences of Philadelphia, December 16, 1834*, Benjamin H. Coates (Published by order of the Academy, Printed by W. P. Gibbons, Philadelphia, 1835) p. 8, 11, 14, 16-17, 19.

[3] "Our Foreigners, a Chronicle of Americans in the Making" by Samuel P. Orth, in *The Chronicles of America*, Allen Johnson, Editor (Yale University Press, New Haven, Conn., 1920) p. 95.

Scarlet Hurricanes. See Davis and Elkins College

Schalk, Raymond W.

Raymond W. Schalk, who was born at Harvel, Ill., on August 12, 1892, and who was outstanding as a catcher in major league baseball, was nicknamed *Cracker.*[1]

[1] *Who's Who in Major League Base Ball*, comp. by Harold (Speed) Johnson (Buxton Publishing Company, Chicago, 1933) p. 480.

Scharein, Arthur Otto

Scoop[1] is the sobriquet applied to Arthur Otto Scharein, who was born at Decatur, Ill., on June 300, 1906, and who played infield in major league baseball.

[1] *Who's Who in Major League Base Ball*, comp. by Harold (Speed) Johnson (Buxton Publishing Company, Chicago, 1933) p. 345.

Schauffler, Henry Albert

Henry Albert Schauffler, Congregationalist clergyman, was widely known as the *Apostle to the Slavs.*[1] From 1882 until his death in 1905, he was an active missionary among many Slavic-Americans living in Cleveland, Ohio, and in Chicago, Ill. He established numerous Congregational churches, missions, and church schools for the spiritual and practical benefit of these immigrants and their families and in every way possible assisted them in adjusting to the benefits and duties of a religious freedom to which many of them were unaccustomed.

Henry Albert Schauffler was born at Constantinople (Istanbul), Turkey, on September 4, 1837, and died at Cleveland, Ohio, on February 15, 1905.

[1] *Dictionary of American Biography under the Auspices of the American Council of Learned Societies*, ed. by Dumas Malone (Charles Scribner's Sons, New York, 1935) vol. 16, p. 420.

Schenectady, New York

Schenectady is called the *City That Lights and Hauls the World*[1] because it is the site of the main plants of the General Electric Company and of the American Locomotive Company.

[1] *The World Book Encyclopedia* (The Quarrie Corporation, Chicago, 1938) vol. 15, p. 6411.

Schley, Winfield Scott

An article in the *Age-Herald*, a newspaper published at Birmingham, Ala., on July 24, 1898, was entitled the *Mephistopheles of the Ocean*. This was a review of Rear Admiral Winfield Scott Schley's life and his accomplishments in the Spanish-American War, and acclaimed him particularly for having destroyed the fleet of the Spanish Admiral Cervera on July 3, 1898, thus assuring the American conquest of Cuba. The article concluded that Schley was called the *Mephistopheles of the Ocean*[1] by the Spaniards because he had defeated them by means of his skillfully-conducted naval expeditions. This sobriquet was an allusion to Mephistopheles, one of the seven chief devils of mediavel demonology, who was known for his relentless campaigns against mankind.

Winfield Scott Schley was born near Frederick, Md., on October 9, 1839, and died at New York City, on October 3, 1911.

[1] *The Age-Herald*, Birmingham, Ala., July, 24, 1898, p. 9.

Scholar of the Georgia Bar. See Hill, W. B.

Schoolboy Rowe. See Rowe, L. T.

Schoolmaster in Politics. See Wilson, Woodrow

Schroeder, Henry

Minnesota's Potato King[1] was a familiar nickname for Henry Schroeder throughout the northwestern part of the United States. He was described thus because he was known as one of the largest potato producers in the Northwest, and was called to Washington, D.C., during World War I to confer with Herbert Hoover, the wartime food administrator, with regard to the production and distribution of this important staple during the war. Schroeder managed five of the largest potato farms in Minnesota in 1917, and won two World's Fair medals that year for the quality of his produce.

Henry Schroeder was born at Rensberg, in Schleswig-Holstein, Germany, on August 31, 1855, and died at St. Paul, Minn., on August 11, 1928.

[1] *Encyclopedia of American Biography: American Biography, a New Cyclopedia*, comp. under the editorial supervision of a notable advisory board (Published under the direction of The American Historical Society, Inc., New York, 1931) vol. 47, p. 364.

Schuble, Henry George, Junior

Heinie [1] is the nickname given to Henry George Schuble, Jr., who was born at Houston, Tex., on November 1, 1908, and who played infield in major league baseball. *Heinie*, or *Heinrich*, is the German term for Henry, Schuble being of German descent.

[1] *Who's Who in Major League Base Ball*, comp. by Harold (Speed) Johnson (Buxton Publishing Company, Chicago, 1933) p. 346.

Schulmerich, Edward Wesley

While he was playing full-back for the Oregon State College football team, Edward Wesley Schulmerich broke through the opposing team in such a manner that the nickname *Ironhorse* [1] suggested itself to his colleagues.

Edward Wesley Schulmerich was born at Hillsboro, Ore., on August 21, 1902, and played outfield in major league baseball.

[1] *Who's Who in Major League Base Ball*, comp. by Harold (Speed) Johnson (Buxton Publishing Company, Chicago, 1933) p. 347.

Schumann-Heink, Mme. Ernestine

Mme. Ernestine Schumann-Heink was widely known as the *Grand Old Lady of Opera*, the *Mother of All the Doughboys*, and the *Mother of the American Legion*. Mme. Schumann-Heink was one of America's most famous and beloved opera stars and in later life was truly the *Grand Old Lady of Opera*. Her nicknames, *Mother of All the Doughboys*, and *Mother of the American Legion*, commemorate her generosity during the World War from 1914 to 1918 when she performed countless times before American soldiers both in camp and concert hall.

Mme. Schumann-Heink (Ernestine Roessler), the world's most famous contralto operatic singer, was born near Prague, Czechoslovakia, on June 15, 1861, and died at her home in Hollywood, Calif., on November 17, 1936.

Schuyler, Philip John

Soon after he was appointed a Major General and placed in command of the military department of New York, with headquarters at Albany, on June 19, 1775, Philip John Schuyler became known as the *Great Eye*.[1] This nickname was given to him because while serving in this capacity, Schuyler kept a vigilant and accurate watch on the movements of the British in the northern colonies.

Philip John Schuyler was born at Albany, N.Y., on November 20, 1733, and died there on November 18, 1804.

[1] *A Political History of the State of New York, 1774-1832*, De Alva Stanwood Alexander (Henry Holt and Company, New York, 1906) vol. 1, p. 18.

Scoop. See Scharein, A. O.

Scots. See Alma College; Carnegie Institute of Technology; Macalester College; Maryville College

Scott, Robert Walter

Throughout the southern states, Robert Walter Scott was widely known as *Farmer Bob* [1] or *Farmer Bob Scott*.[1] He was a capable legislator and faithful to the interests of the farmer, serving in 1929 in the North Carolina State Assembly as Chairman of the Committee on Agriculture, and from 1901 to 1929 as a member of the North Carolina State Board of Agriculture. He was chiefly responsible for procuring the appropriation for the agricultural building of the North Carolina State College, at Raleigh, and he devoted his entire life as a master farmer toward raising agriculture to a higher level of usefulness, dignity, and prosperity throughout the state of North Carolina.

Robert Walter Scott was born at Hawfield, near Mebane, N.C., on July 24, 1861, and died at Burlington, N.C., on May 16, 1929.

[1] *Encyclopedia of American Biography: American Biography, a New Cyclopedia*, comp. under the editorial supervision of a notable advisory board (Published under the direction of The American Historical Society, Inc., New York, 1929) vol. 53, p. 78-80.

Scott, Winfield

The *Hero of Chippewa* and *Old Fuss and Feathers* are nicknames of Lieutenant General Winfield Scott.

Hero of Chippewa [1] fittingly describes Scott's personal gallantry and brilliant leadership at the Battle of Chippewa in Canada, on July 5, 1814, at which time the British

Scott, Winfield—Continued

forces were severely repulsed. In his official report Major General Jacob Brown, who was in general command of the American troops at this time, highly complimented Scott's courage and valor, declaring that more credit was due to Lieutenant General Scott than to any other person for the American victory.[2]

He was nicknamed *Old Fuss and Feathers*[3] by his soldiers and subordinate officers because of his formality and his strict disciplinary policy in dealing with them. Scott was also known by this sobriquet[4] to his other associates because of his rather pompous manner and resplendent dress.

Winfield Scott was born near Petersburg, Va., on June 13, 1786, and died at West Point, N.Y., on May 29, 1866.

[1] *A Book of Nicknames*, John Goff (Courier-Journal Job Printing Company, Louisville, Ky., 1892) p. 25.

[2] *Great Commanders, General Scott*, General Marcus J. Wright, ed. by James Grant Wilson (D. Appleton and Company, New York, 1894) p. 32.

Life and Services of General Winfield Scott, Including the Siege of Vera Cruz, the Battle of Cerro Gordo, and the Battles in the Valley of Mexico, to the Conclusion of Peace, and His Return to the United States, Edward D. Mansfield (A. S. Barnes and Company, New York, 1852) p. 104-10.

[3] *The Encyclopedia Americana* (Americana Corporation, New York and Chicago, 1932) vol. 24, p. 446.

The "Also Rans," Great Men Who Missed Making the Presidential Goal, Don C. Seitz (Thomas Y. Crowell Company, New York, 1928) p. 134.

[4] *The End of an Era*, John S. Wise (Houghton Mifflin and Company, New York and Boston, 1899) p. 103-4.

Scott County, Virginia

Scott County, located in the southwestern part of Virginia, and on the Tennessee border, is sometimes called the *Great Kingdom of Scott*.[1] It has an area of five hundred and forty-three square miles, with picturesque mountains and fertile valleys, and its rich residual limestone soil makes the county outstanding for agricultural and grazing pursuits. The people of Scott County raise burley tobacco, cattle, corn, and wheat.

[1] *Virginia Journal of Education* (Virginia Education Association, Richmond, Va., 1937) vol. 31, December, 1937, p. 116.

Scotties. See Maryville College

Scourge of the District Police. See Blanton, T. L.

Scranton, Pennsylvania

Scranton, in northeastern Pennsylvania, is sometimes designated the *City of Black Diamonds*[1] because it is in the heart of the anthracite coal region of the United States.

It was nicknamed the *Electric City*[2] when the Scranton Suburban Electric Railway began to operate electric cars for passenger service on November 29, 1886.

[1] *Compton's Pictured Encyclopedia* (F. E. Compton and Company, Chicago, 1933) vol. 13, p. 51.

[2] *The Source Book* (Source Research Council, Inc., Chicago, 1936) vol. 6, p. 2586.

Famous First Facts, Joseph Nathan Kane (The H. W. Wilson Company, New York, 1933) p. 495.

Screaming Eagle Division. See One Hundred and First Airborne Division of World War II

Screeno. See Bailey, H. H.

Screen's Bad Girl. See West, Mae

Screen's Greatest Lover. See Valentino, Rudolph

Scribe of the Revolution. See Jefferson, Thomas

Scrub Race

The *Scrub Race*[1] is the nickname applied to the presidential campaign of 1824 in which the following candidates participated: Andrew Jackson of Tennessee, William Harris Crawford of Georgia, John Quincy Adams of Massachusetts, and Henry Clay of Virginia. A scrub race is an impromptu event for which the contestants have not trained beforehand. The nickname is apt in view of the fact that each candidate was representative of a faction rather than the standard-bearer of a united party and none of them was strong enough to obtain a majority electoral vote. The contest was finally thrown into the House of Representatives where Clay rallied his strength to Adams and elected him.

[1] *Encyclopedic Dictionary of American History*, J. Franklin Jameson and J. W. Buel (American History Society, Washington, D.C., 1900) vol. 2, p. 204.

Sculptor of American History. See Kelly, J. E.

Seabees

The *Seabees* is the nickname of the construction battalions of the United States Navy, working chiefly in the Pacific from 1942 to 1943. The nickname originated in the abbreviation of "construction battalions," *C.B.'s*.

[1] *Time: The Weekly Magazine*, Chicago, Illinois, April 19, 1943, Column 1, page 65.

Sears, Isaac

Isaac Sears was popularly called *King Sears*.[1] He was a wealthy merchant, eminent in colonial society, and occupied a prominent place in the political activities of the colonies during the Revolutionary War.

He was born at Norwalk, Conn., in 1729, and died at Canton, China, on October 28, 1786.

[1] *History of Long Island from Its Discovery and Settlement to the Present Time*, Benjamin F. Thompson, Third Edition, revised and greatly enlarged with additions and a biography of the author by Charles J. Werner (Robert H. Dodd, New York, 1918) vol. 4, p. 255.

Seasiders. See Hampton Institute

Seattle's Sensational Son. See Zioncheck, M. A.

Second Infantry Division of World War II

The *Indian Head Division* [1] was the nickname of the Second Infantry Division of the Combat Divisions of World War II.

[1] *Combat Divisions of World War II* (Army of the United States), Army Times Publishing Company, Washington, D.C., 1946, p. 8.

Second William Jennings Bryan. See Lee, J. B.

Sectional President. See Lincoln, Abraham

Sedgwick, John

Although a strict disciplinarian, Major General John Sedgwick was consistently interested in the welfare of his men, and considerate of them in time of battle. His kindness and generosity to them on all occasions, caused the soldiers under his command to affectionately nickname him *Uncle John*.[1]

John Sedgwick was born at Cornwall, Conn., on September 13, 1813, and fell in the battle at Spottsylvania Court House, Va., on May 9, 1864.

[1] *The Portrait Gallery of the War, Civil, Military, and Naval: A Biographical Record*, ed. by Frank Moore (G. P. Putnam, New York, 1864) p. 324.

Seed-corn Battalion

On May 15, 1864, at the Battle of New Market in Virginia, the cadets from Virginia Military Institute at Lexington aided the Confederate soldiers under the command of Major General John Cabell Breckenridge in repulsing the Union forces. At this engagement the cadets, young boys ranging from fourteen to twenty years of age, were designated the *Seed-corn Battalion*.[1]

See also *Seed-corn of the Confederacy.*

[1] *The New Market Campaign, May, 1864*, Edward Raymond Turner (Whittet and Shepperson, Richmond, Va., 1912) p. 85.

Seed-corn of the Confederacy

During the Civil War, Jefferson Davis, President of the Confederacy, spoke of the cadets at Virginia Military Institute in Lexington, Va., as the *Seed-corn of the Confederacy*.[1] They were considered a select group of young soldiers from whom would spring a new stock of leaders to champion the Confederate cause like the seed-corn which is set apart for planting a new crop.

[1] *The End of an Era*, John S. Wise (Houghton Mifflin and Company, New York and Boston, 1889) p. 260.

Seeds, Robert I.

Robert I. Seeds, who was born at Ringgold, Tex., on February 24, 1908, and who played outfield in major league baseball, is nicknamed *Suitcase*,[1] because he always seemed to be traveling from one team to another.

[1] *Who's Who in Major League Base Ball*, comp. by Harold (Speed) Johnson (Buxton Publishing Company, Chicago, 1933) p. 350.

Official Encyclopedia of Baseball, Jubilee Edition, Hy Turkin and S. C. Thompson, (A. S. Barnes and Company, New York, 1951) p. 585.

Seer and Sage of Mississippi College. See Aven, A. J.

Semmes, Raphael

The sobriquet, *Paul Jones of the South*,[1] was applied to Raphael Semmes, because of his daring in sea fighting. He was in command of the steamer *Sumter*, the first vessel of the Confederate Navy, with which he successfully captured much of the northern commerce.

Raphael Semmes was born in Charles County, Md., on September 27, 1809, and died at Mobile, Ala., on August 30, 1877.

[1] *A Book of Nicknames*, John Goff (Courier-Journal Job Printing Company, Louisville, Ky., 1892) p. 26.

Senator. See Grimes, B. A.

Senators. See Davis and Elkins College; Washington American League Baseball Club

Señor. See Neily, Harry

Sergeant. See York, A. C.

Serving Knight. See McConnell, J. P.

Seton, Ernest Thompson

Ernest Thompson Seton acquired his nickname *Wolf* [1] because he had been a noted wolf hunter during his life in the West and most of his drawings and pictures for salon exhibition were of wolf subjects.

Seton, a remarkable combination of scientist, artist, and sportsman,[1] was born Ernest Evan Seton-Thompson at South Shields, England, on August 14, 1860, and died on October 23, 1946, in America.

[1] *The National Cyclopaedia of American Biography* (James T. White and Company, New York, 1907) vol. 9, p. 56.

Seven Days. See Salem College

Seven Mule Barnum. See Barnum, W. H.

Seven Mules Harrington. See Harrington, V. F.

Seven Pillars

Following a careful and deliberate procedure, the colonists of New Haven, Conn., adopted their plan of government on June 4, 1639. At the meeting held for this purpose, John Davenport, a clergyman, discussed in a sermon the principles of civil government and described what he believed to be the necessary qualifications of a righteous officer-holder. He used as the text of his sermon the passage of Scripture which says, "Wisdom hath builded her house, she hath hewn out her seven pillars." A rather literal interpretation of these words led those present at the meeting to decide to choose from their number twelve men prominent in church work. These in turn were to select seven from their group of twelve as the *Seven Pillars* [1] upon whose shoulders would rest the responsibility of inaugurating the Government of the New Haven Colony, of selecting its officers, and of attending to civil and religious duties. Later Milford and Guilford were organized under seven men vested with power or authority similar to that of the *Seven Pillars* named above.

[1] *The New Complete History of the United States of America*, Official Edition, John Clark Ridpath (The Jones Brothers Publishing Company, Cincinnati, Ohio, 1906) vol. 2, p. 991-2.

Seven Sisters

The *Seven Sisters* [1] is an appellation popularly applied to the seven bills designed to bring about trust reforms passed by the Legislature of New Jersey in 1913, and signed by Woodrow Wilson, then Governor of that state.

[1] *A Short History of the United States, 1492-1920*, John Spencer Bassett (The Macmillan Company, New York, 1921) p. 855.

Seventeenth Airborne Division of World War II

The *Golden Talon Division* [1] was the nickname of the Seventeenth Airborne Division of the Combat Divisions of World War II. This division was also called the *Thunder from Heaven Division*.

[1] *Combat Divisions of World War II* (Army of the United States), Army Times Publishing Company, Washington, D.C., 1946, p. 93.

Seventh Armored Division of World War II

The *Lucky Seventh* [1] was the nickname of the Seventh Armored Division of the Combat Divisions of World War II.

[1] *Combat Divisions of World War II* (Army of the United States), Army Times Publishing Company, Washington, D.C., 1946, p. 81.

Seventh Infantry Division of World War II

The *Hourglass Division* [1] was the nickname of the Seventh Infantry Division of the Combat Divisions of World War II.

[1] *Combat Divisions of World War II* (Army of the United States), Army Times Publishing Company, Washington, D.C., 1946, p. 13.

Seventieth Infantry Division of World War II

The *Trailblazer Division* [1] was the nickname of the Seventieth Infantry Division of the Combat Divisions of World War II because it was activated on June 15, 1943, at Camp Adair, Oregon, which suggests the Oregon Trail.

[1] *Combat Divisions of World War II* (Army of the United States), Army Times Publishing Company, Washington, D.C., 1946, p. 42.

Seventy-eight Infantry Division of World War II

The *Lightning Division* [1] was the nickname of the Seventy-eighth Infantry Division of the Combat Divisions of World War II, because in World War I the French likened the action of the Seventy-eighth Division to a bolt of lightning.

Audaciter (*Boldly*) [1] was the motto of the Seventy-eighth Infantry Division of the Combat Divisions of World War II supposedly because of their daring in action.

[1] *Combat Divisions of World War II* (Army of the United States), Army Times Publishing Company, Washington, D.C., 1946, p. 47.

Seventy-ninth Infantry Division of World War II

The *Cross of Lorraine Division* [1] was the nickname of the Seventy-ninth Infantry Division of the Combat Divisions of World War II because of its daring accomplishments at Cherbourg and other battles in France. The Cross of Lorraine is the symbol of Alsace Lorraine in France.

[1] *Combat Divisions of World War II* (Army of the United States), Army Times Publishing Company, Washington, D.C., 1946, p. 48.

Seventy-seventh Infantry Division of World War II

The *Statue of Liberty Division* [1] and *New York's Own* [2] were the nicknames of the Seventy-seventh Infantry Division of the Combat Divisions of World War II because the division was made up of men from New York City. Their shoulder insignia depicted the Statue of Liberty which stands in the city's harbor.

[1] *Combat Divisions of World War II* (Army of the United States), Army Times Publishing Company, Washington, D.C., 1946, p. 46.
[2] *History of New York State, 1523-1927*, James Sullivan, Editor-in-chief, and Melvin Williams, Benedict Fitzpatrick, and Edwin P. Conklin, Associate Editors (Lewis Historical Publishing Company, Inc., New York and Chicago, 1927) vol. 4, p. 1333.

Seventy-sixth Infantry Division of World War II

The *Onaway Division* [1] was the nickname of the Seventy-sixth Infantry Division of the Combat Divisions of World War II supposedly because the division song is *Onaway*.

[1] *Combat Divisions of World War II* (Army of the United States), Army Times Publishing Company, Washington, D.C., 1946, p. 45.

Sewall, Joseph

Because of his highly emotional style of preaching, Joseph Sewall was designated the *Weeping Prophet*.[1] Sewall supported George Whitfield in introducing Methodism in America.

Joseph Sewall was born at Boston, Mass., on August 15, 1688, and died there on June 27, 1769.

[1] *The National Cyclopedia of American Biography* (James T. White and Company, New York, 1899) vol. 2, p. 37.

Seward, William Henry

The statesman, William Henry Seward, was called the *Sage of Auburn* [1] because of his mature judgment and wisdom, and because his later years were spent at Auburn.

Seward was governor of New York from 1839 to 1843 and a United States Senator from 1849 to 1861. A prominent anti-slavery advocate, he is famous for the declaration in a speech made in 1858 that the antagonism between freedom and slavery was an "irrepressible conflict" between opposing and enduring forces. He was Secretary of State from 1861 to 1869.

William Henry Seward was born at Florida, N.Y., on May 16, 1801, and died at Auburn, N.Y., on October 10, 1872.

[1] *Political Americanisms*, Charles Ledyard Norton (Longmans, Green and Company, New York and London, 1890) p. 98.

Seward's Folly. See Alaska

Seward's Ice Box. See Alaska

Shad. See Rhem, C. F.

Shake-rag. See Mineral Point, Wis.

Shakespeare Clown. See Rice, Daniel

Shanghai Bill. See Hickok, J. B.

Shank, Samuel Lewis

Samuel Lewis Shank was nicknamed the *Auctioneer Mayor*, the *Indianapolis Potato Mayor*, and the *Potato Mayor*.[1] In 1910, during his first year of office as Mayor of Indianapolis, Ind., he sold at auction on the front steps of the City Hall such farm commodities as potatoes, pears, and other farm products in an attempt to decrease forcibly the prices of food supplies to the consumers of that city. Shank was Mayor of Indianapolis from 1910 until his resignation during the latter part of 1913. He was again Mayor from 1922 until 1926.

Samuel Lewis Shank, lecturer, vaudeville actor, and politician, was born at Indianapolis, Ind., on January 23, 1872, and died at his home, Golden Hill Drive, in Indianapolis, on September 24, 1927.

[1] *The Indianapolis News*, Indianapolis, Ind., September 24, 1927, cols. 1 and 2, p. 4.

Shanty. See Hogan, J. F.

Sharp Knife. See Jackson, Andrew

Shaute, Joseph Benjamin

Joseph Benjamin Shaute, who was born at Peckville, Pa., on August 1, 1900, and who was a pitcher in major league baseball, was nicknamed *Lefty* [1] because he both pitched and batted the ball left-handed.

[1] *Who's Who in Major League Base Ball*, comp. by Harold (Speed) Johnson (Buxton Publishing Company, Chicago, 1933) p. 353.

Shaw, Howard Elwin

The *Silver-tongued Orator of Lamoille* [1] was the nickname given to Howard Elwin Shaw for his eloquence in public speaking.

Shaw's chief business was the manufacture of hardwood novelties; but in addition to this he owned several sawmills at Sterling and at Stowe, Vt., and large tracts of timberland in the state. He was a representative from Lamoille County to the Vermont legislature from 1910 to 1911.

Howard Elwin Shaw was born at Stowe, Vt., on May 26, 1827, and died there on September 26, 1924.

[1] *The National Cyclopedia of American Biography* (James T. White and Company, New York, 1932) vol. 22, p. 153.

Shaw-nee-aw-kee. See Kinzie, John

Sheboygan, Wisconsin

Sheboygan was termed the *Evergreen City* [1] because, when it was settled in 1836, the plateau on which it was founded was "dotted with little groves of second-growth pine."

[1] *An Illustrated History of the State of Wisconsin. . . .*, Charles Richard Tuttle (B. B. Russell, Boston, 1875) p. 691.

Sheets, Frederick Hill

Frederick Hill Sheets, clergyman, was known to his many friends and acquaintances as the *Happy Warrior* [1] because his work in championing the cause of the missionary Church was characterized by cheerfulness, vigor, and devotion.

He was born at Mount Morris, Ill., on December 25, 1859, and died at Dixon, Ill., on August 11, 1928.

[1] *The National Cyclopedia of American Biography* (James T. White and Company, New York, 1931) vol. 21, p. 176.

Sheffield, George St. John

As a tribute to George St. John Sheffield's enthusiasm and interest in rowing at Yale University, an appreciative alumni and student body have affectionately designated him the *Grandfather of Yale Rowing.* [1]

From about 1860, at which time he entered Yale University and became a member of the class crew, until the time of his death in 1924, Sheffield contributed generously of his time, money, and advice in behalf of the Yale crews. He worked tirelessly every year in shaping the crews for the intercollegiate regattas, having served for years as timekeeper during outstanding boat races, and he succeeded in giving rowing at Yale such an eminent status that Yale crews became internationally prominent.

George St. John Sheffield was born at New Haven, Conn., on April 2, 1842, and died at Providence, R.I., on December 14, 1924.

[1] *Encyclopedia of American Biography: American Biography, a New Cyclopedia*, comp. under the editorial supervision of a notable advisory board (Published under the direction of The American Historical Society, Inc., New York, 1927) vol. 30, p. 7, 8.

Sheffield, Alabama

Sheffield is called the *Iron City on the Tennessee River* [1] because it is located on the Tennessee River, and its chief industry is the production of iron and steel.[2]

[1] *King's Handbook of the United States*, planned and ed. by Moses King, text by M. F. Sweetser (The Matthews-Northrup Company, Buffalo, N.Y., 1896) p. 39.

[2] *History of Alabama and Dictionary of Alabama Biography*, Thomas McAdory Owen (The S. J. Clarke Publishing Company, Chicago, 1921) vol. 2, p. 124.

Shelby's Man of Faith. See Anthony, J. A.

Shenandoah Valley

The Indian word, *Shenandoah*, signifies *daughter of the stars*,[1] and is thus applied to the Shenandoah Valley in Virginia.

The Shenandoah Valley "begins at the Potomac River and extends south-westward between the Blue Ridge Mountains on the east and the Alleghenies on the west, to the eminence of land between Staunton and Lexington," [2] covering an area about a hundred and fifty miles long and varying in width from twenty to thirty miles. It is famed for its rich farmland and scenic beauty. It is historically significant as the scene of many hard-fought battles during the Civil War: with its resources of grain, hay and live-stock, it was a chief supply source for Lee's army until the Confederate troops were driven out by the Federal troops under Sheridan.

[1] *The Diamond Chatterbox*, Washington, D.C., June 4 to June 10, 1939, p. 18.
[2] *The Encyclopaedia Britannica*, Fourteenth Edition (Encyclopaedia Britannica, Inc., New York and Chicago, 1938) vol. 20, p. 490.

Sheppard, Morris

Because of his unceasing efforts to secure the adoption of the Eighteenth Amendment to the Constitution, The Honorable Morris Sheppard was nicknamed the *Father of the Eighteenth Amendment*.[1]

Morris Sheppard was born at Wheatville, Tex., on May 28, 1875, and was elected a Senator from Texas to the United States Congress in 1913, serving continuously until his death in Washington, D.C., on April 9, 1941.

[1] *The Washington Post Magazine*, Washington, D.C., March 4, 1934, p. 4.

Sheridan, Philip Henry

The sobriquet, *Little Phil*,[1] was sometimes applied to General Philip Henry Sheridan by his soldiers because he was one of the youngest officers of high rank in the Union Army, and because he was only of medium height and slight of build.

Philip Henry Sheridan was born at Albany, N.Y., on March 6, 1831, and died at Norquitt, Mass., on August 5, 1888.

[1] *Men and Things I Saw in Civil War Days*, James F. Rusling (Eaton and Mains, New York, 1899) p. 125, 126.

Sheriff. See Blake, J. F.; Harris, D. S.; Lee, H. B.

Sherman, Henry

About 1842 [1] Henry Sherman and his two brothers, William and Peter, established a grocery store and liquor shop at Pottowotamie Creek, in Franklin County, Kans. The brothers were of German descent, and were commonly called *Dutch Henry*,[2] *Dutch Bill* [3] and *Dutch Pete*.[3]

Henry Sherman, a pro-slavery man, was said to have been murdered [3] in the so-called Pottowotamie massacre, of May 23 or 24, 1856. At this time about five pro-slavery men were killed by a group of free-state men led by John Brown. Eye-witnesses of the affair have disagreed as to whether or not Sherman's brother, William, was also killed at this time.

[1] *A Standard History of Kansas and Kansans*, written and comp. by William Elsey Connelley (Lewis Publishing Company, New York and Chicago, 1918) vol. 1, p. 576.
[2] *Kansas Historical Collections: Transactions of the Kansas State Historical Society, 1903-1904; together with Addresses at Annual Meetings, Miscellaneous Papers, and a Roster of Kansas for Fifty Years*, ed. by George W. Martin, Secretary (George A. Clark, State Printer, Topeka, Kans., 1904) vol. 8, p. 276, 280.
[3] *A Standard History of Kansas and Kansans*, written and comp. by William Elsey Connelley (Lewis Publishing Company, New York and Chicago, 1918) vol. 1, p. 572, 574, 576, 577.

Sherman, John (Clergyman)

When John Sherman entered Cambridge University, because he refused to "subscribe to the articles, acknowledging the supremacy of the Church of England" he was called a *College Puritan*.[1]

In 1634 he came to American and settled at Watertown, Mass., where he became assistant pastor, and ten years later, pastor, of the Watertown Society.

John Sherman was born at Dedham, England, on December 26, 1613, and died at Watertown, Mass., on August 8, 1685.

[1] *The National Cyclopedia of American Biography* (James T. White and Company, New York, 1897) vol. 7, p. 75.

Sherman, John (Legislator)

John Sherman was a member of the House, the Senate, and two presidential Cabinets, from 1855 to 1900. Because he was so prominent in shaping or determining the great financial measures of the United States while serving in these offices, he was called the *Great Financier*.[1]

He was a Representative from Ohio to the United States Congress from 1855 to 1861, and from 1861 to 1877 he was a Senator from Ohio to the United States Congress.

John Sherman was born at Lancaster, Ohio, on May 10, 1823, and died at Washington, D.C., on October 22, 1900.

[1] *A Book of Nicknames*, John Goff (Courier-Journal Job Printing Company, Louisville, Ky., 1892) p. 22.
U.S. "Snap Shots"; An Independent, National, and Memorial Encyclopedia. . . ., Oliver McKee (A. M. Thayer and Company, Boston, 1892) p. 242.

Sherman, Roger

Roger Sherman, a prominent legislator, who was born at Newton, Mass., on April 19, 1721, and who died at New Haven, Conn., on July 23, 1793, has been called

Sherman, Roger—Continued

the *Learned Shoemaker* [1] because during his youth he worked with his father at shoe-making.

[1] *A Book of Nicknames*, John Goff (Courier-Journal Job Printing Company, Louisville, Ky., 1892) p. 29.

Sherman, William Tecumseh

The *Great Marcher, Mad Tom, Old Billy, Old Tecumseh,* and *Uncle Billy* are nicknames which have been applied to William Tecumseh Sherman.

Because of his historical march to the sea in 1864, he has become known as the *Great Marcher.* [1]

Sherman was nicknamed *Mad Tom* [2] probably in allusion to his bold and daring activities as a Brigadier General in the Civil War. *Tom* is "often a generic name for a male representative of the common people."

He was called *Old Billy* [3] and *Old Tecumseh* [4] by his soldiers in admiration of his courageous spirit and his military ability.

About 1865 the nickname *Old Billy* was supplanted by that of *Uncle Billy,* [5] his soldiers using it in a spirit of affection and appreciation for his interest in their welfare.

William Tecumseh Sherman was born at Lancaster, Ohio, on February 8, 1820, and died at New York City, on February 14, 1891.

[1] *A Book of Nicknames*, John Goff (Courier-Journal Job Printing Company, Louisville, Ky., 1892) p. 25.

[2] *Americanisms; The English of the New World*, M. Schele De Vere (Charles Scribner and Company, New York, 1872) p. 250.

[3] *New American History*, Albert Bushnell Hart (American Book Company, New York, 1933) p. 456.

[4] *Manual of Useful Information*, comp. under the direction of J. C. Thomas (The Werner Company, Chicago, 1893) p. 23.

[5] *Sherman: Soldier—Realist—American*, B. H. Liddell Hart (Dodd, Mead and Company, New York, 1930) p. 130, 331.

Sherman's Bummers

In 1864, while the army of General William Tecumseh Sherman was making its memorable march from Atlanta to Savannah, Ga., a number of stragglers trailed along with it who came to be contemptuously nicknamed *Sherman's Bummers.* [1] The sobriquet arose because the stragglers maintained a livelihood by plundering homes, and stealing farm products and other possessions belonging to Southerners living along the route traversed by Sherman's army.

[1] *Scribner's Popular History of the United States from the Earliest Discoveries of the Western Hemisphere by the Northmen to the Present Time*, William Cullen Bryant, Sidney Howard Gay, and Noah Brooks (Charles Scribner's Sons, New York, 1896) vol. 5, p. 279.

Sherman's Neckties

During General William Tecumseh Sherman's march from Atlanta to Savannah, Ga., from September 1 to December 23, 1864, his men destroyed parts of the Southern Railway. In order to make the rails useless after they had been taken from the road beds, Sherman had his soldiers twist them around trees. The spectacle of the rails twisted in this manner caused them to be known as *Sherman's Neckties.* [1]

[1] *Jefferson Davis, Political Soldier*, Elisabeth Cutting (Dodd, Mead and Company, New York, 1930) p. 231.

Sherman's Whip-cracker

During the Civil War the army with which General William Tecumseh Sherman captured and burned Atlanta, Ga., on November 17, 1864, was composed of three units, one being the Army of the Tennessee. Because this army was chiefly composed of veteran soldiers who had been under General Sherman's command for a long period of time, and because it was led by officers with whom General Sherman was intimately acquainted, he repeatedly used it with quick, decisive, and effective results. In view of this fact the soldiers spoke of it figuratively as *Sherman's Whip-cracker* [1] because, whenever he used his entire army as a whip in lashing the Confederates, the Army of the Tennessee snapped into action as its cracker."

[1] *The Life and Services of Brevet Brigadier-general Andrew Jonathan Alexander, United States Army; a Sketch from Personal Recollections, Family Letters and the Records of the Great Rebellion*, James Harrison Wilson (New York, 1887) p. 124.

She-wolf. See Lincoln, M. T.

Shirt Tail Flag

During the second or third decades of the nineteenth century, the men at Point Loma in what is now California were accustomed to raise over their hide house fortification a flag [1] patterned somewhat after the national flag of today, but made out of red, white, and blue shirt tails of the men, hence the name *Shirt Tail Flag.*

[1] *Where California Began*, Winifred Davidson (McIntyre Publishing Company, San Diego, Calif., 1929) p. 93.

Shoe-string. See King and Queen County, Va.

Sholes, Christopher Latham

Christopher Latham Sholes has been designated *The Father of the Typewriter*.[1] He invented the first crudely-built machine in 1867. Improvements were made upon it until 1873, when it was considered practical to begin extensive manufacture of these machines. Throughout the remaining years of his life, Sholes consistently worked to improve the typewriter over the original model and added to it many useful features.

Christopher Latham Sholes was born in Columbia County, Pa., on February 14, 1819, and died at Milwaukee, Wis., on February 17, 1890.

[1] *The National Cyclopedia of American Biography* (James T. White and Company, New York, 1893) vol. 3, p. 316.

Sho' Men. See Washington College

Shoremen. See Washington College

Short, Dewey

Dewey Short, a Representative from Missouri to the United States Congress, is nicknamed *Jenny, The Laughing-gas Man*, and *The Preacher*. The first sobriquet was given to Short during his school days.[1] The second nickname was attributed to him because his wit and humor are much appreciated by his colleagues both in informal conversation and on the floor of Congress. He was nicknamed the *Preacher*[2] by his colleagues in the House of Representatives because he was formerly pastor of a Methodist Church.

He was a Republican Representative from Missouri to the United States Congress from 1929 until 1931, and since his reelection in 1935 has served through eight succeeding Congresses.

Dewey Short was born at Galena, Mo., on April 7, 1898.

[1] *The Senator*, Washington, D.C., February 18, 1939, p. 16, cols. 2-3.

[2] An interview with Captain Victor Hunt Harding, Secretary of the National Democratic Congress Reelection Committee, Washington, D.C., April 10, 1939.

Short Bobs. See *Long Bobs*

Shotton, Burton Edwin

Burton Edwin Shotton, who was born at Brownhelm, Ohio, on October 18, 1884, and who was a manager in major league baseball, is nicknamed *Barney*.[1]

[1] *Who's Who in Major League Base Ball*, comp. by Harold (Speed) Johnson (Buxton Publishing Company, Chicago, 1933) p. 355.

Shovel Stiffs

The Irishmen who emigrated to America during the first decades of the nineteenth century were often forced of necessity to take employment shovelling dirt to build the railroad beds, and were, in consequence, nicknamed *Shovel Stiffs*.[1] Stiff is a common slang word for a working man.

[1] *The Romance of the Rails; The Story of the American Railroads*, Agnes C. Laut (Tudor Publishing Company, New York, 1936) p. 116.

Show Me State. See Missouri

Shrouds. See Gustavus Adolphus College

Sibley, Henry Hastings

The Sioux Indians nicknamed Henry Hastings Sibley *Tall Pine, Tall Trader*, and *Wah-ze-o-man-nee*, or *Walker in the Pines*.

Because he seemed to tower over other men of his times in his dignity of manner and because he excelled as a hunter and trapper Sibley was called *The Tall Pine*[1] and the *Tall Trader*[1] by the Indians.

He was known as *Wah-ze-o-man-nee*, or *Walker in the Pines*[1] because he could travel rapidly on foot without becoming physically exhausted.

Henry Hastings Sibley was born at Detroit, Mich., on February 20, 1811, and died at St. Paul, Minn., on February 18, 1891.

[1] *My Minnesota*, Antoinette E. Ford (Lyons and Carnahan, New York and Chicago, 1929) p. 81.

Sickles, Daniel Edgar

Daniel Edgar Sickles, congressman, soldier, and diplomat, was nicknamed the *Yankee King* while he was the Minister of the United States to Spain in 1869 because his official actions were so aggressive and vigorous that the Spaniards felt he was not a diplomat, but a self-willed man who assumed too much authority. Sickles fought in the Union Army during the Civil War as Brigadier General of the Excelsior Brigade of New Yorkers. He was a representative from New York to the United States Congress from 1857 until 1861.

Daniel Edgar Sickles was born at New York City, on October 20, 1825, and died there on May 3, 1914.

[1] *Dictionary of American Biography under the Auspices of the American Council of Learned Societies*, ed. by Dumas Malone (Charles Scribner's Sons, New York, 1935) vol. 17, p. 151.

Sigourney, Lydia Huntley

Mrs. Lydia Huntly Sigourney has been characterized as the *American Hemans*.[1] Like Felicia Hemans, her contemporary in Britain, she was a prolific contributor of articles to periodicals, and she composed numerous poems lyrical, graceful, and descriptive in style, and colored by religious sentiment.

Lydia Huntley Sigourney was born at Norwich, Conn., on September 1, 1791, and died at Hartford, Conn., on June 10, 1865.

[1] *The National Cyclopedia of American Biography* (James T. White and Company, New York, 1898) vol. 1, p. 154.
The Encyclopedia Americana (Americana Corporation, New York and Chicago, 1927) vol. 14, p. 86-7.

Silent Cal. See Benge, R. A.; Coolidge, Calvin

Silent Charley. See Murphy, C. F.

Silent Man. See Grant, U. S.

Silent Senator. See Sturgeon, Daniel

Silent Smith. See Smith, J. H.

Silk-stocking Reformers

Abraham Lincoln, the sixteenth President of the United States, designated as *Silk-stocking Reformers*[1] those persons of high social standing who made loud demands for political reforms and constantly criticized those endeavoring to secure them, but themselves stopped short of active participation in the correction of political abuses.

[1] *Theodore Roosevelt, an Autobiography* (The Macmillan Company, New York, 1913) p. 96.

Silliman, Benjamin

Because he possessed marked wisdom and experience as a scientist, Benjamin Silliman's contemporaries and associates nicknamed him the *Nestor of American Science*[1] in allusion to Nestor, the legendary Greek king, whose age and experience caused him to be classed as the wisest of the Greeks.

Benjamin Silliman was born in Trumbull, Conn., on August 8, 1779, and died at New Haven, Conn., on November 24, 1864. He contributed much to the field of science through his lectures and through his brilliantly written articles which appeared in scientific journals.

[1] *The National Cyclopedia of American Biography* (James T. White and Company, New York, 1899) vol. 2, p. 386.

Silver City. See Meriden, Conn.

Silver Dick. See Bland, R. P.

Silver Grays

The *Silver Grays* were a faction of conservative Whigs who in 1850 abandoned the Whig Party at its National Convention at Syracuse, N.Y. Francis Granger, who presided over this convention, left[1] the hall abruptly when resolutions were adopted protesting slavery and praising William Henry Seward. This constituted a criticism of President Millard Fillmore's administration, of which Granger was a loyal supporter. As he departed, followed by several conservative delegates, it is said an onlooker[2] called out that there went the "silver grays," meaning that most of these men were white-haired. Francis Granger, however, is more generally credited with having originated the nickname[3] for this faction because of his own silver-gray hair. He was born at Suffield, Conn., on December 1, 1792, and died at Canandaigua, N.Y., on August 28, 1868.

[1] *The Life of Thurlow Weed, Volume II: Memoir of Thurlow Weed by His Grandson Thurlow Weed Barnes* (Houghton Mifflin and Company, New York and Boston, 1884) vol. 2, p. 186-7.
[2] *Political Americanisms*, Charles Ledyard Norton (Longmans, Green and Company, New York and London, 1890) p. 101.
[3] *Dictionary of American Biography under the Auspices of the American Council of Learned Societies*, ed. by Allen Johnson and Dumas Malone (Charles Scribner's Sons, New York, 1931) vol. 7, 483.

Silver Greys

When war with Great Britain seemed imminent about 1807, a unit of homeguards was organized at Richmond, Va. The members of this group were popularly called the *Silver Greys*[1] because, being rather advanced in age, most of them had gray hair.

[1] *Richmond, Its People and Its Story*, Mary Newton Stanard (J. B. Lippincott Company, Philadelphia and London, 1923) p. 76.

Silver Heels. See Marshall, John

Silver Heresy

During the candidacy of William McKinley for President of the United States in 1896, the Republican party committed itself to the maintenance of the gold standard. Many Republicans, however, throughout the western, and a few in the southern part of the United States favored the free and unlimited coinage of silver. This advocacy of free silver was nicknamed the *Silver Heresy* [1] and the Republicans favoring it were called *Silver Republicans.* [1]

[1] *Twenty Years of the Republic, 1885-1905,* Harry Thurston Peck (Dodd, Mead and Company, New York, 1907) p. 480, 504.

Silver Man. See Kinzie, John

Silver Sage. See Thomas, Elmer

Silver Spoon Butler. See Butler, B. F.

Silver State. See Colorado; Nevada

Silver tongued and golden hearted. See Willard, F. E.

Silver-tongued Josh. See Lee, J. B.

Silver-tongued Orator. See Bell, J. F.; Bryan, W. J.; Dougherty, Daniel; Kirkpatrick, J. M.; Rollins, J. S.

Silver-tongued Orator of Lamoille. See Shaw, H. E.

Silver-tongued Orator of the South. See Baker, Alpheus

Silver-tongued Spellbinder of the Pacific Coast. See Delmas, D. M.

Silverines. See Coloradans

Simms, William Gilmore

The *Cooper of the South* [1] is a sobriquet applied to William Gilmore Simms because, like James Fenimore Cooper, he wrote novels about Indians.

William Gilmore Simms was born at Charleston, S.C. on April 17, 1806, and died there on June 11, 1870.

[1] *A Book of Nicknames,* John Goff (Courier-Journal Job Printing Company, Louisville, Ky., 1892) p. 30.

Simon. See Allgood, M. C.

Simpson College

The *Redmen* [1] is the sobriquet given to the athletic teams of Simpson College, at Indianola, Iowa, about 1930. The appropriateness of the nickname seems to be borne out by the name of the town and by "the

famous 'Scalp Song' written some years ago by Everett Olive, an alumnus of Simpson and at that time a member of the Conservatory faculty." [1]

[1] A letter from John L. Horsley, Publicity Director at Simpson College, Indianola, Iowa, June 19, 1935.

Simpson, Jerry

Jerry Simpson was called at various times *Sockless Jerry,* the *Sockless Sage, Sockless Simpson, Sockless Socrates,* and the *Sockless Statesman.*

In 1890 he was a candidate of the Peoples Party ticket for Representative from Kansas to the United States Congress, and his Republican opponents accused him of being a clown, an ignoramus, and a ragamuffin. In replying to these accusations, Simpson nicknamed his opponent, Colonel James Hallowell, *Prince Hal,* [1] and spoke of him as wearing silk stockings, which Simpson said he himself could not afford to wear. In writing up Simpson's account of Hallowell, Victor Murdock, a reporter for the Wichita *Daily Eagle,* applied the sobriquet *Sockless Jerry* [1] to Simpson.

Hamlin Garland spoke of Jerry Simpson as the *Sockless Sage;* [1] William Jennings Bryan states that he was nicknamed *Sockless Simpson* [1] and the *Sockless Statesman* [1] by the eastern newspapers when he became Representative from Kansas to the United States Congress in 1891; and Annie L. Diggs says that William Allen White gave Simpson the nickname *Sockless Socrates.* [1]

Jerry Simpson was born in Westmorland County, New Brunswick, Canada, on March 31, 1842, and died at Wichita, Kans., on October 23, 1905.

[1] *The Story of Jerry Simpson,* Annie L. Diggs (Jane Simpson, Publisher, Wichita, Kans., printed and bound by the Hobson Printing Company, Wichita, Kans., 1908) p. 108, 109, 230, 248.

Simpson, John Nicholas

Because he marked his cattle with the brand of a hashknife, *Hashknife Simpson* [1] was the nickname applied to John Nicholas Simpson, a prominent cattle herder living at Weatherford, Tex., in 1876.

[1] *Theodore Roosevelt: An Autobiography* (The Macmillan Company, New York, 1913) p. 122.

Singing Bishop. See McCabe, C. C.

Singing Chaplain. See McCabe, C. C.

Singing City. See Sylacauga, Ala.

Singing Secretary. See McCabe, C. C.

Single Speech Hemphill. See Hemphill, Joseph

Sink the Track and Arch It Over. See Hopkins, F. T.

Sioussat, Jean Pierre
French John [1] was the commonly-known sobriquet of Jean Pierre Sioussat. He was of French descent, and his name in English becomes John. Jean Pierre Sioussat was born in St. Paul's Parish, Paris, France, on September 22, 1781. He began his connection with the White House retinue as doorkeeper during the presidency of James Madison, but later he became the Master of Ceremonies. Because he understood the finer points of French etiquette, he was of invaluable aid [2] to Mrs. Madison in arranging and keeping the White House in order and in assisting her in correctly handling the numerous official social affairs which took place at the White House during President Madison's administration.

[1] *Dolly Madison, the Nation's Hostess*, Elizabeth Lippincott Dean (Lothrop, Lee and Shepard Company, Boston, 1928) p. 119, 138.
[2] "The First Master of Ceremonies of the White House" by John H. McCormick, in *Records of the Columbia Historical Society, Washington, D.C.*, comp. by the Committee on Publication and the Recording Secretary (Published by the Society at the Press of the New Era Printing Company, Lancaster, Pa., 1904) vol. 7, p. 176-7.

Sioux. See University of North Dakota; Wesley College

Sioux Braves. See Sioux Falls College

Sioux Falls College
The athletic teams of Sioux Falls College, at Sioux Falls, S.D., are popularly known as the *Sioux Braves*.[1] Cliff Whitfield of Sioux Falls suggested the sobriquet in 1923 in a contest sponsored by the Alumni Association because it is "in keeping with the Indian legendary theme" [1] of the college.

[1] A communication from M. L. Woods, Secretary to the President of Sioux Falls College, Sioux Falls, S.D., November 20, 1935.

Sioux State. See North Dakota

Sir Veto. See Johnson, Andrew

Siren of the Screen. See West, Mae

Sirovich, William Irving
William Irving Sirovich, a New York physician and congressman, was nicknamed the *Savior of the Arts* by his colleagues in the House of Representatives. He strongly advocated a department of Science, Art, and Literature in the President's Cabinet.

He was a Democratic Representative from the Fourteenth Congressional District of New York State to the United States Congress from 1927 to 1939.

William Irving Sirovich was born at York, Pa., on March 18, 1882, and died December 17, 1939.

[1] An interview with Captain Victor Hunt Harding, Secretary of the National Democratic Congress Re-election Committee, Washington, D.C., April 10, 1939.

Sisk, John
John Sisk, who played halfback in major-league football, was nicknamed *Big Train*.[1] The sobriquet was attributed to him by his fellow athletes on the Marquette University team, in Milwaukee, Wis., while he was making his famous record for touchdowns on that team from 1929 until 1932. *Big Train* undoubtedly was suggested because it once belonged to Walter Johnson, outstanding baseball pitcher with an equally impressive record.

John Sisk was born at New Haven, Conn., on December 11, 1906.

[1] *Who's Who in Major League Football*, comp. by Harold (Speed) Johnson and Wilfrid Smith (B. V. Callahan, Chicago, 1935) p. 23.

Sit-down Striker. See Hoffman, C. E.

Sitting Bull. See Lawson, J. D.; Morton, O. H. P. T.; Summerall, C. P.

Siwashes. See Knox College

Six-shooters
During western frontier days especially, revolvers that fired six times without reloading were called *Six-shooters*.[1] They are still spoken of as such in many localities today.

[1] *The Adventures of Buffalo Bill*, Colonel William F. Cody (Buffalo Bill) (Harper and Brothers, New York, 1904) p. 16.

Sixth Armored Division of World War II
The *Super Sixth* [1] was the nickname of the Sixth Armored Division of the Combat Divisions of World War II.

[1] *Combat Divisions of World War II* (Army of the United States) Army Times Publishing Company, Washington, D.C., 1946, p. 80.

Sixth Infantry Division of World War II

The nickname of the Sixth Infantry Division of the Combat Divisions of World War II was the *Red Star Division*.[1]

[1] *Combat Divisions of World War II* (Army of the United States) Army Times Publishing Company, Washington, D.C., 1946, p. 12.

Sixty-fifth Infantry Division of World War II

The *Battle Axe Division*[1] was the nickname of the Sixty-fifth Infantry Division of the Combat Divisions of World War II.

[1] *Combat Divisions of World War II* (Army of the United States) Army Times Publishing Company, Washington, D.C., 1946, p. 39.

Sixty-ninth Infantry Division of World War II

The *Fighting Sixty-ninth*[1] was the nickname of the Sixty-ninth Division of the Combat Divisions of World War II because of its fierce fighting.

[1] *Combat Divisions of World War II* (Army of the United States) Army Times Publishing Company, Washington, D.C., 1946, p. 41.

Sixty-sixth Infantry Division of World War II

The *Black Panther Division*[1] was the nickname of the Sixty-sixth Infantry Division of the Combat Divisions of World War II.

[1] *Combat Divisions of World War II* (Army of the United States) Army Times Publishing Company, Washington, D.C., 1946, p. 40.

Sixty-third Infantry Division of World War II

The *Blood and Fire Division*[1] was the nickname of the Sixty-third Division of the Combat Divisions of World War II. This nickname originated from a statement at the Casablanca Conference to the effect that the enemy would bleed and burn.

[1] *Combat Divisions of World War II* (Army of the United States) Army Times Publishing Company, Washington, D.C., 1946, p. 38.

Skibos. See Carnegie Institute of Technology

Skillful Neily. See Neily, Harry

Skinner, Otis

The actor, Otis Skinner, was nicknamed the *Dean of the American Theatre*[1] because he was prominent as an actor, manager, producer and playwright from the time of his professional debut in Philadelphia, Pa., in 1877.

Otis Skinner was born at Cambridge, Mass., on June 28, 1858, and died January 4, 1942.

[1] *Newsweek: The Magazine of News Significance,* Rockefeller Center, N.Y., February 6, 1939, col. 2, p. 6.

Skinners

The *Skinners*[1] were bands of plunderers sympathetic to the colonial patriots, who robbed and harassed the British invaders and their Tory friends during the Revolutionary War, and who often engaged in skirmishes with the *Cowboys,* the partisans of the British. The *Skinners* operated in New York State and were doubtless so-called because they were adept at stripping their victims of their money or property. It has been suggested that the British designated the American raiders *Skinners*[2] because they did not leave behind even the skins of the animals they confiscated.

[1] *Dictionary of United States History, 1492-1900: Four Centuries of History, Written Concisely and Arranged Alphabetically in Dictionary Form,* J. Franklin Jameson (History Publishing Company, Boston, 1900) p. 602.
[2] *History of the State of New York,* Charles F. Horne (D. C. Heath and Company, New York and Chicago, 1916) p. 270.

Skullions. See Bettis Academy

Skyagunsta. See Pickens, Andrew

Slater, Samuel

Samuel Slater is known as the *Father of American Manufacture*[2] in recognition of his contribution to the establishment[1] of cotton manufacturing in the United States.

In England, Slater had been apprenticed to a business associate of Richard Arkwright, but upon hearing that a bounty was offered in the United States for cotton-spinning machinery, he embarked for this country. British patent laws forbade the exportation of drawings of cotton-spinning machinery, and Slater was forced to rely upon his memory in designing the cotton-spinning machines which he created and set up at Pawtucket, R.I., in 1790. In later years his interests were extended to include the manufacture of woolen cloth, textiles, and iron products.

Slater, Samuel—Continued

He was born at Belper, Derbyshire, England, on June 9, 1768 and died at Webster, Mass., on April 21, 1835.

[1] *Cotton Manufacture: Memoir of Samuel Slater, The Father of American Manufactures, Connected with a History of the Rise and Progress of the Cotton Manufacture in England and America, with Remarks on the Moral Influence of Manufactories in the United States,* Second Edition, George S. White (Printed at No. 46, Carpenter Street, Philadelphia, 1836) p. 95-7.

[2] *Samuel Slater and the Early Development of the Cotton Manufacture in the United States,* William R. Bagnall (J. S. Stewart, Middletown, Conn., 1890) p. 25.

Sleepy Phil. See Knox, P. C.

Slicker Campaign

About 1845, when horse thieves and counterfeiters were doing a prosperous business in Lincoln County, Mo., the courts were unable to convict them because of the alibis established by witnesses whom the thieves had engaged beforehand to testify in their behalf. The citizens of this county organized a company of vigilantes who visited suspected persons and, if convinced that such persons were guilty of crimes, "slicked them down" with hickory sprouts and gave them a definite number of hours in which to leave the county. By such procedures the vigilantes were able to rid their county of troublesome characters which the law had been unable to handle. The eliminating of objectionable characters from Lincoln County by this means was nicknamed the *Slicker Campaign,*[1] the term being derived from the slang word *slick* which is applied to the act of thrashing an individual.

[1] *Centennial History of Missouri (The Center State) One Hundred Years in the Union 1820-1921,* Walter B. Stevens (The S. J. Clarke Publishing Company, St. Louis, Mo., and Chicago, 1921) vol. 2, p. 239.

Slinging Sammy. See Baugh, S. A.

Slingshot Charley. See Taylor, Charley

Slippery Dick. See Connolly, Richard

Slippery Sam. See Tilden, S. J.

Sloan, James Forman

James Forman Sloan, the celebrated jockey, was nicknamed *Toad*[1] by his father while Sloan was a child because he was so small. This sobriquet was transformed into *Tod* by his playmates and in later life he signed himself Todhunter in order to give a more ornamental account of his nickname.

Sloan made internationally famous the seat in the saddle which revolutionized modern race riding. Lying along the neck and shoulders of his mounts, the position was first jeered at as a "monkey-on-a-stick" attitude until his outstanding record of victories resulted in imitation of his methods.

James Forman Sloan was born near Kokomo, Ind., on August 10, 1874, and died at San Francisco, Calif., on December 21, 1933.

[1] *Dictionary of American Biography under the Auspices of the American Council of Learned Societies,* ed. by Dumas Malone (Charles Scribner's Sons, New York, 1935) vol. 17, p. 211.

Slogan Man. See Smythe, J. H., Jr.

Slogan Smythe. See Smythe, J. H. Jr.

Sloppy. See Thurston, H. J.

Slugger. See Burns, J. I.

Smiling Jim. See Farley, J. A.

Smith, Alfred Emanuel

It is said that at the suggestion of Justice of the New York State Supreme Court Joseph Meyer Proskauer,[1] Franklin Delano Roosevelt used the phrase the *Happy Warrior,*[2] in reference to Alfred Emanuel Smith in a speech delivered by Roosevelt at the 1928 Democratic Convention.

The expression refers to William Wordsworth's poem entitled *Character of the Happy Warrior.* Roosevelt described Smith as a leader of men whose integrity and courage had brought him constant victory,[3] traits of character similar to those possessed by the *Happy Warrior* of Wordsworth's poem.

Alfred Emanuel Smith was born at New York City, on December 30, 1873, and died October 4, 1944.

[1] *Franklin D. Roosevelt, a Career in Progressive Democracy,* Ernest K. Lindley (The Bobbs-Merrill Company, Indianapolis, Ind., 1931) p. 223.

[2] *Torchlight Parades, Our Presidential Pageant,* Sherwin Lawrence Cook (Minton, Balch and Company, New York, 1929) p. 281.

[3] *The Happy Warrior, Alfred E. Smith, a Study of a Public Servant,* Franklin D. Roosevelt (Houghton Mifflin Company, New York and Boston, 1928) p. 40.

Smith, Ellison DuRant

Ellison DuRant Smith, Democratic Senator from South Carolina, was nicknamed *Cotton Ed.*[1] Himself owner of a cotton plantation in Lee County, S.C., he strove to secure legislation for the cotton farmer.

Smith organized the cotton farmers of South Carolina into the Farmers Protective Association to fight the boll weevil in 1901. He also was one of the chief organizers of the Boll Weevil Convention which met at Shreveport, La., in 1905.

He served as Democratic Senator from South Carolina to the United States Congress from 1909 until his defeat in 1944. Although a Democrat, he was a bitter critic of the New Deal.[2]

Ellison DuRant Smith was born in Lee County, S.C., on August 1, 1866, and died November 17, 1944.

[1] *Washington Herald*, Washington, D.C., July 31, 1932, col. 2, p. B-7.

[2] *Current Biography, Who's News and Why, 1945*, ed. by Anna Rothe (The H. W. Wilson Company, New York, 1946) p. 556.

Smith, Erasmus

Deaf Smith[1] was a nickname applied to Erasmus Smith because his hearing was impaired from early childhod throughout his entire life. Smith having been important in the early annals of Texas, the *Houston Telegraph* said of him at his death: " 'This singular individual was one whose name bears with it more of respect than sounding titles. Major, Colonel, General, sink into insignificance before the simple name of Deaf Smith. That name is identified with the battlefields of Texas. His eulogy is inseparably interwoven with the most thrilling annals of our country, and will long yield to our traditional narrative a peculiar interest.' "[2]

[1] *Our First War in Mexico*, Farnham Bishop (Charles Scribner's Sons, New York, 1916) p. 51.

[2] *A Pictorial History of Texas, from the Earliest Visit of European Adventurers, to A.D., 1879*, Fifth Edition Carefully Revised, Homer S. Thrall (N. D. Thompson and Company, St. Louis, Mo., 1879) p. 621.

Smith, Francis Henney

The students in the Virginia Military Institute at Lexington, Va., where many of the officers in the Confederate Army were stationed during the winter of 1862-3, nicknamed Francis Henney Smith *Old Spex*[1] doubtless because he wore spectacles.

In 1833 Smith was graduated from the United States Military Academy, at West Point, N.Y. When the Virginia Military Institute, at Lexington was organized in 1839, he was appointed its Superintendent. He served in this capacity until 1890. at which time he became Professor Emeritus. Smith was also a colonel in the Confederate Army.

Francis Henney Smith was born at Norfolk, Va., on October 18, 1812, and died at Lexington, Va., on March 21, 1880.

[1] *The End of an Era*, John S. Wise (Houghton Mifflin and Company, New York and Boston, 1889) p. 261.

Smith, Francis Marion

Francis Marion Smith was known both nationally and internationally as *Borax Smith*[1] or *The Borax King*.[1] He was the owner of immense borax mines near Columbus, Nev., and in Death Valley, Calif., and as the world's greatest producer of borax and boracic acid controlled the borax markets of the world for many years.

He was born at Richmond, Wis., on February 2, 1846, and died at Oakland, Calif., on August 27, 1931.

[1] *Encyclopedia of American Biography: American Biography, A New Cyclopedia*, comp. under the editorial supervision of a notable advisory board (Published under the direction of The American Historical Society, Inc., New York, 1932) vol. 51, p. 76-8.

Smith, James Henry

James Henry Smith, a New York multimillionaire, was generally designated *Silent Smith*[1] because he lived quietly and was always extremely reticent about himself and his business affairs. His friends said they looked upon him as a "man who locked up his own soul."[2] Although Smith was silent, he was not a hermit for he held membership in several exclusive New York clubs. He lived during the latter part of the nineteenth century and into the twentieth, marrying the former Mrs. Rhinelander Stewart in 1906. He died in Tokyo, Japan, during his wedding trip, on March 27, 1907.

[1] *The New York Times*, New York, March 28, 1907, col. 5, p. 9.

[2] *The Washington Post*, Washington, D.C., March 28, 1907, col. 3, p. 1. Col. 5, p. 12

Smith, James Monroe

James Monroe Smith, former President of Louisiana State University, was nicknamed *Jingle Money Smith*[1] by journalists soon after he had resigned the presidency of the University on June 25, 1939. The sobriquet refers to Dr. Smith's speculative activities with University funds, for which he was indicted on the charge of embezzlement.

He was Dean of the College of Education at Southwest Louisiana Institute from 1920 to 1930, and President of Louisiana State University from 1930 until 1939 when he resigned the post and fled to Canada.

Smith, J. M.—Continued

He was arrested there and returned to Louisiana on the charge of embezzling $100,000 of University funds. He was also indicted thirty-six times on similar charges, and was put in jail at New Orleans, La. He was a part of the Huey Long regime in Louisiana.

James Monroe ·Smith was born in Jackson Parish, La., on October 9, 1888. He was released from the penitentiary, February 6, 1946, and died May 26, 1949.

[1] *Time: The Weekly Newsmagazine*, Chicago, July 31, 1939, col. 3, p. 12.

Smith, John

Captain John Smith has been called the *Father of Virginia*.[1]

He took an active part in establishing the first permanent English settlement in the New World, the Jamestown settlement of 1607. Smith, who had a genius for leadership and a good deal of practical military experience, so effectively organized this colony that its settlers were able to provide themselves with food, clothing, shelter, and protection from hostile Indians.

John Smith was born at Willoughby, Lincolnshire, England, in 1580, and died at London, in June, 1631.

[1] *Barnes' Popular History of the United States of America from Prehistoric America to the Present Time*, Revised to Date, Joel Dorman Steele and Esther Baker Steele (A. L. Burt Company, New York, 1914) p. 34.

Smith, Joseph

Joseph Smith, the founder of the Church of Jesus Christ of Latter Day Saints, is designated the *Father of the Mormons*.[1] He organized the Mormon Church at Fayette, N.Y., on April 6, 1830.

Joseph Smith was born at Sharon, Vt., on December 23, 1805, and died at the hands of a mob in Carthage, Ill., on June 27, 1844.

[1] *A Book of Nicknames*, John Goff (Courier-Journal Job Printing Company, Louisville, Ky., 1892) p. 29.

Smith, Rodney

The Reverend Rodney Smith, one of the most famous English and American evangelists, is commonly designated *Gypsy Smith*.[1] When he began to preach in 1877, in order to distinguish him from his father and two uncles, who were also traveling preachers known as the *Three Gypsy Brothers* or the *Three Converted Gypsies*, Rodney Smith was called the *Gypsy Boy*.

Rodney Smith was born of gypsy parents near London, in Essex county, England, on March 31, 1869.

[1] *Gipsy Smith: His Life and His Work*, Rodney Smith (Free National Church Council, London, 1924) p. 122.

Smith, Thomas Vernon

Thomas Vernon Smith, Congressman from Illinois, was nicknamed *Philosophy Smith*,[1] or the *Political Philosopher*, by his colleagues in the House of Representatives. He was formerly a Professor of Philosophy at Texas Christian University, Fort Worth, Tex., at the University of Texas, Austin, Tex., and at the University of Chicago.

He was a Democratic Senator in the Illinois Legislature from 1935 until 1938, and was a Senator at large from Illinois to the United States Congress from 1939 to 1941. He has been Maxwell Professor of Citizenship and Philosophy at Syracuse University since 1948.

Thomas Vernon Smith was born at Blanket, Tex., on April 26, 1890.

[1] An interview with Captain Victor Hunt Harding, Secretary of the National Democratic Congress Reelection Committee, Washington, D.C., April 10, 1939.

Smith, Walter Bedell

Walter Bedell Smith, appointed by President Eisenhower in February 1953 as Under Secretary of State, is familiarly known as *Beetle*[1] or *Beedle*.[2]

Smith's middle name is pronounced with the stress on the first syllable and from this the nicknames consequently developed. Smith also acquired a nickname from Sir Winston Churchill during World War II. At that time, General Smith was serving as first secretary of the Anglo-American combination guiding joint military policy. His tenacity in disputing suggestions with which he disagreed was much admired by Churchill who affectionately tagged him *Bulldog*.[1]

Walter Bedell Smith was born October 5, 1895, in Indianapolis, Ind. During World War II he was assistant secretary and later secretary to the War Department General Staff, and subsequently first secretary of the Combined Chiefs of Staff in London. After the war he was Ambassador to Moscow during the Truman administration.

[1] *New York Times Magazine*, March 1, 1953, p. 11, p. 44.

[2] *Current Biography 1944, Who's News and Why*, ed. by Anna Rothe (The H. W. Wilson Company, New York, 1945) p. 640.

Smith, William

William Smith who, in his youth, helped to capture a pirate band in Canarsie, N.Y., and who lived to a venerable age, was nicknamed *Uncle Billy*[1] by his fellow-townsmen.

In 1830, Smith was instrumental in the identification and capture of a sea pirate named Gibbs and his accomplices. Gibbs, who was a murderer, was the last sea pirate to be executed in New York.

William Smith was born in Rahway, N.J., on December 27, 1809, and died at Canarsie, N.Y., on February 24, 1907.

[1] *The Washington Post*, Washington, D.C., February 25, 1907, col. 1, p. 3.

Smith, William (Jurist)

William Smith, who was born in Northhamptonshire, England, on February 2, 1655, and who died in Suffolk County, Va., on February 18, 1705, was nicknamed *Tangiers Smith*.[1] About 1685, he held the post of governor of Tangiers in Africa.

[1] *The National Cyclopaedia of American Biography* (James T. White and Company, New York, 1904) vol. 12, p. 252.

Smith, William (Politician)

The nickname, *Extra Billy*,[1] originated while William Smith was a mail contractor. In 1827 he obtained from the Government a contract to transport mail in Culpepper County, Va. In 1831 this contract was renewed and extended to carrying mail from Washington, D.C., to Milledgeville, Ga. In addition to the salary fixed by the contract, extra pay was allowed for additional service performed relative to the carrying of the mail, the added expenditures being noted "in the Blue Book or official register of the United States Government." As Smith's route expanded, his entries of this nature were rather numerous. During a Congressional controversy in 1834, with regard to the administration of Postmaster General W. Barry, Smith's extra duties and extra compensations were commented upon by Senator Benjamin Watkins Leigh, who tactfully avoided an outright mention of Smith but referred to him as *Extra Billy*,[2] a nickname so explicit that his colleagues knew of whom he was speaking. Thereafter, William Smith was popularly known as *Extra Billy*.

William Smith, who was born in King George County, Va., on September 6, 1796, and who died at Warrenton, Va., on May 18, 1887, was governor of Virginia from 1846 to 1849.

[1] *Memoirs of Governor William Smith of Virginia, His Political, Military, and Personal History*, John W. Bell (The Moss Engraving Company, New York, 1891) p. 96-7, 98, 130.

Smith, William Farrar

When William Farrar Smith entered the United States Military Academy at West Point, N.Y., in 1841, he was nicknamed *Baldy*[1] by his fellow-cadets, the purpose of the sobriquet having been to distinguish him from other young men of the same Christian name. It is not said just why this particular nickname was chosen; but it may have been an allusion to Smith's bold, militant, and brave nature, which qualities could have caused him to be compared to the bald eagle, a bird noted for its ability to fight. Pictures of Major General Smith portray him as having had a goodly amount of hair upon his head even as an elderly man, which would eliminate the possibility of an allusion to a bald head.

During the Civil War Major General Smith commanded a division of the Army of the Potomac from about 1861 to 1863, and in 1863 he became the Chief Engineer of the Army of the Cumberland. In this capacity he planned several of the most outstanding battles in which the Army of the Cumberland participated.

William Farrar Smith was born at St. Albans, Vt., on February 17, 1824, and died at Philadelphia, Pa., on February 28, 1903.

[1] *Heroes of the Great Conflict: Life and Services of William Farrar Smith, Major-general, United States Volunteers in the Civil War*, James Harrison Wilson (The John M. Rogers Press, Wilmington, Del., 1904) p. 17.
General Kirby-Smith, Arthur Howard Noll (The University Press, Sewanee, Tenn., 1907) p. 17.

Smith, William Russell

William Russell Smith, a legislator, who was born at Russelville, Ky., on March 27, 1815, and who died at Washington, D.C., on February 26, 1896, was affectionately called *Little Billy*[1] by his numerous friends in allusion to his small physique.

[1] *The National Cyclopaedia of American Biography* (James T. White and Company, New York, 1904) vol. 12, p. 294.

Smith, William Sooy

Sookey Smith[1] was a widely known sobriquet of William Sooy Smith. *Sookey* may be a playful mispronunciation of his middle

Smith, W. S.—Continued
name; it is also an old-fashioned nickname
for Susan.

In 1862 Smith became a Brigadier General and was put in command of the Second
Division of the Army of the Ohio. Later
he became commander of the First Division
of the Sixteenth Army Corps and of the
Cavalry Division of the Department of the
Tennessee. In 1864 he resigned from army
life because of ill health.[2]

William Sooy Smith was born at Tarlton,
Ohio, on July 22, 1830, and died at Medford, Ore., on March 4, 1916.

[1] *Bedford Forrest and His Critter Company*, Andrew
Nelson Lytle (Minton, Balch and Company, New York,
1931) p. 257.
[2] *The National Cyclopaedia of American Biography*
(James T. White and Company, New York, 1897)
vol. 4, p. 498.

Smith's Guerrillas

During the Civil War, the Union soldiers
in the Sixteenth Corps of the Military Division of the Mississippi forces came to be
known as *Smith's Guerrillas*.[1] In 1863 or
1864, while they were under the command
of Major General Andrew Jackson Smith,
taking part in the Federal campaigns in the
Mississippi Valley, they searched that region
thoroughly for food for themselves and their
horses. This marauding caused them to be
compared to guerrillas, or irregular soldiers
who, in time of war, secure provisions by
pillaging along the route of their activities.
The nickname was originated by Major General Nathaniel Prentiss Banks who, during
the Red River Campaign in the southwestern
part of the United States in 1864 asked
General William Tecumseh Sherman for ten
thousand soldiers. When he learned that
the majority of the men assigned to him
were members of the Sixteenth Corps, Banks
remarked bitterly that instead of getting ten
thousand of the best soldiers in General
Sherman's army, he was getting ten thousand guerrillas, for he had previously heard
of the poor discipline of this corps. The
soldiers of the Sixteenth Corps instead of
becoming offended accepted the term with
pride and thereafter spoke of themselves as
Smith's Guerrillas.

[1] *The Bravest Five Hundred of '61; Their Noble
Deeds Described by Themselves, together with an Account of Some Gallant Exploits of Our Soldiers in Indian Warfare; How the Medal of Honor Was Won*,
comp. by Theophile F. Rodenbough (G. W. Dillingham,
New York, 1891) p. 219.

Smoky City. See Pittsburgh, Pa.

Smythe, John Henry, Jr.

John Henry Smythe, Jr., America's most
famous slogan writer, was nicknamed *Slogan
Smythe* and the *Slogan Man*. He is the au-
thor of over one thousand slogans and
battle cries.[1] He was nicknamed the *Slogan
Man* [2] during the 1924 Republican National
Convention. Smythe's work may be classi-
fied: (1) war slogans, (2) battle cries, (3)
Liberty and Victory bond slogans, and (4)
political slogans. He is the author of such
well-known slogans as *Do Your Bit to Keep
It Lit! Lend to Defend! Keep the Faith!
Buy and Keep the Liberty Bonds!*, and *Keep
Coolidge—He Keeps Faith!* Smythe is a
Republican, and his political slogans are
written for that party.

John Henry Smythe, Jr., was born in
Philadelphia, Pa., on October 10, 1883.

[1] *The Washington Post*, Washington, D.C., January
18, 1937, cols. 2 and 3, p. 3.
[2] *Who's Who in America: A Biographical Dictionary
of Notable Living Men and Women of the United States*,
1938-1939, ed. by Albert Nelson Marquis (The A. N.
Marquis Company, Chicago, 1938) vol. 20, p. 2320.

Snappers

Under the leadership of David B. Hill,
Governor of New York, the Democratic
State Committee called a convention to as-
semble in Albany on February 22, 1892, to
elect delegates at large to attend the Democratic National Convention scheduled to
meet in Chicago, on June 21. The New
York state convention, called two months
earlier than usual, was held so that Hill
might secure control of the New York dele-
gation to the national convention in order
to further his own nomination as the Democratic candidate for the office of President
of the United States. The *Snappers*,[1] par-
ticipants in the "snap convention" [2] meant
to give impetus to Hill's campaign, were opposed by *Anti-Snappers*, Democrats who favored the nomination of Grover Cleveland.

[1] *Twenty Years of the Republic, 1885-1905*, Harry
Thurston Peck (Dodd, Mead and Company, New York,
1907) p. 280-1.
[2] *Grover Cleveland, A Study in Courage*, by Allan
Nevins (Dodd, Mead and Company, New York, 1932)
p. 483, 485, 486.

Snapping Turtle. See Glass, G. C.

Snipe. See Hansen, R. F.

Snivel-service Reform

The Civil Service Reform measure adopted by Congress in 1871 was nicknamed the
Snivel-service Reform [1] by those politicians

who had been accustomed to appointing their friends and political favorites to Government positions. This measure gave the President of the United States power to appoint a Civil Service Commission to formulate whatever regulations they saw fit governing the appointing of persons to Government positions, their regulations being subject to the President's approval. "Influential party leaders on both sides despised it."

[1] *Twenty Years of the Republic, 1885-1905,* Harry Thurston Peck (Dodd, Mead and Company, New York, 1907) p. 67, 68.

Snorting Race Horses. See *Black Dragons*

Snow Baby. See Peary, M. A.

Snowshoe Thompson. See Thompson, J. A.

Snozz. See Lombardi, E. N.

Snyder, Christopher

Christopher Snyder was called by his compatriots the *First Martyr of the Revolution.*[1] In Boston, Mass., in 1770 there was much agitation regarding the continued sale by some merchants of certain British merchandise, which the majority of the colonists had decided not to buy or sell. One of these importers was Theophilus Lillie who, because he was selling British merchandise, had incurred the displeasure of a large group of persons, chiefly young boys. Ebenezer Richardson, a friend of Lillie's, seized a musket and in a moment of anger fired a shot at random amidst the boys, which fatally wounded Christopher Snyder, the "son of a poor widow." The townspeople simultaneously proclaimed Richardson a murderer and Snyder the first martyr in the impending struggle for independence. Richardson was imprisoned for two years, after which he was pardoned by King George III.

Christopher Snyder was born about 1755, and died in Boston, Mass., on February 23, 1770.

[1] *Appleton's Cyclopaedia of American Biography,* ed. by James Grant Wilson and John Fiske (D. Appleton and Company, New York, 1888) vol. 5, p. 603.

Snyder, Frank J.

Frank J. Snyder, who has been coach of the New York Giants since 1933, is popularly known as *Pancho.*[1]

[1] *Who's Who in Major League Base Ball,* comp. by Harold (Speed) Johnson (Buxton Publishing Company, Chicago, 1933) p. 432.

Sockless Jerry. See Simpson, Jerry

Sockless Sage. See Simpson, Jerry

Sockless Simpson. See Simpson, Jerry

Sockless Socrates. See Simpson, Jerry

Sockless Statesman. See Simpson, Jerry

Soda Ash Johnny. See Horan, J. M.

Soda Water Bottle

A smooth bore gun invented by Admiral John Adolf Dahlgren, of the United States Navy, was nicknamed the *Soda Water Bottle*[1] because of its resemblance in shape to a soda water bottle.

[1] *The Encyclopaedia Britannica,* Fourteenth Edition (Encyclopaedia Britannica, Inc., New York, 1932) vol. 6, p. 975.

Softs

While Senator Thomas Hart Benton was advocating the exclusive use of gold and silver currency about 1934, opponents of his policy were called *Softs*[1] because they favored paper currency, as distinguished from hard currency.

[1] "Thomas Hart Benton" by Theodore Roosevelt, in *American Statesmen,* ed. by John T. Morse, Junior (Houghton Mifflin and Company, New York and Boston, 1903) p. 342.

Soldier Parson. See Caldwell, James

Soldier's Friend. See Curtin, A. G.; Ward, M. L.

Solid City. See St. Louis, Mo.

Solid Man. See Muldoon, William

Solters, Julius Joseph

Julius Joseph Solters, who was born at Pittsburgh, Pa., on March 22, 1908, and who played outfield in major league base-

Solters, J. J.—Continued
ball, was nicknamed *Lemons* [1] by his fellow
athletes because of his liking for that fruit.

[1] *Who's Who in The Major Leagues*, 1935 Edition,
Harold (Speed) Johnson (B. E. Callahan, Chicago,
1935) p. 48.

Sommerville, Andrew
The appellations, *Faithful Andy* [1] and
Handy Andy,[1] were given by Mrs. Mary
Ann Ball Bickerdyke to Andrew Sommer-
ville, a Union soldier appointed by Major
General Ulysses Simpson Grant to attend
Mrs. Bickerdyke in nursing wounded Fed-
eral soldiers. These sobriquets describe Som-
merville's consistent loyalty, faithfulness, and
trustworthiness while he was assisting Mrs.
Bickerdyke's nursing activities during the
Civil War.

[1] *Mary A. Bickerdyke, "Mother,"* Julia A. Chase (Pub-
lished under the Auspices of the Women's Relief Corps,
Department of Kansas, by the Journal Publishing House,
Lawrence, Kans., 1896) p. 27, 41, 45.

Son Jimmy. See Roosevelt, James

Sookey Smith. See Smith, W. S.

Sooner State. See Oklahoma

Sooners. See Oklahomans; University of
Oklahoma

Sorebacks. See Virginians

Sorrell, Victor Garland
Victor Garland Sorrell's baseball comrades nicknamed him *Ace, Baby-doll, Lawyer,* the *Philosopher,* and *Vic.*[1]
He was born on a plantation in North
Carolina on April 9, 1902, and played in
major league baseball.

[1] *Who's Who in The American League*, 1935 Edition,
Harold (Speed) Johnson (B. E. Callahan, Chicago,
1935) p. 16.

Soul Stealers
During the period of colonization in
America, the sobriquet *Soul Stealers* [1] was
applied to those men in England who worked
for shipowners and others interested in securing colonists to come to America. The
members of this group were known as *Soul
Stealers* because they often caused emigrants
to come to America by causing them to believe that opportunities here were much
more favorable for accumulating wealth than

they were in England. The newcomers, however, were often reduced to a state of de-
pendency by the venture.

[1] *A History of the United States*, Henry Eldridge
Bourne and Elbert Jay Benton (D. C. Heath and Company, New York and Boston, 1913) p. 113.

Sound Money Glass. See Glass, G. C.

Souphouse Charlie. See Bonaparte, C. J.

Sousa, John Philip
John Philip Sousa, bandmaster, conductor,
and composer, was nicknamed the *March
King* [1] because he has written such a vast
number of superior marches. For many
years before his death he was widely known
both in Europe and in America by this
sobriquet. He composed more than fifty
marches to be played by his own band.
His composition *Semper Fidelis* became the
official march of the United States Marine
Corps in 1888.

John Philip Sousa was born at Washington, D.C., on November 6, 1856, and died
at Reading, Pa., on March 6, 1932. His
father was Portuguese and his mother Ba-
varian.

[1] *Washington Herald*, Washington, D.C., March 6,
1932, col. 3 p. 1.

South Carolina
The sobriquets of South Carolina are:
the *Game-cock,* the *Harry Percy of the
Union,* the *Iodine State,* the *Keystone of
the South Atlantic Seaboard,* the *Palmetto
State,* the *Rice State,* the *Sandlapper State,*
and the *Swamp State.*

Because South Carolina so bitterly opposed the abolition of slavery and the coercion of the southern states by the northern
states to remain in the Union, and because
it was the first of the southern states to
secede from the Union in 1860, it has been
called the *Game-cock* [1] and the *Harry Percy
of the Union.*[1] Both these nicknames imply
an impulsive, determined course of action,
the game-cock being a fighter, and Harry
Percy being a fiery-tempered English soldier
who lost his life in a rebellion against Henry
IV at the Battle of Shrewbury on July 21,
1403.

South Carolina is designated the *Iodine
State* because the plants grown there contain
a high percentage of iodine.[2]

The palmetto grows abundantly in South Carolina, especially along the coast, and is pictured on her coat of arms; hence the nickname *Palmetto State*.[3]

South Carolina is also called the *Keystone of the South Atlantic Seaboard* because of its position in the group of states along the coast, and the *Rice State* from the enormous quantities of rice it produces and handles each year.

The *Sandlapper State* is given as a nickname to South Carolina, probably from the fact that some of its poorer inhabitants live on the sandy ridges covered with scrubby pine forest where it would seem that they must lap up sand for sustenance.

The *Swamp State* is applied to South Carolina in reference to the fields where the rice is grown and other swampy areas.

[1] *Andrew Johnson, Plebian and Patriot*, Robert W. Winston (Henry Holt and Company, New York, 1928) p. 162.

[2] *Legislative Manual of the Seventy-ninth General Assembly of South Carolina*, J. Wilson Gibbs, Clerk of the House of Representatives (The State Company, Columbia, S.C., 1931) p. 207.

[3] *A New Dictionary of Americanisms*, Sylva Clapin (Louis Weiss and Company, New York, 1903) p. 299.

South Carolina Gamecock. See Sumter, Thomas

South Carolinians

South Carolinians have been called *Clay-eaters, Palmettoes, Rice-birds, Sandhillers, Sandlappers*, and *Weasels*. Several of these terms have been used derisively in reference to the poorer white class. Poor people living in some of the remoter districts are said to have eaten abundantly of the white clay found in the vicinity when they could get no more substantial food, hence the nickname *Clay-eaters*.[1] For the origin and the significance of *Palmettoes* and *Sandlappers*, see the previous narrative about South Carolina. *Rice-birds* is a nickname given to the well-to-do rice planters and the inhabitants of the rich rice section of the state. The country surrounding Beaufort, S.C., "embraces the best rice fields of the South, so proverbially so indeed that . . . [those] 'up country' are accustomed to call the aristocratic inhabitants of the region *rice-birds*."[2] *Sandhillers* was applied especially to the poor decendants of the laboring white people who were driven out of the pine woods to the sandy hills of South Carolina when slave labor was introduced,[3] and there became skinny and cadaverous-looking. They are said to have skins the color of the sand of their habitat.[4] The name might have been derived from the sand-hill crane (*Grus canadensis*) a longlegged species[2] found commonly in the sections of the country in which these people live. *Sandlappers* is the nickname given to the people living in the pine barrens.[5]

The people living in the out-of-the-way sections of the State are called *Weasels*.[2]

[1] *A New Dictionary of Americanisms*, Sylva Clapin (Louis Weiss and Company, New York, 1903) p. 121.

[2] *U.S.: An Index to the United States of America*, comp. by Malcolm Townsend (D. Lothrop Company, Boston, 1890) p. 80.

[3] *More About Names*, Leopold Wagner (T. Fisher Unwin, London, 1893) p. 26.

[4] *A Journey in the Seaboard Slave States with Remarks on Their Economy*, Frederick Law Olmstead (Dix and Edwards, New York, 1856) p. 506.

[5] *The Forayers*, William Gilmore Simms (Redfield, New York, 1855) p. 391.

South Dakota

South Dakota has the following nicknames: the *Artesian State*, the *Blizzard State*, the *Coyote State*, the *Land of Plenty*, and the *Sunshine State*.

The great number of artesian wells in South Dakota cause it to be called the *Artesian State*.

The nickname *Blizzard State* was given to South Dakota because of the terrific northerly gales laden with fine snow which sweep over portions of the state.

The great number of coyotes or small wolves on the territorial prairie gave the nickname, *Coyote State*, to South Dakota.

In discussing the expression, the *Land of Plenty*, Johnson says that "with an average of over four hundred acres of land for every family in the state, having ability to support in comfort several times the present population, South Dakota certainly deserves the title."[1]

South Dakota is known as the *Sunshine State* because of the great percentage of sunny weather it has during the year. North and South Dakota together are frequently called the *Twin Sisters*.

[1] *South Dakota: A Republic of Friends*, Willis E. Johnson (The Capital Supply Company, Pierre, S.D., 1917) p. 13.

South Dakota State School of Mines

The *Hardknockers*,[1] *the Miners*,[1] and the *Wildcats*[1] are nicknames given to the athletic teams of South Dakota State School of Mines, at Rapid City, S.D. *Hardknockers* "is the name applied to miners who blast their ore from rocks";[1] but this nickname

South Dakota State School of Mines
—Continued

went out of use in 1935. The nickname, the *Miners*, came into current use because the school was originally a college of mining.[1] The fact that the call letters of the broadcasting station at the college are WCAT[1] gave rise to the nickname *Wildcats.*

[1] A communication from R. D. Hahn, Director of Athletics at South Dakota State School of Mines, Rapid City, S.D., June 8, 1935.

Southern Finger of the United States.
See Florida

Southern Gateway of New England.
See Providence, R.I.

Southern Methodist University
The athletic teams of Southern Methodist University, Dallas, Tex., were nicknamed *Mustangs*[1] in 1915. Mustang ponies are to be found on cattle ranches all over Texas. Miss Dorothy Amann, College Librarian, notes that during the first year of the existence of the college, the athletic teams were composed of students without consideration of their rank or their athletic training." When they came out on the athletic field for the first time (in the fall), they looked just like half-broken ponies." This fact suggested the nickname to her mind.

[1] A letter from Dorothy Amann, Librarian at Southern Methodist University, Dallas, Tex., June 21, 1935.

Southwest Baptist College
The nickname, the *Bear Cats,*[1] was given to the members of the basketball teams of Southwest Baptist College, situated at Bolivar, Mo., in 1922, by a vote of the members of the student body. The idea was to select a name with the college initials.

[1] A communication from C. R. Alexander, Coach of the Athletic Teams, Southwest Baptist College, Bolivar, Mo., December 14, 1935.

Southwest Virginia. See *Mountain Empire*

Southwestern College (Kansas)
The athletic teams of Southwestern College, Winfield, Kans., are popularly known as the *Moundbuilders.*

Southwestern College (Tennessee)
The athletic teams of Southwestern College, Memphis, Tenn., are popularly designated *Lynxes*[1] and *Bobcats,*[1] the former nickname is for members of the upper classmen teams, and the latter for the freshmen teams.

[1] A communication from P. N. Rhodes, Faculty Chairman of Athletics at Southwestern College, Memphis, Tenn., November 22, 1935.

Southwestern Louisiana Institute
It is believed that the teams of the Southwestern Louisiana Institute, Lafayette, La., were nicknamed the *Bulldogs,*[1] in 1915, by C. J. McNaspy, the first athletic coach at the college, perhaps for their tenacity.

[1] A letter from E. L. Stephens, President of Southwestern Louisana Institute, Lafayette, La., June 18, 1935.

Southwestern University
The athletic teams of Southwestern University, Los Angeles, Calif., were designated *Bisons*[1] by the members of the Athletic Committee about 1925.

[1] A communication from Rollin L. McNitt, President of Southwestern University, Los Angeles, Calif., November 18, 1935.

Sower, Christopher
During the American Revolution, as an adherent of the doctrine of universal peace, the clergyman Christopher Sower refused actively to aid either the Revolutionists or the British, with the result that he was persecuted by both parties, his property confiscated, and himself imprisoned. However, despite his own scanty means, he was everwilling to unselfishly share his sustenance with the needy families of poverty-stricken soldiers. His paternal anxiety to provide them with the essentials of life caused him to be nicknamed the *Bread-father*[1] or *Der Brod-vater.*

Christopher Sower was born at Laasphe, near Marburg, Germany, on September 26, 1721, and died at Methatchen, Pa., on August 4, 1784.

[1] *The National Cyclopaedia of American Biography* (James T. White and Company, New York, 1906) vol. 13, p. 346.

Spaniards. See New Jerseyans

Spanish Indians. See New Mexicans

Spanish State. See New Mexico

Spartan Band
About 1856 Democrats in Richmond, Va., were so few in number that they are said to have been designated the *Spartan Band.*[1]

The allusion is to the small number of Spartans who defended the pass of Thermopylae under the leadership of Leonidas the First against the attack of Xerxes' hosts in 480 B.C.

[1] *The End of an Era*, John S. Wise (Houghton Mifflin and Company, New York and Boston, 1899) p. 58.

Spartans. See Michigan State College; University of Dubuque

Spaulding, Elbridge Gerry

Father of Greenbacks [1] is the nickname of Elbridge Gerry Spaulding. He framed the act which provided for the legal issuing of notes, bonds, and paper currency by the United States Government, which came to be called *greenbacks* because of the green ink used in printing. This act was passed by Congress on February 25, 1862, and was signed by President Abraham Lincoln on this same day.

Elbridge Gerry Spaulding was born at Sumner Hill, N.Y., on February 24, 1809, and died at Buffalo, N.Y., on May 5, 1897.

[1] *The National Cyclopaedia of American Biography* (James T. White and Company, New York, 1929) vol. 6, p. 355.

Speaker, Tristram

Tristram Speaker, who was born at Hubbard, Tex., on April 4, 1888, and who is a part owner of the Kansas City American Association Baseball Club, was occasionally nicknamed *Spoke*,[1] probably as a play on his last name. Tris Speaker, as he was usually called while he was one of the best outfielders in the game, was elected to the Baseball Hall of Fame in 1937.

[1] *Who's Who in Major League Base Ball*, comp. by Harold (Speed) Johnson (Buxton Publishing Company, Chicago 1933) p. 467.

Spearhead Division. See Third Armored Division of World War II

Speed Magee. See Johnson, Harold

Spencer, Elihu

Elihu Spencer, clergyman, and missionary to the Oneida Indians, won the nickname *Ready Money Spencer* [1] for the fluency and readiness of his speech.

Elihu Spencer was born at East Haddam, Conn., on February 12, 1721, and died at Trenton, N.J., on December 27, 1784.

[1] *The National Cyclopaedia of American Biography* (James T. White and Company, New York, 1907) vol. 5, p. 221.

Spendthrift Congress. See *Rubber Stamp Congress*

Sphinx. See Roosevelt, F. D.

Sphinx of the Rock Island. See Moore, W. H.

Spiders. See University of Richmond

Spindle City. See Lowell, Mass.

Spokane, Washington

Spokane is often designated the *Minneapolis of the West* [1] because it is the site of numerous great flour mills which ship to the markets of the world their products made from the excellent quality of wheat grown in the interior of the Columbia River Valley. Its location amidst a wheat producing region and its many flour mills make it comparable to Minneapolis, Minn.

[1] *Dodge-Lackey Advanced Geography*, Richard Elwood Dodge and Earl Emmet Lackey (Rand McNally and Company, New York, Chicago, and San Francisco, 1932) p. 197.

Spoke. See Speaker, Tristram

Spoon Butler. See Butler, B. F.

Spoon Stealer. See Bulter, B. F.

Spot Resolutions

About April 28, 1846, Major General Zachary Taylor and his army were encamped on the east side of the Rio Grande River which forms the southern boundary of Texas, where they were attacked by Mexican forces and sixteen of General Taylor's men were killed. In reporting the battle to Congress, President James K. Polk said that the blood of American citizens had been shed on American territory, and that a state of war existed between Mexico and the United States. Abraham Lincoln, a Representative from Illinois to the United States Congress at that time, introduced resolutions in Congress requesting President Polk to locate the spot where the blood of American citi-

Spot Resolutions—Continued

zens had been shed, thereby calling attention to the fact that the men killed were armed soldiers sent by order of the President to the place where they were killed and that in all probability they should not have been there. Because Lincoln's resolutions requested President Polk to locate the spot of bloodshed, they have since been called by historians the *Spot Resolutions.*[1]

[1] *A History of the American People*, Arthur Gilman (D. Lothrop and Company, Boston, 1883) p. 456-7.

Spotswood, Alexander

According to the Old Testament, as recorded in Genesis, 4:22, Tubal-cain, the son of Lamech and Zilliah, was the first artificer in brass and iron, hence Governor Alexander Spotswood was appropriately nicknamed *Tubal Cain,*[1] inasmuch as he was the first manufacturer of iron in Virginia.

He was Governor of the Virginia Colony from 1710 to 1722, and actively encouraged and developed the iron industry in Virginia, setting up an iron foundry at Germania, on the Rappahanock River in 1714.

Alexander Spotswood was born at Tangier, Africa, in 1676, and died at Annapolis, Md., on June 7, 1740.

[1] *History of the United States*, Charles A. Beard and Mary R. Beard (The Macmillan Company, New York, 1921) p. 31.

Sprague, Achsa W.

Achsa W. Sprague was widely known as the *Preaching Woman*[1] because she was a trance medium and lectured on spiritualism. She was afflicted with scrofulous disease of the joints, was bedridden for a number of years, but was finally apparently restored to health by what she considered angelic powers. After her recovery she went throughout the eastern section of the United States lecturing on spiritualism and humanitarian reforms, magnetic healing, and hypnotism. She died as the result of a recurrence of her affliction.

Achsa W. Sprague was born on a farm at Plymouth Notch, Vt., about 1828, and died at Plymouth, Vt., on July 6, 1862.

[1] *Dictionary of American Biography under the Auspices of the American Council of Learned Societies*, ed. by Dumas Malone (Charles Scribner's Sons, New York, 1935) vol. 17, p. 470.

Spreckels, Claus

Claus Spreckels, sugar manufacturer and capitalist, was nicknamed the *Sugar King* because for several years he had practically a monopoly on the manufacturing and selling of "refined sugar on the Pacific Coast." After successfully operating a wholesale and retail grocery business in New York City for one year, he moved to San Francisco, Calif., where in 1856, he and his brother organized the Bay Sugar Refining Company. After two years he sold his stock in the company, and went to Europe where he made an intensive study of sugar manufacturing. In 1867, he returned to California where he established the California Sugar Refinery. During the interval from 1881 until 1883, he built a gigantic sugar refinery in San Francisco. He finally became the oustanding manufacturer of sugar on the Pacific Coast, and even in America.

Claus Spreckels was born at Lamstedt, Germany, on July 9, 1828, and died at San Francisco, Calif., on December 26, 1908.

[1] *Dictionary of American Biography under the Auspices of* the American Council of Learned Societies, ed. by Dumas Malone (Charles Scribner's Sons, New York, 1935) vol. 17, p. 478.

Springfield, Illinois

Springfield is known as the *Flower City*[1] because of the particular attention given by its residents to the profuse production of select flowers in the numerous gardens throughout the city. Its general attractiveness is due to the "masses of old fashioned flowers" seen about some of the old homes, and the artistic appearance of the lawns about some of the newer homes, occasioned by effective landscape gardening.

[1] *Historical Encyclopedia of Illinois*, ed. by Newton Bateman and Paul Selby, and *History of Sangamon County*, by special authors and contributors, Paul Selby, editor (Munsell Publishing Company, Chicago, 1912) vol. 2. part 1. p. 845.

Springfield, Missouri

Springfield, standing in all of the splendor of a queen amidst its spacious orchards of stately fruit trees, has been fittingly designated the *Queen City of the Ozarks.*[1]

[1] *Seeing the Middle West*, John T. Faris (J. B. Lippincott Company, Philadelphia, 1923) p. 133.

Springfield, Ohio

Springfield has been nicknamed the *Champion City*[1] because of its location, its natural resources, and its transportation.

[1] *A Book of Nicknames*, John Goff (Courier-Journal Job Printing Company, Louisville, Ky., 1892) p. 15.

Springfield, Vermont

Springfield terms itself the *Cradle of Industry*[1] because it was one of the earliest of the New England cities to engage in industrial manufacturing, in manufacturing the mechanical apparatus necessary to industrial plants in other places, in the training of mechanical engineers, and in encouraging and developing a "spirit of inquiry and invention" beneficial to industrial progress.

[1] *The Vermont of Today, with Its Historic Background, Attractions and People,* Arthur F. Stone (Lewis Historical Publishing Company, Inc., New York, 1929) vol. 1, p. 408.

Sproat, Ebenezer

The Indians at Marietta, Ohio, nicknamed Colonel Ebenezer Sproat the *Big Buckeye*.[1] On September 2, 1788, Colonel Sproat was leading a procession of judges to conduct court at Marietta when a group of Indians looking on shouted "Hetuck!"[2] "Hetuck!", which meant *Big Buckeye.* The stalwart physique of Colonel Sproat perhaps suggested to them a buckeye tree. Colonel Sproat was an unusually tall man, six feet, four inches in height, and carried himself with an imposing bearing which made him outstanding among the other men in the parade.

Ebenezer Sproat was born at Middleborough, Mass., in 1752, and died at Marietta, Ohio, in February 1805.

[1] *Appleton's Cyclopaedia of American Biography,* ed. by James Grant Wilson and John Fiske (D. Appleton and Company, New York, 1888) vol. 5, p. 640.
[2] *Ohio the Beautiful and Historic,* Charles Edwin Hopkins (L. C. Page and Company, Boston, printed by the Colonial Press. Inc., Boston, 1931) p. 256.

Sproul, William Cameron

William Cameron Sproul, manufacturer and politician, was nicknamed the *Father of Good Roads*[1] because as a Senator in the Pennsylvania Legislature from 1896 until 1916. and later as Governor of that state, he actively advocated the construction of good roads. While he was a member of the State Senate, he was largely instrumental in getting the Pennsylvania Legislature to appropriate $100,000,000 for the construction of highways. Sproul organized The Seaboard Casting Company, located at Chester, Pa., in 1900. He was the president of several railroads and other large corporations. He was Republican Governor of Pennsylvania from 1919 until 1923.

William Cameron Sproul was born at Octoraro, Pa., on September 16, 1870, and died near Chester, Pa., on March 21, 1928.

[1] *Dictionary of American Biography under the Auspices of the* American Council of Learned Societies, ed. by Dumas Malone (Charles Scribner's Sons, New York, 1935) vol. 17, p. 485.

Spud. See Davis, V. L.

Spurious Governor. See Livingston, William

Spy of the Cumberland. See Cushman, Pauline

Squatter State. See Kansas

Squaw Campaign

In the fall of 1777 Brigadier General Edward Hand, a Revolutionary soldier, conducted an armed force against the Indians at Sandusky in what is now Ohio. This expedition was humorously nicknamed the *Squaw Campaign*[1] because it resulted only in the invasion of two Indian villages located on Beaver Creek which were "occupied chiefly by squaws."

[1] *Indiana and Indianans, a History of Aboriginal and Territorial Indiana and the Century of Statehood,* Jacob Piatt Dunn (The American Historical Society, New York and Chicago, 1919) vol. 1, p. 141.

Squeaky. See Bluege, O. A.

Squibob. See Derby, G. H.

Squire of Hyde Park. See Roosevelt, F. D.

Squirrel Hunters

In the summer of 1862 a body of approximately twelve hundred armed citizens hastily recruited throughout Ohio was assembled at Cincinnati for the purpose of defending that city against the contemplated attack by Lieutenant General Edmund Kirby Smith and his Confederate Army. This group was popularly called the *Squirrel Hunters*[1] because many of the men composing it were farmers accustomed to hunting small game and carried a variety of guns, some of which were doubtless better suited for squirrel hunting than for use in battle.

[1] *History of the Eighty-third Ohio Volunteer Infantry, the Greyhound Regiment,* T. B. Marshall (Published by the Eighty-third Ohio Volunteer Infantry Association, Cincinnati, Ohio, 1912) p. 21
Ohio in the War, Her Statesmen, Generals and Soldiers, Whitelaw Reid (Eclectic Publishing Company, Columbus, Ohio, 1893) vol. 1, p. 837.

Stadium of The Salinas Packers Football Club

The *Lettuce Bowl*[1] is the nickname attributed by sports writers to the stadium of The Salinas Packers Football Club, located at

Stadium of The Salinas Packers Football Club—Continued

Salinas, Calif. Salinas, county seat of Monterey County, is in Salinas valley, a great lettuce-producing section of California.

[1] A communication from George S. Halas, President-treasurer of The Chicago Bears Football Club, Inc., Chicago, Ill., March 21, 1939.

Stalking Library. See Mitchell, S. M.

Stalwarts

The *Stalwarts* [1] were a faction of the Republican party which during Grant's two administrations had built up a very strong "machine." It opposed Civil Service reform and in 1880 strove to nominate Grant for a third term. The Republican nominating convention, however, chose James A. Garfield, with Chester A. Arthur as his running mate. Garfield was shot, after four months as President, by a disappointed office seeker who boasted, "I am a Stalwart; Arthur is now President." [2]

[1] *A History of the American Nation*, New Edition, Andrew C. McLaughlin (D. Appleton and Company, New York and Chicago, 1916) p. 468.
[2] *The Growth of the American Republic*, by Samuel Eliot Morison and Harry Steele Commager (Oxford University Press, New York, 1950) vol. 2, p. 221.

Standard Oil King. See Rockefeller, J. D.

Standish, Miles

The *Hero of New England* [1] and *Little Indian Fighter* [1] are nicknames by which Captain Standish was called. He successfully defended the settlers against Indian attacks and was a fearless and courageous leader in various other activities and enterprises of the Massachusetts Bay Colony.

Miles Standish was born at Lancashire, England, about 1584, emigrated to the Massachusetts Bay Colony from Leyden, Holland, with the Puritans on the Mayflower, in 1620, and died at Duxbury, in what is now Massachusetts, on October 3, 1656.

[1] *Lives of Celebrated Americans: Comprising Biographies of Three Hundred and Forty Eminent Persons*, Benson J. Lossing (Thomas Belknap, Hartford, Conn., 1869) p. 13.

Standpatters

While William Howard Taft was President of the United States from 1909 to 1913, a conservative faction of the Republican party was sarcastically designated the *Standpatters* [1] because they refused to align themselves with the policies of the more liberal or progressive-minded Republicans. *To stand pat* is an expression used by poker players, signifying their intention of playing their hands just as they had been dealt "without drawing other cards." [2] Today *standpatters* are those who take a stand on some issue and refuse to change their views or convictions.

[1] *Our Country's History*, Paul L. Haworth and Alfred W. Garner (The Bobbs-Merrill Company, Indianapolis, Ind., 1926) p. 556.
[2] *A New English Dictionary*, ed. by James A. H. Murray (The Clarendon Press, Oxford, England, 1914) vol. 9, p. 802.

Stand-up-law

In 1801 a law was passed in the Connecticut Legislature providing that in case there were a division in the votes cast for the councilmen or the members of the upper house, the freemen were required to rise and stand until they had been counted. The law was nicknamed the *Stand-up-law*. [1] It was repealed about 1817.

[1] *Attractions and People*, Arthur F. Stone (Lewis Historical Publishing Company, Inc., New York, 1929) vol. 1, p. 408.

Stanford, Leland. See *Big Four*

Stanford University

The athletes of Stanford University, in California, are designated the *Cardinals* [1] and the *Indians*. [1] One of the college colors is cardinal. The origin of the second nickname is not known.

[1] A letter from Don E. Liebendorfer, Director of the News Service of Stanford University, Stanford University, Calif., December 3, 1935.

Star City. See Lafayette, Ind.

Stark, Albert D.

Albert D. Stark, a National League umpire, was nicknamed *Dolly*. [1]

[1] *Who's Who in Major League Base Ball*, comp. by Harold (Speed) Johnson (Buxton Publishing Company, Chicago, 1933) p. 446.

Stark, John

The sobriquet, *Leonidas of America*, [1] has been attributed to John Stark because he so nobly defended the pass at the bridge over Walloomsac River, in the southwestern part of Vermont, in which respect he was comparable to Leonidas the First, who defended the pass of Thermopylae against Xerxes and his Persian forces in 480 B.C.

John Stark, who led the colonial forces in the Battle of Bennington, on August 16,

1777, was born at Londonderry, N.H., on August 28, 1728, and died at Manchester, N.H., on May 2, 1822.

[1] "The Battle of Bennington: An Address before the Vermont Historical Society," Delivered in the Representatives' Hall, in *Vermont Historical Society Proceedings* (Argus and Patriot Press, Montpelier, Va., 1896) vol. 55, p. 46.

Stark, Lloyd Crow

Lloyd Crow Stark, former Governor of Missouri, was nicknamed *Molly* [1] by his classmates at the United States Naval Academy, while he was a student there from 1904 until 1908. The inspiration for the nickname came from a remark of Governor Stark's ancestor, General John Stark, at the Battle of Bennington in 1775, who said to the soldiers under his command, "Boys, we must beat the redcoats or Molly Stark's a widow tonight."

Lloyd Crow Stark was born near Louisiana in Pike County, Mo., on November 23, 1886.

[1] A communication from Governor Lloyd Crow Stark, Jefferson City, Mo., May 17, 1939.
Life, Chicago, April 24, 1939, p. 18.

Starr, Frederick

The anthropologist, Frederick Starr, was nicknamed the *Lone Star* [1] because while he was Professor of Anthropology at the University of Chicago from 1895 until 1896, he refused to add other instructors in his department, although his classes were the most popular and the most crowded in the University. He traveled over many foreign countries as well as over the various parts of the United States collecting anthropological specimens. He did much work classifying and labeling "collections in the department of ethnology in the American Museum of Natural History," in New York City.

Frederick Starr was born at Auburn, N.Y., on September 2, 1858, and died at Tokyo, Japan, on August 14, 1933.

[1] *Dictionary of American Biography under the Auspices of the American Council of Learned Societies*, ed. by Dumas Malone (Charles Scribner's Sons, New York, 1935) vol. 17, p. 532.

Starr, Raymond Francis

Because he has great physical endurance, having pitched two double-headers on two days in succession, Raymond Francis Starr was popularly called *Ironman*. [1] He was born at Nowata, Okla., on April 23, 1907, and pitched in major league baseball.

[1] *Who's Who in Major League Base Ball*, comp. by Harold (Speed) Johnson (Buxton Publishing Company. Chicago, 1933) p. 364.

Starvation Parties

About 1864 during the latter part of the Civil War, the officers who were encamped near Richmond or Petersburg, Va., often attended dances and other social functions in these cities. At these affairs no refreshments were served because of the scarcity of food, and they were humorously designated *Starvation Parties*. [1]

[1] *History of the United States of America, under the Constitution*, James Schouler (Dodd, Mead and Company, New York, 1889) vol. 6, p. 575.

State College of Washington

Cougars [1] is the appellation given to the athletic teams of the State College of Washington, Pullman, Wash., in 1915 by sports writers. In reporting the game between the teams of the State College of Washington and those of the University of Southern California at Los Angeles in that year, they described "the fierceness and strength" which the teams displayed during the contest.

[1] A letter from J. Fred Bohler, Director of Physical Education at the State College of Washington, Pullman, Wash., July 2, 1935.

State of Camden and Amboy. See New Jersey

State of Spain. See New Jersey

State of Treasure and Opportunity. See Montana

State University of Iowa

Iowa being nicknamed the *Hawkeye State,* the athletic teams of the State University are called *Hawkeyes*. [1]

[1] A letter from Charles S. Galiher, Business Manager of the University of Iowa, Iowa City, Iowa, June 18, 1935.

State University of Montana

The athletic teams of the State University of Montana, at Missoula, Mont., were designated *Grizzlies* [1] probably by sports writers about 1912 or 1913.

[1] A communication from E. K. Badgley, Graduate Manager of Athletics at the State University of Montana, Missoula, Mont., June 21, 1935.

Statesmen. See Massachusetts State College

Statue of Liberty Division. See Seventy-seventh Infantry Division of World War II

Staunch Buckingham. See Buckingham, W. A.

Steadman, Vera
Vera Steadman, born at Monterey, Calif., on June 23, 1900, was nicknamed the *Original Bathing Girl* [1] because she was the first girl to perform as a swimmer in the movies.

[1] *The Blue Book of the Screen*, Ruth Wing, Editor (The Blue Book of the Screen, Inc., Hollywood, Calif., 1923) p. 240.

Stearns, Frederick Kimball
Detroit's Greatest Traveler [1] is an appellation by which Frederick Kimball Stearns was known to his contemporaries. He traveled extensively to the remotest parts of the world, covering a total distance of nearly half a million miles in his journeys.

Frederick Kimball Stearns was born at Buffalo, N.Y., on December 6, 1854, and died at Beverly Hills, Calif., on June 7, 1928.

[1] *Encyclopedia of American Biography: American Biography, a New Cyclopedia*, comp. under the editorial supervision of a notable advisory board (Published under the direction of The American Historical Society, Inc., New York, 1925) vol. 23, p. 156.

Stebbins, Grant Case
Grant Case Stebbins won the odd sobriquet, *Dry Hole Stebbins,* [1] because he drilled for oil twenty-eight times in succession in Tulsa, Okla., before he was successful in finding it.

Grant Case Stebbins was born in Manlius Township, Ill., on March 27, 1862, and died at Kansas City, Kans., on March 21, 1925.

[1] *Encyclopedia of American Biography: American Biography, a New Cyclopedia*, comp. under the editorial supervision of a notable advisory board (Published under the direction of The American Historical Society, Inc., New York, 1925) vol. 31, p. 71.

Steel City. See Pittsburgh, Pa.

Steel State. See Pennsylvania

Steele, Franklin
In 1838, following the news that the United States Government had sanctioned a treaty with the Indians making the land in Fort Snelling and vicinity Government property, prospectors rushed to the spot, renamed St. Anthony, to stake out their claims. They found the first cabin already built by Franklin Steele, who thus acquired his nickname, the *First Citizen of St. Anthony.* [1]

[1] *My Minnesota*, Antoinette E. Ford (Lyons and Carnahan, New York and Chicago, 1929) p. 279-80.

Steelers. See Pittsburgh Pirates Football Club

Steers. See Texas College

Stefan, Karl
Karl Stefan, a Nebraska radio announcer and politician was nicknamed the *Voice of the Radio* [1] by his colleagues in the National House of Representatives. Before he was elected to the United States Congress, he was a radio announcer and commentator.

He was a Republican Representative from the Third Congressional District of Nebraska to the United States Congress from 1935 to 1949.

Karl Stefan, who was born on a farm near Zebravkov, Bohemia-Austria, on March 1, 1884, emigrated to the United States with his father and mother in 1885.

[1] An interview with Captain Victor Hunt Harding, Secretary of the National Democratic Congress Re-election Committee, Washington, D.C., April 10, 1939.

Stengel, Charles Dillon
Charles Dillon Stengel, who manages in major league baseball, is nicknamed *Casey,* [1] presumably for Kansas City, Mo., his birthplace. He was born there on July 30, 1891.

[1] *Who's Who in Major League Base Ball*, comp. by Harold (Speed) Johnson (Buxton Publishing Company, Chicago, 1933) p. 428.
Official Encyclopedia of Baseball, Jubilee Edition, Hy Turkin and S. C. Thompson, (A.S. Barnes and Company, New York, 1951) p. 585.

Stepfather of His Country. See Washington, George

Stephens, Alexander Hamilton
Alexander Hamilton Stephens, the Vice President of the Confederacy, was called the *Dwarf Statesman,* [1] and *Little Aleck* because he was thin, frail, and small of stature.

The latter nickname, which is widely known, evidently began to be applied to Stephens at Crawfordsville,[2] Ga., where he began to practice law in 1834 at the age of twenty-two.

Alexander Hamilton Stephens was born at Crawfordsville, Ga., on February 11, 1812, and died at Atlanta, Ga., on March 4, 1883.

See also Alexander Hamilton Stephens and Robert Toombs.

[1] *A Book of Nicknames*, John Goff (Courier-Journal Job Printing Company, Louisville, Ky., 1892) p. 24.
[2] *Little Aleck: A Life of Alexander H. Stephens, the Fighting vice-president of the Confederacy*, E. Ramsay Richardson (The Bobbs-Merrill Company, Indianapolis, Ind.. 1832) p. 59, 75.

Stephens, Alexander Hamilton, and Robert Toombs

The sobriquet, the *Castor and Pollux of Georgia*,[1] was given to Alexander Hamilton Stephens and Robert Toombs because they were both Georgians, and were almost inseparable in their friendship, and in their political activities both for Georgia and for the South.

In Greek mythology Castor and Pollux were twin brothers. Pollux was immortal and Castor was mortal. When Castor was killed Pollux grieved so over being separated from his brother that Zeus allowed them to spend alternate days on earth and on Mount Olympus.

[1] *Little Aleck: A Life of Alexander H. Stephens, the Fighting Vice President of the Confederacy*, E. Ramsay Richardson (The Bobbs-Merrill Company, Indianapolis, Ind., 1932) p. 77.

Stephenson, Jackson Riggs

Old Hoss and *Stevie* are sobriquets given to Jackson Riggs Stephenson.

He is known as *Old Hoss*[1] because he is so dependable and trustworthy. *Stevie* is a diminutive of his last name.

Jackson Riggs Stephenson was born at Akron, Ala., on January 5, 1899, and played outfield in major league baseball.

[1] *Who's Who in Major League Base Ball*, comp. by Harold (Speed) Johnson (Buxton Publishing Company, Chicago, 1933) p. 365.

Stephenson, John

Because of his honesty and integrity of character, John Stephenson was nicknamed *Honest John Stephenson*.[1] This nickname originated during the money panic of 1837, when Stephenson went bankrupt and was obliged to settle with his creditors at the rate of fifty cents on every dollar that he owed. He then concentrated his attention on the manufacture and sale of coaches and omnibuses, succeeding in paying off all of his debts in seven years. One of his creditors, Jordan L. Mott, who would not take the cash money with which Stephenson insisted on paying his former debtors, was given a large four-horse truck by Stephenson. Mott then put a sign on the truck which read, "This is the way one bankrupt pays his debts," and paraded the truck down Broadway in New York City. This popularized more than ever Stephenson's nickname.

John Stephenson was born in northern Ireland, on July 4, 1809, and died at New Rochelle, N.Y., on July 31, 1893.

[1] *The National Cyclopaedia of American Biography* (James T. White and Company, New York, 1897) vol. 7, p. 364.

Stevens, John H.

In 1850, in order to operate a ferry across the Mississippi River, at St. Anthony Falls, Minn., John H. Stevens settled on land near the falls. In 1851 people from St. Anthony went to the present site of Minneapolis, Minn., and staked out claims. The community thus built up centered about Stevens' land, and he was subsequently called the *Father of Minneapolis*.[1]

John H. Stevens was born at Brompton Falls, Quebec, Canada, on June 13, 1820, and died at Minneapolis, Minn., on May 28, 1900.

[1] *My Minnesota*, Antoinette E. Ford (Lyons and Carnahan, New York and Chicago, 1929) p. 284.

Stevens, Thaddeus

The following appellations have been attributed to Thaddeus Stevens: the *American Pitt*, the *Arch Priest of Anti-Masonry*, the *Chief Old Woman*, the *Great American Commoner*, and the *Old Commoner*.

Stevens has been designated the *American Pitt*[1] because of his uncompromising position on subjects and issues with which he aligned himself, in which respect he was comparable to William Pitt, the great English parliamentary orator and statesman, who lived from 1759 to 1806.

The nicknames, the *Arch Priest of Anti-Masonry*[2] and the *Chief Old Woman*,[2] originated while he was a member of the Pennsylvania House of Representatives from 1833 to 1835. Stevens introduced a measure on December 7, 1835, to repress secret societies or fraternal organizations of the nature of Freemasonry. On December 19, 1835, a committee was appointed with Stevens as its Chairman to inquire into the activities of the Freemasons in Pennsylvania. This procedure created a great deal of interest; and, when a number of Freemasons were brought before the House to answer certain questions regarding the activities of their organization, crowds of people went there hoping to have the secrets of the society revealed to them. At this time, Stevens' opponents described him as the *Arch Priest of Anti-Masonry* and the *Chief Old Woman* in allusion to his denunciation of Freemasonry, and his alleged old-woman-like curiosity regarding the secret proceedings of the society. The committee which had attempted to investigate the business of the Freemasons was ridiculed as an *Old Woman's Curiosity Convention*.[2]

Stevens, Thaddeus—Continued

He was affectionately called the *Great American Commoner* [3] and the *Old Commoner* [3] because he ardently and energetically championed the right and liberties of the common man throughout his entire life. Further evidence of his personal feelings is found in the epitaph which he wrote for himself containing the phrase, "equality of man before his Creator." [4]

Thaddeus Stevens was born at Danville, Vt., on April 4, 1792, and died at Washington, D.C., on August 11, 1868.

[1] *A Book of Nicknames*, John Goff (Courier-Journal Job Printing Company, Louisville, Ky., 1892) p. 21.
[2] *The Life of Thaddeus Stevens: a Study in American Political History, Especially in the Period of the Civil War and Reconstruction*, James Albert Woodburn (The Bobbs-Merrill Company, Indianapolis, Ind., 1913) p. 23.
[3] *Biographical Sketches of Prominent Americans*, Frederick G. Harrison (E. W. Walker Company, Boston, 1892) vol. 2, p. 130.
[4] *Thaddeus Stevens: Commoner*, Edward B. Callender (A. Williams and Company, Boston, 1882) p. 163.

Stevie. See Stephenson, J. R.

Stewart, Alexander Peter

Alexander Peter Stewart, a soldier and educator, was designated *Old Straight* [1] by the Confederate soldiers under his command during the Civil War both because of his excellent posture and because of the fair treatment which he accorded his soldiers and fellow officers. On June 23, 1864, he was commissioned a Lieutenant General in the Confederate Army and was afterwards in command of the Army of the Tennessee. In 1874, he was made Chancellor of the University of Mississippi, retaining that office until 1886. During this period the students at the University revived the sobriquet, *Old Straight,* because he still bore himself splendidly erect and because he administered justice impartially to the school.

Alexander Peter Stewart was born at Rogersville, Tenn., on October 2, 1821, and died at Biloxi, Miss., on August 30, 1908.

[1] *Dictionary of American Biography under the Auspices of the American Council of Learned Societies*, ed. by Dumas Malone (Charles Scribner's Sons, New York, 1936) vol. 18, p. 3.

Stewart, Alexander Turner

Alexander Turner Stewart has been designated the *Prince of Merchants* [1] because, having accumulated a vast fortune by his mercantile activities, he was generous and philanthropic with his fellow-men.

He was born near Belfast, Ireland, on October 12, 1803, and died at New York City, on April 10, 1876.

[1] *A Book of Nicknames*, John Goff (Courier-Journal Job Printing Company, Louisville, Ky., 1892) p. 30.

Stewart, Andrew

Andrew Stewart, a legislator and business executive was nicknamed *Tariff Andy* [1] because, particularly while he was a member of the United States Congress, he was extremely active in advocating a high protective tariff which would encourage and prosper domestic manufacturing. His speeches on the subject before that body were so forceful that they were printed by the hundred thousands and were widely used by the proponents of protection for American industries. He was a Representative from Pennsylvania to the United States Congress from 1831 until 1835, and held that same office from 1843 until 1849.

Andrew Stewart was born near Uniontown, Pa., on June 11, 1791, and died there on July 16, 1872.

[1] *Dictionary of American Biography under the Auspices of the American Council of Learned Societies*, ed. by Dumas Malone (Charles Scribner's Sons, New York, 1936) vol. 18, p. 6.

Stewart, Charles

The sobriquet, *Old Ironsides,* [1] was applied to Rear Admiral Charles Stewart because his strength, endurance, and seeming invincibility suggested comparison to his ship, *Constitution,* widely known as *Old Ironsides.* Stewart commanded this vessel in 1813 and in 1815, during which time he captured a number of British merchant vessels and other British ships.

Charles Stewart was born at Philadelphia, Pa., on July 28, 1778, and died at Bordentown, N.J., on November 6, 1869.

[1] *Appleton's Cyclopaedia of American Biography*, ed. by James Grant Wilson and John Fiske (D. Appleton and Company, New York, 1888) vol. 5, p. 684.

Stewart, Eliza Daniel

Eliza Daniel Stewart, a humanitarian and advocate of temperance, was nicknamed *Mother Stewart* [1] during the Civil War because of her diligence in collecting and sending medical supplies to the men in the Union Armies, and because of her activities in nursing the sick and wounded soldiers on the battlefields. At the close of the Civil War in 1865, she devoted the remainder of her life to temperance work and to lecturing and writing against intemperance. She organized anti-saloon leagues throughout the United States, in Scotland, and in Ireland. The sobriquet, *Mother Stewart*, was continually applied to her throughout her later life.

Eliza Daniel Stewart was born at Piketon, Ohio, on April 25, 1816, and died at Hicksville, Ohio, on August 6, 1908.

[1] *Dictionary of American Biography under the Auspices of the American Council of Learned Societies*, ed. by Dumas Malone (Charles Scribner's Sons, New York, 1936) vol. 18, p. 8, 9.

Stewart, Humphrey John

The *Walter Damrosch of the Pacific Coast* [1] is a nickname by which Dr. Humphrey John Stewart, composer and musician, has been designated. Dr. Stewart, like Walter Damrosch, used to preface his recitals with interesting and attractively presented information regarding the composers of the selections played.

From 1915 to 1916 Dr. Stewart was the official organist of the Panama California Exposition, at San Diego, Calif. In 1917 [2] he was appointed to play the organ built especially for out-of-door use at San Diego.

Humphrey John Stewart was born at London, England, on May 22, 1854, and was the municipal organist at San Diego, Calif. He died December 28, 1932.

[1] *Encyclopedia of American Biography: American Biography, a New Cyclopedia*, comp. under the editorial supervision of a notable advisory board (Published under the direction of The American Historical Society, Inc., New York, 1931) vol. 49, p. 228.
[2] *Baker's Biographical Dictionary of Musicians*, Third Edition, revised and enlarged by Alfred Remy (G. Schirmer, New York and Boston, 1919) p. 911.

Stiegel, Henry William

Henry William Stiegel, ironmaster, glassmaker, and real estate promoter, was popularly called *Baron* or *Baron von Stiegel* [1] because his wealth and his princely manner of living was reminiscent of the life led by the noblemen of Germany, from which country he had emigrated to the United States in August, 1750. From 1760 until 1764 Stiegel was one of the greatest ironmasters in the country; from 1764 until 1772, he was equally prominent in the manufacturing of glass. He then suffered such business reverses that by the time of his death he was poverty-stricken.

Henry William Stiegel was born near Cologne, Germany, on May 13, 1729, and died at Charming Forge, Pa., on January 10, 1785.

[1] *Dictionary of American Biography under the Auspices of the American Council of Learned Societies*, ed. by Dumas Malone (Charles Scribner's Sons, New York, 1936) vol. 18, p. 16, 17.

Stiles, Rolland Mays

The appellation, *Lena* [1] has been given to Rolland May Stiles, who was born at Ratcliff, Ark., on November 12, 1906, and who pitched in major league baseball.

[1] *Who's Who in Major League Base Ball*, comp. by Harold (Speed) Johnson (Buxton Publishing Company, Chicago, 1933) p. 367.

Stilwell, Joseph Warren

General Joseph W. Stilwell was known as *Vinegar Joe, Uncle Joe* and *Old Tu'key Neck*.

He became universally known as *Vinegar Joe* [1] during World War II while he was in command of the China-Burma-India theater of war operations because of his honest and often acidulous appraisals of the problems involved in British-Chinese-American cooperation in that area.

He enjoyed a reputation as a demanding but very fair general who looked after his men, to whom he was known as *Uncle Joe*.[2]

He was of a wiry and very durable constitution, with a weatherbeaten face and a sunburned neck, sometimes referring to himself as *Old Tu'key Neck*. [1]

Joseph W. Stilwell was born in Palatka, Fla., on March 19, 1883. He saw action on the Western Front in 1918. He was an expert linguist, mastering several Chinese dialects. During World War II, he held simultaneously three responsible positions: commander of all American forces in the China-Burma-India theater, chief of staff of Chiang Kai-Shek, and deputy to Lord Louis Mountbatten of the British Army. He was routed from Burma in 1942, but returned there in 1944 to defeat the Japanese.

General Stilwell died, following a liver operation, in San Francisco on October 12, 1946.

[1] *Time*, the Weekly Newsmagazine, October 21, 1946, p. 27-28.
[2] *Current Biography, Who's News and Why*, 1942, ed. by Maxine Block (The H. W. Wilson Company, New York, 1943) p. 809-810.

Stilwell, Silas Moore

Silas Moore Stilwell, a lawyer and politician, was nicknamed *King Caucus* [1] in 1835 at which time he was the Chairman of the

Stilwell, S. M.—Continued
Board of Aldermen of New York City. The sobriquet originated in the fact that in this capacity he was generally called on to cast the decisive vote on the appointments made by the members of that board, who were so evenly divided politically when they came to cast their ballots that it took Stilwell's vote to break the tie. From 1837 until 1841, Stilwell was the United States Marshal of the Southern District of New York State, after which time he practiced law and wrote several pamphlets dealing with matters of finance.

Silas Moore Stilwell was born at New York City, on June 6, 1800, and died there on May 16, 1881.

[1] *Appleton's Cyclopaedia of American Biography*, ed. by James Grant Wilson and John Fiske (D. Appleton and Company, New York, 1888) vol. 5, p. 691.

Stimson, Henry Lewis
Henry Lewis Stimson, Secretary of State in President Hoover's Cabinet from 1929 to 1933, and Secretary of War from 1940 to 1945, under President F. D. Roosevelt, was nicknamed *Stimy*.[1] He was born at New York City on September 21, 1867, and died on October 20, 1950.

[1] *The Literary Digest, January to March, 1930* (Funk and Wagnalls Company, New York, 1930) vol. 104, March 8, 1930, p. 41.

Stimy. See Stimson, H. L.

Stinky. See Davis, H. A.

Stocking-foot Orator. See McKinley, William

Stockton, Richard
Richard Stockton was widely known as the *Duke*.[1] He was prominent in New Jersey as a lawyer and legislator of unusual ability, and influential in the social life of his community. He was a Senator from New Jersey to the United States Congress from 1796 until 1799, and a Representative from New Jersey to Congress from 1813 until 1815.

Richard Stockton was born near Princeton, N.J., on April 17, 1764, and died there on March 17, 1828.

[1] *Appleton's Cyclopaedia of American Biography*, ed. by James Grant Wilson and John Fiske (D. Appleton and Company, New York, 1888) vol. 5, p. 694.

Stoddard, Charles Warren. See Coolbrith, Ina Donna, Bret Harte, and Charles Warren Stoddard

Stokes, William Brickly
William Brickly Stokes, a soldier and lawyer, was popularly called the *Eagle Orator*.[1] He was a man of impressive personal appearance, and noted as a learned and entertaining speaker. He was a Representative from Tennessee to the United States Congress from 1866 until 1871.

He was born in Cheatham County, N.C., on September 9, 1814, and died at Liberty, Tenn., on March 20, 1897.

[1] *Appleton's Cyclopaedia of American Biography*, ed. by James Grant Wilson and John Fiske (D. Appleton and Company, New York, 1900) vol. 7, p. 256.

Stone, Frederick Mather
Frederick Mather Stone's nickname, *Rocks*,[1] was originated by Theodore Roosevelt in 1879. At that time Roosevelt was a junior and Stone a freshman at Harvard University. It was the custom for freshmen members of *The Dickey*, a secret organization, when they met an older member, to introduce themselves by fanciful names which had been given them by the upper classmen. These names were sometimes amusing and often quite obscene. One day Theodore Roosevelt, meeting Stone, and hearing him give his vulgar sobriquet, told him that if he so desired, he could from that time on say to inquiring Dickeymen that his name was " 'Rocks, by God!" and that he was to say that Roosevelt would vouch for the correctness of this statement. Stone followed this advice, and *Rocks* became his permanent nickname.[2]

Stone was a member of the Federal Food Administration under Herbert Hoover. He served in this capacity until 1919, at which time he resumed his practice of law at Boston.

Frederick Mather Stone was born at Brookline, Mass., on October 19, 1861, and died at Milton, Mass., on April 8, 1932.

[1] *Roosevelt, the Story of a Friendship, 1880-1919,* Owen Wister (The Macmillan Company, New York, 1930) p. 10.
[2] *Harvard College: Harvard University Class of 1882, Seventh Report of the Secretary, 1882-1932* (Harvard University Press, Cambridge, Mass., 1932) p. 217.

Stone, John Thomas
John Thomas Stone, who was born at Mulberry, Tenn., on October 10, 1906, and who played outfield in major league base-

ball, is popularly known as *Rocky*,[1] probably suggested by his last name.

[1] *Who's Who in Major League Base Ball*, comp. by Harold (Sneed) Johnson (Buxton Publishing Company, Chicago, 1933) p. 368.

Stone Fleet

The *Stone Fleet*[1] was the name for a score of old battleships heavily laden with stone which were sunk in the channels at the harbor of Charleston, S.C., on December 20, 1861. The sinking of the *Stone Fleet* was effected chiefly by the British in sympathy with the Confederates so as to hinder navigation of ships and render them unable to gain entrance to Charleston or to capture that Confederate stronghold.

[1] *The History of Our Navy from Its Origin to the Present Day, 1775-1897, in Four Volumes*, John R. Spears (Charles Scribner's Sons, New York, 1897) vol. 4, p. 470-1.

Stonewall Jackson. See Jackson, T. J.

Storm King. See Espy, J. P.

Stormy Petrels. See Oglethorpe University

Stout, Allyn McClelland

While Allyn McClelland Stout was once on a fishing trip in Florida, a "plug with nine hooks landed on his forehead." Ever since that happening, *Fish Hooks*[1] has been his nickname. Stout was born at Peoria, Ill., on October 31, 1904, and pitched in major league baseball.

[1] *Who's Who in Major League Base Ball*, comp. by Harold (Speed) Johnson (Buxton Publishing Company, Chicago, 1933) p. 370.

Stove Brigade

The *Stove Brigade*[1] was a nickname applied to a group of Federal officers who, during the Civil War, were imprisoned at the Confederate Military Prison at Danville, Va. The private soldiers confined in this prison designated the officers the *Stove Brigade* because they took it upon themselves to superintend the making of fires in the few stoves allotted the prisoners during the winter season, and because they grouped themselves in a body around these stoves.

[1] *Lights and Shadows in Confederate Prisons; a Personal Experience, 1864-5*, Homer B. Sprague (G. P. Putnam's Sons, New York and London, 1915) p. 79.

Straight Tongue. See Whipple, H. B.

Stranahan, James Samuel Thomas

The *First Citizen of Brooklyn*[1] was a popular sobriquet applied to James Samuel Thomas Stranahan by the people of that city. During his residence there for approximately half a century, he was prominent in the execution of a number of enterprises for the economic and civic welfare of Brooklyn, such as obtaining parks and playgrounds, and generously aiding organizations of a philanthropic nature.

James Samuel Thomas Stranahan was born at Peterboro, N.Y., on April 25, 1808, and died at Saratoga, N.Y., on September 3, 1898.

[1] *The National Cyclopaedia of American Biography* (James T. White and Company, New York, 1893) vol. 3, p. 434.

Stratton, Charles Sherwood

General Tom Thumb, or *Tom Thumb*, and the *Pet of the Palace* are the popular nicknames of Charles Sherwood Stratton.

Stratton was named *General Tom Thumb*,[1] by his employer, Phineas T. Barnum, proprietor of the American Museum in New York City. In Stratton's early adult life he was only about twenty-eight inches high weighing about fifteen pounds, and was a man in miniature like the *Tom Thumb* of nursery rhymes. Barnum first exhibited Stratton in New York City on December 8, 1842,[2] and later carried him abroad to all of the principal countries of Europe, where he was a great favorite. About 1847 he visited the palace of the King of England so much and was so well liked by the royal family that he became the *pet of the palace*.[1]

Charles Sherwood Stratton was born at Bridgeport, Conn., on January 4, 1838, and died at Middleborough, Mass., on July 15, 1883. It is said that prior to his death Stratton attained a height of forty inches and a weight of about seventy pounds. In 1862 he met Lavinia Warren, also a dwarf, and married her on February 10, 1863, at New York City.

[1] *Sketch of the Life, Personal Appearance, Character, and Manners of Charles S. Stratton, the Man in Miniature, Known as General Tom Thumb, Twenty-eight inches high, Weighing Only Fifteen Pounds, with Some Account of Remarkable Dwarfs, Giants, and Other Human Phenomena, of Ancient and Modern Times, Also General Tom Thumb's Songs* (Van Norden and Amerman, Printers, New York, 1847) p. 4-24.
[2] *Appleton's Cyclopaedia of American Biography*, ed. by James Grant Wilson and John Fiske (D. Appleton and Company, New York, 1888) vol. 5, p. 717.

Straus, Nathan

The singular nickname, *Savior of Babies*,[1] attributed to Nathan Straus originated in

Straus, Nathan—Continued

the fact that he established milk stations in the slum districts of New York City where pasteurized milk was sold at reduced rates, enabling poor mothers in the tenement districts to get pure, wholesome milk for their babies. A notable result of Straus' plan was the marked decrease in the high rate of infant mortality in these sections of New York City, with a marked increase in the health and vigor of the babies and growing children; out of sincere affection and gratitude, the mothers gave Straus his sobriquet.

The success of Straus' achievement in New York City was noted by people of many other cities both in the United States and in Europe, and they, too, with his valuable and hearty coöperation, adopted the policy of distributing pure milk at reasonable rates in the poorer sections of the cities.

[1] *Our Foreign-Born Citizens: What They Have Done for America,* Annie E. S. Beard, revised and enlarged by Frederic Beard (Thomas Y. Crowell Company, New York, 1932) p. 372, 374.

Strawberry Townsend. See Townsend, J. G., Jr.

Street, Charles Evard

Because he was so noisy while catching in a baseball game, *Gabby* [1] is the sobriquet by which Charles Evard Street is popularly known. He, himself, says that he became nicknamed *Gabby* because he used to call "porters (by) that (sobriquet) to attract their attention."

Charles Evard Street was born at Huntsville, Ala., on September 30, 1882, and is a manager in major league baseball.

[1] *Who's Who in Major League Base Ball,* comp. by Harold (Speed) Johnson (Buxton Publishing Company, Chicago, 1933) p. 371.

Stripp, Joseph Valentine

Joseph Valentine Stripp, who was born at Harrison, N.J., on February 3, 1903, and who played infield in major league baseball, is nicknamed *Jersey Joe* [1] because he was born in the State of New Jersey.

[1] *Who's Who in Major League Base Ball,* comp. by Harold (Speed) Johnson (Buxton Publishing Company, Chicago, 1933) p. 372.

Strong Boy of Boston. See Sullivan, J. L.

Strong Man of Wall Street. See Whitney, Richard

Stuart, Gilbert

In commemoration of the several fine portraits of presidents which he painted during his lifetime, Gilbert Stuart has been called the *Painter of Presidents,* [1] or the *Portrait Painter of Presidents.* [2] Six American presidents sat for Stuart: John Adams, John Quincy Adams, Thomas Jefferson, James Madison, James Monroe, and George Washington.

Gilbert Stuart was born at Narragansett, R.I., on December 3, 1755, and died at Boston, Mass., on July 27, 1828.

[1] *Dolly Madison, The Nation's Hostess,* Elizabeth Lippincott Dean (Lothrop, Lee and Shepard Company, Boston, 1928) p. 104.
[2] *Famous Painters of America,* Joseph Walker McSpadden (Dodd, Mead and Company, New York, 1916) p. 73.

Stuart, James Ewell Brown

The following appellations have been given to James Ewell Brown Stuart: *Beauty Stuart,* the *Bible-class Man, Jeb Stuart,* the *Knight of the Golden Spurs, Old Jeb,* the *Plumed Knight of the Confederacy,* and the *Prince Rupert of the Confederacy.*

While he attended the United States Military Academy, at West Point, N.Y., from 1850 to 1854, Stuart was nicknamed *Beauty Stuart* and *Bible-class Man* by his fellow-cadets. The first nickname arose from his practice of going clean-shaven, which was regarded somewhat sarcastically by some of his fellow-students. [3] This nickname continued to be attributed to Stuart even after he had graduated from the Academy, and was, indeed, appropriate because he possessed a splendid physique, a cheerful disposition, charming manners, and wore rich and tasteful attire. In commemoration of Stuart's religious nature, evidenced by his high standards of moral conduct and his participation in the school's religious activities, he was called the *Bible-class Man.* [1]

Stuart, himself, originated the sobriquet *Knight of the Golden Spurs.* [2] He was a mounted cavalry officer, and his rich and dashing attire was set off by a pair of gold spurs presented to him by certain admiring ladies of Baltimore, Md.

James Ewell Brown Stuart was affectionately called *Jeb Stuart* [4] or *Old Jeb* by his soldiers, the nickname being composed of his initials J. E. B.

The appellations, the *Plumed Knight of the Confederacy* and *Prince Rupert of the Confederacy,* [1] commemorated the fact that

Major General Stuart as the leader of a brigade of Virginia cavalry, was the most outstanding Confederate cavalry officer of the Civil War. Stuart's service during the Civil War in the United States was compared with that of Prince Rupert of Bavaria during the Civil War in England from 1642 to 1646, when the prince was in command of a corps of Royalist cavalry, in which capacity he distinguished himself as the greatest cavalry officer of that rebellion. Prince Rupert was born at Prague, on December 18, 1619, and died at London, England, on November 29, 1682.

James Ewell Brown Stuart was born in Patrick County, Va., on February 6, 1833, and died at Richmond, Vt., on May 12, 1864.

[1] *The Life of the Gallant Pelham*, Philip Mercer (The J. W. Burke Company, Macon, Ga., 1929) p. 43, 45.
[2] *Life of J. E. B. Stuart*, Mary L. Williamson (B. F. Johnson Publishing Company, Richmond, Va., 1914) p. 20, 45.
[3] *Lee of Virginia: A Biography*, William E. Brooks (The Bobbs-Merrill Company, Indianapolis, Indiana, 1932) p. 166.
[4] *The Makers of America*, New Edition, Revised and Enlarged, James A. Woodburn and Thomas F. Moran (Longmans, Green and Company, New York and Boston, 1922) p. 292.

Stuart, Moses

Because he was an outstanding Biblical scholar and a prominent theologian in the history of early American religious education, Moses Stuart was deservedly called the *Father of Biblical Learning in America*.[1]

In 1809 Stuart entered Andover Theological Seminary, at Andover, Mass., as a Professor of Sacred Literature, a position he occupied for nearly forty years. During this time, he outlined numerous courses in Biblical study, introduced German theological views into American theology, his own understanding of those foreign doctrines making him widely respected by the most able controversialists of that time, and he utilized his thorough knowledge of the German and the Hebrew language in the classroom and in the production of a Hebrew grammar which was the basis of instruction in the study of Hebrew throughout America for approximately half a century.

Moses Stuart was born at Wilton, Conn., on March 26, 1780, and died at Andover, Mass., on January 4, 1852.

[1] *The National Cyclopaedia of American Biography* (James T. White and Company, New York, 1929) vol. 6, p. 244.

Stuart, Robert

As commissioner for the Indians in the Northwest Territory from about 1819 to 1834, and simultaneously in charge of activities of the American Fur Company, at Mackinaw, Mich., Robert Stuart came into constant contact with the Indians of this region. The Indians were so impressed by his fairness, tactfulness, and reliability in dealing with them that they respectfully nicknamed him *Friend of the Indian*.[1]

Robert Stuart was born in Callender, Scotland, on February 19, 1785, and died at Chicago, Ill., on October 28, 1848.

[1] *The National Cyclopaedia of American Biography* (James T. White and Company, New York, 1906) vol. 13, p. 141.

Stubtoe State. See Montana

Student Nurse of Danville. See Burchard, S. D.

Student Princes. See Heidelburg College

Stuffed Prophet. See Cleveland, Grover

Stuhldreyer, Harry. See Four Horsemen

Sturgeon, Daniel

While Daniel Sturgeon was a Senator from Pennsylvania to the United States Congress from 1839 until 1851, it is said that he made only one brief speech before the Senate, that one having been to reiterate a remark he had made in a committee meeting. His unusual reticence, taciturnity, and nonparticipation in debate caused him to be designated the *Silent Senator*.[1]

Daniel Sturgeon was born in Adams County, Pa., on October 27, 1789, and died at Uniontown, Pa., on July 2, 1878. He was Treasurer of the United States Mint at Philadelphia, Pa., from 1853 to 1858.

[1] *The National Cyclopaedia of American Biography* (James T. White and Company, New York, 1909) vol. 11, p. 83.

Stuyvesant, Peter

Hard-headed Pete, Headstrong Peter, or *Hardkopping Piet, Old Silver Leg,* or *Old Silver Nails,* the *One-legged Governor,* and *Wooden Leg* are sobriquets which have been applied to Peter Stuyvesant.

Peter Stuyvesant defended his convictions on all matters in a characteristically vigorous and obstinate manner, causing him to be nicknamed *Hard-headed Pete*[1] and *Headstrong Peter*[2] or *Hardkopping Piet*.

He was nicknamed *Old Silver Leg*[3] or *Old Silver Nail*,[4] and *Wooden Leg*[5] because

Stuyvesant, Peter—Continued

of the silver nails and the polished silver bands studding and encircling his wooden leg.

The *One-legged Governor* [7] lost a leg as the result of a wound received while he was attacking [8] Saint Martin, a Portuguese island in 1644. He was the Dutch Governor of New Amsterdam from 1647 to 1664.

[1] *A Short History of the United States*, Justin Huntly M'Carthy (Herbert S. Stone and Company, New York and Chicago, 1898) p. 66.
[2] *Barnes' Popular History of the United States: A Popular History of the United States of America*, Revised and Enlarged Edition, Joel Dorman Steele and Esther Baker Steele (A. S. Barnes and Company, New York, 1902) p. 57.
 Young Folks' History of the United States, Thomas Wentworth Higginson (Longmans, Green and Company, New York, 1903) p. 97.
[3] *The Essential Facts of American History*, Lawton B. Evans (Benjamin H. Sanborn and Company, New York and Boston, 1917) p. 78.
[4] *The American Colonies*, Mary G. Kelty (Ginn and Company, New York and Boston, 1932) p. 143.
[5] *Life and Times of Peter Stuyvesant*, Hendrik Van Loon (Henry Holt and Company, New York, 1928) p. 325.
[6] *Hail Columbia, the Life of a Nation: Hail Columbia*, Marie A. Lawson (Doubleday Doran and Company, Garden City, N.Y., 1931) p. 37.
[7] *A Book of Nicknames*, John Goff (Courier-Journal Job Printing Company, Louisville, Ky., 1892) p. 23.
[8] *Peter Stuyvesant*, John S. C. Abbott (Dodd, Mead and Company, New York, 1898) p. 122.

Sublime Dandy. See Lewis, Meriwether

Subsidy Pomeroy. See Pomeroy, S. C.

Subterraneans

The members of the American or *Know-nothing Party* were often called the *Subterraneans* [1] in allusion to their policy of carefully concealing their meeting places and the inner activities of their party.

[1] *History of Alabama and Her People*, Albert Burton Moore (The American Historical Society, Inc., New York and Chicago, 1927) vol. 1, p. 273.

Sucker State. See Illinois

Suckers. See Illinois Inhabitants

Sue Mundy. See Clark, M. J.

Sufferers' Lands

During the process of adjusting state boundary lines after the Revolutionary War, Connecticut in 1786 ceded to the United States vast territory which the British King had granted it as a colony, the crown grant being approximately "three thousand miles in length." In return for this, Connecticut received a large tract of land in northeastern

Ohio of about three and a half million acres which was called the Western Reserve of Connecticut. In 1792 Connecticut set aside about five hundred thousand acres of this Reserve land for those settlers who, during the Revolutionary War, had had their property burned and plundered by the British soldiers. Because of this fact the Reserve land was popularly designated the *Sufferers' Lands*.[1]

[1] *This Cleveland of Ours*, Wilfred Henry Alburn and Miriam Russell Alburn (The S. J. Clarke Publishing Company, Chicago and Cleveland, Ohio, 1933) vol. 1, p. 20.

Sugar. See Cain, M. P.

Sugar Beets. See Cummings, Fred

Sugar Bowl

The extensive sugar plantations in the lower part of the state of Louisiana, have caused this section of the state to be nicknamed the *Sugar Bowl*.[1] Louisiana has the distinction of being about the only state in the Union which grows sugar cane to produce sugar.

[1] *The World Book Encyclopedia* (The Quarrie Corporation, Chicago, 1938) vol. 10, p. 4126.

Sugar Bowl. See Tulane Football Stadium

Sugar Bowl of Michigan

The Saginaw Valley in Michigan is popularly called the *Sugar Bowl of Michigan* [1] because this region is devoted almost exclusively to the raising of sugar beets, and immense sugar factories are located in the valley.

[1] *History of Saginaw County, Michigan, Historical, Commercial, Biographical*, James Cooke Mills (Seemann and Peters, Saginaw, Mich., 1918) vol. 1, p. 468.

Sugar Cain. See Cain, M. P.

Sugar King. See Spreckels, Claus

Sugar Senators

The nickname, *Sugar Senators*,[1] was given to the United States senators who, while the Dingley Tariff Bill was being debated before the Senate in 1897, attempted to modify the bill so as to disguise the concessions to the sugar trusts.

[1] *Twenty Years of the Republic, 1885-1905*, Harry Thurston Peck (Dodd, Mead and Company, New York, 1907) p. 527.

Sugar State. See Louisiana

Suitcase. See Seeds, R. I.

Sullivan, James

James Sullivan was accustomed to come into the ring to fight his opponent with an American flag around his waist, hence his nickname *Yankee Sullivan.*[1] He was born of Irish parentage in London, England, and was the American champion prize-fighter from 1841 to 1853.

[1] *Ten—and Out!: The Complete Story of the Prize Ring in America,* Alexander Johnston with a foreword by Gene Tunney (Ives Washburn, New York, 1927) p. 24.

Sullivan, John Lawrence

Early in his career, John Lawrence Sullivan, the champion prize fighter, was called the *Strong Boy of Boston,*[1] or the *Boston Strong Boy.* He was born at Boston, Mass., on October 15, 1858, and died at West Arlington Mass.[2] on February 2, 1918.

[1] *John L. Sullivan,* R. F. Dibble (Little, Brown and Company, Boston, 1925) p. xiv.
[2] *Encyclopedia Americana,* 1952 ed. vol. 25, P. 819-20.

Sullivan, Timothy Daniel

Timothy Daniel Sullivan, a politician, was commonly called by his friends and supporters *Big Tim*[1] and the *Big Feller*[1] because he was unusually large of stature and was a jovial and generous man. He was in the service of the Tammany politicians while he was still a youth. He either owned or had an interest in several saloons by the time he was of age. He owned an interest in various theatres, and was influential in the boxing activities in New York State. He came to be one of the most influential politicians in New York City from 1900 until 1910. He was a Representative from New York State to the United States Congress from 1902 until 1906 when he retired.

Timothy Daniel Sullivan was born at New York City, on July 23, 1862, and died near Eastchester, N.Y., on August 31, 1913.

[1] *Dictionary of American Biography under the Auspices of the American Council of Learned Societies,* ed. by Dumas Malone (Charles Scribner's Sons, New York, 1936) vol. 18, p. 189.

Sullivan, Timothy P.

Timothy P. Sullivan, a Tammany Hall politician and alderman, was nicknamed *Boston Tim, Little Feller,* and *Little Tim.*

The sobriquet, *Boston Tim,* was applied to him to distinguish him from other Timothy Sullivans soon after he had returned to New York City from Boston, Mass.

After he had become prominent in the political affairs of New York City and of New York State, he was designated the *Little Feller* and *Little Tim*[2] to keep from confusing him with his cousin, Timothy Daniel Sullivan, also a New York legislator and Tammany Hall politician.

Timothy P. Sullivan was born either in New York City or in Boston, Mass., and died in New York City on December 22, 1909.

[1] *The New York Times,* New York, December 23, 1909, col. 1, p. 1, col. 5, p. 2.

Sulphur King. See Frasch, Herman

Sultan of Swat. See Ruth, G. H.

Summerall, Charles Pelot

General Charles Pelot Summerall was nicknamed *Sitting Bull*[1] because that was his "telephone exchange in France during the World War."[1]

He was graduated from the United States Military Academy in 1892 and was promoted rapidly in the Army during World War I. He became a Colonel in May 1917, Brigadier General on February 18, 1919, General and Chief of Staff February 23, 1919, and was retired with the rank of General on March 31, 1931.

Charles Pelot Summerall was born at Lake City, Fla., on March 4, 1867.

[1] *The Literary Digest, January to March, 1930* (Funk and Wagnalls Company, New York, 1930) vol. 104, March 8, 1930, p. 41.

Summerville, South Carolina

The *Flower Town in the Pines*[1] is a sobriquet descriptive of Summerville with its many beautiful gardens and flowers. One of the most conspicuous of the flowering plants in the early spring is the wisteria which climbs and falls in garlands from the pine trees over the drives in the vicinity of the town.

[1] *Street Strolls around Charleston, South Carolina, America's Most Historic City, Giving the History, Legends, Traditions,* Miriam Bellangee Wilson (The name of the publisher is not given. Charleston, S.C., 1930) Booklet No. 2, Blue and Gray Historical Series, p. 50.

Summit City. See Akron, Ohio

Summit of the World. See Yellowstone National Park

Sumner, Charles

Bull of the Woods [1] was a sobriquet applied to Charles Sumner, Senator from Massachusetts noted for his vitriolic attacks upon slavery. One such speech made during the battle over Kansas resulted in a physical assault on Sumner by Senator Preston S. Brooks of South Carolina (*q.v.* on p. 59 of this volume).

Charles Sumner was born at Boston, Mass., on January 6, 1811, and died at Washington, D.C., on March 11, 1874.

[1] *Americanisms: The English of the New World.* M. Schele De Vere (Charles Scribner and Company, New York, 1872) p. 250.

Sumter, Thomas

The *Carolinian Gamecock*, or the *South Carolina Gamecock*, and the *Gamecock* are appellations given to the American Revolutionary officer, Thomas Sumter.

In the summer of 1780, while Brigadier General Sumter was engaged in raising troops against the British, it is said that he stopped one day at the residence of the Gillespie family, in the vicinity of Charlotte, N.C. The men of the family were fond of cockfighting and among their collection of Blue Hen's Chickens was a cock known as Tuck noted for his aggressiveness and for the fact that he habitually won. Coming upon the men as they were watching a furious cockfight, Sumter joined them as an interested spectator. After the fight, he adroitly suggested that, if they but followed him, he could show them some real fighting with men as the combatants. The Gillespie brothers acclaimed him as another Tuck, or gamecock of the Blue Hen's Chickens, and Sumter was popularly known thereafter as the *Gamecock.* [1]

Sir Bonastre Tarleton, Sumter's adversary in the South Carolina campaign of the Revolution, is credited with having nicknamed Sumter the *South Carolina Gamecock.* During Sumter's successful campaign against the British in the Carolinas in 1780, at which time he displayed the best qualities of a fighting gamecock, Sumter became known as the *Carolinian Gamecock,* [2] or the *South Carolina Gamecock,* [3] being aggressive, audacious, plucky, determined, and cheerful under the most trying conditions.

Thomas Sumter was born near Charlottesville, Va., on August 14, 1734, and died at Charleston, S.C., on June 1, 1832.

[1] *Thomas Sumter,* Anne King Gregorie (The R. L. Bryan Company, Columbia, S.C., 1931) p. 103-4.
[2] *The Pictorial Field-Book of the Revolution; or, Illustrations by Pen and Pencil, of the History, Biography, Scenery, Relics, and Traditions of the War for Independence,* Benson J. Lossing (Harper and Brothers, New York, 1852) vol. 2, p. 653.
The Encyclopedia Americana (Americana Corporation, New York and Chicago, 1929) vol. 26, p. 19.
[3] *The National Cyclopaedia of American Biography* (James T. White and Company, New York, 1898) vol. 1, p. 79.

Sun Bowl. See Football Stadium, Texas College of Mines and Metallurgy

Sunburst Colonels

About 1882 Lawrence Yates Sherman, later a United States senator and always a gifted coiner of political slang, nicknamed the members of the governor of Ohio's staff *Sunburst Colonels* [1] because of their resplendent uniforms.

[1] *The National Cyclopaedia of American Biography* (James T. White and Company, New York, 1916) vol. 15, p. 101.

Sunburst Division. See Fortieth Infantry Division of World War II

Sun Dodgers. See University of Washington

Sunflower State. See Kansas

Sunflowers. See Kansans

Sunny Jim. See Watson, J. E.

Sunny South

The southern part of the United States, that is, the region south of the Mason and Dixon Line, is often referred to as the *Sunny South* [1] in allusion to the bright, sunny weather generally characteristic of this section of the country.

[1] *The Seventy-ninth Highlanders; New York Volunteers in the War of Rebellion, 1861-1865,* William Todd (Press of Brandow, Barton and Company, Albany, N.Y., 1886) p. 99.

Sunrise Conference

The *Sunrise Conference* [1] is the name given by newspaper men of Washington, D.C., to the conference held in the White House on February 23 or 24, 1916, at seven-thirty in the morning. This meeting was attended by President Woodrow Wilson, and Representatives Claude Kitchin, Henry D. Flood, and Champ Clark.[1] As reporter Gilson Gardner[1] knew this story, "it was at this conference that President Wilson announced his intention to put the United States into war and to do so immediately." (The United States entered World War I on April 6, 1917.) The meeting was called the *Sunrise Conference* because it took place very early in the morning to escape the attention of newspaper men and the general public.[2]

[1] *Woodrow Wilson; the Man, His Times, and His Task*, William Allen White (Houghton, Mifflin Company, Boston and New York, 1924) p. 328, 329.
[2] *The Strangest Friendship in History, Woodrow Wilson and Colonel House*, George Sylvester Viereck (Liveright Inc., New York, 1932) p. 182.

Sunrise Poet. See Lanier, Sidney

Sunset Cox. See Cox, S. S.

Sunset Land. See Arizona

Sunset Law
During the period of Reconstruction following the close of the Civil War, a number of unscrupulous white men in the southern states established small stores for the purpose of receiving stolen cotton, corn, or other farm products in return for whiskey, cheap jewelry, sweets, or other commodities. In order to eliminate the profitable activities of such places, many of the Southern legislatures enacted what became known as the *Sunset Law*[1] because it forbade the proprietors of stores to make any purchases of farm products "after sunset" unless a full record was made of the transaction.

[1] *Documentary History of Reconstruction, Political, Military, Social, Religious, Educational, and Industrial, 1865 to the Present Time*, Walter L. Fleming (The Arthur H. Clark Company, Cleveland, Ohio, 1907) vol. 2, p. 318.

Sunset State. See Arizona; Oregon

Sunshine City. See St. Petersburg, Fla.

Sunshine State. See New Mexico, South Dakota

Super Sixth. See Sixth Armored Division of World War II

Surgeon Scout. See Powell, D. F.

Surveyor President. See Washington, George

Susquehanna University
The *Little Crusaders*[1] is the appellation given to the athletic teams of Susquehanna University, at Selinsgrove, Pa., in 1924. This University is a Lutheran College, which fact connects the players on these teams with "the idea of the early Christian Crusaders."[1]

[1] A communication from Luther D. Grossman, Director of Athletics at Susquehanna University, Selinsgrove, Pa., June 24, 1935.

Sutphin, William Halstead
The nickname, *Barnacle Bill*,[1] applied to William Halstead Sutphin was a humorous allusion to the fact that he represented the Third District of New Jersey in the United States Congress, which is a coastal region where quantities of barnacles abound.

William Halstead Sutphin was born at Brownstown, N.J., on August 30, 1887, resides at Matawan, N.J., and was a Democratic Representative from New Jersey to the United States Congress from 1931 to 1943.

[1] *The Washington Post Magazine*, Washington, D.C., March 4, 1934, p. 4.

Swamp Fox of Mississippi. See Forrest, N. B.

Swamp Fox of South Carolina. See Marion, Francis

Swamp Fox of the Tennessee Valley. See Roddey, P. D.

Swamp State. See South Carolina

Swanson, Claude Augustus
Because he believed in building up rather than decreasing the strength of the United States Navy, Claude Augustus Swanson has been nicknamed *Big-Navy Claude*.[1] He was born at Swansonville, Va., on March 31, 1862, and was Secretary of the Navy from 1933 until 1939. He died July 7, 1939.

[1] *Washington and the Revolutionists: A Characterization of Recovery Policies and of the People Who Are Giving Them Effect*, Roger W. Babson (Harper and Brothers, New York and London, 1934) p. 184.

Swarthmore College

For many years the athletic teams of Swarthmore College, at Swarthmore, Pa., have been designated the *Garnets* [1] because the college color is garnet.

[1] A communication from Samuel Nalmer, Director of Athletics at Swarthmore College, Swarthmore, Pa., August 26, 1935.

Swearing Jack Waller. See Waller, John

Swedes. See Bethany College (Lindsborg, Kans.)

Sweet Gum Battery

During the period from March 27 to April 9, 1865, at Spanish Fort, Ala., cannons made of sweet gum logs bound at the muzzle and at the breech with iron bands were used by the soldiers in Company C of the Thirty-third Regiment of Missouri Volunteers, commanded by Captain A. J. Campbell. These cannons were designated the *Sweet Gum Battery*.[1]

[1] *Centennial History of Missouri (The Center State) One Hundred Years in the Union, 1820-1921*, Walter B. Stevens (The S. J. Clarke Publishing Company, St. Louis, Mo., and Chicago, 1921) vol. 2, p. 292.

Sweetheart of the Foxholes. See Lamour, Dorothy

Sweetheart of the Treasury. See O'Reilly, M. M.

Sweet-spirited Advocate of Justice, Love, and Humanity. See Mott, Lucretia

Swift Bird. See Hare, W. H.

Switzerland of America. See Colorado; Maine; New Hampshire; New Jersey; West Virginia

Sword of the Confederacy. See Jackson, T. J.

Sword of the Revolution. See Washington, George

Sycamore City. See Terre Haute, Ind.

Sylacauga, Alabama

Sylacauga, Ala., was nicknamed the *Singing City* [1] because of the music program given by the school children of that city, and because of the civic and other school musical programs given there. The Sylacauga Civic Male Chorus is said to be one of the finest nonprofessional male choruses in the South. Also contributing to Sylacauga's musical fame is the Robed Chorus consisting of thirty-six high school pupils.

[1] *The Peabody Reflector*, published by George Peabody College for Teachers, Nashville, Tennessee, July, 1948, p. 278.

Syracuse, New York

Syracuse is known as the *Central City, City of Conventions, City of Isms, City of the Plains*, and *Salt City*, or the *City of Salt*.

This city, located midway between Albany and Buffalo, has come to be called the *Central City*.[1] It is termed the *City of Conventions* [2] because it has been the scene of many political and other conventions, and the *City of Isms* because it was formerly the "meeting place of Abolitionists and reformers." During the earlier days of its existence it was nicknamed the *City of the Plains* because it was situated in that part of the state known as the plains. Because the city has numerous salt boiling works it is called *Salt City*, or the *City of Salt*.

[1] *King's Handbook of the United States*, planned and ed. by Moses King, text by M. F. Sweetser (The Matthews-Northrup Company, Buffalo, N.Y., 1896) p. 604.
[2] *Syracuse and Its Environs: A History*, Franklin H. Chase (Lewis Historical Publishing Company, Inc., New York and Chicago, 1924) vol. 1, p. 287.

Syracuse University

The two nicknames, the *Orangemen* and the *Saltine Warriors*, have been applied to the athletic teams of Syracuse University, at Syracuse, N.Y. The appellation, *Orangemen*,[1] originated because orange is the college color and is also the color of the uniforms worn by the teams. *Saltine Warriors*,[1] had its origin in the facts that "Syracuse was famous at one time for its salt wells and the city was known as Salt City, and that it is located on a famous old Indian site." [1]

[1] A letter from James H. Decker, Director of Athletic Publicity at Syracuse University, Syracuse, N.Y., December 2, 1935.

T

Tadpole Ditch

Lawrence Yates Sherman, who was born in Miami County, Ohio, on November 8, 1858, held many positions of public trust from member of the State Legislature to United States senator. While he was a young lawyer at Springfield, Ohio, about 1882, he became noted for his caustic political epigrams which were eagerly circulated by the journalists of the day and which are still often repeated.

It was Sherman who gave the nickname *Tadpole Ditch* [1] to the Illinois and Michigan Canal. He made use of this term perhaps because the Illinois and Michigan Canal was in the process of construction for such a long time (1836-1848) that frogs laid their eggs there.

[1] *The National Cyclopaedia of American Biography* (James T. White and Company, New York, 1916) vol. 15, p. 101.

Tadpoles. See Mississippians

Taft, Robert Alphonso

Some time in 1949, during the precampaign activity for the 1950 senatorial elections, the nickname *Mr. Republican* began to be widely applied in newspapers and magazines to Senator Robert A. Taft as one of the chief exponents of Republican party principle and policy. The nickname continued to be used throughout Senator Taft's campaign in 1952 for the Republican nomination for President of the United States. When President Eisenhower took office in January, 1953, Taft was named the majority leader in the Senate. He had been a Senator from Ohio to the United States Congress since 1939.

Robert A. Taft, son of William Howard Taft, twenty-seventh President of the United States, was born at Cincinnati, Ohio, on September 8, 1889 and died on July 31, 1953, in New York City.

Talcott, John

John Talcott, a soldier and public official, was nicknamed the *Indian Fighter*.[1] During King Philip's War in 1675-76 in colonial Connecticut, Talcott became widely known for his bravery, resourcefulness, and success in subduing the Indians. He attained the rank of Lieutenant Colonel in the standing army of Connecticut which fought the Indians until the war was ended by the killing of King Philip at Bristol, Conn., on August 12, 1676.

John Talcott was born at Braintree, England, about 1630, and died at Hartford, Conn., on July 23, 1688.

[1] *Appleton's Cyclopaedia of American Biography*, ed. by James Grant Wilson and John Fiske (D. Appleton and Company, New York, 1894) vol. 6, p. 23.

Talkative Tom. See Blanton, T. L.

Tall Pine. See Sibley, H. H.

Tall Sycamore of the Wabash. See Voorhees, D. W.

Tall Trader. See Sibley, H. H.

Tallulah's Papa. See Bankhead, W. B.

Tama Jim. See Wilson, James (Legislator)

Tamer of Lightning. See Franklin. Benjamin

Taney, Roger Brooke

Roger Brooke Taney, chief justice of the United States and author of the Dred Scott decision, was nicknamed *King Coody* because he was a leader in the dissenting faction of the Federalist party known as the *Coodies* [1] (*q.v.*). This group separated from the Federalist party over the issue of supporting the United States Government during the War of 1812 with England, the Coodies favoring support.

Taney became Chief Justice of the United States Supreme Court in 1836, filling the vacancy left by the death of Chief Justice John Marshall.

Roger Brooke Taney was born in Calvert County, Md., on March 17, 1777, and died at Washington, D.C., on October 12, 1864.

[1] *Dictionary of American Biography under the Auspices of the American Council of Learned Societies*, ed. by Dumas Malone (Charles Scribner's Sons, New York, 1936) vol. 18, p. 290.

Tangiers Smith. See Smith, William (Jurist)

Tangipahoa of the Crimson Carpet. See Tangipahoa Parish, La.

Tangipahoa Parish, Louisiana

Tangipahoa Parish in Louisiana has been nicknamed *Tangipahoa of the Crimson Carpet* [1] because it is situated in the center of the strawberry-raising belt of the state.[1]

[1] *The World Book Encyclopedia* (The Quarrie Corporation, Chicago, 1938) vol. 10, p. 4128.

Tanner President. See Grant, U. S.

Tar Bucket Nights

The people of Maine celebrate the night of Washington's birthday, February 22, with merry-making. The scenes of these gatherings are illuminated by great bonfires, hence the nickname *Tar Bucket Nights.*[1]

[1] *Maine of the Sea and Pines,* Nathan Haskell Dole and Irwin Leslie Gordon (L. C. Page and Company, Boston, 1928) p. 289.

Tarbuckets

Military cadets speak of full dress hats as *Tarbuckets,*[1] supposedly because they are black and somewhat bucket-shaped.

[1] *Unit Projects in Modern Literature* (Educational Press, Inc., Columbus, Ohio), March 1-14, 1935, p. 12.

Tarheel State. See North Carolina

Tar Heels. See University of North Carolina

Tarheels. See North Carolinians

Tariff Andy. See Stewart, Andrew

Tariff of Abominations

From the end of the War of 1812, a series of laws had been enacted for increasingly higher protective tariffs. When Andrew Jackson became President of the United States in 1829, the tariff act of 1828 then in force imposed exceedingly high tariffs on all imported goods. The people of the South were much displeased by this, inasmuch as their chief product was cotton for export, and their manufactured commodities were purchased either in Europe or the North. In the campaign to make their grievances heard, Southerners nicknamed the law the *Tariff of Abominations.*[1]

[1] *Andrew Jackson, the Fighting President*, Helen Nicolay (The Century Company, New York, 1929) p. 288.

Tarkio College

The athletic teams of Tarkio Callege, at Tarkio, Mo., are designated the *Owls* [1] and the *Tarks.*[1]

[1] A communication from N. P. Kyle, Director of Athletics at Tarkio College, Tarkio, Mo., July 5, 1935.

Tarks. See Tarkio College

Taunton Turkey

In the vicinity of Taunton, Mass., the cod fish is humorously designated *Taunton Turkey.*[1] See also *Marblehead Turkey.*

[1] *Dictionary of Americanisms,* Fourth Edition, John Russell Bartlett (Little, Brown and Company, New York, 1924) p. 364-72.

Tars. See Norfolk Baseball Club; Rollins College

Tartans. See Carnegie Institute of Technology

Tartars. See Wayne University

Tater Town. See Gleason, Tenn.

Taterville. See Gleason, Tenn.

Tattooed Knight. See Blaine, J. G.

Tattooed Man. See Blaine, J. G.

Taylor, Alfred Alexander

Alfred Alexander Taylor, former Governor of Tennessee, was nicknamed the *Knight of the Red Rose*, the *Sage of Happy Valley*, and *Uncle Alf*. He was nicknamed the *Knight of the Red Rose* during the gubernatorial contest of 1886 in Tennessee when both Alfred and his brother, Robert Love Taylor, (*q.v.*) were seeking the election on the Republican and Democratic tickets respectively. Alfred Taylor was called the *Sage of Happy Valley* [2] because he was born and lived the greater part of his life in Happy Valley in Carter County, Tenn. Because people loved and respected him so much in his later life he was popularly known as *Uncle Alf*.[3]

He was a Republican Representative from Tennessee to the United States Congress from 1889 until 1895, and was elected Governor of Tennessee in 1920 for the term which expired on January 1, 1923. He was then seventy-two years old.

Alfred Alexander Taylor was born in Carter County, Tenn., on August 6, 1848, and died at Johnson City, Tenn., on November 25, 1931.

[1] *The Nashville Banner*, Nashville, Tenn., April 1, 1912, col. 3, p. 7.
[2] *The Nashville Tennesseean*, Nashville, Tenn., November 27, 1931, col. 6, p. 1.
[3] *The Nashville Banner*, Nashville, Tenn., November 25, 1931, col. 4, p. 1.
The Nashville Tennesseean, Nashville, Tenn., November 26, 1931, col. 7, p. 1.

Taylor, Benjamin Franklin

The *London Times* gave the sobriquet, *Oliver Goldsmith of America*,[1] to Benjamin Franklin Taylor because much of his poetry was concerned with reproducing the life and times of a past generation, and because his verse was picturesque, fanciful, and displayed humor and pathos, yet was unpretentious, in which respect it was comparable to the poetry of the eighteenth-century Irish poet and writer Oliver Goldsmith.

Benjamin Franklin Taylor was born at Lowville, N.Y., on July 18, 1819, and died at Cleveland, Ohio, on February 24, 1887.

[1] *The National Cyclopaedia of American Biography* (James T. White and Company, New York, 1909) vol. 11, p. 160.

Taylor, Charley

Charley Taylor, a champion slingsman in the United States, and a hunting guide on Reelfoot Lake in Tennessee, was nicknamed *Slingshot Charley*[1] because of his ability with a slingshot. He was such an expert marksman that he could kill coots, ducks, and geese as they swam on the lake after hunters had shot them down, or even kill them in flight. He has appeared on programs at fairs and other public gatherings and has been featured in motion pictures.

Charley Taylor was born at Como, Tenn., on February 2, 1894, and lives on his farm on Reelfoot Lake, Obion County, Tenn., where he hunts, farms, fishes, and guides hunters on the lake.

[1] This biographical data about Taylor was obtained for the author by Paul Thorne, Troy, Tenn., April 24, 1939.

Taylor, James Wren

James Wren Taylor, who was born at Yulee, Fla., on July 27, 1898, and who catches in major league baseball, is popularly known as *Zack*[1] because his last name

reminded people of President Zachary Taylor who was familiarly called *Zach*.

[1] *Who's Who in Major League Base Ball*, comp. by Harold (Speed) Johnson (Buxton Publishing Company, Chicago, 1933) p. 379.

Taylor, Robert

Robert Taylor (Spangler Arlington Brugh), a motion picture actor born at Tilley, Neb., Aug. 5, 1915, was nicknamed *Beautiful Bob* at the beginning of his film career. He is a man of splendid physique and handsome facial features and is considered one of the most attractive motion-picture actors.

[1] *Washington Times-Herald*, Washington, D.C., November 26, 1937, col. 3, p. 10.

Taylor, Robert Love

Robert Love Taylor, Governor of Tennessee, was nicknamed the *Apostle of Sunshine, Fiddling Bob*, the *Knight of the White Rose*, and *Our Bob*. He was designated the *Apostle of Sunshine*[1] because of his congenial and jovial personality. The sobriquet, *Fiddling Bob*,[2] was given to him in 1878 while he was campaigning the First District of Tennessee, an overwhelmingly Republican district, against his Republican opponent, Major A. H. Pettibone, for election as Representative to the Tennessee Legislature. Instead of attempting to meet the arguments advanced by his opponent in serious debate, Taylor "would break off into jig time music on his fiddle, sweeping the audience off its feet."[2] While Taylor was campaigning Tennessee in 1886 with his Republican brother, Alfred Alexander, each seeking election as Governor, a train wreck near Chattanooga caused them to spend the night in a small hotel at Bridgeport, Ala. Next morning before the Taylor brothers and their entourage left the hotel, the proprietress went into the garden, cut a red and a white rose, and gave the white one to Robert and the red one to Alfred, in order to honor their mother. She said, "I know she is proud of two sons who can differ so in politics and still love each other."[3] Henceforth, Robert Love Taylor was nicknamed the *Knight of the White Rose*, his brother, the *Knight of the Red Rose*, and their political campaign, the *War of the Roses*.[4] The popularity of ex-Governor Taylor with all classes of people throughout the state and their appreciation of him as a man and as a politician caused

Taylor, R. L.—Continued

them to nickname him *Our Bob*,[4] a sobriquet widely applied during his state and national political campaigns.

He was Governor of Tennessee from 1887 until 1891 and again from 1897 until 1899, and was a Democratic Senator from Tennessee to the United States Congress from 1907 until 1912.

Champ Clark once said that Taylor was "a strange commingling of wit, humor, philosophy, pathos, eloquence, common sense, and good morals."

Robert Love Taylor was born in Carter County, Tenn., on July 31, 1850, and died at Washington, D.C., on March 31, 1912.

[1] *The Nashville Banner*, Nashville, Tenn., April 4, 1912, col. 4, p. 15.
[2] *The Nashville Tennesseean*, Nashville, Tenn., April 1, 1912, col. 3, p. 1.
Washington Herald, Washington, D.C., March 30, 1912, col. 3, p. 1.
[3] *The Nashville Tennesseean*, Nashville, Tenn., November 26, 1931, col. 3, p. 5.
[4] *The Nashville Banner*, Nashville, Tenn., April 1, 1912, col. 4, p. 1, col. 3, p. 7.

Taylor, Thomas

At the time of his death in 1833, Colonel Thomas Taylor was called the *Patriarch of Columbia*.[1] He had lived to the age of ninety, and had taken a very active part in the founding and developing of the civic, religious, educational, and commercial interests of Columbia, S.C.

Thomas Taylor was born in Virginia, on September 10, 1743, and died at Columbia, S.C., on November 16, 1833.[2] During the Revolutionary War, he was a Colonel in Brigadier General Thomas Sumter's brigade from December 1, 1780, to July 29, 1781.

[1] *The National Cyclopaedia of American Biography* (James T. White and Company, New York, 1904) vol. 12, p. 165.
[2] *A History of Richland County, 1732-1805*, Edwin L. Green (The R. L. Bryan Company, Columbia, S.C., 1932) vol. 1, p. 173.

Taylor, Zachary

Old Buena Vista, *Old Rough and Ready*, and *Old Zach* are appellations by which Zachary Taylor has been designated.

The crushing defeat administered to the Mexicans at the Battle of Buena Vista, near Saltillo, Mexico, on February 23, 1847, caused Major General Taylor to be affectionately and appreciatively nicknamed *Old Buena Vista*.[1]

Zachary Taylor was popularly known as *Old Rough and Ready*[2] by his soldiers.

This sobriquet apparently came into popular usage during the war between Mexico and the United States from 1846 to 1847 when Major General Taylor capably served the United States, proving his worth as a soldier even though his dress and manner were somewhat crude.

He was sometimes familiarly called *Old Zach*[3] by his friends and associates. This nickname was widely used by Taylor's fellow-officers and his soldiers during his campaigns against the Seminole Indians in Florida from 1832 to 1837, and it was also applied to him while he was in the war with Mexico in 1847.

Zachary Taylor, the twelfth President of the United States, was born in Orange County, Va., on September 24, 1784, and died at Washington, D.C., on July 9, 1850.

[1] U.S. *"Snap Shots": An Independent, National, and Memorial Encyclopedia . . .* , Oliver McKee (A. M. Thayer and Company, Boston, 1892) p. 309.
[2] *Old Rough and Ready: Young Folks' Life of General Zachary Taylor*, John Frost (Lee and Shepard, Boston, 1887) p. 46-7, 207.
Pen Pictures of the Presidents, Fred T. Wilson (Southwestern Company, Nashville, Tenn., 1932) p. 199-200.
[3] *Taylor and Fillmore: Life and Public Services of Major-general Zachary Taylor; also, the Life and Services of Honorable Millard Fillmore* (Belknap and Hammersley, Hartford, Conn., 1848) p. 47.

Teacher President. See Garfield, J. A.

Tech Hawks. See Armour Institute of Technology

Telegraphers. See Western Union College

Telescope Teddy. See Roosevelt, Theodore

Templars. See Temple University

Temple University

The athletic teams of Temple University, at Philadelphia, Pa., are popularly known as *Owls*,[1] *Red Devils*,[1] and *Templars*.[1] The sobriquet *Owls*, was given to the teams by a vote of the students in 1924.[1] The Publicity Department of the University nicknamed the teams *Red Devils* in 1930 because they wore red uniforms.[1] Newspaper men in recent years coined the sobriquet, *Templars*.

[1] A communication from Robert V. Geasey, Director of Publicity at Temple University, Philadelphia, June 17, 1935.

Ten-cent Jimmy. See Buchanan, James

Tenderfoot

The sobriquet, *Tenderfoot*,[1] was applied by cowboys and ranchmen to newcomers from the East. The nickname signifies that the newcomer would suffer actual bodily pain from the hardships of western life.

[1] *Jungle Roads and Other Trails of Roosevelt*, Daniel Henderson (E. P. Dutton and Company, New York, 1920) p. 85.

Tenmilers. See Salem College

Tennessee

The following are the nicknames of Tennessee: the *Big Bend State*, the *Lion's Den State*, the *Hog and Hominy State*, the *Monkey State*, the *Mother of Southwestern Statesmen*, and the *Volunteer State*.

The first of these, no doubt, originated in the expression *River with the Big Bend*, which is the Indian name for the Tennessee River.[1]

J. C. Thomas gives the sobriquet, *Lion's Den State*,[2] to Tennessee; but he does not say how it originated. Probably its origin and application to this state are in some way connected with the life and activities of Andrew Jackson.

The corn and pork production of Tennessee reached [1] such great proportions between 1800 and 1840, that the land received the designation (now obsolete) of the *Hog and Hominy State*.[3]

Tennessee has been called the *Monkey State* [4] by writers in newspapers and magazines since the passage of a bill in the Tennessee House of Representatives [5] "prohibiting the teaching of the Evolution Theory in all the universities, normals, and all other public schools of the state, which are supported in whole or in part, by the public school funds" provided by the state.

This bill, was approved on March 25, 1925.

Tennessee, having furnished the United States three presidents and a number of distinguished statesmen, has come to be designated the *Mother of Southwestern Statesmen*.

On May 26, 1847, Governor Aaron V. Brown called for three regiments of soldiers to serve in the Mexican War. Thirty thousand volunteered at once, hence the nickname *Volunteer State*.[6]

[1] *Origin and History of the American Flag*, George Henry Preble (Nickholas L. Brown, Philadelphia, 1917), vol. 2, p. 638.

[2] *Manual of Useful Information*, comp. under the direction of J. C. Thomas (The Werner Company, Chicago, 1893) p. 22.
[3] *King's Handbook of the United States*, planned and ed. by Moses King, text by M. F. Sweetser (The Matthews-Northrup Company, Buffalo, N.Y., 1896) p. 797.
[4] *Washington Herald*, Washington, D.C., February 1, 1935, cols. 1 and 2, p. 3.
[5] *Public Acts of the State of Tennessee, Passed by the Sixty-fourth General Assembly, 1925*, published by authority (Printing Department of the Tennessee Industrial School, Nashville, Tenn., 1925) p. 50-1.
[6] *Tennessee, The Volunteer State, 1796-1923*, John Trotwood Moore and Austin P. Foster (The S. J. Clarke Publishing Company, Chicago and Nashville, Tenn., 1923) vol. 1, p. 437.

Tennessee Polytechnic Institute

The *Eagles* [1] is the nickname given to the athletic teams of Tennessee Polytechnic Institute, at Cookeville, Tenn., in 1923 by a vote of the student body.

[1] A communication from P. V. Overall, Director of Athletics at the Tennessee Polytechnic Institute, Cookeville, Tenn., June 19, 1935.

Tennessee Valley. See Happy Valley

Tennessee Wesleyan College

The athletic teams of Tennessee Wesleyan College, at Athens, Tenn., were nicknamed *Bulldogs* [1] in 1920 by G. F. Stewart, Coach of Athletics at the College at that time.

[1] A communication from James L. Robb, President of Tennessee Wesleyan College, Athens, Tenn., November 18, 1935.

Tennesseeans

Tennesseeans are nicknamed *Big-benders, Butter-nuts, Mudheads*, and *Whelps*. The first nickname is derived from the Tennessee River, called by the Indians the *River with the Big Bend*, referring in all probability to Moccasin bend at the foot of Lookout Mountain, in Chattanooga, Tenn. The name *Butter-nuts* was first given to the soldiers of Tennessee during the Civil War from the tan color of their uniforms,[1] and later came to be applied to the people of the entire state. *Mud-heads* [2] is given as a nickname to the Tennesseeans by more than one writer, but its origin and significance are not explained. The sobriquet *Whelps* [3] applied to the Tennesseeans is not generally accepted by the people of the state.

[1] *U.S.: An Index to the United States of America*, comp. by Malcolm Townsend (D. Lothrop Company, Boston, 1890) p. 80.
[2] *Americanisms—New and Old*, John Stephen Farmer (Privately Printed by Thomas Poulter and Sons, London, 1889) p. 376.
[3] *U.S.: An Index to the United States of America*, comp. by Malcolm Townsend (D. Lothrop Company, Boston, 1890) p. 81.

Tennis Cabinet

While Theodore Roosevelt was President of the United States from 1901 to 1909, he often exercised by taking long walks or rides or by playing tennis. The friends who were his companions on these occasions came to be designated members of the *Tennis Cabinet*.[1]

[1] *Theodore Roosevelt, an Autobiography* (The Macmillan Company, New York, 1913) p. 51.

Tenskwatawa

In November 1805, Tenskwatawa, a Chief of the Shawnee Indians, addressed a group of Wyandot, Ottowa, Seneca, and Shawnee Indians at Wapakonetta, on the Auglaize River, in northern Ohio. The old Shawnee Indian prophet, Penagashega, meaning *The-Change-of-Feathers*, had died in this year, and immediately following the death of this prophet, Tenskwatawa claimed that he had made a journey through the clouds, at which time the Great Spirit had given him the power of prophecy. Previous to the above-mentioned meeting, Tenskwatawa's name had been Laulewasikaw; but following his speech to the group, he changed his name to Tenskwatawa, signifying the *Open Door*, and having appointed himself to take the place of the dead prophet, he was called the *Prophet*[1] by the Indians.

Later he became widely known to both the Indians and the white men by this sobriquet.

[1] *Tecumseh and the Shawnee Prophet Including Sketches of George Rogers Clark, Simon Kenton, William Henry Harrison, Cornstalk, Blackfoot, Bluejacket, the Shawnee Logan, and Others famous in the Frontier Wars of Tecumseh's Time*, Edward Eggleston and Lillie Eggleston Seelye (Dodd, Mead and Company, New York, 1878) p. 105-17.

Tenth Armored Division of World War II

The *Tiger Division*[1] was the nickname of the Tenth Armored Division of the Combat Divisions of World War II.

[1] *Combat Divisions of World War II*, (Army of the United States), Army Times Publishing Company, Washington, D.C., 1946, p. 84.

Tenth Mountain Division of World War II

The *Mountaineer Division*[1] was the nickname of the Tenth Mountain Division of the Combat Divisions of World War II because the tenth was composed of expert woodsmen, skiers, mountaineers, and experimented with new mountain equipment.

[1] *Combat Divisions of World War II*, (Army of the United States), Army Times Publishing Company, Washington, D.C., 1946, p. 16.

Tenth Muse. See Bradstreet, Anne

Ten Thousand Dollar Beauty. See Kelly, M. J.

Terrapin State. See Maryland

Terrapins. See Marylanders; University of Maryland

Terre Haute, Indiana

Terre Haute has sometimes been called the *Sycamore City*[1] because of the fine specimens of sycamore trees along its streets and in its parks. Most of these trees[2] were native to the midwestern region of the United States in which Terre Haute is situated, some of them having been used in marking new streets when the city was laid out in 1816.

[1] *Richard W. Thompson, Memorial*, copyrighted by D. W. Henry (A. B. Morse, St. Joseph, Mich., 1906) p. 158.
[2] *History of Terre Haute: The History of Early Terre Haute from 1816 to 1840*, Blackford Condit (A. S. Barnes and Company, New York, 1900) p. 33.

Terrible Swedes. See Bethany College (Lindsborg, Kans.)

Terrible Turk. See Reed, T. B.

Terriers. See Wofford College

Terror of the House. See Hardin, Benjamin

Terror of the Tories. See Clinch, Joseph

Terrors. See Western Maryland College

Terry, William Harold

William Harold Terry, who was born at Atlanta, Ga., on October 30, 1898, and who was manager of teams in major league baseball, was nicknamed *Memphis Bill*[1] because his estate is near Memphis, Tenn.

[1] *Who's Who in Major League Base Ball*, comp. by Harold (Speed) Johnson (Buxton Publishing Company, Chicago, 1933) p. 380.

Teutons. See Wartburg College

Tex. See Carleton, J. O.; Garms, D. C.; Irvin, C. P.

Texans

The Texans are called *Beef-heads*,[1] *Cowboys*,[1] *Rangers*, and *Blizzards*.[1] The first three are easily accounted for by the fact that Texas is a great cattle-raising country. Texans are called *Blizzards* for the same reason the state is nicknamed the *Blizzard State*.

[1] *U.S.: An Index to the United States of America*, comp. by Malcolm Townsend (D. Lothrop Company, Boston, 1890) p. 81.
A Book of Nicknames, John Goff (Courier-Journal Job Printing Company, Louisville, Ky., 1892) p. 20.

Texarkana, Arkansas—Texas

Texarkana is known as the *Twin Cities*[1] because it is made up of two distinct political municipalities due to the fact that the state line separating Texas from Arkansas, divides Texarkana into two separate units, one in Texas, and the other in Arkansas.

[1] *The Geography of Texas, Physical and Political*, Revised Edition, Frederic William Simonds (Ginn and Company, New York and Boston, 1914) p. 201-2.

Texas

The state of Texas is designated the *Banner State, Beef State, Blizzard State, Jumbo State*, and the *Lone Star State*.

The sobriquet, *Banner State*, is applied to Texas, probably, from the fact that she polls a large vote in national elections. Norton says under the name *Banner State*: "The state, county, town, or other political subdivision that gives the largest vote for a party candidate is termed the 'banner state.' . . ."[2]

Beef State commemorates the fact that Texas has been, and still is, noted for her cattle raising.

Blizzard State, was applied to Texas undoubtedly on account of the frequent wind storms which sweep over the state.

The largest African elephant ever kept in captivity was called Jumbo and all unusually large things have since taken his name. Texas is the largest state in the Union, hence the *Jumbo State*.

Texas is called the *Lone Star State* because it was "once a province of Mexico, then an independent republic, bore a single star in its coat of arms, and being for a time left to struggle unaided against the whole power of her formidable enemy, became then honorably known as the *Lone Star State*—a name which she has ever since retained."[1]

[1] *Americanisms; The English of the New World*, M. Schele De Vere (Charles Scribner and Company, New York, 1872) p. 661.
[2] *Political Americanisms*, Charles Ledyard Norton (Longmans, Green and Company, New York and London, 1890) p. 10.

Texas. See Grant. U. S.

Texas Christian University

The *Horned Frogs*[1] is the nickname given to the athletic teams of Texas Christian University, at Fort Worth, Tex., about 1912, the sobriquet having been taken from *The Horned Frog*, the name of the college annual.

[1] A communication from Colby D. Hall, Dean of Texas Christian University, Fort Worth, Tex., June 20, 1935.

Texas College

The sobriquet, *Steers*,[1] was given to the athletic teams of Texas College, at Tyler, Tex., in 1926 because "many years ago long-horned steers"[1] were numerous in that section of Texas.

[1] A communication from W. H. Martin, Acting Dean of Texas College, Tyler, Tex., November 26, 1935.

Texas College of Arts and Industries

The athletic teams of the Texas College of Arts and Industries, at Kingsville, Tex., were popularly designated the *Javelinas*[1] in 1925 by a committee composed of students and faculty members. The javelina (the Collared Peccary) "is a vicious little animal in this vicinity."[1]

[1] A communication from E. W. Seale, President of Texas College of Arts and Industries, Kingsville, Tex., November 21, 1935.

Texas College of Mines and Metallurgy

The athletic teams of Texas College of Mines and Metallurgy, at El Paso, Tex., are popularly designated *Muckers* perhaps because their mining studies often cause them to come in contact with decayed peat or black swampy earth, that is, muck.

Texas Division. See Thirty-sixth Infantry Division of World War II

Texas Guinan. See Guinan, M. L. C.

Texas Technological College

The *Matadors* and the *Red Raiders* are sobriquets attributed to the athletic teams of Texas Technological College, at Lubbock, Tex. *The Matadors*,[1] the most-widely used of these two nicknames, was selected by Mrs. E. Y. Freeland, the wife of the first Coach of Athletics at the College, because Spanish architecture and names were used a great deal in the early history of the college.[1] The *Red Raiders* [1] was applied to the athletes in 1934 by sports writers of the *Los Angeles Times* in writing up the game with Loyola University of Los Angeles because the colors of the Texas College uniforms are red with black trimmings.

[1] A letter from Bradford Knapp, President of Texas Technological College, Lubbock, Tex., November 21, 1935.

Texas Tom. See Connally, T. T.

Textbook of Seamanship. See Sailor's Bible

Thalberg, Irving Grant

Because at the age of twenty-two, Irving Grant Thalberg began producing successful motion pictures, he was called the *Boy Producer*.[1]

He was born at Brooklyn, N.Y., on May 30, 1899, and died at Santa Monica, Calif., on September 14, 1936.

[1] *Doug and Mary and Others*, Allene Talmey (Macy-Masius, New York, 1927) p. 165.

That Candid Spoilsman. See Farley, J. A.

That Man in the White House. See Roosevelt, F. D.

Thatcher, Moses

In 1861 Moses Thatcher made his home at Logan in the Cache Valley of Utah, and there became Captain of about fifty men belonging to Captain Thomas E. Ricks' *Minute Men*, a local military organization established for the purpose of protecting Logan and other nearby settlements from the ravages of cattle thieves and wandering Indians. During this time, Thatcher was often associated with the Indians, and they nicknamed him the *Little Chief* [1] because he was considerate in his treatment of them, and because he possessed the qualities of

character common to a leader among his own men and to an Indian chieftain.

Moses Thatcher was born in Sangamon County, Ill., on February 2, 1842, and died [2] at Logan, Utah, on August 21, 1909.

[1] *The National Cyclopaedia of American Biography* (James T. White and Company, New York, 1897) vol. 7, p. 396.
Utah Since Statehood: Historical and Biographical, Noble Warrum (The S. J. Clarke Publishing Company, Chicago and Salt Lake City, Utah, 1919) vol. 1, p. 779.
[2] *Utah, the Storied Domain: A Documentary History of Utah's Eventful Career, Comprising the Thrilling Story of Her People from the Indians of Yesterday to the Industrialists of Today*, J. Cecil Alter (The American Historical Society, Inc., New York and Chicago, 1932) vol. 1, p. 491.

Thayer, John

John Thayer, a Roman Catholic missionary, was nicknamed *John Turncoat* [1] soon after 1783 because in that year he joined the Roman Catholic Church at Paris, France, although he had been previously a licensed minister in the Congregational Church. In 1790 he returned to the United States eager to convert his countrymen to the Catholic faith, but his over-zealousness and lack of tact, together with the bitter hostility of the people of the New England States toward Catholicism, prevented him from attaining success in his undertaking. As an itinerant Roman Catholic missionary, however, he did manage to hold the first Catholic meetings tolerated in the New England towns.

John Thayer was born at Boston, Mass., on May 15, 1758, and died at Limerick, Ireland, on February 17, 1815.

[1] *Dictionary of American Biography under the Auspices of the American Council of Learned Societies*, ed. by Dumas Malone (Charles Scribner's Sons, New York, 1936) vol. 18, p. 407.

Thayer, Simeon

Major Simeon Thayer was designated the *Hero of Fort Mifflin* [1] because of his gallant and meritorious conduct in defending Fort Mifflin, near the mouth of the Schuylkill River, against a British fleet.

He was born at Meriden, Mass., on April 30, 1737, and died, apparently at Providence, R.I., on October 14, 1800.

[1] *The National Cyclopaedia of American Biography* (James T. White and Company, New York, 1924) vol. 8, p. 110.

Thayer, Sylvanus

While he was serving as Superintendent of the United States Military Academy, at West Point, N.Y., from 1817 to 1833, Brigadier General Sylvanus Thayer overhauled and reorganized the entire management and operation of that institution so that it became one of the foremost of its kind in the world, and he became known as the *Father of the United States Military Academy.*[1]

Sylvanus Thayer was born at Braintree, Mass., on June 9, 1785, and died at South Braintree, Mass., on September 7, 1872.

[1] *Nelson's Encyclopaedia* (Thomas Nelson and Sons, New York, 1907) vol. 12, p. 29.

Theodore the Meddler. See Roosevelt, Theodore

Thermopylae of America. See Alamo

Thermopylae of Middle Tennessee. See Tullahoma, Tenn.

Thiel College

The athletic teams of Thiel College, at Greenville, Pa., were nicknamed *Tom Cats*[1] in honor of Doctor Tommy Hollerose, former Coach of athletics at Thiel College.

[1] A communication from J. B. Stoeber, Director of Athletics at Thiel College, Greenville, Pa., June 18, 1935.

Third Armored Division of World War II

The Spearhead Division[1] was the nickname of the Third Armored Division of the Combat Divisions of World War II because it was the first to fire on German soil, to enter Germany, and to capture a German city.

[1] *Combat Divisions of World War II,* (Army of the United States), Army Times Publishing Company, Washington, D.C., 1946, p. 77.

Third Infantry Division of World War II

The Third Infantry Division was nicknamed the *Marine Division*[1] because in World War II this division took part in four amphibious invasions; namely, North Africa, Sicily, Anzio and France.

[1] *Combat Divisions of World War II,* (Army of the United States), Army Times Publishing Company, Washington, D.C., 1946, p. 9.

Thirteenth Armored Division of World War II

The *Black Cat Division*[1] was the nickname of the Thirteenth Armored Division of the Combat Divisions of World War II because the tanks of this division were

variations of the caterpillar tractors used in road building, called cats.

[1] *Combat Divisions of World War II,* (Army of the United States), Army Times Publishing Company, Washington, D.C., 1946, p. 87.

Thirty-eighth Infantry Division of World War II

The *Cyclone Division*[1] was the nickname of the Thirty-eighth Infantry Division of the Combat Divisions of World War II because while the division was in training at Camp Shelby, Miss., during World War I its tents were blown down by a storm.

[1] *Combat Divisions of World War II,* (Army of the United States), Army Times Publishing Company, Washington, D.C., 1946, p. 31.

Thirty-fifth Infantry Division of World War II

The *Santa Fe Division*[1] was the nickname of the Thirty-fifth Division of World War II because the ancestors of the men of this division blazed the old Santa Fe Trail.

[1] *Combat Divisions of World War II,* (Army of the United States), Army Times Publishing Company, Washington, D.C., 1946, p. 28.

Thirty-first Infantry Division of World War II

The *Dixie Division*[1] was the nickname of the Thirty-first Infantry Division of the Combat Divisions of World War II because it was organized at Camp Wheeler, Ga., in Oct., 1917, and was inducted into service from Camp Blanding, Fla., on Nov. 25, 1940.

[1] *Combat Divisions of World War II,* (Army of the United States), Army Times Publishing Company, Washington, D.C., 1946, p. 24.

Thirty-fourth Infantry Division of World War II

The *Red Bull Division*[1] was the nickname of the Thirty-fourth Infantry Division of Combat Divisions of World War II supposedly because it was originally organized at Camp Cody, N.M., on October 17, 1917.

[1] *Combat Divisions of World War II,* (Army of the United States), Army Times Publishing Company, Washington, D.C., 1946, p. 27.

Thirty-second Infantry Division of World War II

The *Red Arrow Division*[1] was the nickname of the Thirty-second Infantry Division of the Combat Divisions of World War II because it was said to pierce all enemy lines it faced and as a symbol of this the shoulder

Thirty-second Infantry Division of World War II—Continued

patch bore a red line shot through with a red arrow.

[1] *Combat Divisions of World War II*, (Army of the United States), Army Times Publishing Company, Washington, D.C., 1946, p. 25.

Thirty-seventh Infantry Division of World War II

The *Buckeye Division* [1] was the nickname of the Thirty-seventh Infantry Division of the Combat Divisions of World War II because it was composed of men from Ohio, the *Buckeye State*.

[1] *Combat Divisions of World War II*, (Army of the United States), Army Times Publishing Company, Washington, D.C., 1946, p. 30.

Thirty-sixth Infantry Division of World War II

The *Texas Division* [1] was the nickname of the Thirty-sixth Infantry Division of the Combat Divisions of World War II because this division was originally organized at Camp Bowie, Texas, in July, 1917, and was inducted into the Combat Divisions from Camp Bowie, Texas, November 1940.

[1] *Combat Divisions of World War II*, (Army of the United States), Army Times Publishing Company, Washington, D.C., 1946, p. 29.

Thirty-third Infantry Division of World War II

The Thirty-third Infantry Division of the Combat Divisions of World War II was nicknamed the *Illinois Division* [1] and the *Prairie Division* because Illinois is called the *Prairie State* and the division was made up of Illinois National Guard units.

[1] *Combat Divisions of World War II*, (Army of the United States), Army Times Publishing Company, Washington, D.C., 1946, p. 26.

Thomas, David

About 1840 David Thomas succeeded in manufacturing, on an extensive scale, pig-iron which was produced in blast furnaces fired with anthracite coal. His pioneer work in this enterprise, and his continued interest in, and beneficial contributions to, the process of manufacturing iron by this method caused him to be named the *Father of the American Anthracite Iron Industry*.[1]

David Thomas was born near Neath, South Wales, on November 3, 1794, and died at Catasauqua, Pa., on June 20, 1882.

[1] *The National Cyclopaedia of American Biography* (James T. White and Company, New York, 1893) vol. 3, p. 360.

Thomas, Elmer (John William Elmer Thomas)

Elmer Thomas, an Oklahoma lawyer and politician, was nicknamed the *Silver Sage* [1] by his colleagues in the United States Senate because he so strongly advocated silver legislation.

He was a Democratic Senator from the Sixth Congressional District of Oklahoma to the United States Congress from 1923 to 1949.

Elmer Thomas was born at Greencastle, Ind., on September 8, 1876.

[1] An interview with Captain Victor Hunt Harding, Secretary of the National Democratic Congress Re-election Committee, Washington, D.C., April 10, 1939.

Thomas, George Henry

The soldiers and officers under the command of Major General Thomas respectfully nicknamed him *Old Pap Safety*,[1] *Old Reliable, Pap Thomas*, and *Uncle George*. General Thomas was a cautious and deliberate strategist and a dependable, trustworthy leader. Also he displayed a deep paternal interest in the welfare of those who served under his command during battle. General Thomas was also widely known as *Old Slow Trot* [2] because when engrossed in thought, his more impatient attendants would dash on ahead of him only to be recalled by his command to "Slow trot" with bearing befitting the rank of a general.

The nicknames, *Lion-hearted Thomas* [3] and the *Rock of Chickamauga* [4] were applied to him for his courage, his cool and deliberate judgment, and his heroic defense of the Union forces at the Battle of Chickamauga, near Chattanooga, Tenn., on September 19 and 20, 1863.

The sobriquet *George Washington* [5] was given to General Thomas by his schoolmates at United States Military Academy, West Point, New York, because it was imagined that he bore a likeness to Washington both in physical appearance and in character.

George Henry Thomas was born in Southampton County, Va., on July 31, 1816, and died at San Francisco, Calif., on March 28, 1870.

[1] *Noble Living and Grand Achievement: Giants of the Republic, Embracing the Lives, Deeds, and Personal Traits of Eminent Statesmen, Great Generals, Noted Reformers, Successful Men of Business, Distinguished Literary Men, and Famous Women*, Hamilton W. Mabie, John S. C. Abbott, W. M. Birdsall, J. H. Vincent, James Parton, Frances W. Willard, Henry Ferris, W. Fletcher Johnson, and others, with an introduction by Edward Everett Hale (John C. Winston and Company, Philadelphia, 1895), p. 351.

[2] *Our Army in the Great Rebellion: Heroes and Battles of the War of 1860-65*, J. T. Headley (E. B. Treat, New York, 1891), p. 269.
[3] *History of The United States of America, under the Constitution*, James Schouler (Dodd, Mead and Company, New York, 1889) vol. 6, p. 559.
[4] *The Life of Major-general George H. Thomas*, Thomas B. Van Horne (Charles Scribner's Sons, New York, 1882) p. 144.
[5] *Appleton's Cyclopaedia of American Biography*, ed. by James Grant Wilson and John Fiske (D. Appleton and Company, New York, 1889) vol. 6, p. 79.

Thomas, John Parnell

John Parnell Thomas, a New Jersey salesman and politician, was nicknamed *Impeachment Thomas* [1] by his colleagues in the National House of Representatives because he introduced into Congress, on January 24, 1939, the bill to impeach Frances Perkins, (Mrs. Paul Cadwell Wilson), the Secretary of Labor in President Franklin Delano Roosevelt's Cabinet.

He was Mayor of Allendale, N.J., from 1926 until 1930, Republican Representative to the New Jersey Legislature from 1935 until 1937, and served as Republican Representative from the Seventh Congressional District of New Jersey to the United States Congress from 1937 until his resignation in 1950. He was convicted on charges of fraud and conspiracy in December 1949 and sentenced to serve six to eighteen months in prison and to pay a fine of $10,000.

John Parnell Thomas was born at Jersey City, N.J., on January 16, 1895.

[1] An interview with Captain Victor Hunt Harding, Secretary of the National Democratic Congress Re-election Committee, Washington, D.C., April 10, 1939.

Thompson, Charlie

Charlie Thompson, the Irish-born Secretary of the Continental Congress for fifteen years, was nicknamed by the members of this Congress the *Perpetual Secretary* and the *Hand and Pen of the Congress*.[1] Thompson was selected by the members of the Continental Congress to carry the news to General George Washington of his election as President of the United States in 1789.

Charlie Thompson was born in Maghera, Derby County, Ireland, on November 29, 1729, and died at Lower Merion in Montgomery County, Pa., on August 16, 1824.

[1] *The Sunday Star*, Washington, D.C., May 28, 1939, pt. 2, col. 3, p. C-2.

Thompson, Dorothy

The newspaper columnist and commentator, Dorothy Thompson, acquired the nicknames *Cassandra of the Columnists* [1] and the *Contemporary Cassandra* [1] while she was writing her widely-syndicated column, *On The Record*, during the 1930's. She made many analyses of world politics during that period, in particular forewarning her readers of the menace she saw in the rise of Nazism. Inasmuch as her words did not stir people to action, while later events proved the truth of many of her predictions, she may be compared to Cassandra, daughter of King Priam of Troy, who possessed the gift of prophesy and foretold the fall of Troy, but whose warnings people failed to believe.

Dorothy Thompson was born at Lancaster, N.Y., on July 9, 1894.

[1] *Life*, Chicago, Ill., April 24, 1939, col. 4, p. 24.

Thompson, Frederick F.

Frederick F. Thompson is said to have been called *Uncle Fred* [1] by Vassar students because of his benevolence to them and his financial assistance to Vassar College, Poughkeepsie, N.Y. He was born at New York City, in 1836, and died there on April 16, 1899.

[1] *The National Cyclopaedia of American Biography* (James T. White and Company, New York, 1896) vol. 6, p. 141.

Thompson, John A.

From 1856 to 1876 John A. Thompson carried mail from Placerville, Calif., to Carson Valley, Nev., a distance of ninety miles through a desolated, snowbound stretch of the Sierra Nevada Mountains. Thompson's faithful discharge of his sometimes perilous task called for personal daring, and great endurance on snow-shoes, and eventually he was appropriately known as *Snowshoe Thompson*.[1]

John A. Thompson was born at Upper Tins, ·in Prestijeld, Norway, on April 30, 1827, and died at his home in Diamond Valley, thirty miles south of Carson City, Nev., on May 15, 1876.

[1] *Heroes of California, the Story of the Founders of the Golden State as Narrated by Themselves or Gleaned from Other Sources*, George Wharton James (Little, Brown and Company, Boston, 1910) p. 199-205.
The Overland Mail, 1849-1869; Promoter of Settlement, Precursor of Railroads, LeRoy R. Hafen (The Arthur H. Clark Company, Cleveland, Ohio, 1926) p. 65.

Thompson, Philip Burton, Sr. See
Thompson, P. B., Jr.

Thompson, Philip Burton, Jr.

Little Phil [1] was a popular sobriquet applied to Philip Burton Thompson, Jr., in order to distinguish him from his father Philip Burton Thompson, Sr., both men having been prominent in the political affairs of their native state. The elder Thompson was likewise familiarly called *Old Phil*.[1]

Philip Burton Thompson, Jr., was born at Harrodsburg, Ky., on October 15, 1845, died at Washington, D.C., on December 15, 1909, and was a Representative from Kentucky to the United States Congress from 1879 to 1885.

Philip Burton Thompson, Sr., was born at Harrodsburg, Ky., on January 8, 1821, and for many years was one of the most able criminal lawyers in that state.

[1] *My Quarter Century of American Politics*, Champ Clark (Harper and Brothers, New York and London, 1920) vol. 1, p. 388.
[2] *A History of Kentucky and Kentuckians, the Leaders and Representative Men in Commerce, Industry, and Modern Activities*, E. Polk Johnson (The Lewis Publishing Company, New York and Chicago, 1912) vol. 3, p. 1694.

Thoreau, Henry David

The *Poet Naturalist* and the *Sage of Walden Pond* are nicknames which have been given to Henry David Thoreau.

He was called the *Poet Naturalist* [1] because he was "in spirit a poet as well as a naturalist." [1]

The sobriquet, *Sage of Walden Pond*,[2] was applied to Thoreau because for some time he lived at Walden Pond, near Concord, Mass., where he wrote *Walden*, defining his highly individual philosophy of life.

Henry David Thoreau was born at Concord, Mass., on July 12, 1817, and died there on May 6, 1862.

[1] *American Literary Readings*, Leonidas Warren Payne, Junior (Rand McNally and Company, Chicago and New York, 1917) p. 317.
[2] *Compton's Pictured Encyclopedia* (F. E. Compton and Company, Chicago, 1931) vol. 14, p. 3492.

Thorobreds. See Kentucky State Industrial College

Three Chopped Way

The highway from Milledgeville, Ga., to Natchez, Miss., by way of St. Stephens, Ala., was long known as the *Three Chopped Way* [1] because, when the road was first blazed as a bridle trail about 1800, three notches were cut into the trees bordering this path.

[1] *School History of Mississippi for Use in Public and Private Schools*, Franklin L. Riley (B. F. Johnson Publishing Company, Richmond, Va., 1900) p. 128.

Three Finger Brown. See Luchese, Thomas

Three Fingered Brown. See Brown, M. P. C.

Three-hundred-dollar-men

During the latter part of the Civil War, in order to obtain fighting men for the army, the North offered a bounty to each immigrant on condition that he would enlist in the Union Army. A goodly number of men took improper advantage of this offer for no sooner had they collected their bounty in one county than they were off to another part of the country to get another bounty, sometimes collecting a dozen payments, more or less, before they were apprehended by the law.

The bounties ranged from one hundred to five hundred dollars for each man, three hundred dollars being the average bounty offered as an inducement to enlist in the Union Army. Those who accepted this money as payment for enlisting in the Army were contemptuously called *Three-hundred-dollar-men* [1] by soldiers who at the outbreak of the Civil War had voluntarily offered their services to the North. The Federal Government passed the Conscription Act establishing the bounty in March 1863.

[1] *Andersonville: A Story of Rebel Military Prisons, Fifteen Months a Guest of the So-called Southern Confederacy; a Private Soldier's Experience in Richmond, Andersonville, Savannah, Millen, Blackshear, and Florence*, John McElroy (D. R. Locke, Toledo, Ohio, 1879) p. 87.

Three-minute Brumm. See Brumm, George Franklin

Thunder and Lightning Williams. See Williams, D. R.

Thunder from Heaven Division. See Seventeenth Airborne Division of World War II

Thunder Makers

About 1805 the Snake Indians in northeastern Utah nicknamed the men in the Lewis and Clark Expedition *Thunder Makers*.[1] An old Snake Indian who was doing sentinel duty for a group of Shoshoni Indians tried to escape when he saw a company of white men approaching. Some of the men in the expedition caught him and fired off their guns in his presence, after which they let him go. He told the story to his tribe when he returned. They did not believe him, and in order to exonerate himself before his tribesmen, he led them to the place where the expedition was encamped. There the Indians saw the pale-faced men and heard the *Thunder Makers* with their own ears.

[1] *The Trail of Lewis and Clark, 1804-1904: A Story of the Great Exploration across the Continent in 1804-6; with a Description of the Old Trail, Based upon Actual Travel over It, and of the Changes Found a Century Later,* Olin D. Wheeler (G. P. Putnam's Sons, New York, 1904) vol. 2, p. 48-9.

Thunderbird Division. See Forty-fifth Infantry Division of World War II

Thunderboldts. See Humboldt State College

Thunderbolt Division. See Eighty-third Industry Division of World War II; Eleventh Armored Division of World War II

Thunderbolts. See Humboldt State College

Thundering Herd. See Marshall College

Thundering Jimmy. See Jenkins, James

Thurman, Allan Granberry

The appellations, the *Noblest Roman of Them All, Old Bandanna,* the *Old Roman,* and *Right-angled, Tri-angled Thurman,* have been attributed to Allan Granberry Thurman.

He was nicknamed the *Noblest Roman of Them All* [1] and the *Old Roman* because he spent about fifty years of his life in the political service of his state or of his nation.

Thurman was a Representative from Ohio to the United States Congress from 1845 to 1847; Associate Justice of the Supreme Court of Ohio from 1851 to 1854; Chief Justice of the Supreme Court of Ohio from 1854 to 1856; and Senator from Ohio to the United States Congress from 1869 to 1881.

While he was a Senator from Ohio to the United States Congress from 1869 to 1881,

Allan Granberry Thurman was often called *Old Bandanna* [2] by his colleagues because he habitually carried a red bandanna handkerchief.

Thurman was unusually proficient in the study of mathematics and was humorously nicknamed *Right-angled, Tri-angled Thurman* [3] by his schoolmates.

Allan Granberry Thurman was born at Lynchburg, Va., on November 13, 1813, and died at Columbus, Ohio, on December 13, 1895.

[1] *U.S. "Snap Shots": An Independent, National, and Memorial Encyclopedia . . . ,* Oliver McKee (A. M. Thayer and Company, Boston, 1892) p. 243.
[2] *Ohio Archaeological and Historical Quarterly,* Published by the Society (The F. J. Heer Printing Company, Columbus, Ohio, 1928) vol. 37, *April-July,* 1928, nos. 2 and 3, p. 239-40.
[3] *The National Cyclopaedia of American Biography* (James T. White and Company, New York, 1893) vol. 3, p. 144.

Thurston, Charles Mynn

Charles Mynn Thurston was nicknamed the *Warrior Parson.* [1] He was pastor of an Episcopal Church in Clarke County, Va., at the outbreak of the Revolutionary War, and raised a company of soldiers over whom he was first commissioned Captain and later Lieutenant Colonel. At the close of the War, he was a judge and later a legislator. He moved from Virginia to Louisiana in 1808.

Charles Mynn Thurston was born in Gloucester County, Va., in 1738, and died near New Orleans, La., in 1812.

[1] *Appleton's Cyclopaedia of American Biography,* ed. by James Grant Wilson and John Fiske (D. Appleton and Company, New York, 1894) vol. 6, p. 107.

Thurston, Hollis John

The sobriquet, *Sloppy,* [1] was applied to Hollis John Thurston because, as he explains, while he was a youngster whenever he drank milk, he habitually spilled it on himself. He was born at Fremont, Neb., on June 2, 1899, and pitched in major league baseball.

[1] *Who's Who in Major League Base Ball,* comp. by Harold (Speed) Johnson (Buxton Publishing Company, Chicago, 1933) p. 383.

Tichenor, Isaac

Isaac Tichenor was nicknamed *Jersey Slick,* [1] in somewhat uncomplimentary reference to his home state and his charming manners.

He was born in New Jersey but went to Vermont in 1777 in the service of the Continental Army and took up residence there which he maintained for the rest of

Tichenor, Isaac—Continued

his long life. He was a Representative in the Vermont legislature from 1781 until 1785; and served as agent to the Continental Congress from 1782 until 1785. He was Governor of Vermont from 1797 until 1809.

Isaac Tichenor was born at Newark, N.J., on February 8, 1754, and died at Bennington, Vt., on December 11, 1838.

[1] *Dictionary of American Biography under the Auspices of the American Council of Learned Societies,* ed. by Dumas Malone (Charles Scribner's Sons, New York, 1936) vol. 18, p. 523.

Tiger Division. See Tenth Armored Division of World War II

Tigers. See Depauw University; Detroit American League Baseball Company; Louisiana State University; Princeton University; University of Missouri; University of the South

Tilden, Samuel Jones

The following nicknames have been attributed to Samuel Jones Tilden: *Old Usufruct,* the *Sage of Gramercy Park,* the *Sage of Greystone,* and *Slippery Sam.*

Old Usufruct probably had its origin in the cartoons drawn by Thomas Nast appearing in *Harper's Weekly* in 1876 while Tilden, as Democratic candidate for the presidency, was running against Rutherford B. Hayes. The cartoonist lampooned Tilden's reform policies as primarily designed to promote his own personal interests. Reform was one of the major issues of the 1876 campaign as popular attention was concentrated on evidences of the widespread corruption during the preceding eight years of Grant's administration. Tilden spoke out particularly against the venality then prevalent in the Civil Service.

The election of 1876 was highly disputed but the electoral votes were finally counted against Tilden. He continued, however, to be a leader in the Democratic party, and his opinions and judgment on political questions, both state and national, were eagerly sought and highly valued. His nicknames, *Sage of Greystone* [1] and *Sage of Gramercy Park* denote the respect in which he was held.

Slippery Sam [1] was a sobriquet applied to Tilden by his political enemies.

Samuel Jones Tilden was born at New Lebanon, N.Y., on February 9, 1814, and

died at his country home, Greystone, near Yonkers, N.Y., on August 4, 1886.

[1] *U.S. "Snap Shots": An Independent, National, and Memorial Encyclopedia . . . ,* Oliver McKee (A. M. Thayer and Company, Boston, 1892) p. 246.
[2] *Harper's Weekly: A Journal of Civilization* (Harper and Brothers, New York, 1876) vol. 202, *July-December, 1876,* p. 729, 749, 769, 789.

Tillman, Benjamin Ryan

The *Agricultural Moses, Pitchfork Ben,* and *Pitchfork Tillman* are appellations by which Benjamin Ryan Tillman has been designated.

As Senator from South Carolina, an endeavor to better the economic condition of farmers of his state and of other southern states, Tillman proposed the establishment of experimental farms, and formation of farmers' associations to secure legislation favorable to their interests. During the ensuing controversy over these proposals, Tillman was dubbed the *Agricultural Moses.* [1] In Biblical history Moses led his people out of Egyptian bondage into the "promised land" of Canaan.

It has been said that the nickname, *Pitchfork Ben,* [2] originated as a result of Tillman's rancorous and violent speeches against Grover Cleveland. He was also a bitter opponent of Theodore Roosevelt.

Tillman was a Senator from South Carolina to the United States Congress from 1894 to 1918. As a representative of the small farmer, he favored free coinage of silver, and took a vigorous part in the Battle of the Standards during the congressional elections of 1894 and the Bryan-McKinley contest of 1896.

According to one source [3] the sobriquet *Pitchfork Tillman* was applied to him because he was constantly digging up or spreading, as with a pitchfork, uncomplimentary stories concerning his political opponent. In spite of his harsh, outspoken, and aggressive manner, he was respected by many people during his later years for his efforts to champion the interests of the common man.

Benjamin Ryan Tillman was born in Edgefield County, S.C., on August 11, 1847, and died at Washington, D.C., on July 3, 1918.

[1] *The National Cyclopaedia of American Biography* (James T. White and Company, New York, 1904) vol. 12, p. 181.
[2] *The Encyclopedia Americana* (Americana Corporation, New York and Chicago, 1927) vol. 26, p. 627.
[3] *Roosevelt in the Rough,* Jack Willis, as told to Horace Smith (Ives Washburn, New York, 1931) p. 127.

Timberwolf Division. See One Hundred and Fourth Infantry Division of World War II

Times-That-Made-Chattanooga

Due to the leadership of Adolph Simon Ochs as manager of the *Chattanooga Times* this newspaper has exerted such a tremendous influence in the development both of the city of Chattanooga and of the New South that it has come to be designated the *Times-That-Made-Chattanooga.*[1]

[1] *The National Cyclopaedia of American Biography* (James T. White and Company, New York, 1924) current volume A, p. 77.

Tin Bucket Brigade

The sobriquet, *Tin Bucket Brigade,*[1] was originated about 1860 or 1870 by attorney Robert Green Ingersoll during a case involving mortgage foreclosure on the Chicago and Alton Railroad. The nickname was used by him to designate the workmen employed by railroads, probably suggested by the fact that the men generally carried their lunches in small tin buckets. Ingersoll used the expression "paying the Tin Bucket Brigade first" in describing an Illinois court ruling that those who foreclosed mortgages on the Chicago and Alton Railroad were first to take care of the back pay due the workmen, and then to pay the bondholders. Ingersoll spoke as attorney for the bondholders.

[1] *Life of Walter Quinton Gresham, 1832-1895,* Matilda Gresham (Rand McNally and Company, Chicago, 1919) vol. 1, p. 374, 377.

Tin-clads

During the latter part of the Civil War, when Union soldiers were transported on the Cumberland and Tennessee rivers by river boat, several steamers would act as an armed escort. The convoys were nicknamed *Tin-clads*[1] because the protective armor over their lower decks was a thin sheet of iron plating which was bullet-proof but could easily be pierced by the balls from heavy guns. *Tin-clads* implied that this inefficient iron plating was about as protective as one made of tin.

[1] "Naval Actions and History, 1799-1898," in *Papers of the Military Historical Society of Massachusetts* (Published for the Military Historical Society of Massachusetts by Griffith-Stillings Press, Boston, 1902) vol. 12, p. 303.

Tin Horn Village. See Newton, Mass.

Tinkham, George Holden

George Holden Tinkham, a Massachusetts politician, was nicknamed the *Big-game Hunter,*[1] the *Lion Hunter,*[1] and *Wiskers*[1] by his colleagues in the National House of Representatives. The first two nicknames refer to his avocation, big-game hunting in Africa, and to his practice of keeping a stuffed giraffe and many other trophies in his suite at the Arlington Hotel in Washington, D.C., which he refused to move when Government officials took over the hotel for offices. His beard gave rise to the sobriquet *Wiskers.*

He was a Republican Representative from the Eleventh Congressional District of Massachusetts to the United States Congress from 1915 to 1943.

George Holden Tinkham was born at Boston, Mass., on October 29, 1870.

[1] An interview with Captain Victor Hunt Harding, Secretary of the National Democratic Congress Re-election Committee, Washington, D.C., April 10, 1939.

Tire City of the United States. See Akron, Ohio

Titans. See Illinois Wesleyan University; University of Detroit

Toad. See Sloan, J. F.

Tobacco State. See Kentucky

Tobin, Daniel Joseph

Daniel Joseph Tobin was born in Ireland in 1875, and became President of the International Brotherhood of Teamsters in 1907. He is nicknamed *Big Dan* and *Uncle Dan.*[1]

[1] *Current Biography,* The H. W. Wilson Company, N.Y., November, 1945, p. 52-54.

Tod Sloan. See Sloan, J. F.

Todd, Chapman C.

While in command of a small fleet during the Spanish-American War in 1898, Commander Chapman C. Todd captured nine Spanish vessels at Manzanillo, west of Santiago, Cuba. His resourcefulness in this affair won for him the nickname *Dewey of Manzanillo.*[1] The eminent American naval commander of the Spanish-American War, Admiral George Dewey, distinguished

Todd, C. C.—Continued

himself at the Battle of Manila Bay, on May 1, 1898, by destroying the Spanish squadron anchored there.

[1] *Young People's History of the War with Spain*, Prescott Holmes (Henry Altemus, Philadelphia, 1900) p. 175.

Todd, Payne

While he was touring Europe in 1813, Europeans nicknamed Payne Todd the *Prince of America* [1] because his bearing was commanding and aristocratic, and he was the step-son of James Madison, President of the United States.

[1] *Dolly Madison, The Nation's Hostess*, Elizabeth Lippincott Dean (Lothrop, Lee and Shepard Company, Boston, 1928) p. 123.
Women of Colonial and Revolutionary Times: Dolly Madison, Maud Goodwin (Charles Scribner's Sons, New York, 1896) p. 212.

Toilers. See Detroit Institute of Technology

Toledo, Ohio

Toledo is nicknamed the *Corn City*.[1] Its location on both sides of the Maumee River, six miles from Lake Erie, makes it easily accessible to lake freight vessels by means of the Government strait channel. This city ships vast quantities of wheat, corn, and other grains each year and has been doing so as far back as 1851.

[1] *A Book of Nicknames*, John Goff (Courier-Journal Job Printing Company, Louisville, Ky., 1892) p. 16.

Toledo War

The dispute between the people of the territory of Michigan and the people of Ohio in 1835 and in 1836 over the strip of fertile land on which Toledo is located is commonly designated the *Toledo War*.[1] The United States Congress settled the matter in 1836 by deciding that this border-line strip should belong to the state of Ohio. To compensate for this decision, when Michigan became a state in 1837, it was extended to include the so-called Upper Peninsula, forming the northern section of Michigan, extending north and east from Wisconsin between Lakes Superior and Michigan to the Ontario border.

[1] *The World Book Encyclopedia* (The Quarrie Corporation, Chicago, 1938) vol. 11, p. 4466.

Tom Cats. See Thiel College

Tom the Tinker

On March 3, 1791, the Congress of the United States passed a law taxing the distillation of whiskey within the United States, ranging from seven to eighteen cents a gallon based on the quality of the liquor. In the four counties of southwestern Pennsylvania, Allegheny, Fayette, Washington, and Westmoreland, the people so strongly resented this revenue that they roughly used the revenue collectors, often tore up their books, destroyed their commissions, or forced them to resign and to publish their resignations in the *Pittsburgh Gazette*. Parties of masked men often visited such persons as those who gave information about the location of stills, or those who rented their houses to revenue collectors. These masked parties were designated by the nickname *Tom the Tinker*.[1] The sobriquet appeared on handbills, signs, and notices given to persons who were threatened by them and on other forms of publicity which they gave out.

[1] *A History of the People of the United States, from the Revolution to the Civil War*, John Bach McMaster (D. Appleton and Company, New York, 1885) vol. 2, p. 190.

Tom Thumb

In 1830 the first steam engine used on the Baltimore and Ohio railroad was called *Tom Thumb* [1] because it was so small, in honor of the real *Tom Thumb*, Charles Sherwood Stratton.

[1] *The Growth of the American People and Nation*, Mary G. Kelty (Ginn and Company) New York and Boston, 1931) p. 123.

Tommy the Cork. See Corcoran, T. G.

Tom Thumb. See Stratton, C. S.

Tonguepoint Mott. See Mott, J. W.

Tony Piet. See Pietruszka, A. F.

Tony the Silent. See Pietruszka, A. F.

Toombs, Robert

The *Georgia Fire-eater* [1] is a sobriquet applied to Robert Toombs because of his bitter opposition to those against the secession of the southern states, and because of his firm and uncompromising attitude on questions with which he aligned himself.

Robert Toombs was born in Wilkes County, Ga., on July 2, 1810, and died at Washington, Ga., on December 15, 1885.

See also Stephens, Alexander Hamilton and Robert Toombs.

[1] *A Book of Nicknames,* John Goff (Courier-Journal Job Printing Company, Louisville, Ky., 1892) p. 22.

Toothpick State. See Arkansas

Toothpicks. See Arkansans

Top of New England. See White Mountains

Torchy. See Hamilton, J. D. M.

Tories' Den

A cave in Chippen's Hill, near Bristol, Conn., is known as the *Tories' Den* [1] because it was used as a retreat or hiding place for the Tories of Bristol and its vicinity prior to, and during the Revolutionary War. Bristol was settled about 1727 and was a Loyalist or Tory stronghold during the Revolutionary War.

[1] *The Source Book* (Source Research Council, Inc., Chicago, 1936) vol. 1, p. 386.

Tornado. See Wayne, Anthony

Tory Traitor. See Honeyman, John

Tough Ombres. See Ninetieth Infantry Division of World War II

Tower City. See Chicago, Ill.

Town of Many Opportunities. See Uvalde, Tex.

Town That Moved Overnight. See Hibbing, Minn.

Townsend, Haworth Nottingham

Because he was recognized both nationally and internationally as an authority on matters of marine insurance, Haworth Nottingham Townsend was designated the *King of the Marine Insurance Business* [1] by his friends and business associates in New York City.

Haworth Nottingham Townsend was born at Lancashire, England, on October 1, 1864, and died apparently at New York City, on July 21, 1927.

[1] *The Century Biographical Encyclopedia* (The Historical Press Association, Inc., New York, 1928) vol. 3, p. 27.

Townsend, John G., Jr.

John G. Townsend, Jr., a politician, was nicknamed *Strawberry Townsend* [1] by his colleagues in the United States Senate. He is a fruit grower who lives in the strawberry-raising section of Delaware and once or twice each year he would distribute on "Strawberry Day" large quantities of this fruit to congressmen and to the proprietors of restaurants in the national capital.

He was a Republican Senator from Delaware to the United States Senate from 1929 to 1941.

John G. Townsend, Jr., was born in Worcester County, Md., on May 31, 1871, and lives at Selbyville, Del.

[1] An interview with Captain Victor Hunt Harding, Secretary of the National Democratic Congress Re-election Committee, Washington, D.C., April 10, 1939.

Trader, Ella King Newsom

During the Civil War, Mrs. Ella King Newsom Trader was called the *Florence Nightingale of the Southern Army* [1] because of her devoted and efficient service as a nurse in this army. Florence Nightingale, the great English war-nurse and humanitarian was her contemporary.

Mrs. Ella King Newsom Trader was born at Brandon, in Rankin County, Miss.

[1] *The Florence Nightingale of the Southern Army; Experiences of Mrs Ella K. Newsom, Confederate Nurse in the Great War of 1861-65,* J. Fraise Richard (Broadway Publishing Company, New York and Baltimore, 1914) p. 13, 15.

Trailblazer Division. See Seventieth Infantry Division of World War II

Traynor, Harold Joseph

Harold Joseph Traynor, who was born at Framingham, Mass., on November 11, 1899, and who played infield in major league baseball, was nicknamed *Pie* [1] because he was so fond of pie as a youngster.

[1] *Who's Who in Major League Base Ball,* comp. by Harold (Speed) Johnson (Buxton Publishing Company, Chicago, 1933) p. 386.

Treadwell, John

John Treadwell, fourth governor of Connecticut (1809-11), justly deserves the title, *Father of the System of Common-School*

Treadwell, John—Continued

Education.[1] He assisted in the sale of Connecticut's Western Reserve land in Ohio, by which the Connecticut school fund was created, and drew up the measure for the application of the fund.

He was born at Farmington, Conn., on November 23, 1745 and died there on August 19, 1823.

[1] *The National Cyclopaedia of American Biography* (James T. White and Company, New York, 1900) vol. 10, p. 331.

Treason House

Treason House [1] was a nickname applied to Joshua Smith's residence, a two-story wooden house located between Stony Point and Haverstraw, N.Y., which Benedict Arnold used in 1780 when he drew up his plans to deliver West Point to the British.

[1] *The Manors and Historic Homes of the Hudson Valley,* Harold Donaldson Eberlin (J. B. Lippincott Company, Philadelphia and London, 1924) p. 311.

Treasure State. See Montana

Treasure State of the Rockies. See Colorado

Tree Planters State. See Nebraska

Tribesmen. See Hartwick College

Tribune of the People. See Adams, Samuel

Tri-cities. See Davenport, Iowa, Moline and Rock Island, Ill.

Trimountain City. See Boston, Mass.

Trinity University

The athletic teams of Trinity University, at Waxahachie, Tex., were nicknamed the *Tigers* [1] in 1908 by E. A. Werner, Coach of Athletics at the University.

[1] A communication from L. J. Wilkins, Director of Athletics at Trinity University, Waxahachie, Tex., December 3, 1935.

Triple-headed Monster

When the Constitution of the United States was before the various states for ratification, many who were not in favor of its adoption called it a *Triple-headed Monster,*[1]

referring to the three aspects of government that it embodied, the legislative, judicial, and executive.

[1] *A History of the People of the United States, from the Revolution to the Civil War,* John Bach McMaster (D. Appleton and Company, New York, 1883) vol. 1, p. 482.

Triple Threat. See Lea, C. F.

Trojan. See Evers, J. J.

Trojans. See University of Southern California; Virginia State College for Negroes

Tropic Lightning Division. See Twenty-fifth Infantry Division of World War II

Trotting Twelfth

During the Civil War the Twelfth Regiment of Rhode Island Volunteer Infantrymen was humorously nicknamed the *Trotting Twelfth* [1] because this unit was continuously marched from place to place.

[1] *State of Rhode Island and Providence Plantations at the End of the Century; A History Illustrated with Maps, Fac-similes of Old Plates and Paintings and Photographs of Ancient Landmarks,* ed. by Edward Field (The Mason Publishing Company, Boston and Syracuse, N.Y., 1902) vol. 1, p. 521.

Trousdale, William

The sobriquet, *Warhorse of Sumner County,*[1] was attributed to William Trousdale because he fought bravely in both the Seminole War in 1836, and the Mexican War in 1847.

William Trousdale was born in Orange County, N.C., on September 23, 1790, and died at Nashville, Tenn., on March 27, 1872.

[1] *A History of Tennessee from 1663 to 1924,* Gentry R. McGee, revised and enlarged by C. B. Ijams (American Book Company, New York, 1924) p. 171-2.

Troy, New York

The *Collar Capital of the World* [1] is the nickname applied to Troy because in this city are manufactured about ninety per cent of the men's collars used in the United States. It was in Troy that the detachable linen collar was invented in 1819.

[1] *The Source Book* (Source Research Council, Inc., Chicago, 1936) vol. 7, p. 2932.

Trumbull, John. See *Hartford Wits*

Trumbull, Jonathan

Brother Jonathan and the *Rebel Governor* are the nicknames given to Jonathan Trumbull.

General George Washington affectionately called him *Brother Jonathan*,[1] by which sobriquet Trumbull later became widely known.

During the Revolutionary War, Jonathan Trumbull was designated the *Rebel Governor*,[1] by the British and their Tory sympathizers, because he was the only colonial governor who actively supported the rebelling colonists, contributing much of his personal fortune to that cause. He was Governor of Connecticut from 1760 until he resigned in 1783.

Jonathan Trumbull was born at Lebanon, Conn., on October 12, 1710, and died there on August 17, 1785.

[1] *History of Eastern Connecticut, Embracing the Counties of Tolland, Windham, Middlesex, and New London,* Pliny LeRoy Harwood (The Pioneer Historical Publishing Company, Chicago and New Haven, Conn., 1932) vol. 2, p. 694.

Trust-buster. See Roosevelt, Theodore

Trust-busting President. See Roosevelt, Theodore

Tryon, William

The Indians along the New England frontiers nicknamed William Tryon the *Great Wolf* [1] because his dealings with them were characterized by cruelty and rapaciousness.

William Tryon was born in Ireland, in 1725, and died at London, England, on December 27, 1788.

[1] *The National Cyclopaedia of American Biography* (James T. White and Company, New York, 1897) vol. 7, p. 514-15.

Tubal Cain. See Spotswood, Alexander

Tubbs, Alice

Alice Tubbs, a professional gambler in the pioneer West, was nicknamed *Poker Alice Tubbs*.[1] She was a familiar figure in gold-mining towns during the Black Hills gold rush about 1875 and 1876 and for a number of years thereafter.

Alice Ivers came from England in 1856, migrated to the western part of the United States in 1876, and married a mining engineer named Frank Duffield. After her husband's death in a mine explosion Alice began to gamble for a livelihood. Later she married W. G. Tubbs, a gambler. She became an intimate friend of Martha Jane Canary, commonly nicknamed Calamity Jane, and a number of other persons who gambled for a living.

Alice Tubbs was born in England, on February 17, 1853, and died in Sturgis, S.D., in March 1930.

[1] *The Washington Post,* Washington, D.C., March 17, 1929, col. 2, 3 and 4, p. 8.

Tubman, Harriet

During the Civil War, Harriet Tubman, who was prominent as an abolitionist, a spy, and a nurse in sympathy with the Union cause, became widely known as *Moses*,[1] or the *Negro Moses*.[1] The nickname is descriptive of her chief work, which was to lead Negro slaves out of bondage by means of the "underground railway" system, spiriting them out of Maryland to New York and then to Canada. Harriet Tubman was credited with the escape of about three hundred slaves in this manner, and irate Southerners offered a large reward for her capture.

Harriet Tubman was born a slave in Dorchester County, Md., about 1821, and died at Auburn, N.Y., on March 10, 1913.

[1] *The National Cyclopaedia of American Biography* (James T. White and Company, New York, 1907) vol. 9, p. 547.
Homespun Heroines and Other Women of Distinction, comp. and ed. by Hallie Q. Brown (The Aldine Publishing Company, Xenia, Ohio, 1926) p. 64-7.

Tuckahoes. See Virginians

Tucker, John Randolph

John Randolph Tucker, a naval officer first in the United States Navy and, upon the secession of Virginia, a commander in the short-lived Confederate States Navy, was known to sailors as *Handsome Jack*.[1] He was tall, and of imposing presence, with the reputation of a fine seaman, disciplinarian and fighter.

He was taken prisoner in 1865 at the battle of Sailor's Creek. His later career included service as rear admiral in the Peruvian navy, and a successful survey of the upper waters of the Amazon commissioned by the Peruvian government.

John Randolph Tucker was born at Alexandria, Va., on January 31, 1812, and died at Petersburg, Va., on June 12, 1883.

[1] *Dictionary of American Biography under the Auspices of the American Council of Learned Societies,* ed. by Dumas Malone (Charles Scribner's Sons, New York, 1936) vol. 19, p. 34.

Tucker, Saint George

The nickname, the *American Blackstone*,[1] sometimes applied to Saint George Tucker commemorates his reputation as one of the foremost lawyers in Virginia. For several years he was Professor of Law at the College of William and Mary. He was on a committee which revised and compiled the Virginia statutes; and he served ably as a judge in state and federal courts. He was thus likened to the renowned English lawyer Sir William Blackstone.

Saint George Tucker was born at Port Royal, Bermuda, on July 9, 1752, and died in Nelson County, Va., on November 10, 1827.

[1] *The National Cyclopaedia of American Biography* (James T. White and Company, New York, 1897) vol. 7, p. 136.

Tuckoes. See North Carolinians

Tudor, Frederic

Frederic Tudor, a merchant, was known nationally and internationally as the *Ice King*[1] because of his initiative and success in establishing the ice industry in the United States. From his headquarters in Boston, Mass., he procured ice from the numerous ponds and lakes in that section of the United States. He began to ship ice from his storehouses by boat to tropical and semitropical cities in 1806. Despite ridicule, competition, and imprisonment for debt, Tudor persevered in his undertaking until by 1856 he was shipping about one hundred and forty-six thousand tons of ice to such distant places as the East and West Indies, the Philippine Islands, China, and Australia.

Frederic Tudor was born at Boston, Mass., on September 4, 1783, and died there on February 6, 1864.

[1] *Dictionary of American Biography under the Auspices of the American Council of Learned Societies*, ed. by Dumas Malone (Charles Scribner's Sons, New York, 1936) vol. 19, p. 47, 48.
Lost Men of American History, by Stewart H. Holbrook (The Macmillan Company, New York, 1946) p. 114-23.

Tuffy Leemans. See Leemans, Alphonso

Tufts College

The *Jumbos*[1] is the sobriquet given to the athletic teams of Tufts College, at Medford, Mass., by newspaper writers about 1920. P. T. Barnum gave the skin of Jumbo, the famous elephant, to the college museum.

[1] A communication from Clarence P. Houston, Director of Athletics at Tufts College, Medford, Mass., June 18, 1935.

Tugwell, Rexford Guy

During 1935 and 1936 newspaper writers[1] called Dr. Rexford Guy Tugwell, then Undersecretary of Agriculture in President Franklin Delano Roosevelt's Cabinet, the *Barrymore of the Brain Trust* and *Mr. American*.[1] Dr. Tugwell, one of the most forthright spokesman for President Roosevelt's New Deal policy, was noted for his manly good looks.

Rexford Guy Tugwell was born at Sinclairville, N.Y., on July 10, 1891. He was Undersecretary of Agriculture from 1934 to 1937; governor of Puerto Rico from 1941 to 1946, and since then has been professor of political science at the University of Chicago.

[1] *The Washington Post*, Washington, D.C., November 19, 1936, col. 5, p. 2.

Tulane Football Stadium

The football stadium of Tulane University, at New Orleans, La., is widely known as the *Sugar Bowl*.[1] Because New Orleans is located in the chief sugar-producing section of the United States, the sobriquet was given to the football stadium by the sponsors of the post-season football game known as the *Sugar Bowl Game*, which is played in the stadium each New Year's day.

[1] A communication from Horace Remgar, Publicity Director of Athletics at Tulane University, New Orleans, La., March 10, 1939.

Tulane University

The athletic teams of Tulane University, at New Orleans, La., were designated the *Rolling Green Waves*[1] about 1921, in commemoration of the song entitled *The Rolling Green Wave*, written by Edward Earl Sparling who graduated from Tulane in 1921.

[1] A communication from Horace Remgar, Director of Athletics at Tulane University, New Orleans, La., June 19, 1935.

Tullahoma, Tennessee

During the Civil War, Tullahoma, in Coffee County, Tenn., became nicknamed the *Thermopylae of Middle Tennessee*.[1] This sobriquet was originated by the Confederate general, Braxton Bragg, who, early in 1863, stationed his army at this place in the foothills of the Blue Ridge Mountains. General Bragg used the phrase because Tullahoma served as a gateway for that section of the state, and as an entrance to the states south of it. Its strategic military location caused General Bragg to compare it with the famous mountain pass at Thermopylae in Greece which, according to ancient history, was the only means by which an army could go from northern into southern Greece. In 480 B.C. this was the scene of the battle in which Leonidas the First and his three hundred Spartans sacrificed themselves in the attempt to withstand Xerxes' invading Persian soldiers.

[1] *Representative Men: Sketches of Representative Men, North and South; Representatives of Modern Progress, of the Press, of the Pulpit, the Bench, the Bar, the Army and Navy, of Legislation, Invention, and the Great Industrial Interests of the Country,* ed. by Augustus C. Rogers (Atlantic Publishing Company, New York, 1872) p. 463.

Tulsa, Oklahoma

Tulsa has been appropriately nicknamed the *Oil Capital of the World*.[1] It is the headquarters of the mid-continent oil industry and the hub of pipe lines carrying oil and natural gas from Oklahoma to cities of northern and eastern United States. Tulsa's oil fields produce about one sixth of the world's supply of crude oil.[2]

[1] *Columbia Lippincott Gazetteer of the World,* ed. by Leon E. Seltzer, (Columbia University Press, New York, 1952) p. 1958.
[2] *The World Book Encyclopedia* (W. F. Quarrie and Company, Chicago, 1937) vol. 16, p. 7291.

Tunney, James Joseph (Gene Turney)

Former heavyweight champion boxer Jamés Joseph (Gene) Tunney was sometimes nicknamed the *Fighting Marine* [1] because his fighting career began while he was a member of the United States Marines with the American Expeditionary Forces in World War I.

In 1926 Tunney defeated Jack Dempsey and became heavyweight champion of the world. He retained his title the following year in a return bout, although the decision was disputed because of the "long count" given Tunney when Dempsey would not return to a neutral corner of the ring after knocking him down. Tunney fought once more, in 1928, defeating Tom Heeney by a technical knockout, and then retired from the ring as undefeated champion.

Gene Tunney was born in Greenwich Village, New York City, N.Y., on May 25, 1898.

[1] *Post Boxing Record* (Post Sports Records Corporation, New York, 1935) p. 82.

Tunstall, Alfred Moore

The three nicknames, *Dean of the Alabama Legislature,* the *Gentleman from Hale,*[2] and *Uncle Alf,*[3] were attributed to Alfred Moore Tunstall, an Alabama statesman.

The first sobriquet commemorates his prominence as a member of the State Legislature for approximately thirty-nine years, and as Speaker of the House of Representatives twice during that time. The second nickname referred to his gentility of manner typical of the Old South. He represented Hale County in the State Legislature for a long time, having been a Representative from Hale County to the Alabama Legislature for nine terms, and a Senator from Hale and Greene Counties for one term. The third nickname was given to him during the later years of his life. He lived to be seventy-one, and was one of Alabama's foremost citizens and statesmen.

He was born at Greensboro, Ala., on October 2, 1863, and died there on May 28, 1935.

[1] *The Montgomery Advertiser,* Montgomery, Ala., May 29, 1935, col. 7, p. 1.
[2] *Alabama Official and Statistical Register, 1935* (Department of Archives and History, Mrs. Marie B. Owen, Director, Wetumpka Printing Company, Wetumpka, Ala., 1935) p. 7.
[3] *Alabama Official and Statistical Register, 1935* (Department of Archives and History, Mrs. Marie B. Owen, Director, Wetumpka Printing Company, Wetumpka, Ala., 1935) p. 9.

Turkey Gobblers

Turkey Gobblers [1] was a nickname given to the soldiers in Rush's Lancers, a Pennsylvania regiment encamped near Falmouth, Va., on April 8, 1863. The members of the regiment carried lances surmounted by small red flags or banners, which so suggested strutting turkey gobblers to other soldiers that they would often utter sounds like the gobbling of a turkey-cock as the Lancers passed.

[1] *War Diary and Letters of Stephen Minot Weld, 1861-1865,* Stephen Minot Weld (Privately printed at the Riverside Press,, Cambridge, Mass., 1912) p. 170.

Turnbull's Fort

Turnbull's Fort [1] was a term given to the log house of John Turnbull in Lincoln

Turnbull's Fort—Continued
County, Mo., in which he defended himself against a group of men who formed a unit about 1845 to rid the county of people convicted or suspected of being horse-thieves. John Turnbull was suspected of being a member of such a gang because his son had been friendly with one of the robbers. Turnbull, who claimed that he was innocent, refused to leave his home, and defended himself so effectively in his log cabin that the men abandoned their attempt to force him to leave the county.

[1] *Centennial History of Missouri (The Center State) One Hundred Years in the Union, 1820-1921,* Walter B. Stevens (The S. J. Clarke Publishing Company, St. Louis, Mo., and Chicago, 1921) vol. 2, p. 239.

Turner, Alfred L.

Alfred L. Turner, a major league football player, was nicknamed *Warhorse* [1] by his schoolmates while he was playing center on the football team of the Port Arthur High School, at Port Arthur, Tex., from 1926 until 1929, for his vigor, strength, and fighting ability.

He was born at Westberry, Tex., on December 1, 1911; attended Purdue University, and played center for the Pittsburgh Pirates of the National Football League.

[1] *Who's Who in Major League Football,* comp. by Harold (Speed) Johnson and Wilfrid Smith (B. V. Callahan, Chicago, 1935) p. 43.

Turpentine State. See North Carolina

Turpin, C. Murray

C. Murray Turpin sometimes is called *Ben Turpin* [1] jokingly in allusion to the comedian of that name, the sobriquet doubtless suggested by the identical surname.

C. Murray Turpin was born at Kingston, Pa., on March 4, 1878, and was a Representative from Pennsylvania to the United States Congress from 1933 to 1935.

[1] *The Washington Post Magazine,* Washington, D.C., March 4, 1934, p. 4.

Tuscaloosa, Alabama

Tuscaloosa is known as the *Athens of Alabama* and the *City of Oaks,* or the *Druid City. Athens of Alabama* [1] refers to the city's colleges and intellectual activities. It is termed *City of Oaks,* [2] or the *Druid City,* [2] because numerous massive water oaks

line the streets and avenues, adding much to its attractiveness.

[1] *Tuscaloosa, Alabama: The City of Tuscaloosa, Its Many Advantages as a Manufacturing Point and as a Place of Residence, the Facts that Make It the Pittsburgh of the South, Including a Prospectus of the Tuscaloosa Coal, Iron and Land Company, Organized January 15, 1887* (Keating and Company, Cincinnati, Ohio, 1887) p. 49.
[2] *Tuscaloosa, Alabama: Tuscaloosa; the Origin of Its Name, Its History, etc; A Paper Read Before the Alabama Historical Society, July 1, 1876,* Thomas Maxwell (Tuscaloosa Gazette, Tuscaloosa, Ala., 1876) p. 69, 85.

Tuscarora John. See Barnwell, John

Tusselburgh. See Alton, Ill.

Tutwiler, Julia Strudwick

The *Angel of the Prisons* [1] is a sobriquet by which Julia Strudwick Tutwiler was often designated in recognition of her services in having secured, chiefly through state legislation, a number of needed reforms in the prisons of Alabama, particularly those relating to the convict-lease system. The nickname originated while she was engaged in giving religious and educational guidance to the prison inmates and in ameliorating as much as possible the unfavorable conditions of their environment.

Julia Strudwick Tutwiler was born at Tuscaloosa, Ala., and died at Birmingham, Ala., on March 24, 1916.

[1] *History of Alabama and Dictionary of Alabama Biography,* Thomas McAdory Owen (The S. J. Clarke Publishing Company, Chicago, 1921) vol. 4, p. 1695.

TVA Rankin. See Rankin, J. E.

Twelfth Armored Division of World War II

The *Hellcat Division* [1] was the nickname of the Twelfth Armored Division of the Combat Divisions of World War II.

[1] *Combat Divisions of World War II,* (Army of the United States), Army Times Publishing Company, Washington, D.C., 1946, p. 86.

Twenty-eighth Infantry Division of World War II

The *Keystone Division* [1] was the nickname of the Twenty-eighth Infantry Division of Combat Divisions of World War II because it was inducted into service at Indiantown Gap, in Pennsylvania, the *Keystone State.* This division was also called by the Germans the *Bloody Bucket Division* because of the fury of its assaults launched on Normandy beaches July 22, 1945.

[1] *Combat Divisions of World War II,* (Army of the United States), Army Times Publishing Company, Washington, D.C., 1946, p. 21.

Twentieth Century Moses. See Chaplin, C. S.

Twenty-fifth Infantry Division of World War II

The *Tropic Lightning Division*[1] and the *Pineapple Division* were the nicknames of the Twenty-fifth Infantry Division of the Combat Divisions of World War II.

[1] *Combat Divisions of World War II,* (Army of the United States), Army Times Publishing Company, Washington, D.C., 1946, p. 18.

Twenty-fourth Infantry Division of World War II

The *Victory Division*[1] was the nickname of the Twenty-fourth Infantry Division of the Combat Divisions of World War II because from November 10 to December 4, 1944 when they were on Leyte, in the Philippines, the Filipinos greeted them with the V sign, and also because the landing of this division in Dutch New Guinea on April 22, 1944, has been called a perfect tactical operation.

[1] *Combat Divisions of World War II,* (Army of the United States), Army Times Publishing Company, Washington, D.C., 1946, p. 17.

Twenty-nigger Law

In order to secure soldiers for participation in the Civil War, in April, 1862, the Congress of the Southern Confederacy passed a conscription law requiring all able-bodied men between the ages of eighteen and thirty-five to enlist in the Confederate Army. The law, however, provided for a number of exemptions, one of them being that if a man were the overseer of twenty or more Negro slaves, he was relieved from army service. This particular exemption was obnoxious to the poorer classes who owned no slaves, and was derisively called by them the *Twenty-nigger Law.*[1]

[1] *The Oxford History of the United States, 1783-1917,* Samuel E. Morison (Oxford University Press, London, 1927) vol. 2, p. 267.
High Stakes and Hair Trigger; the Life of Jefferson Davis, Robert W. Winston (Henry Holt and Company, New York, 1930) p. 223.

Twenty-ninth Infantry Division of World War II

The *Blue and Gray Division*[1] was the nickname of the Twenty-ninth Infantry Division of the Combat Divisions of World War II because the men composing it came from ancestors who fought partly for the North and partly for the South in the Civil War.

[1] *Combat Divisions of World War II,* (Army of the United States), Army Times Publishing Company, Washington, D.C., 1946, p. 22.

Twenty-seventh Division of World War II

The *New York Division*[1] was the nickname of the Twenty-seventh Division of the Combat Divisions of World War II because it was originally composed of New York National Guards.

[1] *Combat Divisions of World War II,* (Army of the United States), Army Times Publishing Company, Washington, D.C., 1946, p. 20.

Twenty sixth Infantry Division of World War II

The *Yankee Division*[1] was the nickname of the Twenty-sixth Infantry Division of the Combat Divisions of World War II because the division was originally composed of National Guard troops from New England.

[1] *Combat Divisions of World War II,* (Army of the United States), Army Times Publishing Company, Washington, D.C., 1946, p. 19.

Twiggs, David Emanuel

David Emanuel Twiggs, a soldier and officer, was nicknamed *Old Davy,*[1] the *Horse,*[1] and *Bengal Tiger*[1] by his soldiers because of his tremendous reserves of physical energy. He was Captain of the Eighth United States Infantry during the War with Great Britain in 1812, and later Major of the Twenty-eighth United States Infantry. He fought in the War with Mexico, and was Military Governor of Vera Cruz from December 1847 until March 1848.

David Emanuel Twiggs was born in Richmond County, Ga., on July 15, 1790, and died in Augusta, Ga., on September 15, 1862.

[1] *Dictionary of American Biography under the Auspices of the American Council of Learned Societies,* ed. by Dumas Malone (Charles Scribner's Sons, New York, 1936) vol. 19, p. 83.

Twin City. See Bristol, Va. and Tenn.; St. Paul and Minneapolis, Minn.; Winston-Salem, N.C.

Twin Cities. See Champaign and Urbana, Ill.; Central Falls and Pawtucket, R. I.; St. Paul and Minneapolis, Minn.; Texarkana, Arkansas-Texas; Winston-Salem, N.C.

Twin Sisters. See South Dakota

Twin Villages. See Damariscotta and Newcastle, Me.

Twins. See St. Paul and Minneapolis, Minn.

Two-edged Knife. See Bilbo, T. G.

Two-gun Girl. See Guinan, M. L. C.

Tycoon. See Lincoln, Abraham

Tyler, John

When William Henry Harrison died soon after his inauguration as President of the United States in 1841, Vice President John Tyler, automatically became President, thus acquiring the nicknames *Accidental President* [1] and *His Accidency* [2] from his political opponents.

John Tyler was born at Greenwat, Va., on March 29, 1790, and died at Richmond, Va., on January 18, 1862. He was the tenth President of the United States, in office from 1841 to 1845.

[1] *Monument to John Tyler: Address Delivered in Hollywood Cemetery at Richmond, Virginia, on October 12, 1915, at the Dedication of the Monument Erected by the Government to John Tyler, Tenth President of the United States*, Armistead Gordon (Government Printing Office, Washington, D.C., 1916) p. 21.
[2] *The Heart of Roosevelt; an Intimate Life-story of Theodore Roosevelt*, Wayne Whipple (The John C. Winston Company, Chicago and Philadelphia, 1924) p. 163.

Tyler Lilliputians

Practically all the members in the Cabinet of President John Tyler resigned in 1841 in protest over Tyler's rejection of Henry Clay's proposed bank bill. In the breach which developed between the Chief Executive and Congress, Tyler proceeded to fill the Cabinet with men of his own choice. These were derisively spoken of as the *Tyler Lilliputians*.[1]

[1] *The Godlike Daniel*, Samuel Hopkins Adams (Sears Publishing Company, Inc., New York, 1930) p. 265.

Tytler, James

James Tytler was commonly nicknamed *Balloon Tytler* [1] because he was the first person in Scotland to ascend in a balloon inflated with smoke. He belonged to the organization, The Friends of the People,

and was forced to flee from Scotland to Ireland about 1793 to avoid political persecution. He emigrated from Ireland to the United States in 1796.

James Tytler was born at Brechin, Scotland, in 1747, and was drowned near Salem, Mass., in 1805.

[1] *Appleton's Cyclopaedia of American Biography*, ed. by James Grant Wilson and John Fiske (D. Appleton and Company, New York, 1894) vol. 6, p. 204.

Typhoid Mary. See Mallon, Mary

Typical American. See Roosevelt, Theodore

Tyrant. See Lincoln, Abraham

U

Uhlans. See Valparaiso University

Unbleached American

The American Negro used to be humorously nicknamed the *Unbleached American* [1] because of the color of his skin.

[1] *The New International Encyclopaedia*, Second Edition (Dodd, Mead and Company, New York, 1916) vol. 16, p. 615.

Uncle Abe. See Lincoln, Abraham

Uncle Alf. See Taylor, A. A.; Tunstall, A. M.

Uncle Billy. See Sherman, W. T.; Smith, William; Workman, W. H.

Uncle Dan. See Tobin, D. J.

Uncle Dick. See Oglesby, R. J.; Thompson, R. W.

Uncle Fred. See Thompson, F. F.

Uncle George. See Georgia Power Company; Perkins, G. D.; Thomas, G. H.

Uncle Jerry. See Rusk, J. M.

Uncle Jimmie. See Doughty, J. P.

Uncle Joe. See Cannon, J. G.; Stilwell, J. W.

Uncle John. See Sedgwick, John

Uncle Jumbo. See Cleveland, Grover

Uncle Remus. See Harris, J. C.

Uncle Robert. See Lee, R. E.

Uncle Sam

Uncle Sam is a personification of the United States Government. It is said to have originated during the war of 1812 at which time it was the popular sobriquet of Samuel Wilson of Troy, N.Y.[1] Wilson, a merchant in the slaughtering business, in association with Elbert Anderson, a government contractor, shipped large quantities of meat and other commodities from Troy to American forces stationed in various places in the North. These shipments were commonly marked E.A.U.S., the initials of the shipper, Anderson, and of the consignee, the United States Government. Soldiers from Troy recognized the origin of goods so marked and jokingly spoke of the meat as "Uncle Sam's beef." This expression was quickly adopted by their fellow-soldiers and was applied by them to all property of the United States Government.

The appellation as applied to the national government has become widely used in America and abroad. The figure of a tall, "spare old gentleman with a kind face," dressed in apparel similar to the civilian costume of 1812 is the national cartoon figure symbolical of the United States and is said to have been patterned after the likeness of Samuel Wilson.

[1] *Troy and Rensselaer County, New York, a History,* Rutherford Hayner (Lewis Historical Publishing Company, Inc., New York and Chicago, 1925) vol. 1, p. 175-6.
History of the Valley of the Hudson, River of Destiny, 1609-1930; Covering the Sixteen New York State Hudson River Counties of New York, Bronx, Westchester, Rockland, Orange, Putnam, Dutchess, Ulster, Greene, Columbia, Albany, Rensselaer, Saratoga, Washington, Warren, Essex, ed. by Nelson Greene (The S. J. Clarke Publishing Company, Chicago, 1931) vol. 1, p. 122.

Uncle Sam Grant. See Grant, U. S.

Uncle Sam's Crib

The Treasury of the United States is frequently designated *Uncle Sam's Crib*[1] because as a storehouse of money it is similar to a farmer's crib which is a storehouse for his corn and grain.

[1] *Americanisms; The English of the New World,* M. Schele De Vere (Charles Scribner and Company, New York, 1872) p. 263.

Uncle Sam's Favorite Niece. See Lamour, Dorothy

Uncle Sam's Hounds

The abolitionist, John Brown, gave the nickname *Uncle Sam's Hounds*[1] to the Government officials who sought his whereabouts after he had led the raid which resulted in the deaths of five proslavery men at Pottawatomie, Kans., on May 25, 1856.

John Brown was born at Torrington, Conn., on May 9, 1800. He was convicted of treason for seizing the government arsenal at Harper's Ferry, Va., and was hanged at Charlestown, West Virginia, on December 2, 1859.

[1] *The Life and Letters of John Brown, Liberator of Kansas and Martyr of Virginia,* ed. by F. B. Sanborn (Roberts Brothers, Boston, 1885) p. 382, 511.

Uncle Sam's Pocket Handkerchief. See Delaware

Uncle Shylock

The United States of America or its government is familiarly personified as *Uncle Sam.* About 1920 this was varied to *Uncle Shylock.*[1] The derogatory change occurred at the time that repayment of World War I loans to *Uncle Sam* by debtor nations was being urged.

Shylock is the moneylender in Shakespeare's *Merchant of Venice* who stipulated to the merchant, Antonio, that, if his loan was not repaid by a certain date, Shylock might cut for himself a pound of flesh from any part of Antonio's body. The application of the name to the United States infers that the United States is a moneylending nation which rigorously exacts the payment of loans by nations in its debt.

[1] *The American Scene,* Edwin C. Hill (Witmark Educational Publications Department of M. Witmark and Sons, New York, 1933) p. 412.

Uncle Toby. See Cross, W. L.

"Uncle Tom's Cabin" of the Indians

Helen Maria Fiske Hunt Jackson's novel, *Ramona,* published in 1884, has been nicknamed the *"Uncle Tom's Cabin" of the Indians*[1] because in this fictitious narrative Mrs. Jackson set forth the ill-treatment which the western Indians and Spanish-Americans suffered at the hands of the United States Government. In this respect the novel is comparable to Mrs. Harriet

"Uncle Tom's Cabin" of the Indians
—Continued

Beecher Stowe's novel, *Uncle Tom's Cabin*, which portrays the ill-treatment of the Negro slaves prior to the Civil War.

[1] *The World Book Encyclopedia* (The Quarrie Corporation, Chicago, 1938) vol. 9, p. 3604.

Unconditional Surrender. See Grant, U. S.

Uncrowned King. See Blaine, J. G.

Underground Railroad

Before the slaves were freed in the Civil War, active antislavery people in the United States organized a system for helping fugitive Slaves escape to the North or to Canada. Operations were necessarily carried on in secret and relied on the complete cooperation of all parties concerned. The route of escape was organized so that there were "stations," "junctions," and "conductors" along the way, and was known as the *Underground Railroad*.[1]

[1] *The Story of American Democracy, Political and Industrial*, Willis Mason West (Allyn and Bacon, New York and Boston, 1922) p. 505.

Uniformed Soldier. See Grant, U. S.

Unintentional Defaulter. See Webster, Daniel

Union College

The members of the athletic teams of Union College, Schenectady, N.Y., were nicknamed the *Dutchmen*[1] in 1932 by the students writing for the college paper. This sobriquet had its origin in the song entitled the *College on the Hill* written by H. R. Knight in 1917 and also in the fact that "the college was founded by early Dutch settlers in 1795." [1]

[1] A communication from F. A. Wyatt of Union College, Schnectady, N.Y., November 21, 1935.

Union Safeguard. See Grant, U. S.

Union University

The athletes of Union University, at Jackson, Tenn., were designated the *Bulldogs* in 1924 by a vote of the student body because of the tenacity and determination displayed by the foot-ball squad. The freshman teams are dubbed *Bullpups*.

Union University. See Botany Bay

Union's Grand Old Man. See Savage, G. M.

Union-savers

Those who opposed secession before and during the Civil War were designated the *Union-savers*.[1]

[1] *American History and Government, a Text-book on the History and Civil Government of the United States*, James Albert Woodburn and Thomas Francis Moran (Longmans, Green and Company, New York, 1908) p. 320.

United States Coast Guard Academy

The students of the athletic teams of the United States Coast Guard Academy, at New London, Conn., were given the appellation *Cadets*[1] or *Kaydets*[1] because "the enlisted men's teams aboard service ships at New London necessitated a distinctive name."

[1] A communication from John S. Merriman, Jr., Director of Athletics at United States Coast Guard Academy, New London, Conn., June 17, 1935.

United States Grant. See Grant, U. S.

United States Military Academy

The athletic squads at the United States Military Academy, at West Point, N.Y., are called the *Army Team*[1] presumably because cadets at the Academy are in training to become officers of the United States Army.

[1] A letter from L. D. Worsham, Major, C. E., Graduate Manager of Athletics at the United States Military Academy, West Point, N.Y., June 17, 1935.

United States Naval Academy

Middies is the nickname often attributed by sports writers to the athletic teams of the United States Naval Academy, at Annapolis, Md., the sobriquet being an abbreviation of *midshipmen*. The midshipmen themselves refer to their teams as the *Navy*.[1]

[1] A letter from T. T. Patterson, Lieutenant Commander, Aide to the Superintendent of the United States Naval Academy, Annapolis, Md., November 21, 1935.

University of Akron

The athletic teams of the University of Akron, at Akron, Ohio, were designated the *Zippers* by a unanimous vote of the student body; but the college authorities[1] did not say when or why this sobriquet was given to the members of the teams.

[1] A communication from H. E. Simmons, President of the University of Akron, Akron, Ohio, November 20, 1935.

United States of America. See *Melting Pot; Uncle Sam; Uncle Shylock;* and *Young Industrial Giant of the West*

United States Treasury. See *Uncle Sam's Crib*

University City. See Cambridge, Mass.

University of Alabama

The athletic teams of the University of Alabama, at Tuscaloosa, were nicknamed the *Crimson Tides* [1] about 1920 by the sports editor of the *Birmingham News*. The University colors are crimson and white, and the sight of the football team surging about the field in these colors presumably suggested the metaphor.

[1] A communication from H. G. Crisp, Director of Athletics at the University of Alabama, Tuscaloosa, Ala., July 24, 1935.

University of Arizona

The *Wildcats* [1] is the sobriquet given to the athletic teams of the University of Arizona, at Tucson, Ariz., in 1914 by the students of the University. William Henry, a student reporter at the University for the *Los Angeles Times*, had said in his report of a game in 1914 between the members of the University team and those of Occidental College that "the Arizona team fought like wildcats." [1]

[1] A letter from J. F. McKale, Director of Physical Education for men at the University of Arizona, Tucson, Ariz., June 19, 1935.

University of Arkansas

The athletic teams of the University of Arkansas, at Fayetteville, were designated the *Razorbacks* [1] about 1909, because Arkansas is widely known as the home of the razorback hog, and the college has adopted this animal as its mascot. [1]

[1] A letter from W. J. Lemke, Director of the News Bureau at the University of Arkansas, Fayetteville, Ark., June 19, 1935.

University of Baltimore

The athletic teams of the University of Baltimore, in Maryland, are called *Maroons* and *Bees*. *Maroons* [1] was originated by B. Herbert Brown, Jr., Director of Athletics at the University of Baltimore in 1929 because the University colors are maroon and white. The sobriquet was changed to *Bees* [1] in 1932 because the letter B is the University award. The change was made in order to differentiate the athletic teams of this University from those of another state college also called *Maroons*.

[1] A letter from Merrill L. Carroll, Head of the Publicity Department of the University of Baltimore, Baltimore, Md., November 20, 1935.

University of Buffalo

Bisons [1] and *Bulls* [1] are the appellations given to the athletic teams of the University of Buffalo, in New York State. These sobriquets were originated by sports writers [1] of the *Buffalo Evening News* about 1930, and were suggested [1] by the name Buffalo.

[1] A communication from the Director of Athletics at the University of Buffalo, Buffalo, N.Y., November 23, 1935.

University of California

The athletic teams of the University of California, at Berkeley, Calif., are nicknamed the *California Bears* [1] or the *Golden Bears* "because the California State Flag is the Bear Flag." [1]

[1] A communication from Robert G. Sproul, President of the University of California, Berkeley, Calif., November 18, 1935.

University of California Agricultural College

Mustangs [1] is the sobriquet given to the athletic teams of the University of California Agricultural College, at Davis, Calif., in 1917 by the members of the student body.

[1] A communication from I. F. Toomey, Director of Athletics at the University of California Agricultural College, Davis, Calif., July 1, 1935.

University of California at Los Angeles

The athletic teams of this school, situated at Los Angeles, Calif., were nicknamed *Bruins* [1] in 1927 by the lettermen's society. As a branch of the University of California at Berkeley, whose athletic teams are known as the *Golden Bears*, the University teams at Los Angeles felt that *Bruins* would be appropriate for them.

[1] A communication from William C. Ackerman, Graduate Manager of Athletics at the University of California, Los Angeles, Calif., June 12, 1935.

University of Chattanooga

The athletic teams of the University of Chattanooga, in Tennessee were designated the *Moccasins* [1] because of the moccasin plants which are found by the Tennessee River.

[1] A communication from W. M. Keyser, Graduate Manager of Athletics at the University of Chattanooga, Chattanooga, Tenn., June 18, 1935.

University of Chicago

The *Maroons*[1] and the *Midwayites*[1] are the sobriquets applied to the athletic teams of the University of Chicago. The former sobriquet was attributed to them about 1894 by a vote of the student body because the college color is maroon. *Midwayites*[1] was suggested because this university is "located on the Midway Plaisance connecting Washington and Jackson parks."

[1] A letter from Amos Alonzo Stagg, Football Coach at College of The Pacific, Stockton, Calif., June 24, 1935.

University of Cincinnati

Bearcats is the appellation popularly given to the athletic teams of the University of Cincinnati, in Ohio.

University of Colorado

The athletic teams of the University of Colorado, at Boulder, were designated the *Buffalo*[1] in the fall of 1935 by a student vote. The buffalo is an animal native to the state of Colorado.

[1] A communication from Harry S. Carlson, Director of Athletics at the University of Colorado, Boulder, Colo., August 1, 1935.

University of Dayton

The athletic teams of the University of Dayton, at Dayton, Ohio, were nicknamed the *Flyers*[1] in 1923 because Dayton was the home of aviation pioneers Orville and Wilbur Wright.

[1] A communication from Lou Tachudi, Assistant to the Athletic Director at the University of Dayton, Dayton, Ohio, June 17, 1935.

University of Delaware

The athletic teams of the University of Delaware, at Newark, Del., are popularly known as the *Blue Hen's Chickens*[1] doubtless from the fact that Delaware is called the *Blue Hen State* or the *Blue Hen's Chickens State*.

[1] A communication from Walter Hullihen, President of the University of Delaware, Newark, Del., December 16, 1935.

University of Denver

The *Pioneers*[1] is the sobriquet given to the athletic teams of the University of Denver, at Denver, Colo., in 1927 by a vote of the student body because "the University of Denver is the pioneer institution of higher learning in Colorado."[1]

[1] A communication from L. H. Mahony, Director of Athletics at the University of Denver, Denver, Colo., June 19, 1935.

University of Detroit

The athletic teams of the University of Detroit, in Michigan, were nicknamed the *Titans*[1] in 1923 by Stanley Brink, sports reporter for the *Detroit Free Press*, because "so many of the foot-ball players at Detroit during that season were physical giants, wherefore their resemblance to the Titans of mythology."[1]

[1] A communication from Charles E. Dorais, Director of Athletics at the University of Detroit, Detroit, Mich., June 17, 1935.

University of Dubuque

The sobriquet, *Spartans*,[1] was attributed to the athletic teams of the University of Dubuque, at Dubuque, Iowa. This nickname was selected by a popular vote registered in the student newspaper in 1929 because "it represents something of the fighting spirit"[1] of the teams.

[1] A communication from W. B. Zuker, vice-president of the University of Dubuque, Dubuque, Iowa, November 13, 1935.

University of Florida

The athletic teams of the University of Florida, at Gainesville, Fla., are popularly designated *Alligator*[1] or, in shortened form, *Gators*,[1] propably "because the state is the habitat of the alligator."[1]

[1] A letter from John J. Tigert, President of the University of Florida, Gainsville, Fla., November 15, 1935.

University of Georgia

The athletic teams of the University of Georgia, at Athens, Ga., were nicknamed *Bulldogs*[1] in 1921 by newspaper men writing for the Atlanta newspaper.

[1] A communication from H. J. Stegeman, Director of Athletics at the University of Georgia, Athens, Ga., June 17, 1935.

University of Houston

The athletic teams of the University of Houston, at Houston, Tex., were designated the *Cougars*[1] in the fall of 1927 by a committee at the University which selected the sobriquet from the many nicknames suggested through the local papers.

[1] A communication from N. K. Dupre, Dean of the University of Houston, Houston, Tex., November 22, 1935.

University of Idaho

Vandals[1] is the sobriquet attributed to the athletic teams of the University of Idaho, at Moscow, Idaho. It was first used to designate the members of the basketball team. A year or two later it was applied to

all the college athletic teams. The sport editor of *The Argonaut*, the college paper,
originated the nickname "because the spirit
which pervades all Idaho intercollegiate
activities is analogous to the spirit shown
by the ancient Vandals in their fierce con-
quests." [1]

[1] A communication from Rafe Gibbs, Graduate Manager of Athletics at the University of Idaho, Moscow,
Idaho, August 23, 1935.

University of Illinois

The athletic teams of the University of
Illinois, at Champaign, Ill., were designated
the *Fighting Illini* [1] about 1922 or 1923 in
commemoration of the Illini Indians who
once dwelt in Illinois.

[1] A letter from L. M. Tobin, Director of Athletic
Publicity at the University of Illinois, Champaign, Ill.,
June 20, 1935.

University of Iowa

The athletic teams of the University of
Iowa, at Iowa City, Iowa, are popularly
designated *Hawkeyes* because Iowa is known
as the *Hawkeye State*.

University of Kansas

The *Jayhawks* [1] and the *Jayhawkers* [1] are
the nicknames given to the teams of the
University of Kansas, at Lawrence, Kans.,
about 1890, doubtless because Kansas is
called the *Jayhawker State*.

[1] A communication from E. H. Lindley, Chancellor of
the University of Kansas, Lawrence, Kans., November
18, 1935.

University of Kentucky

The sobriquet, *Wildcats*, [1] was given to
the athletic teams of the University of Kentucky, at Lexington, Ky., about 1909. The
sobriquet originated in a statement made
by someone after the game with the University of Illinois in 1909 when he said
the members of the Kentucky team fought
like wildcats. [1]

[1] A communication from S. A. Boles, Director of
Athletics at the University of Kentucky, Lexington, Ky.,
June 18, 1935.

University of Louisville

The athletic teams of the University of
Louisville, at Louisville, Ky., are called
Cardinals supposedly because the cardinal
is the state bird of Kentucky.

University of Maine

The athletic teams of the University of
Maine, at Orono, Me., are designated *Black
Bears* [1] because in 1915 a bear cub was
donated as mascot to the University.

[1] A communication from T. S. Curtis, Faculty Manager of Athletics at the University of Maine, Orono,
Me., June 24, 1935.

University of Maryland

The *Old Liners* and the *Terrapins* are
nicknames attributed to the athletic teams
of the University of Maryland, at College
Park. Maryland is known as the *Old Line
State* and the *Terrapin State*.

University of Michigan

The sobriquet, *Wolverines*, [1] was applied
to the athletic teams of the University of
Michigan, at Ann Arbor, because Michigan
is called the *Wolverine State*.

[1] A letter from Phil C. Pack, Law Offices of Payne,
Mellot, and Pack, Ann Arbor, Mich., June 17, 1935.

University of Minnesota

The athletic teams of the University of
Minnesota at Minneapolis, were nicknamed
Gophers [1] by the newspaper writers be-
cause Minnesota is the *Gopher State*.

[1] A letter from L. L. Schroeder, Ticket Manager for
Athletics at the University of Minnesota, Minneapolis,
Minn., June 19, 1935.

University of Mississippi

The *Ole Miss Teams*, [1] the *Red and Blues*,
and the *Floods* [1] are the appellations of the
athletic teams of the University of Mississippi, at Oxford, (University of Mississippi), Miss. The first sobriquet had its
origin in the fact that the University of
Mississippi is usually spoken of as *Ole
Miss*. The nickname, *Red and Blues*, [1] refers to the college colors. The football
teams are sometimes called the *Floods*, [1] in
reference to the floods of the Mississippi
River.

[1] A letter from Alfred Hume, Chancellor of the University of Mississippi, Oxford (University of Mississippi), Miss., November 18, 1935.

University of Missouri

The athletic teams of the University of
Missouri, at Columbia, Mo., are designated
the *Tigers*. [1] This sobriquet came into use
even before the days of intercollegiate
athletics from an organization formed by
students, faculty, and townspeople during
the Civil War. This group, nicknamed the
Missouri Tigers, enlisted and served under

University of Missouri—Continued
that name. It was afterwards conferred on
the athletic teams of the University.

[1] A letter from C. L. Brewer, Director of Athletics at
the University of Missouri, Columbia, Mo., July 2,
1935.

University of Nebraska
The athletic teams of the University of
Nebraska, at Lincoln, Neb., were designated
Cornhuskers [1] about 1900 probably because
Nebraska is a prominent corn-growing state.

[1] A communication from S. J. Selleck, Director of
Athletics at the University of Nebraska, Lincoln, Neb.,
November 21, 1935.

University of Nevada
The athletic teams of the University of
Nevada, at Reno, are popularly known as
Sagehens [1] and *Wolves*.[1] In 1921 the members of the student body of the University
voted [1] to change the nickname from *Sagehens* to *Wolves* because they felt that the
former sobriquet was not appropriate.

[1] A communication from J. E. Martie, Director of
Athletics at the University of Nevada, Reno, Nev., June
28, 1935.

University of New Hampshire
Wildcats [1] is the appellation applied in
1924 to the athletic teams of the University of New Hampshire, at Durham. The
wildcat is the mascot of the University,
and "is noted for its fighting qualities, particularly when it is cornered," [1] in which
respect it is comparable to the teams of the
University of New Hampshire.

[1] A communication from Edward M. Lewis, President
of the University of New Hampshire, Durham, N.H.,
November 18, 1935.

University of New Mexico
The athletic teams of the University of
New Mexico, at Albuquerque, were designated the *Lobos* [1] in 1921 or 1922 because
a lobo wolf was team mascot at that time.[1]

[1] A communication from M. Moulder, Faculty Manager of Athletics at the University of New Mexico,
Albuquerque, N.M., December 2, 1935.

University of North Carolina
Tar Heels is the nickname of the athletic
teams of the University of North Carolina,
at Chapel Hill, supposedly because the state
is popularly called the *Tarheel State*.

University of North Dakota
Flickertails,[1] *Nodaks*,[1] and *Sioux* [1] are
sobriquets attributed to the athletic teams
of the University of North Dakota, at

Grand Forks, N.D. The older appellation,
the *Flickertails*, has been in use for a long
time probably by association with North
Dakota as the *Flickertail State*. *Nodaks* is
a contraction of North Dakota. The *Sioux*
was selected by members of the student
body and alumni in 1930 because "the
Sioux Indians formerly made the state their
hunting grounds." [1]

[1] A communication from Frank J. Webb, Director of
the Bureau of Alumni Relations, University of North
Dakota, Grand Forks, N.D., June 20, 1935.

University of Notre Dame
Ramblers, Rockets, and the *Fighting
Irish* are the nicknames attributed to the
athletic teams of the University of Notre
Dame, at Notre Dame, Ind. *Ramblers* and
Rockets are used by members of the stu-
dent body or the staff of the University.

There are two versions of the origin of
the appellation, *The Fighting Irish*, approved by the officials of the University.
One theory is that during the early days
most of the students at the University were
Irish. During this time the members of the
teams were losing a game when one of the
full backs "came up to the line and said,
'What's the matter? You're all Irish and
you're not fighting.' " [1] According to this
theory the nickname originated in this incident and saying.

The other theory is that the appellation
was originated and applied as a term of
derision by the opponents of the members
of the teams, it being synonymous with the
expression, *The Fighting Catholics*.[1]

[1] A communication from the Director of the Department of Sports Publicity at the University of Notre
Dame, Notre Dame, Ind., November 13, 1935.

University of Oklahoma
The athletic teams of the University of
Oklahoma, at Norman, Okla., are popularly
known as the *Sooners* doubtless because
Oklahoma is called the *Sooner State*.

University of Oregon
Webfeet [1] is the sobriquet given to the
athletic teams of the University of Oregon,
at Eugene, in 1921 because Oregon is
known as the *Webfoot State*.

[1] A letter from N. Thomas Stoddard, Manager of Athletics at the University of Oregon, Eugene, Ore., July
11, 1935.

University of Pittsburgh
The fifty-two story building housing all
the departments of the University of Pitts-

burgh except the School of Dentistry and the School of Medicine is known as the *Cathedral of Learning* [1] because it is a modern adaptation of a Gothic tower. The first floor of the *Cathedral* is occupied by sixteen classrooms, the decor of each expressing in material and design the nobility of a particular nation and its contribution to humanity. [2] The building is located on a campus in the center of Pittsburgh, Pa.

The athletic teams of the University of Pittsburgh, Pennsylvania, were nicknamed *Panthers* [3] about 1914 by local sports writers because there are stone panthers "guarding each end of Panther Bridge near the campus." [2]

[1] *The Source Book* (Source Research Council, Inc., Chicago, 1936) vol. 5, p. 2268.
[2] *The Key Reporter*, the Phi Beta Kappa News Magazene, vol. XVIII, no. 3, May 1953.
[3] A communication from W. D. Harrison, Director of Athletics at the University of Pittsburgh, Pittsburgh, Pa., June 12, 1935.

University of Portland

Cliff-dwellers, the *Irish*, and the *Pilots* are nicknames attributed to the athletic teams of the University of Portland, in Oregon, known until February 15, 1935, as Columbia University. [1] *Cliff-dwellers*, [1] applied to its athletic teams, was "originated by a student publicity man in 1924 or 1925. The name seemed appropriate because the University is on a cliff overlooking the Willamette River." The athletic teams are frequently called the *Irish* most likely because "the University of Portland is conducted by the Congregation of the Holy Cross, who also conduct the University of Notre Dame at Notre Dame, Ind. The *Pilots* is the most widely used appellation for the teams, but the college officials did not state when or why it was selected.

[1] A letter from E. J. Fitzpatrick, Registrar of the University of Portland, Portland, Ore., November 21, 1935.

University of Redlands

The *Bulldogs* [1] is the appellation given to the athletic teams of the University of Redlands, at Redlands, Calif., in 1914 or 1915 by the sports writers because of the teams' tenacity and determination in athletic contests.

[1] A communication from Ashel Cunningham, Director of Athletics at the University of Redlands, Redlands, Calif., June 21, 1935.

University of Richmond

The athletic teams of Richmond University, at Richmond, Va., are popularly designated *Spiders*. [1] This sobriquet had its origin as follows: "Between thirty and forty years ago Mr. Evan R. Chesterman, an alumnus of Richmond College, was a reporter on the old Richmond *Dispatch*, and in addition to his regular work of reporting wrote special articles signed, 'The Idle Reporter.' In one of his articles Mr. Chesterman dubbed the Richmond College baseball team 'Spiders,' for the reason, as he suggested, that the players with their long arms and legs reminded him of spiders. The name struck popular fancy and stuck to the team, and since that time not only" [1] the members of the baseball teams, but the constituents of the other athletic teams as well have been designated the *Spiders*. The students of this University have universally accepted this nickname.

[1] A letter from F. W. Boatwright, President of the University of Richmond, Richmond, Va., January 2, 1936.

University of San Francisco

The *Dons* [1] is the nickname of the athletic teams of the University of San Francisco, in California. This sobriquet was selected in 1931 in a contest. The nickname was suggested by John Rhode, at that time a freshman at the college. As San Francisco was founded by the Spanish Dons, the adoption of this name by San Francisco's own University expressed the determination and fighting spirit of these early settlers as well as the glamor and romance of the city and its background." [1]

[1] A communication from John T. Forde, University of San Francisco, San Francisco, Calif., July 31, 1935.

University of Santa Clara

The athletic teams of the University of Santa Clara, at Santa Clara, Calif., are known as the *Broncos*.

University of South Carolina

Game Cocks [1] is the nickname which was given to the athletic teams of the University of South Carolina, at Columbia, S.C., about 1902 by sports writers because of the courageous playing done by the men on these teams despite the fact that they were very light in weight.

[1] A letter from R. K. Foster, Director of Student Activities at the University of South Carolina, Columbia, S.C., June 17, 1935.

University of South Dakota

The athletic teams of the University of South Dakota, at Vermillion, are popularly

University of South Dakota—Cont.

called *Coyotes*[1] doubtless because the coyote is found on the plains of South Dakota.

[1] An unsigned communication from the University of South Dakota, Vermillion, S.D., November 14, 1935.

University of Southern California

The athletic teams of the University of Southern California, at Los Angeles, Calif., were nicknamed the *Trojans*[1] in 1916 because someone watching the team remarked that "they play like Trojans."[1]

[1] A communication from Willis O. Hunter, Director of Athletics at the University of Southern California, Los Angeles, Calif., June 20, 1935.

University of Tennessee

The *Volunteers*[1] is the nickname given to the athletes comprising the teams of the University of Tennessee, at Knoxville, because Tennessee is the *Volunteer State*.

[1] A communication from P. B. Parker, Director of Athletics at the University of Tennessee, Knoxville, Tenn., June 17, 1935.

University of Texas

The *University of Texas Longhorns* is the sobriquet given to the athletic teams of the University of Texas, at Austin, probably because the famous longhorn steer is native to Texas.

University of the South

The *Tigers*[1] is the appellation of the athletic teams of the University of the South, at Sewanee, Tenn. This sobriquet was given to members of these teams in 1891 by "Elwood Wilson and other Princeton men who"[1] initiated football at the University of the South and who patterned their teams after the Princeton squads.

[1] A communication from Gordon M. Clark, Graduate Manager of Athletics at the University of the South, Sewanee, Tenn., June 17, 1935.

University of Telephony. See New York City

University of Texas Longhorns. See University of Texas

University of Toledo

The athletic teams of the University of Toledo at Toledo, Ohio, were designated the *Rockets*[1] in 1924 or 1925 by Pittsburgh sports writers because of the rapid plays they made by means of forward passes in a game with Carnegie Institute of Technology, at Pittsburgh, Pa., in 1924.

[1] A communication from David Connelly, Director of Athletics at the University of Toledo, Toledo, Ohio, June 28, 1935.

University of Tulsa

The athletic teams of the University of Tulsa, in Oklahoma, were nicknamed the *Golden Hurricanes*[1] in 1922 after they had defeated Texas Agricultural and Mechanical College by a score of 13-0. The sobriquet was probably originated by Howard Archer, then coach of the teams, and by some Dallas newspaper writers supposedly because of this defeat, and because the college colors are gold and black.

[1] A communication from W. E. Morris, Junior, Publicity Director of Athletics at the University of Tulsa, Tulsa, Okla., June 22, 1935.

University of Utah

Redskins[1] and *The Utes*[1] are the nicknames given to the athletic teams of the University of Utah, at Salt Lake City. *Redskins* originated because red sweaters are part of the uniform. *Utes* is an abbreviation of the state name.

[1] A communication from Theron Parmelle, General Manager of Student Activities at the University of Utah, Salt Lake City, Utah, June 28, 1935.

University of Vermont

The students playing on the teams of the University of Vermont, at Burlington, were nicknamed *Catamounts*,[1] in 1925 by the student senate. The members of the student body had selected the expression, probably because the catamount is a native of the hilly or mountainous sections of the state.

[1] A communication from Sabin C. Abell, Graduate Manager of Athletics at the University of Vermont, Burlington, Vt., June 18, 1935.

University of Virginia

Cavaliers[1] is the sobriquet attributed to the athletic teams of the University of Virginia, at Charlottesville, in 1923 in commemoration of the song entitled *Cavalier Song,* written by Lawrence Lee, Jr.

[1] A communication from F. Selden, Secretary to the General Athletic Association, University of Virginia, Charlottesville, Va., June 25, 1935.

University of Washington

Huskies,[1] *Purple Tornadoes,*[1] and *Sun Dodgers*[1] are sobriquets of the athletic teams of the University of Washington, at Seattle, Wash. The *Huskies* was given as a nickname to the teams in 1922 by Max Muller because this sobriquet "represented the rugged, loyal, fearless dog of the Northlands." [1] The University of Washington is the furthest north of any institution on the West Coast. *Purple Tornadoes* was apparently given to the teams because the college colors are purple and gold. Formerly the teams were designated *Sun Dodgers* in honor of the college monthly magazine [1] of that name.

[1] A communication from Roy G. Rosenthal, Director of Publicity at the University of Washington, Seattle, Wash., June 19, 1935.

University of Wichita

The athletic teams of the University of Wichita, at Wichita, Kans., are popularly designated the *Farmers* [1] and the *Wheatshockers*.[1] These sobriquets were adopted in 1901 because students of the University were accustomed to earn extra money during the summer months by following up the wheat harvest [1] and shocking wheat.

[1] A communication from Bliss Isely, University of Wichita, Wichita, Kans., June 12, 1935.

University of Wisconsin

The athletic teams of the University of Wisconsin, at Madison, are popularly called *Badgers* [1] because "early settlers in the southern part of the state discovered and worked lead deposits. The burrowing by pick and shovel into the ground earned for them the name of *Badgers* because of the burrowing habits of this animal."

[1] A communication from the University of Wisconsin, Madison, Wis., July 22, 1930.

University of Wyoming

Cowboys [1] is the nickname given to the athletic teams of the University of Wyoming, at Laramie, Wyo., about 1908 by the members of the Athletic Association of the University. Cattle ranching [1] was the chief industry of the state for many years.

[1] A letter from E. Deane Hunton, Dean of the Division of Athletics at the University of Wyoming, Laramie, Wyo., July 23, 1935.

Upper Iowa University

The sobriquet *Peacocks* [1] has been given to the athletic teams of Upper Iowa University, at Fayette, Iowa, because the college color is peacock blue; the peacock is the emblem [1] of the University; and, when the University was founded in 1857, the

site was near a farm "upon which peacocks were cultured." [1]

[1] A communication from Arthur E. Bennett, President of Upper Iowa University, Fayette, Iowa, November 14, 1935.

Unprecedented Strategist. See Grant, U. S.

Ursinus College

The athletic teams of Ursinus College, at Collegeville, Pa., were designated the *Bears* [1] in 1927 by President G. L. Omwake. Ursinus is Latin for "pertaining to a bear." [1]

[1] A communication from R. C. Johnson, Director of Athletics at Ursinus College, Collegeville, Pa., June 14, 1935.

Unquestionably Skilled. See Grant, U. S.

Unreconstructed Rebel. See Glass, G. C.

Upholder of the Constitution. See Webster, Daniel

Useless Grant. See Grant, U. S.

Utah

Utah is known as the *Bee Hive State*, the *Deseret State*, the *Land of the Mormons*, the *Land of the Saints*, the *Mormon State*, and the *Salt Lake State*.

The *Bee Hive State* commemorates Utah's coat of arms which depicts "a conical beehive, with a swarm of bees round it, emblematical of the industry of the people." [1]

Deseret State recalls the fact that the Mormons first called their settlement the State of Deseret, this being the official name of the colony from 1849 to 1850, at which time the Territory of Utah was organized. The word Deseret, meaning *the honeybee*, is taken from the *Book of Mormons*.

Utah is called the *Land of the Mormons* because a great percentage of the Mormons of the United States live there; the *Land of the Saints* because the Mormons called themselves Latter-Day Saints; and the *Mormon State*, because it was founded by the Mormons.

Salt Lake State refers to the fact that the Great Salt Lake is located in Utah.

[1] *Political Americanisms*, Charles Ledyard Norton (Longmans, Green and Company, New York and London, 1890) p. 64.

Utah Inhabitants

The people of Utah were formerly called *Polygamists* [1] from the fact that until recent years polygamy was permitted to be practiced throughout the state. The sobriquets *Mormons* and *Saints* are both applied to the people of Utah because the state was originally settled by members of the Church of Jesus Christ of Latter-Day Saints,[1] unofficially known as Mormons. People of Utah were also called *Polygamists* [2] because polygamy was once part of the Mormon Code.

[1] *More About Names*, Leopold Wagner (T. Fisher Unwin, London, 1893) p. 36.
[2] *Manual of Useful Information*, comp. under the direction of J. C. Thomas (The Werner Company, Chicago, 1893) p. 23.

Utah State Agricultural College

The athletic teams of Utah State Agricultural College, at Logan, Utah, are popularly known as the *Farmers*.[1]

[1] A communication from Elmer G. Peterson, President of Utah State Agricultural College, Logan, Utah, November 20, 1935.

Utes. See University of Utah

Uvalde, Texas

Uvalde possesses the two nicknames *City Beautiful* [1] and *Town of Many Opportunities* [2] because it is an attractive and prosperous community.

[1] *The Geography of Texas, Physical and Political*, Revised Edition, Frederic William Simonds (Ginn and Company, New York and Boston, 1914) p. 215.
[2] *Texas As It Is Today*, Alfred E. Menn (Gemmel's Book Store, Austin, Tex., 1925) p. 224.

Uvalde Jack. See Garner, J. N.

V

V for 5th and Victory. See Fifth Armored Division of World War II

Vacationist's Paradise. See Virginia Beach

Valentine State. See Arizona

Valentino, Rudolph (Rudolpho Guglielmi Valentino)

The *Screen's Greatest Lover* [1] was an appellation given to Rudolph Valentino because his great popularity as an actor was based on his ability to portray a lover in motion pictures.

Rudolph Valentino was born at Castellaneto, Italy, on May 6, 1895, and died in New York City, on August 23, 1926.

[1] *Twinkle, Twinkle, Movie Star*, Harry T. Brunbridge (E. P. Dutton and Company, Inc., New York, 1930) p. 71.

Valley Forge of Connecticut

While the American Revolution was in progress, Major General Israel Putnam and the several brigades of Continental soldiers under his command, encamped during the winter of 1778-79 at Redding, near Danbury in Fairfield County, Conn. This camp became known as the *Valley Forge of Connecticut* [1] because the soldiers stationed there, unpaid, were practically destitute of food and clothing, sheltered in crude, poorly-heated huts, and were discouraged by their countrymen's seeming lack of interest in them. These conditions also prevailed in the winter of 1777-78 at General George Washington's camp at Valley Forge in Chester County, Pa.

[1] *Life and Times of David Humphreys, Soldier-Statesman-Poet*, Frank Landon Humphreys (G. P. Putnam's Sons, New York and London, 1917) vol. 1, p. 121.

Valley of Humiliation

During the Civil War the Shenandoah Valley in the State of Virginia was called the *Valley of Humiliation* [1] by the soldiers belonging to the Union Army. The valley was the scene of a number of humiliating defeats for the Federal soldiers especially in the winter of 1861-62, at which time the brilliant Shenandoah Valley campaign of Stonewall Jackson disrupted General McClellan's campaign and brought momentary victory to the Confederates.

[1] *Lee and His Lieutenants; Comprising the Early Life, Public Services, and Campaigns of General Robert E. Lee and His Companions in Arms, with a Record of Their Campaigns and Heroic Deeds*, Edward A. Pollard (E. B. Treat and Company, New York, 1867) p. 472.

Valley of the Shadow of Death

In 1863 the Eleventh Regiment of Kansas Volunteers was forced to camp at Crane Creek, "thirty miles south of Springfield," Mo., during which time an epidemic of measles and other diseases caused so many of the soldiers to die that the encampment was called the *Valley of the Shadow of Death*.[1]

[1] *The Life of Preston B. Plumb*, William Elsey Connelley (Browne and Howell Company, Chicago, 1913) p. 134.

Valley of Wonders

The *Valley of Wonders* [1] is a nickname often applied to the Yellowstone National Park "in the northwestern part of Wyoming and extending into Idaho and Montana" [2] because of its many natural phenomena.

[1] *Seeing the Far West*, John T. Faris (J. B. Lippincott Company, Philadelphia, 1920) p. 176.
[2] *The Encyclopedia Americana* (Americana Corporation, New York and Chicago, 1927) vol. 29, p. 630.

Valli, Virginia

Virginia Valli, who was born at Chicago, Ill., in 1899, was called *The Outdoor Girl of the Films*.[1] She acted on outdoor sets, and was very fond of outdoor sports. She is the wife of movie and television actor Charles Farrell.

[1] *The Blue Book of the Screen*, Ruth Wing, Editor (The Blue Book of the Screen, Inc., Hollywood, Calif., 1923) p. 265.

Valparaiso University

The members of the athletic teams of Valparaiso University, Valparaiso, Ind., were designated *Uhlans* [1] by sports writers several years ago. The editors of the yearbook in 1933 officially adopted the name by calling that book the *Uhlan*.[1] This nickname, "perhaps, originated because the great majority of the students" are of German-American extraction and the teams "display the Uhlan fighting spirit." [1]

[1] A letter from O. C. Kreinheder, President of Valparaiso University, Valparaiso, Ind., November 15, 1935.

Van Alstine, Mrs. Martin J.

Mrs. Martin J. Van Alstine donated food, clothing, and other necessities of life to the early settlers in the Mohawk Valley, and she served bravely and unflinchingly as a mediator between the Indians and the white settlers. She also did much missionary work among the Indians, bringing many of them to accept the Christian religion. In commemoration of these activities, she was appropriately designated the *Patriot Mother of the Mohawk Valley*.[1]

Mrs. Van Alstine moved into the Mohawk Valley, in what is now the State of New York, about 1751. She was particularly busy during the winter of 1780, at which time the Indians in the neighborhood began to murder the people and to plunder the settlements in the Valley. She bravely defended her family and their property against these Indian attacks. Later she succeeded in getting her neighbors to withdraw from the settlement to an island nearby where she concealed them from the Indians. After the Indians had taken practically all of the food, stock, and furnishings from her home, Mrs. Van Alstine went with her son to the Indian encampment and succeeded in bringing back much of the stolen property by outwitting the Indian women left in charge.

[1] *Women on the American Frontier, a Valuable and Authentic History of the Heroism, Adventures, Privations, Captivities, Trials, and Noble Lives and Deaths of the "Pioneer Mothers of the Republic,"* William W. Fowler (S. S. Scranton and Company, Hartford, Conn., 1877) p. 114.

Van Buren, John

John Van Buren went to England in 1831 as secretary to his father, Martin Van Buren, who had been appointed Envoy Extraordinary and Minister Plenipotentiary to the Court of Saint James on August 1,[1] 1831. On July 25, 1832, Queen Victoria gave a court dinner to which John Van Buren was invited. When a list of the guests at this dinner was published in *The Courier*,[2] the British court journal, Van Buren's name appeared in the roster among the princes. The Whig publications in America, referring to this roster, derisively spoke of young Van Buren as *Prince John*,[3] and the nickname continued to be applied to him throughout the remaining part of his life.

He was born at Hudson, N.Y., on February 18, 1810, and died at sea, on October 13, 1866.

[1] *Encyclopedia of Biography of New York: A Life Record of Men and Women of the Past Whose Sterling Character and Energy and Industry Have Made them Preeminent in Their and Many Other States*, Charles Elliot Fitch (The American Historical Society, New York and Boston, 1916) vol. 1, p. 350.
[2] *An Epoch and a Man: Martin Van Buren and His Times*, Denis Tilden Lynch (Horace Liveright, New York, 1929) p. 421.
[3] *The National Cyclopaedia of American Biography* (James T. White and Company, New York, 1893) vol. 3, p. 386.

Van Buren, Martin

The eighth President of the United States (1837-1841) had the following nicknames: the *Enchanter*, the *Fox, Kinderhook Fox, King Martin the First, Little Magician, Little Van, Machiavellian Belshazzar, Matty, Mistletoe Politician, Petticoat Pet, Red Fox, Sage of Kinderhook, Sage of Lindenwald, Wizard of Kinderhook*, and the *Wizard of the Albany Regency*.

Van Buren's political opponents nicknamed him the *Enchanter* [1] in reference to his great personal and political influence

Van Buren, Martin—Continued

over Andrew Jackson during the latter's presidency. Their association was unique in view of their dissimilar backgrounds and temperament, Jackson being representative of the American frontier, possessing a fiery and forthright personality, and Van Buren being a scion of a New York patroon family and an adroit politician. It was Van Buren's shrewd and skillful handling of political affairs which gave him the nicknames *Fox* [2] and *Little Magician*.[3] *Kinderhook Fox* [3] and *Red Fox* [3] are variations on the theme referring to his home in Kinderhook, N.Y., and to his red hair.

In a famous campaign poster of 1832, Andrew Jackson was dubbed "King Andrew the First" by his opponents in an effort to discredit his alleged autocratic policies. Van Buren, who was Jackson's own choice to succeed him, and who was elected on the strength of Jackson's popularity, inevitably received the title *King Martin the First*.[3]

Little Van [4] refers to Van Buren's physical stature.

Van Buren was called a *Machiavellian Belshazzar* [1] by those hostile to him because of his opulent New York origins and his cleverness as a political strategist.

He was often called *Mat* [5] in his youth. During his campaign for the presidency in 1836, his Whig opponents displayed cartoons in which they labeled him *Matty* and represented him as a child receiving "pap from a spoon in the hand of" Andrew Jackson. In 1840, when he was candidate for reelection, the country was still suffering from the effects of the panic of 1837, and the Whigs promised a return to better times by comparing "Matty's policy, fifty cents a day and French Soup" with their policy, "two dollars a day and roast beef." [6]

Van Buren was a widower with no family and his popularity in Capitol social circles gave rise to the nicknames *Mistletoe Politician* [1] and *Petticoat Pet*.[1]

He was called the *Sage of Kinderhook*,[7] *Sage of Lindenwald*,[8] and *Wizard of Kinderhook* when he had retired from public life to Lindenwald, his estate in Kinderhook, N.Y.

The title, *Wizard of the Albany Regency*,[9] marks his leadership in that group. The Albany Regency was a junto of Democratic politicians meeting at Albany between 1820-50, controlling Democratic party patronage in the state and exerting great influence in national politics as well.

Martin Van Buren was born at Kinderhook, N.Y., on December 5, 1782, and died there on July 24, 1862.

[1] *Andrew Jackson, the Fighting President*, Helen Nicolay (The Century Company, New York, 1929) p. 283.
[2] *National Cyclopaedia of American Biography* (James T. White and Company, New York, 1896) vol. 6, p. 434.
[3] *U.S. "Snap Shots": An Independent, National, and Memorial Encyclopedia. . . ,* Oliver McKee (A. M. Thayer and Company, Boston, 1892) p. 309.
[4] *The Godlike Daniel*, Samuel Hopkins Adams (Sears Publishing Company, Inc., New York, 1930) p. 215.
[5] *An Epoch and a Man: Martin Van Buren and His Times*, Denis Tilden Lynch (Horace Liveright, New York, 1929) p. 28, 36.
"History of the Life, Administration, and Times of Martin Van Buren, Eighth President of the United States; Seven Years' Seminole War, and Period of Great Financial Convulsions" by John Robert Irelan in *The Republic, or, a History of the United States in the Administrations from the Monarchic Colonial Days to the Present Times*, John Robert Irelan (Fairbanks and Palmer Publishing Company, Chicago, 1887) p. 190, 610.
[6] "Martin Van Buren" by Edward M. Shepard in *American Statesmen*, ed. by John T. Morse, Jr. (Houghton Mifflin and Company, Boston and New York, 1900) p. 388.
[7] *Heroes of the Nation: Embracing the Lives and Distinguished Achievements of, Book I, The Great Founders of the Republic, Book II, The Noble Builders of Our Union, Book III, The Great Generals of the Civil War, North and South, Book IV, The Heroes of the American Navy, from 1776 to 1898, Book V, Our Great Presidents and Statesmen, Washington to McKinley, Book VI, Our Giants of Inventive Achievement, from Fulton to Edison, Book VII, Our Successful Men of Business, from Astor to Wanamaker, Book VIII, The Political Leaders of the Present Day, Book IX, Heroes of the Spanish-American War*, William Wilfred Birdsall, William Garnett, W. Fletcher Johnson and others, with an introduction by Edward Everett Hale (Neither the name of the publishers, the place, nor the date of publication is given) P. 425.
[8] *Encyclopedia of Biography of New York: A Life Record of Men and Women of the Past Whose Sterling Character and Energy and Industry Have Made Them Preeminent In Their and Many Other States*, Charles Elliott Fitch (The American Historical Society, New York and Boston, 1916) vol. 1, p. 350.
[9] *The Eagle's History of Poughkeepsie, from the Earliest Settlements, 1683 to 1905*, Edmund Platt (Platt and Platt, Poughkeepsie, N.Y., 1905) p. 103.

Vance, Arthur Charles

It is said that the nickname, *Dazzy*,[1] was applied to Arthur Charles Vance because in mocking a boy calling his cow named *Daisy*, Vance could not say Daisy, but instead, said *Dazzy*.

During the height of his pitching career this nickname often became *Dazzler* because of the sheer speed of his delivery.[2]

Arthur Charles Vance was born at Orient, Iowa, on March 4, 1893, and pitched in major league baseball.

[1] *Who's Who in Major League Base Ball*, comp. by Harold (Speed) Johnson (Buxton Publishing Company, Chicago, 1933) p. 390.
[2] *Baseball Personalities*, by Jimmy Powers (Rudolph Field, New York, 1949) p. 131-38.

Van Cortlandt, Philip

In 1779 Philip Van Cortlandt participated in a campaign against the Indians in the western part of New York. He displayed an almost uncanny knowledge of woodcraft, was dexterous and deadly in his use of firearms, subtle, cunning and resourceful in his transactions with the aborgines, and in the only actual engagement with the Indians, Van Cortlandt led his regiment to a decisive victory. These qualities caused the Indians respectfully to refer to him as the *Great White Devil.*[1]

Philip Van Cortlandt was born at Cortlandt Manor, in Westchester County, N.Y., on September 1, 1749, and died there on November 5, 1831.

[1] *The National Cyclopaedia of American Biography* (James T. White and Company, New York, 1907) vol. 5, p. 533.

Vandals. See University of Idaho

Vanderbilt, Gloria

Gloria Vanderbilt was nicknamed the *Poor Little Rich Girl*[1] by newspapermen during her childhood because, although she was the heir to four million dollars from her father's estate, she had no home life with her mother, Mrs. Reginald C. Vanderbilt, and was finally placed by the courts in the custody of her aunt, Mrs. Harry Payne Whitney.

Gloria Vanderbilt was born in New York City on February 29, 1924. At the time of her first marriage (to Pasquale De Cicco, Jr.) in 1941, she received from her estate about twelve hundred dollars each month.

[1] *Times-Herald*, Washington, D.C., January 19, 1942, col. 2, p. 1.

Vanderbilt University

The athletic teams of Vanderbilt University, at Nashville, Tenn., are popularly known as the *Commodores*[1] in honor of Commodore Cornelius Vanderbilt.

[1] A letter from M. B. Wolfe, Secretary to Dan E. McGugin, Director of Athletics at Vanderbilt University, Nashville, Tenn., June 18, 1935.

Van Dyke, Walter

Walter Van Dyke was called the *Father of the Union Party of California.*[1] He was the chairman of the Union party's first convention, which met at Sacramento, California, in June, 1862. The purpose of this party was to promote loyalty to the Union and to discourage any tendency that favored disloyalty and eventual secession of the state during the Civil War.

He was born at Tyre, N.Y., on October 3, 1823, and died at Los Angeles, Calif., in 1905.

[1] *Los Angeles and Vicinity: Historical and Biographical Record of Los Angeles and Vicinity, Containing a History of the City from Its Earliest Settlement as a Spanish Pueblo to the Closing Year of the Nineteenth Century, Also Containing Biographies of Well-known Citizens of the Past and Present*, James M. Guinn (Champam Publishing Company, Chicago, 1901) p. 628.

Van Santvoord, Alfred

During his life-long association with facilities for water transportation, Alfred Van Santvoord attained an outstanding position in the steamship industry, in which respect he was comparable to a commodore, who is the senior captain of a line of merchant vessels; consequently, he was called *Commodore Van Santvoord.*[1]

Alfred Van Santvoord was born at Utica, N.Y., on January 23, 1819, and died in the harbor of New York City, on July 20, 1901.

[1] *The National Cyclopaedia of American Biography* (James T. White and Company, New York, 1932) vol. 22, p. 221.

Van Vechten, Abraham

Having been admitted to the New York Bar in October, 1785, Abraham Van Vechten was the first attorney granted the right to practice law after the State Constitution of New York had been adopted. Because of this fact, and because during his lifetime he was one of the most distinguished jurists in New York State, Abraham Van Vechten has been designated the *Father of the Bar of the State of New York.*[1]

Abraham Van Vechten was born at Catskill, N.Y., on December 5, 1762, and died at Albany, N.Y., on January 6, 1837.

[1] *The National Cyclopaedia of American Biography* (James T. White and Company, New York, 1907) vol. 9, p. 163.

Van Zant, James E.

James E. Van Zant was nicknamed the *Father of the Bonus*[1] by his colleagues in the National House of Representatives because he took an active part in securing bonus legislation and because he was three times Commander of the Veterans of Foreign Wars.

He was a Republican representative from the Twenty-third Congressional District of Pennsylvania to the United States Congress from 1939 to 1949.

Van Zant, J. E.—Continued

James E. Van Zant was born at Altoona, Pa., on December 18, 1898.

[1] An interview with Captain Victor Hunt Harding, Secretary of the National Democratic Congress Re-election Committee, Washington, D.C., April 10, 1939.

Vaughan, Floyd E.

Floyd E. Vaughan, who was born at Clifty, Ark., on March 9, 1912, and who played infield in major league baseball, was nicknamed *Arkie* [1] because he was born in Arkansas.

[1] *Who's Who in Major League Base Ball*, comp. by Harold (Speed) Johnson (Buxton Publishing Company, Chicago, 1933) p. 391.

Veep. See Barkley, A. W.

Vermont

De Vere says that "Vermont is generally, by simple translation of [Verd Mont] the original name given by the French settlers, called the *Green Mountain State*, the principal ridge of mountains within its boundaries being known by that name." [1]

[1] *Americanisms: The English of the New World*, M. Schele De Vere (Charles Scribner and Company, New York, 1872) p. 662.

Vermonters

Vermonters are called *Green Mountain Boys* because many of its inhabitants live among the Green Mountains.[1]

[1] *U.S.: An Index to the United States of America*, comp. by Malcolm Townsend (D. Lothrop Company, Boston, 1890) p. 81.

Vesey, Denmark

Because he sacrificed his life in an effort to free his people from slavery, Denmark Vesey was called the *Black John Brown*.[1]

On October 16, 1859, with only a few followers, John Brown made a futile attempt to seize the government arsenal near Harper's Ferry, in what is now West Virginia, in order that he and his followers might arm a group of runaway slaves for revolt. However, the plan failed and John Brown was executed for treason against the United States Government. Like this white man, but with a large number of Negroes, Denmark Vesey formed a conspiracy to seize the arsenal near Charleston, S.C., and then to attack the city in order to free the slaves. Vesey was betrayed by one of the conspirators and hanged.

Denmark Vesey was a slave until he purchased his freedom at Charleston, S.C., in 1800, when he was about thirty-four years of age.

[1] *Men of Mark: Eminent, Progressive and Rising*, William J. Simmons (The Rewell Publishing Company, Baltimore, Md., and Cleveland, Ohio, 1891) p. 231-2.
  The Colored Patriots of the American Revolution, with Sketches of Several Distinguished Colored Persons: to Which Is Added a Brief Survey of the Tradition and Prospects of Colored Americans, William C. Nell, with an introduction by Harriet Beecher Stowe (Published by Robert F. Wallcut, Boston, 1855) p. 253-5.

Veto Governor. See Cleveland, Grover; Winston, J. A.

Veto Mayor. See Cleveland, Grover

Veto President. See Johnson, Andrew

Vic. See Sorrell, V. G.

Vicksburg, Mississippi

Vicksburg is called *Gibraltar of America, Gibraltar of Louisiana, Gibraltar of the South*, and the *Key City*.

All these nicknames are in allusion to its location [1] on a high bank at the junction of the Mississippi and the Yazoo Rivers. The nickname, *Gibraltar of Louisiana*,[3] had its origin while Mississippi was still a part of the province of Louisiana, in reference to a fort that the Spanish built north of the site of the present city of Vicksburg. Its commanding position made it an important military base during the Civil War,[2] and its land and water facilities serve western Mississippi and the surrounding country.[4]

[1] *History of Mississippi, the Heart of the South*, Dunbar Rowland (The S. J. Clarke Publishing Company, Chicago and Jackson, Miss., 1925) vol. 2, p. 847.
[2] *With Grant at Fort Donelson, Shiloh, and Vicksburg, and an Appreciation of General U. S. Grant*, Wilbur F. Crummer (E. C. Crummer and Company, Oak Park, Ill., 1915) p. 92.
[3] *In and About Vicksburg: An Illustrated Guide Book to the City of Vicksburg, Mississippi: Its History: Its Appearance: Its Business, to Which is Added a Description of the Resources and Progress of the State of Mississippi, as an Inviting Field for Immigration and Capital*, Lee Richardson, Junior, and Thomas D. Godman (The Gibraltar Publishing Company, Vicksburg, Miss., 1890) p. 24, 48.
  Vicksburg, Mississippi, and the Yazoo Delta: Picturesque Vicksburg: A Description of the Resources and Prospects of That City and the Famous Yazoo Delta, Its Agricultural and Commercial Interests, to Which is Attached a Series of Sketches of Representative Industries, H. P. Chapman and J. F. Battaile (Vicksburg Printing and Publishing Company, Vicksburg, Miss., 1895) p. 10.
[4] *Manual of Useful Information*, comp. under the direction of J. C. Thomas (The Werner Company, Chicago, 1893) p. 23.

Victor. See Edison, T. A.

Victory and OK Division. See Ninety-fifth Infantry Division of World War II

Victory Division. See Twenty-fourth Infantry Division of World War II

Vikings. See Lawrence College; Saint Olaf College

Villanova College

Main-liners,[1] *Villanovanes,*[1] and *Wildcats*[1] are popular sobriquets by which the athletic teams of Villanova College, at Villanova, Pa., are frequently designated. In 1936 the senior class at Villanova College conducted a contest to select a suitable sobriquet for the athletic teams. *Wildcats* became the official nickname.

[1] A letter from Paetrus F. Banmiller, Registrar at Villanova College, Villanova, Pa., November 22, 1935.

Vinegar Joe. See Stilwell, J. W.

Violets. See New York University

Virginia

Virginia is nicknamed the *Ancient Dominion,* or the *Old Dominion,* the *Cavalier State, Down Where the South Begins,* the *Mother of Presidents,* the *Mother of States,* the *Mother of Statesmen.*

The nicknames, the *Ancient Dominion* and *The Old Dominion,* are still widely applied to Virginia, having originated in the days of the Colony of Virginia. About the year 1663, after Charles Stuart had become King of England, he quartered the Arms of Virginia on his royal shield; thus ranking Virginia along with his other four dominions, England, Scotland, France, and Ireland. Historians say that the new king elevated Virginia to the position of a dominion "by quartering its arms (the old seal of the Virginia Company) on his royal shield with the arms of England, Scotland, and Ireland, (and that) the burgesses were very proud of this distinction and, remembering that they were the oldest as well as the most faithful of the Stuart settlements in America, adopted the name of 'The Old Dominion.' "[1] Colonel Richard Lee, of the Colony of Virginia, is said to have visited Charles Stuart while he was in exile in Brussels, Belgium, about 1658. Charles was proclaimed King Charles II of England on May 8, 1660, and the Virginians accepted him as

their king on September the 20th following his ascension.[2] This pleased King Charles so much that he referred to the people of this colony as "the best of his distant children,"[1] and elevated the Colony of Virginia to the position of a dominion.

Fiske says that "after the restoration of Charles II, a new seal for Virginia, adopted about 1663, has the same motto (*En dat Virginia Quintam*) the effect of which was to rank Virginia by the side of his Majesty's other four dominions, England, Scotland, 'France,' and Ireland. We are told by the younger Richard Henry Lee that in these circumstances originated the famous epithet 'Old Dominion.' "[2]

Virginia's nickname, the *Cavalier State,* is derived from the Cavaliers who came over and settled there during, and shortly after the time of Charles I.

Her sobriquet, the *Mother of Presidents,* alludes to the fact that so many of the early presidents of the United States were native Virginians.

Virginia was called the *Mother of States* because she was the first of the states to be settled,[3] and because the original territory of Virginia was split up to make West Virginia, Ohio, Kentucky, Illinois, Indiana, Wisconsin and a part of Minnesota. Because she has produced such a great number of statesmen, she is called *The Mother of Statesmen.*

[1] *An American History,* David Saville Muzzey (Ginn and Company, New York, 1929) p. 32-3.
[2] *Old Virginia and Her Neighbors,* John Fiske (Houghton, Mifflin and Company, Boston and New York, 1897) vol. 2, p. 20-1, 22-3.
[3] *The New International Encyclopaedia,* Second Edition (Dodd, Mead and Company, New York, 1930) vol. 21, p. 464.

Virginia Beach

Virginia Beach, a middle Atlantic seaside resort located on the Atlantic Ocean in Princess Anne County, Va., is frequently designated the *Vacationist's Paradise*[1] because its miles of sandy beach make it attractive and desirable for bathing; because it has scenic beauty, numerous hotels and cottages, and because thousands of tourists and vacationists visit it each year.

[1] *Diamond Chatterbox* (Published by the Diamond Cab Company, Washington, D.C., August 7 until August 13, 1938) p. 20.

Virginia Dynasty

The United States Government was at one time described as the *Virginia Dynasty*[1] because from 1801 to 1825 the office of the

Virginia Dynasty—Continued
President of the United States was continuously filled by Virginians: Thomas Jefferson, James Madison, and James Monroe.

[1] *My Quarter Century of American Politics*, Champ Clark (Harper and Brothers, New York and London, 1920) vol. 2, p. 246.

Virginia Judge. See Kelly, W. C.

Virginia Military Institute
Flying Cadets [1] and *Flying Squadrons* [1] are nicknames given to the athletic teams of the Virginia Military Institute, at Lexington, Va., in 1920. In that year they played without a defeat and "displayed so much speed and scoring power both on long runs and forward passes that Eastern sports writers gave them the sobriquets.

During the Civil War Virginia Military Institute was nicknamed the *West Point of the Confederacy* [2] or the *West Point of the South*,[2] because it furnished several outstanding officers for the Confederate Army and a number of leaders of the Southern Confederacy. Its cadets were often employed to drill newly recruited troops in the military tactics of warfare, and many of the cadets were from the most prominent and distinguished families of the South. In these respects it was comparable to the United States Military Academy, at West Point, N.Y., which in a similar manner contributed its men to the services of the Union Army, and which trains officers for the Army of the United States today.

[1] A letter from B. B. Clarkson, Director of Athletics at Virginia Military Institute, Lexington, Va., June 18, 1935.
[2] *The Military History of the Virginia Military Institute from 1839 to 1865, with Appendix, Maps and Illustrations*, Jennings C. Wise (J. P. Bell Company, Lynchburg, Va., 1915) p. 396, 576.

Virginia, Minnesota
Virginia is nicknamed the *Queen City of the Iron Range* [1] because, located in the great mining center of the Mesabi iron range in St. Louis County, it was formerly heavily wooded and possessed much wealth and natural beauty.

[1] *My Minnesota*, Antoinette E. Ford (Lyons and Carnahan, New York and Chicago, 1929) p. 252.

Virginia Polytechnic Institute
The athletic teams of Virginia Polytechnic Institute, at Blacksburg, Va., were nicknamed the *Gobblers* [1] in 1909 by a former athletic coach. There was a secret organization at the college at that time called the *Gobblers*.

[1] A letter from Mel Jeffries, Department of Publicity, Virginia Polytechnic Institute, Blacksburg, Va., June 15, 1935.

Virginia Rebel. See Bacon, Nathaniel

Virginia State College for Negroes
The *Trojans* [1] is the sobriquet attributed to the athletic teams of Virginia State College for Negroes, at Petersburg, Va. Lawrence Milburn Johnson originated this appellation in 1932. He applied it to the members of the teams "because of the pluck, endurance and determination displayed" by them in athletic contests.

[1] A letter from W. A. Rogers, Secretary of Virginia State College for Negroes, Petersburg, Va., November 20, 1935.

Virginia Union University
Panthers is the nickname given to the athletic teams of the Virginia Union University, at Richmond, Va.

Virginians
Virginians are nicknamed *Beagles* or *Beadles, Cavaliers, FFV's, Sorebacks*, and *Tuckahoes*. The sobriquet *Beadles* or *Beagles* originated during the colonial days when Virginians, following English custom, used beadles in their courts.[1] *Cavaliers* alludes to Virginia's English Cavalier settlers, and *FFV's* stands for the *First Families of Virginia*, a designation of which the people of the state have been and are very proud. "The abbreviation was of northern origin, and was in common use prior to the Civil War." [2]

Tradition gives two accounts of the origin of the nickname, *Sorebacks*. One is that the Virginians are so hospitable that they slap one another on the backs until their backs become sore; the other is that the people in the southern part of the state raise so much cotton that it makes their backs sore to pick it. North Carolinians seem to be the originators of this account. *Tuckahoes* was originally applied only to the poorer white people living in the lower part of the state. This nickname was often heard during the Civil War because poverty often drove the Virginians to eat tuckahoe,[1] i.e., any bulbous root used as food.

[1] *A New Dictionary of Americanisms*, Sylva Clapin (Louis Weiss and Company, New York, 1903) p. 43, 409.
[2] *Political Americanisms*, Charles Ledyard Norton (Longmans, Green and Company, New York and London, 1890) p. 43.

Voice of Silver. See Pittman, Key

Voice of the Radio. See Stefan, Karl

Voice of the Revolution. See Henry, Patrick

Voltiguers

During the battles which took place at the City of Mexico from August 20 to September 14, 1847, the nickname *Voltiguers*[1] was given to members of the special skirmishing group accompanying the American Tenth Infantry, who mounted the walls of the city by means of ladders. The sobriquet is transferred from the French use of the word. A voltiguer was "formerly in the French army, a member of a special skirmishing company attached to each regiment of infantry."[2]

[1] *Our First War in Mexico*, Farnham Bishop (Charles Scribner's Sons, New York, 1916) p. 194.
[2] *A New English Dictionary*, James A. H. Murray (The Clarendon Press, Oxford, England) vol. 10, p. 298.

Volunteer State. See Tennessee

Volunteers. See University of Tennessee

Voorhees, Daniel Wolsey

The *Tall Sycamore of the Wabash*[1] was a very fitting sobriquet attributed to Daniel Wolsey Voorhees because he was six feet and one inch tall and, although born in Ohio, he was moved to Indiana while he was an infant and lived there during the remainder of his life. The Wabash River is in Indiana.

He was a Representative from Indiana to the United States Congress from 1861 to 1866, and again from 1869 to 1873. He was also a Senator from this state to the United States Congress from 1877 until a few months prior to his death in 1897.

Daniel Wolsey Voorhees was born at Liberty, Ohio, on September 26, 1827, and died at Washington, D.C., on April 10, 1897.

[1] *The Cyclopaedia of American Biography, New Enlarged Edition of Appleton's Cyclopaedia of American Biography*, originally ed. by General James Grant Wilson and John Fiske, *Revision to 1914* completed under editorial supervision of Honorable Charles Dick, former United States Senator and James E. Homans, Author and Editor (The Press Association Compilers, Inc., New York, 1915) vol. 6, 155.

W

Wabash College

The athletic teams of Wabash College, at Crawfordsville, Ind., were designated the *Little Giants*[1] in 1904 by the writers[1] of the Indianapolis *News* because, though the athletes of Wabash College were much lighter[1] weight than their opponents, they were exceptionally strong in playing ability[1] and in scoring.

[1] *Wabash College The First Hundred Years, 1832-1932*, James Insley Osborne and Theodore Gregory Gronert (R. E. Banta, Crawfordsville, Ind., 1932) p. 256-7.

Waco, Texas

Waco is known as the *Athens of Texas* and the *Queen of the Brazos*. It is called the *Athens of Texas*[1] in allusion to the many public and private institutions[1] of learning located there. It is frequently called *Queen of the Brazos*[2] because it is located on the Brazos River, one of the most fertile parts of the state.

[1] *The Geography of Texas, Physical and Political*, Revised Edition, Frederic William Simonds (Ginn and Company, New York and Boston, 1914) p. 191.
The Encyclopedia Americana (Americana Corporation, New York and Chicago, 1932) vol. 28, p. 204.
[2] *Flashlights on Texas*, Lillie Terrell Shaver and Willie Williamson Rogers (A. C. Baldwin and Sons, Austin, Tex., 1928) p. 91.

Waddel, James

James Waddel, though handicapped by blindness, was considered the most eloquent pulpit orator in Virginia during his lifetime, and was known as the *Blind Preacher*.[2]

James Waddel was born at Newry, Ireland, in July, 1730, and died in Orange County, Va., on September 17, 1805.

[1] *In the Picturesque Shenandoah Valley*, Armistead C. Gordon, with an introduction by Philip Alexander Bruce (Garret and Massie, Inc., Richmond, Va., 1930) p. 139.
The National Cyclopaedia of American Biography (James T. White and Company, New York, 1899) vol. 2, p. 259.

Waddell, George Edward

George Edward Waddell was of a gangling build, well over six feet, with long arms, and his rustic appearance as he strode to the pitchers' mound caused baseball fans to hail him vociferously with "*Hey, Rube,*"[1] a salutation he always acknowledged with a polite bow.

Rube Waddell was noted for his strikeout achievements during the more than 200 victories of his major league career,[2] He was born at Bradford, Pa., on October 13, 1876, and died at San Antonio, Tex., a victim of tuberculosis, on April 1, 1914.

[1] *Who's Who in Major League Base Ball*, comp. by Harold (Speed) Johnson (Buxton Publishing Company, Chicago, 1933) p. 476.
[2] *My 66 years in the Big Leagues*, by Connie Mack (The John C. Winston Company, Philadelphia, 1950) p. 92-6, 131.

Wade, Benjamin Franklin

Bluff Ben Wade and *Old Ben Wade* are nicknames of Benjamin Franklin Wade, Senator from Ohio (1851-69) and leader of an antislavery group in the Senate.

Bluff Ben Wade[1] alluded to his brusqueness, energy, and fearlessness.

Later he was known as *Old Ben Wade*,[2] because of his long years of honest and sincere participation in the political activities of the country.

Benjamin Franklin Wade was born at Feeding Hills, near West Springfield, Mass., on October 27, 1800, and died at Jefferson, Ohio, on March 2, 1878.

[1] *The Age of Hate, Andrew Johnson and the Radicals*, George Fort Milton (Coward-McCann, Inc., New York, 1930) p. 26.
[2] *The National Cyclopaedia of American Biography* (James T. White and Company, New York, 1899) vol. 2, p. 95.

Wagner, John Henry

John Henry Wagner was nicknamed the *Flying Dutchman* and *Honus* or *Hans* by his colleagues in baseball who recognized him as the best shortstop in the game and a deadly hitter at the plate.

Wagner's remarkable and varied skills as outfielder, shortstop, catcher, third baseman, and hitter made him a formidable opponent, and he hurled his ungainly figure around the ball field so energetically and to such good purpose that he seemed literally to be a *Flying Dutchman*.[1] *Honus*[2] and *Hans*[2] are also nicknames derived from Wagner's German ancestry, being abbreviated forms of *Johann* or John.

Honus Wagner was born John Henry Wagner on February 24, 1874, at Mansfield, Pa.

[1] *The Story of Baseball*, by John Durant (Hastings House, New York, 1947) p. 48.
[2] *Who's Who in Major League Base Ball*, comp. by Harold (Speed) Johnson (Buxton Publishing Company, Chicago, 1933) p. 458.

Wagner Memorial Lutheran College

The athletic teams of Wagner Memorial Lutheran College, at Staten Island, N.Y., were designated the *Green Waves*[1] by the student body[1] in 1928 because the college color is green.

[1] A communication from Frederic Sutter, Acting President of Wagner Memorial Lutheran College, Staten Island, N.Y., November 21, 1935.

Wagon Boy. See Corwin, Thomas

Wah-ze-o-man-nee. See Sibley, H. H.

Wait-a-bit Treaties

The *Wait-a-bit Treaties*[1] was a term applied to the peace treaties made between the United States and thirty other nations while William Jennings Bryan was Seretary of State from 1913 to 1915 during Woodrow Wilson's administration. Each of the signatory countries agreed to wait a year before declaring war upon any of the others. The object of the wait was to provide enough time for the peaceful settling of any misunderstanding or controversy that might arise among them.

[1] *Mace-Bogardus History of the United States*, William H. Mace and Frank S. Bogardus (Rand McNally and Company, New York and San Francisco, 1933) p. 549, 589.

Waite, David Hanson

While he was Governor of Colorado from 1893 to 1894, David Hanson Waite made a speech on the dispute then raging between the miners and mine owners of the Colorado Fuel and Iron Company, in which he used the phrase: "I am prepared to ride in blood up to my bridles!" Henceforth he was called *Bloody Bridles Waite*.[1]

David Hanson Waite was born at Jamestown, N.Y., on April 9, 1825, and died at Aspen, Colo., on November 28, 1901.

[1] *Twenty Years of the Republic, 1885-1905*, Harry Thurston Peck (Dodd, Mead and Company, New York, 1907) p. 452.

Wake Forest College

The athletic teams of Wake Forest College, at Wake Forest, N.C., are popularly called *Deacons* and *Demon Deacons* supposedly from the fact that it is a Baptist college.

Walberg, George

Rube[1] was the nickname applied to George Walberg by his baseball associates because, when he first entered professional baseball, he was a tall, overgrown lad. He was born at Seattle, Wash., on July 27, 1900, and pitched in major league baseball.

[1] *Who's Who in Major League Base Ball*, comp. by Harold (Speed) Johnson (Buxton Publishing Company, Chicago, 1933) p. 394.

Waldo, Hiram H.

The appellation, *Father of Baseball in the West*,[1] was attributed to Hiram H. Waldo because he was a pioneer in organizing and developing baseball in the middlewestern part of the United States, and was the leader of one of the first baseball clubs organized in the Middlewest: the Forest City Baseball Club of Rockford, Ill.

Hiram H. Waldo made his home at Rockford, Ill., for approximately sixty years, and died there on April 26, 1912.

[1] *Baseball and Baseball Players, a History of the National Game of America and Important Events Connected Therewith From Its Origin Down to the Present Time*, Elwood A. Roff (E. A. Roff, Chicago, 1912) p. 251.

Walk-on-the-Water. See Fire Canoes

Walker, Charles Thomas

In 1894 the newspapers of New York City designated the Negro clergyman, Charles Thomas Walker, the *Black Spurgeon of America*[1] because of his outstanding success as a preacher in the Negro Baptist Church, his leadership in this church, and his honest and faithful execution of his duties. This sobriquet was an allusion to Charles Haddon Spurgeon, a prominent English Baptist preacher, who lived from 1834 until 1892.

Charles Thomas Walker was born at Hepzibah, Va., on January 11, 1858.

[1] *The National Cyclopaedia of American Biography* (James T. White and Company, New York, 1906) vol. 13, p. 36.

Walker, Fred

Fred Walker, who was born on a Georgia plantation on September 24, 1910,

and who played outfield in major league baseball, is called *Dixie*.[1]

[1] *Who's Who in Major League Base Ball*, comp. by Harold (Speed) Johnson (Buxton Publishing Company, Chicago, 1933) p. 395.

Walker, Gilbert Carlton

While he was Governor of Virginia from 1869 to 1874, Gilbert Carlton Walker became nicknamed the *Political Savior of Virginia*[1] because he sternly enforced law and order throughout the state, and served ably and efficiently in promoting the general welfare of the people of Virginia during the trying years of the period of Reconstruction.

Gilbert Carlton Walker was born at Binghamton, N.Y., on August 1, 1833, and died at New York City, on May 11, 1885.

[1] *The National Cyclopaedia of American Biography* (James T. White and Company, New York, 1907) vol. 5, p. 454.

Walker, James J.

Father of the New York State Boxing Bill, the *Playboy of New York*, and the *Wisecracker* are nicknames which have been applied to James J. Walker.

About 1918, Walker introduced a boxing bill in the New York State Legislature and strongly fought for its passage, hence he was called the *Father of the New York State Boxing Bill*.[1]

The *Playboy of New York*, refers to the easy-going and congenial life that he led in New York City, especially as its mayor. The *Wisecracker* refers to Walker's talent for repartee, the newspapermen with whom he quipped having named him thus.

James J. Walker, who was born in Greenwich Village, New York City, on May 1, 1881, was formerly the Mayor of New York City.

[1] *The Ring, the World's Foremost Boxing Magazine* February, 1922, to January, 1923 (The Sportsmen's Publishing Company, New York, 1922) March 15, 1922, p. 6.

Walker, William

William Walker, filibuster and adventurer of the early nineteenth century, was nicknamed the *Grey-eyed Man of Destiny, Honey*, and *Missy*.

The singular sobriquet, *Grey-eyed Man of Destiny*,[1] originated in the following manner. In June, 1855, having taken advantage of the insurrections in Nicaragua, William Walker went to that country with a small expedition of his own, captured

Walker, William—Continued

Granada, established himself Generalissimo, and in 1856, in absolute control of Nicaragua, had himself proclaimed its President. Later Walker set up a printing press there and issued a weekly paper called *El Nicaraguense.* In one edition of this paper there appeared an article recalling a legend that for many years the native Indians had believed that fate would send them a "greyeyed man" from a northern country to deliver them from oppressive Spanish rule and to restore peace and happiness. In 1850 this tradition had appeared in Frederick Crowe's book entitled *The Gospel in Central America,* and now it began again to be circulated freely among the Nicaraguan natives who saw in Walker the *Grey-eyed Man of Destiny.* The fact that Walker's grey eyes were unusually large and luminous made the old prophecy even more significant, and soon, not only the natives, but also Walker's followers and those interested in his filibustering activities, called him by this nickname.

Walker's actions as a filibuster, that is, one who had organized a group of armed men for hostile "operations in a foreign country" [2] with which his native country was at peace led eventually to his destruction. In 1857 his rule in Nicaragua was overthrown, and in 1860, in an attempt to establish himself as a power in British Honduras, he was captured, condemned by court-martial at Trujillo, and shot.

During his childhood this soldier-adventurer is said to have been nicknamed *Honey* [2] and *Missy* [2] by his schoolmates who had considered him girlish because of his devotion to books, his lack of participation in athletics or boyish pranks, and his effeminate manners.

William Walker was born at Nashville, Tenn., on May 8, 1824, and died at Trujillo, Honduras, on September 12, 1860.

[1] *Filibusters and Financiers, the Story of William Walker and His Associates,* William O. Scroggs (The Macmillan Company, New York, 1916) p. 128-9. *William Walker, Filibuster,* Merritt Parmelee Allen (Harper and Brothers, New York and London, 1932) p. 5, 7, 14.

Walker in the Pines. See Sibley, H. H.

Walking-purchase

About 1737 William Penn made a treaty with the Indians in the region of the Delaware River to the effect that Penn was to have as much land as he could walk around in three days. Penn, however, stopped after he had walked leisurely for a day and a half. About fifty years later, Penns' descendants, having become dissatisfied with his actions in the matter and with the amount of land he had obtained, demanded that the walking be resumed for another day and a half in order that the time allowed by the contract might be fulfilled. They engaged professional walkers who walked so rapidly and covered so much territory in the day and a half allotted that the Indians were angered at having to give Penn's heirs so much additional land. In commemoration of these facts, the treaty has been called the *Walking-purchase.* [1]

[1] *The United States: A History of Three Centuries, 1607-1904, Population, Politics, War, Industry, Civilization, in Ten Parts,* William Estabrook Chancellor and Fletcher Willis Hewes (G. P. Putnam's Sons, New York and London, 1905) vol. 2, p. 87.

Wall Street of Chicago

La Salle Street in Chicago, Ill., is commonly designated the *Wall Street of Chicago.* [1] Like Wall Street in New York City, La Salle Street is the financial district of the Illinois metropolis.

[1] *The World Book Encyclopedia* (The Quarrie Corporation, Chicago, 1938) vol. 3, p. 1354.

Wall Street of Detroit

Griswold Street, in Detroit, Mich., has been nicknamed the *Wall Street of Detroit* [1] because the great banks and office buildings of the city are located on this street, in which respect it is comparable to Wall Street in New York City.

[1] *The World Book Encyclopedia* (The Quarrie Corporation, Chicago, 1938) vol. 4, p. 1920.

Wallace, Henry Agard

The sobriquet, *Plow 'Em Under Wallace,* [1] attributed to Henry Agard Wallace, originated when he advocated and put into operation the movement of plowing under growing crops, widely practiced by farmers of the United States during the years 1933 and 1934.

Henry Agard Wallace was born in Adair County, Iowa, on October 7, 1888, formerly was Secretary of Agriculture in the Cabinet of President Franklin Delano Roosevelt and Vice President during Roosevelt's third term.

[1] *The Washington Post,* Washington, D.C., February 6, 1935, col. 3, p. 8.

Waller, John

John Waller was nicknamed the *Devil's Adjutant* and *Swearing Jack Waller*[1] because he was so notoriously wicked in his youth. He was especially hostile to Baptists, and was one of the grand jury that prosecuted the Reverend Lewis Craig, a Baptist clergyman, for preaching. At the trial, Craig's address to the jury caused Waller's conversion. Waller later became a Baptist preacher.

John Waller was born in Spottsylvania County, Va., on December 23, 1741, and died at Abbeville, S.C., on July 4, 1802.

[1] *Appleton's Cyclopaedia of American Biography*, ed. by James Grant Wilson and John Fiske (D. Appleton and Company, New York, 1894) vol. 6, p. 337.

Wallis, Frank Edwin

The humorous appellation, *Colonial Wallis*,[1] was applied to Frank Edwin Wallis because he was considered an authority on the American Colonial or Georgian style of architecture. He caused a revival of interest in Colonial architecture throughout the country by his personal enthusiasm and his partiality for this style; he was the author of several excellently illustrated publications dealing with Colonial American architecture, furnishings, and decorations; and he received a number of awards for his exhibits in the United States and in Paris, France.

Frank Edwin Wallis was born at Eastport, Me., on June 14, 1862, and died at Paris, France, on March 21, 1929.

[1] *The National Cyclopaedia of American Biography* (James T. White and Company, New York, 1932) vol. 22, p. 208.

Walsh, Edward A.

Edward A. Walsh, who was born at Plains, Pa., on May 19, 1881, was nicknamed *Big Moose*[1] during his baseball days.

[1] *Who's Who in Major League Base Ball*, comp. by Harold (Speed) Johnson (Buxton Publishing Company, Chicago, 1933) p. 477.

Walter Damrosch of the Pacific Coast.

See Stewart, H. J.

Walthall, Henry B.

Because of his unusual skill and ability as an actor, the *Mansfield of the Screen*[1] was a sobriquet applied to Henry B. Walthall, who was born in Shelby County, Ala., on March 16, 1870. Richard Mansfield appeared on the English and American stage during the latter nineteenth century, and was famous for his varied characterizations.

[1] *The Blue Book of the Screen*, Ruth Wing, Editor (The Blue Book of the Screen, Inc., Hollywood, Calif., 1923) p. 268.

Wandering Mansion

The *Wandering Mansion*[1] is the nickname attributed to the large frame house in which the Arkansas exhibits were displayed at the World's Fair held in St. Louis, Mo., in 1904. After the Fair had closed, A. F. Wolf bought the "rambling three-story structure," moved it to Fayetteville, Ark., and rebuilt it on a plot of ground overlooking the downtown section of the city. Each part of the building was numbered before it was moved from St. Louis to make sure that it would be properly reconstructed. In the spring of 1939, it was demolished.

[1] *Times-Herald*, Washington, D.C., May 21, 1939, col. 7, p. A-3.

Waner, Lloyd James and Waner, Paul Glee

Lloyd James Waner is nicknamed *Little Poison*[1] and his brother Paul Glee Waner is called *Big Poison*[1] because both were such effective ball players, and because Paul Glee is the elder. They were also popularly known as the *Poison Twins* because they made such formidable opponents.

Muscles is another sobriquet applied to Lloyd James Waner in allusion to his great physical strength.

Lloyd James Waner was born at Harrah, Okla., on March 16, 1906, and played outfield in major league baseball.

Paul Glee Waner was born at Harrah, Okla., on April 16, 1903, and played outfield in major league baseball.

[1] *Who's Who in Major League Base Ball*, comp. by Harold (Speed) Johnson (Buxton Publishing Company, Chicago, 1933) p. 398, 399

Wanton, John

The sobriquet, the *Fighting Quaker*,[1] was attributed to John Wanton because, though he was a Quaker, he often sanctioned and aided activities of a militaristic nature, contrary to Quaker religious teachings.

Both in 1706 and in 1709, Wanton had taken an active part in a naval fight with the ship of a French privateer, for which

Wanton, John—Continued

act he was practically excommunicated from the Society of Friends. However, in 1712 he rejoined this religious organization. In May, 1734, he was elected Governor of Rhode Island and the Providence Plantations, which office he held until 1740. During that time, although he continued to be an active member of the Quaker sect, and one of their most eloquent preachers, Wanton remained loyal to the English Royal Government and commissioned [2] a number of privateers who harassed the French ships off the New England Coast.

John Wanton was born at Scituate, Mass., in 1672, and died at Newport, in what is now the State of Rhode Island, on July 5, 1740.

[1] *The National Cyclopaedia of American Biography* (James T. White and Company, New York, 1900) vol. 10, p. 12.
[2] *Rhode Island, a Study in Separatism*, Irving Berdine Richman (Houghton Mifflin and Company, New York and Boston, 1906) p. 96.

War Governor. See Morton, O. H. P. T.

War Hawks

After the election of 1811, John Randolph (of Roanoke) is credited with having given the sobriquet, *War Hawks*,[1] to the group of ardently patriotic young Republicans newly elected to the national House of Representatives. These members, comprising about half the number who came into office, firmly believed in territorial expansion and advocated war with England to eliminate the latter's influence on the frontier. That war came in 1812. The nickname, *War Hawks*, signifies that they desired war much as a hawk desires its prey. The *War Hawks* were mostly representatives of the South and West, and were opposed by representatives of New England and the Middle States, who dubbed them the *War Party*.[2]

[1] *History of the American People*, David Saville Muzzey (Ginn and Company, New York and Boston, 1927) p. 211.
[2] *The Growth of Our Country, the Story of America for Young Americans*, Smith Burnham and Theodore H. Jack (The John G. Winston Company, Chicago and San Francisco, Calif., 1934) pt. 2, p. 40.

Ward, Marcus Lawrence

The *Soldier's Friend* [1] is a nickname applied to Marcus Lawrence Ward. During the Civil War he relinquished his business affairs and devoted his time, money, and energy toward diminishing as much as possible the suffering and destitution of the soldiers upon the battlefield, and in alleviating the privations of their families at home.

Marcus Lawrence Ward was born at Newark, N.J., on November 9, 1812, and died there on April 25, 1884.

[1] *The National Cyclopaedia of American Biography* (James T. White and Company, New York, 1907) vol. 5, p. 209-10.

Ward, Samuel

The author and diplomat, Samuel Ward, was nicknamed *King of the Lobby* [1] because, after he settled in Washington, D.C., following his return from Paraguay on a diplomatic mission for the United States Government in 1862, his skill as a host, his brilliance as a conversationalist, and his persuasive manner enabled him to exert tremendous influence over the members of Congress.

Samuel Ward was born at New York City, on January 27, 1814, and died at Pegli, Italy, on May 19, 1884.

[1] *Appleton's Cyclopaedia of American Biography*, ed. by James Grant Wilson and John Fiske (D. Appleton and Company, New York, 1894) vol. 6, p. 354.

Wares, Clyde

Buzzy [1] is a popularly known sobriquet of Clyde Wares, who was born in Newberg Township, Mich., on March 23, 1886, and who played in major league baseball.

[1] *Who's Who in Major League Base Ball*, comp. by Harold (Speed) Johnson (Buxton Publishing Company, Chicago, 1933) p. 427.

Warhorse. See Turner, A. L.

Warhorse of Sumner County. See Trousdale, William

Warhorse of the Confederacy. See Longstreet, James

Warneke, Lonnie

Lonnie Warneke, who was born at Mt. Ida, Ark., on March 28, 1909, and who pitched in major league baseball, was called *Dixie,* [1] *Country* and *Ol' Arkansas.* Later his team-mates dubbed him the *Arkansas Humming Bird* because of his musical bent as a member of Pepper Martin's "Mudcat

Band" while on the St. Louis Cardinal team in the 1930's. He is now an umpire.

[1] *Who's Who in Major League Base Ball*, comp. by Harold (Speed) Johnson (Buxton Publishing Company, Chicago, 1933) p. 400.
[2] *Baseball Register*, 1952 ed. comp. by J. G. Taylor Spink (published by *the Sporting News*) p. 281.

Warner, Glenn Scobey

Pop Warner [1] was the widely known appellation of Glenn Scobey Warner. He is a highly respected and esteemed figure in American football.

Glenn Scobey Warner was born at Springville, N.Y., on April 5, 1871, and was a football coach at Stanford University, in Palo Alto, Calif. He died at Palo Alto on September 7, 1954.

[1] *Pop Warner's Book for Boys*, Glenn S. "Pop" Warner (Robert M. McBride and Company, New York, 1934) p. x-xi.

Warren, Josiah

Josiah Warren, reformer and author, was called the *Father of Anarchy*.[1] He joined the experimental socialist community at New Harmony, Ind., in 1825, but later advocated the idea of individual sovereignty. His theory of society was based on the interchange of goods and services instead of the payment of money or wages. In 1827 he put this theory into practice, operating for two years an "equity" store at Cincinnati, Ohio, with moderate success. He sold his wares at a profit of seven per cent above cost in order to pay the expense of running the business. His theories are recorded in his work *True Civilization*. He is regarded as the founder of philosophical anarchism in America.[2]

[1] *Famous First Facts*, Joseph Nathan Kane (The H. W. Wilson Company, New York, 1933) p. 30.
[2] *Webster's Biographical Dictionary*, 1st ed. (G. & C. Merriam, Springfield, Mass., 1943, 1948) p. 1546.

Warren, Lindsay Carter

Lindsay Carter Warren of North Carolina was nicknamed *Accounts Warren* [1] by his colleagues in the National House of Representatives because he was Chairman of the House Committee on Accounts.

He became a Democratic representative from the First Congressional District of North Carolina to the United States Congress in 1925 and served until 1940. Lindsay Carter Warren was born at Washington, N.C., on December 16, 1889.

[1] An interview with Captain Victor Hunt Harding, Secretary of the National Democratic Congress Reelection Committee, Washington, D.C., April 10, 1939.

Warrenton Babies

At the outbreak of the Civil War in 1861, the members of a company of infantrymen from Warrenton, Va., were jocularly called the *Warrenton Babies* [1] in allusion to their youthfulness. The majority of this company, which belonged to the Seventeenth Infantry of Virginia, were boys about sixteen and seventeen years of age.

[1] *Southern Generals, Their Lives and Campaigns*, William Parker Snow (Charles B. Richardson, New York, 1866) p. 362.

Warrior Parson. See Thurston, C. M.

Warriors. See Hartwick College; Hendrix College; Midland College

Warstler, Harold Benton

The nickname, *Rabbit*,[1] has been applied to Harold Benton Warstler, who was born at North Canton, Ohio, on September 15, 1904, and who played infield in major league baseball.

[1] *Who's Who in Major League Base Ball*, comp. by Harold (Speed) Johnson (Buxton Publishing Company, Chicago, 1933) p. 402.

Wartburg College

The athletic teams of Wartburg College, at Clinton, Iowa, have been designated *Burgers, Hilltoppers,, Teutons,* and *Knights. Burgers* [1] doubtless comes from the last part of *Wartburg. Hilltoppers* refers to the location of the college. *Teutons* [1] is derived from the fact that the founders of the college were of German descent, and *Knights* is in memory of the first Teuton Knights.[1]

[1] A communication from O. L. Proehl, President of Wartburg College, Clinton, Iowa, November 15, 1935.

Washburn College

The nicknames *Ichabods* and *Blues* have been given to the athletic teams of Washburn College, at Topeka, Kans. *Ichabods* [1] was attributed to the teams about 1905 because the college was named after Ichabod Washburn [1] of Worcester, Mass., in 1865. The *Blues* [1] originated in the fact that the college color is Yale blue.[1]

[1] A letter from J. Fred Zimmerman, Director of Publicity at Washburn College, Topeka, Kans., December 13, 1935.

Washburne, Elihu Benjamin

While Elihu Benjamin Washburne was a Representative from Illinois to the United

Washburne, E. B.—Continued
States Congress (1853-1869), he served for
some time as the Chairman of the Committee on Appropriations. His zealous watch
over the disbursements of the United States
Treasury Departments caused him to be
appreciatively nicknamed the *Watchdog of
the Treasury*.[1]

[1] *Israel, Elihu and Cadwallader Washburn; a Chapter
in American Biography,* comp. by Gaillard Hunt (The
Macmillan Company, New York, 1925) p. 189.

Washington, George
The following appellations have been
given to George Washington: the *American
Fabius, Atlas of America, Cincinnatus of
the West, Deliverer of America, Farmer-
President, Father of His Country, Father of
Pittsburgh*, the *Old Fox, Sage of Mt. Ver-
non, Savior of His Country, Stepfather of
His Country, Surveyor President*, and *Sword
of the Revolution*.

He was called the *American Fabius* because the system of countermarches which
he used against the British during the
Revolutionary War was comparable to tactics
of Quintus Maximus Fabius, a Roman
general, in his attacks on Hannibal in the
Second Punic War.

The *Atlas of America*[1] was applied to
George Washington because on him rested
the major responsibility for the newly-
formed American government, in which respect he was similar to Atlas, the mythological giant who supported the world on
his shoulders.

After he had retired to his estate at
Mount Vernon, Washington was called back
to take command of the United States Army
when it looked as if the nation would go
to war with France in 1798. In this respect he was comparable to Lucius Quintius
Cincinnatus, who is reported to have been
called twice from his farm in order to become the dictator of Rome, once in 458 and
again in 459 B.C., hence Washington was
sometimes called the *Cincinnatus of the
West*.[1]

George Washington was nicknamed the
Deliverer of America[1] and the *Savior of
His Country*[1] because of his service, during
the Revolutionary War, as Commander-in-
chief of the Continental Army.

Washington owned and operated a vast
plantation on the Potomac River in Vir-

ginia, and has been called the *Farmer-Presi-
dent*.[2]

The origin of the sobriquet, *Father of
His Country*,[3] is accredited to Francis
Bailey[4] a printer for the Continental Congress during the Revolutionary War, who
published an almanac in 1779, in which he
described Washington in this way because
he had taken such an active part in shaping
America into an independent nation, had
been prominent in molding its policies, and
had created a great respect for its government and policies both at home and abroad.

In November, 1752, George Washington
selected the present site of the city of Pittsburgh, Pa., for the location of a military
post. In April, 1754, while the fort was
under construction, an attack was made by
superior French and Indian forces. After
several sharp encounters, the British and
colonial troops succeeded in taking possession of Fort Duquesne, which the French
had erected in the immediate vicinity, and
upon the capture of Fort Duquesne it was
renamed Pittsburgh, the name having been
suggested by Washington.[5] Because of this
fact, he was designated the *Father of Pittsburgh*.[6]

The English General, Charles Cornwallis
is accredited with having nicknamed General Washington the *Old Fox*[7] because
Washington's military judgment was so
shrewd.

During the latter part of his life at
Mount Vernon, he was called the *Sage of
Mount Vernon*.[2]

Washington's political enemies described
him as the *Stepfather of His Country*,[1]
sarcastically implying that, as President of
the United States Washington was in the
position of one who takes over the work
started by another, or the duties and responsibilities left unfinished by another, and it
also implied that his rule was tyrannical.

During his youth George Washington
was a surveyor, and has been called the
Surveyor President.[4]

Commander-in-chief of the Continental
Army, prominent in so many battles of the
Revolution, he was designated the *Sword
of the Revolution*.[8]

George Washington, who was born in
Wakefield, the family homestead at Bridges
Creek, in Westmoreland County, Va., on
February 22, 1732, and who died at Mount

Vernon, Va., on December 14, 1799, was the first President of the United States.

[1] *U.S. "Snap Shots": An Independent, National, and Memorial Encyclopedia . . . ,* Oliver McKee (A. M. Thayer and Company, Boston, 1892) p. 308.
[2] *A Book of Nicknames,* John Goff (Courier-Journal Job Printing Company, Louisville, Ky., 1892) p. 23, 27.
[3] *American History for Grammar Schools,* Revised Edition, Marguerite Stockman Dickson (The Macmillan Company, New York, 1926) p. 264.
[4] *Old Churches and Meeting Houses In and Around Philadelphia,* John T. Faris (J. B. Lippincott and Company, Philadelphia and London, 1926) p. 59.
[5] *The Encyclopedia Americana* (Americana Corporation, New York and Chicago, 1927) vol. 22, p. 133.
[6] *Historic Towns of the Middle States,* ed. by Lyman P. Powell (G. P. Putnam's Sons, New York and London, 1899) p. 393.
[7] *The American People and Nation,* Rolla M. Tryon and Charles R. Lingley (Ginn and Company, New York and Boston, 1929) p. 191.
A Book of Nicknames, John Goff (Courier-Journal Job Printing Company, Louisville, Ky., 1892) p. 23.
[8] *Virginia, Rebirth of the Old Dominion,* Philip Alexander Bruce (The Lewis Publishing Company, New York and Chicago, 1929) vol. 1, p. 393.

Washington

The *Chinook State* was given as a nickname to the state of Washington because it was formerly the home of the "principal tribe of the Lower Chinook division of North American Indians." [1]

The sobriquet, the *Evergreen State,* suggests the continual green of the big firs in the state of Washington.

[1] *The Century Cyclopedia of Names,* ed. by Benjamin E. Smith (The Century Company, New York, 1914) vol. II, p. 246.

Washington, D.C.

Washington, D.C., is called: the *Capital City,* the *City of Houses Without Streets, City of Magnificent Distances, City of Receptions, City of Streets Without Houses, Executive City, Federal City,* the *Great Dismal,* and the *Wilderness City.*

It is universally known as the *Capital City* [1] because it is the seat of the capital of the United States. The sobriquet, the *City of Magnificent Distances,* [2] was jocularly bestowed upon it in 1816 by Jose Correa da Serra, then Portuguese Minister to the United States. When the city was first laid out, great distances intervened between the proposed public buildings, parks, and avenues. Charles Joseph Latrobe in 1836 spoke of Washington as the *City of Magnificent Distances* in the following paragraph:

"At Washington, 'the city of magnificent distances,' with the haste and eagerness of a new comer you visit the lions;—ascend to the capitol;—criticise its architecture, whether properly authorized to do so or

not;—listen to the proceedings in either House for an hour or two;—pay your respects to the President;—visit the country-seat and grave of our great and good opponent, Washington. You plan, but do not execute, an excursion to the Falls of the Potomac;—get more and more bewildered with the study of the city, which seems to have been contrived with an eye for the especial advantage of the hackney coachmen. . . ." [3]

Washington is called the *City of Receptions* because of the great number of these functions given in the social life of the capital. Authorities differ as to who originated the expression, *A City of Houses without Streets,* or *A City of Streets without Houses,* which is applied to this city. One authority says that Jean-Jacques Ampère [4] originated the term, another that a visiting Frenchwoman referred to Washington as *A City of Streets without Houses* and to Georgetown as *A City of Houses without Streets.* [5]

Washington is appropriately nicknamed the *Executive City* because it is the seat of the United States Government.

It is frequently spoken of as the *Federal City.* [6] This sobriquet is closely connected with the naming of the city, the use of the name being older in point of time [7] than the present name of the city. George Washington himself was accustomed to refer to the seat of the National Government as the *Federal City.* [8]

Daniel Webster is said to have called this city the *Great Dismal,* [9] probably by way of comparing it to the Great Dismal Swamp, because the city, in the early decades of the nineteenth century when Webster lived there, was poorly lighted, poorly paved, very damp and muddy, and quite unhealthful. [9]

Mrs. John Adams is said to have termed Washington *Wilderness City* [10] because, during the time her husband was President, the town was sparsely settled with vast stretches of wooded land where much of the city is today.

[1] *A Book of Nicknames,* John Goff (Courier-Journal Job Printing Company, Louisville, Ky., 1892) p. 15.
[2] *The Life of James Monroe,* George Morgan (Small, Maynard, and Company, Boston, 1921) p. 411.
Women of Colonial and Revolutionary Times: Dolly Madison, Maud Wilder Goodwin (Charles Scribner's Sons, New York, 1896) p. 135.
[3] *The Rambler in North America,* Second Edition, Charles Joseph Latrobe (Published by R. B. Seeley and W. Burnside, and Sold by L. and G. Seeley, London, MDCCCXXXVI) p. 28-9.

Washington, D.C.—Continued

[4] *Historical Documents Institut Français de Washington, Cahier III, L'Enfant and Washington 1791-1792, Published and Unpublished Documents Now Brought together for the First Time*, Elizabeth S. Kite, introduction by J. J. Jusserand, Ambassador of France to the United States (1902-1925) foreword by Charles Moore, Chairman of the National Commission of Fine Arts (The Johns Hopkins Press, Baltimore, Md., 1929) p. 28.
[5] *Our Capital on the Potomac*, Helen Nicolay (The Century Company, New York, 1924) p. 60.
[6] *Americanisms: The English of the New World*, M. Schele De Vere (Charles Scribner and Company, New York, 1872) p. 665.
[7] *Historical Documents Institut Français de Washington, Cahier III, L'Enfant and Washington 1791-1792, Published and Unpublished Documents Now Brought together for the First Time*, Elizabeth S. Kite, introduction by J. J. Jusserand, Ambassador of France to the United States (1902-1925) foreword by Charles Moore, Chairman of the National Commission of Fine Arts (The Johns Hopkins Press, Baltimore, Md., 1929) p. 21.
[8] *Standard History of the City of Washington from a Study of the Original Sources*, William Tindall (H. W. Crew and Company, Knoxville, Tenn., 1914) p. 70, 84, 87, 88, 116-19, 125, 133, 183.
[9] *The Godlike Daniel*, Samuel Hopkins Adams (Sears Publishing Company, Inc., New York, 1930) p. 80, 81.
[10] *A Souvenir of the Federal Capital and of the National Drill and Encampment at Washington, D.C., May 23 to May 30, 1887*, Stilson Hutchins and J. W. Moore (W. P. Morse, Washington, D.C., and Atlanta, Ga., Gibson Brothers, Printers, Washington, D.C., 1887) p. 51.

Washington American League Baseball Club

Nationals[1] and *Senators*[1] are the nicknames of the Washington American League Baseball Club. The former sobriquet was given to this group in 1912 by Clark Griffith, the president of the club, because this club represents the national capital.[2] The latter nickname was given to the club in honor of the United States Senators.

[1] *Who's Who in Major League Base Ball*, comp. by Harold (Speed) Johnson (Buxton Publishing Company, Chicago, 1933) p. 44, 281.
[2] A communication from E. B. Eynon, Jr., Secretary of The Washington American League Baseball Club, Washington, D.C., June 26, 1935.

Washington and Jefferson College

The teams of Washington and Jefferson College, at Washington, Pa., were designated the *Presidents*[1] in 1916 by a sports writer who made use of the sobriquet, remembering that the teams of Washington and Lee University are designated the *Generals*.

[1] A communication from W. F. Henry, Director of Athletics at Washington and Jefferson College, Washington, Pa., June 18, 1935.

Washington and Lee University

The upper-classmen athletic teams of Washington and Lee University, at Lexington, Va., are popularly called the *Generals*.[1] The University is named for George Washington and Robert E. Lee, two great American generals. The freshman athletic teams of the University are nicknamed *Brigadiers*[1] and *Little Generals*[1] signifying that later as members of the varsity teams they will be *Generals*.

[1] A communication from Richard P. Carter, Director of the Washington and Lee News Bureau, Lexington, Va., November 18, 1935.

Washington Club of the National Football League

The nickname, *Washington Redskins*,[1] is commonly attributed to the teams of the Washington Club of the National Football League, at Washington, D.C. This sobriquet was given to the club by its president in 1933, before it moved from Boston to Washington, the group at that time having been nicknamed the *Boston Redskins*. The sobriquet "typified the fighting Americans and was not being used by any other football team at that time." After the Club had moved to Washington the sobriquet was changed to the *Washington Redskins*.

[1] A communication from George P. Marshall, President-treasurer of The Washington Club of The National Football League, Washington, D.C., March 20, 1939.

Washington College

The athletic teams of Washington College, at Chestertown, Md., although they have no official nicknames, are frequently designated *Sho'men*[1] or *Shoremen*[1] by sports writers[1] because the site of the college is on the Eastern Shore of Maryland.[1]

The basket-ball teams were formerly called the *Flying Pentagon*[1] because the pentagon is the emblem of "the ranking honor society on the campus"[1] called the Silver Pentagon.

[1] A communication from Gilbert W. Mead, President of Washington College, Chestertown, Md., November 18, 1935.

Washington Inhabitants

Inhabitants of the state of Washington have been nicknamed *Clam Grabbers*[1] doubtless from the fact that they gather vast quantities of clams annually from the shallow waters of Puget Sound and of Wallapa Harbor.

[1] *The Lincoln Library of Essential Information*, Thoroughly Revised at Each New Printing (The Frontier Press Company, Buffalo, N.Y., 1937) p. 2068.

Washington of the West. See Clark, G. R.; Harrison, W. H.

Washington Redskins. See Washington Club of the National Football League

Washington University

The appellations, *Pikers*[1] and *Bears*,[1] were given to the athletic teams of Washington University, at Saint Louis, Mo. The former nickname originated in the fact that the pikeway of the 1904 World's Fair was the present site of Washington University. *Bears* was selected as a sobriquet for the teams because they felt that it would be appropriate.

[1] A communication from James D. Conselman, Head Football Coach at Washington University, Saint Louis, Mo., June 21, 1935.

Washington's First Mayoress. See Norton, M. T.

Wasps. See Emory and Henry College

Watchdog of Central Park. See Ochs, A. S.

Watchdog of the Treasury. See Blanton, T. L.; Cannon, J. G.; Gallatin, Albert; Hagner, Peter; Holman, W. S.; McCarl, J. R.; Washburne, E. B.

Watered Stock

Watered Stock[1] is the term for the capital stock of any corporation or organization which has been increased by additional salable shares without adding a proportionate amount of value as assets to the original capital of the concern. It is difficult to account for the origin of the nickname, but tradition tells of a man who, while driving his cattle to market, fed them all the dry feed stuff that they would eat. Before putting them on the market, he allowed the cattle to drink as much water as they desired, thereby increasing their weight. Because he was selling his cattle by the pound, the added weight naturally increased the amount he received. This traditional account probably had something to do with creating the term, *Watered Stock*, and with its application to the nominal increase of capital stock.

[1] *Twenty Years of the Republic, 1885-1905,* Harry Thurston Peck (Dodd, Mead and Company, New York, 1907) p. 314.

Watrous, Harry Wilson

Harry Wilson Watrous has been called the *American Meissonier*[1] because his paintings are of a small size, exquisitely finished, and sometimes of unusual subject matter and design, in which respects he is comparable to the French genre painter of the nineteenth century, Jean Louis Ernest Meissonier.

Harry Wilson Watrous was born at San Francisco, Calif., on September 17, 1857, and died May 9, 1940.

[1] *The National Cyclopaedia of American Biography* (James T. White and Company, New York, 1906) vol. 13, p. 369.

Watson, James Eli

James Eli Watson, formerly Senator from Indiana, was nicknamed *Sunny Jim* and the *Wooden-shoe Statesman.* The former sobriquet[1] was given to him for his congenial disposition. He was nicknamed the *Wooden-shoe Statesman*[2] in 1894 because he wore a pair of wooden shoes when he made a political speech at Spades, Ind., while campaigning to be elected a Representative from Indiana to the United States Senate. Watson had been speaking at Andersonville and other Indiana towns until he was tired and almost exhausted when he reached the home of Dr. G. B. Vincent at Sunman in Ripley County, Ind. Here he rested and relaxed a few hours. After he had started to Spades, Ind., to resume his speaking, he complained to Dr. Vincent who was accompanying him that his feet were cold. Vincent took Watson back to his house and gave him a pair of wooden shoes lined with wool, which Watson wore to make his speech. As his speech was delivered in a country store filled with German people, he was quickly nicknamed the *Wooden-shoe Statesman.*

He was a Representative from Indiana to the United States Congress from 1895 until, 1897, and again from 1899 until 1900. He was a Republican Senator from Indiana to the United States Congress from 1916 until 1933. He was a delegate to the Republican National Conventions in 1912, 1920, 1924, 1933, and in 1936.

James Eli Watson was born at Winchester, Ind., on November 2, 1864, and died in Washington, D.C., on July 29, 1948.

[1] *Washington Herald,* Washington, D.C., May 12, 1934, col. 3, p. 16.
[2] *As I Knew Them: Memoirs of James E. Watson* (Bobbs-Merrill Company, Indianapolis, Ind., 1936) p. 23.

Watson, Milton

Milton Watson, a major league baseball pitcher, was nicknamed *Mule Watson.*[1]

Watson, Milton—Continued

The sobriquet had its origin during his youth because of his stubborness. When he was a boy, Watson was working at a saw mill where he accidentally pushed two fingers on his left hand against a revolving circular saw cutting off the ends of the fingers. After his hand had been bandaged, Watson refused to go home until the mill closed down for the night. Watson became a pitcher for the Saint Louis National League Baseball Club in July, 1917.

Milton Watson was born on a farm near Indian Springs, Ga., on January 19, 1894.

[1] *Baseball Magazine* (The Baseball Magazine Company, New York, 1917-1918) vol. 20-21, May 1918, p. 168.

Watson, Thomas Edward

Thomas Edward Watson's political life began in 1890 when he was elected to the National House of Representatives on the Farmers' Alliance ticket. As an agrarian, he declared himself a Populist during his first term, and was the Populist nominee for vice president of the United States in 1896 and for president in 1904. He was a United States senator in 1921-22.

Most of his nonpolitical life was spent on his estate, Hickory Hill, in McDuffie County, Ga., and he was known as the *Sage of Hickory Hill* or the *Sage of McDuffie*.[1]

Thomas Edward Watson was born at Thomson, Ga., on September 5, 1856, and died at Washington, D.C., on September 26, 1922.

[1] *The Life of Thomas E. Watson*, William W. Brewton (Published by the Author, Atlanta, Georgia, 1926) p. 306, 346, 352.

Watters, Henry Eugene

The appellation, *HE Watters*, was attributed to Dr. Henry Eugene Watters by his students at Hall-Moody Institute, in Martin, Tenn., the sobriquet being taken from his initials.

Henry Eugene Watters was born in Graves County, Ky., on September 14, 1876. He was President of the Hall-Moody Institute from 1903 to 1915; President of Union University, at Jackson, Tenn., from 1918 to 1931; and from 1931 to 1934, he was President of Georgetown College, at Georgetown, Ky. Dr. Watters died April 15, 1938.

Watterson, Henry

Henry Watterson, journalist, and politician, was nicknamed *Henry of Navarre*, *Light Horse Harry*, and *Marse Henry*. He was designated *Henry of Navarre* and *Light Horse Harry*[1] because of "his dashing [journalistic] style." The nickname, *Marse Henry*[1] "is said to have been bestowed [upon him] by Charles F. Grainger of Louisville, [Ky.] in the days when the editor frequently visited a club maintained by Mr. Grainger and others in the old Courier-Journal Building."

He served with the Confederate Army in the Civil War. In 1868 he became the editor of the newly-formed *Courier-Journal* which position he continued to hold until he retired from active life on August 6, 1918.

Watterson was considered one of the most outstanding editors in American journalism. He was one of the most famous phrasemakers of America, and was said to have been "the last of the great personal editors." He maintained a strictly democratic attitude toward his employees, and never rebuked or expressed resentment toward them. His style of writing was basically "founded upon the English of Macaulay's school, but the superstructure he built upon that of his own architecture." He said, "Any faculty I have for writing, I attribute . . . to my ear for music; my appreciation of cadence. I do not write by rule of thumb, but by ear. If the sentence, the paragraph, the column has the right ring, it is the right thing."

He was the author of the phrase, "To Hell with the Hohenzollern and the Hapsburgs,"[2] which he first used in the *Courier-Journal* on April 6, 1915. His war editorials, *Vae Victis*, published on April 7, 1917, and *War Has Its Compensation*, published on April 10, 1917, won the Pulitzer Prize for that year. He sold his interest in the *Courier-Journal* and the *Louisville Times* to Judge Robert N. Bingham on August 6, 1918.

Henry Watterson was born at Washington, D.C., February 16, 1840, and died at Jacksonville, Fla., on December 22, 1921.

[1] *The Courier-Journal*, Louisville, Ky., December 23, 1921, col. 1, p. 2, 4, 6.

Wayne, Anthony

Anthony Wayne has been designated *Big Thunder*, the *Black Snake*, the *Chief Who Never Sleeps*, *Dandy Wayne*, *Drover Wayne*, the *Hero of Stony Point*, *Mad Anthony*, the *Tornado*, and the *Wind*.

The Indians of the Northwest Territory, in the region of the Ohio River, against whom Anthony Wayne waged a fierce campaign from 1793 to 1794, nicknamed him *Big Thunder*,[1] *Tornado*, and the *Wind*.[3] These singular appellations alluded to Wayne's fighting, which they felt had the same devastating effect as the thunderstorms or tornadoes of the West.

The sobriquet, *Black Snake*,[2] was applied to Major General Wayne by the Indians because of Wayne's skill and energy in dealing with them and because of his adeptness at concealing the movements of his troops so as to confuse them.[4]

These same Indians also described Wayne as the *Chief Who Never Sleeps* in commemoration of his ceaseless vigilance, his energy, wariness, and determination with them.

In allusion to his fastidious grooming, Wayne was called *Dandy Wayne*[2] by the men under his command during the Revolutionary War.

During the writer of 1778 the enemies of Anthony Wayne nicknamed him *Drover Wayne*[7] in wry tribute to his zeal in foraging for cattle for the soldiers of the Continental Army at Valley Forge, in Pennsylvania.

Wayne was called the *Hero of Stony Point*[8] after his brilliant and daring leadership in capturing the seemingly impregnable British fort, Stony Point, on the night of July 15, 1779. He was injured in the bayonet charge, but his valor, temerity, and skill inspired his men to a victory which came at a most opportune time to renew the courage of the colonists.

There is a diversity of opinion as to the origin of the sobriquet *Mad Anthony*. Washington Irving[10] believes that the nickname was applied to Wayne because of his reckless courage in military action.

John R. Spears[5] says that it was first used by a Pennsylvania Irishman whom General Wayne used to his great advantage in securing information concerning the enemy's plans.

By orders of General Wayne, the Irishman had been taken to the guard house at Yorktown, Pa., for unruly behavior. Upon his release, the Irishman learned that General Wayne had been greatly displeased with his disorderly conduct, and that he had not ordered him imprisoned merely as a joke. The Irishman then replied that Anthony must

have been mad, and asked them to clear the coast for him, "mad Anthony's friend." Jealous of his accomplishments, General Wayne's enemies sneeringly used the expression, *Mad Anthony*, when referring to him, and it soon became a permanent nickname.

Anthony Wayne was born at Eastown, Pa., on January 1, 1745, and died at Presque Isle, now Erie, Pa., on December 15, 1796.

[1] *Historic Towns of the Western States*, ed. by Lyman P. Powell (G. P. Putnam's Sons, New York and London, 1901) p. 70.
[2] *The Story of the Revolution*, Henry Cabot Lodge (Charles Scribner's Sons, New York, 1898) vol. 2, p. 131, 132.
A Gentleman Rebel: The Exploits of Anthony Wayne, John Hyde Preston (Farrar and Rinehart. Inc., New York, 1930) p. 290.
[3] *Major-General Anthony Wayne, Third General-in-Chief of the United States Army Since the Adoption of the Constitution*, J. Watts De Peyster (Steinman and Hensel, Lancaster, Pa., 1886) p. 6.
Sketches of the Civil and Military Services of William Henry Harrison, Colonel Charles S. Todd, and Benjamin Drake, revised and enlarged by James H. Perkins (J. A. and U. P. James, Cincinnati, Ohio, 1847) p. 14.
[4] *The Peace of Mad Anthony: An Account of the Subjugation of the North-Western Indian Tribes and the Treaty of Greeneville by Which the Territory Beyond the Ohio was Opened for Anglo-Saxon Settlement*, Fraser Ells Wilson (Charles R. Kemble, Greeneville, Ohio, 1909) p. 92.
[5] *Anthony Wayne, Sometimes Called "Mad Anthony,"* John R. Spears (D. Appleton and Company, New York, 1903) p. 182-3, 233.
[6] *A History of the United States and Its People for the Use of Schools*, Edward Eggleston (American Book Company, New York and Chicago, 1931) p. 217.
A School History of the United States, Revised Edition, William H. Mace (Rand McNally and Company, New York and London, 1922) p. 226.
[7] *Major-General Anthony Wayne and the Pennsylvania Line in the Continental Army*, Charles J. Stillé (J. B. Lippincott Company, Philadelphia, 1893) p. 130, 189-200.
[8] *The Hero of Stony Point, Anthony Wayne*, James Barnes (D. Appleton and Company, New York and London, 1916) p. 1.
[9] *Life and Services of General Anthony Wayne, Founded on Documentary Evidence Furnished by His Son, Colonel Isaac Wayne*, H. N. Moore (Leary, Getz and Company, Philadelphia, 1845) p. 94-102.
[10] *The Life of George Washington*, Washington Irving (G. P. Putnam and Company, New York, 1856) vol. 3, p. 503.

Wayne University

The nicknames, *Munies* and *Tartars*, have been applied to the athletic teams of Wayne University, at Detroit, Mich. Wayne University is a municipal university, hence the abbreviation *Munies*.[1]

The students selected the appellation, *Tartars* to replace the former nickname.

[1] A letter from David L. Holmes, Director of Athletics at Wayne University, Detroit, Mich., November 23, 1935.

Waynesburg College

Yellow Jackets[1] is the nickname applied in 1922 or 1923 to the athletic teams of Waynesburg College, at Waynesburg, Pa.,

Waynesburg College—Continued

because they wore jerseys striped with burnt orange and black, the college colors.

[1] A communication from J. M. Miller, Director of Athletics at Waynesburg College, Waynesburg, Pa., June 20, 1935.

Wayward Sisters

In a letter to William Henry Seward on March 3, 1864, Lieutenant General Winfield Scott offered several suggestions as to what action should be taken in regard to the slave-holding states which had seceded from the Union. Scott's fourth or last suggestion was that, rather than precipitate a civil war, these *Wayward Sisters* [1] should be allowed to "depart in peace." The expression was thereafter often applied by northerners to the states which seceded from the Union because they were considered to have strayed from the proper course of action.

[1] *Memoirs of Lieutenant-general Scott, Written by Himself* (Sheldon and Company, New York, 1864) vol. 2, p. 628.

Wearin, Otha Donner

Otha Donner Wearin, Iowa farmer and politician, was nicknamed *Red Necktie* [1] by his colleagues in the National House of Representatives while he was a member of that legislative body from 1933 until 1939 because he habitually wore a "flaming red bow necktie."

He was a Democratic Representative to the Iowa State Legislature from 1928 until 1932, and was a New Deal Democratic Representative from the Seventh Congressional District of Iowa to the United States Congress from 1933 until 1939.

Otha Donner Wearin was born on a farm near Hastings, Iowa, on January 10, 1903.

[1] An interview with Captain Victor Hunt Harding, Secretary of the National Democratic Congressional Reelection Committee, Washington, D.C., April 10, 1939.

Weasels. See South Carolinians

Weaver, Monte Morton

Because he taught mathematics before he became a professional baseball player, *Prof* [1] is the nickname given to Monte Morton Weaver, who was born at Hilton, N.C., on June 15, 1908, and who pitched in major league baseball.

[1] *Who's Who in Major League Base Ball*, comp. by Harold (Speed) Johnson (Buxton Publishing Company, Chicago, 1933) p. 404.

Weaver, Zebulon

Zebulon Weaver, North Carolina lawyer and politician, was nicknamed *Old Zeb* by his colleagues in the National House of Representatives.

He was a Democratic Representative from the Eleventh Congressional District of North Carolina to the United States Congress from 1917 until 1929, and was a Democratic Representative from the same district to the United States Congress from 1931 to 1947.

Zebulon Weaver was born at Weaverville, N.C., on May 12, 1872, and died in Asheville, N.C., October 29, 1948.

[1] An interview with Captain Victor Hunt Harding, Secretary of the National Democratic Congressional Reelection Committee, Washington, D.C., April 10, 1939.

Webfeet. See Oregonians; University of Oregon

Webfoot State. See Oregon

Webster, Daniel

The great American orator, Daniel Webster, was singularly well-endowed for his role by an extraordinary speaking voice and a magnificent presence which served to heighten his intellectual powers. His generation attested to the impression he made by the great many nicknames which they applied to him during his lifetime: *All Eyes, Black Dan*, the *Black Giant, Defender of the Constitution, Defender of the Union, Eagle of the East, Expounder of the Constitution*, the *God-like Daniel*, the *Great Interpreter*, the *Great Stone Face*, the *Illustrious Defender, Immortal Webster, Indian Dan, Little Black Dan*, the *Massachusetts Giant*, the *Massachusetts Thunderer*, the *Modern Sisyphus, New England Cicero, New Hampshire Demosthenes*, the *Old Titanic Earth-son*, the *Pillar of the Constitution*, the *Unintentional Defaulter*, and the *Upholder of the Constitution* and the *Whig Gulliver*.

While he was a young man, Daniel Webster was called *All Eyes* [1] by his friends and associates in allusion to his extraordinary large and brilliant black eyes, made more prominent by dark heavy eyebrows, and accentuated by Webster's lean face and slender figure. Webster himself used the epithet [2] in describing how he looked in his youth.

The nicknames *Black Giant*, [3] *Black Dan*, [4] and *Indian Dan* [4] allude to his black hair and eyes, his dark complexion and lithe figure, and his impressive platform presence.

Black Dan and *Indian Dan* seem to have been used most widely during his school days at Dartmouth College.

Because he upheld and defended [5] the Constitution against any and all attacks which might have lessened its power as a binding force of the Union, Daniel Webster was designated *Defender of the Constitution,*[6] *Upholder of the Constitution,*[3] and *Pillar of the Constitution.*[3]

He is known as the *Defender of the Union* [7] because he vehemently opposed the doctrine of States Rights,[8] and his persuasive arguments imbued his listeners with a strong sense of nationalism.[8]

The Eagle of the East [3] is a poetic reference to his magnificent flights of oratory on numerous occasions in defense of the Constitution, the preservation of the Union, and other famous issues of the early nineteenth century in the United States.

Webster was called the *Expounder of the Constitution* [9] because he so actively defended and expounded that document when it was the subject of many heated controversies.

The God-like Daniel [8] was descriptive of Webster's physical and mental characteristics and of his dominant personality. The nickname is said to have originated after Webster's great speech called the "Reply to Hayne." [10] The zenith of Webster's speaking career seems to have been reached in this speech in which he defined so magnificently the character of the Union as it existed in 1830.

Daniel Webster has been called the *Great Interpreter* [3] for his ability to grasp and interpret the fundamental principles of any subject to which he turned his attention.[1]

The *Great Stone Face* [3] referred to Webster's massive head and forehead and his bronzed complexion which reminded one of "a transparent bronze statue." [8]

For his able defenses of any position he took, he was nicknamed the *Illustrious Defender.*[3] His reputation as a lawyer, statesman, diplomat, and the most famous orator of his age won him the title of the *Immortal Webster.*[3]

Little Black Dan derives from his youth in Salisbury, N.H.[10]

Because he lived practically all of his adult life in Massachusetts, Daniel Webster is known as the *Massachusetts Giant* [11] and the *Massachusetts Thunderer,*[3] the latter nickname referring to his resonant and sonorous voice.

Webster was nicknamed the *Modern Sisyphus* [3] in reference to his long and arduous defense of the Federal Constitution, a task of large-scale proportions in the pre-Civil War era, and comparable, therefore, to the labors of the mythological Sisyphus who constantly rolled a stone uphill, but never succeeded in getting it to its destination.

Webster was designated the *New England Cicero* [3] in recognition of his services as a representative of the New England states and as an outstanding orator,[12] recalling the great Roman orator, Marcus Tullius Cicero. The *New Hampshire Demothenes* [3] is another comparison to a great orator of the past and commemorates Webster's birthplace.

Ralph Waldo Emerson bestowed the epithet the *Old Titanic Earth-son* [6] on Webster in poetic reference to the latter's great intellectual powers and his ability to reason through weighty issues.

At the time Webster resigned as Secretary of State in President John Tyler's Cabinet, there was a deficit of funds that he was unable to completely account for, which amount he personally reimbursed, hence the nickname the *Unintentional Defaulter.*[3]

Webster was called the *Whig Gulliver* [3] while he was Secretary of State in President Tyler's Cabinet. The dissension between the Whig President Tyler and the Whigs in Congress was climaxed by Tyler's veto of the Bank Bill in 1841,[13] and Tyler's entire cabinet, except for Webster, resigned in repudiation of the President's action. This was followed by unparalleled denunciation of the President by the members of his own party. In this situation, Webster chose to stand by Tyler; he believed that Tyler's position on the Bank issue was valid, that the Cabinet members had acted unfairly, and that other important international issues would be jeopardized by his resignation as Secretary of State.[14] Webster alone amidst hostile Whig politicians was compared to Lemuel Gulliver among the Lilliputians in Swift's *Gulliver's Travels.*

Daniel Webster was born at Salisbury, N.H., on January 18, 1782, and died at Marshfield, Mass., on October 24, 1852.

See also *Great Triumvirate.*

[1] *Old Rough and Ready Series: The Great Expounder, Young Folk's Life of Daniel Webster*, John Frost (Lee and Shepard, Boston, 1887) p. 74, 205.
[2] *The Private Life of Daniel Webster*, Charles Lanman (Harper and Brothers, New York, 1852) p. 31.

Webster, Daniel—Continued

[3] *The Godlike Daniel*, Samuel Hopkins Adams (Sears Publishing Company, Inc., New York, 1930) p. 19, 73, 74, 105, 181, 188, 265, 291, 325-30, 338.
[4] *The Private Correspondence of Daniel Webster*, ed. by Fletcher Webster (Little, Brown and Company, Boston, 1857) vol. 1, p. 5-6.
[5] "Daniel Webster" by Henry Cabot Lodge, in *American Statesmen*, ed. by John T. Morse, Junior (Houghton Mifflin and Company, New York and Boston, 1883) p. 179, 191-2.
[6] *Commonwealth History of Massachusetts*, ed. by Albert Bushnell Hart (The States History Company, New York, 1930) vol. 4, p. 104, 118, 119, 130, 132.
[7] *Daniel Webster, Defender of the Union*, Mabel Mason Carlton (John Hancock, Mutual Life Insurance Company, Boston, 1923) p. 3.
[8] *Great Senators of the United States Forty Years Ago (1848 and 1849) with Personal Recollections and Delineations of Calhoun, Benton, Clay, Webster, General Houston, Jefferson Davis, and Other Distinguished Statesmen of That Period*, Oliver Dyer (Robert Bonner's Sons, New York, 1889) p. 251, 253-4, 260-4, 295-6.
[9] *Daniel Webster, the Expounder of the Constitution*, Everett Pepperrell Wheeler (G. P. Putnam's Sons, New York, 1905) p. 1.
[10] *The "Also Rans," Great Men Who Missed Making the Presidential Goal*, Don C. Seitz (Thomas Y. Crowell Company, New York, 1928) p. 110, 114.
[11] *A Book of Nicknames*, John Goff (Courier-Journal Job Printing Company, Louisville, Ky., 1892) p. 22.
[12] *The Real Daniel Webster*, Elijah R. Kennedy (Fleming H. Revell Company, New York and Chicago, 1924) p. 195-7.
[13] "Daniel Webster" by Frederick Austin Ogg, in *American Crisis Biographies*, ed. by Ellis Paxson Oberholtzer (George W. Jacobs and Company, Philadelphia, 1914) p. 299-300.
[14] *Life of Daniel Webster*, George Ticknor Curtis (D. Appleton and Company, New York, 1870) vol. 2, p. 80-1.

Webster, Daniel, and Hugh Lawson White

John Quincy Adams is credited with having called Daniel Webster and Hugh Lawson White the *Golden Calves of the People*.[1] Webster and White, distinguished contemporaries in the United States Senate, were held in high esteem by the general public. The sobriquet implied that the people's respect for them was comparable to the idolatry of the children of Israel for their Golden Calf at Mount Sinai. Adams was frequently in vehement opposition to Webster and White over political issues.

[1] *The Godlike Daniel*, Samuel Hopkins Adams (Sears Publishing Company, Inc., New York, 1930) p. 206.

Wedded Poets. See Piatt, J. J., and Piatt, S. M. B.

Wedgwood, Edgar A.

While he was scarcely more than youth, Edgar A. Wedgwood was elected sheriff of Hall County, Neb., hence the nickname the *Kid Sheriff of Nebraska*.[1]

For many years Wedgwood was an eminent lawyer at Salt Lake City, Utah, specializing in legal cases dealing with irrigation and mining problems.

Edgar A. Wedgwod was born at Lowell, Mass., on May 2, 1856, and died at Salt Lake City, Utah, on January 31, 1920.

[1] *The National Cyclopaedia of American Biography* (James T. White and Company, New York, 1926) vol. 19, p. 304.

Weeden, Charles Foster

Charles Foster Weeden's numerous and varied activities both as a pastor and as a prominent church worker and official, covering a wide field of Congregational church work in the United States and the British Isles, made appropriate the sobriquet, *Bishop of Congregational Churches*,[1] by which he has been designated.

He was born at Providence, R.I., on December 18, 1856, was ordained a minister in the Congregational Church in 1888, and died at Athol, Mass., on June 18, 1928.

[1] *The National Cyclopaedia of American Biography* (James T. White and Company, New York, 1931) vol. 21, p. 427.

Weeping Prophet. See Sewall, Joseph

Weinberger, Moses

Moses Weinberger, an Oklahoma pioneer and saloon keeper, had two sobriquets, the *Same Young Mose* and the *Same Old Mose*. According to the columnist W. A. S. Douglas, Weinberger was nicknamed the *Same Young Mose*[1] by homesteaders in Oklahoma on April 22 and 23, 1889. On the previous day Weinberger had bought a limited stock of bananas from Arkansas City, Ark., to the scene of the Oklahoma homesteading to sell to the settlers. Weinberger sold out his entire store the first day, but, returning to Arkansas City during the night, he arrived at the settlement early on the second day with a fresh supply of bananas, riding the engine-tender of a railroad train. When the settlers discovered that he was back ready to sell them bananas again, they shouted, "It's the same young Mose who sold us bananas yesterday." For a number of years Weinberger continued to be called the *Same Young Mose*. In a recent communication from Mr. Weinberger to the writer, he stated that he did not know how he acquired this nickname.[2]

In July 1890, Bill Reese, a horse trader from Wichita, Kans., came into Weinberger's saloon at Guthrie, Okla. He had not seen Weinberger for about six and a half years, they having become acquainted while they both lived at Wichita. Reese exclaimed, "By gosh; here is the *Same Old Mose*." [1] This sobriquet became widely applied to Weinberger· and has continued to be applied to him ever since.

Moses Weinberger was born at Bagdany, a village in Hungary on April 8, 1859.

[1] *Times-Herald*, Washington, D.C., May 15, 1939, col. 4, p. 7.
[2] A communication from Moses Weinberger, Guthrie, Okla., May 28, 1939.

Well-born

In 1787 when the newly-formed states dere deciding whether to ratify the new Constitution creating a strong federal government, they were split into Federalist and Anti-Federalist factions. The former were derisively referred to as the *Well-born* [1] as a result of an unfortunate remark by John Adams in his *Defense of the Constitutions of Government of the United States of America* [2] in which he recommended the advantages of a bicameral national legislature: "The rich, the well-born, and the able, acquire an influence among the people, that will soon be too much for simple honesty and plain sense, in a House of Representatives. The most illustrious of them must therefore be separated from the mass, and placed by themselves in a Senate; that is, to all honest and useful intents, an ostracism." This recommendation, in terms of class distinction, was not in keeping with the principles of the Declaration of Independence and was so displeasing to Anti-Federalists that they seized upon the expression as a term of ridicule.

[1] *A History of the People of the United States, from the Revolution to the Civil War*, John Bach McMaster (D. Appleton and Company, New York, 1883) vol. 1, p. 469.
[2] *A Defense of the Constitutions of Government of the United States of America, against the Attack of M. Turgot in His Letter to Dr. Price, Dated the Twenty-second Day of March, 1778*, Third Edition, John Adams (Budd and Bartram, Philadelphia, 1797) vol. 1, p. xi.

Well-digger. See Matthews, J. W.

Wellhouse, Frederick

In 1890 Frederick Wellhouse harvested about eighty thousand bushels of apples which he sold for over fifty thousand dollars. Because this crop and the amount of the sale was the best ever to have been attained by any individual apple grower in the middlewestern part of the United States, Wellhouse was nicknamed the *Apple King*. [1] His orchards, covering several thousand acres of land, were located at Fairmount, Glenwood, Leavenworth, Miami, Osage, and Summit, Kans.

Frederick Wellhouse was born in Chippewa Township, Ohio, on November 16, 1828, and died at Leavenworth, Kans., on January 10, 1911. For ten years he was President of the Kansas State Horticultural Society.

[1] *The National Cyclopaedia of American Biography* (James T. White and Company, New York, 1916) vol. 15, p. 153.

Welsh Parson. See Davis, J. J.

Welsh Wonder. See Wilde, Jimmy

Wene, Elmer H.

Elmer H. Wene, a New Jersey poultryman and politician, was nicknamed the *Day-old Chick* [1] by his colleagues in the National House of Representatives because he owns and operates a baby-chick hatchery.

He was President of the International Baby Chick Association in 1933, and served as a Democratic Representative from the Second Congressional District of New Jersey to the United States Congress from 1937 to 1939 and again from 1941 to 1945.

Elmer H. Wene was born on a farm near Pittstown, N.J., on May 1, 1892.

[1] An interview with Captain Victor Hunt Harding, Secretary of the National Democratic Congressional Reelection Committee, Washington, D.C., April 10, 1939.

Wentworth, John

Because he was six feet, seven inches tall, John Wentworth was humorously called *Long John*. [1]

From 1836 to 1861 he was editor of the *Democrat*, a leading newspaper of that day published at Chicago, Ill. In 1857 he was made mayor of Chicago, and in 1860 he was again elected to that office.

John Wentworth was born at Sandwich, N.H., on March 5, 1815, and died at Chicago, Ill., on October 16, 1888.

[1] *The National Cyclopaedia of American Biography* (James T. White and Company, New York, 1900) vol. 10, p. 482.

Wesley College

The athletic teams of Wesley College, at Grand Forks, N.D., are popularly designated *Flickertails, Nodaks*, and *Sioux*. Prior to 1930 the teams were nicknamed *Flickertails* [1] doubtless from the fact that North

Wesley College—Continued

Dakota is the *Flickertail State*. The sobriquet, *Nodaks*,[1] originated by contracting the name, North Dakota, because "many felt that it was difficult to play up the lowly flickertail."[1] The student body and the Alumni Association in the fall of 1930 called the teams *Sioux*[1] because "the Sioux Indians made this state their hunting grounds, also because the physique and vigor of the Sioux Indian is ideal for publicity purposes."[1] The *Sioux* is the commonly-preferred and most widely used nickname for the teams.

[1] A communication from Frank J. Webb, Director of the Bureau of Alumni Relations at Wesley College, Grand Forks, N.D., June 20, 1935.

West, Mae

Mae West, stage and screen actress and dramatic author, has been nicknamed the *Baby Vamp, Diamond Lil*, the *Screen's Bad Girl*, and the *Siren of the Screen*, and has, in turn, given her own name to an inflated life-preserver developed for use by the United States armed forces in World War II, and to a figure-eight-shaped cruller.

The *Baby Vamp*[1] was Miss West's childhood nickname, acquired because she had made such a success playing a vamp at a church social when she was five years old and because at the same age in a play staged by a stock company in Brooklyn she first used the free-wheeling walk for which she later became famous. She was nicknamed *Diamond Lil*[2] after her stage-play of the same name, because she seemed to carry over into real life the flamboyant and voluptuous personality of the heroine. The play was made into a movie, and drew crowds into theatres around the country. In Miss West's movies, the scenarios of which she frequently wrote herself, her portrayals of lusty and alluring women who are never at a loss for a retort have enjoyed huge success. As a result she is known as the *Screen's Bad Girl*[3] and the *Siren of the Screen*.[4] Her screenplays, however, are not in the serious vein of the silent screen melodramas of siren-vampires but are, rather, travesties on the power of sex-appeal.

Mae West was born in Brooklyn, N.Y., on August 17, 1892.

See also Mae West.

[1] *The Washington Daily News*, Washington, D.C., September 8, 1934, col. 5, p. 16.
[2] *The Washington Post*, Washington, D.C., February 17, 1937, col. 2, p. 10.

[3] *The Washington Daily News*, Washington, D.C., September 7, 1934, p. 25.
[4] *The Washington Post*, Washington, D.C., January 7, 1937, col. 5, p. 2.

West, William Henry

Blind Man Eloquent[1] was a widely-known sobriquet applied to William Henry West because, though handicapped by blindness, he was in constant demand at political conventions and at public meetings as an eloquent[2] and learned speaker.

William Henry West was born at Millisboro, Pa., on February 9, 1824, and died at Bellefontaine, Ohio, on March 14, 1911.

[1] *Past and Present of Knox County, Ohio*, Albert B. Williams, Editor-in-chief (B. F. Bowen and Company, Indianapolis, Ind., 1912) vol. 1, p. 399.
[2] *Ohio Archaeological and Historical Quarterly, October, 1911*, Published Quarterly by the Society Office (Press of The F. J. Heer Printing Company, Columbus, Ohio, 1911) vol. 20, no. 4, p. 407.

West Virginia

West Virginia merits the designation the *Mountain State* because more than one third of the state is on a high plateau of the Allegheny Mountains. It is also known as the *Panhandle State* because its shape resembles a pan with a handle on it. The region of the handle is called the *Panhandle Section*, or simply the *Panhandle of West Virginia*.[1]

Switzerland of America is another nickname applied to West Virginia because of her picturesque mountain scenery.

[1] *U.S.: An Index to the United States of America*, comp. by Malcolm Townsend (D. Lothrop Company, Boston, 1890) p. 81.

West Virginia State College

The athletes playing on the teams of West Virginia State College, at Institute, W.Va., were designated *Yellow Jackets*[1] because there are "thousands of yellow jackets and hornets seen in the vicinity of the college during the summer of each year."[1]

[1] A communication from E. S. Jamison, Director of Athletics at West Virginia State College, Institute, W.Va., December 2, 1935.

West Virginia University

The *Mountaineers*[1] is the sobriquet given to the athletic teams of West Virginia University, at Morgantown, W.Va., about 1891 because West Virginia is nicknamed the *Mountain State*.

[1] A letter from H. A. Stansburg, Assistant Director of Athletics at West Virginia University, Morgantown, W.Va., June 21, 1935.

West Virginia Wesleyan College

The athletic teams of West Virginia Wesleyan College, at Buckhannon, W.Va., are popularly called *Bobcats* and *Methodists*.

West Virginians

West Virginia folk are called *Pan-han-dleites* because they come from the *Pan-handle State*.

See West Virginia.

West Point of the Air. See Randolph Field; San Antonio, Tex.

West Point of the Confederacy. See Virginia Military Institute

West Point of the South. See Virginia Military Institute

Western Maryland College

The athletic teams of Western Maryland College, at Westminster, Md., are commonly called the *Terrors*.

Western Reserve University

The *Red Cats* [1] is the nickname given to the athletic teams of Western Reserve University, at Cleveland, Ohio, in 1928 by a vote of the student body because their college paper is called the *Red Cat*.

[1] A letter from Karl Davis, Director of Publicity at Western Reserve University, Cleveland, Ohio, June 18, 1935.

Western State College of Colorado

The athletic teams of Western State College of Colorado, at Gunnison, Colo., were designated *Mountaineers* [1] about 1916 or 1917.

[1] A communication from H. L. Dotson, vice-president of Western State College of Colorado, Gunnison, Colo., November 14, 1935

Western Union College

The *Golden Eagles* [1] and the *Telegraphers* [1] are sobriquets attributed to the athletic teams of Western Union College, at Le Mars, Iowa. The former appellation was given to the teams in 1930 by the Student Association in order "to keep the press writers from calling the Western Union teams the *Telegraphers*." [1]

[1] A communication from D. O. Kemie, Western Union College, Le Mars, Iowa, June 19, 1935.

Westminster College

The athletic teams of Westminster College, at Fulton, Mo., were nicknamed *Blue Jays* [1] in 1903 by a vote of the student body "acting on the report of a committee appointed" to select the colors and a totem for the college.

"In 1903 the colors of the college were changed from yellow and white to Oxford blue, one color. This color was chosen because it is the traditional color of Presbyterianism and for economical reasons in the purchasing of stockings, jerseys, etc.

"At the time the colors were changed, every Missouri college had its colors, but with the single exception of the University of Missouri (whose teams bore the title of 'Tigers') there was then no institution in Missouri which had a 'totem' or nickname. The blue jay was almost the only specimen of the animal kingdom which approached the Westminster color, its pugnacious disposition also being an inducement for its selection as the totem; thus the nickname, *Blue Jays*, is the oldest collegiate nickname in this state." [1]

[1] A letter from Charles F. Lamkin, Alumni Secretary of Westminster College, Fulton, Mo., December 3, 1935.

Westmoreland County, Virginia

Westmoreland County, Va., is called the *Athens of Virginia* [1] because it is the birthplace of a "long line of illustrious men," [1] hence is comparable to Athens, Greece. Prominent Virginians born in Westmoreland County include George Washington, Robert E. Lee, and James Monroe.

[1] *Virginia*, comp. and ed. by Charlotte Allen (Published by the Department of Agriculture and Immigration of the State of Virginia under the direction of George W. Koiner, Commissioner, Department of Purchase and Printing, Richmond, Va., 1937) p. 257.

Wet Quakers

The *Wet Quakers* [1] was the sobriquet attributed to the *Quakers* in Philadelphia during the latter half of the eighteenth century because at times, contrary to their prevalent custom of wearing plain and dull colored clothing, they could not resist wearing the fashionable and colorful dress of their contemporaries. The term implied that this discrepancy in their dress was necessary because they had gotten wet and had to change their clothes.

[1] *Women of Colonial and Revolutionary Times: Dolly Madison*, Maud Wilder Goodwin (Charles Scribner's Sons, New York, 1896) p. 21.

Wheat, Chatham Roberdeau

About 1859 to 1860, while Major Chatham Roberdeau Wheat served in Italy in the army of the renowned Italian patriot, Giuseppe Garibaldi, who was waging his campaign for Italian independence, European newspapers designated Wheat the *Murat of America* [1] because he was a brave, gallant, and resourceful leader of Garibaldi's cavalry troops. This sobriquet was an allusion to Joachim Murat, the French cavalry leader who distinguished himself in Napoleon's military campaigns.

In 1861 Major Wheat returned to the United States from Italy, and raised a battalion of five hundred Confederate cavalrymen known as the *Louisiana Tigers.* [1]

Chatham Roberdeau Wheat was born at Alexandria, Va., on April 9, 1826, and died at the battle of Gaines' Mill, Va., on June 27, 1862.

[1] *The National Cyclopaedia of American Biography* (James T. White and Company, New York, 1907) vol. 9, p. 168.

Wheat State. See Minnesota

Wheaton College

The *Crusaders* is the sobriquet given to the athletic teams of Wheaton College, at Wheaton, Ill.

Wheatshockers. See University of Wichita

Wheel-horse of the Senate. See Ruggles, Benjamin

Wheeler, Burton Kendall

Burton Kendall Wheeler, Senator from Montana, was nicknamed the *Great Liberal* [1] by his colleagues in the United States Senate because he was considered a great Democratic liberal before the New Deal came into power in 1933.

During his term of service as a Democratic Senator from 1923 to 1947 he was, however, one of the bitterest foes of New Deal legislation.

Burton Kendall Wheeler was born at Hudson, Mass., on February 27, 1882.

[1] An interview with Captain Victor Hunt Harding, Secretary of the National Democratic Congress Re-election Committee, Washington, D.C. April 10, 1939

Wheeler, Joseph

Fighting Joe, the *Little Hero,* and *Little Joe* are nicknames of Joseph Wheeler, general in the Confederate Army, later a member of the House of Representatives and widely known for his efforts to promote complete reconciliation between North and South.

He won the nickname, *Fighting Joe,* [1] at the Battle of Shiloh, Tenn., on April 6 and 7, 1862.

He was often called the *Little Hero* [2] and *Little Joe* [3] in reference to his medium height and build, and his soldierly courage during the Civil War. The sobriquet, *Little Hero,* originated in 1862 while Wheeler, then Brigadier General, was defending forces in the vicinity of Nashville, Tenn., during which time he successfully engaged in numerous daring, original attacks upon the enemy.

Joseph Wheeler was born at Augusta, Ga., on September 10, 1836, and died at Brooklyn, N.Y., on January 25, 1906.

[1] *The National Cyclopaedia of American Biography* (James T. White and Company, New York, 1907) vol. 9, p. 19.
[2] *Lee and His Lieutenants; Comprising the Early Life, Public Services, and Campaigns of General Robert E. Lee and His Companions in Arms, with a Record of Their Campaigns and Heroic Deeds,* Edward A. Pollard (E. B. Treat and Company, New York, 1867) p. 697.
[3] *Confederate Military History, a Library of Confederate States History, in Twelve Volumes, Written by Distinguished Men of the South and Edited by General Clement A. Evans of Georgia* (Confederate Publishing Company, Atlanta, Ga., 1899) vol. 1, p. 707.

Wheeling, West Virginia

Wheeling is termed the *Nail City* [1] because of its extensive manufacturing of cut nails.

[1] *History of Greater Wheeling and Vicinity, a Chronicle of Progress and a Narrative Account of the Industries, Institutions and People of the City and Tributary Territory,* Charles A. Wingerter, Editor-in-chief (The Lewis Publishing Company, Chicago and New York, 1912) vol. 1, p. 296.
King's Handbook of the United States, planned and ed. by Moses King, text by M. F. Sweetser (Moses King Corporation, Buffalo, N.Y., 1891) p. 884.

Whelps. See Tennesseeans

Where Mexico Meets Uncle Sam. See Brownsville, Tex.

Whig Gulliver. See Webster, Daniel

Whipple, Henry Benjamin

The Indians in Minnesota nicknamed Henry Benjamin Whipple *Straight Tongue* [1] to describe his sincerity, truthfulness, and directness with them.

He was consecrated the first Bishop of the Episcopalian Church in Minnesota, on

October 13, 1859, took an active and prominent part in promoting the growth of the church; and he was noted for his work in establishing mission schools for the Indians.

Henry Benjamin Whipple was born at Adams, N.Y., on February 15, 1822, and died in Faribault, Minn., on September 16, 1901.

[1] *Appleton's Cyclopaedia of American Biography*, ed. by James Grant Wilson and John Fiske (D. Appleton and Company, New York, 1889) vol. 6, p. 461.

Whipple, Squire

The civil engineer, Squire Whipple was aptly nicknamed the *Father of American Bridge Building*.[1] In 1840 Whipple designed and patented the first iron highway bridge truss; his *Treatise on Bridge Building*, published in 1847, was a thorough and accurate discussion of the elementary principles of framed bridge structures; in 1852 he constructed the type known as the Whipple trapezoid bridge; and in 1872 he obtained a patent for a lift drawbridge. This type of bridge and several others built according to Whipple's principles of construction were erected over the Erie Canal.

Squire Whipple was born at Hardwick, Mass., on September 16, 1804, and died at Albany, N.Y., on March 15, 1888.

[1] *The National Cyclopaedia of American Biography* (James T. White and Company, New York, 1907) vol. 9, p. 35.

Whisky Boys

See Whisky Rebellion.

Whisky Rebellion

The four western counties of Pennsylvania particularly resented the Excise Act of 1791 which imposed a tax on all whisky distilled within the United States. The farmers of that region used distillation as a practical method of disposing of excess corn as well as making it more easily transportable. The rebels, known as the *Whisky Boys*,[1] harassed the tax collectors, formed masked groups to force conformity with their views, and in other ways demonstrated their resistance until President Washington called out the state militia to put down this *Whisky Rebellion*,[2] as it was humorously called. The rebellion melted away before the coming of the militia in the summer of 1794, most of its ringleaders fleeing to the hills and a few receiving presidential pardon. The *Whisky Rebellion* provided the first test of the enforcement of Federal law by the Federal Government.

[1] *A History of the People of the United States, from the Revolution to the Civil War*, John Bach McMaster (D. Appleton and Company, New York, 1885) vol. 2, p. 194.
[2] *The American People and Nation*, Rolla M. Tryon and Charles R. Lingley (Ginn and Company, New York and Boston, 1929) p. 251.
When America Became a Nation, Tudor Jenks (Thomas Y. Crowell and Company, New York, 1910) p. 42-3.

Whisky Ring

In 1875 a group of revenue officers, some at St. Louis, Mo., and some at Washington, D.C., conspired with distillers in the western part of the United States to defraud the Government of its revenue on whisky. The league was designated the *Whisky Ring*[1] after its purpose had been exposed.

[1] *History of Our Country, a Text-book for Schools*, Oscar H. Cooper, Harry F. Estill, and Leonard Lemmon (Ginn and Company, Boston and London, 1903) p. 422.

Whisky Town. See Peoria, Ill.

Whistler, George Washington

While he attended the United States Military Academy, at West Point, N.Y., from 1814 to 1819, George Washington Whistler was nicknamed *Pipes*[1] by his schoolmates because he was an unusually skillful performer on the flute.

Whistler was graduated from West Point in 1819 as an engineer. On loan from the government he worked for the railroad corporations then badly in need of trained personnel for the railroad era just beginning. Whistler's major contributions to civil engineering were made from 1829 to 1839 in the United States.

In 1842 he was invited to Russia as consulting engineer on the proposed St. Petersburg-Moscow railroad. For his work on this project he was much honored by the Russian government who consulted him also about the arsenal and docks at Kronstadt and the iron bridge over the Neva.

George Washington Whistler was born at Fort Wayne, Ind., on May 19, 1800, and died at St. Petersburg, Russia, two years before the opening of the railroad, on April 9, 1849. He was the father of the noted American artist, James McNeill Whistler.

[1] *The National Cyclopaedia of American Biography* (James T. White and Company, New York, 1898) vol. 1, p. 277.

White, Hugh Lawson

Hugh Lawson White was known to his contemporaries as the *Cato of America*[1] or the *Cato of the Senate*.[2]

He was elected to complete Andrew Jackson's uncompleted term as Senator from Tennessee in 1825 and continued to hold that post until his resignation in 1840. The nickname was acquired because White discharged his senatorial duties with a sense of solemn responsibility recalling that of the ancient Roman senators, a similarity heightened by the stately dignity of White's personal presence. Though not an eloquent or a frequent speaker, his utterances were characterized by their thoroughness and temperateness of tone, a rarity in the turbulent congressional debates of that day.

Hugh Lawson White was born in Iredell County, N.C., on October 30, 1773, and died at Knoxville, Tenn., on April 10, 1840.

See also Webster, Daniel and Hugh Lawson White.

[1] *Andrew Johnson, Plebeian and Patriot*, Robert W. Winston (Henry Holt and Company, New York, 1928) p. 26.
[2] *Party Battles of the Jackson Period*, Claude G. Bowers (Houghton Mifflin Company, Boston and New York, 1922) p. 427-433.

White, James

James White, a frontiersman and scout, serving in Brigadier General Philip H. Sheridan's expedition against the Sioux in 1876, was nicknamed *Buffalo Chips*[1] because he was a great friend and admirer of William Frederick Cody, commonly known as *Buffalo Bill*, and imitated the latter's dress, speech, and mannerisms. In his *True Tales of the Plains*, Cody corroborates this story, adding that General Sheridan[2] first applied the sobriquet to White.

James White was sometimes called Jonathan or Charles White. His place and time of birth are not known, but he was killed near Whitewood Creek in the Land of the Dakotas, on September 10, 1876, during a fight with the Sioux Indians.

[1] *Campaigning with Crook and Stories of Army Life*, Charles King (Harper and Brothers, New York, 1890) p. 94, 114.
South Dakota Historical Collections, comp. by the State Historical Society (Will A. Beach Printing Company, Sioux Falls, S.D., 1912) vol. 6, p. 517.
[2] *True Tales of the Plains*, Buffalo Bill (William F. Cody) (Cupples and Leon Company, New York, 1908) p. 225.

White, Joyner

Joyner White, who was born at Union City, La., on June 1, 1909, and who played outfield in major league baseball, is popularly called *Jo-Jo*.[1]

[1] *Who's Who in Major League Base Ball*, comp. by Harold (Speed) Johnson (Buxton Publishing Company, Chicago, 1933) p. 411.

White, William Allen

The journalist and writer, William Allen White, was known as the *Sage of Emporia*.[1] From 1895, as editor and proprietor of the Emporia *Gazette*, he made that paper notable for the quality of its editorial style and thought, reflecting the personality of the editor. It is said that he very much disliked the nickname, for to him a sage was a "bug-eyed, long-haired creature that has no contact with reality."[1]

William Allen White was born at Emporia, Kans., on February 10, 1868, and died January 24, 1944.

[1] *The Evening Star*, Washington, D.C., December 29, 1937, col. 5, p. A-14.

White Beaver. See Powell, D. F.

White City. See Chicago, Ill.

White Dog

From 1840 to 1843, a great period of depression, the city of St. Louis, Mo., became "flooded with paper currency from other states." Some of this paper money, worthless as such, was humorously nicknamed *White Dog*[1] because its borders were decorated with pictures of white dogs.

[1] *Centennial History of Missouri (The Center State) One Hundred Years in the Union, 1820-1921*, Walter B. Stevens (The S. J. Clarke Publishing Company, St. Louis, Mo., and Chicago, 1921) vol. 2, p. 447.

White House

The official residence of the President of the United States is known as the *White House*.[1]

Authorities differ as to when or why this famous building was first called the *White House*. Rufus Rockwell Wilson[1] accepts the traditional theory that George Washington designated it the *White House* in honor of his wife's early home located on the Pamunky River in Virginia. It is thought by some[3] that after the partial destruction of the President's home by fire when the British invaded Washington, D.C., in 1814, the building was repaired and painted white in order to conceal smoke-damage, thus giving rise to the sobriquet.

Other authorities [4] reject this theory, citing instances of the use of the nickname prior to 1814.

[1] *Dolly Madison, the Nation's Hostess*, Elizabeth Lippincott Dean (Lothrop, Lee and Shepard Company, Boston, 1928) p. 151.
[2] *Washington, the Capital City and Its Part in the History of the Nation*, Rufus Rockwell Wilson (J. B. Lippincott Company, Philadelphia, 1901) vol. 1, p. 27.
[3] *Records of the Columbia Historical Society, Washington, D.C.*, comp. by the committee on publication and the Recording Secretary (Published by the Society at the press of The New Era Printing Company, Lancaster, Pa., 1906) vol. 9, p. 31-2.
[4] *A History of the National Capital from Its Foundation, through the Period of the Adoption of the Organic Act*, Wilhelmus Bogart Bryan (The Macmillan Company, New York, 1914) vol. 1, p. 313, 627.

White House Pet. See O'Day, C. G.

White House Tommy. See Corcoran, T. G.

White Mountain Giant. See Crawford, E. A.

White Mountain State. See New Hampshire

White Mountains
The White Mountains, which extend across southern Maine into New Hampshire, have been called the *Top of New England* [1] because they constitute the highest land in the New England States.

[1] *The World Book Encyclopedia* (The Quarrie Corporation, Chicago, 1938) vol. 18, p. 7750.

White Pine King
The largest white pine tree ever grown in Idaho, according to available records, was nicknamed the *White Pine King*.[1] This giant tree grew in Latah County, near Bovill, Idaho. When it was cut down on December 12, 1911, it was two hundred and seven feet high, had a diameter of six feet and nine inches, was 425 years old, and contained 28,900 board feet of lumber, approximately enough to build two average-sized five-room houses.

[1] *Idaho, Its Symbols, Its Capitol, and Some Outstanding Dates in Idaho History* (Idaho State Chamber of Commerce, Boise, Idaho, 1937) a folder.

White Plains Bears Football Club
The *Bears* [1] is the nickname of this club, a member of the American Professional Football Association, at White Plains, N.Y. It was given to the club by sports writers because it was short [1] and easy to write.

[1] A communication from Michael Bambara, Manager of The White Plains Bears Football Club, White Plains, N.Y., April 3, 1939.

White Robe. See Roberts, John

White Savage. See Girty, Simon

White Sox. See Chicago American League Baseball Company

White Stockings. See Chicago American League Baseball Company

Whiteman, Paul
The orchestra leader, Paul Whiteman, has been popularly nicknamed the *Dean of American Popular Music* [1] and the *King of Jazz* [1] because his orchestras and bands specialize in popular music and because his efforts contributed to the acceptance of jazz as a genuine form of musical expression. He has conducted two transcontinental symphonic jazz tours in the United States, and made a similar tour of England and other European countries.

Paul Whiteman was born in Denver, Colo., in 1891.

[1] *The Free Lance-Star*, Fredericksburg, Va., January 7, 1938, col. 1, p. 7.

Whitey. See Pietruszka, A. F.; Young, L. F.

Whitfield of Nova Scotia. See Alline, Henry

Whiting, William Henry Chase
William Henry Chase Whiting, the Confederate soldier and officer, was nicknamed *Little Billy* [1] by the soldiers under his command because he was small of stature, sinewy, and well liked by everyone. He was graduated from the United States Military Academy, at West Point, but resigned from the Union Army on February 20, 1861, and enlisted in the Confederate Army in which, soon afterwards, he was appointed Major. He was active in the Confederate Army throughout the Civil War.

William Henry Chase Whiting was born at Biloxi, Miss., on March 22, 1824, and died at Fort Columbus on Governor's Island, N.Y., on March 10, 1865.

[1] *Dictionary of American Biography under the Auspices of the American Council of Learned Societies*, ed. by Dumas Malone (Charles Scribner's Sons, New York, 1936) vol. 20, p. 137.

Whitman College

The *Missionaries* [1] is the nickname of the athletic teams of Whitman College, at Walla Walla, Wash.

[1] A communication from R. V. Borleske, Director of Athletics at Whitman College, Walla Walla, Wash., June 21, 1935.

Whitman, John Lorin

The *Boy Guard* and the *Beloved Jailer* were nicknames of John Lorin Whitman.

When Whitman became a guard at the Cook County Jail, Chicago, Ill., he was about twenty-eight years of age, slender in build, and seemed a mere boy to the prisoners, hence the nickname *Boy Guard*.[1]

In 1895, Whitman was appointed jailer at this institution and came to be called the *Beloved Jailer* [1] because he was kind, humane, and compassionate in his treatment of the prisoners, and succeeded in procuring a number of very beneficial reforms in the administration of prison affairs.

On June 1, 1907, he was made Superintendent of the House of Correction, at Chicago, and, although no longer a jailer, his reputation for kindness had preceded him so that he was known at this institution also as the *Beloved Jailer*.

John Lorin Whitman was born at Sterling, Ill., on July 23, 1862, and died at Chicago, Ill., on December 13, 1926.

[1] *Encyclopedia of American Biography: American Biography, a New Cyclopedia,* comp. under the editorial supervision of a notable advisory board (Published under the direction of The American Historical Society, Inc., New York, 1929) vol. 37, p. 24-5.

Whitman, Walt

Because he was gray-headed in the latter part of his life, and because so many people admired his poetry, Walt Whitman has been called the *Good Gray Poet*.[1]

He was born at West Hills, Long Island, N.Y., on May 31, 1819, and died at Camden, N.J., on March 26, 1892.

[1] *American Literary Readings,* Leonidas Warren Payne, Jr. (Rand McNally and Company, Chicago and New York, 1917) p. 70.

Whitney, Arthur Carter

Arthur Carter Whitney, who was born at San Antonio, Tex., on January 2, 1908, and who played third base in major league baseball, is nicknamed *Pinkey*.[1]

[1] *Who's Who in Major League Base Ball,* comp. by Harold (Speed) Johnson (Buxton Publishing Company, Chicago, 1933) p. 413.

Whitney, Eli

Because he invented the cotton gin in 1793, Eli Whitney has been designated the *Father of the Cotton Gin*.[1] He was born at Westborough, Mass., on December 8, 1765, and died at New Haven, Conn., on January 8, 1825.

[1] *A Book of Nicknames,* John Goff (Courier-Journal Job Printing Company, Louisville, Ky., 1892) p. 29.

Whitney, Richard

Richard Whitney, former president of the New York Stock Exchange, was nicknamed the *Strong Man of Wall Street* [1] prior to his arrest and imprisonment for grand larceny and for misappropriating securities in 1938. The nickname referred to his marked leadership in American financial affairs, and to the unlimited confidence his business associates had in him.

From 1928 to 1930 Whitney was vice president, and from 1930 to 1935 president, of the New York Stock Exchange. During this period he headed most of the important standing committees of this organization. He was convicted of grand larceny by a jury of the Criminal Court of New York City on April 11, 1938, and sentenced to serve a five-to ten-year-sentence in prison.

He was sent to Sing Sing on April 12, 1938, and was paroled in 1941. He managed a dairy farm for several years after his release, and then became president of Ramie Mills of Florida, Inc., an organization for the growing and processing of ramie for fiber. Ramie Mills is at Zeelwood, Fla., where Whitney has lived for several years.[2]

[1] *Newsweek: The Magazine of News Significance,* Rockefeller Center, N.Y., March 21, 1938, col. 1, p. 37.
[2] *Newsweek: The Magazine of News Significance,* Rockefeller Center, N.Y., April 19, 1948, vol. 31, p. 11.

Whittier, John Greenleaf

The *Burns of America,* the *Poet Laureate of New England,* the *Puritan Poet,* and the *Quaker Poet* are nicknames which have been attributed to John Greenleaf Whittier.

He was sometimes called the *Burns of America* [1] because he was the son of a farmer, suffering many hardships during his youth, and because he wrote in simple language about rural life, in which respects he was comparable to the Scotch poet, Robert Burns.

Because he was considered the outstanding poet of New England rural life, Whittier was also widely known as the *Poet Laureate of New England*,[1] and the *Puritan Poet*.[2]

The Quaker Poet [2] referred to Whittier's membership in the Quaker Church.

John Greenleaf Whittier was born at Haverhill, Mass., on December 17, 1807, and died at Hampton Falls, N.H., on September 7, 1892.

[1] *American Literary Readings*, Leonidas Warren Payne, Jr. (Rand McNally and Company, Chicago and New York, 1917) p. 262.
[2] *Municipal History of Essex County in Massachusetts; a Classified Work, Devoted to the County's Remarkable Growth in All Lines of Human Endeavor, More Especially to Within a Period of Fifty Years*, Tercentenary Edition, Benjamin F. Arrington, Editor-in-chief (Lewis Historical Publishing Company, New York, 1922) vol. 1, p. 197.

Whittier College

The athletic teams of Whittier College, at Whittier, Calif., are designated the *Poets*, doubtless because the name of the college is the same as the last name of the nineteenth century American poet, John Greenleaf Whittier.

Whitworth College

The *Preachers* and the *Pirates* are the nicknames of the athletic teams of Whitworth College, at Spokane, Wash. Whitworth College is a Presbyterian institution and the athletic teams were inevitably designated the *Preachers*. The nickname *Pirates*,[1] was selected by the student body in 1926 because they wished to have a sobriquet more befitting an athletic team, and because the college colors are red and black with which they felt the nickname, *Pirates*, would harmonize.[1]

[1] A communication from Estella Baldwin, Alumni Secretary of Whitworth College, Spokane, Wash., November 21, 1935.

Whyte, William Pinkney

William Pinkney Whyte, lawyer and politician, was nicknamed the *Grand Old Man from Maryland* [1] because of his long and active public services to the people of that state. He was elected a Representative from Baltimore County to the Maryland House of Delegates in 1846, Comptroller of the Maryland Treasury in 1851, and Democratic Governor of Maryland in 1871. He was a Senator from Maryland to the United States Congress from 1875 until 1881. He was appointed a Senator from Maryland to fill the vacancy occasioned by the death of Senator Arthur Pue Gorman, and was still

in office when he died. He held many other public offices in Maryland during his lifetime.

William Pinkney Whyte was born at Baltimore, Md., on August 9, 1824, and died there on March 17, 1908.

[1] *Dictionary of American Biography under the Auspices of the American Council of Learned Societies*, ed. by Dumas Malone (Charles Scribner's Sons, New York, 1936) vol. 20, p. 179.

Wichita, Kansas

Wichita was formerly called the *Magic Mascot of the Plains* [1] in allusion to its rapid growth and development, one of its most progressive decades being that of 1900 to 1910,[2] during which time the population more than doubled.

[1] *King's Handbook of the United States*, planned and ed. by Moses King, text by M. F. Sweetser (The Matthews-Northrup Company, Buffalo, N.Y., 1896) p. 271-2.
[2] *Kansas: A Cyclopedia of State History, Embracing Events, Institutions, Industries, Counties, Cities, Towns, Prominent Persons, etc.*, ed. by Frank W. Blackmar (Standard Publishing Company, Chicago, 1912) vol. 2, p. 913.

Wickliffe, Charles Anderson

Charles Anderson Wickliffe, a lawyer, was sometimes called the *Duke*,[1] a nickname applied to him because he was rich and haughty. He was a Representative from Kentucky to the United States Congress from 1823 until 1833, and again from 1861 until 1863.

Charles Anderson Wickliffe was born at Bardstown, Ky., on June 8, 1788, and died at Howard County, Md., on October 31, 1869.

[1] *Appleton's Cyclopaedia of American Biography*, ed. by James Grant Wilson and John Fiske (D. Appleton and Company, New York, 1888) vol. 6, p. 449.

Wide-awakes

In the presidential campaign of 1860 Abraham Lincoln and Stephen A. Douglas were the candidates. Torchlight processions were then in vogue and on one occasion the Republicans at Hartford, Conn., conducted such a parade. Among those participating in it were several clerks from the dry-goods store belonging to Talcott and Post of that city. In order to protect their clothing from the dripping of the candles used in the procession, the clerks provided themselves with glazed-cloth caps and capes. This action suggested to others that these thoughtful individuals were wide-awake. The Republicans were pleased with the idea and at a meeting of the members of the

Wide-awakes—Continued

party on March 7, 1860, adopted for themselves the name *Wide-awakes*.[1] It is said
that the Democrats who favored the election
of Douglas also adopted the nickname.

[1] *The Lyon Campaign in Missouri, Being a History of the First Iowa Infantry, and of the Causes Which Led up to Its Organization, and How It Earned the Thanks of Congress Which It Got, together with a Birdseye View of the Conditions in Iowa Preceding the Great Civil War of 1861*, E. F. Ware (Crane and Company, Topeka, Kans., 1907) p. 66.

Wigwam

Wigwam is traditional in the United States
for any large structure used for political
conventions. *The Wigwam* usually refers to
Tammany Hall.

It is also used in reference to Andrew
Jackson's pre-inaugural headquarters in
Washington, D.C. Because of the death of
his wife only three months before, Jackson
avoided as much as possible the gay crowds
and importunate office-seekers who had
thronged into the capital to celebrate his
inauguration. His hotel-room, where he attended to business details and quietly but
courteously received his many callers, was
known as the *Wigwam*.

[1] *Andrew Jackson, the Fighting President*, Helen Nico-
lay (The Century Company, New York, 1929) p. 256.
Andrew Jackson, Portrait of a President, by Marquis
James (The Bobbs-Merrill Company, Indianapolis, New
York, 1937) p. 182.

Wilberforce University

Bulldogs, the *Green Wave from Ohio*,
and the *Forces* are the nicknames commonly
given to the athletic teams of Wilberforce
University, at Wilberforce, Ohio. Gilbert
H. Jones, former president of Wilberforce
University, originated the sobriquet *Bulldogs*.[1] In 1930 the teams "played three
games in eight days, winning them all with
high scores," and winning the designation
the *Green Wave from Ohio*[1] by the sports
writers of the Atlanta papers. The campus
nickname for the teams is the *Forces*.[1]

[1] A communication from J. Aubrey Lane, Chairman of
the Athletic Committee at Wilberforce University, Wilberforce, Ohio, November 18, 1935.

Wild Bill. See Hickok, J. B.

Wild Bill the Pony Express Rider.
See Cody, W. F.

Wildcat Currency

Wildcat is colloquial American parlance
for any unreliable enterprise without sound

backing. Prior to 1863, in which year the
National Bank Act was passed, many institutions issued bank notes without sufficient
capital stock to redeem them. The banks
were called wildcat banks and the notes they
issued *Wildcat Currency*, or *Wildcat
Money*.[1] Such a bank was the Columbia
Bank established in Washington, D.C., between 1850 and 1852.[1]

[1] *Records of the Columbia Historical Society, Washington, D.C.*, comp. by the Committee of Publication and
the Recording Secretary (Published by the Society, Washington, D.C., at the Press of The New Era Printing
Company, Lancaster, Pa., 1917) vol. 20, p. 181.

Wildcat Division

During World War I the nickname *Wildcat Division*[1] was applied to the 81st Division of the 321st Infantry of the American
Expeditionary Forces stationed at Camp
Jackson, Columbia, S.C. Camp Jackson was
situated on "Wildcat Creek" from which
the division took its name. The term also
refers to the fierce manner in which the members of the division fought. The nickname
was retained during World War II.

[1] *The 321st Infantry, "Wildcats," 81st Division: The
History of the 321st Infantry with A Brief Historical
Sketch of the 81st Division, Being a Vivid and Authentic
Account of the Life and Experiences of American Soldiers
in France, While They Trained, Worked, and Fought to
Help Win the World War*, Clarence Walton Johnson
(The R. L. Bryan Company, Columbia, S.C., 1919)
p. 133, 137.

Wildcat Money. See *Wildcat Currency*

Wildcats. See South Dakota State School
    of Mines; University of Arizona; Uni-
    versity of Kentucky; University of
    New Hampshire; Villanova College;
    Wiley College

Wilde, Jimmy

Because he was born in Wales, and be-
cause he was an outstanding prize-fighter,
Jimmy Wilde was known as the *Welsh
Wonder*.[2]

Jimmy Wilde was born at Quaker's Yard,
Marthy's Valley, Wales, in May, 1892.

[1] *The Ring, World's Foremost Boxing Magazine* (Published monthly by The Ring, Inc., Dunellen, N.J.,
1931) p. 33.

Wilderness City. See Washington, D.C.

Wild Horse Charlie. See Alexander,
    C. W.

Wild Horses

During Grover Cleveland's return to office as President of the United States from 1893 to 1897 the Democratic members of the House of Representatives who opposed his party leadership and the legislative measures which he advised, were nicknamed *Wild Horses* [1] because, just as wild horses cannot be restrained by harness, they could not be kept within the political traces. Two of the most outstanding members of this group were Joseph C. Sibley from Pennsylvania, and Richard P. Bland from Missouri.

[1] *Twenty Years of the Republic, 1885-1905,* Harry Thurston Peck (Dodd, Mead and Company, New York, 1907) p. 456.

Wiles, Greenbury F.

The soldiers of the Seventy-eighth Regiment of Ohio Volunteer Infantrymen humorously nicknamed Brigadier General Greenbury F. Wiles *Old Whiskers* [1] in allusion to his long, bushy whiskers.

On October 26, 1861,[2] at the age of thirty-six, Wiles entered the Union Army, apparently having been commissioned Captain of Company C of the Seventy-eighth Regiment at that time. On November 29, 1862, he became a Lieutenant Colonel in the regiment, and on March 13, 1865, he was made a brevet Brigadier General of the regiment, having been mustered out of service with this rank on July 11, 1865.

[1] *Andersonville: A Story of Rebel Military Prisons, Fifteen Months a Guest of the So-called Southern Confederacy; a Private Soldier's Experience in Richmond, Andersonville, Savannah, Millen, Blackshear, and Florence,* John McElroy (D. R. Locke, Toledo, Ohio, 1879) p. 279.
[2] *Official Roster of the Soldiers of the State of Ohio in the War of the Rebellion, 1861-1866, Compiled under the direction of the roster commission: Joseph B. Foraker, Governor; James S. Robinson, Secretary of State; and H. A. Axline, Adjutant-general, Published by Authority of the General Assembly* (The Werner Printing and Manufacturing Company, Akron, Ohio, 1888) vol. 6, p. 351.

Wiley College

The *Wildcats* is the nickname of the athletic teams of Wiley College, at Marshall, Tex.

Willard, Frances Elizabeth

The educator and reformer Frances Elizabeth Willard was designated *The silver tongued and golden hearted* [1] because of her ability to speak her convictions to the public and because of her humanitarian attitude which brought about temperance reforms.

Frances Elizabeth Willard was born at Churchville, N.Y., on September 28, 1839.

From 1874 she devoted her life to the temperance movement, becoming national president of the Women's Christian Temperance Union in 1879 and world president of the organization in 1891. She died at New York City, on February 18, 1898. She was elected to the American Hall of Fame in 1910.

[1] *A Book of Nicknames,* John Goff (Courier-Journal Job Printing Company, Louisville, Ky., 1892) p. 30.

Willbanks, Alexander

Alexander Willbanks, preacher and evangelist pastor of a Negro Baptist church at Washington, D.C., during the early decades of the twentieth century, was commonly nicknamed the *Black Billy Sunday* [1] because many of his mannerisms and devices were imitative of the evangelist Billy Sunday.

[1] *Washington City and Capital: Federal Writers' Project,* American Guide Series, 1937 (Government Printing Office, Washington, D.C., 1937) p. 86.

William Jennings Bryan University

The men's basket-ball teams at William Jennings Bryan University, Dayton, Tenn., are designated the *Commoners* [1] and *Bryan Lions* [1] because William Jennings Bryan for whom the University was named was called the *Great Commoner* and the lion is the school mascot.[1] The women's basketball teams of the University are nicknamed the *Bryan Lassies.*[1]

[1] A letter from D. W. Ryther, Junior, Dean of the William Jennings Bryan University, Dayton, Tenn., November 26, 1935.

William Jewell College

The athletic teams of William Jewell College, at Liberty, Mo., were nicknamed *Cardinals* [1] by the sports editor of the *Kansas City Star and Times,* probably because the college colors are cardinal and black.

[1] A communication from William Jewell College, Liberty, Mo., September 24, 1937.

Williamette University

Bearcats is the nickname which was given to the athletic teams of Williamette University, at Salem, Ore.

Williams, Alex

Andrew Johnson called Dr. Alex Williams *Alexander the Great* [1] because the latter exerted great political influence, owned

Williams, Alex—Continued

many slaves, and a spacious home and large tracts of land.

Alex Williams was a wealthy and prominent man who lived in Greenville, Tenn., about 1826.

[1] *Andrew Johnson, Plebeian and Patriot,* Robert W. Winston (Henry Holt and Company, New York, 1928) p. 17.

Williams, David Rogerson

David Rogerson Williams, pioneer manufacturer, congressman, and Governor of South Carolina, was nicknamed *Thunder and Lightning Williams* [1] because he spoke his convictions in an intensely dramatic manner and did not hesitate to be vocal about his personal feelings on any question. He was a Democratic Representative from South Carolina to the United States Congress from 1801 until 1809, and again from 1811 until 1813. He was a Brigadier General in the War of 1812. He was governor of South Carolina from 1814 until 1816.

David Rogerson Williams was born near Society Hill, N.C., on March 8, 1776, and was killed by falling timbers on November 17, 1830, while supervising the building of a bridge at Witherspoon's Ferry, S.C.

[1] *Dictionary of American Biography under the Auspices of the American Council of Learned Societies,* ed. by Dumas Malone (Charles Scribner's Sons, New York, 1936) vol. 20, p. 254.

Williams, Israel

Israel Williams was nicknamed the *Monarch of Hampshire* [1] because he exerted much political power in Hampshire County, Mass., from about 1758 until 1767. He had great ability, but his arrogant and dictatorial manner made him very unpopular with those with whom he came in contact. He was a judge of the Hampshire County Court of Common Pleas from 1758 until 1774; a Representative from Hatfield, Mass., to the Massachusetts Legislature almost continuously from 1761 until 1767; and a member of the Council of the Governor of Massachusetts from 1761 until 1767. During the Revolutionary War, he was an outstanding Loyalist.

Israel Williams was born at Hatfield, Mass., on November 30, 1709, and died there on January 10, 1788.

[1] *Dictionary of American Biography under the Auspices of the American Council of Learned Societies,* ed. by Dumas Malone (Charles Scribner's Sons, New York, 1936) vol. 20, p. 266.

Williams, James Douglas

Because he wore clothing made of blue jean, James Douglas Williams was nicknamed *Blue Jeans Williams.* [1]

James Douglas Williams was born in Pickaway County, Ohio, on January 16, 1808, was Governor of the State of Indiana from 1877 until 1880, and died at Indianapolis, Ind., on November 20, 1880.

[1] *Indiana and Indianans,* Jacob Piatt Dunn (The American Historical Society, Chicago and New York, 1919) vol. 2, p. 708.

Williams, John

John Williams was captured during an Indian attack on Deerfield, Mass., on February 29, 1704, and after two years of captivity, was freed and allowed to return to members of his family still alive at Deerfield. He published a book entitled *The Redeemed Captive Returning to Zion,* after which he became known as the *Redeemed Captive.*

John Williams was born at Roxbury, Mass., on December 10, 1664, and died at Deerfield, Mass., on June 12, 1729.

[1] *The National Cyclopaedia of American Biography* (James T. White and Company, New York, 1898) vol. 1, p. 258.

Williams, Lewis

While he was a Representative from North Carolina to the United States Congress from 1815 to 1842, Lewis Williams was nicknamed the *Father of the House* [1] in allusion to his long and continuous service in office.

Lewis Williams was born in Surry County, N.C., on February 1, 1786, and died at Washington, D.C., on February 23, 1842.

[1] *The National Cyclopaedia of American Biography* (James T. White and Company, New York, 1893) vol. 3, p. 508.

Williams, Roger

Roger Williams was called the *Banished Preacher,* the *Indian's Friend,* and the *Rebel of Salem.*

While he was serving as a minister in Salem, Mass., Williams disagreed with the clergy and the civil authorities of the Massachusetts Colony on the question of liberty of conscience, maintaining that the civil government had no jurisdiction over a person's freedom of conscience. Because of this conviction, and his advocacy of the separation of church and state and of payment to the Indians for land taken from them, Roger

Williams was banished from the Massachusetts Colony. In June 1636, he began the settlement of Providence, in what became later the State of Rhode Island, and was designated the *Banished Preacher* [1] and the *Rebel of Salem*.[1]

He was called the *Indian's Friend* [2] because he dealt justly and honestly with the Indians with whom he came in contact, and appreciative of his kindness, they held him in great esteem.

Roger Williams was born at London, England, probably in 1607, and died at Providence, R.I., in March 1684.

[1] "Roger Williams" by Clifford Smyth, in *Builders of America* (Funk and Wagnalls Company, New York and London, 1931) vol. 6, p. 95.
[2] *The American Portrait Gallery: Containing Correct Portraits and Brief Notices of the Principal Actors in American History; Embracing Distinguished Women, Naval and Military Heroes, Statesmen, Civilians, Jurists, Divines, Authors, and Artists; together with Celebrated Indian Chiefs, from Christopher Columbus down to the Present Time*, A. D. Jones (J. M. Emerson and Company, New York, 1855) p. 307.

Wilmington College

The athletic teams of Wilmington College, at Wilmington, Ohio, are called *Fighting Quakers* and *Green Tornadoes*, the former nickname being applied to the football teams and the latter to the basketball teams. *Fighting Quakers* [1] was the nickname selected by the student body about 1910 because the college is owned and operated by the Society of Friends, and because the teams that year went through the season undefeated. *Green Tornadoes* [1] was adopted by the student body in 1925 because the college colors are green and white.

[1] A letter from Walter L. Collings, President of Wilmington College, Wilmington, Ohio, November 19, 1935.

Wilson, Charles Moseman

The amusing sobriquet, the *One Man Trust Company*,[1] was applied .to lawyer Charles Moseman Wilson because he often was requested to act as administrator of estates and as advisor of the deceased's family. Wilson's legal training, integrity, and his strength of character made people turn to him for these responsible duties.

Charles Moseman Wilson was born at Ionia, Mich., on October 10, 1858, and died at Grand Rapids, Mich., on June 20, 1917.

[1] *The National Cyclopaedia of American Biography* (James T. White and Company, New York, 1922) vol. 18, p. 380.

Wilson, Edith Bolling

Mrs. Edith Bolling Wilson was called the *First Lady of the World* [1] when she accompanied her husband, President Woodrow Wilson, on his first trip to Europe at the close of the World War in 1918. On this trip, President Wilson was feted and publicly honored as one of the outstanding world leaders. As the wife of the President, Mrs. Wilson was already the *First Lady of the Land* in the United States, and shared in the homage and respect paid to her husband by the nations they visited. On his first trip abroad, President Wilson left the United States on December 4, 1918, and left France to return to the United States on February 15, 1919.

[1] *The Strangest Friendship in History, Woodrow Wilson and Colonel House*, George Sylvester Viereck (Liveright, Inc., New York, 1932) p. 235.

Wilson, Henry

The *Cobbler* [1] or the *Natick Cobbler* [2] were popular nicknames of Henry Wilson because as a young man he worked at shoemaking [3] at Natick, Mass., in order to support himself and to accumulate enough money to attend school. He became Vice President of the United States in 1872, having been Ulysses S. Grant's running-mate in the latter's second presidential campaign. He was an ardent abolitionist and the author of the "History of the Rise and Fall of the Slave Power in America."

Henry Wilson was born at Farrington, N.H., on February 12, 1812, and died at Washington, D.C., on November 22, 1875.

[1] *History of the Cabinet of the United States of America from President Washington to President Coolidge, an Account of the Origin of the Cabinet, a Roster of the Various Members with the Term of Service, and Biographical Sketches of Each Member, Showing Public Offices Held by Each*, William Henry Smith (The Industrial Printing Company, Baltimore, Md., 1925) p. 504.
[2] *A Book of Nicknames*, John Goff (Courier-Journal Job Printing Company, Louisville, Ky., 1892) p. 29.
[3] *The National Cyclopaedia of American Biography* (James T. White and Company, New York, 1897) vol. 4, p. 13-14.

Wilson, James (Athlete)

James Wilson, who was born at Philadelphia, Pa., on June 23, 1900, and who was a catcher in major league baseball, is nicknamed *Ace*.[1]

[1] *Who's Who in Major League Base Ball*, comp. by Harold (Speed) Johnson (Buxton Publishing Company, Chicago, 1933) p. 415.

Wilson, James (Legislator)

James Wilson was widely known as *Tama Jim*.[1] From 1855 until his death in 1920,

Wilson, James (Legislator)—Continued
he made his home at Traer, in Tama County, Iowa, and was one of that county's most distinguished citizens.

Wilson devoted practically his entire life to a sincere and earnest attempt to secure better conditions for the American farmer. He was a Representative from Iowa to the United States Congress from 1873 to 1877, and again from 1883 to 1885. From 1891 to 1897 he was the director of the Agricultural Experimental Station at Iowa Agricultural College, at Ames, Iowa, and was also professor of Agriculture at this institution. From 1897 until 1913, he served as Secretary of Agriculture in the Cabinets of Presidents William McKinley, Theodore Roosevelt, and William Howard Taft. During this time a marked increase in the assumption of new responsibilities and in efficiency took place in that department.

James Wilson was born at Ayrshire, Scotland, on August 16, 1835, and died at Traer, in Tama County, Iowa, on August 26, 1920.

[1] *Tama Jim,* Earley Vernon Wilcox, with the collaboration of Flora H. Wilson (The Stratford Company, Boston, 1930) p. 1, 2, 5-15, 17, 31.

Wilson, James Falconer
James Falconer Wilson, Senator from Jefferson County, Iowa, was nicknamed *Jefferson Jim* [1] to distinguish him from James Wilson, Representative from Iowa, who was serving in Congress at the same time (1883-1885). James Falconer Wilson was a member of the Constitutional Convention of Iowa in 1856. He was a Republican Representative from Iowa to the United States Congress from 1861 until 1869, and Republican Senator from Iowa to the United States Congress from 1883 until 1895.

James Falconer Wilson was born at Newark, Ohio, on October 19, 1828, and died at Fairfield, Iowa, on April 22, 1895.

[1] *Dictionary of American Biography under the Auspices of the American Council of Learned Societies,* ed. by Dumas Malone (Charles Scribner's Sons, New York, 1936) vol. 20, p. 331.

Wilson, John
About 1822 a pioneer named John Wilson came to Miller County, Mo., to settle with his family. Not having the time, or probably the means, to build a cabin, he lived in a cave on Tavern creek during the first winter of his residence there, hence he was nicknamed *Cave Wilson.* [1]

It is said that Wilson later became a very prosperous man, popular with the people of the surrounding Ozark Territory, and that he was buried in the cave which had been his first Missouri home.

[1] *Centennial History of Missouri (The Center State) One Hundred Years in the Union, 1820-1921,* Walter B. Stevens (The S. J. Clarke Publishing Company, St. Louis Mo., and Chicago, 1921) vol. 2, p. 546.

Wilson, John Alfred Baynum
From 1883 to 1887 while he was in charge of the Salisbury District, centering about Salisbury, Md., John Alfred Baynum Wilson was designated the *Phenomenal Presiding Elder.* [1] As the sobriquet signifies, Doctor Wilson possessed unusual endurance in performing the arduous duties connected with his work, traveling over vast distances and speaking to large audiences every day, often three or four times on Sunday.

He was born at Milton, Del., on September 14, 1848, and was prominent in the activities of the Methodist Episcopal Church South.

[1] *The National Cyclopaedia of American Biography* (James T. White and Company, New York, 1897) vol. 7, p. 135.

Wilson, Lewis Robert
Lewis Robert Wilson, who was born at Elwood City, Pa., on April 26, 1900, and who played outfield in major league baseball, is nicknamed *Hack.* [1]

[1] *Who's Who in Major League Base Ball,* comp. by Harold (Speed) Johnson (Buxton Publishing Company, Chicago, 1933) p. 416.

Wilson, Samuel. See *Uncle Sam*

Wilson, William Abner
At Houston, Tex., William Abner Wilson was familiarly known as the *Builder of the City of Houston* [1] because he unsparingly gave of his time and ability to the execution of projects which advanced the civic and moral standing of Houston. In particular he devoted much time to the Young Men's Christian Association and to the Houston Chamber of Commerce, and he was prominent in the development of several suburb additions at Houston, having gained a national reputation for planning and building a city of beautiful homes.

William Abner Wilson was born at Syracuse, N.Y., on November 29, 1864, and died at Houston, Tex., on June 24, 1928.

[1] *Encyclopedia of American Biography: American Biography, a New Cyclopedia,* comp. under the editorial supervision of a notable advisory board (Published under the direction of The American Historical Society, Inc., New York, 1928) vol. 43, p. 85.

Wilson, Woodrow

At various times throughout his life Woodrow Wilson was designated a *Coiner of Weasel Words*,[1] a *Phrasemaker*,[1] and the *Schoolmaster in Politics.*

The last-mentioned nickname, which is the most widely-known, referred to Wilson's status as an intellectual and scholar, which many people felt unfitted him for the harsh realities of practical politics. The major portion of his adult life was spent in the teaching profession, from 1875 to 1902 as a college instructor, and from 1902 to 1910 as president of Princeton University.

Wilson's capacity for well-expressed thought was noted by his detractors as well as admirers and gave rise to such nicknames as *Coiner of Weasel Words* and *Phrasemaker.*

Woodrow Wilson was born at Staunton, Va., on December 28, 1856, and died at Washington, D.C., on February 3, 1924. He was the twenty-eighth President of the United States, having served from 1913 to 1921.

See also *Big Four, Big Three.*

[1] *Wilson the Unknown: An Explanation of an Enigma of History*, Wells Wells (pseudonym) (Charles Scribner's Sons, New York, 1931) p. 1, 19.
The Life of Woodrow Wilson, 1856-1924, Josephus Daniels (The John C. Winston Company, Chicago and Philadelphia, 1924) p. 42.

Wilson, Woodrow, and Edward Mandell House

Woodrow Wilson and his personal representative to European nations during World War I, Colonel Edward Mandell House, were designated the *Duumvirate*[1] or the *Duumvirs.*[1]

These expressions, in Roman antiquity, meant that two Roman officers were united in the administration of one public office. In the present application, they refer to Colonel House's close association with Wilson for almost the whole period of his administration, as a confidant and agent. The *Duumvirate* is said to have been most powerful from 1913 until June 1919, at which time Wilson and House, both in Paris for the Peace Conference, became somewhat estranged.

[1] *The Strangest Friendship in History, Woodrow Wilson and Colonel House*, George Sylvester Viereck (Liveright, Inc., New York, 1932) p. xiii, p. 37, 44, 78,

Winchell, Walter

Walter Winchell, newspaper columnist, one-time vaudeville actor, dramatic critic, and radio commentator, is commonly designated *America's One-man Newspaper* because his reporting covers fields of diversified news interest.

Walter Winchell was born at New York City on April 7, 1897.

Wind. See Wayne, Anthony

Windy City. See Chicago, Ill.

Windy Month

March, the third month of the year, has been nicknamed the *Windy Month*[1] because it is the connecting month between winter and spring and is characterized by boisterous, blustery winds.

[1] *The World Book Encyclopedia* (The Quarrie Corporation, Chicago, 1938) vol. 11, p. 4284.

Wing, Joseph Elwyn

Joseph Elwyn Wing, farmer, agricultural journalist, and lecturer, was nicknamed *Alfalfa Joe*.[1] He was the first to advocate raising alfalfa in the Central and Eastern States of the United States, and was a reliable authority on the cultivation of the alfalfa crop.

Joseph Elwyn Wing was born at Hinsdale, N.Y., on September 14, 1861, and died at Marion, Ohio, on September 10, 1915.

[1] *Dictionary of American Biography under the Auspices of the American Council of Learned Societies*, ed. by Dumas Malone (Charles Scribner's Sons, New York, 1936) vol. 20, p. 387.

Winged Victory Division. See Forty-third Infantry Division of World War II

Winona, Minnesota

Winona, the fourth largest city in Minnesota, is nicknamed the *Gate City*[1] because its excellent location on the Mississippi River, about one hundred miles below St. Paul, Minn., at the junction of five great northwestern railway lines, and a number of highways, makes it a gateway for trade and transportation to various places throughout northwestern United States.

[1] *Minnesota and Its People*, ed. by Joseph A. A. Burnquist (The S. J. Clarke Publishing Company, Chicago, 1924) vol. 2, p. 409.

Winston, John Anthony

While he was Governor of Alabama from 1853 to 1856, John Anthony Winston was nicknamed the *Veto Governor*[1] because he

Winston, J. A.—Continued

consistently opposed and vetoed measures providing for the granting of subsidies to railroads and other private companies while the state was in debt.

John Anthony Winston was born in Madison County, Ala., on September 4, 1812, and died at Mobile, Ala., on December 21, 1871.

[1] *The Encyclopedia Americana* (Americana Corporation, New York and Chicago, 1927) vol. 29, p. 401.

Winston-Salem, North Carolina

Winston-Salem has been termed the *Twin City*,[1] or *Twin Cities*,[2] because the cities of Winston and Salem, formerly two separate municipalities but closely related commercially and industrially, are now consolidated into one city, named Winston-Salem.

[1] *Winston-Salem, North Carolina, Authorized and Endorsed by the Directors of the Board of Trade and Endorsed by the Aldermen and Commissioners of Winston-Salem, the Natural Geographical Gateway from the Coal Fields of Virginia, Ohio, and Pennsylvania, the Grain and Meat Markets of the Northwest to the South Atlantic, and Gulf States, and Panama Canal*, Colonel G. Webb and L. E. Norryce (The Stone Printing and Manufacturing Company, Roanoke, Va., 1910) p. 2.
[2] *Souvenir of the Twin Cities of North Carolina, Winston-Salem, Forsythe County, Descriptive and Historical*, Mrs. A. V. Winkler (Blums' Steam Power Press Print, Salem, N.C., 1890) p. 6.

Winthrop, John

The *American Nehemiah* and the *Father of Massachusetts* are appellations given to John Winthrop.

He was called the *American Nehemiah*[1] in allusion to his piety and to his prophetic insight into the future of the Massachusetts Bay Colony.

The sobriquet, *Father of Massachusetts*,[2] was applied to John Winthrop because he was the founder of the Massachusetts Bay Colony, served as its first governor, and because his life and fortunes from 1630 when he left England, were devoted to the affairs of the Puritan commonwealth.

John Winthrop was born near Groton, England, on January 12, 1588, and died at Boston, Mass., on March 26, 1649.

[1] *The Pulpit of the American Revolution: or, the Political Sermons of the Period of 1776, with Historical Introduction, Notes, and Illustrations*, John Wingate Thornton (Gould and Lincoln, Boston, 1860) p. 491.
[2] *The National Cyclopaedia of American Biography* (James T. White and Company, New York, 1896) vol. 6, p. 202.

Wire King of America. See Gates, J. W.

Wiregrass Counties

Coffee, Covington, Geneva, Henry, and Houston Counties in Alabama are commonly designated the *Wiregrass Counties*,[1] because they grow an abundance of wire grass, a slender-stemmed meadow grass with both wiry leaves and roots.

[1] *History of Alabama and Her People*, Albert Burton Moore, Author and Editor (The American Historical Society, Inc., New York and Chicago, 1927) vol. 1, p. 757.

Wirz, Henry

While he was Superintendent of the Confederate Military Prison at Andersonville, Ga., the inmates of that prison nicknamed Captain Henry Wirz *Death on a Pale Horse*[1] because he usually dressed in a suit of white duck and rode upon a white horse, thereby having suggested a resemblance to the specter of death riding a ghost-horse.

Henry Wirz was born at Zurich, Switzerland, in 1822, and died at Washington, D.C., on November 10, 1865.

[1] *Andersonville: A Story of Rebel Military Prisons, Fifteen Months a Guest of the So-called Confederacy, a Private Soldier's Experience in Richmond, Andersonville, Savannah, Millen, Blackshear, and Florence*, John McElroy (D. R. Locke, Toledo, Ohio, 1879) p. 244.

Wisconsin

The origin of Wisconsin's sobriquet, the *Badger State*, is as follows: This term was applied to the early lead miners, who on coming to a new location dug into the side of a hill and lived underground much as the badger in his burrow. Reuben Gold Thwaites speaks of Wisconsin as the "land of the Badgers." Moses M. Strong, in a letter published in the *Madison State Journal* for December 10, 1879, says: "The term 'Badger' —according to tradition—was first applied to the occupants of these temporary subterranean residences in derision . . . and afterward to all the inhabitants of the lead-mine region, and by a not unnatural adaptation, has been applied to the people of the state and to the state itself."[2]

Wisconsin's nickname, the *Copper State*, refers to the copper mines in the northern part of the state.

[1] "The Story of Wisconsin," in *The Story of the States*, Reuben Gold Thwaites (D. Lothrop Company, Boston, 1890) p. 205.
[2] "Wisconsin's Emblems and Sobriquets" Reuben Gold Thwaites, in the *Proceedings of the State Historical Society of Wisconsin at Its Fifty-fifth Annual Meeting Held November 7, 1907* (Published by the Society, Democrat Printing Company, State Printers, Madison, Wis., 1908) p. 304.

Wisconsin Inhabitants

The people of Wisconsin are frequently called *Badgers*. Relative to the origin of this nickname, Professor James D. Butler, in speaking of the early miners in Wisconsin says: "Those from Southern Illinois went home to winter; those from the east could not, but dodged the cold in such dug-outs as they could hurry up. The eastern men were hence nicknamed *Badgers*, as if burrowing in similar holes with those animals.[1]

[1] "Tay-Cho-Pe-Rah—The Four Lake Country—First White Foot-Prints There" by Professor James D. Butler, in *Report and Collections of the State Historical Society of Wisconsin, for the Years 1883, 1884, and 1885* (Democrat Printing Company, State Printers, Madison, Wis., 1888) vol. 10, p. 79.
    For a similar account of the origin of this nickname see also "The Cornish in Southwest Wisconsin" by Louis Albert Copeland, in *Collections of the State Historical Society of Wisconsin* (Democrat Printing Company, Madison, Wis., 1898) vol. 14, p. 305.

Wise, Henry Alexander

The *Harry Percy of the House* and *Old Chinook* were nicknames attributed to Henry Alexander Wise.

While he was a Representative from Virginia to the United States Congress from 1833 to 1844, Wise was accustomed to expressing himself forcibly and eloquently on the subjects debated in the House. His impetuous [1] and ardent participation in these controversies caused them to nickname him, the *Harry Percy of the House,*[1] in allusion to Henry Percy, an English soldier also known as Hotspur, who lived in the fourteenth century. Both Wise and Percy were critical, aggressive, inclined to be rash in words and actions, and were of an excitable temper and disposition.

The students in the Virginia Military Institute at Lexington, Va., where Captain Henry Alexander Wise and several other officers in the Confederate Army were quartered during the winter of 1862-3, nicknamed Captain Wise *Old Chinook,*[2] but it seems to be not definitely known why.

Henry Alexander Wise was born at Drummondtown, Va., on December 3, 1806, and died at Richmond, Va., on September 12, 1876.

[1] *The Life of Henry A. Wise of Virginia, 1806-1876, by His Grandson, The Late Barton H. Wise* (The Macmillan Company, New York and London, 1899) p. 56, 58-9.
[2] *The End of an Era,* John S. Wise (Houghton Mifflin and Company, New York and Boston, 1889) p. 261.

Wise, Isaac Mayer

Isaac Mayer Wise was designated the *Moses of America*[1] because like Moses, he was a leader of the Jewish people. Rabbi Wise came to America in the early nineteenth century and exerted great influence for progressive Judaism among American Jews.

Wise was born at Steingrub, Bohemia, on March 29, 1819, and died at Cincinnati, Ohio, on March 26, 1900.

[1] *The National Cyclopaedia of American Biography* (James T. White and Company, New York, 1900) vol. 10, p. 116.

Wise Charlie. See McNary, C. L.

Wisecracker. See Walker, J. J.

Wiskers. See Tinkham, G. H.

Wisner, Edward

Because he was a pioneer in initiating the reclamation of land on an extensive scale, and because the success of his projects served to inspire both private and state interest in land reclamation, Edward Wisner has been fittingly called the *Father of Reclamation.*[1]

About 1888, Wisner went to Louisiana, settling in Franklin Parish, in the northern part of that state. Here he bought about five thousand acres of land, and, having lost his money during the panic of 1893, he began to investigate the possibilities of reclaiming portions of the several million acres of wet lands in Louisiana. Convinced by careful study that the continuous deposits of silt by the Mississippi River upon these lands had made them exceedingly fertile in a comparatively short time, he had bought nearly one and a half million acres of this wet land. In 1902 he began to drain and develop his tracts for farm use, and soon succeeded in converting immense areas of former wasteland into splendidly cultivated farms.

Edward Wisner was born at Athens, Mich., on February 27, 1860, and died at New Orleans, La., on March 8, 1915.

[1] *The National Cyclopaedia of American Biography* (James T. White and Company, New York, 1916) vol. 15, p. 243.

Witch House

At 310 Essex Street in Salem, Mass., stands a house associated with the witchcraft delusion about 1692. The house contains some of the timbers that originally were in the building used for the imprisonment of those accused of witchcraft, hence it is known as the *Witch House,*[1] or the *Witch Jail.*[1] Edmund H. Garrett states that while the house, once the property of Roger

Witch House—Continued

Williams, is traditionally associated with the witchcraft delusion, the actual building used for the purpose is at 315 Essex Street.[2]

[1] *Historical Markers Erected by Massachusetts Bay Colony Tercentenary Commission, Text of Inscriptions as Revised by Samuel Eliot Morison* with a foreword by Charles Knowles Bolton (The Commonwealth of Massachusetts, Boston, 1930) p. 30.
[2] *Romance and Reality of the Puritan Coast,* Edmund H. Garrett (Little, Brown and Company, Boston, 1913) p. 131.

Witchcraft City. See Salem, Mass.

Wittenberg College

Fighting Lutherans and the *Red Devils of Wittenberg* are nicknames given to the athletic teams of Wittenberg College, at Springfield, Ohio. The *Fighting Lutherans* [1] commemorates the facts that the college is a Lutheran school and that in 1917 a vast number of the students enlisted in the United States Army. *Red Devils of Wittenberg,*[1] was originated by a sports writer in 1932 because the teams began to wear red uniforms, [1] including headgear and footgear.

[1] A communication from Rees E. Tulloss, President of Wittenberg College, Springfield, Ohio, November 18, 1935.

Witz. See Dingell, J. D.

Wizard of Kinderhook. See Van Buren, Martin

Wizard of Menlo Park. See Edison, T. A.

Wizard of the Albany Regency. See Van Buren, Martin

Wizard of the American Drama. See Belasco, David

Wizard of the Saddle. See Forrest, N. B.

Wizard of the Wires. See Edison, T. A.

Wizard of Tomassee. See Pickens, Andrew

Wizard of Word Music. See Poe, E. A.

Wobblies. See Industrial Workers of the World

Wofford College

The athletic teams of Wofford College, at Spartanburg, S.C., were designated *Terriers* [1] about 1915.

[1] A communication from Henry N. Snyder, President of Wofford College, Spartanburg, S.C., November 20, 1935.

Wolf, George

The *Father of the Public School System of Pennsylvania* [1] was the sobriquet attributed to George Wolf in commemoration of his services in having induced the Legislature of Pennsylvania to adopt a measure in 1834 to establish a system of public schools throughout that state.

George Wolf was born in Allen Township, in Northampton County, Pa., on August 12, 1777, and died at Philadelphia, Pa., on March 17, 1840.

[1] *The National Cyclopaedia of American Biography* (James T. White and Company, New York, 1899) vol. 2, p. 286.

Wolf Putnam. See Putnam, Israel

Wolf Thompson. See Seton, E. T.

Wolverine State. See Michigan

Wolverines. See Detroit American League Baseball Company; Michigan Inhabitants; University of Michigan

Wolves. See University of Nevada

Woman Who Always Prays. See Duchesne, R. P.

Woman Who Always Speaks Her Mind. See Oliver, E. M.

Wonder City of the World. See Miami, Fla.

Wonder Devils on Wheels. See *Black Dragons*

Wonder State. See Arkansas

Wonderland of America. See Yellowstone National Park

Wood, Mrs. Mary Ramsey Lemons

Mrs. Mary Ramsey Lemons Wood of Hillsboro, Ore., was nicknamed *Mother*

Wood [1] and the *Queen Mother of Oregon*.[1]
She was over 120 years old at her death and
was one of the oldest survivors among Oregon's first settlers. She was crowned the
Queen Mother of Oregon at Portland, Ore.,
on July 4, 1907, as a special feature of festivities held in that city.

Mary Ramsey, daughter of Richard Ramsey, a brick mason of Knoxville, Tenn.,
pursued a westward course throughout her
life. She married Jacob Lemons at Knoxville, Tenn., in 1804, and moved with him
from Tennessee to Alabama, and from Alabama to Georgia in 1838. Mr. Lemons died
there in 1839. Mrs. Lemons went to Missouri in 1849 and in 1852 moved from
there to Oregon, riding the entire distance
across the plains on a mare which she called
Martha Washington Pioneer.[2] She finally
settled in Washington County, Ore., where
she married John Wood on May 28, 1854.

[1] *The Washington Post,* Washington, D.C., January
2, 1908, col. 4, p. 3.
[2] *The Morning Oregonian,* Portland, Ore., December
2, 1908, col. 3, p. 1.

Woodbridge, Timothy

Timothy Woodbridge, known as the *Blind
Minister* [1], lost his sight while a student in
Williams College, Massachusetts, in 1799.
He studied law after he had been graduated
from Williams College in 1803, but gave
this up to enter Andover Theological Seminary in 1810. He was graduated from there
the following year and became the pastor
of the Presbyterian Church at Green River,
N.Y., in 1816, remaining in this position
until 1842 when he moved to Spencertown,
N.Y., to become the pastor of the Presbyterian Church there. It is said that in spite
of his blindness, Woodbridge was a diligent
student, a most interesting preacher, and a
cheerful and active man.

Timothy Woodbridge was born at Stockbridge, Mass., on November 23, 1784, and
died at Spencertown, N.Y., on December 7,
1862.

[1] *Appleton's Cyclopaedia of American Biography,* ed.
by James Grant Wilson and John Fiske (D. Appleton
and Company, New York, 1894) vol. 6, p. 599.

Wooden Gods of Sedition

By 1798 a period of intense internal strife
had developed in the United States as Americans took sides in the struggles then taking
place between France and England. The
Republicans of that day still favored the
French as recent allies who in 1789 had

followed the example of the American Revolution, while the Federalists believed that
more advantage could be gained for America
by siding with the British. Dissension between the partisans became increasingly violent. Evidences of pro-French feeling were
anathematized, Federalists wore a black
cockade as opposed to the French tri-color,
drowned out the French revolutionary tunes
with "Hail Columbia" and other hymns of
nationalist fervor, and nicknamed the lib-
erty-poles set up in preceding years as symbols of the American and French revolu-
tions, *Wooden Gods of Sedition*.[1]

[1] *A History of the People of the United States, from
the Revolution to the Civil War,* John Bach McMaster
(D. Appleton and Company, New York, 1885) vol. 2,
p. 403.

Wooden Leg. See Stuyvesant, Peter

Wooden Nutmegs. See Connecticut Inhabitants

Wooden-shoe Statesman. See Watson,
J. E.

Wooden Walls of Columbia

After Captain Isaac Hull had encountered
the British fleet and had fought and destroyed the British frigate, *Guerrière*, off
Cape Race at the southeast extremity of Newfoundland, on August 19, 1812, he set sail
for Boston, anchoring in Boston Bay on
August 30.

He was welcomed enthusiastically by the
Bostonians, who saw him as a heroic representative of the Federalist party cause, and
furthermore as a Yankee captain of a Yankee frigate fresh from victory over the
English. Toasts were drunk throughout the
city to the Federalist Congress, the President
and the Navy. The latter was poetically
referred to as the *Wooden Walls of Columbia,* [1] a metaphor explained by the fact that
ships of that day were made of wood and
that the poetic name for America is Columbia.

[1] *A History of the People of the United States, from
the Revolution to the Civil War,* John Bach McMaster
(D. Appleton and Company, New York, 1895) vol. 4,
p. 76.

Wood-Pulp Miller. See Miller, Warner

Woodrum, Clifton Alexander

Clifton Alexander Woodrum was popularly called the *Choirmaster of the House* [1]

Woodrum, C. A.—Continued
by his fellow-congressmen because he generally conducted the singing when the House indulged in that activity.

He was born at Roanoke, Va., on April 27, 1887, now resides there, and was a Representative from Virginia to the United States Congress from 1923 until his resignation on December 31, 1945.

[1] *The Washington Post Magazine*, Washington, D.C., March 4, 1934, p. 4.

Woodstock Races

After the Battle of Tom's Brook at the rear of Fisher's Hill in Virginia on October 9, 1864, the retreat of Confederate forces under Brigadier General Jubal Anderson Early was called the *Woodstock Races* [1] because the soldiers moved rapidly toward Woodstock, Va., a distance of about sixteen miles.

In speaking of this battle, General Early says: "I halted at New Market with the infantry, but Rosser and Lomax moved down the Valley in pursuit, and skirmished successfully with the enemy's cavalry on the 8th; but on the 9th they encountered his whole cavalry force at Tom's Brook, in rear of Fisher's Hill, and both of their commands were driven back in considerable confusion, with a loss of some pieces of artillery—nine were reported to me as the number lost, but Grant claims eleven." [2]

General Sheridan, in reporting this victory to General Grant, said: "I directed Torbert to attack at daylight this morning, and finish this 'Savior of the Valley'. . . . The enemy, after being charged by our gallant cavalry, were broken and ran." [3]

[1] *General Sheridan*, General Henry E. Davies (D. Appleton and Company, New York, 1895) p. 177.
[2] *A Memoir of the Last Year of the War for Independence in the Confederate States of America, Containing an Account of the Operations of His Commands in the Years 1864 and 1865*, Lieutenant-general Jubal A. Early (Printed by Lovell and Gibson, Toronto, Canada, 1866) p. 105.
[3] *The Shenandoah Valley in 1864*, George E. Pond (Charles Scribner's Sons, New York, 1883) p. 203.

Woody. See Jensen, Forrest

Woof-woof

The cadets at a military school designate the Sergeant Major of a battalion a *Woof-woof*. [1] This being the sound made by a more powerful animal, to frighten smaller animals, the implication in the nickname is that the appearance of the Sergeant Major,

a superior officer, would be calculated to have a similar effect upon the cadets.

[1] *Unit Projects in Modern Literature* (Educational Press, Inc., Columbus, Ohio), March 1-14, 1935, p. 12.

Wool-carder President. See Fillmore, Millard

Wooly Bob. See Rich, R. F.

Wooly-head. See Julian, G. W.

Worcester, Massachusetts

Worcester has been designated the *City of Prosperity*. [1] It is the second largest city in Massachusetts, and a rail and industrial center.

[1] *Worcester, City of Prosperity*, Donald Tulloch (The Commonwealth Press, Worcester, Mass., 1914) p. 31.

Worcester Polytechnic Institute

For the last twenty-five years the athletic teams of Worcester Polytechnic Institute, at Worcester, Mass., have been nicknamed *Engineers*. [1]

[1] A communication from P. R. Carpenter, Director of Athletics at Worcester Polytechnic Institute, Worcester, Mass., November 18, 1935.

Workman, William Henry

In Los Angeles, Calif., William Henry Workman was popularly known as *Uncle Billy*. [1] As one of the earliest residents of Los Angeles, and having lived there for sixty-four years, Workman possessed a large circle of friends and acquaintances. To these people he was ever-willing to give advice, encouragement, or financial aid; he took an active part in any civic affairs which promoted the welfare of the city's inhabitants; and he was so kind and thoughtful that many people felt free to call him *Uncle Billy*.

William Henry Workman was born at Boonville, Mo., on January 1, 1839, and died at Los Angeles, Calif., on February 21, 1918.

[1] *The National Cyclopaedia of American Biography* (James T. White and Company, New York, 1926) vol. 19, p. 221.

World War Croesus. See McAdoo, W. G.

World's Egg Basket. See Petaluma, Calif.

World's Sweetheart. See Pickford, Mary

World's Workshop. See Pittsburgh, Pa.

Would-be-Cromwell of America. See Adams, Samuel

Wrackensackers

It is said that the soldiers in General William Tecumseh Sherman's Army designated men from Arkansas *Wrackensackers* [1] about 1862. This nickname is formed by transposing the letters in Arkansas. *Wrackensackers* are given credit for rarely deserting.

[1] *Camp Court and Siege: A Narrative of Personal Adventure and Observation during Two Wars, 1861-1865, 1870-1871,* Wickham Hoffman (Harper and Brothers, New York, 1877) p. 72.

Wright, Benjamin

Benjamin Wright, senior engineer of the Erie Canal, was nicknamed the *Father of American Engineering* [1] because of his outstanding work in the field of engineering, especially in his successful planning and building of the Erie Canal.

Benjamin Wright was born at Wethersfield, Conn., on October 10, 1770, and died at New York City, on August 24, 1842.

[1] *Dictionary of American Biography under the Auspices of the American Council of Learned Societies,* ed. by Dumas Malone (Charles Scribner's Sons, New York, 1936) vol. 20, p. 544.

Wright, Charles Barstow

The life of financier and railroad president Charles Barstow Wright was characterized by industry, perseverance and honesty, and he is generally recognized as a noble example of the successful businessman. As president of the Tacoma Land Company he was greatly revered throughout the Northwest and his nickname, the *Father of Tacoma,* was given in recognition of his efforts in behalf of that city's development.

Charles Barstow Wright was born in Wysox Valley, in Bradford County, Pa., on January 8, 1822, and died at Philadelphia, Pa., on March 23, 1898.

[1] *The National Cyclopaedia of American Biography* (James T. White and Company, New York, 1900) vol. 8, p. 440.

Wright, Forrest Glenn

Forrest Glenn Wright, who was born at Archie, Mo., on February 6, 1902, and who played shortstop in major league baseball,

is nicknamed *Buckshot* [1] because he got the ball away again so swiftly when he caught it.

[1] *Who's Who in Major League Base Ball,* comp. by Harold (Speed) Johnson (Buxton Publishing Company, Chicago, 1933) p. 418.

Wright, Silas

While he was a Senator from New York to the United States Congress from 1833 to 1844, Silas Wright was called the *Cato of the Senate* [1] by Thomas Hart Benton because Wright was a persuasive and skillful debater and orator in the Senate, and was recognized as a statesman anxious to serve his country to the best of his ability. In these qualities Benton compared Wright to Marcus Porcius Cato, known as Cato the Younger, Roman soldier and statesman who lived from 95 B.C. to 46 B.C.

Silas Wright was born at Amherst, Mass., on May 24, 1795, and died at Canton, Ohio, on August 27, 1847.

[1] *The National Cyclopaedia of American Biography* (James T. White and Company, New York, 1893) vol 3, p. 47.

Wrong-way Corrigan. See Corrigan, D. G.

Wyoming

Wyoming is known as the *Equality State* because it was a pioneer in woman suffrage.

Sagebrush State, as Wyoming is sometimes called, refers to the wild sage (*Artemisia tridentata*) which grows on the desert sections of this state.

X

Xavier University

The athletic teams of Xavier University, at Cincinnati, Ohio, were designated the *Musketeers* [1] in 1925 by a resolution suggested by Reverend Francis J. Finn, S.J. This sobriquet " 'typifies the spirit and characteristics of the members of the various teams of Xavier University.' " [1]

[1] A communication from G. J. Sterman, Director of Publicity at Xavier University, Cincinnati, Ohio, July 8, 1935.

XYZ Affair

Having been angry with the United States for not allying herself with the French against Great Britain in 1793 and for mak-

XYZ Affair—Continued
ing Jay's Treaty with England in 1794
France began to capture American merchant
vessels wherever she found them on the sea.
In 1796 France withdrew her minister to
the United States. In an attempt to adjust
matters, President John Adams sent three
American representatives to France: Charles
Cotesworth Pinckney of South Carolina,
John Marshall of Virginia, and Elbridge
Gerry of Massachusetts. When they arrived,
the French Directory would not receive
them, but three private representatives of
the French Government called on the American envoys and told them that they would
not be accepted, nor would existing relations
be adjusted until the American Government
had made a loan of a certain sum of money
to the French Treasury and had given a
bribe or tribute to the chief officials of the
French Directory. The commission reported
this treatment to President Adams who laid
the whole matter before Congress, substitut-
ing X, Y, and Z for the names of the French
agents. The correspondence of Talleyrand,
the French Minister, and the three French
agents was published under the name of
XYZ Papers in 1798, and the whole pro-
ceeding became known as the *XYZ Affair*.[1]

[1] *The United States*, Theodore Calvin Pease (Harcourt,
Brace and Company, New York, 1927) p. 235.
   The American People and Nation, Rolla M. Tryon
and Charles R. Lingley (Ginn and Company, New York
and Boston, 1932) p. 260.

Y

Yale University
The athletes composing the teams of Yale
University, at New Haven, Conn., are called
the *Elis* in honor of Elihu Yale for whom
the University was named.

Yancey, William Lowndes
William Lowndes Yancey was nicknamed
the *Orator of Secession*[1] because he spoke
in both northern and southern states from
about 1848 until the outbreak of the Civil
War in defense of the rights of the southern states, and strove diligently in 1850 to
persuade Georgia, his home state, to secede
from the Union.

William Lowndes Yancey was born at
Ogeechee Shoals, Ga., on August 10, 1814,
and died near Montgomery, Ala., on July
28, 1863.

[1] *The World Book Encyclopedia* (The Quarrie Corporation, Chicago, 1938) vol. 18, p. 7927.

Yankee
Lexicographers generally agree that the
origin of the word, *Yankee,* is uncertain.
Its origin, however, has been accounted for
by several authorities, three of which are
given below. Thomas Anburey, an officer
in the British Army under the command
of General John Burgoyne, says that the
term "is derived from a Cherokee word,
eankke, which signifies coward and slave.
This epithet of yankee," he further states,
"was bestowed upon the inhabitants of New
England by the Virginians, for not assisting
them in a war with the Cherokees, and they
have always been held in derision by it.
But the name has been more prevalent since
the commencement of hostilities; the sol-
diery at Boston used it as a term of reproach; but after the affair at Bunker's
Hill, the Americans gloried in it. *Yankee-
doodle* is now their paean, a favorite of
favorites, played in their army, esteemed
as war-like as the Grenadier's March—it is
the lover's spell, the nurse's lullaby. After
our rapid successes, we held the Yankees
in great contempt; but it was not a little
mortifying to hear them play this tune,
when their army marched down to our
surrender." [1]

The *Century Dictionary and Cyclopedia*,
in discussing the Indian origin of the word,
says that "according to common statement,"
the word *Yankees* [2] is a variation of the Indian word *Yenkees, Yengees,* or *Yanghees,*
which were names applied to the English
Colonists by the Indians in Massachusetts in
their attempts to say the word *English*.

William Gordon says, "You may wish to
know the origin of the term *Yankee*. Take
the best account of it which your friend can
procure. It was a cant, favorite word with
farmer Jonathan Hastings, of Cambridge,
[Mass.], about 1713. Two aged ministers,
who were at the college in that town, have
told me [that] they remembered it to have
been then in use among the students, but
had no recollection of it before that period.
The inventor used it to express excellency.
A Yankee good horse, or Yankee cider, and
the like were an excellent good horse, and
excellent cider. The students used to hire
horses of him; their intercourse with him,

and his use of the term upon all occasions, led them to adopt it, and they gave him the name of Yankee Jon. He was a worthy honest man, but no conjurer. This could not escape the notice of the collegiates. Yankee probably became a by-word among them, to express a weak, simple, awkward person; was carried from the college with them when they left it, and was in that way circulated and established through the country (as was the case in respect to Hobson's choice, by the students at Cambridge, in Old England) till, from its currency in New England, it was at length taken up and unjustly applied to the New Englanders in common, as a term of reproach." [3]

Whatever the origin of the name may have been, it was first used to refer to the people of New England. During the Civil War, the Confederate soldiers extended the nickname to apply to all Northern soldiers, and during World Wars I and II, American soldiers were called *Yanks* or *Yankees*. English writers and speakers had been accustomed to designate Americans as *Yankees* long before 1914.

See also New York American League Baseball Company.

[1] *Travels through the Interior Parts of America; in a Series of Letters*, A New Edition, Thomas Anburey (Printed for William Lane, London, 1791) vol. 2, p. 46-7.
[2] *The Century Dictionary and Cyclopedia* (The Century Company, New York, 1906) vol. 8, p. 7008.
[3] *The History of the Rise, Progress, and Establishment of the Independence of the United States of America: Including an Account of the Late War, and of the Thirteen Colonies, from Their Origin to That Period*, The Third American Edition, William Gordon (Printed for Samuel Campbell by John Woods, New York, 1801) vol. 1, p. 312-13.

Yankee Buzzard

The eagle carried by Company C of the Eighth Regiment of Wisconsin Infantry Troops during the Civil War was designated the *Yankee Buzzard* [1] by the Confederate troops as an expression of their contempt for the Union symbol.

[1] *The Wisconsin Magazine of History*, ed. by Milo Milton Quaife (Publications of The State Historical Society of Wisconsin, Madison, Wis., 1918) September, 1918, vol. 2, no. 1, p. 82-4.

Yankee Cheese Box on a Raft. See
Cheese Box on a Raft

Yankee Division. See Twenty-sixth Infantry Division of World War II

Yankee Hill. See Hill, G. H.

Yankee King. See Sickles, D. E.

Yankee Land of the South. See Georgia

Yankee Palace

During the War of 1812 the British soldiers somewhat derisively spoke of the White House at Washington, D.C., as the *Yankee Palace* [1] because it was the official residence of the President of the United States. The inhabitants of this country were designated *Yankees* by the British invaders.

[1] *The Heart of Roosevelt; an Intimate Life-story of Theodore Roosevelt*, Wayne Whipple (The John C. Winston Company, Chicago and Philadelphia, 1924) p. 172.

Yankee Slayers

Because of the scarcity of steel in the South during the Civil War, southerners often converted the blades of scythes into large knives which they designated *Yankee Slayers* [1] in grim allusion to the formidable purpose for which they were intended.

[1] *Recollections of a Varied Career*, William F. Draper (Little, Brown and Company, Boston, 1908) p. 66.

Yankee State. See Ohio

Yankee Sullivan. See Sullivan, James

Yankton College

The athletic teams of Yankton College, at Yankton, S.D., were designated *Greyhounds* [1] in 1922 by Miss Alice Kingsbury, a teacher in the college, because the athletic color was gray and because Miss Kingsbury said that they ran like greyhounds.

[1] A communication from C. I. Youngworth, Director of Athletics at Yankton College, Yankton, S.D., June 19, 1935.

Yeatman, James E.

Because of his active work in connection with the Western Sanitary Commission, which came into existence in September 1861, James E. Yeatman was called *Old Sanitary*.[1]

James E. Yeatman was born in Bedford County, Tenn., on August 27, 1818, and moved to St. Louis, Mo., about 1842, where he spent the remainder of his life.

[1] *Centennial History of Missouri (The Center State) One Hundred Years in the Union, 1820-1921*, Walter B. Stevens (The S. J. Clarke Publishing company, St. Louis, Mo., and Chicago, 1921) vol. 1, p. 787.

Yellowhammer State. See Alabama

Yellowhammers. See Alabamians

Yellow Jackets. See Randolph-Macon College; Waynesburg College; West Virginia State College

Yellowstone National Park

The Indians in Wyoming designated Yellowstone National Park the *Summit of the World.*[1]

Yellowstone National Park, located chiefly in "northwestern Wyoming, and extending into Idaho and Montana," is often called the *Wonderland of America.*[2] Its delicate or boldly colored rock and clay formations, the mineral rock pinnacles of fantastic shapes, the sun-tinted lakes and waterfalls, and the spouting geysers, are of a nature to excite wonder and admiration.

[1] *Seeing the Far West,* John T. Faris (J. B. Lippincott Company, Philadelphia, 1920) p. 176.
[2] *Tarr and McMurry's Geographies; a Complete Geography,* Ralph S. Tarr and Frank M. McMurry (The Macmillan Company, New York and London, 1902) p. 147.

Yeomen. See Oberlin College

Yoakum, Texas

Yoakum is the possessor of three sobriquets: the *City by Accident, City of Homes, Schools, and Churches,* and the *Hub City of South Texas.* The unusual nickname *City by Accident,* had its origin in the fact that this city encouraged the San Antonio and Arkansas Pass Railroad Company to locate its shops and headquarters there. The subsequent growth of the city having occurred as the result of this move, the place was termed the *City by Accident.*[1]

The second sobriquet applied to Yoakum is descriptive of its many fine homes, churches, and well-attended schools.[1]

This city is nicknamed the *Hub City of South Texas*[1] because it is the focal point of the San Antonio and Arkansas Pass Railroad, and the junction of branch lines and highway routes, it is located approximately midway between San Antonio and Houston, and offers many opportunities for prospective sites to manufacturing concerns because of its location in southern Texas.

[1] *Texas as It Is Today,* Alfred E. Menn (Gammel's Book Store, Austin, Tex., Printed and bound by The Bunker Printing Products Corporation, Fort Worth, Tex., 1925) p. 232-3.

York, Alvin Cullum

On October 8, 1918, during the Battle of Argonne, Alvin Cullum York fought a German machine-gun battalion singlehanded with the result that he and seven private soldiers captured and marched into the American lines one hundred and thirty-two German prisoners. Although a bill was passed by the Senate of the United States which made him a Major and retired him with a major's pay, and although Albert H. Roberts, former Governor of Tennessee, appointed him a life-time Colonel, York prefers to sign his name with the term *Sergeant* prefixed. He is widely known throughout his home-section of Tennessee as the *Sergeant.*

Alvin Cullum York was born at Pall Mall, Tenn., on December 13, 1887.

York College

Panthers[1] is the sobriquet given to the athletic teams of York College, at York, Neb., in 1921 by John Riddell, former Coach of Athletics at the College. The University of Pittsburgh's athletic teams, *The Panthers,*[1] were unusually successful in their athletic contests that year, and Coach Riddell adopted their nickname for the teams at York College because it was expressive of their spirit and fighting qualities.[1]

[1] A communication from J. R. Overmiller, President of York College, York, Neb., November 28, 1935.

York's Tall Son. See Porter, W. T.

Yost, Fielding Harris

Fielding Harris Yost was familiarly known as *Hurry Up Yost*[1] because in training his football teams, he emphasized rapidity in thought and action on the part of the players, constantly telling them to "hurry up."[2]

In addition to serving as football coach at the University of Michigan, since 1921,[3] Yost was the Director of Intercollegiate Athletics, the director of the four-year physical education course, and also the director of the physical training course for athletic coaching and administration given at this University.

He was born at Fairview, W.Va., on April 30, 1871, and died August 20, 1946, at Ann Arbor, Mich.

[1] *Encyclopedia of American Biography: American Biography, a New Cyclopedia,* comp. under the editorial supervision of a notable advisory board (Published under the direction of The American Historical Society, Inc., New York, 1930) vol. 40, p. 152.
[2] *Football for Player and Spectator,* Fielding H. Yost (University Publishing Company, Ann Arbor, Mich., 1905) p. 270-2.
[3] *Who's Who in America: A Biographical Dictionary of Notable Living Men and Women of the United States, 1932-1933,* ed. by Albert Nelson Marquis (The A. N. Marquis Company, Chicago, 1932) vol. 17, p. 2531.

Young, Denton True

Denton True Young was nicknamed *Cy,* a nickname frequently used to designate a tall, gangling country fellow.[1] In Young's case, however, it is suggested that it was short for "cyclone" because he was a phenomenal pitcher.[2] He was elected to the Baseball Hall of Fame as the "only pitcher in first hundred years of baseball to win 500 games. . . . He pitched a perfect game May 5, 1904, no opposing batsman reaching first base."

Young was born on March 29, 1867, in Gilmor, Ohio.

[1] *Who's Who in Major League Base Ball,* comp. by Harold (Speed) Johnson (Buxton Publishing Company, Chicago, 1933) p. 481.
[2] *Official Encyclopedia of Baseball,* by Hy Turkin and S. C. Thompson, (A. S. Barnes and Company, New York, 1951) p. 303, 585.

Young, Lemuel Floyd

Pep and *Whitey* are appellations given to Lemuel Floyd Young, outfielder.

The nickname, *Pep,*[1] was applied to Young because he was such a swift ball player. *Whitey*[1] referred to his heavy mass of blond hair.

Lemuel Floyd Young was born at Jamestown, N.C., on August 29, 1907, and played outfield in major league baseball.

[1] *Who's Who in Major League Base Ball,* comp. by Harold (Speed) Johnson (Buxton Publishing Company, Chicago, 1933) p. 420.

Young, William Hamilton

William Hamilton Young, a veteran telegrapher of Washington, D.C., was widely known as *Ham Young,*[1] the sobriquet having been a shortened form of his given name, Hamilton.

He began his work in telegraphy as a messenger boy in the office of the Washington and New Orleans Telegraph Company, located at Washington, D.C., in 1854, and was the sole operator in charge of the Capitol branch office of the company, situated in the gallery of the National House of Representatives from 1858 until 1861. In 1861 he became chief operator in the main office of the company.

In 1864 Young was appointed Assistant Manager of the United States Telegraph Company, in Washington, and when the Western Union Telegraph Company later leased the lines and other equipment of this company, Young became chief operator for this company. He was in Chicago, Ill., on duty for the Western Union Telegraph and Telephone Company at the Republican National Convention when he died. He was a familiar personage at all national conventions.

William Hamilton Young was born at Washington, D.C., in 1836, and died at Chicago, on June 19, 1908.

[1] *The Washington Post,* Washington, D.C., June 20, 1908, col. 1, p. 5.

Young Hickory. See Hill, D. B.; Polk, J. K.

Young Hotspur. See Ingersoll, R. I.

Young Industrial Giant of the West

The United States has been nicknamed the *Young Industrial Giant of the West*[1] because this country, situated in the Western Hemisphere, leads all other nations in the manufacturing industry, being the world's greatest consumer, as well as producer, of manufactured goods.

[1] *Our World Today; a Textbook in the New Geography,* De Forest Stull and Roy W. Hatch (Allyn and Bacon, New York and Boston, 1932) p. 576.

Young Thunderbolt. See Lea, Luke

Young Torquemada. See Mitchel, J. P.

Youngstown College

Penguins,[1] is the sobriquet of the athletic teams of Youngstown College, at Youngstown, Ohio.

[1] A communication from W. Sporer, Secretary of Youngstown College, Youngstown, Ohio, November 16, 1935.

Z

Zack. See Taylor, J. W.

Zenith City, or Zenith City of the Unsalted Seas. See Duluth, Minn.

Zeus. See Sanders, D. J.

Zioncheck, Marion A.

The *Congressional Playboy,*[1] and *Seattle's Sensational Son*[2] are the sobriquets by which Marion A. Zioncheck was designated by the newspaper men. Both of these nicknames

Zioncheck, M. A.—Continued

originated in the reckless manner of living in which Representative Zioncheck engaged during his stay in Washington, D.C., in 1935 and 1936. Congressman Zioncheck indulged in many playboy pranks, and was arrested and fined for speeding through Washington streets.

Marion A. Zioncheck, Representative from Washington to the United States Congress from 1933 to 1935, was born in a village in Poland, in 1900, and committed suicide at Seattle, Wash., on June 7, 1936.

[1] *The Washington Post*, Washington, D.C., June 2, 1936, col. 2, p. 1.
[2] *Washington Herald*, Washington, D.C., August 8, 1936, cols. 8 and 9, p. 3.

Zippers. See University of Akron

Zukor, Adolph

The sobriquet, *Pop,*[2] is affectionately applied to Adolph Zukor in recognition of his paternal interest in his employees, his generous contributions for philanthropic purposes, and his work as a pioneer in the establishment of the moving picture industry in the United States.

Adolph Zukor was born at Ricse, Hungary, on January 7, 1873. He is chairman of the board of Paramount Pictures Corporation.

[1] *Twenty-one Americans, Being Profiles of Some People Famous in Our Time, Together with Silly Pictures of Them Drawn by De Miskey*, Niven Busch (Doubleday, Doran and Company, Inc., Garden City, N.Y., 1930) p. 251.

Current Biography, Who's News and Why, 1950, ed. by Anna Rothe (The H. W. Wilson Company, New York, 1951) p. 639-641.